HOW TO USE THIS BOOK

Supplying lesbians and gays with the variety of information they need to make travel decisions means providing the gay and lesbian answers to the key questions every traveler asks. Those perennial questions are the headings to the various sections in this book.

Where to Go?

Destinations Index

Under each destination is a list of companies offering that destination and the page number for each.

What to Do?

Activities Index

From "birdwatching" to "honeymoon" to "yachting," each activity listed is followed by a list of companies offering it, and the page number for each.

Who to Call?

Alphabetical Index

This index lists all tour companies in alphabetical order by name and the page numbers where you can find information on each company.

Global Tour Directory

The Global Tour Directory lists each company by name and briefly describes its specialty. Information is based on personal interviews by the editor with each company.

Detailed Company Listings

If a company sent us more detailed information after our interview, we included a full column describing their offerings in more detail. For companies offering many destinations, these columns appear in alphabetical order on pages 83 to 109.

FYI Features

If a company specializes in a single destination, we have placed their full column right along with the other local information about that destination. To make them stand out, we placed the heading "FYI" above the column and included a light gray tint behind the text. The page number of each FYI is cited in the indexes for reader convenience.

Gender Symbols

Every tour entry carries gender symbols to indicate whether the company serves gay men ♂, lesbians ♀, or both ♀♂.

Membership in Gay Travel Associations

Members are indicated by abbreviations. "IGTA" or the symbol IGTA is for the International Gay Travel Association in the US. "AGLTA" or the symbol aglta is for the Australian Gay & Lesbian Travel Association. "EGLTA" is for the European Gay & Lesbian Travel Association.

Reservation Services

See pages 110 to 111

Travel Agents

See pages 112 to 133

When to Go?

Trips & Events Calendar

Every trip and event of which we were aware at presstime, is listed in order by date. An index on page 134 lists all the events by name and gives the date by which to find each in the calendar, where details are provided.

Having A Good Time

City-by-City Listings

Local information is arranged by region, country, state/province, city and finally category. See the index by country, page 5 or the outside back cover. Wherever applicable, the following categories always appear and in this order: Information, Excursions/Tours, Accommodations, Camping/RV, Bars, Dance Bars, Cafes, Saunas/Health Clubs, Restaurants, Retail & Bookstores, Leathers/Piercing and Erotica.

Listings include name (with a star after it for popular places), address, telephone, fax, 800 number, e-mail, web address, and brief description. Pictorial Gay International Symbols allow quick search for specific attributes. (See Key to Symbols in English, German, French, Spanish, Italian & Chinese, page 6).

Listings are updated individually, many by telephone as close as 1 week before presstime. This concentrated effort toward making the Ferrari Guides the most accurate and up-to-date gay guides available is unique in the industry and can be dramatically felt when using the guide.

Destination Features

Feature-length articles on local gay lifestyle appear under the heading, "Ferrari Destination Feature." They are contributed by local gay publications, local gay and lesbian writers or writers with a knowledge of the locale.

FERRARI GUIDES' GAY TRAVEL A to Z - 18th EDITION

Ferrari Guides' Gay Travel A to Z™

18th edition

Published by

> Ferrari International Publishing, Inc.
> PO Box 37887
> Phoenix, AZ 85069 USA
> (602) 863-2408 Fax: (602) 439-3952
> EMAIL: ferrari@q-net.com

Published
> April, 1997

Ferrari Guides is a trademark of Ferrari International Publishing, Inc.

Ferrari, Marianne
> Ferrari Guides' Gay Travel A to Z

> Includes Index
> ISBN 0-942586-59-X

Copyright © 1997 by Ferrari International Publishing, Inc.

All rights reserved. No part of this book may be reproduced in any form, or by any means, electronic or mechanical, including photocopying, recording, or by any information storage and retrieval system, without the express written permission of the publisher.

Opinions expressed in the articles in this book are those of the authors and do not necessarily reflect those of the management of Ferrari International Publishing, Inc. or its employees. Listing of a group, organization or business in *Ferrari Guides' Gay Travel A to Z*™ does not indicate that the sexual orientation of owners or operators is homosexual, nor that the sexual orientation of any given member of that group or client of that business is homosexual, nor that the organization or business specifically encourages membership or patronage of homosexuals as a group. This book is sold without warranties or guarantees of any kind, expressed or implied, and the authors and publisher disclaim any liability for loss, damage or injury in connection with it.

SPECIAL SALES - Purchases of 10+ copies of any of the Ferrari guides can be made at special discounts by businesses and organizations.

Printed in the United States of America

Ferrari International Publishing, Inc. is a proud member of:

International Gay Travel Association   Australian Gay & Lesbian Travel Association

FERRARI GUIDES
Gay Travel AtoZ™

Published Annually Since 1980

Worldwide Gay & Lesbian Travel Guide

Ferrari International Publishing, Inc.
PO Box 37887
Phoenix, AZ 85069 USA
(602) 863-2408

Editor & Publisher
Marianne Ferrari

Member AGLTA & IGTA
Australian Gay & Lesbian Travel Assn.
& International Gay Travel Assn.

Feature Contributors

Costa Rica, Rich Rubin, Genre Magazine

France, Gai Pied

Hong Kong, Matthew Link, Matt's Rainbow Tours

Iceland, Sue Rider Scott, L'Arc en Ciel Voyages

Maui, Hawaii, Barry Fried, Open Eye Tours & Photos

Mexico, Mundo Maya Turquesa

Mykonos, Greece, Pam Taylor, Windmill Travel & Tourism

Russia, Igor Svetlov, Kremlin Tours

Rafting in Siberia, Robert Hayes, Hawk, I'm Your Sister

Scuba Diving, Chris Winkle, Undersea Expeditions

Vancouver, BC, Canada, Rick Hurlbut, Xtra! West

On The Cover

Australia was the first nation whose government travel organization recognized the value of the gay travel market. Our cover photo is part of a major promotional photo shoot which was organized by the Australian Tourism Commission late last year. The roots of Australia's interest in gay travel date back over a decade.

It all started with the Sydney Gay Mardi Gras, the gigantic gay party which increasingly attracted overseas gay travelers throughout the 80's. Related events like Octobers' gay Sleaze Ball and Melbourne's Midsumma party event added to the interest. When Australian gay travel professionals combined forces with gay professionals overseas, starting in 1993, Meet fruit bats, butterflies and exotic birds up-close and personal at fascinating wildlife attractions. Melbourne has they de-

Photo courtesy of Australian Tourist Commission

veloped a host of gay travel options for Australia, making the country really explode in popularity as a gay destination.

Gay and lesbian travelers to Australia now have many kinds of Australian vacations to choose from. Tour groups of all kinds are built around Sydney's Gay Mardi Gras, many with optional add-ons to other parts of Australia and to Pacific islands. Gay tour companies in many countries are offering such tours. Most companies also offer independent travel packages, which combine accommodations and various excursions.

Australia's geographical diversity provides vacation options for people with very different tastes. You can get back to nature and hike through jungles in the Northern Territory. Scuba or snorkel vacations on the Great Barrier Reef can be combined with gay and lesbian resort relaxation in Cairns, Queensland. In the Red Centre, made famous by the movie "The Adventures of Priscilla, Queen of the Desert," which was filmed there, off-road jeep trips will take you, in comfort, to Ayers Rock and other attractions.

For those who like to stay in the city, Melbourne offers excellent fine dining and ethnic neighborhoods to explore. Nearby Daylesford, Australia's answer to California's Russian River, offers gay guest houses and hot springs. Sydney's photogenic harbor can be experienced on various harbor cruises and the Opera House is always an attraction. Both cities have active gay communities which offer a wide variety of gay venues.

TABLE OF CONTENTS

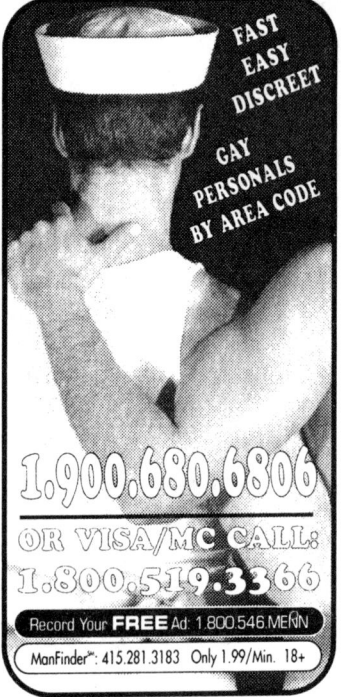

INTRODUCTION
How To Use This Book 1
Contributors 3
On the Cover 3
Table of Contents 4
Index by Country 5
Key to Symbols 6
Order Form 512

WHERE TO GO
Destination Index 8

WHAT TO DO
Activities Index 30

WHO TO CALL
Tour Company Index 43
Tour Company Directory 45
Tour Company Details 83
Reservation Services 110
Travel Agents 112

WHEN TO GO
Events Index 134
Calendar of Trips & Events ... 136

HAVING A GOOD TIME
City by City Listings 173

DESTINATION FEATURES

ASIA
HONG KONG
The Merry Widow 177

FRANCE
Gay France 205

GREECE
MYKONOS
Islands of the Gods 241

ICELAND
Hidden Treasure
   of the North! 245

RUSSIA
Gay Russia:
   Winds of Change 267
Russia's Wild West 269

PACIFIC ISLANDS
Gay and Lesbian Scuba Diving -
   The Urge to Submerge 321

CANADA
Vancouver: Spectacular by
   Nature 325

LATIN AMERICA
Costa Rica 349
The Mayan World 355

UNITED STATES
Off the Map on Maui 423

INDEX BY COUNTRY

AFRICA
KENYA	173
MOROCCO	173
NAMIBIA	174
NIGERIA	174
SOUTH AFRICA	174
ZIMBABWE	176

ASIA
BANGLADESH	187
CHINA	176
HONG KONG	179
INDIA	187
INDONESIA	188
JAPAN	179
KOREA, SOUTH	185
MALAYSIA	188
NEPAL	187
PAKISTAN	187
PHILIPPINES	189
SINGAPORE	189
SRI LANKA	187
TAIWAN	185
THAILAND	189
VIETNAM	192

EUROPE
ALBANIA	193
AUSTRIA	193
BELGIUM	194
CZECH REPUBLIC	198
DENMARK	200
ESTONIA	201
FINLAND	201
FRANCE	202
GERMANY	217
GREECE	237
HUNGARY	243
ICELAND	244
IRELAND	244
ITALY	248
LATVIA	254
LIECHTENSTEIN	254
LUXEMBOURG	254
NETHERLANDS	254
NORWAY	263
POLAND	263
PORTUGAL	265
RUSSIA	268
SLOVAKIA	271
SLOVENIA	271
SPAIN	272
SWEDEN	278
SWITZERLAND	280
TURKEY	283
UK (ENGLAND)	284
UK (N. IRELAND)	301
UK (SCOTLAND)	302
UK (WALES)	303
UKRAINE	304

MIDDLE EAST
ISRAEL	305

PACIFIC REGION
AUSTRALIA	306
NEW ZEALAND	317
COOK ISLANDS	320
FIJI ISLANDS	320
FRENCH POLYNESIA / TAHITI	320
GUAM	320

CANADA
ALBERTA	323
BRITISH COLUMBIA	324
MANITOBA	329
NEW BRUNSWICK	329
NOVA SCOTIA	329
ONTARIO	330
QUEBEC	333
SASKATCHEWAN	336
YUKON	336

CARIBBEAN & ATLANTIC ISLANDS
BRITISH WEST INDIES	337
CUBA	338
DOMINICAN REPUBLIC	338
DUTCH WEST INDIES	338
FRENCH WEST INDIES	338
PUERTO RICO	338
VIRGIN ISLANDS	342

LATIN AMERICA
ARGENTINA	343
BOLIVIA	345
BRAZIL	345
CHILE	351
COSTA RICA	351
EL SALVADOR	353
GUATEMALA	353
HONDURAS	353
MEXICO	354
NICARAGUA	360
PANAMA	361
PERU	361
URUGUAY	361
VENEZUELA	361

USA
ALABAMA	362
ALASKA	363
ARIZONA	364
ARKANSAS	368
CALIFORNIA	369
COLORADO	393
CONNECTICUT	397
DELAWARE	398
DISTRICT OF COLUMBIA	399
FLORIDA	401
GEORGIA	417
HAWAII	419
IDAHO	428
ILLINOIS	428
INDIANA	432
IOWA	433
KANSAS	435
KENTUCKY	435
LOUISIANA	436
MAINE	439
MARYLAND	442
MASSACHUSETTS	443
MICHIGAN	449
MINNESOTA	451
MISSISSIPPI	453
MISSOURI	453
MONTANA	455
NEBRASKA	457
NEVADA	458
NEW HAMPSHIRE	459
NEW JERSEY	460
NEW MEXICO	462
NEW YORK	464
NORTH CAROLINA	473
NORTH DAKOTA	476
OHIO	476
OKLAHOMA	480
OREGON	480
PENNSYLVANIA	483
RHODE ISLAND	486
SOUTH CAROLINA	487
SOUTH DAKOTA	488
TENNESSEE	488
TEXAS	490
UTAH	495
VERMONT	497
VIRGINIA	498
WASHINGTON	500
WEST VIRGINIA	503
WISCONSIN	504
WYOMING	507

KEY TO SYMBOLS

ENGLISH · DEUTSCH · FRANÇAIS · ESPAÑOL · ITALIANO · CHINESE

♂ Mostly men
Männer
hommes
hombres
uomini
男同志佔多

♀ Mostly women
Frauen
femmes
mujeres
donne
女同志佔多

⚥ Both men & women, well-mixed (50/50 or 60/40)
Männer und Frauen
hommes/femmes
hombres y mujeres
uomini e donne
男女同志比率和約
(50/50或60/40)

A non-gay place (gay- friendly, if noted)
Hetero
plutôt hétérosexuelle
clientela hetero-sexual
clientela mista
非同志場所
(如有記號,對同志友善)

Mature clientele 30's, 40's (NO longer "wrinkle room")
für Ältere
plutôt agées
personas mayores
non troppo giovane
成熟型30岁40岁
(非年老同志)

Black and white clientele
Schwarze/Weisse
noirs et blancs
negros y blancos
bianchi e neri
黑人和白人同志

Neighborhood-style bar
Stammbar
bar du quartier
bar de vecindad
bar del quartiere
本地式酒吧

樂 Asian clientele
Asiaten
asiatique
asiaticos
asiatici
華人同志

Ñ Hispanic clientele
Mexikanisch
latins
hispánicos
latinoamericani
西班牙人同志

Very young clientele
für sehr Junge Leute
très jeunes
muy joven
molto giovane
青少年同志

Professional clientele
Geschäftsmann
frau hommes
femmes d'affairs
profesionales
uomini
donne d'affari
事業型同志

Cruise-type bar
gut zum Abschleppen
lieu de drague
vacilar
molto movimento
釣魚吧

Levi bar or clientele
Westernkneipe
costumes levi
tipo vaquero
jeans
穿牛仔褲吧

Leather bar or clientele
Leder
cuir
cuero
leather
穿皮革吧

Uniforms (sometimes indicates dress code)
Uniformen
uniformes
uniformes militares
uniformi
制服
(某些酒吧會指定制服)

U Country & Western bar
Country & Western
western
tipo oeste
tipo Far West
牛仔吧

Dancing (disco only if under Dance Bar category)
Tanzen
danse
bailar
ballare
的士高
(如在跳舞目錄下只作的士高)

Male or female "go go" dancers or strippers
go go
go go
bailarines exoticos
ballerini esotici
有男或女 "Go Go"
舞蹈員 或脫衣舞

Female impersonator shows
Transvestitenshow
spectacles travestis
imitar a las estrellas
spettacoli di travestiti
人妖表演

Live entertainment
live Unterhaltung
spectacles
espectáculos
spettacoli
現場表演

Both liquor & beer available (only exceptions noted for bars)
Cocktailbar
alcool
cocteles
liquori
提供酒類或其它飲品(如非在酒吧欄內有特別記載)

Beer, or beer & wine, only
nur Bier und Wein
bière et vin
cerveza y vino
solo birra e vino
只提供酒類飲品

Bring your own "booze" (BYOB)
alkoholisch
Getränkeürfen mitgebracht werden
apporter boissons
traer bebidas alcoholicas
portare tutto da bere
可自攜飲品

No alcohol permitted
Getränke verboten
pas d'alcool
no se permite alcohol
divieto di bere alcool
不提供任何酒精飲品

Snacks and/or sandwiches served
Imbiss
collation
comidas colazione
tramezzini
只提供小食或三文治

Nudity permitted
Nacktheit erlaubt
nudisme permis
se permite desnudo
permesso andare nudo
准許裸體

Swimming (lake, ocean, pool, etc)
Schwimmen, piscine
mer piscina
mar, piscina
mare
游泳(湖,海灘,泳池…其它)

$ Frequented by hustlers
Stricher
commerciaux
prostitución masculina
prostituzione maschile
有男妓或妓女出沒

A popular place
sehr beliebten Ort
endroit branché
recomendado
popular de ambiente
受歡迎場所

WHERE TO GO

DESTINATION INDEX

ABACO
Island Hoppers Tours .... 59, FYI 341
ABU SIMBEL
2Afrika 45, 83
ACAPULCO
Gay Mexico Travel .... 56, FYI 358
Tours to Paradise .... 75, FYI 189
ACRE
Gay Guided Tours of Israel .... 56, FYI 305
ADELAIDE
Air & Adventure Tours (AAA) ...... 46, FYI 312
ADIRONDACK MTNS
Adventures for Women .... 45, FYI 461
AEGEAN
Cruise World 52, 89
AEGEAN COAST
Adventure Bound Expeditions 45, 85
AFRICA
2Afrika 45, 83
Adventure Associates 45, 84
Adventure Bound Expeditions 45, 85
Archipelago Holidays 48, 87
Baobab Safari Co. 48
Beau Séjour .... 49, FYI 173
Beyond the Blue .... 49, FYI 307
Big Five Tours 49, 88
De Gay Krant Reisservice .... 52, FYI 256
Embassy Travel 54
Frauen Unterwegs 55, 91
Holigays 58, 92
Mantrav International 61
Our Family Abroad 65, 98
Silke's Travel .... 71, FYI 308
Toto Tours 75, 102
Travel Affair 75, 103
Travel Man 76, 104
Voyages & Expeditions 78, 106
Wild Women 79, 106
Woodswomen 81, 108
Worldwide Vacations Inc. 81
Xeno Tours/Mantours 81
AFRICA - NORTH
2Afrika 45, 83
Different Strokes Tours 53
Explorer Tours .... 55, FYI 190
Heritage Tours .... 58, FYI 283
ALASKA
AAD All About Destinations 45
Adventure Associates 45, 84
Alaska Women of the Wilderness 46, 86
Blue Moon Explorations 49
Cloud Canyon Backpacking 50, 88
Common Earth Adventures 51, 89
Izarra Cruises .... 59, FYI 502
Mercury Cruise & Tour 62
Ocean Voyager 64, 97

Oceanwomyn Kayaking .... 64, FYI 357
OutWest Adventures .... 66, FYI 455
Puffin Family Charters .... 68, FYI 363
Rainbow Adventures 68
Remote Possibilities .... 69, FYI 426
Thanks, Babs 74, 102
Toto Tours 75, 102
Travel Club, The 76, 103
T.R.I.P. Tours 76
Voyages & Expeditions 78, 106
Women in the Wilderness 81, 108
Women Sail Alaska .... 81, FYI 363
Woodswomen 81, 108
ALBERTA
Pangaea Expeditions .... 66, FYI 456
Rocky Mountaineer Railtours ...... 69, FYI 328
Super Natural Adventure Tours .. 73, FYI 328
ALBERTON GORGE
Pangaea Expeditions .... 66, FYI 456
ALGARVE
In Touch Holidays Ltd. 59
Pearl Selections/Welcome Abroad 67, 99
Uranian Travel .... 77, FYI 105
ALICE SPRINGS
Todd River Tours 75
ALPS
Alternative Holidays 47, 86
ALPS - FRENCH
French Touch .... 56, FYI 210
ALSACE
French Touch .... 56, FYI 210
AMAZON
Anderson International Tours ...... 47, FYI 346
Beyond Nirvana .... 49, FYI 342
Mercury Cruise & Tour 62
Stockler Expeditions 73
AMAZON RAINFOREST
Women in the Wilderness 81, 108
AMAZON RIVER
Amazon Tours & Cruises 47
Anderson International Tours ...... 47, FYI 346
Hanns Ebensten Travel 57, 92
AMERICAN RIVER
Mariah Wilderness Expeditions 61, 96
AMSTERDAM
Above & Beyond Tours 45, 83
Archipelago Holidays 48, 87
David's Trips and Tours 52, 89
De Gay Krant Reisservice .... 52, FYI 256
Frauen Unterwegs 55, 91
Gaygantic Tours 56
IMTC, Inc. 58, 94
L'Arc en Ciel Voyages 61, 94
Men on Vacation 62, 96
Our Family Abroad 65, 98
Pearl Selections/Welcome Abroad 67, 99

Rainbowworld Custom Tours .... 69, FYI 256
Robin Tyler's Women's Tours,
    Cruises & Events 69
RSVP Travel Productions/
    Club RSVP 70, 100
R&S Travel 70, 100
Stonewall Connection Travel & Tours 73, 101
Teddy Travel 74, 101
Toto Tours 75, 102
Tower Travel 75
Travel Club, The 76, 103
Travel Keys Tours 76, 104
Uranian Travel 77, 105
Wolff + Zink Travel Services 80, 106
Xeno Tours/Mantours 81
ZMAX Travel & Tours Inc. 82, 109
ANAHEIM
Tourmark's Gay Way America Tours .. 75, 103
ANDALUSIA
Heritage Tours .... 58, FYI 283
Terramundo Travels Int'l 74, 102
ANDES
Spirit Journeys 72, 101
Stonewall 69 .... 73, FYI 344
Women in the Wilderness 81, 108
ANDROS
Island Hoppers Tours .... 59, FYI 341
ANKARA
Heritage Tours .... 58, FYI 283
ANNAPOLIS
Sailing Affairs .... 70, FYI 468
ANTARCTICA
Big Five Tours 49, 88
Stonewall 69 .... 73, FYI 344
Voyages & Expeditions 78, 106
ANTIGUA
Mercury Cruise & Tour 62
Mundo Maya Turquesa 64
Tall Ship Adventures, Inc. .... 74, FYI 340
Windjammer Barefoot Cruises 79
ANTILLES
East-West Tours .... 53, FYI 322
ARAD
Gay Guided Tours of Israel .... 56, FYI 305
ARCHES NAT'L PARK
Lizard Head Backcountry Tours .. 61, FYI 495
ARCTIC
Big Five Tours 49, 88
Oceanwide Expeditions 64
ARCTIC CIRCLE
Archipelago Holidays 48, 87
ARGENTINA
Arcadia Turismo Internacional 48
Mercury Cruise & Tour 62
Mix Travel .... 63, FYI 344

8   FERRARI GUIDES' GAY TRAVEL A to Z - 18th EDITION

WHERE TO GO

DESTINATION INDEX

RSVP Travel Productions/Club RSVP 70, 100
Stonewall 69 .... 73, FYI 344
Terramundo Travels Int'l 74, 102

ARIZONA
Alaska Women of the Wilderness 46, 86
Canyon Calling Tours .... 50, FYI 366
Common Earth Adventures 51, 89
Desert Vision Tours 52
Grand Canyon Field Institute 57
Hanns Ebensten Travel 57, 92
Lizard Head Backcountry Tours .. 61, FYI 495
Passage to Utah .... 67, FYI 496
Rainbow Adventures 68
Scenic Air Tours .... 70, FYI 386
Sedona Rainbow Adventure Tours .... 71, FYI 367
Spirit Journeys 72, 101
Tourmark's Gay Way America Tours .. 75, 103
Women in Motion 80, 107
Woodswomen 81, 108

ARUBA
Worldwide Vacations Inc. 81

ASIA
Anywhere Travel 47
Beyond the Blue .... 49, FYI 307
China Voyages .... 50, FYI 176
Destination World 53, 90
Gaygantic Tours 56
Himalayan High Treks .... 58, FYI 186
Travel Man 76, 104
Voyages & Expeditions 78, 106
Woodswomen 81, 108
Worldwide Vacations Inc. 81

ASIA - EAST
Envoy Travel .... 54, FYI 176
L'Arc en Ciel Voyages 61, 94
Our Family Abroad 65, 98
Passport Travel Mgt, Inc. 67
R&S Travel 70, 100
Silke's Travel .... 71, FYI 308
Ventus Reisen 77

ASIA - SOUTH
Lois Lane Expeditions 61
Our Family Abroad 65, 98
Rainbow Adventures 68
Wild Women 79, 106
Woodswomen 81, 108

ASIA - SOUTHEAST
Adventures Unlimited .... 46, FYI 190
Adventures With Flair 46, 85
Beyond the Blue .... 49, FYI 307
BreakOut Tours .... 50, FYI 308
David's Trips and Tours 52, 89
Different Strokes Tours 53
Envoy Travel .... 54, FYI 176
Explorer Tours .... 55, FYI 190
Hanafi Tour and Travel .... 57, FYI 188
Hanns Ebensten Travel 57, 92

Jornada 59, 94
L'Arc en Ciel Voyages 61, 94
Otto Travel Hawaii 65
Our Family Abroad 65, 98
Passport Travel Mgt, Inc. 67
Pearl Selections/Welcome Abroad ... 67, 99
Progressive Travels 68, 99
R&S Travel 70, 100
Silken East Ltd. .... 71, FYI 186
Tours to Paradise .... 75, FYI 189
Travel Affair 75, 103
Travel Man 76, 104
VeloAsia Cycling Adventures 77, 105
Worldwide Vacations Inc. 81

ASPEN
De Gay Krant Reisservice .... 52, FYI 256
Lizard Head Backcountry Tours .. 61, FYI 495
OutWest Adventures .... 66, FYI 455
Travel Man 76, 104

ASWAN
2Afrika 45, 83

ATHABASCAR GLACIER
Pangaea Expeditions .... 66, FYI 456

ATHENS
Hellkamp Reisen 58, 92
IMTC, Inc. 58, 94
Windmills Travel & Tourism .... 80, FYI 239

ATLANTA
Destination Management .... 53, FYI 436
Tourmark's Gay Way America Tours .. 75, 103

ATLANTIC CITY
Sailing Affairs .... 70, FYI 468

ATLANTIC OCEAN
Best of Both Worlds .... FYI 474

ATLAS MTNS
Heritage Tours .... 58, FYI 283

AUCKLAND
Off the Map 65, 97

AUSTRALASIA
Beyond the Blue .... 49, FYI 307
Bushwise Women .... 50, FYI 318
G'day Tours .... 57, FYI 310

AUSTRALIA
Above & Beyond Tours 45, 83
Adventures With Flair 46, 85
Air & Adventure Tours (AAA) .... 46, FYI 312
Alaska Women of the Wilderness 46, 86
Alyson Adventures 47, 87
Archipelago Holidays 48, 87
Atlantis Events 48, 87
Atlantis Travel .... 48, FYI 232
Aust Pac Travel 48
Australian & New Zealand Travel Hdqtrs .. 48
Beyond the Blue .... 49, FYI 307
Bogong Horseback Adventures 49
BreakOut Tours .... 50, FYI 308

Destination Downunder .... 53, FYI 309
Destination World 53, 90
Gaygantic Tours 56
Gaylink Travel Services 56
Graylink Tours .... 57, FYI 310
G'day Tours .... 57, FYI 310
Hawkesbury Expeditions 58
Holidays at Sea/Sunquest 58
Holigays 58, 92
Inter-Rainbow Turismo .... 59, FYI 347
Izarra Cruises .... 59, FYI 502
Jornada 59, 94
Land Voyages 60
Landmark (South Pacific) Pty Ltd 60
L'Arc en Ciel Voyages 61, 94
Men on Vacation 62, 96
Mount Cook Tours 63
Mount'n Beach Safaris 63
North American Travel Specialists 64, 97
Off the Map 65, 97
Out Touring Australia 66
Oz Dive/Passport to Paradise 66
Pacific Experience 66
Pearl Selections/Welcome Abroad 67, 99
Silke's Travel .... 71, FYI 308
Sirius Adventures .... 72, FYI 314
Surfers Paradise Gay Vacations 73
Thanks, Babs 74, 102
Toto Tours 75, 102
Travel Affair 75, 103
Travel Man 76, 104
Undersea Expeditions, Inc. 77, 104
Voyages & Expeditions 78, 106
Wanderlust Ventures 78
Witchencroft 4WD & Bushwalking Tours .. 80, FYI 312
Xeno Tours/Mantours 81

AUSTRALIA - CENTRAL
Todd River Tours 75

AUSTRALIA - SOUTHERN
Southern Discovery Tours .... 72, FYI 315

AUSTRALIA - TOP END
Graylink Tours .... 57, FYI 310

AUSTRIA
Adventures for Women .... 45, FYI 461
Allegro Travel 46, 86
David's Trips and Tours 52, 89
Departures International .... 52, FYI 266
Gaygantic Tours 56
IMTC, Inc. 58, 94
L'Arc en Ciel Voyages 61, 94
Off the Map 65, 97
Our Family Abroad 65, 98
Rail Europe .... 68, FYI 286
R&S Travel 70, 100
Ski Connections .... 72, FYI 194
Travel Affair 75, 103
Wolff + Zink Travel Services 80, 106
Worldwide Vacations Inc. 81

FERRARI GUIDES' GAY TRAVEL A to Z - 18th EDITION

WHERE TO GO

DESTINATION INDEX

AYERS ROCK
Destination Downunder .... 53, FYI 309
AZORE ISLANDS
Paths Less Taken .... 67, FYI 264
BAHAMAS
Olivia Cruises & Resorts 65, 98
Pleasure Travel...Cruise Again Too! .. 68, FYI 339
Port Yacht Charters .... 68, FYI 339
Spirit Journeys 72, 101
Undersea Expeditions, Inc. 77, 104
BAHIA
De Gay Krant Reisservice .... 52, FYI 256
Stonewall 69 .... 73, FYI 344
BAJA MEXICO
AAD All About Destinations 45
Adventure Associates 45, 84
Alaska Women of the Wilderness 46, 86
Club Hommes/Worldguest .... 51, FYI 204
Earth, Wind & Water .... 53, FYI 354
Gay Baja Tours .... 56, FYI 358
Gay Mexico Travel .... 56, FYI 358
Mariah Wilderness Expeditions 61, 96
Oceanwomyn Kayaking .... 64, FYI 357
Paddling South & Saddling South 66, 99
Pangaea Expeditions .... 66, FYI 456
Rainbow Adventures 68
Toto Tours 75, 102
Wild Women 79, 106
Women in the Wilderness 81, 108
BALI
Adventure Associates 45, 84
Beyond the Blue .... 49, FYI 307
Explorer Tours .... 55, FYI 190
Hanafi Tour and Travel .... 57, FYI 188
Hellkamp Reisen 58, 92
Jornada 59, 94
Otto Travel Hawaii 65
Our Family Abroad 65, 98
R&S Travel 70, 100
Tours to Paradise .... 75, FYI 189
Travel Man 76, 104
BALTIC STATES
David's Trips and Tours 52, 89
BALTIMORE
Sailing Affairs .... 70, FYI 468
BANFF
Pangaea Expeditions .... 66, FYI 456
Super Natural Adventure Tours .. 73, FYI 328
BANGKOK
R&S Travel 70, 100
Tours to Paradise .... 75, FYI 189
BANIAS
Gay Guided Tours of Israel .... 56, FYI 305

BARBADOS
Club Le Bon .... 51, FYI 341
Mercury Cruise & Tour 62
RSVP Travel Productions/Club RSVP 70, 100
BARBUDA
Tall Ship Adventures, Inc. .... 74, FYI 340
BARCELONA
Gaygantic Tours 56
Heritage Tours .... 58, FYI 283
Pearl Selections/Welcome Abroad 67, 99
Xeno Tours/Mantours 81
BEARTOOTH WILDERNESS
OutWest Adventures .... 66, FYI 455
BEAUFORT
Best of Both Worlds .... FYI 474
BEERSHEBA
Gay Guided Tours of Israel .... 56, FYI 305
BEIJING
China Voyages .... 50, FYI 176
Envoy Travel .... 54, FYI 176
BELGIUM
IMTC, Inc. 58, 94
Jetman International Gay Travel 59
Rail Europe .... 68, FYI 286
Stonewall Connection Travel & Tours 73, 101
Vaarschool Grietje .... 77, FYI 258
BELIZE
Beyond Nirvana .... 49, FYI 342
Mariah Wilderness Expeditions 61, 96
Mundo Maya Turquesa 64
Undersea Expeditions, Inc. 77, 104
Wild Women 79, 106
Women in Motion 80, 107
BERLIN
Gaygantic Tours 56
Hellkamp Reisen 58, 92
IMTC, Inc. 58, 94
L'Arc en Ciel Voyages 61, 94
Pearl Selections/Welcome Abroad 67, 99
R&S Travel 70, 100
Teddy Travel 74, 101
Travel Keys Tours 76, 104
Wolff + Zink Travel Services 80, 106
BERMUDA
Mercury Cruise & Tour 62
Pied Piper Travel .... 67, FYI 338
BET SHEAN
Gay Guided Tours of Israel .... 56, FYI 305
BETHLEHEM
Gay Guided Tours of Israel .... 56, FYI 305
BHUTAN
Himalayan High Treks .... 58, FYI 186
BIG PINE
We Love the Florida Keys Visitor Center . 78, FYI 408

BIG SKY MONTANA
OutWest Adventures .... 66, FYI 455
BIG SUR
Travel Club, The 76, 103
BIMINI
Island Hoppers Tours .... 59, FYI 341
BITTERROOT MTN RANGE
Pangaea Expeditions .... 66, FYI 456
BLACKFOOT RIVER
Pangaea Expeditions .... 66, FYI 456
BLOCK ISLAND
Sailing Affairs .... 70, FYI 468
BLUE LAGOON
Olivia Cruises & Resorts 65, 98
Pleasure Travel...Cruise Again Too! .. 68, FYI 339
BLUE MTNS
Mount'n Beach Safaris 63
BOCA GRANDE
Whelk Women .... 79, FYI 402
BOCA RATON
Connections Tours 51
BOLIVIA
Our Family Abroad 65, 98
Silke's Travel .... 71, FYI 308
Terramundo Travels Int'l 74, 102
BORA BORA
Travel Man 76, 104
BORDEAUX
French Touch .... 56, FYI 210
BOSPHORUS
Adventure Bound Expeditions 45, 85
BOSTON
Hellkamp Reisen 58, 92
Sailing Affairs .... 70, FYI 468
BOTSWANA
2Afrika 45, 83
Baobab Safari Co. 48
Big Five Tours 49, 88
Embassy Travel 54
Travel Man 76, 104
Wild Women 79, 106
BRAZIL
Adventures With Flair 46, 85
Amazon Tours & Cruises 47
Anderson International Tours .... 47, FYI 346
Archipelago Holidays 48, 87
Beyond Nirvana .... 49, FYI 342
De Gay Krant Reisservice .... 52, FYI 256
Fiesta Tours .... 55, FYI 346
Hanns Ebensten Travel 57, 92
Inter-Rainbow Turismo .... 59, FYI 347
Mercury Cruise & Tour 62
Rio Roma Travel 69

10   FERRARI GUIDES' GAY TRAVEL A to Z - 18th EDITION

WHERE TO GO

DESTINATION INDEX

RSVP Travel Productions/Club RSVP 70, 100
Stockler Expeditions 73
Stonewall 69 .... 73, FYI 344
Sundance Travel 73
Terramundo Travels Int'l 74, 102
Travel Man 76, 104

BRIGHTON
Above & Beyond Tours 45, 83
R&S Travel 70, 100
Teddy Travel 74, 101

BRITAIN
Kenny Tours 60

BRITISH COLUMBIA
Blue Moon Explorations 49
Eat Quiche Tour & Travel Accomm. 54
Envision Charters .... 54, FYI 324
Fair Choices 55, 90
Izarra Cruises .... 59, FYI 502
Lodestar Adventures 61
Oceanwomyn Kayaking .... 64, FYI 357
Onn the Water 65
Progressive Travels 68, 99
Rainbow Adventures 68
Rocky Mountaineer Railtours ..... 69, FYI 328
Super Natural Adventure Tours .. 73, FYI 328
Toto Tours 75, 102
Travel Man 76, 104

BRITISH VIRGIN ISLANDS
Tall Ship Adventures, Inc. .... 74, FYI 340

BRITISH WEST INDIES
Travel Man 76, 104

BRITTANY
French Touch .... 56, FYI 210

BRUGES
IMTC, Inc. 58, 94

BRUSSELS
IMTC, Inc. 58, 94

BRYCE CANYON NAT'L PARK
Rainbow Country Tours & B&B ... 69, FYI 496

BUDAPEST
David's Trips and Tours 52, 89
Hellkamp Reisen 58, 92
IMTC, Inc. 58, 94
Kremlin Tours .... 60, FYI 266
Off the Map 65, 97
Wolff + Zink Travel Services 80, 106

BUENOS AIRES
Arcadia Turismo Internacional 48
Mix Travel .... 63, FYI 344
RSVP Travel Productions/Club RSVP 70, 100
Stonewall 69 .... 73, FYI 344

BURGUNDY
French Touch .... 56, FYI 210

BURMA
Otto Travel Hawaii 65

Silken East Ltd. .... 71, FYI 186
Travel Affair 75, 103

CABO SAN LUCAS
Fair Choices 55, 90
Gay Baja Tours .... 56, FYI 358

CAESAREA
Gay Guided Tours of Israel .... 56, FYI 305

CAIRNS
Australian & New Zealand Travel Hdqtrs .. 48
Beyond the Blue .... 49, FYI 307
Destination Downunder .... 53, FYI 309
Inter-Rainbow Turismo .... 59, FYI 347
Men on Vacation 62, 96
Off the Map 65, 97
Out Touring Australia 66
Pearl Selections/Welcome Abroad 67, 99
Silke's Travel .... 71, FYI 308
Witchencroft 4WD &
  Bushwalking Tours .... 80, FYI 312

CAIRO
2Afrika 45, 83
Allegro Travel 46, 86

CALIFORNIA
Ahwahnee Whitewater 46, 85
Call of the Wild 50
Common Earth Adventures 51, 89
Connections Tours 51
Destination Discovery .... 52, FYI 378
Fair Choices 55, 90
Gay Baja Tours .... 56, FYI 358
Hellkamp Reisen 58, 92
Inter-Rainbow Turismo .... 59, FYI 347
Lizard Head Backcountry Tours .. 61, FYI 495
Mariah Wilderness Expeditions 61, 96
Men on Vacation 62, 96
Merlyn's Journeys .... 63, FYI 370
Milu Tours 63
Off the Map 65, 97
Pearl Selections/Welcome Abroad 67, 99
RSVP Travel Productions/Club RSVP 70, 100
R&S Travel 70, 100
Scenic Air Tours .... 70, FYI 386
Ski Connections .... 72, FYI 194
Teddy Travel 74, 101
Tourmark's Gay Way America Tours .. 75, 103
Travel Club, The 76, 103
Victorian Home Walk .... 77, FYI 386
Women in Motion 80, 107
Woodswomen 81, 108
Xeno Tours/Mantours 81

CAMBODIA
Otto Travel Hawaii 65
Passport Travel Mgt, Inc. 67
Silken East Ltd. .... 71, FYI 186
VeloAsia Cycling Adventures 77, 105

CANADA
Beyond the Blue .... 49, FYI 307
Blue Moon Explorations 49

Connections Tours 51
Eat Quiche Tour & Travel Accommodations 54
Envision Charters .... 54, FYI 324
Fair Choices 55, 90
Frauen Unterwegs 55, 91
Hellkamp Reisen 58, 92
Lodestar Adventures 61
Lois Lane Expeditions 61
New England Vacation Tours 64
North American Travel Specialists 64, 97
Oceanwomyn Kayaking .... 64, FYI 357
Onn the Water 65
Pangaea Expeditions .... 66, FYI 456
Pied Piper Travel .... 67, FYI 338
Progressive Travels 68, 99
Rainbow Adventures 68
Rocky Mountaineer Railtours ..... 69, FYI 328
Stonewall Connection Travel & Tours 73, 101
Super Natural Adventure Tours .. 73, FYI 328
Thanks, Babs 74, 102
Travel Man 76, 104
Wild Women 79, 106
Wild Women Expeditions .... 79, FYI 330
Women in the Wilderness 81, 108

CANADA - MAJOR CITIES
North American Travel Specialists 64, 97

CANADA - NORTHERN
Wild Women Expeditions .... 79, FYI 330

CANADA - WESTERN
Lodestar Adventures 61
Rocky Mountaineer Railtours ..... 69, FYI 328
Super Natural Adventure Tours .. 73, FYI 328

CANADIAN ROCKIES
Lois Lane Expeditions 61
Super Natural Adventure Tours .. 73, FYI 328

CANARY ISLANDS
De Gay Krant Reisservice .... 52, FYI 256
Discus Travel 53
Milu Tours 63
Our Family Abroad 65, 98
Sapphire Travel & Tours 70

CANCUN
Advance Damron Vacations 45, 84
Fair Choices 55, 90
Gay Mexico Travel .... 56, FYI 358
Mundo Maya Turquesa 64
Olivia Cruises & Resorts 65, 98
Travel Affair 75, 103
Windjammer Barefoot Cruises 79

CANNES
French Touch .... 56, FYI 210

CANYON COUNTRY
Cloud Canyon Backpacking 50, 88
Common Earth Adventures 51, 89

CANYONLANDS
Desert Vision Tours 52
Rainbow Country Tours & B&B ... 69, FYI 496

FERRARI GUIDES' GAY TRAVEL A to Z - 18th EDITION   11

WHERE TO GO

DESTINATION INDEX

CANYONLANDS NAT'L PARK
Lizard Head Backcountry Tours .. 61, FYI 495
OutWest Adventures .... 66, FYI 455

CAPE COD
New England Vacation Tours 64

CAPE HATTERAS NAT'L SEA-SHORE
Best of Both Worlds .... FYI 474

CAPE LOOKOUT
Best of Both Worlds .... FYI 474

CAPE MAY
Sailing Affairs .... 70, FYI 468

CAPE TOWN
2Afrika 45, 83
Beau S,jour .... 49, FYI 173
David's Trips and Tours 52, 89
Mantrav International 61

CAPERNAUM
Gay Guided Tours of Israel .... 56, FYI 305

CAPITOL REEF NAT'L PARK
Rainbow Country Tours & B&B ... 69, FYI 496

CAPPADOCIA
Adventure Bound Expeditions 45, 85
Heritage Tours .... 58, FYI 283

CAPRI
Men on Bikes .... 62, FYI 248

CARIBBEAN
AAD All About Destinations 45
Advance Damron Vacations 45, 84
Anywhere Travel 47
Archipelago Holidays 48, 87
Atlantis Events 48, 87
Atlantis Travel .... 48, FYI 232
Beyond Nirvana .... 49, FYI 342
BVI Charters 50
Club Hommes/Worldguest .... 51, FYI 204
Club Le Bon .... 51, FYI 341
Connections Tours 51
Conson Holidays 51
Different Strokes Tours 53
East-West Tours .... 53, FYI 322
Fair Choices 55, 90
Five Star Travel Services 55
Gayventures 56
Hellkamp Reisen 58, 92
Island Hoppers Tours .... 59, FYI 341
Jetman International Gay Travel 59
Journeys by Sea Yacht Charters 60, FYI 337
Kam Tours Int'l 60
Mercury Cruise & Tour 62
Mundo Maya Turquesa 64
Ocean Voyager 64, 97
Oceanwide Expeditions 64
Olivia Cruises & Resorts 65, 98
Our Family Abroad 65, 98
Pied Piper Travel .... 67, FYI 338

Pleasure Travel...Cruise Again Too! .. 68, FYI 339
Port Yacht Charters .... 68, FYI 339
Rainbow Adventures 68
RSVP Travel Productions/Club RSVP 70, 100
R&S Travel 70, 100
Sea Sense .... 71, FYI 398
Spirit Journeys 72, 101
Tall Ship Adventures, Inc. .... 74, FYI 340
Terramundo Travels Int'l 74, 102
Thanks, Babs 74, 102
Toto Tours 75, 102
Travel Affair 75, 103
Travel Man 76, 104
Undersea Expeditions, Inc. 77, 104
VeloAsia Cycling Adventures 77, 105
Voyages & Expeditions 78, 106
Whitney Yacht Charters .... 79, FYI 340
Windjammer Barefoot Cruises 79
Women in Motion 80, 107
Women in the Wilderness 81, 108
Worldwide Vacations Inc. 81
Xeno Tours/Mantours 81
ZMAX Travel & Tours Inc. 82, 109

CARRIACOU
RSVP Travel Productions/Club RSVP 70, 100

CASABLANCA
Heritage Tours .... 58, FYI 283

CASCADES
Lizard Head Backcountry Tours .. 61, FYI 495

CASTRO AREA
Cruisin' the Castro .... 52, FYI 388

CAT ISLAND
Island Hoppers Tours .... 59, FYI 341

CATALINA
Tourmark's Gay Way America Tours .. 75, 103

CATARACT CANYON
Mariah Wilderness Expeditions 61, 96
OutWest Adventures .... 66, FYI 455

CENTRAL AMERICA
American Adventures 47
Archipelago Holidays 48, 87
Beyond Nirvana .... 49, FYI 342
Big Five Tours 49, 88
De Gay Krant Reisservice .... 52, FYI 256
Experience Plus 55, 90
Gayventures 56
Kam Tours Int'l 60
Mariah Wilderness Expeditions 61, 96
Milu Tours 63
Mundo Maya Turquesa 64
Ocean Voyager 64, 97
Olivia Cruises & Resorts 65, 98
Rainbow Adventures 68
R&R Eco Tours 70
Stockler Expeditions 73
Terramundo Travels Int'l 74, 102

Thanks, Babs 74, 102
Toto Tours 75, 102
Travel Club, The 76, 103
Undersea Expeditions, Inc. 77, 104
Way to Go Costa Rica .... 78, FYI 352
Wild Women 79, 106
Women in Motion 80, 107
Woodswomen 81, 108

CENTRAL EUROPE
Different Strokes Tours 53

CEPHALONIA
Peddlers .... 67, FYI 238

CHAMONIX
Ski Connections .... 72, FYI 194

CHANTILLY
Promenades de Style .... 68, FYI 212

CHESAPEAKE BAY
Sailing Affairs .... 70, FYI 468
Sea Sense .... 71, FYI 398

CHIANG MAI
R&S Travel 70, 100
Tours to Paradise .... 75, FYI 189

CHICAGO
Fair Choices 55, 90
Teddy Travel 74, 101

CHILE
Big Five Tours 49, 88
Mercury Cruise & Tour 62
Stonewall 69 .... 73, FYI 344
Terramundo Travels Int'l 74, 102

CHINA
China Voyages .... 50, FYI 176
Envoy Travel .... 54, FYI 176
Passport Travel Mgt, Inc. 67
Ventus Reisen 77

CHRISTCHURCH
Off the Map 65, 97

CLARK FORK RIVER
Pangaea Expeditions .... 66, FYI 456

CLEARWATER
It's Our Nature .... 59, FYI 416

COCOS ISLANDS
Undersea Expeditions, Inc. 77, 104

COLOGNE
Gaygantic Tours 56
R&S Travel 70, 100
Teddy Travel 74, 101
Wolff + Zink Travel Services 80, 106

COLOMBIA
Terramundo Travels Int'l 74, 102

COLORADO
Colorado Women in the Wilderness 51, 88
De Gay Krant Reisservice .... 52, FYI 256
Desert Vision Tours 52

WHERE TO GO

DESTINATION INDEX

Experience Plus 55, 90
Lizard Head Backcountry Tours .. 61, FYI 495
McNamara Ranch .... 62, FYI 396
Never Summer Nordic .... 64, FYI 396
OutWest Adventures .... 66, FYI 455
Travel Club, The 76, 103
Travel Man 76, 104
Women in the Wilderness 81, 108

COLORADO RIVER
Hanns Ebensten Travel 57, 92
Mariah Wilderness Expeditions 61, 96
OutWest Adventures .... 66, FYI 455

CONNECTICUT
Sailing Affairs .... 70, FYI 468
Sea Sense .... 71, FYI 398

CONSTANTINOPLE
Heritage Tours .... 58, FYI 283

COOK ISLANDS
Open Eye Tours & Photos .... 65, FYI 425

COPACABANA
Travel Man 76, 104

COPENHAGEN
Off the Map 65, 97
Pearl Selections/Welcome Abroad 67, 99
Wolff + Zink Travel Services 80, 106

COPPER CANYON
Earth, Wind & Water .... 53, FYI 354
Gay Mexico Travel .... 56, FYI 358
Thanks, Babs 74, 102

CORFU
Fine Travel & Yachting .... 55, FYI 240

COSTA DEL SOL
Heritage Tours .... 58, FYI 283

COSTA RICA
Adventure Associates 45, 84
American Adventures 47
Archipelago Holidays 48, 87
Big Five Tours 49, 88
De Gay Krant Reisservice .... 52, FYI 256
Experience Plus 55, 90
Kam Tours Int'l 60
Mariah Wilderness Expeditions 61, 96
Mercury Cruise & Tour 62
Milu Tours 63
Olivia Cruises & Resorts 65, 98
Rainbow Adventures 68
R&R Eco Tours 70
Stockler Expeditions 73
Terramundo Travels Int'l 74, 102
Thanks, Babs 74, 102
Toto Tours 75, 102
Travel Club, The 76, 103
Undersea Expeditions, Inc. 77, 104
Way to Go Costa Rica .... 78, FYI 352
Women in Motion 80, 107
Woodswomen 81, 108

COTE D'AZUR
French Touch .... 56, FYI 210

COZUMEL
Advance Damron Vacations 45, 84
Fair Choices 55, 90
Gay Mexico Travel .... 56, FYI 358
Mundo Maya Turquesa 64
Olivia Cruises & Resorts 65, 98

CRESTED BUTTE
Lizard Head Backcountry Tours .. 61, FYI 495

CRETE
Trek Out 76

CUBA
Mundo Maya Turquesa 64
VeloAsia Cycling Adventures 77, 105

CYCLADIC ISLANDS
Fine Travel & Yachting .... 55, FYI 240

CZECH REPUBLIC
Above & Beyond Tours 45, 83
David's Trips and Tours 52, 89
Frauen Unterwegs 55, 91
Hellkamp Reisen 58, 92
IMTC, Inc. 58, 94
Kremlin Tours .... 60, FYI 266
Off the Map 65, 97
Our Family Abroad 65, 98
R&S Travel 70, 100
Wolff + Zink Travel Services 80, 106

C.I.S. COUNTRIES
Kremlin Tours .... 60, FYI 266

DAINTREE
Silke's Travel .... 71, FYI 308

DALLAS
Tourmark's Gay Way America Tours .. 75, 103

DARWIN
Graylink Tours .... 57, FYI 310

DAYTONA BEACH
Connections Tours 51
Good Time Tours .... 57, FYI 412

DEAD SEA
Gay Guided Tours of Israel .... 56, FYI 305

DEATH VALLEY
Common Earth Adventures 51, 89

DENALI PARK
Alaska Women of the Wilderness 46, 86
Remote Possibilities .... 69, FYI 426

DENMARK
Frauen Unterwegs 55, 91
Off the Map 65, 97
Pearl Selections/Welcome Abroad 67, 99
Wolff + Zink Travel Services 80, 106

DENVER
Lizard Head Backcountry Tours .. 61, FYI 495

DISNEY WORLD
Good Time Tours .... 57, FYI 412

DISNEYLAND
Travel Club, The 76, 103

DOMINICAN REPUBLIC
R&S Travel 70, 100
Worldwide Vacations Inc. 81
Xeno Tours/Mantours 81

DUBAI
Travel Man 76, 104

DUBLIN
L'Arc en Ciel Voyages 61, 94
Travel Man 76, 104
Uranian Travel 77, 105

EASTER ISLAND
Hanns Ebensten Travel 57, 92

EASTERN EUROPE
Departures International .... 52, FYI 266
IMTC, Inc. 58, 94
Kremlin Tours .... 60, FYI 266
Off the Map 65, 97
Wolff + Zink Travel Services 80, 106

ECUADOR
Adventure Associates 45, 84
Big Five Tours 49, 88
Lois Lane Expeditions 61
Mercury Cruise & Tour 62
Terramundo Travels Int'l 74, 102

EDINBURGH
IMTC, Inc. 58, 94

EGYPT
2Afrika 45, 83
Allegro Travel 46, 86
Big Five Tours 49, 88
Frauen Unterwegs 55, 91
Global Affair 56
Hanns Ebensten Travel 57, 92
Our Family Abroad 65, 98
Rainbow Destinations 69
Travel Affair 75, 103
Woodswomen 81, 108
Zeus Tours & Yacht Cruises 81, 109

EILAT
Gay Guided Tours of Israel .... 56, FYI 305

EIN GEDI
Gay Guided Tours of Israel .... 56, FYI 305

EL SALVADOR
Mercury Cruise & Tour 62

ELBA
Frauen Unterwegs 55, 91

ELEUTHERA
Island Hoppers Tours .... 59, FYI 341

EMERALD ISLE
Best of Both Worlds .... FYI 474

FERRARI GUIDES' GAY TRAVEL A to Z - 18th EDITION

WHERE TO GO

ENGLAND
Above & Beyond Tours 45, 83
Anderson International Tours .... 47, FYI 346
Anywhere Travel 47
Best of Both Worlds Travel Ltd. 49
Beyond the Blue .... 49, FYI 307
Club Hommes/Worldguest .... 51, FYI 204
Cruise World 52, 89
European Luxury Hotel Barge Cruises54, FYI 208
Fair Choices 55, 90
Frauen Unterwegs 55, 91
Gaygantic Tours 56
Hellkamp Reisen 58, 92
IMTC, Inc. 58, 94
London Handling Ltd. 61, 96
L'Arc en Ciel Voyages 61, 94
Off the Map 65, 97
Our Family Abroad 65, 98
Pied Piper Travel .... 67, FYI 338
Rail Europe .... 68, FYI 286
RSVP Travel Productions/Club RSVP70, 100
R&S Travel 70, 100
Stonewall Connection Travel & Tours 73, 101
Teddy Travel 74, 101
Timeout Tours & Travel 74
Travel Keys Tours 76, 104
Virgin Vacations 78, 105
Zone One 82

ENGLAND - SOUTH
Best of Both Worlds Travel Ltd. 49

ENSENADA
Gay Baja Tours .... 56, FYI 358

EPERNAY
Promenades de Style .... 68, FYI 212

ESCALANTE CANYON
Lizard Head Backcountry Tours .. 61, FYI 495

ESTONIA
David's Trips and Tours 52, 89

ETHIOPIA
Adventure Bound Expeditions 45, 85

EUROPE
Above & Beyond Tours 45, 83
Adventures for Women .... 45, FYI 461
Adventures With Flair 46, 85
Alternative Holidays 47, 86
Alyson Adventures 47, 87
Amphitrion Holidays 47
Anderson International Tours .... 47, FYI 346
Anywhere Travel 47
Archipelago Holidays 48, 87
Atlantis Travel .... 48, FYI 232
Beyond the Blue .... 49, FYI 307
Club Hommes/Worldguest .... 51, FYI 204
Cruise World 52, 89
De Gay Krant Reisservice .... 52, FYI 256
Departures International .... 52, FYI 266
Destination World 53, 90

Discus Travel 53
East-West Tours .... 53, FYI 322
Easy Way 54
Embassy Travel 54
European Luxury Hotel Barge Cruises54, FYI 208
Eurway Tour & Cruise Club .... 54, FYI 238
Experience Plus 55, 90
Fair Choices 55, 90
Fine Travel & Yachting .... 55, FYI 240
Five Star Travel Services 55
Frauen Unterwegs 55, 91
French Touch .... 56, FYI 210
Gaygantic Tours 56
GPSC Charters .... 57, FYI 240
Hanns Ebensten Travel 57, 92
Hellkamp Reisen 58, 92
Holigays 58, 92
IMTC, Inc. 58, 94
In Touch Holidays Ltd. 59
Jetman International Gay Travel 59
Jornada 59, 94
Kenny Tours 60
London Handling Ltd. 61, 96
L'Arc en Ciel Voyages 61, 94
Men on Bikes .... 62, FYI 248
Men on Vacation 62, 96
Milu Tours 63
Ocean Voyager 64, 97
Oceanwide Expeditions 64
Olivia Cruises & Resorts 65, 98
Our Family Abroad 65, 98
Paths Less Taken .... 67, FYI 264
Pearl Selections/Welcome Abroad 67, 99
Peddlers .... 67, FYI 238
Pied Piper Travel .... 67, FYI 338
Players Express .... 67, FYI 458
Progressive Travels 68, 99
Rail Europe .... 68, FYI 286
Rainbow Adventures 68
Rainbowworld Custom Tours .... 69, FYI 256
Robin Tyler's Women's Tours, Cruises & Events 69
RSVP Travel Productions/Club RSVP70, 100
Sapphire Travel & Tours 70
Sea Sense .... 71, FYI 398
Sensations .... 71, FYI 292
Ski Connections .... 72, FYI 194
Sounds & Furies .... 72, FYI 244
Spirit Journeys 72, 101
Stonewall Connection Travel & Tours 73, 101
Syosset Travel 74
Teddy Travel 74, 101
Terramundo Travels Int'l 74, 102
Thanks, Babs 74, 102
Timeout Tours & Travel 74
Toto Tours 75, 102
Tower Travel 75
Travel Affair 75, 103
Travel Keys Tours 76, 104
Travel Man 76, 104

Trek Out 76
Uranian Travel 77, 105
Vaarschool Grietje .... 77, FYI 258
Ventus Reisen 77
Virgin Vacations 78, 105
Voyages & Expeditions 78, 106
Windmills Travel & Tourism .... 80, FYI 239
Wolff + Zink Travel Services 80, 106
Women in Motion 80, 107
Women in the Wilderness 81, 108
Woodswomen 81, 108
Worldwide Vacations Inc. 81
Xeno Tours/Mantours 81
Zeus Tours & Yacht Cruises 81, 109
Zipper Travel Association .... 82, FYI 252
ZMAX Travel & Tours Inc. 82, 109
Zone One 82

EUROPE - CAPITALS
Above & Beyond Tours 45, 83
Virgin Vacations 78, 105

EUROPE - CENTRAL
Different Strokes Tours 53

EUROPE - EASTERN
David's Trips and Tours 52, 89
Departures International .... 52, FYI 266
IMTC, Inc. 58, 94
Kremlin Tours .... 60, FYI 266
Off the Map 65, 97
Wolff + Zink Travel Services 80, 106

EXUMA
Island Hoppers Tours .... 59, FYI 341

FAR EAST
Anywhere Travel 47
China Voyages .... 50, FYI 176

FEZ
Heritage Tours .... 58, FYI 283

FIJI
Above & Beyond Tours 45, 83
Beyond the Blue .... 49, FYI 307
BreakOut Tours .... 50, FYI 308
Destination Downunder .... 53, FYI 309
Destination World 53, 90
G'day Tours .... 57, FYI 310
Men on Vacation 62, 96
Oz Dive/Passport to Paradise 66
Silke's Travel .... 71, FYI 308
Travel Man 76, 104
Undersea Expeditions, Inc. 77, 104

FINLAND
Allegro Travel 46, 86
Departures International .... 52, FYI 266
Frauen Unterwegs 55, 91
Off the Map 65, 97
Women in the Wilderness 81, 108

FIRE ISLAND
Travel Club, The 76, 103
Travel Man 76, 104

WHERE TO GO

DESTINATION INDEX

FLORENCE
Allegro Travel 46, 86
Off the Map 65, 97
Travel Affair 75, 103
Zipper Travel Association .... 82, FYI 252

FLORIANOPOLIS
RSVP Travel Productions/Club RSVP 70, 100

FLORIDA
Aquatic Adventures Charter Service . 47, FYI 404
Archipelago Holidays 48, 87
Clione Charters .... 50, FYI 408
Connections Tours 51
Fair Choices 55, 90
Good Time Tours .... 57, FYI 412
Hellkamp Reisen 58, 92
In Touch Holidays Ltd. 59
Inter-Rainbow Turismo .... 59, FYI 347
Island Hoppers Tours .... 59, FYI 341
It's Our Nature .... 59, FYI 416
Men on Vacation 62, 96
Milu Tours 63
Olivia Cruises & Resorts 65, 98
Pearl Selections/Welcome Abroad ... 67, 99
Port Yacht Charters .... 68, FYI 339
RSVP Travel Productions/Club RSVP 70, 100
R&S Travel 70, 100
Sapphire Travel & Tours 70
Sea Sense .... 71, FYI 398
Sensations .... 71, FYI 292
Spirit Journeys 72, 101
Teddy Travel 74, 101
Tourmark's Gay Way America Tours .. 75, 103
Uranian Travel 77, 105
We Love the Florida Keys Visitor Center . 78, FYI 408
Whelk Women .... 79, FYI 402
Xeno Tours/Mantours 81
ZMAX Travel & Tours Inc. 82, 109

FLORIDA KEYS
Aquatic Adventures Charter Service . 47, FYI 404
Good Time Tours .... 57, FYI 412
Island Hoppers Tours .... 59, FYI 341
Sea Sense .... 71, FYI 398
We Love the Florida Keys Visitor Center . 78, FYI 408

FLORIDA - EAST COAST
Good Time Tours .... 57, FYI 412

FLORIDA - WEST COAST
Good Time Tours .... 57, FYI 412

FONTAINEBLEAU
Promenades de Style .... 68, FYI 212

FORBIDDEN CITY
Envoy Travel .... 54, FYI 176

FORT LAUDERDALE
Archipelago Holidays 48, 87

Hellkamp Reisen 58, 92
R&S Travel 70, 100

FRANCE
Above & Beyond Tours 45, 83
Alternative Holidays 47, 86
Alyson Adventures 47, 87
Club Hommes/Worldguest .... 51, FYI 204
Cruise World 52, 89
David's Trips and Tours 52, 89
De Gay Krant Reisservice .... 52, FYI 256
Different Strokes Tours 53
Easy Way 54
European Luxury Hotel Barge Cruises 54, FYI 208
Experience Plus 55, 90
Fair Choices 55, 90
Frauen Unterwegs 55, 91
French Touch .... 56, FYI 210
Gaygantic Tours 56
GPSC Charters .... 57, FYI 240
Hellkamp Reisen 58, 92
IMTC, Inc. 58, 94
Jetman International Gay Travel 59
L'Arc en Ciel Voyages 61, 94
Men on Vacation 62, 96
Mistral Tours .... 63, FYI 203
Off the Map 65, 97
Our Family Abroad 65, 98
Pearl Selections/Welcome Abroad ... 67, 99
Progressive Travels 68, 99
Rail Europe .... 68, FYI 286
RSVP Travel Productions/Club RSVP 70, 100
R&S Travel 70, 100
Sea Sense .... 71, FYI 398
Ski Connections .... 72, FYI 194
Stonewall Connection Travel & Tours 73, 101
Teddy Travel 74, 101
Travel Affair 75, 103
Travel Keys Tours 76, 104
Uranian Travel 77, 105
Vaarschool Grietje .... 77, FYI 258
Women in Motion 80, 107
Xeno Tours/Mantours 81

FRANCE - CHAMPAGNE COUNTRY
Promenades de Style .... 68, FYI 212

FRANK CHURCH WILDERNESS
Pangaea Expeditions .... 66, FYI 456

FRANKFURT
IMTC, Inc. 58, 94

FRENCH POLYNESIA
Australian & New Zealand Travel Hdqtrs .. 48
G'day Tours .... 57, FYI 310
Oz Dive/Passport to Paradise 66
Travel Man 76, 104
Worldwide Vacations Inc. 81

FRENCH RIVIERA
Easy Way 54

FT LAUDERDALE
Connections Tours 51
Olivia Cruises & Resorts 65, 98
Pearl Selections/Welcome Abroad 67, 99
Teddy Travel 74, 101

GALAPAGOS
Adventure Associates 45, 84
Big Five Tours 49, 88
East-West Tours .... 53, FYI 322
Hanns Ebensten Travel 57, 92
Mercury Cruise & Tour 62
Stockler Expeditions 73
Undersea Expeditions, Inc. 77, 104
Woodswomen 81, 108

GALVESTON
After Five Charters .... 46, FYI 492

GAMBIA
Frauen Unterwegs 55, 91

GARNET - GHOST TOWN
Ten Thousand Waves .... 74, FYI 457

GENOA
Allegro Travel 46, 86

GEORGIA
Destination Management .... 53, FYI 436
Tourmark's Gay Way America Tours .. 75, 103

GERMANY
Above & Beyond Tours 45, 83
Fair Choices 55, 90
Frauen Unterwegs 55, 91
Gaygantic Tours 56
Hellkamp Reisen 58, 92
IMTC, Inc. 58, 94
Jetman International Gay Travel 59
L'Arc en Ciel Voyages 61, 94
Milu Tours 63
Our Family Abroad 65, 98
Pearl Selections/Welcome Abroad ... 67, 99
Rail Europe .... 68, FYI 286
R&S Travel 70, 100
Ski Connections .... 72, FYI 194
Stonewall Connection Travel & Tours 73, 101
Teddy Travel 74, 101
Travel Affair 75, 103
Travel Club, The 76, 103
Travel Keys Tours 76, 104
Wolff + Zink Travel Services 80, 106
Worldwide Vacations Inc. 81

GLACIER BAY
Remote Possibilities .... 69, FYI 426

GLACIER COUNTRY
Wild Rockies Tours .... 79, FYI 457

GLACIER NAT'L PARK
Pangaea Expeditions .... 66, FYI 456
Rainbow Adventures 68

GOING TO THE SUN ROAD
Pangaea Expeditions .... 66, FYI 456

FERRARI GUIDES' GAY TRAVEL A to Z - 18th EDITION   15

WHERE TO GO

GOLAN HEIGHTS
Gay Guided Tours of Israel .... 56, FYI 305

GOLD COUNTRY - CALIF
Merlyn's Journeys .... 63, FYI 370

GOLD RUSH COUNTRY
Mariah Wilderness Expeditions 61, 96

GRAN CANARIA
De Gay Krant Reisservice .... 52, FYI 256
Discus Travel 53
Hellkamp Reisen 58, 92
In Touch Holidays Ltd. 59
Pearl Selections/Welcome Abroad 67, 99
R&S Travel 70, 100
Sapphire Travel & Tours 70
Sensations .... 71, FYI 292
Uranian Travel 77, 105
Xeno Tours/Mantours 81

GRANADA
Heritage Tours .... 58, FYI 283

GRAND BAHAMA
Island Hoppers Tours .... 59, FYI 341

GRAND CANYON
Common Earth Adventures 51, 89
Grand Canyon Field Institute 57
Hanns Ebensten Travel 57, 92
Lizard Head Backcountry Tours .. 61, FYI 495
Rainbow Adventures 68
Scenic Air Tours .... 70, FYI 386
Sedona Rainbow Adventure Tours .... 71, FYI 367
Toto Tours 75, 102
Tourmark's Gay Way America Tours .. 75, 103

GRAND CAYMAN
Olivia Cruises & Resorts 65, 98

GRAND TETONS
Adventure Associates 45, 84
Bar H Ranch .... 48, FYI 506

GREAT BARRIER REEF
Above & Beyond Tours 45, 83
Atlantis Events 48, 87
Australian & New Zealand Travel Hdqtrs .. 48
Beyond the Blue .... 49, FYI 307
Destination Downunder .... 53, FYI 309
G'day Tours .... 57, FYI 310
Izarra Cruises .... 59, FYI 502
Men on Vacation 62, 96
Off the Map 65, 97
Out Touring Australia 66
Oz Dive/Passport to Paradise 66
Pearl Selections/Welcome Abroad 67, 99
Silke's Travel .... 71, FYI 308

GREECE
Adventure Associates 45, 84
Adventures With Flair 46, 85
Amphitrion Holidays 47
Beyond the Blue .... 49, FYI 307

Cruise World 52, 89
Discus Travel 53
East-West Tours .... 53, FYI 322
Eurway Tour & Cruise Club .... 54, FYI 238
Fine Travel & Yachting .... 55, FYI 240
Frauen Unterwegs 55, 91
GPSC Charters .... 57, FYI 240
Hanns Ebensten Travel 57, 92
Hellkamp Reisen 58, 92
IMTC, Inc. 58, 94
In Touch Holidays Ltd. 59
Jetman International Gay Travel 59
L'Arc en Ciel Voyages 61, 94
Milu Tours 63
Ocean Voyager 64, 97
Olivia Cruises & Resorts 65, 98
Our Family Abroad 65, 98
Pearl Selections/Welcome Abroad 67, 99
Peddlers .... 67, FYI 238
Rainbow Adventures 68
R&S Travel 70, 100
Sapphire Travel & Tours 70
Sea Sense .... 71, FYI 398
Sensations .... 71, FYI 292
Spirit Journeys 72, 101
Stonewall Connection Travel & Tours 73, 101
Sundance Travel 73
Syosset Travel 74
Thanks, Babs 74, 102
Trek Out 76
Uranian Travel 77, 105
Windmills Travel & Tourism .... 80, FYI 239
Women in the Wilderness 81, 108
Xeno Tours/Mantours 81
Zeus Tours & Yacht Cruises 81, 109

GREEK ISLANDS
Adventures With Flair 46, 85
Amphitrion Holidays 47
Eurway Tour & Cruise Club .... 54, FYI 238
Peddlers .... 67, FYI 238
Players Express .... 67, FYI 458
Thanks, Babs 74, 102
Uranian Travel 77, 105
Voyages & Expeditions 78, 106
Windmills Travel & Tourism .... 80, FYI 239
Worldwide Vacations Inc. 81

GRENADA
RSVP Travel Productions/Club RSVP 70, 100
Tall Ship Adventures, Inc. .... 74, FYI 340
Toto Tours 75, 102
Windjammer Barefoot Cruises 79

GRENADINES
Journeys by Sea Yacht Charters 60, FYI 337
Tall Ship Adventures, Inc. .... 74, FYI 340

GUADALAJARA
Beyond Nirvana .... 49, FYI 342
Gay Mexico Travel .... 56, FYI 358
South of the Border Tour & Travel 72, FYI 358

GUANAJUATO
Gay Mexico Travel .... 56, FYI 358

GUATEMALA
Mundo Maya Turquesa 64
Terramundo Travels Int'l 74, 102
Women in Motion 80, 107

GULF ISLANDS
Envision Charters .... 54, FYI 324

HAIFA
Gay Guided Tours of Israel .... 56, FYI 305

HAMBURG
R&S Travel 70, 100
Wolff + Zink Travel Services 80, 106

HARARE
2Afrika 45, 83

HARBOUR ISLAND
Island Hoppers Tours .... 59, FYI 341

HAVANA
Mundo Maya Turquesa 64

HAWAII
Alaska Women of the Wilderness 46, 86
Beyond Nirvana .... 49, FYI 342
Club Hommes/Worldguest .... 51, FYI 204
Dave's Island Pride Driver, Guide 52, FYI 427
Fair Choices 55, 90
G'day Tours .... 57, FYI 310
Hellkamp Reisen 58, 92
Kayak Historical Discovery Tours 60, FYI 420
Liquid Crystal Divers .... 60, FYI 422
L'Arc en Ciel Voyages 61, 94
Matt's Rainbow Tours .... 62, FYI 421
Maui Surfing School .... 62, FYI 422
Olivia Cruises & Resorts 65, 98
Open Eye Tours & Photos .... 65, FYI 425
Pacific Ocean Holidays .... 66, FYI 427
Pearl Selections/Welcome Abroad 67, 99
Pied Piper Travel .... 67, FYI 338
Pleasant Holidays 67
Remote Possibilities .... 69, FYI 426
Royal Hawaiian Weddings .... 70, FYI 425
RSVP Travel Productions/Club RSVP 70, 100
R&S Travel 70, 100
Teddy Travel 74, 101
Thanks, Babs 74, 102
Toto Tours 75, 102
Travel Man 76, 104
Tropical Tune-ups 76
Women in Motion 80, 107
Woodswomen 81, 108

HAWAII - BIG ISLAND
Kayak Historical Discovery Tours 60, FYI 420
Matt's Rainbow Tours .... 62, FYI 421
Open Eye Tours & Photos .... 65, FYI 425
Pacific Ocean Holidays .... 66, FYI 427
Pleasant Holidays 67
RSVP Travel Productions/Club RSVP 70, 100
Tropical Tune-ups 76

16   FERRARI GUIDES' GAY TRAVEL A to Z - 18th EDITION

WHERE TO GO

DESTINATION INDEX

HEIDELBERG
IMTC, Inc. 58, 94
HELSINKI
Allegro Travel 46, 86
HILO
Olivia Cruises & Resorts 65, 98
HOLLAND
Our Family Abroad 65, 98
Rainboworld Custom Tours .... 69, FYI 256
HOLLYWOOD - FL
Connections Tours 51
HONA
Olivia Cruises & Resorts 65, 98
HONDURAS
Terramundo Travels Int'l 74, 102
Undersea Expeditions, Inc. 77, 104
Women in the Wilderness 81, 108
Woodswomen 81, 108
HONG KONG
Allegro Travel 46, 86
China Voyages .... 50, FYI 176
Envoy Travel .... 54, FYI 176
L'Arc en Ciel Voyages 61, 94
Our Family Abroad 65, 98
Passport Travel Mgt, Inc. 67
R&S Travel 70, 100
HONOLULU
Dave's Island Pride Driver, Guide 52, FYI 427
Pacific Ocean Holidays .... 66, FYI 427
Pearl Selections/Welcome Abroad 67, 99
Pleasant Holidays 67
RSVP Travel Productions/Club RSVP 70, 100
HONOLULU BAY
Liquid Crystal Divers .... 60, FYI 422
HOUSTON
After Five Charters .... 46, FYI 492
Tourmark's Gay Way America Tours .. 75, 103
HUNGARY
David's Trips and Tours 52, 89
Frauen Unterwegs 55, 91
Hellkamp Reisen 58, 92
IMTC, Inc. 58, 94
Kremlin Tours .... 60, FYI 266
Off the Map 65, 97
Our Family Abroad 65, 98
Wolff + Zink Travel Services 80, 106
IBERIA
Terramundo Travels Int'l 74, 102
IBIZA
Discus Travel 53
Hellkamp Reisen 58, 92
Heritage Tours .... 58, FYI 283
In Touch Holidays Ltd. 59
Pearl Selections/Welcome Abroad 67, 99
R&S Travel 70, 100

Sapphire Travel & Tours 70
Sensations .... 71, FYI 292
Uranian Travel 77, 105
Xeno Tours/Mantours 81
ICELAND
L'Arc en Ciel Voyages 61, 94
Off the Map 65, 97
IDAHO
Bar H Ranch .... 48, FYI 506
Lizard Head Backcountry Tours .. 61, FYI 495
Mariah Wilderness Expeditions 61, 96
Middle Fork River Expeditions 63
Pangaea Expeditions .... 66, FYI 456
Wild Women 79, 106
IGUAÇU FALLS
Mix Travel .... 63, FYI 344
Stockler Expeditions 73
Stonewall 69 .... 73, FYI 344
ILLINOIS
Fair Choices 55, 90
Teddy Travel 74, 101
Tourmark's Gay Way America Tours .. 75, 103
INDIA
Big Five Tours 49, 88
Himalayan High Treks .... 58, FYI 186
Our Family Abroad 65, 98
INDIAN RUINS
Pangaea Expeditions .... 66, FYI 456
INDONESIA
Adventure Associates 45, 84
Beyond the Blue .... 49, FYI 307
David's Trips and Tours 52, 89
Different Strokes Tours 53
Envoy Travel .... 54, FYI 176
Explorer Tours .... 55, FYI 190
G'day Tours .... 57, FYI 310
Hanafi Tour and Travel .... 57, FYI 188
Hanns Ebensten Travel 57, 92
Hellkamp Reisen 58, 92
Jornada 59, 94
Passport Travel Mgt, Inc. 67
R&S Travel 70, 100
Tours to Paradise .... 75, FYI 189
Travel Man 76, 104
VeloAsia Cycling Adventures 77, 105
INNSBRUCK
Ski Connections .... 72, FYI 194
INTRACOASTAL WATERWAY
Best of Both Worlds .... FYI 474
IRELAND
Frauen Unterwegs 55, 91
Kenny Tours 60
L'Arc en Ciel Voyages 61, 94
Off the Map 65, 97
Rail Europe .... 68, FYI 286
Sounds & Furies .... 72, FYI 244

Travel Man 76, 104
Uranian Travel 77, 105
Woodswomen 81, 108
ISLA CONVOY
Mundo Maya Turquesa 64
ISLA HOLBOX
Mundo Maya Turquesa 64
ISLA MARGARITA
Worldwide Vacations Inc. 81
ISLA MUJERES
Advance Damron Vacations 45, 84
Club Le Bon .... 51, FYI 341
Mundo Maya Turquesa 64
ISLAMORADA
We Love the Florida Keys Visitor Center . 78, FYI 408
ISLAND DESTINATIONS
Pacific Ocean Holidays .... 66, FYI 427
Tall Ship Adventures, Inc. .... 74, FYI 340
We Love the Florida Keys Visitor Center . 78, FYI 408
Windjammer Barefoot Cruises 79
Windmills Travel & Tourism .... 80, FYI 239
ISRAEL
De Gay Krant Reisservice .... 52, FYI 256
Gay Guided Tours of Israel .... 56, FYI 305
L'Arc en Ciel Voyages 61, 94
Toto Tours 75, 102
Woodswomen 81, 108
Zeus Tours & Yacht Cruises 81, 109
ISTANBUL
Adventure Bound Expeditions 45, 85
Heritage Tours .... 58, FYI 283
IMTC, Inc. 58, 94
Teddy Travel 74, 101
Travel Man 76, 104
ITALY
Allegro Travel 46, 86
Cruise World 52, 89
Easy Way 54
Experience Plus 55, 90
Fair Choices 55, 90
Frauen Unterwegs 55, 91
Gaygantic Tours 56
GPSC Charters .... 57, FYI 240
Hellkamp Reisen 58, 92
IMTC, Inc. 58, 94
Jetman International Gay Travel 59
L'Arc en Ciel Voyages 61, 94
Men on Bikes .... 62, FYI 248
Off the Map 65, 97
Our Family Abroad 65, 98
Progressive Travels 68, 99
Rail Europe .... 68, FYI 286
Rainbow Adventures 68
Stonewall Connection Travel & Tours 73, 101
Teddy Travel 74, 101

FERRARI GUIDES' GAY TRAVEL A to Z - 18th EDITION

WHERE TO GO

DESTINATION INDEX

Travel Affair 75, 103
Woodswomen 81, 108
Xeno Tours/Mantours 81
Zeus Tours & Yacht Cruises 81, 109
Zipper Travel Association .... 82, FYI 252

IXTAPA
Gay Mexico Travel .... 56, FYI 358

JACKSON HOLE
Bar H Ranch .... 48, FYI 506

JAMAICA
Beyond Nirvana .... 49, FYI 342
Fair Choices 55, 90
Island Hoppers Tours .... 59, FYI 341
Travel Man 76, 104

JAPAN
L'Arc en Ciel Voyages 61, 94
Passport Travel Mgt, Inc. 67

JASPER
Super Natural Adventure Tours .. 73, FYI 328

JASPER NAT'L PARK
Pangaea Expeditions .... 66, FYI 456

JAVA
Archipelago Holidays 48, 87

JERICHO
Gay Guided Tours of Israel .... 56, FYI 305

JERUSALEM
Gay Guided Tours of Israel .... 56, FYI 305

JOHANNESBURG
2Afrika 45, 83
David's Trips and Tours 52, 89
Mantrav International 61

JORDAN
Ventus Reisen 77

JUNEAU
Women Sail Alaska .... 81, FYI 363

KAKADU
Sirius Adventures .... 72, FYI 314

KAMPUCHIA
Passport Travel Mgt, Inc. 67

KANGAROO ISLAND
Air & Adventure Tours (AAA) ...... 46, FYI 312

KAUAI
Olivia Cruises & Resorts 65, 98
Open Eye Tours & Photos .... 65, FYI 425
Pacific Ocean Holidays .... 66, FYI 427
Pleasant Holidays 67
RSVP Travel Productions/Club RSVP70, 100
Toto Tours 75, 102
Women in Motion 80, 107

KEALAKEKUA BAY
Kayak Historical Discovery Tours 60, FYI 420

KENAI FJORDS
Alaska Women of the Wilderness 46, 86

Puffin Family Charters .... 68, FYI 363

KENYA
2Afrika 45, 83
Adventure Associates 45, 84
Baobab Safari Co. 48
Big Five Tours 49, 88
De Gay Krant Reisservice .... 52, FYI 256
Embassy Travel 54
Our Family Abroad 65, 98
Travel Affair 75, 103
Xeno Tours/Mantours 81

KEY LARGO
We Love the Florida Keys Visitor Center . 78, FYI 408

KEY WEST
Clione Charters .... 50, FYI 408
Connections Tours 51
Good Time Tours .... 57, FYI 412
Hellkamp Reisen 58, 92
Island Hoppers Tours .... 59, FYI 341
Olivia Cruises & Resorts 65, 98
Pearl Selections/Welcome Abroad 67, 99
RSVP Travel Productions/Club RSVP70, 100
Teddy Travel 74, 101
Tourmark's Gay Way America Tours .. 75, 103
Travel Club, The 76, 103
Uranian Travel 77, 105
We Love the Florida Keys Visitor Center . 78, FYI 408
Xeno Tours/Mantours 81
ZMAX Travel & Tours Inc. 82, 109

KIEV
Departures International .... 52, FYI 266

KILIMANJARO
2Afrika 45, 83

KILLARNEY PROVINCIAL PARK
Wild Women Expeditions .... 79, FYI 330

KIMBERLEY MTNS
Silke's Travel .... 71, FYI 308
Sirius Adventures .... 72, FYI 314

KINGS RIVER
Mariah Wilderness Expeditions 61, 96

KINGSTON
Island Hoppers Tours .... 59, FYI 341

KOH SAMUI
R&S Travel 70, 100

KOREA
L'Arc en Ciel Voyages 61, 94
Passport Travel Mgt, Inc. 67

KRUGER NAT'L PARK
2Afrika 45, 83

LAGO ARGENTINO
Mix Travel .... 63, FYI 344
Stonewall 69 .... 73, FYI 344

LAGUNA BEACH
Tourmark's Gay Way America Tours .. 75, 103

LAKE CHAPALA
South of the Border Tour & Travel72, FYI 358

LAKE HURON
Wild Women Expeditions .... 79, FYI 330

LAKE MICHIGAN
Sea Sense .... 71, FYI 398

LAKE PLACID
Eclectic Excursions .... 54, FYI 466

LAKE TAHOE
Common Earth Adventures 51, 89
Merlyn's Journeys .... 63, FYI 370
Ski Connections .... 72, FYI 194

LANAI
Liquid Crystal Divers .... 60, FYI 422

LAOS
Otto Travel Hawaii 65
Passport Travel Mgt, Inc. 67
Silken East Ltd. .... 71, FYI 186

LAPLAND
Women in the Wilderness 81, 108

LAS VEGAS
Players Express .... 67, FYI 458
R&S Travel 70, 100
Tourmark's Gay Way America Tours .. 75, 103
Women in Motion 80, 107

LATIN AMERICA
Adventures With Flair 46, 85
Amazon Tours & Cruises 47
American Adventures 47
Anderson International Tours ...... 47, FYI 346
Archipelago Holidays 48, 87
Beyond Nirvana .... 49, FYI 342
Big Five Tours 49, 88
De Gay Krant Reisservice .... 52, FYI 256
Doin' It Right - in Puerto Vallarta 53
Earth, Wind & Water .... 53, FYI 354
Experience Plus 55, 90
Fair Choices 55, 90
Fiesta Tours .... 55, FYI 346
Gay Baja Tours .... 56, FYI 358
Gay Mexico Travel .... 56, FYI 358
Gayventures 56
Hanns Ebensten Travel 57, 92
Hawk, I'm Your Sister .... 58, FYI 463
Inter-Rainbow Turismo .... 59, FYI 347
Journeys by Sea Yacht Charters 60, FYI 337
Kam Tours Int'l 60
Mariah Wilderness Expeditions 61, 96
Milu Tours 63
Mix Travel .... 63, FYI 344
MTC (Multinational Travel Corp) 64
Mundo Maya Turquesa 64
Oceanwomyn Kayaking .... 64, FYI 357
Olivia Cruises & Resorts 65, 98

18   FERRARI GUIDES' GAY TRAVEL A to Z - 18th EDITION

WHERE TO GO

DESTINATION INDEX

Our Family Abroad 65, 98
Paddling South & Saddling South 66, 99
Pangaea Expeditions .... 66, FYI 456
Players Express .... 67, FYI 458
Pleasant Holidays 67
Port Yacht Charters .... 68, FYI 339
Rainbow Adventures 68
Rio Roma Travel 69
RSVP Travel Productions/Club RSVP70, 100
R&R Eco Tours 70
R&S Travel 70, 100
Silke's Travel .... 71, FYI 308
South of the Border Tour & Travel72, FYI 358
Spirit Journeys 72, 101
Stag Travel & Tours 73
Stockler Expeditions 73
Stonewall 69 .... 73, FYI 344
Sundance Travel 73
Terramundo Travels Int'l 74, 102
Thanks, Babs 74, 102
Toto Tours 75, 102
Tours to Paradise .... 75, FYI 189
Travel Affair 75, 103
Travel Club, The 76, 103
Travel Man 76, 104
Undersea Expeditions, Inc. 77, 104
VeloAsia Cycling Adventures 77, 105
Voyages & Expeditions 78, 106
Way to Go Costa Rica .... 78, FYI 352
Wild Women 79, 106
Women in Motion 80, 107
Women in the Wilderness 81, 108
Woodswomen 81, 108
Xeno Tours/Mantours 81

LATVIA
David's Trips and Tours 52, 89

LESBOS
Milu Tours 63
Pearl Selections/Welcome Abroad 67, 99
Windmills Travel & Tourism .... 80, FYI 239

LESOTHO
2Afrika 45, 83

LISBON
Hellkamp Reisen 58, 92
Heritage Tours .... 58, FYI 283

LITHUANIA
Allegro Travel 46, 86
David's Trips and Tours 52, 89

LOIRE VALLEY
French Touch .... 56, FYI 210

LONDON
Above & Beyond Tours 45, 83
Anderson International Tours .... 47, FYI 346
Anywhere Travel 47
Best of Both Worlds Travel Ltd. 49
Club Hommes/Worldguest .... 51, FYI 204
Gaygantic Tours 56
Hellkamp Reisen 58, 92

IMTC, Inc. 58, 94
London Handling Ltd. 61, 96
L'Arc en Ciel Voyages 61, 94
Off the Map 65, 97
Our Family Abroad 65, 98
RSVP Travel Productions/Club RSVP70, 100
R&S Travel 70, 100
Teddy Travel 74, 101
Timeout Tours & Travel 74
Tower Travel 75
Virgin Vacations 78, 105
Zone One 82

LONG ISLAND
Sailing Affairs .... 70, FYI 468

LONG ISLAND SOUND
Sea Sense .... 71, FYI 398

LOS ANGELES
Fair Choices 55, 90
Men on Vacation 62, 96
RSVP Travel Productions/Club RSVP70, 100
Teddy Travel 74, 101
Tourmark's Gay Way America Tours .. 75, 103
Xeno Tours/Mantours 81

LOS CABOS
Club Hommes/Worldguest .... 51, FYI 204

LOUISIANA
David's Trips and Tours 52, 89
Destination Management .... 53, FYI 436
Inter-Rainbow Turismo .... 59, FYI 347
RSVP Travel Productions/Club RSVP70, 100
Teddy Travel 74, 101
Tourmark's Gay Way America Tours .. 75, 103
Women in Motion 80, 107

LUXEMBOURG
Rail Europe .... 68, FYI 286

LUXOR
2Afrika 45, 83
Allegro Travel 46, 86

MACCHU PICCHU
Hawk, I'm Your Sister .... 58, FYI 463
Spirit Journeys 72, 101
Women in the Wilderness 81, 108

MADAGASCAR
2Afrika 45, 83

MADRID
Gaygantic Tours 56
Heritage Tours .... 58, FYI 283
Teddy Travel 74, 101

MAINE
Sailing Affairs .... 70, FYI 468

MAJORCA
Pearl Selections/Welcome Abroad 67, 99
Sapphire Travel & Tours 70
Sensations .... 71, FYI 292

MALAWI
2Afrika 45, 83

MALAYSIA
Envoy Travel .... 54, FYI 176
Our Family Abroad 65, 98
Passport Travel Mgt, Inc. 67
R&S Travel 70, 100

MALDIVES
East-West Tours .... 53, FYI 322
R&S Travel 70, 100
Worldwide Vacations Inc. 81

MALLORCA
Hellkamp Reisen 58, 92
R&S Travel 70, 100

MALTA
Frauen Unterwegs 55, 91
Hellkamp Reisen 58, 92
Jetman International Gay Travel 59
Worldwide Vacations Inc. 81

MANCHESTER
Teddy Travel 74, 101

MANDALAY
Silken East Ltd. .... 71, FYI 186
Travel Affair 75, 103

MAR DEL PLATA
Mix Travel .... 63, FYI 344
Stonewall 69 .... 73, FYI 344

MARATHON
Aquatic Adventures Charter Service . 47, FYI 404
We Love the Florida Keys Visitor Center . 78, FYI 408

MARGARITA ISLAND
Kam Tours Int'l 60

MARRAKECH
Heritage Tours .... 58, FYI 283

MARTHA'S VINEYARD
Sailing Affairs .... 70, FYI 468

MARYLAND
Sailing Affairs .... 70, FYI 468

MASSACHUSETTS
Hellkamp Reisen 58, 92
New England Vacation Tours 64
Sailing Affairs .... 70, FYI 468
Tourmark's Gay Way America Tours .. 75, 103
Travel Club, The 76, 103
Woodswomen 81, 108

MASSADA
Gay Guided Tours of Israel .... 56, FYI 305

MAUI
Club Hommes/Worldguest .... 51, FYI 204
Liquid Crystal Divers .... 60, FYI 422
Maui Surfing School .... 62, FYI 422
Olivia Cruises & Resorts 65, 98

FERRARI GUIDES' GAY TRAVEL A to Z - 18th EDITION   19

WHERE TO GO

DESTINATION INDEX

Open Eye Tours & Photos .... 65, FYI 425
Pacific Ocean Holidays .... 66, FYI 427
Pleasant Holidays 67
Remote Possibilities .... 69, FYI 426
Royal Hawaiian Weddings .... 70, FYI 425
RSVP Travel Productions/Club RSVP70, 100
R&S Travel 70, 100
Toto Tours 75, 102

MAURITIUS
2Afrika 45, 83
Big Five Tours 49, 88
Worldwide Vacations Inc. 81

MAZATLAN
Gay Mexico Travel .... 56, FYI 358

MEDITERRANEAN
Adventure Bound Expeditions 45, 85
Amphitrion Holidays 47
Cruise World 52, 89
Eurway Tour & Cruise Club .... 54, FYI 238
Fine Travel & Yachting .... 55, FYI 240
Global Affair 56
GPSC Charters .... 57, FYI 240
Hanns Ebensten Travel 57, 92
Hellkamp Reisen 58, 92
Heritage Tours .... 58, FYI 283
IMTC, Inc. 58, 94
In Touch Holidays Ltd. 59
Jetman International Gay Travel 59
Journeys by Sea Yacht Charters 60, FYI 337
L'Arc en Ciel Voyages 61, 94
Men on Bikes .... 62, FYI 248
Milu Tours 63
Ocean Voyager 64, 97
Off the Map 65, 97
Olivia Cruises & Resorts 65, 98
Our Family Abroad 65, 98
Pearl Selections/Welcome Abroad 67, 99
Peddlers .... 67, FYI 238
Players Express .... 67, FYI 458
Port Yacht Charters .... 68, FYI 339
Progressive Travels 68, 99
Sapphire Travel & Tours 70
Sea Sense .... 71, FYI 398
Sensations .... 71, FYI 292
Spirit Journeys 72, 101
Stonewall Connection Travel & Tours 73, 101
Sundance Travel 73
Syosset Travel 74
Teddy Travel 74, 101
Thanks, Babs 74, 102
Travel Affair 75, 103
Trek Out 76
Uranian Travel 77, 105
VeloAsia Cycling Adventures 77, 105
Voyages & Expeditions 78, 106
Whitney Yacht Charters .... 79, FYI 340
Windmills Travel & Tourism .... 80, FYI 239
Women in the Wilderness 81, 108
Woodswomen 81, 108
Worldwide Vacations Inc. 81

Xeno Tours/Mantours 81
Zeus Tours & Yacht Cruises 81, 109
Zipper Travel Association .... 82, FYI 252

MEGIDDO
Gay Guided Tours of Israel .... 56, FYI 305

MELBOURNE
Australian & New Zealand Travel Hdqtrs .. 48
Beyond the Blue .... 49, FYI 307
Off the Map 65, 97
Southern Discovery Tours .... 72, FYI 315

MENDOCINO
Merlyn's Journeys .... 63, FYI 370

MERCED RIVER
Mariah Wilderness Expeditions 61, 96

MERIDA
Gay Mexico Travel .... 56, FYI 358
Mundo Maya Turquesa 64

MEXICO
AAD All About Destinations 45
Advance Damron Vacations 45, 84
Adventure Associates 45, 84
Alaska Women of the Wilderness 46, 86
Archipelago Holidays 48, 87
Atlantis Events 48, 87
Atlantis Travel .... 48, FYI 232
Beyond Nirvana .... 49, FYI 342
Club Hommes/Worldguest .... 51, FYI 204
Club Le Bon .... 51, FYI 341
Connections Tours 51
Doin' It Right - in Puerto Vallarta 53
Earth, Wind & Water .... 53, FYI 354
Fair Choices 55, 90
Gay Baja Tours .... 56, FYI 358
Gay Mexico Travel .... 56, FYI 358
Journeys by Sea Yacht Charters 60, FYI 337
Mariah Wilderness Expeditions 61, 96
Mercury Cruise & Tour 62
Mundo Maya Turquesa 64
Olivia Cruises & Resorts 65, 98
Our Family Abroad 65, 98
Paddling South & Saddling South 66, 99
Pangaea Expeditions .... 66, FYI 456
Players Express .... 67, FYI 458
Pleasant Holidays 67
Port Yacht Charters .... 68, FYI 339
Rainbow Adventures 68
R&S Travel 70, 100
South of the Border Tour & Travel 72, FYI 358
Spirit Journeys 72, 101
Stag Travel & Tours 73
Sundance Travel 73
Terramundo Travels Int'l 74, 102
Thanks, Babs 74, 102
Toto Tours 75, 102
Tours to Paradise .... 75, FYI 189
Travel Affair 75, 103
Travel Club, The 76, 103
Undersea Expeditions, Inc. 77, 104

Wild Women 79, 106
Windjammer Barefoot Cruises 79
Women in Motion 80, 107
Women in the Wilderness 81, 108
Woodswomen 81, 108
Xeno Tours/Mantours 81

MEXICO CITY
Gay Mexico Travel .... 56, FYI 358

MEXICO - COPPER CANYON
Adventure Associates 45, 84

MIAMI
Connections Tours 51
Fair Choices 55, 90
Hellkamp Reisen 58, 92
Inter-Rainbow Turismo .... 59, FYI 347
Olivia Cruises & Resorts 65, 98
Pearl Selections/Welcome Abroad 67, 99
R&S Travel 70, 100
Xeno Tours/Mantours 81

MIAMI BEACH
Good Time Tours .... 57, FYI 412
In Touch Holidays Ltd. 59
RSVP Travel Productions/Club RSVP70, 100
Tourmark's Gay Way America Tours .. 75, 103
Uranian Travel 77, 105

MICHIGAN - UPPER
Toto Tours 75, 102

MIDDLE EAST
De Gay Krant Reisservice .... 52, FYI 256
Global Affair 56
Hanns Ebensten Travel 57, 92
Our Family Abroad 65, 98
Rainbow Destinations 69
Toto Tours 75, 102
Travel Affair 75, 103
Ventus Reisen 77
Woodswomen 81, 108
Worldwide Vacations Inc. 81
Zeus Tours & Yacht Cruises 81, 109

MILAN
Allegro Travel 46, 86
Gaygantic Tours 56
Men on Bikes .... 62, FYI 248
Xeno Tours/Mantours 81
Zipper Travel Association .... 82, FYI 252

MINNESOTA
Wintermoon .... 80, FYI 452
Women in the Wilderness 81, 108
Woodswomen 81, 108

MISSISSIPPI
Alyson Adventures 47, 87

MISSOULA
Pangaea Expeditions .... 66, FYI 456
Ten Thousand Waves .... 74, FYI 457

MOAB
Lizard Head Backcountry Tours .. 61, FYI 495

WHERE TO GO

DESTINATION INDEX

MOLOKAI
Liquid Crystal Divers .... 60, FYI 422
Open Eye Tours & Photos .... 65, FYI 425
Pacific Ocean Holidays .... 66, FYI 427

MONGOLIA
Ventus Reisen 77

MONTANA
Lizard Head Backcountry Tours .. 61, FYI 495
OutWest Adventures .... 66, FYI 455
Pangaea Expeditions .... 66, FYI 456
Rainbow Adventures 68
Ten Thousand Waves .... 74, FYI 457
Wild Rockies Tours .... 79, FYI 457
Wild Women 79, 106

MONTEGO BAY
Island Hoppers Tours .... 59, FYI 341

MONTEREY
Tourmark's Gay Way America Tours .. 75, 103

MONTREAL
Eat Quiche Tour & Travel Accomm. 54
Fair Choices 55, 90
Hellkamp Reisen 58, 92
New England Vacation Tours 64
Travel Man 76, 104

MOROCCO
Adventure Associates 45, 84
Different Strokes Tours 53
Explorer Tours .... 55, FYI 190
Hanns Ebensten Travel 57, 92
Heritage Tours .... 58, FYI 283
Our Family Abroad 65, 98

MOSCOW
Above & Beyond Tours 45, 83
Allegro Travel 46, 86
Departures International .... 52, FYI 266
Kremlin Tours .... 60, FYI 266
Milu Tours 63
Off the Map 65, 97

MONTEVIDEO
RSVP Travel Productions/Club RSVP 70, 100

MOZAMBIQUE
2Afrika 45, 83

MT RAINIER
Adventure Associates 45, 84

MT TABOR
Gay Guided Tours of Israel .... 56, FYI 305

MUNICH
Above & Beyond Tours 45, 83
Gaygantic Tours 56
R&S Travel 70, 100
Teddy Travel 74, 101
Tower Travel 75
Travel Keys Tours 76, 104
Wolff + Zink Travel Services 80, 106

MYANMAR
Passport Travel Mgt, Inc. 67
Silken East Ltd. .... 71, FYI 186

MYKONOS
Beyond the Blue .... 49, FYI 307
Discus Travel 53
Eurway Tour & Cruise Club .... 54, FYI 238
Hellkamp Reisen 58, 92
In Touch Holidays Ltd. 59
Milu Tours 63
Pearl Selections/Welcome Abroad 67, 99
R&S Travel 70, 100
Sapphire Travel & Tours 70
Sensations .... 71, FYI 292
Sundance Travel 73
Uranian Travel 77, 105
Windmills Travel & Tourism .... 80, FYI 239
Xeno Tours/Mantours 81

MYSTIC
Sailing Affairs .... 70, FYI 468

NAMIBIA
2Afrika 45, 83
Archipelago Holidays 48, 87
Big Five Tours 49, 88
Embassy Travel 54
Wild Women 79, 106

NANTUCKET
Sailing Affairs .... 70, FYI 468

NAPA VALLEY
Destination Discovery .... 52, FYI 378

NASSAU
Olivia Cruises & Resorts 65, 98
Pleasure Travel...Cruise Again Too! .. 68, FYI 339

NAZARETH
Gay Guided Tours of Israel .... 56, FYI 305

NEGRIL
Island Hoppers Tours .... 59, FYI 341

NEPAL
Adventure Associates 45, 84
Alaska Women of the Wilderness 46, 86
Big Five Tours 49, 88
BreakOut Tours .... 50, FYI 308
Himalayan High Treks .... 58, FYI 186
Lois Lane Expeditions 61
Our Family Abroad 65, 98
Passport Travel Mgt, Inc. 67
Rainbow Adventures 68
Silke's Travel .... 71, FYI 308
Wild Women 79, 106
Woodswomen 81, 108

NETHERLANDS
Above & Beyond Tours 45, 83
Archipelago Holidays 48, 87
Beyond the Blue .... 49, FYI 307
David's Trips and Tours 52, 89

De Gay Krant Reisservice .... 52, FYI 256
European Luxury Hotel
  Barge Cruises .... 54, FYI 208
Fair Choices 55, 90
Frauen Unterwegs 55, 91
Gaygantic Tours 56
IMTC, Inc. 58, 94
Jetman International Gay Travel 59
Kenny Tours 60
L'Arc en Ciel Voyages 61, 94
Men on Vacation 62, 96
Our Family Abroad 65, 98
Pearl Selections/Welcome Abroad 67, 99
Rail Europe .... 68, FYI 286
Rainbowworld Custom Tours .... 69, FYI 256
Robin Tyler's Women's Tours, Cruises &
  Events 69
RSVP Travel Productions/Club RSVP 70, 100
R&S Travel 70, 100
Stonewall Connection Travel & Tours 73, 101
Teddy Travel 74, 101
Toto Tours 75, 102
Travel Affair 75, 103
Travel Club, The 76, 103
Travel Keys Tours 76, 104
Uranian Travel 77, 105
Vaarschool Grietje .... 77, FYI 258
Wolff + Zink Travel Services 80, 106
Xeno Tours/Mantours 81
ZMAX Travel & Tours Inc. 82, 109

NEVADA
Lizard Head Backcountry Tours .. 61, FYI 495
Players Express .... 67, FYI 458
R&S Travel 70, 100
Tourmark's Gay Way America Tours .. 75, 103
Women in Motion 80, 107

NEVIS
Tall Ship Adventures, Inc. .... 74, FYI 340

NEW BERN
Best of Both Worlds .... FYI 474

NEW ENGLAND
Journeys by Sea Yacht Charters 60, FYI 337
New England Vacation Tours 64
Port Yacht Charters .... 68, FYI 339
Sea Sense .... 71, FYI 398
Whitney Yacht Charters .... 79, FYI 340

NEW JERSEY
Adventures for Women .... 45, FYI 461
Sailing Affairs .... 70, FYI 468

NEW MEXICO
Desert Vision Tours 52
Hawk, I'm Your Sister .... 58, FYI 463
Lizard Head Backcountry Tours .. 61, FYI 495
Spirit Journeys 72, 101
Women in Motion 80, 107

NEW ORLEANS
David's Trips and Tours 52, 89
Destination Management .... 53, FYI 436

FERRARI GUIDES' GAY TRAVEL A to Z - 18th EDITION

WHERE TO GO

DESTINATION INDEX

Inter-Rainbow Turismo .... 59, FYI 347
RSVP Travel Productions/Club RSVP70, 100
Teddy Travel 74, 101
Tourmark's Gay Way America Tours .. 75, 103
Women in Motion 80, 107

NEW SOUTH WALES
Above & Beyond Tours 45, 83
Aust Pac Travel 48
Destination Downunder .... 53, FYI 309
G'day Tours .... 57, FYI 310
Hawkesbury Expeditions 58
Holidays at Sea/Sunquest 58
Inter-Rainbow Turismo .... 59, FYI 347
Jornada 59, 94
Land Voyages 60
Mount'n Beach Safaris 63
Off the Map 65, 97
Pacific Experience 66
Pearl Selections/Welcome Abroad 67, 99
Travel Affair 75, 103

NEW YORK
Adventures for Women .... 45, FYI 461
Archipelago Holidays 48, 87
Eclectic Excursions .... 54, FYI 466
Fair Choices 55, 90
Hellkamp Reisen 58, 92
In Touch Holidays Ltd. 59
Men on Vacation 62, 96
Pearl Selections/Welcome Abroad 67, 99
RSVP Travel Productions/Club RSVP70, 100
R&S Travel 70, 100
Sailing Affairs .... 70, FYI 468
Teddy Travel 74, 101
Tourmark's Gay Way America Tours .. 75, 103
Travel Club, The 76, 103
Travel Man 76, 104
V.I.P. Tours of New York .... 78, FYI 468
Xeno Tours/Mantours 81

NEW ZEALAND
Above & Beyond Tours 45, 83
Adventure Associates 45, 84
Australian & New Zealand Travel Hdqtrs .. 48
Beyond the Blue .... 49, FYI 307
Bushwise Women .... 50, FYI 318
Cloud Canyon Backpacking 50, 88
Destination Downunder .... 53, FYI 309
Destination World 53, 90
Gaylink Travel Services 56
G'day Tours .... 57, FYI 310
Holidays at Sea/Sunquest 58
Landmark (South Pacific) Pty Ltd 60
L'Arc en Ciel Voyages 61, 94
Men on Vacation 62, 96
Mount Cook Tours 63
Off the Map 65, 97
Oz Dive/Passport to Paradise 66
Pacific Experience 66
Silke's Travel .... 71, FYI 308
Travel Man 76, 104
Womantours/Artemis Sailing 80, 107

Woodswomen 81, 108

NEWPORT
Sailing Affairs .... 70, FYI 468

NEWPORT BEACH
Tourmark's Gay Way America Tours .. 75, 103

NICARAGUA
Terramundo Travels Int'l 74, 102

NICE
French Touch .... 56, FYI 210
Pearl Selections/Welcome Abroad 67, 99

NILE RIVER
2Afrika 45, 83

NORFOLK
Sailing Affairs .... 70, FYI 468

NORTH AFRICA
Hanns Ebensten Travel 57, 92
Heritage Tours .... 58, FYI 283
Our Family Abroad 65, 98

NORTH AMERICA
Progressive Travels 68, 99

NORTH CAROLINA
Best of Both Worlds .... FYI 474
Spirit Journeys 72, 101

NORTHERN ROCKIES
Women in Motion 80, 107

NORTHERN TERRITORY
Graylink Tours .... 57, FYI 310
Sirius Adventures .... 72, FYI 314
Todd River Tours 75
Wanderlust Ventures 78

NORTHWEST TERRITORIES
Women in the Wilderness 81, 108

NORTHWOODS
Wintermoon .... 80, FYI 452

NORWAY
Oceanwide Expeditions 64
Off the Map 65, 97
Travel Affair 75, 103

NUREMBERG
Wolff + Zink Travel Services 80, 106

OAHU
Dave's Island Pride Driver, Guide 52, FYI 427
Pacific Ocean Holidays .... 66, FYI 427
Pleasant Holidays 67

OAXACA
Spirit Journeys 72, 101

OCHO RIOS
Island Hoppers Tours .... 59, FYI 341

OCRACOKE
Best of Both Worlds .... FYI 474

ONTARIO
Eat Quiche Tour & Travel Accomm. 54

Hellkamp Reisen 58, 92
New England Vacation Tours 64
Travel Man 76, 104
Wild Women Expeditions .... 79, FYI 330
Women in the Wilderness 81, 108

OREGON
Experience Plus 55, 90
Lizard Head Backcountry Tours .. 61, FYI 495
Mariah Wilderness Expeditions 61, 96
Merlyn's Journeys .... 63, FYI 370
Progressive Travels 68, 99

ORLANDO
Connections Tours 51
Good Time Tours .... 57, FYI 412
Hellkamp Reisen 58, 92
Inter-Rainbow Turismo .... 59, FYI 347
It's Our Nature .... 59, FYI 416
Men on Vacation 62, 96
Mercury Cruise & Tour 62
R&S Travel 70, 100
Teddy Travel 74, 101
Uranian Travel 77, 105
Xeno Tours/Mantours 81

OSLO
Off the Map 65, 97

OUTER BANKS
Best of Both Worlds .... FYI 474

PACIFIC
Hanns Ebensten Travel 57, 92
Matt's Rainbow Tours .... 62, FYI 421
Pacific Ocean Holidays .... 66, FYI 427
Pleasant Holidays 67
Remote Possibilities .... 69, FYI 426
Royal Hawaiian Weddings .... 70, FYI 425
Thanks, Babs 74, 102
Toto Tours 75, 102

PACIFIC ISLANDS
Archipelago Holidays 48, 87
Beyond the Blue .... 49, FYI 307
East-West Tours .... 53, FYI 322
Gaylink Travel Services 56
G'day Tours .... 57, FYI 310
Journeys by Sea Yacht Charters 60, FYI 337
Men on Vacation 62, 96
Oz Dive/Passport to Paradise 66
Silke's Travel .... 71, FYI 308
Travel Man 76, 104
Undersea Expeditions, Inc. 77, 104
VeloAsia Cycling Adventures 77, 105
Worldwide Vacations Inc. 81

PACIFIC NORTHWEST
Lois Lane Expeditions 61
Onn the Water 65

PAGAN
Silken East Ltd. .... 71, FYI 186

PALM SPRINGS
Gay Baja Tours .... 56, FYI 358

22   FERRARI GUIDES' GAY TRAVEL A to Z - 18th EDITION

WHERE TO GO

DESTINATION INDEX

Hellkamp Reisen 58, 92
Pearl Selections/Welcome Abroad 67, 99
RSVP Travel Productions/Club RSVP 70, 100
R&S Travel 70, 100
Tourmark's Gay Way America Tours .. 75, 103
Women in Motion 80, 107

PALMA DE MALLORCA
In Touch Holidays Ltd. 59
Uranian Travel 77, 105

PAMLICO SOUND
Best of Both Worlds .... FYI 474

PAMPAS
Mix Travel .... 63, FYI 344
Stonewall 69 .... 73, FYI 344

PANAMA
Mercury Cruise & Tour 62
Terramundo Travels Int'l 74, 102

PANTANAL
Stockler Expeditions 73

PARADISE
We Love the Florida Keys Visitor Center . 78, FYI 408

PARAGUAY
Terramundo Travels Int'l 74, 102

PARIS
Above & Beyond Tours 45, 83
Club Hommes/Worldguest .... 51, FYI 204
Cruise World 52, 89
David's Trips and Tours 52, 89
Different Strokes Tours 53
French Touch .... 56, FYI 210
Gaygantic Tours 56
Hellkamp Reisen 58, 92
IMTC, Inc. 58, 94
L'Arc en Ciel Voyages 61, 94
Men on Vacation 62, 96
Off the Map 65, 97
Our Family Abroad 65, 98
Pearl Selections/Welcome Abroad 67, 99
Promenades de Style .... 68, FYI 212
RSVP Travel Productions/Club RSVP 70, 100
R&S Travel 70, 100
Teddy Travel 74, 101
Travel Affair 75, 103
Uranian Travel 77, 105
Women in Motion 80, 107
Xeno Tours/Mantours 81

PARIS ENVIRONS
Promenades de Style .... 68, FYI 212

PATAGONIA
Mix Travel .... 63, FYI 344

PATTAYA
R&S Travel 70, 100
Tours to Paradise .... 75, FYI 189

PENNSYLVANIA
Adventures for Women .... 45, FYI 461

Tourmark's Gay Way America Tours .. 75, 103

PENSACOLA
Connections Tours 51
Good Time Tours .... 57, FYI 412

PERU
Big Five Tours 49, 88
Hawk, I'm Your Sister .... 58, FYI 463
Mercury Cruise & Tour 62
Our Family Abroad 65, 98
Silke's Travel .... 71, FYI 308
Spirit Journeys 72, 101
Stonewall 69 .... 73, FYI 344
Terramundo Travels Int'l 74, 102
Women in the Wilderness 81, 108

PHILADELPHIA
Tourmark's Gay Way America Tours .. 75, 103

PHILIPPINES
R&S Travel 70, 100

PHNOM PENH
Silken East Ltd. .... 71, FYI 186

PHOENIX
Desert Vision Tours 52

PHUKET
R&S Travel 70, 100
Tours to Paradise .... 75, FYI 189

PLAYA BLANCA
Gay Mexico Travel .... 56, FYI 358

PLAYA DEL CARMEN
Mundo Maya Turquesa 64
Olivia Cruises & Resorts 65, 98

PLAYA DEL INGLES
Xeno Tours/Mantours 81

POINT REYES
Merlyn's Journeys .... 63, FYI 370

POLAND
Frauen Unterwegs 55, 91
Jetman International Gay Travel 59

PORT ANTONIO
Island Hoppers Tours .... 59, FYI 341

PORTUGAL
Club Hommes/Worldguest .... 51, FYI 204
Experience Plus 55, 90
Frauen Unterwegs 55, 91
Hellkamp Reisen 58, 92
Heritage Tours .... 58, FYI 283
IMTC, Inc. 58, 94
In Touch Holidays Ltd. 59
L'Arc en Ciel Voyages 61, 94
Off the Map 65, 97
Paths Less Taken .... 67, FYI 264
Pearl Selections/Welcome Abroad 67, 99
Progressive Travels 68, 99
Rail Europe .... 68, FYI 286
Sensations .... 71, FYI 292
Terramundo Travels Int'l 74, 102

Uranian Travel 77, 105

PRAGUE
Above & Beyond Tours 45, 83
David's Trips and Tours 52, 89
Hellkamp Reisen 58, 92
IMTC, Inc. 58, 94
Kremlin Tours .... 60, FYI 266
Off the Map 65, 97
R&S Travel 70, 100
Uranian Travel 77, 105
Wolff + Zink Travel Services 80, 106

PRETORIA
2Afrika 45, 83
Mantrav International 61

PRINCE WILLIAM SOUND
Alaska Women of the Wilderness 46, 86

PROVENCE
Club Hommes/Worldguest .... 51, FYI 204
Mistral Tours .... 63, FYI 203

PROVINCETOWN
Hellkamp Reisen 58, 92
New England Vacation Tours 64
Sailing Affairs .... 70, FYI 468
Tourmark's Gay Way America Tours .. 75, 103
Travel Club, The 76, 103

PUERTO RICO
Conson Holidays 51
Fair Choices 55, 90
Olivia Cruises & Resorts 65, 98
R&S Travel 70, 100
Teddy Travel 74, 101

PUERTO VALLARTA
Doin' It Right - in Puerto Vallarta 53
Fair Choices 55, 90
Gay Mexico Travel .... 56, FYI 358
Players Express .... 67, FYI 458
Sundance Travel 73

PUNTA DEL ESTE
RSVP Travel Productions/Club RSVP 70, 100

QUEBEC
Eat Quiche Tour & Travel Accomm. 54
Fair Choices 55, 90
Hellkamp Reisen 58, 92
New England Vacation Tours 64
Travel Man 76, 104

QUEBEC CITY
Eat Quiche Tour & Travel Accomm. 54

QUEENSLAND
Above & Beyond Tours 45, 83
Australian & New Zealand Travel Hdqtrs .. 48
Beyond the Blue .... 49, FYI 307
Destination Downunder .... 53, FYI 309
G'day Tours .... 57, FYI 310
Holidays at Sea/Sunquest 58
Inter-Rainbow Turismo .... 59, FYI 347
Izarra Cruises .... 59, FYI 502

FERRARI GUIDES' GAY TRAVEL A to Z - 18th EDITION

WHERE TO GO

DESTINATION INDEX

Men on Vacation 62, 96
Off the Map 65, 97
Out Touring Australia 66
Oz Dive/Passport to Paradise 66
Pearl Selections/Welcome Abroad 67, 99
Silke's Travel .... 71, FYI 308
Surfers Paradise Gay Vacations 73
Witchencroft 4WD & Bushwalking Tours .. 80, FYI 312

QUEENSTOWN
Off the Map 65, 97

QUETICO
Wild Women Expeditions .... 79, FYI 330

QUINTANA ROO
Mundo Maya Turquesa 64

QUMRAN
Gay Guided Tours of Israel .... 56, FYI 305

RANGOON
Silken East Ltd. .... 71, FYI 186

RED ROCK COUNTRY
Sedona Rainbow Adventure Tours .... 71, FYI 367

RED SEA
Undersea Expeditions, Inc. 77, 104
Worldwide Vacations Inc. 81

REIMS
Promenades de Style .... 68, FYI 212

RESURRECTION BAY
Puffin Family Charters .... 68, FYI 363

REYKJAVIK
L'Arc en Ciel Voyages 61, 94

RHODE ISLAND
Sailing Affairs .... 70, FYI 468

RHODOS
Seaborne Safaris (Croisieres d'Il en II) 71

RIGA
Allegro Travel 46, 86
David's Trips and Tours 52, 89

RIO DE JANEIRO
Anderson International Tours .... 47, FYI 346
Archipelago Holidays 48, 87
De Gay Krant Reisservice .... 52, FYI 256
Fiesta Tours .... 55, FYI 346
Inter-Rainbow Turismo .... 59, FYI 347
Mercury Cruise & Tour 62
RSVP Travel Productions/Club RSVP 70, 100
Stockler Expeditions 73
Sundance Travel 73
Travel Man 76, 104

RIO GRANDE
Spirit Journeys 72, 101

RIVER OF NO RETURN
Pangaea Expeditions .... 66, FYI 456

RIVIERA - FRENCH
French Touch .... 56, FYI 210

ROATAN
Woodswomen 81, 108

ROCKIES - CANADIAN
Rainbow Adventures 68

ROCKIES - NORTHERN
Wild Women 79, 106
Women in Motion 80, 107

ROCKIES - SOUTHERN
Women in Motion 80, 107

ROCKY MTNS
Lizard Head Backcountry Tours .. 61, FYI 495
McNamara Ranch .... 62, FYI 396
Never Summer Nordic .... 64, FYI 396
Pangaea Expeditions .... 66, FYI 456
Wild Rockies Tours .... 79, FYI 457

ROGUE RIVER
Mariah Wilderness Expeditions 61, 96

ROME
Allegro Travel 46, 86
Easy Way 54
Gaygantic Tours 56
Hellkamp Reisen 58, 92
IMTC, Inc. 58, 94
Men on Bikes .... 62, FYI 248
Off the Map 65, 97
Teddy Travel 74, 101
Travel Affair 75, 103
Zipper Travel Association .... 82, FYI 252

ROSH HANIKRA
Gay Guided Tours of Israel .... 56, FYI 305

RUSSIA
Above & Beyond Tours 45, 83
Allegro Travel 46, 86
Anywhere Travel 47
David's Trips and Tours 52, 89
Departures International .... 52, FYI 266
Different Strokes Tours 53
Five Star Travel Services 55
Hawk, I'm Your Sister .... 58, FYI 463
Jetman International Gay Travel 59
Kremlin Tours .... 60, FYI 266
L'Arc en Ciel Voyages 61, 94
Milu Tours 63
Off the Map 65, 97
Our Family Abroad 65, 98
Rail Europe .... 68, FYI 286
Travel Man 76, 104
Ventus Reisen 77

RUSSIAN RIVER
Off the Map 65, 97
Women in Motion 80, 107

SABA
Tall Ship Adventures, Inc. .... 74, FYI 340

SAFED
Gay Guided Tours of Israel .... 56, FYI 305

SAHARA DESERT
Heritage Tours .... 58, FYI 283

SALAVADOR
Terramundo Travels Int'l 74, 102

SALMON RIVER
Mariah Wilderness Expeditions 61, 96
Middle Fork River Expeditions 63
Pangaea Expeditions .... 66, FYI 456

SALT LAKE CITY
Tourmark's Gay Way America Tours .. 75, 103

SALVADOR
Stockler Expeditions 73

SALZBURG
Allegro Travel 46, 86
IMTC, Inc. 58, 94
Wolff + Zink Travel Services 80, 106

SAMOA - WESTERN
Open Eye Tours & Photos .... 65, FYI 425

SAN ANTONIO
After Five Charters .... 46, FYI 492
Tourmark's Gay Way America Tours .. 75, 103

SAN DIEGO
Hellkamp Reisen 58, 92
R&S Travel 70, 100
Tourmark's Gay Way America Tours .. 75, 103
Travel Club, The 76, 103
Women in Motion 80, 107
Xeno Tours/Mantours 81

SAN FRANCISCO
Connections Tours 51
Cruisin' the Castro .... 52, FYI 388
Fair Choices 55, 90
Hellkamp Reisen 58, 92
Inter-Rainbow Turismo .... 59, FYI 347
Men on Vacation 62, 96
Pearl Selections/Welcome Abroad 67, 99
RSVP Travel Productions/Club RSVP 70, 100
R&S Travel 70, 100
Scenic Air Tours .... 70, FYI 386
Teddy Travel 74, 101
Tourmark's Gay Way America Tours .. 75, 103
Travel Club, The 76, 103
Victorian Home Walk .... 77, FYI 386
Women in Motion 80, 107
Xeno Tours/Mantours 81

SAN JOSE
Way to Go Costa Rica .... 78, FYI 352

SAN JUAN
Conson Holidays 51
Olivia Cruises & Resorts 65, 98
RSVP Travel Productions/Club RSVP 70, 100
R&S Travel 70, 100

FERRARI GUIDES' GAY TRAVEL A to Z - 18th EDITION

WHERE TO GO

DESTINATION INDEX

SAN JUAN ISLANDS
Adventure Associates 45, 84
Blue Moon Explorations 49
Izarra Cruises .... 59, FYI 502
Merlyn's Journeys .... 63, FYI 370
Oceanwomyn Kayaking .... 64, FYI 357

SAN JUAN RIVER
OutWest Adventures .... 66, FYI 455
Pangaea Expeditions .... 66, FYI 456

SAN SALVADOR
Mercury Cruise & Tour 62

SANTA BARBARA
Tourmark's Gay Way America Tours .. 75, 103

SANTA FE
Spirit Journeys 72, 101
Women in Motion 80, 107

SAO PAOLO
Inter-Rainbow Turismo .... 59, FYI 347

SARASOTA
Connections Tours 51
It's Our Nature .... 59, FYI 416

SCANDINAVIA
Frauen Unterwegs 55, 91
L'Arc en Ciel Voyages 61, 94
Oceanwide Expeditions 64
Off the Map 65, 97
Our Family Abroad 65, 98
Travel Affair 75, 103
Women in the Wilderness 81, 108

SCOTLAND
Anderson International Tours .... 47, FYI 346
Frauen Unterwegs 55, 91
IMTC, Inc. 58, 94
Off the Map 65, 97
Our Family Abroad 65, 98
Rail Europe .... 68, FYI 286
Rainbow Adventures 68
Toto Tours 75, 102

SCOTTSDALE
Tourmark's Gay Way America Tours .. 75, 103

SEA OF CORTEZ
Earth, Wind & Water .... 53, FYI 354
Mariah Wilderness Expeditions 61, 96

SEA OF GALILEE
Gay Guided Tours of Israel .... 56, FYI 305

SEATTLE
Lizard Head Backcountry Tours .. 61, FYI 495
Toto Tours 75, 102

SEDONA
Canyon Calling Tours .... 50, FYI 366
Sedona Rainbow Adventure Tours .... 71, FYI 367
Tourmark's Gay Way America Tours .. 75, 103
Women in Motion 80, 107

SENEGAL
Frauen Unterwegs 55, 91

SEQUOIA NATIONAL PARK
Mariah Wilderness Expeditions 61, 96

SEWARD
Puffin Family Charters .... 68, FYI 363

SEYCHELLES
2Afrika 45, 83
Big Five Tours 49, 88
Worldwide Vacations Inc. 81

SHANGHAI
China Voyages .... 50, FYI 176

SIBERIA
Hawk, I'm Your Sister .... 58, FYI 463
Ventus Reisen 77

SICILY
Men on Bikes .... 62, FYI 248

SIENA
Allegro Travel 46, 86
Zipper Travel Association .... 82, FYI 252

SIERRA NEVADA
Adventure Associates 45, 84
Common Earth Adventures 51, 89
Lizard Head Backcountry Tours .. 61, FYI 495

SINGAPORE
Envoy Travel .... 54, FYI 176
Our Family Abroad 65, 98
R&S Travel 70, 100

SIRACUSA
Men on Bikes .... 62, FYI 248

SITGES
Discus Travel 53
Hellkamp Reisen 58, 92
Heritage Tours .... 58, FYI 283
In Touch Holidays Ltd. 59
Milu Tours 63
Pearl Selections/Welcome Abroad 67, 99
R&S Travel 70, 100
Sapphire Travel & Tours 70
Sensations .... 71, FYI 292
Uranian Travel 77, 105
Xeno Tours/Mantours 81

SOLOMON ISLANDS
East-West Tours .... 53, FYI 322

SOMBRERO KEY
We Love the Florida Keys Visitor Center . 78, FYI 408

SOUTH AFRICA
2Afrika 45, 83
Archipelago Holidays 48, 87
Beau Séjour .... 49, FYI 173
Big Five Tours 49, 88
David's Trips and Tours 52, 89
Embassy Travel 54
Mantrav International 61
Travel Man 76, 104
Wild Women 79, 106
Worldwide Vacations Inc. 81

SOUTH AMERICA
Adventures With Flair 46, 85
Amazon Tours & Cruises 47
Anderson International Tours ...... 47, FYI 346
Arcadia Turismo Internacional 48
Archipelago Holidays 48, 87
Beyond Nirvana .... 49, FYI 342
Beyond the Blue .... 49, FYI 307
Big Five Tours 49, 88
De Gay Krant Reisservice .... 52, FYI 256
Fiesta Tours .... 55, FYI 346
Gayventures 56
Hanns Ebensten Travel 57, 92
Hawk, I'm Your Sister .... 58, FYI 463
Inter-Rainbow Turismo .... 59, FYI 347
Kam Tours Int'l 60
Mercury Cruise & Tour 62
Mix Travel .... 63, FYI 344
MTC (Multinational Travel Corp) 64
Our Family Abroad 65, 98
Rio Roma Travel 69
RSVP Travel Productions/Club RSVP 70, 100
Silke's Travel .... 71, FYI 308
Spirit Journeys 72, 101
Stockler Expeditions 73
Stonewall 69 .... 73, FYI 344
Sundance Travel 73
Terramundo Travels Int'l .... 74, FYI 102
Travel Man 76, 104
Voyages & Expeditions 78, 106
Women in the Wilderness 81, 108
Woodswomen 81, 108

SOUTH AUSTRALIA
Wanderlust Ventures 78

SOUTH BEACH
Connections Tours 51
In Touch Holidays Ltd. 59

SOUTH OF FRANCE
Mistral Tours .... 63, FYI 203

SOUTH PACIFIC
Above & Beyond Tours 45, 83
Adventures With Flair 46, 85
Alyson Adventures 47, 87
Archipelago Holidays 48, 87
Atlantis Events 48, 87
Atlantis Travel .... 48, FYI 232
Aust Pac Travel 48
Australian & New Zealand Travel Hdqtrs .. 48
Beyond the Blue .... 49, FYI 307
Bogong Horseback Adventures 49
BreakOut Tours .... 50, FYI 308
Bushwise Women .... 50, FYI 318
Cloud Canyon Backpacking 50, 88
Destination Downunder .... 53, FYI 309
Destination World 53, 90
East-West Tours .... 53, FYI 322

FERRARI GUIDES' GAY TRAVEL A to Z - 18th EDITION

WHERE TO GO

DESTINATION INDEX

Frauen Unterwegs 55, 91
Gaygantic Tours 56
Gaylink Travel Services 56
Graylink Tours .... 57, FYI 310
G'day Tours .... 57, FYI 310
Hanafi Tour and Travel .... 57, FYI 188
Hawkesbury Expeditions 58
Holidays at Sea/Sunquest 58
Holigays 58, 92
Izarra Cruises .... 59, FYI 502
Jornada 59, 94
Journeys by Sea Yacht Charters 60, FYI 337
Landmark (South Pacific) Pty Ltd 60
L'Arc en Ciel Voyages 61, 94
Men on Vacation 62, 96
Mount Cook Tours 63
North American Travel Specialists 64, 97
Off the Map 65, 97
Out Touring Australia 66
Oz Dive/Passport to Paradise 66
Pacific Experience 66
Port Yacht Charters .... 68, FYI 339
Silke's Travel .... 71, FYI 308
Sirius Adventures .... 72, FYI 314
Surfers Paradise Gay Vacations 73
Thanks, Babs 74, 102
Todd River Tours 75
Toto Tours 75, 102
Travel Affair 75, 103
Travel Man 76, 104
Undersea Expeditions, Inc. 77, 104
Voyages & Expeditions 78, 106
Wanderlust Ventures 78
Witchencroft 4WD & Bushwalking Tours .. 80, FYI 312
Womantours/Artemis Sailing 80, 107
Worldwide Vacations Inc. 81
Xeno Tours/Mantours 81

SOUTH PACIFIC ISLANDS
Australian & New Zealand Travel Hdqtrs .. 48

SOUTHEAST ASIA
Otto Travel Hawaii 65
Tours to Paradise .... 75, FYI 189

SOUTHERN ROCKIES
Women in Motion 80, 107

SPAIN
Anderson International Tours ...... 47, FYI 346
De Gay Krant Reisservice .... 52, FYI 256
Different Strokes Tours 53
Discus Travel 53
Experience Plus 55, 90
Fair Choices 55, 90
Frauen Unterwegs 55, 91
Gaygantic Tours 56
Hellkamp Reisen 58, 92
Heritage Tours .... 58, FYI 283
IMTC, Inc. 58, 94
In Touch Holidays Ltd. 59
Jetman International Gay Travel 59

Kremlin Tours .... 60, FYI 266
L'Arc en Ciel Voyages 61, 94
Milu Tours 63
Off the Map 65, 97
Our Family Abroad 65, 98
Paths Less Taken .... 67, FYI 264
Pearl Selections/Welcome Abroad 67, 99
Progressive Travels 68, 99
Rail Europe .... 68, FYI 286
R&S Travel 70, 100
Sapphire Travel & Tours 70
Sensations .... 71, FYI 292
Stonewall Connection Travel & Tours 73, 101
Teddy Travel 74, 101
Terramundo Travels Int'l 74, 102
Uranian Travel 77, 105
Xeno Tours/Mantours 81

SPANISH RIVER
Wild Women Expeditions .... 79, FYI 330

SPITSBERGEN
Oceanwide Expeditions 64

SRI LANKA
Hellkamp Reisen 58, 92

ST BARTHELEMY
Club Hommes/Worldguest .... 51, FYI 204
Different Strokes Tours 53
Journeys by Sea Yacht Charters 60, FYI 337

ST BART'S
Tall Ship Adventures, Inc. .... 74, FYI 340

ST CROIX
Hellkamp Reisen 58, 92

ST EUSTATIUS
Tall Ship Adventures, Inc. .... 74, FYI 340

ST KITTS
Tall Ship Adventures, Inc. .... 74, FYI 340

ST LUCIA
RSVP Travel Productions/Club RSVP 70, 100
Toto Tours 75, 102

ST MAARTEN
Tall Ship Adventures, Inc. .... 74, FYI 340

ST MAARTIN
Fair Choices 55, 90
Windjammer Barefoot Cruises 79

ST MORITZ
Ski Connections .... 72, FYI 194

ST PETE
Connections Tours 51

ST PETERSBURG
Above & Beyond Tours 45, 83
Allegro Travel 46, 86
David's Trips and Tours 52, 89
Departures International .... 52, FYI 266
Kremlin Tours .... 60, FYI 266
Milu Tours 63
Off the Map 65, 97

Travel Man 76, 104

ST THOMAS
BVI Charters 50
Fair Choices 55, 90
Olivia Cruises & Resorts 65, 98

ST TROPEZ
French Touch .... 56, FYI 210

ST VINCENT
RSVP Travel Productions/Club RSVP 70, 100
Tall Ship Adventures, Inc. .... 74, FYI 340

STOCKHOLM
Off the Map 65, 97

SUDAN
Archipelago Holidays 48, 87

SUDBURY
Wild Women Expeditions .... 79, FYI 330

SUMATRA
Otto Travel Hawaii 65
VeloAsia Cycling Adventures 77, 105

SUN CITY - AFRICA
2Afrika 45, 83

SURFERS PARADISE
Australian & New Zealand Travel Hdqtrs .. 48
Surfers Paradise Gay Vacations 73

SURINAM
Terramundo Travels Int'l 74, 102

SWAZILAND
2Afrika 45, 83

SWEDEN
Frauen Unterwegs 55, 91
Off the Map 65, 97

SWITZERLAND
Alyson Adventures 47, 87
Experience Plus 55, 90
Gaygantic Tours 56
L'Arc en Ciel Voyages 61, 94
Rail Europe .... 68, FYI 286
Rainbow Adventures 68
Ski Connections .... 72, FYI 194
Woodswomen 81, 108

SYDNEY
Above & Beyond Tours 45, 83
Atlantis Events 48, 87
Atlantis Travel .... 48, FYI 232
Australian & New Zealand Travel Hdqtrs .. 48
Beyond the Blue .... 49, FYI 307
BreakOut Tours .... 50, FYI 308
Destination Downunder .... 53, FYI 309
Gaygantic Tours 56
G'day Tours .... 57, FYI 310
Holidays at Sea/Sunquest 58
Inter-Rainbow Turismo .... 59, FYI 347
Jornada 59, 94
Off the Map 65, 97
Pacific Experience 66

WHERE TO GO

Pearl Selections/Welcome Abroad 67, 99
Toto Tours 75, 102
Travel Affair 75, 103

SYMI
Seaborne Safaris (Croisieres d'Il en II) 71

SYRIA
Ventus Reisen 77

TAHITI
Australian & New Zealand Travel Hdqtrs .. 48
Destination Downunder .... 53, FYI 309
Destination World 53, 90
East-West Tours .... 53, FYI 322
G'day Tours .... 57, FYI 310
Journeys by Sea Yacht Charters 60, FYI 337
Oz Dive/Passport to Paradise 66
Travel Man 76, 104
Worldwide Vacations Inc. 81

TAIWAN
Envoy Travel .... 54, FYI 176

TALLINN
Allegro Travel 46, 86
David's Trips and Tours 52, 89

TAMPA
Connections Tours 51
It's Our Nature .... 59, FYI 416

TANZANIA
2Afrika 45, 83
Adventure Associates 45, 84
Baobab Safari Co. 48
Big Five Tours 49, 88
Embassy Travel 54
Our Family Abroad 65, 98
Toto Tours 75, 102

TAORMINA
Men on Bikes .... 62, FYI 248

TAOS
Women in Motion 80, 107

TASHKENT
Departures International .... 52, FYI 266

TAVERNIER
We Love the Florida Keys Visitor Center . 78, FYI 408

TEL AVIV
Gay Guided Tours of Israel .... 56, FYI 305

TELLURIDE
Lizard Head Backcountry Tours .. 61, FYI 495

TEMAGAMI
Wild Women Expeditions .... 79, FYI 330

TENERIFE
Hellkamp Reisen 58, 92

TETONS
Bar H Ranch .... 48, FYI 506
Toto Tours 75, 102

TEXAS
After Five Charters .... 46, FYI 492
Spirit Journeys 72, 101
Tourmark's Gay Way America Tours .. 75, 103

THAILAND
Adventures Unlimited .... 46, FYI 190
Adventures With Flair 46, 85
Explorer Tours .... 55, FYI 190
Hanns Ebensten Travel 57, 92
Jornada 59, 94
Otto Travel Hawaii 65
Our Family Abroad 65, 98
Passport Travel Mgt, Inc. 67
Pearl Selections/Welcome Abroad 67, 99
Progressive Travels 68, 99
R&S Travel 70, 100
Tours to Paradise .... 75, FYI 189
Travel Affair 75, 103

THAILAND - NORTHERN
Silken East Ltd. .... 71, FYI 186

THE HAGUE
IMTC, Inc. 58, 94

TIBERIAS
Gay Guided Tours of Israel .... 56, FYI 305

TIBET
Himalayan High Treks .... 58, FYI 186

TIERRA DEL FUEGO
Mix Travel .... 63, FYI 344
Stonewall 69 .... 73, FYI 344

TIJUANA
Gay Baja Tours .... 56, FYI 358
Gay Mexico Travel .... 56, FYI 358

TOBAGO
RSVP Travel Productions/Club RSVP 70, 100

TONGA ISLANDS
Bushwise Women .... 50, FYI 318

TORONTO
Eat Quiche Tour & Travel Accomm. 54
Hellkamp Reisen 58, 92
New England Vacation Tours 64
Travel Man 76, 104
Wild Women Expeditions .... 79, FYI 330

TORREMOLINOS
Sensations .... 71, FYI 292

TORTOLA
Windjammer Barefoot Cruises 79

TSIPORRI
Gay Guided Tours of Israel .... 56, FYI 305

TUCSON
Tourmark's Gay Way America Tours .. 75, 103

TULUM
Mundo Maya Turquesa 64

TUOLUMNE RIVER
Mariah Wilderness Expeditions 61, 96

TURKEY
Adventure Bound Expeditions 45, 85
Cruise World 52, 89
Different Strokes Tours 53
Global Affair 56
GPSC Charters .... 57, FYI 240
Hanns Ebensten Travel 57, 92
Heritage Tours .... 58, FYI 283
IMTC, Inc. 58, 94
Jetman International Gay Travel 59
L'Arc en Ciel Voyages 61, 94
Ocean Voyager 64, 97
Olivia Cruises & Resorts 65, 98
Our Family Abroad 65, 98
Progressive Travels 68, 99
Seaborne Safaris (Croisieres d'Il en II) 71
Syosset Travel 74
Teddy Travel 74, 101
Travel Man 76, 104
VeloAsia Cycling Adventures 77, 105
Zeus Tours & Yacht Cruises 81, 109

TURKOISE
Atlantis Events 48, 87

TURQUOISE COAST
Seaborne Safaris (Croisieres d'Il en II) 71

UGANDA
Big Five Tours 49, 88

UKRAINE
Departures International .... 52, FYI 266
Kremlin Tours .... 60, FYI 266
Off the Map 65, 97

UNITED KINGDOM
Rail Europe .... 68, FYI 286

URUGUAY
Stonewall 69 .... 73, FYI 344
Terramundo Travels Int'l 74, 102

USA
AAD All About Destinations 45
Adventure Associates 45, 84
Adventures for Women .... 45, FYI 461
After Five Charters .... 46, FYI 492
Ahwahnee Whitewater 46, 85
Alaska Women of the Wilderness 46, 86
Alyson Adventures 47, 87
Archipelago Holidays 48, 87
Atlantis Travel .... 48, FYI 232
Bar H Ranch .... 48, FYI 506
Best of Both Worlds .... FYI 474
Beyond Nirvana .... 49, FYI 342
Beyond the Blue .... 49, FYI 307
Blue Moon Explorations 49
Call of the Wild 50
Canyon Calling Tours .... 50, FYI 366
Cloud Canyon Backpacking 50, 88
Club Hommes/Worldguest .... 51, FYI 204
Colorado Women in the Wilderness 51, 88
Connections Tours 51
Dave's Island Pride Driver, Guide 52, FYI 427

FERRARI GUIDES' GAY TRAVEL A to Z - 18th EDITION 27

WHERE TO GO

DESTINATION INDEX

De Gay Krant Reisservice .... 52, FYI 256
Destination Discovery .... 52, FYI 378
Destination Management .... 53, FYI 436
Easy Way 54
Eclectic Excursions .... 54, FYI 466
Experience Plus 55, 90
Fair Choices 55, 90
Frauen Unterwegs 55, 91
Gay Baja Tours .... 56, FYI 358
Gaygantic Tours 56
Good Time Tours .... 57, FYI 412
Grand Canyon Field Institute 57
Hanns Ebensten Travel 57, 92
Hawk, I'm Your Sister .... 58, FYI 463
Hellkamp Reisen 58, 92
Holigays 58, 92
In Touch Holidays Ltd. 59
Inter-Rainbow Turismo .... 59, FYI 347
Island Hoppers Tours .... 59, FYI 341
It's Our Nature .... 59, FYI 416
Jetman International Gay Travel 59
Jornada 59, 94
Journeys by Sea Yacht Charters 60, FYI 337
Kayak Historical Discovery Tours 60, FYI 420
Lois Lane Expeditions 61
L'Arc en Ciel Voyages 61, 94
Mariah Wilderness Expeditions 61, 96
Men on Vacation 62, 96
Merlyn's Journeys .... 63, FYI 370
Milu Tours 63
New England Vacation Tours 64
North American Travel Specialists 64, 97
Ocean Voyager 64, 97
Oceanwomyn Kayaking .... 64, FYI 357
Off the Map 65, 97
Olivia Cruises & Resorts 65, 98
Pacific Ocean Holidays .... 66, FYI 427
Pearl Selections/Welcome Abroad 67, 99
Pied Piper Travel .... 67, FYI 338
Pleasant Holidays 67
Progressive Travels 68, 99
Puffin Family Charters .... 68, FYI 363
Remote Possibilities .... 69, FYI 426
Royal Hawaiian Weddings .... 70, FYI 425
RSVP Travel Productions/Club RSVP70, 100
R&S Travel 70, 100
Sapphire Travel & Tours 70
Scenic Air Tours .... 70, FYI 386
Sea Sense .... 71, FYI 398
Sensations .... 71, FYI 292
Ski Connections .... 72, FYI 194
Spirit Journeys 72, 101
Teddy Travel 74, 101
Thanks, Babs 74, 102
Toto Tours 75, 102
Tower Travel 75
Travel Club, The 76, 103
Travel Man 76, 104
Tropical Tune-ups 76
T.R.I.P. Tours 76
Uranian Travel 77, 105

Voyages & Expeditions 78, 106
V.I.P. Tours of New York .... 78, FYI 468
We Love the Florida Keys Visitor Center . 78, FYI 408
Whelk Women .... 79, FYI 402
Whitney Yacht Charters .... 79, FYI 340
Wild Women 79, 106
Wintermoon .... 80, FYI 452
Womantours/Artemis Sailing 80, 107
Women in Motion 80, 107
Women in the Wilderness 81, 108
Women Sail Alaska .... 81, FYI 363
Woodswomen 81, 108
Xeno Tours/Mantours 81
Zipper Travel Association .... 82, FYI 252
ZMAX Travel & Tours Inc. 82, 109
Zone One 82

USA AND CANADA ONLY
North American Travel Specialists 64, 97

USA - ALL STATES
Tourmark's Gay Way America Tours .. 75, 103

USA - MAJOR CITIES
North American Travel Specialists 64, 97

USA - MOUNTAIN STATES
Passage to Utah .... 67, FYI 496

USA - NORTHEAST
New England Vacation Tours 64
Port Yacht Charters .... 68, FYI 339
Sailing Affairs .... 70, FYI 468
Whitney Yacht Charters .... 79, FYI 340
Woodswomen 81, 108

USA - NORTHWEST
Adventure Associates 45, 84
Merlyn's Journeys .... 63, FYI 370
Onn the Water 65
Progressive Travels 68, 99
Toto Tours 75, 102

USA - SOUTHWEST
Canyon Calling Tours .... 50, FYI 366
Common Earth Adventures 51, 89
Rainbow Adventures 68
Rainbow Country Tours & B&B ... 69, FYI 496

USA - WESTERN
Lizard Head Backcountry Tours .. 61, FYI 495
Mariah Wilderness Expeditions 61, 96
McNamara Ranch .... 62, FYI 396
Middle Fork River Expeditions 63
Never Summer Nordic .... 64, FYI 396
OutWest Adventures .... 66, FYI 455
Pangaea Expeditions .... 66, FYI 456
Passage to Utah .... 67, FYI 496
Players Express .... 67, FYI 458
Rainbow Adventures 68
Rainbow Country Tours & B&B ... 69, FYI 496
Ten Thousand Waves .... 74, FYI 457
Wild Rockies Tours .... 79, FYI 457

UTAH
Cloud Canyon Backpacking 50, 88
Desert Vision Tours 52
Experience Plus 55, 90
Lizard Head Backcountry Tours .. 61, FYI 495
Mariah Wilderness Expeditions 61, 96
OutWest Adventures .... 66, FYI 455
Pangaea Expeditions .... 66, FYI 456
Passage to Utah .... 67, FYI 496
Rainbow Adventures 68
Rainbow Country Tours & B&B ... 69, FYI 496
Toto Tours 75, 102
Tourmark's Gay Way America Tours .. 75, 103
Woodswomen 81, 108

UTAH DESERTS
Women in the Wilderness 81, 108

UZBEKISTAN
Departures International .... 52, FYI 266
Ventus Reisen 77

VAIL
Lizard Head Backcountry Tours .. 61, FYI 495

VANCOUVER
Eat Quiche Tour & Travel Accomm. 54
Envision Charters .... 54, FYI 324
Fair Choices 55, 90
Super Natural Adventure Tours .. 73, FYI 328
Toto Tours 75, 102
Travel Man 76, 104

VANCOUVER ISLAND
Oceanwomyn Kayaking .... 64, FYI 357
Super Natural Adventure Tours .. 73, FYI 328

VAUX LE VICOMTE
Promenades de Style .... 68, FYI 212

VENEZUELA
Kam Tours Int'l 60
Mercury Cruise & Tour 62
RSVP Travel Productions/Club RSVP70, 100
Terramundo Travels Int'l 74, 102

VENICE
Allegro Travel 46, 86
IMTC, Inc. 58, 94
Men on Bikes .... 62, FYI 248
Travel Affair 75, 103
Zipper Travel Association .... 82, FYI 252

VERACRUZ
Gay Mexico Travel .... 56, FYI 358

VERONA
Zipper Travel Association .... 82, FYI 252

VERSAILLES
Promenades de Style .... 68, FYI 212

VICTORIA
Australian & New Zealand Travel Hdqtrs .. 48
Beyond the Blue .... 49, FYI 307
Bogong Horseback Adventures 49
G'day Tours .... 57, FYI 310
Holidays at Sea/Sunquest 58

WHERE TO GO

Off the Map 65, 97
Southern Discovery Tours .... 72, FYI 315
Toto Tours 75, 102
Wanderlust Ventures 78

VICTORIA FALLS
2Afrika 45, 83

VIENNA
Allegro Travel 46, 86
David's Trips and Tours 52, 89
Gaygantic Tours 56
IMTC, Inc. 58, 94
Off the Map 65, 97
R&S Travel 70, 100
Wolff + Zink Travel Services 80, 106

VIENTAINE
Silken East Ltd. .... 71, FYI 186

VIETNAM
BreakOut Tours .... 50, FYI 308
L'Arc en Ciel Voyages 61, 94
Otto Travel Hawaii 65
Passport Travel Mgt, Inc. 67
VeloAsia Cycling Adventures 77, 105
Worldwide Vacations Inc. 81

VILNIUS
Allegro Travel 46, 86
David's Trips and Tours 52, 89

VIRGIN ISLANDS
BVI Charters 50
Fair Choices 55, 90
Hellkamp Reisen 58, 92
Journeys by Sea Yacht Charters 60, FYI 337
Sea Sense .... 71, FYI 398
Tall Ship Adventures, Inc. .... 74, FYI 340
Women in the Wilderness 81, 108

VIRGINIA
Spirit Journeys 72, 101

WAIKIKI
Pacific Ocean Holidays .... 66, FYI 427

WALES
Cruise World 52, 89

WASHINGTON
Blue Moon Explorations 49
Lizard Head Backcountry Tours .. 61, FYI 495
Oceanwomyn Kayaking .... 64, FYI 357
Progressive Travels 68, 99

WASHINGTON DC
Sailing Affairs .... 70, FYI 468
Tourmark's Gay Way America Tours .. 75, 103

WASHINGTON STATE
Adventure Associates 45, 84
Izarra Cruises .... 59, FYI 502
Merlyn's Journeys .... 63, FYI 370
Toto Tours 75, 102
Woodswomen 81, 108

WATERTON NATIONAL PARK
Pangaea Expeditions .... 66, FYI 456

WEST PALM BEACH
Connections Tours 51

WESTERN AUSTRALIA
Sirius Adventures .... 72, FYI 314

WHITSUNDAY ISLANDS - CANADA
Izarra Cruises .... 59, FYI 502

WINE COUNTRY - CALIF
Merlyn's Journeys .... 63, FYI 370

WISCONSIN
Sea Sense .... 71, FYI 398
Women in the Wilderness 81, 108
Woodswomen 81, 108

WYOMING
Adventure Associates 45, 84
Bar H Ranch .... 48, FYI 506
Lizard Head Backcountry Tours .. 61, FYI 495
Passage to Utah .... 67, FYI 496
Rainbow Adventures 68
Wild Women 79, 106
Woodswomen 81, 108

XIAN
China Voyages .... 50, FYI 176
Envoy Travel .... 54, FYI 176

YELLOWSTONE NAT'L PARK
Adventure Associates 45, 84
Bar H Ranch .... 48, FYI 506
OutWest Adventures .... 66, FYI 455
Rainbow Adventures 68
Toto Tours 75, 102

YOSEMITE NAT'L PARK
Common Earth Adventures 51, 89
Mariah Wilderness Expeditions .. 61, 96
Merlyn's Journeys .... 63, FYI 370
Scenic Air Tours .... 70, FYI 386

YUCATAN
Gay Mexico Travel .... 56, FYI 358
Mundo Maya Turquesa 64

YUKON
Rainbow Adventures 68

ZAMBIA
2Afrika 45, 83
Big Five Tours 49, 88

ZIMBABWE
2Afrika 45, 83
Baobab Safari Co. 48
Big Five Tours 49, 88
Embassy Travel 54
Travel Man 76, 104
Wild Women 79, 106

ZION CANYON
Lizard Head Backcountry Tours .. 61, FYI 495

ZURICH
Gaygantic Tours 56

DESTINATION INDEX

FERRARI GUIDES' GAY TRAVEL A to Z - 18th EDITION

WHAT TO DO

ACTIVITY INDEX

ABORIGINES
Todd River Tours 75

ACTIVE TRAVEL
Experience Plus 55, 90

ADVENTURE SCHOOL
Pangaea Expeditions .... 66, FYI 456

ADVENTURE TRAVEL
2Afrika 45, 83
Adventure Associates 45, 84
Adventure Bound Expeditions 45, 85
Bushwise Women .... 50, FYI 318
Cloud Canyon Backpacking 50, 88
Destination World 53, 90
Earth, Wind & Water .... 53, FYI 354
G'day Tours .... 57, FYI 310
Heritage Tours .... 58, FYI 283
Lizard Head Backcountry Tours .. 61, FYI 495
Lodestar Adventures 61
Lois Lane Expeditions 61
Mercury Cruise & Tour 62
Off the Map 65, 97
OutWest Adventures .... 66, FYI 455
Oz Dive/Passport to Paradise 66
Progressive Travels 68, 99
Rainbow Adventures 68
Sirius Adventures .... 72, FYI 314
Stockler Expeditions 73
Tall Ship Adventures, Inc. .... 74, FYI 340
Way to Go Costa Rica .... 78, FYI 352
Wild Rockies Tours .... 79, FYI 457
Wild Women Expeditions .... 79, FYI 330
Wintermoon .... 80, FYI 452
Women in Motion 80, 107
Women Sail Alaska .... 81, FYI 363
Woodswomen 81, 108

AIR TOURS
Air & Adventure Tours (AAA) .... 46, FYI 312
Scenic Air Tours .... 70, FYI 386
Todd River Tours 75

AMAZON CRUISE
Anderson International Tours ...... 47, FYI 346

ANIMAL TRACKING
Women in the Wilderness 81, 108

ANTIQUE - AUCTIONS
Travel Keys Tours 76, 104

ANTIQUE - BUYING
Travel Keys Tours 76, 104

ANTIQUE - MARKETS
Travel Keys Tours 76, 104

ANTIQUES
Beau Séjour .... 49, FYI 173

ANTIQUES - ENGLAND
European Luxury Hotel Barge Cruises54, FYI 208

ANTIQUITIES
Travel Man 76, 104

ARCHAEOLOGICAL DIGS
Gay Guided Tours of Israel .... 56, FYI 305

ARCHAEOLOGICAL TOURS
Women in the Wilderness 81, 108

ARCHAEOLOGY
GPSC Charters .... 57, FYI 240
Rainbow Destinations 69
Silken East Ltd. .... 71, FYI 186

ARCHITECTURAL TOURS
Our Family Abroad 65, 98
Victorian Home Walk .... 77, FYI 386
V.I.P. Tours of New York .... 78, FYI 468

ARCHITECTURE
Beau Séjour .... 49, FYI 173
David's Trips and Tours 52, 89
Heritage Tours .... 58, FYI 283
Rainboworld Custom Tours .... 69, FYI 256
Silken East Ltd. .... 71, FYI 186

ART
David's Trips and Tours 52, 89

ART DECO TOURS
Good Time Tours .... 57, FYI 412

ART DECO WKND PKGS
Connections Tours 51

ART GALLERIES
Sedona Rainbow Adventure Tours .... 71, FYI 367

ART GROUPS
Departures International .... 52, FYI 266
European Luxury Hotel Barge Cruises54, FYI 208

ART TOURS
Departures International .... 52, FYI 266
IMTC, Inc. 58, 94
Off the Map 65, 97
Women in Motion 80, 107

ART - RENAISSANCE
Rainboworld Custom Tours .... 69, FYI 256

ARTISTS' STUDIOS
Open Eye Tours & Photos .... 65, FYI 425

ARTS/CRAFTS
Silken East Ltd. .... 71, FYI 186
Wild Women Expeditions .... 79, FYI 330

BACKPACKING
Adventure Associates 45, 84
Alaska Women of the Wilderness 46, 86
Bushwise Women .... 50, FYI 318
Call of the Wild 50
Cloud Canyon Backpacking 50, 88
Colorado Women in the Wilderness 51, 88
Common Earth Adventures 51, 89
Grand Canyon Field Institute 57
G'day Tours .... 57, FYI 310
Lizard Head Backcountry Tours .. 61, FYI 495
Lois Lane Expeditions 61

OutWest Adventures .... 66, FYI 455
Pangaea Expeditions .... 66, FYI 456
Rainbow Adventures 68
Super Natural Adventure Tours .. 73, FYI 328
Tours to Paradise .... 75, FYI 189
Wild Rockies Tours .... 79, FYI 457
Wild Women 79, 106
Women in Motion 80, 107
Woodswomen 81, 108

BALLOONING
2Afrika 45, 83

BARGE TRIPS
Our Family Abroad 65, 98

BATTLEFIELD TOURS
Silken East Ltd. .... 71, FYI 186

BEACH RESORTS
2Afrika 45, 83
Good Time Tours .... 57, FYI 412
Tours to Paradise .... 75, FYI 189

BEACH VACATIONS
American Adventures 47
Anderson International Tours ...... 47, FYI 346
Archipelago Holidays 48, 87
Best of Both Worlds .... FYI 474
Beyond the Blue .... 49, FYI 307
Good Time Tours .... 57, FYI 412
G'day Tours .... 57, FYI 310
Pacific Ocean Holidays .... 66, FYI 427
Stonewall 69 .... 73, FYI 344
Surfers Paradise Gay Vacations 73
Tall Ship Adventures, Inc. .... 74, FYI 340
Uranian Travel 77, 105

BEACHCOMBING
Open Eye Tours & Photos .... 65, FYI 425

BEACHES
Good Time Tours .... 57, FYI 412

BEACHES - REMOTE
Kayak Historical Discovery Tours 60, FYI 420

BEDOUIN HOSPITALITY
Gay Guided Tours of Israel .... 56, FYI 305

BICYCLE TOURS
Lizard Head Backcountry Tours .. 61, FYI 495
Paths Less Taken .... 67, FYI 264
Peddlers .... 67, FYI 238
Women in Motion 80, 107
Woodswomen 81, 108

BICYCLING
Alyson Adventures 47, 87
Archipelago Holidays 48, 87
Experience Plus 55, 90
Men on Bikes .... 62, FYI 248
Off the Map 65, 97
Pangaea Expeditions .... 66, FYI 456
Peddlers .... 67, FYI 238
Progressive Travels 68, 99
Super Natural Adventure Tours .. 73, FYI 328

FERRARI GUIDES' GAY TRAVEL A to Z - 18th EDITION

WHAT TO DO

Todd River Tours 75
VeloAsia Cycling Adventures 77, 105
Womantours/Artemis Sailing 80, 107
Women in Motion 80, 107

BICYCLING - MEN'S
Men on Bikes .... 62, FYI 248

BIG GAME
2Afrika 45, 83

BIKING
Alyson Adventures 47, 87
European Luxury Hotel Barge Cruises 54, FYI 208
Frauen Unterwegs 55, 91
Gay Guided Tours of Israel .... 56, FYI 305
Men on Bikes .... 62, FYI 248
Off the Map 65, 97
OutWest Adventures .... 66, FYI 455
Pangaea Expeditions .... 66, FYI 456
Passage to Utah .... 67, FYI 496
Paths Less Taken .... 67, FYI 264
Peddlers .... 67, FYI 238
Rainbow Country Tours & B&B ... 69, FYI 496
Toto Tours 75, 102
VeloAsia Cycling Adventures 77, 105
Women in Motion 80, 107

BIKING - MOUNTAIN
Lizard Head Backcountry Tours .. 61, FYI 495
Never Summer Nordic .... 64, FYI 396
OutWest Adventures .... 66, FYI 455
Paddling South & Saddling South 66, 99
Pangaea Expeditions .... 66, FYI 456
Wild Rockies Tours .... 79, FYI 457
Women in Motion 80, 107

BIKING - ROAD
Pangaea Expeditions .... 66, FYI 456

BIRDWATCHING
2Afrika 45, 83
American Adventures 47
Archipelago Holidays 48, 87
Bushwise Women .... 50, FYI 318
Gay Guided Tours of Israel .... 56, FYI 305
It's Our Nature .... 59, FYI 416
Kayak Historical Discovery Tours 60, FYI 420
Mix Travel .... 63, FYI 344
Open Eye Tours & Photos .... 65, FYI 425
Stonewall 69 .... 73, FYI 344
Todd River Tours 75
Wild Rockies Tours .... 79, FYI 457
Women Sail Alaska .... 81, FYI 363

BLACK HERITAGE
Stockler Expeditions 73

BOAT CHARTERS
Super Natural Adventure Tours .. 73, FYI 328

BOAT RACES
We Love the Florida Keys Visitor Center . 78, FYI 408

BOATING
Gay Guided Tours of Israel .... 56, FYI 305
Oz Dive/Passport to Paradise 66
Progressive Travels 68, 99
Sailing Affairs .... 70, FYI 468
Sea Sense .... 71, FYI 398

BOBSLED
Eclectic Excursions .... 54, FYI 466

BOLSHOI
Allegro Travel 46, 86

BREATHING WORKSHOPS
Adventures for Women .... 45, FYI 461

BUDDHIST RETREATS
Silken East Ltd. .... 71, FYI 186

BUDDHIST STUDIES
Lois Lane Expeditions 61

BULLFIGHTS
Mundo Maya Turquesa 64

BUNGEE JUMPING
2Afrika 45, 83
American Adventures 47
Oz Dive/Passport to Paradise 66

BURIAL MOUNDS
Sounds & Furies .... 72, FYI 244

BUS TOURS
Land Voyages 60

BUS - FLY PKGS
New England Vacation Tours 64

BUS - VAN CHARTERS
After Five Charters .... 46, FYI 492

BUSH MEDICINE
Todd River Tours 75

BUSHWALKING
Sirius Adventures .... 72, FYI 314
Todd River Tours 75
Wanderlust Ventures 78
Witchencroft 4WD & Bushwalking Tours .. 80, FYI 312

BUTTERFLY WATCHING
American Adventures 47
Earth, Wind & Water .... 53, FYI 354

CAMEL SAFARIS
Heritage Tours .... 58, FYI 283

CAMEL TOURS
Gay Guided Tours of Israel .... 56, FYI 305

CAMPING
Adventure Associates 45, 84
Adventure Bound Expeditions 45, 85
Alyson Adventures 47, 87
Bogong Horseback Adventures 49
Bushwise Women .... 50, FYI 318
Cloud Canyon Backpacking 50, 88
Earth, Wind & Water .... 53, FYI 354

Frauen Unterwegs 55, 91
G'day Tours .... 57, FYI 310
Kayak Historical Discovery Tours 60, FYI 420
McNamara Ranch .... 62, FYI 396
Merlyn's Journeys .... 63, FYI 370
OutWest Adventures .... 66, FYI 455
Oz Dive/Passport to Paradise 66
Paddling South & Saddling South 66, 99
Pangaea Expeditions .... 66, FYI 456
Sirius Adventures .... 72, FYI 314
Wanderlust Ventures 78
Wild Rockies Tours .... 79, FYI 457
Woodswomen 81, 108

CAMPING - SNOW
Common Earth Adventures 51, 89

CAMPING - SUMMER
Lizard Head Backcountry Tours .. 61, FYI 495

CAMPING - WINTER
Lizard Head Backcountry Tours .. 61, FYI 495

CAMPOUTS
Rainbow Country Tours & B&B ... 69, FYI 496

CANCER SURVIVORS' RETREATS
Women in the Wilderness 81, 108

CANOE INSTRUCTION
Women in the Wilderness 81, 108

CANOEING
Adventures for Women .... 45, FYI 461
Hawk, I'm Your Sister .... 58, FYI 463
Pangaea Expeditions .... 66, FYI 456
Rainbow Adventures 68
Silke's Travel .... 71, FYI 308
Sirius Adventures .... 72, FYI 314
Super Natural Adventure Tours .. 73, FYI 328
Wild Rockies Tours .... 79, FYI 457
Wild Women 79, 106
Wild Women Expeditions .... 79, FYI 330
Women in Motion 80, 107
Women in the Wilderness 81, 108
Woodswomen 81, 108

CANOEING - WHITEWATER
Women in the Wilderness 81, 108

CANOEING - WILDERNESS
Wild Women Expeditions .... 79, FYI 330

CANYONEERING
Lizard Head Backcountry Tours .. 61, FYI 495

CARNAVAL IN RIO
Fiesta Tours .... 55, FYI 346
Mercury Cruise & Tour 62
Stockler Expeditions 73
Sundance Travel 73

CARNIVAL IN COLOGNE
Teddy Travel 74, 101

ACTIVITY INDEX

FERRARI GUIDES' GAY TRAVEL A to Z - 18th EDITION

WHAT TO DO

ACTIVITY INDEX

CASINOS
2Afrika 45, 83
Thanks, Babs 74, 102

CASTLES
Travel Keys Tours 76, 104
Travel Man 76, 104

CATTLE DRIVE
OutWest Adventures .... 66, FYI 455

CATTLE RANCH
Bar H Ranch .... 48, FYI 506

CHARTERS
2Afrika 45, 83
After Five Charters .... 46, FYI 492
Aquatic Adventures Charter Service . 47, FYI 404
BVI Charters 50
Clione Charters .... 50, FYI 408
Envision Charters .... 54, FYI 324
Hawkesbury Expeditions 58
L'Arc en Ciel Voyages 61, 94
Our Family Abroad 65, 98
Seaborne Safaris (Croisieres d'Il en Il) 71
Thanks, Babs 74, 102
Whelk Women .... 79, FYI 402

CHARTERS - BOAT
We Love the Florida Keys Visitor Center . 78, FYI 408

CHARTERS - CAPTAINED
Best of Both Worlds .... FYI 474
Tall Ship Adventures, Inc. .... 74, FYI 340

CHARTERS - CUSTOM
We Love the Florida Keys Visitor Center . 78, FYI 408

CHARTERS - DIVE
We Love the Florida Keys Visitor Center . 78, FYI 408

CHARTERS - FISHING
Puffin Family Charters .... 68, FYI 363
We Love the Florida Keys Visitor Center . 78, FYI 408

CHARTERS - SNORKELING
We Love the Florida Keys Visitor Center . 78, FYI 408

CHARTERS - YACHT
GPSC Charters .... 57, FYI 240

CHATEAU ACCOMMODATIONS
French Touch .... 56, FYI 210

CHEESE MAKING
Beau Séjour .... 49, FYI 173

CHI GONG
It's Our Nature .... 59, FYI 416

CHRISTIAN HERITAGE
Heritage Tours .... 58, FYI 283

CHRISTMAS SHOPPING
Wolff + Zink Travel Services 80, 106

CIRCUIT PARTIES - PKGS
Connections Tours 51
ZMAX Travel & Tours Inc. 82, 109

CIRCUS WORKSHOPS
Atlantis Events 48, 87

CITY SIGHTSEEING
Victorian Home Walk .... 77, FYI 386

CITY TOURS
American Adventures 47
Departures International .... 52, FYI 266
Frauen Unterwegs 55, 91
French Touch .... 56, FYI 210
Gay Mexico Travel .... 56, FYI 358
Good Time Tours .... 57, FYI 412
Mistral Tours .... 63, FYI 203
Our Family Abroad 65, 98
Promenades de Style .... 68, FYI 212
R&R Eco Tours 70
Southern Discovery Tours .... 72, FYI 315

CLIMBING
Adventure Associates 45, 84
Alyson Adventures 47, 87
Lois Lane Expeditions 61
Wild Women 79, 106
Women in Motion 80, 107

CLIMBING INSTRUCTION
Lois Lane Expeditions 61

CLIMBING - MOUNTAIN
Big Five Tours 49, 88

CLIMBING - ROCK
Woodswomen 81, 108

CLUB MED
2Afrika 45, 83
Alternative Holidays 47, 86
Atlantis Events 48, 87
Olivia Cruises & Resorts 65, 98
Women in Motion 80, 107

COACH TOURS
Land Voyages 60

COFFEE PLANTATIONS
American Adventures 47
Matt's Rainbow Tours .... 62, FYI 421

COLOGNE CARNIVAL '97
Wolff + Zink Travel Services 80, 106

COMMITMENT CEREMONIES
Olivia Cruises & Resorts 65, 98
Royal Hawaiian Weddings .... 70, FYI 425
Tall Ship Adventures, Inc. .... 74, FYI 340
Windmills Travel & Tourism .... 80, FYI 239

CONCERTS - CLASSICAL
Worldwide Vacations Inc. 81

CONCIERGE SERVICE
Tourmark's Gay Way America Tours .. 75, 103

CONDOMINIUMS
Gay Mexico Travel .... 56, FYI 358
Good Time Tours .... 57, FYI 412

COOKING
Mistral Tours .... 63, FYI 203

COOKING SCHOOL
Progressive Travels 68, 99
Rainbow Adventures 68

CRAFTS PEOPLE
Desert Vision Tours 52

CREATIVE ARTS
Wild Women Expeditions .... 79, FYI 330

CRUISES
AAD All About Destinations 45
Advance Damron Vacations 45, 84
Adventure Associates 45, 84
Amazon Tours & Cruises 47
American Adventures 47
Anywhere Travel 47
Beyond the Blue .... 49, FYI 307
China Voyages .... 50, FYI 176
Cruise World 52, 89
Departures International .... 52, FYI 266
East-West Tours .... 53, FYI 322
Eurway Tour & Cruise Club .... 54, FYI 238
Explorer Tours .... 55, FYI 190
Fine Travel & Yachting .... 55, FYI 240
GPSC Charters .... 57, FYI 240
G'day Tours .... 57, FYI 310
Hanns Ebensten Travel 57, 92
L'Arc en Ciel Voyages 61, 94
Mantrav International 61
Mercury Cruise & Tour 62
Ocean Voyager 64, 97
Off the Map 65, 97
Olivia Cruises & Resorts 65, 98
Our Family Abroad 65, 98
Pearl Selections/Welcome Abroad 67, 99
Pied Piper Travel .... 67, FYI 338
Players Express .... 67, FYI 458
Pleasure Travel...Cruise Again Too! .. 68, FYI 339
RSVP Travel Productions/Club RSVP 70, 100
Seaborne Safaris (Croisieres d'Il en Il) 71
Super Natural Adventure Tours .. 73, FYI 328
Tall Ship Adventures, Inc. .... 74, FYI 340
Teddy Travel 74, 101
Thanks, Babs 74, 102
Travel Affair 75, 103
T.R.I.P. Tours 76
Uranian Travel 77, 105
Voyages & Expeditions .... 78, FYI 106
Windjammer Barefoot Cruises 79
Worldwide Vacations Inc. 81
ZMAX Travel & Tours Inc. 82, 109

WHAT TO DO

ACTIVITY INDEX

CRUISES - ALL-GAY
Advance Damron Vacations 45, 84

CRUISES - AMAZON
Amazon Tours & Cruises 47

CRUISES - CANAL
Vaarschool Grietje .... 77, FYI 258

CRUISES - NILE
2Afrika 45, 83

CRUISES - NUDIST
GPSC Charters .... 57, FYI 240
Thanks, Babs 74, 102

CRUISES - RIVER
Off the Map 65, 97
Out Touring Australia 66
Silken East Ltd. .... 71, FYI 186
Travel Affair 75, 103

CRUISES - TALL SHIP
Thanks, Babs 74, 102

CRUISES - WOMEN'S
Olivia Cruises & Resorts 65, 98

CUISINE
David's Trips and Tours 52, 89
Off the Map 65, 97

CUISINE TOURS
Mistral Tours .... 63, FYI 203
Progressive Travels 68, 99
Thanks, Babs 74, 102

CUISINE - AFRICAN
2Afrika 45, 83

CUISINE - EUROPE
Mistral Tours .... 63, FYI 203
Ski Connections .... 72, FYI 194

CULTURAL
2Afrika 45, 83
Beau Séjour .... 49, FYI 173
Canyon Calling Tours .... 50, FYI 366
David's Trips and Tours 52, 89
Earth, Wind & Water .... 53, FYI 354
GPSC Charters .... 57, FYI 240
Heritage Tours .... 58, FYI 283
L'Arc en Ciel Voyages 61, 94
Paddling South & Saddling South 66, 99
Paths Less Taken .... 67, FYI 264
Rainboworld Custom Tours .... 69, FYI 256
Silken East Ltd. .... 71, FYI 186
Sounds & Furies .... 72, FYI 244
Terramundo Travels Int'l 74, 102
Thanks, Babs 74, 102
Worldwide Vacations Inc. 81

CULTURAL ENRICHMENT
Toto Tours 75, 102

CULTURAL TOURS
Adventure Associates 45, 84
Adventure Bound Expeditions 45, 85
Adventures Unlimited .... 46, FYI 190
American Adventures 47
Departures International .... 52, FYI 266
Different Strokes Tours 53
French Touch .... 56, FYI 210
Gay Mexico Travel .... 56, FYI 358
G'day Tours .... 57, FYI 310
Lois Lane Expeditions 61
Mix Travel .... 63, FYI 344
Our Family Abroad 65, 98
Stonewall 69 .... 73, FYI 344
Tours to Paradise .... 75, FYI 189

CULTURE - ABORIGINAL
Destination Downunder .... 53, FYI 309
Todd River Tours 75

CULTURE - HAWAIIAN
Open Eye Tours & Photos .... 65, FYI 425

DANCE
Wild Women Expeditions .... 79, FYI 330

DANCE PARTIES
Beyond the Blue .... 49, FYI 307

DAY SAILS
Best of Both Worlds .... FYI 474
Clione Charters .... 50, FYI 408
Olivia Cruises & Resorts 65, 98

DELUXE ADVENTURE TRAVEL
G'day Tours .... 57, FYI 310
Voyages & Expeditions 78, 106

DELUXE PKGS
Departures International .... 52, FYI 266
Gay Mexico Travel .... 56, FYI 358
Good Time Tours .... 57, FYI 412

DELUXE TRAVEL
Good Time Tours .... 57, FYI 412
Voyages & Expeditions 78, 106

DESERT EXPEDITIONS
Heritage Tours .... 58, FYI 283

DESERTS
Earth, Wind & Water .... 53, FYI 354

DINNER CRUISES
We Love the Florida Keys Visitor Center . 78, FYI 408

DISABLED TRAVELERS
Thanks, Babs 74, 102

DISNEY WORLD
R&S Travel 70, 100

DOGSLEDDING
Alaska Women of the Wilderness 46, 86
Thanks, Babs 74, 102
Wintermoon .... 80, FYI 452
Women in the Wilderness 81, 108
Woodswomen 81, 108

DOLPHIN WATCHING
Kayak Historical Discovery Tours 60, FYI 420
Oz Dive/Passport to Paradise 66

DRAMA
Wild Women Expeditions .... 79, FYI 330

DRUM MAKING
Alaska Women of the Wilderness 46, 86

DUDE RANCH
McNamara Ranch .... 62, FYI 396
OutWest Adventures .... 66, FYI 455

DUNGEONS
Travel Keys Tours 76, 104

ECOTRAVEL
2Afrika 45, 83
American Adventures 47
Beyond the Blue .... 49, FYI 307
Bushwise Women .... 50, FYI 318
Gay Mexico Travel .... 56, FYI 358
G'day Tours .... 57, FYI 310
It's Our Nature .... 59, FYI 416
Mariah Wilderness Expeditions 61, 96
Mercury Cruise & Tour 62
Oz Dive/Passport to Paradise 66
Thanks, Babs 74, 102
Toto Tours 75, 102
Wild Rockies Tours .... 79, FYI 457
Women Sail Alaska .... 81, FYI 363
Woodswomen 81, 108

EDUCATIONAL TRIPS
Lois Lane Expeditions 61
Mistral Tours .... 63, FYI 203

ELEPHANT RIDES
Tours to Paradise .... 75, FYI 189

ELEPHANT TREKKING
Explorer Tours .... 55, FYI 190
Progressive Travels 68, 99
Silken East Ltd. .... 71, FYI 186

EURAIL PASSES
Rail Europe .... 68, FYI 286

EUROPE PACKAGES
Anderson International Tours ...... 47, FYI 346

EUROPEAN CAPITALS
Pearl Selections/Welcome Abroad 67, 99

EUROPEAN CITYBREAKS
Uranian Travel 77, 105

EUROPEAN GAY CITY PKGS
Uranian Travel 77, 105

EUROPEAN GAY RESORTS
De Gay Krant Reisservice .... 52, FYI 256
Uranian Travel 77, 105

EUROPRIDE '97
Above & Beyond Tours 45, 83
Travel Affair 75, 103

EXOTIC TRAVEL
Olivia Cruises & Resorts 65, 98
Voyages & Expeditions 78, 106

FERRARI GUIDES' GAY TRAVEL A to Z - 18th EDITION   33

WHAT TO DO

ACTIVITY INDEX

EXPLORING
Mariah Wilderness Expeditions 61, 96

EXPRESSIVE ARTS
Wild Women Expeditions .... 79, FYI 330

FAMILY VACATIONS
American Adventures 47
Club Le Bon .... 51, FYI 341
Good Time Tours .... 57, FYI 412
Tall Ship Adventures, Inc. .... 74, FYI 340

FANTASY FEST
We Love the Florida Keys Visitor Center . 78, FYI 408

FANTASY FEST CRUISE
ZMAX Travel & Tours Inc. 82, 109

FARM HOLIDAYS
Terramundo Travels Int'l 74, 102

FISHING
Alaska Women of the Wilderness 46, 86
American Adventures 47
Bar H Ranch .... 48, FYI 506
Best of Both Worlds .... FYI 474
Explorer Tours .... 55, FYI 190
McNamara Ranch .... 62, FYI 396
Middle Fork River Expeditions 63
Out Touring Australia 66
OutWest Adventures .... 66, FYI 455
Passage to Utah .... 67, FYI 496
Puffin Family Charters .... 68, FYI 363
We Love the Florida Keys Visitor Center . 78, FYI 408
Wild Women 79, 106

FISHING - DEEPSEA
American Adventures 47
Mundo Maya Turquesa 64
Olivia Cruises & Resorts 65, 98
Oz Dive/Passport to Paradise 66
We Love the Florida Keys Visitor Center . 78, FYI 408

FISHING - FLY
Adventure Associates 45, 84
Rainbow Adventures 68

FISHING - NIGHT
Mundo Maya Turquesa 64

FISHING - OFFSHORE
We Love the Florida Keys Visitor Center . 78, FYI 408

FISHING - SPEAR
We Love the Florida Keys Visitor Center . 78, FYI 408

FLOAT TRIPS
Pangaea Expeditions .... 66, FYI 456

FLOWER FARMS
Open Eye Tours & Photos .... 65, FYI 425

FLOWERS
Rainboworld Custom Tours .... 69, FYI 256

FOOD TOURS
Mistral Tours .... 63, FYI 203

FORBIDDEN CITY
China Voyages .... 50, FYI 176

FORESTS - ANCIENT
Merlyn's Journeys .... 63, FYI 370

FOURWHEEL TOURS
Heritage Tours .... 58, FYI 283
Mount'n Beach Safaris 63
Out Touring Australia 66
Passage to Utah .... 67, FYI 496
Todd River Tours 75
Wanderlust Ventures 78
Witchencroft 4WD & Bushwalking Tours .. 80, FYI 312

FRENCH CHATEAUX
European Luxury Hotel Barge Cruises 54, FYI 208
Our Family Abroad 65, 98

FUNDRAISING TOURS
Good Time Tours .... 57, FYI 412

GAMBLING
2Afrika 45, 83
Women in Motion 80, 107

GARDENS
Rainbowworld Custom Tours .... 69, FYI 256

GAUCHO LIFE
Arcadia Turismo Internacional 48
Mix Travel .... 63, FYI 344
Stonewall 69 .... 73, FYI 344

GAY AND GRAY TOURS
Good Time Tours .... 57, FYI 412
Mistral Tours .... 63, FYI 203

GAY ARCTIC CRUISE
Oceanwide Expeditions 64

GAY DAY AT DISNEY
Mercury Cruise & Tour 62

GAY DAY AT DISNEY PKGS
Connections Tours 51
Good Time Tours .... 57, FYI 412

GAY FAMILY VACATIONS
Club Le Bon .... 51, FYI 341

GAY GAMES
De Gay Krant Reisservice .... 52, FYI 256
IMTC, Inc. 58, 94
Kam Tours Int'l 60
L'Arc en Ciel Voyages 61, 94
Rainbowworld Custom Tours .... 69, FYI 256
Stonewall Connection Travel & Tours 73, 101
Thanks, Babs 74, 102
Women in Motion 80, 107
ZMAX Travel & Tours Inc. 82, 109

GAY HISTORICAL TOURS
Cruisin' the Castro .... 52, FYI 388

GAY PARTIES
Beyond the Blue .... 49, FYI 307
Good Time Tours .... 57, FYI 412

GAY PRIDE PKGS
Men on Vacation 62, 96

GAY RESORT VACATIONS
Alternative Holidays 47, 86
Atlantis Events 48, 87
Atlantis Travel .... 48, FYI 232
Beyond the Blue .... 49, FYI 307
De Gay Krant Reisservice .... 52, FYI 256
Discus Travel 53
Eclectic Excursions .... 54, FYI 466
Good Time Tours .... 57, FYI 412
G'day Tours .... 57, FYI 310
Hellkamp Reisen 58, 92
Holigays 58, 92
Pearl Selections/Welcome Abroad 67, 99
Teddy Travel 74, 101
Travel Man 76, 104
Uranian Travel 77, 105
Women in Motion 80, 107
Xeno Tours/Mantours 81

GAY SKI WEEK
Alternative Holidays 47, 86
Eclectic Excursions .... 54, FYI 466
New England Vacation Tours 64
OutWest Adventures .... 66, FYI 455
Thanks, Babs 74, 102
Travel Man 76, 104

GAY SKI WEEKEND - WINTER GAMES
Eclectic Excursions .... 54, FYI 466

GEOLOGY
Lizard Head Backcountry Tours .. 61, FYI 495

GEOLOGY - JADE MINES
Silken East Ltd. .... 71, FYI 186

GEOLOGY - RUBY MINES
Silken East Ltd. .... 71, FYI 186

GEOLOGY - SILVER MINES
Silken East Ltd. .... 71, FYI 186

GHOST TOWNS
Desert Vision Tours 52
Ten Thousand Waves .... 74, FYI 457

GIRLS' CAMPS
Alaska Women of the Wilderness 46, 86

GLACIER TRAVEL
Alaska Women of the Wilderness 46, 86
G'day Tours .... 57, FYI 310
Lois Lane Expeditions 61
Our Family Abroad 65, 98
Stonewall 69 .... 73, FYI 344

GLASS-BOTTOMED BOATS
We Love the Florida Keys Visitor Center . 78, FYI 408

WHAT TO DO

GODDESS TOURS
Global Affair 56

GOLF
2Afrika 45, 83
Best of Both Worlds .... FYI 474
Destination World 53, 90
Heritage Tours .... 58, FYI 283
L'Arc en Ciel Voyages 61, 94
Mistral Tours .... 63, FYI 203
Silken East Ltd. .... 71, FYI 186
Women in Motion 80, 107

GOLF PACKAGES
Good Time Tours .... 57, FYI 412
G'day Tours .... 57, FYI 310
Mistral Tours .... 63, FYI 203

GOURMET
Destination World 53, 90
Experience Plus 55, 90
Heritage Tours .... 58, FYI 283
L'Arc en Ciel Voyages 61, 94
Off the Map 65, 97
Paths Less Taken .... 67, FYI 264

GOURMET DINING
We Love the Florida Keys Visitor Center . 78, FYI 408

HANDICRAFT MARKETS
American Adventures 47

HAWAII SIGHTSEEING TOURS
Dave's Island Pride Driver, Guide 52, FYI 427

HEALTH
Destination Discovery .... 52, FYI 378

HELICOPTER TOURS
Mundo Maya Turquesa 64
Sedona Rainbow Adventure Tours .... 71, FYI 367

HEMINGWAY HOUSE
We Love the Florida Keys Visitor Center . 78, FYI 408

HERO PARTY
Destination Downunder .... 53, FYI 309
Men on Vacation 62, 96

HIGH COUNTRY
Never Summer Nordic .... 64, FYI 396

HIKING
2Afrika 45, 83
Adventure Associates 45, 84
Adventure Bound Expeditions 45, 85
Adventures for Women .... 45, FYI 461
Alyson Adventures 47, 87
Archipelago Holidays 48, 87
Bar H Ranch .... 48, FYI 506
Beyond the Blue .... 49, FYI 307
Bushwise Women .... 50, FYI 318
Call of the Wild 50
Cloud Canyon Backpacking 50, 88
Experience Plus 55, 90

Frauen Unterwegs 55, 91
Gay Guided Tours of Israel .... 56, FYI 305
G'day Tours .... 57, FYI 310
Heritage Tours .... 58, FYI 283
Himalayan High Treks .... 58, FYI 186
It's Our Nature .... 59, FYI 416
Kayak Historical Discovery Tours 60, FYI 420
Lizard Head Backcountry Tours .. 61, FYI 495
Lodestar Adventures 61
Lois Lane Expeditions 61
Matt's Rainbow Tours .... 62, FYI 421
Merlyn's Journeys .... 63, FYI 370
Never Summer Nordic .... 64, FYI 396
Off the Map 65, 97
Open Eye Tours & Photos .... 65, FYI 425
OutWest Adventures .... 66, FYI 455
Pangaea Expeditions .... 66, FYI 456
Passage to Utah .... 67, FYI 496
Progressive Travels 68, 99
Rainbow Adventures 68
Rainbow Country Tours & B&B ... 69, FYI 496
Remote Possibilities .... 69, FYI 426
Sirius Adventures .... 72, FYI 314
Spirit Journeys 72, 101
Stockler Expeditions 73
Super Natural Adventure Tours .. 73, FYI 328
Ten Thousand Waves .... 74, FYI 457
Toto Tours 75, 102
Travel Club, The 76, 103
Wanderlust Ventures 78
Wild Rockies Tours .... 79, FYI 457
Women in Motion 80, 107
Women in the Wilderness 81, 108
Women Sail Alaska .... 81, FYI 363
Woodswomen 81, 108

HIKING LITE
Bushwise Women .... 50, FYI 318
Call of the Wild 50
Canyon Calling Tours .... 50, FYI 366

HIKING - DESERT
Lizard Head Backcountry Tours .. 61, FYI 495

HIKING - LODGE BASED
Earth, Wind & Water .... 53, FYI 354

HIKING - VOLCANOES
Blue Moon Explorations 49

HISTORICAL
David's Trips and Tours 52, 89
L'Arc en Ciel Voyages 61, 94

HISTORICAL TOURS
GPSC Charters .... 57, FYI 240
IMTC, Inc. 58, 94
It's Our Nature .... 59, FYI 416
Open Eye Tours & Photos .... 65, FYI 425
Paths Less Taken .... 67, FYI 264
Timeout Tours & Travel 74
V.I.P. Tours of New York .... 78, FYI 468
Wild Rockies Tours .... 79, FYI 457

HISTORY
Beau Séjour .... 49, FYI 173
Departures International .... 52, FYI 266
Mistral Tours .... 63, FYI 203
Our Family Abroad 65, 98
Thanks, Babs 74, 102
Travel Club, The 76, 103

HOLIDAY GETAWAYS
Good Time Tours .... 57, FYI 412

HONEYMOONS
American Adventures 47
Good Time Tours .... 57, FYI 412
G'day Tours .... 57, FYI 310
Tall Ship Adventures, Inc. .... 74, FYI 340

HORSEBACK RIDING
Bar H Ranch .... 48, FYI 506
Big Five Tours 49, 88
Bogong Horseback Adventures 49
McNamara Ranch .... 62, FYI 396
Merlyn's Journeys .... 63, FYI 370
Mix Travel .... 63, FYI 344
Mundo Maya Turquesa 64
Olivia Cruises & Resorts 65, 98
Out Touring Australia 66
OutWest Adventures .... 66, FYI 455
Rainbow Adventures 68
Rainbow Country Tours & B&B ... 69, FYI 496
Spirit Journeys 72, 101
Stonewall 69 .... 73, FYI 344
Ten Thousand Waves .... 74, FYI 457
Terramundo Travels Int'l 74, 102
Toto Tours 75, 102
Travel Club, The 76, 103
Way to Go Costa Rica .... 78, FYI 352
Windmills Travel & Tourism .... 80, FYI 239
Woodswomen 81, 108

HORSEPACKING
Alaska Women of the Wilderness 46, 86
Bar H Ranch .... 48, FYI 506
Bogong Horseback Adventures 49
Paddling South & Saddling South 66, 99
Super Natural Adventure Tours .. 73, FYI 328

HORSERIDING - TRAIL
McNamara Ranch .... 62, FYI 396

HOSTELLING
Pangaea Expeditions .... 66, FYI 456

HOT AIR BALLOONING
Travel Club, The 76, 103

HOT SPRINGS
Merlyn's Journeys .... 63, FYI 370
Pangaea Expeditions .... 66, FYI 456

HOT TUBS
Travel Club, The 76, 103

HOTEL BARGING
Our Family Abroad 65, 98

WHAT TO DO

HOTEL PACKAGES
Good Time Tours .... 57, FYI 412
HOUSEBOATING
Toto Tours 75, 102
ICE SKATING
Eclectic Excursions .... 54, FYI 466
IDITAROD RACE
Thanks, Babs 74, 102
INCARCERATION PARTY
Destination Downunder .... 53, FYI 309
INVESTMENT TOURS
Doin' It Right - in Puerto Vallarta 53
ISLAMIC ARCHITECTURE
Heritage Tours .... 58, FYI 283
ISLAND VACATIONS
Island Hoppers Tours .... 59, FYI 341
Oz Dive/Passport to Paradise 66
Pacific Ocean Holidays .... 66, FYI 427
JAZZ
Thanks, Babs 74, 102
JEEP TOURS
Gay Guided Tours of Israel .... 56, FYI 305
Mistral Tours .... 63, FYI 203
Mount'n Beach Safaris 63
Rainbow Country Tours & B&B .. 69, FYI 496
Wanderlust Ventures 78
JEWISH HERITAGE
Heritage Tours .... 58, FYI 283
JOURNAL WRITING
It's Our Nature .... 59, FYI 416
JUNGLE EXCURSIONS
R&R Eco Tours 70
JUNGLE EXPEDITIONS
American Adventures 47
JUNGLE SAFARIS
R&R Eco Tours 70
JUNGLE TRAINING
Archipelago Holidays 48, 87
JUNGLE TREKKING
Anderson International Tours ...... 47, FYI 346
KAYAK INSTRUCTION
Pangaea Expeditions .... 66, FYI 456
KAYAKING
Ahwahnee Whitewater 46, 85
American Adventures 47
Archipelago Holidays 48, 87
Bushwise Women .... 50, FYI 318
Common Earth Adventures 51, 89
Explorer Tours .... 55, FYI 190
Gay Guided Tours of Israel .... 56, FYI 305
Kayak Historical Discovery Tours 60, FYI 420
Lizard Head Backcountry Tours .. 61, FYI 495
Matt's Rainbow Tours .... 62, FYI 421

Oceanwomyn Kayaking .... 64, FYI 357
Pangaea Expeditions .... 66, FYI 456
Spirit Journeys 72, 101
Ten Thousand Waves .... 74, FYI 457
Toto Tours 75, 102
Wild Women 79, 106
Wintermoon .... 80, FYI 452
Women in Motion 80, 107
Women Sail Alaska .... 81, FYI 363
KAYAKING - CAVE
Matt's Rainbow Tours .... 62, FYI 421
KAYAKING - FLATWATER
It's Our Nature .... 59, FYI 416
KAYAKING - SEA
Adventure Associates 45, 84
Alaska Women of the Wilderness 46, 86
Blue Moon Explorations 49
Bushwise Women .... 50, FYI 318
Earth, Wind & Water .... 53, FYI 354
Mariah Wilderness Expeditions 61, 96
Oceanwomyn Kayaking .... 64, FYI 357
Oz Dive/Passport to Paradise 66
Paddling South & Saddling South 66, 99
Pangaea Expeditions .... 66, FYI 456
Rainbow Adventures 68
Silke's Travel .... 71, FYI 308
Super Natural Adventure Tours .. 73, FYI 328
Wild Women 79, 106
Women in the Wilderness 81, 108
Woodswomen 81, 108
KIBBUTZ TOURS
Gay Guided Tours of Israel .... 56, FYI 305
KIDS
Thanks, Babs 74, 102
KINK
Rainboworld Custom Tours .... 69, FYI 256
KIROV THEATER
Allegro Travel 46, 86
LANGUAGE SCHOOL
Paddling South & Saddling South 66, 99
LEADERSHIP TRAINING
Women in the Wilderness 81, 108
Woodswomen 81, 108
LEARNING VACATIONS
Experience Plus 55, 90
LEATHER
Rainboworld Custom Tours .... 69, FYI 256
LEATHER PRIDE
Rainboworld Custom Tours .... 69, FYI 256
LEATHER SCENE
Travel Keys Tours 76, 104
LEATHER WEEK - IBIZA
Teddy Travel 74, 101

LEATHER WEEK - SYDNEY
BreakOut Tours .... 50, FYI 308
Destination Downunder .... 53, FYI 309
LEATHERMAN'S TOURS
Tall Ship Adventures, Inc. .... 74, FYI 340
Travel Keys Tours 76, 104
LESBIAN EVENTS PKGS
Thanks, Babs 74, 102
LESBIAN RESORT VACATIONS
Beyond the Blue .... 49, FYI 307
Club Le Bon .... 51, FYI 341
Olivia Cruises & Resorts 65, 98
Remote Possibilities .... 69, FYI 426
Women in Motion 80, 107
LIMOUSINE SERVICE
Promenades de Style .... 68, FYI 212
LINE DANCING
Olivia Cruises & Resorts 65, 98
LINGUISTICS
David's Trips and Tours 52, 89
LLAMA PACKING
Alaska Women of the Wilderness 46, 86
Colorado Women in the Wilderness 51, 88
LLAMA TREKKING
Lodestar Adventures 61
LOBSTERING
We Love the Florida Keys Visitor Center . 78,
FYI 408
LUGE
Eclectic Excursions .... 54, FYI 466
LUXURY TRAVEL
Departures International .... 52, FYI 266
G'day Tours .... 57, FYI 310
Olivia Cruises & Resorts 65, 98
Voyages & Expeditions 78, 106
Way to Go Costa Rica .... 78, FYI 352
MACADAMIA NUT PLANTATIONS
Matt's Rainbow Tours .... 62, FYI 421
MACCHU PICCHU
Mercury Cruise & Tour 62
MAGIC KINGDOM
R&S Travel 70, 100
MASSAGE
Matt's Rainbow Tours .... 62, FYI 421
Merlyn's Journeys .... 63, FYI 370
MEDIEVAL
Rainboworld Custom Tours .... 69, FYI 256
MEDIEVAL CITIES
Heritage Tours .... 58, FYI 283
MEN'S OUTDOOR ADVENTURES
Adventure Bound Expeditions 45, 85
Earth, Wind & Water .... 53, FYI 354
Eclectic Excursions .... 54, FYI 466

36   FERRARI GUIDES' GAY TRAVEL A to Z - 18th EDITION

WHAT TO DO

Tall Ship Adventures, Inc. .... 74, FYI 340
MEN'S RESORT VACATIONS
Jetman International Gay Travel 59
R&S Travel 70, 100
Sapphire Travel & Tours 70
Sensations .... 71, FYI 292
MEN'S TRAVEL CLUB
Club Hommes/Worldguest .... 51, FYI 204
MEXICO - MARDI GRAS
Gay Baja Tours .... 56, FYI 358
MIDSUMMA FESTIVAL
Destination Downunder .... 53, FYI 309
Men on Vacation 62, 96
MILITARY HISTORY
Silken East Ltd. .... 71, FYI 186
MOTHER - DAUGHTER ADVENTURES
Alaska Women of the Wilderness 46, 86
Canyon Calling Tours .... 50, FYI 366
Tall Ship Adventures, Inc. .... 74, FYI 340
Women in the Wilderness 81, 108
MOTOR COACH TOURS
Departures International .... 52, FYI 266
Our Family Abroad 65, 98
MOTORCYCLE TOURS
Todd River Tours 75
MOTORCYCLE TREKS
Tours to Paradise .... 75, FYI 189
MOUNTAINEERING
Lizard Head Backcountry Tours .. 61, FYI 495
Lois Lane Expeditions 61
Wild Rockies Tours .... 79, FYI 457
Woodswomen 81, 108
MOUNTAINEERING INSTRUCTION
Lois Lane Expeditions 61
MOUNTAINS
Explorer Tours .... 55, FYI 190
MR DRUMMER
Rainboworld Custom Tours .... 69, FYI 256
MR LEATHER IBIZA
Teddy Travel 74, 101
MUD BATHS
Beyond Nirvana .... 49, FYI 342
MULTI-SPORT TRIPS
Adventure Associates 45, 84
MURDER MYSTERY TOURS
L'Arc en Ciel Voyages 61, 94
MUSEUMS
American Adventures 47
Beau Séjour .... 49, FYI 173

MUSIC FESTIVAL PKGS
Thanks, Babs 74, 102
NATIONAL PARKS
American Adventures 47
Bushwise Women .... 50, FYI 318
OutWest Adventures .... 66, FYI 455
Stonewall 69 .... 73, FYI 344
Women in Motion 80, 107
NATIVE AMERICANS
Desert Vision Tours 52
NATIVE SPIRITUALITY
Wild Women Expeditions .... 79, FYI 330
NATURAL HISTORY
G'day Tours .... 57, FYI 310
Paddling South & Saddling South 66, 99
NATURE CRUISES
Big Five Tours 49, 88
NATURE STUDY
Women in the Wilderness 81, 108
NATURE TOURS
Adventure Associates 45, 84
Bushwise Women .... 50, FYI 318
Earth, Wind & Water .... 53, FYI 354
G'day Tours .... 57, FYI 310
Mix Travel .... 63, FYI 344
Stonewall 69 .... 73, FYI 344
NEW ORLEANS MARDI GRAS
Destination Management .... 53, FYI 436
NEW YEAR TOURS
Departures International .... 52, FYI 266
NEW YEARS 1999
Travel Affair 75, 103
NEW YEARS IN RIO
Sundance Travel 73
NIGHTLIFE
Anderson International Tours ...... 47, FYI 346
NIGHTLIFE - EUROPE
Ski Connections .... 72, FYI 194
Uranian Travel 77, 105
Windmills Travel & Tourism .... 80, FYI 239
NIGHTLIFE - RUSSIA
Departures International .... 52, FYI 266
NILE RIVER
Rainbow Destinations 69
NUDIST
Journeys by Sea Yacht Charters 60, FYI 337
Thanks, Babs 74, 102
OCEAN EXPEDITIONS
Oceanwide Expeditions 64
OKTOBERFEST
Travel Keys Tours 76, 104
Wolff + Zink Travel Services 80, 106

OKTOBERFEST - LEATHER MEET
Travel Keys Tours 76, 104
OLYMPICS 2000
Destination Downunder .... 53, FYI 309
OPERA
2Afrika 45, 83
Allegro Travel 46, 86
Off the Map 65, 97
Worldwide Vacations Inc. 81
OPERA - FINLAND
Allegro Travel 46, 86
OPERA - FRANCE
European Luxury Hotel Barge Cruises 54, FYI 208
Mistral Tours .... 63, FYI 203
ORCHID FARMS
Matt's Rainbow Tours .... 62, FYI 421
OUTBACK
Oz Dive/Passport to Paradise 66
Wanderlust Ventures 78
OUTDOOR ADVENTURE
Air & Adventure Tours (AAA) ...... 46, FYI 312
Canyon Calling Tours .... 50, FYI 366
Earth, Wind & Water .... 53, FYI 354
Off the Map 65, 97
Oz Dive/Passport to Paradise 66
Passage to Utah .... 67, FYI 496
Paths Less Taken .... 67, FYI 264
Progressive Travels 68, 99
Rainbow Country Tours & B&B .. 69, FYI 496
Sailing Affairs .... 70, FYI 468
Sirius Adventures .... 72, FYI 314
Wild Rockies Tours .... 79, FYI 457
Wild Women Expeditions .... 79, FYI 330
OUTDOOR SPORTS
Lizard Head Backcountry Tours .. 61, FYI 495
PAGAN SITES
Sounds & Furies .... 72, FYI 244
PAINTING VACATIONS
Trek Out 76
PANNING FOR GOLD
Travel Club, The 76, 103
PARAGLIDING
Archipelago Holidays 48, 87
PARENT - CHILD TRIPS
Good Time Tours .... 57, FYI 412
Tall Ship Adventures, Inc. .... 74, FYI 340
PARIS BY NIGHT
Promenades de Style .... 68, FYI 212
PHOTOGRAPHY
2Afrika 45, 83
Baobab Safari Co. 48
Big Five Tours 49, 88

ACTIVITY INDEX

FERRARI GUIDES' GAY TRAVEL A to Z - 18th EDITION

WHAT TO DO

Bushwise Women .... 50, FYI 318
Heritage Tours .... 58, FYI 283
Oz Dive/Passport to Paradise 66
Robin Tyler's Women's Tours, Cruises &
    Events 69

PHOTOGRAPHY - NATURE
It's Our Nature .... 59, FYI 416

PICNICS
Open Eye Tours & Photos .... 65, FYI 425

PLANTATIONS
Open Eye Tours & Photos .... 65, FYI 425

POETRY
Wild Women Expeditions .... 79, FYI 330

POWER BOAT RACES
We Love the Florida Keys Visitor Center . 78,
    FYI 408

POWER BOATING
Sea Sense .... 71, FYI 398

PRIDE EVENTS
Doin' It Right - in Puerto Vallarta 53
L'Arc en Ciel Voyages 61, 94

PRIVATE CAR/DRIVER
Destination World 53, 90

PYRAMIDS
2Afrika 45, 83
Hanns Ebensten Travel 57, 92
Rainbow Destinations 69
Travel Affair 75, 103

QUEENS BIRTHDAY BALL
Destination Downunder .... 53, FYI 309

QUEENSDAY
Rainboworld Custom Tours .... 69, FYI 256

RAFTING
Adventure Associates 45, 84
Ahwahnee Whitewater 46, 85
Alyson Adventures 47, 87
American Adventures 47
Archipelago Holidays 48, 87
Big Five Tours 49, 88
Colorado Women in the Wilderness 51, 88
Gay Guided Tours of Israel .... 56, FYI 305
Hawk, I'm Your Sister .... 58, FYI 463
Mariah Wilderness Expeditions 61, 96
Men on Vacation 62, 96
Mercury Cruise & Tour 62
Merlyn's Journeys .... 63, FYI 370
Middle Fork River Expeditions 63
Off the Map 65, 97
Olivia Cruises & Resorts 65, 98
Out Touring Australia 66
OutWest Adventures .... 66, FYI 455
Pangaea Expeditions .... 66, FYI 456
Passage to Utah .... 67, FYI 496
Progressive Travels 68, 99
Rainbow Adventures 68
Remote Possibilities .... 69, FYI 426

Silken East Ltd. .... 71, FYI 186
Spirit Journeys 72, 101
Super Natural Adventure Tours .. 73, FYI 328
Ten Thousand Waves .... 74, FYI 457
Terramundo Travels Int'l 74, 102
Toto Tours 75, 102
Travel Club, The 76, 103
Way to Go Costa Rica .... 78, FYI 352
Wild Women 79, 106
Women in Motion 80, 107
Women in the Wilderness 81, 108
Woodswomen 81, 108

RAFTING - OVERNIGHT TRIPS
Pangaea Expeditions .... 66, FYI 456

RAIL TRAVEL
Earth, Wind & Water .... 53, FYI 354
OutWest Adventures .... 66, FYI 455
Rail Europe .... 68, FYI 286
Rocky Mountaineer Railtours ..... 69, FYI 328

RAINFOREST
2Afrika 45, 83
American Adventures 47
Bushwise Women .... 50, FYI 318
Explorer Tours .... 55, FYI 190
Mercury Cruise & Tour 62
Olivia Cruises & Resorts 65, 98
Oz Dive/Passport to Paradise 66
Stockler Expeditions 73
Thanks, Babs 74, 102
Way to Go Costa Rica .... 78, FYI 352

RANCH LIFE
Bar H Ranch .... 48, FYI 506
McNamara Ranch .... 62, FYI 396
OutWest Adventures .... 66, FYI 455
Stonewall 69 .... 73, FYI 344

RANCH VACATION
G'day Tours .... 57, FYI 310
McNamara Ranch .... 62, FYI 396
Open Eye Tours & Photos .... 65, FYI 425
Super Natural Adventure Tours .. 73, FYI 328

RANCH - DUDE
McNamara Ranch .... 62, FYI 396

RANCH - GAUCHO LIFE
Mix Travel .... 63, FYI 344

RAPELLING
Gay Guided Tours of Israel .... 56, FYI 305

RED RAW PARTY
Destination Downunder .... 53, FYI 309

REEF TRIPS
Out Touring Australia 66

RELIGIOUS PILGRIMAGES
L'Arc en Ciel Voyages 61, 94

RESORT PKGS
Good Time Tours .... 57, FYI 412

RESORT VACATIONS
We Love the Florida Keys Visitor Center . 78,
    FYI 408

RETIREMENT IN MEXICO
South of the Border Tour & Travel 72, FYI 358

RETREATS
Destination World 53, 90
Spirit Journeys 72, 101

RIVER RUNNING
Passage to Utah .... 67, FYI 496

ROCK CLIMBING
Lizard Head Backcountry Tours .. 61, FYI 495
Pangaea Expeditions .... 66, FYI 456
Woodswomen 81, 108

RODEO
McNamara Ranch .... 62, FYI 396
OutWest Adventures .... 66, FYI 455

ROPES COURSE
Common Earth Adventures 51, 89

RUINS - INDIAN
Kayak Historical Discovery Tours 60, FYI 420

RUINS - ROMAN
Hanns Ebensten Travel 57, 92
Heritage Tours .... 58, FYI 283

SAFARIS
2Afrika 45, 83
Adventure Associates 45, 84
Archipelago Holidays 48, 87
Baobab Safari Co. 48
David's Trips and Tours 52, 89
De Gay Krant Reisservice .... 52, FYI 256
Embassy Travel 54
Mantrav International 61
Robin Tyler's Women's Tours, Cruises &
    Events 69
Silke's Travel .... 71, FYI 308
Travel Affair 75, 103

SAFARIS - AIR
Big Five Tours 49, 88

SAFARIS - DESERT
Explorer Tours .... 55, FYI 190

SAFARIS - DRIVEN
Big Five Tours 49, 88

SAFARIS - POLAR BEAR
Big Five Tours 49, 88

SAFARIS - WALKING
Big Five Tours 49, 88

SAILING
Advance Damron Vacations 45, 84
Adventure Associates 45, 84
Aquatic Adventures Charter Service . 47, FYI
    404
Best of Both Worlds .... FYI 474
BVI Charters 50

WHAT TO DO

Clione Charters .... 50, FYI 408
East-West Tours .... 53, FYI 322
Envision Charters .... 54, FYI 324
Fine Travel & Yachting .... 55, FYI 240
Gay Guided Tours of Israel .... 56, FYI 305
G'day Tours .... 57, FYI 310
Hawkesbury Expeditions 58
Izarra Cruises .... 59, FYI 502
Journeys by Sea Yacht Charters 60, FYI 337
Mariah Wilderness Expeditions 61, 96
Merlyn's Journeys .... 63, FYI 370
Mundo Maya Turquesa 64
Olivia Cruises & Resorts 65, 98
Onn the Water 65
Paddling South & Saddling South 66, 99
Port Yacht Charters .... 68, FYI 339
Puffin Family Charters .... 68, FYI 363
Rainbow Adventures 68
Sailing Affairs .... 70, FYI 468
Sea Sense .... 71, FYI 398
Seaborne Safaris (Croisieres d'Il en Il) 71
Syosset Travel 74
Tall Ship Adventures, Inc. .... 74, FYI 340
Toto Tours 75, 102
Vaarschool Grietje .... 77, FYI 258
We Love the Florida Keys Visitor Center . 78, FYI 408
Whelk Women .... 79, FYI 402
Whitney Yacht Charters .... 79, FYI 340
Windjammer Barefoot Cruises 79
Womantours/Artemis Sailing ..... 80, FYI 107
Women in the Wilderness 81, 108
Women Sail Alaska .... 81, FYI 363

SAILING AROUND THE WORLD
East-West Tours .... 53, FYI 322

SAILING CHARTERS
Eurway Tour & Cruise Club .... 54, FYI 238
Good Time Tours .... 57, FYI 412
Hawkesbury Expeditions 58
Izarra Cruises .... 59, FYI 502
Journeys by Sea Yacht Charters 60, FYI 337
Oz Dive/Passport to Paradise 66
Sailing Affairs .... 70, FYI 468
Tall Ship Adventures, Inc. .... 74, FYI 340
Whitney Yacht Charters .... 79, FYI 340

SAILING INSTRUCTION
Best of Both Worlds .... FYI 474
Sea Sense .... 71, FYI 398
Vaarschool Grietje .... 77, FYI 258

SAILING SCHOOL
Sea Sense .... 71, FYI 398

SAILING VACATIONS
Port Yacht Charters .... 68, FYI 339

SAILING - TALL SHIPS
Windjammer Barefoot Cruises 79

SALES INCENTIVES
Good Time Tours .... 57, FYI 412

SALZBURGER FESTSPIELE
Wolff + Zink Travel Services 80, 106

SCHOONER CRUISES
Tall Ship Adventures, Inc. .... 74, FYI 340

SCUBA DIVING
2Afrika 45, 83
Advance Damron Vacations 45, 84
Alyson Adventures 47, 87
Aquatic Adventures Charter Service . 47, FYI 404
Archipelago Holidays 48, 87
Beyond the Blue .... 49, FYI 307
Destination World 53, 90
Explorer Tours .... 55, FYI 190
Fair Choices 55, 90
Gay Baja Tours .... 56, FYI 358
Gay Guided Tours of Israel .... 56, FYI 305
G'day Tours .... 57, FYI 310
Hanafi Tour and Travel .... 57, FYI 188
Hawk, I'm Your Sister .... 58, FYI 463
Journeys by Sea Yacht Charters 60, FYI 337
Liquid Crystal Divers .... 60, FYI 422
Mariah Wilderness Expeditions 61, 96
Mercury Cruise & Tour 62
Mundo Maya Turquesa 64
Olivia Cruises & Resorts 65, 98
Out Touring Australia 66
Oz Dive/Passport to Paradise 66
Paddling South & Saddling South 66, 99
Port Yacht Charters .... 68, FYI 339
Sailing Affairs .... 70, FYI 468
Toto Tours 75, 102
Undersea Expeditions, Inc. 77, 104
Way to Go Costa Rica .... 78, FYI 352
We Love the Florida Keys Visitor Center . 78, FYI 408
Windmills Travel & Tourism .... 80, FYI 239
Women in Motion 80, 107
Woodswomen 81, 108
Worldwide Vacations Inc. 81

SCUBA WITH SHARKS
Archipelago Holidays 48, 87

SHIP CHARTERS
Olivia Cruises & Resorts 65, 98
Tall Ship Adventures, Inc. .... 74, FYI 340
Voyages & Expeditions 78, 106
Windjammer Barefoot Cruises 79

SHOOTING
Sedona Rainbow Adventure Tours .... 71, FYI 367

SHOPPING
Beau Séjour .... 49, FYI 173
David's Trips and Tours 52, 89
Gay Guided Tours of Israel .... 56, FYI 305
G'day Tours .... 57, FYI 310
Mistral Tours .... 63, FYI 203
Our Family Abroad 65, 98
Travel Club, The 76, 103

SHOPPING TOURS
Doin' It Right - in Puerto Vallarta 53
Good Time Tours .... 57, FYI 412
Stonewall 69 .... 73, FYI 344

SIGHTSEEING
Departures International .... 52, FYI 266
L'Arc en Ciel Voyages 61, 94
Matt's Rainbow Tours .... 62, FYI 421
Mix Travel .... 63, FYI 344
Olivia Cruises & Resorts 65, 98
Open Eye Tours & Photos .... 65, FYI 425
Our Family Abroad 65, 98
Stonewall 69 .... 73, FYI 344
Travel Club, The 76, 103

SIGHTSEEING TOURS
Good Time Tours .... 57, FYI 412

SIGHTSEEING - AIR
Scenic Air Tours .... 70, FYI 386

SILK SPINNING
China Voyages .... 50, FYI 176

SKI TOURS
Ski Connections .... 72, FYI 194

SKI WEEK
Eclectic Excursions .... 54, FYI 466
Lois Lane Expeditions 61

SKIING
Adventure Associates 45, 84
Alternative Holidays 47, 86
Alyson Adventures 47, 87
Archipelago Holidays 48, 87
De Gay Krant Reisservice .... 52, FYI 256
Eclectic Excursions .... 54, FYI 466
Fair Choices 55, 90
Frauen Unterwegs 55, 91
G'day Tours .... 57, FYI 310
Himalayan High Treks .... 58, FYI 186
Lois Lane Expeditions 61
Never Summer Nordic .... 64, FYI 396
Off the Map 65, 97
Olivia Cruises & Resorts 65, 98
OutWest Adventures .... 66, FYI 455
Pearl Selections/Welcome Abroad 67, 99
Ski Connections .... 72, FYI 194
Stonewall 69 .... 73, FYI 344
Super Natural Adventure Tours .. 73, FYI 328
Thanks, Babs 74, 102
Travel Affair 75, 103
Travel Man 76, 104
Wild Women 79, 106
Worldwide Vacations Inc. 81

SKIING IN JULY
Mix Travel .... 63, FYI 344
Stonewall 69 .... 73, FYI 344

SKIING - ALPINE
Lizard Head Backcountry Tours .. 61, FYI 495

FERRARI GUIDES' GAY TRAVEL A to Z - 18th EDITION

WHAT TO DO

SKIING - BACKCOUNTRY
Lizard Head Backcountry Tours .. 61, FYI 495

SKIING - CROSSCOUNTRY
Adventure Associates 45, 84
Adventures for Women .... 45, FYI 461
Bushwise Women .... 50, FYI 318
Common Earth Adventures 51, 89
Eclectic Excursions .... 54, FYI 466
Lizard Head Backcountry Tours .. 61, FYI 495
Lois Lane Expeditions 61
Mix Travel .... 63, FYI 344
Never Summer Nordic .... 64, FYI 396
OutWest Adventures .... 66, FYI 455
Ski Connections .... 72, FYI 194
Stonewall 69 .... 73, FYI 344
Women in Motion 80, 107
Women in the Wilderness 81, 108
Woodswomen 81, 108

SKIING - DUNE
Archipelago Holidays 48, 87

SKIING - EUROPE
Ski Connections .... 72, FYI 194

SKIING - GLACIER
Ski Connections .... 72, FYI 194

SKIING - HELI SKIING
Ski Connections .... 72, FYI 194

SKIING - WATER
Port Yacht Charters .... 68, FYI 339

SLEAZE BALL
Above & Beyond Tours 45, 83
Destination Downunder .... 53, FYI 309
G'day Tours .... 57, FYI 310
Oz Dive/Passport to Paradise 66

SNORKELING
2Afrika 45, 83
Advance Damron Vacations 45, 84
Aquatic Adventures Charter Service . 47, FYI 404
Blue Moon Explorations 49
Clione Charters .... 50, FYI 408
GPSC Charters .... 57, FYI 240
Hanafi Tour and Travel .... 57, FYI 188
Hanns Ebensten Travel 57, 92
Hawk, I'm Your Sister .... 58, FYI 463
Journeys by Sea Yacht Charters 60, FYI 337
Kayak Historical Discovery Tours 60, FYI 420
Mariah Wilderness Expeditions 61, 96
Matt's Rainbow Tours .... 62, FYI 421
Men on Vacation 62, 96
Mercury Cruise & Tour 62
Mundo Maya Turquesa 64
Olivia Cruises & Resorts 65, 98
Open Eye Tours & Photos .... 65, FYI 425
Oz Dive/Passport to Paradise 66
Paddling South & Saddling South 66, 99
Port Yacht Charters .... 68, FYI 339
Sailing Affairs .... 70, FYI 468

Tall Ship Adventures, Inc. .... 74, FYI 340
Toto Tours 75, 102
Travel Man 76, 104
Undersea Expeditions, Inc. 77, 104
Way to Go Costa Rica .... 78, FYI 352
We Love the Florida Keys Visitor Center . 78, FYI 408
Women in Motion 80, 107
Woodswomen 81, 108

SNOWBOARDING
Eclectic Excursions .... 54, FYI 466
Ski Connections .... 72, FYI 194
Women in Motion 80, 107

SNOWMOBILING
Departures International .... 52, FYI 266
Eclectic Excursions .... 54, FYI 466
Thanks, Babs 74, 102

SNOWSHOEING
Eclectic Excursions .... 54, FYI 466
Lizard Head Backcountry Tours .. 61, FYI 495
Thanks, Babs 74, 102
Women in Motion 80, 107
Women in the Wilderness 81, 108

SOFT ADVENTURE
Australian & New Zealand Travel Hdqtrs .. 48
Big Five Tours 49, 88
Bushwise Women .... 50, FYI 318
Earth, Wind & Water .... 53, FYI 354
Explorer Tours .... 55, FYI 190
G'day Tours .... 57, FYI 310
Mercury Cruise & Tour 62
Oz Dive/Passport to Paradise 66
Passage to Utah .... 67, FYI 496
Super Natural Adventure Tours .. 73, FYI 328
Tall Ship Adventures, Inc. .... 74, FYI 340
Voyages & Expeditions 78, 106
Women in Motion 80, 107

SPA
Gay Guided Tours of Israel .... 56, FYI 305

SPA VACATIONS
2Afrika 45, 83
Beyond Nirvana .... 49, FYI 342
Off the Map 65, 97

SPACE CAMP
Travel Club, The 76, 103

SPECIAL ITINERARIES
Bushwise Women .... 50, FYI 318
Departures International .... 52, FYI 266
Gay Mexico Travel .... 56, FYI 358
Good Time Tours .... 57, FYI 412
G'day Tours .... 57, FYI 310
Our Family Abroad 65, 98
Stonewall 69 .... 73, FYI 344

SPECIALTY TOURS
Paths Less Taken .... 67, FYI 264

SPECIAL-INTEREST TOURS
Departures International .... 52, FYI 266
Olivia Cruises & Resorts 65, 98
Our Family Abroad 65, 98

SPIRITUAL
Alaska Women of the Wilderness 46, 86
Wild Women Expeditions .... 79, FYI 330

SPIRITUAL QUESTS
Cloud Canyon Backpacking 50, 88

SPORTS INSTRUCTION
Lizard Head Backcountry Tours .. 61, FYI 495

STONE CIRCLES
Sounds & Furies .... 72, FYI 244

STUDENT TOURS
GPSC Charters .... 57, FYI 240

SUBMARINE - GLASS BOTTOMED
Mundo Maya Turquesa 64

SUB-TROPICAL ISLANDS
We Love the Florida Keys Visitor Center . 78, FYI 408

SUNSET CELEBRATIONS
We Love the Florida Keys Visitor Center . 78, FYI 408

SUNSET CRUISES
Best of Both Worlds .... FYI 474
Olivia Cruises & Resorts 65, 98
We Love the Florida Keys Visitor Center . 78, FYI 408

SURFING INSTRUCTION
Maui Surfing School .... 62, FYI 422
Royal Hawaiian Weddings .... 70, FYI 425

SWIM WITH DOLPHINS
Mundo Maya Turquesa 64

SWIMMING
Clione Charters .... 50, FYI 408
Matt's Rainbow Tours .... 62, FYI 421
We Love the Florida Keys Visitor Center . 78, FYI 408

SYDNEY MARDI GRAS
Above & Beyond Tours 45, 83
Atlantis Events 48, 87
Atlantis Travel .... 48, FYI 232
Australian & New Zealand Travel Hdqtrs .. 48
Beyond the Blue .... 49, FYI 307
BreakOut Tours .... 50, FYI 308
Destination Downunder .... 53, FYI 309
Gaygantic Tours 56
G'day Tours .... 57, FYI 310
Holidays at Sea/Sunquest 58
Jornada 59, 94
Men on Vacation 62, 96
Oz Dive/Passport to Paradise 66
Travel Man 76, 104

WHAT TO DO

S/M
Rainboworld Custom Tours .... 69, FYI 256
TAI CHI
It's Our Nature .... 59, FYI 416
Trek Out 76
TALL SHIPS
Thanks, Babs 74, 102
TANGO
Arcadia Turismo Internacional 48
TELEMARKING
Lois Lane Expeditions 61
TEMPLES - HAWAIIAN
Matt's Rainbow Tours .... 62, FYI 421
THEME TRIPS
French Touch .... 56, FYI 210
TOBOGGAN
Eclectic Excursions .... 54, FYI 466
TORTURE CHAMBERS
Travel Keys Tours 76, 104
TRAIL RIDING
Bar H Ranch .... 48, FYI 506
TRAIN EXCURSIONS
Rocky Mountaineer Railtours ..... 69, FYI 328
TRAIN - LUXURY
2Afrika 45, 83
TREKKING
2Afrika 45, 83
Adventure Associates 45, 84
Adventure Bound Expeditions 45, 85
Alaska Women of the Wilderness 46, 86
G'day Tours .... 57, FYI 310
Heritage Tours .... 58, FYI 283
Lodestar Adventures 61
Lois Lane Expeditions 61
Silken East Ltd. .... 71, FYI 186
Silke's Travel .... 71, FYI 308
Stonewall 69 .... 73, FYI 344
Terramundo Travels Int'l 74, 102
Tours to Paradise .... 75, FYI 189
Wild Women 79, 106
Woodswomen 81, 108
TREKKING - ELEPHANT
Adventures Unlimited .... 46, FYI 190
TROPICAL VACATION PACKAGES
Pacific Ocean Holidays .... 66, FYI 427
TROPICS
We Love the Florida Keys
Visitor Center .... 78, FYI 408
TUBING
Gay Guided Tours of Israel .... 56, FYI 305

TULIP TIME
European Luxury Hotel Barge Cruises 54, FYI 208
TURTLE WATCHING
American Adventures 47
TWO STEPPING
Olivia Cruises & Resorts 65, 98
UPSCALE TOURS
Departures International .... 52, FYI 266
Mistral Tours .... 63, FYI 203
Our Family Abroad 65, 98
UPSCALE TRAVEL
Club Hommes/Worldguest .... 51, FYI 204
Destination World 53, 90
VAN TOURS
Paths Less Taken .... 67, FYI 264
VETERANS
L'Arc en Ciel Voyages 61, 94
VICTORIA FALLS
Travel Man 76, 104
VILLAS
American Adventures 47
Gay Mexico Travel .... 56, FYI 358
Journeys by Sea Yacht Charters 60, FYI 337
Mistral Tours .... 63, FYI 203
Uranian Travel 77, 105
VOLCANO TOURS
Mercury Cruise & Tour 62
VOLCANOES
American Adventures 47
Open Eye Tours & Photos .... 65, FYI 425
WAHINE WEEK - LESBIAN
Remote Possibilities .... 69, FYI 426
WALKING
Adventures for Women .... 45, FYI 461
Beyond the Blue .... 49, FYI 307
Bushwise Women .... 50, FYI 318
Earth, Wind & Water .... 53, FYI 354
Experience Plus 55, 90
G'day Tours .... 57, FYI 310
It's Our Nature .... 59, FYI 416
Kayak Historical Discovery Tours 60, FYI 420
Lois Lane Expeditions 61
Merlyn's Journeys .... 63, FYI 370
Off the Map 65, 97
Progressive Travels 68, 99
Rainbow Adventures 68
Todd River Tours 75
Trek Out 76
WALKING TOURS
Canyon Calling Tours .... 50, FYI 366
Cruisin' the Castro .... 52, FYI 388
Himalayan High Treks .... 58, FYI 186
Victorian Home Walk .... 77, FYI 386

WATER SKIING
Olivia Cruises & Resorts 65, 98
WATERFALLS
Open Eye Tours & Photos .... 65, FYI 425
WATERSPORTS
2Afrika 45, 83
Fair Choices 55, 90
WEDDINGS
Royal Hawaiian Weddings .... 70, FYI 425
WELLNESS VACATIONS
Destination Discovery .... 52, FYI 378
G'day Tours .... 57, FYI 310
Tropical Tune-ups 76
WHALE WATCHING
2Afrika 45, 83
Archipelago Holidays 48, 87
Blue Moon Explorations 49
Earth, Wind & Water .... 53, FYI 354
Gay Baja Tours .... 56, FYI 358
Gay Mexico Travel .... 56, FYI 358
Kayak Historical Discovery Tours 60, FYI 420
Mix Travel .... 63, FYI 344
Olivia Cruises & Resorts 65, 98
Our Family Abroad 65, 98
Rainbow Adventures 68
Stonewall 69 .... 73, FYI 344
Toto Tours 75, 102
Women Sail Alaska .... 81, FYI 363
WILD FLOWERS
Lizard Head Backcountry Tours .. 61, FYI 495
WILD WEST
Sedona Rainbow Adventure Tours .... 71, FYI 367
WILDERNESS
Wild Women Expeditions .... 79, FYI 330
WILDERNESS RETREATS
Bushwise Women .... 50, FYI 318
Women in the Wilderness 81, 108
WILDLIFE
2Afrika 45, 83
Adventure Bound Expeditions 45, 85
Baobab Safari Co. 48
Big Five Tours 49, 88
Bushwise Women .... 50, FYI 318
Rainbow Adventures 68
Todd River Tours 75
Women Sail Alaska .... 81, FYI 363
Woodswomen 81, 108
WILDLIFE ENCOUNTERS
Air & Adventure Tours (AAA) .... 46, FYI 312
WILDLIFE SAFARIS
Toto Tours 75, 102
WILDLIFE VIEWING
Super Natural Adventure Tours .. 73, FYI 328

ACTIVITY INDEX

FERRARI GUIDES' GAY TRAVEL A to Z - 18th EDITION

WHAT TO DO

WINDSURFING
Gay Guided Tours of Israel .... 56, FYI 305
Worldwide Vacations Inc. 81

WINE
Off the Map 65, 97

WINE CRUISES
European Luxury Hotel
    Barge Cruises .... 54, FYI 208

WINE FESTIVALS
Gay Baja Tours .... 56, FYI 358

WINE TOURS
Beau Séjour .... 49, FYI 173
Mistral Tours .... 63, FYI 203
Mix Travel .... 63, FYI 344
Stonewall 69 .... 73, FYI 344
Travel Club, The 76, 103
Wolff + Zink Travel Services 80, 106

WINE - CHEESE FLOAT TRIPS
Pangaea Expeditions .... 66, FYI 456

WINE - EUROPE
Ski Connections .... 72, FYI 194

WINERIES
2Afrika 45, 83
Southern Discovery Tours .... 72, FYI 315
Thanks, Babs 74, 102

WINERIES - AUSTRALIAN
Destination Downunder .... 53, FYI 309

WINETASTING
2Afrika 45, 83
Air & Adventure Tours (AAA) .... 46, FYI 312
David's Trips and Tours 52, 89
Holidays at Sea/Sunquest 58
Mistral Tours .... 63, FYI 203
Women in Motion 80, 107

WINTER CAMPING
Lois Lane Expeditions 61

WINTER PARTY PKGS
Connections Tours 51

WINTER SUN HOLIDAYS
Uranian Travel 77, 105

WINTERDAZE DANCE PARTY
Destination Downunder .... 53, FYI 309

WOMEN OVER 60 PROGRAMS
Alaska Women of the Wilderness 46, 86

WOMENFEST KEY WEST PKGS
Connections Tours 51

WOMEN'S CULTURAL
Frauen Unterwegs 55, 91
Ventus Reisen 77

WOMEN'S FESTIVALS
Women in Motion 80, 107

WOMEN'S LIFESTYLES
Ventus Reisen 77

WOMEN'S OUTDOOR
2Afrika 45, 83
Adventure Associates 45, 84
Adventures for Women .... 45, FYI 461
Beyond the Blue .... 49, FYI 307
Blue Moon Explorations 49
Bushwise Women .... 50, FYI 318
Canyon Calling Tours .... 50, FYI 366
Cloud Canyon Backpacking 50, 88
Colorado Women in the Wilderness 51, 88
Earth, Wind & Water .... 53, FYI 354
Eclectic Excursions .... 54, FYI 466
Frauen Unterwegs 55, 91
Global Affair 56
Grand Canyon Field Institute 57
G'day Tours .... 57, FYI 310
Hawk, I'm Your Sister .... 58, FYI 463
Lodestar Adventures 61
Lois Lane Expeditions 61
McNamara Ranch .... 62, FYI 396
Oceanwomyn Kayaking .... 64, FYI 357
Onn the Water 65
OutWest Adventures .... 66, FYI 455
Pangaea Expeditions .... 66, FYI 456
Rainbow Adventures 68
Sea Sense .... 71, FYI 398
Tall Ship Adventures, Inc. .... 74, FYI 340
Trek Out 76
Wild Women 79, 106
Wild Women Expeditions .... 79, FYI 330
Wintermoon .... 80, FYI 452
Witchencroft 4WD & Bushwalking Tours .. 80, FYI 312
Women in Motion 80, 107
Women Sail Alaska .... 81, FYI 363
Woodswomen 81, 108

WOMEN'S RESORT VACATIONS
Club Le Bon .... 51, FYI 341
Cornerstone Associates 51
Olivia Cruises & Resorts 65, 98
Women in Motion 80, 107

WOMEN'S SPIRITUALITY
Wild Women Expeditions .... 79, FYI 330

WOMEN'S TRAVEL CLUB
Women's Travel Club 81

WORLD HERITAGE SITES
Heritage Tours .... 58, FYI 283

WORLD WAR II - PILGRIMAGES
Silken East Ltd. .... 71, FYI 186

WRITING RETREATS
Hawk, I'm Your Sister .... 58, FYI 463

WRITING WORKSHOPS
Women in the Wilderness 81, 108

YACHT CHARTERS
Eurway Tour & Cruise Club .... 54, FYI 238
Fine Travel & Yachting .... 55, FYI 240
GPSC Charters .... 57, FYI 240
G'day Tours .... 57, FYI 310
Hawkesbury Expeditions 58
Journeys by Sea Yacht Charters 60, FYI 337
Oz Dive/Passport to Paradise 66
Port Yacht Charters .... 68, FYI 339
Sailing Affairs .... 70, FYI 468
Seaborne Safaris (Croisieres d'Il en Il) 71
Syosset Travel 74
Tall Ship Adventures, Inc. .... 74, FYI 340
Voyages & Expeditions 78, 106
Whitney Yacht Charters .... 79, FYI 340
Womantours/Artemis Sailing 80, 107

YOGA
Call of the Wild 50
Trek Out 76

YOGA RETREATS
Destination Discovery .... 52, FYI 378

YOUNG WOMEN'S LEADERSHIP TRIPS
Wild Women 79, 106

YOUTH PROGRAMS
Departures International .... 52, FYI 266
Gay Mexico Travel .... 56, FYI 358
Stonewall 69 .... 73, FYI 344

WHO TO CALL

Index to Gay & Lesbian Tour, Cruise & Excursion Companies

All companies covered in this book are listed in alphabetical order below. Each company is briefly described in the "Who to Call" global list of tour companies on pages 45-82. For companies that are featured in more detail, additional pages are cited. The initials "FYI" (For Your Information) indicate that a special feature is included on the indicated page.

2Afrika 45, 83	Canyon Calling Tours .... 50, FYI 366	Fine Travel & Yachting .... 55, FYI 240
AAD All About Destinations 45	China Voyages .... 50, FYI 176	Five Star Travel Services 55
Above & Beyond Tours 45, 83	Clione Charters .... 50, FYI 408	Frauen Unterwegs 55, 91
Advance Damron Vacations 45, 84	Cloud Canyon Backpacking 50, 88	French Touch .... 56, FYI 210
Adventure Associates 45, 84	Club Hommes/Worldguest .... 51, FYI 204	Gay Baja Tours .... 56, FYI 358
Adventure Bound Expeditions 45, 85	Club Le Bon .... 51, FYI 341	Gay Guided Tours of Israel .... 56, FYI 305
Adventures for Women .... 45, FYI 461	Club Voyage Josee 51	Gay Mexico Travel .... 56, FYI 358
Adventures Unlimited .... 46, FYI 190	Colorado Women in the Wilderness .. 51, 88	Gaygantic Tours 56
Adventures With Flair 46, 85	Common Earth Adventures 51, 89	Gaylink Travel Services 56
After Five Charters .... 46, FYI 492	Connections Tours 51	Gayventures 56
Ahwahnee Whitewater 46, 85	Conson Holidays 51	Global Affair 56
Air & Adventure Tours (AAA) .... 46, FYI 312	Cornerstone Associates 51	Good Time Tours .... 57, FYI 412
Alaska Women of the Wilderness 46, 86	Cruise World 52, 89	GPSC Charters .... 57, FYI 240
Allegro Travel 46, 86	Cruisin' the Castro .... 52, FYI 388	Grand Canyon Field Institute 57
Alternative Holidays 47, 86	Dave's Island Pride	Graylink Tours .... 57, FYI 310
Alyson Adventures 47, 87	Driver, Guide .... 52, FYI 427	G'day Tours .... 57, FYI 310
Amazon Tours & Cruises 47	David's Trips and Tours 52, 89	Hanafi Tour and Travel .... 57, FYI 188
American Adventures 47	De Gay Krant Reisservice .... 52, FYI 256	Hanns Ebensten Travel 57, 92
Amphitrion Holidays 47	Departures International .... 52, FYI 266	Hawkesbury Expeditions 58
Anderson International Tours .... 47, FYI 346	Desert Vision Tours 52	Hawk, I'm Your Sister .... 58, FYI 463
Anywhere Travel 47	Destination Discovery .... 52, FYI 378	Hellkamp Reisen 58, 92
Aquatic Adventures	Destination Downunder .... 53, FYI 309	Heritage Tours .... 58, FYI 283
Charter Service .... 47, FYI 404	Destination Management .... 53, FYI 436	Himalayan High Treks .... 58, FYI 186
Arcadia Turismo Internacional 48	Destination World 53, 90	Holidays at Sea/Sunquest 58
Archipelago Holidays 48, 87	Different Strokes Tours 53	Holigays 58, 92
Atlantis Events 48, 87	Discus Travel 53	IMTC, Inc. 58, 94
Atlantis Travel .... 48, FYI 232	Doin' It Right - in Puerto Vallarta 53	In Touch Holidays Ltd. 59
Aust Pac Travel 48	Earth, Wind & Water .... 53, FYI 354	Inter-Rainbow Turismo .... 59, FYI 347
Australian & New Zealand	East-West Tours .... 53, FYI 322	Island Hoppers Tours .... 59, FYI 341
Travel Hdqtrs 48	Easy Way 54	It's Our Nature .... 59, FYI 416
Baobab Safari Co. 48	Eat Quiche Tour & Travel	Izarra Cruises .... 59, FYI 502
Bar H Ranch .... 48, FYI 506	Accommodations 54	Jetman International Gay Travel 59
Beau Séjour .... 49, FYI 173	Eclectic Excursions .... 54, FYI 466	Jornada 59, 94
Best of Both Worlds .... FYI 474	Embassy Travel 54	Journeys by Sea
Best of Both Worlds Travel Ltd. 49	Envision Charters .... 54, FYI 324	Yacht Charters .... 60, FYI 337
Beyond Nirvana .... 49, FYI 342	Envoy Travel .... 54, FYI 176	Kam Tours Int'l 60
Beyond the Blue .... 49, FYI 307	European Luxury Hotel	Kayak Historical Discovery
Big Five Tours 49, 88	Barge Cruises .... 54, FYI 208	Tours .... 60, FYI 420
Blue Moon Explorations 49	Eurway Tour & Cruise Club ...... 54, FYI 238	Kenny Tours 60
Bogong Horseback Adventures 49	Experience Plus 55, 90	Kremlin Tours .... 60, FYI 266
BreakOut Tours .... 50, FYI 308	Explorer Tours 55, 190	Land Voyages 60
Bushwise Women .... 50, FYI 318	Fair Choices 55, 90	Landmark (South Pacific) Pty Ltd 60
BVI Charters 50	Fiesta Tours .... 55, FYI 346	Liquid Crystal Divers .... 60, FYI 422
Call of the Wild 50	Fiesta Tours 55	Lizard Head Backcountry Tours 61, FYI 495

FERRARI GUIDES' GAY TRAVEL A to Z - 18th EDITION

WHO TO CALL

Lodestar Adventures 61
Lois Lane Expeditions 61
London Handling Ltd. 61, 96
L'Arc en Ciel Voyages 61, 94
Mantrav International 61
Mariah Wilderness Expeditions 61, 96
Matt's Rainbow Tours .... 62, FYI 421
Maui Surfing School .... 62, FYI 422
McNamara Ranch .... 62, FYI 396
Men on Bikes .... 62, FYI 248
Men on Vacation 62, 96
Mercury Cruise & Tour 62
Merlyn's Journeys .... 63, FYI 370
Middle Fork River Expeditions 63
Milu Tours 63
Mistral Tours .... 63, FYI 203
Mix Travel .... 63, FYI 344
Mount Cook Tours 63
Mount'n Beach Safaris 63
MTC (Multinational Travel Corp) 64
Mundo Maya Turquesa 64
Never Summer Nordic .... 64, FYI 396
New England Vacation Tours 64
North American Travel Specialists ... 64, 97
Ocean Voyager 64, 97
Oceanwide Expeditions 64
Oceanwomyn Kayaking .... 64, FYI 357
Off the Map 65, 97
Olivia Cruises & Resorts 65, 98
Onn the Water 65
Open Eye Tours & Photos .... 65, FYI 425
Orion Travel Tours 65
Otto Travel Hawaii 65
Our Family Abroad 65, 98
Out Touring Australia 66
OutWest Adventures .... 66, FYI 455
Oz Dive/Passport to Paradise 66
Pacific Experience 66
Pacific Ocean Holidays .... 66, FYI 427
Paddling South & Saddling South 66, 99
Pangaea Expeditions .... 66, FYI 456
Passage to Utah .... 67, FYI 496
Passport Travel Mgt, Inc. 67
Paths Less Taken .... 67, FYI 264
Pearl Selections/Welcome Abroad 67, 99
Peddlers .... 67, FYI 238
Pied Piper Travel .... 67, FYI 338
Players Express .... 67, FYI 458
Pleasant Holidays 67

Pleasure Travel...
   Cruise Again Too! .... 68, FYI 339
Port Yacht Charters .... 68, FYI 339
Progressive Travels 68, 99
Promenades de Style .... 68, FYI 212
Puffin Family Charters .... 68, FYI 363
Rail Europe .... 68, FYI 286
Rainbow Adventures 68
Rainbow Country Tours
   & B&B .... 69, FYI 496
Rainbow Destinations 69
Rainboworld Custom Tours ...... 69, FYI 256
Remote Possibilities .... 69, FYI 426
Rio Roma Travel 69
Robin Tyler's Women's Tours,
   Cruises & Events 69
Rocky Mountaineer Railtours ... 69, FYI 328
Royal Hawaiian Weddings .... 70, FYI 425
RSVP Travel Productions/
   Club RSVP 70, 100
R&R Eco Tours 70
R&S Travel 70, 100
Sailing Affairs .... 70, FYI 468
Sapphire Travel & Tours 70
Scenic Air Tours .... 70, FYI 386
Sea Sense .... 71, FYI 398
Seaborne Safaris (Croisieres d'Il en Il) 71
Sedona Rainbow Adventure
   Tours .... 71, FYI 367
Sensations .... 71, FYI 292
Silken East Ltd. .... 71, FYI 186
Silke's Travel .... 71, FYI 308
Sirius Adventures .... 72, FYI 314
Ski Connections .... 72, FYI 194
Sounds & Furies .... 72, FYI 244
South of the Border
   Tour & Travel .... 72, FYI 358
Southern Discovery Tours .... 72, FYI 315
Spirit Journeys 72, 101
Stag Travel & Tours 73
Stockler Expeditions 73
Stonewall 69 .... 73, FYI 344
Stonewall Connection
   Travel & Tours 73, 101
Sundance Travel 73
Super Natural Adventure
   Tours .... 73, FYI 328
Surfers Paradise Gay Vacations 73
Syosset Travel 74
Tall Ship Adventures, Inc. .... 74, FYI 340
Teddy Travel 74, 101

Ten Thousand Waves .... 74, FYI 457
Terramundo Travels Int'l 74, 102
Thanks, Babs 74, 102
Timeout Tours & Travel 74
Todd River Tours 75
Toto Tours 75, 102
Tourmark's Gay Way
   America Tours 75, 103
Tours to Paradise .... 75, FYI 189
Tower Travel 75
Travel Affair 75, 103
Travel Club, The 76, 103
Travel Keys Tours 76, 104
Travel Man 76, 104
Trek Out 76
Tropical Tune-ups 76
T.R.I.P. Tours 76
Undersea Expeditions, Inc. 77, 104
Uranian Travel 77, 105
Vaarschool Grietje .... 77, FYI 258
VeloAsia Cycling Adventures 77, 105
Ventus Reisen 77
Victorian Home Walk .... 77, FYI 386
Virgin Vacations 78, 105
Voyages & Expeditions 78, 106
V.I.P. Tours of New York .... 78, FYI 468
Wanderlust Ventures 78
Way to Go Costa Rica 78, 352
We Love the Florida Keys
   Visitor Center .... 78, FYI 408
Whelk Women .... 79, FYI 402
Whitney Yacht Charters .... 79, FYI 340
Wild Rockies Tours .... 79, FYI 457
Wild Women 79, 106
Wild Women Expeditions .... 79, FYI 330
Windjammer Barefoot Cruises 79
Windmills Travel & Tourism .... 80, FYI 239
Wintermoon .... 80, FYI 452
Witchencroft 4WD &
   Bushwalking Tours .... 80, FYI 312
Wolff + Zink Travel Services 80, 106
Womantours/Artemis Sailing 80, 107
Women in Motion 80, 107
Women in the Wilderness 81, 108
Women Sail Alaska .... 81, FYI 363
Women's Travel Club 81
Woodswomen 81, 108
Worldwide Vacations Inc. 81
Xeno Tours/Mantours 81
Zeus Tours & Yacht Cruises 81, 109
Zipper Travel Association .... 82, FYI 252
ZMAX Travel & Tours Inc. 82, 109
Zone One 82

◐ Wholesale/Retail (Call Direct or Have Travel Agent Contact)

WHO TO CALL

♀♂	◐	**2Afrika** 2663 E Sunrise Blvd #167 Ft Lauderdale, FL 33304 USA (800) 2AFRIKA (800-223-7452), Fax: (305) 466-0873, E-mail: 2afrika@safari.net, Web: www.travelfile.com/get/2afrk.html.	From Cape Town to Cairo, they know the African continent. Extensive gay and lesbian individual and group programs. Johannesburg, Cape Town, Swaziland, Maasai cultural experience, Zimbabwe, Victoria Falls, game lodges, South Africa's gay scene, special program for gays and lesbians of African descent, all "at prices that cannot be beaten."	*Bookings:* Call travel agent or direct. *Est:* 1984. *TAC:* 10. *Pymt:* Checks, major credit cards. *Member:* ASTA, IATA, ATA IGTA
♀♂	◐	**AAD All About Destinations** 3819 N 3rd St, Gallery 3 Plaza Phoenix, AZ 85012-2074 USA (602) 277-2703, (800) 375-2703, Fax: (602) 277-2786, E-mail: proudmembr@aol.com, www.pcslink.com/~aad/cruisefr.htm.	Gay and lesbian groups on mainstream cruise ships, Baja, Caribbean, Alaska.	*Bookings:* Call travel agent or direct.
♀♂	◐	**Above & Beyond Tours** 330 Townsend St #107 San Francisco, CA 94107 USA (415) 284-1666, (800) 397-2681, Fax: (415) 284-1660, E-mail: info@abovebeyondtours.com , Web: www.abovebeyondtours.com.	Often imitated - never duplicated, we do things a little differently, Europe, Australia, New Z'land, Fiji, Sydney Mardi Gras & Sleaze Ball, Man Friday Resort in Fiji, Amsterdam Floating Gay Pride.	*Bookings:* Call travel agent. *Est:* 1991. *TAC:* 10+. *Pymt:* Check, Visa, MC. *Member:* ASTA IGTA aglta
♀♂	◐	**Advance Damron Vacations** One Greenway Plaza #890 Houston, TX 77046 USA (713) 888-1023, (800) 695-0880, Fax:(713) 888-1010, E-mail: Donnie@Advance-Damron.com, Web: www.advance-damron.com.	Annual all-gay Halloween cruise, spring Mexico all-gay cruise, Windjammer fleet, Cozumel, Cancun, Isla Mujeres, Dress Code: NONE! Toga party, Halloween costume party.	*Bookings:* Call travel agent or direct. *Est:* 1978. *Comm:* 10% plus overrides. *Pymt:* Cash, check, credit cards. *Member:* ARC, IATA, CLIA IGTA
♀	◐	**Adventure Associates** PO Box 16304 Seattle, WA 98116 USA (206) 932-8352, Fax: (206) 938-2654, E-mail: AdvntrAssc@aol.com.	Worldwide outdoor adventures, hiking, kayaking, climbing, skiing, backpacking, safaris, cultural tours, personally-designed itineraries, Africa, NW US, Greece, Pacific, no experience needed.	*Bookings:* Call travel agent or direct. *Est:* 1987; *Comm:* Varies with program. *Pymt:* Visa, MC, for trip deposit only.
♂	◐	**Adventure Bound Expeditions** 711 Walnut St Boulder, CO 80302 USA (303) 449-0990, Fax:(303) 449-9038, E-mail: ADVENTBDEX@aol.com.	Exclusively for gay men, outdoor adventure tours, destinations worldwide, hiking in mountains, interaction with exotic, cultures, Turkey, Ethiopia, Greece.	*Bookings:* Call travel agent or direct. *Comm:* 10. *Pymt:* Checks.
♀	○	**Adventures for Women** PO Box 515 Montvale, NJ 07645 USA Tel/Fax: (201) 930-0557.	Wilderness challenges, hiking, skiing, canoeing, contemplation weekends, breathing workshops, NY, New Jersey, Pennsylvania, Austrian Alps, Adirondacks.	*Bookings:* Call direct. *Est:* 1981. *Pymt:* Checks.

FERRARI GUIDES' GAY TRAVEL A to Z - 18th EDITION

TOUR COMPANIES

WHO TO CALL

○ Retail (Call Direct)   ● Wholesale (Travel Agent Must Contact)

♂	◐	**Adventures Unlimited** PO Box 33924 San Diego, CA 92163 USA (619) 669-0968, Fax:(619) 669-6901, E-mail: au4travel@aol.com, Web: www.wsai.com/adventures/.	Thailand specialist, small groups of gay men, daytime cultural activities, evening gay nightlife, Bangkok, Chiang Mai, Pattaya.	*Bookings:* Call travel agent or direct. *Est:* 1996. *Comm:* 10%. *Pymt:* VISA, MC for airfares, checks for land pkgs. **IGTA**
♂	◐	**Adventures With Flair** Williamson Rd, PO Box 2926 Pikeville, KY 41502 USA (606) 432-7109, (800) 463-5247, Fax: (606) 432-0059	Gay travel...in style, top international airlines, first-class & deluxe hotels, custom-designed tours, Thailand, Greek Isles, Australia, Amsterdam, Copenhagen, Rio.	*Bookings:* Call travel agent or direct. *Est:* 1988. *Comm:* varies. *Pymt:* Checks. *Member:* IATAN, ARC
♀♂	◐	**After Five Charters** 2602 Killder Ln Humble, TX 77396-1826 USA (281) 441-1369, (800) 335-1369, Fax: (281) 441-1275, E-mail: Afterfive@onramp.net, Web: rampages.onramp.net/~AFTER/	In Houston: Airport pick-up, gay nightlife tours, special itineraries, van & bus charters, also Galveston, San Antonio.	*Bookings:* Call travel agent or direct. *Est:* 1994. *Comm:* 10-12. *Pymt:* Checks, Discover card. *Member:* USTO **IGTA**
♀♂	◐	**Ahwahnee Whitewater** PO Box 1161 Columbia, CA 95310 USA (209) 533-1401, (800) 359-9790, Fax: (209) 533-1409.	Whitewater rafting in California, departures 7 days a week, exceptional guides, can arrange gay/lesbian & women's trips, our rivers are "mild" to "wild," Yosemite & Lake Tahoe areas.	*Bookings:* Call travel agent or direct. *Est:* 1960;s. *Comm:* 10-12%. *Pymt:* Checks, Visa, MC, Amex, Dis.
♀♂	◐	**Air & Adventure Tours (AAA)** 12 Sheridan Ct. Salisbury Hights, SA 5109 Australia (61 8) 8281-0530, Fax:(61 8) 8281-9301, E-mail: aaatours.senet.com.au.	Luxury aircraft tours, winetasting excursions, stand near wild kangaroos, sea lions, champagne flights over Adelaide, Adelaide coach tours.	*Bookings:* Call travel agent or direct. *Est:* 1991. *Comm:* 10%.
♀	◐	**Alaska Women of the Wilderness** PO Box 773556 Eagle River, AK 99577 USA (907) 688-2226, Fax:(907) 688-2285, E-mail: akwow@alaska.net.	Women's wilderness trips, Alaska, Baja, Nepal, Hawaii, backpacking, climbing, skiing, kayaking, girls' camps, elderhostel programs, healing drumming programs.	*Bookings:* Call travel agent or direct. *Est:* 1984. *Comm:* 10%. *Pymt:* Checks, Visa, MC. *Member:* Women Outdoors, Assoc. Experiential Education, Sound Healers Assoc., Reiki Master.
♀♂	◐	**Allegro Travel** 900 West End Ave #12-C New York, NY 10025 USA (212) 666-6700, (800) 666-3553, Fax: (212) 666-7451, E-mail: allegro@mail.idt.net.	North America's only agent for Bolshoi & Kirov tickets, guaranteed orchestra seats, opera, music and cultural tours, Russia, Egypt, Finland, Lithuania, Hong Kong. Vienna, Salzburg, Florence.	*Bookings:* Call travel agent or direct. *Est:* 1972. *Comm:* 10%. *Pymt:* Checks.

TOUR COMPANIES

◐ Wholesale/Retail (Call Direct or Have Travel Agent Contact)

WHO TO CALL

♂	◐	**Alternative Holidays** 21 Russell Gardens Mews London W14 8EU England (44-7000) 782 267 (tel/fax), E-mail: alternatives@mail.bogo.co.uk, Web: www.bogo.co.uk/alternatives.	Europe Gay Ski Week, in the French Alps, high-altitude skiing, parties & entertainment, January, 1998, other gay Club Med resort events planned.	*Bookings:* Call travel agent or direct. *Est:* 1995. *Comm:* 10%. *Pymt:* Visa, Amex, Eurocard, bank transfer. **IGTA**
♀♂	◐	**Alyson Adventures** PO Box 180179 Boston, MA 02118 USA (617) 247-8170, (800) 825-9766, E-mail: AlyVenture@aol.com, Web: www.channel1.com/alyson.	Fun & excitement outdoors, for gays & lesbians, hiking in switzerland, cycling the Natchez Trace, diving in the Caribbean, HIV+ men's trip - Sedona, AZ.	*Bookings:* Call travel agent or direct. *Est:* 1995. *Comm:* 10%. *Pymt:* Checks. **IGTA**
♀♂	◐	**Amazon Tours & Cruises** 8700 W Flagler St #190 Miami, FL 33174 USA (305) 227-2266, (800) 423-2791, Fax (305) 227-1880.	Amazon River cruises, air-conditioned ships, rainforest side trips, visits to Indian encampments.	*Bookings:* Call travel agent or direct. **IGTA**
♀♂	◐	**American Adventures** PO Box 1015-1007 Centro Colón San José Costa Rica (506) 292-1233, (506) 292-4608, Fax: (506) 292-4598.	Customized Costa Rica itineraries, individuals and groups.	*Bookings:* Call travel agent or direct. **IGTA**
♀♂	◐	**Amphitrion Holidays** 1506 21st St NW #100-A Washington, DC 20036 USA (202) 872-9878, (800) 424-2471, Fax: (202) 872-8210, E-mail: amphitvl@aol.com.	Specializing in Greece, mainstream tour operator, will customize gay tours, packages with air, hotels.	*Bookings:* Call travel agent or direct.
♀♂	◐	**Anderson International Tours** 2740 E Lansing Dr East Lansing, MI 48823 USA (517) 337-1300, (800) 723-1233, Fax: (517) 337-8561. E-mail: travela@pilot.msu.edu.	Rio de Janeiro specialists, Rio nightlife sizzles! Air/hotel packages, optional Amazon tours, Manaus, Recife, Sao Paulo, all-inclusive Europe packages.	*Bookings:* Call travel agent or direct. *Est:* 1975. *Comm:* 10%. *Pymt:* Checks, Visa, MC, Amex, Discover. *Member:* ASTA, ARC, IATAN, ARTA, WATA **IGTA**
♀♂	◐	**Anywhere Travel** 1326 Plainfield St Cranston, RI 02920 USA (401) 943-3300, Fax: (401) 943-1052, E-mail: joecruise@aol.com.	Gay and lesbian group cruises, worldwide destinations, Caribbean, Europe, Russia, far east, high volume bookings with major cruise lines assures low prices, In 1997, September gay cruise to London, ask for Joe Cruise.	*Bookings:* Call travel agent or direct. *Est:* 1972. *Comm:* Not reported. *Pymt:* All major cards.
♀♂	◐	**Aquatic Adventures Charter Service** PO Box 522540 Marathon Shores, FL 33052 USA (305) 743-2421	Scuba, snorkel and fishing excursions, Marathon, Florida and the Florida Keys, custom-designed dive or fishing vacations, new comfortable boat, half-day to multi-day excursions available, gay-friendly.	*Bookings:* Call travel agent or direct. *Est:* 1991. *Comm:* 10%. *Pymt:* MC, Visa, Amex. *Member:* Marthon COC

TOUR COMPANIES

FERRARI GUIDES' GAY TRAVEL A to Z - 18th EDITION   47

WHO TO CALL

○ Retail (Call Direct)   ● Wholesale (Travel Agent Must Contact)

♀♂	◐	**Arcadia Turismo Internacional** Florida 142, 6th Floor #N Buenos Aires, Argentina (54-1) 326 4910, Fax: (54-1) 326 8449, Email: arcadia@mainet.com.ar.	Gay & lesbian itineraries throughout Argentina.	IGTA
♀♂	○	**Archipelago Holidays** 2 Alexandra Ave London SW11 4DZ England (44-171) 622 7773, Fax: (44-171) 978 2615.	Worldwide adventure tours, laid-back beach holidays, diving, safaris, skiing, hiking, dune skiing, kayaking, each tour personalized, US, Europe, Africa, Pacific.	*Bookings:* Call direct. *Est:*1996. *Pymt:* Checks, bank transfers, cash, soon: credit cards. *Member:* ATCL
♀♂	◐	**Atlantis Events** 9060 Santa Monica Blvd #310 West Hollywood, CA 90069 USA (310) 281-5450, (800) 628-5268, Fax: (310) 281-5455.	All-gay resort vacations, Caribbean, Mexico, Australia, Sydney Gay Mardi Gras, intensive circus workshops, new in 1997: Club Atlantis, our own Mexican resort.	*Bookings:* Call travel agent or direct. IGTA
♀♂	◐	**Atlantis Travel** Pestalozzistr 17 Munich 80469 Germany (49-89) 23 6660-0, Fax:(49-89) 23 6660-55, E-mail: tommi@atlantis-travel.de, Web: www.atlantis-travel.de.	Upscale tour operator and travel agency in Munich, Germany, European representative of Atlantis Events gay resort vacations, located in the gay area of central Munich, motto: "Only the best is good enough for our clients."	*Bookings:* Call travel agent or direct. *Est:* 1996. *Comm:* Varies. *Pymt:* Credit cards, transers, eurochecks. *Member:* IATA IGTA
♀♂	○	**Aust Pac Travel** 20 Emily St Leichhardt, NSW 2040 Australia (61-2) 9660 3199, (800) 151 051, Fax: (61-2) 9660 8662.	Retail and inbound operator. Unusual destinations, individual itineraries group and cruise specialists.	*Bookings:* Call direct. agta
♀♂	◐	**Australian & New Zealand Travel Hdqtrs** 332 Pine St #700 San Francisco, CA 94104 USA (415) 956-2990, (800) 453-6636, Fax: (415) 956-2886, E-mail: GOWOMBAT@aol.com.	Gay & gay-friendly, independent and group customized itineraries, Australia, New Zealand, South Pacific Islands, gay and gay-friendly accommodations, soft adventure activities, wholesaler of international air, wholesale domestic airpasses.	*Bookings:* Call travel agent or direct. *Est:* 1945. *Comm:* negotiable. *Member:* ARC-Appointed, PATA IGTA
♀♂	●	**Baobab Safari Co.** 210 Post St #911 San Francisco, CA 94108 USA (415) 391-5788, (800) 835-3692, Fax: (415) 391-3752.	Safari wildlife and photography trips, customized itineraries for small groups and couples, kenya, tanzania, zimbabwe, botswana.	*Bookings:* Call travel agent.
♀	◐	**Bar H Ranch** Box 297 Driggs, ID 83422 USA (208) 354-2906, (800) 247-1444.	Women's trail riding in Wyoming & Idaho, wilderness horse packing, check fences - move cattle, deluxe ranch accommodations, rustic tipi accommodations, saddle your own horse.	*Bookings:* Call travel agent or direct. *Est:* 1980. *Comm:* 10%. *Pymt:* Cash, checks.

TOUR COMPANIES

◐ Wholesale/Retail (Call Direct or Have Travel Agent Contact) ## WHO TO CALL

♀♂	◐	**Beau Séjour** PO Box 44642 Claremont, WCP 7735 South Africa (27 21) 788-2710 (tel/fax), cellular: (27 82) 556 8175.	Cape Town culture, wine & cheese tasting, gay nIghtlife tours, local architecture, antiques and museums, unconventional approach, we relate equally to men and women.	*Bookings:* Call travel agent or direct. *Est:* 1994. *Comm:* 15%. *Pymt:* Cash, check. *Member:* TOAC, SATOUR
♀	◐	**Best of Both Worlds** PO Box 763 Bridgeton, NC 28519 USA (919) 322-5804.	Women learn to sail, North Carolina's Coast, day trips & overnights, deepsea fishing, shelling, golf, uncrowded beaches, handle an oceangoing sloop.	*Bookings:* Call direct. *Comm:* 10%. *Pymt:* Checks.
♂	◐	**Best of Both Worlds Travel Ltd.** 117 Phyllis Ave New Malden, Surrey KT3 6LB England (44-181) 942 0533 (tel/fax), E-mail: WorldCroll@aol.com.	Tailor-made guided tours showing both sides of London — tourist attractions and gay night life – and the south of England, for gay men. Gay and gay-friendly hotel arrangements and theatre tickets.	*Bookings:* Call travel agent or direct. IGTA
♀♂	●	**Beyond Nirvana** 12670 NW Barnes Road #104 Portland, OR 97229-6016 USA (800) 532-0526, Fax:: (503) 643-8965, E-mail: nirvana@spiritone.com, Web: www.spa-traveler.com.	First exclusively gay spa vacations, massage, herbal wraps, facials, fango (mud) baths, health-enhancing activity tours, yoga, Tai Chi, biking, hiking, meditation, Mexico, Caribbean, Belize, Hawaii.	*Bookings:* Call travel agent or direct. *Est:* 1996. *TAC:* 11-15. *Pymt:* Visa, MC, Discover, Amex. IGTA
♀♂	◐	**Beyond the Blue** 275 Alfred St #205 North Sydney, NSW 2060 Australia (61 2) 9955 6755, Fax: (61 2) 9922 6036. E-mail: btb@msn.com. North American office: 2030 Dexter Ave N #273, Seattle, WA 98109, (206) 285-8637, Fax: (206) 283-7095, E-mail: btb_usa@msn.com, Web: www.beyondblue.com.	Whether TO or FROM Australia! Airfares, gay accommodations, soft adventure, Gay Mardi Gras, groups from 1 to 500 People, offices in Sydney & Seattle! Wholesaler for Man Friday, Fiji.	*Bookings:* Call travel agent or direct. *Established:* 1993; *Comm:* 10-12%; *License No.:* 2TA003912; *Payment:* Checks, Visa, MC, Amex. *Member:* ASTA, AFTA, NZGLTA IGTA aglta
♀♂	●	**Big Five Tours** 819 S. Federal Hwy #103 Stuart, FL 34994 USA (561) 287-7995, (800) 244-3483, Fax:(561) 287-5990, E-mail: bigfive@gate.net, Web: www.bigfive.com.	A soft adventure pioneer, travel in utmost comfort, African wildlife, Galapagos, Antarctica, India & Nepal, Peru, Chile and Costa Rica, pkgs & personalized Itineraries.	*Bookings:* Call travel agent. *Est:* 1973. *Comm:* From 12%. *Pymt:* Check or credit cards. *Member:* IATA, ASTA, APTA IGTA
♀♂	◐	**Blue Moon Explorations** PO Box 2568 Bellingham, WA 98227 USA Tel/Fax: (360) 856-5622, (800) 966-8806.	Hiking, kayaking, whale watching, Alaska, British Columbia, San Juan Islands, WA, snorkel with dolphins, hike active volcanoes, reasonable prices.	*Bookings:* Call travel agent or direct. *Est:* 1988. *Comm:* 10%. *Pymt:* Cash or check. *Member:* TASK
♀♂	◐	**Bogong Horseback Adventures** Spring Spur, Mountain Creek Rd Tawonga, VIC 3699 Australia (61-3) 5754 4849, Fax: (61-3) 5754 4181, Mobile: (61-18) 572 993.	High-country horse tours. From 1/2-day to 7-day horsepack tours in Victoria's mountain wilderness. Traditional Australian camping. Group tours by arrangement.	*Bookings:* Call travel agent or direct. aglta

FERRARI GUIDES' GAY TRAVEL A to Z - 18th EDITION   49

TOUR COMPANIES

WHO TO CALL

○ Retail (Call Direct) ● Wholesale (Travel Agent Must Contact)

♀♂	●	**BreakOut Tours** 10 Roseby St Marrickville, NSW 2204 Australia (61 2) 9558 8229, Fax:(61 2) 9558 7140, E-mail: brkout@world.net, Web: http://breakout.com.au.	Exclusively gay, days and overnights within Australia, Nepal, Fiji and Vietnam tours, Sydney Mardi Gras, Ayers Rock, Sydney Leather Week.	*Bookings:* Call travel agent or direct. *Est:* 1990. *Comm:* 12% (day tours up to 30). *Pymt:* MC, Visa, Bankcard, Amex, cheques. **aglta**
♀	●	**Bushwise Women** PO Box 28010 Christchurch, New Zealand Tel/Fax: (64 3) 332 4952.	Women's wilderness adventures, New Zealand's unspoilt wilderness, explore rainforest, mountains, lakes, learn bushcraft skills, canoeing, kayaking, goldpanning, maximum of 8 women, any age.	*Bookings:* Call travel agent or direct. *Est:* 1992. *Comm:* 10%. *License No:* WC097401. *Pymt:* Visa, Bankcard.
♀♂	●	**BVI Charters** PO Box 11156 St Thomas, USVI 00801 (809) 494-4289, Fax:(809) 494-6552, E-mail: sailbvi@caribsurf.com.	Sailing charters in Virgin Islands.	*Bookings:* Call travel agent or direct.
♀	○	**Call of the Wild** 2519 Cedar St Berkeley, CA 94708 USA (510) 849-9292, (800) 742-9494, Fax: (510) 644-3811, E-mail: callwild@vdn.com.	Women's outdoor adventures, backpacking, hiking "lite," "fit" trips with low-fat food & yoga sessions, mostly in California, most participants straight women, gay women are welcome.	*Bookings:* Call direct.
♀	●	**Canyon Calling Tours** 215 Disney Lane Sedona, AZ 86336 USA (520) 282-0916, (800) 664-8922, 'Fax: (520) 282-3586.	Women's southwest adventure, five beautiful canyons, swim at Supai waterfalls, Monument Valley, Rainbow Bridge, Anasazi ruins and petroglyphs, fine hotels, restaurants.	*Bookings* Call travel agent or direct. *Est:* 1996. *Comm:* 10%. *Pymt* Checks, Visa, MC.
♀♂	●	**China Voyages** 582 Market St #605 San Francisco, CA 94104 USA (415) 398-2244, (800) 914-9133, Fax: (415) 399-0827, E-mail: Jack@chinavoyages.com, Web: www.chinavoyages.com.	Exclusively gay China & Hong Kong group tours, independent customized travel, discounted hotel bookings, discounted air tickets to China, extensive guided tours, China visa processing.	*Bookings:* Call travel agent or direct.
♂	○	**Clione Charters** PO Box 1874 Key West, FL 33041 USA (305) 296-1433, (305) 745-4519	All-male day sails off Key West, sailing, snorkeling, swimming, small groups up to 8 people, free limo service, equipment and instruction.	*Bookings* Call direct. *Est:* 1981. *Member* Key West Bus. Guild
♀	○	**Cloud Canyon Backpacking** PO Box 41359 Santa Barbara, CA 93140 USA (805) 969-0982, E-mail: areitz@silcom.com.	Women's hiking adventures, lighthearted & easygoing, women of all skills welcome, groups of 6-8 women of all ages, Utah, Alaska, New Zealand, backpacking, spiritual quests.	*Bookings:* Call travel agent or direct. *Est:* 1991. *Pymt:* Checks.

TOUR COMPANIES

◐ Wholesale/Retail (Call Direct or Have Travel Agent Contact)

WHO TO CALL

♂	◐	**Club Hommes/Worldguest** 224 W 4th St New York, NY 10014 USA (212) 206-6900, (800) 429-6969, Fax: (212) 206-6904, E-mail: club@worldgucst.com, Web: www.worldguest.com. Worldguest: #8 75th St, North Bergen, NJ 07047, (201) 861-5059, Fax: (201) 861-4983, E-mial:: tours@worldguest.com.	An upscale men's travel club offering sophisticated travel experiences for small groups of gay men, France, England, Mexico, Caribbean, Hawaii, membership free when you fill out traveler survey.	*Bookings:* Call travel agent or direct. *Est:* 1995. *TAC:* 10. *Pymt:* Major credit cards, checks. **IGTA**
♀	○	**Club Le Bon** PO Box 444 Woodbridge, NJ 07095 USA (908) 826-1577, (800) 836-8687, Fax: (908) 826-1577. E-mail: clublebon@aol.com, Web: www.provincetown.com/clublebon.	Lesbian tropical resort vacations, all-inclusive prices, no crowds - 30-100 lesbians, Barbados & Mexico locations, swim with dolphins, white sand beaches.	*Bookings:* Call direct.
♂	●	**Club Voyage Josee** 157 est Jean Talon Montreal, QC H2R 1S8 Canada (514) 270-4376, Fax: (514) 270-1077.	Wholesaler.	**IGTA**
♀	◐	**Colorado Women in the Wilderness** Box 399 Telluride, CO 81435 USA (970) 728-4538.	Women's adventure travel, hiking, backpacking, rafting, mountains, canyon country, ocean island healing retreats, customized group trips, highly experienced women guides.	*Bookings:* Call travel agent or direct. *Est:* 1990. *Comm:* 10%. *Pymt:* Checks.
♀	○	**Common Earth Adventures** PO Box 1191 Fairfax, CA 94978 USA (415) 455-0646, Fax: (415) 454-3967.	Women's adventure travel, backpacking, kayaking, x-country skiing, snow camping, ropes course Arizona, California & Alaska, sliding fee scale.	*Bookings:* Call direct. *Est:* 1992. *Pymt:* Checks.
♀♂	◐	**Connections Tours** 169 Lincoln Rd #302 Miami Beach, FL 33139 USA (305) 673-3153, (800) OUT-TIME (688-8463), Fax: (305) 673-6501, E-mail: connectfl@aol.com.	Packages to Florida circuit parties, South Beach, Winter Gayla, Winter Party, Gay Day at Disney, Art Deco Wknd, Womenfest Key West, also Calif, Carib, Canada, Mexico, North American gay pride packages.	*Bookings* Call travel agent or direct. *Est:* 1995. *TAC:* 15%. *Pymt:* Checks, wire transfers, major credit cards (TAC 10%). *Member:* UFA, SBBG, SAVE, SBAD, GMCVB
♀♂	●	**Conson Holidays** 954 Ponce de Leon Ave #309 San Juan, PR 00907 (809) 725-5940, (800) 981-5940, Fax: (809) 725-1263.	Specialty: the Caribbean, introducing gay vacation pkgs, individuals and groups, Puerto Rico and San Juan, will customize Itineraries.	*Bookings:* Call travel agent. **IGTA**
♀	○	**Cornerstone Associates** PO Box 1055 Northampton, MA 01061 USA (413) 268-7363, (800) 798-6877, Fax: (413) 268-9294.	Women's resort vacations, geared to the tastes of professionals, reserves entire resort, individuals travel at group rates, scheduled programs & independent itineraries.	*Bookings:* Call direct.

TOUR COMPANIES

FERRARI GUIDES' GAY TRAVEL A to Z - 18th EDITION

WHO TO CALL

○ Retail (Call Direct)   ● Wholesale (Travel Agent Must Contact)

Cruise World
901 Fairview Ave # A-150
Seattle, WA 98109 USA
(206) 343-0221, (800) 340-0221, Fax:(206) 343-0771.

Cruise/tours specialists, England, Mediterranean, Greece, the Aegean, Italy, some with day trips included.

Bookings: Call direct. *Est:* 1990. *Pymt:* Checks, most major credit cards. *Member:* GSEA, CLIA, NACOA

Cruisin' the Castro
375 Lexington St
San Francisco, CA 94110 USA
(415) 550-8110, E-mail: trvrhailey@aol.com.

Fascinating San Fran Castro walking tours, learn gay history, 3 1/2 hr tours include brunch, available Tues-Sat & holidays, guided by Trevor Hailey.

Bookings: Call travel agent or direct. *Est:* 1989. *TAC:* 10% (15%-IGTA). *Pymt:* Cash & checks. *Member:* SFCVB, IGTA

Dave's Island Pride Driver, Guide
3151 Monsarrat #402
Honolulu, HI 96815 USA
(808) 732-6518, E-mail: ishow4u@aol.com.

Gay Honolulu sightseeing tours, honeymoon package, customized nightlife tours, airport pick-ups, luxury mini-van transport, experienced, certified guide.

Bookings: Call travel agent or direct. *Est:* 1994. *TAC:* 10%. *Pymt:* Cash, check.

David's Trips and Tours
310 Dahlia Place, Suite A
Corona del Mar, CA 92625-2821 USA
(714) 723-0699, Toll Free (888) 723-0699, Fax: (714) 723-0666, E-mail: davidtours@aol.com, Web: http://home.aol.com/davidtours.

Paris for Euro Gay Pride, spa stays in Czech Republic, New Years in gay Cape Town, Gay Games in Amsterdam, Halloween party - New Orleans, many luxurious extras.

Bookings: Call travel agent or direct. *Comm:* 10%. *Pymt:* Checks, Visa, MC, Amex. IGTA

De Gay Krant Reisservice
Kloveniersburgwal 40
Amsterdam 1012 CW The Netherlands
(31 20) 421 00 00, Fax: (31 20) 620 62 17 (in Belgium, phone: (32-14) 37 24 40), E-mail: reis@gayworld.nl, Web: www.gayworld.nl/reis/index.html.

Amsterdam gay experts, Gay Games packages, European gay resort pkgs, USA skiing & beach pkgs, Gran Canaria, Ibiza, Mykonos, also Kenya, USA, Thailand.

Bookings: Call direct. *Est:* 1985. *Pymt:* Checks, credit cards. *Member:* ANUR, SGR IGTA

Departures International
1793 Union St
San Francisco, CA 94123 USA
(415) 563-5959, (800) 509-5959, Fax: (415) 563-5935.

Russia & CIS experts, 50 years experience, good connections for hotels, staff of 70 is on site, Moscow, St Ptsbg, Kiev offices, business & vacation travel.

Bookings: Call travel agent or direct. *Est:* 1989; *TAC:* 10%; *Pymt:* Checks; *Member:* ASTA, IATAN

Desert Vision Tours
PO Box 5754
Carefree, AZ 85377 USA
(602) 488-4645 (tel/fax).

Adventures in Arizona, Colorado, Utah and New Mexico, visits to native American nations, ghost towns of the old west, old mines and canyonlands, visits with crafts people, insights into desert landscape.

Bookings: Call travel agent or direct. aging, enjoy

Destination Discovery
P.O. Box 614
St Helena, CA 94574 USA
(707) 963-0543, (800) 954-5543, Email: DDISCOVERY@aol.com.

Take mud baths, practice yoga, visit wineries & learn wellness, stress management and succeful aging, enjoy wineries, mineral soaks, hikes, separate sessions for HIV+ Men and for lesbian & bi women.

Bookings: Call travel agent or direct. *Est:* 1991. *TAC:* 10%. IGTA

TOUR COMPANIES

52   FERRARI GUIDES' GAY TRAVEL A to Z - 18th EDITION

◐ Wholesale/Retail (Call Direct or Have Travel Agent Contact)

WHO TO CALL

♀♂	●	**Destination Downunder** Level 10, 130 Elizabeth St Sydney, NSW 2000 Australia (61 2) 9268 2111, Fax: (61 2) 9267 9733, In US: (415) 284-1666, (800) 397-2681. E-mail: atssyd@s054.aone.net.au, Web: http://ddu.com.au.	Packages to all Australian gay festivals and events, award-winning Australian tour company, Mardi Gras, Sleaze Ball, Queens Birthday, Red Raw Dance Party, Midsumma, Sydney Leather Week, etc., book in US and Australia.	*Bookings:* Call travel agent or direct. *Est:* 1991. *TAC:* from 10%. *Pymt:* All credit cards. *Member:* SLGBA, SGLMG IGTA agita
♀♂	◐	**Destination Management** 610 S. Peters #200 New Orleans, LA 70130 USA Individuals call: (800) 366-8882, (504) 524-5030, Fax: (504) 529-1405. Groups, agents call: (800) 471-8222, (504) 592-0500, Fax: (504) 592-0529, E-mail: info@new.orleans.com, Web: www.new.orleans.com.	New Orleans specialist, specialized programs, special event packages, New Orleans Mardi Gras, Air tickets to hotels to riverboat cruises.	*Bookings:* Call travel agent or direct. *Est:* 1989. *TAC:* 10%. *Pymt:* Checks, AX, V, MC, agent MCOs validated on Delta. *Member:* TIAA, NTA, AS, ASTA, IGTA
♀♂	●	**Destination World** PO Box 1077 Santa Barbara, CA 93102 USA (805) 569-9385, (800) 426-3644, Fax: (805) 569-3795, E-mail: world@destinationworld.com.	Personalized upscale Itineraries, for celebrity & deluxe market, chauffered limousine transport, custom-designed programs, South Pacific, Europe, Asia, Africa, South America.	*Bookings:* Call travel agent. *Est:* 1976. *TAC:* 10%. *Pymt:* Checks. *Member:* AFTA
♀♂	●	**Different Strokes Tours** 1841 Broadway #1207 New York, NY 10023 USA (212) 262-3860, (800) 688-3301, Fax: (212) 262-3865.	Gay and lesbian cultural tours, created for intellectually adventurous, Turkey, Indonesia, Scandinavia, Spain, Russia, Morocco, Paris.	*Bookings:* Call travel agent. IGTA
♂	◐	**Discus Travel** Schwetzinger Str 93 Mannheim 68165 Germany (49 621) 40 9627, Fax: (49 621) 44 1340.	Men's resort vacation packages, Mykonos, Ibiza, Sitges, Gran Canaria.	*Bookings:* Call travel agent or direct. IGTA
♀♂	◐	**Doin' It Right Travel** PO Box 192212 San Francisco, CA 94119 USA (415) 621-3584, (800) 936-3646, Fax: (415) 621-3576, E-Mail: PVDoinIt@aol.com.	Gay Puerto Vallarta tour packages, air, transfers, hotels, condos, apartments, villas, B&Bs, gay tours, excursions, LA and SF pride parade packages.	*Bookings:* Call travel agent or direct. *Est:* 1993. *TAC:* 10%. *Pymt* Checks, money orders. *Member:* CLIA IGTA
♀♂	◐	**Earth, Wind & Water** 176 E 81st St, #3-A New York, NY 10028 USA (212) 744-3177, (800) 555-0977, Fax:(212) 744-8755, E-mail: earthww@aol.com, Web: www.earthww.com.	Soft adventure in Mexico, Copper Canyon, Baja, whale watching, camping, kayaking, hiking, train rides, comfortable lodgings, breathtaking wilderness.	*Bookings:* Call travel agent or direct. *Est:* 1993. *TAC:* 10. *Pymt:* Checks. IGTA
♀♂	◐	**East-West Tours** 17, avenue Hoche Paris 75008 France (33 1) 53 89 13 33, Fax: (33 1) 53 89 13 34, Web: www.east.west.worldtour.com.	Sail around the world, depart from Tahiti, crew for entire 14 months, or choose from 6 2-month legs, Galapagos, Maldives, Salomons, Antilles, Greece, Fr. Polynesia.	*Bookings:* Call travel agent or direct. *Est:* 1996. *Comm:* 10%. *Pymt:* Credit cards, checks.

TOUR COMPANIES

FERRARI GUIDES' GAY TRAVEL A to Z - 18th EDITION 53

WHO TO CALL

○ Retail (Call Direct)   ● Wholesale (Travel Agent Must Contact)

♀♂	●	**Easy Way** 350 Fifth Ave #6608 New York, NY 10118 USA (212) 629-0964, (800) 223-5799, Fax:(212) 629-3647, E-mail: easywayusa@aol.com.	USA packages for travelers from Italy, France, Germany and Spain, Europe packages for travelers from USA to French Riviera and Italy, will customize itineraries for gay and lesbian individuals and groups.	*Bookings:* Call travel agent. **IGTA**
♀♂	◐	**Eat Quiche Tour & Travel Accommodations** 42 ave des Pins ouest #2 Montreal, QC H2W 1R1 Canada (514) 845-4188, (800) 575-6955, Fax: (800) 575-6855, E-mail:EQuiche@aol.com	Travel packages to major Canadian Cities, exclusively gay & lesbian, gay and gay-friendly accommodations, welcome pack with map, local discounts.	*Bookings:* Call travel agent or direct. *Est:* 1996. *TAC:* 10%. *Pymt:* Visa, MC. **IGTA**
♀♂	○	**Eclectic Excursions** 2045 Hunters Glen Drive Dunedin, FL 34698 USA (813) 734-1111, (800) 447-5224 ext 114, Fax:(813) 734-1111	Seventh annual Gay Ski East, March 7 to March 10, 1997, Lake Placid, New York, packages include accommodation, skiing, other winter sports and Saturday night dance event.	*Bookings:* Call travel agent or direct.
♀♂	◐	**Embassy Travel** 906 N Harper Ave #B West Hollywood, CA 90046 USA (213) 656-0743, (800) 227-6668, Fax: (213) 650-6968.	Specializes in safaris, individuals and groups, Kenya, South Africa, Tanzania, Botswana, Namibia, Zimbabwe, experts on gay life in South Africa.	*Bookings:* Call travel agent or direct. *Est:* 1987. *TAC:* 10%. *Member:* IATA, ASTA **IGTA**
♀♂	○	**Envision Charters** Box 201 125A 1030 Denman St Vancouver, BC V6G 2M6 Canada (604) 688-7245, cellular: (604) 657-2893.	Sailing off Vancouver, BC, evening cruises, BBQ dinners, weekend getaways, Gulf Islands, Sunshine Coast, commitment ceremonies, other cruising ideas welcome.	*Bookings* Call direct. *Est:* 1997. *Pymt:* Visa, MC, money orders.
♀♂	◐	**Envoy Travel** 740 N Rush St Chicago, IL 60611 USA (312) 787-2400, (800) 443-6869, Fax: (312) 787-7109.	China travel experts, individual tours at group prices, your own guide and driver, four- to 9-day packages, customized journeys.	*Bookings:* Call travel agent or direct. **IGTA**
♀♂	●	**European Luxury Hotel Barge Cruises** 106 Calvert St Harrison, NY 10528 USA A service of Kemwell's Premier Selections, (800) 234-4000, Fax: (914) 835-5449.	Wholesaler of luxury barge cruises in France and England. A range of prices is available to tour operators or travel agents who put together gay groups. Entire boats can be chartered or mixed travel is available.	*Bookings:* Call travel agent. *Est:* 1991. *TAC:*10%. *Pymt:* Checks, Visa, MC, Amex.
♀♂	◐	**Eurway Tour & Cruise Club** 26 6th St #260 Stamford, CT 06905 USA (203) 967-1611, (800) 938-7929, Fax: (203) 969-0799, E-mail: aegeanvisions@msn.com.	Athens, Greek Isles,Turkey, exclusively for gays & lesbians, yacht charters, villas, resorts, special 7-day cruise/ tour packages, customized itineraries. *Bookings:* Call travel agent or direct.	*Est:* 1979. *TAC:* 12+. *Pymt:* Checks, MC, Visa. **IGTA**

TOUR COMPANIES

54   FERRARI GUIDES' GAY TRAVEL A to Z - 18th EDITION

Wholesale/Retail (Call Direct or Have Travel Agent Contact)

WHO TO CALL

♀♂	◐	**Experience Plus** 1925 Wallenberg Dr Ft Collins, CO 80526 USA (970) 484-8489 (tel/fax), (800) 685-4565, E-mail: tours@xplus.com, Web: www.xplus.com.	Bicycling, walking, hiking tours, gourmet & culinary tours, Italy, France, Spain, Portugal, Costa Rica, United States, guided and self-guided, quality lodgings, gay-friendly company, customizes vacations for gay groups.	*Bookings:* Call travel agent or direct. *Est:* 1972. TAC: 10%. *Pymt:* Amex, Visa, MC (agents: business checks). *Member:* LAB, AHS, ES, CFT.
♀♂	◐	**Explorer Tours** PO Box 3710 San Diego, CA 92163 USA (619) 543-9100, Fax: (619) 291-8819, E-mail: explortrs@aol.com.	Personalized tours to exotic cultures, for the adventurous traveler, Thailand, Bali (Indonesia), Morocco, sightseeing, architecture combined with soft adventure, elephant treks, diving, fishing, kayaking, cruises.	*Bookings:* Call travel agent or direct. *Est:* 1990. *Comm:* 10%. *Pymt:* Visa, MC, Amex. *Member:* PATA
♀♂	○	**Fair Choices** 1120 Capital of Texas Hwy South, Bldg 3 #300 Austin, TX 78746 USA (512) 329-7260, Fax: (512) 329-7269, E-mail: jayjuba@inetport.com.	Travel for airline employees, discount travel opportunities, gay and lesbian vacation packages, major hotel properties, resorts, cruises, tours, resorts, value-added packages.	*Bookings:* Call direct. *Est:* 1996. *Pymt:* All credit cards. *Member:* CLIA IGTA
♀♂	○	**Fiesta Tours** 323 Geary St #619 San Francisco, CA 94102 USA (415) 986-1134, (800) 200-0582, Fax: (415) 986-3029. E-mail: brazusa@primenet.com.	Gay and lesbian tours to Brazil, Carnaval and New Years, South American destinations, special-interest groups.	*Bookings:* Call direct. *Est:* 1979. *Pymt:* most types. *Member:* IATAN, ARC, ASTA IGTA
♀♂	◐	**Fiesta Tours** Paseo Infanta Isabel 21, 8-10 Madrid 28014 Spain (34-1) 551 5294, Fax: (34-1) 501 1835, E-mail: aki@sarenet.es.	Tour operator and wholesaler.	IGTA
♀♂	○	**Fine Travel & Yachting** 145 Kountouriotou St Piraeus 185 32 Greece (30 1) 412 2324, Fax:(30 1) 417 0137.	All services in area of yachting, chartering yachts, motor sailers, scheduled Greek Island cruises, seminars, incentives, events, product promotion, presentation, hotels, apts, villas, car rental, excursions throughout Greece.	*Bookings:* Call travel agent or direct. *Est:* 1983. *Comm:* 15%. *Pymt:* Checks, Visa, MC, Amex. *Member:* ASTA, GYBCA IGTA
♀♂	◐	**Five Star Travel Services** 164 Newbury St Boston, MA 02116 USA (617) 536-1999, (800) 359-1999, Fax: (617) 236-1999, startrvl@aol.com.	One or two trips per year, destinations like Caribbean, Europe, Russia.	IGTA
♀	◐	**Frauen Unterwegs** Potsdamerstr 139 1028 Berlin, Germany (49 30) 215 1022, Fax: (49 30) 216 9852.	Women-only cultural and soft adventure tours from Germany to worldwide destinations. Women from all countries are welcome, but trips are intended mainly for German speakers. This is the oldest women's travel company, in operation since 1984.	*Bookings:* Call travel agent or direct. *Est:* 1984.

TOUR COMPANIES

FERRARI GUIDES' GAY TRAVEL A to Z - 18th EDITION

WHO TO CALL

○ Retail (Call Direct)   ● Wholesale (Travel Agent Must Contact)

♀♂ ●	**French Touch** 13 rue Stephenson Paris 75018 France (33 1) 41 10 38 37 Fax: (33 1) 41 10 39 55.	Paris-based gay tour company, 15 years travel experience, theme trips in France, gay & lesbian cultural tours, convention and incentive planner, specialized gay group tours.	*Bookings:* Call travel agent. *Est:* 1994. *Comm:* Low net rates. *Pymt:* Int'l wire. IGTA
♀♂ ◐	**Gay Baja Tours** 511 E San Ysidro Blvd #311 San Ysidro, CA 92173 USA (52-61) 76 4958 (tel/fax), (888) 225-2429, E-mail: rdblack@compunet.com.mx.	Specializing in gay and lesbian vacations in Baja, Mexico, Carnaval in Ensenada, whale watching in Guerrero Negro, Tijuana Pride celebration, diving in the Sea of Cortez, wine festival in Ensenada, Christmas in Cabo San Lucas and others.	*Bookings:* Call travel agent or direct.
♀ ◐	**Gay Guided Tours of Israel** PO Box 10497 Jerusalem, Israel (972-2) 673-3987 (tel/fax).	Customized gay Israel vacations, guides Have 10 years experience, licensed by Israeli Ministry of Tourism, private or group tours, niblical sites to snorkeling, camel rides to mud baths.	
♀♂ ◐	**Gay Mexico Travel** Avenida Mexico 99 PB, Col. Hipódromo Condesa Mexico DF 06170 Mexico (52 5) 264 0822, Fax: (52 5) 264 2827.	Customized gay and lesbian Mexican itineraries, gay-friendly hotels and escursions, referrals to gay-friendly bars and restaurants, any location in Mexico, friendly and professional service, English spoken.	*Bookings:* Call travel agent or direct. *Established:* 1980; *Comm:* 10%; *Payment:* Checks, money orders; *Member:* IATA
♀♂ ◐	**Gaygantic Tours** Neptun Reisen & Touristik GmbH, Dom-Pedro-Str 16 Munich 80637 Germany (49 89)1591 9086, Fax: (49 89) 1575 834, E-mail: Neptun.Reisen@T-Online.de.	Gay and lesbian city packages to Europe's major cities, Australia, USA and Asia vacations.	*Bookings:* Call travel agent or direct. *Est:* 1992. *Comm:* 10%. *Pymt:* Credit cards.
♀♂ ◐	**Gaylink Travel Services** PO Box 11-584 Wellington 6001 New Zealand (64-4) 384 1877, Fax: (64-4) 384 5187, E-mail: gts@clear.net.nz, Web: http://webnz.com/tpac/gay.	Individual independent gay and lesbian travel packages, New Zealand, Australia, South Pacific.	IGTA
♀♂ ◐	**Gayventures** 2009 SW 9th St Miami, FL 33135 USA (305) 541-6141, (800) 940-7757, Fax: (305) 541-8003.	Affordable vacation packages, for gay and lesbian couples, Caribbean and Latin America.	*Bookings:* Call travel agent or direct.
♀ ○	**Global Affair** 285 E 5th Ave Eugene, OR 97401 USA (541) 343-8595, (800) 755-2753, Fax: (541) 343-3891	Upscale women's tours, outdoor adventure trips, destinations worldwide, specializing in small groups.	*Bookings:* Call direct. *Pymt:* Checks, all credit cards.

TOUR COMPANIES

○ Wholesale/Retail (Call Direct or Have Travel Agent Contact)

WHO TO CALL

♀♂	●	**Good Time Tours** 450 W 62nd St Miami Beach, FL 33140 USA (305) 864-9431, (888) 429-3527, Fax: (305) 866-6955, E-mail: gayfla@bridge.net or gayfla@aol.com, Web: www.gayday.com.	Gay Florida ONLY! Groups and individual travelers, fabulous Florida custom itineraries, the ONLY official tour operator for Gay Day at Disney, provides Gay Fun Packs to the area you'll visit.	*Bookings:* Call travel agent. *Est:* 1991. *Comm:* unusually generous to agents. *Pymt:* Checks, wire transfers. *Member:* ASTA, TAG IGTA
♀♂	◐	**GPSC Charters** 600 Saint Andrews Road Philadelphia, PA 19118 USA (215) 247-3903, (800) 732-6786, Fax: (215) 247-1505, E-mail: corr@gpsc.com, Web: www.gpsc.com.	All-inclusive Greek sailing vacations, including air from New York, hotels, transfers, guide and others, private crewed sailing yachts or bareboat charters, 1997 Gay Adventure sail July 20-August 2.	*Bookings* Call travel agent or direct. *Est:* 1976. *TAC* 10-20%. IGTA
♀	○	**Grand Canyon Field Institute** PO Box 399 Grand Canyon, AZ 86023 USA (520) 638-2485, Fax: (520) 638-2484.	Women's backpacking trips, Grand Canyon, Arizona, beginners to advanced backpackers, all ages welcome, mainstream women's trips, lesbians most welcome.	*Bookings:* Call direct.
♀♂	●	**Graylink Tours** PO Box 3826 Darwin, NT 0801 Australia (61 8) 894 80089, Fax: (61 8) 894 72807, E-mail: graylink@ozemail.com.au.	Visit Australia's "Top End," Darwin, Northern Territory, Kakadu National Park, Katherine Gorge and birdlife, Aboriginal culture and crocodiles, arranges everything from outdoor adventures to transportation to luxury accommodations.	*Bookings:* Call travel agent. IGTA agta
♀♂	◐	**G'day Tours** A division of Swain Travel Services, Inc., 6 W Lancaster Ave Ardmore, PA 19003 USA (610) 896-9595, (800) 272-1149, Fax: (610) 896-9592. E-mail: SWAINAUST@AOL.COM.	Certified Australia specialists, detailed customized South Pacific iitineraries, Australia, New Zealand, Pacific islands, experienced US, New Zealand and Aussie staffs.	*Bookings:* Call travel agent or direct. *Est:* 1986; *Comm:* 10%/12%. Certified Aussie Specialists on land and air packages; *Pymt:* Checks, Visa, MC, Amex, Discover, Diners Club; *Member:* ASTA, IATAN, ARC, PATA IGTA
♀♂	○	**Hanafi Tour and Travel** Poppies Lane 1, #77 Kuta 80361, Bali, Indonesia (62 361) 756 454, Fax: (62 361) 752 561.	A friendly gay and lesbian welcome in Bali, airport pick-up, sightseeing excursions, "gay" bars & beach, transportation and arrangements for snorkeling, scuba diving, para-sailing, etc., even hotel arrangements. Call or fax direct.	*Bookings:* Call direct. *Est:* 1990. *TAC* Not reported, but may be available. *Pymt:* Cash or funds transfer.
♂	◐	**Hanns Ebensten Travel** 513 Fleming St Key West, FL 33040 USA (305) 294-8174, Fax: (305) 292-9665.	This is the man who invented gay tours, renowned for excellence in gay travel, author of the book, Volleyball with the Cuna Indians, his autobiography, mostly male-only tours, several mixed trips each year, worldwide destinations, historical, cultural and archaeolgical tours, cruises.	*Bookings:* Call travel agent or direct. *Est:* 1972; *TAC:* Depends on circumstances; *Lic* 47148-0008414; *Pymt:* Checks; *Member:* IATAN, ARC

TOUR COMPANIES

FERRARI GUIDES' GAY TRAVEL A to Z - 18th EDITION

WHO TO CALL

○ Retail (Call Direct)   ● Wholesale (Travel Agent Must Contact)

♀	○	**Hawk, I'm Your Sister** PO Box 9109-F Santa Fe, NM 87504-9109 USA (505) 984-2268.	Women's wilderness canoeing, learn wilderness skills, visit ancient sites, like Macchu Picchu, raft in Siberia, wilderness writing retreats and seminars.	*Bookings:* Call direct. *Est:* 1983. *Pymt:* Checks, money orders, travelers checks, cash.
♀♂	◐	**Hawkesbury Expeditions** 33 Point Road Mooney Mooney, NSW 2254 Australia (61-2) 9985 9349, Fax: (61-2) 9985 9349.	Tour and charter boat company. Individually tailored itineraries for the travel industry and the public. Private charters available for minimum of five passengers.	*Bookings:* Call travel agent or direct. **aglta**
♂	◐	**Hellkamp Reisen** Hellkamp 17 Hamburg 20255 Germany (49-40) 491 9054, Fax: (49 40) 491 9100, E-mail: hellkamp@aol.com, Web: www.gaytravel.do.	Worldwide gay itineraries, city pkgs & men's resort vacations, Europe, USA, Caribbean, Canada, Ibiza, Mykonos, Key West, Provincetown, Berlin, London, Toronto, Miami, Rome, San Francisco, Prague, Montreal.	*Bookings:* Call travel agent or direct. *Est:* 1990. *TAC:* 10. *Pymt:* Checks, wire transfer CC on $ rates. *Member:* IATA **IGTA**
♀♂	◐	**Heritage Tours** 57 West 93rd St #6-G New York, NY 10025 USA (212) 749-1339, Fax: (212) 749-4317, E-mail: heritagejz@earthlink.net.	Top-quality, in-depth tours, Morocco, Spain & Turkey, planned and independent travel, architecture, history, culture, soft adventure, hiking, trekking, private car and driver, finest accommodations, dining, full-time guide/translator.	*Bookings:* Call travel agent or direct. *Est:* 1994. *TAC:* Varies.
♀♂	◐	**Himalayan High Treks** 241 Dolores St San Francisco, CA 94103-2211 USA (415) 861-2391, (800) 455-8735. E-mail: effie@well.com Internet: http://www.com/user/effie	Trekking in the Himalayas, hike with views of the hIghest mountains, visit local monasteries and homes, experience indigenous Buddhist and Hindu cultures, from walking tours to strenuous ski tours, departures throughout the year.	*Bookings:* Call travel agent or direct. *Est:* 1988; *TAC:* 10%; *Pymt:* checks, visa, MC, Amex; *Member:* PATA, Ecotourism Society
♀♂	◐	**Holidays at Sea/Sunquest** 1208 Fourth St Santa Rosa, CA 95404-4012 USA (707) 573-8300, (800) 444-8300, Fax: (707) 573-9992, E-mail: 105000.1424@compuserve.com, Web: www.travelhub.com/sea/.	Certified Aussie specialist, wholesales customized tours to Australia and New Zealand, groups from 1 to 100, personalized arrangements, not fixed packages, ask for Jonas.	*Bookings* Call travel agent or direct. *Est:* 1986. *TAC:* 10%. *Member:* CLIA, ICTA, IATAN, CAS
♀♂	●	**Holigays** Schwalbengasse 46 Cologne 50667 Germany (49-221) 925 891 13, Fax: (49-221) 257 69 43. US address: 14 Dartmouth St, Malden, MA 02148, (617) 321-6100.	Worldwide gay tours and packages, exclusively gay & lesbian, for those deparing from or visiting Germany, vacations in Europe, USA, Australia, Africa, Central America, comprehensive color brochure.	*Bookings:* Call travel agent. *Est:* 1994. *TAC:* 10%. *Pymt:* Checks, transfers, all major cards. **IGTA**
♀♂	◐	**IMTC, Inc.** 3025 Maple Drive #5 Atlanta, GA 30305 USA (404) 240-0949, (800) 790-4682, Fax: (404) 240-0948, E-mail: imtc@mindspring.com.	European vacation packages, Atlanta, Amsterdam and Vienna offices, superior, first-class and deluxe hotels, Gay Games '97 packages, personal assistance on the spot, independent travel itineraries. Europe to US, US to Europe.	*Bookings:* Call travel agent or direct. *Est:* 1992. *TAC:* Net. *Pymt:* Check. No credit cards. *Member:* SITE, ASI **IGTA**

TOUR COMPANIES

◐ Wholesale/Retail (Call Direct or Have Travel Agent Contact)

WHO TO CALL

♂ ○	**In Touch Holidays Ltd.** 24 Chiswick High Rd London W4 1TE England (44 181) 742 7749, Fax: (44 181) 742 7407.	Inclusive air/hotel packages, gay resorts throughout Europe, Gran Canaria, Mykonos, Spain, Algarve, USA, selling direct to the public.	*Bookings:* Call direct. IGTA	
♀♂ ◐	**Inter-Rainbow Turismo** Rua Xavier de Toledo, 264 #137, 13o Andar Sao Paulo 01048.904 Brazil (55 11) 214 0380 (tel/fax).	For international visitors: Rio and Sao Paulo packages, including hotel, sightseeing, nightlife, for gay Brazilians, worldwide tours & cruises, Australia, USA, Russia, Caribbean.	*Bookings:* Call travel agent or direct. *Est:* 1992. *TAC:* 10%. *Pymt:* Transfers. IGTA	
♀♂ ●	**Island Hoppers Tours** 3501 W Vine St #388 Kissimmee, FL 34741 USA (407) 933-4333, (800) 467-7595, Fax: (407) 933-0005, E-mail: kalikmon@digital.net, Web: http://islandhoppers.com.	Island-hopping vacations, Jamaica and the Bahamas, choose a single island or hop to other islands, scuba and cultural programs, day trips from Florida.	*Bookings:* Call travel agent. *Est:* 1994. *TAC:* 10-12. *Pymt:* Major credit cards. *Member:* Caribbean Tourism Org.	
♀ ◐	**It's Our Nature** 929 Bay Esplanade Clearwater, FL 34630 USA (813) 441-2599 (tel/fax). E-mail: itsrnature@aol.com, Web: www.itsournature.com.	Women's nature hikes and kayaking, Tampa Bay area of Florida, move quietly thru slash pine forest, natural history told in storybook fashion, virgin forests, bird sanctuaries, beach habitats, lifelong naturalist guide.	*Bookings:* Call travel agent or direct. *Est:* 1996. *TAC:* 10. *Pymt:* Checks, cash. *Member:* Gulf Beaches COC.	
♀ ◐	**Izarra Cruises** 2442 NW Market St #467 Seattle, WA 98107 USA (206) 789-2175.	Women's Sailing Adventures, NW US, British Columbia waters, cruising amongst the San Juan Islands and to Alaska, 1997 features sailing the Great Barrier Reef Sept 24-Oct 8, the Izarra is smoke-free, holds 4 women plus Coast Guard-licensed skipper, learn sail trimming, helmswomanship, navigation, etc.	*Bookings:* Call travel agent or direct. *Est:* 1990. *TAC:* 10. *Pymt:* Checks, money orders.	
♂ ◐	**Jetman International Gay Travel** c/o Bon(n) Voyage Touristik, Thomas-Mann-Str 56 Bonn D-53111 Germany (49-228) 98518-0, Fax: (49-228) 9851818.	Gay men's tours, cruises, worldwide destinations.	*Bookings:* Call travel agent or direct. *Est:* 1992.	
♀♂ ◐	**Jornada** Level 1, 53 Cross St Double Bay, NSW 2028 Australia (61 2) 9362 0900, Fax: (61 2) 9362 0788, E-mail: justask@jornada.com.au.	Australia's largest gay travel company, worldwide tours, cruises, hotel and resort packages, custom independent itineraries a specialty, Australia, New Zealand, South Pacific, Europe, Thailand, Bali, USA.	*Bookings:* Call travel agent or direct. *Est:* 1995. *TAC:* 10. *Pymt:* Amex, Visa, Diners, MC, transfers, *Member:* IATA, AFTA IGTA agta	

TOUR COMPANIES

FERRARI GUIDES' GAY TRAVEL A to Z - 18th EDITION   59

WHO TO CALL

○ Retail (Call Direct)   ● Wholesale (Travel Agent Must Contact)

♀♂ ◐	**Journeys by Sea Yacht Charters** 1402 E Las Olas Blvd #122 Ft. Lauderdale, FL 33301 USA (954) 730-8585, (800) 825-3632, Fax: (954) 730-8586, E-mail: journeys@safari.net, Web: www.safari.net/~journeys.	A floating gay resort, meals and bar included, gourmet chef onboard, you decide ports of call, Caribbean, Mediterranean, worldwide, snorkeling, scuba, water ski, priced competitively with resort hotel stays.	*Bookings:* Call travel agent or direct. *Est:* 1989. *TAC:* 10. *Pymt:* Checks, credit cards.
♀♂ ●	**Kam Tours Int'l** 135 W 18th St New York, NY 10011 USA (212) 886-6685, (800) 326-0339, Fax: (212) 229-2216, E-mail: kamtours@aol.com.	Vacation packages to Costa Rica and Margarita Island (Venezuela), beaches, volcanoes, rainforests, approved consolidators for Viasa, Servivensa, Lacsa and United Airlines to Central and South America, also Gay Games 1998 packages.	*Bookings:* Call travel agent. *Est:* 1992. *TAC:* 12-15. *Pymt:* Checks, Ax, MC, VI. *Member:* IATAN IGTA
♀♂ ○	**Kayak Historical Discovery Tours** 87-3187 Honu Moe Road Captain Cook, HI 96704 USA (808) 328-8911.	Kayak off Hawaii's Big Island, 1/2-day and 2-day to 5-day trips, camp & kayak beautiful bays called Kealakekua or Keauhou, snorkel, see dolphins and whales, eat fresh-caught grilled fish on the beach, equipment & guide provided.	*Bookings:* Travel agent or call direct. *Est:* 1991. *TAC:* 15. *Pymt:* Checks, cash. *Member:* Hawaii Visitors Bureau, Ecotourism Assoc.
♀♂ ●	**Kenny Tours** 106 Market Ct Stevensville, MD 21666-2192 USA (410) 643-9200, (800) 648-1492, Fax: (410) 643-8868.	Ireland, Britain, Netherlands specialists, customized individual and group packages.	*Bookings:* Call travel agent. IGTA
♀♂ ◐	**Kremlin Tours** PO Box 44 105318 Moscow E-318 Russia (7 095) 274 74 21 (tel/fax) or fax: (7 095) 464 18 14, E-mail: kremln@dol.ru, Web: www.gayrussia.msk.ru.	Russia's first gay tour company, group tours and individual itineraries, supplier to the travel industry, Russia, Eastern Europe, Ukraine, special guides, private gay parties, gay nightlife, businessmen's arrangements, deluxe VIP services available, qualified guide/interpreters.	*Bookings:* Call travel agent or direct. *Est:*1992. IGTA
♀♂ ◐	**Land Voyages** PO Box 831 Strathfield, NSW 2135 Australia (61-2) 9763 1611, Fax: (61-2) 9763 1677, Mobile: (61-15) 270 566.	Luxury coach tours. One-day to several days. Available for charter.	*Bookings:* Call travel agent or direct. agta
♀♂ ●	**Landmark (South Pacific) Pty Ltd** c/o World Mktg Group, 4444 W Lake Harriet Pkwy #10 Minneapolis, MN 55410 USA (612) 925-4432, (800) 347-6447, Fax: (612) 925-0955.	Supplier to the travel industry, customizes programs to Australia and New Zealand, groups of 10 or more.	*Bookings:* Call travel agent only. IGTA
♀ ◐	**Liquid Crystal Divers** PO Box 628 Makawao, HI 96768 USA (808) 572-4774. E-mail: aquasong@sprynet.com.	Women's SCUBA diving in Maui, female guides are veterans of over 6,000 dives, minimal training allows underwater exploration of reefs from shore, beginners to certification to advanced instruction, day and night dives, boat dives, shore dives, checkout dives.	*Bookings:* Call travel agent or direct. *Est:* 1983. *TAC:* 15. *Pymt:* Cash or checks.

TOUR COMPANIES

Wholesale/Retail (Call Direct or Have Travel Agent Contact) — **WHO TO CALL**

♀♂ ●	**Lizard Head Backcountry Tours** 1280 Humboldt St #32 Denver, CO 80218 USA (303) 831-7090, (888) 540-2737, Fax: (303) 831-7079, E-mail: info@lizardhead.com, Web: http://lizardhead.com.	Learn self-reliance in the wilderness, hiking, mountain biking, skiing, snowshoeing, rock climbing, desert foraging, Colorado, Utah, Arizona, N Mexico, all skill levels, beginner to expert, exclusively gay and lesbian.	*Bookings:* Call travel agent. *Est:* 1995. *TAC:* 10-15. *Pymt:* Checks, Visa, MC. IGTA
♀♂ ○	**Lodestar Adventures** Box 84 Procter, BC V0G 1V0 Canada (250) 229-5354, E-mail: mgrove@netidea.com.	Gay/lesbian llama treks, llama-assisted backpacking, mountain bike tours, multi-activity, small-group adventure excursions in British Columbia, Canada. "Wir schicken Ihnen gerne Information in deutsch."	*Bookings:* Call direct.
♀ ○	**Lois Lane Expeditions** 2622 Franklin Ave East Seattle, WA 98102 USA (206) 726-2676, Fax: (360) 732-4096. E-mail: LOISLANE@DAKA.COM.	Women's outdoor adventures, worldwide destinations, Nepal, Ecuador, Canadian Rockies, USA, skiing, hiking, climbing, snow camping, glacier travel, women's mountaineering, hands-on practice and experience.	*Bookings:* Call direct.
♀♂ ●	**London Handling Ltd.** 12 Kendrick Mews London SW7 3HG England (44 171) 589-2212, Fax: (44 171) 225-1033.	Gay and lesbian group packages for overseas travelers visiting London and England, including accommodations, excursions.	*Bookings:* Call travel agent. *Est:* 1978. IGTA
♀♂ ◐	**L'Arc en Ciel Voyages** PO Box 234 Wayne, PA 19087-0234 USA (610) 964-7888, (800) 965-LARC (5272), Fax: (610) 964-8220. E-mail: larc@galaxytours.com.	Preferred sales agent for the 1998 Amsterdam Gay Games, custom-designs personalized group tours, over 36 years experience in over 60 countries, will custom-design gay/lesbian group adventures for any group.	*Bookings:* Call travel agent or direct. *Est:* 1960. *TAC:* 10+. *Pymt:* Checks, MC, Visa, Discover, Amex. *Member:* ASTA, IATAN, ARC, IGTA
♂ ◐	**Mantrav International** PO Box 378 Pretoria, Gauteng 0001 South Africa (27-1464) 77354 (tel/fax), E-mail: mantrav@ilink.nis.za, Web: www.nis.za/homepgs/mantrav/home.htm.	Gay tours and safaris in South Africa, group getaways for South African gays, gay cruises.	*Bookings:* Call travel agent or direct. *Est:* 1993. agta
♀♂ ◐	**Mariah Wilderness Expeditions** PO Box 248 Point Richmond, CA 94807 USA (510) 233-2303, (800) 462-7424, Fax: (510) 233-0956, E-mail: rafting@mariahwe.com, Web: www.mariahwe.com.	California's only women-owned whitewater rafting company, a pioneer of women's whitewater rafting trips, high-quality adventure travel, Costa Rica and Baja Mexico rafting, kayaking and beaches, rafting on California, Idaho, Oregon and Utah rivers.	*Bookings:* Call travel agent or direct. *Est:* 1982. *TAC:* 10. *Pymt:* MC, Visa, checks, cash. IGTA

TOUR COMPANIES

WHO TO CALL

○ Retail (Call Direct) ● Wholesale (Travel Agent Must Contact)

♀♂	○	**Matt's Rainbow Tours** 87-3202 Guava Rd. Captain Cook, HI 96704 USA (808) 328-8406, (tel/fax), E-mail: MrLinkk@aol.com.	Casual, personalized kayak, snorkel and massage therapy package, on the Big Island of Hawaii, writer, filmmaker Matt Link is your guide, paddle an easy, 3-seat beginner's kayak to a clothing-optional black-sand beach, snorkel and swim coral reef with colorful fish, after kayaking, snorkeling enjoy swedish massage therapy overlooking the ocean.	*Bookings:* Call direct. *Est:* 1994. *Pymt:* Cash, checks.
♀♂	◐	**Maui Surfing School** PO Box 424 Puunene, HI 96784 USA (808) 875-0625, (800) 851-0543, Fax: (808) 875-0623, E-mail: andrea@maui.net, Web: www.mauisurf.com.	You can surf in ONE lesson! Maui Surfing School specializes in beginners and cowards. most students stand up on their first wave. Lessons are fun, safe and easy for all ages, shapes and sizes. Gay-friendly.	*Bookings:* Call travel agent or direct. *Est:* 1980. *TAC:* 10. *Pymt:* Visa, MC, Discover, cash.
♀	○	**McNamara Ranch** 4620 County Rd 100 Florissant, CO 80816 USA (719) 748-3466.	Stay on a working women's ranch, ride horses above timberline, rides are tailored to your stamina, camp overnight or return to ranch house for good food, shear sheep, move sheep from pasture to pasture, feed newborn lambs, go trout fishing, relax in hot tub under the stars, nearby rodeos, gambling town.	*Bookings:* Call direct. *Est:* 1991.
♂	◐	**Men on Bikes** 1265 Beach Grove Court Delta, BC V4L 1N5 Canada Canada office: (604) 943-9260, Fax: (604) 948-2703, Rome office: Via Rosa 36, Ariccia (RM) Italy, (39-6) 934 8459 (tel/fax), E-mail: pblackman@pcg.telpress.it.	Biking vacations in Italy for gay men. Choose Mantua to Venice, San Marino to Florence, Syracuse to Taormina, Rome to Capri. Join up with Italian gay biking groups, experience Italian gay culture.	*Bookings:* Call travel agent or direct. IGTA
♂	●	**Men on Vacation** 4715 30th St #6 San Diego, CA 92116 USA (619) 641-7085, (800) 959-4636, Fax: (619) 641-7088, special Gay Games line: (800) 854-7688, E-mail: MenOnVacat@aol.com.	One of the larger suppliers of Australian gay group vacations, provides tour packages for men, usually involving major gay party events, packages for Sydney Gay Mardi Gras, Gay Games Amsterdam, Twelve Gods Party (Mykonos), Gay Pride in NY, SF, LA, Euro Pride Paris, also tropical resort vacations at Man Friday Resort Pkgs (Fiji).	*Bookings:* Call travel agent. *Est:* 1992. *TAC:* 13. *Pymt:* Checks, MC, Visa. IGTA aglta
♀♂	◐	**Mercury Cruise & Tour** 625 S. Hwy 427 Longwood, FL 32750 USA (407) 831-7379, (800) 624-6192, Fax: (407) 831-9895, E-mail: latintrvl@aol.com.	Cruises and tours mainly in the Caribbean, Central and South America. Gay groups on mainstream cruises.	*Bookings:* Call travel agent or direct. *Est:* 1996. *TAC:* 10-12. *Pymt:* Checks, Visa, MC, Amex. IGTA

TOUR COMPANIES

Wholesale/Retail (Call Direct or Have Travel Agent Contact) **WHO TO CALL**

Merlyn's Journeys
PO Box 277
Altaville, CA 95221 USA
(209) 736-9330, (800) 509-9330, Fax: (209) 736-4651, E-mail: merlyns@goldrush.com.

Outdoor getaways for city-weary women, short 2- to 4-day trips, breathe fresh air, travel to where you can see the stars at night, hiking, swimming, hot tub soaking, relaxing by cozy fires, friendly, nurturing, spontaneous groups, fabulous home-cooked meals, massages and yoga optional.

Bookings: Call direct.

Middle Fork River Expeditions
1615 -21 Avenue East
Seattle, WA 98112 USA
(206) 324-0364, (800) 801-5146.

Gay-friendly whitewater rafting specialist, interested in customizing gay and lesbian group rafting trips.

Bookings: Call travel agent or direct.

Milu Tours
Motzstrasse 23
Berlin 10777 Germany
(49 30) 217 6488, Fax: (49 30) 214 3374.

Gay and lesbian vacation packages, Germany, Havana, Mykonos Sitges, Barcelona, Prague, Baltic coast, Hiddensee Island in Eastern Germany, Berlin packages for gay visitors to Germany.

Bookings: Call travel agent or direct. *Est:* 1994. *Pymt:* Visa, MC, Amex, Eurocard.

Mistral Tours
Ile de la Barthelasse
Avignon 84000 France
(33) 4 90 85 86 41 (tel/fax), E-mail: drbusiness@avignon-pacwan.net.

Gay and lesbian day excursions in the South of France, specialized arrangements for small groups, Half- and full-day excursions to principal historic sites, major towns, unusual or less-accessible attractions, visit fine wineries not always open to the public, transportation in air-conditioned Land Rover.

Bookings: Call travel agent or direct. *Est:* 1994. *Pymt:* Cash, checks.

Mix Travel
Maipu 971 5-C
Buenos Aires 1006 Argentina
(54 1) 312 3410, Fax: (54 1) 375-4586 or (54 1) 313 4432.

Live the gaucho life on colonial estancia, ride horses in the Andes. hike trails of the Conquistadores, visit Iguaçu Falls, the glaciers of the south or the tango bars of Buenos Aires or rugged Patagonia...Mix Travel offers unusual, unique experiences in a gay-friendly environment, specialty: individual travel, groups on request.

Bookings: Call travel agent or direct. *Est:* pre-1967. *TAC:* Net to agents. *Pymt:* Wire to bank in US$.
IGTA

Mount Cook Tours
1960 Grand Ave #910
El Segundo, CA 90245 USA
(310) 648-7067, (800) 468-2665, Fax: (310) 640-2823.

Customized itineraries for individuals and for groups of 15 or more, Australia and New Zealand, supplier to the travel industry.

Bookings: Call travel agent.

Mount'n Beach Safaris
1 Plunkett St
Narembum, NSW 2065 Australia
(61-2) 9267 5899, Fax: (61-2) 9437 5744, E-mail: mbstour@ozemail.com.au, Mobile: (61-4) 1843 3275.

Four-wheel-drive excursions departing from Sydney. See natural sights and wildlife in the Blue Mtns of New South Wales.

Bookings: Call travel agent or direct.
agta

FERRARI GUIDES' GAY TRAVEL A to Z - 18th EDITION

WHO TO CALL

○ Retail (Call Direct) ● Wholesale (Travel Agent Must Contact)

♀♂ ●	**MTC (Multinational Travel Corp)** 16 E 53rd St, 4th Floor New York, NY 10022 USA (212) 371-8887, (800) 634-6487, Fax: (212) 644-8709.	Customized individual and group travel to South America.	*Bookings:* Call travel agent or direct.
♀♂ ●	**Mundo Maya Turquesa** Centro Comercial Plaza América,, Loc A-24, S.M. 4 Cancun 77500 Mexico (52-98) 87 63 21, (52-98) 87 57 75, Fax: (52-98) 87 67 78, E-mail: turquesa @cancun.rce.com.mx.	Private and group tours, bilingual and mostly-gay staff, Cuba, Mexico (Playa del Carmen, Cancun, Cozumel, Isla Mujeres), Belize, other Latin American destinations,	*Bookings:* Call travel agent or direct. *Est:* 1990. *TAC:* 10-13. *Pymt:* Visa, MC Amex. Member: AMAV IGTA
♀♂ ●	**Never Summer Nordic** PO Box 1983 Ft Collins, CO 80522 USA (970) 482-9411, Web: www.nsnyurts.com.	Hike, ski or bike to a cozy yurt shelter, located in Colorado's Rocky-Mountain Medicine Bow Range, yurts have wood stove, kitchen, beds, tables, chairs, getting there is half the fun, one yurt is auto- wheelchair-accessible, Endless trail systems to hike, bike and ski.	*Bookings:* Call direct. *Est:* 1986. *TAC:* Inquire. *Pymt:* Checks, MC, Visa.
♀♂ ●	**New England Vacation Tours** PO Box 560, Mount Snow Village West Dover, VT 05356-0560 USA (802) 464-2076, (800) 742-7669, Fax: (802) 464-2629.	Bus and fly packages, New England and eastern Canada destinations, Memorial Day Wknd in Provincetown, July 4th in Toronto, Labor Day Wknd in Montreal, and a gay ski week.	*Bookings:* Call travel agent or direct.
♀♂ ●	**North American Travel Specialists** Suite 1, 478 High Street Maitland, NSW 2320 Australia (61 49) 342 088, Fax: (61 49) 347 522.	USA & Canada ONLY! Tailor-made independent itineraries, gay and gay-friendly hotels and excursions utilized, from one night to multi-week itineraries, supplier to the industry, buying power = big discounts off regular rates.	*Bookings:* Call travel agent or direct. *Est:* 1986. *TAC:* 10. *Pymt:* Net cheques. *Member:* TIA IGTA aglta
♀♂ ●	**Ocean Voyager** 1717 N Bayshore Drive #3246 Miami, FL 33132-1167 USA (305) 379-5722, (800) 435-2531, Fax: (305) 379-4417.	Hosted gay groups on mainstream cruise lines. Destinations that appeal to gay and lesbian travelers. Caribbean, Alaska, Transatlantic, Greek Islands, Turkey. Intimate, small gay and lesbian groups.	*Bookings:* Call travel agent or direct. *Est:* 1995. *TAC:* 10. *Pymt:* Major credit cards, checks. IGTA
♀♂ ●	**Oceanwide Expeditions** Badhuisstraat 148-150 Vlissingen 4382 AP Netherlands (31-118) 410 410, Fax: (31-118) 415 068, E-mail: Expeditions@ocnwide.com	Gay and lesbian ocean expeditions, Gay Arctic Circle Cruise 1997 from Spitsbergen Island, Norway.	*Bookings:* Call travel agent or direct. IGTA
♀ ○	**Oceanwomyn Kayaking** (206) 325-3970.	The first women's company to offer all-womyn's sea kayaking adventures, Baja Mexico, British Columbia, San Juan Islands, Alaska, great for beginners, no experience necessary, expert lesbian guides/instructors, vegetarian cuisine and great coffee on the beach.	*Bookings:* Call direct. *Est:* 1984.

TOUR COMPANIES

◐ Wholesale/Retail (Call Direct or Have Travel Agent Contact) **WHO TO CALL**

Off the Map
3990 Old Town Ave #100-C
San Diego, CA 92110 USA
(619) 293-7096, (800) 633-8436, Fax:
(619) 293-7026, E-mail:
fish@offthemap.com, Web:
www.offthemap.com.

Custom individual and group vacations, all of Europe, Russia, South Pacific, partial & whole boat charters, regional experts for each destination, specialists for group and for individual travel, if you can imagine it, we can create it!

Bookings: Call travel agent or direct. *Est:* 1988. *TAC:* 10-12-14-15 depending on volume. *Pymt:* Checks, MC, Visa, Amex, Discover.

Olivia Cruises & Resorts
4400 Market St
Oakland, CA 94608 USA
(510) 655-0364, (800) 631-6277, Fax:
(510) 655-4334. E-mail: olivia@eor.com.
Web:www.oliviatravel.com.

Largest US women's travel company, has taken more than 12,000 women on vacations, destinations like the Caribbean, Alaska, Greece, the Riviera, the Galapagos, Canada, the Bahamas, and Mexico.

Bookings: Call travel agent or direct. *Est:* 1973. *TAC:* 10. *Pymt:* Checks, Visa, MC, interest-free pymt plans. **IGTA**

Onn the Water
PO Box 173
Gig Harbor, WA 98335 USA
(206) 851-5259.

Women's sailing adventures, USA's Pacific Northwest and Canada's British Columbia.

Bookings: Call direct.

Open Eye Tours & Photos
PO Box 324
Makawao, HI 96768 USA
(808) 572-3483, E-mail:
openeye@aloha.net.

Not a tourist-type tour, each customized to client's interests and abilities, trips to most Hawaiian islands, sightseeing, hiking, walking, monuments and museums, upcountry villages and exotic gardens, birdwatching and tasting medicinal plants, swimming beneath a waterfall and swimming in a secluded ocean cove, or beautiful views, visits to artists' studios and unique shops.

Bookings: Call travel agent or direct. *Est:* 1983. *TAC:* 10. *Pymt:* Checks, cash.

Orion Travel Tours
7858 Burns Ct
El Cerrito, CA 94530 USA
(510) 524-1133, (800) 552-3326, Fax:
(510) 524-0631.

Gay and lesbian tours, worldwide destinations.

Bookings: Call travel agent or direct.

Otto Travel Hawaii
1560 Kanunu St #1407
Honolulu, HI 96814-3205 USA
(808) 944-8618 (tel/fax).

Southeast Asia specialist, "unorthodox tour programs" for gay groups and independent travelers, Vietnam, Laos, Cambodia, Malaysia, Java, Myanmar, Thailand, Sumatra, Burma, Bali, all gay or gay-friendly accommodations.

Bookings: Call travel agent or direct. *Est:* 1980. *TAC:* 6-10. *Pymt:* Checks, money orders, travellers' checks.

Our Family Abroad
40 W 57th St, #430
New York, NY 10019-4001 USA
(212) 459-1800, (800) 999-5500, Fax:
(212) 581-3756.

Global touring for gay men and women, the best of Europe, Asia, Latin America, Africa, Morocco and Egypt, stay in first-class hotels, talented guides escort each tour, gay-owned & -operated, EuroPride 1997 in Paris.

Bookings: Call travel agent or direct. *Est:* 1993. *TAC:* 10. *License #:* 13-3743313. *Pymt:* Checks, Visa, MC, Amex, Discover. *Member:* ASTA **IGTA**

TOUR COMPANIES

FERRARI GUIDES' GAY TRAVEL A to Z - 18th EDITION 65

WHO TO CALL

○ Retail (Call Direct) ● Wholesale (Travel Agent Must Contact)

Out Touring Australia
PO Box 1214
Cairns, QLD 4870 Australia
(61-70) 511 483, Fax: (61-70) 521 478, E-mail: shar@internetnorth.com.au.

Gay and lesbian tour service for tropical North Queensland and the Great Barrier Reef. Customizes packages including accommodation, sightseeing, excursions like diving, fishing, helicopters, 4WD adventures, limousines, rafting, river cruises, reef trips, even information on places to dine.

Bookings: Call travel agent or direct.

OutWest Adventures
PO Box 1050
Red Lodge, MT 59068 USA
(406) 446-1533, (800) 743-0458, Fax: (406) 446-1338, E-mail: OutWestAdv@aol.com.

Exclusively gay and lesbian, outdoor vacations in the US far west, experienced guides, hiking, biking, horseback riding, fishing, sightseeing, whitewater rafting, backpacking, ranch stays, camping, skiing.

Bookings: Call travel agent or direct. *Est:* 1994. *TAC:* 10. *Pymt:* Visa, MC, checks. IGTA

Oz Dive/Passport to Paradise
37 Pidgeon Hill Dr #150
Sterling, VA 20165 USA
(703) 406-2703, (800) 4-PARADISE, (472-7234), Fax: (703) 406-2704, E-mail: OZDIVE@worldnet.att.net.

Gay and lesbian vacations in the South Pacific, Australia, New Zealand, Fiji, Tahiti, Sydney Mardi Gras, Sleaze Ball packages, resorts to outdoor adventure, scuba diving & snorkeling vacations, twice-annual gay scuba charter to the Great Barrier Reef.

Bookings: Call travel agent or direct. *Est:* 1992. *TAC:* 10. *Pymt:* Checks. *Member:* CLIA, DTIA, DEMA, NZPAL, PADI IGTA

Pacific Experience
Suite 3 65 Nicholson St
St Leonards, NSW 2065 Australia
(61-2) 9438 5755, Fax: (62-2) 9438 5667, Mobile: (61-18) 230 099.

Inbound wholesale tour arrangements to the South Pacific. Special emphasis on personalized programming.

Bookings: Call travel agent. IGTA aglta

Pacific Ocean Holidays
PO Box 88245-F
Honolulu, HI 96830-8245 USA
(808) 923-2400, (800) 735-6600, Fax: (808) 923-2499. E-mail: poh@hi.net, Web: http://gayhawaii.com.

Exclusively Hawaii vacation packages, exclusively gay and lesbian, widest selection of gay and gay-friendly Hawaii hotels, bed and breakfasts, condos, year-round customized vacations, visiting one or more islands, vacations not escorted, so sightsee at your leisure.

Bookings: Call travel agent or direct. *Est:* 1982. *TAC:* 10. *License No.:* Hawaii #TAR-1193. *Pymt:* Visa, MC, Amex, Discover/Novus IGTA

Paddling South & Saddling South
4510 Silverado Tr
Calistoga, CA 94515 USA
Tel/Fax: (707) 942-4550.

Sea kayaking and horse packing adventures, Baja, Mexico, mostly mixed, two women-only trips per year.

Bookings: Call travel agent or call direct. *Est:* 1983. *TAC:* Not reported. *Pymt:* Visa, MC, checks.

Pangaea Expeditions
PO Box 5753
Missoula, MT 59806 USA
(406) 721-7719, (888) 721-7719, E-mail: wildwomenz@aol.com, Web: bigsky.net/pangaea.

Missoula-based gay and lesbian rafting company, 2-hour wine and cheese float trips, variety of rafting, mountain biking in Canadian Rockies, Baja sea kayaking, Montana climbing, backpacking, rafting, kayaking and Wild Women adventure trips.

Bookings: Call direct. *Est:* 1989. *TAC:* 10. *Pymt:* Checks, Visa, MC. *Member:* America Outdoors IGTA

TOUR COMPANIES

66 FERRARI GUIDES' GAY TRAVEL A to Z - 18th EDITION

◐ Wholesale/Retail (Call Direct or Have Travel Agent Contact) **WHO TO CALL**

♂	◐	**Passage to Utah** PO Box 520883 Salt Lake City, UT 84152 USA (801) 582-1896, (800) 677-0553, Fax: (801) 281-1868 (faxes attn: Mike), E-mail: Passage2ut@aol.com.	Utah's only gay men's river trips, Grand Staircase and Escalante, Bryce Canyon and Capitol Reef Nat'l Parks, Westwater Canyon, Desolation Canyon (Hell's Half Mile), Lodore Canyon, abundant wildlife, hiking.	*Bookings:* Call travel agent or direct. *Est:* 1992. *TAC:* 10. *Pymt:* MC, Visa, Amex, cash, check.
♀♂	◐	**Passport Travel Mgt, Inc.** 1503 W Busch Blvd #A Tampa, FL 33612 USA (813) 931-3166, (800) 950-5864, Fax: (813) 933-1670, E-mail: TMG@juno.com, Web: http://pages.prodigy.com/passport.	Customized independent travel itineraries, all Asia destinations, gay-friendly mainstream company.	*Bookings:* Call travel agent or direct. *Est:* 1990. *TAC:* 10. *Pymt:* Credit cards, checks. *Member:* IGTA
♀♂	◐	**Paths Less Taken** Rua Dra. Iracy Doyle 9-3E Cascais 2750 Portugal (351 1) 486 2044, Fax: (351 1) 486 14 09, E-mail: jcabdo@ip.pt.	Portugal, Spain, the Azores, less-traveled routes, wines & cheeses of Portugal, bicycle or van travel, upgraded accommodations, will customize itineraries.	*Bookings:* Call travel agent or direct. *Est:*1987. *TAC* 10%. *Pymt:* Checks, bank transfers, money orders.
♀♂	○	**Pearl Selections/Welcome Abroad** 121 Kirby Rd Leicester LE3 6BE England (44-116) 233 7555, (44-116) 233 6655, Fax: (44-116) 233 6660	Gay and lesbian vacation packages. European and US beach vacation resorts & city packages, skiing and cruises. Well-established English company. Dedicated to offering lowest possible prices. Call their reservation hotline for current prices.	*Bookings:* Call direct.
♀♂	◐	**Peddlers** Book through Destinations & Adventures Int'l, (800) 659-4599, (213) 650-7267, Fax: (213) 650-6902, E-mail: DAITravel@AOL.com.	Civilized Cycling on Greek island of Cephalonia, rIde on well-paved, quiet roads, panoramic views of the coastline, pass through Greek Villages unchanged since ancient times, beginners through advanced cyclists, no experience necessary.	*Bookings:* Call travel agent or direct. *TAC:* 10.
♀♂	◐	**Pied Piper Travel** 330 W 42nd St #1804 New York, NY 10036 USA (212) 239-2412, (800) 874-7312, Fax: (212) 239-2275, E-mail: 73170.410@compuserve.com.	Gay cruises aboard the Queen Elizabeth 2 and other gay-friendly ships, Caribbean, transatlantic crossings, Hawaii, New England, Canada, welcome-aboard cocktail party, other special gay events included.	*Bookings:* Call travel agent or direct. *Est:* 1990. *TAC:* 10. *Pymt:* major credit cards. *Member:* CLIA IGTA
♀♂	◐	**Players Express** 2980-A W. Meade Ave Las Vegas, NV 89102 USA (702) 257-5034, (800) 458-6161 (groups: (800) 848-4877), Fax: (702) 362-5594.	Affordable gay vacation packages with gay visitor's guide and discount coupon pack, Las Vegas, Puerto Vallarta, Cancun, Hawaii, Florida, discounts on major airlines worldwide, competitive group pricing, 1997 Greek Isle cruise.	*Bookings:* Call travel agent or direct. *TAC:* 10-12. *Pymt:* All major cards, cashiers checks, money orders. *Member:* ASTA, IATAN
♀♂	●	**Pleasant Holidays** 2404 Townsgate Rd Westlake Village, CA 91361 USA (818) 991-3390, Fax: (805) 495-4972.	Suppliers to the travel industry of Hawaii and Mexico packages.	*Bookings:* Call travel agent. IGTA

TOUR COMPANIES

FERRARI GUIDES' GAY TRAVEL A to Z - 18th EDITION   67

WHO TO CALL

◯ Retail (Call Direct)   ● Wholesale (Travel Agent Must Contact)

♀♂ ◯	**Pleasure Travel...Cruise Again Too!** 4837 Cedar Springs #216 Dallas, TX 75219 USA (214) 526-1126, (800) 583-3913, Fax: (214) 526-1109.	Several cruises per year, for 1997: three 3-day cruises in the Bahamas, visiting Nassau, Blue Lagoon, Miami, Key West.	*Bookings:* Call direct. IGTA
♀♂ ◐	**Port Yacht Charters** 9 Belleview Ave Port Washington, NY 11050 USA (516) 883-0998 (tel/fax), (800) 213-0465, E-mail: KenYachts@afl.com, Web: www.paw.com/sail/port/.	"Tie the knot" aboard a gay yacht, or just vacation on a gay or gay-friendly sailing vessel, Caribbean, Mediterranean, South Pacific, New England, gourmet cuisine, first-class accommodations, about the same cost as resort vacation or cruise.	*Bookings:* Call travel agent or direct. *Est:* 1986. *TAC:* 10-12. *Pymt:* Checks, credit cards.
♀♂ ◐	**Progressive Travels** 224 W Galer #C Seattle, WA 98119 USA (206) 285-1987, (800) 245-2229, Fax: (206) 285-1988, E-mail: progressivetravel@aol.com, Web: www.progressivetravels.com.	Gay and lesbian active adventures, adventure travel worldwide, gay-owned & -operated company, experienced in adventure travel since 1984, bicycling, cruises, yachting, walking, hiking, rafting, cooking school, Europe, North America, Thailand.	*Bookings:* Call travel agent or direct. *Est:* 1984. *TAC:* 10+. IGTA
♀♂ ◐	**Promenades de Style** 52 Rue de Faubourg Poissonnière Paris 75010 France (33 1) 4671 7335, Fax: (33 1) 4671 6170, e-mail: 100442.423@compuserve.com.	Tour Paris in extreme comfort in a 1964 vintage Lincoln Continental convertible, carries up to five people, gay-owned company, city tours both daytime and by night, excursions outside Paris to chateaux like Versailles and Fountainebleau, and the champagne country.	*Bookings:* Call travel agent or direct. *Est:* 1992. *TAC:* 15. *Pymt:* Amex, cash, traveller's checks.
♀♂ ◯	**Puffin Family Charters** Box 90743 Anchorage, AK 99509 USA (907) 278-3346, (800) 978-3346.	Sightseeing and fishing charters, for gays and lesbians, Alaska's Resurrection Bay and Kenai Fjords, whales, seals, otters, porpoises, puffins, magnificent views of glaciers and mountains, abundant fish, halibut, salmon, black bass, red snapper, 30-foot charter boat, fully electronic, heated cabin.	*Bookings:* Call direct. *Est:* 1993. *Pymt:* Visa, MC, cash.
♀♂ ◐	**Rail Europe** 500 Mamaroneck Ave. Harrison, NY 10528 USA US: (800) 438-7245, Canada: (800) 361-7245, Fax: (800) 432-1329, E-mail: webmaster@raileurope.com, Web: www.raileurope.com.	The leading supplier to North America of European rail and related travel is gay-friendly, Eurailpass, Europass, Rail 'n Drive, regular point-to-point rail tickets, customized business and leisure packages including air, car rental, rail, hotel, 24-Hour Toll-Free information lines have fares, schedules.	*Bookings:* Call travel agent or direct. *Est:* 1930. *TAC:* 8-12. *Pymt:* Amex, MCI, Visa, Diners. *Member:* ACTA, ARTA, ASTA, IBTA, NBTA, USTOA
♀ ◯	**Rainbow Adventures** 15033 Kelly Canyon Rd Bozeman, MT 59715 USA (406) 587-3883, (800) 804-8686, Fax: (406) 587-9449.	Worldwide outdoor adventure vacations, for women over 30, gay women are welcome, but most particpants are married women, NO lesbian-only trips.	*Bookings:* Call direct.

TOUR COMPANIES

Wholesale/Retail (Call Direct or Have Travel Agent Contact)

WHO TO CALL

Rainbow Country Tours & B&B
PO Box 333
Escalante, UT 84726 USA
(801) 826-4567 (tel/fax), (800) 252-8824 (tel/fax).

Exploring canyon country in comfort, combining home-base B&B with half-day and full-day tours, jeep ride to trail head, petrified forests, towering rock formations, narrow canyons, aspens' color change turns mountains "gold" in september, trail shuttle available for independent hikers, also horseback riding, biking, campouts.

Bookings: Call travel agent or direct.

Rainbow Destinations
PO Box 776
Southbury, CT 06488 USA
(203) 791-1535, (800) 387-2462, Fax: (203) 791-1535.

Gay and lesbian Ancient Egypt tour and Nile cruise. Tour is accompanied by an Egyptologist.

Bookings: Call travel agent or direct. *Est:* 1995. *TAC:* 5. *Pymt:* Credit cards.

Rainboworld Custom Tours
PO Box 275
Indian Hills, CO 80454 USA
(303) 697-6956, (800) 969-2268, E-mail: rwctours@tde.com, Web: www.tde.com/~rwctours.

Customized Amsterdam tours, geared to orienting visitors so they can explore in-depth on their own, airport pickup, unique bicycling city tours, gay history tour, canal boat trips, gay party event packages.

Bookings: Call travel agent or direct. *Est:* 1996. *TAC:* 10+. *Pymt:* Visa, MC, no checks, please.
IGTA

Remote Possibilities
PO Box 1851, Wailuku
Maui, HI 96793 USA
(808) 875-7438, (800) 511-3121, Fax: (808) 875-4557, E-mail: remotepo@maui.net, Web: www.remotepo.com.

Lesbian tour company, organizers of Wahine Week, a luxury lesbian resort week on Maui, also offers lesbian weddings on Maui with lesbian ministers, new for 1998: two adventure tours and a cruise in Alaska.

Bookings: Call travel agent or direct.
IGTA

Rio Roma Travel
2211 Lombard St
San Francisco, CA 94123 USA
(415) 921-3353, (800) 227-2745, Fax: (415) 921-3557.

Consolidator of discount air/hotel packages to Brazil, operates two gay Brazil group departures annually.

Bookings: Call travel agent.

Robin Tyler's Women's Tours, Cruises & Events
15842 Chase St
North Hills, CA 91343 USA
(818) 893-4075, (800) 936-8514, Fax: (818) 893-1593, E-mail: RobinTyler@aol.com.

Women's tours and cruises, worldwide destinations, current offering is women's tour to Amsterdam Gay Games 1998.

Bookings: Call travel agent or direct. *Est:* 1980. *TAC:* 10. *Pymt:* Visa, MC, checks.

Rocky Mountaineer Railtours
1150 Station St 1st floor
Vancouver, BC V6A 2X7 Canada
(604) 606-7200, (800) 665-7245, Fax: (604) 606-7201, E-mail: rkymtn@fleethouse.com, Web: www.rkymtnrail.com.

The most spectacular train trip, passes through miles of glacier-clad mtns, begins in Spectacular train trip through Canada's Rocky Mtns, forests, glaciers...begins in Vancouver, Calgary, Banff or Jasper...Signature Service is non-smoking, has spacious recliners, picture windows, Gold Leaf Service has bi-level dome coach on upper level, open-air observation platform on lower level, dining lounge, designated smoking areas, attendant provides commentary.

Bookings: Call travel agent or direct. *Est:* 1990. *TAC:* 10. *Pymt:* Amex, MC, Visa, JCB, Diners Club of Japan. *Member:* ABA, ASTA, ACTA, NTA
IGTA

TOUR COMPANIES

FERRARI GUIDES' GAY TRAVEL A to Z - 18th EDITION 69

WHO TO CALL

○ Retail (Call Direct)   ● Wholesale (Travel Agent Must Contact)

♀♂	○	**Royal Hawaiian Weddings** PO Box 424 Puunene, Maui, HI 96784 USA (808) 875-8569, (800) 659-1866, Fax: (808) 875-0623. E-mail: andrea@maui.net.	Gay and lesbian weddings, commitment ceremonies on Maui, all arrangements coordinated, can include airport lei greeting, "just-married" limo service, secluded beach and tropical settings, candle-light dinner, champagne, photographer, photo album, flower leis, also luaus, snorkeling, surfing adventures.	*Bookings:* Call travel agent or direct. *Est:* 1980. *TAC:* 10. *Pymt:* Checks. Visa, MC Discover. **IGTA**
♀♂	●	**RSVP Travel Productions/Club RSVP** 2800 University Ave SE Minneapolis, MN 55414 USA (612) 379-4697, (800) 328-7787, Fax: (612) 379-0484, E-mail: rsvptvl@skypoint.com, Web: www.rsvp.net.	Gay and lesbian tour company, offers three kinds of vacations, cruises, Club RSVP resort vacations, PLAANET RSVP hotel and air packages, group or independent travel, air provided by American Airlines, RSVP always reserves an entire ship or resort.	*Bookings:* Call travel agent. *TAC:* 10. *Pymt:* Visa, MC, Amex, agency check. **IGTA**
♀♂	○	**R&R Eco Tours** SJO 1715, PO Box 025216 Miami, FL 33102-5216 USA Dial Int'l. access # (506) 228-4627 (located in Costa Rica, mailing address in Miami).	Custom gay and lesbian Costa Rica itineraries, individuals and groups, city tours, 2-hour aerial tramway rides through jungle canopy, 10-day jungle "safaris."	*Bookings:* Call travel agent or direct.
♂	○	**R&S Travel** Solothurner Str. Heilbronn 74072 Germany (49-7131) 991 2420, Fax: (49-7131) 991 2426.	Gay German tour company with large, comprehensive brochure of gay men's vacations, geared toward German speakers (brochure in German only), but non-German speakers can book their tours, Thailand, Malaysia, Hong Kong, Bali, Philippines, Mallorca, Ibiza, Gran Canaria, Mykonos, capitals of Europe, New York, Florida, California, Las Vegas, Hawaii, Mexico, Dominican Republic. Best to fax them.	*Bookings:* Call direct. **IGTA**
♀♂	○	**Sailing Affairs** 404 E 11th St New York, NY 10009 USA (212) 228-5755, Fax: (212) 228-8512, E-mail: sailingaff@aol.com.	Gay yacht sailing the U.S. east coast, sunset sails on NY Harbor, custom yacht vacations on east coast and sometimes winter Caribbean vacations, summer eastern seaboard sailing schedule, join the yacht at any point, stay any number of days.	*Bookings:* Call travel agent or direct. *Est:* 1984. *TAC:* 15. *Pymt:* Check, cash. **IGTA**
♂	○	**Sapphire Travel & Tours** 98 High Street Rayleigh, Essex SS6 7BY England (44 1268) 777 667, Fax: (44 1268) 777 687.	Gay men's holidays, departing from England, worldwide destinations, Australia's Sydney Mardi Gras, Mykoknos, Sitges, Ibiza, Majorca, Gran Canaria, Florida, etc.	*Bookings:* Call direct. **IGTA**
♀♂	○	**Scenic Air Tours** PO Box 471287 San Francisco, CA 94147 USA (415) 922-2386, (800) 95-SCENIC (957-2364), Fax: (415) 346-6940, E-mail: scenicair.com.	Air sightseeing over San Franciso, day trips to Yosemite and Grand Canyon, including free pick-up and delivery at your downtown SF hotel, Yosemite includes ground tour with lunch extra, Grand Canyon includes South Rim ground tour, lunch and show at IMAX theater, custom air excursions also arranged.	*Bookings:* Call travel agent or direct. *Est:* 1993. *TAC:* 20. *Pymt:* Visa, MC, cash.

TOUR COMPANIES

Wholesale/Retail (Call Direct or Have Travel Agent Contact)

WHO TO CALL

♀	◐	**Sea Sense** 25 Thames St New London, CT 06320 USA (860) 444-1404, (800) 332-1404, E-mail: seasense@aol.com, Web: http://members.aol.com/seasense/index.htm.	Women's sailing school, summer and winter locations, New London, CT, Miami, Florida Keys, Caribbean, Florida's Gulf Coast, captains have over 50 yrs experience, locations chosen for variety of sailing challenges and beautiful anchorages.	*Bookings:* Call travel agent or direct. *Est:* 1989. *TAC:* 10. *Pymt:* Visa, MC, checks.
♂	◐	**Seaborne Safaris (Croisieres d'Il en Il)** Doseme Market, Keci Buku, Orhaniye Marmaris 48700 Turkey (90-252) 487 10 71 (tel/fax), E-mail: seaborne@unimedya.net.tr.	A new company offering custom sailing cruises. Captain is a gay man. Crew is a woman. Learn sailing or relax. Snorkel, scuba, etc. Honeymoons on board. Archaeological trips. Will arrange for all interests. Sailing Turkey's Turguoise Coast with side trips to Rhodos and Symi, Greece. All on traditional 40-foot Turkish sailing boat accommodating 4 passengers. Three boats available. Minimum one week.	*Bookings:* Call travel agent or direct. *Est:* 1996. *TAC:* 20 on booking. *Pymt:* Cash on cruise derparture.
♀♂	◐	**Sedona Rainbow Adventure Tours** PO Box 10147 Sedona, AZ 86339 USA (520) 204-9967, (888) 282-9967, Fax: (520) 204-1399.	Half- and full-day tours by the Rainbow Rangers. Gay and lesbian. Tour Grand Canyon and Sedona, Arizona. Grand Canyon helicopter tours. Shooting tours with colt .45s. Art gallery tours.	*Bookings:* Call travel agent or direct.
♂	○	**Sensations** 22 Blenheim Terrace, St John's Wood London NW8 0EB England (44-171) 625 6969, Fax: (44-171) 624 0167.	European gay beach holidays, Sitges, Ibiza, Mykonos, Sitges, Gran Canaria, Torremolinos, Majorca, also Florida. Full pkgs from London or hotel only, international clients welcome, customer service a specialty.	*Bookings:* Call direct. *Pymt:* All major cards. *Member:* GBA, ABTA, ATOL.
♀♂	◐	**Silken East Ltd.** 36-C Sisters Ave London SW11 5SQ England (44-171) 223 8987 (tel/fax).	The only tour company with unique access to all areas of Burma. Tours are conducted by the author of the definitive "Guide to Burma," who says Burma and Thailand "have proved exceedingly gay-friendly, "owing to their strong Buddhist cultures." Extentions to Thailand, Laos and Cambodia available.	*Bookings:* Call travel agent or direct. *Est:* 1992. *TAC:* 10. *Pymt:* Checks.
♀♂	◐	**Silke's Travel** 263 Oxford St Darlinghurst, NSW 2010 Australia (61-2) 9380 6244, Fax: (61-2) 9361 3729. E-mail: silba@magna.com.au, Web: www.outinsydney.com.au.	A tour company "devoted to women's travel." Accredited Sydney Mardi Gras tour operator whose packages include Mardi Gras tickets. "Cairns for Women" program includes Great Barrier Reef and women's accommodations. Worldwide tours for 1997 include Macchu Picchu, an Annapurna trek and a safari in East Africa.	*Bookings:* Call travel agent or direct. *Est:* 1994. *TAC:* 10. *Pymt:* credit cards, bank transfers, bank cheques. IGTA agta

TOUR COMPANIES

WHO TO CALL

○ Retail (Call Direct)   ● Wholesale (Travel Agent Must Contact)

♀♂ ●	**Sirius Adventures** PO Box 1130 Kununurra, WA 6743 Australia (61-8) 9168 2110 (tel/fax).	Customized lesbian and gay bushwalks in Western Australia and Northern Territory. Lesbian guide plans itinerary to fit interests and skill levels of participants. See the Kimberley, one of the world's last wilderness areas, where you can still drink water from streams. Also visits famous Kakadu Nat'l Park.	*Bookings:* Call travel agent or direct. *Est:* 1996. *TAC:* 15. *Pymt:* Visa, MC, Bankcard, cash.
♀♂ ●	**Ski Connections** 10356 Airport Rd, Hanger 1 Truckee, CA 96161 USA (916) 582-1889, (800) SKI-1888, Fax: (916) 582-0568.	Quality gay European skiing vacations at great prices, individual and group gay itineraries, travel anytime or choose annual all-gay, all-inclusive skiing vacation, usually in Innsbruck. They make frequent inspection visits to every European ski area.	*Bookings:* Call travel agent or direct. IGTA
♀ ○	**Sounds & Furies** PO Box 21510, 1850 Commercial Dr Vancouver, BC V5N 4A0 Canada (604) 253-7189, Fax: (604) 253-2191	For women, a journey into mystical Ireland. Visit ancient stone circles, pagan sites and burial mounds. Stay in a Georgian mansion near Cork, walk green meadows and misty woods to Blarney, touch history with your own hands, discover different perspectives, visit the beautiful Dingle Peninsula and Galway with 20 other women.	*Bookings:* Call direct.
♀♂ ●	**South of the Border Tour & Travel** 40 Fourth St #203 Petaluma, CA 94952 USA (707) 765-4573, (800) 922-TRAV (8728), Fax: (707) 778-1080.	For those considering retiring in Mexico, factfinding vacations to Guadalajara and Lake Chapala, gay-friendly location of 40,000 American retirees...seminars cover immigration, health care, real estate, banking, investment opportunities, possibilities to meet local gay retirees, share their knowledge and experiences.	*Bookings:* Call travel agent or direct.
♀♂ ●	**Southern Discovery Tours** 437 Napier St Fitzroy, VIC 3065 Australia (61-3) 9419 5230 (tel/fax), E-mail: mleaney@rainbow.net.au.	Exclusively gay & lesbian. City tours and excursions in Melbourne, Australia and environs. Up to 4 passengers in a luxury 4-wheel drive vehicle. Winery tours, Great Ocean Road, Melbourne Gay Orientation, city tours, and Fairy Penguins. "Forget about driving on the left side of the road—that's what we're here for."	*Bookings:* Call travel agent or direct. *Est:* 1995. *TAC:* 10-20. *Pymt:* Visa, MC, Bankcard, cash. IGTA agta
♀♂ ●	**Spirit Journeys** PO Box 3046 Asheville, NC 28802 USA (704) 258-8880, Fax: (704) 281-0334, E-mail: spiritjourneys@worldnet.att.net.	Journeys of self-discovery for gay men. Can include swimming with dolphins, hiking or canoeing, or meditation, ceremony and exchanges with indigenous people, Rio Grande, North Carolina, Greece, New Mexico, Peru, Mexico, Arizona. For men of all types, all ages.	*Bookings:* Call travel agent or direct.

TOUR COMPANIES

FERRARI GUIDES' GAY TRAVEL A to Z - 18th EDITION

Wholesale/Retail (Call Direct or Have Travel Agent Contact)

WHO TO CALL

Stag Travel & Tours
A.P. 6-962, col. Juárez, .
Mexico D.F. 06602 Mexico
(52 5) 525 4658 (tel/fax), E-mail:
74563.2046@compuserve.com.

Fully-escorted individualized gay Mexico tours, complete land packages can include monuments, active outdoor adventures, beach resorts, villa rentals.

Bookings: Call travel agent or direct. *Est:* 1994. *TAC:* 10-12. *Pymt:* Wire transfers.

Stockler Expeditions
10266 NW 4th Court
Plantation, FL 33324 USA
(954) 472-7163, (800) 591-2955, Fax: (954) 472-7579.

Tailor-made programs for independent gay and lesbian travelers to Brazil, the Galapagos and Costa Rica. Amazon trips include Guanavenas Jungle Lodge, most beautiful in the area. Cruise the Amazon on the Dedsafio, a secure and comfortable boat. Visit the Galapagos accompanied by a professional naturalist. Fly over Costa Rica in a balloon.

Bookings: Call travel agent or direct. *Est:* 1987. *TAC:* 10. *Pymt:* Checks. *Member:* IATAN, ASTA

Stonewall 69
Carlos Pellegrini 1055 3#A
Buenos Aires 1011 Argentina
(54 1) 394-6832, Fax: (54 1) 328-6480.
Send mail to: 7891 W Flager St #54-119, Miami, FL 33144, USA.

Argentina's first gay-owned and -operated tour operator and travel agency. Full program of itineraries in Argentina for international gay and lesbian travelers. Worldwide travel packages for Argentine gays and lesbians traveling abroad.

Bookings: Call travel agent or direct. *Est:* 1996. *TAC:* Net prices to agents. *Pymt:* Checks, wire transfers. IGTA

Stonewall Connection Travel & Tours
#320 3545 32nd Ave NE
Calgary, AB T1Y 6M6 Canada
(403) 250-3061, (888) 228-7477, Fax: (403) 250-1041, E-mail: stonewall@canuck.com, Web: www.canuck.com/stonewall.

Official Gay Games tour operator in Canada, exclusively gay & lesbian tour company, offers a variety of travel packages to many gay events. Gives background info on gay accommodations. Both individual and group gay tours.

Bookings: Call travel agent or direct. *Est:* 1993. *TAC:* 10. *Pymt:* Visa, MC, Amex, DC, Direct Access. *Member:* IATA, ACTA IGTA

Sundance Travel
19800 MacArthur Blvd #100
Irvine, CA 92612 USA
(714) 752-5456, (800) 424-3434, Fax: (714) 553-3253, E-mail: royer@sunnet.attmail.com.

Specializing in value-priced group trips that give the traveler total independence, along with the security of being part of a group. New Years and Carnaval in Rio de Janeiro are featured annually. In late August, 1997, Mykonos and Athens, Greece. Year-round Puerto Vallarta villa packages, including air.

Bookings: Call travel agent or direct. *Est:* 1981. *TAC:* 10. *Pymt:* Credit cards, checks.

Super Natural Adventure Tours
626 W Pender St
Vancouver, BC V6B 1V9 Canada
(604) 683-5101, (800) 263-1600, Fax: (604) 683-5129.

Soft adventure specialists, British Columbia and Alberta, all manner of outdoor activities and transportation. Accommodations, rental cars, all vacation arrangements. Gay-friendly company personalizes itineraries for gay and lesbian individuals and groups.

Bookings: Call travel agent or direct., *Est:* 1990. *Pymt:* Visa, Amex, checks.

Surfers Paradise Gay Vacations
PO Box 7260, Gold Coast Mail Centre
Bundall, QLD 4217 Australia
(61 75) 922 223, Fax: (61 75) 922 209.

Gay air/hotel packages to Surfers Paradise, Australian urban beach resort in Queensland.

Bookings: Call direct. *Est:* 1991. *Pymt:* All major cards.

TOUR COMPANIES

FERRARI GUIDES' GAY TRAVEL A to Z - 18th EDITION

WHO TO CALL

○ Retail (Call Direct)   ● Wholesale (Travel Agent Must Contact)

♀♂ ● **Syosset Travel** 15 Jackson Ave Syosset, NY 11791 USA (516) 496-0534, Fax: (516) 496-3514.	Cruises on private yachts or ships, Greek Islands, Turkey, gay-friendly company.	*Bookings:* Call travel agent or direct. *Est:* 1980. *TAC:* 10. *Pymt:* Checks, credit cards. *Member:* IATA, ASTA, ARC
♀♂ ● **Tall Ship Adventures, Inc.** 1389 S Havana St Aurora, CO 80012 USA (303) 755-7983, (800) 662-0090, Fax: (303) 755-9007, E-mail: info@tallshipadventures.com, Web: www.tallshipadventures.com.	Cruise the Caribbean on an authentic "tall ship" built in 1917, interior remodeled to modern standards. Visits British Virgin Islands and other Caribbean ports of call. Gay-friendly all year and books several gay tour groups per year.	*Bookings:* Call travel agent or direct. *Est:* 1988. *TAC:* 10. *Pymt:* Checks, Visa, MC, Amex. **IGTA**
♀♂ ● **Teddy Travel** Mathiasstr. 4-6 Cologne 50676 Germany (49-221) 219 886 (for gays and lesbians), (49-221) 234 967 (for everybody), Fax: (49-221) 241 774, E-mail: teddy-travel@t-online.de.	Europe's oldest and largest gay tour company. Exclusively gay and lesbian program includes gay resort vacations in Europe and USA, city packages, tour packages for Mr. Leather Ibiza and Chicago, Cologne Gay Pride packages, including event tickets.	*Bookings:* Call travel agent or direct. *Est:* 1983. *TAC:* 8-10. *Pymt:* Checks, money orders, Visa, bank transfers. **IGTA**
♀♂ ● **Ten Thousand Waves** PO Box 7924 Missoula, MT 59807 USA (406) 549-6670, (800) 537-8315.	Rafting and kayaking in western Montana. Departures daily between April 15 and October 15 annually. Paddle raft, sit-on-top kayaks or instruction standard kayaks. Also offers ghost town tours in the Bob Marshall Wilderness.	*Bookings:* Call travel agent or direct. *Est:* 1989. *TAC:* 10. *Pymt:* Checks, cash, all cards.
♀♂ ● **Terramundo Travels Int'l** Binnen Dommersstraat 21-23 Amsterdam 1013 HK The Netherlands (31 20) 420 1122, Fax: (31 20) 622 6912.	A gay-friendly company specializing in Latin America, Spain and Portugal. Always seeks unusual accommodations with interesting atmosphere, trekking, climbing, mtn biking, fly-drives, hacienda stays, offers lowest prices possible (example: 8-day trek in Bolivia with guide, transport at US$370 per person).	*Bookings:* Call travel agent or direct. *Est:* 1994. *TAC:* 10. *Pymt:* all major credit cards. *Member:* IATA, UFTAA, LATA
♀ ● **Thanks, Babs** 3938 19th St San Francisco, CA 94114 USA (415) 552-1791, (888) 969-2227, Fax: (415) 522-0791, E-mail: ThanksBabs@aol.com, Web: www.ThanksBabs.com.	Women's group and independent travel worldwide, golfing in Puerto Vallarta, skiing in Alaska, cruising the Caribbean. Tours and independent, air-inclusive packages to 50 global destinations. Women-friendly destinations with affordable pricing and value.	*Bookings:* Call travel agent or direct. *Est:* 1996. *TAC:* 10 + incentives. *Pymt:* credit cards, checks, transfers. **IGTA**
♀♂ ● **Timeout Tours & Travel** 68 Wilberforce Rd London N4 2SR England (44 171) 354 0535, Fax: (44 171) 354 2606.	Private tours of London, England for gays and lesbians.	*Bookings:* Call travel agent or direct. *Est:* 1993. *TAC:* 10. *Pymt:* Bank checks, wire transfers.

TOUR COMPANIES

Wholesale/Retail (Call Direct or Have Travel Agent Contact) **WHO TO CALL**

♀♂	☽	**Todd River Tours** PO Box 3779 Alice Springs, NT 0871 Australia (61-8) 8953 2747, Fax: (61-8) 8953 4448, mobile: (61-15) 187 243, E-mail: ozytours@taunet.net.au.	Private, personalized gay-friendly itineraries in Australia's Northern Territory (central Australia). Bushwalking, aboriginal culture, cycling & motorcycle tours, air tours, learning bush medicine and bush "tucker" (food finding), 4-wheel drive tours, wildlife. Accommodations also arranged.	*Bookings:* Call direct.
♀♂	☽	**Toto Tours** 1326 W Albion #3-W Chicago, IL 60626-4753 USA (773) 274-8686, (800) 565-1241, Fax: (773) 274-8695, E-mail: tototours@aol.com, Web: www.tototours.com.	The gay and lesbian adventure travel company, active vacations in the US and worldwide. Hike into volcanoes, kayak in Maui, safari in Africa, swim with sea lions in Baja, Mexico. In 1997, Toto Tours' first women-only trip: Rafting the Grand Canyon. Participants in most trips are mostly men.	*Bookings:* Call travel agent or direct. *Est:* 1990. *TAC:* 10. *Pymt:* Checks only. **IGTA**
♀♂	●	**Tourmark's Gay Way America Tours** 125 Park Ave 2nd Floor New York, NY 10017 USA (212) 949-0017, (888) 868-7627, Fax: (212) 949-0321.	In cooperation with American Airlines, gay and lesbian air/hotel holidays throughout the US. Each client gets local information packet, use of Tourmark's Concierge Service and toll-free Assistance Line. For special group prices, have your travel agent contact them. Quotes returned within 24 hours of receipt.	*Bookings:* Call travel agent. *Est:* 1993. *TAC:* 10. *Pymt:* Checks, Visa, MC, Amex. *Member:* TIA, RSA **IGTA**
♂	☽	**Tours to Paradise** PO Box 3656 Hollywood, CA 90078-3656 USA (213) 962-9169, Fax: (213) 962-3236. E-mail: sjiservices@earthlink.net.	Thailand specialists since 1990. Quality tours for individuals or groups. Single-occupancy hotel with air conditioning and private bath. All Thailand transfers, transportation and local taxes. Over 12 excursions in Thailand with sightseeing, cultural and historical aspects, dining, recreation, chartered boat trip on the Bay of Siam, English-speaking guides. $1,390 plus round-trip air at deeply discounted rates. They also handle gay packages to Acapulco, Mexico.	*Bookings:* Call travel agent or direct. *TAC:* 10. *Escrow Acct:* Yes. *License No.:* In Calif: 020550-40. In Thailand: 51-044. *Pymt:* Credit cards for purchase of air tickets only, checks for land/air packages. **IGTA**
♀♂	☽	**Tower Travel** Tower Square, 600 N Colony Rd Wallingford, CT 06492 USA (203) 284-8747, (800) 229-8693, Fax: (203) 284-3322.	Escorted gay and lesbian vacations inside the United States and from the US to Europe. Three or four trips per year.	*Bookings:* Call travel agent or direct. **IGTA**
♀♂	☽	**Travel Affair** 1069 Juniper St Atlanta, GA 30309 USA (404) 892-9400, (800) 332-3417, Fax: (404) 876-9791.	Specializing in gay travel for the last 12 years, they offer monthly gay and lesbian group departures for worldwide destinations. Special New Years packages are already available for 1999. Choose New Years Eve in Sydney, by the pyramids in Egypt or Paris.	*Bookings:* Call travel agent or direct. **IGTA**

TOUR COMPANIES

FERRARI GUIDES' GAY TRAVEL A to Z - 18th EDITION   75

WHO TO CALL

○ Retail (Call Direct) ● Wholesale (Travel Agent Must Contact)

♂	○	**Travel Club, The** City Centre Box 128 Monroe City, IN 47557 USA Tel/Fax: (812) 743-2919, E-mail: kerry@in.net.	Gay men's travel club Members vote on destinations. Usually stay in multi-BR villas and homes so members can save money by cooking. Newsletter sent in plain, or even security envelope, if desired. Usually travel in the off-season or shoulder season to keep rates down. Accommodation usually averages $35-$60pp per night, plus tax.	*Bookings:* Call direct. *Est:* 1991. *Pymt:* Checks, Ames, Optima, Diners Club.
♂	◐	**Travel Keys Tours** PO Box 162266 Sacramento, CA 95816-2266 USA (916) 452-5200 (tel/fax).	Two specialized, unique European tours. Choose antique buying trip in Britain, France (no gender requirements) with guides who take you to best markets and help negotiate purchases. Or choose the Leatherman's Dungeons & Castles trip (leathermen only), which includes Berlin & Amsterdam Leather Scene and Munich's Oktoberfest Leather Meeting. Accommodations in both modern big-city hotels and in castles & ancient Inns in medieval walled towns.	*Bookings:* Call travel agent or direct. *Est:* 1984. *TAC:* 10. *Pymt:* Checks, Visa, MC, Amex, Discover. IGTA
♂	◐	**Travel Man** Postfach 1543 Koenigstein 61455 Germany (49 6174) 931 873, Fax: (49 6174) 252 90, E-mail: travelhouse@t-online.de	German-Based tour operator for both men and women. Gay & lesbian independent travel arrangements to exotic destinations worldwide. Their motto: "Travel in Style." They seek out unusual, interesting and quality accommodations. All tours are tailormade. No fixed packages.	*Bookings:* Call travel agent or direct. *Est:* 1991. *TAC:* 10. *Pymt:* Bank transfers, Eurochecks. *Member:* PATA
♀	◐	**Trek Out** 19 Roundham Grove, Leeds West Yorkshire L58 4DR England (44-1132) 621 407, Fax: (44 171) 498 4756.	Women's walking tours on Crete. Located in an area untouched by tourism. Tai, Chi, yoga and painting holidays. Moderately-paced treks are designed for women who enjoy 2-4 hours of rough country walking.	*Bookings:* Call travel agent or direct.
♀	◐	**Tropical Tune-ups** PO Box 390847 Kailua-Kona, HI 96739 USA (541) 935-1829 (tel/fax), (800) 587-0405, E-mail: SoundBodyMind@worldnet.att.net, Web: http://tropicaltuneups.com.	Hawaiian wellness retreats for women with vegetarian meals, accommodations and a program of activities included. Breathing, massage, yoga, spirituality, meditation on a live volcano, kayaking, swimming, swimming with dolphins and sea turtles, bathing in warm lava pools. Relax and unwind.	*Bookings:* Call travel agent or direct. *Est:* 1997. *TAC:* 10. *Pymt:* Checks.
♀♂	◐	**T.R.I.P. Tours** 11 Grace Ave Great Neck, NY 11021 USA (800) 448-8834.	Gay and lesbian cruises to Alaska.	*Bookings:* Call travel agent or direct. IGTA

TOUR COMPANIES

76   FERRARI GUIDES' GAY TRAVEL A to Z - 18th EDITION

◐ Wholesale/Retail (Call Direct or Have Travel Agent Contact)   **WHO TO CALL**

♀♂	◐	**Undersea Expeditions, Inc.** PO Box 9455 San Diego (Pacific Beach), CA 92169 USA (619) 270-2900, (800) 669-0310, Fax: (619) 490-1002, E-mail: underseax@aol.com, Web: www.mindfood.com/gaydiving.html.	Gay and lesbian scuba diving in exotic dive locations worldwide. Beginners to advanced divers, men and women. Packages include air, hotel and diving. Mexico, Caribbean, Red Sea, Galapagos, Papua New Guinea, Australia, Tahiti, and others.	*Bookings:* Call travel agent or direct. *Est:* 1991. *TAC:* 10-12. *Pymt:* Checks, wire transfers. *Member:* DEMA **IGTA**
♀♂	○	**Uranian Travel** Infocus House, 111 Kew Rd Richmond, Surrey TW9 2PN England (44 181) 332 1022, Fax: (44 181) 332 1619. In Manchester: (44 161) 236 9339. E-mail: info@uranian.co.uk. http://www.uranian.co.uk.	Europe's largest, oldest tour operator (22 years), exclusively gay & lesbian packages, Mykonos, Gran Canaria, Ibiza, Sitges, Mallorca, Key West, Miami, city breaks to Amsterdam, Dublin, Paris. Low-cost car hire in all locations.	*Bookings:* Call direct. *Est:* 1974. *Pymt:* Checks, Visa, MC, Amex, Access, Eurocard. *Member:* ABTA #V1407, IATA, ATOL #1941. **IGTA**
♀	○	**Vaarschool Grietje** Prinsengracht T/O 187 Amsterdam 1015 AZ The Netherlands (31 20) 625 91 05 (tel/fax).	Sail the canals of Holland, Belgium and France on a women's ship. Get a different view of these countries from the water. Summer, 1997: Sail north and south Holland. In July, sail to France via Maastricht, Belgium and the French Ardennes. Handle the ship, maneuver through locks or relax. The ship accommodates four women with rustic amenities.	*Bookings:* Call direct. *Est:* 1994. *Pymt:* Cash, bank transfers.
♀♂	◐	**VeloAsia Cycling Adventures** 1271 43rd Ave., San Francisco, Ca 94122 (800) 884 ASIA (2742), Tel/Fax: (415) 664-6779, Email: veloasia@aol.com.	Adventure cycling tours in places unusual and interesting. Vietnam, Cambodia, Sumatra, Turkey, Cuba. They handle logistics. You enjoy an enthralling way to explore. Small groups of 10. Cooking and language lessons, delicious meals, comfortable hotels. Proven safety record, emergency evacuation insurance.	*Bookings:* Call travel agent or direct. *Est:* 1991. *TAC:* 11. *Pymt:* Checks only.
♀	◐	**Ventus Reisen** Krefelder Str 8 Berlin D-10555 Germany (49 30) 393 2031, (49 30) 399 6093, Fax: (49 30) 399 5587.	Customizes women's cultural tours for women's organizations and travel agents. Destinations include China, Russia, Uzbekistan, Siberia, Mongolia, Syria, Jordan. Itineraries include meetings with local businesswomen and families to provide participants an experience of women's lifestyles in the destination country. Though mainly wholesale, Ventus offers one trip to individuals each year. Groups need not be German speakers, as guides speaking any language can be arranged.	*Bookings:* Call travel agent or direct.
♀♂	◐	**Victorian Home Walk** 2226 15th St San Francisco, CA 94114 USA (415) 252-9485, Fax: (415) 863-7577, E-mail: jay@victorianwalk.com, Web: www.victorianwalk.com.	San Francisco walking tours, view Victorian homes, easy pace, low-impact walking, spectacular views of the bay, see Mrs. Doubtfire's Victorian, learn about Victorian styles.	*Bookings:* Call travel agent or direct. *Est:* 1995. *Comm:* 10%. *Pymt:* Cash, checks. **IGTA**

TOUR COMPANIES

FERRARI GUIDES' GAY TRAVEL A to Z - 18th EDITION

WHO TO CALL

○ Retail (Call Direct)   ● Wholesale (Travel Agent Must Contact)

♀♂	●	**Virgin Vacations** 599 Broadway New York, NY 10012 USA (800) 364-6466, Fax: (800) 364-6657.	Independent tour packages to Britain and Europe. Include air, transfers, entry to some of London's hottest gay clubs, passes for London's Tube and buses. Optional add-on sightseeing. Or choose fly/drive package including accommodations in any of 170 Minotels around Britain. Travel on to Europe with Virgin partner airline British Midland, staying in first-class hotels.	*Bookings:* Call travel agent or direct. *Est:* 1994. *TAC:* 10. *Pymt:* MC, Amex, Discover. IGTA
♀♂	●	**Voyages & Expeditions** 8323 SW Freeway #800 Houston, TX 77074 USA (713) 776-3438, (800) 818-2877, Fax: (713) 771-9761.	Gay-owned company, specializing in luxury travel to exotic destinations for discerning, value-conscious clients. Individuals or any size group. Cruise on the Crystal Symphony or take a tented "Hemingway safari" or around the world on Concorde. For 1997, Grand European cruise on The Island Princess.	*Bookings:* Call travel agent or direct. *Est:* 1982. *TAC:* Varies. *Pymt:* Credit cards, checks. IGTA
♀♂	●	**V.I.P. Tours of New York** The Osborne, 205 W 57th St New York, NY 10019 USA (212) 247-0366, (800) 300-6203, Fax: (212) 397-0851.	In-depth, gay- and lesbian-oriented tours of New York City. Private meetings with gay and lesbian actors, singers, performers. Behind-the-Scenes visits to places like Carnegie Hall and Lincoln Center. Architectural tours of Greenwich Village, and many more insiders' views of NYC. Tours are customized to the interests and budget of individuals and groups.	*Bookings:* Call travel agent or direct. *Est:* 1988. *TAC:* 12+. *Pymt:* Checks. *Member:* NYCVB, SITE IGTA
♀♂	●	**Wanderlust Ventures** PO Box 253 Bridgewater, SA 5155 Australia SA: (61-8) 8339 7099 (tel/fax), NT: (61-8) 8962 2731 (tel/fax).	Bushwalking, camping, four-wheel-drive tours in Flinders Ranges, South Australia, the Grampians in Victoria and Northern Territory's Outback. Equipment, meals, accommodation, transport provided. Challenging, but non-intimidating, adventures.	*Bookings:* Call travel agent or direct. agta
♀♂	●	**Way to Go Costa Rica** 2801 Blue Ridge Rd Raleigh, NC 27607 USA (919) 782-1900, (800) 835-1223, Fax: (919) 787-1952, E-mail: hlasky@internetmci.com, Web: www.datasolv.com/costarica/waytogo.html.	Multilingual, gay-friendly Costa Rica experts customize individual and group gay-escorted tours including gay-friendly hotels, cruises and resort companies in Costa Rica. Activities include sport fishing, scuba diving, snorkeling. Bulk airfares are available from major US cities.	*Bookings:* Call travel agent. *Est:* 1993. *TAC:* 11. *Pymt:* Visa, MC, Amex. IGTA
♀♂	●	**We Love the Florida Keys Visitor Center** PO Box 504443 Marathon, FL 33050 USA (305) 289-1400, (800) 403-2154, Fax: (305) 289-4334.	Attractive prices for gay-exclusive and gay-friendly accommodations and excursions in the Florida Keys and Key West. In addition to accommodations, call them for sunset sails, snorkeling, scuba diving, parasailing, jet skiing, glass-bottomed boat ridees, fishing. They even make restaurant reservations!	*Bookings:* Call travel agent or direct. *Est:* 1994. *TAC:* 10. *Pymt:* Visa, MC, Discover, checks, cash. *Member:* Key West Bus. Guild

TOUR COMPANIES

◐ Wholesale/Retail (Call Direct or Have Travel Agent Contact)

WHO TO CALL

♀	○	**Whelk Women** PO Box 1006 Boca Grande, FL 33921 USA (941) 964-2027.	Sailing for women among barrier islands off Florida's west coast. Watch dolphins and many birds. Eagles, osprey, pelicans and others. Fish and collect shells, swim, sun. Stay in rustic cabin or tent. Bring food, bedding, towels. Camping gear supplied.	*Bookings:* Call direct. *Est:* 1983. *Pymt:* Checks, cash.
♀♂	◐	**Whitney Yacht Charters** 4065 Crockers Lake Blvd #2722 Sarasota, FL 34238 USA (941) 927-0108, (800) 223-1426, Fax: (941) 922-7819, E-mail: whtney673@aol.com.	Gay-friendly and 35 years in business. They know the yachts and crews. Can recommend the perfect combination for your particular group. Gay or very gay-friendly crews available. Yacht in the Caribbean, Mediterranean or New England. Their motto: "We see every yacht we charter. We do not charter every yacht we see."	*Bookings:* Call travel agent or direct. *Est:* 1963. *TAC:* 10.ad *Pymt:* Checks. IGTA
♀♂	◐	**Wild Rockies Tours** Box 8184 Missoula, MT 59807 USA (406) 728-0566, fax coming soon.	Canoe trips in remote wild country of Montana, soaks in hot springs. Originating from Great Falls or Missoula. Missouri, Lower Clark Fork, Blackfoot and Yellowstone Rivers. Mountaineering trips include climbing class-3 peaks in Selway-Bitterroot Wilderness. Day trips include canoeing, mountain biking, hiking. Gay-friendly.	*Bookings:* Call travel agent or direct. *Est:* 1993. *TAC:* 15. *Pymt:* Checks, cash.
♀	○	**Wild Women** PO Box 8743 Missoula, MT 59807 USA (406) 543-3747, Fax: (406) 728-4134, E-mail: wve@wildrockies.org.	A non-profit project of Women's Voices for the Earth. Young women's leadership development, learning wilderness survival skills. Learning to adapt those skills to everyday life. Rafting, kayakijng, canoeing, trekking, fishing, hiking, climbing, backpacking. Rocky Mountains, Montana, Canada, Idaho, Wyoming, Baja, Belize, Zimbabwe, South Africa, Botswana, Namibia, Nepal.	*Bookings:* Call direct. *Est:* 1993. *Pymt:* Checks, cash, money orders, no cards.
♀	◐	**Wild Women Expeditions** PO Box 145, Station B Sudbury, ON P3E 4N5 Canada (705) 866-1260.	Women's 3- to 7-day canoe trips in Ontario's wilderness. By car: 5 hours from Toronto, 3 hrs from Michigan's border. Spectacular wilderness abounds. Less demanding 3- to 7-day vacations are at the riverside base camp with cozy cabins. Gourmet vegetarian meals and massage therapist on-site.	*Bookings:* Call travel agent or direct.
♀♂	●	**Windjammer Barefoot Cruises** 7985 Santa Monica Blvd #109-424 West Hollywood, CA 90046 USA (800) 864-6567, (213) 654-7700, Fax: (213) 654-7909.	Tall ship cruises. One gay cruise per year, others gay-friendly. Caribbean, Mexico, Tortola, St. Maartin, Antigua, Grenada.	*Bookings:* Call travel agent. IGTA

TOUR COMPANIES

FERRARI GUIDES' GAY TRAVEL A to Z - 18th EDITION

WHO TO CALL

○ Retail (Call Direct)   ● Wholesale (Travel Agent Must Contact)

♀♂	●	**Windmills Travel & Tourism** PO Box 154 Mykonos 84600 Greece (30 289) 23877/26555/26556/26557, Fax: (30 289) 22066 (ONLY fax is operative November to March), E-mail: windmills@travelling.gr.	For individual travelers looking for the right hotel. For travel agents seeking professional assistance with reservations for valued clients. Your personal contact on Mykonos is Pam Taylor. She is an accommodations, transportation, and excursions expert for Mykonos, the Cycladic Islands, and Greece. Windmills is Official Tour Operator for the 12 Gods Party, a gay and lesbian event.	*Bookings:* Call travel agent or direct. *Est:* 1979. IGTA
♀	○	**Wintermoon** 3388 Petrell Brimson, MN 55602 USA (218) 848-2442.	Alaskan Huskies love to run and pull a sled. Learn dogsledding 50 miles north of Duluth. Kathleen Anderson has mushed for 12 years. She bred and trained her 28 dogs. Stay in a rustic log cabin, with sauna, wood heater, solar power, hand pump for well water, outhouse. All trips include lodging, meals, instruction.	*Bookings:* Call direct.
♀	●	**Witchencroft 4WD & Bushwalking Tours** PO Box 685 Atherton, QLD 4883 Australia (61-70) 912 683, E-mail: jj@bushnet.qld.edu.au.	Four-wheel-drive tours and bushwalking for women. In rural Queensland, guided by a 4th-generation North Queenslander. Stay at Witchencroft Australia's oldest women's guest house. Climate virtually guarantees fine weather.	*Bookings:* Call travel agent or direct. *Est:* 1987. *TAC:* 10. *Pymt:* Travelers checks, cash, bank transfers.
♀♂	●	**Wolff + Zink Travel Services** Hans-Sachs-Strasse 22 Munich 80469 Germany (49 89) 260-6330, Fax: (49 89) 260-5962.	German-based gay travel company and tour operator since 1989. Monthly gay group trips visit several European cities. For individuals, Gay City Tours packages offer arrangements for Amsterdam, Berlin, Budapest, Cologne, Frankfurt, Hamburg, Munichy, Paris, Prague, Rome, Salzburg. Eleven different South African tours booked and operated from a branch office in South Africa.	*Bookings:* Call travel agent or direct. *Est:* 1989. *TAC:* 10. *Pymt:* Checks, bank drafts. *Member:* BBP IGTA
♀	●	**Womantours/Artemis Sailing** PO Box 931 Driggs, ID 83422 USA (208) 354-2906, (800) 247-1444.	Bicycling and sailing trips for women, bike Natchez Trace, Utah, Canadian Rockies, Yellowstone, sail Tahiti, Tonga, Caribbean, all routes researched.	*Bookings:* Call travel agent or direct. *Est:* 1993. *Comm:* 5%.
♀	●	**Women in Motion** PO Box 4533 Oceanside, CA 92052-4533 USA (619) 754-6747, (888) GO-WOMEN (469-6636), Fax: (619) 754-8066. E-mail: eventsrus@aol.com, Web: http://gowomen.com.	Active vacations for women, with women, by women. You choose the vacation. You set the pace. Rafting, kayaking, golfing, packages to women's festivals, cycling, rock climbing.	*Bookings:* Call travel agent or direct. *Est:* 1987. *TAC:* 10. *Pymt:* MC, Visa, checks, interest-free pymt plans.

TOUR COMPANIES

ZMAX
GAY TRAVEL WORLDWIDE
Your Gay Travel Specialists

Gay owned and operated full-service American Express travel agency in Miami Beach.

ZMAX arranges Gay Tours and Cruises, Circuit Party Travel, RSVP, Atlantis, Toto, Men on Vacation, Our Family Abroad, Above and Beyond, Olivia, Mariah, Out West Adventures, safaris, and preferred cruise lines, including Seabourn, Crystal, Royal Caribbean, Norwegian, Carnival, Holland America, Radisson Seven Seas, and Windstar.

South Beach/Miami Beach, USA
1-800-TO-GO-GAY · FAX 1-800-538-0776
Australia 0014-800-124-012 France 0-800-90-1753; Germany 0130-81-7295; Italy 1678-73182; Spain 900-94-1162; Switzerland 155-0078; UK 0800-96-0827.

Z·M·A·X
TRAVEL & TOURS INC

AMERICAN EXPRESS Travel Agency Representative

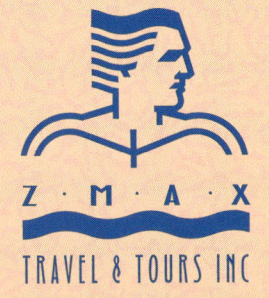

305-532-0111 · FAX 305-532-1222
420 Lincoln Rd., Ste. 239, Miami Beach, Florida, 33139

OUR WORLD

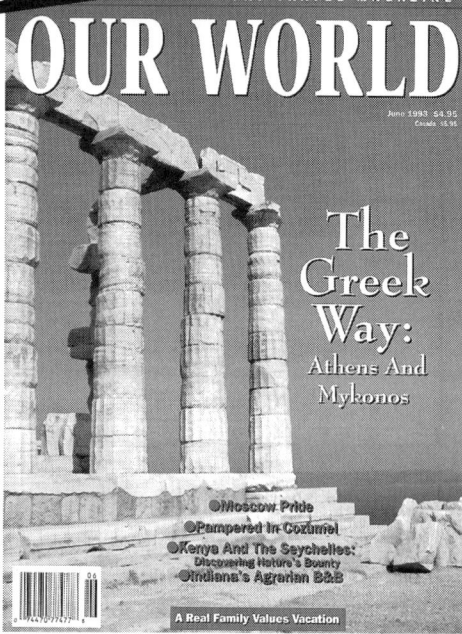

ONLY $35 FOR 10 ISSUES

The #1 Magazine For Gay and Lesbian Travelers

➥ **Exciting Articles & Features**
➥ **Color Photos That Take You There**
➥ **Informative Monthly Departments**
➥ **USA & Worldwide Destinations**
➥ **Exclusive Travel Listings**

OUR WORLD is the recognized monthly magazine for travel enthusiasts. Unlike other publications, you'll find everything you need to know about gay and lesbian travel in our 56-page, all-glossy format – including color photography.

It's all here: from New York to L.A.; London to Moscow; Thailand to Tahiti; the Caribbean to the Amazon; and Key West to Alaska. So don't be left out, join 50,000 other readers and subscribe to OUR WORLD magazine before you go!

1 year (10 issues) $35. Send check, money order, or VISA, MasterCard to:

OUR WORLD,
1104 North Nova Road, Suite 251, Daytona Beach, FL 32117
Tel: (904) 441-5367   Fax: (904) 441-5604
Internet: http://www.ourworldmag.com

Money-back guarantee. First issue mails in 6 weeks in plain envelope. Outside USA send US$45 (surface) or US$70 (airmail).

member aglta

member IGTA

◐ Wholesale/Retail (Call Direct or Have Travel Agent Contact) **WHO TO CALL**

♀	◐	**Women in the Wilderness** 566 Ottawa Ave St Paul, MN 55107 USA (612) 227-2284, Fax: (612) 227-4028	Teaches women skills to really enjoy the wilderness. Canoeing, kayaking, dog sledding, snowshoeing. Learn to be at home in the wilds. Worldwide destinations, like Finland's Lapland, Peru's Macchu Picchu and Amazon rainforest, Utah's canyons, Minnesota's northwoods and waterways. Nearly 20 years experience guiding women's adventure trips.	*Bookings:* Call travel agent or direct.
♀	◐	**Women Sail Alaska** PO Box 20348 Juneau, AK 99802 USA (907) 463-3372, (888) 272-4525.	Sailing excursions for women, around Juneau, Alaska, sheltered anchorages among barrier islands, abundant wildlife, hiking, beachcombing, fishing, catch halibut or salmon for dinner, view pods of whales, sea lions, bears. Groups of up to 4 women.	*Bookings:* Call travel agent or direct. *Est:* 1995. *TAC:* 20. *Pymt:* Cash, check.
♀	○	**Women's Travel Club** 21401 NE 38th Ave Aventura, FL 33180 USA (305) 936-9669, (800) 480-4448, Fax: (305) 937-7649, E-mail: womantrip@aol.com.	Women's travel club with members nationwide. Specializing in cultural tours to domestic and international destinations. Roomshare is guaranteed — never a single supplement charge. Meetings in NY, Chicago and several Florida cities, monthly newsletter.	Bookings: Call direct. *Est:* 1992. *Pymt:* Credit cards, checks. *Member:* ASTA.
♀	◐	**Woodswomen** 25 W Diamond Lake Rd Minneapolis, MN 55419 USA (612) 822-3809, (800) 279-0555, Fax: (612) 822-3814.	Oldest, largest women's outdoor adventure travel company. All ages, skill and fitness levels welcome. Flexible pace, easy group interaction. Exotic destinations worldwide, canoeing, bicycling, backpacking, hiking, kayaking, climbing, etc.	*Bookings:* Call travel agent or direct. *Est:* 1977. *TAC:* 10. *Pymt:* Check, Visa, MC.
♀♂	◐	**Worldwide Vacations Inc.** 1400 East Oakland Park Blvd #216 Ft Lauderdale, FL 33334 USA (954) 630-0242, (800) 841-8222, Fax: (954) 630-9420, E-mail: worldvac@gate.net, Web: www.worldtours.com.	Customized gay-friendly, individual tour packages catering to various interests, scuba diving, opera, classical concerts, skiing, windsurfing, cruises, Caribbean, Maldives, Red Sea, Austria, Aruba, Dominican Republic, Greece, Vietnam and others.	*Bookings:* Call travel agent or call direct. *Est:* 1994. *TAC:* 10. *Pymt:* Credit cards. *Member:* ASTA, PATA IGTA
♂	○	**Xeno Tours/Mantours** Passauerplatz 6 Wien 1010 Austria (43 1) 533 0660, Fax: (43 1) 533 0650.	Individual gay travel packages, 90% male clientele, European gay men's resorts like Ibiza, Mykonos, Gran Canaria, and cities like Berlin. Austrian outlet for Holigays travel packages.	*Bookings:* Call direct.
♀♂	●	**Zeus Tours & Yacht Cruises** 209 W 40th St New York, NY 10018 USA (212) 221-0006, (800) 447-5667, Fax: (212) 764-7912.	Specializing in Greece, Turkey, Egypt, Israel, Italy. Supersaver packages, customized tours, gay-exclusive and gay-friendly itineraries. Tours, cruises, yacht cruises, Athens, Greek Isles.	*Bookings:* Call travel agent. IGTA

TOUR COMPANIES

WHO TO CALL

○ Retail (Call Direct)   ● Wholesale (Travel Agent Must Contact)

♀♂	●	**Zipper Travel Association** Via Francesco Carletti, 8 Rome 00154 Italy Main office: (39 6) 578 3170. Operating office: Via Castelfidardo 18, Rome 00185, Italy. (39 6) 488 2730, Fax: (39 6) 488 2729. E-mail: tptravel@aconet.it.	Italy's exclusively gay and lesbian travel company, customized, individualized itineraries, for overseas visitors: Italian Gay Discovery Tour, Venice, Florence, Rome, Siena, for Italian gays going abroad: fun gay and lesbian adventures and business travel arrangements.	*Bookings:* Call travel agent or direct. **IGTA**
♂	●	**ZMAX Travel & Tours Inc.** 420 Lincoln Rd Miami Beach, FL 33239 USA (305) 532-0111, (800) 864-6429, Fax: (305) 532-1222, E-mail: zmaxtravel@aol.com.	Fantasy Fest Cruise, Miami to Key West, Oct 24-27, 1997. Experts on the party circuit, with packages available. Several Gay Games packages for 1998.	*Bookings:* Call travel agent or direct. *Est:* 1995. *TAC:* 10. *Pymt:* Amex, Visa, MC. **IGTA**
♀♂	●	**Zone One** 140 Buckingham Palace Road London SW1 W9SA England (44-171) 730-2347, Fax: (44-171) 730-9756.	For overseas travelers visiting England and for English gays and lesbians traveling overseas, a full program of gay and lesbian itineraries and travel arrangements.	*Bookings:* Call travel agent or direct. *Est:* 1997. *Member:* EGLTA

Indulgent Vacations for Men

Club Hommes™

Paris & *LeCordonBleu l'Art Culinaire* • Silversea Voyages • New Year's on Maui • 1998 Amsterdam GayGames Rhine River Cruise • The Vineyards of Châteauneuf-du-Pape • The Rainbow Golf Classic™ on Miami Beach • The Lesser Antilles • Costa Rica • China • The Galapagos Islands • St. Barthélemy • The Millenium

224 West 4th Street NYC 10014
212/206-6900 • 800/429-6969
club@worldguest.com
www.worldguest.com/club

IGTA
we're a proud member of the
International Gay Travel Association

TOUR COMPANIES

Wholesale/Retail (Call Direct or Have Travel Agent Contact)

WHO TO CALL

TOUR COMPANY DETAILS

2Afrika

- **Cape Town to Cairo, We Know Africa!**
- **Gay & Lesbian Group, Indiv'l Tours**
- **Cruise Cape Town's Gay Scene**
- **View Big Game/Victoria Falls**
- **Maasai Cultural Experience, Swaziland**
- **Luxury Blue Train Across South Africa**

We give you the best Africa has to offer at a price that cannot be beaten. Our South African tours include Johannesburg, Kruger National Park, Sun City (with its famed Palace), a night with a traditional African family at Lesedi Cultural Village, and glorious, sun-drenched Cape Town with its bustling gay nightlife. Optional extensions feature neighboring Zimbabwe. Traveling with us through Kenya includes Nairobi, exotic game reserves and the East African coastline at Mombassa and Malindi. Our Egypt tours encompass Cairo, Luxor, Aswan and Abu Simbel, with a luxurious Nile cruise linking these cities adorned with one fifth of the world's antiquities.

Ride the Rave Wave, Madiba, City Pack Hotel Pkgs, Day Tours, Lesedi Cultural Village, Game Lodges, Luxury Blue Train, Kruger Nat'l Park, Africa Alive, Garden Route, Zimbabwe, Namibia, Gary Player Golf Tours, Maasai Cultural & Wildlife Experience, East Africa—Trekking Mt. Kenya, Kilimanjaro, Swahili expedition, Maasai adventure, Sangara experience

---

2Afrika
2663 E Sunrise Blvd #167
Ft Lauderdale, FL 33304 USA
(800) 2AFRIKA (800-223-7452), Fax: (305) 466-0873, E-mail: 2afrika@safari.net, Web: www.travelfile.com/get/2afrk.html.

♀♂ ◐

Above & Beyond Tours

- **Often Imitated - Never Duplicated**
- **We Do Things A Little Differently**
- **Europe/Aust./New Z'land, Fiji**
- **Sydney Mardi Gras/Sleaze Ball**
- **Crusoe's Resort in Fiji**
- **Amsterdam Floating Gay Pride**

At *Above & Beyond Travel*, we believe a straight tour that is "gay" one week of the year is just not good enough. Labels belong on clothes and don't change the identity of a travel product. That's why we design our travel packages with you in mind, from the ground up. From the moment of your arrival, your arrangements are coordinated by gay-owned or -operated tour companies intent on introducing you to their destination. Our hotels are chosen because they are centrally located to gay activiites, represent a good value, and cater to gay and lesbian travelers. Professional gay tour guides share the sights of the city while giving insight to the gay lifestyle of their country. And we balance organized activity with lots of leisure time. Choose from 31 scheduled group departures, many of which can be combined with others, to destinations in Europe and the South Pacific.

— 1997 —

Fe 08 - 18	Pre-Mardi Gras at Crusoe's Resort
Fe 12 - Mr 06	Best of South Pacific
Fe 15 - 21	New Zealand Adventure
Fe 19 - Mr 03	Party! Party! Package (S. Pacific)
Fe 23 - Mr 03	Sydney Gay and Lesbian Mardi Gras
Mr 01 - 15	Mardi Gras Recovery at Crusoe's Resort
Mr 03 - 08	Dive the Great Barrier Reef
Mr 15 - 24	Treasures of Italy
Ap 01 - 12	Tom Bianchi & Friends at Crusoe's Resort
Ap 27 - Ma 02	Queens Day Amsterdam
Ma 23 - Jn 01	Costa Rica Coast to Coast
Jn 10 - 17	Women's Golf Week at Crusoe's Resort
Jn 20 - 25	London & Brighton
Jn 20 - Jy 07	Grand Europe #1
Jn 25 - 30	EuroPride Paris
Jn 30 - Jy 07	Amsterdam & Cologne Gay Pride
Jy 05 - 12	Women's Week at Crusoe's Resort
Jy 19 - 23	St. Petersburg, Russia
Jy 19 - Ag 11	Grand Europe #2
Jy 23 - Ag 01	Utopia '97—Russia's White Nights
Ag 01 - 04	Floating Pride Amsterdam
Ag 01 - 11	Great Britain & Edinburgh Festival
Se 05 - 14	Costa Rica Coast to Coast
Se 11 - Oc 10	Best of South Pacific
Se 13 - 20	Fall in Fiji at Crusoe's Resort
Se 23 - Oc 02	Iberian Capitals
Se 23 - Oc 20	Grand Europe #3
Se 26 - Oc 06	Incarceration
Oc 01 - 06	Sydney Sleaze Ball
Oc 02 - 11	Prague, Vienna, Budapest
Oc 11 - 20	Treasures of Italy
No 21 - 27	London Theater
No 22 - 29	Thanksgiving at Man Friday Resort
No 23 - De 12	Dive Fiji
No 27 - 30	Thanksgiving in Amsterdam
De 23 - Ja 02	Christmas DownUnder
De 29 - Ja 02	New Years in Paris

Above & Beyond Tours
330 Townsend St #107
San Francisco, CA 94107 USA
(415) 284-1666, (800) 397-2681, Fax: (415) 284-1660, E-mail: info@abovebeyondtours.com, Web: www.abovebeyondtours.com.

♀♂ ◐

FERRARI GUIDES' GAY TRAVEL A to Z - 18th EDITION

WHO TO CALL

○ Retail (Call Direct)　● Wholesale (Travel Agent Must Contact)

TOUR COMPANY DETAILS

Advance Damron Vacations

- **Annual All-Gay Halloween Cruise**
- **Spring Mexico All-Gay Cruise**
- **Windjammer Fleet**
- **Cozumel, Cancun, Isla Mujeres**
- **Dress Code: NONE!**
- **Toga party, Halloween Costume Party**

Explore the Mexican Caribbean with *Advance Damron Vacations,* aboard Windjammer's S/V Fantome. Sun-drenched beaches, awesome Mayan ruins and fabulous ports-of-call...are waiting for you to explore. There's no better place to call "home" for the week than the largest 4-masted stay-sail schooner in the world. Join us and 127 other gays as we climb aboard the pride of the Windjammer fleet.

For eight glorious days, you'll enjoy outrageous costume parties, campy evening extravaganzas, dancing, beach parties and more! All the clothing you really need to bring is your swim suit! Activities include an hilarious Toga party, Halloween costume party, entertainment, sightseeing, shopping and watersports. Three hearty meals each day, late-night snacks, luncheon buffets and fun beach parties, brunch, morning Bloody Marys, evening rum and swizzles. Dress code: NONE! *Plus, we've thrown in an extra night free!!* Now you'll enjoy an entire week of fun and adventure in the fabulous Mexican sunshine!

— 1997 —

Mr 07 - 09	Winter Party '97 Package
Ap 20 - 26	Caribbean Windjammer Cruise
Oc 26 - No 02	Halloween All-Gay Windjammer Cruise

Advance Damron Vacations
One Greenway Plaza #890
Houston, TX 77046 USA
(713) 888-1023, (800) 695-0880, Fax:(713) 888-1010, E-mail: Donnie@Advance-Damron.com, Web: www.advance-damron.com.
♀♂ ◐

Adventure Associates

- **Worldwide Outdoor Adventures**
- **Hiking, Kayaking, Climbing, Skiing,**
- **Backpacking, Safaris, Cultural**
- **Personally-designed Itineraries**
- **Africa, NW US, Greece, Pacific**
- **No Experience Needed**

In 1997, we celebrate our Tenth Anniversary! Over the past decade, we have explored both the "well-known" and "little-known" corners of this spectacular planet with hundreds of fun-loving, curious and adventure-spirited travelers. From the golden savannas of East Africa to the snow-capped mountains of the North Cascades to the gleaming islands of Greece, our programs are beyond the beaten path, active, educational, and always great fun! Each of our trip itineraries is personally designed by us — we don't simply contract out to other companies to run our programs. We are committed to traveling in small groups, so you'll enjoy the camaraderie and convenience of a well-organized trip without the regimentation of a "standard" tour. Whether you're a seasoned adventure traveler or just beginning to venture out, single or with a companion, 25 or 75 years old, you'll be in the good company of other like-spirited travelers. Typically, *no experience is needed* to participate in any of our programs and you do not need to be an athlete. Our seasoned guides are experts! Bring your sense of adventure, your desire to discover, and your love of wild places and leave the logistics to us!

Call or write now for your free brochure.

— 1997 —

June	Whale Watch Kayak Weekends, WA
Jn 21 - Jy 06	Tanzania Wildlife Cultural Safari
Jn 23 - 27	Rafting Deschutes River, OR
Jn 30 - Jy 06	Cruise Alaska Inside Passage
Jy 12 - 18	N Cascades Hike, Raft, Bike
Jy 18 - 20	Mt. Rainier Retreat-Hike, Kayak, Bike
Jy 20 - 25	San Juan Isles Multi-Sport Trip
Jy 27 - Ag 01	N Cascades Gourmet Hiking, Lodge
Jy 27 - Ag 01	Sea Kayak San Juan Islands, WA
August	Backpack Olympic Wilderness Coast
Ag 03 - 08	Hiking Grand Tetons, ID Lodge
Ag 03 - 08	Olympic Explorer Lodge-Based Hiking, WA
Ag 03 - 08	Sea Kayak San Juan Islands, WA
Ag 10 - 15	Sea Kayak in San Juan Islands, WA
Ag 11 - 16	Pacific NW Multi-Sport Lodge Trip
Ag 12 - 17	Fly Fishing West Yellowstone
Ag 15 - 31	Sail Greek Isles Private Yacht
Ag 17 - 22	North Cascades Gourmet Hiking
Ag 30 - Se 14	Greece, Turkey Sailing Odyssey
September	Morocco Exotic Kingdoms, High Atlas Hike
Se 07 - 13	High Sierras Hiking (horseback-assisted)
October	Bali, Lombok Island Paradise Adventure
October	EcuadorAdventure/Galapagos Cruise
October	Trek Mt. Everest Area, Nepal
October	Trek Royal Villages Himalayas—Nepal
November	New Zealand Adventure
De 26 - Ja 05	Costa Rica - New Year's in the Tropics

— 1998 —

Ja 09 - 18	Costa Rica Caribbean Adventure
Ja 17 - 25	Costa Rica Pacific Adventure
February	Copper Canyon Mexico Mule Trek
February	Crosscountry Skiing Yellowstone

Adventure Associates
PO Box 16304
Seattle, WA 98116 USA
(206) 932-8352, Fax: (206) 938-2654, E-mail: AdvntrAssc@aol.com.
♀ ◐

FERRARI GUIDES' GAY TRAVEL A to Z - 18th EDITION

◐ Wholesale/Retail (Call Direct or Have Travel Agent Contact)

WHO TO CALL

Adventure Bound Expeditions

- **Exclusively for Gay Men**
- **Outdoor Adventure Tours**
- **Destinations Worldwide**
- **Emphasis: Mountain Hiking**
- **Interaction with Exotic Cultures**
- **Turkey, Ethiopia, Greece**

Adventure Bound designs and conducts outdoor adventure tours exclusively for gay men to destinations worldwide. All tours are limited to small groups and emphasize hiking in mountains, interaction with exotic cultures and wildlife viewing. We regularly visit Africa, Asia, Europe and South America.

August, 1997: *Mountain & Ancient Cities of Turkey for Gay Men,* We will follow ancient high alpine trails amongst towering peaks, cobalt blue skies and dense forests. We'll relax on the Aegean coast, visit ancient temples ruins. Istanbul's mosques, palaces, covered bazaar and spice market are followed by a cruise of the Bosphorus on a private boat.

October, 1997: We cruise the Mediterranean along the *Turquoise Coast of Turkey* on a motor sailer yacht, anchor in quiet coves and visit ancient ruins. In Cappadocia we see underground cities.

In October, 1997, we trek for 5 days in the sculptured Simlen Mtns of Ethiopia, a region with mile-deep canyons. We'll visit 12th-century rock-hewn churches and end by rafting the Omo River.

— 1997 —
Ag 02 - 18	Mountains and Ancient Cities of Turkey
Se 06 - 21	Sail Turquoise Coast of Turkey
Oc 18 - No 02	Ehiopinan Mountains & Tribal Cultures

Adventure Bound Expeditions
711 Walnut St
Boulder, CO 80302 USA
(303) 449-0990, Fax:(303) 449-9038, E-mail: ADVENTBDEX@aol.com
♂ ◐

Adventures With Flair

- **Gay Travel...In Style**
- **Top International Airlines**
- **First-Class & Deluxe Hotels**
- **Custom-Designed Tours**
- **Thailand, Greek Isles, Australia**
- **Amsterdam, Copenhagen, Rio**

On an *Adventures With Flair* tour, you'll travel via top international airlines with knowledgeable guides intimately familiar with the local gay scene. And you'll stay in only first-class and deluxe hotels and resorts, not necessarily gay, but always gay-friendly. All tours are custom-designed and always feature destinations that are popular with gay travelers.

Flair's showcase product is the ever-popular Thailand with its world-class hotels, fine dining, unforgettable sightseeing, vibrant, and often outrageous, nightlife, bargain shopping, and a fascinating exotic culture. Weekly departures are available for a 12-day holiday featuring Bangkok and Pattaya with an optional 3-day extention to Chiang Mai.

On Flair's Aegean Odyssey, 24 pampered gay men experience the sun-drenched Greek Isles like true jet-setters — by private yacht. There are leisurely days on the Aegean and exuberant evenings in picturesque island ports, including Mykonos, the gay "mecca" of the Mediterranean. Experience these golden isles at a remarkably affordable cost. Departures in June and October (the best times to visit).

Or join Flair in Amsterdam or Copenhagen in July, scintillating, sexy Rio de Janeiro in October or fabulous Australia in November.

Adventures With Flair
Williamson Rd, PO Box 2926
Pikeville, KY 41502 USA
(606) 432-7109, (800) 463-5247, Fax: (606) 432-0059
♂ ◐

Ahwahnee Whitewater

- **Whitewater Rafting in Calif.**
- **Departures 7 Days A Week**
- **Exceptional Guides**
- **Gay & Women's Trips Arranged**
- **Our Rivers Are 'Mild' to 'Wild'**
- **Yosemite & Lake Tahoe Areas**

Ahwahnee Whitewater guides whitewater rafting trips on the Tuolumne, Cherry Creek, Merced and Carson Rivers in California. We also offer raft-supported trips for kayakers and both beginning and advanced whitewater rafting guide schools. Our rivers are rated "mild' to "wild," and are located near Yosemite and Lake Tahoe, just 2 1/2 to 5 hours from San Francisco. For those wishing a new challenge, we provide solocats on our milder rivers. Choose among half-day, 1-day, 2-day and 3-day trips, or combine two or more rivers for a longer adventure vacation. Book when you like. There are trips seven days a week from April till November! We are happy to arrange gay and lesbian or women-only trips on request.

Our purpose is to provide environmentally-sensitive recreational adventures that are safe, exhilarating and fun. Our guides are personable, experienced, thoughtful, fun-loving men and women who share their knowledge, respect and excitement for the river canyon you are exploring. Many of them guide rivers all year long around the country and around the world. Ahwahnee's exceptional guides keep guests coming back. "The trip itself was awesome and I had a great time. But what really made it such a good day was the people of Ahwahnee." (R. K., 1993)

— 1996 —
Jn 15	Rafting, Merced, Class III-IV
Ag 26 - 27	Rafting, Tuolumne, Class IV-IV+

Ahwahnee Whitewater
PO Box 1161
Columbia, CA 95310 USA
(209) 533-1401, (800) 359-9790, Fax: (209) 533-1409.
♀♂ ◐

TOUR COMPANY DETAILS

WHO TO CALL

○ Retail (Call Direct)　● Wholesale (Travel Agent Must Contact)

TOUR COMPANY DETAILS

Alaska Women of the Wilderness

- Women's Wilderness Trips
- Alaska, Baja, Nepal, Hawain
- Backpacking, Climbing, Skiing
- Kayaking, Girls' Camps
- Elderhostel Programs
- Healing Drumming Programs

Alaska Women of the Wilderness is a non-profit year-round wilderness and spiritual empowerment program for girls and women to explore and deepen their relationship with themselves, with others and with the earth in a supportive and nurturing atmosphere. We provide a supportive and noncompetitive learning environment where women can search for a deeper, richer connection to their own power.

During our thirteen years herstory, over six thousand girls and women have participated in backpacking, llama packing, horsepacking, sea kayaking, rock climbing, dog mushing, glacier travel, ski touring, fishing, mother and daughter adventures, girls' camps, elderhostel courses, spiritual quests, shamanic healing, ritual art and ceremony, meditation classes and women's retreats. Our Sacred Sounds and Inner Rhythms 1997 schedule includes meditations, healing, drumming and toning circles and the "Primal Connections," program, a reawakening of the feminine voice of leadership.

— 1997 —
June	Ancient Voices, Exploring Alaska's Glaciers
Jn 15 - 21	Young Women, Strong Women
Jy 06 - 12	Kayaking in Aialik Bay, Alaska
Jy 10 - 16	Young Women, Strong Women
Jy 25 - 27	Drum-Making Ceremony
August	Hiking in Denali National Park
Ag 13 - 19	Young Women, Strong Women

Alaska Women of the Wilderness
PO Box 773556
Eagle River, AK 99577 USA
(907) 688-2226, Fax:(907) 688-2285, E-mail: akwow@alaska.net.
♀ ☾

Allegro Travel

- Opera, Music, Cultural Tours
- Bolshoi & Kirov Ticket Agent
- Guaranteed Orchestra Seats
- Russia, Egypt, Finland
- Lithuania, Hong Kong
- Vienna, Salzburg, Florence

Allegro Travel is the only authorized ticket agent in North America for the Bolshoi Theater of Moscow, Russia, the Kirov Marlinsky Theater of St. Petersburg, the Finnish National Opera in Helsinki and other theaters. Allegro always provides schedules in advance and guarantees center orchestra seats. (Formerly, travelers to Russia were unable to obtain information in advance as to what performances were being presented or where their seats would be.) Center Orchestra seats at both the Kirov and Bolshoi are $70.00. Finnish National Opera tickets are $65.00. Please call or write to receive our ticket order form.

In addition, as experts in cultural travel, Allegro develops unique travel experiences that are centered on special events worthy of international recognition. Director Terry Jablonski is a specialist in opera, music and cultural travel.

— 1997 —
Ja 24 - Fe 02	Rhapsody on the Nile
Fe 04 - 12	Carnival in Venice
Fe 17 - 27	Russian Winter Gala
Fe 26 - Mr 05	Festival Hong Kong
Ap 28 - Ma 12	Vilnius, Riga, Tallinn, Helsinki, Russia
Ma 09 - 21	Italian Medley — Five Cities
Ma 23 - 31	Vienna & Salzburg
Jn 23 - Jy 08	White Nights Festival
Jn 27 - Jy 08	Grand Palio/Florence, Siena, Milan
Jy 02 - 10	Finnish Festival
October	Aida in Luxor

Allegro Travel
900 West End Ave #12-C
New York, NY 10025 USA
(212) 666-6700, (800) 666-3553, Fax: (212) 666-7451, E-mail: allegro@mail.idt.net.
♀♂ ☾

Alternative Holidays

- European Gay Ski Week
- In the French Alps
- High-Altitude Skiing
- Parties & Entertainment
- January, 1998
- Other Events Planned

Report on European Gay Ski Week 1997: It was a real success with many having to be turned away for lack of space. Only a few Americans attended, and the organizer wants to encourage more Americans to attend in 1998. The event takes place at one of Europe's finest resorts. We take over a Club Med hotel for a complete week of winter sports, parties, entertainment and hassle-free fun. Almost everything is included in the price, from full board (with wine) to your ski pass and tuition. Our ski area is Les Arcs offering some of the finest high-altitude skiing in Europe and a variety of ski terrain. Besides skiing, there are ice skating, paragliding, shopping and cinema close to your hotel. The hotel has well-appointed rooms and a restaurant featuring Club Med's renowned cuisine. There is a spectacular roster of evening entertainment, parties, shows, games, discos and more. For 1998, the company also plans an exclusively-male trip up the Nile in Egypt, a safari in Africa and a summer European Club Med week in Portugal.

TRIP SCHEDULE	
Sep, 1997	Club Med, Mallorca, Spain
Jan, 1998	European Gay Ski Week

Alternative Holidays
21 Russell Gardens Mews
London W14 8EU England
(44-7000) 782 267 (tel/fax), E-mail: alternatives@mail.bogo.co.uk, Web: www.bogo.co.uk/alternatives.
♂ ☾

FERRARI GUIDES' GAY TRAVEL A to Z - 18th EDITION

○ Wholesale/Retail (Call Direct or Have Travel Agent Contact)

WHO TO CALL

TOUR COMPANY DETAILS

Alyson Adventures

- **Fun & Excitement Outdoors**
- **For Gays & Lesbians**
- **Hiking in Switzerland**
- **Cycling the Natchez Trace**
- **Diving in the Caribbean**
- **HIV+ Men's Trip - Sedona, AZ**

Fun, excitement and the thrill of spending time in the great outdoors are three essential ingredients on every *Alyson Adventures* vacation. Whether cycling in France, climbing Wyoming's Grand Teton or visiting Australia for an active vacation at Mardi Gras time, Alyson Adventures' clients enjoy some of the world's greatest outdoor trips, in the company of other gay and lesbian travelers.

In 1997, Sasha Alyson will take groups hiking in Switzerland, diving in the Caribbean, cycling the historic Natchez Trace in Mississippi. A multi-activity trip is also planned for Jackson Hole, Wyoming and a group of active HIV+ men will take an outdoor trip to spectacular Sedona, Arizona.

Director Sasha Alyson, has a wealth of experience in active travel and a wonderful attention to detail that has clients calling their Alyson Adventures vacation "the best trip I've ever taken in my life."

— 1997 —

Fe 20 - Mr 07	Boomerang! Sydney Mardi Gras
Ap 20 - 27	Red Rock HIV+ Single Men's Wk.
Ma 02 - 09	Provencal: Biking S. France
Ma 10 - 17	Mistral - Biking in Provence, France
Ma 18 - 25	Provencal - Biking S. France
Jn 07 - 12	Biking in Central France
Jn 13 - 20	Valley of Kings - Biking in France
Jn 21 - 28	Edelweiss: Hiking in Swiss Alps
Jy 19 - 26	Rafting, Hiking, Climbing in WY
Jy 27 - Ag 03	Grand: Mountaineering in WY

Alyson Adventures
PO Box 180179
Boston, MA 02118 USA
(617) 247-8170, (800) 825-9766, E-mail: AlyVenture@aol.com, Web: www.channel1.com/alyson.
♀♂ ◐

Archipelago Holidays

- **Worldwide Adventure Tours**
- **Laid-Back Beach Holidays**
- **Diving, Safaris, Skiing**
- **Hiking, Dune Skiing, Kayaking**
- **Each Tour Customized**
- **US, Europe, Africa, Pacific**

Archipelago Holidays is a new holiday company promoting ecotourism and offering an exciting range of gay and gay-friendly holidays to destinations around the world.

We specialize in personalized itineraries, and most of our ecotourism holidays in straight or gay destinations are very environmentally friendly and include a high level of adventure activities, e.g. jungle training in Java or whitewater rafting in Costa Rica, as well as scuba diving virtually anywhere in the world.

You can also go on safari in a variety of countries in Africa, laze on the beach in the Caribbean, go whale watching in the Arctic Circle, dive with sharks in South Africa or from a livaboard in Sudan, or the Pacific Islands.

Have an outrageous holiday in San Francisco, New York, Mexico or Amsterdam. Show your body beautiful on the beaches of Fort Lauderdale, Brazil, Australia, the Indian Ocean or the Mediterranean.

We can cater for those who love to overdose on the adrenaline rush of adventure holidays, as well as those who like to take the relaxing, laid-back approach to going on holiday.

Once you have booked and paid for your holiday with Archipelago Holidays, you will automatically become a member of an Exclusive Holidays Reward Card Club.

Archipelago Holidays
2 Alexandra Ave
London SW11 4DZ England
(44-171) 622 7533, Fax: (44-171) 978 2615.
♀♂ ○

Atlantis Events

- **All-Gay Resort Vacations**
- **Caribbean, Mexico, Australia**
- **Sydney Gay Mardi Gras**
- **New: Club Atlantis**
- **Intensive Circus Workshops**
- **First-Class Resorts**

Atlantis vacations are designed for the way we enjoy ourselves today — Vacations at first-class resorts with an emphasis on friendship, community and camaraderie...places where you can always be yourself and always have fun. By popular request, we're back in the Caribbean in 1997, where you'll experience Turkoise, a complete Caribbean resort. For Sydney Gay Mardi Gras, we've added a private week at Daydream Island, right on the Great Barrier Reef. And you'll discover a new way to vacation at our very own Club Atlantis in Mexico this spring.

ATLANTIS
THE WAY WE PLAY.

We've added more sports, from scuba diving to intensive circus workshops, more destinations, exciting new entertainment and new lower prices. Atlantis was founded on a very simple principle — to create an exclusive, all-gay experience at some of the finest resorts in the world. We set high standards for ourselves and work only with well-recognized companies.

— 1997 —

Ja 18 - 25	Club Med Turkoise
Fe 24 - Mr 08	Sydney Mardi Gras
Ap 26 - Ma 03	Club Atlantis - Blue Bay Village, Mexico
Ma 03 - 10	Club Atlantis - Blue Bay Village, Mexico

Atlantis Events
9060 Santa Monica Blvd #310
West Hollywood, CA 90069 USA
(310) 281-5450, (800) 628-5268, Fax: (310) 281-5455.
♀♂ ◐

FERRARI GUIDES' GAY TRAVEL A to Z - 18th EDITION

WHO TO CALL

○ Retail (Call Direct) ● Wholesale (Travel Agent Must Contact)

TOUR COMPANY DETAILS

Big Five Tours

- **Soft Adventure Pioneer**
- **Travel in Utmost Comfort**
- **African Wildlife, Galapagos**
- **Antarctica, India & Nepal**
- **Peru, Chile and Costa Rica**
- **Pkgs & Personal Itineraries**

Big Five first opened its doors in Kenya in 1973, as a small African safari operation dedicated to introducing clients to the wonders of Africa whilst traveling in utmost comfort and style. Today, the gay-friendly company, which is entirely family-owned and -operated, remains a pioneer and a leader in the field of authentic soft adventure tours. Its name is derived from the famous African "Big Five" animals of the bygone hunting days: Leopard, Rhinoceros, Buffalo, Lion and Elephant.

Trips now include other exotic parts of the world, such as the Galapagos and Ecuador, Antarctica, Chile and Peru, India and Nepal, Costa and the Seychelles. In addition to its own established tour packages, Big Five designs and executes new and inventive programs for organizations and personalized itineraries for those not wishing to join a group. They report that they are constantly praised for tour quality and high standards, the personal service of on-site offices, the knowledgeable and accommodating guides, the price value of the tours and the intimate, unhurried nature of their in-depth itineraries.

Big Five Tours
819 S. Federal Hwy #103
Stuart, FL 34994 USA
(561) 287-7995, (800) 244-3483, Fax:(561) 287-5990, E-mail: bigfive@gate.net, Web: www.bigfive.com.
♀♂ ●

Cloud Canyon Backpacking

- **Women's Hiking Adventures**
- **Lighthearted & Easygoing**
- **Women of All Skills Welcome**
- **Groups of 6-8 Women All Ages**
- **Utah, Alaska, New Zealand**
- **Backpacking, Spiritual Quests**

Women of all skill levels are welcome. From the basics of loading and adjusting your backpack, to using a map and compass for cross-country route-finding, we will help you increase your level of self-confidence and enjoyment of the wilderness while viewing some of the world's most beautiful, untamed country. Groups are of 6-8 diverse and interesting women ranging in age from early 20s to mid 60s. Older women are welcome!

Cloud Canyon recognizes that everyone who goes into the wilderness goes on two trips, the inner trip and the outer trip. Every Cloud Canyon trip is a chance to explore the inner questions (like "Who am I?" "What are my true strengths?" What do I bring home to the rest of my life?") in a lighthearted, accepting, easygoing atmosphere.

— 1997 —

Mr 08 - 28	Backpacking in New Zealand
Jn 01 - 07	Backpacking in Utah
Jn 22 - 28	Backpacking in Utah
Ag 27 - Se 06	Backpacking in Alaska
Se 21 - 27	Backpacking in Utah
Se 29 - Oc 07	Backpacking in Utah

Cloud Canyon Backpacking
PO Box 41359
Santa Barbara, CA 93140 USA
(805) 969-0982, E-mail: areitz@silcom.com.
♀ ○

Colorado Women in the Wilderness

- **Women's Adventure Travel**
- **Hiking, Backpacking, Rafting**
- **Mountains, Canyon Country**
- **Ocean Island Healing Retreats**
- **Customized Group Trips**
- **Experienced Women Guides**

This program introduces women of all ages to the outdoor world in a supportive, non-competitive environment where participants can learn the basic skills needed to discover and explore the backcountry at their own pace.

If you are in reasonably good condition and have a sense of adventure, this program is designed for you. Options include hiking with llamas, backpacking the Colorado Trail and river rafting in Utah's canyon country. Each trip is designed to allow ample time to slow down into the rhythm of the wilderness, to listen to the voices of nature and to listen to each other and to oneself. Rita and Ulli are highly-experienced outdoor guides, and, beyond the regular program, they can design custom trips for families, moms and kids or for any group. If you are seeking a more challenging adventure, they can match a trip to your level of ability. We are also affiliated with the Southwest Institute for Women's Healing Journeys, which offers wilderness experiences on an island off the coast of Santa Barbara, California.

Colorado Women in the Wilderness
Box 399, Telluride, CO 81435 USA
(970) 728-4538.
♀ ◐

Wholesale/Retail (Call Direct or Have Travel Agent Contact)

WHO TO CALL

TOUR COMPANY DETAILS

Common Earth Adventures

- **Women's Adventure Travel**
- **Backpacking, Kayaking**
- **Skiing, Snow Camping**
- **Ropes Course**
- **Arizona, California & Alaska**
- **Sliding Scale Fee**

Common Earth is a non-profit, educational adventure program for women and youth. We offer a unique sliding-scale fee for each kayak, ropes course, backpack and cross-country ski trip. Common Earth opens the door to the natural world to a broader spectrum of women and youth-at-risk. Expert guides provide knowledge, a sense of humor, ecological awareness, and a safe environment in which participants can take risks.

— 1997 —

Mr 07 - 09	Sierra Ski & Snow Camping
Mr 17 - 22	Writing and Hiking-Death Valley
Ap 03 - 06	Singing & Hiking With Joanne Rand
Ap 18 - 20	Retreat for Women with Life Threatening Illnesses
Ap 18 - 27	Desert Women's Quest
Ma 16 - 18	Council of All Cultures
Ma 22 - 26	Spring Sierra Nevada Trek
Jy 24 - 27	Yosemite Skills Course
Ag 21 - 24	Writing & Hiking-Yosemite
Se 08 - 13	Trinity Alps Backpacking
Se 26 - Oc 05	Desert Women's Quest

Common Earth Adventures
PO Box 1191
Fairfax, CA 94978 USA
(415) 455-0646, Fax: (415) 454-3967.

Cruise World

- **Cruise/Tours Specialists**
- **England, Mediterranean**
- **Greece, the Aegean, Italy**
- **Day Trips Included**

As this book goes to press, *Cruise World* has two Cruise/Tours scheduled for 1997. An additional three or four will be scheduled by February, 1997. The company places gay groups on mainstream cruises.

A Week in London (Departs 9/1697) Seven-night theater package to London with escorted sightseeing and an all-day trip to Brighton with lunch. Optional tours available to Paris, Wales and Southern England. Gay escorts assigned to gay and lesbian groups.

Aegean & Mediterranean (10/10/97) Fifteen-night cruise tour. Air from US to Barcelona with deluxe hotel and 1/2-day city tour. Cruise on the Marco Polo to Cannes...Civitavecchia (Rome), Italy...Sorrento (Capri), Italy...Taormina, Sicily...Santorini, Greece...Piraeus (Athens)... Delos... Mykonos...Heraklion... Rhodes... Kusadasi (Ephesus) and Istanbul, Turkey. Two nights in Istanbul with half-day city tour. Price includes 3 hotel nghts, a 12-night cruise, transfers, baggage handling and the Captain's cocktail parties.

Cruise World
901 Fairview Ave # A-150
Seattle, WA 98109 USA
(206) 343-0221, (800) 340-0221, Fax:(206) 343-0771.

David's Trips and Tours

- **Budapest-Vienna-Prague**
- **Hungary & The Czech Rep.**
- **New Year's in South Africa**
- **Life Ball & Euro Pride**
- **Halloween Party - New Orleans**
- **Many Luxurious Extras**

David's Trips & Tour creates custom-designed tours for the discerning independent traveler who previously avoided group travel. Each tour is meticulously researched to assure affordable luxury and casual sophistication. Your vacation will have balance between planned activiites and free time. We rarely have early-morning departures, and most hotel stays last several nights. By inviting our

David's Trips and Tours

network of local friends to join us for cocktail and dinner parties, we create a unique international environment where our clients meet well-educated, English-speaking local people with diverse backgrounds, interests and careers.

Tours coincide with major international and special events to which our clients have pre-arranged access. Tours include exceptional guides, excellent, centrally-located hotels, many great meals with fine dining at "sought-after" spots, and many luxurious extras.

— 1997 —

Ma 03 - 18	Hungary-Austria & Czech Rep.
Jn 14 - 30	Hungary-Vienna, Czech Republic, Paris
Ag 16 - Se 01	Hungary, Vienna, The Czech Republic & Czech Spa
Oc 30 - No 02	New Orleans Halloween Parties
De 27 - Ja 11	New Year's In South Africa

David's Trips and Tours
310 Dahlia Place, Suite A
Corona del Mar, CA 92625-2821 USA
(714) 723-0699, Toll Free (888) 723-0699, Fax: (714) 723-0666, E-mail: davidtours@aol.com, Web: http://home.aol.com/davidtours.

FERRARI GUIDES' GAY TRAVEL A to Z - 18th EDITION

WHO TO CALL

○ Retail (Call Direct)　● Wholesale (Travel Agent Must Contact)

Destination World

- **Personalized Upscale Itineraries**
- **For Celebrity & Deluxe Market**
- **Chauffered Limo Transport**
- **Custom-Design Programs**
- **South Pacific, Europe, Asia**
- **Africa, South America**

Destination World is an Australian-owned and -operated tour wholesaler with a difference: We design itineraries for those who have been captivated by the extraordinary and will not rest until they experience it again. It is about the best in custom-designed programs from mid-range to deluxe, catering to independent travelers, groups and the incentive tour market, and the motto: "Treat Your Clients like Gold."

DESTINATION WORLD

Our aim is to create unique, personal experiences for our clients, so we pay particular attention to detail and creative tour design, treat each file with kid gloves and demand the same treatment from our local suppliers.

Besides the South Pacific, Destination World covers Europe, Asia, Africa and South America for the deluxe market. In these areas, transportation and touring is by chauffer-driven limousine. For our celebrity and political clients, we can, upon request, provide private planes, body guards, private chefs, etc.

Our associates throughout the world are constantly researching for unique products and services to add to our collection. They share our enthusiasm and relentless pursuit of hidden treasures. We provide a program way beyond their expectations.

Destination World
PO Box 1077
Santa Barbara, CA 93102 USA
(805) 569-9385, (800) 426-3644, Fax: (805) 569-3795, E-mail:
world@destinationworld.com.
♀♂ ●

Experience Plus

- **Bicycling & Walking Tours**
- **Gourmet & Culinary Tours**
- **Italy, France, Spain, Portugal**
- **Costa Rica, United States**
- **Guided and Self-Guided,**
- **Quality Lodgings**

Since 1972, Experience Plus! has delivered the best and most unique bicycling and walking vacations in the world. We offer tours throughout Europe, Costa Rica and the US, and are always adding new tours in exotic and beautiful locations...so you'll never get bored visiting the same places over and over.

Enjoy pasta-making lessons in Italy's Emilia-Romagna, explore the Provencal landscape of Van Gogh's France, or just relax beneath a palm tree in sunny Costa Rica. All tours feature quality lodging in comfortable, local-style inns, and gourmet meals. Guided, self-guided and custom tours are available. All feature use of a 21-speed hybrid or racing-style bicycle and a luggage shuttle to move your bags from inn to inn. Guided tours include a "sag" wagon to assist tired cyclists and hikers along the route.

Experience Plus will customize vacations for gay groups. Tours include: Bike Across Italy (Venice-Pisa), Italian Culinary Cycling Circus, Heart of Switzerland, (walking/hiking), Provençe, So. of France (cycling, walking), Costa Rica Butterflies & Beaches, (cycling/walking)

Experience Plus
1925 Wallenberg Dr
Ft Collins, CO 80526 USA
(970) 484-8489 (tel/fax), (800) 685-4565, E-mail: tours@xplus.com, Web: www.xplus.com.
♀♂ ◐

Fair Choices

- **Travel for Airline Employees**
- **Discount Travel Opportunities**
- **Gay/Lesbian Vacation Pkgs**
- **Major Hotel Properties**
- **Cruises, Tours, Resorts,**
- **Value-Added Packages**

Fair Choices specializes in vacation packages for gay and lesbian airline employees. The program features highly desirable vacation destinations like Cancun, Puerto Vallarta, Cabo San Lucas, Cozumel, St. Thomas, Jamaica, Puerto Rico, Hawaii, Montreal and many European destinations.

The operative word is "discounts." The company has formalized marketing agreements with several major hotel chains, including Intercontinental, Hyatt, Sheraton and Choice. These hotel chains, which own and operate hundreds of properties worldwide, will be promoted as "gay-friendly" establishments and offered to gays and lesbians for year-round individual and group travel.

Fair Choices has also developed vacation programs, including cruises, tours and special-event packages, working with gay-owned hotel properties and established gay-friendly tour operators. The company operates a frequent traveler program, provides "value-added" packages and encourages travel during off-season periods, when suppliers are likely to make their best rates available.

Fair Choices
1120 Capital of Texas Hwy South, Bldg 3 #300
Austin, TX 78746 USA
(512) 329-7260, Fax: (512) 329-7269, E-mail: jayjuba@inetport.com.
♀♂ ○

○ Wholesale/Retail (Call Direct or Have Travel Agent Contact)

WHO TO CALL

Frauen Unterwegs

- **Women-Only Vacations**
- **For German Speakers**
- **City Pkgs & Soft Adventure**
- **Europe, Eqypt, Africa**
- **Canoeing, Sailing, Hiking**
- **Biking, Skiing, Retreats**

Frauen Unterwegs, ("Women on the Move") is a German tour operator and one of the largest women tour operators in Europe. Established in 1984, we now yearly organize nearly two hundred women-only tours and trips. Our schedule lists a wide range of activiites for both winter and summer...city tours (for example Berlin, Paris, London, Rome,

FRAUEN UNTERWEGS

Prague) focusing on women's history and women's projects, as well as contryside vacations throughout Europe where we stay in women's inns and get in contact with local women.

We also offer workshops, language courses, sports and outdoor activities, such as camping, canoeing, sailing, hiking, biking, skiing.

Frauen Unterwegs calendar for 1997 does not appear in the calendar section, rather, it is provided in German below:

Mai

1-4	Weimar, Stadt der Frauen
7-11	Amsterdam, bunt und eigenwillig
7-21	Malta, matriarchats-Studienreise
10-19	Barcelona und Guara-Naturpark
14-21	La Palma, Wander- und Geniesserinnentour
16-20	Niederrhein, Massage-Workshop
16-20	Emsland, Kanuwandern u. Frauengeschichte
17-23	Holland, Schiffsreise mit Rad, Kanu
17-31	Griech, Inseln, Segeln im Mittelmeer
18-6/1	Andalusische Reise, Rundreise
24-6/7	Sardinien, Inselferien
25-31	Ostsee, Ausbildungstörn Segeln
28-6/1	Mecklenburg, Kanufahren
29-6/5	Glasgow/Edinburgh - Schottische Kontraste
31-6/14	Elba, Entspannung und Verwöhnung

Juni

7-14	Langeland, Inselferien
14-21	Piemont, Kurwoche
21-28	Äolische Inseln, Inselferien
21-7/5	Spanische Pyrenäen, Wandern
21-7/6	Schottland, Inselferien
21-7/12	Schweden, Mittsommersegeln
22-29	Rom— Römische Impressionen
26-7/6	New York, New York
27-7/12	Kanada, kanu und Kajak
29-7/6	Prag, Metropole zwischen Ost, West

Juli

3-17	Sierra Nevada, Wandern
4-6	Holland, Hausboot
5-12	Costa Dorada, Badeurlaun
6-16	Hohe Tatra, Wandern
6-20	Newfundland, Entdeckungsreise
10-13	Dresden, Mit dem Elbdampfer nach Meissen
12-19	Münsterland, Literarische Radkult(o)ur
12-19	Rügen, Segeln
12-27	Irland, Studienreise
13-26	Schweden, Segeln
14-18	Holland, Hausboot
18-22	Amsterdam, bunt und eigenwillig
18-25	Holland, Segeln
18-8/3	Schweden, Paddeln
19-26	Rügen, Segeln
19-8/2	Span.Pyrenäen, Höhenweg-Wanderung
20-26	Hiddensee, Inselurlaun
20-8/3	Island, Rundreise
21-25	Holland, Hausboot
25-8/1	Holland, Segeln und Massage
26-8/1	Hiddensee, Inselurlaun
26-8/3	London, ladies and ladies
26-8/3	Mecklenburg, Kanufahren
26-8/9	Insel Bornholm, Segeln
27-8/2	Worpswede, Weltdorf der Kunst
29-8/3	Emsland, Kanufahren für Frauen u. Kinder

August

2-9	Gardasee, Dolce Vita
2-9	Graubünden, Wanderstudienreise
2-16	Devon, Englisxh-Sprachkurs
2-17	Masuren, Radtouir
2-17	Schottland, Inselferien
7-10	Dreseden, Mit dem Elbdampfer nach Meissen
9-16	Toskana, Exkursion zum Tarotgarten
9-22	Finnland, Radeln und Paddeln
10-24	Neufundland, Entdeckungsreise
16-23	Rügen, Segeln
23-9/6	Spanische Pyrenäen, Wandern
29-9/5	Holland, Segeln
29-9/7	Saurland, Steinbildhauen
30-9/6	Rom, Römisch Impressionen
30-9/1	Südwestfrankreich, Französisch-Sprachkurs
31-9/13	Dänemark, Segeln

September

6-13	Harz, Wandern und Exkursionen
6-20	Malta, Matriarchats-Studienreise
7-14	Umbrien, Die schöne Unbekannte
7-21	Mallorca, Verwöhnung
7-21	Andalusische Reise, Rundreise
11-18	Zypern, Wandern
13-27	Sardinien, Inselferien
13-278	Devon, Englisch-Sprachkurs spezial
14-20	Ostsee, Segeln
15-24	Span. Pyrenäen, Tai Chi und Wandern
20-10/4	Elba, Wandern und Sonnegeniessen
20-10/4	Griech. Inseln, Segeln im Mittelmeer
26-10/5	Barcelona und Guara-naturpark
27-10/4	Piemont, Kulinaria
28-10/4	Ostsee, Ausbildungstörn Segeln
28-10/5	Glasgow/Edinburgh, Schottische Kontraste

Oktober

1-5	Niederrhein, Qigong-Workshop
2-5	Weimar, Stadt der Frauen
2-9	Zypern, Wandern
3-5	Berlin, Museumsführungen
3-8	Hiddensee, Inselurlaun
3-17	Stromboli, Inselferien
4-12	Wien, Facetten einer Stadt
4-18	Mallorca, Literatur und Wandern
4-18	Portugal, Entdeckungsreise Algarve
4-18	Griech. Inseln, Segeln im Mittelmeer
5-19	Sinai, Wandern in der Wüste
11-18	Venedig—das andere Vanedig
11-18	Krakau—Du Schöne!
11-18	Andalusien, Sonne, Meer und Palmen
12-18	Budapest, Bäderreise
13-17	Emsland, Frauenkloster
18-25	Föhr, Inselferien
18-25	Piemont, Kurwoche
18-25	Prag, Metropole zwischen Ost, West
19-26	Venedig—das andere Venedig
20-24	Emsland, Frauenkloster
22-29	La Palma, Wander- und Geniesserinnentour
23-30	Zypern, Wandern
26-11/1	Paris, Das künstlerische Schaffen von Frauen

November

1-15	Devon, Englisch-Sprachkurs spezial
2-16	Lanzarote, Badeurlaun
13-20	Zypern, Wandern
14-29	Senegal und Gambia, Frauen treffen Frauen
19-26	La Palma, Wander- und Geniesserinnentour

Frauen Unterwegs
Potsdamerstr 139
1028 BerlinGermany
(49 30) 215 1022, Fax: (49 30) 216 9852.
♀ ◐

TOUR COMPANY DETAILS

FERRARI GUIDES' GAY TRAVEL A to Z - 18th EDITION

WHO TO CALL

○ Retail (Call Direct)   ● Wholesale (Travel Agent Must Contact)

TOUR COMPANY DETAILS

Hanns Ebensten Travel

- Man Who Invented Gay Tours
- Renowned in the Industry
- Mostly Male-Only Tours
- Several Mixed Trips/Year
- Worldwide Destinations
- History, Culture, Archaeology

We are the world's leading operator of meaningful tours, cruises and expeditions for men, which have, since 1972, attracted participants from all over North America and from other continents, who enjoy traveling together and seeing interesting places in congenial company under expert guidance. Many of our valued clients have traveled with us more than a dozen times, some of them three or four times a year; and an annual tour, cruise, or expedition with us has become an enriching and rewarding part of their lives. All of them appreciate the advantages of traveling in comfort and style with a well-informed organization.

Some of our tour members are in their twenties, but most are around 30 to 50 — successful men at the top of their professions who live up to our high standards, just as we live up to theirs. All our travel programs are accompanied by knowledgeable leaders and "The Advocate" neatly summed up what we do when it described our "decidedly refined adventures" as being "synonymous with quality in the field of gay travel."

— 1997 —
Ma 31 - Jn 14   Islands of Indonesia
Jn 26 - Jy 05   Great Amazon Adventure Cruise
Ag 14 - 23   Cruise the Galapagos Islands in Style
Ag 31 - Se 14   Sailing Cruise in Turkey
Se 14 - 28   Expedition to Vilcabamba
Oc 27 - No 07   Expedition to Easter Island
Oc 27 - No 07   Expedition to Easter Island
De 18 - 27   Christmas in Marrakech

Hanns Ebensten Travel
513 Fleming St
Key West, FL 33040 USA
(305) 294-8174, Fax: (305) 292-9665.
♂ ◐

Hellkamp Reisen

- Worldwide Gay Itineraries
- City Pkgs & Men's Resorts
- Europe, US, Caribbean, Canada
- Ibiza, Mykonos, Key West
- Berlin, London, Toronto, Miami
- Rome, SF, Prague, Montreal

A full line of gay itineraries to destiinations in Europe, North America, Asia and the Caribbean. While the brochures are in German, Hellkamp is fully equipped to assist English-speaking travelers. A description of the New York City package from their brochure (in German) follows:

New York New York
Berühmt-berüchtigt und immer wieder faszinierend. Erleben Sie eine Weltstadt mit Ihrem faszinierend *Reiseziele für Gays* vielfältigen Angebot. Lassen Sie sich einfach treiben, inspiriert von der quirligen Atmosphäre des "Big Apple." Das hervorragende U-Bahn-Netz ermöglicht Ihnen ausserdem, Ihre ganz individuellen Wünsche zu planen: 5th Avenue, Museen, Musicals, "MET," Restaurants — was auch immer Sie suchen: Sie werden es finden.

Mit den Reiseunterlagen erhalten Sie einen Reiseführer, der zahlreiche Tips enthält. Unsere Mitarbeiter kennen die Stadt fast alle persönlich, so können wir Ihnen beste Beratung garantieren. Durch unseren INTERNET-Zugang zur offiziellen Datenbank des Fremdenverkehrsamts von New York können wir Ihnen auch spezielle Fragen beantworten.

Hellkamp Reisen
Hellkamp 17
Hamburg 20255 Germany
(49-40) 491 9054, Fax: (49 40) 491 9100, E-mail: hellkamp@aol.com, Web: www.gaytravel.do.
♂ ◐

Holigays

- Worldwide Gay Tours, Pkgs
- Exclusively Gay & Lesbian
- Europe, USA, Australia
- Africa, Central America,
- Comprehensive Color Brochure
- Pink Cruise—Greece Oct '97

Holigays offers travel packages throughout the world. The fantastic full-color brochure 1997 includes Gran Canaria, Ibiza, Mallorca, Sitges, Portugal, Mykonos, Zandvoort, Brighton, Amsterdam, London, Paris, Madrid, Barcelona, Nice, Prague, Berlin, Frankfurt, Munich, Cologne, Vienna, Copenhagen. We also offer a great variety of superb

holigays
weltweit reisen

gay and gay-friendly hotels throughout the USA (Miami Beach, Ft. Lauderdale, Key West, New York, San Francisco, Los Angeles, San Diego and New Orleans). Special packages to Mexico, Costa Rica, Puerto Rico, Australia, Bali and South Africa are also available.

— 1997 —
September   Twelve Gods Party Packages
October   South Africa Tour
Oc 17 - 27 Pink Cruise (Venice-Greek Isles)

— 1998 —
February   Sydney Mardi Gras Package

Holigays
Schwalbengasse 46
Cologne 50667 Germany
(49-221) 925 891 13, Fax: (49-221) 257 69 43. US address: 14 Dartmouth St, Malden, MA 02148, (617) 321-6100.
⚥ ●

Wholesale/Retail (Call Direct or Have Travel Agent Contact)　　　　　　　　　**WHO TO CALL**

TOUR COMPANY DETAILS

JUST ASK JORNADA

Jornada is Australia's largest gay and lesbian international travel company. Our innovative and responsive approach has made us a market leader. We specialise in tailoring individual and group packages to Australia, the South Pacific and Asia at very competitive prices.

JORNADA

Phone 61 2 9362 0900　　Fax 61 2 9362 0788
EMAIL sales@jornada.com.au
Commission payable to agents. AFTA & IATA member.
LEVEL 1, 53 CROSS STREET, DOUBLE BAY, SYDNEY, NSW 2028 AUSTRALIA

aglta — australian gay & lesbian tourism association

MEMBER IGTA — INTERNATIONAL • GAY • TRAVEL • ASSOCIATION

Indulgent Vacations for Men

Club Hommes™

Paris & *LeCordonBleu l'Art Culinaire* • Silversea Voyages • New Year's on Maui • 1998 Amsterdam GayGames Rhine River Cruise • The Vineyards of Châteauneuf-du-Pape • The Rainbow Golf Classic™ on Miami Beach • The Lesser Antilles • Costa Rica • China • The Galapagos Islands • St. Barthélémy • The Millenium

224 West 4th Street NYC 10014
212/206-6900 • 800/429-6969
club@worldguest.com
www.worldguest.com/club

IGTA
we're a proud member of the
international Gay Travel Association

FERRARI GUIDES' GAY TRAVEL A to Z - 18th EDITION

WHO TO CALL

○ Retail (Call Direct) ● Wholesale (Travel Agent Must Contact)

TOUR COMPANY DETAILS

IMTC, Inc.

- European Land Packages
- Atlanta, Amst'dam, Vienna Offices
- Superior, 1st Class, Deluxe Hotels
- Gay Games '97 Packages
- Personal Assistance on the Spot
- Independent Travel Itineraries

IMTC is a wholesale travel company, with offices in Atlanta, Amsterdam, and Vienna, offering outstanding net rates in superior tourist, first-class, and deluxe hotels throughout Europe as well as tailor-made group itineraries and special FIT packages.

"The Amsterdam Way:" 3-night land-only package includes superior tourist class hotel, gay welcome gift, canal cruise, daily breakfast buffet, service charges, taxes ($269 pp, double occ. ref: #AW1).

"Deluxe Benelux" ($599 pp, double occ) 5-day unlimited railpass in Benelux, 5-nights at Sofitel Hotel, The Hague, one dinner, welcome gift, coupons valued at $50, daily breakfast buffet, service charges, and taxes (ref: DB2).

Gay-exclusive guided deluxe tours in Portugal's wine and cheese country. For the 1998 Gay Games in Amsterdam, now is the time for you to start making arrangements to attend. With offices in both the United States and Amsterdam, we are the one wholesaler that can handle all your requests. You can count on *IMTC's* friendly and reliable staff — in Atlanta for information and reservations, and in Europe with personal assistance on the spot. We are your gay Europe and Gay Games experts.

IMTC, Inc.
3025 Maple Drive #5
Atlanta, GA 30305 USA
(404) 240-0949, (800) 790-4682, Fax: (404) 240-0948, E-mail: imtc@mindspring.com.
♀♂ ●

Jornada

- Australia's Largest Gay Travel Co.
- Worldwide Tours, Cruises
- Hotel & Resort Packages
- Custom Independent Travel
- Australia, NZ, S Pacific, USA
- Europe, Thailand, Bali

Innovative Travel—Jornada is Australia's largest gay and lesbian international travel company. Our "Unique Journeys" collection of tours cruises, hotels and resorts are especially chosen for gay and lesbian travellers. We have spent a great deal of time researching each tour and cruise, and have personally chosen each and every hotel in our programme. From charming gay hotels to gay-friendly hotels worldwide, you will discover a wide range of boutique hotels where a genuinely open and warm welcome awaits you.

We specialize in tailoring individual, special-interest and group packages to Australia, the South Pacific and Asia at very competitive prices. Jornada is also the Australian/South Pacific sales agent for Our Family Abroad. The friendly team at Jornada has many years experience in the travel industry and is proud of its reputation as Australia's foremost provider of gay and lesbian travel services. Let us show you the wonders of Australia and the South Pacific.

— 1997 —
ALL Departing From Australia

June	Euro Pride Pkg
June	Los Angeles Pride Pkg
June	New York Pride Pkg
June	San Francisco Pride Pkg
July	London Pride Pkg
September	Folsom St. Fair Pkg
October	Castro St Fair Pkg
October	Sydney Sleaze Ball Pkg

Jornada
Level 1, 53 Cross St
Double Bay, NSW 2028 Australia
(61 2) 9362 0900, Fax: (61 2) 9362 0788, E-mail: justask@jornada.com.au.
♀♂ ○ (See Ad on Page 93)

L'Arc en Ciel Voyages

- Gay Games Preferred Agent
- Custom-Designed Group Travel
- 36+ Years Experience
- Special-Interest Tours
- Incentive Travel & Seminars
- Design Your Own Group Trip

Our experienced staff can custom-design the right trip for your gay and lesbian group. It's easy to form your own group tour! (Are you active in MCC or Dignity? Organize a trip to the Holyland). Your travel adventures are limited only by your imagination! The first company appointed a Preferred Sales Agent for Gay Games Amsterdam and the first to make registration available, we are the only company offering guaranteed prices and free insurance to early registrants—Register in 1997 and pay 1997 prices, saving hundreds of dollars. Our credentials are impeccable and we're known throughout the industry. Individuals can join any of our scheduled departures, and in some cases, we can design custom individual travel. We're only a phonecall away, toll-free.

— 1997 —

Ap 01 - 15	Steps of St. Paul, Turkey
Ap 25 - Ma 03	Queen's Day Tulip Festival - Amsterdam
Ma 13 - 20	Berlin Gay Pride 100th Anniversary
Jn 02 - 12	World War II European History
Jn 17 - 24	Eurogames 1997
Jn 25 - 29	Nordic Gay Pride
Jn 26 - 30	Euro Pride 1997
Jy 11 - 15	Bastille Day in Paris
Ag 17 - 24	Five-Country Land Cruise
Oc 01 - 05	Ladies-Only Hike, Swim, Spa Adventure
De 04 - 10	Christmas Shopping in London

— 1998 —

Ag 01 - 08	Gay Games in Amsterdam

L'Arc en Ciel Voyages
PO Box 234, Wayne, PA 19087-0234 USA
(610) 964-7888, (800) 965-LARC (5272), Fax: (610) 964-8220. E-mail:larc@galaxytours.com.
♀♂ ●

○ Wholesale/Retail (Call Direct or Have Travel Agent Contact)

WHO TO CALL

TOUR COMPANY DETAILS

L'Arc en Ciel™ Voyages
presents
CUSTOM-DESIGNED TOUR PROGRAMS
for the
GAY & LESBIAN COMMUNITY

*Four Decades of international, group travel experience in 100 nations
*Personalization of all tour programs, to incorporate unique interests & desires of tour members
*Both *group & individual* travel programs
*All tours *fully escorted* insuring VIP treatment & worry-free travel
*Exclusive Time-Payment Plan for long-term travel purchases including <u>free</u> insurance!
*Donations made to AIDS-related organizations for all passengers!
*Travel as Fundraising opportunities for all types of groups (MCCs, PFLAGS, sports teams & more!)

Unique gay & lesbian travel <u>opportunities such as our:</u>
5-country European "land cruise"
World War II History Tour
Murder-Mystery Tour
Nordic Gay Pride
Ladies Only Spa Package
Queens Day & Tulip Time
Christian Pilgrimages

Both scheduled departures & custom-designed programs available!

The 1998 Amsterdam Gay Games

- First appointed Preferred Sales Agent for the Games
- First to offer pre-registration for the Games
- Only company to offer Guaranteed Prices & Free Insurance
- Only company to offer fund-raising assistance to Teams!
- All-inclusive packages available for participants <u>and</u> spectators!

<u>EXCLUSIVE GAY BERLIN PACKAGE</u>
Developed in cooperation with the city of Berlin and the German National Tourist Office! Includes special prices & travel opportunities! Ask for details!

U.S. REPRESENTATIVE FOR THE ONLY <u>GAY BED & BREAKFAST IN ICELAND!</u>
A delightful country with cheerful citizens and partnership laws in force! A must-see for any gay or lesbian traveller!

We're here to fill all your travel needs!
Call us, toll-free, at 1-800-965-LARC

FERRARI GUIDES' GAY TRAVEL A to Z - 18th EDITION

WHO TO CALL

○ Retail (Call Direct) ● Wholesale (Travel Agent Must Contact)

TOUR COMPANY DETAILS

London Handling Ltd.

- **London, Britain Specialists**
- **Complete Gay/Lesb Programs**
- **Computerized Reservations**
- **Hotels from 2 to 5 Stars**
- **Conference Programs**

Five Nights in London Gay & Lesbian Group Itinerary. We can customize ANY itinerary to Britain.

Day 1 —
Arrival at Airport. Time to check out Soho and the Pink Village.

Day 2 —
Morning sightseeing at the Houses of Parliament, westminster Abbey, Changing of the Guard outside Buckingham Palace. Afternoon free for shopping. Dinner in an Earls Court gay restaurant, then Soho and a cabaret evening at Madame Jo Jo's.

Day 3 —
Continental breakfast. A 3-hour cruise on the Thames, including lunch and a unique view of London's most famous landmarks. Afternoon visit to the Tower of London and Crown Jewels. Evening: Seats at a top musical or drama.

Day 4 —
Continental breakfast. A day in Brighton, Britain's popular gay seaside resort (1-hour by train). Brighton's Royal Pavilion, shops in the "Lanes," strolling the sea front, lunch in one of Brighton's best restaurants, afternoon free to explore gay-friendly pubs and coffee shops. Return by evening train.

Day 5 —
Continental breakfast. The day free to explore London at your own pace.

Day 6 —
Continental breakfast. Departure.

London Handling Ltd.
12 Kendrick Mews
London SW7 3HG England
(44 171) 589-2212, Fax: (44 171) 225-1033.
♀♂ ●

Mariah Wilderness Exp.

- **Women-Owned Rafting Co.**
- **Pioneered Women's Rafting**
- **High-Quality Adventure Travel**
- **Sea Kayaking in Baja Mexico**
- **Costa Rica Rafting, Kayaking**
- **Rafting Many American Rivers**

Gay and lesbian and women's whitewater rafting on California, Idaho, Oregon and Utah rivers. We are proud that we pioneered whitewater rafting trips for women 16 years ago, helping this sport become a popular activity for all women, regardless of age or degree of experience. As women continue to exercise their rights to seek more purposeful travel, and experience more outdoor adventures that are unusual and exotic, we have sought to remain on the cutting edge of providing the discerning traveler with a high-quality adventure travel experience. Owners Donna Hunter and Nancy Byrnes bring a wealth of outdoor, people-oriented experiences to Mariah. So please be our guest and join us.

— 1997 —

Ap 26 - 27	Rafting S. Fork Amer. R., Calif
Ma 09	Rafting Merced R., Calif
Ma 10 - 11	Raft Kings R., California
Ma 23	Raft the Merced R., California
Jn 14 - 15	Raft American R., California
Jn 25 - 30	Raft Main Salmon R., Idaho
Jn 27 - 28	Rafting S & Mid. Fork, Amer. R.
Jn 28 - Jy 06	Costa Rica Adventure, Raft, Kayak, Bike
Jy 19 - 20	Rafting S. Fork Amer. R., Calif
Jy 19 - 22	Raft Rogue R., Oregon
Ag 03 - 05	Raft Tuolumne R., California
Ag 11 - 14	Raft Green R., Utah
Ag 22 - 24	Raft Mid. Fork Amer. R.
Ag 29 - 30	Raft Mid. Fork, Amer. R., Calif.
No 01 - 11	Costa Rica Raft, Sea Kayak, Beaches
De 26 - Ja 06	Sea of Cortez Baja Sea Kayaking

Mariah Wilderness Expeditions
PO Box 248
Point Richmond, CA 94807 USA
(510) 233-2303, (800) 462-7424, Fax: (510) 233-0956, E-mail: rafting@mariahwe.com, Web: www.mariahwe.com.
♀♂ ◐

Men on Vacation

- **Gay Games Amsterdam Pkgs**
- **12 Gods Party Pkgs (Mykonos)**
- **Sydney Gay Mardi Gras**
- **Gay Pride Packages-NY, SF, LA**
- **Man Friday Resort Pkgs (Fiji)**
- **Euro Pride Paris**

Men On Vacation is known throughout the gay and lesbian community for its travel packages to the South Pacific. Many tour packages involve important gay party events like the 12 Gods Party or Sydney Gay Mardi Gras or Gay Pride events in large cities, such as New York. Men On Vacation has been named an official American tour operator for Gay Games Amsterdam, which will take place in August, 1998.

— 1997 —

Fe 13 - 24	Ultimate New Zealand Adv. Tour
Fe 19 - 24	Hero the Party-New Zealand
Fe 21 - Mr 03	Sydney Gay Mardi Gras
Mr 03 - 05	Post-Mardi Gras Rock, Reef, Rainforest
Mr 05 - 08	Barrier Reef Recovery-After Syd Mardi Gras
Mr 08 - 09	Fitzroy Fantasy-1st Annual Bash
June	Los Angeles Gay Pride Pkgs
June	New York Gay Pride Pkgs
June	San Francisco Gay Pride Pkgs
Jn 06 - 09	Gay Day in Orlando
Jn 21 - 28	EuroPride Paris
September	12 Gods Party Pkgs (Mykonos)
December	New Year's Downunder

— 1998 —

January	Melbourne Midsumma Fest, Red Raw Dance
August	Gay Games Amsterdam Pkgs

Men on Vacation
4715 30th St #6
San Diego, CA 92116 USA
(619) 641-7085, (800) 959-4636, Fax: (619) 641-7088, special Gay Games line: (800) 854-7688, E-mail: MenOnVacat@aol.com.
♂ ●

WHO TO CALL

North American Travel Specialists

- **USA & Canada ONLY!**
- **Custom Independent Itineraries**
- **Gay, Gay-Friendly Properties**
- **From One Night to Many**
- **Supplier to the Industry**
- **Buying Power = Big Discounts**

North American Travel Specialists are Australia's leading fully-independent travel wholesaler, with more than 3,000 hotels and resorts, rental cars, bus tours, sightseeing trips, whitewater rafting trips, adventure holidays and other products throughout the USA and Canada. We do not offer pre-packaged holidays. Our strength lies in the way we tailor-make exactly the holiday the client wants, whether it's just one night in one hotel, or a complete itinerary for 4 weeks. We handle ONLY the US and Canada, and our buying power is second to none, allowing us to pass savings of 30-50% on to our clients.

Whilst we do not have any exclusively gay and lesbian travel packages, we have an experienced staff ready, willing and able to help our gay and lesbian clients create the holiday they want. Our network of contacts in North America gives us access to gay and gay-friendly hotels and resorts throughout the US and Canada, and our membership with the International Gay Travel Assn (IGTA), allows us contact with a wide range of gay and gay-friendly travel products.

North American Travel Specialists
Suite 1, 478 High Street
Maitland, NSW 2320 Australia
(61 49) 342 088, Fax: (61 49) 347 522.

♀♂ ☽

Ocean Voyager

- **Passionate About Cruising!**
- **Hosted Gay Group Cruises**
- **Mainstream Cruise Lines**
- **Popular Gay Destinations**
- **Caribbean, Alaska, Atlantic**
- **Greek Islands & Turkey**

Our groups, both escorted and non-escorted, sail on a variety of well-known cruise lines to stimulating destinations throughout the year. Our cruises are not all-gay charters. Our concept is to provide the gay traveler with the company of other gay men and women aboard the highest quality ships, featuring fine dining, spacious accommodations, elegant surroundings and gracious service. We choose the most interesting and exciting itineraries that include destinations popoular with gay travelers. Our groups are small and intimate, so that we can get to know each other quickly. This way, from the first day, we can share the special moments that only a cruise vacation can offer!

Contact Ocean Voyager at (305) 379-5722, (800) 435-2531, Fax: (305) 379-4417.

— 1997 —

Mr 15 - 22	Eastern Caribbean Cruise
Ma 24 - 31	East Caribbean Cruise
Jy 11 - 18	Alaska Cruise on the Rotterdam
Se 01 - 10	Transatlantic Crossing on the Norway
Oc 06 - 18	Greek Isles & Turkey Cruise
No 22 - 29	South Caribbean Cruise on the Galaxy
De 20 - 27	West Caribbean/Central America Xmas Cruise
De 20 - Ja 02	Christmas/New Years Caribbean Cruise
De 27 - Ja 02	Christmas/New Years Caribbean Cruise

Ocean Voyager
1717 N Bayshore Drive #3246
Miami, FL 33132-1167 USA
(305) 379-5722, (800) 435-2531, Fax: (305) 379-4417.

♀♂ ☽

Off the Map

- **Custom Group, Individual Tours**
- **Europe, Russia, South Pacific**
- **Partial & Whole Boat Charters**
- **Regional Destination Experts**
- **Group & Individual Travel**
- **You Imagine it, We Create It!**

Off the Map specializes in creative custom group and individual tours to all of Europe, Russia and the South Pacific. Ours are more than the standard variety of sightseeing tours. Our staff consists of regional experts with over 125 years of combined professional experience. We **know** our destinations and are able to assist you in experiencing the true character of these destinations and their people. We offer accommodations at unusual properties and tours crafted to your desires. Travel agents use us, a division of Legend Tours, with complete confidence.

The world is big and wide with untold travel experiences to choose from...Perhaps you're interested in a walking tour of England's beautiful Cotswolds area, a tour of the manor houses of Britain, kayaking the islands of Fiji, luxuriating in a spa town in Tuscany, feasting on a wine or food tour of Provence, cycling in Ireland, taking the wilderness train in Sweden, exploring the fjords of Norway, camping in Australia. Our answer is, "If you can imagine it, we can create it!"

Off the Map
3990 Old Town Ave #100-C
San Diego, CA 92110 USA
(619) 293-7096, (800) 633-8436, Fax: (619) 293-7026, E-mail: fish@offthemap.com, Web: www.offthemap.com.

♀♂ ☽

TOUR COMPANY DETAILS

FERRARI GUIDES' GAY TRAVEL A to Z - 18th EDITION

WHO TO CALL

○ Retail (Call Direct) ● Wholesale (Travel Agent Must Contact)

TOUR COMPANY DETAILS

Olivia Cruises & Resorts

- **Redefining Women's Vacations**
- **Since 1990**
- **Largest US Women's Travel Co.**
- **Caribbean, Greece, Alaska**
- **Women's Entertainers**
- **Adventure, Luxury, Romance**

For the past 7 years, *Olivia*, the largest US women's travel company, has been designing and redefining vacations for women. We've taken more than 12,000 women on vacations to locations like the Caribbean, Alaska, Greece, the Riviera, the Galapagos, Canada, the Bahamas, and Mexico.

We charter entire cruise ships and resorts to ensure your privacy and comfort. This most important ingredient guarantees you a vacation where you are free to be yourself. We provide an exceptional level of service. Even the entertainment is special! World-class entertainers join us on every vacation to complete the customization of your travel experience.

One of our previous travelers said: "Thank you so much for what you do. You have created a way for lesbians, like myself, to travel with other women in an environment that is safe and caring. With Olivia, I can see the most exciting places in the world, meet other fabulous women, and be fully who I am. There's nothing else like you, Olivia!" — Laura, Illinois.

— 1997 —
Ap 14 - 21	Mexican Caribbean Cruise
Jy 04 - 11	Greek Isles/Turkey Cruise
Oc 25 - No 01	Club Med Huatulco, Mexico
De 13 - 20	Hawaii Cruise

— 1998 —
Fe 14 - 21	Costa Rica Cruise
Ap 12 - 19	Eastern Caribbean Cruise

Olivia Cruises & Resorts
4400 Market St, Oakland, CA 94608 USA
(510) 655-0364, (800) 631-6347, Fax: (510) 655-4334. E-mail: olivia@eor.com.
Web: www.oliviatravel.com.

♀ ☽

Our Family Abroad

- **Global Gay /Lesbian Touring**
- **Best of Europe, Asia, Africa**
- **Stay in First-Class Hotels**
- **Escorted by Talented Guides**
- **Gay-Owned & -Operated**
- **EuroPride 1997 in Paris**

Congenial companionship. It's what makes the difference between an ordinary trip and a great vacation. *Our Family Abroad*, gay-owned and -operated, will show you the best of Europe, Asia, Africa including Egypt and Morocco, the Caribbean and Latin America and Alaska escorted by the most talented guides, staying in first-class hotels, all in the relaxed company of fellow travelers who share a similar lifestyle. Celebrate Europride '97 in Paris. Experience the glories of Ancient Egypt. See the scenic wonders of Alaska, including Glacier Bay and the Inside Passage cruise. Let us show you Bangkok, Singapore, Bali and Hong Kong on our Southeast Asia tour. Travel the trail of the Incas from Bolivia and through Peru. Let India cast its spell. Or explore Europe on one of our single- or multi-country tours. Your money is safe with Our Family Abroad. Most of our tours are operated by members of the United States Tour Operators Assn (USTOA) who participate in the USTOA $1 Million Consumer Protection Plan. In addition, all tours are covered by Our Family Abroad's $1 million professional liability insurance. What's more, you won't pay one penny more for the privilege of traveling in our uniquely gay-friendly environment. Travel with Our Family Abroad just once, and you'll come back again and again.

— 1997 —
Fe 09 - 16	Carnival in Las Palmas
Mr 14 - 25	Ancient Egypt
Ap 26 - Ma 03	Morocco With Our Family Abroad
Ma 24 - 31	Moscow and St. Petersburg
Jn 21 - Ag 04	Imperial Capitals
Jn 24 - 30	EuroPride '97 in Paris Tour
Jn 27 - Jy 11	Italian Holiday-Our Family Abroad
Jn 28 - Jy 13	European Panorama
Jy 01 - 12	Classical Greece & Turkey
Jy 09 - 15	Bastille Day in Paris
Jy 12 - 21	England, Scotland & Wales
Jy 22 - Ag 03	Spain Tour with Our Family Abroad
Jy 23 - 31	Alaska & Inside Passage Cruise
Ag 02 - 17	Scandinavia & Russia Cruise
Ag 09 - 24	European Panorama
Ag 23 - Se 02	Legacy of the Incas
Ag 23 - Se 05	Imperial Capitals
Ag 26 - Se 06	Classical Greece & Turkey
Se 06 - 15	England, Scotland & Wales
Se 12 - 25	Italian Holiday-Our Family Abroad
Se 19 - 28	Turkey With Our Family Abroad
Se 20 - Oc 03	Germany With Our Family Abroad
Se 20 - Oc 03	Imperial Capitals
Se 20 - Oc 05	European Panorama
Oc 12 - 28	South East Asia
Oc 14 - 25	Classical Greece & Turkey
Oc 14 - 26	Spain Tour with Our Family Abroad
Oc 17 - 27	Ancient Egypt
Oc 17 - 30	Italian Holiday-Out Family Abroad
Oc 25 - No 01	Morocco With Our Family Abroad
No 07 - 17	Ancient Egypt
No 08 - 16	Yucatan & Mexico City
No 15 - 30	Kenya & Tanzania Safari
No 21 - De 01	Ancient Egypt
No 24 - De 03	Caribbean Explorer
De 19 - 29	Ancient Egypt

— 1998 —
Ja 19 - 28	Caribbean Explorer
Ja 25 - Fe 08	India & Nepal
Ja 31 - Fe 08	Yucatan & Mexico City
Fe 14 - Mr 01	Kenya & Tanzania Safari
Fe 22 - Mr 01	Carnival in Las Palmas

Our Family Abroad
40 W 57th St, #430
New York, NY 10019-4001 USA
(212) 459-1800, (800) 999-5500, Fax: (212) 581-3756.

♀♂ ☽

FERRARI GUIDES' GAY TRAVEL A to Z - 18th EDITION

◐ Wholesale/Retail (Call Direct or Have Travel Agent Contact)

WHO TO CALL

TOUR COMPANY DETAILS

Paddling South & Saddling South

- Sea Kayaking & Horse Packing
- In Baja California, Mexico
- Mixed & Women-Only Trips
- Ride Horses to Remote Ranches
- Local Culture & Folklore
- No Experience Necessary

Paddling South began running kayak tours in the early '80s. Our trips offer wilderness adventure and close cultural contact with friends and families in the areas we visit. An afternoon hike to Chita's palm-thatched kitchen to make tortillas, or sharing a cup of campfire coffee with panga fishermen, is often a highlight for guests. Our 8- to 10-day trips will introduce you to basic skills used in Baja-style touring. No previous kayaking experience is necessary. Most days, we kayak 5-10 miles to one of many beautiful beaches. After setting up camp, we explore wilderness beaches and canyons before ending the trip at a small fishing village and remote roadhead. Private groups scheduling dates in advance can request any area and length of trip.

Get to know the real Baja, Mexico by horse and mule. In November, we ride to ranches and cave paintings in the foothills of the Sierra de Guadalupe...in December, to the San Javier historical festival...in spring, we visit a sugarcane candymaking village or climb the highest peak in central Baja for a spectacular view of both coasts. Local culture and folklore highlight our days of riding and the wonderful miles of unfenced desert landscapes we enjoy.

— 1997 —
Mr 02 - 09   Sea Kayaking in Baja, Mexico
Mr 30 - Ap 06 Sea Kayaking in Baja, Mexico
Ma 04 - 11   Sea Kayaking in Baja, Mexico

Paddling South & Saddling South
4510 Silverado Tr
Calistoga, CA 94515 USA
Tel/Fax: (707) 942-4550.
♀♂ ◐

Pearl Selections/Welcome Abroad

- Gay & Lesbian Vacation Pkgs
- Dedicated to Low Prices
- All the Gay European Resorts
- US Beach Vacation Cities
- Cruises, Skiing and More
- Call "Res" Hotline for Prices

Pearl Selections is a division of Welcome Abroad Travel, a well-established England-based gay travel company. Our main objective is to offer you the lowest possible prices. We try every possible way to reduce your holiday costs and, as we don't spend your money on producing expensive brochures, we can offer you even better deals! Holiday prices fluctuate frequently, therefore confirmed prices are absent from our brochure, so we can offer you the most up-to-date special-offer prices. Once you have chosen your destination and accommodation, simply call our reservations hotline for the current cost. All accommodations featured are either gay-exclusive or gay-friendly. Our production team is constantly busy finding new destinations and accommodations worldwide. Unlike others, we don't prepackage your holiday. We tailor it to allow you to choose when and how you wish to travel. We ahve access to hundreds of tour operators an airlines and can even book the most complicated round-the-world itinerary.

Current Destinations: Amsterdam, Paris, Copenhagen, Berlin, New York, Toronto, Barcelona, Majorca, Ibiza, Algarve, Gran Canaria, Sitges, San Francisco, Palm Springs, Honolulu, Miami, Key West, Ft Lauderdale, Thailand, Sydney, Perth, Cairns, Mykonos, Lesbos, Nice, Spain, cruises, skiing and more.

Pearl Selections/Welcome Abroad
121 Kirby Rd
Leicester LE3 6BE England
(44-116) 233 7555, (44-116) 233 6655, Fax: (44-116) 233 6660
♀♂ ○

Progressive Travels

- G & L Active Adventures
- Adventure Travel Worldwide
- Gay-Owned & -Operated
- Bicycling, Cruises, Walking
- Hike, Raft, Cooking School
- Europe, N. America, Thailand

This year marks the first year that Progressive Travels has a brochure of tours and destinations specifically for our gay and lesbian clients. Progressive Travels is not new to gay travel and certainly not new to adventure travel. Gay-owned and -operated, Progressive Travels has operated active vacations since 1984. Since we began featuring them in 1991, many have experienced our gay and lesbian adventures, which have included bicycle tours in Provence, Dordogne and Tuscany, a cruise through the Panama Canal and a yachting voyage along Turkey's Turquoise Coast. The Gay and Lesbian Active Adventures for 1997 are designed to appeal to different interests and are offered at various times of the calendar year.

— 1997 —
Ma 28 - Jn 03 Walking tour of Burgundy, France
Jn 19 - 25   Bicycling Tour of Provençe, France
Jy 02 - 12   Istanbul & Yachting Turkey's Turquoise Coast
Jy 20 - 26   Walking Tour of Olympic Peninsula, WA
Se 07 - 13   Walking Tour of Burgundy, France
Oc 01 - 11   Istanbul & Yachting Turkey's Turquoise Coast
No 05 - 18   Cooking School, Elephant Trek, Rafting-Thailand

— 1998 —
Fe 10 - 22   Cooking School, Elephant Trek, Rafting-Thailand

Progressive Travels
224 W Galer #C
Seattle, WA 98119 USA
(206) 285-1987, (800) 245-2229, Fax: (206) 285-1988, E-mail: progressivetravel@aol.com, Web: www.progressivetravels.com.
♀♂ ◐

FERRARI GUIDES' GAY TRAVEL A to Z - 18th EDITION

WHO TO CALL

○ Retail (Call Direct) ● Wholesale (Travel Agent Must Contact)

TOUR COMPANY DETAILS

R&S Travel

- Gay German Tour Company
- Thailand, Malaysia, Hong Kong, Bali
- Philippinen, Mallorca, Ibiza, Gran Canaria
- Mykonos, London, Paris, und und und
- New York, Florida, California, Las Vegas
- Hawaii, Mexico, Dom. Republik,

R&S Travel has one of the largest, most comprehensive gay travel brochures including hundreds of itineraries. Their program involves gay men's vacations, mostly in warm places, with city tours to the capitals of Europe and New York City, and is geared toward the German-speaking market, with a brochure entirely in German. They can book non-German speakers on any of their itineraries, though communication will not be the smoothest for English speakers. Excerpts from the brochure (in German) follow:

R&S Das können wir für Sie tun

Sie wollen mal raus aus dem Altagstrott - etwas anderes sehen, Horizonte erweitern, Aufregendes erleben oder einfach nur ein paar Tage entspannen und Resorts von Ihrer schönsten Seite entdecken. Sie haben die Qual der Wahl! Sie möchten reisen, wann Sie Zeit haben. Nicht an einem festgesetzten Termin, sondern dann und solange wie Sie möchten. Die Entscheidung liegt bei Ihnen. Sie wählen die Fluggesellschaft Ihres Vertrauens und los gehts in Ihren Urlaub. Mit dem Helikopter über die Skyline von Manhattan, der Besuch eines Pariser Nachtclubs, ein Chauffeur in Bangkok, Karten für ein Musical in London oder ein Ausflug nach Macau während Ihrer Hongkong-Reise? Kein Problem. Wenn Sie das Besondere lieben, etwas anderes machen wollen als es Andere tun oder sich selbst ein Highlight Ihrer Reise schenken wollen, sind Sie bei uns richtig. Wenn Sie Sonderwünsche haben, fragen Sie uns! Vielleicht machen wir das Unmögliche möglich!

Alles Ist Möglich

Jeder Kunde hat seine eigenen, individuellen Vorstellungen von seinem Traumurlaub. Unsere Auswahl, so hoffen wir, hat für jeden etwas. Hip und Hop in New York, Tempel in Bangkok, CSD in Amsterdam, Sonne in Key West, Karnaval in Köln, Oktoberfest in München und und und. Vor Ort lassen wir Sie nicht alleine. Erfahrene Partner vor Ort sprechen Englisch, zumeist sogar Deutsch. Wenn Sie einen Tip für einen Restaurantbesuch benötigen, Hinweise auf kulturelle Höhepunkte oder Veranstaltungen erfragen möchten oder jemanden brauchen der Ihnen mit Rat und Tat zur Seite steht, dann sind Sie bei unseren Partneragenturen richtig. Die Kontaktadresse mit der jeweiligen Telefonnummer entnehmen Sie bitte Ihren Reiseunterlagen.

R&S Travel
Solothurner Str.
Heilbronn 74072 Germany
(49-7131) 991 2420, Fax: (49-7131) 991 2426.

♂ ◐

RSVP Travel Prod./Club RSVP

- **World's Leading Gay Tour Co.**
- **Takes Entire Ship or Resort**
- **Three Kinds of Vacations**
- **Club RSVP, PLAANET RSVP**
- **Groups & Independent Pkgs**
- **Air by American Airlines**

RSVP Travel Productions is the worlds' leading gay and lesbian tour company. RSVP offers three kinds of the worlds best vacations, RSVP Cruises, Club RSVP resorts and PLAANET RSVP hotel or air-and-hotel packages. RSVP takes the entire ship or resort on an RSVP Cruises or at a Club RSVP resort. Doing it all means RSVP designs the whole event specifically for you. RSVP entertainment, parties, amenities and games are unique, but c maraderie that happens is what r ally makes a great vacation. PLAANET RSVP vacation is an i dependent package to one of the popular vacation destinations. (Wi an option to vacation with a grou in London and Paris). Wi PLAANET RSVP, choose either h tel packages or air-and-hotel packag at great rates that fit your schedul .. Air is provided by American Airlines, the gay and lesbian airline of choice and PLAANET PERKS packets aer sent to travelers containing great information and values for each destination.

PLAANET RSVP—Daily departures to NYC, SF, LA, Palm Springs, New Orleans, San Juan, Key West, Miami, Hawaii, Amsterdam, London, Paris.

— 1997 —

Mr 01 - 08	Clipper Caribbean Cruise
Mr 21 - 29	South American Cruise
Jn 21 - 28	Europride '97 Cruises
Jn 22 - 28	Europride '97 London & Paris
Jn 28 - Jy 05	Europride '97 Cruises
No 08 - 15	Club RSVP—Puerto Vallarta

RSVP Travel Productions/Club RSVP
2800 University Ave SE
Minneapolis, MN 55414 USA
(612) 379-4697, (800) 328-7787, Fax: (612) 379-0484, E-mail: rsvptvl@skypoint.com,
Web: www.rsvp.net. ♀♂

○ Wholesale/Retail (Call Direct or Have Travel Agent Contact) **WHO TO CALL**

Spirit Journeys

- Self-Discovery for Gay Men
- Themed Weekend Workshops
- Leisurely, Fun-Filled Retreats
- Meditative Journeys
- Interaction Cuts Superficiality
- Sacred Sites, Indigenous People

We sponsor events for gay men that encourage self-discovery and passion for life. Themed weekend workshops encourage in-depth personal exploration. Retreats offer rejuvenation, relaxation and self-discovery in a fun-filled environment. Some journeys include adventure activities like canoeing, swimming with dolphins and hiking in the canyonlands. Others include meditation, ceremony, wandering sacred sites and exchanges with indigenous people.

Participants are both singles and couples, Americans and people from abroad, from 20- to 70-year-olds. We keep a healthy balance between scheduled activities and personal time. All events provide meaningful interaction which cuts through superficiality. A frequent comment: "I can't believe how comfortable I feel with a group of men I've just met."

— 1997 —

Ma 02 - 04	3-Part Men's Self-Exploration
Ma 10 - 16	Dolphin Encounters, Bahamas
Jn 21 - Jy 04	Journey to Ancient Greece
Ag 12 - 17	Men's R&R New Mexico Summer Retreat
Se 08 - 22	Pilgrimage to Mystic Andes, Macchu Picchu
Oc 09 - 21	Peru, Macchu Picchu, Mystic Andes
Oc 12 - 19	Arizona Autumn Quest, Chanting, Rituals
No 07 - 09	Men's Couples Workshop
De 27 - Ja 03	New Years in Oaxaca, Mexico

Spirit Journeys
PO Box 3046
Asheville, NC 28802 USA
(704) 258-8880, Fax: (704) 281-0334, E-mail: spiritjourneys@worldnet.att.net.
♀♂ ○

Stonewall Connection Travel & Tours

- Official Gay Games Agent
- Exclusively Gay & Lesbian
- Pkgs to Many Gay Events
- Destination Information
- Individual & Group Gay Tours
- Serving All of North America

Stonewall Connection tours of Calgary is an official Canadian tour operator for Gay Games 1998.

Their Gay Games package includes: 9 night's accommodations in your choice of hotels (double occupancy with private facilities); Breakfast daily (continental or buffet, depending on hotel); Tickets to Opening and Closing Ceremonies; Round-trip transfers between Schiphol Airport to hotel; 8-day public transportation pass in Amsterdam; Half-day Amsterdam sightseeing tour; One-hour gay history canal cruise; Stonewall representative on site in Amsterdam; Stonewall Connection survival kit.

Available options that can be added to the package include: Tickets to other events planned around the Games; Tickets to midnight parties; Additional sightseeing excursions; Pre- and post-Games tours to other European destinations.

These packages are subjected to certain terms and conditions. Contact Stonewall for more information.

— 1998 —

Ag 01 - 08	Gay Games Amsterdam Package

Stonewall Connection Travel & Tours
#320 3545 32nd Ave NE
Calgary, AB T1Y 6M6 Canada
(403) 250-3061, (888) 228-7477, Fax: (403) 250-1041, E-mail: stonewall@canuck.com, Web: www.canuck.com/stonewall.
♀♂ ○

Teddy Travel

- Oldest European Gay Tour Co.
- Exclusively Gay/Lesbian
- Gay Resort Vacations
- City Pkgs in Europe, USA
- Leather Event Tours
- Cologne Gay Pride

Founded in 1983, Teddy Travel is one of the oldest and largest gay travel companies in Europe. Their winter program includes Europe's main gay men's resorts, featuring special gay bungalow complexes, where they have guaranteed contracts. They also offer other warm resort destinations worldwide. The summer program Mediterranean beach vacations and city packages to London, Manchester, Brighton, Cologne, Munich, Ft Lauderdale (Florida), Key West, Orlando, LA and San Francisco, plus Hawaii and Puerto Rico and special weekly tours in the Caribbean.

— 1997 —

Fe 28 - Mr 02	Gay Barcelona Group Tour
Ma 18 - 25	Leather Week, Mr. Leather in Ibiza
Ma 22 - 27	Mr Leather Chicago Pkg for Overseas Visitors
Jy 04 - 06	Cologne Gay Pride Package (Hotel & Event Tickets)
Oc 17 - 26	Pink Cruise Venice to Greek Islands

— 1998 —

February	Colgne Carnival Hotel & Event Package

Teddy Travel
Mathiasstr. 4-6
Cologne 50676 Germany
(49-221) 219 886 (for gays and lesbians), (49-221) 234 967 (for everybody), Fax: (49-221) 241 774, E-mail: teddy-travel@t-online.de.
♀♂ ○

TOUR COMPANY DETAILS

WHO TO CALL

○ Retail (Call Direct) ● Wholesale (Travel Agent Must Contact)

TOUR COMPANY DETAILS

Terramundo Travels Int'l

- Gay-Friendly Dutch Co.
- Latin Amer., Iberia Specialists
- Unusual Accommodations
- Offers Lowest Prices Possible
- Trekking, Climbing, Mtn Biking
- Fly-Drives, Hacienda Stays

We are a Dutch company specializing in customized, tailor-made individual and group itineraries throughout Latin America, Spain and Portugal and the Caribbean. We cover all the countries in this area and offer treks through the jungle and the mountains in small international groups with English-speaking guides from the country of destination. Whenever possible, we try to offer unusual accommodations, rather than regular hotels, for instance, haciendas in Mexico and estancias in Argentina, Chile and Uruguay. The atmosphere of an accommodation is for us a lot more important than the number of stars or category.

We keep costs as low as possible, for example, an 8-day jungle trek with full board in Bolivia, including hiking guide, transport, etc., goes from US $370 per person (ask for current pricing when you call). Our activities include mountain biking forever downhill in Peru, Inca hiking trails, rafting in all countries with big rivers, hot air ballooning, mountain climbing, fly and drive arrangements throughout Mexico, Panama, Costa Rica, Guatemala, Argentina and Uruguay, hikes to unspoiled Indian tribes deep in the jungle, airpasses throughout Central and South America. We answer all faxed requests within 2 days.

Terramundo Travels Int'l
Binnen Dommersstraat 21-23
Amsterdam 1013 HK The Netherlands
(31 20) 420 1122, Fax: (31 20) 622 6912.
♀♂ ●

Thanks, Babs

- Escorted Lesbian Group Travel
- Independent Air-Inclusive Pkgs
- Over 50 Global Destinations
- Resorts to Adventure Travel
- Caribbean, Alaska, Hawaii,
- Golf, Skiing, Kayaking, Cruises

After five years of developing vacation packages for more than 10,000 lesbian travelers with the USA's premiere women's cruise and resort company, Babs Daitsch has now created her own adventures of a lifetime. Group tours are escorted by the knowledgeable and friendly "Thanks, Babs" team. For independent travelers, Thanks, Babs offers air-inclusive hotel and land packages to more than 50 global gay-friendly destinations. Using the buying power of one of the strongest mainstream destination wholesaler of air-inclusive packages, Babs can recommend women-friendly destinations with affordable pricing and value.

— 1997 —

Ma 24 - 31	Cruise-Caribbean
Jn 05 - 09	Gay Day in Orlando Pkg
Jn 19 - 30	Paris and Europride Paris '97
Jn 28 - Jy 06	Femmes Fatale for the 4th, SF
July	Alaskan Native Expeditions
July	Mademoiselles in Montreal
Jy 05 - 12	Fiji Women's Week
August	Denali Rail/Inside Passage Adv.
September	Hiking, Kayaking, Hawaii
September	Paris Walking Tour
October	Yuppies in Yucatan—Cancun
November	Babes Aboard to Baja, Mexico
December	Wahine Week in Wailea

— 1998 —

January	Sapphos In the Snow, Idaho
February	Sydney Mardi Gras, Australia
February	Women's Golf Tourn., Mexico
March	Dykes & Dogs—Iditarod
April	NYC—Lucy & Ethel's Easter Caper, A Lesbian Event

Thanks, Babs
3938 19th St, San Francisco, CA 94114 USA
(415) 552-1791, (888) 969-2227, Fax: (415) 522-0791, E-mail: ThanksBabs@aol.com,
Web: www.ThanksBabs.com. ♀ ○

Toto Tours

- Gay/Lesbian Adventure Travel
- USA and Worldwide Dest.
- Hike Volcanoes, Kayak Maun
- Safari in Africa
- Raft Grand Canyon
- 1997:Our 1st Women-Only Tour

Toto Tours is known for unusual, reasonably-priced adventures in the US and abroad, such as rafting the Grand Canyon, galloping through surf in Costa Rica, hiking into a volcano on Maui, kayaking and swimming with sea lions in Baja or hoisting the sails aboard a classic schooner in the Caribbean, Participants appreciate the physical, mental and emotional benefits derived from participating in new and sometimes unnerving activities within a small group of like-minded people. Incredible adventures, indelible memories, life-long friendships — these are the promise of every Toto Tour! What are you waiting for? Le't go adventuring!

— 1997 —

Mr 20 - 26	Sea Kayaking, Baja Mexico
Ap 02 - 11	Slice of Kauai, Hawaii Prime Beef
Jn 09 - 22	Giraffic Park African Photo Safari
Jn 12 - 23	Hiking Scottish Highlands
Jn 21 - 28	Nat'l Parks SW, Utah
Jn 27 - Jy 08	Call of the Wild-Alaskan Safari
Jy 01 - 08	Rafting Grand Canyon (Men)
Jy 06 - 12	Yellowstone Sampler
Jy 26 - Ag 02	Hike-Intensive Grand Can. Raft
Ag 09 - 16	Rafting Grand Canyon (Women)
Ag 21 - 29	Sailing Inland Seas of Holland
Ag 23 - 30	Emerald Cities -Pacific NW
Se 28 - Oc 04	Hiking, Biking Fall Colorsin Upper Mich.
No 06 - 16	Unorthodox Pilgrimage to Israel
No 21 - De 01	Thanksgiving in Costa Rica

Toto Tours
1326 W Albion #3-W
Chicago, IL 60626-4753 USA
(773) 274-8686, (800) 565-1241, Fax: (773) 274-8695, E-mail: tototours@aol.com, Web: www.tototours.com.
♀♂ ●

Wholesale/Retail (Call Direct or Have Travel Agent Contact)

WHO TO CALL

TOUR COMPANY DETAILS

Tourmark's Gay Way America Tours

- American Airlines Holidays
- For Gay and Lesbian Travelers
- Throughout the United States
- Special Group Costings
- Free Use of Concierge Service
- Toll-Free Assistance Line

In cooperation with American Airlines, Tourmark has developed both group and independent air/hotel packages specifically designed for gays and lesbians. Groups are always led by a professional gay or gay-friendly tour guide. All hotels in the program were selected on the basis of: 1) Understanding the gay and lesbian travel market. 2) Quality of service. 3) Location. 4) Value, relative to price category.

Each client receives a welcome letter highlighting special events scheduled during their stay, plus detailed information getting around the city, restaurants and clubs, sightseeing and shopping. New for 1997, each client can use Tourmark's Concierge Service Centers and the Tourmark toll-free assistance line for guidance and assistance. For special ad hoc groups of any kind, have your travel agent call Tourmark to receive a custom group costing within 24 hours of receipt. Tourmark recognizes the importance of the gay and lesbian community, particularly in the ongoing fight against AIDS. Until a cure is found, and we no longer have to fear this disease, we will continue to donate a portion of our proceeds to organizations like the Names Project, GMHC and God's Love We Deliver. Tourmark strives to exceed your expectations.

Tourmark's Gay Way America Tours
125 Park Ave 2nd Floor
New York, NY 10017 USA
(212) 949-0017, (888) 868-7627, Fax: (212) 949-0321.♀♂ ●

Travel Affair

- Gay & Lesbian Group Tours
- 12 Years in Gay Travel
- Focus on Service, Quality, Value
- Ski Austria, Tour Italy, Europride
- Book Now for New Years 1999:
- Paris, Sydney or the Pyramids

Travel Affair has provided gays and lesbians with tour packages for 12 years. Focusing on service, quality and value, we offer monthly gay and lesbian group departures to destinations such as the Caribbean, Europe, asia, Australia and within the US. River cruises on Germany's Rhine River and in Burma are planned for 1997.

Travel Affair is already planning ahead to the last New Years of this decade. For the Millenium, three special tours are planned with New Years Eve taking place in unique locations. Early reservations are already being taken for the New Years of the Millenium.

— 1997 —
Mr 08 - 16	Austria Ski Trip
Ap 17 - 20	Pools/Pumps '97, Cancun, Mex.
Ap 19 - 25	Tulip Time in Holland
Ma 19 - 28	Venice Simplon-Orient Express European Holiday
Jn 24 - 30	Europride '97 in Paris & Scandinavian Cruise
Jy 20 - Ag 03	Grand Safari to Kenya during Migration Season
Ag 16 - 23	Summer Cruise in Western Caribbean
September	Road to Mandalay Cruise, Burma & Thailand
Oc 11 - 18	Fall Wine Cruise Along the Rhine River
No 22 - 29	Thanksgiving in Italy—Rome, Florence, Venice
De 23 - Ja 03	French Country Xmas & New Year's Eve in Paris

— 1999 —
December	New Years '99 at the Pyramids
December	New Years '99 in Paris
December	New Years '99 in Sydney, Aust.

Travel Affair
1069 Juniper St
Atlanta, GA 30309 USA
(404) 892-9400, (800) 332-3417, Fax: (404) 876-9791.
♀♂ ◐

Travel Club, The

- Gay Men's Travel Club
- Members Vote on Destinations
- Stay in Multi-BR Villas, Homes
- Newsletter in Plain Envelope
- Travel in Off/Shoulder Seasons
- Accommodation Usually $35-$60pp

Members are from every part of the US. Ages range from 18 to 80 (most 29-49). About 75% are single. Almost every profession is represented. We are certain that you will return from any of our vacations with a lot of new friends. On any one vacation, about half are repeat members. Our newsletter always arrives in a plain envelope, and you can request a "security" envelope, if desired. We do horseback riding, hiking, bicycling, sightseeing, shopping. If two or three participants decide to climb some snowcovered mountaintop or take a day trip to some hidden beach, that's great. Vehicles are usually available. We usually rent multi-bedroom villas, condos or homes so members can save money by cooking. We usually have a few great chefs along just waiting to be taken advantage of. Couples can always get a private bedroom, and, if we must put two people in a bedroom together, we make every effort to pair people who are compatible. Accommodation usually cost $35-$60 per person per night, plus tax.

    Each Aug – NYC/Fire Island
    Fall/Spring – San Diego/Mexico
    Jan – Key West
    Sep – Europe
    Fall – Wyoming
    Winter – Orlando
    Fall/Winter – Orlando
    Winter – Hawaii
    And lots more voted on by YOU!

Travel Club, The
City Centre Box 128
Monroe City, IN 47557 USA
Tel/Fax: (812) 743-2919, E-mail: kerry@in.net.
♂ ○

WHO TO CALL

○ Retail (Call Direct) ● Wholesale (Travel Agent Must Contact)

TOUR COMPANY DETAILS

Travel Keys Tours

- Two Specialized, Unique Tours
- Europe Antique Buying Tour
- Dungeons & Castles (Leather)
- Berlin/Amst'd'm Leather Scene
- Munich's Oktoberfest (Leather)
- Stay in Unique Castles & Inns

Our tours are small — never over 20 people. Rather, it's as if a good friend were showing you the best.

Dungeons & Castles of Europe: The Leatherman's Tour

For leathermen. We explore centuries-old castles, dungeons, torture chambers and museums of criminal justice and enjoy the lively leather nightlife of Amsterdam, Berlin and Munich's amazing Oktoberfest Leather Meeting. We stay in rural castles, ancient inns and modern hotels.

Buying Antiques in Europe

For any antique collector. You can still find great antiques throughout Europe, both grand art and all types of collectibles. We'll get you to the best antique markets, specialist dealers and auctions in Britain and France, overwhelming you with great variety and fabulous selection. Mornings are almost always devoted to the markets, finding antiques, while afternoons are often free for the pursuit of specialized items. Bilingual guides can help you negotiate purchases. Shipping is available at extra cost.

— 1997 —
| Se 11 - 24 | Dungeons & Castles, Europe: The Leatherman's Tour |
| Oc 02 - 14 | Buying Antiques in European Markets |

— 1998 —
| September | Dungeons & Castles of Europe |
| October | Buying Antiques in European Markets |

Travel Keys Tours
PO Box 162266,
Sacramento, CA 95816 USA
(916) 452-5200 (tel/fax). ♂ ☾

Travel Man

- German-Based Tour Operator
- Gay/Lesbian Indep't Travel
- Our Motto: Travel in Style
- Exotic Destinations Worldwide
- Unusual, Quality Hotels
- Tailormade Tours/No Fixed Pkgs

Travelman is a German tour operator specializing in gay and lesbian travel. Our motto is "Travel in Style" and we take it seriously: Faced with a good, gay-friendly hotel and a bad gay hotel, we choose the mixed one! We seek out hotels with an extra element of interest. Our hotel in Bali is a member of "Leading Hotels of the World." Our Irish castle is the oldest in Europe. Our Istanbul hotel was once part of a sultan's palace. All our tours are tailormade. There are no fixed packages. Most of our clients are couples who enjoy traveling in style and exploring the special charisma of the country visited.

We do NOT offer the typical Mediterranean, Canary Island, Florida or NY gay beach destinations favored by our competitors. We have sought out exotic destinations like Tahiti, the Cook Islands, Fiji, Botswana, Zimbabwe, South Africa, Hawaii, Istanbul, Dubai, Jamaica, Australia, New Zealand, Rio, Bali and Canada. The Ireland and St Petersburg, Russia trips include cultural elements. Outdoor activities available on our tours range from whitewater rafting to snorkeling and scuba diving, trekking, biking and wilderness canoeing.

Travel Man
Postfach 1543
Koeningstein 61455 Germany
(49 6174) 931 873, Fax: (49 6174) 252 90, E-mail: travelhouse@t-online.de
♂ ☾

Undersea Expeditions, Inc.

- Gay/Lesbian Scuba Diving
- Exotic Locations Worldwide
- Including Air, Hotel, Dive
- Beginners to Advanced Divers
- Mexico, Caribbean, Red Sea
- Galapagos, Papua New Guinea

Gay and lesbian scuba divers no longer have to "go straight." Undersea Expeditions, the exclusively gay and lesbian scuba dive travel company, was established in 1991 to offer gay-friendly options for divers. Undersea offers group adventures to the world's most exotic dive locations. Undersea often has special airfares to its destinations, and with one call, you can book your dive package and your flight. We are specialists and take care of all the details. Beginners get their dive certification on many of our trips, and experienced divers appreciate the exotic ports of call and liveaboard dive opportunities. Meet new dive buddies and enjoy diving with "family."

— 1997 —
May in Bahamas	Snorkel & Scuba with Dolphins
August	Dive Sea of Cortez, La Paz, Mexico
Se 13 - 20	Scuba Dive in Fiji
October Honduras	All-Girl's Scuba Dive in Roatan,
No 22 - 29	Dive Reefs of Honduras

— 1998 —
September	Dive the Red Sea
November	Dive Reefs of Belize
De 25 - Ja 01	New Years Dive, Belize
De 28 - Ja 06	New Years Dive, Galapagos

— 1999 —
| January | Dive Cocos Islands, Costa Rica |

Undersea Expeditions, Inc.
PO Box 9455
San Diego (Pacific Beach), CA 92169 USA
(619) 270-2900, (800) 669-0310, Fax: (619) 490-1002, E-mail: underseax@aol.com, Web: www.mindfood.com/gaydiving.html.
♀♂ ☾

FERRARI GUIDES' GAY TRAVEL A to Z - 18th EDITION

◐ Wholesale/Retail (Call Direct or Have Travel Agent Contact)

WHO TO CALL

TOUR COMPANY DETAILS

Uranian Travel

- Europe's Largest, Oldest
- Exclusively Gay & Lesbian
- Mykonos, Gran Canaria, Ibiza
- Spain, Key West, Miami
- Amsterdam, Dublin, Paris
- Low-Cost Car Hire

In business for more than 22 years, *Uranian Travel* is the largest, most experienced gay tour operator in Europe. Our experience gives us great insight into the requirements of our clients, whose word-of-mouth recommendations have built *Uranian's* reputation as a successful, reliable, and friendly gay tour company.

Uranian's main sunshine resorts in Europe are: **Ibiza,** the colorful Mediterranean island off Spain. **Sitges,** on Spain's Mediterranean Coast near Barcelona. **Magical Palma,** capital of Mallorca. **Playa del Ingles,** on Gran Canaria off the northwest coast of Africa, and the most popular gay holiday playground of all. **Mykonos** in the Aegean Sea, the ever-popular gay island resort.

Uranian's famous Citybreaks: Amsterdam's exciting gay night life; Dublin, Ireland's laid-back capital; Paris restaurants, pavement cafes and gay nightlife. Uranian's low-cost car hire is available at all destinations.

Uranian Travel
Infocus House, 111 Kew Rd
Richmond, Surrey TW9 2PN England
(44 181) 332 1022, Fax: (44 181) 332 1619. In Manchester: (44 161) 236 9339. E-mail: info@uranian.co.uk. http://www.uranian.co.uk.
♀♂ ○

VeloAsia Cycling Adventures

- Bicycling in Unusual Places
- Vietnam, Cambodia, Sumatra
- Planning First Trip to Cuba
- An Enthralling Way to Explore
- Cooking & Language Lessons
- Snorkeling, Hiking

VeloAsia organizes adventure cycling tours in places unusual and interesting. We were the first to organize a bicycle tour of Vietnam and are the only company to offer Sumatra. We are currently organizing the first bicycle tour of Cuba. Bicycling is an enthralling way to experience and explore, removing barriers and putting you in direct contact with people and sights along the way. The journey, not the destination, becomes the focus. We choose destinations especially suited for this form of travel, taking care of the logistics, so you are free to enjoy what would otherwise be a demanding travel experience. Our tours feature small groups of no more than 10, co-led by native and western guides. Cooking and language lessons, snorkeling or hiking and spontaneous events are all part of the tour. We excel at providing delicious meals and comfortable hotels to keep you well-fueled and rested. Our tours are designed to accommodate everyone, whether they want to ride just a few miles or all day. Our van is always nearby. We have a proven record of safety and offer emergency evacuation insurance.

-1997-
May 6-26	Turkey
July 14-27	Sumatra, Indonesia
Nov 19-30	Vietnam Rainforest
Dec 11-16	Cambodia

VeloAsia Cycling Adventures
1271 43rd Ave
San Francisco, CA 94122 USA
(800) 884-ASIA (2742), Tel/Fax: (415) 664-6779, E-mail: veloasia@aol.com.
♀♂ ◐

Virgin Vacations

- Gay-Friendly Britain Pkgs
- Include Air, Transfers, &
- Entry to Hot Gay Clubs
- Sightseeing Add-ons
- Fly/Drive Packages in Britain
- Travel On to Gay Europe

Virgin Vacations offers flexible, independent tour packages to Britain and Europe that can be customized to any taste. And you'll find our packages are gay-friendly, with free admission to some of the hottest gay and lesbian clubs in London.

All of our London packages include round-trip air on Virgin Atlantic Airways, meet-and-greet service on arrival and transfers to and from your hotel in London. Our winter program includes extras like a full day open-top bus tour of London and unlimited use of the Underground and buses. Additional sightseeing options let you plan activities before your departure.

Spring and summer offer a fly-drive program in conjunction with Minotel establishments. With this package, you can choose your own itinerary, staying at any of the over 170 charming Minotels as you travel. From London, Virgin Vacationers can travel on to popular gay European destinations via the Channel Tunnel, or our partner airline, British Midland. In all of these cities, you'll enjoy first-class accommodations and a choice of sightseeing options.

Virgin Vacations
599 Broadway
New York, NY 10012 USA
(800) 364-6466, Fax: (800) 364-6657.
♀♂ ◐

FERRARI GUIDES' GAY TRAVEL A to Z - 18th EDITION

WHO TO CALL

○ Retail (Call Direct) ● Wholesale (Travel Agent Must Contact)

Voyages & Expeditions

- **Gay-Sensitive Luxury Travel**
- **Exotic Destinations Worldwide**
- **Individuals and Any-Size Group**
- **Attention to Detail**
- **Cruise (Crystal Symphony)**
- **Tented "Hemingway Safari"**

Voyages & Expeditions is a gay-owned travel organization with 15 years experience in luxury travel planning for discerning value-conscious clients. Travel to exotic destinations from Alaska to Antarctica and Bali to the Black Sea, in gay-friendly style and comfort is a V&E specialty. In addition to personalized individual cruise and tour planning, V&E also makes travel arrangements for groups of any size from a few friends traveling together to full-ship charters. Many V&E travelers prefer gay-friendly over exclusively gay vacations. Whatever your desire in exotic deluxe travel, be it a world cruise on the Crystal Symphony or around the world on the Concorde, a week on a luxury hotel barge in France or on a yacht in the Greek Isles, a nostalgic rail journey on the Orient Express, or a legendary Blue Train, a tented "Hemingway Safari" in Kenya or Tanzania, or an expedition voyage to the Galapagos or the Spice Islands of Indonesia, V&E has the expertise, facilities and worldwide contacts to make your dream a carefree reality. Quality, value and attention-to-detail service is the trademark of Voyages & Expeditions.

— 1997 —
Ap 25 - Ma 07   Grand European Odyssey Cruise on Island Princess

Voyages & Expeditions
8323 SW Freeway #800
Houston, TX 77074 USA
(713) 776-3438, (800) 818-2877, Fax: (713) 771-9761.
♀♂ ●

Wild Women

- **Wilderness for Young Women**
- **Wilderness Survival Skills**
- **Rafting, Kayaking, Canoeing**
- **Backpacking, Climbing, Hiking**
- **Skiing, Trekking, Fishing**
- **Worldwide Locations**

WILD Women (Wilderness Institute for Leadership Development in Women), a non-profit educational project of Women's Voices for the Earth, provides women with exceptional wilderness adventures especially designed to inspire a deep respect of the natural world and enhance self-esteem, healing, interdependence and leadership skills in the participants.

Equality, safety and enjoyment are the cornerstones of our trips. In a society that has not socialized women to be alone or to take risks, WILD Women provides access to the wilderness in a way in which women will feel safe emotionally, spiritually and physically.

Stepping into the wilderness has been painted as a scary, intimidating and uncomfortalbe event. WILD Women recognizes a woman's experience in the wilderness as unique. While trips are physical in nature, intense physical strength is de-emphasized. Guides joyfully and passionately share their knowledge of wilderness skills needed to survive in a primitive environment, and together we examine the way in which these skills can be incorporated into our everyday lives. Trips include rafting, kayaking, canoeing, fishing, backpacking, trekking, climbing, skiing, and wildlife viewing.

— 1997 —
Ag 02 - 07   Rafting Salmon R., Idaho (Young Women's Leadership
October   Zimbabwe & South Africa
November   Polar Bear Ecology Trip, Hudson Bay

Wild Women
PO Box 8743, Missoula, MT 59802 USA
(406) 543-3747, Fax: (406) 728-4734, E-mail: wve@wildrockies.org.
♀ ○

Wolff + Zink Travel Services

- **Gay Munich's Oktoberfest**
- **Euro Games & Euro Pride**
- **Group Tours European Cities**
- **Individual Gay Europe Pkgs**
- **Special Series of 11 South African Tours**

• Branch Office in South Africa
We are *Wolff & + Zink* Travel Services, your European travel partner. We book your hotel rooms, work out your itinerary, make your rental car arrangements or get your train tickets, and provide you with information about the gay scenes.

This year's highlights are the Euro Games and Euro Pride in Paris in June, Cologne's Carnival in February and in September, Munich's Oktoberfest, which becomes gayer every year. From May to October, we also offer monthly 10-day group tours, each visiting 3 or 4 European cities. Our individual Gay City Tour program, available year-round, offers arrangements for Amsterdam, Berlin, Budapest, Cologne, Frankfurt, Hamburg, Munich, Paris, Prague, Rome, Salzburg and Vienna. We now operate a travel office in South Africa, from which we book and operate 11 different tours in South Africa for groups and individuals.

All of our packages use gay tour guides and gay and gay-friendly accommodations wherever possible.

— 1996 —
Se 12 - 24   Oktoberfest
No 29 - De 08   Christmas Shopping in Bavaria

Wolff + Zink Travel Services
Hans-Sachs-Strasse 22
Munich 80469 Germany
(49 89) 260-6330, Fax: (49 89) 260-5962.
♀♂ ●

TOUR COMPANY DETAILS

◐ Wholesale/Retail (Call Direct or Have Travel Agent Contact)

WHO TO CALL

TOUR COMPANY DETAILS

Womantours/Artemis Sailing

- **Bicycling and Sailing Trips**
- **For Women**
- **Bike Natchez Trace, Utah**
- **Canadian Rockies, Yellowstone**
- **Sail Tahiti, Tonga, Caribbean**
- **All Routes Researched**

Gloria Smith, your *WomanTours* tour leader, has enjoyed 10 years of cycle touring, and her enthusiasm has inspired her to share her adventures with other women. She has personally researched and toured the routes we offer to ensure that you will have an exciting, but safe and comfortable experience. Natchez Trace: From the green, rolling hills of the Apalachians through thick forests to the lowlands of the Mississippi River Basin. Yellowstone: While snow lingers on the peaks, the lower country comes alive with flowers and wildlife. Southwest Canyons: Zion and Bryce National Parks on bikes or by foot with spectacular views. Canadian Rockies: Indian summer among glaciers, hot springs, lake views.

With *Artemis Sailing Charters* Gloria offers

7- to 14-day vacations in Tahiti, Tonga, the Sea of Cortez and the Caribbean for women of all ages. You can take the helm, learn to set and trim sails, tack, steer and anchor. We sail 3-5 hours daily, allowing plenty of time for beachcombing, snorkeling, scuba diving.

— 1997 —

Ma 24 - 31	Women Bike Zion, Bryce Canyons
Jn 07 - 15	Women Bike Yellowstone-Idaho Loop
Ag 30 - Se 05	Women Bike Canadian Rockies
Se 20 - 28	Women Bike Zion, Grand Canyon
Oc 10 - 18	Women Bike Natchez Trace
Oc 27 - 31	Women Bike Calif Wine Country

Womantours/Artemis Sailing
PO Box 931
Driggs, ID 83422 USA
(208) 354-2906, (800) 247-1444.

♀ ◐

Women in Motion

- **Active Vacations for Women**
- **Travel Exclusively with Women**
- **Worldwide Destinations**
- **YOU Set the Pace**
- **Adventure Travel**
- **Women's Fests**
- **Gay Games in Amsterdam**

Women in Motion organizes active vacations for women, with women, by women. Our specialty is exciting and fun adventure vacations for those seeking new challenges and/or to increase skills. For pure, exciting R&R, we run superb tour-style vacations to various locations around the world.

Women in Motion

YOU choose the vacation that's right for you, and YOU set the pace. In the process, you make new friends on trips that are perfect for singles and couples, young and old, participant and spectator. An important element is the freedom to be yourself, to enjoy the comfort and energy level of adventure, active vacations and to travel exclusively with other women.

— 1997 —

Ja 30 - Fe 02	Cross Country Skiing, Yosemite Valley
Fe 20 - 23	Downhill Skiing, Big Bear Lake, CA
Mr 02 - 09	Cycle Costa Rica/Inn Tour
Mr 16 - 21	Cross Country Skiing/Inn Tour, Canadian Rockies
Mr 21 - 23	Rosarito Beach Resort, Mexico
Mr 27 - 31	Dinah Shore Women's Festival, Palm Spring, CA
Ap 25 - 27	Imperial Wildlife Refuge Canoe Trip, CA/AZ border
Ma 09 - 11	Las Vegas Social, Las Vegas, NV
Jn 13 - 15	Sea Kayaking, Catalina Island, CA
Jn 20 - 22	Golf Weekend, San Diego
Jy 10 - 13	Yosemite Nat'l Park, California
Jy 18 - 20	Biking in Big Bear, California
Jy 18 - 20	Rock Climbing, Big Bear Lake, CA
Ag 02 - 08	Scuba & Tour Kauai, Hawaii
Ag 24 - 28	Tour Santa Fe & Taos, New Mexico
Se 05 - 07	Whitewater Rafting (Beg & Interm) No. Calif
Se 15 - 20	Paris Women's Tour
Oc 11 - 17	Scuba, Tour Big Island, Hawaii
November	Cycle Across America "Peddle for the Cure"
De 31 - Ja 03	New Year's Eve in San Francisco

— 1998 —

Fe 05 - 08	Crosscountry Skiing in Yosemite
Fe 19 - 22	Downhill Ski & Snowboard Big Bear Lake, CA
Mr 15 - 22	Cycling Costa Rica
Mr 21 - 28	Adventure Cruise to Belize, Guatemala
Mr 26 - 30	Dinah Shore Women's Festival
April	Cooking School in San Diego
April	New Orleans Jazz Festival Social
Ma 01 - 04	Russian River Women's Festival
Ma 29 - 31	Advanced Rafting, Northern California
August	Gay Games Amsterdam Package
De 30 - Ja 02	New Year's Eve 1998 in San Francisco

Women in Motion
PO Box 4533
Oceanside, CA 92052-4533 USA
(619) 754-6747, (888) GO-WOMEN (469-6636), Fax: (619) 754-8066. E-mail: eventsrus@aol.com, Web: http://gowomen.com.

♀ ◐

FERRARI GUIDES' GAY TRAVEL A to Z - 18th EDITION

WHO TO CALL

○ Retail (Call Direct)   ● Wholesale (Travel Agent Must Contact)

Women in the Wilderness

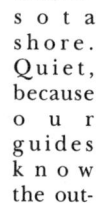

- **Women's Outdoor Adventures**
- **From the Arctic to the Equator**
- **Canoe, Hike, Climb, Kayak**
- **Lapland, Amazon, USA's MN**
- **Macchu Picchu, Utah's Cnyns**
- **20 Yrs Experience**

We teach women the skills to really enjoy the wilderness: canoeing, kayaking, snowshoeing, dog sledding, and just being at home in the wilds. Join us, in a dugout canoe in the rainforest, in a Sami tent in Finland, dancing in a tavern in Crete, or watching northern lights on a quiet Minnesota shore. Quiet, because our guides know the out-of-the-way places the Department of Tourism hasn't found and advertised to the whole world. Many of us have been guiding women's trips for almost 20 years and know how to see that you have fun and meet the goals that you came for.

— 1997 —

January	Dogsledding in Minnesota
February	Dogsledding in Minnesota
February	Whale Watching, Sea Kayaking, Baja California
Fe 08 - 22	Peru: Machu Picchu and the Andes
Fe 24 - Mr 02	Writers' Workshop, Skiing, Snowshoeing, Minnesota
March	Dogsledding in Minnesota
Mr 01 - 08	Sailing in the Virgin Islands
Ap 04 - 15	Rainforest of Honduras Rafting, Mule Travel
Ma 03 - 04	Whitewater Canoe Instruction, Wisconsin
Ma 10 - 11	Whitewater Canoe Instruction, Wisconsin
Ma 17 - 18	Whitewater Canoe Instruction, Wisconsin
Ma 24 - 25	Whitewater Canoe Instruction, Wisconsin
Ma 31 - Jn 01	Whitewater Canoe Instruction, Wisconsin
Jn 24 - Jy 06	Canoeing, Sea Kayaking, Lake Superior (Ontario)
Jn 26 - 29	Sailing Lake Superior, Apostle Islands
Jy 13 - 19	Friends & Family Canoe Trip, North Minnesota
Jy 23 - 27	Hiking, Canoeing, Wolf Ecology, Minnesota
Jy 25 - 27	Solo Canoe Instruction, Northern Minnesota
Jy 31 - Ag 03	Sailing Lake Superior, Apostle Islands
Ag 01 - 05	Reading About Wilderness & Canoeing Retreat
Ag 07 - 10	Northwoods Canoe Retreat for Elders
Ag 21 - 24	Northwoods Retreat, Superior Nat'l Forest, MN
Se 05 - 14	Finnish Lapland: Sami Culture, Wilderness Canoeing
Se 11 - 14	Northwoods Retreat, Superior Nat'l Forest, MN
Se 11 - 14	Sailing Lake Superior, Apostle Islands
Oc 04 - 11	Canoeing Labyrinth Canyon, Utah
Oc 04 - 18	Amazon Rainforest in Peru
Oc 12 - 18	Rafting San Juan River, Utah, Wild'ness Literature

— 1998 —

January	Weekend Dogsledding, Northern Minnesota
February	Northwoods Retreat for Survivors of Cancer
February	Weekend Dogsledding in Northern Minnesota
Fe 07 - 20	Macchu Picchu, Andes and Amazon Rainforest
March	Sailing in the Virgin Islands
March	Weekend Dogsledding in Northern Minnesota
April	Writers' Workshop with Carol Bly
June	Rambles in Greece with Greek Woman Guide
July	Whitewater Canoeing, Missinaibi River, Ontario

Women in the Wilderness
566 Ottawa Ave
St Paul, MN 55107 USA
(612) 227-2284, Fax: (612) 227-4028

♀ ◐

Woodswomen

- **Women's Outdoor Adventures**
- **For All Skill & Fitness Levels**
- **Visiting Exotic Destinations**
- **Himalayas, Grand Canyon, Italy**
- **Alaska, Canada's Wilds, Utah**
- **Vegetar'n Cuisine Under the Stars**

As the oldest, largest women's adventure travel company, *Woodswomen's* organizes outdoor trips for women of all skill and fitness levels to beautiful and exotic places. It's like traveling with a small, congenial group of friends. With flexible pace and easy group interaction, we have time for side trips and gazing at sunsets. Our cuisine under the stars has gourmet touches, is all vegetarian and gets superb reviews. On international vacations, meals are at the finest restaurants, and we stay in unique bed and breakfasts with local folks. We say, "Adventure is the Best Souvenir." Join us for the trip of a lifetime!

— 1997 —

Mr 13 - 22	Exploring Costa Rica
Mr 15 - 21	Vacation in Cozumel
Ap 05 - 12	Climbing, Leadership, California
Ap 05 - 12	Joshua Tree Rock Climbing
Ap 19 - 20	Integrated leadership - Minnesota
Ma 02 - 04	St. Croix Spring Hike, Wisconsin
Ma 09 - 11	Canoeing Namekagon R., Wisconsin
Ma 11 - 17	Backpacking Desert Slickrock, Utah
Ma 30 - Jn 01	Learn to Bicycle Tour - Wisconsin
Jn 07 - 14	Creative Dynamics Canoe & Leadership- MN
Jn 07 - 14	Rafting Cataract Canyon, Utah
Jn 13 - 16	Horseback Riding in Wisconsin
Jn 20 - 22	Canoeing, Cycling Red Cedar Trail, Wis.

FERRARI GUIDES' GAY TRAVEL A to Z - 18th EDITION

○ Wholesale/Retail (Call Direct or Have Travel Agent Contact)

WHO TO CALL

TOUR COMPANY DETAILS

Jy 04 - 10	Mountaineering, Glacier Travel, Washington State
Jy 06 - 12	Canoeing Northern Lakes Loop, MN
Jy 12 - 18	Mountaineering NW Washington
Jy 13 - 19	Canoeing (Lakes, Rivers, Pictographs) in MN
Jy 13 - 25	Bicycling in Tuscany, Italy
Jy 20 - 26	Backpacking Olympic Nat'l Park, WA
Jy 26 - 31	Sea Kayaking Kenai Fjords, Alaska
Jy 27 - Ag 02	Canoeing Northern Lakes Loop, MN
Ag 02 - 08	Hiking in Denali Park
Ag 03 - 09	Backpacking Mt., Rainier, Washington
Ag 03 - 16	Canoeing Canadian Wilds - MN, Canada
Ag 10 - 16	Hiking in Denali Park, Alaska
Ag 17 - 23	Backpacking Isle Royale, Michigan
Ag 22 - 25	Horseback Riding in Wisconsin
Ag 24 - 28	Sea Kayaking San Juan Islands, Washington
Ag 31 - Se 06	Autumn Canoeing in Minnesota
Se 11 - 14	Backpacking North Shore in Minnesota
Se 20 - 26	Backpacking & Leadership- Grand Canyon, AZ
Se 28 - Oc 03	Bicycling Wine Country in California
Se 28 - Oc 04	Backpacking Grand Canyon, Arizona
Oc 03 - 09	Bicycling & Whale Watching - Provincetown
No 01 - 08	Scuba, Wildlife in Roatan
No 08 - 09	Integrated Leadership Seminar - Minnesota

— 1998 —

February	Galapagos Island Cruise, Snorkel, Wildlife
February	New Zealand Bicycle Tour
March	Vacation in Cozumel - Snorkeling, Cycling
August	Magic & Mythology of Ireland — Bicycling
October	Kilimanjaro & Serengeti - Mouintain Trek, Safari
October	Trekking in Himalayas

Woodswomen
25 W Diamond Lake Rd
Minneapolis, MN 55419 USA
(612) 822-3809, (800) 279-0555, Fax: (612) 822-3814.
♀ ○

Zeus Tours & Yacht Cruises

- **Gay and Gay-Friendly**
- **Supersaver Pkgs & Tours**
- **Greece, Israel, Turkey, Egypt**
- **Individuals & Groups**
- **Reserve Thru Travel Agent**
- **Air from NYC, Cruises, Hotels**

The Supersaver to Greece (Gay-Friendly) Includes air from JFK, 3 nights in a first-class Athens hotel with buffet breakfast, half-day Athens sightseeing tour, 3-day cruise to Greek Isles and Turkey on the MV Aegean Dolphin, all round-trip transfers, all hotel service charges and port taxes, VIP service in Greece. (Departing: May 15, June 5, Sept 4, Oct 6).

Aegean Yacht Cruise (Gay-Exclusive) Includes air from JFK, 3 nights in a first-class Athens hotel with buffet breakfast, half-day Athens sightseeing tour, 7-day cruise to the Greek Isles aboard Zeus Yacht Cruises, outside cabin, all round-trip transfers, all hotel service charges and port taxes, VIP service in Greece. (Gay-exclusive departures: Aug 14, Oct 9, Gay-friendly departures: May 8, Jun 5, Oct 16).

Island Lover (Gay-Friendly) Includes: Air from JFK, continental breakfast daily, 2 nights first-class Athens hotel, 3 nights first-class Mykonos hotel, 3 nights first-class Santorini hotel, half-day Athens sightseeing tour, all inter-island transportation and transfers, all hotel service charges and port taxes, VIP service in Greece. (Departing: June 9, Aug 25, Sept 29, Oct 13).

Zeus will customize any itinerary for Greece, Israel, Egypt, Turkey or Italy.

Zeus Tours & Yacht Cruises
209 W 40th St
New York, NY 10018 USA
(212) 221-0006, (800) 447-5667, Fax: (212) 764-7912.
♀♂ ●

ZMAX Travel & Tours Inc.

- **Fantasy Fest Cruise**
- **October 24-27, 1997**
- **From Miami to Key West**
- **To Bahamas to Miami**
- **Including Fantasy Fest-ivities**
- **Experts on the Party Circuit**

Experience Fantasy Fest on the M/S Leeward (NCL). The ship departs Miami on Friday, October 24, 1997. On Saturday, it arrives in Key West at 8:00 am, well in time for you to participate in the Fantasy Fest Parade and other festivities. The theme for Fantasy Fest is "TV Jeebies." Dress as your favorite TV character from the past. Parade ends at 10:00 pm on Saturday, giving you plenty of time to get back to the ship, where festivities will continue! The ship will travel through the night, arriving at Stirrup Cay in the Bahamas at noon on Sunday. You'll have the entire afternoon to enjoy this private Bahamian island before departure for Miami.

ZMax also offers several Gay Games Amsterdam packages, which include upgraded tickets to opening and closing ceremonies, as well as accommodations, sightseeing excursions and local assistance.

Zmax's specialty has become the Party Circuit. They not only book them, they are literally the experts on circuit parties.

— 1997 —

Oc 24 - 27	Fantasy Fest Cruise Miami to Key West

— 1998 —

Ag 01 - 09	Gay Games Packages

ZMAX Travel & Tours Inc.
420 Lincoln Rd, Miami Beach, FL 33239 USA
(305) 532-0111, (800) 864-6429, Fax: (305) 532-1222, E-mail: zmaxtravel@aol.com.
♂ ○ (See ad between Pages 80 & 81)

FERRARI GUIDES' GAY TRAVEL A to Z - 18th EDITION

WHO TO CALL

RESERVATION SERVICES

AIRZONA TRAILS B&B RESERVATION SERVICE
(602) 837-4284, (888) 799-4284, Fax: (602) 816-4224.

Gay and gay-friendly B&Bs in Arizona. Personally inspected.

ALTERNATIVE TRAVEL
42 Pine Ave W #2, Montreal, PQ H2W 1R1 Canada, (514) 845-7769, Fax: (514) 845-8421.

Gay-friendly reservation service for accommodations & local events in Montreal.

BED & BREAKFAST CALIFORNIA
PO Box 282910, San Francisco, CA 94128-2910 USA, (415) 696-1690, Fax: (415) 696-1699.

Gay-friendly accommodations reservation service.

BED & BREAKFAST INN ARIZONA
Gallery 3 Plaza, 3819 N 3rd St, Phoenix, AZ 85012 USA, (602) 265-9511, (800) 266-STAY (7829).

Inns, B&Bs, hotels, resorts, dude ranches, apartments & condos throughout Arizona! Discounts available on self-drive autos. Gay-friendly.

BIG EASY/GULF COAST RESERVATIONS
(504) 433-2563, (800) 368-4876, Fax: (504) 391-1903.

Gay-friendly reservations for New Orleans and the Gulf Coast.

CALIFORNIA RIVIERA 800
914 N. Coast Hwy, Laguna Beach, CA 92651 USA, (714) 376-0305, (800) 621-0500, Fax: (714) 497-9077.

Reservation service for hotels, resorts, B&Bs and vacation rentals along the southern California coastline. Gay-friendly.

CARITAS BED & BREAKFAST NETWORK
75 E Wacker Dr #3600, Chicago, IL 60601 USA, (312) 857-0801, Fax: (312) 857-0805.

B&B accommodations in gay homes throughout America for both the discriminating traveler and the budget minded. Each host carefully screened.

CITYWIDE RESERVATION SERVICES
25 Huntington Ave #607, Boston, MA 02116 USA, (617) 267-7424, (800) 468-3593.

Reservations at gay and non-gay locations in Boston and New England, Quebec, Washington DC and southern Florida, Open 9am-9pm or 10:30am-6pm weekends. Gay-friendly.

C.A.N. RESERVATIONS
PO Box 42 Stn M, Montreal, QC H1V 3L6 Canada, (514) 254-1250 ext. 2.

♀♂ Gay-owned and -operated reservation service for all of Canada.

DESTINNATIONS
572 Rte 28, West Yarmouth, MA 02673 USA, (508) 790-0566, (800) 333-4667, Fax: (508) 790-0565

♀♂ Reservations at gay-friendly inns throughout New England.

FRENCH QUARTER RESERVATION SERVICE
940 Royal St #263, New Orleans, LA 70116 USA, (504) 523-1246, Fax: (504) 527-6327, E-mail: fqrsinc@linknet.net.

Specialize in finding accommodations in small hotels, inns and private guest-homes in the historic French Quarter & famous Garden District of New Orleans.

GREATER BOSTON HOSPITALITY
PO Box 1142, Brookline, MA 02146 USA, (617) 277-5430.
B&B reservations throughout the Boston area. Gay-friendly.

HOME SUITE HOM
PO 762 Succ C, Montréal, QC H2L 4L6 Canada, (514) 523 6107, (800) 429 4983 (US & Canada).

International gay housing club - hospitality exchange at other members' homes.

HOMESTAY BY THE BAY
PO Box 2116, Berkeley, CA 94702 USA, (510) 869-4395.

Local lesbians and gay men invite you to vacation in their homes. Enjoy breakfasts, gay events, resources, fun. You can network, meet friends in the community and make connections. Accommodations are available throughout San Francisco, Berkeley and Oakland. All host homes are visited and approved, and come with free references.

ITS CARS & HOTELS
3332 NE 33rd St, Ft Lauderdale, FL 33308 USA, (954) 566-7111, (800) 521-0643, Fax: (954) 566-0036

European car rentals & worldwide hotel reservations. Gay-friendly.

KEY WEST BUSINESS GUILD
Box 1208, Key West, FL 33041 USA, (305) 294-4603, (800) 535-7797.

Specializing in gay & lesbian travel in Key West.

KEY WEST RESERVATION SERVICE
PO Drawer 1689, Key West, FL 33041 USA, (305) 296-7753, (800) 327-4831 (USA & Canada), Fax: (305) 296-6291.

Info. on gay & straight Key West accommodations.

LESBIAN & GAY HOSPITALITY EXCHANGE
PO Box 612, Stn C, Montréal, QC H2L 4K5 Canada, Tel/Fax: (514) 523-1559. E-mail: lghei@odyssee.net.

♀♂ $25/yr membership includes an annual directory and supplementary list. Use these to find hosts in 40 countries for up to two nights free lodging in homes of other members.

MI CASA SU CASA
PO Box 10327, Oakland, CA 94610 USA, (510) 268-8534, (800) 215-CASA (2272), Fax: (510) 265-8534, E-mail: homeswap@aol.com.

International and domestic home exchange and hospitaltity network, specializing in short- and long-term exchanges for lesbian and gay and gay-friendly travelers. The Mi Casa Su Casa confidential member catalog connects you with gay and lesbian people around the world. For an agreed time period, you enjoy their home and community while they enjoy yours. Member IGTA.

WHO TO CALL

PALM SPRINGS VISITORS INFORMATION CENTER
2781 N. Palm Canyon Dr, Palm Springs, CA (760) 778-8418, (800) 347-7746.

The city's Division of Tourism offers information on all accommodations (gay included). Palm Springs, CA...the destination for everyone.

PROVINCETOWN BUSINESS GUILD
PO Box 421, 115 Bradford St, Provincetown, MA 02657 USA, (508) 487-2313.

Gay & lesbian customers welcome. Provincetown gay visitor information.

PROVINCETOWN RESERVATIONS
293 Commercial St #5, Provincetown, MA 02657 USA, (508) 487-2021, (800) 648-0364 (US & Canada), Fax: (508) 487-4887.

♀♂

RENT A VILLA
6 Fredon Dr, Livingston, NJ 07039 USA, (201) 533-6863, (800) 533-6863, Fax: (201) 740-8833.

♀♂ Wide range of reservations in the Virgin Islands. Gay-friendly.

RIVER SPIRIT RETREAT B&B SERVICE
187 W 19th St, Alton, IL 62002 USA, (618) 462-4051, (314) 569-5795.

Nationwide reservations for women.

ROYAL COMMAND INC. NETWORK
108 Mohican Cir, Boca Raton, FL 33487-1520 USA, (407) 994-3558, (800) 71-ROYAL (76925), Fax: (407) 994-3634.

Reservations for B&B's throughout the UK and Europe. No Fee.

SOUTH FLORIDA HOTEL NETWORK
1688 Meridian Ave #1016, Miami Beach, FL 33139 USA, (305) 538-3616, (800) 538-3616.

♀♂ Free service, over 500 South Florida hotels to choose from. Airlines, tours, cruises, car rentals.

VHR WORLDWIDE
235 Kensington Ave, Norwood, NJ 07648 USA, (201) 767-9393, (800) 633-3284, Fax: (201) 767-5510. E-mail: klyu87a@prodigy.com.

♀♂ Custom-tailored reservations to gay-friendly accommodations in the Bahamas, Caribbean, Mexico, and Central America, Europe, and parts of the United States. VHR Worldwide takes pride in personalized service.

WAIKIKI STUDIOS
3242 Kaohinani, Honolulu, HI 96817 USA, (808) 595-7533, (800) 288-4666, Fax: (808) 595-2030.

Studios, hosted rentals and B&B reservation service throughout the islands.

WAIKIKI VACATION RENTALS
1860 Ala Moana Blvd #108, Honolulu, HI 96815 USA, (808) 946-9371, (800) 543-5663.

Fully-furnished condominium rentals in central Waikiki, from budget to deluxe, near to bars and beach.

RESERVATION SERVICES

There's a Number of Things To Know About Gay & Lesbian Travel.

Fortunately, You Have Only One Number to Remember:

1-800-448-8550

CRUISES • TOURS • RESORTS

No matter where you want to go, how you want to get there and where you want to stay, The International Gay Travel Association's worldwide network of over 1000 gay & lesbian community-based travel agents can professionally guide you with the latest information on hot, new travel opportunities. For an IGTA travel agent or IGTA accommodations worldwide call today!

International Gay Travel Association
IGTA

PROVIDING A WORLD OF ANSWERS FOR GAY & LESBIAN TRAVELERS
AOL Gay/Lesbian Forum • www.rainbow-mall.com

FERRARI GUIDES' GAY TRAVEL A to Z - 18th EDITION

WHO TO CALL

AFRICA
SOUTH AFRICA
CHRIS ALEC TRAVEL, Suite 2512, 25th fl, 320 West St, Durban 4001, South Africa, (27 31) 307 5361.

EQUATOR TRAVEL, 33 Long St, Cape Town, South Africa, 8000, (27 21) 247344, (27 21) 249672, Fax: (27 21) 249662.

GAY ESCAPE, 7 Castle St, Cape Town, South Africa, 8001, (27-21) 239 001, (27-21) 235 907. *Member:* IGTA

TRAVEL CONSULTANT, THE, 1118 Pretorius St, Hatfield 0083, Pretoria, South Africa, (27 12) 342-4385/6, Fax: (27 12) 342-4567. Specializing in gay and lesbian travel, ask for Ken. Mail to: PO Box 6424, Pretoria 0001.

EAST ASIA
JAPAN
EAST WEST TRAVEL, 1082-1 Ochiai, Tama-shi, Tokyo, Japan, (81 423) 73-6284. Gay-friendly.

SOUTHEAST ASIA
THAILAND
RAINBOW TOURS, Unit 5/2, 403/29 Silom SO1 5, Bangkok, Thailand, 10500, (66 2) 234 2180, Fax: (66 2) 266 5479.

VIETNAM
ATLAS TRAVEL & TOURS, district 1,, 41-43 Nam Ky Khoi Nghia, Ho Chi Minh City, Vietnam, (84-8) 822 4122, fax: (84-8) 829 8604. *Member:* IGTA

EUROPE
CZECH REPUBLIC
TGT, Sokolská 56, 120 00 Prague 2, Czech Republic, (42 2) 24 91 33 31, (42 2) 24 91 41 37, Fax: (42 2) 29 57 00.

DENMARK
INTER-TRAVEL, Frederiksholms Kanal 2, 1220 Kobenhavn K, Denmark, (45) 33 15 00 77.

FRANCE
ACTITUDE, 33 rue du Petit Musc, Paris 75004, France, (33 1) 4887 7744, Fax: (33 1) 4887 7879.

BOUSSOLE BLEUE, 15 rue de la Baume, 75383 Paris Cedex 8, France, (33-1) 53 93 53 67, fax: (33-1) 40 75 03 03. Ask for Irene.

EUROGAYS TRAVEL, 23 rue Bourg-Tibourg, Paris, France, (33-1) 48 87 37 77, (33-1) 48 87 39 99. *Member:* IGTA

FRENCH TOUCH, 13 Rue Stephenson, Paris 75018, France, (33 1) 41 10 38 37, Fax: (33-1) 41 10 39 55. *Member:* IGTA

PRIEURE DES GRANGES, 15 Rue des Fontaines, 37510 Savonnieres, Tours, France, (33 47) 50 09 67, Fax: (33 47) 50 06 43.

VISTAMAR TRAVEL, 34 Helio Village, Cap d'Agde 34308, France, (33 67) 26 0341.

GERMANY
AAD WELTWEIT REISEN, Schanzweg 8, 86845 Grossaitingen, Germany, (49-820) 396 0611, fax: (49-820) 396 0660. *Member:* IGTA

BON(N) VOYAGE, Thomas Mann Str 56, Bonn, Germany, (49-228) 985 1813 (tel/fax).

EVENT & TRAVEL, Knobeldorffstr. 39, Berlin, Germany, (49-30) 326 5313.

FLYING TICKET, Reisecenter, Flamingoweg 1, Stuttgart, Germany, (49-711) 953 7931, (49-711) 539 0297.

GABLENGER REISEBÜRO, Gablenger Hauptstr. 64, Stuttgart, Germany, (49-711) 480 0535, (49-711) 480 0434.

GLOCKENBACH REISEN, Hans Sachs Str. 8, 80469 Munich, Germany, (49 89) 260 9952, (49 89) 260 9828.

HORIZONT REISEN, Bahnhofstr. 11, 26122 Oldenburg, Germany, (49 441) 261 33, Fax: (49 441) 264 66.

KRIS REISEN, Radlsteg 2 (TAL), 80331 Munich, Germany, (49 89) 291 129, Fax: (49 89) 221 047.

MÄNNER NATÜRLICH, Im Mühlenbach 81, Bonn, Germany, (49-228) 254 434, (49-228) 254 219, men-only.

NEPTUN REISEN & TOURISTIK, Dom Pedro Str 16, 80637 Munich, Germany, (49 89) 157 5802, Fax: (49 89) 157 5834.

NEUE WELT REISEN, Pfalzburger Str 72, 1000 Berlin 15, Germany, (49 30) 883 1946.

OUR WORLD TRAVEL, Muellerstrasse 43, 80469 Munich, Germany, (49-89) 260 5571, Fax: (49-89) 260 5576. *Member:* IGTA

R&S REISESERVICE, Solothurnerstr 24, 74072 Heilbronn, Germany, (49 7131) 991 2420, Fax: (49-7131) 991 2426. *Member:* IGTA

REISEBURO SCHNEIDER, Hohenzollernplatz 3, 80769 Munich, Germany, (49 89) 300 9007. Ask for Michael.

REISEBÜRO AM HELLKAMP, Hellkamp 17, 20255 Hamburg, Germany, (49 40) 401 92121, Fax: (49 40) 491 9100. *Member:* IGTA

RTS REISE & TOURISTIC SERVICE, Schoenhauser Allee, 130, 10437 Berlin, Germany, (49 30) 609 7786, Fax: (49 30) 609 7872.

SCHWULE MITFAHRZENTRALE, Yorckstrasse 52, Berlin, Germany, (49-30) 216 4020.

STATTREISEN HAMBURG, Bartelstr. 12, Hamburg, Germany, (49-40) 430 7429, (49-40) 430 7429.

SUNRISE TRAVEL SERVICE, Kruenerstr. 104, 81377 Munich, Germany, (49-89) 7414 1847, fax: (49-89) 7414 1848. *Member:* IGTA

TE ANAU REISEN, Klosterallee 67, 20144 Hamburg, Germany, (49 40) 420 5500, Fax: (49 40) 420 1550.

TEDDY TRAVEL, Mathiasstrasse 4-6, 50676 Köln, Germany, (49 221) 234 967, Fax: (49 221) 241 774.

TICKET KONTOR, Feldstr. 37, Hamburg, Germany, (49-40) 430 1076.

TICKETKONTOR, Fleischhauerstr. 80, Lübeck, Germany, (49-451) 702 0774, (49-451) 702 0799.

VEDEMA REISEN, Prenzlauer Allee 61, Berlin, Germany, (49-30) 425 0156.

WORLDWIDE ENCOUNTERS, Eisenzahnstr 59, 10709 Berlin, Germany, (49 30) 891 8656, Fax: (49 30) 232 1661.

GREECE
BLUE MOON TRAVEL & TOURISM, 29 Agiou Efthmiou St, Mykonos, Greece, 846 00, (30 2) 892 2042, Fax: (30 2) 893 3276.

MYKONOS ACCOMMODATION CENTER, PO Box 58, Mykonos, Greece, 84600, (30 289) 23160, Fax: (30 289) 2 4137. *Member:* IGTA

WINDMILLS TRAVEL & TOURISM, Mykonos, Greece, Tel/fax: (30 289) 23877, Fax: (30-289) 22066. *Member:* IGTA

ITALY
A.M.A. VIAGGI, Piazza Velasca 5, Milan, Italy, 20100, (39 2) 809 166.

VAG VIAGGI, (39 6) 980 50 20, Fax: (39 6) 980 71 47.

LATVIA
BALTA, Elizabetes iela 63, Riga, 1050, (371) 728 6349, Fax: (371) 882 0179.

NETHERLANDS
DE GAY KRANT TRAVEL, Kloveniersburgwal 40, Amsterdam, Netherlands, 1012 CW, (31 20) 421 0000, Fax: (31 20) 620 6217. *Member:* IGTA

WENS REIZEN, Baronielaan 103, 4818 PD Breda, Netherlands, (31 76) 5226340, Fax: (31 76) 5221931. *Member:* IGTA

RUSSIA
POLEFF TOURS, PO Box 70, 191025 St. Petersburg, Russia, (7-812) 272 6538, fax: (7-812) 272 6562. *Member:* IGTA

SPAIN
CCJ TRAVEL PLUS, Quintana 20, 3-B, 28008 Madrid, Spain, (34-1) 542 6009, fax: (34-1)542 8928. *Member:* IGTA

GAY FRIENDS HOLIDAYS (MAGIC TRAVEL), Benet Mercade 9-11, Barcelona 08012, Spain, (34 3) 238 0356, Fax: (34 3) 415 4097. *Member:* IGTA

LAMBDA VIAJES, Fuencarral 43, 28004 Madrid, Spain, (34-1) 532 7833, fax: (34-1) 532 5162. *Member:* IGTA

PAISAJES AGENCIA DE VIAJES, Gran Vía 80 #507, 28013 Madrid, (34-1) 541 0099 (tel/fax).

SWEDEN
HALVAR PRODUCTION, Orvar odds V-51, Stockholm, Sweden, 11254, (46 8) 213 0522, Fax: (46 8) 210 708.

RESEBUTIKEN NOBLE TRAVEL, Bjorngardsgatan 1B, 118 52 Stockholm, Sweden, (46-8) 644 7456, fax: (46-8) 644 2423. *Member:* IGTA

SWITZERLAND
GO TRAVEL, Wuhre 19, 8001 Zurich, Switzerland, (41 1) 212 3103, Fax: (41 1) 212 3113. *Member:* IGTA

JEKAMI REISEN, Markt Gasse 5, 4th floor, 3011 Bern, Switzerland, (41 31) 312 4040, Fax: (41 31) 312 40. Specializing in gay and lesbian travel.

TOP AIR TRAVEL, Marktgasse 5/4, 3011 Bern, Switzerland, (41-31) 312 4040, fax: (41-31) 312 4042. *Member:* IGTA

TRAVEL ETC, Schulstr 3, 8153 Zurich, Switzerland, (41 1) 818 0546, Fax: (41-1) 818 0649. *Member:* IGTA

UK (ENGLAND)
ALTERNATIVE HOLIDAYS, 21 Russell Gardens Mews, London W14 8EU, England, (44 171) 602 6867, Fax: (44 171) 602 7964. *Member:* IGTA

EUROVILLIAGE, 64 Old Compton St, 2nd Floor, London W1V 6ER, England, (44 171) 287 3334.

TRAVEL AGENTS

WHO TO CALL

FREEDOM VACATIONS, Palace House, 62 Pall Mall, London SW1Y 5HZ, England, (44 171) 394-0070, Fax: (44 171) 976-2121.

GI JOHN DARRAH CORP, 53 Manor Park, London SE1 35RA, England, (44 181) 318 5590. Apts, B&B, holiday pkgs in London.

GI TRAVEL, Unit 2, 124 Rossmore Rd, Parkstone Poole, Dorest BH12 2HJ, England, (44 202) 734 100, Fax: (44 202) 732 525. *Member:* AGLTA

MAN AROUND LTD, 89 Wembley Park Dr, Wembley Park, Middlesex, England, HA9 8HS, (44 181) 795 1411, Fax: (44 181) 903 7357. *Member:* IGTA

NOW VOYAGER, 7/11 Kensington High St, London GU34 3QT, England, (44 171) 938 3390, Fax: (44 171) 937 4550. *Member:* AGLTA

PRIDE TRAVEL, Devonshire Mns, Devonshire Pl, Brighton, England, BN2 1QH, (44 1273) 606 656, Fax: (44 1273) 624 584. *Member:* IGTA

SAPPHIRE TRAVEL & TOURS, Central Chambers, 98 High St, Rayleigh, Essex SS6 7BY, England, (44 1268) 777 667, Fax: (44-01268) 777 687. *Member:* IGTA

TICKETS ANYWHERE, 5 Vigo St, London W1X 1AH, England, (44 171) 434 0367, Fax: (44 171) 437 0828.

TRIANGLE TRAVEL, Workshop 4, The Leadmill, 6/7 Leadmill Road, Sheffield S1 4SF, England, (44 1742) 722 990.

AUSTRALIA

AUST. CAPITAL TERRITORY

BRADDON TRAVEL, 3 Lonsdale St, Braddon 2601 ACT, Australia, Tel/Fax: (61 6) 247 5788.

JAPAN SPECIALIST TRAVEL, PO Box 122, O'Conner 2602 ACT, Australia, (61 6) 247 5400, Fax: (61 6) 247 5788.

JUST TRAVEL, Ste 2, RSPCA House 6 Napier Close, Deakin 2600 ACT, Australia, (61 6) 285 2644, Fax: (61 6) 285 2430. *Member:* IGTA AGLTA

NEW SOUTH WALES

AFRICA TRAVEL CENTRE, 456 Kent St, level 11, Sydney 2000 NSW, Australia, (61 2) 9267 3048, Fax: (61 2) 9267 0247.

ALUMNI TRAVEL, GPO Box 1368, Sydney 2001 NSW, Australia, (61 2) 9290-3856, Fax: (61 2) 9290-3857. *Member:* IGTA AGLTA

ASTRAL TRAVEL & TOURS, #7 Level 3, 250 Pitt St, Sydney 2000 NSW, Australia, (61 2) 9283 2718, Fax: (61 2) 9264 1674.

AUST PAC TRAVEL, 20 Emily St, Leichhardt 2040 NSW, Australia, (61 2) 9660 3199, Fax: (61 2) 9660 8662. *Member:* IGTA AGLTA

F.O.D. TRAVEL, 2nd Fl, 77 Oxford St, Darlinghurst 2010 NSW, Australia, (61 2) 9360 3616, Fax: (61 2) 9332-3326. *Member:* AGLTA

FIORELLA TRAVEL, 92 Pitt St, Sydney 2000 NSW, Australia, (61 2) 9231 4099, Fax: (61 2) 9231 2472.

H.H.K. TRAVEL, 50 Oxford St, Paddington 2021 NSW, Australia, (61 2) 9332 4299, Fax: (61 2) 9360 2164. *Member:* AGLTA

JETSET TRAVEL BONDI, 219 Bondi Rd, Bondi, Australia, (61 2) 9300 0243.

JORNADA, Level 1 53 Cross St, Double Bay, Sydney 2028 NSW, Australia, (61 2) 9362-0900,
Fax: (61 2) 9362-0788. *Member:* AGLTA

KPK SAMPSONS TRAVEL INTERNATIONAL, PO Box 415, Nowra 2541 NSW, Australia, (61 44) 210 522, Fax: (61 44) 213 869. *Member:* IGTA AGLTA

LAP OF LUXURY, PO Box 600, Milsons Point 2061 NSW, Australia, (61-2) 9959 5931, (61-2) 9959 5931. *Member:* AGLTA

LIFESTYLE TOURS, PO Box 343, Punchbowl 2196 NSW, Australia, (61 2) 9740 6130, Fax: (61 2) 9759 8972.

OUT AND ABOUT TRAVEL, 259 George St, level 25, Sydney 2000 NSW, Australia, (61 2) 9251 2500, Fax: (61 2) 9251 2526.

OXFORD STREET FLIGHT CENTRE, 26 Oxford St, Woollahra 2025 NSW, Australia, (61 2) 9360 2277, Fax: (61 2) 9360 5665. *Member:* AGLTA

SILKE'S TRAVEL, 263 Oxford St, Sydney 2010 NSW, Australia, (61 2) 9380 6244, Fax: (61 2) 9361 3729. *Member:* IGTA AGLTA

SOMEWHERE TRAVEL, Level 5, 46-56 Holt St, Surrey Hills 2010 NSW, Australia, (61 2) 9310 5555, Fax: (61 2) 9319 3039. *Member:* IGTA AGLTA

STA TRAVEL, 9 Oxford St, Paddington NSW, Australia, (61 2) 9360 1822.

THOMAS COOK, GPO Box 62, Sydney 2001 NSW, Australia, (61 2) 9248 6288, Fax: (61 2) 9262 2340. *Member:* AGLTA

TOURS COORDINATION WORLD TRAVEL SERVICE, 2 Cross St, Ste. 1, Double Bay 2028 NSW, Australia, (61 2) 9327-6600, Fax: (61 2) 9362 4989.

TRAVEL CALL, 20 Bay St, level 4, Double Bay 2028 NSW, Australia, (61 2) 9326 1711, Fax: (61 2) 9327 5049.

TRAVEL CONSULTANT, 63 Arthur St, Surry Hills 2010 NSW, Australia, (61 2) 9360 9880.

TRAVEL OZ (Greyhound/Pioneer Australia), 7/4 Llankelly Place, Potts Point 2011 NSW, Australia, (61 2) 9368 1284, Fax: (61 2) 9357-4639.

TRAVELAND, Oxford St at Riley St, Darlinghurst 2010 NSW, Australia, (61-2) 9352 6955, (61-2) 9352 6957. *Member:* AGLTA

TRAVELLERS, 182 George St, level 7, Sydney 2000 NSW, Australia, (61 2) 9256 4470, Fax: (61 2) 9233 2273.

WIEDEMANN TRAVEL, PO Box 736, North Sydney 2060 NSW, Australia, (61-2) 9955 0000, (61-2) 9954 5913. *Member:* AGLTA

NORTHERN TERRITORY

DUCKET TOURS & TRAVEL SHOP, PO Box 3826, Darwin 0801 NT, Australia, (61 89) 819 321, Fax: (61 89) 810 777.

QUEENSLAND

JETSET TRAVEL CAIRNS, PO Box 2356, Cairns 4870 QLD, Australia, (61-70) 517 177, (61-70) 519 175. *Member:* AGLTA

OUT TOURING, PO Box 1214, Cairns 4870 QLD, Australia, (61 70) 511 483, Fax: (61 70) 521 942.

PEREGIAN TRAVEL, PO Box 115, Peregian Beach, Australia, 4573, (61-7) 54 482770, fax (61-7) 54 482775.

PLATYPUS TRAVEL, PO Box 696, Kirwan 4817 QLD, Australia, (61 77) 232811, Fax: (61 77) 231656.

STA TRAVEL, University of Queensland, Union
Bldg, ground floor, St. Lucia QLD, Australia, (61 7) 371 2433.

TRAVELAND FORTITUDE VALLEY, 669 Ann St, Brisbane, QLD, Australia, 4006, (61-7) 3852 1870, (61-7) 495 4493. *Member:* IGTA

TRAVELAND NOOSA, Shop 11, The Palms Centre, Lanyana Way, Noosa Junction 4567 QLD, Australia, (61-74) 472 722, (61-74) 472 349. *Member:* AGLTA

TRIANGLE VACATIONS, PO Box 162, Albion, QLD, Australia, 4010, (61-7) 3862 2490, Fax: (61-7) 3262 6422. *Member:* IGTA AGLTA

SOUTH AUSTRALIA

O'CONNELL TRAVEL, 163 O'Connell St, N Adelaide 5006 SA, Australia, (61-8) 8239 2555, (61-8) 8239 251. *Member:* AGLTA

PARKSIDE TRAVEL, 70 Glen Osmond Rd, Parkside 5063 SA, Australia, (61 8) 8274 1222, Fax: (61 8) 8272 7371. *Member:* AGLTA

PRESTIGE TRAVEL, 447 Portrush Rd, Shop 13,, Burnside Village,, Glendside SA, Australia, (61) 8338 12 23

PRIDE TRAVEL, 3A, 28 Hindley St, Adelaide 5000 SA, Australia, (61 8) 8212 3833, Fax: (61 8) 8231 3145.

STA TRAVEL, 235 Rundle St, Adelaide SA, Australia, (61 8) 8223 2426.

VICTORIA

AMERICA YOUR WAY TRAVEL, 93 Jenkins St, Northcote 3070 VIC, Australia, (61 3) 9481 5218, Fax: (61 3) 9482 5158.

CORONA TRAVEL, 146 Station St, Fairfield 3070 VIC, Australia, (61 3) 9489 3989.

FBI TRAVEL, 204 Balaclava Rd, Caulfield 3161 VIC, Australia, (61 3) 9576 0900, Fax: (61 3) 9525 2975. *Member:* IGTA AGLTA

JETSET TRAVEL, Level 9, 5 Queens Rd, Melbourne 3004 VIC, Australia, (61 3) 9828-8904, Fax: (61 3) 9828 8998. *Member:* AGLTA

JETSET TRAVEL BRIGHTON, 254 Bay St, Brighton 3186 VIC, Australia, (61 3) 9596 3566, Fax: (61 3) 9596 7761. *Member:* IGTA

STA TRAVEL, 222 Faraday St, Carlton 3053 VIC, Australia, (61 3) 9347 6911, Fax: (61 3) 9347 0608.. *Member:* IGTA

STA TRAVEL, 142 Acland St, St. Kilda VIC, Australia, (61 3) 9525 3188.

THAILAND DO IT RIGHT, PO Box 338, World Trade Centre, Melbourne 3005 VIC, Australia, Tel/Fax: (61 3) 9521 2889.

TRAVEL OZ, 205 Spencer St, Melbourne 3000 VIC, Australia, (61 3) 9600 1687, Fax: (61 3) 9642 1173.

TRAVELMARVEL, 283 Drummond St, Carlton 3053 VIC, Australia, (61 3) 9288 0000, Fax: (61 3) 9349 1542.

WINGS OF DESIRE, 8/176 Commercial Rd, Prahran 3181 VIC, Australia, (61 3) 9521 1544, Fax: (61 3) 9521 3944. *Member:* IGTA AGLTA

WESTERN AUSTRALIA

STA TRAVEL, 100 James St, Northbridge WA, Australia, (61 9) 227 7569.

NEW ZEALAND

EUROLYNX TRAVEL PLANNERS, 20 Fort St, 3rd fl, Auckland, New Zealand, (64 9) 3799716, Fax: (64 9) 3798874.

FERRARI GUIDES' GAY TRAVEL A to Z - 18th EDITION

WHO TO CALL

GAYLINK INTERNATIONAL, PO Box 11-582, Wellington, New Zealand, (64 4) 384 1877, Fax: (64 4) 384 1787.

GREY LYNN TRAVEL, 555 Great North Rd, Grey Lynn, New Zealand, (64 9) 376 3556.

METRO UNITED TRAVEL, 6 Lorne St, Auckland, New Zealand, (64 9) 309 6655.

MILBROOK TRAVEL, 2nd floor, Vulcan Ln, Auckland, New Zealand, (64 9) 358-2220, Fax: (64 9) 358-2221.

TRAVEL DESK NEW ZEALAND, 2nd floor of the OUT! Centre, 45 Anzac Ave, Auckland, New Zealand, (64 9) 3779 031, Fax: (64 9) 3777 767.

TRAVEL PLANNERS LTD, 3rd Floor, 20 Fort St, Auckland 1, New Zealand, (64 9) 379 9716.

CANADA

ALBERTA

ALGONQUIN TRAVEL, 17303 Stony Plain Rd, Edmonton, AB, T5S 1B5, (403) 483-8778, Fax: (403) 481-5206. *Member:* IGTA

ALL WORLD TRAVEL (1992), 818 3rd Ave S, Lethbridge, AB, T1J 0H7, (403) 328-9614, Fax: (403) 328-2166. *Member:* IGTA

FLETCHER SCOTT TRAVEL LTD, 333 5th Ave SW #220, Calgary, AB, T2P 3B6, (403) 232-1180, Fax: (403) 232-0211. *Member:* IGTA

HAROLD SMITH TRAVEL, 10200 102nd Ave #1274, Edmonton, AB, T5J 4B7, (403) 429-2233, fax: (403) 424-2649. *Member:* IGTA

HAT TRAVEL CENTRE, 51 Tweed Ave NW, Medicine Hat, AB, T1A 6W3, (403) 528-2821. Ask for Rick.

HOLIDAY SHOPS, #125, 3604 52nd Ave NW, Calgary, AB, T2L 1V9, (403) 220-0008, fax: (403) 220-0010. *Member:* IGTA

LET'S TALK WORLDWIDE TRAVEL, 4428 16th Ave NW, Calgary, AB, T3B 0M4, (403) 247-0600, (403) 247-1652. *Member:* IGTA

MACK TRAVEL,, Stanley Tech Centre #1240, 1122 4th St SW,, Calgary, AB, T2R 1M1, (403) 233-8700, Fax: (403) 233-8705.

NEWPORT PACIFIC TRAVEL, 10180-101 St #1860, Edmonton, AB, T5J 3S4, (403) 424 5700, Fax: (403) 428 5100. *Member:* IGTA

STONEWALL CONNECTION TRAVEL & TOURS, #320 3545-32nd Ave NE, Calgary, AB, T1Y 6M6, (403) 250-3061, (800) 360-8773 (North America), Fax: (403) 250-1041. *Member:* IGTA

TRIANGLE TOURS, LTD, 717 7th Ave SW #1000, Calgary, AB, T2P 0Z3, (403) 234-0463, Fax: (403) 269-5370.

UNIGLOBE SWIFT TRAVEL, STE 112, 908 17th Ave SW, Calgary, AB, T2T 0A3, (403) 244-7887, Fax: (403) 229-2611.

BRITISH COLUMBIA

AMEX CANADA INC, 666 Burrard St, Park Place, Vancouver, BC, V6C 2X8, (604) 669-2813, (800) 772-4473, Fax: (604) 669-3207. *Member:* IGTA

ASSOCIATED TRAVEL CONSULTANTS, 105 389-12th St, Courtenay, BC, V9N 8V7, (604) 334-8529, (800) 856-4777, Fax: (604) 334-8539. *Member:* IGTA

CARLSON WAGONLIT TRAVEL, 329000 S Feaser Way #332, Abbotsford, BC, V2T 5A6, (604) 853-9111, fax: (604) 853-8621. *Member:* IGTA

ENGLISH BAY TRAVEL, 1267 Davie St, Vancouver, BC, V6E 1N4, (604) 687-8785, Fax: (604) 682-1027. *Member:* IGTA

ENSING TRAVEL, James Bay Sq 3-C, 435 Simcoe St, Victoria, BC, V8V 4T4,

FLIGHT CENTER DAVIE STREET, 1232 Davie St, Vancouver, BC, V6E 1N3, (604) 681-9992,Fax: (604) 681-9998.

HARBOUR CENTRE TRAVEL, PO Box 12030, Vancouver, BC, V6B 4N4, (604) 689-9100, fax: (604) 689-5073. *Member:* IGTA

HUME HOLIDAYS, 100-1281 W Georgia St, Vancouver, BC, V6E 3J7, (604) 682-7581, Fax: (604) 681-2651. Ask for Mike.

MARLIN TRAVEL (BC), 116A 1950 Harvey Ave, Kelowna, BC, V1Y 8J8, (604) 860-7887, Fax: (604) 861-3808.

MARLIN TRAVEL (BC), 2009 S Park Royal, West Vancouver, BC, V7T 1A1, (604) 922-9301, Fax: (604) 922-2961. Ask for Denni.

P. LAWSON TRAVEL, Suite 150, 409 Granville St, Vancouver, BC, V6C 1T4, (604) 682-4272, Fax: (604) 682-7492.

PRIDE ENTERPRISES, 3514 E 27th Ave, Vancouver, BC, V5R 1R1, (604) 435-4576, fax: (604) 435-9630. *Member:* IGTA

PRIDE TRAVEL NETWORK, 910 Mainland St #815, Vancouver, BC, V6B 1A9, (604) 687-4323, Fax: (604) 685-9397. *Member:* IGTA

PROGRESSIVE TRAVEL INC, 1120 Davie St, Vancouver, BC, V6E 1N2, (604) 687-3837, Fax: (604) 687-7937. *Member:* IGTA

ROCKY MOUNTAINEER RAILTOURS, 1150 Station St, 1st Floor, Vancouver, BC, V6A 2X7, (604) 984-3131, (800) 665-7245, Fax: (604) 984-3112. *Member:* IGTA

TDI TRAVEL DIMENSIONS, 1200 Burrard St #220, Vancouver, BC, V6Z 1Z2, (604) 685-8636, Fax: (604) 685-8616. *Member:* IGTA

TEAM TRAVEL, 1140 W Pender St #1800, Vancouver, BC, V6E 4G1, (604) 688-9655, Fax: (604) 688-0902.

TRAVEL CLINIC, THE, 1033 Davie St #411, Vancouver, BC, V6E 1M7, (604) 669-3321, Fax: (604) 669-3323. *Member:* IGTA

UNIGLOBE SPECIALTY TRAVEL, 626 W. Pender St, Vancouver, BC, V6B 1V9, (604) 688-8816, Fax: (604) 688-8317.

YALETOWN TRAVEL, DBA TRIANGLE TRAVEL GROUP, 777 W Broadway #800, Vancouver, BC, V5Z 4J7, (604) 877-1660, (604) 975-8487. *Member:* IGTA

MANITOBA

FLAIR TRAVEL, 1120 Grant Ave #320, Winnipeg, MB, R3M 2A6, (204) 284-9682, fax: (204) 452-5594. *Member:* IGTA

GOLIGER'S TRAVEL, 125 Garry St #100, Winnipeg, MB, R3L 3P2, (204) 943-6224, Fax: (204) 947-0479.

OUT 'N ABOUT TRAVEL, 100 Osborne St S #207, Winnipeg, MB, R3L 1V5, (204) 477-6799, (800) 254-5552 (in Canada), Fax: (204) 475-9493. *Member:* IGTA

TRAVEL VISION, 102-698 Carydon Ave, Winnipeg, MB, R3M 0X9, (204) 957-8888, Fax: (204) 957-8891.

NEW BRUNSWICK

TIME LINES TRAVEL, 210 Park St, Moncton, NB, E1C 2B8, (506) 382-7171, fax: (506) 854-3868. *Member:* IGTA

WILDWOOD EASTERN TRAVEL INC, 210 Park St, Moncton, NB, EIC 2B8, (506) 382-7171, (800) 622-8111, Fax: (506) 854-3868.

ONTARIO

ADMIT TRAVEL, 1050 Broadview Ave PH#1, Toronto, ON, M4K 253, (416) 921-7171, Fax: (416) 921-5533. *Member:* IGTA

ALGONQUIN TRAVEL, 1105 Wellington Rd S, London, ON, N6E 1V4, (519) 668-8479, Fax: (519) 668-0700.

BRANT HERITAGE TRAVEL, 155 Brant Ave, Brantford, ON, N3T 3H6, (519) 759-1990, (800) 661-4207, Fax: (519) 759-2871.

CANATOURS INC, 360 Park St West, Windsor, ON, N9A 5V1, (519) 258-9700, Fax: (519) 258-9544.

CARLSON WAGONLIT TRAVEL, 224 Central Ave, London, ON, N6A 1M8, (519) 679-8520, fax: (519) 679-2437. *Member:* IGTA

CLINTON'S TRAVEL, 540 Talbot St, St. Thomas, ON, N5P 1C4, (519) 631-6400, (800) 303-7404, Fax: (519) 631 6550. Ask for Shirley.

CREATIVE TRAVEL GROUPS/CLARKE WAY TRAVEL, 36 Toronto St, Toronto, ON, M5C 2C5, (416) 364-0782, fax: (416) 364-0458. *Member:* IGTA

ESCAPE TRAVEL, 469 Church St, Toronto, ON, M4Y 2C5, (416) 962-4833, Fax: (416) 962-4101.

FAR HORIZONS, 190 McLaren St, Ottawa, ON, K2P 0L6, (613) 234-6116, Fax: (800) 555-5719, (613) 563-2593.

GETAWAY TRAVEL, 380 Elgin St, Ottawa, ON, K2P 1N1, (613) 230-2250, Fax: (613) 230-3396.

GOLIGER'S TRAVEL, 322 King St West, Toronto, ON, M5V 1J2, (416) 979-1313, Fax: (416) 979-8384. *Member:* IGTA

LAFABULA TRAVEL & TOURS, 551 Church St, Toronto, ON, M4Y 2E5, (416) 920-3229, Fax: (416) 920-9484. *Member:* IGTA

MANOTICK TRAVEL & CRUISE CENTRE, 1160 John St, Box 610, Manotick, ON, K4M 1A6, (613) 692-2521. *Member:* IGTA

NIAGARA TRAVEL CENTER, 7000 McLeod Rd, Niagara Falls, ON, L2G 7K3, (905) 357-2330, Fax: (905) 357-2331.

OPEN DOOR TRAVEL, 815A Queen St East, Toronto, ON, M4M 1H8, (416) 463-7400, (416) 463-7670. *Member:* IGTA

PLANET TRAVEL, 154B Caroline St S, Hamilton, ON, L8P 3K9, (709) 256-9385, (800) 667-2642, Fax: (709) 256-9375.

REGAL CRUISES & TRAVEL, 45 Godrich Rd Unit 5, Hamilton, ON, L8E 4W8, (905) 578-9888, Fax: (905) 578-9895, Toll-free: (800) 461-7447 (Canada & USA), (0800) 897613 (Great Britain). Ask for Christine.

ROBERT Q'S TRAVEL, 1240 Commissioners Rd W, London, ON, N6K 1C7, (519) 474-7979, Fax: (519) 474-0809.

ROBERT Q'S TRAVEL MART, 105 Wharncliffe Rd S, London, ON, N6J 2K2, (519) 672-9020, Fax: (519) 673-1935.

TALK OF THE TOWN TRAVEL, 565 Sherbourne St, Toronto, ON, M4X 1W7, (416) 960-1393, Fax:

WHO TO CALL

(416) 960-6379. Ask for Henry. *Member:* IGTA

TCB TRAVEL, 600 Doon Village Rd, Kitchener, ON, N2P 1G6, (519) 748-0850, Fax: (519) 748-0852. Ask for Linda.

TRAVEL CLINIC, THE, 506 Church St #200, Toronto, ON, M4Y 2C8, (416) 962-2422, Fax: (416) 962-6621. *Member:* IGTA

TRAVEL SEARCH, 1050 Broadview Ave PH#1, Toronto, ON, M4K 253, (416) 920-9107, Fax: (416) 920-3210.

TTI ADMIRAL TRAVEL AGENCIES LTD, 731 Belfast Rd, Ottawa, ON, K1G 3T8, (613) 244-1234, Fax: (613) 244-0413. *Member:* IGTA

UNIGLOBE CANADIAN TRAVEL CENTER, 2230 Queensway Dr, Burlington, ON, L7R 3T1, (905) 634-8811, (800) 263-8811, Fax: (905) 639-3315. *Member:* IGTA

UPTOWN TRAVEL, 104 King St South, Waterloo, ON, N2J 1P5, (519) 886-3320, (519) 886-8328. *Member:* IGTA

WHOLESALE TRAVEL GROUP, 82 Adelaide St East, Toronto, ON, M5C 1K9, (416) 366-1000, fax: (416) 449-6078. *Member:* IGTA

YOULTEN TRAVEL, Box 2133, Timmins, ON, P4N 7X8, (705) 268-6449, Fax: (705) 267-1337.

QUEBEC

AGENCE DE VOYAGES CAA QUEBEC, 1555 Place Jean XXIII, Trois Rivieres, QC, G9C 1A2, (819) 379-2732 (tel/fax). *Member:* IGTA

ALTERNATIVE TRAVEL, 42 Pine Ave W Ste 2, Montreal, QC, H2W 1R1, (514) 845-7769, Fax: (514) 845-8421. *Member:* IGTA

CLUB VOYAGES, 920 Maisonneuve est, Montreal, PQ, H2L 1Z1, (514) 521-2155, Fax: (514) 521-9991.

CLUB VOYAGES DU PLATEAU, 981 rue Duluth est, Montreal, QC, H2L 1B9, (514) 521-3320, Fax: (514) 526-0369.

CLUB VOYAGES JOSEE, 157 Est Jean Talon, Montreal, QC, H2R 1S8, (514) 270-4376, Fax: (514) 270-1077. *Member:* IGTA

M.A.P. TRAVEL, 410 St-Nicolas Ste 118, Montreal, QC, H2Y 2P5, (514) 287-7446, Fax: (514) 287-7375.

QT, 4002 Laval Ave, Montreal, QC, H2W 2J2, (514) 286-7527, Fax: (514) 289-9058.

SUPERIOR TRAVEL, 590 Avenue Beaumont, Montreal, QC, H3N 1T7, (514) 277-8677, Fax: (514) 277-2542. *Member:* IGTA

TERRE DES HOMMES, 1122 Blvd de Maisonneuve Est, Montreal, QC, H2L 1Z5, (514) 522 2225, Fax: (514) 522 7987. *Member:* IGTA

VOYAGES AQUANAUTES, 1551 Montarville, St. Bruno, QC, J3V 3T8, (514) 461-0110, Fax: (514) 461-3199.

VOYAGES LORRAINE, 153 rue Principale, Aylmer, QC, J9H 3M9, (819) 684-3536, Fax: (819) 684-0185.

VOYAGES OTTAWA, Place du Centre, 200, Prm du Portage, Hull, QC, J8X 4B7, (819) 770-4441.

VOYAGES SOLARIS, 215 Boul. Concord, Laval, QC, H7G 2C9, (514) 667-7711, Fax: (514) 667-8670.

VOYAGES VIAU MARLIN, 1356 Blu Cure Labelle #234, Blainville, QC, J7C 2P2, (514) 971-5511, (514) 971-5512. *Member:* IGTA

WORLD BEAT TRAVEL, 1221 St Hubert #300, Montreal, QC, H2L 3Y8, (514) 286-9014, fax: (514) 286-2897. *Member:* IGTA

SASKATCHEWAN

JUBILEE TRAVEL, Circle 8 Centre, #108-3120 8th St E, Saskatoon, SK, S7H 0W2, (306) 373-9633, Fax: (306) 374-5878.

CARIBBEAN
PUERTO RICO

CONNECTIONS TRAVEL, Tetuan 257, PO Box 71, San Juan, PR, 00902, (787) 721-5550, (800) 973-5550, Fax: (787) 721-7123. *Member:* IGTA

CONSON HOLIDAYS, 954 Ponce De Leon Ave #309, Santurce, PR, 00907, (809) 725-5940, Fax: (809) 725-1263. *Member:* IGTA

DARLINGTON TRAVEL, 1007 Monoz Rivera Ave, Rio Piedras, PR, (787) 765-1760, (787) 765-1745. *Member:* IGTA

JUST 4U TRAVEL, PO Box 70359, San Juan, PR, 00936, (787) 257-3575, (888) GAYSTORE, fax: (787) 781-8242.

RUMY TRAVEL, 931 Eider St, Contry Club Rio Piedras, PR, 00924, (787) 257-1650, Fax: (787) 257-6100.

TRAVEL MAKER INTERNATIONAL TOURS, San Claudio Mail Stations, Box 224, Rio Piedras, PR, 00926, (787) 755-5878, Fax: (787) 755-5850. *Member:* IGTA

VIRGIN ISLANDS

CALPARRIO INT'L TRAVELS, W. 67 King St, Frederiksted, Saint Croix, 00840, (809) 772-9822, Fax: (809) 772-9677.

LATIN AMERICA
ARGENTINA

MIX TRAVEL, Maipú 971 5-C, Buenos Aires 1006, Argentina, (54 1) 312-3410, Fax: (54 1) 315 4586 or 313 4432. *Member:* IGTA

BRAZIL

GET TOGETHER RIO, Ave N.S. de Copacabana 435-Cj 411, Rio de Janeiro, Brazil, 22020-000, (55 21) 237 6369, Fax: (55 21) 237 63 69.

GET TOGETHER TRAVEL, R. da Consolaçao 222 cj. 809, Sao Paulo, Brazil, 01302-910, (55 11) 258 6701, Fax: (55 11) 256 0124. Specializing in gay travel.

GUIRLANDA VIAGENS E TURISMO, Av Franklin Roosevelt #23/1302, 20021-120 Rio de Janeiro, Brazil, (55-21) 2207162, (55-21) 220-7162. *Member:* IGTA

INTER-RAINBOW TURISMO, Av. Ipiranga 104 #71, Sao Paulo, Brazil, 01046-918, (55 11) 214 5898, Fax: (55 11) 258 7693.

O.G. TRAVEL TOURS, Rua Barata Ribeiro 383 #201, Rio de Janeiro, Brazil, 22040, (55 21) 255 9449, Fax: (55 21) 235 6733.

OUTGOING TOURS & TRAVEL, Rua Constante Ramos #44, Rio de Janeiro, Brazil, 22051-010, (55 21) 256 3932, Fax: (55 21) 257 6714.

CHILE

CASTING CHILE, Napoleon 3310 #132, Santiago, Chile, (56 2) 332 170, Fax: (56 2) 520 198.

COLOMBIA

VIAJES Y EVENTOS CLAVE, Calle 64 #4-08, 55253 Bogota, Colombia, (57-1) 346 4896, (57-1) 346 4896. *Member:* IGTA

MEXICO

AM & LN DE VIAJES COORDINADORES, Ingres No 134 101, Col. Nonoalco, Mexico City, Mexico, 03700, (52 5) 611 2149, Fax: (52 5) 611 2149.

LAREDO ASESORES, Rio Danubio 63 #5, Col. Cuauhtemoc, Mexico City, Mexico, 06500, (52 5) 525 8903, Fax: (52 5) 207 5078. *Member:* IGTA

PLANTUR, Avda. Mexico 99 #PB, Mexico City, Mexico, 06170, (52 5) 264 0822, Fax: (52 5) 264 2827. *Member:* IGTA

STAG TRAVEL & TOURS, Hamburgo 214-31, Col. Juarez, Mexico City, Mexico, 06600, (52 5) 525-4658, Fax: (52 5) 525-4658.

TURISMO DIFERENTE, Ingres No. 134, 101, Col. Nonoalco, Mexico City, Mexico, 03700, (52 5) 611 2149, Fax: (52 5) 611 2149. *Member:* IGTA

TURISMO PERINORTE SA DE CV, Canada NBR, 11 Mezz 4, Plaza de L, Edo de Tlalnepantla, Mexico City, Mexico, 54080, (52 5) 397-7117, Fax: (52 5) 397-2211.

VIAJES HELENA, Blvd. 31 Oriente #1612, Puebla Pue., Mexico, 72540, (52 22) 45 89 79, (52 22) 33 50 04, Fax: (52 22) 44 08 65. Ask for Ramón.

VENEZUELA

NEW LIFE TOURS, Apto Postal 68110, 1062 Caracas, Venezuela, (58-2) 286 2927, Fax: (58-2) 285 3827. *Member:* IGTA

UNITED STATES
ALABAMA

A WORLD OF TRAVEL, 2101 Civic Center Blvd, Birmingham, AL, 35203, (205) 458-8888, (800) 458-3597, Fax: (205) 458-8889.

EXOTIC TRAVEL INC, 1406 17th St S, Birmingham, AL, 32505, (205) 930-0911, (205) 933-7063. *Member:* IGTA

USTRAVEL STERLING TRAVEL AGENCY, 720 Madison St, Huntsville, AL, 35801, (205) 533-1301, Fax: (205) 536-3914. *Member:* IGTA

VILLAGE TRAVEL, 1929 Cahaba Rd, Birmingham, AL, 35223, (205) 870-4866, Fax: (205) 871-6114.

ALASKA

ALASKA RIDGE RIDERS, PO Box 357, Healy, AK, 99753, (907) 683-2580, (800) 713-6163, Fax: (907) 683-2580. *Member:* IGTA

AMERICAN EXPRESS TRAVEL, PO Box 1769, Nome, AK, 99762, Attn: John or Mickey.

AMERICAN EXPRESS TRAVEL, 5530 E Northern Lights Blvd, Anchorage, AK, 99504, (907) 333-8585, Fax: (907) 337-7341.

APOLLO TRAVEL SERVICE, 1207 West 47th Ave, Anchorage, AK, 99503, (907) 561-0661, Fax: (907) 561-5802. *Member:* IGTA

ARIZONA

ADVENTURE BOUND TRAVEL, 2100 W Chandler Blvd #38, Chandler, AZ, 85224, (602) 963-2506, Fax: (602) 899-9898.

ALL ABOUT DESTINATIONS, 3819 N 3rd St, Phoenix, AZ, 85012-2074, (602) 277-2703, (800) 375-2703, Fax: (602) 277-2786. E-mail: proudmember@aol.com. *Member:* IGTA

ALL HOURS TRAVEL, 8120 E McDowell, Scottsdale, AZ, 85257, (602) 970-3545, Fax: (602) 970-3510.

FERRARI GUIDES' GAY TRAVEL A to Z - 18th EDITION

115

WHO TO CALL

ALL POINTS TRAVEL, 3001 Stockton Hill Rd #5, Kingman, AZ, 86401, (602) 753-7878, (800) 719-7878. Ask for Brandy.
ARIZONA TRAVEL CENTER, 2502 E Grant Rd, Tucson, AZ, 85716, (520) 323-3250, Fax: (520) 325-0560. Member: IGTA
CARLSON TRAVEL NETWORK (AZ), 13628 N 99th Ave, Sun City, AZ, 85351, (602) 974-3668, Fax: (602) 977-9115.
CASABLANCA TRAVEL, 3030 N Central #106, Phoenix, AZ, 85012, (602) 631-9050, (800) 321-1807, Fax: (602) 631-9054. Member: IGTA
CENTURY TRAVEL WEST, 2280 N Oracle Rd, Tuscon, AZ, 85705-5431, (602) 624-7458, Fax: (602) 622-1497.
DOLPHIN TRAVEL SERVICES, 10632-B N Scottsdale Rd, Scottsdale, AZ, 85254, (602) 998-9191, Fax: (602) 998-1110. Member: IGTA
EAGLE TRAVEL, 121 N Cortez, Prescott, AZ, 86301, (520) 445-5492, (800) 821-6844, Fax: (520) 445-5498. Ask for Harvey.
FIFTH AVENUE TRAVEL, 7007 5th Ave, Scottsdale, AZ, 85251, (602) 949-1919, (800) 336-2242, Fax: (602) 941-3718.
FIRSTRAVEL LTD, 5150 N 7th St, Phoenix, AZ, 85014, (602) 265-0666, Fax: (602) 265-0135.
FULL SPECTRUM TRAVEL, 3801 N Swan Rd, Tucson, AZ, 85718, (520) 577-0645, (520) 577-1195. Member: IGTA
MANALI TRAVEL, 1041 N Firewood Place, Tucson, AZ, 85742, (520) 290-1054, (800) 649-9639.
MOUNTAIN VIEW TRANSPORTATION, 3149 E Prince Rd, Tucson, AZ, 85716-1227, (602) 326-8670, Fax: (602) 622-4488.
PINNACLE PEAK TRAVELER, 8700 E Pinnacle Peak Rd #106, Scottsdale, AZ, 85255, (602) 585-0033.
PRISM WORLD TRAVEL, 5625 E Indian School Rd, Phoenix, AZ, 85018, (602) 941-8600, (800) 253-2852, Fax: (602) 994-3650.
PSI TRAVEL, 2100 N Wilmot #203, Tucson, AZ, 85712, (520) 296-3788.
ROMANTIC HAWAII VACATIONS, 3310 W Bell Rd, Ste 242, Phoenix, AZ, 85023, (602) 861-0771, Fax: (602) 866-7759.
SELECT TRAVEL SERVICES, INC, 77 E Weldon Ave, Ste 280, Phoenix, AZ, 85012-2076, (602) 279-7500, (800) 743-3550, Fax: (602) 279-7600.
SUN KACHINA TRAVEL, 1987 McCullich #108, Lake Havasu City, AZ, 86403, (520) 855-0066, Fax: (520) 855-7412. Member: IGTA
TGI TRAVEL AGENCY, 5540 W Glendale Ave #A-102, Glendale, AZ, 85301, (602) 939-1445.
TRAVEL EASY, 1133 E Glendale Ave, Phoenix, AZ, 85020, (602) 277-1995, (800) 769-2446, Fax: (602) 277-0170.
TREK, 6451 N Lena Pl, Tucson, AZ, 85741, (520) 742-2862.
VICTORY VACATIONS, PO Box 11429, Tucson, AZ, 85734, (602) 295-1173.
WORLD TRAVEL, 1377 N Scottsdale Rd, Scottsdale, AZ, 85257, (602) 949-1995, (800) 699-3894, Fax: (602) 949-1891.

ARKANSAS

TRAVEL BY PHILLIP, Box 250119, Little Rock, AR, 72225-5119, (501) 227-7690, Fax: (501) 224-8638. Member: IGTA

TRAVEL SERVICES OF FORT SMITH, 4120 Rogers Ave, Fort Smith, AR, 72903, (501) 782-6000, (501) 782-9603. Member: IGTA
WORLDWIDE TRAVEL, 3810 Front St #8, Fayetteville, AR, 72703, (501) 521-3440, (800) 262-4545, Fax: (501) 521-1124. Ask for Marty. Member: IGTA

CALIFORNIA

800 I FLY GAY, 5440 Morehouse #2000, San Diego, CA, 92121, (800) 435-9429, fax: (619) 450-6932. Member: IGTA
A & D TRAVEL, 2547 W Shaw #108, Fresno, CA, 93711, (209) 224-1200, Fax: (209) 224-1213. Ask for Helen. Member: IGTA
A RAINBOW OF TRAVEL, 407 W Imperial Hwy, Brea, CA, 92821, (714) 670-1897, fax: (310) 697-7504. Member: IGTA
A TO Z TRAVEL PLANNERS, INC, 5533 Snell Ave, Ste 100, San Jose, CA, 95123-1526, (408) 363-9966, (408) 365-9555, Fax: (408) 363-9967.
AACTION TRAVEL SERVICE, 6416 Del Amo Blvd, Lakewood, CA, 90713, (310) 420-3316, fax: (310) 420-1976. Member: IGTA
ABC TRAVEL SERVICES, 6160 Mission Gorge Rd #102, San Diego, CA, 92120-3425, (619) 280-9986, Fax: (619) 280-9989.
ABOVE AND BEYOND TRAVEL, 330 Townsend St #107, San Francisco, CA, 94107, (415) 284-1666, (800) 397-2681, Fax: (415) 284-1660. Member: IGTA
ADVENTURE TRAVEL, PO Box 669, Aptos, CA, 95001, (408) 688-9400. Member: IGTA
ADVENTURES WITH A RAINBOW, PO Box 293055, Sacramento, CA, 95829-3055, (916) 383-0123, Fax: (916) 383-0124.
AFFORDABLE TRAVEL, 8680 Navajo Rd #106, San Diego, CA, 92119, (619) 460-6400, Fax: (619) 460-3624. Ask for Ed.
ALADDIN TRAVEL, 818 K Street Mall, Sacramento, CA, 95814, (916) 446-0633, CA: (800) 433-5386. Ask for Rob Thorbin.
ALL ABOUT CRUISING 'N TOURS, PO Box 992583, Redding, CA, 96099, (916) 245-0511 (tel/fax). Member: IGTA
ALL CONTINENTS TRAVEL,, 5250 W Century Blvd #626,, Los Angeles, , CA, 90045, (310) 645-7527, (800) 995-7997, (310) 645-1071. Member: IGTA
ALL DESTINATIONS TRAVEL, 2500 E Imperial Hwy #102, Brea, CA, 92621, (714) 529-4400, (800) 283-1203, Fax: (714) 529-5400. Member: IGTA
ALL POINTS TRAVEL, 615A Stockton Ave, San Jose, CA, 95126, (408) 288-3280, Fax: (403) 993-8134.
ALL TRAVEL, 2001 S Barrington Ave #150, Los Angeles, CA, 90025, (213) 312-3368.
ALPHA PACIFIC TRAVEL, 915 Redondo Ave, Long Beach, CA, 90804, (310) 987-2626. Member: IGTA
ALTERNATIVE VACATIONS TRAVEL, 584 Castro #413, San Francisco, CA, 94114, (415) 440-8609 (tel/fax). Member: IGTA
AMERICAN EXPRESS TRAVEL, 2011 N Shoreline Blvd, MS 724, Mountain View, CA, 94043, (415) 933-1093, (415) 964-3844. Member: IGTA
AMERICAN EXPRESS TRAVEL RELATED

SERVICES, 525 Market St, Ste 3800, San Francisco, CA, 94105, (415) 543-1144.
AMERICAN EXPRESS TRAVEL SERVICE, 180 Montgomery St, 13th Fl, San Francisco, CA, 94104, (415) 398-4090, (800) 942-2438, Fax: (415) 398-5490.
AMERICAN EXPRESS TRAVEL SERVICE, 237 Post St, San Francisco, CA, 94108, (415) 955-5641, (800) 461-8484, Fax: (415) 296-0906.
AMERICAN EXPRESS TRAVEL SERVICE, 201 Mission St #2020, San Francisco, CA, 94105, (415) 536-2662 (Ask for Steve), (415) 536-2670 (Ask for Jim), (800) 461-8484, Fax: (415) 974-1403.
AMERICAN EXPRESS TRAVEL SERVICE, 8493 W 3rd St, Los Angeles, CA, 90048, (310) 659-1682, (310) 659-1151. Member: IGTA
AMERICAN EXPRESS TRS, 91 Broadway Ln, Walnut Creek, CA, 94596, (510) 938-0800, Fax: (510) 938-4362.
AMERICAN WAY TOURS, 8110 W Norton Ave #8, West Hollywood, CA, 90046, (213) 654-9098.
ANCIENT MARINER TRAVEL, 14145 Red Hill Ave, Tustin, CA, 92680, (714) 838-9780, Fax: (714) 838-9796.
ANDERSON TRAVEL SERVICE, 700 E Tahquitz Canyon Dr #A, Palm Springs, CA, 92262, (760) 325-2001, (760) 325-5127. Member: IGTA
AP TRAVEL SERVICES, 30 Spring St, Salinas, CA, 93901, (408) 758-2212.
ARCO IRIS TRAVEL SERVICES, 1286 University Ave #154, San Diego, CA, 92103, (619) 297-0897, fax: (619) 297-6419.
ART OF TRAVEL, THE, 2902 Dove St, San Diego, CA, 92103-5543, (619) 294-3598, Fax: (619) 683-7772. Member: IGTA
ASTRA TRAVEL SERVICE, 1164 Chestnut St, Menlo Park, CA, 94025, (415) 323-8080, Fax: (415) 324-4869. Ask for Basil.
ATLAS SERVICES & TRAVEL, 8923 S Sepulveda Blvd, Los Angeles, CA, 90045, (310) 670-3574, Fax: (310) 670-0725. Ask for Rose. Member: IGTA
AURORA WORLDWIDE TRAVEL, 75 Woodhaven Dr, Laguna Niguel, CA, 92677, Tel/Fax: (714) 661-0223.
AUSTRALIA & NEW ZEALAND TRAVEL HEADQUARTERS, 120 Montgomery St #1280, San Francisco, CA, 94104, (415) 956-2990, (800) 453-6636, Fax: (415) 956-2886. Member: IGTA
AVB TRAVEL, 1548 Palos Verdes Mall, Walnut Creek, CA, 94596, (510) 977-4034.
AZZURRO TRAVEL, 7985 Santa Monica Blvd #206, West Hollywood, CA, 90046, (213) 654-3700, Fax: (213) 654-7909. Member: IGTA
BEHIND THE SCENES TRAVEL, 5200 Lankershim Blvd #240, North Hollywood, CA, 91602, (818) 762-5200, Fax: (818) 761-5200.
BERKELEY'S NORTHSIDE TRAVEL., 1824 Euclid Ave, Berkeley, CA, 94709, (510) 843-1000, Fax: (510) 843-7537.
BEST OF BELIZE AND BEYOND, 31F Commercial Blvd, Novato, CA, 94949, (415) 884-2325, (800) 735-9520, Fax: (415) 884-2339. Member: IGTA
BEYOND THE BAY, 726 Polk St, San Francisco, CA, 94109, (415) 441-3440.
BLAZE TRAVEL, 1349 E Broadway, Long Beach,

WHO TO CALL

CA, 90802, (310) 628-0555, Fax: (310) 628-0550. *Member:* IGTA

BON VOYAGE TRAVEL, 5955 Ball Rd, Cypress, CA, 90630, (714) 236-9094, Fax: (714) 527-1713. *Member:* IGTA

BOTTOM LINE TRAVEL, 1236 Castro St, San Francisco, CA, 94114, (415) 826-8600, (800) 456-9833, Fax: (415) 826-8698. *Member:* IGTA

BRYAN INTERNATIONAL TRAVEL, 98 Battery St #302, San Francisco, CA, 94111, (415) 731-8411, Fax: (415) 433-5208.

CALIFORNIA TRAVEL, 1117 Texas St, Fairfield, CA, 94533, (707) 427-1117, (888) 427-1117, (707) 427-1121. E-mail: ctravel@juno.com.

CALIG WORLD TRAVEL, 4873 Topanga Canyon Blvd, Woodland Hills, CA, 91364, (818) 703-0100.

CANYON TRAVEL, 67-555 Hwy 111, #C-110, Cathedral City, CA, 92234, (760) 324-3484, Fax: (760) 324-0298. *Member:* IGTA

CARLSON TRAVEL NETWORK (CA), 5975 Topanga Canyon Blvd, Woodland Hills, CA, 91367, (818) 703-8871, Fax: (818) 703-0849.

CASSIS TRAVEL SERVICES, 9200 W Sunset Blvd #320, West Hollywood, CA, 90069-3505, (310) 246-5400, Fax: (310) 246-5499. *Member:* IGTA

CASTRO TRAVEL COMPANY, 435 Brannan St. #214, San Francisco, CA, 94107, (415) 357-0957, (800) 861-0957, Fax: (415) 357-0221. E-mail: castrotrvl@aol.com. *Member:* IGTA

CHASE TRAVEL, 316 E Broadway, Glendale, CA, 91209-3060, (818) 246-1661, (213) 245-7611. Ask for Patty.

CLASSIC CRUISE & TRAVEL, 19626 Ventura Blvd Ste 216, Tarzana, CA, 91356, (818) 708-7288, Fax: (818) 708-2928. *Member:* IGTA

CLASSIC TRAVEL, 7985 Santa Monica Blvd #103, West Hollywood, CA, 90046-5112, (213) 650-8444, Fax: (213) 650-5135 *Member:* IGTA

CLUB TRAVEL, 8739 Santa Monica Blvd, West Hollywood, CA, 90069, (310) 358-2207, Fax: (310) 358-2122. *Member:* IGTA

COAST TRAVEL, 1355 N Harbor Dr, San Diego, CA, 92101, (619) 239-9973, Fax: (619) 238-4283.

CONFIDENT TRAVEL, 1499 Bayshore Hwy #126, Burlingame, CA, 94010, (415) 697-7274, (800) 872-7252, Fax: (415) 697-0499. *Member:* IGTA

COUNCIL TRAVEL, 220 Montgomery St #2630, San Francisco, CA, 94104, (415) 863-8553.

COUNCIL TRAVEL, 530 Bush St, Ground Fl, San Francisco, CA, 94108-3623, (415) 693-8780, Fax: (415) 247-5603.

COUNCIL TRAVEL LOS ANGELES, 1600 S Bentley Ave #1, Los Angeles, CA, 90025, (310) 312-0176, Fax: (310) 208-4407.

COUNTRY HILLS TRAVEL, 1210 DW Imperial Hwy Ste D, La Habra, CA, 90631, (714) 871-9896, Fax: (310) 691-9210. *Member:* IGTA '

CRAIG'S TRAVEL SERVICE, 12089 Euclid St, Garden Grove, CA, 92840, (714) 638-7381, Fax: (714) 638-3713. *Member:* IGTA

CREATIVE JOURNEYS, 5329 Skylane Blvd, Santa Rosa, CA, 95403, (707) 526-5444, Fax: (707) 528-3217.

CRUISE & TRAVEL INTERNATIONAL, 1313 N H St #E, Lompoc, CA, 93436, (805) 737-9668, fax: (805) 737-9666. *Member:* IGTA

CRUISE COMPANY OF SAN DIEGO, 3145 Rosecrans, San Diego, CA, 92110, (619) 224-7303, Fax: (619) 224-8276.

CRUISE HOLIDAYS, 224 S Robertson Blvd, Beverly Hills, CA, 90211, (213) 652-8521, Fax: (213) 652-8524.

CRUISE TIME, 1 Hallidie Plaza, #406, San Francisco, CA, 94102, (415) 677-0777, (800) 338-0818, Fax: (415) 391-1856.

CUPERTINO TRAVEL, 1211 B Kentwood Ave, San Jose, CA, 95129, (408) 255-6900, Fax: (408) 255-7340.

CUSTOM CRUISES INTERNATIONAL, 482 Greathouse Dr, Milpitas, CA, 95035, (408) 945-8286, Fax: (408) 945-8989.

DAVISVILLE TRAVEL, 420 2nd St, Davis, CA, 95616, Ask for Karen.

DBA TRAVEL 800, 3530 Camino del Rio N, #300, San Diego, CA, 92108, (619) 624-2000, Fax: (619) 624-2050.

DE ROSE TRAVEL GROUP, PO Box 170609, San Francisco, CA, 94117, (415) 864-1600, Fax: (415) 864-1692.

DEEDS & DAILY WORLD TRAVEL, 311 9th Ave, San Francisco, CA, 94118, (415) 221-6760, Fax: (415) 221-5905. *Member:* IGTA

DIMENSIONS IN TRAVEL INC, 2 Commercial Blvd Ste 101, Novato, CA, 94949, (415) 883-3245, Fax: (415) 883-7671.

DISCOVERY COSTA TRAVEL, 886 Overlook Dr, San Marcos, CA, 92069, (619) 744-6536, fax: (619) 744-5765. *Member:* IGTA

DON WILSON TRAVEL, 2332 Steiner St, San Francisco, CA, 94115, (415) 567-1009.

DOOLITTLE & CO. TRAVEL, 354 N Coast Hwy, Laguna Beach, CA, 92651, (714) 497-0566, (800) 445-0461, Fax: (714) 497-4511.

DREAMQUEST, 9446 Laguna Lake Way, Elk Grove, CA, 95758, Tel/Fax: (916) 683-1728.

DREAMS DO COME TRUE, 520 Bonita Ct, Vallejo, CA, 94591, (707) 558-0544, (800) 305-0544, Fax: (707) 644-7860.

ELECTRA TRAVEL SERVICES CO, 1258 N Highland Ave #302, Los Angeles, CA, 90038, (213) 962-8456.

ELITE DESTINATIONS, 13969 Marquesas Way #217, Marina del Rey, CA, 90292, (310) 448-1942, fax: (310) 448-1941. *Member:* IGTA

EMBASSY TRAVEL, 906 N Harper Ave #B, Los Angeles, CA, 90046, (213) 656-0743, (800) 227-6669, Fax: (213) 650-6968.

ESCAPE ARTIST TOURS, INC, 150 Tiller Ct, Half Moon Bay, CA, 94019, (415) 726-7626, (800) 728-1384, Fax: (415) 726-7647.

EUROPEAN TRAVEL, 442 Post St #301, San Francisco, CA, 94102, (415) 981-5518, Fax: (415) 986-5166. *Member:* IGTA

EXPRESS TRAVEL, 1425 Treat Blvd, Walnut Creek, CA, 94596, (510) 939-4300, Fax: (510) 947-4876.

EZE TRAVEL, 1480 N Lakeview Ave, Anaheim, CA, 92807, (714) 701-3680, Fax: (714) 777-2360.

FAIRYLAND TRAVEL,, PO Box 15128,, Santa Rosa,, CA, 95402, (707) 793-2172.

FESTIVE TOURS, 1220 N Coast Hwy, Laguna Beach, CA, 92651, (714) 494-6670.

FIESTA RIVIERA TRAVEL, 230 E 17th St #230, Costa Mesa, CA, 92627, (714) 722-8754, Fax: (714) 642-1972. Ask for Terry.

FIRSTWORLD TRAVEL, 7443 Mission Gorge Rd, San Diego, CA, 92120, (619) 265-1916, Fax: (619) 265-1930.

FIRSTWORLD TRAVEL EXPRESS, 1990 S Bundy Dr #175, West Los Angeles, CA, 90025, (310) 820-6868, (800) 366-0815, Fax: (310) 820-2807. *Member:* IGTA

FOUR WINDS TRAVEL, 3663 The Barnyard, Carmel, CA, 93923, (408) 622-0800, Fax: (408) 622-9467. *Member:* IGTA

FRANCISCAN TRAVEL, 323 Geary St #701, San Francisco, CA, 94102, (415) 391-6592, Fax: (415) 391-6674. *Member:* IGTA

FRIENDS OF DOROTHY CRUISES, TOURS AND GREAT ADVENTURES, 290 Roosevelt Way #2, San Francisco, CA, 94114, (415) 864-1600, Fax: (415) 864-1692. E-mail: derose@sirius.com. *Member:* IGTA

FRIENDS TRAVEL, 322 Huntley Dr. #100, West Hollywood, CA, 90048, (310) 652-9600, (800) GAY-0069, Fax: (310) 652-5454.

GHELLER-VERS TRAVEL, 1074 East Ave Ste H, Chico, CA, 95926, (916) 891-1633, Fax: (916) 891-0388. *Member:* IGTA

GLOBAL COMMUNICATIONS NETWORK, 12750 Ventura Blvd #202, Studio City, CA, 91604, (818) 755-9589, Fax: (818) 755-9593. Ask for Scott.

GO AWEIGH! TRAVEL, 2584 Carbon Ct #2, Colton, CA, 92324, (909) 370-4554, Fax: (909) 824-8644. *Member:* IGTA

GOLD COAST TRAVEL PLUS, PO Box 4518, Saticoy, CA, 93007, (805) 525-3351, fax: (805) 525-3355. *Member:* IGTA

GOLD RIVER TRAVEL & TOURS, 1949 Zinfandel Dr, Rancho Cordova, CA, 95670, (916) 638-2749, Fax: (916) 635-9770.

GOLDEN EAGLE TRAVEL, 17412 Beach Blvd, Huntington Beach, CA, 92647, (714) 848-9090, Fax: (714) 842-6494.

GR TRAVEL & TOURS, 1949 Zinfandel Dr, Rancho Cordova, CA, 95670, (916) 638-8800, Fax: (916) 635-9770.

GREAT ESCAPES TRAVEL, 663 Trancas St, Napa, CA, 94558, (707) 255-6600, (707) 255-2294. *Member:* IGTA

GREGORY HOWELL & ASSOC, 118 King St #530, San Francisco, CA, 94107-1916, (415) 541-5388, Fax: (415) 541-9347. *Member:* IGTA

GULLIVER'S WORLD TRAVEL, 2465 S Winchester Blvd, Campbell, CA, 95008-4801, (408) 379-0822, (800) 621-2966, Fax: (408) 379-5308.

GUNDERSON TRAVEL, 8543 Santa Monica Blvd, West Hollywood, CA, 90069, (310) 657-3944, Fax: (310) 652-4301. *Member:* IGTA

HERE, THERE & EVERYWHERE, 626 Santa Monica Blvd #56, Santa Monica, CA, 90401, (310) 453-7552, fax: (310) 453-6865. *Member:* IGTA

HILLCREST TRAVEL, 431 Robinson Ave, San Diego, CA, 92103, (619) 291-0758, Fax: (619) 291-3151. *Member:* IGTA

HOUSE OF TRAVEL, 1107 L St, Sacramento, CA, 95814, (916) 442-0743, fax: (916) 442-5656. *Member:* IGTA

HUGHLIN TRAVEL, 1139 Kansas St, San Francisco, CA, 94107.,

TRAVEL AGENTS

FERRARI GUIDES' GAY TRAVEL A to Z - 18th EDITION

WHO TO CALL

I.T.S. TRAVEL, 8833 Sunset Blvd #302, Los Angeles, CA, 90069, (310) 855-1445, Fax: (310) 855-0840.

ICT TRAVEL, 201 N Figueroa St #1410, Los Angeles, CA, 90012, (213) 482-3374, (800) 532-5821, Fax: (213) 482-5843.

JACKSON TRAVEL SERVICE LTD, 1829 Polk St, San Francisco, CA, 94109, (415) 928-2500, Fax: (415) 928-2510. Member: IGTA

JERRY & DAVID'S TRAVEL, 1025 W Laurel St, San Diego, CA, 92101, (619) 233-5199, (800) 748-6968, Fax: (619) 231-0641. Member: IGTA

JETSET TOURS, 5120 W Goldleaf Circle #310, Los Angeles, CA, 90056, (213) 290-5800, Fax: (213) 294-0434.

JP TRAVEL, 11632 Luanda St, Sylmar, CA, 91342, (818) 834-2125, Fax: (818) 890-0734. Member: IGTA

JUST CORPORATE A TRAVEL COMPANY, 510 5th St, Santa Rosa, CA, 95401, (707) 525-5105, Fax: (707) 525-5191.

KB TRAVEL & TOURS, 8907 Warner Ave #162, Huntington Beach, CA, 92647, (714) 848-7272, fax: (714) 848-5572. Member: IGTA

KISMET TRAVEL, PO Box 974, Redway, CA, 95560, (707) 986-7205, (800) 926-7205.

LAS PALMAS TRAVEL, PO Box 1930, Palm Springs, CA, 92263, (619) 325-6311, Fax: (619) 325-3542.

LEFT COAST TRAVEL, 1655 Polk St #1, San Francisco, CA, 94109, (415) 771-5353, Fax: (415) 771-5354. Member: IGTA

LEISURETYME TRAVEL/SAN DIEGO TRAVEL, PO Box 95, San Leandro, CA, 94577, (510) 614-6776.

LEMON GROVE TRAVEL, 7735 Pacific Ave, Lemon Grove, CA, 91945-0549, (619) 466-9999, Reservations: (619) 295-1984, Fax: (619) 697-7968.

LENCI CRUISE & TRAVEL, 1005 Terra Nova Blvd, Pacifica, CA, 94044, (415) 355-3919.

LINLI TRAVEL, 19510 Ventura Blvd, #107, Tarzana, CA, 91356, (818) 344-3640, Fax: (818) 344-0078.

LOS GATOS TRAVEL, 644 N Santa Cruz Ave, Los Gatos, CA, 95030, (408) 395-3167, Fax: (408) 395-4671.

LOWE'S WORLD TRAVEL, 141 University Ave #4, San Diego, CA, 92103, (619) 298-8595, Fax: (619) 294-3359.

MAGNUM TRAVEL, 8500 Wilshire Blvd #900, Beverly Hills, CA, 90211, (310) 652-7900, ext 200.

MAGNUM/SELECT TRAVEL, 9056 Santa Monica Blvd #304, West Hollywood, CA, 90069, (310) 887-0930, (800) 782-9429, Fax: (310) 887-0340.

MEGA TOURS, 1456 Jones St, San Francisco, CA, 94109, (415) 474-1941, (800) 900-6342, Fax: (415) 474-5201.

MERIDIAN DESTINATIONS INC, 13400 Riverside Dr Ste 111, Sherman Oaks, CA, 91423, (818) 986-6868, Fax: (818) 986-0608. Member: IGTA

MERRY TRAVEL SERVICES, 1742 Begen Ave, Mountain View, CA, 94040, (415) 967-2964.

MICO MEDIA INTERNATIONAL, 8016 3/4 W Norton Ave, West Hollywood, CA, 90046, (213) 848-8038, (800) 225-5759, Fax: (310) 462-0562.

MISSION CENTER TRAVEL, 3108 Fifth Ave #A, San Diego, CA, 92103-6105, (619) 299-2720.

Member: IGTA

NAVIGATOR TRAVEL, 2047 Market St, San Francisco, CA, 94114, (415) 864-0401. Ask for John.

NEW VENTURE TRAVEL, 404 22nd St, Oakland, CA, 94612, (510) 835-3800, Fax: (510) 835-7865.

NEW VENTURES TRAVEL, 3291 Truxel Rd #32, Sacramento, CA, 95833, (916) 925-4881, in CA (800) 655-1100.

NORTHSIDE TRAVEL, 1824 Euclid Ave, Berkeley, CA, 94709, (510) 843-1000, Fax: (510) 843-7537. Member: IGTA

NOW, VOYAGER TRAVEL, 4406 18th St, San Francisco, CA, 94114, (415) 626-1169, (800) 255-6951, Fax: (415) 626-8626. Member: IGTA

NTS VACATIONS, 523 E Broadway, Long Beach, CA, 90802, (310) 432-6973, (800) 886-2623, Fax: (310) 435-2745.

ODYSSEY TRAVEL, PO Box 8209, Rancho Santa Fe, 92067-8209, (619) 756-0700, Fax: (619) 759-2099. Member: IGTA

ONE WORLD TRAVEL CENTER, 526 N Larchmont Blvd, Los Angeles, CA, 90004, (213) 962-8700, (800) 231-5705, Fax: (213) 962-5856.

ORCHID TRAVEL SERVICES, 4122 20th St, San Francisco, CA, 94114, (415) 552-2468, Fax: (415) 552-9264. Member: IGTA

OUT AND ABOUT TRAVEL, 864 Apricot Ave #D, Campbell, CA, 95008, (408) 369-1739.

OVER THE RAINBOW TRAVEL, 1510 McAllister, Ste 4, San Francisco, CA, 94115, (415) 346-1524, Fax: (415) 346-1324.

PACIFIC COASTLINE, 219 N Broadway Ste 331, Laguna Beach, CA, 92651, (714) 494-1399, Fax: (714) 494-3837. Member: IGTA

PACIFIC HARBOR TRAVEL, 519 Seabright Ave #201, Santa Cruz, CA, 95062, (408) 427-5000, Fax: (408) 425-0709. Member: IGTA

PANORAMA TRAVEL CENTRE, 877 S Tustin Ave, Orange, CA, 92866, (714) 633-4640, (714) 633-4751. Member: IGTA

PASSPORT TICKET TRAVEL, 9048 Brooks Rd South, Windsor, CA, 95492, (707) 838-1557, (800) 443-4134.

PASSPORT TO LEISURE, 2265 Market St, San Francisco, CA, 94114, (415) 621-8300. Ask for Rob.

PATTERSON TRAVEL, 1107 21st St, Sacramento, CA, 95814, (916) 441-1526, Fax: (916) 442-8361. Member: IGTA

PEBBLE BEACH TRAVEL, Lincoln St at 6th Ave, PO Drawer 0, Carmel, CA, 93921, (408) 626-2000, Fax: (408) 626-2006.

PERFECT TRAVEL, 7490 La Jolla Blvd, La Jolla, CA, 92037, (619) 456-2201, (800) 232-2201.

PERNELL CARLSON WAGONLIT TRAVEL, 2616 Hyperion Ave, Los Angeles, CA, 90027, (213) 660-2946, Fax: (213) 661-4518. Member: IGTA

PIEDMONT TRAVEL SERVICE, 2067 Mountain Blvd, Oakland, CA, 94611, (510) 339-8814, (800) 762-5885, Fax: (510) 339-2087. Ask for Jeremy.

PINK TRIANGLE ADVENTURES, 743 Addison St Ste A, Berkeley, CA, 94710-1929, (510) 843-0181, (800) 843-0181, Fax: (510) 843-4066.

PLEASANT HOLIDAYS, 2404 Townsgate Rd, Westlake Village, CA, 91361, (818) 991-3390, (800) 242-9244, Fax: (805) 495-4972.

PRIDE RAIL, 18627 Mescalero St, Rowland Heights, CA, 91748, (800) 414-4297, Fax: (818) 854-9743.

QUALITY TOURS AND SUPERIOR TRAVEL SERVICES, 5003 Palmetto Ave Ste 83, San Francisco, CA, 94044, (415) 994-5054, (415) 992-8033. Member: IGTA

RAINBOW TRAVEL, 1055 Monroe St, Santa Clara, CA, 95050, (408) 246-1414, Fax: (408) 983-0677. Member: IGTA

RANCHO MIRAGE TRAVEL, 71-428 Hwy 111, Rancho Mirage, CA, 92270, (760) 341-7888, (800) 369-1073, Fax: (760) 568-9202. Member: IGTA

RED SHOES TRAVEL, 3241 Folsom Blvd, Sacramento, CA, 95816, (916) 454-4201, Fax: (916) 456-5331.

REEL TRAVEL/HISTOURIES, 298 4th Ave #306, San Francisco, CA, 94118, (415) 281-9948, Fax: (415) 928-8278.

RIO ROMA, 2211 Lombard St, San Francisco, CA, 94123, (415) 921-3353, Fax: (415) 921-3557.

S.G.T.I., 19355 Business Center Dr #2, Northridge, CA, 91324, (818) 701-8777, (800) 447-2036, Fax: (818) 892-4464.

SAN VINCENTE TRAVEL, 451 E Tahquitz Canyon Way, Palm Springs, CA, 92262, (619) 320-8220.

SANTA ROSA TRAVEL, 542 Farmers Lane, Santa Rosa, CA, 95405, (707) 542-0943, Fax: (707) 545-2753.

SCANDIA TRAVEL, 76 Gough St, San Francisco, CA, 94102, (415) 552-5300, Fax: (415) 552-5076.

SF TRAVELERS, 870 Market St #578, San Francisco, CA, 94102, (415) 433-9621, Fax: (415) 433-0618. Member: IGTA

SLOTSY TOURS & TRAVEL, 1821 W Commonwealth #B, Fullerton, CA, 92633, (714) 870-8641, Fax: (714) 870-8241.

SMART TRAVEL, 1728 Union St #309, San Francisco, CA, 94128, (415) 885-0909, Fax: (415) 885-2659. Ask for Jean-Pierre.

SONORA TRAVEL, 2-920 E Cliff Dr, Santa Cruz, CA, 95062, (408) 475-6149, Fax: (408) 475-6182. Member: IGTA

SONY PICTURES TRAVEL, 10202 W Washington Blvd, Culver City, CA, 90232, (310) 280-4873, fax: (310) 280-1833. Member: IGTA

SPECIAL SERVICE TRAVEL, 747 Wimbledon Rd, Walnut Creek, CA, 94598, (510) 939-4300. Member: IGTA

SPORTS LEISURE TRAVEL, 9527-A Folsom Blvd, Sacramento, CA, 95827, (916) 361-2051, Fax: (916) 361-7995. Member: IGTA

STA TRAVEL, 7202 Melrose, Los Angeles, CA, 90046, (213) 934-8722, Fax: (213) 937-6008.

STEWART-COLE TRAVEL EXPRESS, 6761 Sebastopol Ave, Sebastopol, CA, 95472, (707) 823-8402.

SULLIVAN'S TRAVELS, 40 Jeffers Way, Campbell, CA, 95008, (408) 378-6461.

SUN TRAVEL, 3545 Midway Dr, San Diego, CA, 92110, (619) 222-2786, Fax: (619) 222-9591. Member: IGTA

SUNDANCE TOURS & TRAVEL, 1040 University Ave #207, San Diego, CA, 92103-3310, (619) 497-2100, (800) 472-4070, Fax: (619) 293-4615.

SUNDANCE TRAVEL, 19800 MacArthur Blvd Ste 100, Irvine, CA, 92715, (714) 752-5456, Fax: (714)

WHO TO CALL

833-3718.

SUNRISE TRAVEL, 23891 Via Fabricante #603, Mission Viejo, CA, 92691, (714) 837-0620. Ask for Robert.

SUNTRIPS, The SunTrips Bldg, 2350 Paragon Dr, San Jose, CA, 95131, (408) 432-1101, (800) 786-7253, Fax: (408) 436-7825.

SUNVENTURE TRAVEL, 1621 Bridgeway, Sausalito, CA, 94965, (415) 332-6611, Fax: (415) 332-8098.

SUPERIOR TRAVEL ASSOCIATES, 715 N Central #218, Glendale, CA, 91203, (818) 549-8755, (800) 549-8755, Fax: (818) 549-8751.

TEMPO TRAVEL, 1600 McHenry #A, Modesto, CA, 95350, (209) 521-2000, Fax: (209) 521-1197. *Member:* IGTA

THOMAS COOK TRAVEL (CA), 180 Montgomery St, 13th Fl, San Francisco, CA, 94104, (415) 398-4090, (800) 942-2438, Fax: (415) 398-5490.

TICKET QWIK TRAVEL SERVICE, 2665 30th St #102, Santa Monica, CA, 90405, (310) 396-3188, (800) 942-5707, Fax: (310) 396-9503.

TIME TO TRAVEL, 582 Market St, #1201, San Francisco, CA, 94104, (415) 421-3333, (800) 524-3300, Fax: (415) 421-4857.

TIME TRAVELERS INT'L CONSULTANTS, 3841 4th Ave #287, San Diego, CA, 92103, (619) 239-1964, Fax: (619) 298-9150.

TOUCHES OF TRAVEL, 1015 1st St, Manhattan Beach, CA, 90266, (310) 937-6724, Fax: (310) 937-6727. *Member:* IGTA

TR PROFESSIONAL TRAVEL SERVICE, 12946 Valleyheart Dr #211, Studio City, CA, 91604, (818) 789-0751, Fax: (818) 789-7651. *Member:* IGTA

TRAVEL 800, 3530 Camino del Rio N #300, San Diego, CA, 92108, (619) 624-2000, fax: (619) 624-2050. *Member:* IGTA

TRAVEL ADDRESS/GALAXSEA, 6465 N Blackstone Ave, Fresno, CA, 93710, (209) 432-9095, Fax: (209) 432-1565.

TRAVEL ADVISORS, 650 S Brookhurst St, Anaheim, CA, 92804, (714) 535-1174, Fax: (714) 535-3552.

TRAVEL BOUND, 16255 Ventura Blvd #500, Encino, CA, 91436-2394, (818) 906-2121, Fax: (818) 906-3049.

TRAVEL BY GRETA, 17106 Devonshire St, Northridge, CA, 91325, (818) 366-9611.

TRAVEL CONCEPTS, 931 Howe Ave #103, Sacramento, CA, 95825, (916) 506-3771, fax: (916) 927-3623. *Member:* IGTA

TRAVEL CONNECTION, 5450 Alpine Ct, Paradise, CA, 95969, (916) 877-7111.

TRAVEL CONNECTION, THE, 260 Stockton St, 2nd Fl, San Francisco, CA, 94108, (415) 397-3977, Fax: (415) 989-9889.

TRAVEL CONSULTANT (CARLSON TRAVEL NETWORK), 1245 Market St, San Francisco, CA, 94103, (415) 558-9796, Fax: (415) 558-8960.

TRAVEL ETC, 8764 Holloway Dr, West Hollywood, CA, 90069-2244, (310) 652-4430, (800) 652-4430, Fax: (310) 652-1283.

TRAVEL EXPERIENCE ON CALL, PO Box 2588, Aptos, CA, 95001, (408) 464-8035.

TRAVEL FLO, 925 Dartmouth Way, Concord, CA, 94518, (510) 687-0661. Ask for Flo.

TRAVEL LAB, 1943 Hillhurst Ave, Los Angeles, CA, 90027, (213) 660-9811, (800) 747-7026, Fax: (213) 660-9814. *Member:* IGTA

TRAVEL MANAGEMENT GROUP, 832 N LaBrea Ave, Hollywood, CA, 90038, (213) 993-0444, Fax: (213) 993-3777.

TRAVEL ONE, One First St #1, Los Altos, CA, 94022, (415) 949-5222, Fax: (415) 949-0847.

TRAVEL SYNDICATE, 20855 Ventura Blvd #10, Woodland Hills, CA, 91364.,

TRAVEL TIME, One Hallidie Plaza #406, San Francisco, CA, 94102, (415) 677-0799, Fax: (415) 391-1856. *Member:* IGTA

TRAVEL TRENDS, 431 Castro St, San Francisco, CA, 94114, (415) 558-6922, (800) 558-6920, Fax: (415) 558-9338. *Member:* IGTA

TRAVEL WITH EASE, 1065 W Lomita Blvd #322, Harbor City, CA, 90710, (310) 325-8638, Fax: (310) 530-6054.

TRAVEL WITH HAL, 2227 Atlanta St, Anaheim, CA, 92802, (714) 537-1553.

TRAVELER'S EDGE, 9363 Wilshire Blvd #216, Beverly Hills, CA, 90210, (310) 271-2208, fax: (310) 550-1532. *Member:* IGTA

TRAVELER'S EDGE, THE, 9393 Wilshire Blvd #216, Beverly Hills, CA, 90210, (310) 271-2208, (800) 404-8687, Fax: (310) 550-1532. *Member:* IGTA

TRAVELINE, 8721 Santa Monica Blvd #845, Los Angeles, CA, 90069, (213) 654-3000, Fax: (213) 654-1488. *Member:* IGTA

TRAVEX, 1875 Olympic Blvd #100, Walnut Creek, CA, 94596, (510) 932-5276, (800) 392-5439, Fax: (510) 932-6591. *Member:* IGTA

TWO BROTHERS TRAVEL, 2750 Bellflower Blvd #206-B, Long Beach, CA, 90815-1146, (562) 938-8650, Fax: (562) 938-8649. *Member:* IGTA

TZELL TRAVEL, 8383 Wilshire Blvd #922, Beverly Hills, CA, 90211, (213) 651-5557, Fax: (213) 651-5454.

UNIGLOBE EXPO TRAVEL, 2100 Arden Way #220, Sacramento, CA, 95825, (916) 920-1701, (800) 879-8785.

UNIGLOBE PASSPORT TRAVEL, 100 Spear St, San Francisco, CA, 94105, (415) 904-6380, Fax: (415) 904-6390.

UNIGLOBE RAINBOW TRAVEL, 1624 Franklin St #1102, Oakland, CA, 94612, (510) 238-4646, Fax: (510) 238-4656.

UNIGLOBE TOTAL TRAVEL, 2150 Mariner Sq Dr Ste #100, Alameda, CA, 94501, (510) 523-9796, Fax: (510) 523-9260. *Member:* IGTA

UNIVERSAL TRAVEL, 11 Tillman Place #400, San Francisco, CA, (415) 421-1882, fax: (415) 421-2819. *Member:* IGTA

WANDERLUST TRAVEL, 201 N Larchmont Blvd, Los Angeles, CA, 90004, (213) 464-3927, Fax: (213) 464-4603.

WEST HOLLYWOOD TRAVEL, 746 Ashland Ave, Santa Monica, CA, 90405, (310) 452-0506, Fax: (310) 452-0562.

WEST HOLLYWOOD TRAVEL, 801 Larrabee St, West Hollywood, CA, 90069, (310) 289-5900, Fax: (310) 289-8700. *Member:* IGTA

WHERE IN THE WORLD INC, 420 Marine St Unit 3, Santa Monica, CA, 90405, (310) 396-9625.

WHITNEY ROBERTS TRAVEL, 1801 Bush St #106, San Francisco, CA, 94109, (415) 440-1601, (888) 8-LESBIAN (853-7242), fax: (415) 440-1605, e-mail: trvljewel@aol.com. *Member:* IGTA

WILDLIFE SAFARI, 346 Rheem Blvd #107, Moraga, CA, 94556-1588, (800) 221-8118, Fax: (510) 376-5059.

WILSON'S TRAVEL, 9359 Wilshire Blvd, Beverly Hills, CA, 90210, (310) 275-4131, (800) 255-6797, Fax: (310) 550-3991. *Member:* IGTA

WINSHIP TRAVEL, 2321 Market St, San Francisco, CA, 94114-1688, (415) 863-2717, Fax: (415) 863-2473. Ask for Raoul.

WORLD TRAVEL ARRANGERS, 256 Sutter St 7th fl, San Francisco, CA, 94108, (415) 421-4460, Fax: (415) 982-7397.

YANKEE CLIPPER TRAVEL, 413 Monterey Ave, Los Gatos, CA, 95030, (408) 354-6400, (800) 624-2664, Fax: (408) 395-4453. *Member:* IGTA

COLORADO

ACS WORLD TRAVEL, 2255 S. Broadway, Denver, CO, 80210, (303) 871-9600, (800) 234-3453, Fax: (303) 871-9658. Ask for Linda.

ATS TRAVEL SERVICES, 3131 S Vaughn Way #120, Aurora, CO, 80014, (303) 369-8680, Fax: (303) 369-9327.

BUSINESS & LEISURE TRAVEL, 1775 Sherman St, Denver, CO, 80203, (303) 830-8928, Fax: (303) 830-8938. *Member:* IGTA

CARLSON TRAVEL NETWORK (CO), 2032 35th Ave, Greeley, CO, 80634, (303) 339-3311, (303) 339-3770. Ask for Kathryn Freese.

COAST TO COAST TRAVEL, 1400 S Collyer St #183, Longmont, CO, 80501, (303) 772-3894, fax: (303) 444-4772. *Member:* IGTA

COLORADO'S TRAVEL HAVEN, 1905 Yorktown Ave, Ft. Collins, CO, 80526, (303) 484-2139, Fax: (303) 484-8729.

COMPASS TRAVEL, 1001 16th St #A-150, Denver, CO, 80265, (303) 534-1292, Fax: (303) 534-8061. *Member:* IGTA

EXCEL TRAVEL, 2099 Wadsworth Blvd, Lakewood, CO, 80215, (303) 232-4300, Fax: (303) 238-8207.

EXECUTIVE TRAVEL SERVICE, 907 17th St, Denver, CO, 80202, (303) 292-3600, Fax: (303) 292-4645.

FARE DEALS TRAVEL, 9350 E Arapahoe Rd #330, Englewood, CO, 80112, (303) 792-2929, fax: (303) 792-2954. *Member:* IGTA

GATEWAY TRAVEL & GATEWAY TOURS, 3510 W 10th St, Greeley, CO, 80634, (303) 353-2200.

IMPERIAL TRAVEL, 717 17th St, Denver, CO, 80202, (303) 292-1334, Fax: (303) 292-5175.

LET'S TALK TRAVEL (CARLSON TRAVEL NETWORK), 1485 S Colorado Blvd #260, Denver, CO, 80222, (303) 759-1318, Fax: (303) 758-5390. *Member:* IGTA

METRO TRAVEL, 90 Madison St #101, Denver, CO, 80206, (303) 333-6777, (303) 333-6646. *Member:* IGTA

NEW HORIZONS TRAVEL, 3510 W 10th St, Greeley, CO, 80634, (303) 353-2200, Fax: (303) 356-8936.

PARTNERS TRAVEL SERVICE, 1811 S Quebec Way #63, Denver, CO, 80231, (303) 751-2247.

PATH WAYS TRAVEL SERVICE, Crossroads Mall, 1700 28th St #108, Boulder, CO, 80301, (303) 449-0099, Fax: (303) 449-4585.

FERRARI GUIDES' GAY TRAVEL A to Z - 18th EDITION

TRAVEL AGENTS

WHO TO CALL

TRAVEL 16TH STREET, 535 Sixteenth St, Denver, CO, 80202, (303) 820-0312, (303) 820-0311, Fax: (303) 595-0313. Member: IGTA

TRAVEL BOY COMPANY, 201 Steele St #2-B, Denver, CO, 80206, (303) 333-4855, (800) 334-2285, Fax: (303) 333-8559. Men-only travel. Member: IGTA

TRAVEL SQUARE ONE, 608 Garrison St #G, Lakewood, CO, 80215, (303) 233-8457, Fax: (303) 233-8586. Member: IGTA

WIZARD TRAVEL, 200 S Chase St, Lakewood, CO, 80226, (303) 237-5340.

CONNECTICUT

ADLER TRAVEL, 2323 Whitney Ave, Hamden, CT, 06518, (203) 288-8100, Fax: (203) 230-8416. Member: IGTA

ADVANTAGE IN GAY TRAVEL, 109 Broad St, Middletown, CT, 06457, (203) 347-7218, (800) 251-1114, Fax: (203) 346-4877.

ALDIS THE TRAVEL PLANNER, 46 Mill Plain Rd, Danbury, CT, 06811, (203) 778-9399, (800) 369-6528, Fax: (203) 744-1139. Ask for Aldis, Mark or Paul. Member: IGTA

AROUND THE WORLD TRAVEL, 93 Cherry St, New Canaan, CT, 06840, (203) 966-2688, (203) 972-1822. Member: IGTA

CARLSON WAGONLIT EXCEL TRAVEL, 2693 Whitney Ave, Hamden, CT, 06518, (203) 281-7208, fax: (203) 281-3335. Member: IGTA

CONTEMPORARY CRUISE VACATIONS, 444-A Lime Rock Rd, Lakeville, CT, 06039, (203) 435-3534.

COPPER COYOTE CRUISES AND TRAVEL, 978 Pleasant St, Southington, CT, 06489, (860) 620-0776 (tel/fax). Member: IGTA

CORPORATE TRAVEL SERVICES, 412 Cromwell Ave, Rocky Hill, CT, 06067, (203) 563-3288.

CRUISE SHIP VACATIONS, 444-A Lime Rock Rd, Lakeville, CT, 06039, (860) 435-3534 (tel/fax). Member: IGTA

CRUISETIME INC., 35 Point Beach Dr., Milford, CT, 06460, (203) 877-6967, (800) 427-9402, Fax: (203) 877-7087. Member: IGTA

EXCEL TRAVEL SERVICE, 2693 Whitney Ave, Hamden, CT, 06518, (203) 281-7208, Fax: (203) 281-3335.

HAMDEN TRAVEL, 2911 Dixwell Ave #208, Hamden, CT, 06518, (203) 288-7718, Fax: (203) 281-7443. Member: IGTA *

JEN-EL TRAVEL, PO Box 210, New Hartford, CT, 06057, (860) 693-3865, fax: (860) 693-3872. Member: IGTA

KLINGERMAN TRAVEL, 900 Boston Post Rd, Old Saybrook, CT, 06475, (860) 388-1423, (800) 388-6078, Fax: (860) 388-1427. Member: IGTA

KLINGERMAN TRAVEL, 11 Bank St, New London, CT, 06320-6001, (203) 443-2855, Fax: (203) 443-3562.

MAP TRAVEL/DBA FIRST DISCOUNT TRAVEL, 1866 Berlin Turnpike, Wethersfield, CT, 06109, (203) 563-9781, Fax: (203) 563-5919.

MCGREGOR TRAVEL, 40 Country Way, Bridgeport, CT, 06752, (203) 222-6660, Fax: (203) 222-6536.

PARADISE TRAVEL, 104 Waterbury Rd, Prospect, CT, 06712, (203) 758-6132, Fax: (203) 758-6132.

PAUL DAVID TOURS, PO Box 176, East Berlin, CT, 06023, (860) 632-8806, fax: (860) 632-8806. Member: IGTA

PLAZA TRAVEL CENTER, 208 College St, New Haven, CT, 06510, (203) 777-7334, Fax: (203) 787-9553. Member: IGTA

RAINBOW DESTINATIONS, PO Box 776, Southbury, CT, 06488, (203) 791-1535, Fax: (203) 791-1535. Member: IGTA

REKAP TRAVEL, Crystal Mall, 850 Hartford Tpke, Waterford, CT, 06385, (203) 442-7144, Fax: (203) 440-3233.

TOWER TRAVEL, 600 N Colony Rd, Wallingford, CT, 06492, (203) 284-8747, (800) 229-TOWER, Fax: (203) 284-3322. Ask for Alan. Member: IGTA

TRAVEL TRENDS, 454 Main Ave, Norwalk, CT, 06851, (203) 845-0000, Fax: (203) 840-8352.

TRAVELSTAR INC, 15 Apple Tree Trail, Westport, CT, 06880, (203) 227-7233, Fax: (203) 227-3774. Member: IGTA

WARREN TRAVEL GROUP, 320 Post Rd West, Westport, CT, 06880, (203) 454-2034, Fax: (203) 454-8664.

WEBER'S TRAVEL SERVICE, 24 Cedar St, New Britain, CT, 06052, (203) 229-4846.

DELAWARE

ALL AROUND TRAVEL, 911 Orange St, Wilmington, DE, 19801, (302) 657-2104, fax: (302) 657-2106. Member: IGTA

BOSCHO'S TRAVEL, 3000 Dover Mall, Dover, DE, 19901-2292, (302) 734-9210.

FOUR SEASONS TOURS & TRAVEL, 1404 N DuPont St,, Wilmington, DE, 19806, (302) 594-1030, Fax: (302) 655-5280.

GEORGETOWN TRAVEL CENTER, 600 E Market St, Georgetown, DE, 19947, (302) 856-3556.

GULLIVER'S TRAVEL INC., 171 Dupont Hwy, Dover, DE, 19901, (302) 678-3747, (800) 444-4855, Fax: (302) 678-3746. Member: IGTA

TRAVEL COMPANY, 9 S Cleveland Ave, Wilmington, DE, 19805, (302) 652-6263, Fax: (302) 652-2188.

TRAVEL TRAVEL, 146 E Main St, Newark, DE, 19711, (302) 737-5555, (302) 737-5674. Member: IGTA

DISTRICT OF COLUMBIA

ACT TRAVEL, 1629 K St NW #401, Washington, DC, 20006, (202) 463-6300, (800) 433-3577, Fax: (202) 452-8597. Ask for Wayne. Member: IGTA

AMERICAN EXPRESS TRAVEL RELATED SERVICES, 1150 Connecticut Ave NW, Washington, DC, 20036, (202) 457-1325, Fax: (202) 775-0786.

CARLSON WAGONLIT TRAVEL, 3400 International Dr NW, Washington, DC, 20008, (202) 966-5730, Fax: (202) 364-4251.

EXECUTIVE TRAVEL ASSOCIATES, 1101 17th St NW Ste 412, Washington, DC, 20036, (202) 828-3501, (800) 562-0189, Fax: (202) 785-2566. Member: IGTA

FORTE INT'L TRAVEL, 1901 Penn Ave NW #406, Washington, DC, 20006, (202) 833-4167, Fax: (202) 296-8685.

FREEDOM TRAVEL, 1750 K St NW Ste 510, Washington, DC, 20006, (202) 496-1810, Fax: (202) 452-1329. Member: IGTA

GREAT ESCAPE TRAVEL, 1730 K St NW #910, Washington, DC, 20006, (202) 331-3322, (800) 228-0861, Fax: (202) 331-1109.

HERE TODAY THERE TOMORROW, 1901 Penna Ave NW Ste 204, Washington, DC, 20006, (202) 296-6373, Fax: (202) 296-0815.

HERITAGE WORLD TRAVEL, 1611 Connecticut Ave NW #4C, Washington, DC, 20009, (202) 518-5300, fax: (202) 518-5333. Member: IGTA

MITCHELL FITZGERALD & ASSOC. TRAVEL, 1730 K St NW #910, Washington, DC, 20006, (202) 331-3322, (202) 331-1109. Member: IGTA

MULLIN TRAVEL, 2424 Pennsylvania Ave NW #118, Washington, DC, 20037, (202) 296-5966.

PASSPORT EXECUTIVE TRAVEL, 1025 Thomas Jefferson St NW, Washington, DC, 20007, (202) 337-7718, (800) 222-9800, Fax: (202) 342-7475. Member: IGTA

PERSONALIZED TRAVEL, 1325 "G" St NW #915, Washington, DC, 20005, (202) 508-8656, Fax: (202) 637-8454. Member: IGTA

THOMAS COOK TRAVEL (DC), 1776 Eye St NW #725, Washington, DC, 20006, (202) 857-4945. Ask for Matt.

TOUR WORLD USA, 1130 Connecticut Ave NW #310, Washington, DC, 20003, (202) 293-0517.

TRAVEL ADVISOR, 1601 16th St NW #2, Washington, DC, 20009, (202) 667-1182. Member: IGTA

TRAVEL DESIGNERS, 529 14th St NW #200, Washington, DC, 20045, (800) 237-6971, (202) 508-8656, Fax: (202) 508-8668.

TRAVEL ESCAPE, 1725 K St NW, Washington, DC, 20006, (202) 223-9354, Fax: (202) 296-0724. Member: IGTA

TRAVEL ESCAPE, 1601 16th St NW #2, Washington, DC, 20009, (202) 667-1182.

WORLDWIDE ASSISTANCE SERVICES, 1133 15th St NW #400, Washington, DC, 20003, (202) 331-1609, (800) 777-8710, Fax: (202) 828-5886. Ask for George.

FLORIDA

A BEELINE TRAVEL CENTER, 6937 St Augustine Rd, Jacksonville, FL, 32217, (904) 739-3349, Fax: (904) 739-3931. Member: IGTA

A WORLD OF TRAVEL, 3947 Boulevard Center Dr #101, Jacksonville, FL, 32207, (904) 398-6638, Fax: (904) 399-5952. Member: IGTA

A+ TRAVEL OF SARASOTA INC, 327 N Washington Blvd, Sarasota, FL, 34236, (941) 951-6866, Fax: (941) 951-6767. Member: IGTA

ACBS TRAVEL AGENCY, 628 Decatur Ave, Brooksville, FL, 34601, (352) 796-4984, (800) 449-2227, Fax: (352) 799-6049. Member: IGTA

ADVENTURE WORLD TRAVEL, Harbourtown Shopping Village #40, Gulf Breeze, FL, 32561,, (904) 932-9363. Ask for Art or Carla.

AEROSPACE TRAVEL, 205 Parnell St, Merritt Island, FL, 32953, (407) 453-1702, Fax: (407) 453-2846. Member: IGTA

AIRCHARTER WORLD, 1136 Andora Ave, Coral Gables, FL, 33146, (305) 662-9797, (800) 845-8150, Fax: (305) 662-9745.

AKT TRAVEL SERVICES, 6840 SW 40th St, Miami, FL, 33155, (305) 661-1002 (tel/fax). Member: IGTA

ALL SEASONS TRAVEL PROFESSIONALS

WHO TO CALL

INT'L, 405 Central Ave, St. Petersburg, FL, 33701, (813) 898-7411, Fax: (813) 894-0030.
ALL WORLD TRAVEL, 4014 N 46th Ave, Hollywood, FL, 33021, (954) 983-5501.
ALTERNATIVE TRAVEL, 2572 NE Mildred St, Jensen Beach, FL, 34957, (407) 225-2500, Fax: (407) 334-4594.
AMERICAN TRAVEL, 2000 Hendricks Ave, Jacksonville, FL, 32207, (904) 399-4490, (800) 633-6836. Ask for Jack.
AMIGO-ECO TOURS, 1024 E Powhattan Ave #200, Tampa, FL, 33604, (800) 250-7709, Fax: (813) 231-2188.
APEX TRAVEL SERVICE, 1510 S Clark Ave, Tampa, FL, 33629, (813) 289-9197, Fax: (813) 288-4918.
ATLANTIC TRAVEL/FUN VACATIONS, 2430 S Atlantic Ave, Daytona Beach Shores, FL, 32118, (904) 255-0070, (800) 338-9162, Fax: (904) 254-2829.
BEACH TRAVEL SERVICE, 3280 NE 32nd St, Ft Lauderdale, FL, 33308, (954) 564-2323, fax: (954) 563-4922. Member: IGTA
BELLEAIR ADVENTURE TRAVEL, 1530 S Fort Harrison Ave, Clearwater, FL, 34616-2005, (813) 442-4633, Fax: (813) 461-5102.
BEYOND & BACK, INC, 401 Ocean Ave #101, Melbourne Beach, FL, 32951, (407) 725-9720, Fax: (407) 951-2017. Member: IGTA
BOCA EXPRESS TRAVEL, 8177 Glades Rd #14, Boca Raton, FL, 33434-4022, (561) 451-4511, fax: (561) 451-3507. Member: IGTA
BON VOYAGE TRAVEL, 3111 University Dr, Coral Springs, FL, 33065, (954) 752-2430, fax: (954) 752-4552. Member: IGTA
BONITA BEACH TRAVEL, 4365 Bonita Beach Rd Ste 124, Bonita Springs, FL, 33923, (813) 498-0877, Fax: (813) 498-0877. Member: IGTA
BRANDON LAKES TRAVEL, 2020 Brandon Blvd, Brandon, FL, 33511, (813) 661-2988.
CARLSON WAGONLIT/CRT VENTURE TRAVEL, 2561 Countryside Blvd #6, Clearwater, FL, 34621, (813) 796-1539, (813) 797-7894.
CARRIE ME AWAY TRAVEL, 5650 Stirling Road #9, Hollywood, FL, 33021, (954) 987-9770, fax: (954) 987-9771. Member: IGTA
CERTIFIED VACATIONS, 110 E Broward Blvd Fl 10, Ft. Lauderdale, FL, 33301-3503, (941) 522-1440, Fax: (941) 468-4713.
CLIFF PETTIT TRAVEL SERVICE, 1975 E Sunrise Blvd Ste 714, Ft. Lauderdale, FL, 33304, (941) 463-4630, (800) 327-3713, Fax: (941) 463-6270.
CONSOLIDATED TRAVEL GROUP INC, 101 NE 3rd Ave Ste 203, Ft. Lauderdale, FL, 33301, (941) 761-2311, Fax: (941) 761-8842.
CONSOLIDATED TRAVEL GROUP, INC, 7160 W McNab Rd, Tamarac, FL, 33321, (954) 724-2055, (800) 997-1555, Fax: (954) 724-0545.
COPPER COYOTE CRUISES & TRAVEL, 8466 N Lockwood Ridge Rd #325, Sarasota, FL, 34243, (941) 377-7931, Fax: (941) 377-7931.
CRUISE DESTINATIONS, 170 W Spanish River Blvd, Boca Raton, FL, 33431, (407) 338-4203, Fax: (407) 394-0319.
CRUISE MARKET/US TRAVEL, 1300 Riverplace Blvd #400, Jacksonville, FL, 32205, (904) 858-0123, fax: (904) 858-0115. Member: IGTA
CRUISIN WITH PRIDE, 8725 SW 57 St, Cooper City, FL, 33328, (954) 434-5442, Fax: (954) 434-6197.
CTN VISION TRAVEL, 2222 Ponce de Leon Blvd, Coral Gables, FL, 33134, (305) 444-8484, fax: (305) 444-9070. Member: IGTA
CURRENT EVENTS TRAVEL, 443 N Lakemont Ave, Winter Park, FL, 32792, (800) 569-6753, (407) 628-2228, Fax: (407) 628-5444.
DELUXE TRAVEL PROFESSIONALS INT'L, 13186 N Dale Mabry Hwy, Tampa, FL, 33618, (813) 962-0208, fax: (813) 962-8939. Member: IGTA
DESTINATIONS TRAVEL OF PALM CITY, 870 Martin Downs Blvd, Palm City, FL, 34990, (407) 288-4000, Fax (407) 288-4119.
DIPLOMATIC TRAVEL, INC, PO Box 370729, Miami, FL, 33137-0729, (305) 573-8242, (800) 349-4554, Fax: (305) 573-7886.
DISCOVER TRAVEL, 517 Duval St, Key West, FL, 33040, (305) 296-1585, Fax: (305) 296-8747.
DISTINCTIVE TRAVEL COMPANY, 18327 NE 19th Ave, N Miami Beach, FL, 33179, (305) 931-4443, fax: (305) 931-7990. Member: IGTA
DOLPHIN TRAVEL, 2837 NE 22nd St, Ft. Lauderdale, FL, 33305, (941) 566-6539, (800) 272-5585. Member: IGTA
DONITA'S VACATIONS UNLIMITED, 636 SW 34th St, Ft. Lauderdale, FL, 33315, (941) 359-2761, (800) 325-2721 (Canada & USA). Ask for Michael.
ELKIN TRAVEL, 885 E Palmetto Park Rd, Boca Raton, FL, 33432, (407) 368-8788.
EVELINA TRAVEL, 800 West Ave #1-A, Miami Beach, FL, 33139, (305) 673-3141, Fax: (305) 673-3313.
EXOTIC ADVENTURES, 12769 N Kendall Dr, Miami, FL, 33186, (305) 382-7757, (800) 940-7757, Fax: (305) 388-5259.
FAIRBANKS AVE. TRAVEL, 1299 W Fairbanks Ave, Winter Park, FL, 32789, (407) 628-8480, (800) 343-8480, Fax: (407) 628-1138.
FANTASY ADVENTURES TRAVEL, 138 Beach Dr NE, St. Petersburg, FL, 33701-3928, (813) 821-0880, Fax: (813) 822-0892. Member: IGTA
FESTIVE TRAVEL, 35 SW 6th St, Ft Lauderdale, FL, 33004, (954) 927-8697, fax: (954) 927-8098. Member: IGTA
FIRST TRAVEL, 3211 W Swann Ave Apt 1004, Tampa, FL, 33609-4672, (813) 254-2007, Fax: (813) 254-0889.
FLORIDA BEST TRAVEL SERVICES, 1905 Collins Ave, Miami, FL, 33139-1911, (305) 673-0909, Fax: (305) 673-2600.
FOREMOST TOURING ASSOC, 8652 NW 44th St, Sunrise, FL, 33351, (305) 742-2100, (800) 652-8444, Fax: (305) 742-0020. Ask for Al.
FOREST LAKES TRAVEL, 3618 Webber St #101, Sarasota, FL, 34232, (941) 923-6474, (800) 922-4818, Fax: (941) 923-4250. Member: IGTA
FOUR SEASONS TRAVEL, 3528 N Federal Hwy, Ft. Lauderdale, FL, 33308-6223, (954) 566-1900, Fax: (954) 561-8404. Member: IGTA
FUTURE TRAVEL AGENCY, 300 S Luna Ct #4, Hollywood, FL, 33021, (954) 964-7950.
GALAXSEA CRUISES, 6584 Superior Ave, Sarasota, FL, 34231, (941) 921-3456, Fax: (941) 922-1241.
GARDEN TRAVEL, 175 NE 4th Ave, Delray Beach, FL, 33483, (407) 272-5400, Fax: (407) 272-5439.
GERACI TRAVEL, 2132 E First St, Ft Myers, FL, 33901, (941) 334-1161, (941) 334-4251. Member: IGTA
GET OUTTA TOWN! TRAVEL, 2532 Longpine Lane, St. Cloud, FL, 34772, (407) 957-8870, Fax: (407) 957-4493. Member: IGTA
GLOBAL TRAVEL & TOURS, 3018 E Commercial Blvd #103, Ft. Lauderdale, FL, 33308, (941) 771-0204, Fax: (941) 771-0205.
GOLD COAST DISCOUNT TRAVEL, 1822-A University Dr, Plantation, FL, 33322, (305) 474-7755, Fax: (305) 474-7733.
GOOD BUY TRAVEL SERVICES, PO Box 5700815, Miami, FL, 33257, (305) 252-0003.
GREAT ADVENTURE TRAVEL, 2252 Coral Way, Miami, FL, 33145, (305) 858-4347, Fax: (305) 858-7485.
GREAT DESTINATIONS, 11000 70th Ave NW, Seminole, FL, 34642, (813) 398-4683, Fax: (813) 398-4958.
GREAT GETAWAY TOURS, 10330 N Dale Mabry #226, Tampa, FL, 33618, (813) 960-1370, Fax: (813) 264-5351.
GULF BEACH TRAVEL, 14995 Gulf Blvd, Madeira Beach, FL, 33708, (813) 391-9944, Fax: (813) 391-6430.
HAPPY WANDERER, THE, 118 N Ocean Blvd, Pompano Beach, FL, 33062, (954) 782-8668, (800) 329-7447.
HORIZON TRAVEL, 1561 Main St, Sarasota, FL, 34236, (941) 362-0166, fax: (941) 362-3821. Member: IGTA
HOUSE OF TRAVEL, 3905 SW 18th St, Gainesville, FL, 32608, (904) 378-1601, Fax: (904) 372-3308.
INTERCONTINENTAL TRAVEL AGENCY, 3332 NE 33rd St, Ft. Lauderdale, FL, 33308, (941) 566-7111, (800) 521-0643, Fax: (941) 566-0036.
INTERNATIONAL HOUSE OF TRAVEL, 40966 US Hwy 19 N, Tarpon Springs, FL, 34689, (813) 938-1511, Fax: (813) 942-6458.
JACQUIN TRAVEL, 10530 NW 26th St #F-105, Miami, FL, 33172-2174, (305) 592-5882, Fax: (305) 592-6761. Member: IGTA
LEISURE PLANNERS, PO Box 450332, Kissimmee, FL, 34745, (407) 932-500, Fax: (407) 932-4684.
LIBERTY TRAVEL (FL), 2313 N Federal Hwy, Pompano Beach, FL, 33062, (954) 946-0880.
MERCURY CRUISE & TOUR, 625 S Hwy 427, Longwood, FL, 32750, (407) 831-7379, (407) 831-9895. Member: IGTA
MILLENNIUM TRAVEL, 761 S Pinellas Ave, Tarpon Springs, FL, 34689, (813) 944-2000, (813) 942-1704. Member: IGTA
MK TRAVEL & TOURS, 1430 S Bayshore Dr #1207, Miami, FL, 33131, (305) 441-7800, Fax: (305) 448-0655. Member: IGTA
MOLIN TOURS, 1701 W Flagler St #10, Miami, FL, 33135, (305) 649-8811, (800) 356-6546, Fax: (305) 649-3711.

TRAVEL AGENTS

FERRARI GUIDES' GAY TRAVEL A to Z - 18th EDITION

WHO TO CALL

NATION TRAVEL AGENCY, 3900 W Commercial Blvd #100, Ft. Lauderdale, FL, 33309, (941) 484-8486, Fax: (941) 484-3307.

NFE (NOT FOR EVERYBODY) TRAVEL, 5850 Lakehurst Dr #230, Orlando, FL, 32819, (407) 363-0929, Fax: (407) 363-9784. Ask for Joshua. *Member:* IGTA

NOSOTROS G L TRAVEL & TOURS, 5921 NW 199th St, Miami Lakes, FL, 33015, (305) 592-1975, Fax: (305) 592-8432.

OASIS TRAVEL, 3152 Northside Dr #100, Key West, FL, 33040, (800) 872-8208.

OCEAN TRAVEL SERVICE, 885 E Palmetto Park Rd, Boca Raton, FL, 33432, (407) 368-8788, (800) 226-TRIP.

ODYSSEY TRAVEL, 224 E Michigan St, Orlando, FL, 32806, (407) 841-8686, Fax: (407) 649-9471. *Member:* IGTA

OLWELL TRAVEL SERVICE, 100 NE 3rd Ave #110, Ft. Lauderdale, FL, 33301, (954) 764-8510, Fax: (954) 764-7053. *Member:* IGTA

PARK AVENUE TRAVEL, 7563 W Oakland Park Blvd, Lauderhill, FL, 33319, (954) 741-3003, (954) 741-3422. *Member:* IGTA

PEGASUS TRAVEL MANAGEMENT, 2424 S Dixie Highway #100, Coconut Grove, FL, 33133, (305) 859-9955, Fax: (305) 859-8310.

POST HASTE TRAVEL SERVICE INC, 4555 Sheridan Rd, Hollywood, FL, 33021, (954) 966-7690, (954) 966-7706.

PREFERRED TRAVEL, 9144 Glades Rd, Boca Raton, FL, 33434, (407) 852-4400, Fax: (407) 852-1512. *Member:* IGTA

PRIORITY TRAVEL SERVICES, 291 E Altamonte Dr #1, Altamonte Springs, FL, 32701, (407) 830-7198, fax: (407) 830-0154. *Member:* IGTA

PRODUCTIONS AT SEA, 3550 Bicayne Blvd #507, Miami, FL, 33137, (305) 573-5155, fax: (305) 573-7588. *Member:* IGTA

PROFESSIONAL TRAVEL MANAGEMENT, 195 SW 15th Rd #403, Miami, FL, 33129, (305) 858-5522.

RADCLIFF TRAVEL & TOURS INC, 13090 North A1A, Vero Beach, FL, 32963, (407) 388-9035, Fax: (407) 388-9035.

RAINBOW TREK CRUISE & TOUR EMPORIUM, 2606 NW 6th St #N, Gainesville, FL, 32601, (352) 380-0610, fax: (352) 380-0766. *Member:* IGTA

REGENCY TRAVEL, 1075 Duval St C-19, Key West, FL, 33040, (305) 294-0175, Fax: (305) 294-3631. *Member:* IGTA

ROYAL PALM TRAVEL, 223 Sunset Ave, Palm Beach, FL, 33480-3855, (407) 659-6080, Fax: (407) 659-6089.

RUN AWAY TRAVEL, 9913 Miramar Pkwy, Miramar, FL, 33025-2307, (954) 432-4300, fax: (954) 432-4915. *Member:* IGTA

SEA BREEZE TRAVEL, 200 Jody Ct, #A, Largo, FL, 34644, (813) 797-7364, Fax: (813) 797-3973.

SEMINOLE TRAVEL, 7731 Seminole Mall, Seminole, FL, 34642, (813) 392-2202, Fax: (813) 399-1945.

SOUND TRAVEL, 2841 Executive Dr #120, Clearwater, FL, 34622, (813) 572-7004, fax: (813) 572-4289. *Member:* IGTA

SUN-N-FUN TOURS, INC, 2700 W. Oakland Blvd #22B, Ft. Lauderdale, FL, 33311, (941) 731-2579, (800) 316-1370, Fax: (941) 731-1210.

TAMPA BAY TRAVEL CORP, 4830 W Kennedy #148, Tampa, FL, 33609, (813) 286-4202, Fax: (813) 286-4204. *Member:* IGTA

TOP FLIGHT TRAVEL, 300 S Luna Ct #4, Hollywood, FL, 33021, (954) 966-9111, Fax: (954) 966-9122.

TRADEWINDS TRAVEL SERVICE, 811 US Hwy 1, Lake Park, FL, 33403, (561) 845-8951, fax: (561) 845-8953. *Member:* IGTA

TRAVEL ACCESS, 2273 Palm Beach Lakes Blvd, West Palm Beach, FL, 33409, (407) 697-2291, Fax: (407) 697-2303.

TRAVEL ACCESS PLUS, 145 N Grove, Merritt Island, FL, 32953, (407) 452-4749, Fax: (407) 459-9467.

TRAVEL AGENCY, THE, 615 N Main St, Chiefland, FL, 32626, (904) 493-4826, Fax: (904) 493-2606.

TRAVEL AGENTS INT'L (FL), 4507 Gunn Hwy, Tampa, FL, 33624, (813) 968-3600, Fax: (813) 968-3713. *Member:* IGTA

TRAVEL BEYOND, 2525 Pasadena Ave Ste N, St. Petersburg, FL, 33707-4566, (813) 367-3737, Fax: (813) 367-3730. *Member:* IGTA

TRAVEL BUSINESS BUREAU, 100 N Biscayne Blvd #901, Miami, FL, 33132, (305) 374-3366, (305) 374-8473.

TRAVEL BY PEGASUS, 1865 N US #1, Fort Pierce, FL, 34946, (407) 464-6330, Fax: (407) 464-6486. Ask for Jody.

TRAVEL EASY INT'L, International Bldg, 2455 E Sunrise Blvd #900, Ft. Lauderdale, FL, 33304, (941) 564-4561, (800) 542-3279.

TRAVEL HOUSE,, 3801 N Miami Ave,, Miami,, FL, 33137, (305) 576-5550, (800) 878-5473, (305) 576-5567. *Member:* IGTA

TRAVEL NETWORK, 725 Almond St, Clermont, FL, 34711, (904) 394-4040, (800) 269-4040, Fax: (904) 269-1163.

TRAVEL SERVICES UNLIMITED, 726 S Dale Mabry, Tampa, FL, 33609, (813) 877-4040, (800) 874-4711, Fax: (813) 876-6048. *Member:* IGTA

TRAVELCRAFTERS, 1941 University Dr, Coral Springs, FL, 33071-6032, (305) 753-7540, Fax: (305) 753-6035. *Member:* IGTA

TRAVELMASTERS & TOURS, 4225 W Commercial Blvd, Tamarac, FL, 33319, (305) 739-2285. Ask for Frank.

TRAVELMAX INTERNATIONAL, 1222 S Dale Mabry Hwy #303, Tampa, FL, 33629-5009, (813) 286-2333, fax: (813) 286-7783. *Member:* IGTA

TRIANGLES UNLTD TRAVEL, PO Box 5596, Deltona, FL, 32728, (407) 574-3481.

TRIPS ON SHIPS, 3303 Creekridge Rd, Brandon, FL, 33511, (813) 684-4383, (800) 521-8473, Fax: (813) 685-5268.

TUSCAWILLA TRAVEL, 1020 Spring Villas Point, Winter Springs, FL, 32708, (407) 699-4700, (800) 872-8566, Fax: (407) 699-6749. *Member:* IGTA

TWO GUYS TRAVEL, 525 Margaret St, Key West, FL, 33040, (305) 292-9858, Fax: (305) 296-5522. *Member:* IGTA

UNIGLOBE ALL SEASONS TRAVEL, 405 Central Ave, St. Petersburg, FL, 33701, (813) 898-7411.

UNIVERSAL TRAVEL, 215 S Andrews Ave, Ft. Lauderdale, FL, 33301, (941) 525-5000.

UNIVERSAL TRAVEL SERVICES INC, 5728 Major Blvd Ste 611, Orlando, FL, 32819, (407) 345-0368, Fax: (407) 352-8754. *Member:* IGTA

UNIVERSITY PARK TRAVEL, 11640 Spoon Bill Lane, Fort Myers, FL, 33913, (813) 561-4602, Fax: (813) 768-5373.

UP UP AND AWAY, 701 E Broward Blvd, Ft. Lauderdale, FL, 33301, (954) 523-4944, Fax: (954) 463-1154. *Member:* IGTA

USA TRAVEL INVESTMENT INC, 3855 SW 137 Ave #13, Miami, FL, 33175, (305) 229-0501, Fax: (305) 229-0702.

VAGABOND TRAVELS, 601 Northlake Blvd, North Palm Beach, FL, 33408, (561) 848-0648. Fax: (561) 848-0679. *Member:* IGTA

VAGAYTIONERS CLUB, 9423 Tradeport Dr, Orlando, FL, 32827, (407) 240-3600, (800) 929-7387, Fax: (407) 825-2963.

VENTURE TRAVEL, 1322 NE 105th St #10, Miami Shores, FL, 33138, (305) 895-1229, Fax: (305) 892-2881.

VISION TRAVEL, 2222 Ponce de Leon Blvd, Coral Gables, FL, 33134, (305) 444-8484. Ask for Connie.

WORLDWIDE TRAVEL SERVICES, Tamiami Mall, 8784 SW 8th St, Miami, FL, 33174, (305) 223-2323, (800) 441-1954.

ZMAX TRAVEL & TOURS, PO Box 398179, Miami Beach, FL, 33239, (305) 532-0111, Fax: (305) 532-1222. *Member:* IGTA

GEORGIA

AIR SEA WORLDWIDE TRAVEL, 270 Cobb Pkwy S #A-10, Mariette, GA, 30062-8201, (770) 425-3554, fax: (770) 425-1088. *Member:* IGTA

ALL POINTS TRAVEL, 1544 Piedmont Ave, Atlanta, GA, 30324, (770) 873-3631, Fax: (770) 873-3633. *Member:* IGTA

ALTERNATIVE TRAVEL, 9 Dunwoody Park #111, Atlanta, GA, 30338, (770) 698-8444, (800) 875-3363, Fax: (770) 698-0460.

AMERICAN EXPRESS TRAVEL, 400 Pinnacle Way, 460, Norcross, GA, 30071, (404) 246-3500, Fax: (404) 246-3614. *Member:* IGTA

ANZA WORLD TRAVEL, 3533 Chamblee-Tucker Rd #F, Atlanta, GA, 30341, (770) 986-0275.

CARLSON TRAVEL NETWORK/TRIPS UNLIMITED, 1004 Virginia Ave NE, Atlanta, GA, 30306, (770) 872-8747, Fax: (770) 873-1267. *Member:* IGTA

CONTINENTAL TRAVEL, 1794 Willard Way, Snellville, GA, 30278, (404) 972-1187.

CONVENTIONAL TRAVEL, 1658 Lavista Rd NE 6-A, Atlanta, GA, 30329, (770) 315-0107, (800) 747-7107, Fax: (770) 315-0206. *Member:* IGTA

CREATIVE WORLD ADVENTURES, 750 Willoughby Way, Atlanta, GA, 30312, (770) 653-0106, Fax: (770) 653-0036.

CROWN TRAVEL, 1000 Piedmont Ave NE, Atlanta, GA, 30309, (770) 873-2102.

CUMBERLAND TRAVEL SERVICES, INC, 2580 Cumberland Pkwy #455, Atlanta, GA, 30339-3909, (770) 438-2555, (770) 435-8925. *Member:* IGTA

WHO TO CALL

DIFFERENT DIRECTIONS TRAVEL, 314 Pharr Rd NE, Atlanta, GA, 30305, (770) 262-1011, (800) 365-1012, Fax: (770) 262-1013. Ask for Lavonne. *Member:* IGTA

DISCOUNT TRAVEL, Akers Mill Square, 2971 Cobb Pkwy, #E, Atlanta, GA, 30339, (770) 916-0331, (800) 274-6118, Fax: (770) 916-0548.

GEORGE HEARN HOLIDAYS, 1473 Brookvalley Ln NE, Atlanta, GA, 30324, (770) 636-4312, Fax: (770) 982-9161.

GRAND DESTINATION MANAGEMENT, 2255 Cumberland Pkwy #200, Atlanta, GA, 30339, (770) 333-9396, (800) 472-6399, Fax: (770) 333-8846.

HAILEY TRAVEL, 1874 Piedmont Rd 550E, Atlanta, GA, 30324, (770) 874-1692, (800) 366-1692.

KIMELLE KRUISES, 400 Colchester Dr, Stone Mountain, GA, 30088, (770) 879-2535, (800) 880-8982, Fax: (770) 469-2423. E-mail: kimelle@aol.com.

MEETINGS COAST TO COAST, 400 Stone Mountain-Lithania Rd #131, Stone Mountain, GA, 30088, (404) 484-9100.

MIDTOWN TRAVEL CONSULTANTS, 931 Monroe Dr #105, Atlanta, GA, 30308, (770) 872-8308, Fax: (770) 881-6322.

NORTH AMERICAN TRAVEL, 2040 Beaver Ruin Rd, Norcross, GA, 30071, (770) 441-2545, (770) 441-1226. *Member:* IGTA

OUT & ABOUT TRAVEL ADVISORS, 587 Virginia Ave #3A, Atlanta, GA, 30306, (404) 892-8998, (404) 892-7407. *Member:* IGTA

REAL TRAVEL, 3375 Buford Hwy, NE Plaza #1030, Atlanta, GA, 30329-1759, (770) 636-8500, (800) 551-4202, Fax: (770) 636-8639. *Member:* IGTA

SHAW TRAVEL, 3513 Shaw Rd #E, Marietta, GA, 30066, (404) 578-6334.

TRAVEL AFFAIR, 1069 Juniper St, Atlanta, GA, 30309, (404) 892-9400, Fax: (404) 876-9791. *Member:* IGTA

TRAVEL AGENTS INTERNATIONAL (GA), 2971 Cobb Pkwy NW #E, Atlanta, GA, 30339-5910, (770) 916-0331, Fax: (770) 916-0548.

TRAVELERS' CHOICE, 325 Hammond Dr #201, Atlanta, GA, 30328, (770) 256-1818.

UNIGLOBE PREMIER TRAVEL, 600 W Peachtree St #1440, Atlanta, GA, 30308, (770) 885-1122, Fax: (770) 885-9878.

UNIGLOBE VIP TRAVEL, 2970 Clairmount Rd #180, Atlanta, GA, 30329, (404) 982-9100, (404) 634-9824. *Member:* IGTA

VACATIONS UNLIMITED TOURS & TRAVEL, 236 Auburn Ave #206, Atlanta, GA, 30303, (770) 524-2933, Fax: (770) 524-0100.

HAWAII

A PREMIER INTERNATIONAL,, 505 Ward Ave #208, Honolulu,, HI, 96814, (808) 596-9555, (800) 778-4832, Fax: (808) 596-2642. *Member:* IGTA

AMERICAN EXPRESS TRAVEL SERVICE, (808) 947-2607, (808) 926-5441. Ask for Don.

BIRD OF PARADISE TRAVEL, PO Box 4157, Honolulu, HI, 96812-4157, (808) 735-9103, Fax (808) 735-1436. *Member:* IGTA

CARL ERDMAN TRAVEL, 1001 Bishop St #1010, Pauahi Tower, Bishop Sq, Honolulu, HI, 96813, (808) 531-4811.

CHRISTOPHER TRAVEL & TOURS, 134 S Kalaheo Ave, Kailua, HI, 96734-2932, (808) 261-3745, (800) 994-0400, Fax: (808) 261-3765.

CLASSIC TRAVEL, 1413 S King St #201, Honolulu, HI, 96814, (808) 947-3900, Fax (808) 941-5049.

OUTRIGGER INT'L TRAVEL, 150 Kaiulani Ave, Honolulu, HI, 96815, (808) 923-2377, (800) 676-7740. Ask for Mark.

QUEST TRAVEL, The Waialae Bldg, 3660 Waialae Ave #310, Honolulu, HI, 96816, (808) 737-2202. Ask for Verne.

SIMEON DEN EVENTS, 1313 Hoakoa Place, Honolulu, HI, 96821, (808) 732-0550, Fax: (808) 732-3555.

STARLITE EXPLORER A TRAVEL COMPANY, PO Box 949, Wailuku, HI, 96793, (808) 242-5589, Fax: (808) 244-1482.

TICKETS TO GO, 1910 Ala Moana Blvd #B, Honolulu, HI, 96815, (808) 942-7785, Fax: (808) 949-3935.

TRAVEL TRAVEL, 320 Ward Ave #204, Honolulu, HI, 96814, (808) 596-0336, Fax: (808) 591-6639. Ask for Billy. *Member:* IGTA

VACATIONS HAWAII, 1314 S King St #1062, Honolulu, HI, 96814, (808) 524-4711, Fax: (808) 524-7947. *Member:* IGTA

IDAHO

EPIC TRAVEL, PO Box 2810, Hailey, ID, 83333, (208) 788-9551, fax: (208) 788-9561. *Member:* IGTA

ILLINOIS

ACTION TRAVEL, 2256 W Roscoe, Chicago, IL, 60618, (312) 929-4600, Fax: (312) 929-4766. *Member:* IGTA

ALL POINTS TRAVEL SERVICES, 3405 N Broadway, Chicago, IL, 60657, (312) 525-4700, fax: (312) 525-7600. *Member:* IGTA

ALL-WAYS TRAVEL INC, 111 N Canal St River Center Lobby, Chicago, IL, 60606, (312) 258-0909, (800) 926-2350, Fax: (312) 258-3232. *Member:* IGTA

AMBASSADOR TRAVEL, 907 E 31st St, La Grange Park, IL, 60525, (708) 579-3390.

AMERICAN EXPRESS TRAVEL LINCOLN PARK, 625 N Michigan, Chicago, IL, 60611, (312) 435-2570, Fax: (312) 477-8034. *Member:* IGTA

AMERICAN TRAVEL, 2590 E Devon Ave #100, Des Plaines, IL, 60018, (708) 803-5400, Fax: (708) 803-5408.

ARRINGTON TRAVEL CENTER, 1940 N Larrabee, Chicago, IL, 60614, (312) 280-1254. *Member:* IGTA

ASAP TRAVEL SERVICE, 3745 N Halsted, Chicago, IL, 60613, (612) 975-3900, Fax: (312) 975-3995.

BONANZA TRAVEL, 3952 W Touhy, Lincolnwood, IL, 60645, (708) 674-3770, Fax: (708) 674-7174. *Member:* IGTA

BRAVO TRAVEL SERVICES, 325 N Milwaukee #D, Wheeling, IL, 60090, (847) 459-3795, fax: (847) 459-3785. *Member:* IGTA

BUSINESS TRAVEL ADVISORS, 875 N Michigan Ave #1355, Chicago, IL, 60611, (312) 266-8700, (800) 203-8700, Fax: (312) 266-8281. *Member:* IGTA

CARLSON WAGONLIT TRAVEL, 1246 W Northwest Hwy, Palatine, IL, 60067, (708) 991-5666, (800) 925-9848, Fax: (708) 991-0061.

CRC TRAVEL, 2121 N. Clybourn, Chicago, IL, 60614, (312) 525-3800, Fax: (312) 525-8762.

CRC TRAVEL, 2121 N Clybourn, Chicago, IL, 60614, (312) 525-3800, fax: (312) 525-8762. *Member:* IGTA

CRYSTAL TOURS & TRAVEL, 5833 N Paulina, Unit B, Chicago, IL, 60660-3264, (312) 271-1533. Ask for Norma.

DESTINATION INTERNATIONAL, 1520 Kensington Rd #201, Oak Brook, IL, 60521, (708) 954-4758, Fax: (708) 954-2814.

DREAMS & MEMORIES TRAVEL, 1236 S Maple, Berwyn, IL, 60402, (708) 788-3044, Fax: (708) 343-2080.

DUNDEE TRAVEL, 737 S Route 31, Dundee, IL, 60118, (708) 428-3996, (800) 852-1414, Fax: (708) 428-4446.

EDWARDS TRAVEL ADVISORS, 7301 N Lincoln Ave #215, Lincolnwood, IL, 60646, (708) 677-4420, (800) 541-5158, Fax: (708) 677-4434. *Member:* IGTA

ENVOY TRAVEL, 740 N Rush St, Chicago, IL, 60611, (312) 787-2400, 44-ENVOY, Fax: (312) 787-7109. *Member:* IGTA

GONE WITH THE WIND TRAVEL, 212 S Marion #5, Oak Park, IL, 60302, (708) 383-6960, (708) 383-6984. *Member:* IGTA

HEMINGWAY TRAVEL, 1640 N Wells St #201, Chicago, IL, 60614, (312) 440-9870, Fax: (312) 440-9851.

IVORY ISLE TRAVEL, 1 North Franklin #350, Chicago, IL, 60606, (312) 726-8998, Fax: (312) 726-8933.

JORDAN RIVER TOURS & TRAVEL, 207 E Ohio St Ste 239, Chicago, IL, 60611, (708) 429-9490, Fax: (708) 429-4944.

KB TRAVEL & TOURS, 1503 S Coast Dr #309, Elgin, IL, 92626, (714) 434-6196, Fax: (714) 434-6781.

LEADER TRAVEL, One S State St, Corp. Level, Chicago, IL, 60603, (312) 346-9707, Fax: (312) 346-9710.

MARKS TRAVEL SERVICE, 1134 Chicago Ave, Oak Park, IL, 60302, (708) 383-6776, Fax: (708) 383-6876. *Member:* IGTA

NEW HORIZON TRAVEL & TOURS/EXPERTS IN TRAVEL, 5302 1/2 N Milwaukee Ave, Chicago, IL, 60630, (312) 775-4211, Fax: (312) 775-4207.

P.S. TRAVEL, 1783 W Washington St #107, Naperville, IL, 60565-2401, (708) 983-5525, (708) 357-3085. *Member:* IGTA

RENAISSANCE TRAVEL SERVICES, 4S100 Rt 59L, Naperville, IL, 60563, (708) 961-0010, Fax: (708) 961-0018. Ask for Michael.

RIDGEBROOK TRAVEL, 104 Wilmot Rd #100, Deerfield, IL, 60015, (708) 374-0077, Fax: (708) 374-9515. *Member:* IGTA

RIDGEBROOK TRAVEL, 3800 N Lake Shore Dr #6D, Chicago, IL, 60613, (708) 374-0077, (800) 962-0560, Fax: (708) 374-9515.

RIVER NORTH TRAVEL, 432 N Clark St, Chicago, IL, 60610, (312) 527-2269. *Member:* IGTA

ROSENBLUTH INTERNATIONAL, 833 W Buena #1704, Chicago, IL, 60613, (312) 755-4300. *Member:* IGTA

SEVEN SEAS TRAVEL, PO Box 3513,

FERRARI GUIDES' GAY TRAVEL A to Z - 18th EDITION

WHO TO CALL

Bloomington, IL, 61702-3513, (309) 662-8711, Fax: (309) 663-2948.

SHORE TRAVEL, 351 W Hubbard St #105, Chicago, IL, 60610, (312) 329-0015, Fax: (312) 329-0752.

SOUTH HOLLAND TRAVEL & CRUISE, 550 E 162nd St C-East, South Holland, IL, 60473, (708) 333-0360, fax: (708) 333-8561. *Member:* IGTA

SUNSET TRAVEL, 732 W Fullerton Pkwy, Chicago, IL, 60614, (312) 929-8155, Fax: (312) 929-2821. Ask for Stan.

TAN TRAVEL, 107 S Marion St, Oak Park, IL, 60302, (708) 386-6363, (800) 777-8261, Fax: (708) 386-6471.

TELESIS TRAVEL, 730 N Lasalle St #1089, Chicago, IL, 60610-3539, (312) 337-2460, Fax: (312) 337-2464. *Member:* IGTA

TIME TRAVELERS, 822 W Roscoe, Chicago, IL, 60657, (312) 248-8173, (800) 919-7300, Fax: (312) 280-9545.

TRAVEL N.E.T., 1660 N LaSalle St #606, Chicago, IL, 60614, (312) 564-8000. *Member:* IGTA

TRAVEL PROFESSIONALS, 401 N Michigan Ave #206, Chicago, IL, 60611, (312) 321-1450, Fax: (312) 321-0501.

TRAVEL SPIRIT, 2512 N Lincoln Ave, Chicago, IL, 60614, (312) 975-0055, Fax: (312) 975-0085.

TRAVEL WITH US, LTD, 919 N Michigan Ave #3102, Chicago, IL, 60611, (312) 944-2244, (800) 441-9608, Fax: (312) 944-4370. *Member:* IGTA

TRIANGLE TRAVEL, 8501 S 77th Ct, Bridgeview, IL, 60455, (708) 599-0411.

TRIANGLE TRAVEL & CRUISES, PO Box 548, Frankfort, IL, 60423, (815) 464-6460, (800) 214-5514, Fax: (815) 464-6461. Ask for John. *Member:* IGTA

UNITED INVESTORS TRAVEL AGENCY, 5960 N Broadway St, Chicago, IL, 60660-3524, (312) 989-2101, Fax: (312) 989-4896.

VILLAGE TRAVEL, 3008 N Water, Decatur, IL, 62526, (217) 875-5640, Fax: (217) 875-7566. *Member:* IGTA

VIVA TRAVEL & TOURS, 2717 W Cermak Rd, Chicago, IL, 60623, (312) 254-5900. Ask for Juanita.

YELLOW BRICK ROAD, THE TRAVEL AGENCY, 1500 W Balmoral Ave, Chicago, IL, 60640, (312) 561-1800, Fax: (312) 561-4497. *Member:* IGTA

YOUR CUSTOM TRAVEL AGENT, 32-W 151 Anderson Lane, Naperville, IL, 60563, (708) 851-7888, Fax: (708) 961-0018. *Member:* IGTA

INDIANA

ACCESS TRAVEL, 5990 E 71st St #B, Indianapolis, IN, 46220, (317) 577-1220 (tel/fax). *Member:* IGTA

AMBASSADOR CORPORATE CENTER, 5701 Wesbriar Ln, Evansville, IN, 47720, (812) 421-4485, Fax: (812) 421-4493.

ATHENA TRAVEL SERVICES, 1099 N Karwick Rd, Michigan City, IN, 46360, (219) 879-4461, Fax: (219) 873-9860.

EVANSVILLE TRAVEL, 970 S Hebron Ave, Evansville, IN, 47714, (812) 471-4000, Fax: (812) 475-2625.

FANTASY TRAVEL, 3598 Village Ct, Gary, IN, 46408, (219) 663-8144.

GAY & LESBIAN TRAVEL ARTISTS, 119 Mary Claire Ln, Aurora, IN, 47001, (812) 438-3150.

LTM TRAVEL SERVICES, 475 Broadway #111, Gary, IN, 46402, (219) 881-0697, Fax: (219) 886-3827.

TRAVEL AGENT INC, 11562 Westfield Blvd, Carmel, IN, 46032, (317) 846-9619, (800) 347-2512, Fax: (317) 848-3998. Ask for John or Julia.

TRAVEL AGENTS INT'L (IN), 2648 E 10th St, Bloomington, IN, 47408, (812) 333-2262, Fax: (812) 333-7954. Specializes in gay travel. Ask for Marilyn.

UNIGLOBE EVANSVILLE TRAVEL, 970 S Hebron Ave, Evansville, IN, 47714, (812) 471-4000, fax: (812) 475-2625. *Member:* IGTA

WORRALL TRAVEL CRUISES & TOURS, 512 E Court Ave, Jeffersonville, IN, 47130, (812) 283-5000, Fax: (812) 283-5160.

IOWA

ASIA TOURS, 223 E Walnut St, Des Moines, IA, 50309, (515) 244-2071, Fax: (515) 244-1404.

COUNTRYSIDE TRAVEL, 406 E Erie St, Missouri Valley, IA, 51555, (712) 642-2734. Ask for Nancy.

COUNTRYSIDE TRAVEL, 700 1st Ave, Council Bluffs, IA, 51501, (712) 322-7777, Fax: (712) 328-8386.

FIRST TOURS & CRUISES, Clock Tower Square, 900 University, W Des Moines, IA, 50266, (515) 224-1225, fax: (515) 224-1228. *Member:* IGTA

ROYAL APPLE TRAVEL, 512 Nebraska St, Sioux City, IA, 51101, (712) 277-1100, fax: (712) 277-2848. *Member:* IGTA

KANSAS

DENMARK TRAVEL/CJ'S TRAVEL, 6400 W 110th St #102, Overland Park, KS, 66211, (913) 491-5474, fax: (913) 491-1960. *Member:* IGTA

INTERNATIONAL TOURS AND CRUISES, 7202 College Blvd, Overland Park, KS, 66210, (913) 491-8944, (800) 264-8775, Fax: (913) 491-4196.

LR TOUR CONCEPTS, PO Box 8706, Shawnee Mission, KS, 66208-0706, (816) 363-3400, (913) 432-8083. *Member:* IGTA

NEW WORLD TOURS, 10318 Caenen Dr, Overland Park, KS, 66215, (913) 894-6905, (800) 397-0916, Fax: (913) 894-6905.

PERSONAL TOUCH TRAVEL, 714 Poyntz Ave #C, Manhattan, KS, 66502, (913) 539-6233, Fax: (913) 539-1522.

PRESTIGE TRAVEL, PO Box 14985, Lenexa, KS, 66285-4985, (913) 599-3700, Fax: (913) 599-3838. *Member:* IGTA

R&T TRAVEL, 15843 Glenwood, Overland Park, KS, 66223, (913) 681-5831, fax: (913) 681-5831. *Member:* IGTA

KENTUCKY

INTERNATIONAL TOURS & CRUISES, 1235 North Main, Madisonville, KY, 42431, (502) 821-0025, Fax: (502) 821-0028.

JOURNEYS TRAVEL, (606) 331-4844, (800) 852-7439. Ask for Vicki.

PEGASUS TRAVEL, 245 Lexington Ave, Lexington, KY, 40508, (606) 253-1644, fax: (606) 253-0177. *Member:* IGTA

TRAVEL 2000, 981 S Third St #410, Louisville, KY, 40203, (502) 584-1799, Fax: (502) 581-9063. *Member:* IGTA

LOUISIANA

ALTERNATIVE TOURS AND TRAVEL, 1001 Marigny St, New Orleans, LA, 70117, (504) 949-5815, Fax: (504) 949-5917. *Member:* IGTA

AVALON TRAVEL ADVISORS, 1206 Magazine St, New Orleans, LA, 70130, (504) 525-1303, (800) 966-1303, Fax: (504) 525-1306. *Member:* IGTA

FRENCH QUARTER RESERVATION SVC, 940 Royal St Ste 263, New Orleans, LA, 70116, (504) 523-1246, Fax: (504) 527-6327. *Member:* IGTA

GARTRELL TRAVEL SERVICE, 433 Gravier St, New Orleans, LA, 70130, (504) 525-4040, Fax: (504) 581-1378.

GLOBE TOURS & TRAVEL, 1500 Canal St, New Orleans, LA, 70112, (504) 522-6697, (800) 374-8352, Fax: (504) 522-6703. Ask for Lonnie.

OUT & ABOUT TRAVEL, 11528 Old Hammond Hwy #610, Baton Rouge, LA, 70816, (504) 272-7448, Fax: (504) 293-8736. Ask for Lori.

TRAVEL HOTLINE/DMI TRAVEL, 940 Royal St Ste 243, New Orleans, LA, 70116, (504) 523-9338, Fax: (504) 522-9943.

UNIGLOBE ACCESS TRAVEL, 9230 Florida Blvd #B, Baton Rouge, LA, 70815, (504) 923-0587, Fax: (504) 929-6963.

WORLDWIDE TRAVEL & CRUISES, Westside Shopping Center N #19A, Gretna, LA, 70056, (504) 394-8834.

MAINE

ADVENTURE TRAVEL INC, PO Box 6610, Scarborough, ME, 04070-6610, (207) 885-5060, (800) 234-6252, Fax: (207) 885-5062. *Member:* IGTA

PRINCE OF FUNDY CRUISES, PO Box 4216, Portland, ME, 04101-0416, (207) 775-5616, (800) 341-7540, Fax: (207) 773-7403.

TRIANGLE TRAVEL, 288 Cedar St, Ashland, MA, 01721, (508) 881-5019, (800) 254-0304, Fax: (508) 881-5019.

MARYLAND

ADVENTURES IN TRAVEL, 3900 N Charles St, Baltimore, MD, 21218, (410) 467-1161, Fax: (410) 467-1165. Ask for Ron.

ALL COUNTRIES TRAVEL AGENCY, 8635 Philadelphia Rd, Baltimore, MD, 21237, Ask for Isabella.

AMERICAN EXPRESS TRAVEL RELATED SERVICES, 8857 Youngsea Place, Columbia, MD, 21045, (410) 740-9079, Fax: (410) 997-9571. *Member:* IGTA

AMERICAN EXPRESS TRAVEL RELATED SERVICES, 6172 Encounter Row, Columbia, MD, 21045-4346, (410) 715-6826, (410) 715-6828. *Member:* IGTA

FALLS ROAD TRAVEL, 3649 Falls Rd, Baltimore, MD, 21211, (410) 467-2600, Fax: (410) 235-0853. Ask for Michael. *Member:* IGTA

FARE DEALS, 10806 Reiserstown Rd #2C, Owings Mills, MD, 21117, (410) 581-8787, fax: (410) 581-1093. *Member:* IGTA

GALAXSEA CRUISES & VACATIONS, 6400 Baltimore Natl Pike 270-B, Cantonsville, MD, 21228, (410) 747-5204, Fax: (410) 747-6555. *Member:* IGTA

GLOBETROTTER TRAVEL, 3416 Olandwood Ct

WHO TO CALL

#110, Olney, MD, 20832, (301) 570-0800, (301) 570-9514. *Member:* IGTA

INNER HARBOR TRAVEL, 916 Eastern Ave, Baltimore, MD, 21202, (410) 837-2909, Fax: (410) 332-1356. *Member:* IGTA

LAMBDA TRAVEL NETWORK, 8209 Fenton St, Silver Spring, MD, 20910, (301) 565-2345.

LEISURE FOX TRAVEL, PO Box 1127, N Beach, MD, 20714-1127, (410) 257-0300.

MONARCH TRAVEL, 9047 Gaither Rd, Gaithersburg, MD, 20877, (301) 258-0989, Fax: (301) 527-0711. *Member:* IGTA

MT. ROYAL TRAVEL, 1303 N Charles St, Baltimore, MD, 21201, (410) 685-6633, Fax: (410) 783-0243. *Member:* IGTA

OUT THERE TRAVEL/CARLSON WAGONLIT ALL WAYS, 6505 Democracy Blvd, Bethesda, MD, 20817, (508) 349-3794, (508) 349-7207. *Member:* IGTA

SAFE HARBORS TRAVEL, 25 South St, Baltimore, MD, 21202, (301) 547-6565, Fax: (301) 783-1912.

SHIPMATE CRUISE & TRAVEL, 1300 Mercantile Ln #158, Largo, MD, 20774, (301) 925-7041, (800) 925-7041, Fax: (301) 925-8158. *Member:* IGTA

SHOW-ME TRAVEL INC, 245 Tenth St, Pasadena, MD, 21122, (410) 360-6501, Fax: (410) 360-6502. *Member:* IGTA

TRAVEL BY DESIGN, 7516 Belair Rd, Baltimore, MD, 21236, (410) 668-9414, Fax: (410) 668-9762.

TRAVEL CONCEPTS (CARLSON TRAVEL NETWORK), 111 Lexington Rd, Bel Air, MD, 21014, (410) 893-6567.

TRAVEL DESK INC, 6178 Oxon Hill Rd #103, Oxon Hill, MD, 20745, (301) 567-9550, Fax: (301) 567-4153.

TRAVELSMART SERVICES, 4102 Century Towne Rd, Randallstown, MD, 21133-4325, (410) 922-3080, fax: (410) 521-5659. *Member:* IGTA

YOUR TRAVEL AGENT OF BELTSVILLE, 10440 Baltimore Blvd, Beltsville, MD, 20705, (301) 937-0966, Fax: (301) 937-4211. *Member:* IGTA

MASSACHUSETTS

A-1 TRAVEL DEPOT, 2170 Acushnet Ave, New Bedford, MA, 02745, (508) 998-2600. Ask for Lucy.

ABINGTON TRAVEL, 700 Bedford St, PO Box 157, Abington, MA, 02351, (617) 871-1406, Fax: (617) 871-7129.

ADVENTURE TRAVEL, 774 Oak Hill Ave, Attleboro, MA, 02703, (508) 222-3416, (800) 241-3540.

ALL PORTS CRUISE CO, 873 Western Ave, Lynn, MA, 01905, (617) 581-8887, Fax: (617) 593-0882. *Member:* IGTA

ALTERNATIVE TRAVEL, 413 Lowell St, Wakefield, MA, 01880, (617) 246-7480, Fax: (617) 246-3646.

AMERICAN EXPRESS TRAVEL, 12 Melrose St #4, Boston, MA, 02116, (617) 423-2178, (800) 769-5183. *Member:* IGTA

AROUND THE WORLD TRAVEL, Town House Square, Marblehead, MA, 01945, (617) 631-8620, Fax: (617) 639-0775.

ATHOL TRAVEL AGENCY INC, PO Box 340, Athol, MA, 01331, (508) 249-3543, Fax: (508) 249-7175. *Member:* IGTA

ATLANTIC TRAVEL SERVICE, 10 Kelley Square, Worcester, MA, 01610, (508) 798-3744, Fax: (508) 791-5708.

BLUE HILL TRAVEL, 35 Sea St, P.O. Box 31, N Weymouth, MA, 02191-0903, (617) 337-3774, Fax: (617) 337-3710. *Member:* IGTA

CLEVELAND CIRCLE TRAVEL, 1624 Beacon St, Brookline, MA, 02146, (617) 734-2350.

COPLEY PLACE TRAVEL BUREAU, 4 Copley Place #120, Boston, MA, 02116, (617) 266-8349. Ask for Lucil.

CORNERSTONE ASSOCIATES, PO Box 1055, Northampton, MA, 01061, (413) 863-3600, (800) 798-6877, Fax: (413) 863-2209. *Member:* IGTA

ESCAPES, 166 Queen Anne Rd, Harwich, MA, 02645, (508) 430-0666, (800) 540-0808, Fax: (508) 430-0843.

ESCAPES, 35 Vernon St, Hyannis, MA, 02601, (508) 771-6498, Fax: (508) 430-0843.

FISHER TRAVEL, 111 Charles St, Boston, MA, 02114, (617) 367-3490, (800) 745-3490.

FIVE STAR TRAVEL SERVICES, 164 Newbury St, Boston, MA, 02116, (617) 536-1999, (800) 359-1999, Fax: (617) 236-1999.

FOREX TRAVEL, 76 Arlington St, Park Plaza Hotel, Boston, MA, 02116, (617) 482-2900, (800) 962-3637. Ask for Patti or Raphael.

FPT TRAVEL MANAGEMENT GROUP, 186 Alewife Brook Pkwy, Cambridge, MA, 02138-1102, (617) 661-9200, (800) 645-0001.

FRIENDS IN TRAVEL, 5230 Washington St, W Roxbury, MA, 02132, (617) 327-8600, Fax: (617) 327-8602. *Member:* IGTA

GARBER TRAVEL, 20 Gray St, Boston, MA, 02116, (617) 472-6203, Fax: (617) 328-8392. Ask for Dana or Jon.

GIBB TRAVEL CORP, 673 Boylston St, Boston, MA, 02116, (617) 353-0595, Fax: (617) 353-0205. *Member:* IGTA

GOING PLACES TRAVEL, 89 Devonshire St, Boston, MA, 02109, (617) 720-3660, Fax: (617) 523-7579.

HELLER TRAVEL, 146 Massachusetts Ave, Boston, MA, 02115, (617) 236-4300, fax: (617) 236-1284. *Member:* IGTA

HOMEBASE ABROAD, LTD, 29 Mary's Ln, Scituate, MA, 02066, (617) 545-5112, Fax: (617) 545-1808.

IN TOWN RESERVATIONS & TRAVEL, PO Box 1983, 50 Bradford St, Provincetown, MA, 02657, (508) 487-1883, (800) 67P-TOWN, Fax: (508) 487-6140.

NEATO LEISURE GROUP, (617) 247-6752.

NORFOLK TRAVEL, 158 Main St, Norfolk, MA, 02056, (508) 520-1696, (800) 669-0997, Fax: (508) 520-1840. Ask for Cathy.

OMEGA INTERNATIONAL TRAVEL, 99 Summer St (mezzanine), Boston, MA, 02110, (617) 737-8511, Fax: (617) 737-8512.

ON LINE TRAVEL, PO Box 388, Rochester, MA, 02770, (508) 763-3855, Fax: (508) 763-3866. *Member:* IGTA

OUTER CAPE TRAVEL AGENCY, 30 Briar Lane, Wellfleet, MA, 02667-1413, (508) 349-3794, Fax: (508) 349-7207. *Member:* IGTA

PETERS TRAVEL CENTER, 2 Punchard Ave, Andover, MA, 01810, (508) 475-4114, (800) 326-9920.

QUEBEC TOURS, 45 Merrimac St, Newburyport, MA, 01950, (508) 465-5223, (800) 750-6792, Fax:

(508) 463-8674.

SKYLINK INTERNATIONAL, 828 Massachusetts Ave, Arlington, MA, 02174, (617) 646-8527, fax: (617) 646-8003. *Member:* IGTA

STEVEN TRAVELS, 45A Pleasant St, Malden, MA, 02148, (617) 321-6100, (800) 500-6921, Fax: (617) 321-6646. *Member:* IGTA

TARGET SPORT ADVENTURES, 46 Birmingham Pkwy, Boston, MA, 02153-1115, (617) 562-1300, Fax: (617) 254-7277. *Member:* IGTA

TRAVEL AGENCY, THE, 20 Main St, N Reading, MA, 01864, (508) 664-1600, Fax: (508) 664-1602.

TRAVEL MANAGEMENT, 160 Commonwealth Ave, Boston, MA, 02116, (617) 424-1908.

TRAVEL MASTER, 493 Broadway, Everett, MA, 02149, (617) 389-2300, Fax: (617) 394-9030.

TRAVEL PLUS/CRUISE CONNECTION, 1401 Centre St, Boston, MA, 02131, (617) 469-5500, Fax: (617) 469-5505.

TRAVEL YOUR WAY, 281 Needham St, Newton, MA, 02164, (617) 244-4420.

TROY'S TRAVEL AGENCY, 301 Dalton Ave, Pittsfield, MA, 01201, (413) 499-1346, Fax: (413) 499-7396. *Member:* IGTA

WITCH CITY TRAVEL, 2 North St, Salem, MA, 01970, (508) 744-5777, Fax: (508) 744-6660.

WORLD TRAVELERS, 132 Commercial St, Provincetown, MA, 02657, (508) 487-6515, (800) 487-8747, Fax: (508) 487-6517.

YOUR TRAVEL ARRANGEMENTS, 72 Pearl Ave, Revere, MA, 02151, (617) 286-3172.

YOUR WAY TRAVEL, 145 Commercial St, Provincetown, MA, 02657, (508) 487-2992.

MICHIGAN

AIR, SHIP & SHORE, 4791 14 Mile Rd, Rockford, MI, 49341, (616) 696-3000, Fax: (616) VIP-TKTS. Ask for Anne.

ALL-SEASONS TRAVEL, 117 Main St, St. Joseph, MI, 49085, (616) 983-0526, Fax: (616) 983-0529.

ALTERNATIVE LIFESTYLES TRAVEL RESOURCE, 1114 Catalpa Dr, Royal Oak, MI, 48067, (810) 398-7876, (810) 398-7197. *Member:* IGTA

ALTERNATIVE TRAVEL, (810) 238-5217.

AMERICAN TRAVEL SERVICE, 700 E Maple Rd, #203, Birmingham, MI, 48009, (810) 649-0411, Fax: (810) 649-1018.

ANDERSON INTERNATIONAL TRAVEL, 2740 E Lansing Dr, East Lansing, MI, 48823, (517) 337-1300, (800) 723-1233, Fax: (517) 337-8561. *Member:* IGTA

ATS TRAVEL, 26059 Woodward Ave #103, Huntington Woods, MI, 48070, (810) 543-7950, (800) 372-5544, Fax: (810) 399-9396.

BEE KALT TRAVEL SERVICE, PO Box 721245, Royal Oak, MI, 48072, (313) 288-9600, Fax: (313) 435-5370. *Member:* IGTA

CARLSON WAGONLIT TRAVEL/TLC TRAVEL PARTNERS, 2773 44th SW, Wyoming, MI, 49509, (616) 530-5551, fax: (616) 530-9576. *Member:* IGTA

CONLIN - FABER TRAVEL, 601 E William, Ann Arbor, MI, 48104, (313) 677-0900, Fax: (313) 769-6121. *Member:* IGTA

ELLIOTT TRAVEL & TOURS, 46000 Geddes Rd #28, Canton, MI, 48188, (313) 495-1301, Fax: (810) 851-8825.

FERRARI GUIDES' GAY TRAVEL A to Z - 18th EDITION

WHO TO CALL

ESCAPE TRAVEL,, 1640 Haslett Rd #3,, Haslett, MI, 48840, (517) 339-3660, (800) 527-3201, Fax: (517) 339-3379. Exclusively gay & lesbian travel.
FREEDOM TRAVEL, PO Box 399, Douglas, MI, 49406, (616) 857-6068, (616) 857-3418. *Member:* IGTA
GEMINI TRAVEL, 6393 Orchard Lake Rd, W Bloomfield, MI, 48322, (810) 855-3600, (810) 855-4276. *Member:* IGTA
GREAT ESCAPE TRAVEL, 608 S Woodward Ave, Birmingham, MI, 48009, (810) 540-8080, Fax: (810) 540-2701.
HORIZONS TRAVEL, 475 Market Pl, Ann Arbor, MI, 48108, (313) 663-3434.
J. MARTIN TRAVEL, 749 Airport Blvd, Ann Arbor, MI, 48108, (313) 930-2700, fax: (313) 930-6138. *Member:* IGTA
OURWORLD/TRAVEL WORLD, 29269 Dequindre Rd, Madison Heights, MI, 48071-4804, (810) 542-7590, Fax: (810) 399-6753.
PASSAGEWAY TRAVEL & TOURS, 3063 Textile Rd, Ypsilanti, MI, 48197, (313) 467-1801.
PEOPLE'S TRAVEL, 10796 Belleville Rd, Belleville, MI, 48111, (313) 699-3330.
PINK CADILLAC TRAVEL, 27800 Northwestern Hwy #143, Southfield, MI, 48034, (810) 358-5330, (800) 369-8747, Fax: (810) 358-5894.
PRIDE TRAVEL SERVICE, 23315 Woodward Ave, Ferndale, MI, 48220, (810) 584-4004. *Member:* IGTA
ROYAL APPLE TRAVEL, 46000 Geddes Rd #28, Canton, MI, 48188, (313) 495-1301, Fax: (712) 277-2848.
ROYAL INT'L TRAVEL SERVICE, 31455 Southfield Rd, Birmingham, MI, 48025, (313) 644-1600, Fax: (313) 644-1510. *Member:* IGTA
SAUGATUCK CRUISE & TRAVEL, PO Box 672, Saugatuck, MI, 49453, (616) 857-5205.
TRAVEL TOGETHER, PO Box 1453, Midland, MI, 48641, (517) 835-3452, Fax: (517) 835-7355.
TRAVELWORLD, 29269 Dequindre, Madison Heights, MI, 48071, (810) 542-7590, Fax: (810) 399-6753.
VACATION DEPOT, 973 Cherry SE, Grand Rapids, MI, 49506, (616) 454-4339, Fax: (616) 454-4972.
WORLD TRAVEL CENTER, 5446 Schaefer, Dearborn, MI, 48126, (313) 582-1234, fax: (810) 777-0277. *Member:* IGTA
WORLDWISE TRAVEL, 3055 Hayward Dr SE, Grand Rapids, MI, 49546, (616) 942-7065, Fax: (616) 956-7790.
WRIGHT WAY TRAVEL, THE, 24642 Robin, Taylor, MI, 48180, (313) 946-9330. *Member:* IGTA
YOUR GUY FOR TRAVEL, 85 Groveland Rd, Ortonville, MI, 48462-8815, (810) 627-4393, Fax: (810) 627-6097. *Member:* IGTA

MINNESOTA

ADVENT TRAVEL, 330 2nd Ave S #107, Minneapolis, MN, 55401, (612) 333-5559, (612) 333-6010. *Member:* IGTA
ALL AIRLINES TRAVEL, 111 E. Kellogg Blvd. Ste. 225, St. Paul, MN, 55101, (612) 464-2920, (800) 832-0304, Fax: (612) 464-2933.
ALL AIRLINES TRAVEL, 2610 Garfield Ave S #102, Minneapolis, MN, 55408, (612) 872-1706, Fax: (612) 464-2933.
AMERICAN EXPRESS TRAVEL, 200 S 6th St, Minneapolis, MN, 55402, (612) 343-5500, Fax: (612) 343-0866. *Member:* IGTA
AMERICAN EXPRESS TRS, Pillsbury Center, 200 South 6th St, Minneapolis, MN, 55402, (612) 343 5500, Fax: (612) 343 0866. Ask for Douglas.
AWA TRAVEL, 2517 Irving Ave S, Minneapolis, MN, 55405, (612) 991-7825, fax: (612) 904-0391. *Member:* IGTA
FRIENDSHIP TRAVEL, 2610 Garfield Ave S #102, Minneapolis, MN, 55408, (612) 872-1879, (612) 872-1706. *Member:* IGTA
HOT SPOTS TRAVEL, 2150 James Ave, St. Paul, MN, 55105, (612) 699-0403, Fax: (612) 699-0403. *Member:* IGTA
LNBN PARTNERS IN TRAVEL, 825 On the Mall, Minneapolis, MN, 55402-2606, (612) 338-0004, Fax: (612) 338-2396.
MAINLINE CRUISE & TRAVEL, 300 Prairie Ctr Dr, Eden Prairie, MN, 55344, (612) 941-5400, (612) 941-6940.
MAINLINE TRAVEL, 120 S 6th St #202, Minneapolis, MN, 55402, (612) 339-8461, Fax: (612) 339-8467. *Member:* IGTA
NEW DEPARTURES, 625 2nd Ave S Ste 408, Minneapolis, MN, 55402, (612) 305-0025, Fax: (612) 305-0116. *Member:* IGTA
PARTNERS IN TRAVEL LTD, 825 on the Mall, Minneapolis, MN, 55402-2606, (612) 338-0004, Fax: (612) 338-2396. *Member:* IGTA
TIME OUT TRAVEL, 1515 W Lake St, Minneapolis, MN, 55408, (612) 823-7244, Fax: (612) 823-7446.
TRAVEL ABOUT, 406 S Cedar Lake Rd, Minneapolis, MN, 55405, (612) 377-8955, Fax: (612) 377-2826. *Member:* IGTA
TRAVEL CLINIC/FRIENDS IN TRAVEL, 201 Peninsula Rd, Minneapolis, MN, 55441, (612) 591-1948, fax: (612) 591-1964. *Member:* IGTA
TRAVEL COMPANY, THE, 2800 University Ave SE, Minneapolis, MN, 55414-3293, (612) 379-9000, Fax: (612) 379-8258. *Member:* IGTA
TRAVEL QUEST INTERNATIONAL, 245 Aldrich Ave N #305, Mineapolis, MN, 55405-1617, (612) 377-7700, Fax: (612) 374-3888. *Member:* IGTA
UNIGLOBE DIVERSIFIED TRAVEL & CRUISES, 7100 Northland Cl #107, Brooklyn Park, MN, 55428, (612) 537-3132, fax: (612) 537-6977. *Member:* IGTA
VENTURE OUT TRAVEL, 4421 Portland Ave S, Minneapolis, MN, 55407, (612) 823-7803, Fax: (612) 823-5790.

MISSISSIPPI

TRAVEL AFFILIATES, 515 West Live Oak Ave, Pascagoula, MS, 39567, (601) 762-5011, Fax: (601) 762-7837.

MISSOURI

ACTION TRAVEL, 13035 Olive Blvd #218, St. Louis, MO, 63141, (314) 576-9736, (800) 231-8646, Fax: (314) 576-5964. *Member:* IGTA
BON VOYAGE N. TRAVEL & CRUISE CENTER, 7301 NW Tiffany Spring Rd, Kansas City, MO, 64153, (816) 746-5500, Fax: (816) 746-5632.
CREATIVE TRAVEL CONSULTANTS INC, 7948 Warnall Ste 1203, Kansas City, MO, 64114, (816) 363-2787, Fax: (816) 753-7877.
CRUIZN' THE GAY WAY, 7948 Wornall #1203, Kansas City, MO, 64114, (816) 363-CRUS, Fax: (816) 753-7877.
DYNAMIC TRAVEL, 7750 Clayton Rd #105, St. Louis, MO, 63117, (314) 781-8400, Fax: (314) 781-9339. *Member:* IGTA
FIRST DISCOUNT TRAVEL, 1749 Clarkson Rd, Chesterfield, MO, 63017, (314) 532-8888, Fax: (314) 532-8148.
IMPERIAL TRAVEL EXPERTS, 1558 Miller Rd, Imperial, MO, 63052, (314) 464-7077, Fax: (314) 464-7079.
LAFAYETTE SQUARE TRAVEL, 2347 Park Ave Unit C, St. Louis, MO, 63104, (314) 776-8747.
PARK AVENUE TRAVEL SERVICES, 2347 Park Ave, Unit C, St. Louis, MO, 63104, (314) 771-8031, Fax: (314) 773-0900. *Member:* IGTA
PATRIK TRAVEL, 22 N Euclid Ave #101, St. Louis, MO, 63108, (314) 367-1468, Fax: (314) 367-3861. *Member:* IGTA
TRAVEL COMPANY, THE, 11457 Olive Blvd, St. Louis, MO, 63141, (314) 432-6020, Fax: (314) 432-3373.
WILSON TRAVEL, 9262 Blue Ridge Blvd, Kansas City, MO, 64138, (816) 966-1112, Fax: (816) 767-1421. Ask for Donna.
WORLDTREK TRAVEL, 5826 S Grand Blvd, St Louis, MO, 63111, (314) 832-4300, fax: (314) 832-2816. *Member:* IGTA

MONTANA

ALL WAYS TRAVEL, PO Box 987, Bigfork, MT, 59911, (406) 837-5411, Fax: (406) 837-5460.

NEBRASKA

COUNTRYSIDE TRAVEL, 4338 Cass St, Omaha, NE, 68131-1703, (402) 556-1819, Fax: (402) 556-7097. Ask for Dave. *Member:* IGTA
CRUISES INC, 126 N 14th St #5, Lincoln, NE, 68408, (402) 475-7447, fax: (402) 435-1180. *Member:* IGTA
GOOD LIFE TOUR & TRAVEL, 8200 Fletcher Ave, Lincoln, NE, 68507, (800) 233-0404, (402) 467-3900, Fax: (402) 467-5714. Ask for Charles.
MIC/LINCOLN TRAVEL, 233 North 48th Ste F, Lincoln, NE, 68504, (402) 466-1520, Fax: (402) 466-1449.
SINN-FULLY FUN TRIPS, 3443 N Street, Lincoln, NE, 68510, Tel/Fax: (402) 474-3048. Ask for Michael.
TRAVEL CORNER, 4230 S 33rd St #202, Lincoln, NE, 68506, (402) 483-7262, Fax: (402) 483-6389.

NEVADA

A TO Z BARGAIN TRAVEL, 3133 S Industrial Rd, Las Vegas, NV, 89109, (702) 369-8671.
CRUISE-AHOLICS, 2327-A Renaissance Drive, Las Vegas, NV, 89119, (702) 256-8082, (800) 200-3012, Fax: (702) 256-8052. *Member:* IGTA
DELUXE TRAVEL LTD, 102 California Ave, Reno, NV, 89509, (702) 323-4644, Fax: (702) 323-3561. *Member:* IGTA
G&L TRAVEL, 13575 Mt Rainier, Reno, NV, 89506, (702) 677-4139, Fax: (702) 677-2416.
GOOD TIMES TRAVEL, 624 N Rainbow Blvd, Las Vegas, NV, 89107, (702) 878-8900, (800) 638-1066.
SUNRISE TRAVEL, 940 W Moana Ln #101, Reno, NV, 89509,

TRAVEL AGENTS

WHO TO CALL

TAHOE/RENO EXPERIENCE, PO Box 4878, Incline Village, NV, 89450, (702) 831-2023, Fax: (702) 831-2159.
ULTIMATE TRAVEL, 2291 N Green Valley Pkwy, Henderson, NV, 89014, (702) 435-4004, Fax: (702) 435-7001.
UNIGLOBE COMMERCIAL & LEISURE TRAVEL., 1221 Town Center Dr, Ste A, Las Vegas, NV, 89134, (702) 254-4514, (800) 336-1966.

NEW HAMPSHIRE

MARTINELLI TRAVEL, PO Box 1147, Londonberry, NH, 03053, (603) 434-4989, Fax: (603) 434-1696.
STRATHAM TRAVEL, 98 PORTSMOUTH AVE, PO BOX 527, Stratham, NH, 03885, (603) 778-0900.
TRAVEL ABOUT, 7 Main St, Goffstown, NH, 03045, (603) 497-3147, fax: (603) 497-4828. *Member:* IGTA
WORLDWISE TRAVEL, 10 Vaughan Mall #14, Portsmouth, NH, 03108, (603) 430-9060, Fax: (603) 430-9065. *Member:* IGTA

NEW JERSEY

AMBASSADOR WORLD TRAVEL, 118 Westfield Ave #7, Clark, NJ, 07066, (908) 388-9500, (800) 803-9500, Fax: (908) 388-3282. *Member:* IGTA
B'LINE TRAVEL, PO Box 222, Haddonfield, NJ, 08033, (609) 429-3426.
BEACON TRAVEL, 18 Beacon Ln, Brigantine, NJ, 08203, (609) 264-1159, fax: (609) 266-1911. *Member:* IGTA
BERKSHIRE TRAVEL, 64 Oak Ridge Rd, New Foundland, NJ, 07435, (201) 208-1200, (800) 340-6411, Fax: (201) 208-1204. *Member:* IGTA
BUTLER TRAVEL ASSOCIATES, 214 Mayfield Ct, Madison, NJ, 07940, (908) 276-8887, Fax: (908) 276-3312.
CONLEY'S TRAVEL AGENCY, 309 Gordon Ave, Williamstown, NJ, 08094, (609) 262-1111.
CTN/TRAVEL TRENDS BY SAL, 19-03 Maple Ave #1, Fair Lawn, NJ, 07410-1553, (201) 794-9170, Fax: (201) 794-9267.
EMERALD TRAVEL NETWORK, 36 Evesham Rd, Voorhees, NJ, 08043, (609) 424-6677, Fax: (609) 424-0991.
EMPRESS TRAVEL, 226 Rt 37 W, Toms River, NJ, 08755, (908) 244-7771. Ask for Jazmin.
EMPRESS TRAVEL, 43 Versailles Ct, Hamilton, NJ, 08619, (609) 587-1143, fax: (609) 587-3086. *Member:* IGTA
ENTRANCE TO EDEN, 440 Market St, 1st floor, Elmwood Park, NJ, 07407, (201) 794-1931, fax: (201) 794-0699. *Member:* IGTA
FLORHAM PARK TRAVEL, 15 James St, Florham Park, NJ, 07932, (201) 377-1300, Fax: (201) 377-5635. *Member:* IGTA
FODOR'S TRAVEL, 193-B Richey Ave, Collingswood, NJ, 08108, (609) 858-3133 (tel/fax). *Member:* IGTA
FRANKEL TRAVEL, 60 E Hanover Ave, Unit 1 Bldg A,, Morris Plains, NJ, 07950, (201) 455-1111, Fax: (201) 455-0074. *Member:* IGTA
FREE SPIRIT CRUISES, 2133 Price St, Rahway, NJ, 07065, (908) 388-6729, Fax: (908) 381-5529. *Member:* IGTA
FREEDOM TRAVEL, 212 Clifton Country Mall, Clifton Park, NJ, 12065, (518) 371-1866, (518) 731-4659. *Member:* IGTA

FRIENDLY TRAVEL, 309 Gordon Ave, Williamstown, NJ, 08094, (609) 262-1111 (tel/fax). *Member:* IGTA
GALAXSEA CRUISES, 149 Markham Place, Little Silver, NJ, 07739, (908) 219-9600, Fax: (908) 219-5191.
GOOD COMPANIONS TRAVEL & TOURS, 1105 Cooper Ct #200-A, Voorhees, NJ, 08043, (609) 772-9269.
GULLIVER'S TRAVEL, 76 Main St, Woodbridge, NJ, 07095, (908) 636-1120, (800) 836-8687.
INTERNATIONAL TOURS & CRUISES, PO Box 1065, Balmawr, NJ, 08099-5056, (609) 964-0214 (tel/fax). *Member:* IGTA
LA SALLE TRAVEL SERVICES, 70 Taylor Place, South Orange, NJ, 07079-2018, (201) 378-3400, fax: (201) 378-3032. *Member:* IGTA
LIBERTY TRAVEL, 69 Spring St, Ramsey, NJ, 07446, (201) 934-3778, Fax: (201) 934-3792. *Member:* IGTA
MAIN STREET TRAVEL SERVICE, PO Box 864, Marlton, NJ, 08053, (609) 988-0750, Fax: (609) 988-0750.
NEW BRUNSWICK TRAVEL, Church Lane Plaza, 2200 US Hwy 130, N Brunswick, NJ, 08902, (908) 297-7666, Fax: (908) 297-0878. Ask for John.
OVER THE RAINBOW, 450 S Washington Ave, Bergenfield, NJ, 07621, (201) 439-5900, (201) 439-1911. *Member:* IGTA
PARK TRAVEL AGENCY, 2119 Park Ave, South Plainfield, NJ, 07080, (908) 756-3800, Fax: (908) 754-7310. *Member:* IGTA
PRIMA TRAVEL CENTRE, 175-D White Horse Pike, Absecon, NJ, 08201, (609) 485-0900, Fax: (609) 646-1669.
SKYLINE TRAVEL, 35 Kings Hwy E #111, Haddonfield, NJ, 08033, (609) 795-3222. Ask for William.
TM GROUP TRAVEL SERVICES, 875 Kings Hwy #200, Woodbury, NJ, 08096, (609) 853-1919, Fax: (609) 853-0411.
TRAVEL EXPRESSIONS, 382 Centre St, Nutley, NJ, 07110, (201) 667-6624, fax: (201) 667-0440. *Member:* IGTA
TRAVEL FOUR, 1033 Rte 46 East, #A101, Clifton, NJ, 07015, (201) 473-0066, Fax: (201) 473-7441. *Member:* IGTA
TRAVEL NAC, 317 Williams Ave, Hasbrouck Heights, NJ, 07604, (201) 393-0319. Ask for Natalie or Celeste.
TRAVEL REGISTRY, PO Box 589, 127 Washington St, Rocky Hill, NJ, 08553-0589, (609) 921-6900, (800) 346-6901, Fax: (609) 497-6344. *Member:* IGTA
TRAVEL WITH EILEEN, 31 Cornell Dr, Livingston, NJ, 07039, (201) 992-7238, Fax: (201) 992-7238. *Member:* IGTA
TURNER WORLD TRAVEL, 560 Springfield Ave, Westfield, NJ, 07090-1012, (908) 233-3900, Fax: (908) 233-6632. *Member:* IGTA
TWO RIVERS TRAVEL, 113 E River Rd, Rumson, NJ, 07760, (908) 224-0600, fax: (908) 224-1060. *Member:* IGTA
UNIQUE TRAVEL, 331 South Ave, Garwood, NJ, 07027, (908) 789-3303, Fax: (908) 789-3325. *Member:* IGTA
VAGABOND TRAVEL, 542 Prospect Ave, Little

Silver, NJ, 07739, (908) 842-5410.
VIAGGI TRAVEL, PO Box 325, Lyndhurst, NJ, 07071, (201) 438-9019, (201) 438-9219. *Member:* IGTA
VILLAGE TRAVEL, PO Box 310, Fanwood, NJ, 07023, (908) 322-8700, Fax: (908) 322-2020. *Member:* IGTA
WINGS/DIVISION OF STB TRAVEL, 55 Newark St, Hoboken, NJ, 07030, (201) 216-1200, Fax: (201) 216-1212.

NEW MEXICO

AMERICAN EXPRESS TRAVEL, 6600 Indian School Rd, Albuquerque, NM, 87110, (505) 883-3677, Fax: (505) 884-0008.
AMF TRAVEL, 10009 Bryan Ct NW, Albuquerque, NM, 87114, (505) 898-8389, Fax: (505) 897-8654.
ATLAS TRAVEL SERVICE, 1301 Wyoming NE, Albuquerque, NM, 87112, (505) 291-6575.
NORTH & SOUTH TRAVEL, 215 Central Ave NW, Albuquerque, NM, 87102-3363, (505) 246-9100, (800) 456-1497, Fax: (505) 246-2688. *Member:* IGTA
NORTH & SOUTH TRAVEL & TOURS #2, 425 San Lorenzo Ave NW, Albuquerque, NM, 87107, (505) 344-6632, (800) 585-8016, Fax: (505) 344-6616.
PASSARIELLO TRAVEL, 9320-D Menaul NE, Albuquerque, NM, 87112, (505) 296-1584, Fax: (505) 294-5833.
PREMIUM TRAVEL, 6020 Indian School Rd NE, Albuquerque, NM, 87110, (505) 344-3161, Fax: (505) 344-3235.
THOMAS COOK TRAVEL (NM), 6600 Indian School Rd, Albuquerque, NM, 87110, (505) 883-3677, Fax: (505) 884-0008.
UNIGLOBE ABOVE & BEYOND TRAVEL, 2225 E Lohman #A, Las Cruces, NM, 88001, (505) 527-0200, Fax: (505) 527-0366.

NEW YORK

ACE CRUISE MASTERS, 282 Manhattan Ave #3 South, New York, NY, 10026, (212) 749-2626, Fax: (212) 749-5178. *Member:* IGTA
ADONIS TRAVEL, DBA DASELI, 300 Vanderbilt Motor parkway #225, Hauppauge, NY, 11788, (516) 231-4821, Fax: (516) 231-4825.
ADVANCED TRAVEL NETWORK, 1132 Morton Blvd, Kingston, NY, 12401, (914) 336-4655, (800) 841-0703, Fax: (914) 336-4718. *Member:* IGTA
ALL CONTINENT TRAVEL, 227 E 56th St, New York, NY, 10022, (212) 371-7171, Fax: (212) 887-2072.
ALL POINTS TRAVEL, 7396 E Main St, Lima, NY, 14485, (716) 582-1120, Fax: (716) 582-1087. *Member:* IGTA
ALLEGRO ENTERPRISES, 900 West End Ave #12C, New York, NY, 10025-3525, (212) 666-6700. *Member:* IGTA
AMERICAN EXPRESS TRAVEL, 822 Lexington Ave, New York, NY, 10021, (212) 758-6510, (212) 935-7699. *Member:* IGTA
AQUARIUS TRAVEL, 25 Rockledge Ave Ste 603, White Plains, NY, 10601, (914) 682-5663, Fax: (914) 682-5663. *Member:* IGTA
ATLAS TRAVEL CENTER, 1545 Central Ave, Albany, NY, 12205-5044, (518) 464-0271, Fax:

TRAVEL AGENTS

FERRARI GUIDES' GAY TRAVEL A to Z - 18th EDITION   127

WHO TO CALL

(518) 464-0273. Member: IGTA
AVALON TRAVEL, 9421 3rd Ave, Brooklyn, NY, 11209, (718) 833-5500, Fax: (718) 238-3858.
BARD GROUP, THE, 239 W 21st St #3-B, New York, NY, 10011, (212) 242-1165, Fax: (212) 727-9070. Member: IGTA
BON ADVENTURE, 1173A Second Ave #135, New York, NY, 10021, (212) 759-2206, Fax: (212) 593-7612.
BR TRAVEL SERVICE, 3070 Belgium Rd, Baldwinsville, NY, 13027, (315) 635-8722, fax: (315) 635-8724. Member: IGTA
CATHERINE'S TRAVEL SERVICE, 528 Haley Rd, Ontario, NY, 14519, (315) 524-8733. Member: IGTA
CHOICE TRAVEL, 267 S Central Park Ave, Scarsdale, NY, 10530, (914) 993-3300, Fax: (914) 993-0361. Member: IGTA
COMMUNITY TRAVEL CONNECTIONS, 30 Griffen St, Poughquag, NY, 12570, (914) 227-4059, Fax: (914) 227-4059. Member: IGTA
CORTLAND TRAVEL, 1970 Crompond Rd, Peekskill, NY, 10566, (914) 737-7800, Fax: (914) 737-7881.
COURTYARD TRAVEL, 50 Brompton Rd Apt 1C, Great Neck, NY, 11021, (516) 773-3700, Fax: (516) 829-4931.
CRITIC'S CHOICE THEATRE TOURS, 69 Warren St, Brooklyn, NY, 11201, (718) 522-1345, (800) 926-9844, Fax: (717) 522-2203.
D.C. WORLD WIDE TRAVEL, 251 W 19th St #4C, New York, NY, 10011, (212) 243-7529, Fax: (212) 647-1629.
DE PREZ TRAVEL BUREAU, 325 Westminster Rd, Rochester, NY, 14607, (716) 234-3615, Fax: (716) 442-8309. Member: IGTA
DEEP JOURNEYS, 98 Riverside Dr #5H, New York, NY, 10024, (212) 595-9573. Member: IGTA
DESTINATION WORLD, 370 Lexington #1410, New York, NY, 10017, (212) 682-1001, Fax: (212) 682-3130.
DESTINATIONS UNLIMITED, 130 Theater Place, Buffalo, NY, 14202, (716) 855-1955, (800) 528-8877, Fax: (716) 855-0016. Member: IGTA
DEVILLE TRAVEL SERVICE, 7818 3rd Ave, Brooklyn, NY, 11209, (718) 680-2700, Fax: (718) 680-2743.
DISCOVERY TOURS, 40-03 79th St, Elmhurst, NY, 11373, (718) 898-0561, (718) 898-0634, Fax: (718) 335-3099.
DISCRETION, 527 W 143rd St #44, New York, NY, 10031, (212) 368-0717, Fax: (212) 862-9808. Member: IGTA
EARTH TRAVELERS, 683 Dick Rd, Buffalo, NY, 14225, (716) 685-2900, Fax: (716) 685-1170. Member: IGTA
EC TOURS, 265 Southdown Rd, Huntingdon, NY, 11743, (516) 423-2097.
EDLEN TRAVEL, 161 S Middletown Rd, Nanuet, NY, 10954, (914) 624-2100, Fax: (914) 624-2315.
ELEGANT TRAVEL, 83 Constellation Rd, Levittown, NY, 11756, (516) 579-7045, Fax: (516) 520-0813.
EMPRESS TRAVEL, 54 The Crossing Blvd #F-12, Clifton Park, NY, 12065, (518) 371-1155, fax: (518) 371-1591. Member: IGTA
EMPRESS TRAVEL, 188 E 34th St, New York, NY, 10016, (212) 685-1800, fax: (212) 685-8216. Member: IGTA
FANTASTIC TOURS & TRAVEL INC, 6143 Jericho Trnpke, Commack, NY, 11725, (516) 462-6262, Fax: (516) 462-2311. Member: IGTA
FOUR SEASONS TRAVEL, 163 Empire Blvd,, Rochester, NY, 14609, (716) 482-0010, Fax: (716) 482-0053.
FREEDOM TRAVEL, 1075 Portion Rd, Farmingville, NY, 11738, (516) 736-3636, Fax: (516) 736-3655.
GATEWAY TRAVEL, 1300 Hylan Blvd, Staten Island, NY, 10305, (718) 667-1100.
GINMAR TRAVEL, 392 Central Park W, 8th fl, New York, NY, 10025, In U.S.A.: (212) 866-9452, (800) GINMAR-1 (446-6271), Fax: (212) 222-5333. Ask for Robert. In London: call toll-free (0800) 966-554.
GREAT EXPECTATIONS, 41 Landing Rd S, Rochester, NY, 14610, (716) 244-8430, Fax: (716) 244-8749. Member: IGTA
HAGGART TRAVEL, 75 Saint Marks Place, Staten Island, NY, 10301, (718) 981-7015, Fax: (718) 816-4092.
HEIDIES TRAVEL & TOUR, 2308 Seneca St, Buffalo, NY, 14227, (716) 821-1991, Fax: (716) 826-5658.
HISA TRAVEL, 3699 W Henrietta Rd, Rochester, NY, 14623, (716) 334-0941, Fax: (716) 334-4212.
HOLLOWBROOK TRAVEL AT ALLSPORT INC, 17 Old Main St, Fiskill, NY, 12524, (914) 896-0227, Fax: (914) 898-8673.
HOMERIC TOURS, 55 E 59th St, 17th Floor, New York, NY, 10022, (212) 753-1100, (800) 223-5570, Fax: (212) 753-0319.
INDEPENDENT TRAVEL CONSULTANT, 245 8th Ave #233, New York, NY, 10011, (212) 229-1801.
INTERNATIONAL TOURS, 153-04 75 Ave #2E, Flushing, NY, 11367, (212) 242-2277, Fax: (212) 242-2924.
ISLANDERS KENNEDY TRAVEL, 267-10 Hillside Ave, Queens, NY, 11004, (718) 347-7433, Fax: (718) 347-1291. Member: IGTA
KON TRAVEL, 310 Madison Ave, New York, NY, 10017, (212) 286-9410, fax: (212) 286-1924. Member: IGTA
LAKE SHORE TRAVEL, 594 Rte 6, Mahopac, NY, 10541, (914) 628-6522, fax: (914) 628-6544. Member: IGTA
LAPOINT'S HOMETOWN TRAVEL, 94 Bay St, Glens Falls, NY, 12801, (518) 793-3390, Fax: (518) 793-3694.
LE SOLEIL TOURS, 1323 72nd St, Brooklyn, NY, 11228, (718) 232-4060.
LET'S TRAVEL, PO Box 100, Bearsville, NY, 12409, (914) 679-6235, Fax: (914) 679-4157.
LIBERTY TRAVEL, 298 Madison Ave, New York, NY, 10017, (212) 689-5600, Fax: (212) 545-8050. Member: IGTA
LUCY'S TRAVEL, 185 Medford Ave, Patchogue, NY, 11772, (516) 758-0058, Fax: (516) 758-0001.
MAINLINE TRAVEL, 680 Pittsford-Victor Rd, Pittsford, NY, 14534, (716) 248-2530, Fax: (716) 248-2709.
MAJESTY TRAVEL, INC, 41 W 72nd St, New York, NY, 10023, (212) 697-3447, (800) 732-3490, Fax: (212) 986-2940. Member: IGTA
MCGEARY'S TRAVEL, 460 Madison Ave, Albany, NY, 12208, (518) 436-3411, (518) 436-3434. Member: IGTA
MONARCH TRAVEL, 291 Herbertsville Rd, Brick, NJ, 08724-1778, (908) 840-2233, Fax: (908) 840-5511. Member: IGTA
NEW PALTZ TRAVEL CENTER, 7 Cherry Hill Center, New Paltz, NY, 12561, (914) 255-7706, Fax: (914) 255-8015. Member: IGTA
NOAH'S ARK TRAVEL, 33A Roosevelt Dr, W Haverstraw, NY, 10993, (914) 429-7556.
NORTHFORK TRAVEL, 99-2 Rt 25A, PO Box 549, Shoreham, NY, 11786, (516) 821-3400, (516) 821-7810. Member: IGTA
OCEAN VOYAGER CRUISE CONSULTANTS, 404 1/2 Henry St, Brooklyn, NY, 11201-6009, (718) 624-3063, (800) 435-2531, Fax: (718) 624-5437.
ODYSSEUS ENTERPRISES, LTD, Box 1548, Port Washington, NY, 11050, (516) 944-5330, Fax: (516) 944-7540. Member: IGTA
ODYSSEY TRAVEL, INC, 151 7th Ave, Brooklyn, NY, 11215-2298, (718) 636-9000, Fax: (718) 857-3431.
OPTIMA TRAVEL, 460 State St #202, Rochester, NY, 14608, (716) 546-2840, Fax: (716) 458-0620. Ask for Noeme or Ivette.
OUR TIME VOYAGES, 16 E 34th St 3rd fl., New York, NY, 10016, (212) 545-5565, Fax: (212) 251-1486. Member: IGTA
OUT EVERYWHERE, PO Box 4571, Great Neck, NY, 11023, (516) 482-1405, Fax: (516) 466-2847.
OUT THERE TRAVEL, 360 W 55th St #2-S, New York, NY, 10019, (212) 245-3909, (212) 315-4118. Member: IGTA
PARK AVENUE TRAVEL, 25 Buckingham St, Rochester, NY, 14607, (716) 256-3080, Fax: (716) 473-7436.
PARKSIDE TRAVEL AND TOURS, 1116 Parkside Ave, Buffalo, NY, 14214, (716) 446-9630, Fax: (714) 446-9630. Member: IGTA
PEOPLE TRAVEL CLUB, 156 Fifth Ave #1025, New York, NY, 10010, (212) 627-4004, Fax: (212) 645-2891. Member: IGTA
PIED PIPER TRAVEL, 330 West 42nd St #1804, New York, NY, 10036, (212) 239-2412, (800) TRIP-312, Fax: (212) 239-2275. Member: IGTA
RAINBOW TRAVEL, 1109 1st Ave #4A, New York, NY, 10021, (212) 935-7246.
RICH WORLDWIDE TRAVEL, INC, 500 Fifth Ave #325, New York, NY, 10110, (212) 997-1600, (800) 333-7424, Fax: (212) 997-5427. Member: IGTA
RIVERDALE TRAVEL SERVICE, 5705 Mosholu Ave, Riverdale, NY, 10471, (718) 549-5950. Member: IGTA
RMC TRAVEL, 424 Madison Ave Ste 705, New York, NY, 10017, (212) 754-6560, Fax: (212) 754-6571. Member: IGTA
ROBERTA SONNINO TRAVEL INC, 225 W 34th St, New York, NY, 10122, (212) 714-2540, Fax: (212) 239-1494. Member: IGTA
ROGERS TRAVEL AGENCY, 140 Medford Ave, Patchogue, NY, 11772, (516) 289-5252, (800) 753-2400, Fax: (516) 289-4071. Ask for Marta.
SCARSDALE TAN & TRAVEL, 390 Central Park

WHO TO CALL

Ave, Greenville Plaza, Scarsdale, NY, 10583, (914) 472-2273, Fax: (914) 472-6682.
SEA RAPTURE BY MAB, 225 Vandalia Ave Ste 7C, Brooklyn, NY, 11239, (718) 642-0740.
SEALANDAIR TRAVEL, 41 W 72nd St, New York, NY, 10023, (212) 697-3447, Fax: (212) 986-2940.
SILVER SANDS TRAVEL, 1005 Church Ave,, Brooklyn, NY, 11218, (718) 284-5512.
SPA ADVENTURES INC, 325 W 45th St #910, New York, NY, 10036, (212) 399-0700, (800) 955-7737, Fax: (212) 399-0422.
SPECIALTY TRAVEL SERVICE, 185 Medford Ave, Patchogue, NY, 11772, (516) 758-0058, Fax: (516) 758-0001.
STEVENS TRAVEL MGT, 432 Park Ave S, 9th floor, New York, NY, 10016, (212) 696-4300, Fax: (212) 679-5072. *Member:* IGTA
SYOSSET TRAVEL, 15 Jackson Ave, Syosset, NY, 11791, (516) 496-0534, Fax: (516) 496-3514.
T.R.I.P. TOURS, 50 Brompton Rd, 1- C, Great Neck, NY, 11021, (516) 829-5676, Fax: (516) 829-4931. *Member:* IGTA
TIOGA TRAVEL, 189 Main St, Owego, NY, 13827, (607) 687-4144, (800) 542-2349, Fax: (607) 687-4323. Ask for Ricardo. *Member:* IGTA
TOUR DU JOUR, 709 W 176th St, New York, NY, 10033, (212) 795-0131.
TRADE WIND, 6 Jay St, Spring Valley, NY, 10977, (914) 352-4134. Ask for Greg. *Member:* IGTA
TRADEWINDS TRAVEL, 9 Hobby St, Pleasantville, NY, 10570-0298, (914) 769-6804, Fax: (914) 769-5619.
TRAVEL COMPANY OF TROY, 500 Federal St #304, Troy, NY, 12180, (518) 273-2119, Fax: (518) 273-4604, ask for Bobbi. *Member:* IGTA
TRAVEL INNOVATIONS, 1501 Broadway #506, New York, NY, 10036, (212) 354-3100, (800) 321-8264, Fax: (212) 354-3111. *Member:* IGTA
TRAVEL MASTERS OF N.Y., 823 Willow Rd, Franklin Square, NY, 11010, (800) MOR—TVL, (516) 485-0707, (516) 466-7918. Ask for Jesse or Sonya. *Member:* IGTA
TRAVEL TAMMARO, 139-15 83rd Ave #125, Briarwood, NY, 11435, (718) 805-0907.
TRIANGLE DESTINATIONS INC, 1115 E Main St, Rochester, NY, 14609, (716) 288-0560, Fax: (716) 288-0272. *Member:* IGTA
VIRGA'S TRAVEL SERVICE, Rt. 82, PO Box 460, Hopewell Jct., NY, 12533, (914) 221-2455, Fax: (914) 226-6260. *Member:* IGTA
WELCOME TRAVEL AGENCY, 340 Portion Rd, Lake Ronkonkoma, NY, 11779, (516) 585-7070, Fax: (516) 585-7267. *Member:* IGTA
WEST HILLS TRAVEL, 444 W Jericho Turnpike, Huntington, NY, 11743, (516) 692-9800, (800) 291-3313, Fax: (516) 692-9817. *Member:* IGTA

NORTH CAROLINA

ARGO WORLD TRAVEL, 8307 University Exec. Park. #263, Charlotte, NC, 28262, (704) 547-1454, Fax: (704) 547-1457.
ATLANTIS TRAVEL, 4801 E Independence, #711, Charlotte, NC, 28212, (704) 566-9779, Fax: (704) 566-7649.
CAROLINA TRAVEL, 2054 Carolina Circle Mall, Greensboro, NC, 27405, (919) 621-9000, Fax: (919) 621-9004. *Member:* IGTA
CREATIVE ADVENTURE TRAVEL, 136 Harmon Ave, Winston-Salem, NC, 27106, (910) 750-0733, Fax: (910) 724-1272.
FIRST DISCOUNT TRAVEL, 915 Main St #1, N Wilkesboro, NC, 28659, (910) 667-1644, fax: (910) 667-0974. *Member:* IGTA
JOURNEYS, 8 Biltmore Ave, Asheville, NC, 28801, (704) 232-0800, fax: (704) 232-0802. *Member:* IGTA
MAIN STREET TRAVEL, 205 W Main St, Carrboro, NC, 27510, (919) 968-1800, Fax: (919) 968-6984.
MANN TRAVELS, 9009-2 J.M. Keynes Dr, Charlotte, NC, 28262, (704) 547-1240, (800) 849-2028, Fax: (704) 549-4256. *Member:* IGTA
PARADISE TRAVEL & TOURS, 309 W Martin St, Raleigh, NC, 27601, (919) 755-1404.
PINK FAIRY TRAVELS, 1409 East Blvd #6A, Charlotte, NC, 28203, (704) 332-5545, (800) 243-3477, Fax: (704) 332-0482. *Member:* IGTA
PINK TRIANGLE TRAVEL, 309 W Martin St, Raleigh, NC, 27601, (919) 755-1404, Fax: (919) 829-0830.
RAINBOW TRAVEL, PO Box 31288, Raleigh, NC, 27622, (919) 571-9054, (800) 633-9350 ext 430, fax: (919) 782-1936. www.citysearch.com/rou/rainbowtravel. Ask for Rolo. *Member:* IGTA
TRAVEL ASSOCIATES, 100 W Innes St #102, Salisbury, NC, 28144, (704) 637-9000, Fax: (704) 637-9013
TRAVEL BY DESIGN, 2333 Pine Haven Dr, Gastonia, NC, 28054, (704) 864-0631, (800) 210-1274, Fax: (704) 867-2166.
TRAVEL CENTER, THE, 905 W Main St, #5, Durham, NC, 27701, (919) 682-9378, (800) 334-1085, Fax: (619) 687-0903. Ask for Mària.
TRAVEL QUEST, 3030-A S Main St, High Point, NC, 27263, (919) 434-3867, (800) 798-3867, Fax: (919) 434-5329. *Member:* IGTA
UNIGLOBE GATEWAY TRAVEL, 1919 South Blvd, Charlotte, NC, 28203, (704) 377-1957, Fax: (704) 377-1952.
VIDEO BOATIQUE, 5719 Shadow Creek Rd, Charlotte, NC, 28226, (704) 544-1727, (800) 685-BOAT (2628). Cruise-only travel agency.

OHIO

AD'E TRAVEL INTERNATIONAL, PO Box 94198, Cleveland, OH, 44101, (216) 771-5551, Fax: (216) 771-5552.
ALL WORLD TRAVEL SERVICE, 108 W First St, Dayton, OH, 45402, (937) 222-1220, fax: (937) 222-2765. *Member:* IGTA
BROOKSIDE TRAVEL AGENCY, PO Box 89, Brookfield, OH, 44403, (216) 448-4232, Fax: (216) 448-5747.
CARDINAL WORLDWIDE TRAVEL, 4911 Grant Ave, Cleveland, OH, 44125, (216) 341-8333, fax (216) 341-8233. *Member:* IGTA
CHAPEL HILL TRAVEL CENTER, Chapel Hill Mall #477, Akron, OH, 44310, (216) 633-9334, Fax: (216) 633-1697.
CINCINNATI CRUISE CONNECTION, 7485 Colerain Ave, Cincinnati, OH, 45231-5307, (513) 729-2261, Fax: (513) 729-2264.
COMPLETE TRAVEL & TOUR SERVICES, 28704 Chardon Rd, Willoughby Hills, OH, 44092, (216) 944-9200, (216) 944-1529. *Member:* IGTA
CORNERS OF THE WORLD INT'L TRAVEL, 1631 Remington Dr #9, Westlake, OH, 44145, (216) 892-0022, (800) 368-TRIP. Ask for David.
EUCLID TRAVEL, 22078 Lakeshore Blvd, Euclid, OH, 44123, (216) 261-1050, fax: (216) 261-1054. *Member:* IGTA
FIRST DISCOUNT TRAVEL, 323 West Bridge St, Dublin, OH, 43155, (614) 799-8770, Fax: (614) 799-8771. *Member:* IGTA
FIRST DISCOUNT TRAVEL, 628 Leona St, Elyria, OH, 44035, (216) 324-4866, fax: (216) 324-4792. *Member:* IGTA
FIRST DISCOUNT TRAVEL/LANDINGS TRAVEL, 32730 Walker Rd #F4, Avon Lake, OH, 44012, (216) 933-3720, (800) 429-1122, Fax: (216) 933-5227.
GREAT WAYS TRAVEL, 4625 W Bancroft St, Toledo, OH, 43615, (419) 536-8000, Fax: (419) 536-8005. *Member:* IGTA
HMS LEGEND, 42 Victorian Gate Way, Columbus, OH, 43215, (614) 228-0838, (800) 301-7513, Fax: (614) 228-0838.
JUST TRAVEL, 82 S High St, Dublin, OH, 43017, (614) 791-9500.
L.B. BURGER TRAVEL SERVICE, 517 Bank One Bldg, Youngstown, OH, 44503, (216) 744-5035, Fax: (216) 744-4519. *Member:* IGTA
PARKSIDE TRAVEL AKRON OFFICE, 1431 S Main St, Akron, OH, 44301, (330) 773-1816, (330) 724-1800. *Member:* IGTA
PARKSIDE TRAVEL USA, 3310 Kent Rd, Stow, OH, 44224, (330) 688-3334, (800) 552-1647, Fax: (330) 688-2054. *Member:* IGTA
PIER 'N PORT TRAVEL, 2692 Madison Rd #H1, Cincinnati, OH, 45208, (513) 841-9900, Fax: (513) 841-5930.
PLAYHOUSE SQUARE TRAVEL, 1422 Euclid Ave #1160, Cleveland, OH, 44115, (216) 575-0813, (800) 575-0813, Fax: (216) 575-1614. *Member:* IGTA
PROVIDENT TRAVEL, 221 E 4th St, 2800 Atrium II, Cincinnati, OH, 45202, (513) 621-4900, Fax: (513) 621-1814. *Member:* IGTA
RESERVE TRAVEL, 1820 Superior Bldg, 815 Superior Ave E, Cleveland, OH, 44114-2799, (216) 348-6650, (800) 331-2428. Ask for Dale or Robin.
ROFFLER CRUISE & TRAVEL, 2786 Cleveland Rd, Wooster, OH, 44691, (216) 345-7755, Fax: (216) 345-7756. Ask for Neil.
SERENDIB, 11820 Edgewater Drive #619, Lakewood, OH, 44107-2522, (216) 221-3994. *Member:* IGTA
STAR TRAVEL CONSULTANTS, PO Box 345, Loveland, OH, 45140, (513) 677-3022, Fax: (513) 677-3514.
SUN LOVERS' CRUISES & TRAVEL, 11627 Clifton Blvd, Cleveland, OH, 44102-1319, (216) 529-0100, Fax: (216) 529-0111. *Member:* IGTA
TOLEDO TRAVEL CLUB, 4612 Talmadge Rd, Toledo, OH, 43623, (419) 471-2820, Fax: (419) 471-2877.
TRAVEL AGENTS INT'L (OH), 2855 W Market St #115, Akron, OH, 44333, (216) 836-6500, Fax: (216) 836-6506.
TRAVEL EXCHANGE GROUP, 1020 Kingston Pl, Cincinnati, OH, 45204, (513) 471-5772.
TRAVEL EXCHANGE GROUP, THE, 4600

WHO TO CALL

Montgomery Road #105, Cincinnati, OH, 45212, (513) 841-5595. Ask for Melissa.

TRAVEL PLACE, THE (OH), 22965 Lorain Rd, Fairview Park, OH, 44126, (216) 734-1886, Fax: (216) 734-1981. *Member:* IGTA

TRAVELPLEX EAST, PO Box 360956, Columbus, OH, 43236-0956, (614) 337-3155, Fax: (614) 337-3165. *Member:* IGTA

TRAVELPLEX EAST, 760 Morrison Rd #C, Gahanna, OH, 43230, (614) 337-3155, fax: (614) 337-3165. *Member:* IGTA

TROPICAL KNIGHTS TRAVEL & TOURS, 465 Carrie Ave NW, New Philadelphia, OH, 44663, (330) 364-4218, (888) 929-4218, Fax: (330) 364-2718.

UNIGLOBE FIVE STAR TRAVEL, 1160 Hanna Bldg, 1422 Euclid Ave, Cleveland, OH, 44115, (216) 575-0813, (800) 575-0813, Fax: (216) 575-1614.

VICTORIA TRAVEL, 3330 Erie Ave 1A, Cincinnati, OH, 45208, (513) 871-1100, (800) 626-4932, Fax: (513) 871-7344. *Member:* IGTA

OKLAHOMA

ABOVE & BEYOND TRAVEL, 1000 E Alameda St #136, Norman, OK, 73071, (405) 366-7766, Fax: (405) 366-7771.

BOARDING PASS TRAVEL, THE, 1110 W Main St, Norman, OK, 73069, (405) 321-0222, Fax: (405) 321-1711. Ask for Shelia.

INTERNATIONAL TOURS OF CLAREMORE, 5240 SW Brandon Terrace, Claremore, OK, 74017, (918) 341-6866, Fax: (918) 341-8570. *Member:* IGTA

TLC TRAVEL PROFESSIONALS, 1015 S Meridian, Oklahoma City, OK, 73108, (405) 948-1740, (800) 852-1740, Fax: (405) 948-1720.

OREGON

ADVANTAGE TRAVEL SERVICE, 812 SW Washington St #200, Portland, OR, 97205-3210, (503) 225-0186.

AFFORDABLE VACATIONS, 7435 SW Hermosa Way, Tigard, OR, 97223, (503) 684-1236, Fax: (503) 620-5184.

AWAY TO TRAVEL, 7314 NE Fremont, Portland, OR, 97213, (503) 281-1234, Fax: (503) 281-0903. *Member:* IGTA

BARBUR TRAVEL, 9049 SW Barbur Blvd, Portland, OR, 97219, (503) 246-2469, Fax: (503) 246-4689.

CLASSIC WORLD TRAVEL, 656 Charnelton, Eugene, OR, 97401, (541) 343-1992, Fax: (541) 343-2489. *Member:* IGTA

COLUMBIA TRAVEL BUREAU, 700 E Third, The Dalles, OR, 97058, (541) 298-5174, (541) 296-1804. *Member:* IGTA

CORPORATE TRAVELS, American Bank Building, 621 SW Morrison St, Portland, OR, 97205, (503) 220-0351, (800) 446-4117.

GLOBAL AFFAIR, 285 E 5th Ave, Eugene, OR, 97401, (541) 343-8595, (800) 755-2753, Fax: (541) 687-1558.

GULLIVER'S TRAVEL & VOYAGES, 514 NW 9th Ave, Portland, OR, 97209, (503) 221-0013, Fax: (503) 230-0355. *Member:* IGTA

HAWTHORNE TRAVEL COMPANY, 1939 SE Hawthorne Blvd, Portland, OR, 97214, (503) 232-5944, Fax: (503) 232-4662. *Member:* IGTA

HAZEL PHILLIPS TRAVEL, 402 Washington, The Dalles, OR, 97058, (541) 296-6105, fax: (541) 296-6213. *Member:* IGTA

IN TOUCH TRAVEL, 121 SW Morrison #270, Portland, OR, 97204, (503) 223-1062, Fax: (503) 224-4920. *Member:* IGTA

J & M TRAVEL, 4370 NE Halsey, Portland, OR, 97213, (503) 249-0305, Fax: (503) 280-1717.

JOAN SHER TRAVEL CONSULTANTS, 3264 SW Fairmount Blvd, Portland, OR, 97201, (503) 248-9870, (800) 548-8144, Fax: (503) 244-3503. Ask for Joan. *Member:* IGTA

KAZ TRAVEL SERVICES, 1975 SW First Ave #K, Portland, OR, 97201, (503) 223-4585, Fax: (503) 223-2361.

MIKUNI TRAVEL SERVICE, 1 SW Columbia St #1010, Portland, OR, 97258-2011, (503) 227-3639, Fax: (503) 227-0602. *Member:* IGTA

MORRIS TRAVEL, 8285 SW Nimbus #140, Beaverton, OR, 97008, (503) 526-6764, (503) 526-6764. *Member:* IGTA

NOVA TRAVEL INC, 27 S State St #230, Lake Oswego, OR, 97034, (503) 697-4460, Fax: (503) 697-4475. *Member:* IGTA

TRAVEL AGENTS INT'L (OR), 917 SW Washington St, Portland, OR, 97205-2818, (503) 223-1100, Fax: (503) 497-1015. Ask for Rip. *Member:* IGTA

TRAVEL NETWORK, 179 High St, Salem, OR, 97301, (503) 399-4799, Fax: (503) 399-4798. *Member:* IGTA

TRAVEL NETWORK, 29756 Town Center Loop W #C, Wilsonville, OR, 97070, (503) 570-0761, fax: (503) 682-9368. *Member:* IGTA

TRAVEL SHOP, THE, PO Box 0987, Beaverton, OR, 97075, (503) 684-8533, Fax: (503) 624-1339. Ask for Mark for men's travel.

TRAVEL SHOP, THE, 10115 SW Nimbus #600, Tigard, OR, 97223, (503) 684-8533, Fax: (503) 624-1339. *Member:* IGTA

ULTIMATE TRAVELS, 621 SW Morrison St #435, Portland, OR, 97205, (503) 220-0351, fax: (503) 220-0744. *Member:* IGTA

UNIGLOBE LANE TRAVEL, 1211 NW 23, Portland, OR, 97210, (503) 223-6055, Fax: (503) 223-8388.

WE'RE EVERYWHERE TRAVEL, 5725 N Burrage, Portland, OR, 97217-4133, (503) 286-2229, (503) 758-0552. *Member:* IGTA

WORLD TRAVEL, 700 NE Multnomah Ste 478, Portland, OR, 97232, (503) 231-1600, Fax: (503) 235-2338. *Member:* IGTA

PENNSYLVANIA

A GREAT WAY TO TRAVEL, 5824 McKay Ave, Bensalem, PA, 19020, (215) 639-6341, fax: (215) 638-3308. *Member:* IGTA

ALICE'S TRAVEL, 10 North 8th St, Stroudsburg, PA, 18360, (717) 421-9999, Fax: (717) 421-3612.

ALTERNATIVE TRAVELS, 201 9th St, Pittsburgh, PA, 15222, (412) 263-2930, Fax; (412) 471-1594. *Member:* IGTA

BERNIE'S WORLD TRAVEL, 144 E Independence St, Shamokin, PA, 17872, (717) 644-0831.

BON AMI TRAVEL SERVICE, 309 First St, Apollo, PA, 15613, (412) 478-2000, (800) 426-6264, Fax: (412) 478-5226. *Member:* IGTA

CABOT TRAVEL, 8530 Wittmer Rd, Pittsburgh, PA, 15237, (412) 366-1278, Fax: (412) 366-1278.

CAMELOT TRAVEL & TOURS, (814) 835-3434.

CARLSON TRAVEL NETWORK/IOBST TRAVEL SVC, 328 Main St, Emmaus, PA, 18049, (610) 965-9025, Fax: (610) 967-4179.

CRUISES & TOURS MCKNIGHT, 7440 McKnight Rd, 202 Ross Park Centre, Pittsburgh, PA, 15237, (412) 366-7630, (800) 992-7968, Fax: (412) 366-7968. *Member:* IGTA

CRUISES & TOURS MCKNIGHT,, 7440 McKnight Rd,, Pittsburgh, PA, 15237, (412) 366-7630. Fax: (412) 366-7068, (800) 992-7678.

DANCA TRAVEL, 531 N York Rd, Warminster, PA, 18974, (215) 443-5030, Fax: (215) 443-5003. *Member:* IGTA

DOWNINGTON TRAVEL, 123 B East Lancaster Ave, Downington, PA, 19335, (610) 269-3973, fax: (610) 269-4134. *Member:* IGTA

ELAN A TRAVEL COMPANY, 3955 Forbes Ave, Pittsburgh, PA, 15213, (412) 621-4854 (tel/fax). *Member:* IGTA

FLIGHT OF FANCY, PO Box 234, 408 York Road, New Hope, PA, 18938, (215) 862-9665, Fax: (215) 862-9764. *Member:* IGTA

FORUM TRAVEL, 4608 Winthrop St, Pittsburgh, PA, 15213, (412) 681-4099, (800) 888-4099, Fax: (412) 687-6766. *Member:* IGTA

GUARDIAN TRAVEL, 115 Technology Dr #100, Pittsburgh, PA, 15275, (412) 787-7576, (800) 424-6220, Fax: (412) 787-7062. Ask for David. *Member:* IGTA

HOLIDAY TRAVEL INTERNATIONAL, 5832 Library Rd, Bethel Park, PA, 97301, (412) 835-8747, Fax: (412) 835-9149.

HORIZON TRAVEL, 4 Market Place, Logan Square, New Hope, PA, 18938, (215) 862-3373.

INTERNATIONAL TOURS, 8 Cavender Lane, Landenberg, PA, 19350, (215) 255-4862, Fax: (215) 677-1960.

JEWEL TRAVEL, 225 S 15 St #829, Philadelphia, PA, 19102, (610) 546-8747, (800) 755-3935, Fax: (610) 546-8812. Ask for Woody.

LAMBDA TRAVEL, 1903 Walnut St Box 435, Philadelphia, PA, 19103, (215) 636-0880, Fax: (215) 636-0548. *Member:* IGTA

LIBERTY TRAVEL (PA), 9376 Fairmont Terrace, Tobyhanna, PA, 18466, (717) 894-9076, Fax: (717) 476-9099.

LYNN TRAVEL ASSOC, PO Box 300, New Hope, PA, 18938, (215) 862-5015, Fax: (215) 862-0303. *Member:* IGTA

MAKEFIELD TRAVEL, 14 Decision Way West, PO Box 828, Washington Crossing, PA, 18977, (215) 493-2998, (800) 435-4268.

MON VALLEY TRAVEL, 100 Smithfield St, Pittsburgh, PA, 15222, (412) 255-8747, (412) 765-2614. *Member:* IGTA

MORGAN DELFOSSE TRAVEL, 360 Pine Hollow Rd, Level Green, PA, 15085, (412) 372-1846.

ODYSSEY TRAVEL, 1501 Wilmington Pike, West Chester, PA, 19382, (215) 358-0411, Fax: (215) 358-3752.

PITTSBURGH TRAVEL SERVICE, Shops at Station Square, Pittsburgh, PA, 15219, (412) 471-7417.

RUSTY'S TRAVEL AGENCY, 1973 71st Ave, Philadelphia, PA, 19138, (215) 424-3977, fax: (215) 424-2181. *Member:* IGTA

WHO TO CALL

SIGMUND TRAVEL BUREAU, 262 S 12th St, Philadelphia, PA, 19107, (610) 735-0090.
STALBAUM TRAVEL, 349 Montgomery Ave, Bala Cynwyd, PA, 19004, (610) 667-4545, fax: (610) 667-5034. *Member:* IGTA
THOMAS TRAVEL SERVICE, 1235 Main St, Doylestown, PA, 18901, (215) 348-1770, Fax: (215) 340-9390. *Member:* IGTA
THOMAS TRAVEL SERVICE, PO Box 507, 202 Marketplace, Montgomeryville, PA, 18936, (215) 362-1711, Fax: (215) 362-2143. *Member:* IGA
TRAVEL LOFT, 5100 State Rd, Drexel Hill, PA, 19026, (610) 626-6331, fax: (610) 626-4467. *Member:* IGTA
TRAVEL NOW, One Franklin Plaza, Philadelphia, PA, 19103, (610) 988-0848, Fax: (610) 988-0355. Ask for Steve.
WILL TRAVEL, 9693 Pine Rd, Philadelphia, PA, 19115, (610) 741-4492, (800) 443-7460, Fax: (610) 741-5156. Ask for Pat. *Member:* IGTA
WORLD WIDE TRAVEL, 221 Rohrerstown Rd, Lancaster, PA, 17603, (717) 394-6997, fax: (717) 394-7682. *Member:* IGTA
ZELLER TRAVEL/BROWNSTOWN, 4213 Oregon Pike, Ephrata, PA, 17522, (717) 859-4710, (800) 331-4359, Fax: (717) 859-3638. *Member:* IGTA

RHODE ISLAND

AIR-SEA TRAVEL, 135 Sandy Bottom Rd, Coventry, RI, 02816, (401) 826-2040.
ALA-MONTE TRAVEL, 1800 Mineral Spring Ave, North Providence, RI, 02904, (401) 354-6119, Fax: (401) 354-6053.
CONTINENTAL TRAVEL AGENCY, 20 Cedar Swamp Rd, Smithfield, RI, 02917, (401) 232-0980, (800) 234-5209, Fax: (401) 232-0470. Ask for Jeanne.
CWT CONTINENTAL TRAVEL, 20 Cedar Swamp Rd, Smithfield, RI, 02917, (401) 232-0980, fax: (401) 232-0470. *Member:* IGTA
GLOBAL EXCELLENCE, 155 Jefferson Blvd, Warwick, RI, 02888, (401) 732-8080, Fax: (401) 737-7455.
M&L TRAVEL, 691 Atwood Ave, Cranston, RI, 02886, (401) 944-8072. Ask for Lisa.
SOUTH COUNTY TRAVEL, 600 Kingstown Rd, Wakefield, RI, 02879, (401) 789-9731, Fax: (401) 792-3647. Ask for Helen.
TRAVEL CONCEPTS, 84 Lorimer Ave, Providence, RI, 02906, (401) 453-6000, (800) 983-6900, Fax: (401) 453-0222. *Member:* IGTA

SOUTH CAROLINA

ALL AROUND TRAVEL, Rt 1 Box 502, Eutawville, SC, 29408, (803) 854-2475, Fax: (803) 854-2734.
ALL AROUND TRAVEL, 1568 Village Square Blvd, Santee, SC, 29142, (803) 854-2475, Fax: (803) 854-2734. *Member:* IGTA
B & A TRAVEL SERVICE, 2728 Devine St, Columbia, SC, 29205, (803) 256-0547, Fax: (803) 779-4871.
OUT-N-OUT ADVENTURES, 1861 Robin Rd, N. Augusta, SC, 29841, (803) 278-6931, Fax: (803) 278-6931.
RUSSELL TRAVEL SERVICE, 136 S Railroad Ave, Moncks Corner, SC, 29461, (803) 761-6888, Fax: (803) 899-7909. *Member:* IGTA
TRAVEL MASTERS OF COLUMBIA, PO Box 5916, Columbia, SC, 29250, (803) 254-4777.
TRAVEL PROFESSIONALS INTERNATIONAL, 1931 Bull St Ste B, Columbia, SC, 29201, (803) 765-1212, Fax: (803) 931-8040.
TRAVEL UNLIMITED, 612 St Andrews Rd #8, Columbia, SC, 29210, (803) 798-8122, Fax: (803) 798-9339. *Member:* IGTA

TENNESSEE

AMERICAN EXPRESS, 4400 Harding Rd #101, Nashville, TN, 37205, (615) 385-3550, Fax: (615) 269-7403.
BROADHEAD TRAVEL, 2517 Lebanon Rd, Nashville, TN, 37214, (615) 889-5834, Fax: (615) 889-6616.
BRYAN TRAVEL, 5614 Kingston Pike, Knoxville, TN, 37919, (615) 588-8166, (800) 234-8166, Fax: (615) 558-8011. Ask for Mike. *Member:* IGTA
INTERNATIONAL TRAVEL INC, 4004 Hillsboro Rd Ste 214-B, Nashville, TN, 37215, (615) 385-1222, Fax: (615) 385-5704. *Member:* IGTA
PRIDE TRAVEL, 1123 Murfreesboro Rd, Nashville, TN, 37217, (615) 360-8445, (800) 583-3998, Fax: (615) 367-1131. *Member:* IGTA
TRAVELPLEX HILLSBORO, 1602 21st Ave S, Nashville, TN, 37212, (615) 321-3321, Fax: (615) 329-8145.
UNIGLOBE TOTAL TRAVEL, 2601 Elm Hill Pike Ste D, Nashville, TN, 37214, (615) 883-4300, Fax: (615) 883-0025.
VOLUNTEER TRAVEL, 102 S Main St, Erwin, TN, 37650, (423) 743-8863, (423) 743-0711. *Member:* IGTA

TEXAS

ACCENT ON TRAVEL, 10006 Hickory Crossing, Dallas, TX, 75243-4616, (214) 783-9296, (800) 446-5064, Fax: (214) 783-9296. *Member:* IGTA
ACCENT TRAVEL, 15701 Henderson Pass, San Antonio, TX, 78232, (210) 494-3553, fax: (210) 494-0079. *Member:* IGTA
ADVANCE TRAVEL, 10700 NW Freeway #160, Houston, TX, 77092, (713) 682-2002, Fax: (713) 680-3200.
ADVANTAGE PLUS TRAVEL, 800 NW Loop 410 #306-S, San Antonio, TX, 78216, (210) 366-1955, (210) 366-9581. *Member:* IGTA
AFTER FIVE TRAVEL & CRUISES, 2602 Killdeer Ln, Humble, TX, 77396-1826, (713) 441-1369, (800) 335-1369, Fax: (713) 441-1275. *Member:* IGTA
ALEXIS TRAVEL, Cornerstone G&L Center, 1117 Red River, Austin, TX, 78701, (512) 457-1001, (800) 459-9814, fax: (512) 457-1051, e-mail: alexisinc@aol.com. Dedicated to the gay & lesbian traveler.
ALEXIS TRAVEL USA, 1117 Red River, Austin, TX, 78701, (512) 457-1001, fax: (512) 457-1051. *Member:* IGTA
ALTERNATIVE INTERNATIONAL TRAVEL, 7616 LBJ Freeway #524, Dallas, TX, 75251, (214) 980-4540, Fax: (214) 934-9634. *Member:* IGTA
AVANTI TRAVEL, 6449 Blanco Rd, San Antonio, TX, 78216, (210) 344-3364, Fax: (210) 344-4611.
B&B TRAVEL CONNECTIONS, 6303 Silver Fox, San Antonio, TX, 78247, (210) 979-7811 Fax: (210) 366-9581.

BEDFORD WORLD TRAVEL, PO Box 161021, Ft.Worth, TX, 76161-1021, (817) 246-3384, (800) 468-7090, Fax: (817) 246-3384. *Member:* IGTA
BROWN-WILKINS & ASSOC TRAVEL, 3311 Richmond #230, Houston, TX, 77098, (713) 942-0664, Fax: (713) 942-0665.
CAROL'S TRAVEL, 2036 E TC Jester Ste C, Houston, TX, 77008, (713) 862-9888, Fax: (713) 862-3555.
CELEBRATION TRAVEL, 12701 Fuqua #111, Houston, TX, 77034, (713) 941-7686, fax: (713) 922-9328. *Member:* IGTA
CREATIVE TRAVEL CENTER, 8650 Spicewood Springs Rd #210, Austin, TX, 78759, (512) 331-9560, Fax: (512) 331-6230. *Member:* IGTA
CRUISE & EXPEDITION PLANNERS, 8323 Southwest Fwy #800, Houston, TX, 77074, (713) 771-1371, Fax: (713) 771-9761.
D&J TOURS TO GO, 2000 Hwy 157N #112, Mansfield, TX, 76063, (817) 473-4471, (800) 460-9271, Fax: (817) 473-1377.
DAVID PEARSON TRAVEL, 2737 Exposition Blvd, Austin, TX, 78703-1206, (512) 482-8197.
DOUBLE-O-SEVEN TRAVEL, 1120 Nottingham, Cedar Hill, TX, 75104, (214) 291-0133.
EAGLE TRAVEL CONNECTION, 4122 Sarong Dr, Houston, TX, 77025, (713) 666-8256, Fax: (713) 660-0005. *Member:* IGTA
FANTASTIC VOYAGES, 9001 Willoughby Ct, Ft. Worth, TX, 76134-5504, (817) 568-8611, Fax: (817) 568-8617.
FIRST CLASS TRAVEL, 2313 NW Military #101, San Antonio, TX, 78231, (210) 341-6363, Fax: (210) 341-6392. *Member:* IGTA
FUTURE TRAVEL, INC, 16850 Diana Ln, Houston, TX, 77058, (281) 480-1988, Fax: (281) 480-2587. *Member:* IGTA
GATEWAY TRAVEL & TOURS, 1902 W Pioneer Pkwy #100, Arlington, TX, 76013-6107, (817) 548-7222, (800) 466-2742, Fax: (817) 275-6649. *Member:* IGTA
GOLDEN GLOBETROTTERS, 12600 Bissonnet #A4-518, Houston, TX, 77099, (713) 495-2822. *Member:* IGTA
GOOD LIFE ADVENTURES & TRAVEL, PO 19468, Austin, TX, 78760, (512) 276-7870, (512) 276-7349. *Member:* IGTA
GOOD TIMES TRAVEL, PO Box 821352, Ft. Worth, TX, 76182, (817) 577-0041, (800) 484-9020 ext. 0041, Fax: (817) 577-2945. *Member:* IGTA
LONGHORN TRAVEL INTERNATIONAL, 605 W 28th, Austin, TX, 78705-3707, (512) 479-9888, (512) 708-1140. *Member:* IGTA
OCS TICKET TO RIDE, 251 W Renner Pkwy #170, Richardson, TX, 75080, (214) 680-0997, Fax: (214) 680-0815.
ODYSSEY TRAVEL, 11829 Perrin Beitel Rd, San Antonio, TX, 78217-2107, (210) 656-0083, (800) 999-4905, Fax: (210) 656-3980.
ODYSSEY TRAVEL, PO Box 39776, San Antonio, TX, 78219-6776, (210) 655-8722.
OUR TRAVEL, 15600 San Pedro Ave #305, San Antonio, TX, 78232, (210) 496-1776, (210) 496-7644. *Member:* IGTA
P.S. TRAVEL, 3131 Turtle Creek Blvd #620, Dallas, TX, 75219, (214) 526-8866, (800) 448-9029, Fax: (214) 526-0044. *Member:* IGTA

WHO TO CALL

P.S. TRAVEL, 8838 C Viscount Blvd, El Paso, TX, 79925, (915) 598-6188, (800) 432-5152, Fax: (915) 595-5944.

PLANET TRAVEL, 3102 Maple Ave #450, Dallas, TX, 75201, (214) 965-0800, Fax: (214) 965-0805. Member: IGTA

PLAZA TRAVEL INC, 15851 Dallas Pkwy #190, Dallas, TX, 75248, (972) 980-1191, Fax: (972) 980-2877. Member: IGTA

PLEASURE TRAVEL-CRUISE AGAIN TOO, 1373 W Campbell Rd, Richardson, TX, 75080, (214) 644-6242, Fax: (214) 644-5168.

SOJOURNS, 3400 Montrose Blvd #909, Houston, TX, 77006, (713) 528-2299, Fax: (713) 528-6767. Member: IGTA

STRONG TRAVEL SERVICES, 8201 Preston Rd #160, Dallas, TX, 75225, (214) 361-0027, Fax: (214) 361-0139.

SUN TRAVEL, 3100 N Mesa, Ste B, El Paso, TX, 79902, (915) 532-8900, Fax: (915) 533-6887.

SUNSET WORLD TRAVEL INC, 5050 Quorum Dr Ste 743, Dallas, TX, 75240, (214) 386-9835, Fax: (214) 386-9807.

SUPER TRAVEL, 5800 N Mopac Ste 102, Austin, TX, 78731, (512) 302-5800.

TRAVEL DREAMS, PO Box 3571, Austin, TX, 78764-3571, (512) 443-5116, fax: (512) 443-0653. Member: IGTA

TRAVEL EMPORIUM, 3408 Oak Lawn Ave, Dallas, TX, 75219, (214) 520-7678, Fax: (214) 520-1723. Member: IGTA

TRAVEL FRIENDS, 8080 N Central #320, Dallas, TX, 75206, (214) 891-8833, (800) 862-8833, Fax: (214) 891-8873. Member: IGTA

TRAVEL INNOVATIONS, 2711 Market Garden, Austin, TX, 78745, (512) 443-5393, Fax: (512) 442-8515. E-mail: jmc12@io.com.

TRAVEL PARTNERSHIP, THE, 1411-A Bonnie Brae, Houston, TX, 77006-5214, (713) 526-4471, Fax: (713) 524-4733. Member: IGTA

TRAVEL PROFESSIONALS INTERNATIONAL, 700 E Park Blvd #102, Plano, TX, 75074, (214) 881-5517, Fax: (214) 422-7298. Member: IGTA

UNIGLOBE CREATIVE TRAVEL, 13984 Westheimer, Houston, TX, 77077, (713) 496-9600, Fax: (713) 496-9459.

UNIGLOBE DESTINATIONS IN TRAVEL, 2727 Allen Pkwy #PL-02, Houston, TX, 77019, (713) 520-7526, Fax: (713) 520-5346. Member: IGTA

UNIGLOBE FIRST CHOICE TRAVEL, 2236 W Holcombe Blvd, Houston, TX, 77030, (713) 667-0580, Fax: (713) 667-0180. Member: IGTA

UNIGLOBE FOX TRAVEL, 25701 I-45 North #3A, Spring, TX, 77380, (713) 363-0808, Fax: (713) 363-0916.

UNIGLOBE PREMIER TRAVEL, 210 N 10th, McAllen, TX, 78501, (210) 682-3072, Fax: (210) 682-3198.

UNIGLOBE ULTIMATE TRAVEL, 4934 Beechnut St, Houston, TX, 77096, (713) 669-1171, fax: (713) 669-0307. Member: IGTA

UNIGLOBE UNIVERSAL, 14455 Memorial Dr, Houston, TX, 77079, (713) 497-1668, Fax: (713) 497-5844.

WCN-WCT/GM TRAVEL & TOURS, 6618 Billikin Dr, Houston, TX, 77086, (713) 999-7962, Fax: (713) 931-5563. Member: IGTA

WEST AUSTIN TRAVEL, 2737 Exposition Blvd, Austin, TX, 78703-1206, (512) 482-8197, (512) 482-8264. Member: IGTA

WHITE HERON TRAVEL SERVICE, 4849 Greenville Ave #173, Dallas, TX, 75206, (214) 692-0446, (214) 696-6418. Member: IGTA

WINDSOR TRAVEL, 600 Travis #2075, Houston, TX, 77002, (713) 228-1111. Specializing in gay travel.

WOODLAKE TRAVEL, 2513 S Gessner, Houston, TX, 77063, (713) 789-7500, Fax: (713) 789-2951. Member: IGTA

WORLD TRAVEL—THE CRUISE SHOP, 2323 S Shepherd, Houston, TX, 77019, (713) 942-7447, (800) 747-5174, Fax: (713) 523-4297.

UTAH

BEEHIVE TRAVEL, 419 Wakara Way #105, Salt Lake City, UT, 84108, (801) 583-0273, Fax: (801) 583-4103. Ask for Kirk or Mark.

CRUISE & TRAVEL MASTERS, 4905 S 900 E #630, Salt Lake City, UT, 84117-5703, (801) 268-4470, Fax: (801) 268-5703.

JETSTAR TRAVEL, 1740 Meadowmoor Rd, Salt Lake City, UT, 84117, (801) 278-1060.

MORRIS TRAVEL., 240 E Morris Ave, Salt Lake City, UT, 84115-3200, (801) 483-6146, (800) 333-3611, Fax: (801) 483-6198.

SPORTOURS TRAVEL, PO Box 680846, Park City, UT, 84068, (801) 655-0500, (800) 359-9925, Fax: (801) 645-7260. Member: IGTA

TRAVEL ZONE/CRUISE ZONE, 757 E South Temple, Salt Lake City, UT, 84102, (801) 531-1606, Fax: (801) 531-1633. Member: IGTA

VERMONT

AMERICAN-INTERNATIONAL TRAVEL SERVICE, 114 Church St, PO Box 852, Burlington, VT, 05402, (802) 864-9827, Fax: (802) 864-0612. Member: IGTA

CARMEN'S HORIZONS TRAVEL, Broad St, RFD 1, Lyndonville, VT, 05851, (802) 626-8176, Fax: (802) 626-8178.

COTTAGE WORKS, PO Box 907, Chester, VT, 05143, (802) 875-4651, Fax: (802) 875-4672. Member: IGTA

CUSTOM TRAVEL, 431 Pine St, Burlington, VT, 05401, (802) 658-9123, Fax: (802) 658-3100.

TRAVEL NETWORK, 1860 Williston Rd, S Burlington, VT, 05403-6027, (802) 863-4300, Fax: (802) 863-0292. Member: IGTA

VIRGINIA

ADVANCE TRAVEL, 10560 Main St #113, Fairfax, VA, 22030, (703) 352-2440, (703) 352-2107. Member: IGTA

ALEXIS TRAVEL, 1037 Sterling Rd #201, Herndon, VA, 22070, (703) 318-8998, (800) 200-8997, Fax (703) 318-7864, E-mail alexisinc@aol.com.

AMERICAN DREAM CRUISES, 800 Penniman Rd, Williamsburg, VA, 23185-5413, (804) 220-4727, (804) 220-9427. Member: IGTA

CAREFREE CRUISES, Rte 1, Box 24, Midland, VA, 22728-9704, (703) 439-2403, Fax: (703) 439-1610.

CARLSON WAGONLIT TRAVEL, 635 Slaters Ln, Ste 370, Alexandria, VA, 22314, (703) 838-0133, Fax: (703) 683-8642.

COVINGTON INT'L TRAVEL, 4401 Dominion Blvd, Glen Allen, VA, 23060, (804) 747-7077, Fax: (804) 273-0009. Ask for Roy. Member: IGTA

CULPEPER TRAVEL, 763 Madison Rd #208-B, Culpeper, VA, 22701, (703) 825-1258, Fax: (703) 825-1276.

DANSK TRAVEL, 5881 Leesburg Pike #100, Falls Church, VA, 22041, (703) 931-6074, fax: (703) 820-6118. Member: IGTA

DESIGNS TRAVEL, INC, 7632 Michelle Ct, Manassas, VA, 22110-2959, (703) 330-0951, (800) 830-5685, Fax: (703) 257-7104.

DESTINATIONS, 1800 Diagonal Rd Plaza D, Alexandria, VA, 22314, (703) 684-8824, fax: (703) 836-4174. Member: IGTA

EMPRESS TRAVEL, 4533 Duke St, Alex, VA, 22304, (703) 823-0060, Fax: (703) 823-0063.

GAY-LE TRAVEL, 5203 S Laburnum Ave, Richmond, VA, 23231, Member: IGTA

LATITUDES INC, 3 North 19th St, Richmond, VA, 23223, (804) 644-7047, Fax: (804) 644-7050. Member: IGTA

MOORE TRAVEL, 7516 Granby St, Norfolk, VA, 23505, (804) 583-2362, Fax: (804) 583-6384. Member: IGTA

RITA LEWIS TRAVEL SERVICE, 1343 Armory Dr, Franklin, VA, 23851, (757) 562-7000, fax: (757) 562-5986. Member: IGTA

TRAVEL MARKETING SERVICES, 3133 Guysborough Dr, Fairfax, VA, 22031-2615, (703) 280-2527, fax: (703) 280-0327. Member: IGTA

TRAVEL MERCHANTS, 332 N Great Neck Rd #104, Virginia Beach, VA 23454, (804) 463-0014, Fax: (804) 463-3239. Ask for John.

TRAVEL NETWORK, 7632 Michelle Rd, Manassas, VA, 20109, (703) 330-0951, Fax: (703) 257-7104. Member: IGTA

TRAVEL STORE, THE, 5203 S Laburnum Ave, Richmond, VA, 23231, (804) 222-2100, (800) 235-0356, Fax: (804) 226-4759.

TRAVELINK, 1700-H George Washington Hwy, Yorktown, VA, 23693, (804) 599-3000, Fax: (804) 599-6042.

UNIGLOBE DIRECT TRAVEL, 1800 Diagonal Rd Plaza D, Alexandria, VA, 22314, (703) 684-8824, Fax: (703) 836-4174.

VACATIONS VACATIONS, 4605 Pembroke Lake Circle #202, Virginia Beach, VA, 23455, (804) 499-0619, Fax: (804) 499-1267.

VENTURE WORLD CRUISING SOCIETY, 84 Cambridge St, Fredericksburg, VA, 22405, (540) 373-5202, (540) 373-4772. Member: IGTA

WASHINGTON

A BETTER WAY TO TRAVEL, 10006 NW 4th Ave, Vancouver, WA, 98685, (206) 573-4750, Fax: (206) 573-8780.

ALL-AROUND TRAVEL, 4701 42 Ave SW, Seattle, WA, 98116, (206) 938-3030, Fax: (206) 938-8462. Ask for Davyn.

WHO TO CALL

BLACK TIE TRAVEL, 1411 Fourth Ave #920, Seattle, WA, 98101, (206) 622-4409, (800) 776-2930.

BUSINESS TRAVEL NW, 2003 Western Ave #445, Seattle, WA, 98121-2182, (206) 674-4400, (206) 674-4444. *Member:* IGTA

CAPITOL HILL TRAVEL, 401 Broadway E #204, Seattle, WA, 98102, (206) 726-8996, (800) 726-8996, Fax: (206) 726-1004. *Member:* IGTA

COUNCIL TRAVEL, 219 Broadway Ave E, #17, Seattle, WA, 98102, (206) 329-4567, Fax: (206) 329-1982.

CRUISE CENTER, 1703 S 324th St, Federal, WA, 98003, (206) 927-7447, (800) 677-7447, Fax: (206) 927-3528.

CRUISE HOLIDAYS OF SEATTLE CENTRE, 2001 Sixth Ave, Ste 345, Seattle, WA, 98121, (206) 441-7447, (800) 340-7447, Fax: (206) 441-1321. Internet: azrkruzhol@aol.com.

DONNA'S TRAVEL & CRUISE, PO Box 1529, Stanwood, WA, 98292, (206) 629-9751, Fax: (206) 629-9754.

DOUG FOX TRAVEL, 601 Union St #222A, Seattle, WA, 98101, (206) 296-3030, Fax: (206) 296-3077. Ask for Darrell.

DOUG FOX TRAVEL, 701 5th Ave Ste 314, Seattle, WA, 98104, (206) 621-8900, Fax: (206) 621-8291.

EDWARDS LALONE TRAVEL, S 5 Washington, Spokane, WA, 99204, (509) 747-3000, Fax: (509) 747-4733. *Member:* IGTA

ELLENSBURG TRAVEL, 306 N Pine, Ellensburg, WA, 98926, (509) 925-6933.

EUROPE EXPRESS, 4040 Lake Washington Blvd #101, Kirkland, WA, 98033, (800) 927-3876, Fax: (800) 370-0509.

FIRST DISCOUNT TRAVEL, 11700 NE 95th St #110, Vancouver, WA, 98682, (360) 896-6200, Fax: (360) 896-1990. *Member:* IGTA

INTERNATIONAL SENDERS TRAVEL, INC, 9061 NE 34th St, Bellevue, WA, 98004, (206) 453-9889, (800) 278-6017, Fax: (206) 688-0378.

IT'S YOUR WORLD TRAVEL, 1411 E Olive Way, Seattle, WA, 98102, (206) 328-0616, Fax: (206) 324-2512. *Member:* IGTA

JACK ROBERTS COMPANY, PO Box 399, Bothell, WA, 98041, (206) 485-6511, Fax: (206) 486-0692.

LAKE CITY TRAVEL & CRUISES, 12316 Lake City Way NE, Seattle, WA, 98125, (206) 364-0100, Fax: (206) 368-2311. Ask for David.

LAKE UNION TRAVEL/CRUISEWORLD, 901 Fairview Ave N #A150, Seattle, WA, 98109, (206) 343-0221, (800) 340-0221, Fax: (206) 343-0771.

MARY NORTH TRAVEL SERVICE, 3701 SW Alaska St, Seattle, WA, 98126, (206) 935-3404, Fax: (206) 938-2107.

MUTUAL TRAVEL, 600 108th Ave NE #104, Bellevue, WA, 98004, (206) 637-6913, (800) 443-4431, Fax: (206) 637-6999. Ask for Janet.

MUTUAL TRAVEL, 1201 3rd Ave, Seattle, WA, 98101, (206) 205-4991, (800) 348-8800, Fax: (206) 205-4790.

PASSPORT TRAVEL & TOURS, 6270 NE Bothell Way, Seattle, WA, 98155, (206) 483-8687, fax: (206) 485-9568. *Member:* IGTA

ROYALTY TRAVEL, 1200 5th Ave, IBM Plaza Level West, Seattle, WA, 98101, (206) 623-7474, Fax: (206) 623-8283. Ask for Greg or Dwayne. *Member:* IGTA

SCAN EAST WEST TRAVEL, 500 Union #420, Seattle, WA, 98101, (206) 623-2157, Fax: (206) 623-2970.

SECURITY PACK TRAVEL, 1101 Boylston Ave, Seattle, WA, 98101-2818, (206) 322-8305, Fax: (206) 323-5785.

SUNSHINE TRAVEL, 519 N 85th St, Seattle, WA, 98103, (206) 784-8141, Fax: (206) 784-8143. *Member:* IGTA

TRAVEL AGENTS INTERNATIONAL, 412 E Fairhaven Ave, Burlington, WA, 98233, (360) 755-9595, fax: (360) 755-0842. *Member:* IGTA

TRAVEL EXPRESS, 4022 Stoneway North, Seattle, WA, 98103, (206) 545-7300, (800) 451-8097, Fax: (206) 547-8607.

TRAVEL NETWORK KENT, 25619 104th Ave SE, Kent, WA, 98031, (206) 859-2040, Fax: (206) 854-7577. Ask for Bobbi or Alice.

TRAVEL PLACE, THE (WA), 401 E Magesium #117, Spokane, WA, 99208, (509) 624-7434. Ask for Myke.

TRAVEL SOLUTIONS, 4009 Gilman Ave W, Seattle, WA, 98199, (206) 281-7202, (800) 727-1616, Fax: (206) 281-7139. *Member:* IGTA

TRAVEL SOURCE/AMERICAN EXPRESS, 1882-136th Place NE #105, Bellevue, WA, 98005, (206) 747-1900, (206) 641-6911. *Member:* IGTA

TWO MOUNTAINS INC, 1202 E Pike St #1176, Seattle, WA, 98122, (206) 325-3075, Fax: (206) 325-1422. *Member:* IGTA

UNIGLOBE ADVANTAGE TRAVEL, 505 Cedar Ave #C1, Marysville, WA, 98270, (206) 659-8054 ext 6969, (800) 788-3523. Ask for Jared.

VACATION PLACES, PO Box 20457, Seattle, WA, 98102, (206) 324-6996.

VANCOUVER TRAVEL, 516 SE Chkalov Dr #15, Vancouver, WA, 98684-5274, (360) 892-5555, Fax: (360) 896-0145. *Member:* IGTA

VOYAGER TRAVEL COMPANY, 5009 Richey Rd, Yakima, WA, 98908, (509) 575-0805.

VROOMAN TRAVEL MANAGEMENT, 17524 Bothell Way, Bothell, WA, 98011, (206) 485-6511, (206) 486-0692. *Member:* IGTA

WOODSIDE TRAVEL, 3130 E Madison St, Seattle, WA, 98112, (206) 325-1266, Fax: (206) 322-2980. *Member:* IGTA

WEST VIRGINIA

SUNCREST TRAVEL, PO Box 723, Morgantown, WV, 26507-0723, (304) 599-2056, (800) 627-8669, Fax: (304) 599-1500. *Member:* IGTA

WILD WONDERFUL TRAVEL, 1517 Jackson St, Charleston, WV, 25311, (304) 345-0491 (tel/fax). *Member:* IGTA

WISCONSIN

AMERICAN EXPRESS TRAVEL SERVICE, 16620 W Bluemound Rd, Brookfield, WI, 53005, (414) 797-4280, (800) 367-0093, Fax: (414) 797-0705. *Member:* IGTA

AMERICAN EXPRESS TRAVEL SERVICE, 330 E Silver Spring Dr, Milwaukee, WI, 53217, (414) 332-3157, (800) 325-6157, Fax: (414) 332-9946. *Member:* IGTA

AROUND THE GLOBE TRAVEL, 7416 W State St, Wauwatosa, WI, 53213, (414) 257-0199, Fax: (414) 257-0283.

DAN'S TRAVEL, 600 Williamson #C, Madison, WI, 53703, (608) 251-1110, fax: (608) 251-1101. *Member:* IGTA

FAR HORIZONS TRAVEL, 5902 Hwy 51, McFarland, WI, 53558, (608) 258-1600.

HORIZON TRAVEL, N 81 W 15028 Appleton Ave, Menomonee Falls, WI, 53051, (414) 255-0704.

LANDMARK ENTERPRISES, 735 N Water St, Milwaukee, WI, 53211, (414) 276-6355, Fax: (414) 276-9858.

MILWAUKEE TRAVEL, 7665 N Port Washington Rd, Milwaukee, WI, 53217, (414) 351-3010, (414) 351-7059. *Member:* IGTA

TRAVEL CONSULTANTS INC, 2222 N Mayfair, Wauwatosa, WI, 53226, (414) 453-8300, Fax: (414) 453-8305. *Member:* IGTA

TRAVEL EXPERIENCE, 501 E Otjen, Milwaukee, WI, 53207, (414) 744-6020, fax: (414) 744-9221. *Member:* IGTA

TRAVEL PERKS, 501 E Otjen, Milwaukee, WI, 53207, (414) 744-6020, (800) 707-3767, Fax: (414) 744-9221.

TRIO TRAVEL & IMPORTS LTD, 2812 W Forest Home Ave, Milwaukee, WI, 53215, (414) 384-8746.

FERRARI GUIDES' GAY TRAVEL A to Z - 18th EDITION

WHEN TO GO

INDEX TO EVENTS

The following index to events is divided by category. Find the category, then find the event. Following the name is the date of the event. Now, look up this date and name in the calendar, on page 136, for more details about the event.

LEATHER

American Brotherhood Weekend	Apr 25 - 27
Folsom Street Fair	Sep 28
Hamburger Hexenkessel '97	May 07 - 11
Int'l Bear Rendezvous	Feb '98 TBA
Int'l Mr. Leather Contest 1997 (IML)	May 22 - 26
Int'l Ms. Leather Contest	Jul 17 - 19
Int'l Ms. Leather Contest	Jul 17 - 19
Leatherfest IX	Apr 18 - 20
Living in Leather XII, Nat'l Conference	Oct 09 - 12
Mr. Dixie Bell Leather Contest	Mar '98 TBA
Mr. Drummer Contest	Sep 27 - 28
Mr. Kentucky Leather 98	Apr '98 TBA
Mr. Leather Europe & 24th ECMC Conference	Aug 22 - 25
Mr. & Ms New Mexico Leather	Mar '98 TBA
Out of Hibernation '97	Apr 25 - 27
Pantheon of Leather VIII	Feb 12 - 15
Seattle Mr. Leather Contest	Feb '98 TBA
Shipwreck IV	May 02 - 04
Southeast Leatherfest '97	Jun 13 - 15
Up-Your-Alley Fair (Dore Alley Fair)	Jul 27
Washington State Mr. Leather '98	May '98 TBA

OTHER EVENTS

Adventure Camp	Oct 26 - Nov 02
Adventure Camp	Feb 13 - 16
Adventure Camp	Oct 25 - Nov 01
Altitude 98 - Whistler Gay Ski Week	Feb '98 TBA
Aspen Gay Ski Week	Jan 24 - 31
Big Bear Spring Ski & Snowboard Daze 3	Feb '98 TBA
Big Men's Convergence '97	Sep '97 TBA
Black Gay & Lesbian Conference (11th annual)	Feb '98 TBA
Black & White Men Together 17th Convention	Jul 07 - 12
Body Electric	Oct 24 - 26
Body Electric	Feb 06 - 13
Body Electric	Oct 23 - 25
Camp Lesbigay	May 23 - 26
Camp Lesbigay	May 22 - 25
Camp SCWU	Jun '98 TBA
Canadian GALA Choruses: Festival '98	May 15 - 18
Crape Myrtle Festival XVII	Jul 26
Dinah Shore Tournament Week Womens' Events	Mar '98 TBA
Drumfest	May 09 - 11
EPOA - Conference 1997	Oct 31 - Nov 02
Euro Fun Cup '97	Jun '97 TBA
EuroGames V	Jun 19 - 23
EuroPride '97	Jun 19 - 29
EuroPride '98	Jul 18 - 26
EuroSalon Gay Life Fair	Jun 25 - 29
Fantasia Fair (23rd annual)	Oct 19 - 26
Fantasy Fest in Key West	Oct 17 - 26
Fat Women's Gatherings	Jul '97 TBA
Gay Games V	Aug 01 - 08
Gay Marathon of Rome	Apr '98 TBA
Gay Night at Disneyland	Oct '97 TBA
Gay Spirit	Dec 20 - 26
Gay Spirit	Dec 20 - 26
Gay & Lesbian Run in Berlin (8th annual)	May '98 TBA
Gay & Lesbian Soccer World Cup	Sep 23 - 27
Gay & Lesbian Softball World Series '97	Aug '97 TBA
Gays For Patsy Firecracker Hoedown	Jul 03 - 06
Gay/Lesbian Day at Walt Disney World (7th annual)	Jun 05 - 08
Girls in the Snow	Feb 06 - 08
Healing Arts Retreat	May 18 - 24
Healing Arts Retreat	May 17 - 23
Hotlanta River Expo (19th annual)	Aug 07 - 10
Hula Heritage Festival, Hawaii	Apr 13 - 19
Igloo Weekend in Stowe, Vermont	Feb '98 TBA
ILGA World Conference	Jul 04 - 06
Intrepid IV	Jun 28
Int'l Conference of Gay & Lesbian Jews	Jul 04 - 06
Int'l Conference on AIDS (12th annual)	Jun 28 - Jul 03
Int'l Gay Ski Week (SWING) 1998	Mar '98 TBA
Int'l Gay & Lesbian Aquatics Competition	Oct '97 TBA
Int'l Gay & Lesbian Badminton Tournament,	May 08 - 11
Int'l Pride Conference (IAL/GPC)	Sep 11 - 14
Int'l Rainbow Golf Classic	Oct 31 - Nov 02
I-Men	Mar 23 - 29
Jackson Hole 1998 Women's Ski Camp	Jan '98 TBA
K.W.W.F.F.L. Flag-A-Tag National Kickoff	Feb 01
Lambda Literary Awards (9th annual)	May 30
Lesbenwoche (Lesbian Week in Berlin, Germany)	Oct '97 TBA
Lesbian Pride in Paris	Jun 19 - 29
Lesbies Doe-Front Lesbian Day	May '97 TBA
Lesbies Doe-Front Lesbian Day	May '98 TBA
Midsumma 1998	Jan '98 TBA
NAGVA Championships	May 23 - 25
Nat'l Conference of Gay & Lesbian Catholics	Sep 04 - 07
Nat'l Lesbian & Gay Health Conference & HIV Forum	Jul 26 - 30
Nat'l Women and Motorcycling Foundation Conference	Jul 13 - 16
Northalsted Market Days	Aug '97 TBA
NW Gay & Lesbian Summer Sports Festival	Jul 03 - 06
N.W.F.F.A. San Francisco Nat'l Kickoff	Oct 10 - 13
Outwrite '98	Feb 21 - 23
Pacific Men's Gathering	Jul 27 - Aug 02
Pacific Men's Gathering	Jul 26 - Aug 01
Park City Gay Ski Week (3rd annual)	Feb '97 TBA
Pink Monday at the Tilburg Fair	Jul '97 TBA
Pony Express Tour 1998	Jun 29 - Aug 18
Pride (Amsterdam)	Aug 01 - 10
Pride (Atlanta)	Jun 27 - 29
Pride (Berlin)	Jun 20 - 29
Pride (Boston)	Jun 01 - 08
Pride (Brussels)	May 03
Pride (Chicago)	Jun 29
Pride (Denver)	Jun 29
Pride (Fort Lauderdale)	Jun 15
Pride (Hartford)	Jun 21
Pride (Houston)	Jun 19 - 29
Pride (Kansas City)	Jun 07 - 08
Pride (Key West)	Jun 26 - 30
Pride (London)	Jul 05
Pride (Los Angeles)	Jun 21 - 22
Pride (Minneapolis)	Jun 28 - 29
Pride (Oslo)	Jun 15 - 22
Pride (Phoenix)	May 30 - Jun 01
Pride (San Diego)	Jul 25 - 27
Pride (San Francisco)	Jun 28 - 29
Pride (Seattle)	Jun 29
Pride (Washington DC)	Jun 08
Queen's Birthday Weekend in Sydney	Jun '98 TBA
Queen's Day in Amsterdam	Apr 30
San Francisco Int'l. Lesbian & Gay Film Festival	Jun 20 - 29
Sisterfest	Oct 03 - 05
Slide for Pride	Apr '98 TBA
Southern Decadence (25th Anniversary)	Aug 29 - 31
Swim for Life in Provincetown	Sep 06
Sydney Gay & Lesbian Mardi Gras	Feb '98 TBA
Taos Conference on Feminine Spirituality	Aug '97 TBA
The Club Skirts Monterey Bay Women's Weekend	Aug 28 - 31
Tokyo Int'l Lesbian & Gay Film & Video Festival	May 07 - 11
Tokyo Int'l Lesbian & Gay Film & Video Festival	May '98 TBA
We're Funny That Way	Apr 23 - 26
We're Funny That Way	Apr '98 TBA
Winter Gayla '98	Apr '98 TBA
Winterfest Lake Tahoe	Mar '98 TBA
Women's Weekend	May '97 TBA
Women's Weekend II	Sep '97 TBA

WHEN TO GO

PARTY CIRCUIT

Bal des Boys IV	Dec 31
Black Party (New York)	Mar '98 TBA
Black & Blue Party/Festival	Oct 08 - 14
Blue Ball '98	Jan '98 TBA
Cherry Jubilee	Apr 25 - 27
Cherry Jubilee	Apr '98 TBA
Club Skirts/Girl Bar/ Dinah Shore Weekend	Mar '98 TBA
Fire & Ice '97	Nov 07 - 09
Garage Party	May 25
Gay & Lesbian Day at Disney World Party	Jun 07
Gear Party	May '97 TBA
Gear Party	May '98 TBA
GMHC Morning Party	Aug 17
Hearts Party (BOHT)	Feb 13 - 15
Hellball '97	Oct '97 TBA
Hero 8 Festival	Feb '98 TBA
Hotlanta River Expo '97 Parties	Aug 07 - 10
House of Blues	Mar 02
House of Blues	May 25
House of Blues	Jun 22
House of Blues	Jul 27
House of Blues	Dec 22
House of Blues	Apr 20
Int'l Mr. Leather Weekend (IML)	Feb '98 TBA
Laguna Surf 2	Jul 04 - 06
Lesbian Pride Weekend (Denver)	Mar '98 TBA
Luv Ball	Oct 11 - 13
Masquerade '98 - The Purple Party	Feb '98 TBA
Meltdown '97	May 23 - 26
Meltdown '98	May '98 TBA
Miss Fire Island Contest (32nd Annual)	Sep 06
Pensacola Beach Maneuvers 4	May 24 - 26
Pensacola Beach Maneuvers 5	May '98 TBA
Red Heart Party (London)	Apr 10
Red Party	Feb '98 TBA
RIP'D '97	Aug 28 - Sep 01
Rudely Elegant Red Party	Sep 20
Saint-At-Large White Party	Feb '98 TBA
Sleaze Ball	Oct 04
Spin II	Jun 28
Steel Party	Sep '97 TBA
Twelve Gods Party	Sep 03 - 07
Twist IV	Aug 02
Wet Party '97	Jul 05
Wet & Wild Weekend	May '98 TBA
White Party 1998 (Palm Springs)	Apr '98 TBA
White Party (Fire Island)	Jul 26
White Party (Melbourne)	Apr 24
White Party (Miami Beach)	Nov 26 - 30
Wild & Wet Weekend	May 15 - 19
Winter Party South Beach	Mar '98 TBA

RODEOS

Atlantic Stampede Rodeo	Oct 03 - 05
Atlantic Stampede Rodeo	Oct '98 TBA
Bay Area Regional Rodeo	May 30 - Jun 01
Bay Area Regional Rodeo	May '98 TBA
Big Sky Regional Rodeo	Jun '98 TBA
Big Sky Regional Rodeo	Jun 13 - 15
Bighorn Rodeo	Mar '98 TBA
Bighorn Rodeo	Mar 07 - 09
Canadian Rockies Int'l Rodeo	Jun '98 TBA
Canadian Rockies Int'l Rodeo	Jun 27 - 29
Dixieland Regional Rodeo	May '98 TBA
Great Plains Regional Rodeo	May 23 - 25
Great Plains Regional Rodeo	May '98 TBA
Greater Motown Int'l Rodeo	May 16 - 18
Greater Motown Int'l Rodeo	May '98 TBA
Greater NW Int'l Rodeo	Aug '98 TBA
Greater San Diego Rodeo	Sep 26 - 28
Greater San Diego Rodeo	Sep '98 TBA
Heartland Regional Rodeo	Jun 27 - 29
Heartland Regional Rodeo	Jun '98 TBA
I.G.R.A. 1997 Finals Rodeo	Oct 23 - 26
I.G.R.A. 1998 Finals Rodeo	Oct '98 TBA
I.G.R.A. Annual Convention	Jul 24 - 27
I.G.R.A. Annual Convention	Jul '98 TBA
Kansas Gay Rodeo	Aug 09 - 11
L.A. Rodeo '97	Apr 11 - 13
L.A. Rodeo '98	Apr '98 TBA
Missouri Gay Rodeo	Aug 29 - 31
Missouri Gay Rodeo	Aug '98 TBA
North Star Regional Rodeo	Jul 11 - 13
North Star Regional Rodeo	Jul '98 TBA
Palm Springs Regional Rodeo	Oct 31 - Nov 02
Palm Springs Regional Rodeo	Nov '98 TBA
Pikes Peak United Rodeo	Sep 19 - 21
Pikes Peak United Rodeo	Sep '98 TBA
Road Runner Regional Rodeo	Jan '98 TBA
Rocky Mtn. Regional Rodeo	Jul '98 TBA
Rocky Mtn. Regional Rodeo	Jul 18 - 20
Rodeo in the Rock	Apr 25 - 27
Rodeo in the Rock	Apr '98 TBA
Saguaro Regional Rodeo	Mar 21 - 23
Saguaro Regional Rodeo	Mar '98 TBA
Texas Gay Rodeo (14th annual)	Nov 07 - 09
Texas Gay Rodeo (15th annual)	Nov '98 TBA
Windy City Gay Rodeo	Aug '98 TBA
Zia Regional Rodeo	Aug 29 - 31
Zia Regional Rodeo	Aug '98 TBA

WOMEN'S FESTIVALS

Campfest	May 21 - 26
Campfest	Jun '98 TBA
Elderflower Womenspirit Festival (9th annual)	Aug 14 - 17
Femo Prideweek	Jun '98 TBA
Fire Island's Fifth Annual Women's Weekend	Sep 12 - 14
Golden Threads Celebration	Jun '98 TBA
Golden Threads Celebration (11th Annual)	Jun 27 - 29
Gulf Coast Women's Festival (10th annual)	Apr '98 TBA
Hopland Women's Festival	May 30 - Jun 01
Hopland Women's Festival	May '98 TBA
Int'l Goddess Festival	Jul '98 TBA
July 4th Kick-Back	Jul 04 - 06
Lesbian Liberation Rally (7th annual)	May '97 TBA
Maine-ly for You Spring Fling & Autumn Fests	Aug '97 TBA
Maryland Womyn's Gathering	May 15 - 18
Maryland Womyn's Gathering	May '98 TBA
Michigan Womyn's Music Festival 1997	Aug 12 - 17
Midwest Womyn's Autumnfest (3rd annual)	Aug 31
National Women's Music Festival (13th annual)	May 29 - Jun 01
National Women's Music Festival (14th annual)	May 28 - 31
New Hampshire Women's Music Festival (4th annual)	Sep '97 TBA
Ohio Lesbian Festival	Sep '97 TBA
Sisterspace Pocono Weekend, '98	Sep '98 TBA
Veranstaltungen Lesbenfruhlingstreffen	May '98 TBA
Virginia Women's Music Festival	May 30 - Jun 01
Virginia Women's Music Festival	May '98 TBA
West Coast Women's Music Festival	Sep '98 TBA
Wild Western Women's Weekend	Sep 19 - 21
Wiminfest '98	May '98 TBA
Wise Festival	Oct '97 TBA
Women Celebrating Our Diversity	Aug '97 TBA
Womenfest '97	Sep 03 - 09
Women's Week in Provincetown (12th annual)	Oct 12 - 19
Womongathering	Jun 12 - 15
Womongathering	Jun '98 TBA

TRIP/EVENTS CALENDAR

FERRARI GUIDES' GAY TRAVEL A to Z - 18th EDITION

WHEN TO GO

UNDATED EVENTS

TBA ♀♂ **AIDS, Medicine & Miracles,** One- to four-day conferences held throughout the year in the USA & Canada focusing on people living with HIV/AIDS. Workshops and plenary sessions cover topics ranging from research and treatment updates to nutrition and complementary therapies to dealing with grief and loss. Importance is placed on creating a supportive, healing retreat environment for PWAs, their loved ones and caregivers. Contact: Aids, Medicine & Miracles, PO Box 9130, Maxwell Bldg, 311 Mapleton, Boulder, CO 80301-9130, (303) 447-8777, (800) 875-8770, Fax: (303) 447-3902.

TBA ♀ **Camp Sisterspirit 5-Year Reunion,** A family-reunion of visitors and supporters of Camp Sisterspirit since 1993 will take place in either September or October, 1998. Contact: Camp Sisterspirit, PO Box 12, Ovett, MS 39464, (601) 344-1411, tel/fax: (601) 344-2005.

TBA ♀ **Conference For Catholic Lesbians Regional Retreats,** CCL is a national organization for lesbians of Catholic heritage. The group publishes a quarterly newsletter and provides a supportive network. It serves as an advocate for lesbian issues in political and church forums. Regional retreats planned. Contact: (212) 663-2963 or (718) 680-6107.

TBA ♀♂ **Int'l Pride Martial Arts & Judo Tournament,** A rotating event. Call for schedule. Workshops for both martial artists and non-martial artists are also open to the general public. Sample subjects: self defense with weapon attacks, advanced sparring techniques for martial artists, verbal self defense vs. guns, basic Judo throws. Judo tournament and open martial arts tournament and an evening demonstration by gay martial arts masters, including musical forms, team fighting, weapons sparring. Grand championships conclude the event. Contact I.A.G.L.M.A., PO Box 590601, San Francisco, CA 94159-0601, Attn: Karen Lee Leonard.

TBA ♀♂ **Lavender Law V,** Held every 2 years, the National Lesbian & Gay Law Association's national conferencetook place in New Orleans, LA in October, 1996. Sessions cover issues such as civil rights law, criminal law, employment discrimination, family law, activism, immigration and legal practice. Contact: NLGA, Box 77130, National Capital Station, Washington, DC 20013, (202) 389-0161.

TBA ♂ **Leather in Europe,** In Europe, leather club meetings and events at leather bars take place in any given week. Because plans are not made far in advance, contact local bars for current details. Activities at events usually include a Friday reception, a Saturday disco, a bike run and a goodbye drink. Safe-sex parties are held in Amsterdam on a regular basis. For information about any events or local clubs, contact ECMC (European Confederation of Motor Clubs), Postbus 725, Znrich 8025, Switzerland.

TBA ♀♂ **Leather Pride Celebration '97,** A two-week party, with piercings, tattooing, branding demos. Leather men and women from all over North America will attend and senior leather titleholders will appear. Date not yet determined for 1997. Location: Toronto, Ontario, Canada. Contact: MLT, 552 Church St, PO Box 500-48, Toronto, ON Canada M4Y 2H0.

TBA ♀ **Lesbian Events in Sedona, Arizona,** Dances and events especially for lesbians take place throughout the year. Lesbians from around the world are invited to attend. For information call (520) 282-7742

TBA ♀ **MoonSisters Drum Camp,** Moonsisters offers 3-5 camps a year, some of which are attended by as many as 400 womyn drummers. Nurudafina Pili Abena, Carolyn Brandy, Nydia Mata & Mabiba Baegne are among the teachers of rhythms from Africa, Cuba & Brazil. In addition to classes, there are performaces, circles, a marketplace & jams. All levels welcome. Register early, camps will sell out! 1997 camps: Oct. 3-5 in Sausalito, CA & Sept. a location in the Southwest TBA. 1998 camps: the 1st weekends in Apr. & Oct. in Sausalito, CA. Contact: For registration info send SASE to MoonSisters Drum Camp, PO Box 20918, Oakland, CA 94620, (510) 547-8386.

TBA ♀♂ **Sober Spring Break,** An annual Spring Break event for students from the "university of life," as well as those from academia. Activities include working on the memorial garden for Southern activist women, woodworking, discussions of issues such as class, race, regional differences, etc. Location: Camp Sisterspirit. Contact: Contact: Camp Sisterspirit, PO Box 12, Ovett, MS 39464, (601) 344-1411, tel/fax: (601) 344-2005.

TBA ♀ **Ten/Forty Conference,** Held annually in Australia. A conference for feminists who have been in the women's movement at least 10 years & are over 40 years old. This event is held in a different city each year. Contact 10/40 Conference, PO Box 142, Camperdown 2050, Australia.

WHEN TO GO

TRIP/EVENTS CALENDAR

| TBA | ♀ | **Womynspirit,** Womyn's festivals held several times in Australia. Contact RMB, 335 Forest Grove 6286, WA, Australia, (61-97) 577 578. |

If you are interested in a trip or event that has already taken place, call the tour operator or organizer to find out if and when it will take place again. Individual trips and events frequently recur year after year. Some trips have several departures per year, or can be organized expressly for an interested party or group. "FYI" (For Your Information) refers to a special feature about a company.

January 97

TBA	♀	**Dogsledding in Minnesota,** see Women in the Wilderness on page 81, 108
TBA	♀	**Goddess Tour in Turkey,** see Global Affair on page 56
TBA	♀♂	**Midsumma Festival Melbourne,** see Beyond the Blue on page 49, FYI 307
04 - 06	♀	**Arthur's Pass Nat'l Park Tramp,** see Bushwise Women on page 50, FYI 318
04 - 11	♀♂	**Orthodox Christmas in Russia,** see Kremlin Tours on page 60, FYI 266
04 - 11	♀♂	**Roadtown, Tortola to Roadtown, Tortola Cruise,** see Tall Ship Adventures, Inc. on page 74, FYI 340
10 - 18	♀	**Amazon Rainforest,** see Club Le Bon on page 51, FYI 341
11 - 18	♀♂	**Roadtown, Tortola to Roadtown, Tortola Cruise,** see Tall Ship Adventures, Inc. on page 74, FYI 340
12 - 17	♀	**Pack/Paddle, New Year, Bushline Lodge,** see Bushwise Women on page 50, FYI 318
18 - 25	♀♂	**Atlantis Events Club Med Turkoise,** see Atlantis Events on page 48, 87
18 - 25	♀♂	**Best of Russia,** see Kremlin Tours on page 60, FYI 266
18 - 25	♀♂	**Roadtown, Tortola to Roadtown, Tortola Cruise,** see Tall Ship Adventures, Inc. on page 74, FYI 340
24 - 31	♀	**Rees/Dart Tramp Mt. Aspiring Nat'l Park,** see Bushwise Women on page 50, FYI 318
24 - FE 02	♀♂	**Rhapsody on the Nile,** see Allegro Travel on page 46, 86
25 - FE 01	♀♂	**Roadtown, Tortola to Roadtown, Tortola Cruise,** see Tall Ship Adventures, Inc. on page 74, FYI 340
30 - FE 02	♀	**Cross Country Skiing, Yosemite Valley,** see Women in Motion on page 80, 107

February 97

TBA	♀	**Assam, Northeast India,** see Club Le Bon on page 51, FYI 341
TBA	♀♂	**Coach Tours of New Zealand,** see Beyond the Blue on page 49, FYI 307
TBA	♂	**Costa Rica,** see Travel Club, The on page 76, 103
TBA	♀	**Dogsledding in Minnesota,** see Women in the Wilderness on page 81, 108
TBA	♀♂	**Hero Party, Auckland,** see Beyond the Blue on page 49, FYI 307
TBA	♀♂	**International Gay Ski Week,**
TBA	♀♂	**Park City Gay Ski Week (3rd annual),** The resort area of Park City/Deer Valley is the site of this ski event, featuring ski races & competitions, special events, parties and "fun runs". Location: Park City, UT. Call: (800) 429-8747.
TBA	♀♂	**Sydney Gay and Lesbian Mardi Gras,** see Beyond the Blue on page 49, FYI 307
TBA	♀	**Whale Watching, Sea Kayaking, Baja California,** see Women in the Wilderness on page 81, 108
01 - 08	♀♂	**Best of Russia,** see Kremlin Tours on page 60, FYI 266
01 - 08	♀♂	**Roadtown, Tortola to Roadtown, Tortola Cruise,** see Tall Ship Adventures, Inc. on page 74, FYI 340
02 - 09	♀	**Whales of Magdalena Bay, BC—Kayak,** see Blue Moon Explorations on page 49
03 - 17	♂	**Chiang Mai Flower Festival, Thailand,** see Tours to Paradise on page 75, FYI 189
04 - 12	♀♂	**Carnival in Venice,** see Allegro Travel on page 46, 86
04 - 12	♀♂	**Hong Kong's Final Days plus Chinese New Year,** see L'Arc en Ciel Voyages on page 61, 94
07 - 09	♀♂	**Mardi Gras in Ensenada,** see Gay Baja Tours on page 56, FYI 358
08 - 15	♀♂	**Roadtown, Tortola to Roadtown, Tortola Cruise,** see Tall Ship Adventures, Inc. on page 74, FYI 340
08 - 18	♀♂	**Pre-Mardi Gras at Man Friday Resort,** see Above & Beyond Tours on page 45, 83
08 - 22	♀	**Peru: Machu Picchu and the Andes,** see Women in the Wilderness on page 81, 108
09 - 15	♀♂	**Colorado Hike, Snowshoe, Ski,** see Lizard Head Backcountry Tours on page 61, FYI 495
09 - 16	♀♂	**Carnival in Las Palmas,** see Our Family Abroad on page 65, 98
11 - 19	♀♂	**Valentine's Day in Paris,** see L'Arc en Ciel Voyages on page 61, 94
11 - MR 06	♀♂	**Best of South Pacific (Fiji, NZ, Australia),** see Destination Downunder on page 53, FYI 309
12 - MR 06	♀♂	**Best of South Pacific,** see Above & Beyond Tours on page 45, 83
13 - 21	♀♂	**New Zealand Adventure,** see Destination Downunder on page 53, FYI 309
13 - 24	♂	**Ultimate New Zealand Adventure Tour,** see Men on Vacation on page 62, 96
14 - 17	♀♂	**Viking Serenade, Baja Cruise,**

FERRARI GUIDES' GAY TRAVEL A to Z - 18th EDITION

WHEN TO GO

TRIP/EVENTS CALENDAR

14 - 22	♀♂	**Costa Rica: Butterflies, Bicycles, & Beaches,** see Experience Plus on page 55, 90
15 - 21	♀♂	**New Zealand Adventure,** see Above & Beyond Tours on page 45, 83
15 - 22	♀♂	**Best of Russia,** see Kremlin Tours on page 60, FYI 266
15 - 22	♀♂	**Roadtown, Tortola to Roadtown, Tortola Cruise,** see Tall Ship Adventures, Inc. on page 74, FYI 340
16 - 23	♀	**Whales of Magdalena Bay,,** see Blue Moon Explorations on page 49
17 - 27	♀♂	**Russian Winter Gala,** see Allegro Travel on page 46, 86
19 - 24	♂	**Hero the Party-New Zealand,** see Men on Vacation on page 62, 96
19 - MR 03	♀♂	**Party! Party! Package (S. Pacific),** see Above & Beyond Tours on page 45, 83
20 - 23	♀	**Downhill Skiing, Big Bear Lake, CA,** see Women in Motion on page 80, 107
20 - 28	♀	**Hawaii Kayak and Hike Kona Island,** see Blue Moon Explorations on page 49
20 - MR 02	♀♂	**28th Sydney Gay Mardi Gras Parade & Party,** see Destination Downunder on page 53, FYI 309
20 - MR 07	♀♂	**Boomerang! Sydney Mardi Gras,** see Alyson Adventures on page 47, 87
21 - MR 03	♂	**Sydney Gay Mardi Gras,** see Men on Vacation on page 62, 96
22 - MR 01	♀♂	**Roadtown, Tortola to Roadtown, Tortola Cruise,** see Tall Ship Adventures, Inc. on page 74, FYI 340
23 - MR 01		**Canadian Rockies Ski Week,** see Lois Lane Expeditions on page 61
23 - MR 02	♀	**Sea Kayak Rakiura (Stewart Island),** see Bushwise Women on page 50, FYI 318
23 - MR 02	♀	**Whales of Magdalena Bay—Kayak,** see Blue Moon Explorations on page 49
23 - MR 03	♀♂	**Sydney Gay and Lesbian Mardi Gras,** see Above & Beyond Tours on page 45, 83
23 - MR 03	♀♂	**Sydney Mardi Gras Party Pkgs,** see Destination Downunder on page 53, FYI 309
24 - MR 02	♀	**Writers' Workshop, Skiing, Snowshoeing, Minnesota,** see Women in the Wilderness on page 81, 108
24 - MR 08	♀♂	**Atlantis Events Sydney Mardi Gras,** see Atlantis Events on page 48, 87
25 - MR 04	♀	**Sea Kayak Baja Mexico,** see Oceanwomyn Kayaking on page 64, FYI 357
25 - MR 05	♀♂	**Sydney Gay Mardi Gras Tour,** see Australian & New Zealand Travel Hdqtrs on page 48
25 - MR 08	♀♂	**Israel Christian Pilgrimage + Amsterdam,** see L'Arc en Ciel Voyages on page 61, 94
26 - MR 03	♀♂	**Budget Buster Syd Mardi Gras Party Pkg,** see Destination Downunder on page 53, FYI 309
26 - MR 05	♀♂	**Festival Hong Kong,** see Allegro Travel on page 46, 86
28 - MR 02	♂	**Gay Barcelona Group Tour,** see Teddy Travel on page 74, 101

March 97

TBA	♀	**Dogsledding in Minnesota,** see Women in the Wilderness on page 81, 108
TBA	♀♂	**Gay Far East Cruise,** see Anywhere Travel on page 47
TBA	♂	**Key West,** see Travel Club, The on page 76, 103
01 - 08	♀♂	**Clipper Caribbean Cruise,** see RSVP Travel Productions/Club RSVP on page 70, 100
01 - 08	♀♂	**Roadtown, Tortola to Roadtown, Tortola Cruise,** see Tall Ship Adventures, Inc. on page 74, FYI 340
01 - 08	♀♂	**Russian Spring,** see Kremlin Tours on page 60, FYI 266
01 - 08	♀	**Sailing in the Virgin Islands,** see Women in the Wilderness on page 81, 108
01 - 12	♀♂	**Legend of the Seas, Panama Canal Cruise,**
01 - 15	♀♂	**Mardi Gras Recovery at Man Friday Resort,** see Above & Beyond Tours on page 45, 83
02 - 02	♀♂	**House of Blues,** Sunday Tea Dance, Los Angeles' largest party takes place every month and features headlining performers debuting their newest creations. Attendance 1,400. Contact: http://www.jeffreysanker.com/events.htm
02 - 04	♀♂	**Whale Watching in Mexico,** see Gay Baja Tours on page 56, FYI 358
02 - 06	♀	**Canadian Rockies Beginning Ice Climbing,** see Lois Lane Expeditions on page 61
02 - 09	♀	**Cycle Costa Rica/Inn Tour,** see Women in Motion on page 80, 107
02 - 09	♀	**Sea Kayaking in Baja, Mexico,** see Paddling South & Saddling South on page 66, 99
03 - 05	♂	**Post-Mardi Gras Rock, Reef, Rainforest,** see Men on Vacation on page 62, 96
03 - 08	♀♂	**Dive the Great Barrier Reef,** see Above & Beyond Tours on page 45, 83
03 - 08	♀♂	**Gay Dive Boat-Great Barrier Reef,** see Destination Downunder on page 53, FYI 309
03 - 11	♀	**Hawaii Kayak & Hike KonaIsland,** see Blue Moon Explorations on page 49
04 - 17	♂	**Special Tour, Thailand,** see Tours to Paradise on page 75, FYI 189
05 - 08	♂	**Barrier Reef Recovery-After Syd Mardi Gras,** see Men on Vacation on page 62, 96
07 - 09	♀♂	**Bighorn Rodeo,** Las Vegas, NV. Call: NGRA, (702) 732-7559.
07 - 09	♀	**Sierra Ski & Snow Camping,** see Common Earth Adventures on page 51, 89
07 - 09	♂	**Winter Party '97 Package,** see Advance Damron Vacations on page 45, 84

WHEN TO GO

TRIP/EVENTS CALENDAR

Dates		Event
07 - 10	♀♂	**Gay Ski East '97, Lake Placid, NY,** see Eclectic Excursions on page 54, FYI 466
08 - 09	♂	**Fitzroy Fantasy-Join 1st Annual Bash,** see Men on Vacation on page 62, 96
08 - 15	♀♂	**Roadtown, Tortola to Roadtown, Tortola Cruise,** see Tall Ship Adventures, Inc. on page 74, FYI 340
08 - 16	♀♂	**Austria Ski Trip,** see Travel Affair on page 75, 103
08 - 16	♀♂	**Costa Rica: Butterflies, Bicycles, & Beaches,** see Experience Plus on page 55, 90
08 - 17	♀♂	**Italian Gay Discovery Tour,** see Zipper Travel Association on page 82, FYI 252
08 - 28	♀	**Backpacking in New Zealand,** see Cloud Canyon Backpacking on page 50, 88
09 - 15	♀♂	**Desert Wildflowers-Hike Desert in Bloom,** see Lizard Head Backcountry Tours on page 61, FYI 495
09 - 16	♀	**Whales of Magdalena Bay—Kayak,** see Blue Moon Explorations on page 49
10 - 14	♀	**Forest Footing, Bushline Lodge,** see Bushwise Women on page 50, FYI 318
10 - JA 17	♀	**Sea Kakak Baja Mexico,** see Oceanwomyn Kayaking on page 64, FYI 357
13 - 22	♀	**Exploring Costa Rica,** see Woodswomen on page 81, 108
14 - 25	♀♂	**Ancient Egypt,** see Our Family Abroad on page 65, 98
15 - 21	♀	**Vacation in Cozumel,** see Woodswomen on page 81, 108
15 - 22	♀♂	**Best of Russia,** see Kremlin Tours on page 60, FYI 266
15 - 22	♀♂	**Eastern Caribbean Cruise,** see Ocean Voyager on page 64, 97
15 - 22	♀♂	**Roadtown, Tortola to Roadtown, Tortola Cruise,** see Tall Ship Adventures, Inc. on page 74, FYI 340
15 - 24	♀♂	**Treasures of Italy,** see Above & Beyond Tours on page 45, 83
16 - 21	♀	**Cross Country Skiing/Inn Tour, Canadian Rockies,** see Women in Motion on page 80, 107
16 - 23	♀	**Kayak Sea of Cortez, Baja Mexico,** see Blue Moon Explorations on page 49
17 - 22	♀	**Writing and Hiking-Death Valley,** see Common Earth Adventures on page 51, 89
20 - 26	♀♂	**Kayaking Sea of Cortez, Baja Mexico,** see Toto Tours on page 75, 102
21 - 16	♀♂	**Andalusia: Seville to Granada,** see Experience Plus on page 55, 90
21 - 23	♀	**Rosarito Beach Resort, Mexico,** see Women in Motion on page 80, 107
21 - 23	♀♂	**Saguaro Regional Rodeo,** Tucson, AZ. Call: AGRA (Tucson Chapter), (520) 323-0805.
21 - 29	♀♂	**South American Cruise,** see RSVP Travel Productions/Club RSVP on page 70, 100
22 - 24	♀	**Gold Country Getaway,** see Merlyn's Journeys on page 63, FYI 370
22 - 29	♀♂	**Roadtown, Tortola to Roadtown, Tortola Cruise,** see Tall Ship Adventures, Inc. on page 74, FYI 340
24 - AP 04	♀♂	**Expedition to Easter Island,** see Hanns Ebensten Travel on page 57, 92
27 - 31	♀	**Dinah Shore Women's Festival, Palm Spring, CA,** see Women in Motion on page 80, 107
28 - 28	♂	**Red Heart Party (London),** Billed as "Europe's only official Circuit Party," this event was voted one of the circuit's top ten in 1996. Features include: Top-notch sound system, a bevy of DJ's, exquisite production design, multi-system light show, and the invaluable "Red Heart Party Survival Kit." Location: London, England. Contact: The Red Heart Company Ltd., 3rd Floor, 60-62 Old Compton Street, London W1V SPA, England, (0171) 420 0088, Web: http://www.redheart.co.uk
29 - AP 05	♀♂	**Roadtown, Tortola to Roadtown, Tortola Cruise,** see Tall Ship Adventures, Inc. on page 74, FYI 340
30 - AP 06	♀	**Kayak Sea of Cortez, Baja Mexico,** see Blue Moon Explorations on page 49
30 - AP 06	♀	**Sea Kayaking in Baja, Mexico,** see Paddling South & Saddling South on page 66, 99

April 97

Dates		Event
TBA	♀♂	**Players Express Greek Isles Cruise/Tour,** see Players Express on page 67, FYI 458
TBA	♀	**Sailing Alaska - Taku Harbor, Funter Bay, Etc.,** see Women Sail Alaska on page 81, FYI 363
TBA	♂	**San Francisco/Big Sur,** see Travel Club, The on page 76, 103
TBA	♀	**Women of Paris Tour,** see Five Star Travel Services on page 55
01 - 12	♂	**Tom Bianchi & Friends at Man Friday Resort,** see Above & Beyond Tours on page 45, 83
01 - 15	♀♂	**Steps of St. Paul, Turkey,** see L'Arc en Ciel Voyages on page 61, 94
02 - 11	♂	**Slice of Hawaii, Slice of Kauai, Prime Beef,** see Toto Tours on page 75, 102
03 - 06	♀	**Singing & Hiking With Joanne Rand,** see Common Earth Adventures on page 51, 89
04 - 15	♀	**Rainforest of Honduras Rafting, Mule Travel,** see Women in the Wilderness on page 81, 108
05 - 12	♀♂	**Best of Russia,** see Kremlin Tours on page 60, FYI 266
05 - 12	♀	**Climbing, Leadership, California,** see Woodswomen on page 81, 108
05 - 12	♀	**Joshua Tree Rock Climbing,** see Woodswomen on page 81, 108
05 - 12	♂	**Rafting & Canoeing the Rio Grande R., Texas,** see Spirit Journeys on page 72, 101

FERRARI GUIDES' GAY TRAVEL A to Z - 18th EDITION

WHEN TO GO

TRIP/EVENTS CALENDAR

05 - 12 ♀♂ **Roadtown, Tortola to Roadtown, Tortola Cruise,** see Tall Ship Adventures, Inc. on page 74, FYI 340

05 - 12 ♀♂ **Southwest Canyons and Culture,** see Experience Plus on page 55, 90

05 - 20 ♂ **Thai New Year and Water Festival, Thailand,** see Tours to Paradise on page 75, FYI 189

06 - 13 ♀ **Kayak Sea of Cortez, Baja, Mexico,** see Blue Moon Explorations on page 49

07 - JY 21 ♂ **Thai Experience,** see Hanns Ebensten Travel on page 57, 92

10 - 14 ♂ **Spring Break on St Barts,** see Club Hommes/Worldguest on page 51, FYI 204

10 - 15 ♀ **Pack/Paddle, Bush/Beach, Bushline Lodge,** see Bushwise Women on page 50, FYI 318

11 - 13 ♀♂ **L.A. Rodeo '97,** Los Angeles, CA. Call: GSGRA (LA Chapter), (310) 498-1675.

11 - 13 ♀ **Wine Country Getaway,** see Merlyn's Journeys on page 63, FYI 370

12 - 19 ♀♂ **Roadtown, Tortola to Roadtown, Tortola Cruise,** see Tall Ship Adventures, Inc. on page 74, FYI 340

12 - 20 ♀♂ **Coasting to the Algarve,** see Experience Plus on page 55, 90

13 - 20 ♀ **Kayak Sea of Cortez, Baja, Mexico,** see Blue Moon Explorations on page 49

14 - 21 ♀ **Mexican Caribbean Cruise,** see Olivia Cruises & Resorts on page 65, 98

17 - 20 ♀♂ **Pools & Pumps '97, Cancun, Mexico,** see Travel Affair on page 75, 103

18 - 20 ♀♂ **Leatherfest IX,** A thousand people from around the world are expected for this event, which includes a weekend of education and entertainment, receptions, workshops, awards banquet, LeatherTip Square Dance. Location: San Diego, CA. Contact: NLA, San Diego Chapter, PO Box 3092, San Diego, CA 92163, (800) 598-1859, email: Lasher@connectnet.com

18 - 20 ♀ **Retreat for Women with Life Threatening Illnesses,** see Common Earth Adventures on page 51, 89

18 - 27 ♀ **Desert Women's Quest,** see Common Earth Adventures on page 51, 89

19 - 20 ♀ **Integrated leadership - Minnesota,** see Woodswomen on page 81, 108

19 - 25 ♀♂ **Tulip Time in Holland,** see Travel Affair on page 75, 103

19 - 26 ♀♂ **Escorted Costa Rica,** see Way to Go Costa Rica on page 78, FYI 352

19 - 26 ♀♂ **Kool Kids G/L Family Vacation,** see Club Le Bon on page 51, FYI 341

19 - 26 ♀♂ **Roadtown, Tortola to Roadtown, Tortola Cruise,** see Tall Ship Adventures, Inc. on page 74, FYI 340

19 - 27 ♀♂ **Desert Explorations—Hiking, Rafting Utah,** see OutWest Adventures on page 66, FYI 455

19 - 28 ♀♂ **Italian Gay Discovery Tour,** see Zipper Travel Association on page 82, FYI 252

20 - 20 ♀♂ **House of Blues,** (2nd Anniversary) Sunday Tea Dance, Los Angeles' largest party takes place every month and features headlining performers debuting their newest creations. Attendance 1,400. Contact: http://www.jeffreysanker.com/events.htm

20 - 26 ♂ **Caribbean Windjammer Cruise,** see Advance Damron Vacations on page 45, 84

20 - 26 ♀♂ **Hike Utah's Canyon Country,** see Lizard Head Backcountry Tours on page 61, FYI 495

20 - 27 ♂ **Red Rock HIV+ Single Men's Week,** see Alyson Adventures on page 47, 87

22 - 27 ♀ **Autumn Workparty,** see Bushwise Women on page 50, FYI 318

23 - 26 ♀♂ **We're Funny That Way,** Comedians from Canada, USA, Europe, Latin America and Australia are expected to perform at Canada's first international gay & lesbian comedy festival. Approximately 30 acts will be performed in five to seven venues throughout the city. Acts will include individual stand-up, improvisation, sketch comedy, drag and musical comedy. Location: Toronto, Canada. Contact: WFTW Productions Office, 40 Homewood Ave #104, Toronto, ON M4Y 2K2 Canada, (416) 515-1067, Fax: 964-3526

24 - 24 ♀♂ **White Party (Melbourne),** Australia's first international gay & lesbian dance party will be held at the Royal Melbourne Showgrounds in five music arenas. In addition to the White Room, the White Unity Retro Room and the chillout cafe, there will be a room for women only (Vanilla Room) and men only (Cream Room). Location: Melbourne, Australia. Contact: Gay & lesbian businesses in the Melbourne area.

25 - 27 ♀♂ **American Brotherhood Weekend,** Includes three contests: American Leatherman, American Leatherwoman, and American Leatherboy. Host hotel is the Howard Johnson Hotel & Suites and host bar is the Club Improv, both located in the heart of gay businesses in Washington, DC. Contact: ABLE Productions, Inc. P.O. Box 5130, Utica, NY 13505-5130, Email: ABLEprod@aol.com

25 - 27 ♂ **Cherry Jubilee,** This "spring thaw" party heats up our nation's capitol, Washington, D.C. Several pre- and post-events are planned throughout the weekend with the main event on Saturday night. Benefits: Whitman-Walker Clinic and Food & Friends. Contact: (800) 201-0807, Fax: (703) 836-1716.

WHEN TO GO

TRIP/EVENTS CALENDAR

25 - 27 ♀ **Imperial Wildlife Refuge Canoe Trip, CA/AZ border,** see Women in Motion on page 80, 107

25 - 27 ♂ **Journey Into Ourselves, Asheville, NC,** see Spirit Journeys on page 72, 101

25 - 27 ♂ **Men's Couples Workshop, Santa Fe, NM,** see Spirit Journeys on page 72, 101

25 - 27 ♂ **Out of Hibernation '97,** Presented by the Hoosier Bears, this annual event and weekend run is a 3-day event guaranteed to shake off the winter lethargy and welcome spring. Contests include the traditional Mr. Hoosier Bear on Friday and Mr. Midwest Bear on Saturday with after-hours parties both nights. Location: Indianapolis, IN. Contact: (317) 289-0555 or (317) 641-9734, Web: http://www.n2it.com/ooh97/

25 - 27 ♀♂ **Rodeo in the Rock,** Little Rock, AR. Call: DSRA, (501) 562-4466.

25 - 27 ♀ **Santa Cruz Mountains Getaway,** see Merlyn's Journeys on page 63, FYI 370

25 - MA 03 ♀♂ **Queen's Day Tulip Festival - Amsterdam,** see L'Arc en Ciel Voyages on page 61, 94

25 - MA 04 ♀♂ **Queensday in Amsterdam Party Package,** see Rainboworld Custom Tours on page 69, FYI 256

25 - MA 07 ♀♂ **Grand European Odyssey Cruise on Island Princess,** see Voyages & Expeditions on page 78, 106

26 - 27 ♀♂ **Rafting S. Fork American R., Calif,** see Mariah Wilderness Expeditions on page 61, 96

26 - MA 03 ♀♂ **Club Atlantis - Blue Bay Village, Mexico,** see Atlantis Events on page 48, 87

26 - MA 03 ♀♂ **May Celebration in Russia,** see Kremlin Tours on page 60, FYI 266

26 - MA 03 ♀♂ **Morocco With Our Family Abroad,** see Our Family Abroad on page 65, 98

26 - MA 03 ♀♂ **Roadtown, Tortola to Roadtown, Tortola Cruise,** see Tall Ship Adventures, Inc. on page 74, FYI 340

27 - MA 02 ♀♂ **Queens Day Amsterdam,** see Above & Beyond Tours on page 45, 83

28 - MA 01 ♀ **Beginning Backpacking-Grand Canyon,** see Grand Canyon Field Institute on page 57

28 - MA 12 ♀♂ **Vilnius, Riga, Tallinn, Helsinki, Russia,** see Allegro Travel on page 46, 86

30 - MA 13 ♂ **The Nile in Style,** see Hanns Ebensten Travel on page 57, 92

May 97

TBA ♀ **Creative Play Weekend (theme),** see Wilderness of Women on page

TBA ♀♂ **Gear Party,** Detroit, Michigan is the setting for the 4th annual Gear Party. Having established itself as a circuit main stay, "Gear" benefits the Geard for Life organization and is the largest gay and lesbian gathering in Detroit each year. Contact: (810) 358-9849, Email: GEARD4LIFE@aol.com

TBA ♀ **Lesbian Liberation Rally (7th annual),** A day of fun and celebration that is free to all lesbians. Lesbians gather together and play, talk politics. The event includes an afternoon stage with featured musicians, poets, comedians and speakers. There are craftswimmin and food vendors. Location: Northampton, MA. Contact: Lesbians for Lesbians, PO Box 1062, Greenfield, MA 01302.

TBA ♀ **Lesbies Doe-Front Lesbian Day,** Among the many events are a special lesbian theater, authors, workshops, films and photo & art exhibits. Over 800 lesbians are expected to attend. The final event is a huge dance party. Location: Belgium. Contact: Lesbies Doe-Front, Postbus 621, 9000 Gent, Belgium, (32-9) 223 69 29.

TBA ♀♂ **Memorial Day Weekend in Provincetown,** see New England Vacation Tours on page 64

TBA ♀♂ **Scuba Diving Great Barrier Reef,** see Oz Dive/Passport to Paradise on page 66

TBA ♀♂ **Snorkel & Scuba with Dolphins in Bahamas,** see Undersea Expeditions, Inc. on page 77, 104

TBA ♀ **Unlearning Oppressions (workshop),** see Wilderness of Women on page

TBA ♀ **Women's Basic Mountaineering Course,** see Lois Lane Expeditions on page 61

TBA ♀ **Women's Weekend,** A large gathering of thousands of women from around the USA, this event takes place annually in Russian River, CA during the first week of May. Contact: We The People newspaper, (707) 573-8896.

01 ♀ **Sailing Alaska - Taku Harbor, Funter Bay, Etc.,** see Women Sail Alaska on page 81, FYI 363

02 - 04 ♀ **Gold Country Getaway,** see Merlyn's Journeys on page 63, FYI 370

02 - 04 ♀ **Menopausal Women, Bushline Lodge,** see Bushwise Women on page 50, FYI 318

02 - 04 ♂ **Shipwreck IV,** This is the 4th annual celebration of "The Pirate Tradition" presented by the Key West Wreckers Levi/Leather Club. Contact: Key West Wreckers, P.O. Box 4723, Key West, FL 33041-4723, (305) 296-3338, Email: RUBBRONE@aol.com

02 - 04 ♀ **St. Croix Spring HIke, Wisconsin,** see Woodswomen on page 81, 108

02 - 04 ♂ **Three-Part Men's Self-Exploration Series,** see Spirit Journeys on page 72, 101

02 - 09 ♂ **Provencal: Biking Southern France,** see

FERRARI GUIDES' GAY TRAVEL A to Z - 18th EDITION   141

WHEN TO GO

TRIP/EVENTS CALENDAR

02 - 11 ♀♂ **Golden Capitals of Slavs,** see Kremlin Tours on page 60, FYI 266

03 ♀♂ **Pride (Brussels),** Contact local businesses for details.

03 - 04 ♀ **Whitewater Canoe Instruction, Wisconsin,** see Women in the Wilderness on page 81, 108

03 - 10 ♀♂ **Club Atlantis - Blue Bay Village, Mexico,** see Atlantis Events on page 48, 87

03 - 10 ♀♂ **Italy's Cinque Terre: A Walking Tour,** see Experience Plus on page 55, 90

03 - 10 ♀♂ **Roadtown, Tortola to Roadtown, Tortola Cruise,** see Tall Ship Adventures, Inc. on page 74, FYI 340

03 - 10 ♀♂ **Sydney Leather Week Package,** see Destination Downunder on page 53, FYI 309

03 - 10 ♀♂ **Victory Day in Russia,** see Kremlin Tours on page 60, FYI 266

03 - 10 ♀♂ **Wines & Chees of Portugal,** see Paths Less Taken on page 67, FYI 264

03 - 13 ♀♂ **Castles and Corktrees,** see Experience Plus on page 55, 90

03 - 16 ♀ **Peru, Macchu Picchu, Urubamba RIver Raft,** see Hawk, I'm Your Sister on page 58, FYI 463

03 - 18 ♀♂ **Hungary-Austria & Czech Republic,** see David's Trips and Tours on page 52, 89

04 - 11 ♀ **Sea Kayaking in Baja, Mexico,** see Paddling South & Saddling South on page 66, 99

06 - 26 ♀♂ **Bicycling Turkey — Turquoise Coast,** see VeloAsia Cycling Adventures on page 77, 105

07 - 11 ♂ **Hamburger Hexenkessel '97,** Events include: Pre-welcome at Chaps, Welcome evening at Black, Gossip Party at Tom's, Walk over the "Harbours Mile," Uniform Night at Chaps, Black Leather Disco at Black, & LCH Biker Tour. Main event Alyson Adventures on page 47, 87 is a theatrical performance (english translators available) of "Der m"blierte Herr" (gay version). Finally a Brunch at Caf, Spund on Sunday noon. Contact: Leder-Club Hamburg (LCH) e.V. c/o R. H"lscher, Reineckestr. 16, D-22761 Hamburg, Germany. Tel: (49-40) 899-1223, Email: 100773.562@compuserve.com

07 - 11 ♀♂ **Tokyo Int'l Lesbian & Gay Film & Video Festival,** The Tokyo festival is expected to attract 4,000 attendees. From Tokyo, the film festival will travel to Kyoto and Osaka. The 1997 festival is expected to take place in May. Location: Tokyo, Japan. Contact: Tokyo Int'l Gay & Lesbian Film & Video Office, Tel/Fax: (81-3) 5380 5760, http://www.wax.or.jp/L-GFF/. For specific information in English, call (81-3) 3316 1029.

08 - 11 ♀♂ **Int'l Gay & Lesbian Badminton Tournament,,** Europe's largest badminton tournament with various levels of competition, singles, doubles and a championship. Events also include a party and a farewell brunch. Location: Hamburg, Germany. Contact: Schwul/Lesbischer Sportverein Hamburg, Kleinerpulverteich 1721, 20099 Hamburg, Germany, (49-40) 24 03 33.

08 - 12 ♀♂ **Puerto Vallarta Travel Agent/Writer Fam Trip,** see Doin' It Right - in Puerto Vallarta on page 53

09 ♀♂ **Rafting Merced R., Calif,** see Mariah Wilderness Expeditions on page 61, 96

09 - 11 ♀ **Canoeing Namekagon R., Wisconsin,** see Woodswomen on page 81, 108

09 - 11 ♀ **Drumfest,** Drummers of all levels will learn drumming techniques from experienced drummers and participate in performances. There will be time for individual instruction, as well as group participation. On the off hours, you can swim, fish, relax, play volleyball. Location: At InTouch Women's Camping & Events Center, near Ferncliff, VA. Contact: INTOUCH, Rte 2, Box 1096, Kent's Store, VA 23084.

09 - 11 ♀ **Las Vegas Social, Las Vegas, NV,** see Women in Motion on page 80, 107

09 - 21 ♀♂ **Italian Medley — Five Cities,** see Allegro Travel on page 46, 86

10 ♂ **Leather Inquisition Party,** see Destination Downunder on page 53, FYI 309

10 - 11 ♀ **Raft Kings R., California,** see Mariah Wilderness Expeditions on page 61, 96

10 - 11 ♀ **Whitewater Canoe Instruction, Wisconsin,** see Women in the Wilderness on page 81, 108

10 - 16 ♂ **Dolphin Encounters in the Bahamas,** see Spirit Journeys on page 72, 101

10 - 17 ♂ **Mistral - Biking in Provence, France,** see Alyson Adventures on page 47, 87

10 - 17 ♀♂ **Puerto Vallarta Shopping Tours,** see Doin' It Right - in Puerto Vallarta on page 53

10 - 17 ♀♂ **Roadtown, Tortola to Roadtown, Tortola Cruise,** see Tall Ship Adventures, Inc. on page 74, FYI 340

11 - 17 ♀ **Backpacking Desert Slickrock, Utah,** see Woodswomen on page 81, 108

11 - 17 ♀♂ **Pinnacles, Fins, Spires-Hike Utah Canyons,** see Lizard Head Backcountry Tours on page 61, FYI 495

12 - 17 ♀ **Hiking the Marin Coast,** see Merlyn's Journeys on page 63, FYI 370

13 - 20 ♀♂ **Berlin Gay Pride 100th Anniversary,** see L'Arc en Ciel Voyages on page 61, 94

15 - 18 ♀ **Maryland Womyn's Gathering,** Over 160 acres of waterfront, wetlands & woods set the tone for this year's gathering. Events include opening & closing circles, sharing stage, fire circles, drum council, crafts &

WHEN TO GO

TRIP/EVENTS CALENDAR

dancing. Rustic cabins, newly renovated bath houses, camping welcome. Vegetarian meals. Childcare available (boys under 5 years only). Location: Southern Maryland. Contact: In Gaia's Lap, PO Box 39, Maryland Line, MD 21105, (410) 435-3111.

15 - 18 ♀ **Travel Writing and Photography, Bushline Lodge,** see Bushwise Women on page 50, FYI 318

15 - 19 ♂ **Wild & Wet Weekend,** Celebrated on Canada's Victoria Holiday weekend, in Montreal, it is second only in Canada to the Black & Blue party. Produced by Bad Boy Club Montreal (BBCM) this is a weekend packed with events ranging from a "warm-up party" on Thursday, the "weekend launch (leather optional) party" on Friday, the military/uniform party on Saturday, the late afternoon tea-dance and the main event Sunday (dress: as bare as you dare). Contact: BBCM, (514) 875-7026, Fax: (514) 875-9323, Email: bbcm@pop.point-net.com, Web: http://bbcm.org

15 - 22 ♂ **Silversea Monte Carlo-to-Lisbon Cruise,** see Club Hommes/Worldguest on page 51, FYI 204

16 - 18 ♀ **Council of All Cultures,** see Common Earth Adventures on page 51, 89

16 - 18 ♀♂ **Greater Motown Int'l Rodeo,** Detroit, MI. Call: MIGRA, (313) 438-1305.

17 - 18 ♀ **Whitewater Canoe Instruction, Wisconsin,** see Women in the Wilderness on page 81, 108

17 - 24 ♀♂ **Best of Russia,** see Kremlin Tours on page 60, FYI 266

17 - 24 ♀♂ **Red Rocks/Whitewater—Rafting Cataract Canyon,** see OutWest Adventures on page 66, FYI 455

17 - 24 ♀♂ **Roadtown, Tortola to Roadtown, Tortola Cruise,** see Tall Ship Adventures, Inc. on page 74, FYI 340

17 - 26 ♀♂ **Italian Gay Discovery Tour,** see Zipper Travel Association on page 82, FYI 252

18 - 24 ♂ **Healing Arts Retreat,** Health equals learning Hawaiian lomi lomi massage, the basics of huna and elemental breathing and shiatsu while floating in thermal springs, sunrise meditations, yoga and hula. Contact: Kalani Eco-Resort, RR2 Box 4500, Kehena Beach, HI 96778, (808) 965-7828, for reservations only: (800) 800-6886.

18 - 24 ♀♂ **Mountain Biking in Utah's Slick Rock Trails,** see Lizard Head Backcountry Tours on page 61, FYI 495

18 - 25 ♂ **Leather Week, Mr. Leather in Ibiza,** see Teddy Travel on page 74, 101

18 - 25 ♀♂ **Provencal - Biking Sothern France,** see Alyson Adventures on page 47, 87

18 - JN 01 ♀♂ **Transsiberian Express Adventure Tour,** see Kremlin Tours on page 60, FYI 266

19 - 28 ♀♂ **Venice Simplon-Orient Express European Holiday,** see Travel Affair on page 75, 103

19 - 29 ♀♂ **Provence and the South of France,** see Experience Plus on page 55, 90

20 - 27 ♀♂ **Venice to Florence,** see Experience Plus on page 55, 90

20 - JN 02 ♂ **Special Tour, Thailand,** see Tours to Paradise on page 75, FYI 189

21 - 26 ♀ **Campfest,** Five days of magic in a scenic, private camp near Oxford, PA. Workshops, day and evening live entertainment, crafts area, activities for singles, vegetarian and non-vegetarian meals, choice of cabin space or tenting, hot water and flush toilets, dining hall, olympic pool, sports, lake fishing, tennis and more. Held on Memorial Day weekend. Contact: Campfest, PO Box 559, Franklinville, NJ 08322, (609) 694-2037, e-mail: campfest@aol.com.

22 - 26 ♀♂ **Int'l Mr. Leather Contest 1997 (IML),** Leather men and women from all over the world will descend on Chicago on Memorial Day Weekend for a celebration of the leather, SM and fetish lifestyle. The weekend includes non-stop parties at Chicago's infamous leather bars, a leather market, a meet-the-contestants cocktail reception, the legendary Black-and-Blue Ball and the contest, itself. Location: Chicago, IL. Contact: International Mr. Leather, 5015 N Clark St, Chicago, IL 60640, (312) 878-6360, (800) 545-6753, Web: http://www.nycnet.com/gallagher/im1001.htm

22 - 26 ♀ **San Juan Island Whale Watch Kayak,** see Blue Moon Explorations on page 49

22 - 26 ♀ **Spring Sierra Nevada Trek,** see Common Earth Adventures on page 51, 89

22 - 27 ♂ **Mr Leather Chicago Pkg for Overseas Visitors,** see Teddy Travel on page 74, 101

23 ♀ **Raft the Merced R., California,** see Mariah Wilderness Expeditions on page 61, 96

23 - 25 ♀♂ **Great Plains Regional Rodeo,** Oklahoma City, OK. Call: OGRA, (405) 842-0845.

23 - 25 ♀♂ **NAGVA Championships,** The North American Gay Volleyball Association's 15th annual championship tournament, men's & women's play. Location: Philadelphia, PA. Contact: NAGVA, PO Box 223751, Dallas, TX 75222-3751

23 - 26 ♀♂ **Camp Lesbigay,** A fun unity gathering for gay and lesbian adults and our children! Contact: Kalani Eco-Resort, RR2 Box 4500, Kehena Beach, HI 96778, (808) 965-7828, for reservations only: (800) 800-6886.

FERRARI GUIDES' GAY TRAVEL A to Z - 18th EDITION

WHEN TO GO

TRIP/EVENTS CALENDAR

23 - 26 ♀♂ **Meltdown '97,** Celebrated over Memorial Day weekend in Austin, Texas, Meltdown includes 5 events. The main event is Meltdown '97 on Saturday night followed by the Captain Morgan's Rum Run (a flotilla of party boats on lake Travis) on Sunday. Benefits: Helping Hands for Life, Inc. Contact: (512) 478-1210, (512) 419-4763, Web: http://www.partyaustin.com

23 - 31 ♀♂ **Vienna & Salzburg,** see Allegro Travel on page 46, 86

23 - JN 01 ♀♂ **Costa Rica Coast to Coast,** see Above & Beyond Tours on page 45, 83

24 - 25 ♀ **Whitewater Canoe Instruction, Wisconsin,** see Women in the Wilderness on page 81, 108

24 - 26 ♀♂ **Pensacola Beach Maneuvers 4,** On Memorial Day Weekend, Pensacola, Florida (otherwise known as the Gay Riveria) is flooded with over 50,000 gay men and women for the annual "Beach Maneuvers" festivities. Held on the waterfront at the historic Bay Front Auditorium, the Saturday night main event features DJ ABEL of Miami and go go dancers from South Beach. Benefits: White Heat Foundation. Contact: (888) 777-8886, Web: http://www.jeffreysanker.com

24 - 31 ♀♂ **Caribbean Cruise,** see Pied Piper Travel on page 67, FYI 338

24 - 31 ♀♂ **Cruise Miami to Norway (NCL's),** see Pied Piper Travel on page 67, FYI 338

24 - 31 ♀♂ **East Caribbean Cruise,** see Ocean Voyager on page 64, 97

24 - 31 ♀♂ **Moscow and St. Petersburg,** see Our Family Abroad on page 65, 98

24 - 31 ♀♂ **Roadtown, Tortola to Roadtown, Tortola Cruise,** see Tall Ship Adventures, Inc. on page 74, FYI 340

24 - 31 ♀ **Swashbuckling Sisters Treasure Cruise-Caribbean,** see Thanks, Babs on page 74, 102

24 - 31 ♀ **Women Bike Zion, Bryce Canyons,** see Womantours/Artemis Sailing on page 80, 107

24 - JN 01 ♀♂ **Gay & Lesbian Costa Rica Escorted Tour,** see Way to Go Costa Rica on page 78, FYI 352

25 - 25 ♀♂ **Garage Party,** All of Indiana turns out for this events now in its 14th year. Benefits: Indiana Cares, Inc. Contact: (317) 920-1200.

25 - 25 ♀♂ **House of Blues,** Sunday Tea Dance, Los Angeles largest party takes place every month and features headlining performers debuting their newest creations. Attendance 1,400. Contact: http://www.jeffreysanker.com/events.htm

25 - 31 ♀ **Grand Canyon Rim-to-Rim Backpack,** see Grand Canyon Field Institute on page 57

25 - 31 ♀♂ **OutWestern Trails—Gay/Lesb Ranch Week,** see OutWest Adventures on page 66, FYI 455

28 - JN 03 ♀♂ **Walking tour of Burgundy, France,** see Progressive Travels on page 68, 99

28 - JN 07 ♀♂ **Spanish Vacation,** see Kremlin Tours on page 60, FYI 266

29 - JN 01 ♀ **National Women's Music Festival (13th annual),** An all-indoor festival in Bloomington, Indiana on the campus of Indiana University, with evening concerts, writer's and spirituality conferences, a full complement of intensive workshops, an older & young women's series, a performers' series, health, fitness, sexuality and sports series and a video series. Accommodations are on the campus. Contact: National Women's Music Festival, PO Box 1427, Indianapolis, IN 46206-1427, (317) 927-9355.

30 - 30 ♀♂ **Lambda Literary Awards (9th annual),** Awards recognizing excellence in gay and lesbian writing and publishing will be presented during a gala banquet in Chicago, to coincide with the Book Expo America '97 Convention. Location: Chicago, IL. Contact: Lambda Book Report, PO Box 73910, Washington, DC 20056-3910, (202) 462-7924, Fax: (202) 462-5264. E-mail: LBReditor@aol.com.

30 - JN 01 ♀♂ **Bay Area Regional Rodeo,** San Francisco, CA. Call: GSGRA, (415) 985-5200.

30 - JN 01 ♀ **Hopland Women's Festival,** This annual women's festival takes place in a rural California area & features comedy, music and arts & crafts. There is camping available. Location: Hopland, CA. Contact: HWF, PO Box 416, Hopland, CA 95449, (415) 641-5212.

30 - JN 01 ♀ **Learn to Bicycle Tour - Wisconsin,** see Woodswomen on page 81, 108

30 - JN 01 ♀♂ **Pride (Phoenix),** Contact local businesses for details.

30 - JN 01 ♀ **Virginia Women's Music Festival,** Join us for our 8th annual festival held at Intouch for 106 acres of music, workshops, games and fun! Swim, boat & go fishing in 7-acre Towanda Lake. Drumfest prior to festival. Location: 20 miles east of Charlottesville, VA. Contact: Intouch, Rte 2, Box 1096, Kent's Store, VA 23084, (804) 589-6542.

Virginia Women's Music Festival
MAY 30 - JUNE 1, 1997
INTOUCH

30 - JN 08 ♀♂ **Tiptoe Through the Two Lips Party Pkg,** see Rainboworld Custom Tours on page 69, FYI 256

31 - JN 01 ♀ **Whitewater Canoe Instruction, Wisconsin,** see Women in the Wilderness on page 81, 108

WHEN TO GO

TRIP/EVENTS CALENDAR

31 - JN 07 ♀♂ Roadtown, Tortola to Roadtown, Tortola Cruise, see Tall Ship Adventures, Inc. on page 74, FYI 340

31 - JN 14 ♂ Islands of Indonesia, see Hanns Ebenstein Travel on page 57, 92

June 97

TBA ♀ Ancient Voices, Exploring Alaska's Glaciers, see Alaska Women of the Wilderness on page 46, 86

TBA ♀ Basic Skill Development (workshop), see Wilderness of Women on page

TBA ♀ Elder Adventure (theme), see Wilderness of Women on page

TBA ♀ Euro Fun Cup '97, Held in conjunction with Oslo's gay pride week, this tournament is open to all lesbians who play handball. Both teams and singles participate. In addition to lots of sport, there are many social activities and a final Great Cup party planned. Location: Oslo, Norway. Contact: S. Kvalheim, Orknoygt. 4, 0658 Oslo, Norway, (47) 2219 4080.

TBA ♂ Euro Pride Package (depart from Australia), see Jornada on page 59, 94

TBA ♀ Fun in the Woods (theme), see Wilderness of Women on page

TBA ♀♂ Gay Pride in Tijuana Tour, see Gay Baja Tours on page 56, FYI 358

TBA ♀♂ Los Angeles Gay Pride Pkgs, see Men on Vacation on page 62, 96

TBA ♂ Los Angeles Pride Pkg (depart from Australia), see Jornada on page 59, 94

TBA ♀♂ New York Gay Pride Pkgs, see Men on Vacation on page 62, 96

TBA ♂ New York Pride Pkg (depart from Australia), see Jornada on page 59, 94

TBA ♀ Point Adolphus Sailing, Whale Watching, Alaska, see Women Sail Alaska on page 81, FYI 363

TBA ♀ Sail to Tenakee Hot Springs (No one Has Cars), see Women Sail Alaska on page 81, FYI 363

TBA ♀ Sailing Seymour Canal, See Icebergs, Alaska, see Women Sail Alaska on page 81, FYI 363

TBA ♀♂ San Francisco Gay Pride Pkgs, see Men on Vacation on page 62, 96

TBA ♂ San Francisco Pride Pkg (depart from Australia), see Jornada on page 59, 94

TBA ♀ Summer Solstice and Earth Awareness (theme), see Wilderness of Women on page

TBA ♀ Whale Watch Kayak Weekends, WA, see Adventure Associates on page 45, 84

01 ♀ Summer Solstice Sail Admiralty Island, Alaska, see Women Sail Alaska on page 81, FYI 363

01 - 07 ♀ Backpacking in Utah, see Cloud Canyon Backpacking on page 50, 88

01 - 08 ♀♂ Pride (Boston), Contact local businesses for details.

01 - 14 ♀ Trekking & Canoeing in Kimberley Mtns, Australia, see Silke's Travel on page 71, FYI 308

02 - 06 ♀ San Juan Island Whale Watch Kayak, see Blue Moon Explorations on page 49

02 - 12 ♀♂ Provence and the South of France, see Experience Plus on page 55, 90

02 - 12 ♀♂ World War II European History, see L'Arc en Ciel Voyages on page 61, 94

02 - 14 ♀♂ Sardinia: Alghero to Cagliari, see Experience Plus on page 55, 90

05 - 08 ♀♂ Gay Day at Magic Kingdom Packages, see Good Time Tours on page 57, FYI 412

05 - 08 ♀♂ Gay/Lesbian Day at Walt Disney World (7th annual), Over 40,000 gays & lesbians are expected to attend this special gathering at Walt Disney World in Orlando, Florida. Scheduled events include parties, dinner shows & parades. Official Gay Day Tour Operator - Good Time Tours, 1-888-GAYFLAS (888-429-3527), (305) 864-9431, Fax: (305) 866-6955.

05 - 09 ♀♂ Gay Day in Orlando Pkg, see Thanks, Babs on page 74, 102

05 - 16 ♀♂ Mediterranean to Scandinavia Cruise, see Pied Piper Travel on page 67, FYI 338

06 - 08 ♀♂ Bahama Cruise (3-night), see Pleasure Travel...Cruise Again Too! on page 68, FYI 339

06 - 09 ♀♂ Gay Day in Orlando, see Men on Vacation on page 62, 96

07 ♀♂ Gay & Lesbian Day at Disney World Party, Jeffrey Sanker is teaming up with Johnny Chism to bring a slick circuit party to the New York back-lot set of Disney World. Few details were available. Contact: (407) 425-4527, (888) 777-8886, Web: http://www.jeffreysanker.com

07 ♀♂ Queens Birthday Ball-Sydney, see Destination Downunder on page 53, FYI 309

07 - 08 ♀♂ Pride (Kansas City), Contact local businesses for details.

07 - 12 ♀♂ Biking in Central France, see Alyson Adventures on page 47, 87

07 - 14 ♀ Creative Dynamics Canoe & Leadership- MN, see Woodswomen on page 81, 108

07 - 14 ♀ Rafting Cataract Canyon, Utah, see Woodswomen on page 81, 108

07 - 14 ♀♂ Roadtown, Tortola to Roadtown, Tortola Cruise, see Tall Ship Adventures, Inc. on page 74, FYI 340

07 - 14 ♀♂ Russia De Luxe, see Kremlin Tours on page 60, FYI 266

07 - 15 ♀ Women Bike Yellowstone-Idaho Loop, see Womantours/Artemis Sailing on page 80, 107

WHEN TO GO

TRIP/EVENTS CALENDAR

08	♀♂	**Pride (Washington DC),** Contact local businesses for details.
08 - 14	♀♂	**Venice: Flat as a Pancake,** see Experience Plus on page 55, 90
09 - 13	♀	**San Juan Island Whale Watch Kayak,** see Blue Moon Explorations on page 49
09 - 22	♀♂	**Giraffic Park African Wildlife Photo Safari,** see Toto Tours on page 75, 102
10 - 17	♀	**Women's Golf Week at Man Friday Resort,** see Above & Beyond Tours on page 45, 83
12 - 15	♀	**Womongathering,** A warm and friendly festival for womyn only at a scenic, private camp. We feature local and nationally-recognized womyn spiritual leaders presenting intensive, experiential workshops reflecting the diversity of beliefs known as Womyn's Spirituality. The crafts area features womyn-made items, such as crystals, also readers, body workers and herbalists. Rain will not disturb your enjoyment, because our dining and workshop areas are covered. Location: In the Pocono Mts. Contact: Womongathering, Box 559, Franklinville, NJ 08322, (609) 694-2037, e-mail: womongathr@aol.com.
12 - 19	♀	**Revisioning Personal Power- Retreat (NM),** see Hawk, I'm Your Sister on page 58, FYI 463
12 - 23	♀♂	**Scots on the Rocks-Hiking Scottish Highlands,** see Toto Tours on page 75, 102
13 - 15	♀♂	**Big Sky Regional Rodeo,** Billings, MT. Call: BSGRA, (406) 248-2993.
13 - 15	♀	**Carson River Rafting,** see Merlyn's Journeys on page 63, FYI 370
13 - 15	♀	**Sea Kayaking, Catalina Island, CA,** see Women in Motion on page 80, 107
13 - 15	♀♂	**Southeast Leatherfest '97,** This regional event is sponsored by the Atlanta Leatherfest Pride Committee, is a festival celebrating the leather/S&M/fetish lifestyle, and features the Preliminary Southeast Drummer and Drummer Boy and the Mr. & Ms. Georgia Leather contests. Location: Atlanta, GA. Contact:P.O. Box 78974, Atlanta, GA 30357, (888) 285-1955, Email: kyle@crl.com Web: http:www.crl.com/~jeje/
13 - 16	♀	**Horseback Riding in Wisconsin,** see Woodswomen on page 81, 108
13 - 20	♀♂	**Valley of Kings - Biking in France,** see Alyson Adventures on page 47, 87
14	♀	**Alberton Gorge Wild Women Raft Trip,** see Pangaea Expeditions on page 66, FYI 456
14 - 15	♀	**Raft American R., California,** see Mariah Wilderness Expeditions on page 61, 96
14 - 21	♀♂	**Best of Russia,** see Kremlin Tours on page 60, FYI 266
14 - 21	♀♂	**Roadtown, Tortola to Roadtown, Tortola Cruise,** see Tall Ship Adventures, Inc. on page 74, FYI 340
14 - 23	♀♂	**Italian Gay Discovery Tour,** see Zipper Travel Association on page 82, FYI 252
14 - 24	♀♂	**Galicia and the Minho,** see Experience Plus on page 55, 90
14 - 30	♀♂	**Hungary-Vienna, Czech Republic, Paris,** see David's Trips and Tours on page 52, 89
15	♀♂	**Pride (Fort Lauderdale),** Contact local businesses for details.
15 - 21	♀	**Young Women, Strong Women,** see Alaska Women of the Wilderness on page 46, 86
15 - 22	♀♂	**Alaska Cruise,** see Pied Piper Travel on page 67, FYI 338
15 - 22	♀♂	**Pride (Oslo),** Contact local businesses for details.
16 - 20	♀	**San Juan Island Whale Watch Kayak,** see Blue Moon Explorations on page 49
17 - 24	♀♂	**Eurogames 1997,** see L'Arc en Ciel Voyages on page 61, 94
17 - 28	♀♂	**Bike Across Italy: Pisa to Venice,** see Experience Plus on page 55, 90
19 - 23	♀♂	**EuroGames V,** The European gay & lesbian sports championships featuring events such as basketball, soccer, bowling, volleyball, handball, swimming, table-tennis, chess & ballroom dancing. 4,000 people expected to attend. Location: Paris, France. Contact: EuroGames V, BP 120, 75623 Paris Cedex 13, France, (33-1) 48 24 26 88, Fax: (33-1) 48 24 26 87.
19 - 25	♀♂	**Bicycling Tour of Provence, France,** see Progressive Travels on page 68, 99
19 - 29	♀♂	**EuroPride '97,** This annual event, a celebration of gay life in Europe, takes place in a different European country each year. Activities include parties, art exhibits and photography. Various festivals, such as singing, dance and film are highlighted. The event culminates in a large parade. Location: Paris, France. Contact: SOFIGED, 29 rue Bleue, 75009 Paris, France, (33-1) 48 24 26 88, Fax: (33-1) 48 24 26 87.
19 - 29	♀	**Lesbian Pride in Paris,** A gathering of lesbians from all over Europe coinciding with the 1997 EuroGames & EuroPride in Paris. Events will include a concert, a week of films by women filmmakers, a 2-day conference on lesbian political involvement, a lesbian march & a forum involving lesbian & feminist groups from many parts of the world. Location: Paris, France. Contact: Lesbia Magazine, BP 19, 75521

WHEN TO GO

TRIP/EVENTS CALENDAR

		Paris cedex 11, France, (33-1) 43 48 89 54, Fax: (33-1) 43 48 11 79.
19 - 29	♀♂	**Pride (Houston),** Contact local businesses for details.
19 - 30	♀♂	**Bike Across Italy: Pisa to Venice,** see Experience Plus on page 55, 90
19 - 30	♀♂	**Paris and Europride Paris '97,** see Thanks, Babs on page 74, 102
20 - 22	♀	**Canoeing, Cycling Red Cedar Trail, Wis.,** see Woodswomen on page 81, 108
20 - 22	♀	**Golf Weekend, San Diego,** see Women in Motion on page 80, 107
20 - 25	♀♂	**London & Brighton,** see Above & Beyond Tours on page 45, 83
20 - 29	♀♂	**Pride (Berlin),** Contact local businesses for details.
20 - 29	♀♂	**San Francisco Int'l. Lesbian & Gay Film Festival,** The 21st annual event features over 200 films and videos from around the world. Contact: (415) 703-8663 (after 5/28/97)
20 - 30	♀♂	**Gay Arctic Sailing Expedition,** see Oceanwide Expeditions on page 64
20 - 30	♀♂	**LA & SF Gay Pride Package,** see Doin' It Right - in Puerto Vallarta on page 53
20 - JY 07	♀♂	**Grand Europe #1,** see Above & Beyond Tours on page 45, 83
21	♀♂	**Pride (Hartford),** Contact local businesses for details.
21 - 22	♀♂	**Pride (Los Angeles),** Los Angeles Gay and Lesbian Pride Celebration, Sat: noon-mid., Sun: 11am-11pm. Location: West Hollywood, CA, West Hollywood Park. Contact: (213) 860-0701, Email: Lapride@aol.com
21 - 28	♀♂	**Edelweiss: Hiking in Swiss Alps,** see Alyson Adventures on page 47, 87
21 - 28	♂	**EuroPride Paris,** see Men on Vacation on page 62, 96
21 - 28	♀♂	**London, Paris, Amsterdam Europride '97 Cruises,** see RSVP Travel Productions/Club RSVP on page 70, 100
21 - 28	♀♂	**Roadtown, Tortola to Roadtown, Tortola Cruise,** see Tall Ship Adventures, Inc. on page 74, FYI 340
21 - 28	♂	**Westward Ho! Nat'l Parks SW Utah,** see Toto Tours on page 75, 102
21 - AG 04	♀♂	**Imperial Capitals,** see Our Family Abroad on page 65, 98
21 - JY 04	♂	**Journey to Ancient Greece,** see Spirit Journeys on page 72, 101
21 - JY 06	♀♂	**Tanzania Wildlife Cultural Safari,** see Adventure Associates on page 45, 84
22 - 22	♀♂	**House of Blues,** Sunday Tea Dance, Los Angeles largest party takes place every month and features headlining performers debuting their newest creations. Attendance 1,400. Contact: http://www.jeffreysanker.com/events.htm
22 - 28	♀	**Backpacking in Utah,** see Cloud Canyon Backpacking on page 50, 88
22 - 28	♀♂	**Europride '97 London & Paris Tour,** see RSVP Travel Productions/Club RSVP on page 70, 100
22 - 28	♀♂	**Mountain Bike, Raft Big Sky Country,** see Pangaea Expeditions on page 66, FYI 456
22 - JY 01	♀	**Alice with the Lot (A Wildewise/Silke Event),** see Silke's Travel on page 71, FYI 308
23 - 27	♀	**Rafting Deschutes River, OR,** see Adventure Associates on page 45, 84
23 - 28	♂	**Utah Canyons, Rafting, B&B,** see Passage to Utah on page 67, FYI 496
23 - JY 08	♀♂	**White Nights Festival,** see Allegro Travel on page 46, 86
24 - 30	♀♂	**EuroPride '97 in Paris Tour,** see Our Family Abroad on page 65, 98
24 - 30	♀♂	**Europride '97 in Paris & Scandinavian Cruise,** see Travel Affair on page 75, 103
24 - 30	♀	**Writing Retreat with Deena Metzger, New Mexico,** see Hawk, I'm Your Sister on page 58, FYI 463
24 - JY 06	♀	**Canoeing, Sea Kayaking, Lake Superior (Ontario),** see Women in the Wilderness on page 81, 108
25 - 29	♀♂	**EuroSalon Gay Life Fair,** There will be more than 250 exhibitors from all over Europe for this gay life fair, which is part of the celebration around EuroPride '97. Contact: Paris '97 - SOFIGED, 13/15 rue de la Verrerie, F- 75004 Paris, France. English info line: (33-1) 40 50 63 00, French info line: (33-1) 40 50 69 69, Fax: (33-1) 44 54 51 62, E-mail: paris97@hol.fr, Web: www.paris97.com or www.europride.com.
25 - 29	♀♂	**Nordic Gay Pride,** see L'Arc en Ciel Voyages on page 61, 94
25 - 30	♀♂	**EuroPride Paris,** see Above & Beyond Tours on page 45, 83
25 - 30	♀	**Raft Main Salmon R., Idaho,** see Mariah Wilderness Expeditions on page 61, 96
26 - 29	♀	**Sailing Lake Superior, Apostle Islands,** see Women in the Wilderness on page 81, 108
26 - 30	♀♂	**Euro Pride 1997,** see L'Arc en Ciel Voyages on page 61, 94
26 - 30	♀♂	**Pride (Key West),** Contact: (305) 293-0494
26 - JY 05	♂	**Great Amazon Adventure Cruise,** see Hanns Ebensten Travel on page 57, 92
27 - 28	♀♂	**Rafting S & Middle Fork, American R.,** see Mariah Wilderness Expeditions on page 61, 96
27 - 29	♀♂	**Canadian Rockies Int'l Rodeo,** Calgary, AB, Canada. Call: ARGRA, (403) 541-8140.
27 - 29	♀	**Golden Threads Celebration (11th Annual),** A celebration for lesbians over 50 and their friends from the US, Canada, and other countries, held in

FERRARI GUIDES' GAY TRAVEL A to Z - 18th EDITION

WHEN TO GO

TRIP/EVENTS CALENDAR

		Provincetown, MA. There is no age restriction and membership in Golden Threads is not required to participate. Events include workshops, a banquet, dance and live entertainment. Contact: Golden Threads, PO Box 60475, Northampton, MA 01060-0475. Web: http://members.aol.com/goldentred/index.htm
27 - 29	♀♂	**Heartland Regional Rodeo,** Omaha, NE. Call: HGRA, (402) 597-1689.
27 - 29	♀♂	**Pride (Atlanta),** Contact local businesses for details.
27 - 30	♀♂	**San Francisco Gay Pride Package,** see Doin' It Right - in Puerto Vallarta on page 53
27 - JY 01	♀	**Four-Day Canoe Trip in Killarney Prov. Prk, Canada,** see Wild Women Expeditions on page 79, FYI 330
27 - JY 06	♀♂	**Netherlands Gay Pride Party Pkg,** see Rainboworld Custom Tours on page 69, FYI 256
27 - JY 08	♂	**Call of the Wild-Alaskan Wildlife Safari,** see Toto Tours on page 75, 102
27 - JY 08	♀♂	**Grand Palio - Florence, Siena, Milan,** see Allegro Travel on page 46, 86
27 - JY 11	♀♂	**Italian Holiday-Our Family Aborad,** see Our Family Abroad on page 65, 98
28	♂	**Intrepid IV,** The largest party of NYC's Gay Pride weekend. Six thousand gay men will party on the world's largest aircraft carrier, the USS Intrepid. Location: New York, NY. Contact: (800) GAY-3433 or your local IGTA travel agent, Web: http://www.inch.com/~circuitx
28	♂	**Spin II,** Another of Bad Boy Club Montreal's (BBCM) circuit events during Toronto Gay Pride celebration. Location: Toronto, Canada. Contact: (514) 875-7026, Fax: (514) 875-9323 Web: http://www.bbcm.org
28 - 29	♀♂	**Pride (Minneapolis),** Contact local businesses for details.
28 - 29	♀♂	**Pride (San Francisco),** Contact local businesses for details.
28 - JY 03	♀♂	**Int'l Conference on AIDS (12th annual),** Roundtable discussion groups, speakers and workshops on both the scientific and social aspects of AIDS will be featured. There will also be numerous outdoor activities and cultural activities. 12,000 participants from around the world are expected to attend this event. Location: Geneva, Switzerland. Contact Conference Secretariat: Congrex (Sweden) AB, Box 5619, 114 86 Stockholm, Sweden, (46-8) 612 6900, Fax: (46-8) 612 6292.
28 - JY 04	♀♂	**Church Tour of Mexico,** see Mercury Cruise & Tour on page 62
28 - JY 05	♀♂	**Best of Russia,** see Kremlin Tours on page 60, FYI 266
28 - JY 05	♀♂	**London, Paris, Amsterdam Europride '97 Cruises,** see RSVP Travel Productions/Club RSVP on page 70, 100
28 - JY 05	♀♂	**Roadtown, Tortola to Roadtown, Tortola Cruise,** see Tall Ship Adventures, Inc. on page 74, FYI 340
28 - JY 06	♀♂	**Costa Rica Adventure, Raft, Kayak, Bike,** see Mariah Wilderness Expeditions on page 61, 96
28 - JY 06	♀	**Femmes Fatale for the 4th—San Francisco,** see Thanks, Babs on page 74, 102
28 - JY 07	♀♂	**Picos de Europa,** see Experience Plus on page 55, 90
28 - JY 08	♀♂	**Cycling the Dordogne,** see Experience Plus on page 55, 90
28 - JY 13	♀♂	**European Panorama,** see Our Family Abroad on page 65, 98
29	♀♂	**Pride (Chicago),** Contact local businesses for details.
29	♀♂	**Pride (Denver),** Contact local businesses for details.
29	♀♂	**Pride (Seattle),** Contact local businesses for details.
29 - JY 04	♀	**Kayaking South Carolina's Coast,** see Adventures for Women on page 45, FYI 461
29 - JY 05	♀♂	**Montana Big Sky Adventure,** see OutWest Adventures on page 66, FYI 455
30 - JY 04	♀	**Cruise Southern Holland's Canals, Rivers,** see Vaarschool Grietje on page 77, FYI 258
30 - JY 06	♀	**Cruise Alaska Inside Passage,** see Adventure Associates on page 45, 84
30 - JY 07	♀♂	**Amsterdam & Cologne Gay Pride,** see Above & Beyond Tours on page 45, 83

July 97

TBA	♀	**Alaskan Native Expeditions—Anchorage,** see Thanks, Babs on page 74, 102
TBA	♀	**Fat Women's Gatherings,** These are gatherings, for women only, of large-sized women. Workshops, parties, swimming and a representation of vendors specializing in products for large-sized women, especially clothing, are included. This is not a lesbian organization, per se, but all fat women are most welcome. The 1996 event will be held during the 4th weekend in July. Location: Northern New Jersey. For all meetings, contact Carole Campbell, PO Box 1154, New York, NY 10023 (212) 721-8259.
TBA	♀♂	**Fouth of July in Toronto, Canada,** see New England Vacation Tours on page 64
TBA	♀	**Lesbian & Bisexual Women's Celebration (workshop),** see Wilderness of Women on page
TBA	♂	**London Pride Pkg (depart from Australia),** see Jornada on page 59, 94
TBA	♀	**Mademoiselles in Montreal,** see Thanks, Babs on page 74, 102
TBA	♀♂	**Pink Monday at the Tilburg Fair,** This annual gay Monday held in July each year is the gay portion of a larger fair dating back 425 years. Approximately 25,000

WHEN TO GO

TRIP/EVENTS CALENDAR

gays & lesbians attend festivities at local gay establishments and other programmes. Location: Tilburg, The Netherlands. Contact: De GAY Krant, PO Box 10, NL-Best, The Netherlands, (31) 499 391 000, Fax: (31) 499 372 638, E-mail: gaykrant@pop3.worldaccess.nl.

TBA	♀	**Point Adolphus Sailing, Whale Watching, Alaska,** see Women Sail Alaska on page 81, FYI 363
TBA	♀	**Sail to Tenakee Hot Springs (No one Has Cars),** see Women Sail Alaska on page 81, FYI 363
TBA	♀	**Sailing Seymour Canal, See Icebergs, Alaska,** see Women Sail Alaska on page 81, FYI 363
TBA	♀	**Women's Empowerment (workshop),** see Wilderness of Women on page
01 - 05	♀	**San Juan Island Whale Watch Kayak,** see Blue Moon Explorations on page 49
01 - 08	♂	**Swept Away I—Rafting Grand Canyon (Men),** see Toto Tours on page 75, 102
01 - 08	♀♂	**Venice to Florence,** see Experience Plus on page 55, 90
01 - 12	♀♂	**Classical Greece & Turkey,** see Our Family Abroad on page 65, 98
01 - 15	♂	**Summer Teacher's Tour, Thailand,** see Tours to Paradise on page 75, FYI 189
02 - 10	♀♂	**Finnish Festival,** see Allegro Travel on page 46, 86
02 - 12	♀♂	**Istanbul & Yachting Turkey's Turquoise Coast,** see Progressive Travels on page 68, 99
03 - 05	♀♂	**Fourth of July Bahamas Cruise,** see Mercury Cruise & Tour on page 62
03 - 06	♀♂	**Gays For Patsy Firecracker Hoedown,** A weekend long country/western dance party in the heart of Boston, MA held in conjunction with the 4th annual meeting of the Int'l. Assoc. of Gay & Lesbian Country Western Dance Clubs. Contact: Provincetown Reservations (800) 648-0364, Email: gz@pobox.com, Web: http://www.entity.com/gfp/hoedown.html
03 - 06	♀♂	**NW Gay & Lesbian Summer Sports Festival,** Events in 26 different sports, such as softball, volleyball, swimming, diving, sailing & crew, marathons, bowling, croquet and darts, will be held. Special events surrounding the athletics include parties and the annual Orca Boat Cruise. Location: Seattle, WA. Contact: Team Seattle, 1202 E. Pike St #515, Seattle, WA 98112, (206) 322-7769.
03 - 07	♀♂	**Rockies High Country Backpacking,** see Lizard Head Backcountry Tours on page 61, FYI 495
04 - 06	♀♂	**Cologne Gay Pride Package (Hotel & Event Tickets),** see Teddy Travel on page 74, 101
04 - 06	♀♂	**ILGA World Conference,** The 1997 conference will take place in Cologne, Germany. This world conference of the International Lesbian & Gay Assn. ILGA represents over 300 groups worldwide whose aim is to affirm the human rights of the global lesbian and gay community. For information contact: ILGA Administrative Office, Kolenmarkt 81, 1000 Brussels, Belgium, Tel/Fax: (32-2) 502 24 71, E-mail: ilga@glo.be.
04 - 06	♀♂	**Int'l Conference of Gay & Lesbian Jews,** 15th international conference with over 1000 people expected to attend. Events will include workshops, religious services & social events. Location: Dallas, TX. Contact: 14th Int'l. Conference, c/o C.B.S.T. 57 Bethune St, New York, NY 10014, (212) 929-9498.
04 - 06	♀	**July 4th Kick-Back,** Join us for 4 days of playful adventure. Cool off in Towanda Lake with water games, contests, and a luau & live performances on July 6. All other days will be spent in hammocks, lying on the beach, volleyball games & kick-back activities of your choice. No athletic ability is necessary. Camping and cabins are on site. Prizes will be awarded. Location: Ferncliff, VA. Contact: InTouch, Rte 2, Box 1096, Kent's Store, VA 23084, (804) 589-6542.
04 - 06	♀♂	**Laguna Surf 2,** Three days and nights of parties at night...days filled with sun and fun at Laguna Beach, CA. This event brings out the Southern California party crowd by the thousands to enjoy the beautiful beaches and weather. Contact: any Laguna Beach business listed in this guide, Web: http://www.jeffreysanker.com
04 - 06	♀	**Weekend Canal Cruise From Amsterdam,** see Vaarschool Grietje on page 77, FYI 258
04 - 07	♀	**Canoe Trip to Loon Rookery in Canada,** see Wild Women Expeditions on page 79, FYI 330
04 - 10	♀	**Mountaineering, Glacier Travel, Washington State,** see Woodswomen on page 81, 108
04 - 11	♀	**Greek Isles/Turkey Cruise,** see Olivia Cruises & Resorts on page 65, 98
05	♀♂	**Pride (London),** Contact local businesses for details.
05	♂	**Wet Party '97,** This is the second annual Wet Party. Last year's event drew 2,500 hot, sweaty men. Location: Tampa, FL. Contact: (813) 837-4485, Fax (813) 837-0810, Email: TBGMC@aol.com

INTOUCH
JULY 4TH KICK-BACK
July 4-6
1997

FERRARI GUIDES' GAY TRAVEL A to Z - 18th EDITION

WHEN TO GO

TRIP/EVENTS CALENDAR

05 - 12 ♀ **Fiji Women's Week at Man Friday Resort,** see Thanks, Babs on page 74, 102

05 - 12 ♀ **Women-Only 2-Week Vacation at Man Friday-Fiji,** see Silke's Travel on page 71, FYI 308

05 - 12 ♀ **Women's Week at Man Friday Resort,** see Above & Beyond Tours on page 45, 83

06 - 12 ♀ **Canoeing Northern Lakes Loop, MN,** see Woodswomen on page 81, 108

06 - 12 ♀♂ **Home on the Range—Yellowstone Sampler,** see Toto Tours on page 75, 102

06 - 12 ♀ **Kayaking in Aialik Bay, Alaska,** see Alaska Women of the Wilderness on page 46, 86

06 - 12 ♀ **Kenai Fjords Kayaking—Alaska,** see Blue Moon Explorations on page 49

06 - 26 ♀♂ **Bicycle Tour in Canadian Rockies,** see Pangaea Expeditions on page 66, FYI 456

07 - 11 ♀ **Cruise Norhern Holland's Canals,** see Vaarschool Grietje on page 77, FYI 258

07 - 11 ♀ **San Juan Island Whale Watch Kayak,** see Blue Moon Explorations on page 49

07 - 12 ♂ **Black & White Men Together 17th Convention,** This is THE social event of the year, so come early and join our celebration of gay life. This is our 17th anniversary celebration with social activities, workshops & speakers. In Charlotte, NC at the Adams Mark Hotel. Contact: NABMT Convention '97, 1747 Connecticut Ave NW, Washington, DC 20009-1108, (202) 462-3599, (800) NA4-BWMT.

09 - 11 ♀♂ **Three-Day Trek,** see Lodestar Adventures on page 61

09 - 15 ♀♂ **Bastille Day in Paris,** see Our Family Abroad on page 65, 98

10 - 13 ♀ **Yosemite Nat'l Park, California,** see Women in Motion on page 80, 107

10 - 16 ♀ **Young Women, Strong Women,** see Alaska Women of the Wilderness on page 46, 86

10 - 20 ♀♂ **Cycling the Dordogne,** see Experience Plus on page 55, 90

11 - 13 ♀♂ **North Star Regional Rodeo,** St. Paul, MN. Call: NSGRA, (612) 641-0069.

11 - 13 ♀ **Weekend Canal Cruise Amsterdam-Westeinder,** see Vaarschool Grietje on page 77, FYI 258

11 - 15 ♀♂ **Bastille Day in Paris,** see L'Arc en Ciel Voyages on page 61, 94

11 - 18 ♀♂ **Alaska Cruise on the Rotterdam,** see Ocean Voyager on page 64, 97

12 - 18 ♀ **Mountaineering NW Washington,** see Woodswomen on page 81, 108

12 - 18 ♀ **N Cascades Hike, Raft, Bike,** see Adventure Associates on page 45, 84

12 - 19 ♀♂ **Best of Russia,** see Kremlin Tours on page 60, FYI 266

12 - 19 ♀ **Isla Mujeres Lesbian Resort Vacation,** see Club Le Bon on page 51, FYI 341

12 - 21 ♀♂ **England, Scotland & Wales,** see Our Family Abroad on page 65, 98

12 - 21 ♀♂ **Italian Gay Discovery Tour,** see Zipper Travel Association on page 82, FYI 252

13 - 16 ♀ **Nat'l Women and Motorcycling Foundation Conference,** Workshops, informational activities and entertainment. Location: Westerville, OH. Contact: Women's Motorcyclist Foundation, 7 Lent Ave, LeRoy, NY 14482, (716) 768-6054.

13 - 19 ♀ **Canoeing (Lakes, Rivers, Pictographs) in MN,** see Woodswomen on page 81, 108

13 - 19 ♀ **Friends & Family Canoe Trip, North Minnesota,** see Women in the Wilderness on page 81, 108

13 - 25 ♀ **Bicycling in Tuscany, Italy,** see Woodswomen on page 81, 108

14 - 18 ♀ **Cruise Southern Holland's Canals, Rivers,** see Vaarschool Grietje on page 77, FYI 258

14 - 18 ♀ **San Juan Island Whale Watch Kayak,** see Blue Moon Explorations on page 49

14 - 27 ♀♂ **Bicycling Sumatra — Last Frontier,** see VeloAsia Cycling Adventures on page 77, 105

16 - 22 ♀♂ **Montana by Rail & Yellowstone Nat'l Park,** see OutWest Adventures on page 66, FYI 455

17 - 26 ♀ **Wild Women Adventure Trip,** see Pangaea Expeditions on page 66, FYI 456

18 - 20 ♀ **Biking in Big Bear, California,** see Women in Motion on page 80, 107

18 - 20 ♀ **Horseback Riding in the Redwoods,** see Merlyn's Journeys on page 63, FYI 370

18 - 20 ♀ **Mt. Rainier Retreat-Hike, Kayak, Bike,** see Adventure Associates on page 45, 84

18 - 20 ♀ **Rock Climbing, Big Bear Lake, CA,** see Women in Motion on page 80, 107

18 - 20 ♀♂ **Rocky Mtn. Regional Rodeo,** Denver, CO. Call: IGRA, (303) 839-8810.

18 - 27 ♀♂ **North Sea Beach Party Package,** see Rainboworld Custom Tours on page 69, FYI 256

19 - 20 ♀♂ **Rafting S. Fork American R., Calif,** see Mariah Wilderness Expeditions on page 61, 96

19 - 22 ♀ **Raft Rogue R., Oregon,** see Mariah Wilderness Expeditions on page 61, 96

19 - 23 ♀♂ **St. Petersburg, Russia,** see Above & Beyond Tours on page 45, 83

19 - 26 ♀♂ **Rafting, Hiking, Climbing Wyoming,** see Alyson Adventures on page 47, 87

19 - AG 11 ♀♂ **Grand Europe #2,** see Above & Beyond Tours on page 45, 83

FERRARI GUIDES' GAY TRAVEL A to Z - 18th EDITION

WHEN TO GO

TRIP/EVENTS CALENDAR

20 - 24 ♀ **Paddling Adirondack Lake Country,** see Adventures for Women on page 45, FYI 461

20 - 25 ♀ **San Juan Isles Multi-Sport Trip,** see Adventure Associates on page 45, 84

20 - 26 ♀ **Backpacking Olympic Nat'l Park, WA,** see Woodswomen on page 81, 108

20 - 26 ♀♂ **Walking Tour of Olympic Peninsula, WA,** see Progressive Travels on page 68, 99

20 - 26 ♀♂ **Waterfalls & Wildflowers- Hike Colorado,** see Lizard Head Backcountry Tours on page 61, FYI 495

20 - 26 ♀ **Wild Women Adventure Trip,** see Pangaea Expeditions on page 66, FYI 456

20 - 27 ♀ **Canoeing in Quetico, Canada,** see Wild Women Expeditions on page 79, FYI 330

20 - 29 ♀♂ **All-Gay Safari, Costa Rica,** see R&R Eco Tours on page 70

20 - AG 02 ♀♂ **Gay Adventure Charter 1997,** see GPSC Charters on page 57, FYI 240

20 - AG 03 ♀♂ **Grand Safari to Kenya during Migration Season,** see Travel Affair on page 75, 103

21 - 25 ♀ **Cruise Northern Holland Canals,** see Vaarschool Grietje on page 77, FYI 258

21 - 25 ♀ **Inside Passage Whale Watch—BC,** see Blue Moon Explorations on page 49

21 - 26 ♀ **Llama-Assisted Backpacking,** see Lodestar Adventures on page 61

22 - AG 03 ♀♂ **Spain Tour with Our Family Abroad,** see Our Family Abroad on page 65, 98

23 - 26 ♀ **Wild Women Adventure Trip,** see Pangaea Expeditions on page 66, FYI 456

23 - 27 ♀ **Hiking, Canoeing, Wolf Ecology, Minnesota,** see Women in the Wilderness on page 81, 108

23 - 30 ♀♂ **Island Hop the Misty Green Azores,** see Paths Less Taken on page 67, FYI 264

23 - 31 ♀♂ **Alaska & Inside Passage Cruise,** see Our Family Abroad on page 65, 98

23 - AG 01 ♀♂ **Utopia '97—Russia's White Nights,** see Above & Beyond Tours on page 45, 83

24 - 27 ♀♂ **I.G.R.A. Annual Convention,** Salt Lake City, UT. Call: UGRA, (801) 359-7314.

24 - 27 ♀ **Yosemite Skills Course,** see Common Earth Adventures on page 51, 89

25 - 27 ♀ **Drum-Making Ceremony,** see Alaska Women of the Wilderness on page 46, 86

25 - 27 ♀♂ **Pride (San Diego),** Contact local businesses for details.

25 - 27 ♀ **Rafting the American River,** see Merlyn's Journeys on page 63, FYI 370

25 - 27 ♀ **Solo Canoe Instruction, Northern Minnesota,** see Women in the Wilderness on page 81, 108

26 ♀♂ **Crape Myrtle Festival XVII,** Once a party among friends, this festival has evolved into an annual week of events culminating in an outdoor gala. Proceeds from the festival are donated to various Triangle Area AIDS/HIV agencies. Location: Chapel Hill, NC. Contact: (919) 829-1482.

26 ♂ **White Party (Fire Island),** You'll find wall-to-wall beefcake at this traditional summer party. Location: Fire Island, NY. Contact: any Fire Island Business listed in this guide.

26 - 30 ♀♂ **Nat'l Lesbian & Gay Health Conference & HIV Forum,** Over 1300 people will attend the conference, whose theme is "Health Care for the 21st Century: Healthy Families, Healthy Lives, Healthy Communities." About 200 workshops, on such subjects as grant writing, domestic violence, lesbian & gay health, anti-gay violence and substance abuse, will be held. Social activities will surround the event. Location: The Radisson Hotel in Atlanta, GA. Contact: (800) 367-1481.

26 - 31 ♀ **Sea Kayaking Kenai Fjords, Alaska,** see Woodswomen on page 81, 108

26 - AG 02 ♀♂ **Best of Russia,** see Kremlin Tours on page 60, FYI 266

26 - AG 02 ♂ **Swept Away II-Hiking-Intensive Grand Canyon Raft,** see Toto Tours on page 75, 102

27 ♀♂ **Up-Your-Alley Fair (Dore Alley Fair),** San Francisco's Leather Block Party is held at Dore Alley on Folsom between 9th and 10th, from 11am-6pm. Contact: (415) 861-FAIR, Fax: (415) 861-2312. Web: http://www.folsomstfair.com

27 - 27 ♀♂ **House of Blues,** Sunday Tea Dance, Los Angeles largest party takes place every month and features headlining performers debuting their newest creations. Attendance 1,400. Contact: http://www.jeffreysanker.com/events.htm

27 - AG 01 ♀♂ **N Cascades Gourmet Hiking, Lodge,** see Adventure Associates on page 45, 84

27 - AG 01 ♀ **Sea Kayak San Juan Islands, WA,** see Adventure Associates on page 45, 84

27 - AG 02 ♀ **Canoeing Northern Lakes Loop, MN,** see Woodswomen on page 81, 108

27 - AG 02 ♀ **Cruise Holland's Canals Amsterdam to Maastricht,** see Vaarschool Grietje on page 77, FYI 258

27 - AG 02 ♀♂ **Montana Big Sky Adventure,** see OutWest Adventures on page 66, FYI 455

27 - AG 02 ♂ **Pacific Men's Gathering,** A spectrum of adventure, culture & wellness-sharing presented by island men. Hawaiian temple massage, floating shiatsu in thermal springs, volcano lava viewing, traditional but temporary body tattooing, swimming with dolphins, ancient male hula, and more nuture the "aikane" male-

FERRARI GUIDES' GAY TRAVEL A to Z - 18th EDITION   151

WHEN TO GO

male loving that is part of Hawaii's aloha heritage. Contact: Kalani Eco-Resort, RR2 Box 4500, Kehena Beach, HI 96778, (808) 965-7828, for reservations only: (800) 800-6886.

27 - AG 03 ♀♂ **Grand: Mountaineering in Wyoming,** see Alyson Adventures on page 47, 87

28 - 30 ♀♂ **Three-Day Trek in BC — Gay & Lesbian Only,** see Lodestar Adventures on page 61

28 - AG 01 ♀ **Inside Passage Whale Watch—BC,** see Blue Moon Explorations on page 49

28 - AG 01 ♂ **Rafting Desolation Canyon, Utah,** see Passage to Utah on page 67, FYI 496

31 - AG 03 ♀ **Sailing Lake Superior, Apostle Islands,** see Women in the Wilderness on page 81, 108

31 - AG 04 ♀ **Fastwater Canoe Trip, Spanish River, Canada,** see Wild Women Expeditions on page 79, FYI 330

August 97

TBA ♀ **Denali Rail & Inside Passage Adventure,** see Thanks, Babs on page 74, 102

TBA ♀♂ **Dive Sea of Cortez, La Paz, Mexico,** see Undersea Expeditions, Inc. on page 77, 104

TBA ♀ **Earth Awareness (workshop),** see Wilderness of Women on page

TBA ♀ **First Nations and Allies (workshop),** see Wilderness of Women on page

TBA ♀♂ **Gay & Lesbian Softball World Series '97,** Fifty gay & lesbian softball leagues from the USA & Canada send teams to participate in the softball world series. Twenty-two fields are reserved and 2,500 athletes are expected to attend. Location: Minneapolis, MN. Contact: Emerald City Softball Assoc., 1202 E Pike #1177, Seattle, WA 98112, (206) 322-7769.

TBA ♀ **Hiking in Denali National Park,** see Alaska Women of the Wilderness on page 46, 86

TBA ♀ **Maine-ly for You Spring Fling & Autumn Fests,** June and August each year on the premises of a campground with 1800 feet of waterfront, a dock and swimming float. Activities nearby include climbing, canoeing, hiking, water sports. The festivals include women's music, workshops, dancing, crafts, sports. Contact: Maine-ly For You, RR 2 Box 745, Waterford, ME 04088. Oct-May contact: 114 Bennett Ave, Auburn, ME 04210. Tel: (207) 583-6980.

TBA ♀♂ **Northalsted Market Days,** A giant 2-day street fair on Halsted St, Chicago's gayest street. Contact any local gay & lesbian business for information. Location: Chicago, IL.

TBA ♀ **Point Adolphus Sailing, Whale Watching, Alaska,** see Women Sail Alaska on page 81, FYI 363

TBA ♀ **Rites of Passage for Young Women (theme),** see Wilderness of Women on page

TBA ♀ **Sail to Tenakee Hot Springs (No one Has Cars),** see Women Sail Alaska on page 81, FYI 363

TBA ♀ **Sailing Seymour Canal, See Icebergs, Alaska,** see Women Sail Alaska on page 81, FYI 363

TBA ♀♂ **Sea of Cortez Diving,** see Gay Baja Tours on page 56, FYI 358

TBA ♀ **Taos Conference on Feminine Spirituality,** A weekend festival with workshops, crafts & food. This conference investigates the emerging Goddess as alternative spirituality. Speakers have included Z Budapest, Ruth Barrett & Julia Cameron. Rituals will be performed. Both men & women are welcome, but participation is 85% women. Location: Taos, NM. Contact: The Corn Maiden, 127 Bent St, Taos, NM 87571, (505) 751-3739.

TBA ♀ **Wanna Play? (theme),** see Wilderness of Women on page

TBA ♀♂ **Western Caribbean Cruise on Celebrity's Horizon,** see Mercury Cruise & Tour on page 62

TBA ♀ **Women Celebrating Our Diversity,** A multicultural gathering highlighting creative expression with workshops, networking, drumming, camping, movement, sweat and mud pits, volleyball, entertainment and talent shows, dances, dye painting, sharing, writing, drawing, swimming, outdoor gallery. Location: Twin Oaks Community, Louisa, VA. Contact: Twin Oaks Community Women's Gathering, Rte 4, Box 169, Louisa, VA 23093, (703) 894-5126.

TBA ♀ **Backpack Olympic Wilderness Coast,** see Adventure Associates on page 45, 84

01 - 03 ♀ **Camping on Navarro River,** see Merlyn's Journeys on page 63, FYI 370

01 - 04 ♀♂ **Floating Pride Amsterdam,** see Above & Beyond Tours on page 45, 83

01 - 05 ♀ **Reading About Wilderness & Canoeing Retreat,** see Women in the Wilderness on page 81, 108

01 - 06 ♀ **Kenai Fjord Kayaking—Alaska,** see Blue Moon Explorations on page 49

01 - 08 ♀ **Expressive Arts Camp, Dance, Drama, Ont., Canada,** see Wild Women Expeditions on page 79, FYI 330

01 - 10 ♀♂ **Amsterdam Pride Party Package,** see Rainbowworld Custom Tours on page 69, FYI 256

01 - 10 ♀♂ **Pride (Amsterdam),** Contact local businesses for details.

WHEN TO GO

TRIP/EVENTS CALENDAR

01 - 11 ♀♂ **Great Britain & Edinburgh Festival,** see Above & Beyond Tours on page 45, 83

02 ♀♂ **Twist IV,** Bad Boy Club of Montreal (BBCM) celebrates Montreal Pride Weekend (Divers/Cit, 97) with this mid-summer white event party. Dress code: white with a twist. Location: Montreal, Canada. Contact: (514) 875-7026, Fax: (514) 875-9323, Web: http://www.bbcm.org

02 - 07 ♀ **Llama-Assisted Backpacking in BC,** see Lodestar Adventures on page 61

02 - 07 ♀ **Rafting Salmon R., Idaho (Young Women's Leadership,** see Wild Women on page 79, 106

02 - 08 ♀ **Hiking in Denali Park,** see Woodswomen on page 81, 108

02 - 08 ♀ **Scuba & Tour Kauai, Hawaii,** see Women in Motion on page 80, 107

02 - 09 ♀♂ **The Oregon Coast: A Walking Tour,** see Experience Plus on page 55, 90

02 - 14 ♀♂ **To China with Kremlin Tours,** see Kremlin Tours on page 60, FYI 266

02 - 17 ♀♂ **Scandinavia & Russia Cruise,** see Our Family Abroad on page 65, 98

02 - 18 ♂ **Mountains and Ancient Cities of Turkey,** see Adventure Bound Expeditions on page 45, 85

03 - 05 ♀ **Raft Tuolumne R., California,** see Mariah Wilderness Expeditions on page 61, 96

03 - 07 ♀ **Walking Adirondack Lake Country,** see Adventures for Women on page 45, FYI 461

03 - 08 ♀ **Hiking Grand Tetons, ID Lodge,** see Adventure Associates on page 45, 84

03 - 08 ♀ **Olympic Explorer Lodge-Based Hiking, WA,** see Adventure Associates on page 45, 84

03 - 08 ♀♂ **Sea Kayak San Juan Islands, WA,** see Adventure Associates on page 45, 84

03 - 09 ♀♂ **Back country Bliss-Backpack Beartooth Wilderness,** see OutWest Adventures on page 66, FYI 455

03 - 09 ♀ **Backpacking Mt., Rainier, Washington,** see Woodswomen on page 81, 108

03 - 09 ♀ **Sail Canals and Rivers Maastricht-Charleville,** see Vaarschool Grietje on page 77, FYI 258

03 - 09 ♀♂ **Waterfalls & Wildflowers-Hike Colorado,** see Lizard Head Backcountry Tours on page 61, FYI 495

03 - 16 ♀ **Canoeing Canadian Wilds - MN, Canada,** see Woodswomen on page 81, 108

07 - 10 ♀♂ **Hotlanta River Expo (19th annual),** A welcome party and the Miss Hotlanta Contest kicks off the weekend, then there is the Mr. Hotlanta National Finals with contestants from Australia and Canada included. Rafting the Chattahoochee River on Saturday is the main event, with a contest fo the Best Theme Raft '97. A Saturday night party is scheduled afterward. Location: Atlanta, GA. Contact: Hotlanta, PO Box 8375, Atlanta, GA 31106, (404) 874-3976.

07 - 10 ♂ **Hotlanta River Expo '97 Parties,** Atlanta, Georgia is host to the party circuit with its ever-popular "Hotlanta River Expo." This tried-and-true event has parties constantly. Contact: (404) 874-3976, Web: http://www.hotlanta.org/~hotlanta

07 - 10 ♀ **Northwoods Canoe Retreat for Elders,** see Women in the Wilderness on page 81, 108

07 - 11 ♀ **Trail Riding Grand Tetons, Wyoming,** see Bar H Ranch on page 48, FYI 506

08 - 11 ♀ **Beginners Canoe Trip, Canada,** see Wild Women Expeditions on page 79, FYI 330

08 - 11 ♂ **Rafting, Hiking Lodore Canyon, Utah,** see Passage to Utah on page 67, FYI 496

09 - 16 ♀♂ **Best of Russia,** see Kremlin Tours on page 60, FYI 266

09 - 16 ♀ **Swept Away III-Rafting Grand Canyon (Women),** see Toto Tours on page 75, 102

09 - 18 ♀♂ **Italian Gay Discovery Tour,** see Zipper Travel Association on page 82, FYI 252

09 - 19 ♀♂ **The Minho Wine Country,** see Experience Plus on page 55, 90

09 - 24 ♀♂ **European Panorama,** see Our Family Abroad on page 65, 98

10 - 14 ♀ **Hiking Adirondack High Peaks,** see Adventures for Women on page 45, FYI 461

10 - 15 ♀ **Sea Kayak in San Juan Islands, WA,** see Adventure Associates on page 45, 84

10 - 16 ♀♂ **Crested Butte Mountain Biking,** see Lizard Head Backcountry Tours on page 61, FYI 495

10 - 16 ♀ **Hiking in Denali Park, Alaska,** see Woodswomen on page 81, 108

10 - 16 ♀ **Sail French Rivers Charleville to Reims,** see Vaarschool Grietje on page 77, FYI 258

11 - 14 ♀ **Midweek Beginners Canoe Trip, Canada,** see Wild Women Expeditions on page 79, FYI 330

11 - 14 ♀ **Raft Green R., Utah,** see Mariah Wilderness Expeditions on page 61, 96

11 - 15 ♀ **Sailing in San Juan Islands,** see Merlyn's Journeys on page 63, FYI 370

11 - 16 ♀♂ **Pacific NW Multi-Sport Lodge Trip,** see Adventure Associates on page 45, 84

11 - 18 ♀ **All-Women's Multi-Activity Camping Tour, BC,** see Lodestar Adventures on page 61

12 - 17 ♀ **Fly Fishing West Yellowstone,** see Adventure Associates on page 45, 84

FERRARI GUIDES' GAY TRAVEL A to Z - 18th EDITION

WHEN TO GO

TRIP/EVENTS CALENDAR

12 - 17 ♂ **Men's R&R New Mexico Summer Retreat,** see Spirit Journeys on page 72, 101

12 - 17 ♀ **Michigan Womyn's Music Festival 1997,** A 6-day, all-womyn, camping event on 650 acres near Hart, in a beautifully wooded area of northwest Michigan. This is the oldest and largest of the U.S. womyn's music festivals. Activities include 40 performances on 3 stages, 300 workshops and 140 craftswomyn. It is a magical week in a village of womyn's culture, with music, dance, theater, arts, sports and lots of networking. Services for childcare, over-50's camping, differently-abled resources and ASL. 6000-7000 womyn from the US, Canada and many other countries throughout the world will attend. Contact: WWTMC, PO Box 22, Walhalla, MI 49458, (616) 757-4766.

13 - 17 ♀ **Trail Riding Grand Tetons Wyoming,** see Bar H Ranch on page 48, FYI 506

13 - 19 ♀ **Young Women, Strong Women,** see Alaska Women of the Wilderness on page 46, 86

14 - 17 ♀ **Elderflower Womenspirit Festival (9th annual),** Workshops, rituals, movement, crafts, drumming, music, discussions, and fun in the woods for women and girls. A part of the camp is a Clean and Sober area. Tent and cabin camping. Relaxed atmosphere, reasonably rates. Location: Near Mendocino, CA. Contact: Elderflower, PO Box 460790, San Francisco, CA 94146-0790, (916) 658-0697 or (415) 263-5719.

14 - 18 ♀ **Canoe Trip in Temagami Wilderness, Canada,** see Wild Women Expeditions on page 79, FYI 330

14 - 23 ♂ **Cruise the Galapagos Islands in Style,** see Hanns Ebensten Travel on page 57, 92

15 - 19 ♀ **Native Spirituality Workshop, Ontario, Canada,** see Wild Women Expeditions on page 79, FYI 330

15 - 22 ♀♂ **Cruise to Alaska,** see AAD All About Destinations on page 45

15 - 31 ♀ **Sail Greek Isles Private Yacht,** see Adventure Associates on page 45, 84

16 - 23 ♀♂ **Summer Cruise in Western Caribbean,** see Travel Affair on page 75, 103

16 - SE 01 ♀♂ **Hungary, Vienna, The Czech Republic & Czech Spa,** see David's Trips and Tours on page 52, 89

17 ♂ **GMHC Morning Party,** The 15th annual GMHC fundraiser is one of the most exciting dance parties in the world and certainly one of the oldest AIDS fundraisers. Beautifully set along the Fire Island, NY seashore, this party has beautiful men, splashy-costumed groups, and hot dance music. Contact: GMHC (212) 337-3519 early. Tickets sell-out very fast!

17 - 22 ♀ **North Cascades Gourmet Hiking,** see Adventure Associates on page 45, 84

17 - 23 ♀ **Backpacking Isle Royale, Michigan,** see Woodswomen on page 81, 108

17 - 23 ♀ **Sail French Rivers Reims to Charleville,** see Vaarschool Grietje on page 77, FYI 258

17 - 24 ♀♂ **Five-Country Land Cruise,** see L'Arc en Ciel Voyages on page 61, 94

17 - 28 ♀ **Hiking Austria's Vorarlberg Alps,** see Adventures for Women on page 45, FYI 461

18 - 22 ♀ **Hiking in Ancient Forests of Oregon,** see Merlyn's Journeys on page 63, FYI 370

19 - 23 ♀ **Trail Riding Grand Tetons Wyoming,** see Bar H Ranch on page 48, FYI 506

19 - SE 01 ♂ **Umbrella Tour, Thailand,** see Tours to Paradise on page 75, FYI 189

20 - 22 ♀♂ **Three-Day Trek, Kootenays, BC,** see Lodestar Adventures on page 61

20 - 30 ♀♂ **Cycling the Dordogne,** see Experience Plus on page 55, 90

21 - 24 ♀ **Northwoods Retreat, Superior Nat'l Forest, MN,** see Women in the Wilderness on page 81, 108

21 - 24 ♀ **Writing & Hiking-Yosemite,** see Common Earth Adventures on page 51, 89

21 - 27 ♀ **Sea Kayak West Vancouver Island, BC,** see Oceanwomyn Kayaking on page 64, FYI 357

21 - 29 ♂ **Dutch Treat-Sailing Inland Seas of Holland,** see Toto Tours on page 75, 102

22 - 24 ♀♂ **Rafting Middle Fork American R., Cal.,** see Mariah Wilderness Expeditions on page 61, 96

22 - 25 ♀ **Horseback Riding in Wisconsin,** see Woodswomen on page 81, 108

22 - 25 ♂ **Mr. Leather Europe & 24th ECMC Conference,** Held in conjunction with Manchester's Mardi Gras, a popular event celebrating gay sexuality and the fight against HIV and AIDS, with accommodations at the Univ. of Manchester Institute of Science and Technology (UMIST). Located on the edge of Manchester's "gay village" and 1/4 mile from Piccadilly railway station, UMIST provides affordable, safe and clean accommodations. Events include Welcome Buffet, Mardi Gras Parade (biggest gay parade in Europe), ECMC Annual Dinner at "The Town Hall," Mr Leather Europe contest and two European Leather Parties with a farewell fireworks display. Location: Manchester, England. Contact: MSCMSC (ECMC97), P.O. Box 104, Manchester, M6O 1GY, England. Fax: (44 161) 839 3884. Web: http://

WHEN TO GO

TRIP/EVENTS CALENDAR

www.users.dircon.co.uk/~mscmsc/msc97.htm

22 - 26 ♀ **Canoe Trip in Temagami Wilderness, Canada,** see Wild Women Expeditions on page 79, FYI 330

22 - 28 ♀♂ **Alaska Cruise on Celebrity's Horizon,** see Mercury Cruise & Tour on page 62

22 - 31 ♀ **Wild Women Adventure Trip,** see Pangaea Expeditions on page 66, FYI 456

23 ♀ **Alberton Gorge Wild Women Raft Trip,** see Pangaea Expeditions on page 66, FYI 456

23 - 30 ♀♂ **Best of Russia,** see Kremlin Tours on page 60, FYI 266

23 - 30 ♀♂ **Emerald Cities & Enchanted Forests-Pacific NW,** see Toto Tours on page 75, 102

23 - SE 02 ♀♂ **Legacy of the Incas,** see Our Family Abroad on page 65, 98

23 - SE 05 ♀♂ **Imperial Capitals,** see Our Family Abroad on page 65, 98

24 - 28 ♀ **Sea Kayaking San Juan Islands, Washington,** see Woodswomen on page 81, 108

24 - 28 ♀ **Tour Santa Fe & Taos, New Mexico,** see Women in Motion on page 80, 107

24 - 29 ♀♂ **Llama-Assisted Backpacking, BC,** see Lodestar Adventures on page 61

24 - 30 ♀♂ **OutWestern Trails—Gay/Lesb Ranch Week,** see OutWest Adventures on page 66, FYI 455

24 - 30 ♀ **Sail Canals & Rivers Charleville to Maastricht,** see Vaarschool Grietje on page 77, FYI 258

24 - 31 ♂ **Week of Haute Cuisine at Paris's le Cordon Bleu,** see Club Hommes/Worldguest on page 51, FYI 204

25 - 29 ♀ **W Vancouver Island & Clayquot Sound Kayak,** see Blue Moon Explorations on page 49

25 - 31 ♀♂ **Whitewater Rafting Salmon River's Middle Fork,** see Pangaea Expeditions on page 66, FYI 456

25 - 31 ♀ **Wild Women Adventure Trip,** see Pangaea Expeditions on page 66, FYI 456

25 - SE 01 ♀♂ **Alaska Cruise,** see Pied Piper Travel on page 67, FYI 338

26 - SE 02 ♀♂ **San Juan to New York City Cruise,** see Pied Piper Travel on page 67, FYI 338

26 - SE 03 ♀♂ **A Culinary Cycling Circus,** see Experience Plus on page 55, 90

26 - SE 06 ♀♂ **Classical Greece & Turkey,** see Our Family Abroad on page 65, 98

27 - SE 06 ♀ **Backpacking in Alaska,** see Cloud Canyon Backpacking on page 50, 88

28 - 31 ♀ **The Club Skirts Monterey Bay Women's Weekend,** Located at the Hyatt Regency Monterey, this is a stylised women's weekend at a luxury hotel, with evening mega-dances, daily pool parties and a clebrity golf tournament to benefit the Human Rights Campaign Fund. Contact: MT Productions (415) 337-4962 Email: MTPROD1@aol.com

28 - 31 ♀ **Wild Women Adventure Trip,** see Pangaea Expeditions on page 66, FYI 456

28 - SE 01 ♀♂ **Desert Foraging-Ariz. Superstition Mtns,** see Lizard Head Backcountry Tours on page 61, FYI 495

28 - SE 01 ♀♂ **RIP'D '97,** Austin, Texas rolls out its second party of the summer over Labor Day Weekend. There are five different events throughout the weekend including the RIP'D 97 dance party Saturday Night and "Last Splash" on Sunday at Lake Travis. Contact: (514) 478-1210, (512) 419-4763, Web:http://alienz.com/rip

29 - 30 ♀ **Raft Middle Fork, American R., Calif.,** see Mariah Wilderness Expeditions on page 61, 96

29 - 31 ♀♂ **Missouri Gay Rodeo,** Kansas City, MO. Call: (816) 224-6139.

29 - 31 ♀♂ **Southern Decadence (25th Anniversary),** A three-day (Labor Day Weekend) gay Mardi Gras with parties, river cuises, drag queen parade (Sunday) & more. Events take place at or near the French Quarter gay bars. Contact: French Quarter Reservation Service, (504) 523-1246, Fax: (504) 527-6327, Email: fqrs@accesscom.net

29 - 31 ♀♂ **Zia Regional Rodeo,** Albuquerque, NM. Call: NMGRA, (505) 255-5045.

29 - SE 01 ♀♂ **Baja Mexico Cruise-Labor Day Wknd,** see AAD All About Destinations on page 45

29 - SE 01 ♀ **Canoe Trip in Killarney Provincial Park, Canada,** see Wild Women Expeditions on page 79, FYI 330

29 - SE 01 ♀ **Point Reyes Getaway,** see Merlyn's Journeys on page 63, FYI 370

30 - SE 05 ♀ **Women Bike Canadian Rockies,** see Womantours/Artemis Sailing on page 80, 107

30 - SE 14 ♀♂ **Greece, Turkey Sailing Odyssey,** see Adventure Associates on page 45, 84

31 - 31 ♀ **Midwest Womyn's Autumnfest (3rd annual),** A one-day outdoor womyn's music & cultural festival held in a meadow, with workshops, craftswomyn, theater & performing arts. Work exchange available. Approximately 1,500 womyn are expected to attend this 3rd annual event. Electricity & flush toilets on site. Location: Dekalb, IL. Contact: Athena Productions, 217 S 2nd St #193, Dekalb, IL 60115, (815) 748-5359, e-mail: Autumnfest@aol.com.

31 - SE 05 ♀♂ **Gay/Lesbian Llama-Assisted Backpacking in BC,** see Lodestar Adventures on page 61

FERRARI GUIDES' GAY TRAVEL A to Z - 18th EDITION

WHEN TO GO

TRIP/EVENTS CALENDAR

31 - SE 06	♀	**Autumn Canoeing in Minnesota,** see Woodswomen on page 81, 108
31 - SE 06	♀♂	**Church Tour of Alaska,** see Mercury Cruise & Tour on page 62
31 - SE 06	♀♂	**Montana Big Sky Adventure,** see OutWest Adventures on page 66, FYI 455
31 - SE 06	♀	**Sail Canals, Rivers, Maastricht to Amsterdam,** see Vaarschool Grietje on page 77, FYI 258
31 - SE 14	♂	**Sailing Cruise in Turkey,** see Hanns Ebensten Travel on page 57, 92

September 97

TBA	♂	**Bicycling in Italy-Mantua to Venice,** see Men on Bikes on page 62, FYI 248
TBA	♂	**Bicycling in Italy-Rome to Capri, Pompei,** see Men on Bikes on page 62, FYI 248
TBA	♂	**Bicycling in Italy-Syracuse to Taormina,** see Men on Bikes on page 62, FYI 248
TBA	♂	**Big Men's Convergence '97,** A Big Bash presented by Girth and Mirth, a social club for big men and their admirers. This event features hospitality suites and five big events. Contact: GMC-NY, Convergence, '97, PO Box 10, Pelham, NY 10803.
TBA	♂	**Club Med, Mallorca, Spain,** see Alternative Holidays on page 47, 86
TBA	♀	**Earth Based Spirituality (theme),** see Wilderness of Women on page
TBA	♀♂	**Ensenada Pride at the Beach! (Mex),** see Gay Baja Tours on page 56, FYI 358
TBA	♂	**Folsom St. Fair Pkg (depart from Australia),** see Jornada on page 59, 94
TBA	♀♂	**Gay Group Cruise on QE2 to London,** see Anywhere Travel on page 47
TBA	♀	**Hiking, Kayaking & King Kong, Hawaii,** see Thanks, Babs on page 74, 102
TBA	♀♂	**Labor Day Weekend in Montreal,** see New England Vacation Tours on page 64
TBA	♀♂	**Morocco Exotic Kingdoms, High Atlas Hike,** see Adventure Associates on page 45, 84
TBA	♀	**New Hampshire Women's Music Festival (4th annual),** Sponsored by the NH Feminist Connection, this event features NH musicians and includes children's activities, collaborative weaving, vendors, and booths for women's organizations. Held outdoors, rain or shine. Everyone is welcome. Location: At the Highlands Ski area in central New Hampshire. Contact: NH Feminist Connection, PO Box 311, Concord, NH 03302-0311, (603) 225-3501.
TBA	♀	**Ohio Lesbian Festival,** An all-day event from 11am to midnight, with crafts, workshops, performances, volleyball, picnic and play area, market area and cafe. Contact: LBA (Lesbian Business Assn), PO Box 02086, Columbus, OH 43202, (614) 267-3953.
TBA	♀	**Paris Walking Tour,** see Thanks, Babs on page 74, 102
TBA	♀	**River Rafting, Russia,** see Hawk, I'm Your Sister on page 58, FYI 463
TBA	♀♂	**Road to Mandalay Cruise, Burma & Thailand,** see Travel Affair on page 75, 103
TBA	♀	**Sailing Alaska - Taku Harbor, Funter Bay, Etc.,** see Women Sail Alaska on page 81, FYI 363
TBA	♀♂	**Steel Party,** One of the newer additions to the circuit scene, the Steel Party in Pittsburgh, PA is an annual fundraiser for the Persad Center. Events usually include a welcome party on Friday and the main event on Saturday night. Contact: (412) 441-9786.
TBA	♀	**Survivors of Childhood Sexual Abuse (theme),** see Wilderness of Women on page
TBA	♀♂	**Twelve Gods Party Packages,** see Holigays on page 58, 92
TBA	♂	**Twelve Gods Party Pkgs (Mykonos),** see Men on Vacation on page 62, 96
TBA	♀	**Women's Weekend II,** A smaller gathering than the women's weekend in May, this event marks the end of the summer season in Russian River, CA. It usually takes place towards the end of September. Contact: We the People newspaper, (707) 573-8896.
01 - 05	♀	**W Vancouver Island & Clayquot Sound Kayak,** see Blue Moon Explorations on page 49
01 - 10	♀♂	**The Basque Country,** see Experience Plus on page 55, 90
01 - 10	♀♂	**Transatlantic Crossing on the Norway,** see Ocean Voyager on page 64, 97
03 - 07	♂	**Twelve Gods Party,** The first global circuit benefit ever organized for AIDS research will be held on the beautiful island of Mykonos, Greece. A week of festivities is planned for an international crowd of partygoers from the US, Canada, Europe & Australia. Contact: Windmills Travel & Tourism, (30 289) 23877/26555/26556/26557, Fax: (30 289) 22066 (ONLY fax is operative November to March), E-mail: windmills@travelling.gr
03 - 09	♀	**Womenfest '97,** Women take over Key West during this women's week featuring sunset cruises, glass bottom boat rides, a tennis tournament, water & sand volleyball, scuba diving, a film festival, and trolley tours of Key West. There will be a fair with vendors carrying women-oriented products, as well as women's art, live entertainment, food & drink. Location: Key West, FL.

156   FERRARI GUIDES' GAY TRAVEL A to Z - 18th EDITION

WHEN TO GO

TRIP/EVENTS CALENDAR

Contact: Jacqueline Harrington, director, Womenfest '97, 201 Coppitt Rd #106A, Key West, FL 33040, Hdq: (800) 374-2784, (305) 296-4238, KWF Bus. Guild (800) 535-7797.

03 - 13 ♀♂ **Provence and the South of France,** see Experience Plus on page 55, 90

04 - 07 ♀♂ **Nat'l Conference of Gay & Lesbian Catholics,** Over 100 lesbian & gay Catholics and religious & lay ministers gather from across the USA. Discussed are common goals of welcoming gays & lesbians, offering spiritual support, helping reconcile past hurts & providing educational opportunities for parents, clergy & the faith community at large. Location: Long Beach, CA. Contact: NACDLGM, 433 Jefferson St, Oakland, CA 94607, (510) 465-9344, Fax: (510) 451-6998, E-mail: nacdlgm@aol.com.

04 - 08 ♀ **Photography in Killarney Provincial Park, Canada,** see Wild Women Expeditions on page 79, FYI 330

05 - 06 ♀ **Lake Tahoe Getaway,** see Merlyn's Journeys on page 63, FYI 370

05 - 07 ♀ **Whitewater Rafting (Beg & Interm) No. Calif,** see Women in Motion on page 80, 107

05 - 14 ♀♂ **Costa Rica Coast to Coast,** see Above & Beyond Tours on page 45, 83

05 - 14 ♀ **Finnish Lapland: Sami Culture, Wilderness Canoeing,** see Women in the Wilderness on page 81, 108

05 - 26 ♀ **Peru, Macchu Picchu, Bolivia,** see Silke's Travel on page 71, FYI 308

06 - 06 ♂ **Miss Fire Island Contest (32nd Annual),** This annual event at the end of summer on Fire Island, NY is always an interesting affair and features the best in female impersonation. Contact any Fire Island business for more information, or (212) 337-3519.

06 - 06 ♀♂ **Swim for Life in Provincetown,** A 1.4-mile swimathon held in Provincetown Harbor at one of the most famous gay and lesbian resort destinations. Weekend activities include a Mermaid Brunch after the swim. Both leisurely swimmers and real competitors participate in this AIDS benefit. Location: Provincetown, MA. Contact: Provincetown Swim For Life, PO Box 819, Provincetown, MA 02657, (508) 487-3684.

06 - 12 ♀♂ **Mountain Bike, Raft Big Sky Country,** see Pangaea Expeditions on page 66, FYI 456

06 - 14 ♀♂ **Golden Ring Adventure Tour,** see Kremlin Tours on page 60, FYI 266

06 - 15 ♀♂ **England, Scotland & Wales,** see Our Family Abroad on page 65, 98

06 - 15 ♀♂ **Italian Gay Discovery Tour,** see Zipper Travel Association on page 82, FYI 252

06 - 17 ♀♂ **Bike Across Italy: Pisa to Venice,** see Experience Plus on page 55, 90

06 - 21 ♂ **Sail Turquoise Coast of Turkey,** see Adventure Bound Expeditions on page 45, 85

07 - 13 ♀ **High Sierras Hiking (horseback-assisted),** see Adventure Associates on page 45, 84

07 - 13 ♀♂ **Walking Tour of Burgundy, France,** see Progressive Travels on page 68, 99

08 - 12 ♀ **W Vancouver Island & Clayquot Sound Kayak,** see Blue Moon Explorations on page 49

08 - 13 ♀ **R&R Mountain Bike Tour, Kootenays, BC,** see Lodestar Adventures on page 61

08 - 13 ♀ **Trinity Alps Backpacking,** see Common Earth Adventures on page 51, 89

08 - 15 ♀♂ **A Little Tour in Tuscany,** see Experience Plus on page 55, 90

08 - 22 ♂ **Pilgrimage to Mystic Andes, Macchu Picchu,** see Spirit Journeys on page 72, 101

11 - 14 ♀ **Backpacking North Shore in Minnesota,** see Woodswomen on page 81, 108

11 - 14 ♀♂ **Int'l P-FLAG Convention,** The 16th annual convention of Parents & Friends of Lesbians and Gays (P-FLAG) will include keynote speakers and workshops on gay and lesbian issues, such as coalition building, networking, public service announcements, sexual orientation, religious and spiritual issues, AIDS, etc. This year's theme: Love Takes Action — The PFLAG Family Adventure. There will also be entertainment, a special concert and scheduled day trips. Location: Clarion Plaza Hotel in Orlando, FL. Contact: P-FLAG, 1101 14th St NW #1030, Washington, DC 20005, Tel: (202) 638-4200, Fax: (202) 638-0243.

11 - 14 ♀ **Northwoods Retreat, Superior Nat'l Forest, MN,** see Women in the Wilderness on page 81, 108

11 - 14 ♀ **Sailing Lake Superior, Apostle Islands,** see Women in the Wilderness on page 81, 108

11 - 18 ♀♂ **Wines & Cheeses of Portugal,** see Paths Less Taken on page 67, FYI 264

11 - 24 ♂ **Dungeons & Castles, Europe: The Leatherman's Tour,** see Travel Keys Tours on page 76, 104

11 - OC 10 ♀♂ **Best of South Pacific,** see Above & Beyond Tours on page 45, 83

12 - 14 ♀ **Dillon Beach Getaway,** see Merlyn's Journeys on page 63, FYI 370

12 - 14 ♀ **Fire Island's Fifth Annual Women's Weekend,** A full weekend of round-the-clock lesbian activities, entertainment, workshops, vendors and more. Location: Fire Island, NY. Contact any

FERRARI GUIDES' GAY TRAVEL A to Z - 18th EDITION 157

WHEN TO GO

12 - 16	♀	**Creative Writing Workshop, Ontario, Canada,** see Wild Women Expeditions on page 79, FYI 330
12 - 25	♀♂	**Italian Holiday-Our Family Abroad,** see Our Family Abroad on page 65, 98
13 - 20	♀♂	**Fall in Fiji at Man Friday Resort,** see Above & Beyond Tours on page 45, 83
13 - 20	♀♂	**Scuba Dive in Fiji,** see Undersea Expeditions, Inc. on page 77, 104
13 - 23	♂	**Sumatra Overland Escapade,** see Otto Travel Hawaii on page 65
13 - OC 10	♀♂	**Best of the South Pacific,** see Destination Downunder on page 53, FYI 309
14 - 28	♀♂	**Expedition to Vilcabamba,** see Hanns Ebensten Travel on page 57, 92
15 - 20	♀	**Paris Women's Tour,** see Women in Motion on page 80, 107
15 - 25	♀♂	**Provence and the South of France,** see Experience Plus on page 55, 90
18 - 29	♀♂	**Bike Across Italy: Pisa to Venice,** see Experience Plus on page 55, 90
18 - OC 01	♀	**Women's Sacred Journey to Ireland,** see Sounds & Furies on page 72, FYI 244
19 - 20	♀	**Gold Country Getaway,** see Merlyn's Journeys on page 63, FYI 370
19 - 21	♀♂	**Pikes Peak United Rodeo,** Colorado Springs, CO. Call: CGRA, (303) 839-8810.
19 - 21	♀	**Wild Western Women's Weekend,** Learn and show off your two steppin', line dancing, clogging and square dancing. Dance all day and night! What a weekend with live bands playing country & western music all evening! Also Crazy Feats rodeo, contests and a hay ride. Location: At Fire Island Business or (212) 337-3519.

INTOUCH Wild Western Women's Weekend Sept 19-21, 1997

19 - 28	♀♂	**Turkey With Our Family Abroad,** see Our Family Abroad on page 65, 98
20 - 20	♂	**Rudely Elegant Red Party,** This annual event in Columbus, Ohio is the vision of one man and consistently delivers non-stop party action with a flair all its own. This event has been running for 20+ years and draws a crowd of over 2,500. Contact: (614) 297-6453.
20 - 26	♀	**Backpacking & Leadership- Grand Canyon, AZ,** see Woodswomen on page 81, 108
20 - 27	♀♂	**Best of Russia,** see Kremlin Tours on page 60, FYI 266
20 - 28	♀	**Women Bike Zion, Grand Canyon,** see Womantours/ Artemis Sailing on page 80, 107
20 - OC 03	♀♂	**Germany With Our Family Abroad,** see Our Family Abroad on page 65, 98
20 - OC 03	♀♂	**Imperial Capitals,** see Our Family Abroad on page 65, 98
20 - OC 05	♀♂	**European Panorama,** see Our Family Abroad on page 65, 98
21 - 27	♀	**Backpacking in Utah,** see Cloud Canyon Backpacking on page 50, 88
21 - 27	♀♂	**Gay/Lesbian Multi-Activity Adventure Tour in BC,** see Lodestar Adventures on page 61
21 - 27	♀♂	**Hike Utah's Arches & Canyonlands,** see Lizard Head Backcountry Tours on page 61, FYI 495
21 - 27	♀♂	**OutWestern Trails—Gay/ Lesb Ranch Week,** see OutWest Adventures on page 66, FYI 455
21 - 28	♀♂	**Rafting the San Juan River, Utah,** see Pangaea Expeditions on page 66, FYI 456
21 - 28	♂	**Vineyards of Chateauneuf du Pape,** see Club Hommes/ Worldguest on page 51, FYI 204
23 - 27	♀♂	**Gay & Lesbian Soccer World Cup,** Annual international soccer championship with both men's & women's divisions. Location: Washington, DC. Contact: Washington, DC Federal Triangles Soccer Club, PO Box 15563, Washington, DC 20003-0563.
23 - OC 02	♀♂	**Iberian Capitals,** see Above & Beyond Tours on page 45, 83
23 - OC 20	♀♂	**Grand Europe #3,** see Above & Beyond Tours on page 45, 83
26 - 27	♀	**Horseback Riding in the Redwoods,** see Merlyn's Journeys on page 63, FYI 370
26 - 28	♀♂	**Greater San Diego Rodeo,** San Diego, CA. Call: GSGRA (San Diego Chapter), (619) 298-4708.
26 - OC 05	♀	**Desert Women's Quest,** see Common Earth Adventures on page 51, 89
26 - OC 06	♀♂	**Incarceration,** see Above & Beyond Tours on page 45, 83
27	♂	**Incarceration Party- Melbourne, Australia,** see Destination Downunder on page 53, FYI 309
27 - 28	♀♂	**Mr. Drummer Contest,** These are the finals for winners of numerous regional Mr. Drummer contests throughout the world. Each contestant will perform a fantasy skit. Location: San Francisco, CA. Contact: Mr. Drummer Contest, PO Box 410390, San Francisco, CA 94141-0390, (415) 252-1195.
28 - 28	♀♂	**Folsom Street Fair,** A street fair with live bands, dancing, entertainment and booths with leather items for sale. The fair is just one of the many events surrounding the Mr. Drummer Contest Finals, which take place the same weekend. Location: San Francisco, CA. Contact: Drummer Magazine, (415) 252-1195 or SMMILE, (415) 861-FAIR, Fax: (415) 861-2312.

WHEN TO GO

TRIP/EVENTS CALENDAR

28 - OC 03 ♀	**Bicycling Wine Country in California,** see Woodswomen on page 81, 108
28 - OC 04 ♀	**Backpacking Grand Canyon, Arizona,** see Woodswomen on page 81, 108
28 - OC 04 ♀♂	**Hiking, Biking Fall Colors in Upper Michigan,** see Toto Tours on page 75, 102
28 - OC 08 ♀♂	**Galicia and the Minho,** see Experience Plus on page 55, 90
29 - OC 07 ♀	**Backpacking in Utah,** see Cloud Canyon Backpacking on page 50, 88
29 - OC 09 ♀♂	**Provence and the South of France,** see Experience Plus on page 55, 90

October 97

- **TBA** ♀♂ **Aida in Luxor,** see Allegro Travel on page 46, 86
- **TBA** ♀ **All-Girl's Scuba Dive in Roatan, Honduras,** see Undersea Expeditions, Inc. on page 77, 104
- **TBA** ♀♂ **Bali, Lombok Island Paradise Adventure,** see Adventure Associates on page 45, 84
- **TBA** ♂ **Bicycling in Italy-San Marino to Florence,** see Men on Bikes on page 62, FYI 248
- **TBA** ♂ **Castro St Fair Pkg (depart from Australia),** see Jornada on page 59, 94
- **TBA** ♀♂ **EcuadorAdventure/ Galapagos Cruise,** see Adventure Associates on page 45, 84
- **TBA** ♀♂ **Gay Night at Disneyland,** Scheduled for either Oct. 23 or Oct. 31, 8pm-1am, at Disneyland in Anaheim, CA. The general public will not be admitted during this gay and lesbian Private Holiday Party at Disneyland (7000-8,000 gays & lesbians expected). Contact: Odyssey Adventures, (805) 222-7788, Fax: (805) 222-7787, PO Box 221477, Newhall, CA 91322.
- **TBA** ♀ **Hawaii Women's Week,** see Remote Possibilities on page 69, FYI 426
- **TBA** ♀♂ **Hellball '97,** Held over Halloween, Hellball is San Francisco's largest costume/ dance party extravaganza. Large cash prizes for the costume contest draw participants from all over the USA. Benefits Continuum and Halloween San Francisco. Contact: Businesses in San Francisco, or Web: http://206.15.12.13/hellball/info.html
- **TBA** ♀♂ **Int'l Gay & Lesbian Aquatics Competition,** Swimming, diving, synchronized swimming and water polo are among the events featured at this international competiton which takes place on the Columbus Day weekend. Location: San Diego, CA.
- **TBA** ♀ **Lesbenwoche (Lesbian Week in Berlin, Germany),** Held in late Oct. during Lesbian Week in Berlin, the lesbian presence is felt throughout the city. This year's program incudes women's music performances, films, slide shows, poetry readings and thousands of lesbians. Workshops will feature lesbian sexuality, safer sex, lesbian prostitution, lesbians of color, immigreps and exiles and lesbians with AIDS. Accommodation can be arranged. Contact: Berliner Lesbenwoche, c/o Rat und Tat, Schillerpromenade 1, 1000 Berlin 44, Germany (49) (30) 621 47 53.
- **TBA** ♀ **Peak-a-Week Khumbu Traverse,** see Lois Lane Expeditions on page 61
- **TBA** ♀♂ **Scuba Diving Great Barrier Reef,** see Oz Dive/Passport to Paradise on page 66
- **TBA** ♀♂ **South Africa Tour,** see Holigays on page 58, 92
- **TBA** ♀♂ **Sydney Sleaze Ball,** see Beyond the Blue on page 49, FYI 307
- **TBA** ♂ **Sydney Sleaze Ball Pkg,** see Jornada on page 59, 94
- **TBA** ♀♂ **Trek Mt. Everest Area, Nepal,** see Adventure Associates on page 45, 84
- **TBA** ♀♂ **Trek Royal Villages Himalayas—Nepal,** see Adventure Associates on page 45, 84
- **TBA** ♀ **Wise Festival,** Held in October in Western Australia around the full moon. A 4-day full-moon camping festival with workshops, arts, crafts, spirituality & entertainment. Participatory - bring your own music, too. Contact RMB, 335 Forest Grove 6286, WA, Australia, (61-97) 577 578.
- **TBA** ♀ **Yuppies in Yucatan— Cancun, Mexico,** see Thanks, Babs on page 74, 102
- **TBA** ♀ **Zimbabwe & South Africa,** see Wild Women on page 79, 106
- **01 - 05** ♀ **Ladies-Only Hike, Swim, Spa Adventure,** see L'Arc en Ciel Voyages on page 61, 94
- **01 - 06** ♀♂ **Sydney Sleaze Ball,** see Above & Beyond Tours on page 45, 83
- **01 - 09** ♀♂ **Coasting to the Algarve,** see Experience Plus on page 55, 90
- **01 - 11** ♀♂ **Istanbul & Yachting Turkey's Turquoise Coast,** see Progressive Travels on page 68, 99
- **02 - 09** ♀♂ **A Little Tour in Tuscany,** see Experience Plus on page 55, 90
- **02 - 11** ♀♂ **Prague, Vienna, Budapest,** see Above & Beyond Tours on page 45, 83
- **02 - 14** ♂ **Buying Antiques in European Markets,** see Travel Keys Tours on page 76, 104
- **03 - 05** ♀♂ **Atlantic Stampede Rodeo,** Washington, DC. Call: ASGRA, (202) 298-0928.
- **03 - 05** ♀ **Sisterfest,** An annual retreat for Black lesbians sponsored by United Lesbians of African

FERRARI GUIDES' GAY TRAVEL A to Z - 18th EDITION

WHEN TO GO

TRIP/EVENTS CALENDAR

03 - 09 ♀ **Bicycling & Whale Watching - Provincetown,** see Woodswomen on page 81, 108

03 - 12 ♀♂ **Heart of Europe,** see Kremlin Tours on page 60, FYI 266

04 ♀♂ **Sleaze Ball,** An annual theme ball in which participants dress in sleezy costumes. About 17,000 participate annually in the ball. Location: R.A.S. Showgrounds in Sydney, Australia. Contact: Box 1064, Darlinghurst 2010, NSW Australia or call: (61-2) 9557 4332

04 - 11 ♀♂ **Best of Russia,** see Kremlin Tours on page 60, FYI 266

04 - 11 ♀ **Canoeing Labyrinth Canyon, Utah,** see Women in the Wilderness on page 81, 108

04 - 11 ♀ **Isla Mujeres Lesbian Resort Vacation,** see Club Le Bon on page 51, FYI 341

04 - 18 ♀ **Amazon Rainforest in Peru,** see Women in the Wilderness on page 81, 108

05 - 11 ♀♂ **Pinnacles, Fins, Spires-Utah Hiking,** see Lizard Head Backcountry Tours on page 61, FYI 495

06 - 08 ♀♂ **Luxury Hot Springs Llama Trek in BC,** see Lodestar Adventures on page 61

06 - 18 ♀♂ **Greek Isles & Turkey Cruise,** see Ocean Voyager on page 64, 97

07 - 20 ♂ **Banana Festival, Thailand,** see Tours to Paradise on page 75, FYI 189

08 - 14 ♂ **Black & Blue Party/Festival,** Sunday, October 12 is the largest party in North America as Montreal and its infamous Bad Boy Club hosts the mega-event of the year. Planned for the 3-day weekend of US Columbus Day and Canadian Thanksgiving, revelers will have many choices of gay parties and cultural activities. The party itself draws over 10,000 participants. Location: Montreal, Canada. Contact: BBCM, P.O. Box 1253, Station "B", Montreal, QC, Canada H3B 3K9, (514) 875-7026, Fax: (514) 875-9323, Email: bbcm@sim.qc.ca Web: http://www.bbcm.org

09 - 12 ♀♂ **Living in Leather XII, Nat'l Conference,** A conference celebrating the diversity of the pan-sexual leather, SM, fetish community, with panel discussions, seminars, workshops, craftspeople, erotic equipment and literature. Location: Portland, OR. Contact: NLA International, 3439 N.E. Sandy Blvd. #155, Portland, OR 97232, (619) 899-4406, Web: http://www.nla-i.com.

09 - 21 ♀♂ **Peru, Macchu Picchu, Mystic Andes,** see Spirit Journeys on page 72, 101

10 - 13 ♀ **Autumn Outdoor Getaway, Canada,** see Wild Women Expeditions on page 79, FYI 330

10 - 13 ♀ **Yosemite Getaway,** see Merlyn's Journeys on page 63, FYI 370

10 - 17 ♀♂ **A Little Tour in Tuscany,** see Experience Plus on page 55, 90

10 - 18 ♀ **Women Bike Natchez Trace,** see Womantours/Artemis Sailing on page 80, 107

11 - 13 ♂ **Luv Ball,** Vancouver, BC Canada, is the setting for another of Jeffrey Sankers productions in cooperation with local talent Will Gorges. Main event on Saturday night with many events at the local bars. Contact: (888) 777-8886.

11 - 17 ♀ **Scuba, Tour Big Island, Hawaii,** see Women in Motion on page 80, 107

11 - 18 ♀♂ **Fall Wine Cruise Along the Rhine River,** see Travel Affair on page 75, 103

11 - 20 ♀♂ **Italian Gay Discovery Tour,** see Zipper Travel Association on page 82, FYI 252

11 - 20 ♀♂ **Treasures of Italy,** see Above & Beyond Tours on page 45, 83

12 - 18 ♀ **Rafting San Juan River, Utah, Wild'ness Literature,** see Women in the Wilderness on page 81, 108

12 - 19 ♂ **Arizona Autumn Quest, Chanting, Rituals,** see Spirit Journeys on page 72, 101

12 - 19 ♀ **Women's Week in Provincetown (12th annual),** The world's finest lesbian resort goes all out for this week-long, town-wide extravaganza. Special gallery exhibitions, workshops & seminars, the biggest and brightest names in women's entertainment, community dinner and, of course, the formal prom are why thousands of women make this so much fun! Sponsored by the Women Innkeepers of Provincetown. Make reservations early. Location: Provincetown, MA. Contact: Box 573, Provincetown, MA 02657 FMI.

12 - 28 ♀♂ **South East Asia,** see Our Family Abroad on page 65, 98

13 - 15 ♀♂ **Luxury Hot Springs Llama Trek in BC,** see Lodestar Adventures on page 61

14 - 25 ♀♂ **Classical Greece & Turkey,** see Our Family Abroad on page 65, 98

14 - 26 ♀♂ **Spain Tour with Our Family Abroad,** see Our Family Abroad on page 65, 98

17 - 19 ♀♂ **Int'l Pride Conference (IAL/GPC),** InterPride '97 is the annual meeting of the International Association of Gay/Lesbian Pride Coordinators, Inc. and will be held in New York, NY. Contact: Web: http://www.interpride.org

17 - 26 ♀♂ **Fantasy Fest in Key West,** Held on Halloween weekend, this is an island-wide Halloween party, with

WHEN TO GO

TRIP/EVENTS CALENDAR

dances, shows, crowds in the streets, non-stop revelry for men and women. This year's theme is "TV Jebbies" and is the 19th annual event. Location: Key West, FL. Contact any gay business in the Key West listings for information, or call: (305) 296-1817, Web: http://www.gaykeywestfl.com

17 - 26 ♀♂ **Pink Cruise Venice to Greek Islands,** see Teddy Travel on page 74, 101

17 - 27 ♀♂ **Ancient Egypt,** see Our Family Abroad on page 65, 98

17 - 27 ♀♂ **Pink Cruise (Venice-Greek Isles),** see Holigays on page 58, 92

17 - 30 ♀♂ **Italian Holiday-Out Family Abroad,** see Our Family Abroad on page 65, 98

18 - 25 ♀♂ **Best of Russia,** see Kremlin Tours on page 60, FYI 266

18 - 25 ♀♂ **Southwest Canyons and Culture,** see Experience Plus on page 55, 90

18 - 29 ♂ **Destination Laos,** see Otto Travel Hawaii on page 65

18 - NO 02 ♂ **Ehiopinan Mountains & Tribal Cultures,** see Adventure Bound Expeditions on page 45, 85

19 - 26 ♂ **Fantasia Fair (23rd annual),** This 23rd anniversary event is a week of workshops and social events providing practical, social and educational experiences for novice and advanced male-to-femme crossdressers. Topics such as personal grooming and feminine expression are covered, with emphasis on makeup and hairstyling. Seminars cover legal and medical aspects and personal growth. Suppers, a Fantasy Ball, two awards banquets, a fashion show, a kite fly, a picnic and AIDS benefit ball, whale watches, video parties and house parties are included. Location: Provincetown, MA. Contact: Fantasia Fair XXIII, c/o Outreach Institute of Gender Studies, Dept. PI, 126 Western Ave #246, Augusta, ME 04330, Tel/Fax: (207) 621-0858.

23 - 26 ♀♂ **I.G.R.A. 1997 Finals Rodeo,** Phoenix, AZ. Call: AGRA, (602) 265-8166.

24 - 26 ♂ **Body Electric,** Celebrate the Body Erotic with conscious breathwork & sacred rituals. Feel at home in your erotic body. Contact: Kalani Eco-Resort, RR2 Box 4500, Kehena Beach, HI 96778, (808) 965-7828, for reservations only: (800) 800-6886.

24 - 27 ♀♂ **Fantasy Fest Cruise Miami to Key West,** see ZMAX Travel & Tours Inc. on page 82, 109

24 - NO 02 ♂ **Amsterdam Leather Pride Party Pkg,** see Rainboworld Custom Tours on page 69, FYI 256

25 - NO 01 ♀♂ **Halloween Caribbean Cruise,** see AAD All About Destinations on page 45

25 - NO 01 ♀ **Lesbian Spa Resort Vacation-Mexico,** see Club Le Bon on page 51, FYI 341

25 - NO 01 ♀ **Mexico Resort (Club Med Huatulco),** see Olivia Cruises & Resorts on page 65, 98

25 - NO 01 ♀♂ **Morocco With Our Family Abroad,** see Our Family Abroad on page 65, 98

25 - NO 01 ♀♂ **Puerto Vallarta Caring for Caregivers Trip,** see Doin' It Right - in Puerto Vallarta on page 53

25 - NO 13 ♀ **Annapurna Dhanlagiri Trek-Nepal,** see Silke's Travel on page 71, FYI 308

26 - NO 01 ♀♂ **Gay Caribbean Cruise,** see Windjammer Barefoot Cruises on page 79

26 - NO 02 ♂ **Adventure Camp,** A fun frolic in Hawaii's volcanos, waters & forests. Build new friendships, hike to secluded beaches, descend into lava caves, kayak streams into the sea, bathe in crater lakes, etc. Contact: Kalani Eco-Resort, RR2 Box 4500, Kehena Beach, HI 96778, (808) 965-7828, for reservations only: (800) 800-6886.

26 - NO 02 ♂ **Halloween All-Gay Windjammer Cruise,** see Advance Damron Vacations on page 45, 84

27 - 31 ♀ **Women Bike Calif Wine Country,** see Womantours/Artemis Sailing on page 80, 107

27 - NO 07 ♀♂ **Expedition to Easter Island,** see Hanns Ebensten Travel on page 57, 92

27 - NO 07 ♀♂ **Expedition to Easter Island,** see Hanns Ebensten Travel on page 57, 92

28 - NO 04 ♀♂ **Halloween/Day of the Dead in Puerto Vallarta,** see Doin' It Right - in Puerto Vallarta on page 53

30 - NO 02 ♀♂ **New Orleans Halloween Parties,** see David's Trips and Tours on page 52, 89

31 - NO 02 ♀♂ **EPOA - Conference 1997,** The Fourth Annual European Pride Coordinators Conference will be held in Stockholm, Sweden. Contact: Web: http://www.interpride.org

31 - NO 02 ♀♂ **Int'l Rainbow Golf Classic,** The first all-lesbian and -gay international full handicap golf tournament will be held at the legendary Bayshore Golf Club on Miami Beach. Prize awards are valued at $10,000. Also planned are special Halloween events in South Beach, private cocktail parties and a grand awards banquet. Tournament air and hotel packages and sightseeing events are available. Location: Miami Beach, FL. Contact: Vic Ruggiero at the Rainbow Golf Classic info line (212) 206-6900 or (800) 429-6969, Fax: (212) 206 6904, E-mail: club@worldquest.com.

INT'L RAINBOW GOLF CLASSIC
Miami Beach, FL
Oct 31 to Nov 2, 1997

31 - NO 02 ♀♂ **Palm Springs Regional Rodeo,** Palm Springs, CA. Call: GSGRA (Desert Empire Chapter), (619) 320-8686.

FERRARI GUIDES' GAY TRAVEL A to Z - 18th EDITION   161

WHEN TO GO

November 97

TBA	♀	**Babes Aboard to Baja, Copper Canyon, Mexico,** see Thanks, Babs on page 74, 102
TBA	♀	**Cycle Across America "Peddle for the Cure",** see Women in Motion on page 80, 107
TBA	♀	**New Zealand Adventure,** see Adventure Associates on page 45, 84
TBA	♀	**Polar Bear Ecology Trip, Hudson Bay,** see Wild Women on page 79, 106
01 - 08	♀♂	**Follow the Trail of the Moors—Spain,** see Paths Less Taken on page 67, FYI 264
01 - 08	♀♂	**October Revolution's 80th Anniversary Tour,** see Kremlin Tours on page 60, FYI 266
01 - 08	♀♂	**Puerto Vallarta Grief Support Tour,** see Doin' It Right - in Puerto Vallarta on page 53
01 - 08	♀♂	**Puerto Vallarta Pampering/ Shopping Tour,** see Doin' It Right - in Puerto Vallarta on page 53
01 - 08	♀	**Scuba, Wildlife in Roatan,** see Woodswomen on page 81, 108
01 - 11	♀	**Costa Rica Raft, Sea Kayak, Beaches,** see Mariah Wilderness Expeditions on page 61, 96
03 - 17	♂	**Fall Special Tour, Thailand,** see Tours to Paradise on page 75, FYI 189
05 - 18	♀♂	**Cooking School, Elephant Trek, Rafting-Thailand,** see Progressive Travels on page 68, 99
06 - 09	♀	**Las Vegas Hearts of the West Festival Pkg,** see Thanks, Babs on page 74, 102
06 - 16	♀♂	**Unorthodox Pilgrimage to Israel,** see Toto Tours on page 75, 102
07 - 09	♂	**Fire & Ice '97,** This is the fourth annual circuit party in Phoenix, Arizona and it all happens over Veteran's Day Weekend. Last year's attendance topped 2,000 and this three-day event benefits Phoenix Body Positive. A Friday night party kicks off the weekend's events followed by the Fire & Ice party on Saturday night. Top-notch DJs and community participation makes this event a must on the circuit calendar. Contact: (602) 708 FIRE (708-3473), Web: http://www.fireandice.com
07 - 09	♂	**Men's Couples Workshop,** see Spirit Journeys on page 72, 101
07 - 09	♀♂	**Palm Springs Pride Wknd Pkg,** see Gay Baja Tours on page 56, FYI 358
07 - 09	♀♂	**Texas Gay Rodeo (14th annual),** Houston, TX. Call: TGRA (Houston chapter), (713) 777-1444.
07 - 16	♀♂	**Sinterklaas Celebration Party Pkg,** see Rainboworld Custom Tours on page 69, FYI 256
07 - 17	♀♂	**Ancient Egypt,** see Our Family Abroad on page 65, 98
08 - 09	♀	**Integrated Leadership Seminar - Minnesota,** see Woodswomen on page 81, 108
08 - 15	♀♂	**Club RSVP—Puerto Vallarta,** see RSVP Travel Productions/Club RSVP on page 70, 100
08 - 15	♀♂	**Puerto Vallarta Investment Tour,** see Doin' It Right - in Puerto Vallarta on page 53
08 - 16	♀♂	**Yucatan & Mexico City,** see Our Family Abroad on page 65, 98
09 - 15	♂	**Golf & Ocean Villa Vacation, Los Cabos, Mex,** see Club Hommes/ Worldguest on page 51, FYI 204
15 - 22	♀	**Barbados,** see Club Le Bon on page 51, FYI 341
15 - 22	♀♂	**Russia De Luxe,** see Kremlin Tours on page 60, FYI 266
15 - 24	♀♂	**Italian Gay Discovery Tour,** see Zipper Travel Association on page 82, FYI 252
15 - 30	♀♂	**Kenya & Tanzania Safari,** see Our Family Abroad on page 65, 98
16 - 27	♂	**Dream Splendor-Thailand North to South,** see Otto Travel Hawaii on page 65
19 - 30	♀♂	**Bicycling Vietnam — Rainforest Revealed,** see VeloAsia Cycling Adventures on page 77, 105
20 - 26	♀♂	**Gay Costa Rica - 7 Nights,** see Mercury Cruise & Tour on page 62
21 - 27	♀♂	**London Theater,** see Above & Beyond Tours on page 45, 83
21 - DE 01	♀♂	**Ancient Egypt,** see Our Family Abroad on page 65, 98
21 - DE 01	♀♂	**Lush Life—Thanksgiving in Costa Rica,** see Toto Tours on page 75, 102
22 - 29	♀♂	**Dive Reefs of Honduras,** see Undersea Expeditions, Inc. on page 77, 104
22 - 29	♀♂	**South Caribbean Cruise on the Galaxy,** see Ocean Voyager on page 64, 97
22 - 29	♀	**Thanksgiving at Man Friday Resort,** see Above & Beyond Tours on page 45, 83
22 - 29	♀♂	**Thanksgiving in Italy— Rome, Florence, Venice,** see Travel Affair on page 75, 103
23 - 29	♀♂	**Thanksgiving Western Caribbean Cruise,** see Mercury Cruise & Tour on page 62
23 - DE 12	♀♂	**Dive Fiji,** see Above & Beyond Tours on page 45, 83
24 - DE 03	♀♂	**Caribbean Explorer,** see Our Family Abroad on page 65, 98
26 - 30	♂	**White Party (Miami Beach),** The 13th annual White Party at Vizcaya is a benefit for the Health Crisis Network and is often referred to as the "crown jewel" of the international gay party circuit. An entire week of events surround the Sunday night main event. Location: Miami Beach, FL. Contact: (305) 759-6181.

WHEN TO GO

TRIP/EVENTS CALENDAR

Dates		Event
27 - 30	♀♂	**Thanksgiving in Amsterdam,** see Above & Beyond Tours on page 45, 83
28 - 30	♀♂	**Bahama Cruise (3-night),** see Pleasure Travel...Cruise Again Too! on page 68, FYI 339

December 97

Dates		Event
TBA	♀	**Cabin-Based Dogsledding in Minnesota,** see Wintermoon on page 80, FYI 452
TBA	♀♂	**Italian Gay Discovery Tour,** see Zipper Travel Association on page 82, FYI 252
TBA	♀♂	**New Years in Puerto Vallarta,** see Doin' It Right - in Puerto Vallarta on page 53
TBA	♂	**New Year's Downunder,** see Men on Vacation on page 62, 96
TBA	♀♂	**Old Galveston, TX Victorian Festival,** see After Five Charters on page 46, FYI 492
TBA	♀♂	**San Antonio Xmas Festival of Lights,** see After Five Charters on page 46, FYI 492
TBA	♀	**Sled Dog School,** see Wintermoon on page 80, FYI 452
TBA	♀	**Wahine Week in Wailea,** see Thanks, Babs on page 74, 102
01 - 05	♂	**Killing Fields of Cambodia,** see Otto Travel Hawaii on page 65
04 - 10	♀♂	**Christmas Shopping in London,** see L'Arc en Ciel Voyages on page 61, 94
06 - 13	♀♂	**Best of Russia,** see Kremlin Tours on page 60, FYI 266
10 - 17	♀♂	**Puerto Vallarta Travel Agent/Writer Fam Tour,** see Doin' It Right - in Puerto Vallarta on page 53
11 - 16	♀♂	**Bicycling Cambodia, Temples of Angkor,** see VeloAsia Cycling Adventures on page 77, 105
13 - 20	♀	**Hawaii Cruise,** see Olivia Cruises & Resorts on page 65, 98
18 - 27	♂	**Christmas in Marrakech,** see Hanns Ebensten Travel on page 57, 92
19 - 29	♀♂	**Ancient Egypt,** see Our Family Abroad on page 65, 98
20 - 26	♂	**Gay Spirit,** Tribal celebration & transformative alternative to the holidaze. Sway your hula hips to the rhythm of the islands & your spirit will manifest loving brotherhood, abundant nature & healthful living. Contact: Kalani Eco-Resort, RR2 Box 4500, Kehena Beach, HI 96778, (808) 965-7828, for reservations only: (800) 800-6886.
20 - 27	♀♂	**Christmas Caribbean Cruise,** see AAD All About Destinations on page 45
20 - 27	♀♂	**New Year's Eve in Russia,** see Kremlin Tours on page 60, FYI 266
20 - 27	♀♂	**West Caribbean/Central America Xmas Cruise,** see Ocean Voyager on page 64, 97
20 - JA 02	♀♂	**Christmas/New Years Caribbean Cruise,** see Ocean Voyager on page 64, 97
20 - JA 03	♂	**Christmas and New Year,** see Tours to Paradise on page 75, FYI 189
22 - 22	♀♂	**House of Blues,** Sunday Tea Dance, Los Angeles largest party takes place every month and features headlining performers debuting their newest creations. Attendance 1,400. Contact: http://www.jeffreysanker.com/events.htm
23 - 26	♀♂	**Christmas in Cabo San Lucas, Mexico,** see Gay Baja Tours on page 56, FYI 358
23 - JA 02	♀♂	**Christmas DownUnder,** see Above & Beyond Tours on page 45, 83
23 - JA 02	♀♂	**Christmas Downunder Tour,** see Destination Downunder on page 53, FYI 309
23 - JA 03	♀♂	**French Country Xmas & New Year's Eve in Paris,** see Travel Affair on page 75, 103
25 - 31	♀♂	**Xmas Snowshoeing & Skiing-Taos, NM,** see Lizard Head Backcountry Tours on page 61, FYI 495
26 - 28	♀♂	**Bahama Cruise (3-night),** see Pleasure Travel...Cruise Again Too! on page 68, FYI 339
26 - JA 04	♀♂	**Deluxe New Year's Egypt Tour & Nile Cruise,** see Rainbow Destinations on page 69
26 - JA 05	♀♂	**Costa Rica - New Year's in the Tropics,** see Adventure Associates on page 45, 84
26 - JA 06	♀	**Sea of Cortez Baja Sea Kayaking,** see Mariah Wilderness Expeditions on page 61, 96
27 - JA 02	♀♂	**Christmas/New Years Caribbean Cruise,** see Ocean Voyager on page 64, 97
27 - JA 03	♀♂	**New Years Caribbean Cruise,** see AAD All About Destinations on page 45
27 - JA 03	♂	**New Years in Oaxaca, Mexico,** see Spirit Journeys on page 72, 101
27 - JA 11	♀♂	**New Year's In South Africa,** see David's Trips and Tours on page 52, 89
28 - JA 03	♀♂	**Mexican Gay Beaches All-Inclusive,** see Mercury Cruise & Tour on page 62
28 - JA 03	♀	**Romantic Old Mexico-Butterfly Tour,** see Club Le Bon on page 51, FYI 341
29 - JA 02	♀♂	**New Years in Paris,** see Above & Beyond Tours on page 45, 83
31 - 31	♂	**Bal des Boys IV,** The final Bad Boys Club of Montreal (BBCM) event of the year is their now famous, all-night dance party on New Year's Eve. Dress code is black & white. Location: Montreal, Canada. Contact: (514) 875-7026, Fax: (514) 875-9323, Email: bbcm@sim.qc.ca Web: http://www.bbcm.org
31 - JA 03	♀	**New Year's Eve in San Francisco,** see Women in Motion on page 80, 107

FERRARI GUIDES' GAY TRAVEL A to Z - 18th EDITION

WHEN TO GO

TRIP/EVENTS CALENDAR

January 98

TBA ♀ **Blue Ball '98,** Usually the last weekend of January, in Philadelphia, PA, the Blue Ball is a weekend long party benefitting the AIDS Information Network (AIN) The events attended by over 2,000 "boys" include the large Saturday Night dance party and the "diva" of all brunches on Sunday. For more information contact: (215) 575-1110 X108, For tickets: (800) 494-8497.

TBA ♀ **Cabin-Based Dogsledding,** see Wintermoon on page 80, FYI 452

TBA ♂ **European Gay Ski Week,** see Alternative Holidays on page 47, 86

TBA ♀ **Jackson Hole 1998 Women's Ski Camp,** Open to skiers of intermediate skills or better who want to improve their skiing and enjoy the camaraderie of other women. Top female instructors. Location: Jackson Hole, WY. Contact: Jackson Hole 1999 Women's Ski Camp, PO Box 290, Teton Village, WY 83025, (307) 739-2686.

TBA ♂ **Melbourne Midsumma Fest, Red Raw Dance,** see Men on Vacation on page 62, 96

TBA ♀♂ **Midsumma 1998,** Melbourne, Australia's outrageous and incredible summer bash with parties, theater, bus trips, art exhibits, fetish events, drag workshops and forums, AIDS forums, to mention a few. Don't forget, summer "down under" is winter in the northern hemisphere. Contact: Midsumma, 5th floor, 258 Flinders Lane, Melbourne, VIC 3000, Australia, (61-3) 650 6080.

TBA ♀♂ **Midsumma Festival Melbourne,** see Beyond the Blue on page 49, FYI 307

TBA ♀♂ **Road Runner Regional Rodeo,** Phoenix, AZ. Call: AGRA, (602) 265-0618.

TBA ♀ **Sapphos In the Snow—Sun Valley, Idaho,** see Thanks, Babs on page 74, 102

TBA ♀♂ **Sea Kayaking in Baja Mexico,** see Pangaea Expeditions on page 66, FYI 456

TBA ♀ **Weekend Dogsledding, Northern Minnesota,** see Women in the Wilderness on page 81, 108

01 - 23 ♀ **Best of East Africa,** see Silke's Travel on page 71, FYI 308

03 - 10 ♀♂ **Orthodox Christmas in Russia,** see Kremlin Tours on page 60, FYI 266

09 - 18 ♀♂ **Costa Rica Caribbean Adventure,** see Adventure Associates on page 45, 84

17 - 25 ♀♂ **Costa Rica Pacific Adventure,** see Adventure Associates on page 45, 84

19 - 28 ♀♂ **Caribbean Explorer,** see Our Family Abroad on page 65, 98

24 - 31 ♀♂ **Aspen Gay Ski Week,** A full week of skiing and varied activities for gay men and lesbians in Aspen, Colorado, including the "Coors Light World Famous Mountain Bump Your Buns Downhill Costume Party." Over 6000 participants attend. For information on travel, lodging and events, contact: The Aspen Gay & Lesbian Community (AGLC) PO Box 3486, Aspen, CO 81612, (970) 925-4123, Email: aspengay@rof.net, Web: http://www.rof.net/yp/aspengay

25 - FE 08 ♀♂ **India & Nepal,** see Our Family Abroad on page 65, 98

31 - FE 08 ♀♂ **Yucatan & Mexico City,** see Our Family Abroad on page 65, 98

February 98

TBA ♀♂ **Altitude 98 - Whistler Gay Ski Week,** (tentative date: Feb 1-8, 1998) A one-week ski and party event combination for gays and lesbians. Over 2000 participants and 30 eventes. Packages include seven nights lodging, ski pass, admission to parties and events. Location: Whistler, BC, Canada. Contact: Out on the Slopes Productions, P.O. Box 1370, Whistler, BC Canada V0N 1B0, (604) 688-5079, Fax: (604) 688-5033, (888) 258-4883.

TBA ♀ **Big Bear Spring Ski & Snowboard Daze 3,** Escape to the slopes at the end of February every year for a wild weekend of skiing, snowboarding and wild parites. Enjoy the Ski Daze Ball on Saturday night. Contact: Canboy Productions (213) 464-5388 Email: WGORGES@aol.com Web: http://www.gaywired.com/canboy.htm

TBA ♀♂ **Black Gay & Lesbian Conference (11th annual),** One of the largest gatherings of black lesbians and gay men, this event focuses on issues, challenges and the direction of the Black lesbian & gay community. Each year, it attracts hundreds of national & international presenters and attendees. It is always held on President's Day weekend, and is organized by the Black Gay & Lesbian Leadership Forum. Write: BGLLF, 1219 S. La Brea Ave, Los Angeles, CA 90019, (213) 964-7820.

TBA ♀ **Cabin-Based Dogsledding,** see Wintermoon on page 80, FYI 452

TBA ♀♂ **Carnaval in Rio,** see Sundance Travel on page 73

TBA ♀♂ **Colgne Carnival Hotel & Event Package,** see Teddy Travel on page 74, 101

TBA ♀♂ **Copper Canyon Mexico Mule Trek,** see Adventure Associates on page 45, 84

TBA ♀ **Crosscountry Skiing Yellowstone,** see Adventure Associates on page 45, 84

TBA ♀ **Dog Sledding & Wolf Ecology,** see Wintermoon on page 80, FYI 452

FERRARI GUIDES' GAY TRAVEL A to Z - 18th EDITION

WHEN TO GO

TRIP/EVENTS CALENDAR

TBA	♀	**Galapagos Island Cruise, Snorkel, Wildlife,** see Woodswomen on page 81, 108	TBA	♂	**Red Party,** The Red Party weekend features many events including the infamous dance sponsored by the La Foundation B.B.C.M. Location: Montreal, Canada. Contact: (514) 875-7026, Fax: (514) 875-9323.			as it's host to a weekend of festivities celebrating gay pride. Events include a Saturday beach party and open-air dance in the evening. Sunday features the Winter Pride Parade & Festival. Monday morning enjoy the party aboard double decker boats that wind through the "Venice of America." Contact: AAR Productions, Inc., PO. Box 2467, Ft. Lauderdale, FL 33303-2467, (954) 525-4567, Email: aarinc@earthlink.net
TBA	♀♂	**Hero Party, Auckland,** see Beyond the Blue on page 49, FYI 307						
TBA	♀♂	**Igloo Weekend in Stowe, Vermont,** A weekend of gay skiing, parties, snowshoeing hikes, ski lessons, and cross-country ski hikes. This event is usually held in late February or early March. Call for details. Location: Stowe, VT. Contact: Buccaneer Country Lodge (802) 253-4772.	TBA	♂	**Saint-At-Large White Party,** This annual event in New York City is usually held at the Roseland. Contact: (212) 674-8541.			
			TBA	♀♂	**Sea Kayaking in Baja Mexico,** see Pangaea Expeditions on page 66, FYI 456			
TBA	♂	**Int'l Bear Rendezvous,** For bears and their cubs, this international event is held in San Francisco, CA. Activities include pub crawls, workshops, parties, dinners, brunch and the International Bear Competition. Contact: The Leather Zone, 2352 Market St. or The Bear Store, 367 Ninth St, San Francisco, CA. Web: http://www.q.com/bosf	TBA	♂	**Seattle Mr. Leather Contest,** Contact: Generic Leather Productions of Washington, 1202 E. Pike St. #707, Seattle, WA 98122, (202) 325-4275, Email: lthrpride@aol.com	TBA	♀	**Women's Golf Tournament—Puerto Vallarta,** see Thanks, Babs on page 74, 102
						01	♀	**K.W.W.F.F.L. Flag-A-Tag National Kickoff,** Key West Women's Flag Football League. This is the world's largest women's flag football tournament, with 30 teams from the U.S., Canada & South Africa expected to participate. The tournament will provide airline, hotel, water sports and social activities discounts to all teams. Spectators are welcome as well. Location: Key West, FL. Contact: Diane Beruldsen, 1731 Laird St, Key West, FL 33040, Tel/Fax: (305) 293-9315.
			TBA	♀♂	**Sydney Gay & Lesbian Mardi Gras,** A month-long festival of gay and lesbian cultural events, including theatre, cabaret, film festivals, sporting events, exhibitions, parties, dances on the biggest dance floor in the world, harbor cruises, a parade and major entertainment productions. Many gay and lesbian travel agents offer travel packages including this event. Location: Sydney, Australia. Contact: Sydney Gay & Lesbian Mardi Gras, PO Box 1064, Darlinghurst, 2010 NSW, Australia, (61-2) 332 4088, FAX: (61-2) 332 2969.			
TBA	♂	**Int'l Mr. Leather Weekend (IML),** All of Chicago becomes party central surrounding the IML contest. 1997 brought Chicagoland the "House of Blues" by Club BAD. Watch out in 1998 for an even better show. Contact: IML, (800) 233-1234, (312) 986-1234, Web: http://imrl.com, www.hob.com						
						05 - 08	♀	**Crosscountry Skiing in Yosemite,** see Women in Motion on page 80, 107
						06 - 08	♀	**Girls in the Snow,** Women's ski and winter sports weekend in Colorado. Contact: Circles Magazine, (303) 417-1385, Fax: (303) 417-1453.
TBA	♀	**Masquerade '98 - The Purple Party,** Ninth annual Mardi Gras theme celebration in Atlanta, GA, benefiting Project Open Hand. Events include: Friday night gala reception for 1,000 host and VIPs, Satuday night dance with expected crowd of 3,500. Contact: (404) 872-8089.	TBA	♀♂	**Sydney Gay/Lesbian Mardi Gras,** see Beyond the Blue on page 49, FYI 307			
			TBA	♀♂	**Sydney Mardi Gras Package,** see Holigays on page 58, 92	06 - 09	♀	**Gay Ski East,** see Eclectic Excursions on page 54, FYI 466
			TBA	♀	**Sydney Mardi Gras, Australia,** see Thanks, Babs on page 74, 102	06 - 13	♂	**Body Electric,** Celebrate the Body Erotic with conscious breathwork & sacred rituals. Feel at home in your erotic body. Contact: Kalani Eco-Resort, RR2 Box 4500, Kehena Beach, HI 96778, (808) 965-7828, for reservations only: (800) 800-6886.
TBA	♀	**New Zealand Bicycle Tour,** see Woodswomen on page 81, 108	TBA	♀	**Weekend Dogsledding in Northern Minnesota,** see Women in the Wilderness on page 81, 108			
TBA	♀	**Northwoods Retreat for Survivors of Cancer,** see Women in the Wilderness on page 81, 108	TBA	♀♂	**Winter Gayla '98,** Over President's Day weekend, join all of Ft. Lauderdale, FL			

FERRARI GUIDES' GAY TRAVEL A to Z - 18th EDITION

WHEN TO GO

TRIP/EVENTS CALENDAR

06 - 21 ♀♂ **Hero Festival,** The 2-week festival includes a series of parties, gay art exhibits, entertainment, a short-course swim meet, beach parties, nightclub shows, gay church services, and the Gay Day Party on Wahiki Island, including the Mr. Gay New Zealand Competition, all preceding the Hero Parade & Party, New Zealand's biggest bash of the year. Location: Auckland, New Zealand. Contact: New Zealand AIDS Foundation, PO Box 6663, Wellesly St., Auckland, NZ.

07 - 14 ♀ **Romantic Getaway at Secluded Spa,** see Club Le Bon on page 51, FYI 341

07 - 20 ♀ **Macchu Picchu, Andes and Amazon Rainforest,** see Women in the Wilderness on page 81, 108

10 - 22 ♀♂ **Cooking School, Elephant Trek, Rafting-Thailand,** see Progressive Travels on page 68, 99

12 - 15 ♀♂ **Pantheon of Leather VIII,** Annual service awards to men, women and businesses of the leather community. Events include cocktail parties, the award presentation and the Mr. and Ms Olympus Leather 1998 Contest. Sunday Night is the "Black Hearts Ball" a costume party and contest where the top vote getters are crowned King and Queen of the ball. Location: New Orleans, LA. Contact: The Leather Journal, 7985 Santa Monica Blvd #109-368, West Hollywood, CA 90046, (213) 656-5073, Fax: (213) 656-3120, Email: tljandcuir@qol.com

13 - 15 ♀♂ **Hearts Party (BOHT),** This will be the 11th anniversary gala weekend celebration in Chicago, IL, which includes a variety of events that benefit the TPA Network. Events include: Friday night: auction and entertainment & the King of Hearts Ball; Saturday night: 1998 Hearts Party dance; Sunday: Tea dance. Contact: Test Postive Aware Network (TPA), 1258 W. Belmont, Chicago, IL 60657 (773) 404-8726; Party hotline: (773) 404-3784 or Email: BOHT@aol.com

13 - 16 ♂ **Adventure Camp,** A fun frolic in Hawaii's volcanos, waters & forests. Build new friendships, hike to secluded beaches, descend into lava caves, kayak streams into the sea, bathe in crater lakes, etc. Contact: Kalani Eco-Resort, RR2 Box 4500, Kehena Beach, HI 96778, (808) 965-7828, for reservations only: (800) 800-6886.

14 - 21 ♀ **Costa Rica Cruise,** see Olivia Cruises & Resorts on page 65, 98

14 - MR 01 ♀♂ **Kenya & Tanzania Safari,** see Our Family Abroad on page 65, 98

19 - 22 ♀ **Downhill Ski & Snowboard Big Bear Lake, CA,** see Women in Motion on page 80, 107

21 - 23 ♀♂ **Outwrite '98,** Over 2000 writers, editors, publishers, critics & agents meet for this 2-1/2 day conference to discuss the latest trends in lesbian & gay publishing. Event includes panel discussions, keynote speakers & entertainment. Location: Sheraton Hotel in Boston, MA. Contact: Ouwrite '98, 29 Stanhope St, Boston, MA 02116, (617) 262-6969, Fax: (617) 267-0852.

22 - MR 01 ♀♂ **Carnival in Las Palmas,** see Our Family Abroad on page 65, 98

March 98

TBA ♀♂ **Bighorn Rodeo,** Las Vegas, NV. Call: NGRA, (702) 732-7559.

TBA ♂ **Black Party (New York),** Saint-At-Large-Black Party is the largest event in the "Saint's" repertoire of parties. Features sex shows by XXX film stars (and some uninhibited attendees), mega dance floors, leather-clad attendees (although costumes are not required) and a crowd of over 5,000. Location: New York, NY. Contact: (212) 674-8541.

TBA ♀ **Cabin-Based Dogsledding,** see Wintermoon on page 80, FYI 452

TBA ♀ **Club Skirts/Girl Bar/ Dinah Shore Weekend,** In addition to the many other activities associated with Dinah Shore Weekend, Club Skirts & Girl Bar host one of the largest parties for women on the planet. Top-notch DJs are featured and the crowd swells to over 6,000 women. Location: Palm Springs, CA. Contact: (888) 44 DINAH.

TBA ♀ **Dinah Shore Tournament Week Womens' Events,** It is estimated that 8,000 women come to Palm Springs for the multitude of women's parties and events taking place during the week of the Dinah Shore Golf Tournament. Dances, pool parties, breakfasts, lunches, cocktail parties and other events take place. Contact any gay or lesbian business listed in the Palm Springs section of this book for details.

TBA ♀ **Dykes & Dogs—Iditarod Winterfest,** see Thanks, Babs on page 74, 102

TBA ♀♂ **Int'l Gay Ski Week (SWING) 1998,** This event is held in the Swiss Alps each year, attended by skiiers from Europe & the USA. Events include hiking by torchlight, skating, cinema, concerts, disco & a costume ball. The decision on which city and country is never made until after this book goes to press. Contact the organization for the 1998 schedule. Contact: SWING, Wagnerweg 8, 8810 Horgen, Switzerland. Tel: (41-1) 725 44 41.

TBA ♀ **Lesbian Pride Weekend (Denver),** A series of lesbian parties and events, sponsored by Out Front

WHEN TO GO

TRIP/EVENTS CALENDAR

TBA ♂ **Mr. Dixie Bell Leather Contest,** Sponsored by the Kansas City Pioneers. Contact: P.O. Box 413025, Kansas City, MO 64141, or call the Dixie Bell, (816) 471-2424.

TBA ♀♂ **Mr. & Ms New Mexico Leather,** This IML/IMsL qualifying contest is held annually in Albuquerque. Contact: Sandia Leathermen/Leatherwomen, 8900 Central Ave., SE, Albq., NM 87123, (505)275-1616, Email: SandiaLthr@aol.com

TBA ♀♂ **Saguaro Regional Rodeo,** Tucson, AZ. Call: AGRA (Tucson Chapter), (520) 323-0805.

TBA ♀ **Sailing in the Virgin Islands,** see Women in the Wilderness on page 81, 108

TBA ♀ **Vacation in Cozumel - Snorkeling, Cycling,** see Woodswomen on page 81, 108

TBA ♂ **Washington State Mr. Leather 1998,** Seattle, Washington hosts the annual contest to choose the man that will represent them as Mr. Leather. Contact: The Cuff, (206) 323-1525.

TBA ♀ **Weekend Dogsledding in Northern Minnesota,** see Women in the Wilderness on page 81, 108

TBA ♂ **Winter Party South Beach,** March, 1998 in South Beach, FL. A 1-day beach party from noon to sunset, ticket price includes drinks. Benefits Dade County Human Rights Found. Contact: (305) 460-3115, Tickets: (800) 695-0880.

TBA ♀♂ **Winterfest Lake Tahoe,** A gay & lesbian winter festival featuring live entertainment, parties, as well as activities such as skiing, sleighrides, snowmobiling & snowboarding. Location: Lake Tahoe, CA. Contact any IGTA travel agent for details.

13 - 21 ♀♂ **Winterfest Europe 1998 — Innsbruck, Austria,** see Ski Connections on page 72, FYI 194

15 - 22 ♀ **Cycling Costa Rica,** see Women in Motion on page 80, 107

21 - 24 ♀♂ **Winterfest Europe 1998 — Berlin, Germany,** see Ski Connections on page 72, FYI 194

21 - 28 ♀ **Adventure Cruise to Belize, Guatemala,** see Women in Motion on page 80, 107

23 - 29 ♂ **I-Men,** Join the fun. I-Men comes to Kalani with a splash of delicious activities and adventures, au naturel. Contact: Kalani Eco-Resort, RR2 Box 4500, Kehena Beach, HI 96778, (808) 965-7828, for reservations only: (800) 800-6886.

26 - 30 ♀ **Dinah Shore Women's Festival,** see Women in Motion on page 80, 107

April 98

TBA ♂ **Cherry Jubilee,** This "spring thaw" party heats up our nation's capitol, Washington, D.C. Several pre- and post-events are planned thoughout the weekend with the main event on Saturday night. Benefits: Whitman-Walker Clinic and Food & Friends. Contact: (800) 201-0807, Fax: (703) 836-1716.

TBA ♀ **Cooking School in San Diego,** see Women in Motion on page 80, 107

TBA ♂ **Gay Marathon of Rome,** Held annually in April, this is not a sports event, but a running party sponsored by the gay bar Alibi, and taking place every evening for 14 days. Events include a Mister Alibi contest, a Gay Corrida, shows, after hours, male strippers and a 70's disco. Location: Rome, Italy. Contact: Alibi bar in Rome.

TBA ♀ **Gulf Coast Women's Festival (10th annual),** Held on Easter Weekend, '98. Get ready for a laid-back good time! Workshops, women musicians in a jam tent, a nightly dance, campfires, affinity spaces, and craftswomen displaying a variety of unique gifts. Location: North of New Orleans, LA. Contact: Wanda & Brenda Henson, producers, Camp Sisterspirit, PO Box 12, Ovett, MS 39464, (601) 344-1411, tel/fax (601) 344-2005.

TBA ♀♂ **L.A. Rodeo '98,** Los Angeles, CA. Call: GSGRA (LA Chapter), (310) 498-1675.

TBA ♂ **Mr. Kentucky Leather 98,** Contact: Bluegrass C.O.L.T.S., P.O. Box 12403, Lexington, KY or call Crossings, (606) 233-7266.

TBA ♀ **New Orleans Jazz Festival Social,** see Women in Motion on page 80, 107

TBA ♀ **NYC—Lucy & Ethel's Easter Caper, A Lesbian Event,** see Thanks, Babs on page 74, 102

TBA ♀♂ **Queensday Party Package,** see Rainboworld Custom Tours on page 69, FYI 256

TBA ♀♂ **Rodeo in the Rock,** Little Rock, AR. Call: DSRA, (501) 562-4466.

TBA ♀♂ **Slide for Pride,** Athletes from Europe, Canada & USA will participate in this men's & women's winter sports festival. Events include Alpine skiing, snowboard giant slalom, Nordic races, ice hockey & figure skating. Location: Seattle. WA. Contact: Team Seattle, 1202 E Pike St #515, Seattle, WA 98112, (206) 322-7769.

TBA ♀♂ **We're Funny That Way,** Comedians from Canada, USA, Europe, Latin America and Australia are expected to perform at Canada's first international gay & lesbian comedy festival. Approximately 30 acts will be performed in five to seven venues throughout the city. Acts will include individual stand-up, improvisation, sketch comedy, drag and musical comedy. Location:

FERRARI GUIDES' GAY TRAVEL A to Z - 18th EDITION

WHEN TO GO

TRIP/EVENTS CALENDAR

TBA ♂ Toronto, Canada. Contact: WFTW Productions Office, 40 Homewood Ave #104, Toronto, ON M4Y 2K2 Canada, (416) 515-1067, Fax: 964-3526
White Party 1998 (Palm Springs), A national gay desert weekend on Easter weekend each year. Dance and party with over 3,000 gay men. Desert Dance and additional parties throughout the weekend. Contact any gay business listed in the Palm Springs, CA section of this book for details or for info and tickets: White Party 1998, 8344 Melrose Ave. Suite 20, West Hollywood, CA 90069, (888) 777-8886.

TBA ♀ **Writers' Workshop with Carol Bly,** see Women in the Wilderness on page 81, 108

10 - 10 ♂ **Red Heart Party (London),** (Tentative Date) Billed as "Europe's only official Circuit Party," this event was voted one of the circuit's top ten in 1996. Features include: Top-notch sound system, a bevy of DJ's, exquisite production design, multi-system light show, and the invaluable "Red Heart Party Survival Kit." Location: London, England. Contact: The Red Heart Company Ltd., 3rd Floor, 60-62 Old Compton Street, London W1V 5PA, England, (0171) 420 0088, Web: http://www.redheart.co.uk

12 - 19 ♀ **Eastern Caribbean Cruise,** see Olivia Cruises & Resorts on page 65, 98

13 - 19 ♀♂ **Hula Heritage Festival, Hawaii,** Explore traditional dance, chant, myths, crafts & language and attend Hawaii's premiere cultural exposition, Hilo's Merrie Monarch Hula Festival. Reserve now, sold out by February. Location: Island of Hawaii, HI. Contact: Kalani Eco-Resort, RR2 Box 4500, Kehena Beach, HI 96778, (808) 965-7828, for reservations only: (800) 800-6886.

25 - MA 02 ♀ **Caribbean Dive/Snorkel Getaway,** see Club Le Bon on page 51, FYI 341

30 - 30 ♀♂ **Queen's Day in Amsterdam,** A huge gay and lesbian street party in Amsterdam held on April 30 every year. The gay and lesbian community joins in this enormous national celebration as over a million people, both straight and gay, converge on Amsterdam for street fairs, theatre, musical entertainment and partying.

May 98

TBA ♀ **Australian Aboriginal & Red Desert Camp-Out,** see Thanks, Babs on page 74, 102

TBA ♀♂ **Bay Area Regional Rodeo,** San Francisco, CA. Call: GSGRA, (415) 985-5200.

TBA ♀♂ **Dixieland Regional Rodeo,** Atlanta, GA. Call: SEGRA, (404) 760-8126.

TBA ♀♂ **Gay & Lesbian Run in Berlin (8th annual),** All lesbians and gays are invited to participate as athletes and to join us in cultural exchange and celebration. High achievement is not the most important goal of this event, rather it is the centerpiece of a broad spectrum of sporting and fun activities. A wide variety of tourist, cultural and culinary programs will also be available. in the 10,000-meter run, the men and women will start together, but all other events will be separated by gender. Wheelchair participation is encouraged. Accommodation can be arranged in private homes. Location: Berlin, Germany. Contact: Gay & Lesbian Run Berlin, PO Box 420 703, 12067 Berlin, Germany. Call: (49-30) 32 49 348.

TBA ♀♂ **Gear Party,** Detroit, Michigan is the setting for the 4th annual Gear Party. Having established itself as a circuit main stay, "Gear" benefits the Geard for Life organization and is the largest gay and lesbian gathering in Detroit each year. Contact: (810) 358-9849, Email: GEARD4LIFE@aol.com

TBA ♀♂ **Great Plains Regional Rodeo,** Oklahoma City, OK. Call: OGRA, (405) 842-0845.

TBA ♀♂ **Greater Motown Int'l Rodeo,** Detroit, MI. Call: MIGRA, (313) 438-1305.

TBA ♀ **Hopland Women's Festival,** This annual women's festival takes place in a rural California area & features comedy, music and arts & crafts. There is camping available. Location: Hopland, CA. Contact: HWF, PO Box 416, Hopland, CA 95449, (415) 641-5212.

TBA ♀ **Lesbies Doe-Front Lesbian Day,** Among the many events are a special lesbian theater, authors, workshops, films and photo & art exhibits. Over 800 lesbians are expected to attend. The final event is a huge dance party. Location: Belgium. Contact: Lesbies Doe-Front, Postbus 621, 9000 Gent, Belgium, (32-9) 223 69 29.

TBA ♀ **Maryland Womyn's Gathering,** Over 160 acres of waterfront, wetlands & woods set the tone for this year's gathering. Events include opening & closing circles, sharing stage, fire circles, drum council, crafts & dancing. Rustic cabins, newly renovated bath houses, camping welcome. Vegetarian meals. Childcare available (boys under 5 years only). Location: Southern Maryland. Contact: In Gaia's Lap, PO Box 39, Maryland Line, MD 21105, (410) 435-3111.

TBA ♀♂ **Meltdown '98,** Celebrated over Memorial Day weekend in Austin, Texas, Meltdown includes 5 events. The main event is Meltdown '97 on

WHEN TO GO

TRIP/EVENTS CALENDAR

Saturday night followed by the Captain Morgan's Rum Run (a flotilla of party boats on lake Travis) on Sunday. Benefits: Helping Hands for Life, Inc. Contact: (512) 478-1210, (512) 419-4763, Web: http://www.partyaustin.com

TBA ♀♂ **Pensacola Beach Maneuvers 5,** On Memorial Day Weekend, Pensacola, Florida (otherwise known as the Gay Riveria) is flooded with over 50,000 gay men and women for the annual "Beach Maneuvers" festivities. Benefits: White Heat Foundation. Contact: (888) 777-8886, Web: http://www.jeffreysanker.com

TBA ♀♂ **Tiptoe Through the Two Lips Party Pkg,** see Rainboworld Custom Tours on page 69, FYI 256

TBA ♀♂ **Tokyo Int'l Lesbian & Gay Film & Video Festival,** The Tokyo festival is expected to attract 4,000 attendees. From Tokyo, the film festival will travel to Kyoto and Osaka. Location: Tokyo, Japan. Contact: Tokyo Int'l Gay & Lesbian Film & Video Office, Tel/Fax: (81-3) 5380 5760, http://www.wax.or.jp/L-GFF/. For specific information in English, call (81-3) 3316 1029.

TBA ♀ **Veranstaltungen Lesbenfruhlingstreffen,** (Lesbian Spring Gathering). Workshops, seminars, sporting events, social activities, crafts, books, music. Contact last year's organizers: Lesbenfrnhlingstreffen '97, c/o Frauen in Bewegung, Schwarzwaldstrasse 107, D-W-7800 Freiburg, Germany, tel: 49-761-33339 Tues 8-10p.m.

TBA ♀ **Virginia Women's Music Festival,** Join us for our 9th annual festival held at Intouch for 106 acres of music, workshops, games and fun! Swim, boat & go fishing in 7-acre Towanda Lake. Drumfest prior to festival. Location: 20 miles east of Charlottesville, VA. Contact: Intouch, Rte 2, Box 1096, Kent's Store, VA 23084, (804) 589-6542.

TBA ♂ **Wet & Wild Weekend,** Celebrated on Canada's Victoria Holiday weekend, in Montreal, it is second only in Canada to the Black & Blue party. Produced by Bad Boy Club Montreal (BBCM) this is a weekend packed with events ranging from a "warm-up party" on Thursday, the "weekend launch (leather optional) party" on Friday, the military/uniform party on Saturday, the late afternoon tea-dance and the main event Sunday (dress: as bare as you dare). Contact: BBCM, (514) 875-7026, Fax: (514) 875-9323, Email: bbcm@pop.point-net.com, Web: http://bbcm.org

TBA ♀ **Wiminfest '98,** Open mike, fun in the sun, dances, arts and crafts. Reserved seating for performances. Festival passes sell out every year, so reservations are a MUST! There is space ONLY for the number of tickets issued. Single concert tickets may be available at door, call for availability. Memorial Day Weekend. Location: Albuquerque, NM. Contact W.I.M.I.N., PO Box 80204, Albuquerque, NM 87198-0204, (505) 899-3627, (800) 499-5688.

01 - 04 ♀ **Russian River Women's Festival,** see Women in Motion on page 80, 107

15 - 18 ♀♂ **Canadian GALA Choruses: Festival '98,** Canadian gay and lesbian choruses invite singers from across Canada and around the world to Edmonton, Alberta for this event. Hosted by Edmonton Vocal Minority (a mixed-voice chorus of over 100 members), it will feature performances by over a dozen gay and lesbian choruses, including the Vancouver Men's Chorus and Toronto's Singing OUT!.Held during the Victoria Day long-weekend, there will also be workshops and performances by renowned performers such as Heather Bishop, and a Multi-media Extravaganza of dancers, musicians and visual artists. Nearly 1000 visitors are expected to attend. Performances will be held in The Winspear Centre for Music, with the host hotel being the luxurious Hilton Hotel. Contact: Edmonton Vocal Minority, P.O. Box 12091, Main Post Office, Edmonton, Alberta, Canada T5J 3L2, (403) 988-4620, Fax: (403) 425-8543, Email: evm@freenet.edmonton.ab.ca

17 - 23 ♂ **Healing Arts Retreat,** Health equals learning Hawaiian lomi lomi massage, the basics of huna and elemental breathing and shiatsu while floating in thermal springs, sunrise meditations, yoga and hula. Contact: Kalani Eco-Resort, RR2 Box 4500, Kehena Beach, HI 96778, (808) 965-7828, for reservations only: (800) 800-6886.

22 - 25 ♀♂ **Camp Lesbigay,** A fun unity gathering for gay and lesbian adults and our children! Contact: Kalani Eco-Resort, RR2 Box 4500, Kehena Beach, HI 96778, (808) 965-7828, for reservations only: (800) 800-6886.

28 - 31 ♀ **National Women's Music Festival (14th annual),** An all-indoor festival in Bloomington, Indiana on the campus of Indiana University, with evening concerts, writer's and spirituality conferences, a full complement of intensive workshops, an older & young women's series, a performers' series, health, fitness, sexuality and sports series and a video series. Accommodations are on the campus. Contact: National Women's Music Festival, PO

WHEN TO GO

TRIP/EVENTS CALENDAR

Box 1427, Indianapolis, IN 46206-1427, (317) 927-9355.

29 - 31 ♀ **Advanced Rafting, Northern California,** see Women in Motion on page 80, 107

June 98

TBA ♀ **Alaskan Native Expeditions,** see Thanks, Babs on page 74, 102

TBA ♀♂ **Big Sky Regional Rodeo,** Billings, MT. Call: BSGRA, (406) 248-2993.

TBA ♀ **Camp SCWU,** A weekend of assorted activities and seminars, sponsored by Southern California Women for Understanding. Location: Pilgrim Pines, CA, in the San Bernadino Mountains. Contact: Southern California Women for Understanding, 7985 Santa Monica Blvd #207, Los Angeles, CA 90046, (213) 654-SCWU, fax: (213) 654-7268.

TBA ♀ **Campfest,** Five days of magic in a scenic, private camp near Oxford, PA. Workshops, day and evening live entertainment, crafts area, activities for singles, vegetarian and non-vegetarian meals, choice of cabin space or tenting, hot water and flush toilets, dining hall, olympic pool, sports, lake fishing, tennis and more. Held on Memorial Day weekend. Contact: Campfest, PO Box 559, Franklinville, NJ 08322, (609) 694-2037, e-mail: campfest@aol.com.

TBA ♀♂ **Canadian Rockies Int'l Rodeo,** Calgary, AB, Canada. Call: ARGRA, (403) 541-8140.

TBA ♀ **Femmes Fatales for the 4th—San Francisco,** see Thanks, Babs on page 74, 102

TBA ♀ **Femo Prideweek,** The Danish women's FemOcamp, in Maribo, is the setting for an international lesbian week. The themes of this year's event include how to maintain love & intimacy, sex without borders & limits, & being a lesbian in your own country. In addition to workshops, there is plenty of opportunity to participate in sports, sunbathe & relax. During this week English will be the main language. Contact: Foreningen Femo, Kvindehuset, Gothersgade 37, 1123 Copenhagen, Denmark.

TBA ♀ **Golden Threads Celebration,** A celebration for lesbians over 50 and their friends from the US, Canada, and other countries, held in Provincetown, MA. There is no age restriction and membership in Golden Threads is not required to participate. Events include workshops, a banquet, dance and live entertainment. Contact: Golden Threads, PO Box 60475, Northampton, MA 01060-0475. Web: http://members.aol.com/goldentred/index.htm

TBA ♀♂ **Heartland Regional Rodeo,** Omaha, NE. Call: HGRA, (402) 597-1689.

TBA ♀♂ **Kool Kids Family Vacation-Isla Mujeres,** see Club Le Bon on page 51, FYI 341

TBA ♀♂ **Netherlands Gay Pride Party Pkg,** see Rainboworld Custom Tours on page 69, FYI 256

TBA ♀♂ **Queen's Birthday Weekend in Sydney,** A weekend of gay and lesbian parties are held annually in Sydney to commemorate the queen's birthday. Location: Sydney, Australia. Contact: Sydney Gay & Lesbian Mardi Gras, PO Box 1064, Darlinghurst, 2010, NSW, Australia.

TBA ♀ **Rambles in Greece with Greek Woman Guide,** see Women in the Wilderness on page 81, 108

TBA ♀ **Womongathering,** A warm and friendly festival for womyn only at a scenic, private camp. We feature local and nationally-recognized womyn spiritual leaders presenting intensive, experiential workshops reflecting the diversity of beliefs known as Womyn's Spirituality. The crafts area features womyn-made items, such as crystals, also readers, body workers and herbalists. Rain will not disturb your enjoyment, because our dining and workshop areas are covered. Location: In the Pocono Mts. Contact: Womongathering, Box 559, Franklinville, NJ 08322, (609) 694-2037, e-mail: womongathr@aol.com.

29 - AG 18 ♀ **Pony Express Tour 1998,** Modern Day Cowgirls Riding for Breast Cancer Research. 50-60 riders will circumnavigate the perimeter of the U.S. The principal rider must be a woman. Each 300-mile leg will raise $1000 for breast cancer research. As did the Pony Express, each woman will pass a medallion to the next rider. The 50-day tour will stop in key cities where ride-in breakfasts & motorcycle shows will be held along with breast cancer educational presentations. Dates of '98 event may change slightly, call for exact dates. Contact: Women's Motorcyclist Foundation, 7 Lent Ave, LeRoy, NY 14482, (716) 768-6054.

July 98

TBA ♀ **Alaska Cruise,** see Remote Possibilities on page 69, FYI 426

TBA ♀ **Alaskan Native Expeditions, Anchorage,** see Thanks, Babs on page 74, 102

TBA ♀ **Int'l Goddess Festival,** A biannual festival, held during a full moon in spring, on a Santa Cruz, CA mountaintop. A celebration of the returning Goddess culture, music, spirit, body. Lodging in wood cabins or camping,

WHEN TO GO

TRIP/EVENTS CALENDAR

swimming pool and ocean, goddess singers, musicians, actresses, workshops. Contact: Women's Spirituality Forum, PO Box 11363, Piedmont, CA 94611-0383, tel/fax: (510) 444-7724.

TBA ♀♂ **I.G.R.A. Annual Convention,** Call IGRA, (303) 832-4472.

TBA ♀♂ **North Star Regional Rodeo,** St. Paul, MN. Call: NSGRA, (612) 641-0069.

TBA ♀♂ **Rocky Mtn. Regional Rodeo,** Denver, CO. Call: IGRA, (303) 839-8810.

TBA ♀ **Whitewater Canoeing, Missinaibi River, Ontario,** see Women in the Wilderness on page 81, 108

17 - 19 ♀ **Int'l Ms. Leather Contest,** A leather contest for SM women, with a welcome beer bust, play parties and other events. Location: Atlanta, GA. Contact: Int'l Ms. Leather, Inc., 2215-R Market St, San Francisco, CA 94114, (402) 451-7987.

17 - 19 ♀ **Int'l Ms. Leather Contest,** A leather contest for SM women, with a welcome beer bust, play parties and other events. Location: Atlanta, GA. Contact: Int'l Ms. Leather, Inc., 2215-R Market St, San Francisco, CA 94114, (402) 451-7987.

18 - 26 ♀♂ **EuroPride '98,** This annual event, a celebration of gay life in Europe, takes place in a different European country each year. Activities include parties, art exhibits and photography. Various festivals, such as singing, dance and film are highlighted. The event culminates in a large parade. Location: Stockholm, Sweden. Contact: Stockholm Europride '98, Box 45090, 104 30 Stockholm, Sweden.

26 - AG 01 ♂ **Pacific Men's Gathering,** A spectrum of adventure, culture & wellness-sharing presented by island men. Hawaiian temple massage, floating shiatsu in thermal springs, volcano lava viewing, traditional but temporary body tattooing, swimming with dolphins, ancient male hula, and more nuture the "aikane" male-male loving that is part of Hawaii's aloha heritage. Contact: Kalani Eco-Resort, RR2 Box 4500, Kehena Beach, HI 96778, (808) 965-7828, for reservations only: (800) 800-6886.

31 - AG 09 ♀ **Women's Tour to Amsterdam Gay Games,** see Robin Tyler's Women's Tours, Cruises & Events on page 69

August 98

TBA ♀ **Denali Rail & Inside Passage Adventure-Alaska,** see Thanks, Babs on page 74, 102

TBA ♀♂ **Gay Games 98 Party Package,** see Rainboworld Custom Tours on page 69, FYI 256

TBA ♀ **Gay Games Amsterdam Package,** see Women in Motion on page 80, 107

TBA ♀♂ **Gay Games Amsterdam Pkgs,** see Beyond the Blue on page 49, FYI 307

TBA ♂ **Gay Games Amsterdam Pkgs,** see Men on Vacation on page 62, 96

TBA ♀♂ **Greater NW Int'l Rodeo,** Seattle, WA. Call: NWGRA, (206) 233-8931.

TBA ♀ **Magic & Mythology of Ireland — Bicycling,** see Woodswomen on page 81, 108

TBA ♀♂ **Missouri Gay Rodeo,** Kansas City, MO. Call: (816) 224-6139.

TBA ♀♂ **Windy City Gay Rodeo,** Chicago, IL. Call: ILGRA, (312) 883-1880.

TBA ♀♂ **Zia Regional Rodeo,** Albuquerque, NM. Call: NMGRA, (505) 255-5045.

01 - 08 ♀♂ **Gay Games Amsterdam Package,** see Stonewall Connection Travel & Tours on page 73, 101

01 - 08 ♀♂ **Gay Games in Amsterdam,** see L'Arc en Ciel Voyages on page 61, 94

01 - 08 ♀♂ **Gay Games V,** Gay Games V will have the theme of Friendship Through Culture & Sports. Also featured is a cultural festival including artists, theater, film, sculpture, history, architecture, literature, performance art and photography. Location: Amsterdam, Netherlands. Contact: Federation of Gay & Lesbian Games Amsterdam, PO Box 2837, 1000 CV Amsterdam, Netherlands, (31-20) 620 1998, Fax: (31-20) 626 1998. E-mail: info@gaygames.nl.

01 - 09 ♀♂ **Gay Games Packages,** see ZMAX Travel & Tours Inc. on page 82, 109

01 - 15 ♀ **Dikes & Dykes—Gay Games Amsterdam,** see Thanks, Babs on page 74, 102

10 - 16 ♀♂ **Gay Games Recovery Extentions,** see Rainboworld Custom Tours on page 69, FYI 256

September 98

TBA ♀♂ **Dive the Red Sea,** see Undersea Expeditions, Inc. on page 77, 104

TBA ♂ **Dungeons & Castles of Europe,** see Travel Keys Tours on page 76, 104

TBA ♀♂ **Greater San Diego Rodeo,** San Diego, CA. Call: GSGRA (San Diego Chapter), (619) 298-4708.

TBA ♀♂ **Pikes Peak United Rodeo,** Colorado Springs, CO. Call: CGRA, (303) 839-8810.

TBA ♀ **Sisterspace Pocono Weekend, '98,** Cancelled for 1997, this event will next take place in 1998 during the weekend after Labor Day. Join us at a wonderful, private, 1000-acre campground with lake in Canadensis, Pennsylvania, only 2.5 hours from NYC and Philadelphia. There are hiking trails, waterfalls and a

FERRARI GUIDES' GAY TRAVEL A to Z - 18th EDITION 171

WHEN TO GO

TRIP/EVENTS CALENDAR

huge lake with good fishing, swimming, boating, cabins, hot showers, beautiful tenting areas and delicious food for both nonveggie and veggie lovers. Enjoy musicians, theater, speakers, workshops, crafts, sports facilities galore, country and square dancing, disco, heated pools, canoes, arts gallery, etc. Contact Sisterspace, 542A S. 48th St, Philadelphia, PA 19143, (215) 476-8856.

TBA ♀ **West Coast Women's Music Festival,** Thousands of women in the woods, music, comedy, dances, country-western lessons, disco, workshops, crafts, childcare, sports. This event will not be held in 1997. Please write or call for '98 dates. Contact: WCWMF, 15842 Chase St, North Hills, CA 91343, (818) 893-4075, Fax: (818) 893-1593.

October 98

TBA ♀♂ **Amsterdam Leather Pride Party Pkg,** see Rainbowworld Custom Tours on page 69, FYI 256

TBA ♀♂ **Atlantic Stampede Rodeo,** Washington, DC. Call: ASGRA, (202) 298-0928.

TBA ♂ **Buying Antiques in European Markets,** see Travel Keys Tours on page 76, 104

TBA ♀ **Hawaii Women's Week— Fall, 1998,** see Remote Possibilities on page 69, FYI 426

TBA ♀♂ **I.G.R.A. 1998 Finals Rodeo,** Call IGRA, (303) 832-4472.

TBA ♀ **Kilimanjaro & Serengeti - Mouintain Trek, Safari,** see Woodswomen on page 81, 108

TBA ♀ **Nepal, Himalayas,** see Club Le Bon on page 51, FYI 341

TBA ♀♂ **Sydney Sleaze Ball,** see Beyond the Blue on page 49, FYI 307

TBA ♀ **Trekking in Himalayas,** see Woodswomen on page 81, 108

23 - 25 ♂ **Body Electric,** Celebrate the Body Erotic with conscious breathwork & sacred rituals. Feel at home in your erotic body. Contact: Kalani Eco-Resort, RR2 Box 4500, Kehena Beach, HI 96778, (808) 965-7828, for reservations only: (800) 800-6886.

25 - NO 01 ♂ **Adventure Camp,** A fun frolic in Hawaii's volcanos, waters & forests. Build new friendships, hike to secluded beaches, descend into lava caves, kayak streams into the sea, bathe in crater lakes, etc. Contact: Kalani Eco-Resort, RR2 Box 4500, Kehena Beach, HI 96778, (808) 965-7828, for reservations only: (800) 800-6886.

November 98

TBA ♀♂ **Dive Reefs of Belize,** see Undersea Expeditions, Inc. on page 77, 104

TBA ♀♂ **Palm Springs Regional Rodeo,** Palm Springs, CA. Call: GSGRA (Desert Empire Chapter), (619) 320-8686.

TBA ♀♂ **Texas Gay Rodeo (15th annual),** Call: TGRA, (512) 835-5314.

December 98

20 - 26 ♂ **Gay Spirit,** Tribal celebration & transformative alternative to the holidaze. Sway your hula hips to the rhythm of the islands & your spirit will manifest loving brotherhood, abundant nature & healthful living. Contact: Kalani Eco-Resort, RR2 Box 4500, Kehena Beach, HI 96778, (808) 965-7828, for reservations only: (800) 800-6886.

25 - JA 01 ♀♂ **New Years Dive in Belize,** see Undersea Expeditions, Inc. on page 77, 104

28 - JA 06 ♀♂ **New Years Dive in the Galapagos,** see Undersea Expeditions, Inc. on page 77, 104

30 - JA 02 ♀ **New Year's Eve 1998 in San Francisco,** see Women in Motion on page 80, 107

January 99

TBA ♀♂ **Dive the Cocos Islands, Costa Rica,** see Undersea Expeditions, Inc. on page 77, 104

December 99

TBA ♀♂ **New Years '99 at the Pyramids,** see Travel Affair on page 75, 103

TBA ♀♂ **New Years '99 in Paris,** see Travel Affair on page 75, 103

TBA ♀♂ **New Years '99 in Sydney, Australia,** see Travel Affair on page 75, 103

AFRICA

WHO TO CALL

For Tour Companies Serving This Destination
See Africa on page 8

KENYA
COUNTRY CODE: (254)

NAIROBI

■ *Retail & Bookstores*

BINTI LEGACY, THE, Write: PO Box 68077, Nairobi, women's bookstore.

MOROCCO

WHO TO CALL

For Tour Companies Serving This Destination
See Morocco on page 21

Travel for Gays to Morocco

Morocco is an extremely sensual, exotic country with plenty to offer the gay or lesbian traveler...delicious food, colorful markets, exquisite architecture and remarkable landscapes ranging from the largest mountain chain in Africa to the Sahara desert. Moroccans are very friendly and welcoming to foreigners (especially if you bother to venture beyond the normal tourist sites), and eager to please.

Amongst Moroccan men, it is not uncommon to have special and intimate relationships with another male, starting from their teenage years and continuing throughout most of their lives, even after they are married. In general, there is fairly widespread acceptance of homosexuality among Moroccan men. But one does not flaunt it on the street.

During the period of French colonialism (1912-1956), Morocco was famous as a playground for European homosexuals and pedophiles. It was also known for a circle of American gays centered in Tanger around author Paul Bowles (who, now in his 80's, can still be found in a little cafe at the Petit Socco), including Burroughs, Tennessee Williams and countless others.

Upon independence, homosexuality was made illegal. While the police do not bother Moroccan gays, they are not necessarily as lenient with foreigners caught with Moroccans—especially Moroccan teenagers.

Gay sex between Moroccans and foreigners is not uncommon, but the key is to exercise great discretion. Sex is usually for a fee (be sure to settle on a price in advance). If you do find yourself in trouble, a discrete monetary gift to the police may often, but NOT always, help.

Other gay guides list certain cafes and restaurants as gay, but these places are no more and no less gay than any other place. Generally, any public space, be it cafe, restaurant, street or marketplace, is dominated by men and may have a gay undercurrent.

Moroccans are extremely friendly and open to conversation with a foreigner. It is very easy to strike up a friendship that may last through a cup of coffee or for years. In speaking of yourself, remember that homosexuality carries a different set of meanings in a culture vastly different from your own. A vast majority of men who have had sex with other men would never consider themselves homosexual and would never use the term in reference to themselves.

If you do go to Morocco looking for an encounter, it can certainly be found. Just exercise discretion. The towns most famous for gay life are Marrakech, Essaouira and Taroudant in the south and Tanger and Chefchaouon in the north. It is especially easy to meet people at the Jemaa el Fnaa in Marrakech in the early evening.

Reliable AIDS statistics are not easily available. Condoms can be hard to find; bring your own from home!

At all cost, avoid the large, mass-market tour groups. They are terrible. You see shockingly little and get dragged from one cheap bazaar to another, where guides earn high commissions.

Spring and fall are the best times to travel. Winters are moderate, but it can rain. Summers are hot, unless you are at one of the beaches. Morocco is only 12 miles from Spain, and there are regular ferries. There are also direct flights from the US and Canada three times per week (five times per week, during summer).

> This information was provided by Heritage Tours (USA) Inc., a company which specializes in customizing in-depth explorations of Morocco for independent travelers. Contact Heritage at (212) 749-1339, Fax: (212) 749-4317, E-Mail: heritagejz@earthlink.net.

MOROCCO

FYI

Cape Town Cultural Excursions...Wine & Cheese Tasting...Gay Nightlife Tours

Beau Séjour directors, Ken and John say, "Our favourite tours leave Cape Town bound for the countryside beyond the isthmus that connects the Cape Peninsula to the mainland of Africa, with views of some spectacular mountains and valleys. Here is where most of our well-known wine estates are situated, and where we sample some of the fruits of the vine, and local cheeses and fruits."

"Here also are some of our oldest and most beautiful country towns. Stellenbosch is the second-oldest settlement in SA and now a large university town, Franschhoek was originally a Huguenot settlement. Paarl, is the centre of our brandy making industry."

"Another typical tour is a kind of "cradle of culture" driving and walking tour of town and suburbs, looking at the many cultures, religions and societies which make Cape culture so rich: Malay, Indian, Afrikaans, British, Dutch, French, Muslim, etc. And then, of course, there are the legacies of apartheid, the vacant land of a once-thriving District Six, on the one hand, and the thriving, bustling African shanty townships on the outskirts of town. The apartheid era, itself, is "recorded" in the Mayibuye Centre at the U. of Western Cape, which was itself at the centre of the anti-apartheid struggle."

Contact **Beau Séjour** at (27-21) 788-2710 (tel/fax) or cellphone: (27-82) 556-8175.

NAMIBIA

NAMIBIA
COUNTRY CODE: (264)

WHO TO CALL
For Tour Companies Serving This Destination
See Namibia on page 21

WINDHOEK

■ *Information*
UGON, Write: PO Box 21429, Windhoek, United Gay Organization of Namibia.

NIGERIA
COUNTRY CODE: (234)

CALABAR

■ *Information*
GIRLS' POWER INITIATIVE, Write: GPI, PO Box 3663, Unical Post Office, Calabar, group promoting the rights, education, protection & advancement of girls in Nigeria.

SOUTH AFRICA
COUNTRY CODE: (27)

WHO TO CALL
For Tour Companies Serving This Destination
See South Africa on page 25

BENONI

■ *Bars*
BARN, THE, 73 6th Road, Cloverdene, (011) 968 2719.

BLOEMFONTEIN

■ *Bars*
BLOEMFONTEIN CLUB, (051) 228 720, party held by the Gay Association of Bloemfontein, Sat till 03:00.

■ *Dance Bar/Disco*
BUZERANT ESTATE, Ferreira Rd, Orange Grove Farm, (083) 228 3013, Wed 20:00-24:00 (Fri & Sat from 21:00 till later).

CAPE TOWN

■ *Information*
LESBIAN & GAY HELPLINE & AIDS INFO, (021) 215 420, 24hrs.

■ *Accommodations*
HIGH LODGE, in Sea Point, (27-21) 439 87 15, guesthouse with private baths, Jacuzzi, pool on premises.

■ *Bars*
ANGELS, 27 Somerset Rd, Greenpoint, (021) 419 9216, from 20:00, 3-bar complex.
BRONX, 27 Somerset Rd, Greenpoint, at Angels bar complex, (021) 419 9216.
BRUNSWICK TAVERN, 17 Bree St, (021) 25 27 39, 17:00-01:00 (Sat from 10:30, Sun from 18:00).
MURIEL'S, 95 Lower Main St, Observatory, (021) 61 08 32, from 19:30, closed Mon.
OWEN'S GAT PARTY, Temple of Israel Hall, Upper Portswood Rd, Greenpoint, (021) 930 33 99, monthly party, 20:00-01:00. Call for schedule.

■ *Dance Bar/Disco*
DETOUR, 27 Somerset Rd, Greenpoint, at Angels bar complex, (021) 419 9216, from 20:00.
WATER ROOM, Liesbeek Park, Observatory, at the River Club, (021) 448 0192, scheduled monthly women's dance night, upscale atmosphere, call for exact dates.

■ *Cafe*
ALLADDIN COFFEE SHOP, Kloof Rd, at the Nedbank Centre, shop 7, Sea Point, (021) 439 44 28, 08:00-18:00 (Sat till 16:00), Sun 09:00-15:00.
WOMEN'S CAFE NIGHT, at Cafe Erte, 265a Main Rd, Seapoint, (021) 434 6624, Sun 20:00-06:00.

■ *Saunas/Health Clubs*
CLUB WELGELEGEN, 51 William St, Mowbray, (021) 448 6202, from 18:00.
STEAMERS HEALTH & LEISURE CLUB, Old Creda Press, at Wembley & Solan Rds, (021) 461 62 10, 12:00-02:00 (Fri-Sun 24hrs).

■ *Restaurants*
AFRICA CAFE, 213 Lower Main Rd, Observatory, (021) 47 95 53, 18:30-01:00.
CAFE ERTE, 265a Main Rd, Sea Point, (021) 434 6624, restaurant & coffee bar, 20:00-06:00, Sun women's night.
CLEMENTINES, Wolfe St, in Chelsea Village, Wynberg, (021) 797 6168, intimate atmosphere.
DINNER CLUB, THE, 10 Leeuwenhog Roda, Higgovale, (021) 24 08 04, private & arranged-in-advance dinner parties for 6-10 people, monthly murder mystery evenings.
ELAINE'S CURRY BISTRO, 105 Lower Main Rd, Observatory, (021) 472 616, Mon-Fri 12:30-14:30 & 18:30-24:00 (Sat & Sun 18:00-24:00 only).
L'ORIENT, 50 Main Rd, Three Anchor Bay, (021) 439 6572, from 19:00 (closed Mon), Southeast Asian cuisine.
LA RIVIERA, Main Rd, Hout Bay, from 19:00, closed Mon.
LE PETIT PARIS, Green Market Sq, (021) 23 76 48, 07:30-17:00 (Sat till 13:00), closed Sun.

DURBAN

■ *Accommodations*
BREAKAWAY, PO Box 740, Umhlanga Rocks 4320, mornings: (27-31) 207 2093, evenings: (27-31) 5612573. Fully serviced self-catering apartments in coastal town of Umhlanga, just north of Durban, restaurants & bar, beaches nearby.

■ *Bars*
CLUB, THE, 301 Umbilo Rd, (031) 304 4091, bar & restaurant, membership available, closed Wed.
GOSSIPS, 423 West St, at Masonic Grove & West St, from 20:00.
GRUMPY'S BAR, at Grumpy's Complex location, Fri & Sat from 20:00.
GRUMPY'S COMPLEX, Point Road, at the Alexander Hotel, (031) 368 1625, complex with 2 bars, cafe & sauna.
OUR PLACE, at Grumpy's Complex location, daily from 18:30, strippers.
PANDORA'S BY THE SEA, 27 Hunter St, near Brickfield Rd, (031) 368 5337.

■ *Cafe*
LATE NIGHT GALLEON, Nedbank Centre, street level, at Point & West Streets, (031) 32 46 89, 08:00-04:00.
MADHATTER'S COFFEE SHOP, at Grumpy's Complex location, Wed-Sun from 18:30.

■ *Saunas/Health Clubs*
HYDRO HEAVEN, at Grumpy's Complex location, bring your own towel Tues.

■ *Restaurants*
EL GUAPPO, Blue Heights Centre, Italian Quarter Restaurant, Shop 7A, Westville, (031) 267 0424.
TWO MOON JUNCTION, 45 Windermere Rd, Morningside, (031) 303 3078, from 09:00 till late, closed Sun.

EAST LONDON

■ *Bars*
CLUB BYRONS, (0431) 726 9449, call for exact address & opening hours.

■ *Dance Bar/Disco*
THUMPERS, Recreation Rd, (0431) 726 9449, Fri & Sat, call for time.

JOHANNESBURG

■ *Information*
AIDS INFO, (011) 725 6710, or AIDS Life Line: (0800) 0123 22.
GAY & LESBIAN LINE, (011) 643 2311, 19:00-22:00.
GAY LIBRARY, 38 High St, Berea, (011) 643 2311, Tues 19:30-21:30, Sat 14:30-16:30.

SOUTH AFRICA

LESBIAN FORUM, (011) 336 5081, support group for lesbians.

■ Accommodations

COTTAGES, THE, 30 Gill St, Observatory, (27-11) 487 2829, Fax: (27-11) 487 2404. Separate stone & thatched cottages, private baths, country garden, no smoking in dining room, 10 minutes from gay clubs, 50% gay & lesbian clientele.

JOEL HOUSE, 61 Joel Rd (nr Lily Rd), Berea, (11) 642 4426, Fax: 642 5221, gay-friendly guest house with restaurant, private baths, full breakfast, ceiling fans, TV lounge, nearby pool.

ROSLIN HOUSE, (27-11) 487 2402. Gay & lesbian luxury B&B guesthouse 10 minutes from Johannesburg gay nightlife, pool on premises.

THEME GUEST LODGE, 60 Joel Rd, across from Joel House, (011) 484 5730, 70% men, 30% women.

■ Bars

CARDINAL BAR, 430 Louis Botha Ave, at Main St, Rouxville, (082) 551 5285, from 19:00 (Sun 11:00-23:00 & Sun brunch), closed Mon.

CHAMPIONS, Wolmarans St, at Loveday St, Braamfontein, (011) 720 6605, from 13:00.

CLUB ZOO, Hopkins St, beside Shoprite & Checkers, Yeoville, (011) 447 1620, men-only leather bar, Wed-Sat 22:00-05:00. Strictly leather, levi, camouflage, rubber or naked from waist up.

CONNECTIONS WOMEN'S BAR, 1 Pretoria St, Hillbrow, (011) 642 8511, restaurant & women's bar downstairs, men's cruise bar upstairs, daily 11:00-02:00.

CONNECTIONS, 1 Pretoria St, Hillbrow, (011) 642 8511, men's pub upstairs, restaurant & women's bar downstairs, daily 11:00-02:00.

DIVA'S, Old Pretoria Main Rd, at Motor City, upstairs, Midrand, (082) 410 2872, 7 days.

GOTHAM CITY, 58 Pretoria St, Hillbrow, (011) 642 0243, video bar, strippers, theme parties, 23:00-05:00.

PANDORA'S PIANO LOUNGE, 77 Cargo Corner, at Tyrwhitt Ave, Rosebank, (011) 447 3066, bar & restaurant serving light fare, open 6 days from 18:00.

PUNCHLINE, Civic Theatre, Braamfontein, (011) 403 3408, from 19:00 (closed Sun).

SASHAY SOUTH, Johannesburg St at 5th St, La Rochelle, (011) 435 1757, from 16:00.

SKYLINE BAR, Pretoria St, Hillbrow, near Harrison Reef Hotel.

TOGS BAR, Putney Rd, at the Togs Sports & Rec. Centre, Brixton, tea & coffee bar, Sun from 15:00.

■ Dance Bar/Disco

CLUB CACTUS CITY, Catharine Ave at Pretoria St, Hillbrow, near Gotham City bar, (011) 447 1608.

KRYPTON, 17 Constantia Centre, at Tyrwhitt Ave, Rosebank, (011) 442 7372, Wed, Fri-Sat from 18:00.

■ Restaurants

JOJO'S, main entrance of the Civic Theatre, Braamfontein, (011) 403 7373, restaurant & wine bar, Portuguese cuisine.

JOSE'S, 21 4th Ave, Parkhurst, (011) 788 4308, open late 7 days.

PRAVINA'S GUJERATI CUISINE, 83 4th Ave, Melville, (011) 482 6670, vegetarian Indian cuisine.

■ Retail & Bookstores

ESTORIL, Pretoria St, Hillbrow, (011) 643 1613, general bookstore with gay & lesbian section.

EXCLUSIVE BOOKS, Village Walk, (011) 884 7591, general bookstore with gay & lesbian section. Other locations: Hyde Park Corner, Hyde Park; Victoria Wharf, Waterfront, Constantia Village Shopping Centre, Constantia.

PHAMBILI BOOKS, 55 Kruis St, (011) 29 4944, general bookstore with small gay & lesbian section.

SHELDONS BOOKSHOP, Entrance 5, Eastgate Shopping Centre, Bedfordview, (011) 622 4870, general bookstore with gay & lesbian section.

KIMBERLEY

■ Bars

STALLIONS ACTION BAR, Stockdale St, at Queens Hotel, cruisy, 2 bars (1 for men, 1 for women).

■ Restaurants

MARIO'S, Dutoitspan Road, close to Holiday Inn Garden Court, Mon-Sat 10:00-23:00.

KLERKSDORP

■ Bars

CLUB EX, Park St, at Cock St, (018) 464 1268, daily from 20:00.

COTTON CLUB, North St, (018) 462 9924, from 19:00.

NYLSTROOM

■ Accommodations

SHANGRI-LA COUNTRY LODGE, PO Box 262, Nylstroom 0510, (27-14) 717 53 81, fax: (27-14) 717 31 88, gay-friendly country lodge with restaurant & bar, 1 hour north of Pretoria, private baths, buffet breakfast.

PIKETBERG

■ Accommodations

NOUPOORT GUEST FARM, PO Box 101, (0261) 5754, Fax: (0261) 5834. Gay-friendly guest farm with 10 cottages, gay weekends arranged, TV lounge, conference room, BBQ, pool, sauna & basic work-out gym.

PORT ELIZABETH

■ Information

GAY & LESBIAN HELPLINE, (041) 335 6426, 18:00-22:00, ask for GLAC.

■ Bars

RICH'S, Lincoln House, 3rd floor, at Kemp & Strand Streets, Wed, Fri-Sun from 20:00.

■ Restaurants

CUYLER CRESCENT GUESTHOUSE, 19 Cuyler Crescent, (014) 55 36 72, serves breakfast & dinner, Victorian tea garden. Reservations required.

GALLERI, 95 Parliament St, (041) 555 223, daily 16:00-04:00.

PRETORIA

■ Information

AIDS INFO, (012) 313 7988.

GLO-P (GAYS & LESBIANS OF PRETORIA), (012) 469 888, 19:00-22:00.

■ Bars

STEAMERS COMPLEX, Railway St. Ext., at Paul Kruger, (012) 322 6278, complex houses restaurant, 7 bars & 2 dance floors.

■ Saunas/Health Clubs

CLUB 64 64 Steenboklaan, Monument Park, (012) 46 40 71, upscale, be discreet.

SOUTH COAST

■ Accommodations

STARBASE, Port Edward, (03930) 32891, accommodation with bar, restaurant & observatory.

■ Bars

ASTRONAUTS & CONSTELLATIONS AT STARBASE, Port Edward, (03930) 32891, bar & restaurant, Fri & Sat (bar from 19:00).

WARMBATHS

■ Accommodations

ELEPHANT SPRINGS HOTEL, 31 Sutter Rd, Warmbaths 0480, (27-14) 736 2101, fax: (27-14) 736 4812, gay-friendly B&B with restaurant & bar, private baths, full breakfast.

WELKOM

■ Dance Bar/Disco

CLUB EQUESTRIAN, Stateway, (057) 353 2813 or (083) 262 1361, Fri & Sat from 21:00.

ZIMBABWE

FYI

Exclusively Gay Tours to China & Hong Kong

CHINA VOYAGES

With most of its staff having grown up in China, **China Voyages** has a justifiable claim to being knowledgeable about their specialty destination. The company offers exclusively gay tours to China and Hong Kong. The Golden China Tour (15 days) takes you to the "must-see" cities of Beijing, Chengde, Shanghai, Suzou (the Venice of the East) and Guilin, finishing in Hong Kong. The Best of China Tour (21 days) adds more time to savor the splendours of the Forbidden City, the Terracotta Army in Xian, a silk-spinning factory in Hangzhou and the antiques and crafts markets of Guilin, plus a 4-day cruise on the Yangtze River. The company also provides customized independent itineraries, discount hotel and air bookings, extensive guided tours, and China visa processing.

Contact **China Voyages** at (415) 398-2244, (800) 914-9133, Fax: (415) 399-0827, E-mail: Jack@chinavoyages.com, Web: www.chinavoyages.com.

FYI

The China Experts

Having specialized in itineraries to China for fifteen years, the people at **Envoy Travel** have the answers to most of the questions that come up about China travel. Over the years, they have developed itineraries that let you visit China at your own pace. In short, you can arrange your own individual tour at group prices.

When you travel to China with Envoy, you meet your own guide and driver when you disembark from the plane, and travel through this unique culture with an itinerary to suit your interests.

For a first trip to China, Envoy recommends an itinerary including Beijing – site of the Forbidden City, the Imperial Palace Museum, the Temple of Heaven and world-famous Tianamen Square – and Xian – capital of China for eleven dynasties and rich in archaeological treasures – and Guilin – the city of emerald hairpin mountains around the Li River. Visiting all these takes a 9-day trip.

If you have more time, add the exotic experience of five days in Lhasa, capital of Tibet and known as the "rooftop of the world."

Envoy Travel also has first-hand knowledge of, and features itineraries to, many other Asian destinations, such as Hong Kong, Taiwan, Singapore, Malaysia, Indonesia.

Contact **Envoy Travel** at (800) 443-6869, (312) 787-2400, Fax: (312) 787-7109.

ZIMBABWE
COUNTRY CODE: (263)

WHO TO CALL
For Tour Companies Serving This Destination
See Zimbabwe on page 29

HARARE

■ *Information*

GALZ (GAYS & LESBIANS OF ZIMBABWE), Write: Private Bag A6131, Avondale, Harare, gay & lesbian group.

WOMEN'S ACTION GROUP, Write: Box 135, Harare women's organization.

ZWRCN (ZIMBABWE WOMEN'S RESOURCE CENTRE & NETWORK), 288A Herbert Chitepo Ave, 737 435, library Mon-Fri 08:30-12:30, Sat 09:30-12:00. For info write PO Box 2192, Harare.

EAST ASIA

CHINA
COUNTRY CODE: (86)

WHO TO CALL
For Tour Companies Serving This Destination
See China on page 12

BEIJING

■ *Bars*

JJ'S, not a gay bar, but frequented by local gays, ask locally for address.

■ *Dance Bar/Disco*

NIGHTMAN DISCO, not far from the Radisson Hotel, look for red neon sign, not a gay disco, discreetly frequented by gays who stay more to the right of the DJ area.

■ *Cafe*

HALF & HALF CAFE, San Li Tun, South 15 Bldg, Chao Yang District, (10) 6416 6919, not a gay cafe, more gay Wed evening.

Hong Kong — The Merry Widow

by Matthew Link, Rainbow Tours

Not many civilizations can claim knowledge of their own self-destruct date, but one British Crown Colony in Asia has the privilege of foretelling its own future: Hong Kong and July 1, 1997.

Hong Kong's notorious streets of Suzy Wong and Bruce Lee were built upon the principles of free capitalist trade gone wild. From a factory-choked export hub in the 1960's, to a financial and shipping mega-center in the 1990's, Hong Kong is one of Asia's remarkable economic success stories. "As long as someone makes a buck..." was the credo for this capitalistic fantasy city for years - an Asian New York high on MSG, albeit cleaner, safer, and harder working than any Big Apple! Young, suited "Chuppies" (Chinese Yuppies), with the ever present cellular phone in one hand and stock quotes in the other, smoothly weave their way in and out of the convoluted human and automobile jungle that is the heart Hong Kong, while feeble tourists fear for their very lives while crossing marked sidewalks. The Asian metropolis is a dog-eat-dog city, no denying it, and doesn't warm up to people nicely. Yet despite its ruthless reputation, the traveler finds a fanciful and even innocent side to this city, like a proud teenager showing off her newfound body of concrete and metal and money.

The question is: will the current prosperity last past the '97 handover to China? Will China's awful human rights record cripple the freewheeling society? And what's in store for modern gays and lesbians under the banner of the last massive Communist country on the planet? Only China can tell us, if she will.

Up until even last year, the mood in the British Crown Colony was one of denial that the inescapable date of July, 1997 would ever actually happen - everyone was too busy counting their Hong Kong dollars to care. Now this robust city that has given so much to so many is now getting that creeping feeling of abandonment: many British citizens (who may have lived in the colony most of their lives) are headed back to family in London or Manchester for good. The few, fortunate local Chinese that have their own UK passports (Britain stopped issuing them to Hong Kongers in the 1980's) are being told they need to leave the colony during the handover, and then re-enter "China" afterwards. Needless to say, the airlines are already full. It may take a miracle for visitors to be able to fly into the colony for post-handover parties!

China, the current bully of the Asian scene, is doing its best to make a rocky transition even rockier. Still, there are thousands of Americans, Southeast Asians, and Europeans who will remain on Chinese turf (as thousands of foreigners do in other parts of China), and will remain to call Hong Kong home. And stay tuned: China's policies, schizophrenic at best, will change day by day even after the handover.

And so goes the woe and fate

Matthew Link is a writer and filmmaker who resides full-time in Hawaii, where he conducts personal tours for gay visitors through his company Rainbow Tours. Matthew has, at various times, called Micronesia, Papua New Guinea, New Zealand, California, and of course, Hong Kong, home. Feel free to contact Matthew at (808) 328-8406, or by E-mail at MrLinkk @aol.com.

Continued on next page

of Hong Kong. As one character in a popular Chinese film put it, "Hong Kong's like a mistress. Everyone wants to have her but no one wants to marry her."

Hong Kong has been a thorn in China's side ever since China lost the excellent natural port to British forces during the Opium Wars in the late 1800's. Communist China has always looked down in disgust at Hong Kong's opulent capitalism, while at the same time being secretly envious of its stature as a premier world trading center. ("Mainland" Chinese have been escaping into Hong Kong for years - for political freedom, as well as to do some killer shopping.) China has spent most of the last decade mimicking her wealthy little sister to the south, setting up "special economic zones", encouraging "free trade", selling "Gucci" fashions on the streets of Shanghai, munching on Kentucky Fried Chicken in Beijing, snatching up Ferraris smuggled in by the Chinese Mafia (affectionately known as the "Triads"). The secret is that China, for all its posturing, is jealous of its shining sister Hong Kong and wants not to just be like her, but to be *her. A global Jan and Marsha Brady, if you will. And guess what? It's now Jan's turn to tell Marsha what to do.*

As with the rest of China, the future is rushing forward rapidly, yet still up in the air. And regardless of what actually happens in the aftermath of '97, Hong Kong will no doubt remain a vibrant and thriving Chinese center for many years to come.

But what does 1997 mean for gays living in Hong Kong? The best case scenario is that life may go on as normal - "normal" in Hong Kong meaning the continuation of deep closets through the Chinese culture of implicit politeness - and at times, with doors bolted shut. One would think that in a modern Westernized city like Hong Kong, gay life would be like living in the San Francisco of the Orient. But not so fast. There's the little detail of culture to take into account. Even with China's long history of queer emperors, eunuchs, artists, etc., most modern Hong Kong Chinese still think sex between two men is a funny joke. Many people think it is just not possible. The solid and sturdy institution of the Chinese family molds expectations of their children intensely, and patriarchal lineage of a family name is important. Most cramped Hong Kong apartments house at least two generations of relatives, if not more. Although this makes for strong family ties, privacy is at a minimum, and group activities dominate. Marriages aren't exactly arranged, but likely spouses are heavily suggested. Taking just these things into account, the possibility of living some kind of free, exciting homosexual lifestyle is very difficult in this confining city. Even with over six million inhabitants, Hong Kong still feels like a relatively a small town. Since most of the population lives on the island of Hong Kong and neighboring Kowloon peninsula, simply bumping into people you know on the bus or subway everyday is common (no one owns a car and the metro, buses, ferries, and taxis are cheap and plentiful). The concrete forests may seem immense to the visitor, but stay longer than a week and you're sure to experience that lovely Hong Kong feeling of inescapable claustrophobia.

The good news is that in just the last couple of years, gays in Hong Kong have finally awakened to the possible human rights threats of China, and the gay community has been more unified and visible than at any other point in the colony's history, getting involved politically and socially. Many Hong Kong Chinese have gone to school or lived in the West, and being out to them is less of a big deal. And out-and-out liberalism as a retaliatory action has made a comeback in these months before the handover, causing the climate for gays to improve dramatically.

Most gays and lesbians are hoping for the best, since Mainland cities like Shanghai and Beijing are now excessively more "open" economically and socially

Continued on page 507

CANTON

Dance Bar/Disco
PACIFIC NIGHTS, Renmin Zhong Rd, gay Sat evenings. Address may change in '97, ask locally to verify exact address. 🍴♂

SHANGHAI

Bars
BAHAMA MAMAS, ask locally for address, bar & cafe with younger crowd, not a gay, discreetly frequented by gays, till 04:00.

EDDY'S BAR, 890 Weihai Rd, 6247 7235. ♂

LA CAFE, ask locally for address, trendy, not a gay bar, discreetly frequented by gays, more gay after 22:00. 🍴

SHENZHEN

Bars
QUEEN'S PUB, Jianshe Rd, across from Century Plaza Hotel, close to train station & Dragon Hotel, not a gay bar, discreetly frequented by gays.

HONG KONG
COUNTRY CODE: (852)

WHO TO CALL
For Tour Companies Serving This Destination
See Hong Kong on page 17

HONG KONG

Information
AIDS HOTLINE, 2898 4422, Thurs, Sat 19:00-22:00.

CONTACTS MAGAZINE, c/o Island Publishing Co., GPO Box 13427, Hong Kong, 2817 9447, E-mail: BandT@hk.super.net. Launched in Feb '93, this monthly publication is the only title being published by the newly emergent gay community. Published on the 15th of each month, with 32 pages of local & international gay news, reviews, stories, features & personal ads. Annual 12-issue subscription costs HK$300 for local residents & US$70 for overseas residents, including airmail postage. Sample copies cost US$10.

HONG KONG 10%, 2314 8726, gay organization with scheduled socials & events, answers in Chinese only.

HORIZONS, 2815 9268, gay organization, answers Mon-Thurs 19:30-22:30, scheduled socials.

QUEER SISTERS, 2314 4348, lesbian organization, answers in Cantonese, Thurs 19:30-22:00, or tape.

Accommodations
BABYLON VILLA, Lower Cheung Sha 29, Lantau Island, 2980 2872, gay guesthouse.

Bars
BABYLON, 409-413 Jaffe Rd, Kingspower Commercial Bldg, 5th floor, Wanchai, Hong Kong, 2573 3978, karaoke lounge, 20:00-02:00. ♂

CE TOP, 37-43 Cochrane St, 9th floor, Central Hong Kong, 2544 3581, karaoke bar, lounge & dance bar, 18:00-03:00. 🍴♂

CIRCUS CLUB, 2-6 Yee Woo St, Ying Kong Mansions, 11th floor, Causeway Bay, Hong Kong, 2576 5680, biggest karaoke lounge in Hong Kong, 20:00-02:00, younger crowd. ♂

FIRESIDE BAR, 97-43 Cochrane St, Cheung Hing Commercial Bldg, at CE Top bar, Central Hong Kong, karaoke. ♂

GARAGE, 35 Peel St, Central Hong Kong, 2542 1488, bar & restaurant on 2 levels, 12:00-20:00 (closed Sun). ✗♂

H2O, 474-476 Lockhart Rd, Hop Yee Bldg, 2nd floor, Causeway Bay, Hong Kong, 2834 6451, karaoke lounge, 17:00-03:00. ♂

MEMBERS CONNECTION, 5 Lan Fong Rd, 3rd floor, Causeway Bay, Hong Kong, 2890 7731, small karaoke lounge, 19:00-03:00. ♂

VELVET KARAOKE, 220 Gloucester Rd, Causeway Bay, Hong Kong, 2891 1338, karaoke lounge, from 22:00, frequented by many lesbians. ♀♂

WHY NOT, 491-499 Lockhart Rd, Wan Chai, Hong Kong, 2572 7808, karaoke lounge, 20:00-02:00. ♂

XX, Lan Kwai Fong, at Club 64, Central Hong Kong, 1108 18318, women-only socials, last Sun 17:00-20:00. ♀

Dance Bar/Disco
CLUB 97, 9 Lan Kwai Fong, Central Hong Kong, 2810 9333, gay Fri 18:00-22:00. Horizons gay group holds Tea dance 1st Sun. 🍴♀♂

PROPAGANDA DANCE CLUB, ★ 30-32 Wyndham St, Central Hong Kong, 2868 1316, disco & lounge, 21:30-03:30 (usually closed Sun). 🍴♂

ZIP, 2 Glenealy St, Central Hong Kong, 2523 3595, 18:00-02:00. 🍴♂

Saunas/Health Clubs
AA, 19 Lan Fong Rd, 1st floor, Causeway Bay, Hong Kong, 2577 3705, 13:00-02:00. ♂

AE, 114 Thompson Rd, Kwong Ah Bldg, 1st floor, Wan Chai, Hong Kong, 2591 0500, 14:00-01:00. ♂

BA, 25-33 Johnston Rd, Cheung Hong Mansion, 1st floor, flat D, Wanchai, Hong Kong, 2527 7073, 14:00-02:00. ♂

CENTRAL ESCALATOR, 37-43 Cochrane St, Cheung Hing Commercial Bldg, 2nd floor, Central Hong Kong, 2581 9951, 13:00-01:00. ♂

GAME BOY'S, 324 Lockhart Rd, Fook Yee Bldg, 2nd floor, Wanchai, Hong Kong, 2369 8174, 12:00-02:00. ♂

JJ PARK, 51 Patterson St, Fairview Mansion, 3rd floor, flat A, Causeway Bay, Hong Kong, 2882 2399, 15:00-01:00. ♂

Leathers/Piercing
FETISH FASHION, 52-60 Lynhurst Terrace, Central Hong Kong, 2546 5188, men's & women's rubber & leather clothing and accessories.

KOWLOON

Bars
WALLY MATT LOUNGE, 9 Cornwall Ave, Tsim Sha Tsui, 2367 6874. frequented by some gays, 18:00-03:00. ✗🍴

Saunas/Health Clubs
BLUE BLOOD, 20 Austin Ave, Perfect Commercial Bldg, 3rd floor, Tsim Sha Tsui, 2302 0780, 15:00-24:00, rumored to welcome Chinese only. ♂

BOBSON FITNESS CLUB, 35-37 Hankow Rd, Ma Bldg, 3rd floor, Apt D, Tsim Sha Tsui, 2376 2208, 15:30-01:00. ♂

JONATHAN'S FITNESS CLUB, 42 Carnarvon Rd, 2nd floor, Tsim Sha Tsui, 2369 81 74, 18:00-24:00. ♂

KK, 19-21 Jordan Rd, Fuk Kok Bldg, 16th floor, Block A, 2388 6138, 14:00-02:00.

ROME CLUB, 27 Ashley Rd, Chiap Lee Commercial Bldg, 2nd fl, Tsim Sha Tsui, 2376 0602, 15:00-24:00, unfriendly to non-Chinese. ♂

YUK TAK CHEE, 123 Prince Edward Rd, ground level, 2393 9595, 12:00-24:00. ♂

JAPAN
COUNTRY CODE: (81)

WHO TO CALL
For Tour Companies Serving This Destination
See Japan on page 18

GETTING AROUND JAPAN: If you're not sure whether you'll be welcome in a bar, call first. Your language ability in Japanese, English, French, German, etc, may be enough to make you welcome. Otherwise, pick a place where you can be understood & where you can understand what is going on. Not all bars listed here have English-speaking staff; many Japanese are embarassed that they don't speak English well. If you're visiting for several weeks or more, a little Japanese language study on your part may be helpful. Besides, it's a great icebreaker.

JAPAN

AMAGASAKI
Bars
JUN, Kanda, Nakadori 3-77, in the Yamamoto Bldg, 3rd floor, (06) 413 1381, 20:00-05:00. ⑤♂

AOMORI
Bars
ATORIUMU, 1-10-4 Arikata, (0177) 34 7768. ♂

CARAVAN, Hurukawa 1-chome, in the Sun Friend Bldg, (0177) 77 8956, 18:00-24:00. ♂

RENTARO, 2-10-9 Ankata, ♂

BEPPU
Saunas/Health Clubs
DANWASHITSU IKOI, 6-21 Kyomachi, (0977) 22 6460. ♂

FUJISAWA
Information
KANAGAWA WOMEN'S CENTER, 1-11-1 Enoshima, Fujisawa City, (0466) 27 2111.

FUKUOKA
Bars
APOLLON, 4-15-7 Sumiyoshi, Hakata-ku, across from Marion Hotel, (092) 475 6699. ⑤♂

ENJELU (ANGEL), 1-2-22 Kiyokawa, Chuo-ku, (092) 522 5333. ♂

HACHIBAN KAN, 2-13-6 Sumiyoshi, in the Suminoe Bldg #2-103, Hakata-ku, near Sumiyoshi Shrine, (092) 282 6389, 19:00-03:00. ♂

KANCHAN, 2-14-9 Haruyoshi, Chuo-ku, (092) 712 6063. ♂

KANIVALU, 2-6-32 Kiyokawa, Chuo-ku, (092) 524 6554. ♂

KATACHAN, 3-8-5 Watanabe-dori, Chuo-ku, (092) 731 4439. ♂

KUROI-JUN, 4-11-14 Sumiyoshi, Hakata-ku, (092) 472 8411. ♂

SANBANGAI, 2-15-10 Sumiyoshi, Hakata-ku, at Casa Hakata, 1st floor, (092) 291 6578. ♂

YOTCHAN, 3-7-13 Watanabe-dori, Chuo-ku, (092) 711 8057. ♂

Saunas/Health Clubs
HISAMATSU BUSINESS INN, 2-19-3 Haruyoshi, Chuo-ku, (092) 761 4770. ♂

Erotica
BUDO-YA, 9-32-2 Sumiyoshi, 3-chome, Hakata-ku, (092) 272 3628, bookstore.

OKURA GEKIJO, 5-4-1 Higashi-Nakasu, Hakata-ku, (092) 291 4363, cinema.

HAKODATE
Bars
YOROZUYA, 20-9 Matsukaze-cho, (0138) 27 0661. ♂

HAMAMATSU
Bars
ODAMARI GAL, 180-4 Kagimachi, in the Hamamatsu S. Bldg, 4th floor, (0534) 55 0359. ♂

SPACIA, 357-1 Sunayama, (0534) 455 1918, 18:30-24:00, closed Mon. ♂

HIMEJI
Bars
PARU, 65 Sakancho, (0792) 223 445. ♂

HIROSHIMA
Bars
AKADEMIE, 6-10 Shinten-ji, Naka-ku, in Honshu Kaikan Bldg, 4th floor, (082) 244 3041. ♂

CIN CIN, 1-1 Tanaka-machi, Naka-ku, (082) 246 0970. ♂

KAME, 5-3 Nagaregawa-machi, Naka-ku, (082) 246 8018. ♂

MIDORI NO YAKATA, 2-31 Tanaka-cho, (082) 243 5301, 17:00-01:00. ♂

NIROKU (26), Tanaka-machi 1-13, Naka-ku, in the Shoei Bldg, 3rd floor, (082) 249 0013, 18:00-03:00. ♂

PAUL, Shintenchi 1-9, Naka-ku, in the Shintenchi Leisure Bldg, 3rd floor, (082) 243 4087, 19:00-02:00. ♂

TE-II, 5-3 Nagaregawa, Naka-ku, (082) 247 7388. ♂

Saunas/Health Clubs
IABARISHI, 4-32 Higashi Arakami-cho, Minami-ku, (082) 264 2895, closed Mon. ♂

Erotica
MATOBA CINEMA, 2-1-15 Matoba, Minami-ku, (082) 263 7095.

KAGOSHIMA
Bars
HERO, 10-2 Okenoguchi-cho, (099) 227 2182. ♂

KOGUMA, 10-18 Okenoguchi-cho, (099) 223 3154. ♂

LEE 1988, 7-13 Yamanokuchi Hondo, in the Nanei Bldg, 1st floor, (0992) 275 448. ♂

NEW BONDO, 166-2 Tagamicho, (0992) 557 922, 19:00-02:00, closed Sun. ♂

KANAZAWA
Bars
HIRO, 13-18 Oyama-cho, near the Oyama Shrine, (0762) 641 855, 19:00-02:00, closed Sun. ♂

JINAN, 13-20 Oyama-cho, across from Oyama shrine, (0762) 611 881, 18:00-02:00. ♂

K'S (KID'S), 2-29-2 Kata-machi, (0762) 62 9924. ♂

POTETO, 2-12-12 Kata-machi, (0762) 60 0661. ♂

SHINJU GAI, 1-8-23 Kata-machi, (0762) 33 3002. ♂

VIP, 2-22-15 Kata-machi, (0762) 21 8199. ♂

KITAKYUSHU
Bars
HISEN SNACK, at Hisen Kaikan sauna location, (093) 551 1414, snack bar. ♂

P MAN, 10-3 Konyamachi, Kokura, Kita-ku, in the Yamazaki Bldg, 2nd floor, (093) 531 7103, 19:00-03:00, closed Tues. ♂

TECCHAN, 4-3-8 Uomachi, Kita-ku, in the Muhomatsu Bldg, 1st floor, (093) 531 7175, 19:00-03:00. ♂

TOMOI, 6-7 Konya-cho, Kokura, Kita-ku, (093) 522 7163. ♂

Saunas/Health Clubs
HISEN KAIKAN, 2-14 Furusemba, Kokura, Kita-ku, (093) 551 1414, 18:00-22:00 (Sat, Sun 24hrs), snack bar. ♂

KOBE
Bars
HACHIBAN KAN, 4-9-16 Kano-cho, Chuo-ku, close to Kitigami Hotel, (078) 332 6168, 17:00-01:00. ♂

SANBANGAI, 5-3-5 Koto-cho, Chuo-ku at Green Shapo Bldg, B1 floor, (078) 231 0534, 18:00-02:00. ♂

TARO, 4-1-16 Kano-cho, Chuo-ku, in the Kamitani Bldg, 3rd floor, (078) 332 5443, 18:00-02:00, closed Sun. ♂

Saunas/Health Clubs
GENTLEMEN, (078) 577 2724, close to Shinkaichi metro, 14:00-23:00. ♂

KORIYAMA
Bars
POP STAR, 7-8 Naka-machi, Bunka-Mato, (0249) 329 405, 18:00-04:00. ♂

KUMAMOTO
Bars
CD CLUB, 1-11-5 Shimo-dori. ♂

OCTOBER 86, 1-36 Shinshigai, in the Issei Bldg, 4th floor, (096) 355 6600, 17:00-01:00. ♂

POLUKA, 1-9 Shinshigai, (096) 354 6381. ♂

Saunas/Health Clubs
KIRAKU KAIKAN, 2 Kuhonji, Kumamoto-shi, (096) 362 3856. ♂

KYOTO
Information
AIDS POSTER PROJECT, at Artscape gay & lesbian meeting space, (075) 771 6711, call for exact address & schedule of activities. ♀♂

Bars
APPLE, Torishijo Nishikiamachi, Shimokyo-ku, Dai-ichi Kobashi Kaikan, 3rd floor, (075) 256 0258, younger crowd. ♂

JAPAN

C'EST BON, Shijo Kawaramachi dori-Agaru, Futasuji-me, Higashi-iru, 2nd floor North, Nakagyo-ku, (075) 211 0385, older clientele, English spoken. ♂

FRIEND, Kyoto Kanko Bldg, 4th floor, (075) 256 3782. ♂

HIGASHIYAMA, Nakano-machi, Uratera-dori, Shijo Agaru, Nakagyo-ku, (075) 221 6862. ♂

KEN, Hitosuji-me Agaru, Dai-ichi Kobashi, 2nd floor, Shijo, Nishi Kiamachi, Shimokyo-ku, (075) 255 2954, 19:00-03:00. ♂

METRO, take the Keihan train to Marutacho Stn, take exit #2, (075) 752 4765, even Fri from 21:00, some men. ♀

NIGHTCAP, close to C'est Bon bar location, (075) 341 5006, call for exact address. ♂

NOT STRAIGHT, (052) 935 0090, regular parties for men & women, call for schedule. ♀♂

RINGOYA, (075) 255 6989, call for address. ♂

SAMU, Kiyamachi Shiji Agaru, Teruyakoji, 1st floor, Nakagyo-ku, (075) 221 6495, 19:00-03:00. ♂

SHINOBU, Shijo Agaru, Uratera-machi, Nakagyo, (075) 211 5548. ♂

V ZONE, Futasuji Agaru-Nishigawa, Shijo Nishikiya-machi, Nakagyo-ku, (075) 212 1933. ♂

■ *Saunas/Health Clubs*

MIMATSU SAUNA, close to Takashimaya, Shinkyogo-ku. ♂

■ *Retail & Bookstores*

SHOKADO, Nishi-iru, Nishitoin, Shimodachiuri, Kamigyo-ku, Tel/fax: (075) 441 6905, women's bookstore, Mon-Fri 10:00-17:30.

■ *Erotica*

CINE FRIENDS, Senbon Nakadachiori-agaru, Higashi-iru, Kamigyoko, (075) 441 1460, cinema.

NAGASAKI

■ *Bars*

BAN BAN, 1-1 Kabashima-cho, Kuraoka Bldg, 2nd floor, (0958) 229 703, 19:00-03:00. ♂

CHIKI CHIKI, 6-1 Kajiya-machi, (0958) 272 955. ♂

JUNIOR, 2-2 Daikoku-cho, (0958) 27 2984. ♂

NAGOYA

■ *Bars*

AO, 20-15 Tsubaki-cho, Nakamura-ku, (052) 452 1274. ♂

BABANUKI, 4-4-9 Sakae, Naka-ku, Nishishin Bldg, 2nd floor, (052) 261 8508, from 19:30. ♂

BEYAN, 4-4-9 Sakae, Naka-ku, Nishishin Bldg. (052) 241 6135. ♂

CATS, 1-15-5 Nishiki, Naka-ku, (052) 201 1578. ♂

DAIGORO, 4-4-9 Sakae, Naka-ku, Nishishin Bldg, 5th floor, (052) 261 0930. ♂

DAMBO, 4-4-9 Sakae, Naka-ku, (052) 241 5106. ♂

DON FAN, 1-7-4 Sakae, Naka-ku, (052) 222 3647. ♂

HAKUBA, 1-15-5 Nishiki, Naka-ku, in the Grand Nishiki Bldg, (052) 231 8805, 18:00-01:00, closed Wed. ♂

HIPS, 4-11-10 Sakae, Naka-ku, Tokyo Bldg, 1st floor, (052) 265 0904. ♂

JAGAIMO, 1-10-19 Nagoya-s.t. minami, Nakamura-ku, (052) 565 6334. ♂

KIYOSHI, 4-4-9 Sakae, Naka-ku, Nishishin Bldg, 2nd floor, (052) 242 0165. ♂

KURIKO, 4-4-9 Sakae, Naka-ku, Nishishin Bldg, (052) 251 0150, 21:00-04:00. ♂

MEGAMIX, 4-18-3 Ei, Naka-ku, (052) 252-7827. ♂

MEMAI, 1-11-15 Sakae, Naka-ku, (052) 231 9213. ♂

MIKKY, 4-4-9 Sakae, Naka-ku, Nishishin Bldg, (052) 263 0362. ♂

MINAMI, 4-4-9 Sakae, Naka-ku, Nishishin Bldg, (052) 264 4110. ♂

NAN NAN, near Hirokoji Stn, (052) 201 4740, bar only for teenagers, 18:00-02:00, closed Tues. Call for address. ♂

NOBORU, 4-11-10 Sakae, Naka-ku, Tokyo Bldg, 4th floor, (052) 241 2852, 19:00-02:00, closed Sun. ♂

NOBUNAGA, 1-7-4 Sakae, Naka-ku, (052) 223 2405. ♂

OTONBO, 1-15-5 Nishiki, Naka-ku, (052) 203 1988. ♂

RATORI, 3-16-8 Nishiki-cho, Naka-ku, Moriman Bldg, B1 floor, (052) 971 2449, closed Sun. ♂

SACHI, 20-5 Tsubaki-cho, Nakamura-ku, (052) 452 2752. ♂

SADA, 4-4-9 Sakae, Naka-ku, Nishishin Bldg, (052) 241 9675. ♂

TARO, 1-15-5 Nishiki, Naka-ku, (052) 201 7588. ♂

■ *Saunas/Health Clubs*

FUTOGAWA-RYO HOTEL, 2-2 Sanae-cho, Nishi-ku, (052) 451 7667. ♂

NIIGATA

■ *Bars*

NEW SHIRO, 7 Kami Okawamaedori, Sakai Bldg, 2nd floor, (025) 224 1696, 18:00-03:00. ♂

SYOKU, 5-4-34 Mashiro, Tatsumi Bldg, 2nd floor, (025) 243 4930, 19:00-02:00.

OKAYAMA

■ *Bars*

DAN, 4-11 Minami Chuo-cho, in the Chugoku Bldg, (0862) 257 980, small, friendly bar, private rooms, bath, VCR. ✖ ♂

KAZU, 2-5-3 Nodaya-machi, (086) 232 4114. ♂

KOCHI, 1-3-29 Ta-machi, (086) 221 2360. ♂

SUGATA, New Oka Bldg, B1 floor, (0862) 258 922, women-only bar, 18:00-03:00. ♀

OKINAWA

■ *Bars*

AKIRA, (0988) 687 423, 20:00-04:00, call for address. ♂

MURASAKI, 1-10-6 Tsuboya, Naha, (0988) 685 128, 20:00-05:00, closed Sun. ♂

OAK, 1-9-11 Tsuboya, Naha, (098) 864 5730. ♂

RESORT, 1-9-11 Tsubaya, Naha, (098) 866 8924. ♂

SHIKI, 3-7-8 Makishi, Naha, (098) 867 9966. ♂

SHINGO, (0988) 624 031, 22:00-04:00, closed Thurs. ♂

UMI, 3-9-26 Makishi, Naha, (098) 867 0433. ♂

OSAKA

■ *Information*

OSAKA GAY COMMUNITY (OGC), 6-1-26 Tenbigado, Matsubara City, (0723) 30 0870, monthly Sunday discussion groups.

WAKKATTA PLANNING, 5-3 Enoki-cho, Suita-shi, (06) 389 0044, Fax: (06) 389 1139, women's workshops, meeting rooms for rent for parties & events. They also hold their own events. If you don't speak Japanese, bring an interpreter in order to benefit from visit. Have interpreter call ahead.

WOMEN'S INFORMATION CENTER (DAWN CENTER), Otemae2-chome, Chuo-ku, (06) 942 3821, information, library & referral center run by the city government. Can inform you of all women's organizations in the city.

■ *Bars*

ADONIS, 8-18 Doyama-cho, Kita-ku, (06) 312 2429. ♂

BEAR, 8-23 Doyama-cho, Kita-ku, (06) 366 0930. ♂

BOYS, 16-19 Doyama-cho, Kita-ku, in the Iwata Bldg, 2nd floor, (06) 313 4800. [S] ♂

CHECK IN, 1-22-3 Ebisu higashi, 601 My Life Ebisu Bldg, Naniwa-ku, (06) 636 7461. ♂

CHRISTOPHER, 16-4 Doyama-cho, Kita-ku, in the Pearl Leisure Bldg, (06) 315 1380, 19:00-05:00, closed Tues. ♂

CRAZY-8, 632 8010. ♂

DAYARUIN, 2-3-17 Higashi Shinsaibashi, Osaka-shi, Papillon Bldg 3rd fl, Chuo-ku, (06) 212 2084, women only Sat 18:30-23:30. ♀

JAPAN

EAGLE, 8-18 Doyama-cho, Kita-ku, (06) 315 9473. ♂

EURIKAGO, 8-12 Kamiyama-cho, Osaka-fu, Kita-ku, 20:00-09:00 (Mon from 01:00, Sun 19:00-12:00), closed 3rd Sun. ✗♀

FRIEND, 1-4-22 Motomachi, Naniwa-ku, (06) 634 0996, 13:00-23:30. [$]♂

GO BAN GAI, 11-2 Doyama-cho, Kita-ku, in the Matunoki Bldg, (06) 315 1980, from 16:00. [$]♂

HARUKA, 8-14 Kamiyama-cho, Kita-ku, (06) 314 1698. ♂

HOMME, 8-18 Doyama-cho, Kita-ku, in the Kirishima Leisure Bldg, lower level, (06) 311 1936, 16:00-01:00. ♂

IF, in the Naka-dori Leisure Bldg #203, (06) 312 4148, small bar, 18:00-02:00. ♂

IN AND OUT, 633 1525, video room. ♂

JANGLE BOX, 366 4450, dark room. ♂

JUN II, (06) 312 1514, call for address. ♂

JUN, 16-6 Doyama-cho, Building F, Kita-ku (06) 312 8088. ♂

KIDS CLUB, 8-23 Doyama-cho, Kita-ku, at Sanyo Kaikan, (06) 312 2747, from 16:00. [$] ♂

KINTARO, 8-14 Kamiyama-cho, Kita-ku, (06) 363 5310. ♂

KUREY JENNY, 1-4-26 Dojima, Tamaya Bldg B1, Osaka-shi, Kita-ku, (06) 345 5284, 3rd Sat 19:00-24:00. ♀

KURO, 16-6 Doyama-cho, Kita-ku, in the OK Bldg, 1st floor, (06) 313 4665, mature clientele. ♂

KUTCHAN, 8-18 Doyama-cho, Kita-ku, (06) 316 0925. ♂

LESBIAN NIGHT, 3-3-8 Nakazaki Nishi, Osaka-shi, Kita-ku, at Club Down, (06) 373 4919, 3rd Sun 19:00-24:00. ♀

MS. TERIOUS, 1-16-12 Nishi Shinsaibashi, Osaka-shi, New American Plaza 7 FD, Chuo-ku, (06) 281 1066, 19:00-03:00 (closed Tues), some gay men. ♀

NEKO, 16-5 Doyama-cho, Kita-ku, (06) 311 7317. ♂

NEW DON, 16-5 Doyama-cho, Kita-ku, 2nd floor, (06) 315 9312. ♂

NINEN SANKUMI, 11-13 Doyama-cho, in the Daini-koraku Bldg, 2nd floor, (06) 315 0887, prefer Japanese only. [$]♂

PIPELINE, in the Takeda Bldg, lower level, Kita-ku, (06) 362 0441, women welcome. ♂

POPEYE, 6-15 Doyama-cho, Kita-ku, Dai-ichi Matsue Kaikan, (06) 315 1502, from 19:30. ♂

SALOON ROSE, 10-7 Doyama-cho, Kita-ku, (06) 311 1560. ♂

SEX BLOND, 16-4 Doyama-cho, Kita-ku, (06) 365 5957. ♂

SHOW UP PUB, 2-14-10 Sonezaki, Umeda Royal Bldg 4th fl, Kita-ku, (06) 314 3935, closed Sun & national holidays. ♀

SHY BOY, 7-16 Doyama-cho, Kita-ku, in the Kitahachi Bldg, 1st floor, (06) 316 1815, 18:00-02:00. ♂

STORK CLUB, 17-3 Doyama-cho, Kita-ku, in the Stork Bldg, 2nd floor, (06) 361 4484, piano bar. ♂

VERANDA, 16-19 Doyama-cho, Kita-ku, (06) 314 0088. ♂

YACHT, 4-7-9 Nanba, Minami-ku, in the Nanshin Bldg, 2nd floor, (06) 643 6734, 18:00-03:00, videos shown 15:00-18:00. ♂

YOUKIRO, 7-22 Doyama-cho, Kita-ku, (06) 313 0415. ♂

■ *Saunas/Health Clubs*

SPORTSMEN CLUB OSAKA, Airin Kaikan, Nishinari-ku, close to Dobutsuen-mae station, (06) 647 3930, 24hrs. ♂

■ *Retail & Bookstores*

MS. CRAYON HOUSE, 5-3 Enoki-cho, Suita City, (06) 330 8071, Fax: (06) 330 8075, women's bookstore, 11:00-19:00, 7 days.

■ *Erotica*

E.T.C. BOX, 14-22 Kamiyama-cho, Kita-ku, in the Toho Bldg, 2nd floor, (06) 316 0095, 12:00-23:00. ♂

HIGASHI UMEDA ROSE GEKIJO, 17-8 Doyama, Kita-ku, (06) 312 1856, cinema.

PLAZA APPLE INN, 1-11-5 Moto-machi, Naniwa-ku, in the Ishimoto Building, (06) 633 4878, bookstore.

SAPPORO

■ *Bars*

BE BE LU, Minami 5 jyo, Nishi 5-chome, Susukino, Chuo-ku, in Gajiro, 2nd floor, (011) 512 5392. [$]♂

CHAPLIN, Minami 6 jyo, Nishi 6-chome, Chuo-ku, in the S.A. Bldg, 5th floor, (011) 531 1334. ♂

CIAO, Minami 5 jyo, Nishi 6-chome, Chuo-ku, in the Shinmachi Bldg, 2nd floor, (011) 531 9331, 19:00-02:30, young crowd. ♂

JAMES, Minami 6 jyo, Nishi 6-chome, Chuo-ku, in the S.A. Bldg, 1st floor, (011) 512 2997. ♂

LA CAVE, Minami 6 jyo, Nishi 6-chome, Chuo-ku in the S. A. Bldg, 4th floor, (011)531 6734. ♂

MISHIMA, Minami 5 jyo, Nishi 5-chome, Chuo-ku, at Gaijiro Ramen, 2nd floor, (011) 531 1168. ♂

PRISM, Minami 6 jyo, Nishi 6-chome, (011) 513 8465. ♂

TWO-O-THREE (NI ZERO SAN), Minami 5 jyo, Nishi 6-chome, Chuo-ku, (011) 513 1250. ♂

SENDAI

■ *Bars*

ATOMU, 2-1-13 Kokubuncho, Haimato Bldg, 3rd floor, (022) 224 5468, 17:00-02:00, closed Sun. ♂

EIJI, 2-8-1 Kokubuncho, 18 Bldg, 4th floor, (022) 261 4023, 19:00-02:00, closed Sun. ♂

ICHI TEN YON (1.4), 2-8-1 Kokubunjicho, Aoba-ku (022) 224 4014. ♂

LEO, 1-6-1 Kokubuncho, Social Yamaji Bldg, lower level, (022) 265 9647, closed Tues. ♂

MMC (MEN'S CINEMA), Ichiban-cho, 1-chome, Aoba-ku, (022) 262 7580, bar with videos. ♂

TAIHO, Inanikoji, Ichiban-cho, in the Daisan Fujiwaraya Bldg, 3rd floor, (022) 263 0328, from 19:00, closed 2nd & 4th Sun. ♂

URAN, 2-10-7 Kokubu-cho, Aoba-ku, (022) 224 0815. ♂

TAKAMATSU

■ *Bars*

BOYA, 3-4 Hakken-machi, (0878) 210 420, 18:00-01:00. ♂

RAKUGAKI, 4-13 Uchi-machi, (0878) 22 1794. ♂

SCHOOL MATE, 7-4 Hyakken-machi, (0878) 510 836, 19:00-03:00. ♂

YASHIMA, 6-2 Daikumachi, (0878) 212 008. ♂

■ *Saunas/Health Clubs*

BUSINESS INN RAKUEN, 7-5 Marunouchi, (0878) 510 469. ♂

TOKYO

■ *Information*

INT'L FEMINISTS OF JAPAN, 3793 6241. Feminist group, write c/o AGORA, 1-9-6 Shinjuku, Shinjuku-ku, Tokyo. Unverifiable spring '97.

INTERNATIONAL FRIENDS, C.P.O. Box 180, Tokyo 100-91, (03) 5693 4569, E-mail: ferrarijapan@passport.org. Since 1981. The group is a social group with regular monthly meetings on the 3rd Sunday. The group does not: provide escorts, meet planes, or send someone to your hotel. If you have Ferrari with you, you really have enough information to have a good time in Japan. ♂

REGUMI STUDIO TOKYO, c/o JOKI, 3F Nakazawa Bld, 23 Araki-cho, Shinjuku, (03) 3226 8314 (tape machine), lesbian drop-in center every Sat evening. Call first, schedule changes. Women can call Meiko (044) 987 3417 before 21:00.

TOKYO INT'L DRAGON CLUB, Room 207 Nomura Bldg, 5-3 Yochoucho, Shinjuku-ku, (03) 5379 9660, Sat & Sun 10:00-23:00, meeting place for gays & lesbians, offers info to foreigners living in & traveling to Tokyo. ♀♂

TOKYO WOMEN'S FOUNDATION, Tokyo Metropolitan Government, Marunouchi Bldg 6F, 3-8-1 Marunouchi Chiyoda-ku, (03) 3213 0021, Fax: (03) 3213 0185, women's information center run by the city government.

TOKYO WOMEN'S INFORMATION CENTER, Central Plaza 15F, 1-1, Kagurazaki, Shinjuku-ku, (03) 3235 1140, women's information center run by the city government,

JAPAN

Tues-Sat 9:00-20:00 (Sun till 17:00). Approved application necessary for use of facilities. Lobby area open to visitors for informal use.

■ Bars

AJISAI, 3-15-13 Higashi Ueno, Suehiro Bldg 102, Taito-ku, (03) 3835 7490. ♂

ANDERSON, 2-18-10 Shinjuku, Shinjuku-ku, in the Anderson Bldg, 2nd floor, 3341 0392, 16:00-03:00. $ ♂

AOI, 2-46-13 Higashi Ikebukuro, Toshima-ku, 3981 5822. ♂

AOSANGO, 2-18-10 Shinjuku, New Chidori-gai, Shinjuku-ku, (03) 3352 8805. ♂

APACHE, 2-7-3 Shinjuku, Shinjuku-ku, in the Vella Heights Bldg, 1st floor, 3354 6045. ♂

ARTY FARTY, 2-17-4 Shinjuku, Shinjuku-ku 3356 5388, gay bar with USA Southwest atmosphere, 14:00-05:00. ✕ ♂

B'RUSH, 2-7-3 Shinjuku, Shinjuku-ku, at Vella Heights #111, 3350 1956. ♂

BAR FRIDA, 1-7 Yotsuya, Sobi Bldg 1st fl, Shinjuku-ku, (03) 3358 7922, Sat at the Han Gallery Cafe. ♂♀

C'EST BON, 5-4-13 Nishi-Kamata, Morota Bldg 1F, Ohta-ku, (03) 3738 6066. ♂

CALL, 2-14-8 Shinjuku, 3rd Tenkoh Bldg, 3rd fl, Shinjuku-ku, (03) 3354 6267. ♂

CAPTURE, 2-14-7 Shinjuku, Watanabe Bldg 47, Shinjuku-ku, (03) 3357 6962. ♂

CARAVAN, 2-12-14 Shinjuku, New Futami Bldg, Shinjuku-ku, (03) 3352 6006. ♂

CLUB DRAGON, 2-12-4-B1 Shinjuku, Accord Bldg, 3341 0606, bar with dance floor. ▣♂

COLLEGE NO OSAMA (KINGS), 2-15-8 Shinjuku, Shinjuku-ku, in the Nagira Bldg, 2nd floor, 3352 3980, 19:00-02:00. $ ♂

COUPLE, 2-15-13 Shinjuku, Fujita Bldg, 2nd floor, 3350 6180, 18:00-03:00. ♂

DAIFUKU, 1-5-2 Kita Ueno, EKC Bldg, 1st fl, (03) 5828 6266. ♂

DOKKOISHO, 4-32-25 Kitazawa, 1st floor, Setagaya-ku, 3460 8637, 19:00-03:00, videos. ♂

DOROIMO, 2-4-13 Nishi-Asakusa, Nishi Asakusa Bldg 102, (03) 3845 0130. ♂

ELIZABETH CLUB, 5-32-18 Kameido, Koto-ku, 3208 0117, expensive club for transvestites, NOT a gay bar. ♪✕

FITNESS, 2-7-3 Shinjuku, Shinjuku-ku, at Vella Heights Bldg #301, 3341 8994. $ ♂

FUJI, 2-12-16-B104 Shinjuku, Shinjuku-ku, at Sento Four Bldg, lower level, 3354 2707, 19:30-03:00. ♂

GB, 2-12-3 Shinjuku, Shinjuku-ku, at Shinjuku Plaza Bldg, lower level, 3352 8972, many tourists, 20:00-02:00 (Sat till 03:00). ♂

GIREAUD (JIRO), 7-7-13 Ueno, 1st floor, Taito-ku, 3844 4443, 19:00-04:00. $ ♂

GIRO, 1-37-1 Higashi Ikebukuro, Toutsaya Bldg, 1st floor, 5952 0533. ♂

GOSHOGURUMA, 2-25-4 Asakusa, Taito-ku, 3845 1474, 18:00-01:00 (Sun from 15:00), closed Wed. Many Nay-Nov couples. ♂

GOSHU, 2-14-13 Shinjuku, Yuni Bldg 2nd floor, 3350 0566, 19:00-02:00. ♂

HANA, 3-14-5 Hatanodai, 2nd floor, Shinagawa-ku, 3785 3792, 19:00-02:00. ♂

HANABISHI, Asakusa 2-chome, Taito-ku, 3845 0292. ♂

HANAKO, 2-15-8 Shinjuku, Shinjuku-ku, (03) 3352 4862, friendly & cozy bar, 20:00-03:00 (closed Thurs). ♀

HATTEN HACHI (8.8), 2-15-13 Shinjuku, Shinjuku-ku, in the Shigemi Bldg, 2nd floor, 3354 6695. ♂

HIGE (BEARD), 7-7-5 Ueno, Taito-ku, in the Toho Bldg, 3rd floor, Taito-ku, 3844 1261, hirsute men, 19:00-01:00. ✕ ♂

HUG, 2-15-8 Shinjuku, Shinjuku-ku, (03) 5379 5085, butch & femme roles strictly adhered to, 01:00-09:00 (Sat from 24:00), closed Sun. ♀

ICHI, 3-15-13 Nishiasakusa, 5th floor, Taito-ku, 3845 9330, young "short hair" crowd. ♂

ICHIGO ICHIE, 3-8-7 Shinjuku, Yoshikawa Bldg, Shinjuku-ku, (03) 3355 5139. ♂

IGOR, 7-5-6 Ueno, Taito-ku, in the Lion Bldg, 1st floor, 3841 3939. ♂

ISLANDS, 2-15-13 Shinjuku, 3rd Nakae Bldg 2nd fl, Shinjuku-ku, (03) 3359 0540. ♂

J CLUB, Futami #9 Bldg, Shinjuku, 3352 4969, 19:00-04:00, English & Thai spoken. ♂

JANNY SHONENTAI, 2-11-10 Shinjuku, Shinjuku-ku, in the Shinjuku Center Bldg, 3352 6767, 11:00-23:30. $ ♂

JANNY, 2-15-10 Shinjuku, Shinjuku-ku, in the Daiichi Tenka Bldg, 6th floor, 3356 2202. $ ♂

JANNY, 2-14-4 Shinjuku, Shinjuku-ku, in the Daisan Fujiwara Bldg, 3rd floor, 3354 8828. ♂

KAMATA, 5-27-3 Nishi Kamata, 1st floor, Ota-ku, 3735 6927, busy after 23:00, closed Thurs. ♂

KAMEN, 2-10-7 Nishiasakusa, 2nd floor, Taito-ku, 5828 4440. ♂

KASUGA, 2-2-1 Nishi-Asakusa, NAT Bldg, 2nd fl, (03) 3841-2616. ♂

KINSMEN, 2-18-5 Shinjuku, Shinjuku-ku, Oda Bldg, 2nd floor, 3354 4949, popular bar, mostly gay/lesbian clientele, 21:00-05:00 (closed Tues). ♂

KINSWOMYN, 2-15-10 Shinjuku, Shinjuku-ku, in the Daiichi Tenka Bldg, 3rd floor, 3354 8720, women-only bar. ♀

KOBU CHAN, 2-2-1 Nishi-Asakusa, NAT Bldg 301, Taito-ku, (03) 5828 3887. ♂

KOBUTA, 7-2-1 Ueno, Shoei Bldg, 4th fl, Taito-ku, (03) 3844 2717. ♂

KUSUO, 2-17-1 Shinjuku, Shinjuku-ku, at the Sunflower Bldg, 3rd floor, 3354 5050, young "short hair" crowd, 19:00-03:00. ♂

LA MANCHA, 2-17-2 Shinjuku, Shinjuku-ku, 3357 6895. ♂

LAMP POST, 2-12-15 Shinjuku, Shinjuku-ku, at Yamahara Heights, 2nd floor, 3354 0436, from 19:00-03:00, at times a piano bar. ♂

LAX, 2-8 Sakuragaoka, Shibuya-ku, in the Fuyo Bldg, 3rd floor, 3496 4190. ♂

LEO, 2-14-36 Shinjuku, Shinjuku-ku, in the Tsutsui Bldg, 2nd floor, 3354 7699. ♂

LUCKY, 1-19-24 Koiwa, Edogawa-ku, 3650 9970. ♂

LYNCH, THE, ★ 2-10-10 Shinjuku, Shinjuku-ku, (03) 3359 4799, 20:00-05:00. ♂

M&M, 2-14-10 Shinjuku, Shinjuku-ku, in the Wakao Bldg, 2nd floor, 3354 0474, videos. ♂

MADONNA, 2-15-13 Shinjuku, Shinjuku-ku, in the Fujita Bldg, 1st floor, 3354 1330, women-only bar. ♀

MAKI, 2-12-15 Shinjuku, Shinjuku-ku, at Yamahara Heights #404, 3341 8991, 19:00-03:00. ♂

MAMBO MAMA, 2-12-16 Shinjuku, Four Bldg, Shinjuku-ku, (03) 5361 7840. ♂

MANBOH, 2-2-5 Nishi-Asakusa, Igarashi Bldg 1st fl, (03) 3841 0818. ♂

MARS BAR, 2-15-13 Shinjuku, Shinjuku-ku, in the Hosono Bldg, 3rd floor, 3354 7923, women-only bar, a bit expensive. Manager, Mar, speaks good English and is helpful to travelers, phone for directions. ♀

MATSU, 3-1-10 Nishi-Asakusa, Morita Bldg 4th fl, (03) 3845 5094. ♂

MENKURA, 2-14-9 Shinjuku, Shinjuku-ku, in the Shimazaki Bldg, 2nd floor, 3356 0589. ♂

MITAKA, 7-60-9 Nishi Kamata, Ota-ku, 3735 6765, 19:00-02:00. ♂

MITCHAN, 2-2-1 Nishi-Asakusa, NAT Bldg 4th fl, (03) 3847 0349. ♂

MONA LISA PINK, 2-14-6 Shinjuku, Dai 2 Hayakawaya Bldg, B1, Shinjuku-ku, at Bar Delight, (03) 3352 6297, women's party 2nd Fri. For information on Mona Lisa & other women's parties call (03) 3445 7865. ♀

MONA LISA X, women's salon, call (03) 3445 7865 for schedule. ♀

MOONSHINER, near Sunny Bar, (03) 3355 6938, call for address. ♀

MURAMASA, 2-10-2 Shinjuku, Koka Bldg, 3rd fl, Shinjuku-ku, (03) 3355 6887. ♂

MUSO AN, 2-10-3 Shinjuku, Seven Futami Bldg, 2nd fl, Shinjuku-ku, (03) 3352 7210. ♂

NAWA, 2-15-13 Shinjuku, 2nd floor, Shinjuku-ku, 3354 5218, best with local escort. ▣ $ ♂

NEW FACE, 2-14-11 Shinjuku, Shinjuku-ku, 3354 8828. $ ♂

NEW KON, close to the Musashi Koyama station, 3784 9609, 18:00-01:00. ▣ $ ♂

NEW MARILYN, 2-28-16 Kabukicho, 4th fl, Shinjuku-ku, (03) 3200 3168, onabe bar (butch bartenders & hosts, frequented by femme lesbians & straight women), 22:00-07:30. ♀

NEW SAZAE, 2-18-5 Shinjuku, Shinjuku-ku,

JAPAN

in the Ishikawa Bldg, 2nd floor, 3354 1745, busy after 24:00, many women. ♀♂

NEW TOKEI DAI, 4-17-3 Higashi Ueno, Taito-ku, (03) 3847 1819. ♂

NEW TSUKASA, 7-4-3 Ueno, close to Ueno Station, Taito-ku, 3841 5583. ♂

O-EDO, 1-1-16 Nishi Asakasu, Shoko Bldg, Taito-ku, 3841 7233, ask for Koba-san, his English is quite good. 🍴♂

O.M.S., 1-7-25 Hiroo, Minato-ku, 3442 9308. $♂

OGURIN, 2-2-7 Nishi-Asakusa, Taito-ku, (03) 5828 5154. ♂

OJI, 9-2 Yokoyama-cho, 1st floor, Hachioji-shi, (0426) 463 082, 19:00-01:00. ♂

OMOCHABAKO, 2-12-15 Shinjuku, Shinjuku-ku, at Yamara Heights, 2nd floor, 3350 1759, 20:00-01:00, college crowd. ♂

OTAFUKU, 7-7-5 Ueno, Too Bldg 1st fl, Taito-ku, (03) 3844 4312. ♂

OTOKO ISHIMATSU, 2-21-1 Asakusa, Karino Bldg, 2nd fl, (03) 5827 7275. ♂

OTOKO NO SHIRO, 2-21-11 Asakusa, 2nd floor, Taito-ku, 3845 0293, young crowd. ♂

PENTHOUSE, 3-17-6 Shinbashi, Tagawa Bldg 4th fl, Minato-ku, (03) 5401 5004. ♂

PEPPERMINT, 4-20-1 Higashi Ueno, Taito-ku, in the Mimasu Bldg, lower level, 3845 1093, 19:00-04:00, young crowd. ♂

PIERROT, 2-7-3 Shinjuku, Shinjuku-ku, at Vella Heights Bldg #305, 3352 1939, 18:00-03:00. ♂

POPLAR, 2-12-16 Shinjuku, Shinjuku-ku, in the Sentofo Bldg #B103, across hall from Fuji, 3350 6929, 18:00-02:00. 🍴♂

POSITION, 2-12-15 Shinjuku, Yamahara Heights #503, 3341 5980, 19:30-03:00. ♂

PUCHI MARCO, 3-41-3 Kamitakada, 3rd floor, Nakano-ku, 3389 8033, 19:00-02:00, closed Wed. ♂

QUE QUE GO (995), 2-14-5 Shinjuku, Shinjuku-ku, in the Sakagami Bldg #301, 3352 0995. ♂

RATAN, 1-45-5 Higashi-Ikebukura, A-1 Bldg 1st fl, Toshima-ku, (03) 3971 9707. ♂

ROM, 2-14-3 Shinjuku, Ohki Bldg, 3rd fl, Shinjuku-ku, (03) 3354 5680. ♂

RYU, 2-14-5 Shinjuku, Shinjuku-ku, Sakagame Bldg #201, 3354 1680. ♂

SAIGO DON, 2-2-1 Nishi-Asakusa, NAT Bldg 402, Taito-ku, (03) 5828 0644. ♂

SALLY'S, 2-12-15 Shinjuku, Shinjuku-ku, at Yamahara Heights #502, 3356 6409, 20:00-04:00. ♂

SALON POSITIVE, 8-13-19 Imperial Ichibankan B1, Akasaka, Minato-ku, in club Antibes, (03) 3470 7431, monthly party, women only 20:00-23:30, men welcome from 23:30. Call for schedule. ♀

SAMSON, 2-12-15 Shinjuku #603, Shinjuku-ku, 3354 5227. ♂

SATSUMA, 4-17-3 Higashi Ueno, Taito-ku, (03) 3844 6075. ♂

SATURDAY, 2-15-8 Shinjuku, 1st floor, Shinjuku-ku, 3354 0324, videos. ♂

SEBUN (7), 2-10-7 Nishi Asakusa, Makino Bldg, 2nd floor, Taito-ku, 15:00-23:30. ♂

SEN, 2-13-21 Akasaka, Kiyokawa Bldg 201, Minato-ku, (03) 3582 9803. ♂

SENKAWA, 2-10-3 Nishi-Asakusa, Ogawa Bldg, 1st fl, (03) 5828 4847. ♂

SHINOBU, 7-8-21 Ueno, Taito-ku, in the Showa Bldg, 1st floor, 3841 0678. ♂

SHOW, 4-15-8 Shinbashi, Minato-ku, (03) 3431 4870. ♂

SIMON, 2-12-14 Shinjuku, New Futami Bldg, 5th fl, Shinjuku-ku, (03) 3357 1450. ♂

SOUTHERN VENUS, 2-13-6 Shinjuku, Shinjuku-ku, in the Koa Bldg, lower level, 3354 5877, expensive shows (about $100 per person). 🎵♂

SUGI CHAN, 2-10-10 Shinjuku, 6th Tehkoh Bldg, 4th fl, Shinjuku-ku, (03) 3341 4554. ♂

SUNNY BAR, 2-15-8 Shinjuku, 2nd floor, Shinjuku-ku, 3356 0368, very small women-only bar, 14:00-05:00. ♀

T ZONE, 2-18-18 Shinjuku, Kurihara Bldg, 2nd fl, Shinjuku-ku, (03) 3353 9986. ♂

TAC'S KNOT, 3-11-12-202 Shinjuku, Shinjuku-ku, 3341 9404. ♂

TAC, 4-15-8 Shinbashi, Minato-ku, (03) 3431 3214. ♂

TAMAGO BAR, 2-15-13 Shinjuku, Nakae Bldg III, 1st fl, Shinjuku-ku, (03) 3351 4838, karaoke bar, 21:00-05:00. ♂

TENGU, 1-38-1 Higashi Ikebukuro, Toshima-ku, 3987 5512. ♂

TORCH, 2-7-2 Shinjuku, Shinjuku-ku, at the Sani Copo, 1st floor, 3354 9156. ♂

TWENTY FOUR SNACK ASAKUSA, 2-28-18 Asakusa, Taito-ku, 3843 4424, 18:00-02:00 (Sat 16:00-03:00, Sun from 15:00).. ♂

TWENTY FOUR SNACK UENO, 7-7-11 Ueno, Taito-ku, in the Shinei Bldg, 1st floor, 3845 1942, 18:00-02:00. ♂

UTAYA, 4-10-9 Higashi Ueno, Taito-ku, 3844 2358, 19:00-03:00. ♂

WAKANA, 2-11-2 Nishi-Asakusa, (03) 3844 7715. ♂

X, 2-2-7 Ikebukuro, Toshima-ku, in the Daigo Maejima Bldg, 3982 8747, 18:00-02:00, best with escort, backroom. 🍴🎵📺♂

YADORIKI, 2-21-1 Asakusa, Taito-ku, at the Karino Bldg, 1st floor, 3845 3846. ♂

YAJIUMA, 7-60-8 Nishi Kamata, 2nd floor, Ota-ku, 3735 2653, 19:00-02:00. ♂

YAJIUMA, 4-11-5 Shinbashi, Sono Bldg B1, Minato-ku, (03) 3578 8969. ♂

YAMABIKO, 1-9-5 Kami Ikebukuro, Toshima-ku, 3918 5857, professional crowd. ♂

YOUNG MATES, 2-15-10 Shinjuku, First Tenka Bldg, 3rd fl, Shinjuku-ku, (03) 3341 1155. ♂

YU, 7-5-6 Higashi Ueno, Taito-ku, in the Lion Bldg, 3rd floor, 3845 2524. ♂

YUKI, 2-28-18 Asakusa, Taito-ku, (03) 3844 6107. ♂

ZIP, 2-14-11 Shinjuku, 1st floor, Shinjuku-ku, 3356 5029. ♂

ZUKKERO, 2-12-16 Shinjuku, Shinjuku-ku, in the Sentofo Bldg #305, 3354 9174, big men. ♂

■ Dance Bar/Disco

CLUB GAMOS, 2-11-10 Shinjuku, Shinjuku-ku, (03) 3354 5519, open Tues-Sun, some Tues & Wed bar only, Sat men-only dance night. 🍴♂

■ Saunas/Health Clubs

FINLAND SAUNA, 1-20-1 Kabukicho, Shinjuku-ku, 3208 0117, NOT a gay sauna, but discreetly frequented by gays.

HOTEL JINYA, 2-30 Ikebukuro, Toshima-ku, 5951 0995, friendly to foreigners.

ICHIJO, 1-1-5 Negishi, Taito-ku, near Ueno Station, 3844 4567. ♂

QP SAUNA, Higashi Ueno, 3831 8063, NOT a gay sauna, but discreetly frequented by gays.

TWENTY FOUR KAIKAN ASAKUSA, 2-19-16 Asakusa, Taito-ku, close to Sensoji Temple, 3841 7806, 3841 6979, 24hrs. ♂

■ Retail & Bookstores

MS. CRAYON HOUSE, 3-8-15 Kitaaoyama, Minato-ku, (03) 3406 6492, Fax: (03) 3407 9568, women's bookstore, stationery store and restaurant, also children's bookstore, women's crafts.

SABAI, 3-44-18 Koenji-minami, Suginami, (03) 3315 3715, clothing store with cafe (cafe frequented by feminist lesbian women).

■ Erotica

APPLE INN, 1-13-5 Shimbashi, 2nd floor, Minato-ku, 3574 1477, upper level has gay books.

ATENE UENO-TEN, 3-18-12 Ueno, Taito-ku, 3831 8209, bookstore.

BIG GYM, 3-39-7 Higashi Ueno, Maruyama Bldg #202, Taito-ku, (03) 3589 0297, bookstore.

BOOKS ROSE, 2-12-15 Shinjuku, Shinjuku-ku, in Yamahara Heights, lower level, 3341 0600, bookstore, 11:00-03:00.

CAVALIER, 3-11-2 Shinjuku, Shinjuku-ku, in the Muraki Bldg, lower level, 3354 7976, bookstore, 11:00-23:00.

CLIMAX, 1-13-7 Kabukicho, Shinjuku-ku, in Dai 19 Tokyo Bldg, 1st floor, 3200 2246, bookstore.

GINZA BUNKA, 4-4 Ginza, Chuo-ku, in the Hata Bldg, 3rd floor, 3561 0707, cinema, discreetly frequented by some gays. 📺

LUMIERE, 2-17-1 Shinjuku, Shinjuku-ku, in the Sunflower Bldg, 1st floor, 3352 3378, bookstore.

TAIWAN

MEMOIRE, 2-14-8 Shinjuku, Shinjuku-ku, in the Tenko Bldg, 1st floor, 3341 1775, bookstore.
SEKAI KESSAKU GEKIJYO, close to Ueno Station, 3831 0158, cinema.

TOYAMA

■ *Bars*
IKEBUKURO, 2-1 Uchi-Saiwaicho, Matsyoshi Bldg 1st fl, (0764) 33 5333. ♂

YOKOHAMA

■ *Information*
YOKOHAMA WOMEN'S FORUM, 435-1 Kamikuratacho Totsukaku, (045) 862 5050.

■ *Bars*
CHECKMATE, 1-34-2 Noge, Naka-ku, (045) 231 8595. ♂
DARUMA, 2-51 Takagawa, Naka-ku, (045) 242 8385. ♂
FRIEND, 2-66 Nogecho, Naka-ku, (045) 241 7059. ♂
GINREI, 1-5 Noge, 1st Kohsan Bldg 2nd fl, Naka-ku, (045) 231 9391. ♂
JIN, 14-3 Ekimae-Honcho, Kawasaki-ku, in nearby town of Kawasaki, (044) 233 0996. ♂
MONOTONE, (045) 253 3473, call for address. ♂
NEW PORT, (045) 242 8287, call for address. ♂
NEW YORK, 2-68 Noge, Naka-ku, (045) 241 3420, videos. ♂
OH CHAN, 1-53 Noge, Naka-ku, (045) 242 5622. ♂
PEGASUS, (045) 242 9768, 17:00-02:00, closed Wed, mature crowd. ♂
SAHARU, (045) 241 0148, 18:30-02:00, closed Thurs, call for address. ♂
TEPPEI, 1-23-6 Noge, Naka-ku, (045) 251 6518. ♂
THREE BOX, 2-90 Nogecho, Naka-ku, in the Sky Bldg, 2nd floor, (045) 242 4570, 19:00-01:00, young crowd. ♂
TOMO (FRIEND), 1-5 Nogecho, Naka-ku, in the Minato-kosan Bldg, 2nd floor, (045) 231 2236, 18:00-02:00. ♂
TONY, 1-33 Nogecho, Naka-ku, (045) 242 8395, mature crowd, English spoken. ♂
YAKOCHU, 1-53 Nogecho, Naka-ku, (045) 231 8218, from 18:00. ♂

■ *Saunas/Health Clubs*
DOANJI, 3-93 Miyagawa-cho, Naka-ku, close to Hinodecho Station, (045) 242 6255. ♂
RYOSO NOGE, 3-131 Noge-machi, close to Youth Hostel, Naka-ku, (045) 231 2916. ♂
YOKOHAMA CLUB, 48-1 Miyazaki-cho, Nishiki, Naka-ku, (045) 242 3111. ✗♂

KOREA (SOUTH)
COUNTRY CODE: (82)

WHO TO CALL
For Tour Companies Serving This Destination
See Korea on page 18

SEOUL

■ *Information*
SAPPHO KOREA, CPO Box 4589, Seoul 100 645, women's group.

■ *Bars*
AGENT, (02) 32 72 12 88, ask locally for address. ♂
CAFE RIMBAUD, (02) 766 71 58, ask locally for address. ♂

■ *Cafe*
CAFE PRISON, (02) 924 52 04, ask locally for address. ♂
COOL CAFE, (02) 36 73 49 09, ask locally for address. ♂

TAIWAN
COUNTRY CODE: (886)

WHO TO CALL
For Tour Companies Serving This Destination
See Taiwan on page 27

KAOHSIUNG

■ *Bars*
BOLIVIA, Da Jen Rd, 10th floor, 521 7032. ♂
COLOUR PLATE, Tayou St 5, 2nd floor, 551 3757. ♂
MEN'S TALK, 32 Ming Shing St B-1, 211 7049. ♂

■ *Saunas/Health Clubs*
HAN CHIN, Ho Nan 2 Rd, 216 7073, discreetly frequented by gays.

TAIPEI

■ *Bars*
CASABLANCA, Chung Shan North Rd 22, Lane 33, section 1, 563 7895. ♂
CUPID, Po Ai Rd #154 (west side of road), south of Henyang St, lower level, 311 8585, karaoke bar, discreetly frequented by gays. ✗
FUNKY, Hang Chou Rd, B-1 #10, bar & disco, popular Sat. 🎵♂
MING FANG, #70, Lane 85, off Linsen North Rd, 581 5840, karaoke bar, discreetly frequented by gays. ✗
RE DAI YU, #5, Alley 6, lower level, off east side of Chub Shan North Rd, Sector 2, 562 7123, karaoke bar, discreetly frequented by gays. ✗
SOURCE, 190 Nan Chang Rd, section 2, (02) 368 8797, frequented by local gays, 19:00-03:00, some hetero clientele. ♂

■ *Dance Bar/Disco*
MING CHUN, #22, Lane 33, near Chung Shan North Rd, Sector 1, 563 78 95, dance bar & lounge, discreetly frequented by gays. 🎵✗
PARADISE UNDERGROUND CLUB, Sungchiang Rd 23, gay Wed only. 🎵♂

■ *Saunas/Health Clubs*
BAI LE CHI, 61 Yen Ping South Rd, between Han Kou & Wu Chang Streets, 381 8791, 24 hrs, not a gay sauna, discreetly frequented by gay men.
DA FUN SAUNA, 195 Chung Hsiao West Rd, section 1, 5th floor, 381 1859, 24hrs, not a gay sauna, discreetly frequented by gay men.
HANS SAUNA, 120 Shi Ning North Rd, 2nd floor, 311 8681, 24hrs, not a gay sauna, discreetly frequented by gay men.
HUA GONG, 20 Hsi Ning Rd, Sector 2, between Kai Fang & Han Kou Streets, 381 5900, 24hrs, not a gay sauna, discreetly frequented by gay men.

■ *Erotica*
GREENWOOD CO., Tun Hwa South Rd, Section 1, Lane 160 #51, 1-F, videos & gay magazines.

The Burma Westerners Never See

Retrace the footsteps of Kipling to Moulmein, where he lost his heart to the "Burma girl" who was sitting on the steps of the Kyaik-than-lan Pagoda "a-smoking" of a whackin' white cheroot. Journey beyond the Chindwin in a World War II pilgrimage. Be amongst the very first western travellers to scale Mount Victoria in Chin State in a land which prompted Somerset Maugham to declare "its exuberance is captivating."

Valleys teeming with rubies, sapphires, emeralds and jade... the Golden 'Rock and the Burma Road, the Shan Hills and the 804 islands (many uncharted) of the Mergui Archipelago... 135 different ethnic groups speaking more than 100 indigenous languages... this is a microcosm of the "Silken East," an epithet coined by author Scott O'Connor for his fabulous "Record of Life and Travel in Burma," first published in 1904.

Silken East is the only western tour operator with unique access to all areas of Burma (since 1989 officially known as Myanmar). Silken East is a joint venture between the UK's Burma expert Nicholas Greenwood, author of the definitive "Guide to Burma," (Bradt Publications, 1996), and Northern Thai specialist John Boyes, author of "Hmong Voices" and "Opium Fields."

How is it to travel in Burma as a gay person? Greenwood says, "Burma and Thailand, owing to their strong Buddhist cultures, have proved exceedingly gay-friendly, in particular the Burmese, who are undoubtedly the friendliest and most hospitable people I know."

Silken East is a rare commodity amongst tour companies, an operator with a social conscience. "Our aim," says Greenwood, a leading advocate for the people of Burma to determine their own future, "is to enable those with a genuine interest in Burma to develop a greater understanding of a country for which we have a deep passion. By enabling travelers, as opposed to tourists, to visit parts of the country rarely seen by other westerners, we will attempt to increase public awareness of the way of life in present-day Burma." Tour extentions are also available to Northern Thailand, Cambodia and Laos. Clients' monies are fully protected in compliance with the European Union Travel Regulations.

Contact **Silken East** at (44-171) 223 8987 (tel/fax).

Trekking the Himalayas

Himalayan High Treks offers gay-friendly tours to India, Nepal, Bhutan and Tibet. Groups are small (4-8), and economical (land from $65 per day). Owner Effie Fletcher personally researches and leads many treks, using quality equipment and an experienced, dedicated staff. Accommodations are simple, yet comfortable, and the food is good (a choice of local vegetarian dishes or simple western cuisine. Enjoy the thrill of hiking with views of the tallest mountains in the world. Effie says, "Our small groups allow us to get to know the local people. We are often invited into local monasteries and homes. Culturally, same-sex affection is more acceptable here than demonstrative heterosexuals. However, there is little gay culture, as such, and our focus is more on the traditional Buddhist and Hindu culture indigenous to the area." Everything from easy walking tours to super-strenuous ski tours is offered, and departures are throughout the year.

Contact **Himalayan High Treks** at (415) 861-2391, (800) 455-8735. E-mail: effie@well.com.

SOUTH ASIA

BANGLADESH
COUNTRY CODE: (880)

DHAKA

■ Retail & Bookstores

NARIGRANTHA PRABARTANA (FEMINIST BOOKSTORE), 2/8 Sir Syed Rd., Mohammadpur, above saree and handicraft shop. (2) 318428 or 329620, Fax: (2) 813065. Bookstore and meeting place for women, 9:00-21:00.

INDIA
COUNTRY CODE: (91)

For Tour Companies Serving This Destination See India on page 17

AKOLA

■ Information

SAHAYAK GAY GROUP, Write: Laxmi Narayan Sadhan, Prasad Colony, Jathar Peth, Akola 444 004.

BANGALORE

■ Information

GOOD AS YOU, c/o Samraksha, 2nd level, Royal Corner, 1 & 2 Lambaugh Rd, gay group meets Thurs 18:30-20:00.

■ Retail & Bookstores

STREELEKHA, 67, II Floor, Blumoon Complex, Mahatma Gandhi Rd, women's bookstore, library & reading room.

BOMBAY

■ Information

BOMBAY DOST, gay & lesbian group. Publishes Bombay Dost magazine, write: 105A Veena-Beena Shopping Centre, Bandra Station Rd., Bandra (West), Bombay 400 050, India.

HUMSAFAR CENTRE, (22) 972 6913, gay & lesbian drop-in center, call for address.

CALCUTTA

■ Information

COUNSEL CLUB, gay organization, publishes Pravartak magazine, membership fee, write: Post Bag 10237, Calcutta 700 019, India.

NAZ FOUNDATION INDIA TRUST, Calcutta Project, South Asian health organization. Write: NAZ, 468A Block K, New Alipur, Calcutta 700 053, India.

COCHIN

■ Information

MEN INDIA MOVEMENT, gay men's group, write: PO Box 885, Cochin 682 005, India.

DELHI

■ Information

ARAMBH SUPPORT GROUP, gay & lesbian organization. Publishes newsletter, write: PO Box 9522, Delhi 110 095, India.

DEHLI WOMEN'S LEAGUE, 6 Bahagwan Das Rd, women's meeting place.

LUCKNOW

■ Information

FRIENDS INDIA, gay group, publishes bi-monthly newsletter, meets Wed 17:00-18:00. Write for details: PO Box 59, Mahanagar, Lucknow 226 006, India.

NEW DELHI

■ Information

AIDS BHEDBHAV VIRODHI ANDOLAN, organization doing community work involving gay men & lesbians, education, health & legal issues, etc. Write: PO Box 5308, New Delhi 110 053, India.

NAZ PROJECT, D-45 Gulmohar Park, New Delhi 110 049, (11) 667 328, South Asian health organization.

SAHELI WOMEN'S RESOURCE CENTRE, Defence Colony Flyover 105-108, New Delhi 110 024, India, women's meeting place.

SAKHI LESBIAN COLLECTIVE, (11) 462 8970, Write SAKHI, PO Box 3526, Lajapat Nagar, New Delhi 110 024, India.

SAKHI, (11) 462 8970, gay & lesbian group, write: PO Box 3526, Lajpat Nagar, New Delhi 110 024, India.

WOMEN'S NETWORK, lesbian organization, write: PO Box 142, GPO, New Delhi 110 001, India.

■ Women's Accommodations

NAARI, B1/7 Vishal Bhawan, 95 Nehru Place, New Delhi 19, (91-11) 646 5711, Fax: (91-11) 618 7401 or 623 4621. The first women's guesthouse in India. Offers lodgings, meals & woman-guided tours of New Delhi. ♀

SECUNDERABAD

■ Information

EXPRESSION, write: PO Box 5, Bolarum, Secunderabad 500 010, India.

NEPAL
COUNTRY CODE: (977)

For Tour Companies Serving This Destination See Nepal on page 21

KATHMANDU

■ Information

NEPAL QUEER SOCIETY, GPO 8975, EPC 5203, Kathmandu, Nepal, gay organization.

PAKISTAN
COUNTRY CODE: (92)

LAHORE

■ Information

SHIRKAT GAH, 874951, 874947. Women's resource centre, library and centre for women's organizations in Pakistan. Write to 18A Mian Mir Rd, Lahore 54840, Pakistan.

SRI LANKA
COUNTRY CODE: (94)

For Tour Companies Serving This Destination See Sri Lanka on page 26

WATTALA

■ Information

COMPANIONS ON A JOURNEY, 27/3 Anderson Rd, Kalubowilla, (1) 82 78 69, gay & lesbian organization.

FERRARI GUIDES' GAY TRAVEL A to Z - 18th EDITION

INDONESIA

FYI

A Friendly Gay Welcome in Bali

Operating out of two pottery shops, each sporting the pink triangle and the rainbow flag, Hanafi (his first name) has been providing excursion and guide service for travelers for the past 6 years. He proudly reports this year that 60% of his excursion business is gay.

In Bali, he says, don't expect a hopping gay nightlife. But there are a few ever-changing gay-friendly bars where gays congregate on special nights, and he can take you to a beach where gays do congregate. He also knows where to take you for snorkeling, scuba diving, jet skiing, para sailing, bungy jumping, etc.

Services include transportation, sightseeing, arranging meetings with gay locals, and even hotel reservations. Hanafi says he knows Australian sign language and has had some experience escorting blind people on tour.

Contact **Hanafi** at (62 361) 756 454, Fax: (62 361) 752 561.

SOUTHEAST ASIA

INDONESIA
COUNTRY CODE: (62)

WHO TO CALL — For Tour Companies Serving This Destination
See Indonesia on page 17

ISLAND OF BALI

■ *Accommodations*

PONDOK MUTIARA MAS, Jln. P. Aru 1/2, Denpasar, Bali, (62-361) 233 158. Gay-friendly B&B in a small rural area surrounded by rice paddies on the beautiful island of Bali, well-known for its beaches, lush valleys, and intriguing cultures. Its small size ensures an attentive staff who will do their best to please you & help you experience the real Bali. It is a short drive from the Kuta beach & other places of interest.

PURI WIMPY BALI VILLA, Jalan Kayu Aya 15a, Baangkasa, Kuta Beach, (62-361) 730 862 (ask for the manager), bungalow & cottage with AC, many amenities, pool on premises, near beaches & gay venues.

■ *Bars*

CAFE LUNA, Raya Seminyak St, Seminyak area, Kuta, frequented by gays.

GOA 2001, Raya Seminyak St, Seminyak area, Kuta, frequented by gays.

HULU CAFE, close to Padma St, Legian, bar & restaurant, frequent drag shows.

KOALA BLUE, Legian St, Kuta, bar & restaurant, drag shows nightly, except Sun.

■ *Dance Bar/Disco*

DOUBLE SIX, Double Six St, Seminyak area, Kuta, many gays Sat from 24:00.

GADO GADO, Diana Pura St, Seminyak area, Kuta, many gays Fri from 24:00.

ISLAND OF JAVA

■ *Dance Bar/Disco*

KLIMAX, Gajah Mada St, Jakarta, more gay Sun 22:00-02:00.

NEW MOONLIGHT, Hayam Wuruk St, at Manga Besar St, Jakarta.

MALAYSIA
COUNTRY CODE: (60)

WHO TO CALL — For Tour Companies Serving This Destination
See Malaysia on page 19

KUALA LUMPUR

■ *Dance Bar/Disco*

ALIBI WOMEN'S DISCO, Central Square, Jln Hang Kasturi, women-only dance night, 1st Wed.

ALIBI, Central Square, Jln Hang Kasturi, dance bar with karaoke, gay Thurs & Sun from 20:00. Entry is at management's discretion.

BLUE BOY DISCOTHEQUE, next to Regent Hotel, dance bar with karaoke, 21:00-23:00.

■ *Cafe*

COCOMO DAFE, 6 Jalan Telawi, 4 Bangsar, (03) 254 2503; 2nd location at Salem Powerstation, Bukit Bintang Plaza, ground level, Tel: (03) 244 7841. Discreetly frequented by gays.

---

trikone MAGAZINE — Gay & Lesbian South Asians — SINCE 1986
P.O. Box 21354, San Jose, CA 95151 USA
(408) 270-8776 EMAIL: trikone@rahul.net
Subscriptions: $10/Year North America $15/Year Overseas

PHILIPPINES
COUNTRY CODE: (63)

WHO TO CALL
For Tour Companies Serving This Destination
See Philippines on page 23

MANILA

Information
LESBIAN LINE, (2) 921 7229, Mon-Fri 18:00-22:00.

TLC (THE LESBIAN COLLECTIVE), #66-C Scout Ojeda St, Roxas District, Quezon City, (2) 97 28 60, or ask for Giney Villar at (2) 96 92 87, fax: (2) 922 5004. Discussions, social events, women from other countries welcome to attend. Ask about weekly women's parties.

UNIVERSITY CENTER FOR WOMEN'S STUDIES, Univ. of the Philippines, Diliman, Quezon City, (2) 99 50 71, center for women with courses, activities & local information.

WOMEN SUPPORTING WOMEN COMMITTEE, (632) 922 5253, Lesbian group, publishes newsletter, phone answers Mon, Wed, Fri 18:00-20:00, Sat 13:00-20:00. Write: PO Box 43-44, UP Shopping Center, UP Diliman, Quezon City.

Bars
CINE CAFE, Roces Ave, Quezon City, 3 levels, videos. ♂

CLUB 690,★ Retiro St 690, La Loma, Quezon City, 712 3662, bold shows. 🎵♂

CLUB MAGINOO, E. Rodriguez, at Roces St, Quezon City. ♂

LIBRARY, in the area of Remedios Circle, Malate, not a gay bar, but frequented by gays, ask locally for exact address. 🎵

PIGGY & GEN GALI, beside Library bar, 2 bars with one common entrance & exit, not gay, but frequented by local gays, upscale clientele.

Q, Maria Orosa St, beside the Court of Appeals. ♂

ZOO, THE, address not available at presstime, frequented by local gays.

Dance Bar/Disco
103 GAY DISCO BAR, 103 Recto Ave, Santa Cruz, younger crowd. May change in 1997. 🍴♂

CHICOS,★ E. Rodriguez Blvd, Quezon City, 921 1822, some hetero clientele. 🍴🎵♂

Cafe
BLUE CAFE, Nakpil St 610, Malate, close to Remedios Circle, not a gay cafe, but frequented by local gays.

Saunas/Health Clubs
CLUB BATHS, 2456 F. Harrison St, Pasay City.

DATU, E. Rodriquez Ave, Quezon City.

LAKAN, Araneta Ave, Quezon City.

OPEN HOUSE, BLISS Homes, 3rd floor, close to SM City, Quezon City.

SINGAPORE
COUNTRY CODE: (65)

WHO TO CALL
For Tour Companies Serving This Destination
See Singapore on page 25

SINGAPORE

Bars
CONNECTION, 304 Orchard Rd, 6th floor, at the Lucky Plaza. ♂

VINCENT'S LOUNGE, 304 Orchard Rd, 6th story, at the Lucky Plaza, 7361 360. ♂

ZOUK,★ Jiak Kim Road, near Havelock and River Valley roads, not a gay bar, discreetly frequented by gays. 🍴

Dance Bar/Disco
MOONDANCE, 62/64 Tanjong Pagar, Tanjong Pagar Conservation District, 324 29 11, trendy crowd, not a gay disco, discreetly frequented by gays. 🍴

MUSIC WORLD, near the Katong Shopping Center, more popular Wed & Fri-Sun, not a gay disco, discreetly frequented by gays. 🍴

THAILAND
COUNTRY CODE: (66)

WHO TO CALL
For Tour Companies Serving This Destination
See Thailand on page 27

BANGKOK

Information
ALCOHOLICS ANONYMOUS, 253 0305, 253 8411, 253 8578, meetings Tues, Thurs 18:00, Sun 09:30.

ANJAREE LESBIAN GROUP, address mail

THAILAND

FYI

14-Day Thailand Tours

Tours to Paradise has specialized in Thailand since 1990 and are bona fide Thailand specialists. They offer quality tours for both groups or individuals that include Bangkok, Chiang Mai and Pattaya and all of the following: All hotels with single occupancy, private bath, and air conditioning; All intra-Thailand transfers, transportation and local taxes; Over 12 tours with sightseeing, historical and cultural aspects, dining and recreation; A private chartered boat trip, which is a one-day excursion in the beautiful Bay of Siam; English-speaking guides. The cost of the 14-day land package is from $1,390, plus roundtrip airfare which they can get for you at deeply discounted prices. You can also call them for gay travel packages to Acapulco, Mexico.

1997	Tour Schedule
Mar 4-17	Special Tour
Apr 5-20	Thai New Year, Water Festival
May 20-Jun 2	Special Tour
July 1-15	Mid-Summer Tour
Aug 19-Sep 1	Umbrella Tour
Oct 7-20	Banana Festival Tour
Nov 3-17	Fall Special Tour
Dec 20-Jan 3 '98	Xmas/New Years Tour

Contact **Tours to Paradise** at (213) 962-9169, Fax: (213) 962-3236.

FERRARI GUIDES' GAY TRAVEL A to Z - 18th EDITION

ASIA

THAILAND

FYI

Soft Adventure Tours to Thailand & Morocco

THAILAND– On a two-day tour of Bangkok, where we navigate the Chao Phrtaya River and visit the 17th-century landmark, the Watt Phrakeo Royal Palace to observe the classic architecture of gold leaf pagodas and see mythological sculptures, detailed frescos and the Emerald Buddha temple. From Bangkok, we drive through the countryside to visit the busiest floating market in Thailand. Our two-day elephant trek gives us a complete feel of the breathtaking splendors the rainforest has to offer. We finish with a nine-day boat cruise amongst verdant limesone islands on the Andaman Sea with kayaking, diving and fishing and other adventurous activities.

MOROCCO—We visit the main imperial cities where lively narrow streets display a variety of workshops, colorful dye pits and ancient architecture. A two-day scenic drive takes us through the Atlas Mountains, giving us a chance to see the nomad tribes in their natural environment and the ancient Berber villages which accent the fertile landscapes of these high elevations. A five-day excursion shows us the mysterious kasbah trail located in the Sahara region.

Contact **Explorer Tours** at (619) 543-9100, Fax: (619) 291-8819, E-mail: explortrs@aol.com.

FYI

Gay Men's Group Tours to Thailand

Adventures Unlimited specializes in small group tours to Thailand with or without side trips to select Southeast Asian destinations. Tours are designed to allow each adventurer to tailor his activites according to his own tastes. Activities are designed with the self-directed traveler in mind, as well as the traveler who prefers guided or escorted activities.

Adventurers sample the majestic and the mundane. The "3Ts" Thailand Adventure allows the dreamer to make his dreams come true. Daytime activities focus on cultural sites and events. Evening activities focus on the gay social scene, with plenty of opportunities to make new Thai friends. Adventures Unlimited uses the services of young, energetic, bilingual guides and contracts with established and well-known agents and carriers for intra-Thailand travel. The itinerary includes Bangkok, the ancient city of Chiang Mai and hedonistic and exotic Pattaya.

Contact **Adventures Unlimited** at (619) 669-0968, Fax: (619) 669-6901.

only to: Anjaree, PO Box 322, Rajdamnern, Bangkok 10200, Thailand. Group is available for exchange of info, reciprocal visits, networking. They hold a monthly open house on 2nd Sun afternoon. They will mail you directions addressed to: Post Restante, GPO, Bangkok. To receive mailed response outside Thailand, enclose an international postage voucher to cover postage for their response. DO NOT write lesbian on the envelope!

F.A.C.T. AIDS HELPLINE, (02) 574 1100, 574 3461, 09:00-24:00.

WOMEN'S ASSOC. OF THAILAND, 64 Petchabur, Bangkok, Thailand. Umbrella organization for women's groups in Thailand.

■ Accommodations

AQUARIUS, THE, 243 Hutayana, Soi Suanphlu, South Satorn Rd, (662) 286 0217, Tel/Fax: 286 2174, guesthouse with restaurant & bar, AC, TV lounge, some rooms with color TV, room & laundry service, massage in house, private baths, women welcome. ♂

BANGKOK CENTER HOTEL, 1st class businessman's hotel, gay-friendly, book through Tours to Paradise (213) 962-9169 for discount rate.

■ Bars

A-GO-GO, across from Super A. ♂

ACHILLES KARAOKE MUSIC LOUNGE, Hollywood Soi Entertainment Complex, 1st floor, across from Asia Hotel, (02) 208 9299.♂

ADAM, 224/14 Soi Pradipat Sinema, Pradipat Rd, District Saphankwai, 278-1191, cocktail lounge.

ALADDIN, 218/3 Pradipat Soi 18, Saphankwai, (02) 271 0809.

APACHE BOY, 1407/13-14 Pradipat Soi 20, Saphankwai, (02) 278 2756, 20:30-03:00, go go boys.

BARBIERY LOUNGE★, 35, 3-4-5 Thanon Suriwongse, 235-1078, shows at 24:00, 18:00-01:00.

BIG BOY, 1/34 Sukhumvit Soi 11, (02) 251 9582, 12:00-01:00. ♂

BODY ENTERTAINMENT, 43/277 Pahonyotin Rd (enter from Ammarinniwed 1), Bangken, near airport, (02) 521 4267.

BUDDY BOY PUB, Pradipat Rd, across from Pradipat Theatre, Saphankwai. ♂

CHARMING, 2 Soi Tawan Sak, Thanon Pradiphat, Saphan Kwai, 270 1853.

CITY PUB, Sukhumvit Soi 45, between Soi 1 & Soi 3, (02) 251 3262, 13:00-01:00. ♂

COLOUR, Soi Petchaburi, near White Horse bar. ♂

DRAMA WORLD (LOK LA KORN), Pradipat Soi 12, Saphankwai, in back of Mido Hotel, (02) 278 0395, bar with USA Southwest atmosphere, 20:00-02:00. ♂

ELYSEE COCKTAIL LOUNGE, Sukhumvit Soi 11, (02) 253 5142. ♂

THAILAND

FOR FUN COCKTAIL LOUNGE, next to O.A. cinema, Maggasa Pratoonam, in back of Soro bar, 20:00-02:00, go go boys Fri & Sat.

FREE ZONE, Soi Pradipat Theatre, Pradipat Rd, Saphankwai.

GALAXY BOY, Suriwongse Rd, Soi Ton Pho, Ko Kaew Restaurant, 2nd level, (02) 233 7901, go go boys.

GARDEN BAR, at Harries Complex, younger clientele.

GOLDEN COCK LOUNGE, 39,27 Soi Anuman Rajadhon, 236-3859, lounge & go-go bar with relax rooms, 11:00-01:00.

HIPPO DROME, 18 Soi Pradipat, Pradipat Rd, next to Mido Hotel, Saphankwai, (02) 278 0413, cocktail lounge with karaoke.

INTER MOUSTACHE'S HOUSE, 23,12 Sukhumvit Soi 10 (upstairs), 25017212, go-go bar, Fri & Sat 12:00-01:00, Sun-Thurs 18:00-24:00.

IVORY, Sukhumvit Soi 26, Sukhumvit.

JUPITER CLUB, at the Surawong Hotel, Patpong, (02) 237 4050, 19:00-02:00.

JUPITER, Soi Aree, Pahonyotin 13, then turn left, Saphankwai, (02) 270 1708.

K-NUDE, 454 Thanon Phahonyothin, in Saphan Kwai area, around courner from Adam bar, 279-2988.

KING'S HEAVEN, on Soi next to Tanakan Omsin bank, Saphankwai, bar & restaurant.

L'AMOUR, 2/3 Sukhumvit Soi 34, Prakanong, Sukhumvit, (02) 259 7270.

LES BEAUX, Petchaburi Rd, in Soi next to Nakonluangthai Bank office, (02) 254 1360.

MASK, THE, Patpong Soi 2, 2nd level, Patpong, (02) 236 5010.

MASTER CLUB, Silom Soi 2, 3rd floor, (02) 632 7719, karaoke.

MIDNIGHT COWBOY, 17-20 Soi Laleewan, Saphan Kwai area, 279 5712, all-male cabaret show.

MY WAY, 944,4 Thanon Rama 4, 233-9567, older crowd, nightly shows, muscular, macho types, 13:00-01:00.

NEW CENTRE, Patpong Soi 2, 5th floor, across from Foodland, Surawong, Patpong, (02) 234 9106, pub with restaurant & disco.

OASIS, Soi Kaw Toey, Pradipat Rd, Saphankwai, (02) 278 5058, karaoke.

PALAZZO, The, 36/5-36/9 Prachanimit Rd, Pradipat Soi 10, Saphankwai, (02) 279 1518, 19:30-03:00.

PARADISE COCKTAIL LOUNGE, 466/12 Phahonyothin Soi, on Soi next to Tanakan Omsin bank, Saphankwai, (02) 271 0602, 19:00-01:00, go go boys.

PASSPORT KARAOKE, Rama 4 Rd, across from My Way, in back of Khao Shong Coffee Shop, Patong.

PEMPER MOUSSE, 439 Sukhumvit 71, (02) 392 3233, pub with karaoke.

RELAX, 3,8 Phaholyothin Rd, Soi 2, 279-4803, mainly local crowd, 19:00-01:00.

SEVEN NIGHT, Pradipat Rd, next to railroad, Saphankwai, (02) 279 9399.

SPHINX/DIVINE, Silom Soi 4, Patpong, (02) 234 7249, 4 levels, pub, restaurant & disco.

STAX, 5-9 sOI 20, Pradipat Soi, Saphankai, (02) 278 1521, 18:00-05:00, karaoke, go go boys.

STUDIO 982, Sukhumvit Rd, across from Wat Tattong, Sukhumvit, (02) 391 6545.

SUPER LEX LOUNGE, 39,19 Soi Anuman Rajadhon, 236-1636, 19:00-01:00.

TAWAN, Soi Tantawan, Surawong Rd, across from Tawanna Ramada Hotel, Patong, (02) 234 5506, muscle men.

TELEPHONE PUB, ★ 114,11-13 Silom Rd, Soi 4, 234-3279, bar & restaurant, 18:00-03:00.

TELEPHONE, Silom Soi 4, Silom Rd, (02) 234 3279, pub & restaurant, 19:00-02:00.

TURNING POINT, Sukhumvit Soi 23, (02) 662 1103.

UTOPIA, 116/1 Sukhumvit 23, at Soi 23 & Soi Sawaddee, Saphankwai, (02) 259 9619, pub, cafe, gallery & shops. Accommodation available.

WHITE HORSE, Soi T.S. Apartment (Soi Phetchaburi 14), 252-9715, younger crowd, 18:00-01:00.

■ Dance Bar/Disco

DIVINE DISCO, Silom Soi 4, video disco, variety stores, 3 floors.

DJ STATION, Silom Soi 2, from 21:00, late-night disco, younger crowd.

STAX, Pradipat Rd, 9 Soi Ko Toei, Saphankwai, (02) 278 4018, karaoke disco, 19:00-01:00.

■ Saunas/Health Clubs

ADONIS SAUNA, 1025,18 Thanon Ploenchit, 253-7609, bar inside.

ANGELO SAUNA, 1025/10-11 Plern Jit Rd, near Central Chidlom, (02) 252 9176, 16:00-23:00 (Sat, Sun from 13:00).

BABYLON BANGKOK, ★ 50 Soi Atthakarn Prasit, 286-4947, roof garden & bar, outside jacuzzi, gym.

COLONY SAUNA, 117 Ikkamai Soi 5 (Soi Jalernsook), Sukhumvit Rd, Sukhumvit, (02) 391 4393, 15:00-24:00.

COLONY, THE, 117 Ekamai Soi 5, Sukhumvit, (02) 391 4383, from 15:00 (Sat, Sun 12:00-06:00).

DAVID DE BANGKOK, Chao Pha, near Praartid Rd.

G.G. SAUNA, Soi Ronnachai 2, Saphankwai, in back of train station, (02) 279 3807, 15:00-23:00 (Sat, Sun from 12:00).

NOBODY BODY CENTER, 212/9-10, Sukhumvit Soi 12, Sukhumvit Plaza, 4th floor, (02) 251 4367, 12:00-23:00.

OBELISKS, THE, 39/3 Sukhumvit Soi 53, (02) 662 4377, sauna & bar, 17:00-23:30 (Sat, Sun from 14:00).

OTOKO SAUNA, Soi Serksawittaya, Silom Rd.

PHU NIGHT PUB & SAUNA, Saphankwai area, Pradipat Soi, (02) 278 2706 or 279 5236, sauna & bar 20:00-06:00, call for exact location.

SUKHOTHAI SAUNA, Sukhothai Rd, Dusit, Saphankwai, (02) 241 3385, 16:00-23:00 (Sat, Sun from 14:00).

THAIMEX SAUNA ENTERTAINMENT, 17 Pradipat Soi 10, Saphankwai, (02) 271-1173, sauna & bar. Sauna: 15:00-23:00; Bar: 21:00-03:00.

■ Restaurants

BAN CHIANG, 114 Thanon Srivieng, 236-7045, northeastern Thai cuisine, 10:30-14:30 & 16:30-22:30.

GREEN CARNATION, 128,9 Soi Tantawan, 235-3291, bar & restaurant, bar open 19:00-01:00.

J.J. PARK, Silom Rd (opposite Harrie's bar), Thai cuisine.

KOKAEO, 109,80 Phetchaburi Soi 33, 253-2343.

LOOGBUAB, 39,25-26 Soi Anuman Rajadhon, 236-2870, restaurant & bar, Thai & European cuisine.

TELEPHONE, at Telephone Pub.

THANYING, 10 Thanon Pramuan, 236-4361.

CHIANG MAI

■ Information

ALCOHOLICS ANONYMOUS, McCormack Hospital, room 133, meetings daily 18:30 (Sun also 09:30).

■ Tours, Charters & Excursions

SONN TREKKING, (53) 814 069, in USA: (213) 962-9169, knowledgeable guide to the area, can arrange elephant rides, etc. Ask for the guide called Mister Gosonn Vonganuwong. His is the best guide service in northern Thailand and is used exclusively by Tours to Paradise.

■ Accommodations

CHATREE HOTEL, 11/10 Suriyawong Rd, (53) 279 179, fax: 279 085, gay-friendly hotel with restaurant, room service, AC, private baths, pool on premises.

COFFEE BOY COTTAGES, 248 Toong Hotel Rd, tel & fax: 66 53 247021, bar tel: 244 458, luxury Lana-style cottages and a 3-bedroom house, men only, private baths, tropical gardens, water-lily pond, private entrance to Coffee Boy Bar, full American breakfast.

LOTUS HOTEL, 2/25 Soi Viangbua, Tambol Chang-Phuk, Amphur Muang, (53) 215 376, fax 221 340, hotel with bar, restaurant, kiosk shops, go-go boys & drag shows, AC, phone,

THAILAND

refrigerator, color TV, women welcome, some hetero clientele. ♂

■ Bars

ADAM'S APPLE BAR, Soi Viangbua, across from Lotus Hotel, go-go boys. ⌧

BUTTERFLY ROOM, 126 Thanon Loi Khroh, (053) 213-584, small bar, go-go dancers, 20:00-24:00. ⌧♂

CIVILIZED BAR, Chotana Rd, next to Rainbow bar. ♂

COFFEE BOY, 248 Thanon Toonghotel, (053) 244-458, go-go boys, 20:00-02:00. ⌧♂

DOI BOY BAR, 5/40 Soi 4, Chotana Rd, male cabaret. ⌧♂

KRA JIAP, 18/1 Wualai Soi 3, Haiya, restuarant & bar, drag cabaret show, rooftop terrace. ⌧♂

LANTERNS, 25/1 Rajchiangsaen Rd, Soi 2. ⌧♂

LOTUS BAR, downstairs at Lotus Hotel location. ⌧♂

MACHO BAR, 248 Tranon Thung (near the Chatree Hotel), Suriyawong Rd, off boys, full bar, cabaret show. ⌧♂

RAINBOW BAR, 161/90 Chotana Rd. ♂

■ Restaurants

AMERICA RESTAURANT, 402/1-2 Tapae Rd, 232 017, homemade American apple pie & chocolate cake, bottomless coffee cup. ⌧

PATTAYA

■ Accommodations

AMBIANCE HOTEL, 325/91 Pattaya Land Soi 3, South Pattaya, Thailand, (038) 424 099, 425 145, Fax 422 824, 424 626, men only hotel with terrace bar, coffee shop & nightclub on premises, private baths, satellite TV, video channel, Jacuzzi, near gay bars, 150 yards to ocean beach. ♂

CAFE ROYALE HOTEL, LE, 325/102-5 Pattaya Land Soi 3, South Pattaya, (038) 423 515, 428 303, FAX (038) 424 579, hotel with sidewalk cafe & bar, women welcome, private baths, color TV, AC, phone, maid, room & laundry service, near gay beach. ♂

CLASSIC INN, 293/27-28 Moo 10 Soi Buakaew, South Pattaya Rd, Banglamung, Chomburi, Pattaya, 038424159, fax 6622376153, hotel with restaurant & bar, men only, private baths with shower & toilet. ♂

■ Bars

ADAM & EVE COCKTAIL LOUNGE, Soi 2, North Pattaya, 424-672, live shows & cabaret, 20:00-03:00. ♪⌧$♂

AMOUR, Pattayaland Soi 3. ⌧♂

BODYGUARD, Pattayaland Soi 2. ⌧♂

BOYS, BOYS, BOYS, 325,89 Pattayaland Soi 3 at Ambiance Guest House, South Pattaya, 424-099, patio, shows, dancing, go-go boys & shower show 23:00-01:00. Open 19:00-03:00. ⑩♪⌧♂

CAFÉ ROYAL, 325,103-5 Pattayaland Soi 3 at Cafe Royale Hotel, 423-515, piano bar, 21:00 till late. ♂

CHARLIE BOY, Pattayaland Soi 1. ⌧♂

COCABANANA, Pattayaland Soi 3. ♂

COCKPIT GAY BAR, 325,106 Pattayaland Soi 3, next to Boys, Boys, Boys, South Pattaya, go-go dancers, 7 days 19:00-03:00. ⌧$♂

CRUZ 101, Pattayaland Soi 3. ♂

EXECUTIVE CLUB, Pattaya Land Soi 1, South Pattaya. ♂

GENTLEMEN'S BAR, Pattayaland Soi 1. ⌧ ♂

MOONLIGHT, Pattayaland Soi 1, bar with small hotel & restaurant. ⌧♂

TOY BOY BAR, Pattayaland Soi 3. ⌧♂

WHY NOT?, 325,25 Pattayaland Soi 1, South Pattaya, 2nd floor go-go dancers, cabaret, rooms, 19:00-02:00. ♪⌧$♂

■ Restaurants

DOLF RIKS, Sri Nakorn Centre, South Pattaya, 428-269, Indonesian & international cuisine, 11:00-24:00.

JUST A FRIEND, Pattayaland Soi 3. ⌧♂

REUN THAI, Thanon Pattaya 2, South Pattaya, 425-911, Thai seafood, Thai dancing, 11:00-24:00. ♪

PHUKET

■ Accommodations

HOME SWEET HOME GUEST HOUSE & POW-WOW PUB & RESTAURANT, (076) 340 756, Fax: 340 757, guesthouse with restaurant, bar & American Indian jewelry store, women welcome in guesthouse, 50% gay/lesbian in bar & restaurant, private baths, color TV, AC, telephone, maid & laundry service, VCR rental available. ♂

■ Bars

BLACK & WHITE BAR, THE, 81,29 Thanon Bang-La, 321-118, DJ & small dance floor, 19:00-02:00. ⑩$♂

HOLLYWOOD, Patong Beach, ask locally for address. ⌧♂

MAXIM'S, 1/2 block from Uncle Charlie's Boys bar. ⌧♂

MY WAY II, 89,26-28 Soi Permpong Pattana, 321-401, large stage, go-go dancers, rooms available, 16:00-01:00. ⌧$♂

UNCLE CHARLIE'S BOYS, 1 block from Black & White bar. ⌧♂

YOUNG SHARK BOY, ★ 38/6 Sawaddirock Rd, Patong Beach. ⌧♂

VIETNAM

COUNTRY CODE: (84)

WHO TO CALL

For Tour Companies Serving This Destination
See Vietnam on page 29

HANOI

■ Bars

POLITE BAR, not far from Hoan Kiem Lake, ask locally for address, very discreetly frequented by gays.

WHITE BOX, close to VIP Hotel, ask locally for address, very discreetly frequented by gays.

HO CHI MINH CITY

■ Accommodations

THAI THIEN HOTEL, 31 Le Anh Xuan, 1st District, (84-8) 839 1713, Fax: (84-8) 839 1713, very small hotel with AC, satellite TV, some English spoken, gays welcome, but must be VERY discreet.

■ Bars

CAY DUA (COCONUT TREE) COFFEE SHOP, 6a Tu Xuong St, Q3, 20:00-23:00, very discreetly frequented by gays.

CONCERT BAR, Nguyen Hue St, across from Doc Lap Hotel, very discreetly frequented by gays.

Q BAR, in back of the concert hall in the city center, very discreetly frequented by gays.

THAI SON CLUB, 151 Ton That Dam Q-1, 21-F Ton That Thiep St, 821 3227, very discreetly frequented by gays.

■ Dance Bar/Disco

SAM SAN, Le Duan St, very discreetly frequented by gays, Wed only. ⑩

■ Cafe

CHI LANG CAFE, Dong Khoi St, 824 2936, very discreetly frequented by gays.

PHUONG CAC CAFE, 213bis Nam Ky Khoi Nghia St, 829 7484, very discreetly frequented by gays.

THREE-SEVENTY-THREE CAFE, 373/44 CMT 8 St, 842 5997, very discreetly frequented by gays.

AUSTRIA

EUROPE

For Tour Companies Serving This Destination
See Europe on page 14

ALBANIA
COUNTRY CODE: (355)

TIRANA

■ *Information*
SHOQATA GAY ALBANIA, PO Box 104, Tirana, gay group.

AUSTRIA
COUNTRY CODE: (43)

For Tour Companies Serving This Destination
See Austria on page 9

BREGENZ

■ *Information*
AIDS-HILFE VORARLBERG, (05574) 46 5 26.
FRAUENGETRIEBE, Schillerstr. 2, (05574) 455 38, bildungszentrum für frauen (women's info center).

ELBIGENALP

■ *Bars*
ZUR GEIERWALLY St. Urban Stube, (05634) 6405, 11:00-01:00, closed Wed. ♂

GRAZ

■ *Information*
FRAUENINITIATIVE FABRIK, Plüssemanngasse 47, (0316) 47 11 79, women's organization, lesbian group meets here.
ROSAROTE PANTHER, Rapoldgasse 24, (0316) 82 80 80, gay & lesbian center, Thurs & Fri 19:00-23:00. Women's cafe Mon 17:00-23:00.
STEIRISCHE AIDS-HILFE, (0316) 81 50 50.

■ *Bars*
CLUB WERNER, Reitschulgasse 20, (0316) 84 52 48, 21:00-04:00, closed Sun. ♂

■ *Cafe*
BANG, Dreihackengasse 4, (0316) 91 95 49, cafe 20:00-02:00 (Sun till 24:00), disco nights Fri & Sat 21:00-04:00, closed Mon, Tues. [♫]♂

■ *Erotica*
AMERICAN DISCOUNT, Jakoministr. 12.

INNSBRUCK

■ *Information*
AIDS-HILFE TIROL, (0512) 56 36 21.
FRAUENZENTRUM & FRAUENCAFE, Liebeneggstr. 15, (0512) 58 08 39, women's center, Lesbengruppe (lesbian group) meetings and Frauencafe (women's cafe) take place here.
HOSI TIROL, Innrain 100, 1st floor, (0512) 56 24 03, meetings Thurs 20:30-23:00.

■ *Bars*
DIE ALTE PICCOLO, Seilergasse 2, (05222) 58 21 63, 21:00-04:00, closed Sun. ♂
SAVOY STÜBERL, Höttinger Au 26, (05222) 28 78 32, 10:00-01:00, closed Sun. ♂

■ *Erotica*
OLYMPIA KINO, Höttinger Au 26, 10:00-22:00, closed Sun.

KLAGENFURT

■ *Information*
AIDS-HILFE KÄRNTEN, (0463) 55 1 28.
FRAUENZENTRUM, Villacher Ring 21/2, (463) 51 12 48, lesbian group meets 3rd Fri from 19:00.
ROSA TELEFON & GAY HOTLINE, (0463) 50 46 90, Wed 19:00-20:00, gay group meets Thurs 18:00-20:00..

■ *Bars*
NA UND, Burggasse 2, (0463) 51 49 18, 07:30-13:00 & 21:00-02:00 7 days. ♂

LINZ

■ *Information*
AIDS-HILFE OBERÖSTERREICH, (0732) 21 70.
FRAUENZENTRUM LINZ, Altstadt 11, (0732) 21 29, Lesbengruppe (lesbian group) meetings.
HOSI LINZ, Schubertstr. 36, (0732) 60 98 98, meetings Thurs 20:00-22:00. Rosa gay line: Mon 20:00-22:00, Thurs from 18:30. Lesbengruppe (lesbian group) meets 1st Fri from 20:00.

■ *Bars*
STONE WALL, Rainerstr. 22, (0732) 60 04 38, 11:00-03:00 (dance bar Tues, Fri-Sat 22:00-04:00) [♫]♂
WOHIN, Starhembergstr. 11, (0732) 77 80 75, 19:00-04:00 (Sun from 17:00). ♂

■ *Cafe*
COFFEE CORNER (C&C), Bethlehemstr. 30, (0732) 77 08 62, Mon-Fri from 17:00, Sat from 19:00, Sun from 15:00. ♀♂

SALZBURG

■ *Information*
AIDS-HILFE SALZBURG, (0662) 88 14 88.
FRAUENZENTRUM UND FRAUENCAFE, Elisabethstr. 11, (0662) 871 639, women's cultural center and cafe. ♀
HOSI-ZENTRUM, Müllner Hauptstrasse 11, (0662) 43 59 27, Tues from 20:00 & Wed 18:00-24:00, Fri 21:00-24:00, café Sat from 20:00.
ROSA TELEFON, (0622) 43 59 27, Fri 19:00-21:00.

■ *Bars*
KUPFERPFANDL, Paracelsusstr. 14, (0662) 87 57 60, 17:00-04:00. ♂
TIROLER WEINSTUBE, Steingasse 51, (0662) 74 92 54, 21:00-03:00. ♂

■ *Erotica*
AMERICAN DISCOUNT, Alter Markt 1.

WIEN - VIENNA

■ *Information*
AIDS-HILFE WIEN, (1) 408 61 86, Safer Sex Hotline: Mon & Fri 18:00-20:00.
FRAUENBERATUNGSSTELLE, (1) 587 67 50, Wed 18:00-20:00.
FRAUENZENTRUM BEISL, Währinger Str. 59, Stiege 6, 1 Stock, (1) 40 85 057, women's center, Wed & Fri 19:00-24:00.
HOSI-ZENTRUM, Novaragasse 40, (1) 216 66 04, gay & lesbian center with varying schedule of events. Tues cafe evening from 20:00, Wed Lesbengruppe (women's social) from 19:00, Thurs youth group from 20:00.
ROSA LILA TELEFON, (1) 216 66 04, Tues 18:00-20:00, Wed 19:00-21:00. Lesbentelefon (lesbian line) Thurs from 19:00.
ROSA LILA VILLA/TIP, Linke Wienzeile 102, (1) 58 68 150, gay & lesbian center with many activities, lending library, open Mon-Fri 17:00-20:00.
STICHWORT, ARCHIV DER FRAUEN, BIBLIOTHEK, Diefenbachgasse 38, (1) 812 98 86, archive and library for women, Mon, Tues 09:00-14:00, Thurs 15:00-20:00.

■ *Bars*
ALTE LAMPE, Heumühlgasse 13, (1) 587 34

AUSTRIA

Quality Gay European Skiing Vacations at Great Prices

Ski Connections is a company that is serious about its specialty, European ski vacations. Their frequent inspection trips to every one of Europe's ski resorts allow them to make meaningful recommendations based on clients' preferences. Their extensive brochure includes only hotels that meet stringent, and high, minimum standards of comfort. They cultivate and maintain warm, personal relationships with the personnel of these hotels, because they have found this results in more enthusiastic welcomes and prompter service for their clients. Followthrough like that is truly rare in these times!

For the past three years, Ski Connections has offered all-gay ski tours to Innsbruck, Austria, with stops in Munich. (Innsbruck is a place of dramatic backdrops of sheer mountains whose 6 different ski facilities have no problem guaranteeing there WILL be snow for your visit). Ski Connections' gay tour for 1997 was an all-inclusive Gay Carnival tour to Innsbruck. The $1,215 price included round-trip air from NYC or Boston, round-trip transfers, 4-star accommodations in a hotel with casino, buffet breakfast and dinner daily, gay events and parties, other extras and discounts, hotel taxes and gratuities, and a night in Amsterdam on the return. A similar trip is planned for early 1998.

Contact **Ski Connections** at (916) 582-1889, (800) SKI-1888, Fax: (916) 582-0568.

54, piano bar, Wed-Sat 21:00-04:00, Sun 17:00-01:00.
CAFÉ REINER, Kettenbrückengasse 4, (1) 586 23 62, bar, restaurant, cafe, daily 21:00-04:00. ♂
EAGLE, Blümelgasse 1, (1) 587 26 61, daily 21:00-04:00, frequented by some levi & leather clientele, darkroom.
GOLDENER SPIEGEL, Linke Wienzeile 46, (1) 586 66 08, bar & restaurant, 19:00-02:00, closed Mon, Tues. ♂
MANGO BAR, Laimgrubengasse 3, (1) 587 44 48, daily 21:00-04:00. ♂
NANU, Schleifmühlgasse 11, (1) 587 29 87, till 04:00 7 days, very few women. ♂
NIGHTSHIFT, Corneliusgasse 8, (1) 586 23 37, 22:00-04:00 (Fri, Sat till 05:00), darkroom.
STIEFELKNECHT, Wimmergasse 20, (1) 545 23 01, men-only, frequented by leather men, darkroom, daily 22:00-02:00 (Fri, Sat till 04:00).
TRADITIONS BEISL, Zieglergasse 40, bar & restaurant, 18:00-24:00 (Sat till 01:00, Sun from 16:00). ♂

■*Dance Bar/Disco*
HEAVEN U4,★ Schönbrunnerstr. 222, (1) 858 31 85, men's disco night Thurs 23:00-05:00. ♂
LESBIAN DISCO, at the Frauenzentrum, Währingerstr. 59/Stiege 6, (entrance Prechtlgasse), (1) 402 87 54, 1st & 3rd Sat 21:00-05:00 (2nd Sat of month smoke-free disco from 21:00). ♀
WHY NOT, Tiefer Graben 22, (1) 535 11 58, Fri & Sat 22:00-04:00, Sun 21:00-02:00. ♂

■*Cafe*
BERG - DAS CAFÉ, Berggasse 8, enter from Wasagasse, Löwenherz bookstore location, (1) 319 57 20, daily 10:00-01:00.
CAFE HARTAUER, Riemergasse 9, (1) 512 89 81, 08:00-02:00 (Sat from 17:00), closed Sun, frequented by some gays.
CAFE JOY, Franzensgasse 2, (1) 586 59 38. 20:00-04:00.
CAFE SAVOY, Linke Wienzeile 36, (1) 56 73 48, 17:00-02:00, Sat 21:00-02:00 (Sat many women), closed Sun.
CAFE WILLENDORF, Linke Wienzeile 102, (1) 587 17 89, café & restaurant, daily 19:00-02:00, many lesbians. ♀♂
DAS POSIHIVE CAFÉ, Novaragasse 40, at the HOSI gay center, café for people with HIV or AIDS, and their friends, Tues 17:00-22:00.
DAS VERSTECK, Grünangergasse, at Nikolaigasse, (1) 513 40 53, 18:00-24:00 (Sat from 19:00), closed Sun, frequented by some gays.
FRAUENCAFE, Lange Gasse 11, (1) 43 37 54, Mon-Sat 18:00-01:00. ♀
WIENER FREIHEIT, Schönbrunnerstr. 25, (1) 581 58 90, 14:00-04:00 (Fri, Sat till 05:00), closed Sun. ♂

■*Saunas/Health Clubs*
ADONIS SAUNA, Halbgasse 2, (1) 522 98 61, 10:00-18:00 (closed Sun).
AMIGOS CAFE-SAUNA, Müllnergasse 5, (1) 319 05 14, 7 days, 17:00-04:00.
APOLLO CITY SAUNA, Wimbergergasse 34, (1) 523 08 14, daily 14:00-02:00.
KAISERBRÜNDL, Weihburggasse 18-20, (1) 513 32 93, 14:00-24:00 (Fri-Sun till 02:00).
RÖMER SAUNA, Passauerplatz 6, (1) 53 35 318, videos, 14:00-02:00 7 days. ♂

■*Retail & Bookstores*
FRAUENZIMMER BUCHHANDLUNG, Lange Gasse 11, (1) 406 86 78, feminist & lesbian bookshop with a wide selection of titles. Mon-Fri 09:00-18:00 & Sat till 13:00.
LÖWENHERZ, Berggasse 8, enter from Wasagasse, (1) 317 29 82, gay bookstore, 10:00-19:00 (Sat till 13:00), closed Sun.

■*Leathers/Piercing*
TIBERIUS, Lindengasse 2a, (1) 522 04 74, 15:00-19:00 (Sat 10:00-13:00), closed Sun.

■*Erotica*
AMERICAN DISCOUNT, Neubaugasse 39; Rechte Wienzeile 5; Lugner City, Gablenzgasse 5-13; Donauzentrum, Donaustadtstr. 1; SZ, Simmeringer Hauptstr. 96a.
MAN FOR MAN, Hamburgstr. 8, (1) 585 20 64.

BELGIUM
COUNTRY CODE: (32)

WHO TO CALL
For Tour Companies Serving This Destination
See Belgium on page 10

AALST

■ *Information*
GROUP VICE VERSA, Meuleschettestr. 74, (053) 77 25 05, gay & lesbian group, café Wed from 20:30.
PINKLADIES, Michielsplaats 2, (053) 70 05 78.

■ *Bars*
COMPANY, THE, 35 Vrijheidsstraat. ♂
DAENS, 6 Pontstraat. ♀
POES CAFE, 14 Gentsestraat, from 11:00. ♂
SAVARIN, 29 Pontstraat. ♂
TWILIGHT, 38 De Ridderstraat. ♂

BELGIUM

EUROPE

■ *Restaurants*
ALLEGRO, Gentsestraat. 🚾
DE VESTEN, 10 Keizersplein. 🚾
RAAR MAAR WAAR, 11 De Ridderstraat. 🚾
ST. LAZARE, 2 Consciencestraat, from 10:30 (closed Mon). 🚾
WIENERHAUS, Esplanadeplein. 🚾

AARSCHOT

■ *Information*
IMPULS, 47 Leuvensesteenweg, (016) 56 95 68, women's aid & resource center.

■ *Bars*
CHAPLIN, 8 Grote Markt. ♂
DEN BIECHTSTOEL, 23 Tielseweg. ♂
VIERTAP, 1 Molenstraat, gay 2nd Fri & Sun. ♂

■ *Restaurants*
MALIBU, Dorp 2A. 🚾
SCHOLEKEN, 'T, 1 Molenstraat. 🚾

ANTWERP

■ *Information*
ATTHIS, Geuzenstraat 27, (03) 216 37 37, ask about women's cafe & socials. ♀

■ *Women's Accommodations*
KRIS'S ANTWERP WOMEN'S B&B, Dolfijnstraat 69, 2018 Antwerp, (32-3) 271 0613. Antwerp is so strategically located that your stay here will never be boring. Just get up and go to Brussels, Amsterdam or even Paris. Many interesting places are within an hour to three hours' drive or train from here. Have your own bedroom and share the bath in a big, Art Deco-style house and garden. It's close to the city center, and there are cafes, restaurants and cultural activities nearby. Your host, Kris, is a professional translator who speaks Dutch, French, English, German, Russian and Polish. Kris can give you directions to the women's bar in Antwerp, or get you invited to one of the lesbian parties that are frequently held in Antwerp. ♀

■ *Bars*
BACCHUS, Van Schoonhovenstr 28, Fri-Sun from 14:00. ♂
BELIZE, Oude Baan, gay Sun only. ♂
BLITZ, THE, Van Schoonhovenstraat 24, 12:00-06:00. ♂
BOOTS, THE, 22 van Aerdstraat, (03) 23 32 136, private club with backroom, videos, leather & toy shop inside, 22:30-05:00 Fri & Sat. 🚾
BORSALINO, Van Schoonhovenstr 48, from 21:00. ♂
CAPITAN CAVEMAN, Geulinxcstraat 28, 20:00-03:00 (Fri, Sat till 06:00), closed Mon, Tues. 🚾
DEN BAZAAR, Van Schoonhovenstr. 22, 12:00-05:00. ♂

FUNNIES, Lange Beeldekensstraat 12, 21:00-06:00 (closed Mon). ♂
HANKY CODE, 69 Van de Wervestraat, 19:00-02:00 (Fri till 03:00, Sat-Sun from 15:00). 🚾 ♂
KATSHUIS, Grote Pieter Potstraat 18, from 16:00 (Mon-Tues from 20:00). ♂
LADY'S PUB, Waalskaai 56, from 19:00. ♀
NO DIFFERENCE BAR, Van Schoonhovenstr, mainly women. ♀
PLAY BOY, Van Schoonhovenstraat 42, from 17:00. ♂
QUEENS, Van Schoonhovenstraat 4, from 17:30 (closed Wed). ♂
SPAGHETTIWORLD, Oude Koornmarkt 66, Sun from 15:00. ♂
TAVEERNE CHAPLIN, Breidelstraat. ♂
TWILIGHT, Van Schoonhovenstraat 54. from 18:00 (Sun from 15:00). ♂

■ *Dance Bar/Disco*
SHAKESPEARE, Oude Korenmarkt 24, (03) 23 70 473, mostly women, from 20:00 (closed Tues). 🚾 ♀
STRANGE, 161 Dambruggestraat, (03) 226-0072, bar & disco, from 21:00 (Sun from 16:00). 🚾 ♂

■ *Cafe*
COTE COUR, Mechelseplein 21, Tues-Sat from 11:30. ♂
DE KLEINE OPERA, 6 Kipdorpbrug, from 10:00. ♂
HET HESSENHUIS, Falconrui 53.
OGENBLIK, 'T, Grote Markt 12, Wed-Sun 11:00-24:00. ♂
ROSKAM, Vrijdagmarkt 12, from 17:00 (Fri from 08:30, Sat & Sun form 15:00). ♀♂
TAVERNE 'T ROKIN, Melkmarkt 13. ♂

■ *Saunas/Health Clubs*
ADONIS, 174 Dambruggestraat.
DIMITRI, Greinstraat 47, 14:00-23:00 (closed Sat, Sun).
DINGEMAN, Karel de Preterlei 170, (03) 271 04 17, 13:00-24:00.
MACHO 1,★ Florisstraat 10, (03) 22 60 393, bar inside, 15:00-01:00, Fri, Sat 20:00-06:00. 🚾
METROPOLITAN INTERNATIONAL, St. Elisabethstr. 47, 14:00-22:00, Fri till 02:00, Sat till 20:00 (closed Sun).
SPA 55, 55 Sandersstraat, large bath house with gym & bar, 14:00-24:00 (Fri, Sat till 02:00). 🚾

■ *Restaurants*
CASTELLINO, Groenplaats 28, 09:00-23:00. 🚾
DEN BEIAARD, Handschoenmarkt 21, from 10:00.
EILAND, 1 Isabellalei, 09:00-21:00 (closed Sun). 🚾
IN DE SCHADUW VAN DE KATHEDRAAL, Handschoenmarkt 17-21 (03) 232 4014, 12:00-15:00 & 18:00-22:00 (Sun only 12:00-21:30). 🚾
KERTOSONO, Provinciestr. 118, from 18:00. 🚾
L'ANVERS OI, 52 Sint Jacobstraat, retaurant & bar, 18:00-22:00 (Sat till 24:00, Sun from 20:00). 🚾
LUNCH EN SUPPER, 246 L. Lozanastraat, 12:00-15:00 & 19:00-22:00 (Mon only 12:00-15:00, Sat only 19:00-22:00), closed Sun. 🚾

■ *Retail & Bookstores*
BOOKSHOP 'T VERSCHIL, Minderbroedersrui 42.

BERCHEM

■ *Bars*
GROS VISAGE, Spiegelstraat. ♂

■ *Restaurants*
TAFELTJE ROND, Hogeweg 14, 12:00-22:00, closed Sun. 🚾

BERLAAR-HEIKANT

■ *Bars*
DE OUDE SPAR, Aarschotsebaan 2, 19:00-02:00 (Fri, Sat till 05:00), Sun 16:00-04:00. ♂

BOORTMEERBECK

■ *Bars*
LOCOON, 11 Pastorijstraat, Thurs from 21:00. ♂

BRAKEL

■ *Bars*
GODFATHER, 12 Stationspl., from 15:00 (closed Mon). ♂

BRUGGE

■ *Information*
GAY CENTER IDEM DITO, St. Jansstraat 3, (050) 33 47 42, café Sun 15:00-18:00, youth café Fri 20:00-23:00.

An Historic Stop Between Paris & Amsterdam

HOTEL KERLINGA
Brugge, Belgium
(32-50) 41 17 91

BELGIUM

■ Accommodations

HOSTELLERIE TEN LANDE, Reigerlostraat 25, Beernem, (32-50) 79 10 00, fax: (32-50) 79 12 84, gay-friendly hotel with restaurant & bar, private baths, color cable TV, telephone with direct outside lines, fully stocked mini-bar, refrigerator, nearby ocean, pool & river, 50% gay/lesbian clientele.

HOTEL KERLINGA, Kerkstraat 146, Blankenberge, Belgium 8370, (32-50) 41 17 91, Fax: (32-50) 42 99 26. An ideal gay-friendly holiday getaway a short distance from Brugge, the hotel is 600 meters from the beach and within walking distance of the town. Climb to the belfry (366 winding steps), visit the city gates, the windmills, breweries, view exquisite lace & more! Return to a modern, newly furnished room with private bath, phone (TV & minibar on request). A substantial breakfast is served daily, and all meals are prepared by the proprietors, using only the finest-quality foods. Vegetarian and other special diets can be catered for. Groups are also welcome and our rates are very reasonable. See ad Page 195.

■ Women's Accommodations

HUIZE VITA, Gieterijstraat 45, Brugge, 8000, (32-50) 34 25 93. A romantic double room for women only a 5-minute walk from the city centre, available with or without full breakfast. Call or write Ann & Nathalie. We would love to be your guide! ♀

■ Bars

HOLLYWOOD, 't Zand 33, from 14:00, closed Mon. ♂

LOCOMOTIEF, Spoorwegstraat 312, from 10:00, closed Thurs. ♂

MON PARIS, Langestraat 138, from 10:00 (Sun from 14:30). ♂

PASSE PARTOUT, St. Jansstr. 3, from 14:30. ♂

RAVEL, 172 K. d. Stoutelaan, from 22:00 (closed Tues, Thurs). ♂

■ Cafe

GOUDOU, 's Gragenstraat 44, at De Dwarskop, lesbian cafe, Thurs from 20:00. ♀

BRUSSELS

■ Information

ALLO SIDA AIDS HELPLINE, Dutch: (02) 51 22 121, French: Homo Sida 51 14 529.

INFOR-HOMO/LESBIENNES, Ave. de L'Opale 100, (02) 733 10 24, gay & lesbian meeting place & information center.

LES LESBIANAIRES, radical lesbian archives, write Isabel D'Argent, B.P. 2024, 1000 Bxl 1.

TELS QUELS, Kolenmarktstraat 81, (02) 51 24 587, Fri 20:00-22:00, first Sun 15:00-18:00.

■ Accommodations

BRUSSELS GAY MEN'S HOMESTAY, (32-2) 354 1811, ask for Randy. For discreet gay guys traveling in Europe: Enjoy the comforts of our gay home. Bed & breakfast in a beautiful old Belgian home with a secluded setting. Located in a near suburb of Brussels just 15 min by train from the Grande Place. Extensive gay video library. Nude sunbathing is possible on the private patio. ♂

■ Women's Accommodations

CHAMBRE D'HOTE, (32) (02) 420 24 56, women's bed & breakfast, private & shared baths. Both overnight & longer stays available, call far ahead for reservations, open sporadically. ♀

GASTHOF DE GREEF, 136 Rue Th. Verhaegen, (02) 537 00 36, women's guesthouse. ♀

■ Bars

BIG NOISE, 44 Kolenmarkt, at Big Noise men's bar, (02) 512 25 25, women-only bar night Sun from 17:00. ♀

BNG, LE, Kolenmarkt 44, (02) 512 25 25, cruise bar, from 17:00. Sun women only. ♂

CAN CAN, Steenstraat 55, (02) 512-7404, from 12:00 (Sat, Sun from 15:00). ♂

CAPRICORNE, Anderlechtstraat 8. ♀

CENTRE BOULEVART, Anspach 108, from 10:00. ♂

CHEZ MAMAN, Grote Karmelietenstraat 7, 18:00-03:00 (closed Wed). ♂

COCONUTS, Kolenmarkt 100, from 15:00. ♂

COU COU, Olivetenhof 8, from 22:00, closed Mon. ♂

DUQUESNOY, 12 Duquesnoystraat, (02) 502 38 83, bar & café, from 21:00. ♂

FACTORY, 4 Imp. de la Fidelite, gay only Fri, Sat. ♂

HE RIJK DER ZINNEN, 14 Steenstraat, from 11:00 (Fri, Sat from 15:00). ♂

L'EXODUS, Rue de la Fourche 12, (02) 223 0835, 11:00-02:00. ♂

L'HERBE ROUGE, rue des Minimes 34, bar & restaurant, Sat from 19:00, Sun from 16:00. ♀

L'INCOGNITO, Steenstraat 36, from 16:00 (Sun from 15:00). ♂

L'ORANGE BLEU, Rue Antoine Dansaert 29, 19:00-03:00. ♂

LA DOLCE, Kleine Boterstr. 14, (02) 502 78 66, from 15:00. ♂

LA LUNE, Carperbrugstraat 12, from 17:00, closed Mon. ♂

LE CARROUSEL, Fontainaspl. 19, 10:00-23:00 (Fri, Sat 10:00-01:00), closed Sun. ♂

LE FROU FROU, 60 Kolenmarkt, from 15:00. ♂

LE GEMEAU, 12 Rue de Laeken, (02) 219 23 36, Fri-Mon from 20:00. ♂

LE GENTLEMAN, Kartuizerstraat 36, from 22:00. ♂

LE PETIT LOMBARD, 25 Rue du Lombard, (02) 514 0327, 15:00-03:00 (Sat from 17:00). ♂

RESERVE, Kleine Boterstr. 14, Fri-Mon from 11:00. ♂

SAPHO, Rue Borgval, across from Féminin disco, Fri-Sun from 22:00. ♀

TELS QUELS BAR, Kolenmarkt 81, (02) 512 3234, bar, café & gay center, mostly men, Sun-Thurs 17:00-02:00, Fri & Sat till 04:00. ♂

■ Dance Bar/Disco

CERCLE 52, 52 Rue des Chartreux, (02) 514-3078, from 22:00 (closed Mon). ♂

FACTORY, THE, Getrouwhovengang, gay only Fri, Sat 23:00-08:00. ♂

GARAGE, LE, Duquesnoystraat 16-18, (02) 512-6622, Sun from 23:00. ♂

LA DÉMENCE, Rue Blaes 208, Sun 23:00-08:00. ♂

LE FEMININ, Rue Borgval, 9, (02) 511-1709, women-only, Fri-Sun from 22:00. ♀

LE SEPT, 7, Platesteenstraat, (02) 51 31 414, dance & cruise bar, from 21:00 (closed Thurs). ♂

SAPHO, St. Gérystr. 1, Fri, Sat from 22:00. ♂

■ Saunas/Health Clubs

CLUB 3000 MALIBU, Boulevard Jamar 9.

DINANT, 41-43 Dinantstraat, (02) 51 26 251, 12:00-21:00 (Sat till 23:00, Sun 14:00-19:00). ♂

LA LAGON, 86 Livournestraat, from 12:00.

MACHO 2, ★ Kolenmarkt 106, (02) 513-5667, from 12:00 (Sun from 14:00). ♂

OASIS, L' 10 Van Orleystraat, (02) 218-0800, from 11:00. ♂

■ Restaurants

COMPTOIR, 24 Oude Korenh., (02)514-0500, restaurant & bar, from 19:00.

EL PAPAGAYO, Rouppeplaan 6, 19:00-02:00.

L'ANNEXE, at L'Annexe bar. ♂

TROISEME ACTE, Steenstraat 28, (02) 502 5649, 18:00-02:00.

■ Retail & Bookstores

ARTEMYS, Rue St. Jean (inside Galerie Bortier 8), next to the Central Station, (02) 512 0347, lesbian & feminist bookshop with current local information. Tues-Thurs 10:00-18:00, Fri & Sat 10:00-19:00, closed Mon. In summer open from 12:00.

■ Leathers/Piercing

BOUTIQUE MINUIT, Centraal Galerij 6, 10:00-18:00, closed Sun.

MAN TO MAN, 9 R. Klarenstraat, 10:00-18:00, closed Sun, Mon.

DOORNIK

■ Bars

NEW DECLIC, Grote Markt. ♂

BELGIUM

PETIT PELICAN, Brusselsesteenweg 1, 19:00-06:00. ♂

GHENT

Information
AKSENT OP ROZE, Het Geuzenhuis, Kantienberg 19, (09) 31 72 80 or (09) 224 35 82, lesbian organization, socials Sat 21:00-01:00.
CLG, Guinardstr. 34, (09) 25 06 52, women's info.
LESBIAN & GAY SWITCHBOARD, (09) 223 69 29. National switchboard run by the Federatie Werkgroepen Homoseksualiteit lesbian/gay organization.
LESBIES DOE-FRONT, Postbus 621, 9000 Gent, (09) 223 69 29. Lesbian group with current local information for women. Organizers of the annual Lesbian Day.

Women's Accommodations
VROUWENHOTEL KRIS, 93 Baudelostraat, (091) 25 20 45. ♀

Bars
CHERRY LANE, 3 Meersenierstraat, from 20:00 (Fri-Sun from 22:00), closed Wed. ♀
DANDY'S CLUB, Pr. Clemetinalaan 195, from 16:00, closed Mon, Tues. ♂
KING STREET, Kammerstraat 49, 21:00-07:00. ♂
LADY INN, Maaltebruggestraat 23, (09) 222 37 99, Mon-Sat 22:00-05:00. ♀
PETIT PARIS, 183 Smidsestraat, from 21:00 (closed Tues, Wed). ♂
PINTELIER, 76 Pintestraat, from 18:00 (closed Tues). ♂
POR QUE NO, 155 St. Denijsln, from 21:00 (closed Wed). ♂
SWING, 1 Spadestraat, from 18:00, closed Tues. ♂
ZÉNON, St. Veerlepl. 7, 11:00-01:00 (Fri, Sat 14:00-2:00). ♂

Dance Bar/Disco
ROLLS, Ed. Anseelplein 5. ♀♂

Cafe
'T AKSENT OP ROZE, Geuzenhuis Bldg, Kantienberg 19, (09) 31 72 80, women's café, Sat 20:00-02:00. ♀

Saunas/Health Clubs
BOYS AVENUE, 1A Oude Schaapmarkt, 12:00-24:00 (Fri, Sat till 04:00).

Restaurants
AVALON, 37 Geldmunt, 12:00-14:00 (closed Sun).
BUDDHASBELLY, Hoogpoort 30, closed Sun.
LA MALCONTENTA, 7-9 Haringsteeg.
MAXIMILIAAN, 50 Mageleinstraat, 11:00-19:00.
SOL Y SOMBRA, Serpentraat 5, open Wed-Sat.
SOL, Zwartezustersstraat 16, open Mon-Sat.

VIER TAFELS, 6 Plotersgr., 11:00-14:00 & 20:00-24:00.
WALRY, Zwijnaardsesteenweg 6, 08:00-18:00, closed Sun.
WAREMPEL, Zandberg 8, (09) 24 30 62. Women-owned restaurant, Tues-Thurs 12:00-14:00, Fri & Sat 12:00-14:00 & 18:00-22:00.

GHENT AREA

Accommodations
BUNGALOW 'T STAAKSKEN, Staakstraat 136/138A, 9960 Assenede, (32-9) 3340954 (tel/fax). Gay-friendly B&B & self-catering bungalow, panoramic views of garden, lake & surrounding fields, 50% gay & lesbian clientele, shared baths, TV lounge, full breakfast in B&B. Color cable TV, kitchen, laundry service in bungalow.

Bars
CAFE PASSE, Doornend. 1, Assenede, Thurs-Mon from 17:00. ♂

Restaurants
DEN HOEK, 15 Holleken, Assenede, creative dinners, art interior, green surroundings with creeks & dikes, closed Mon-Wed.

HASSELT

Information
L.A.C.H., Wijngaardstraat 1, (011) 21 20 20, gay & lesbian group.

Bars
KASTEELTJE, Steenweg 169, Alken, open Wed-Sun from 21:00. ♂
LES HOMMES, Persoonstraat 10, 21:00-07:00 (Sun from 16:00), closed Tues. ♂
MOUSTIQUE II, St. Truidersteenweg, 16, (011) 22 11 99, women on Fri-Sun from 20:00. ♀
SILVERGATE, Zuivelmarkt 60, 21:00-07:00. ♂

Cafe
VROUWENKAFFE LILEV, p/a Luikersteenweg 94, (011) 24 22 94, women's cafe run by women's organization, 3rd Sat of the month from 21:00.

Restaurants
DE LEVENSBOOM, Leopoldplein 44, 12:00-14:30 & 18:30-21:00 (Sun only 12:00-14:30), closed Mon.

KNOKKE-HEIST

Bars
L'APERO, 3 Zoutelaan, 20:00-05:00. ♂

Restaurants
BOLLE, 62 Vlamingstraat, 11:30-14:30 & 18:30-24:00.

KORTRIJK

Information
DE NIMFEN, at Vrouwencentrum, Plein 52, (056) 20 07 13, women's center, café night Sat from 20:00. ♀

Bars
BRONX, Kasteelkaai 5, from 21:00, closed Tues. ♂
BURNING LOVE, Doornikswijk 113. ♂
DE TENDER, Brugsesteenweg 21, Fri-Sun from 21:30. ♀
DE VALENTINO, Gasstraat 7, from 10:00. ♂
NEW TROPIC, Vercruysselaan 6, from 16:00 (closed Wed). ♂
PINK PANTHER, THE, Papenstraat 9, Fri-Sun 20:00-02:00. ♂
VAGABOND, Meensesteenweg 80, from 22:00 (Fri-Sun from 22:00), closed Wed, Thurs. ♂

Saunas/Health Clubs
KOUROS, Liebaertln. 59, 13:30-24:00.

KUURNE

Bars
AFTER NINE, 120 Brugsesteenweg, Fri-Sun from 21:00. ♂

LENDELEDE

Bars
RICS PUB, 5 Dorpsplein, 15:00-22:00 (closed Tues). ♂

LEUVEN

Information
DE ROZE DREMPEL, Ierse Predikherenstraat 25, (016) 20 06 06, gay & lesbian group, café Thurs from 20:00, youth café Mon from 20:00.
LABYRINT, Martelarenlaan 109, (016) 25 66 76, lesbian group.

Bars
COUPERUS EN COCTEAU, Diestsestraat 245, 20:00-02:00 (closed Tues). ♂
FRENKIES, Schapenstraat, Fri-Tues from 21:00. ♂
OASE, Oude Markt 43. ♂

Restaurants
BEGIJNTJE, Naamsestraat 123, 11:30-15:00 & 17:00-22:00.
DE WITTE OLIFANT, Diestsestraat 180, 11:30-17:30 & 18:30-23:00, closed Tues.

LIEGE

Bars
BRIQUE, 4, Rue Laruelle. ♂
L'AMI GAY, Rue de la Casquette, 33, 41 22 16 26, erotic videos, backroom, frequented by leather men, open from 22:00 7 days. Unverifiable spring '97. ♂
LA SCENE, Rue de la Casquette 1, from 11:00 (Sun from 15:00). ♂
MAMA ROMA, Rue des Célestines 16, Wed-Sun from 22:00. ♂
QUARTIER GENERAL, R.I. Casquette 37, from 19:00. ♂
SPARTACUS CLUB, 12 Rue St. Jean, 22:00-06:00. ♂

FERRARI GUIDES' GAY TRAVEL A to Z - 18th EDITION

BELGIUM

■ Cafe
LA JUNGLE WOMEN'S CAFE, Rue Léon Mignon 20, from 22:00, closed Mon. ♀

LOMMEL

■ Bars
LOMMELS HUISJE, Adelberg 51, 09:00-24:00, closed Sun. ♂
STARS, Lutlommel 24, 21:00-06:00 (Sun from 22:00), closed Mon-Thurs. ♂

■ Restaurants
BISTRO, Kerkhovensesteenweg 449a.

MECHELEN

■ Information
LESBIAN GROUP, 74 Hanswijckstr., ()15) 43 21 20, socials Mon 20:00-01:00.

■ Bars
AMPHORA, Putsesteenweg 46. ♂
SEBASTIAAN, Brusselsesteenweg 205, from 18:00, closed Thurs. ♂

OOSTENDE

■ Bars
BISTRO DALI, St. Franciscusstraat 18. ♂
CALYPSO, Groetenmarkt 15, 16:00-02:00. ♂
DEE LIGHT, Ooststraat 55, (059) 511 892, from 22:00, closed Mon. ♂
LA CROISETTE, 50a Albert 1-prom., closed Thurs. ♂
MEN 4 MEN, St. Franciscusstraat 22, from 21:30-02:00 (closed Wed). ♂
RAPSODY, St. Franciscusstraat 24. ♂
SUN SCHINE, St. Paulstraat 58, from 10:00, closed Tues. ♂
YELLOW SUBMARINE, Zeelaan 101, from 20:00. ♂

■ Saunas/Health Clubs
KOUROS II, P. Benoitstraat 77, (059) 51 34 55, 13:00-24:00 (Sat 14:00-03:00, Sun from 14:00).
THERMOS, 34 Kaaistraat.

ROESELARE

■ Bars
PLAFONNEUR, 25 Sint Jorisstraat, 19:00-01:00 (closed Tues). ♂

■ Cafe
MOIRA, 4 Koornstraat, lesbian cafe Fri from 20:00. ♀

SINT-NIKLAAS

■ Information
GROUP DE ROZE WAAS, Mercatorstr. 95, (03) 776 43 84, gay group, café Tues from 20:00. ♂

TEMSE

■ Bars
EROS, 2 Dijstraat, from 21:00. ♂

TIELT

■ Bars
L'ANGE DECHU, 2-4 Brugstoweg, from 19:00 (Sun from 17:00), Sat disco from 21:00. 🏳‍🌈♂

TORHOUT

■ Bars
PELIKAN, 55 K. Markstraat, from 15:00 (Sat, Sun from 21:00). ♂

TOURNAI

■ Dance Bar/Disco
GEORGE SAND, 10 rue des Maux, (069) 84 14 69, Fri, Sat from 22:00, Sun 17:30-01:00. 🏳‍🌈♀

TURNHOUT

■ Bars
GOMPY'S, Begijnenstraat 15, 11:00-03:00. ♂
KASTEELTJE, 'T, Kasteelpln. 8, from 11:00 (Sun from 14:00), closed Mon. ♂

■ Dance Bar/Disco
K.W.H., Driezenstraat 23, (014) 42 35 83, dance bar, Fri only from 20:00. 🏳‍🌈♀

■ Cafe
DAMESKAFEE, Buurthuis 't Stokt, Kongostr. 76, (041) 41 15 65, lesbian café, 1st Fri from 20:00. ♀

VARSENARE

■ Bars
POPCORN, 14 Kriekelaarstraat, Sat from 22:00. ♂

WEVELGEM

■ Bars
MALBORO, 20 Lauwestraat, from 15:00 (Wed from 12:00, Sat & Sun from 10:00), closed Tues. ♂

ZOTTEGEM

■ Bars
KRYPTON, 2 Ter Kameren, Sat & Sun from 22:00. ♂

CZECH REPUBLIC
COUNTRY CODE: (42)

WHO TO CALL — For Tour Companies Serving This Destination See Czech Republic on page 13

BRNO

■ Information
LAMBDA BRNO, gay & lesbian organization. Men call (05) 57 29 37. Women call 52 37 12.

■ Bars
PHILADELPHIA CLUB, Milady Horakove 1A, 17:00-04:00. ♂

■ Dance Bar/Disco
DISCO MEMPHIS, Vranovská 11, Tues-Sat 21:00-05:00. 🏳‍🌈♀♂
H 46 (HACKO) BAR CLUB, 46 Hybesova, (05) 324 945, 17:00-02:00. 🏳‍🌈♂
SAPFO KLUB, 24 Pekarská, close to the Autoturist building, lesbian disco, call Inge for details: (05) 523 712. 🏳‍🌈♀
SKLIPEK U RICHARDA, Luzova 29, (05) 57 29 37, Fri & Sat 20:00-06:00, open Sept-June. 🏳‍🌈♂

CESKA LIPA

■ Dance Bar/Disco
MARCUS, 28 Rína ul, (0425) 23 518, Tues-Sun 20:00-04:00. 🏳‍🌈♂

CESKÉ BUDEJOVICE

■ Information
LAMBDA CESKÉ BUDEJOVICE, PO Box 33, 389 01 Vodnany, (342) 905 890, gay organization.
STOP AIDS INFO LINE, (038) 32 308.

■ Dance Bar/Disco
JIVAK, 2 Bozeny Nemcove, 2nd & 4th Sat 20:30-04:00. Only operates when local group organizes event. 🏳‍🌈♀♂

CHEB

■ Bars
BERT, Evrobská 30, (166) 33716, daily 18:00-02:00. ♂

HRADEC KRALOVE

■ Bars
THEATER CLUB, Dlouha St, nr main theater, gay-friendly wine bar, discreetly & occasionally frequented by a few gays. 🚫

CZECH REPUBLIC

■ Dance Bar/Disco
U HROZNU, Nerudova 18, (49) 315 15, Sat 20:00-04:00, frequented by some gays.

■ Restaurants
AL DENTE, Velke Namesti, popular with gays.

LIBEREC

■ Information
STOP AIDS INFO LINE, (048) 327, ext 223.

■ Bars
ECHO, ul. Studnicná 13, close to the Vinárna Opera, (048) 27 577, cruise bar 2nd & 4th Sat 19:00-03:00. ♂

LITOMERICE

■ Accommodations
VISCOUNT, Pod Nádrazim 281, Hostka (50 km from Prague), guesthouse with restaurant, coffee bar, sauna & nightclub. ♂

MOST

■ Information
NADACE SOKRATES, Pionyru 2922, (047) 218 3256, gay organization with meetings & discussions Tues-Thurs 18:00-22:00. Disco Fri, Sat 20:00-05:00. Evenings call (035) 278 87; write: PO Box 9a, 434 11 Most. ♂

OSTRAVA

■ Information
KLUB LAMBDA, gay organization, PO Box 377, 730 77 Ostrava 1. Occasionally organizes activities.

■ Bars
U DZBANU, Kurí Rynek, 10:00-24:00 (Fri, Sat 20:00-04:00). ♀♂

■ Dance Bar/Disco
G KLUB, Frydecká 62, videos, 18:00-04:00 (Fri & Sat from 20:00). ♀♂

■ Saunas/Health Clubs
LAZNE CAPKOVA SOKOLOVNA, Trída Osvoboditelu. Not a gay sauna, discreetly frequented by gays. It is important to be discreet. Public swimming pool.

PLZEN

■ Information
HELP LINE, (019) 224 325, Tues 14:00-16:00.

■ Bars
VINARNA U MUSKETYRU, ul. Havlíckova, Fri 19:00-02:00. ♂

PRAHA - PRAGUE

■ Information
AIDS LINE, (02) 2421 0956, Mon-Thurs 13:00-16:00.

GAY & LESBIAN SERVICE INFO LINE, (02) 2491 1104.

LAMBDA PRAHA, gay & lesbian organization. Men write PO Box 13, Rubensova 2180, 100 00 Prague 10. Women write Truhlárská 29, 110 00 Praha 1.

LOGOS G&L CHRISTIAN HELP LINE, (02) 2422 0327, Wed 10:00-22:00.

SOHO, Senovázné nam. 2, (02) 257 891, gay organization, publishes national monthly gay magazine.

■ Accommodations
PENZION DAVID, Holubova 5, (42-2) 900 11 293 or 294, Fax: (42-2) 549 820. Hotel with restaurant, sauna, bar & escorts. Private baths, expanded continental breakfast, colour cable TV, phone, terrace & garden on premises. ♂

PRAGUE HOME STAY, Pod Kotlárkou 14, 150 00 Prague 5, Tel/fax: (42 2) 527 388. Phone may be altered in 1997, for information call (42-2) 5721 0862. Lodging & kitchen privileges in a private home, some hetero clientele, easy tram ride into city, kitchen priveleges available, telephone upon request, shared baths. ♀♂

■ Bars
DRAKE'S, Petrínská 5, enter from Zborovská, (02) 534 909, cruise bar, 24hrs, back room, video cabins/relax rooms, live shows. ♂

INKOGNITO BAR, Prokopova 18, 278 347, Wed-Sat 23:00-08:00. ♂

L CLUB, Lublanská 48, (02) 9000 1189 536, 20:00-04:00 (disco from 22:00). ♀♂

PIANO BAR, Milesovska 10, 16:00-22:00, small bar with artsy crowd, frequented by gays & lesbians.

RAINBOW CLUB CAFE-BAR (DUHOVY KLUB), Kamzíková 6, Old Town, below U Cerveného Páva straight bar, (42-2) 24 23 31 68. Classical & Jazz music, separate room for non-smokers, 12:00-01:00 7 days. Sandwiches, salads, pastries, liquor & coffees. ♂

SAM, Cajkovského 34, S&M bar. ♂

STELLA, Luzicka 10, daily 17:00-04:00, large pub with younger crowd, 40% women. ♀♂

TOM'S BAR, Pernerova 4, (02) 232 1170, men-only bar & disco, 19:00-05:00 (disco from 22:00). ♂

U DUBU, Záhrebská 14, (02) 691 08 89, neighborhood-style pub, daily 18:00-04:00, 90% men.

U STAREGO SONGU, Stitneho 27, 683 7853, 16:00-01:00 (closed Mon). ♂

U STRELCE, Karoliny Svetle 12, 18:00-04:00 (Fri, Sat till 06:00, popular drag shows), 20% women. ♂

U TLUSTY BERTY, Macharovo nam. 418/4, (02) 311 4611, private club outside city center, transportation difficult to this venue, 22:00-05:00 (closed Mon, Tues). Many locals. ♂

ZA BUKEM, Rumunska 7, 9001 0151, 16:00-02:00. ♂

■ Dance Bar/Disco
RADOST, ul. Belehradská 120, discreetly frequented by gays (mostly expatriot American locals). Downstairs cafeteria with American breakfast & natural food items. Also bookshop with American books, posters, etc.

U PETRA VOKA, Na belidle 40, near Andel metro station, occasional drag & strip shows, from 21:00. ♂

■ Saunas/Health Clubs
CHAOS CLUB, ★ Dusni 13b, 242 38510, daily 17:00-05:00.

DAVID FITNESS CENTER, ★ Sokolovská 77, (2) 231 78 82, exclusively gay fitness center & sauna, 14:00-02:00. ♂

INKOGNITO, ★ Strelnicná 1969, (02) 858 6616, exclusively gay 19:00-24:00 daily. ♂

LAZNE ZIZKOV, Husitská 7, (02) 627 89 71, mostly gay sauna complex for men on four floors, including disco, bar, billiards, etc, 16:00-24:00 (closed Sun, Mon).

PLAVECKY STADION PODOLI, Podolská 74, (02) 439 1513. Not a gay place, important to be discreet, popular public swimming pool, 09:00-21:00 (Sat, Sun till 20:00).

■ Erotica
LINDA, Jana Masaryk 43.

SEX SHOP RIAL, Wilsonova ul, Milady Horákové 84; Sokolovská 97; Holesovická trznice (hala c. 12).

VIDEO CENTER, cinemas: Americká 14; Veletrzní 41; Zitná 28.

VIDEO EROTIC STUDIO, cinemas: Borivojova 105; Hrubého 1203; Jana Zajíce 4; Moskevská 50.

PROSTEJOV

■ Bars
G KLUB, Západní 5, 16:00-01:00 (Sat till 02:00), closed Sun, Mon. ♂

SOKOLOV

■ Information
GAY KLUB SOKOLOV, Slavíckova 1691, (0618) 24 254, gay organization.

TEPLICE

■ Information
GAY KLUB TEPLICE, PO Box 17, 415 03 Teplice 3, (0417) 41 058, gay organization.

DENMARK

DENMARK
COUNTRY CODE: (45)

WHO TO CALL
For Tour Companies Serving This Destination
See Denmark on page 13

AALBORG

■ *Cafe*
PAN BLUE GATE, Danmarksgade 27A, cafe 98 12 22 45, Tues & Wed 20:00-01:00, Thurs 20:00-02:00, Fri 22:00-04:00, Sat 22:00-05:00. [!]♀♂

ÅBENRÅ

■ *Cafe*
PAN CAFE, Nygade 55, 74 62 11 48, cafe run by gay organization, Fri, Sat 20:00-24:00. Women meet 1st Fri from 20:00. ♀♂

ÅRHUS

■ *Information*
AIDS INFORMATION, 86 13 65 13, daily 19:00-23:00.

LBL, Jaegergårdsgade 42, 86 13 19 48, gay organization, Mon-Fri 11:00-15:00.

■ *Bars*
A MEN'S CLUB, Ostbanetorvet 8, 86 19 10 89, action & relax rooms, Fri & Sat 21:00-02:00. ♥♫☆♂

PAN KLUB & DISCO, Jaegergårdsgade 42, 86 13 43 80, Café: Mon-Thurs 18:00-01:00, Fri 18:00-06:00, Sat 20:00-06:00, Sun 20:00-01:00. Disco: Wed & Thurs 23:00-03:00, Fri & Sat 23:00-05:00. Women's nights 2nd Fri. [!]♀♂

■ *Cafe*
AKTHIVHUSET, Vestergade 5B, 86 18 16 46, HIV-group tel 86 12 43 13; HIV-café Tues & Thurs 19:00-22:00.

CAFE ARTHUR, Klosterport 2, 86 19 33 00. ♂

CAFÉ PARADIS,★ Paradisgade 7-9, frequented by gays & lesbians. ☆

SAPPHO, Mejigade 71, women's cafe, Tues-Fri 15:00-23:00. ♀

■ *Erotica*
A VIDEO CENTER, Rosenkrantzgade 16, 12:00-24:00.

COPENHAGEN
SEE KOBENHAVN.

ESBJERG

■ *Information*
AIDS INFO, 33 32 58 68.

■ *Cafe*
CAFÉ TULIP, Norrebrogade 102, 75 45 19 48, Thurs 19:30-22:30, party 1st Sat 20:00-24:00. ♂

FREDERICIA

■ *Bars*
CLUB 77, Dalegade 77, 75 93 12 28, Thurs 22:00-02:00, Fri & Sat 23:00-05:00. [!]♀♂

HILLERØD

■ *Information*
SLOTSBIOGRUPPEN, c/o Butikken, Mollestrade 3, group meets last Sat of the month.

HOLBAEK

■ *Bars*
CAFÉ OASEN, Jernbanevej 16, Fri 19:00-24:00. ♀♂

KØBENHAVN - COPENHAGEN

■ *Information*
AIDS INFO FOR GREENLANDERS IN DENMARK, 33 91 47 43, Thurs 16:00-18:00, or tape.

AIDS INFO, 33 91 11 19, daily 09:00-23:00.

BOSSEHUSET, Fristaden Christiania (entrance at Refshålevej 2), 32 95 98 72, gay meeting house, holds different events during summer, including discos with shows, cabaret, many activities for women. Phone answers Mon 20:00-22:00. [!]♫♀♂

GREVINDE DANNER HUSET, Nansengade 1, 31 14 16 76, this shelter for battered women, often has interesting programs for lesbians & parties from time to time.

KVINDEHUSET, Gothersgade 37, 33 14 28 04, women's center with book cafe, Mon-Fri 12:00-17:30, cafe Mon & Thurs 19:00-22:00, attended by many lesbians.

LBL, Teglgårdsstraede 13, in back, 33 13 19 48, Mon-Fri 10:00-15:00. National gay & lesbian organization, also houses Radio Rosa, gay & lesbian archive, library & PAN magazine.

PAN INFO LINE, 33 13 01 12, national gay & lesbian switchboard, Thurs, Sun, Mon 20:00-23:00.

■ *Accommodations*
HOTEL WINDSOR, Frederiksborggade 30, 1360 Kobenhavn K, Denmark, 33 11 08 30, fax 33 11 63 87. Exclusively gay hotel with breakfast restaurant. Certain floors are designated for men only & have a somewhat bath house atmosphere. Private & shared baths, continental breakfast, color cable TV, hotel accessed by stairs, no lift. ♂

■ *Beaches*
BELLVUE STRAND, take local train to Charlottenlund; S-train to Klampenborg, has a nude area.

TISVILDE STRAND (NORTH ZEALAND), take train to Copenhagen via Hillerod, then walk from the station to the large parking lot & continue 2km along the beach. Considered to be the most beautiful gay beach around Copenhagen.

■ *Bars*
AMIGO BAR, Schonbergsgade 4, Fridereiksberg, 31 21 49 15, 20:00-05:00 (Fri-Sun from 22:00). ☆♂

CAFÉ INTIME, Allegade 25, Frederiksberg, 38 34 19 58, intimate, old fashioned atmosphere, live piano, 17:00-02:00 (Sat from 20:00). [!]☆♫♂

CAN CAN, Mikkel Bryggersgade 11, 33 11 50 10, tavern, 11:00-02:00. ♂

CENTRALHJORNET, Kattesundet 18, 33 11 85 49, oldest gay bar in Copenhagen, 11:00-01:00 (Sat & Sun 15:00-01:00, breakfast 05:00-12:00). ☆☆☆$♂

CHECKPOINT, Studiestraede 31, Fri, Sat 23:00-06:00. ♂

MASKEN, Studiestraede 33, 33 91 67 80, 16:00-02:00 (Sat, Sun open for breakfast 05:00-10:00). [!]♂

MEN'S BAR, Teglgårdstraede 3, 33 12 73 03, popular with foreign visitors, leather clientele later in the evening, 15:00-02:00. ♥☆ ♂

NEVER MIND, Norre Voldgade 2, 21:00-05:00 (Fri, Sat till later). [!]♂

QUEEN VICTORIA, Snaregade 4, bar & restaurant. ☓♀♂

SEBASTIAN,★ Hyskenstraede 10, 33 32 22 79, multi-level bar & cafe with changing art exhibits, daily 12:00-02:00, Gay-Time 17:00-21:00. ♫☓♀♂

SLM KOBENHAVN (SCANDANAVIAN LEATHER MEN), Studiestraede 14, Fri 22:00-02:00. ♥☆♂

SMIL, Sorgenfrigade 8a, 31 81 05 50, hetero and gay SM club, Mon 18:00-21:00. ☆

STEDET, Lavendelstraede 13, bar & restaurant. ☓♀♂

■ *Dance Bar/Disco*
BABOOSHKA, at Café Babooshka location, Fri women-only disco night. [!]♀

BLUE NOTE,★ Studiestraede 31. disco, showbar & café, Wed-Sat 23:00-06:00, strippers. Women's social evenings Fri & Sat in the café. [!]♫☆♂

GEOZ, Studiestraede 31, disco & showbar. [!]♂

JEPPES CLUB 48, Allegade 25, Frederiksberg, 31 87 32 48, disco, mostly mature lesbians, some transvestites. [!]♀

■ *Cafe*
CAFÉ BABOOSHKA, Turesensgade 6, 33 15

05 36, cafe, pies, cakes, men welcome, women-run, 10:00-01:00 (Sun from 16:00). Fri women-only disco night. ✕🛇♀

KAFÉ KNUD, Skindergade 26, at the Hivhuset, for HIV positive people & their friends, Wed & Thurs 14:00-22:00. ♂

KRASNAPOLSKI, Vestergade 10, 12:00-05:00. ☒

WOMEN'S CAFE, Gothersgade 37, at the Kvindehuset women's center, Mon & Thurs 19:00-22:00. ♀

■ *Saunas/Health Clubs*

AMIGO SAUNA, Studiestraede 31a, 33 15 33 32, gay men's sauna, daily 12:00-08:00. ♂

COPENHAGEN GAY CENTER, Istedgade 36, 31 22 23 00, gay sauna, daily 10:00-05:00. ♂

■ *Restaurants*

ROSE DE TUNIS, LA, Vesterbrogade 120, 31 24 06 51, Tunisian cuisine, daily 17:00-23:00. ☒

STEDET, Lavendelstraede 13, bar & restaurant, 11:30-24:00 (food served from 12:00), closed Mon. ☒

TEGLKROEN, Teglgårdsstraede 17. ☒

■ *Retail & Bookstores*

PAN BOOKSTORE & LIBRARY, Teglgårdsstraede 13, in back, 33 11 19 61, gay and lesbian bookstore & library, Mon-Fri 17:00-19:00, Sat 13:00-15:00.

ROGER, Studiestraede, second-hand military and leather clothing store.

■ *Leathers/Piercing*

CRUZ LEATHER WORKS, Studiestraede 29.

DET SORTE UNIVERS (BLACK UNIVERSE), Studiestraede 16, S/M shop.

STYX, Nansensgade 42.

■ *Erotica*

BODY BIO, Kingosgade 7.

CLUB KINGO, Kingosgade 5.

COPENHAGEN GAY CENTER, Istedgade 36, 31 22 23 00, 3 minutes from the southern exit of the central station in the hetero red-light district. Sauna, video shows, shop, daily 10:00-5:00.

LOOKY LOOK, Randersgade 49.

MEN'S SHOP, Viktoriagade 24, 31 23 14 93, books, magazines, toys & leather items, 3 large movie rooms with non-stop shows, relax rooms, S&M room, S&M nights. Open 10:00-02:00.

SM SHOP, Studiestraede 12, 33 32 33 03, 10:00-18:30 (Fri till 19:00), Sat 10:00-15:00.

SUBWAVE, Studiestraede, adult shop specializing in rubber clothing.

KOLDING

■ *Cafe*

LOBITO GAY & LESBIAN CAFE, Dyrehavegårdvej 38, 75 54 10 23, Wed 19:00-23:00, Sat 21:00-02:00. ♀♂

NAESTVED

■ *Information*

LBL, Glentevej 23, gay & lesbian group, cafe 1st Tues from 19:00.

ODENSE

■ *Information*

AIDS INFO, 65 91 11 19, 08:00-23:00 (Sat, Sun from 14:00).

LAMBDA, Vindegade 100, lower level, 66 17 76 92, gay/lesbian organization, Cafe: 4th Sat 21:00-02:00 (men-only 3rd Sat), Disco: 1st Sat 22:00-04:00.

SKAGEN

■ *Accommodations*

FINNS PENSION, Ostre Strandvej 63, (45) 98 45 01 55. Hotel with restaurant for guests, some hetero clientele. Telephone, library, lounge, garden, sauna, expanded continental breakfast, nearby ocean beach. ♀ ♂

ESTONIA

COUNTRY CODE: (372)

WHO TO CALL
For Tour Companies Serving This Destination
See Estonia on page 14

TALLINN

■ *Information*

ESTONIAN LESBIAN UNION, (2) 45 56 37, lesbian group, scheduled parties & socials, phone answers Thurs & Sat 18:00-21:00. Write: E.L.U., PO Box 3245, EE0090 Tallinn, Estonia.

■ *Bars*

KASHTAN, 7 Toompuiestee St, 12:00-23:00, busy in evening, popular on weekends. ✕♂

TALLINN, at the Tallinn hotel, lower level, 21:00-03:00, NOT a gay bar, discreetly frequented by gays. ✕

■ *Saunas/Health Clubs*

SAUNA, 23 Raua St, 12:00-22:00, NOT a gay sauna, discreetly frequented by gays. ✕

FINLAND

COUNTRY CODE: (358)

WHO TO CALL
For Tour Companies Serving This Destination
See Finland on page 14

ÅLAND

■ *Information*

VILDROSORNA GAY ORGANIZATION, PO Box 133, 22101 Mariehamn, Aland.

HELSINKI

■ *Information*

AIDS INFO, Hietaniemenkatu 5, 4th floor, (09) 454 2070 or 454 3536.

SETA, Oikokatu 3, (09) 135 83 02, Helsinki gay organization for lesbians & gays, publishes Z Magazine. Also office of Finnish nat'l organization SETA.

■ *Bars*

BLUE BOY ,H Eerikinkatu 14, (09) 608 826, 19:00-02:00, casual atmosphere, terrace in summer, 90% men. ♂

ESCALE, Kansakoulunkatu 3, (09) 693 1533, daily 15:00-02:00. 🛇♀♂

H2O,★ Eerikinkatu 14, (09) 608 826, 19:00-02:00, casual atmosphere, terrace in summer, 90% men. ♂

NALLE PUB, Kaarlenkatu 3-5, (09) 701 5534, daily 15:00-02:00, frequented by women, men very welcome. ♀

NEW FACES, Fabianinkatu 29, at Bar 52, (09) 626 940, women-only bar 1st, 3rd & 5th Sat 21:00-03:00. 🛇♀

STONEWALL,★ Eerikinkatu 3, (09) 694 4034, 2 bars & restaurant, 17:00-02:00 (Fri, Sat till 04:00, Sun till 03:00), closed Mon. Occasional women-only nights. Food served till 24:00, techno music, young/trendy crowd. ✕🛇♀♂

TOM'S CLUB, (09) 680 29 48. Club nights organized by MSC Finland (member ECMC), gay leather, rubber & fetish themes, Fri 23:00-04:00, Sat 00:00-05:00. Dress code, leather women welcome. Near H2O bar, call for exact location. ▼☐☒♂

■ *Dance Bar/Disco*

DARE TO BE, Kaivokatu 12, at Nylon, Mon 22:00-04:00, young & trendy crowd. 🛇♀♂

DON'T TELL MAMA,★ Annankatu 32, next to main bus station, (09) 694 11 22, large disco, 23:00-04:00, closed Mon. 🛇♂

■ *Saunas/Health Clubs*

SVUL (TÖÖLÖN URHEILUTALO), Topeliusenkatu 41a, (09) 417 761, public

FINLAND

bathouse & swimming pool run by the city, discreetly frequented by gays.

TALLI, Porkkalankatu 1, at Lepakko, (09) 694 0148, info: (0400) 786 847, sauna & bar, Wed 20:00-02:00, Sun 18:00-02:00. ♂

YRJÖNKADUN UIMHALLI, Yrjönkatu 21b, (09) 60 981. Roman-style public bathouse run by the city, discreetly frequented by gays & lesbians, men & women use separate pools & saunas. Men: Tues, Wed, Fri 14:00-20:00 (Sat 13:00-19:00). Women: Tues, Wed, Fri 14:00-20:00, closed Sun.

■ Restaurants
LOST & FOUND, Annankatu 6, (09) 680 1010, newest gay restaurant in Helsinki, two bars with dancing in downstairs bar, frequent shows, Mon-Fri 14:00-04:00 (Sat, Sun till 03:00), busy weekends.

■ Retail & Bookstores
BAFFIN BOOKS, Eerikinkatu 15, (09) 694 7078, gay & lesbian bookstore, 10:00-19:00 (Sat till 15:00), closed Sun.

■ Erotica
SIN CITY, Albertinkatu 36, (09) 7002 9204, videos, magazines, piercing, jewelry, leather clothes & equipment, pvc, 11:00-19:00 (Sat till 17:00).

JOENSUU
■ Bars
MOLLY'S, Torikatu 20. ♂

PUB VANHA JOKELA, Torikatu 26, many students. ♂

JYVÄSKYLÄ
■ Information
JYVÄSSEUDUN SETA - PINK CLUB, Yliopistonkatu 26, (014) 310 0660, gay & lesbian organization, answers Wed 18:00-21:00 (tape other times).

■ Bars
PUB HEMINGWAY, Kauppakatu 32, not a gay bar, discreetly frequented by some gays.

KUOPIO
■ Information
KUOPION SEUDUN SETA, Tulliportinkatu 11 (3rd floor), (017) 261 95 56, gay switchboard, Thurs 18:00-20:00. Meetings Wed 18:00-20:00, Sun 15:00-17:00.

■ Bars
HENRY'S PUB, Kauppakatu, near the market square, not a gay bar, discreetly frequented by gay men.

LAHTI
■ Information
PH SETA, (03) 751 79 71, gay & lesbian organization, Wed 14:00-18:00 (switchboard till 21:00), also scheduled parties.

■ Bars
STREET BAR, Aleksanterinkatu 23, not a gay bar, discreetly frequented by gays.

OULU
■ Information
OULUN SETA, Kirkkokatu 19 A 6, (08) 379 458, gay & lesbian organization, switchboard Mon, Wed, Fri 09:00-15:00, Tues & Thurs 09:00-19:00.

■ Bars
DNC CLUB, Asemakatu 28, not a gay bar, frequented by bays.

KUJASEN BAARI, Pakkahuoneenkatu 30, not a gay bar, frequented by women.

MADISON, Isokatu 18, frequented by gays.

ROVANIEMI
■ Information
ROVANIEMI SETA, Hallituskatu 24, (016) 310 141, gay & lesbian organization, Fri 20:00-22:00.

■ Bars
CAN CAN NIGHTCLUB, at the City Hotel, not a gay bar, discreetly frequented by gays.

TAMPERE
■ Information
TAMPEREEN SETA, Hämeenpuisto 41 A 47, (03) 2148 721, gay & lesbian organization, Tues & Fri 20:00-22:00 or tape.

■ Bars
DISCO MIXEI,★ Otavalankatu 3, (03) 222 03 64, bar & disco, 22:00-03:00 (Fri, Sat till 04:00), 80% men, 20% women.

NICE PLACE, Hämeenpuisto 29, (03) 214 09 22, 15:00-01:00 (Fri, Sat till 02:00). ♀♂

■ Saunas/Health Clubs
SORIN SAUNA CLUB, Vuolteenkatu 20, at Cafe Oz, (03) 212 7337, 1st Sat from 24:00, club cards available from Cafe Oz.

TURKU
■ Information
TURUN SEUDUN SETA, Rauhankatu 1 c B 22, (02) 2550 695, gay & lesbian organization.

■ Bars
JACK'S & MIKE'S PUB,★ Kauppiaskatu 4, at Forum Bldg, inner courtyard, daily 16:00-02:00, casual atmosphere.

VAASA
■ Information
VAASANSEUDUN SETA, Wolffintie 36 F 12, room 5, (06) 312 51 30, Fri 19:00-21:00.

FRANCE
COUNTRY CODE: (33)

WHO TO CALL
For Tour Companies Serving This Destination
See France on page 15

AIX-EN-PROVENCE
■ Bars
MP AIX VIDEO PUB, 38 rue des Bernardines, (4) 42 27 66 90, 17:00-02:00. ♂

■ Dance Bar/Disco
LA CHIMERE, Montée d'Avignon, (4) 42 23 36 28, Wed-Sun from 23:30.

■ Saunas/Health Clubs
AIX SAUNA CLUB, 8 bis, rue Annonerie-Vieille, (4) 42 27 21 49, 12:00-20:30, Wed & Fri till 24:00.

ALLUY
■ Accommodations
LE CHATEAU QUENTIN, 58110 Alluy, (3) 86 84 08 95, French gardeners cottage & manor house 40 km from Nevers & 300 km from Paris, modern comforts, central heating, private baths, open fireplaces.

ALSACE
■ Accommodations
ESPACE BALLON D'ALSACE, La Musardière, 90200 Ballon d'Alsace, (3) 84 29 33 22, Fax: (3) 84 23 96 40. A bed & breakfast guesthouse with restaurant & bar, panoramic mountain views, 50% gay / lesbian clientele, private & shared baths, continental breakfast & dinner, color TV, maid service. Location ideal for both summer and winter vacationing, activities include mountain biking, horseback riding, Alpine & Nordic skiing and bobsledding.

ANGOULEME
■ Information
LIBRAIRIE DES FEMMES, 6, rue d'Arcole, (5) 45 38 73 21, women's organization & Les Deux Elles disco, membership. Women's organization: 10:15-20:15 (closed Sun, Mon). Disco: daily from 20:00. ♀

ANNECY
■ Dance Bar/Disco
STUDIO 9, 9, av du Rhône, (3) 50 45 46 30, 22:00-04:30, closed Tues. ♀♂

■ Restaurants
ARC-EN-CIEL, 26, rue de l'Arc-en-Ciel, (3) 50 23 08 86, hotel restaurant, 12:00-14:00 & 19:00-21:00 (Sat, Sun only 12:00-14:00).

FRANCE

ANNEMASSE

Bars
BAR L'APOLLON, 36 Ave de la Gare, (4) 50 95 03 94, from 17:00. ♂

Saunas/Health Clubs
SAUNA LE CLUB, 39, av Jean-Jaurès, (4) 50 38 68 12, 14:00-23:00 (mixed on Tu & Fri). ♂

ANTIBES

Bars
LE RENDEZ-VOUS, 5 cours Massena, (4) 93 34 17 77, 18:00-00:30 (summer till 02:30). ♀♂

Erotica
EROSHOP, 6, rue Vauban, (4) 93 34 09 04. ♂

ARGELES-SUR-MER

Dance Bar/Disco
LE POT CHIC, in the Costa Blanca shopping center, (4) 68 81 08 86, Fri, Sat 23:00-05:00 (summer months, open daily). ♀♂

ARLES

Accommodations
APARTMENTS & STUDIOS BY SCI DE CAMARGUE, Box 7, Salin de Giraud, 13129, (4) 42 48 80 40, Fax: (4) 42 86 89 10, apartments & studios 10 min from gay nudist beach at Piémanson. ♀♂

Beaches
SALIN DE GIRAUD, gay nudist beach in Piémanson, at the mouth of the Rhone river.

AUREC-SUR-LOIRE

Dance Bar/Disco
SAX'S CLUB, (2) 77 35 41 87. Gay only Sat 22:00-04:30. ♂

AVIGNON

Beaches
PISCINE DE LA BARTHELASSE, very popular beach on the Isle of Barthelasse, summer only.

Dance Bar/Disco
L'ESCLAVE BAR, 12, rue du Limas, (4) 90 85 14 91. Dance & video 22:00-05:00. ♂

Saunas/Health Clubs
SAUNA H CLUB, 20, rue Paul-Manivet, (4) 90 85 00 39, 12:00-24:00.

Restaurants
COTÉ JARDIN, rue des Trois Carreaux, (4) 90 82 26 70.

BAYONNE

Bars
LE JAMES DEAN, 11, rue Vieille-Boucherie, (5) 59 59 19 64, 10:30-02:00. ♀♂
LE MONROE, 2 impasse Latournerie, (5) 59 25 41 05, 21:30-05:00 (closed Mon.). ♀♂
LE PIMM'S, Ave. Leon Bonnat, across from gardens, (5) 59 25 76 22, 10:00-02:00. ♀♂

Saunas/Health Clubs
SAUNA SAN MARCO, 20, rue des Faures, (5) 59 59 46 17, 14:00-20:00 (Fri, Sat till 24:00). ♂

Restaurants
RESTAURANT DE LA TOUR, 5, rue des Faures, (5) 59 59 05 67, traditional French cuisine, 12:00-14:30 & 19:00-23:30.

BEAUCAIRE

Dance Bar/Disco
LE COQUEMAR, 2, rue Camille-Desmoulins, (4) 66 59 17 76, Fri-Sun from 22:00.

BESANÇON

Information
AIDS LINE, (3) 81 81 80 00.

Bars
LE BROADWAY, 90 rue des Granges, (3) 81 81 67 51, 18:00-02:00. ♀♂
LE SPIRAL, 3, rue Jean Petit, (3) 81 81 17 90, 18:00-01:00 (Fri, Sat till 02:00), closed Sun, Mon. ♀♂

Dance Bar/Disco
LE PRIVÉ, 1, rue Antide-Janvier, (3) 81 81 48 57. Videos, Tues-Fri & Sun 22:30-04:00. Sat from 22:00. ♂

BEZIERS

Accommodations
CHAMBRES D'HOTE DU MOULIN, Chemin du Moulin, Poilhes, 34310, (4) 67 93 46 22, B&B with swimming pool & terrace, some hetero clientele. ♀♂
HOTEL ALMA UNIC, 41 rue Guilhemon, (4) 67 28 44 31, Fax: (4) 67 28 79 44, gay-owned, gay-friendly hotel, nude sunbathing on the terrace.

Bars
KEPHREN, 5 rue A. Naugaret, (4) 67 49 02 20, 21:30-02:00 (from 19:00 in winter), closed Mon. ♂

Saunas/Health Clubs
SAUNA LE KHÉOPS, 5, rue Berlioz, (4) 67 49 31 37, 12:00-20:00 (weekends till 21:00). ♂

BIARRITZ

Beaches
PLAGE DE MIRAMAR (BY THE LIGHTHOUSE), PLAGE DE L'OCÉAN.

Dance Bar/Disco
CITY'S BAR LE 31, 31, av. de Verdun, (5) 59 24 27 85, 08:00-05:00. ♀♂
LE CAVEAU, 4, rue Gambetta, (5) 59 24 16 17, disco & bar with shows, 17:00-05:00. ♂

BORDEAUX

Information
SAPHOLLES, 29 rue de la Boétie, (5) 56 79 30 75, lesbian group, meets Thurs from 18:00.

Wineries & Restaurants of Provence

For those interested in gourmet dining and fine wine, a visit to Provence in the South of France can be a real event. As a person with an avid interest in gourmet food and wine, Anthony Bird and his company **Mistral Tours** have developed close contacts with wine producers in the area. With Anthony, you can visit some of France's finest wineries which are not always open to the public. He also keeps a data base of restaurants in the area, with notes on which are to be treasured and which avoided.

Each Mistral tour consists of a full- or half-day excursion to major towns and principal historical sites of the region and also to some of the more unusual and less-accessible attractions. The company will design personalized itineraries for groups of two to six people with transport provided in an air-conditioned Land Rover Discovery. Optional activites include walking the rambling paths of the region and horseback riding. Camargue is the land of the horse and the region has several top-quality riding schools. Many boats plow up and down the Rhone River, and bookings can be made year-round.

Contact **Mistral Tours** at (33 4) 90 85 86 41 (tel/fax), E-mail: drbusiness@avignon-pacwan.net.

FERRARI GUIDES' GAY TRAVEL A to Z - 18th EDITION

FRANCE

A Sophisticated New Idea in Gay Men's Travel

The cruise begins on dry land with cocktails at sunset high above the Riviera in the Alps-Maritimes, then dinner in a farmhouse in the village of La Turbie, and ending with an evening to remember in Lisbon. All this is part of the **Club Hommes** Mediterranean Cruise from Monte Carlo to Portugal this May, 1997. In July, they'll indulge in a week of haute cuisine at Paris's le Cordon Bleu - Ecole de Cuisine et de Pâtisserie. The fall will find them tasting the first vintage of 1997 in the vineyards of Châteauneuf du Pape in Provençe. For the 1998 Gay Games in Amsterdam, Club Hommes will bypass the hotel rush. Instead, they'll charter their own ship to sail up the Rhine and dock in Amsterdam, using the ship as their hotel for the Games. After the closing ceremony, they'll take the last train to Berlin for an evening to remember.

There are a few examples of the unique, upscale travel experiences being offered exclusively to Club Hommes members, currently numbering 3000. To join, simply fill out their membership survey. Their affiliate, Worldguest Tours, specializes in custom group travel for gay and lesbian organizations.

Contact **Club Hommes** at (212) 206-6900, (800) 429-6969, Fax: (212) 206-6904, E-mail: club@worldguest.com, Web: www.worldguest.com.

■ Bars
L'ALIBI, 20 rue de la Vieille Tour, (5) 56 52 01 34, 18:00-02:00. ♂

LE MOYEN AGE,★ 8, rue des Remparts, (5) 56 44 12 87, Wed-Mon 22:00-02:00. ♂

LE TH, 15 rue Montbazon, (5) 56 81 38 16, bar & restaurant, 20:00-02:00 (clsd. Mon). ♂

■ Dance Bar/Disco
LE 18, 18, rue Louis-de-Foix, (5) 56 52 82 98, Wed-Mon from 23:00. ♂

LE KEY WEST, 32 rue de Cornac, (5) 56 48 22 13, 22:00-04:00. ♀♂

YELLOW MOON, 6, rue Combes, (5) 56 51 00 79, lounge 18:30-22:00, closed Sun. Dance bar, videos daily 23:00-05:00. ♂

■ Saunas/Health Clubs
SAUNA CLUB 137, 137, quai des Chartrons, (5) 56 43 18 49, 14:00-01:00 (Tues & Fri till 04:00). ♂

SAUNA FERRIERE, 18, rue Ferrière, (5) 56 44 53 01, gay & lesbian sauna, 13:00-20:00. ♀♂

SAUNA THIERS, 329, av. Thiers, (5) 56 32 00 63, 12:00-24:00 (Tues, Fri till 04:00). ♂

■ Restaurants
UN MONDE A PART, 62 rue de la Devise, (5) 56 48 19 92.

■ Erotica
LOVE VIDEO, 221, cours de la Marne, (5) 56 91 68 55.

BRITTANY

■ Women's Accommodations
CHEZ JACQUILINE, Jun-Sept: Jacquiline Boudillet, La Croix Cadio, 22800 St Donan, 96 73 81 22. Oct-May in Paris: 6, rue du Port, 92110 Clichy, (1) 47 39 94 54. Women-only bed & breakfast. Double rooms with shared bath. TV room. ♀

BRIVE LA GAILLARDE

■ Dance Bar/Disco
CRAZY BOY, Château de la Rage, Noailles, by highway exit Noailles south of Brive, (5) 55 85 84 19, Fri-Sun 23:00-06:00. ♂

■ Erotica
CINE VIDEO SHOP, 44, avenue Jean-Juarès, (5) 55 23 19 49.

BURGUNDY REGION

■ Accommodations
LA SALAMANDRE, Au Bourg Grande Rue, Salornay sur Guye 71250, (33) 385 59 91 56, Fax: (33) 385 59 91 67. Gay-owned, gay-friendly guesthouse in a restored 18th-century house surrounded by a large park with old trees. Vineyards nearby and country walks and biking routes. Private baths, expanded continental breakfast. Optional 3-course guest dinner FF 120.

CANNES

■ Information
AIDS INFO, (4) 93 68 98 31.

■ Accommodations
LE CHALIT, 27 av Marechal Galliéni, (33-4) 93 99 22 11, Fax: (33-4) 93 39 00 28. Hostel in downtown Cannes, one hour from winter skiing, summer ocean beaches. Mostly women with men welcome. 31 beds in rooms with 3, 4 & 7 beds (3 rooms for women, 2 dorms for men), 4 shared showers & 4 shared toilets. For people wanting to travel on a small budget. Kitchen privileges available for breakfast & dinner. ♀

TOURING HOTEL, 11 rue Hoche, (4) 93 38 34 40, Fax: (4) 93 38 73 34, gay-friendly hotel in center of Cannes, private baths, continental breakfast, color TV phone, maid & laundry service.

■ Beaches
ILLE STE-MARGUERITE: nude beach on the side facing l'Ille Saint-Honorat. Plage de la Batterie: nude beach between Cannes & Golfe-Juan, near the service station.

PLAGE DE LA BATTERIE, gay nude beach between Cannes & Golf Juan, at the Service Station parking. ♂

■ Bars
EXTÉRIEUR NUIT, 16, rue du Suquet, (4) 93 99 27 36, 1950's style bar, 18:00-02:30, closed Tues. ♀♂

LE ZANZI-BAR, 85, rue Félix-Faure, (4) 93 39 30 75, daily 18:30-05:00. ♂

■ Dance Bar/Disco
LE SEPT, 7, rue Rouguières, (4) 93 39 10 36, 23:00-06:00. ♀♂

LES TROIS CLOCHES, 6, rue du Commandant Vidal, (4) 93 68 32 92, daily from 23:00. ♀♂

■ Restaurants
LA CROISETTE, 15, rue du Commandant André, (4) 93 39 86 06. Fondues & Italian cuisine, Tues-Sat 12:00-14:30 & 19:00-22:30, Sun only 19:00-22:30, closed Mon.

LE BISTROT DE LA GALERIE, 4, rue Saint-Antoine, (4) 93 39 99 38. Seafood, daily 12:00-14:00 & 19:30-23:00, closed Mon.

LE MARAIS, 9, rue du Suquet, (4) 93 38 39 19, 19:30-23:00, closed Mon. ♀♂

LE TREIZE, 13, rue Perissol, (4) 93 39 85 19, French & Swiss cuisine, daily 19:30-24:00. ♀♂

■ Erotica
LE SALON, 13 rue de Mimont, closed Sun.
SEX SHOP, 6, rue Jean Jaurès, (4) 93 68 91 82.

CAP D'AGDE

■ Beaches
MARSEILAN PLAGE, gay nude beach at the right-hand end of the beach, in the dunes between Sete & Cap d'Agde, by the RN 112.

FRANCE

Gay France

Excerpted, with permission, from Gai Pied Guide '96-'97

Every country has its own culture and customs. This may seem obvious, but keeping it in mind is perhaps the first step to making your foreign holidays a success. There's no point in traveling, if you're not willing to encounter the unfamiliar. How you approach the different people, places, mentalities and languages you meet will determine whether your vacation is unforgettable or, on the contrary, something you'd rather forget. Traveling means discovering and adapting oneself to the unexpected. This is the surest way to enrich your travel experience.

You'll no doubt run into people who are rude and unfriendly, just as you would anywhere. But keeping an open mind and a smile on your face will do wonders, often leading you to unforeseen opportunities. It undoubtedly will be easier for you to meet people if you make an effort to learn a few words of French ("bonjour," "s'il vous plaît," "je ne parle pas français"). Don't be timid. Many French speakers will find your accent charming, and trying to speak the language is an excellent ice-breaker. If you're lost or need assistance, don't hesitate to ask for help. There will always be someone willing to lend a hand, and it's one of the ways you can make acquaintances.

At the gay and lesbian establishments and other places listed in this guide, you'll surely encounter people who share your interests, so don't be afraid to start up a conversation, even if you can't speak French well. Many of the French speak a little English, and if words fail, sign language can often be effective.

Laws and the Police

It is important for you to know a little about French law — it may help you avoid useless headaches. The age of sexual majority is 16 years for both males and females. But don't put too much faith in this fact, be-

> Gai Pied is the national gay guide to France, published annually.

cause the official age of full majority is 18. And if you're over 18 yourself, and your young lover is between 16 and 18, you can be accused of corrupting a minor if his or her parents decide to file charges.

As for the French police, if they've got a job to do, they can be testy, so it is advisable always to comply with their orders. Carry your passport or ID card with you at all times. Police checks are frequent, and you can be asked to present your papers on public transportation or in public places at any time. On the other hand, if you're lost or need other assistance, don't hesitate to ask the gendarmes. They are always happy to help.

Cruising

There are cruising areas all over this country. These are public places where gays meet for a quick encounter...a look, a few words, a gesture, and voila! Your partner may want to take you home, or prefer to "play" on the spot. However, cruising does involve a certain number of risks. Homophobic gangs sometimes make incursions into cruising areas for queer bashing. So be cautious. Likewise, some of the young people you may meet merely use their charms to rip you off. In addition, the blue-uniformed national and municipal police sometimes visit these spots to ensure that the rules and regs, and public decency, are respected (regulations are posted at the entry of every park). Paris

Continued on next page

FRANCE

has no municipal police force, but the Public Parks Brigade, in khaki uniforms, can be counted on to step in, in the event of generalized debauchery, unless, of course, they prefer to join the party!

If you're caught breaking the law, you may be asked to present your ID papers and given a ticket. In any event, it is strongly recommended that you obey any orders the police give you. Last, but now least, there are a certain number of things you mustn't do in public parks: It is forbidden to be slovenly or drunk, to play music, sing, take photos, film, or carry signboards. It is also against the law to "offer services free or for a charge."

Going Out On the Town

Most French businesses are open Monday through Saturday from 9am to 7pm, or even later. Small shops and those in the provinces often close for lunch from 12:30 to 2:30pm. Most banks close Friday afternoon for the weekend. National museums (Louvre, Pompidou Center, etc.) are closed on Monday. Remember that the French indicate time on a 24-hour basis, like the American and British military. So when, for example, a bar's hours are 22h00 to 2h00, it means the bar is open from 10pm to 2am. Also remember French holidays! You're likely to find quite a few places closed on May 1, May 8, July 14 and August 15.

Cafe's and bars are veritable institutions in France. You can spend hours quietly sipping a drink reading, or just watching the people go by. The price of drinks varies widely depending on the establishment's location. And the more "fashionable" a place is, the higher the prices. Prices also vary, depending on whether you stand at the bar, have a seat at an inside table, or sit outside. If you take a seat, the waiter will probably assume you're in no hurry, so he won't rush to serve you. This is one of the charms of France. Grin and bear it.

Finally a word about tipping. As a general rule, service is always included in the menu price. So you are never obliged to leave a tip, particularly if the service is the pits. But it is customary to tip in cafes, restaurants, cinemas and theaters (for the ushers), at the hairdresser, and in taxis, by rounding the bill up.

Useful Phone Numbers & Addresses

In the event of an emergency, you can dial the following numbers from anywhere in France for help. These calls are free from any payphone. No coins or telephone card are necessary.

Police: 17 (This number puts you in touch with the nearest police station).

Fire: 18 (The fire brigade also handles minor medical emergencies. Their answering system indicates where you are calling from, so if you don't speak French, just make it clear that you need help, and they can locate you).

Medical: 15 (For an ambulance or paramedical assistance).

Last, but not least, here are the addresses of a few embassies in the capital.

American Embassy, 2, avenue Gabriel 75008 Paris. Metro: Concorde. Tel: 01 43 12 22 22.

Australian Embassy, 4, rue Jean Rey 75015 Paris. Metro: Bir Hakeim. Tel: 01 40 59 33 00.

British Embassy, 35, rue du Faubourg St. Honoré, 75008 Paris. Metro: Concorde. Tel: 01 44 51 31 00.

Canadian Embassy, 35, avenue Montaigne, 75008 Paris. Metro: Franklin D. Roosevelt. Tel: 01 44 43 29 00.

FRANCE

■ Bars
LE LOOK, at Village Naturiste, across from the port. Bar in the most famous nudist village in the world, open Easter thru December 17:00-02:00 (low season weekends only till 01:00).

CLERMONT-FERRAND
■ Information
AIDS LINE, (4) 73 31 31 03, Tues 17:30-19:30.
■ Dance Bar/Disco
CLUB L'EXCLUSIF, 12, rue des Petits Gros, (4) 73 37 87 69, techno music, daily from 24:00, closed Sun.
■ Saunas/Health Clubs
SAUNA LE THERMOS, 77 bis, av Edouard-Michelin, (4) 73 92 93 25, 13:00-20:00.
■ Erotica
PARADIX, 46, av Albert-Elisabeth, (4) 73 90 97 80.

COGNIN
■ Dance Bar/Disco
SIXTIES GAY TEA DANCE, RN 6, Cognin, (4) 79 69 11 22, 22:00-02:00, closed Mon.

COMPIEGNE
■ Dance Bar/Disco
PHUTURE, 14, rue des Boucheries, (3) 44 86 14 44, video disco, daily from 23:30.

DIJON
■ Information
AIDS LINE, (3) 80 30 37 77.
■ Saunas/Health Clubs
SAUNA LE BOSSUET, 25, place Bossuet, (3) 80 49 97 45, 14:00-20:00 (Tues-Thurs till 03:00, Sat till 01:00).
SAUNA RELAX, 97, rue Berbisey, (3) 80 30 14 40, 14:00-20:00, closed Sun.
■ Restaurants
LE BOUFFON, 74, rue Chevreuil, (3) 80 63 74 87, 12:00-15:00 & 19:00-23:00 (Sat only 19:00-23:00), closed Sun.
■ Erotica
LIBRAIRIE EROTIQUE, 64, rue Berbisey, (3) 80 30 74 09.

DINARD
■ Bars
PALACE CAFE, 21 bd Wilson, (2) 99 46 93 50, 10:30-24:00.

DIOU
■ Bars
LE BATACLAN, Ecluse de Putay, (3) 70 42 90 03, Fri-Sun 23:00-04:00.

DOMME
■ Camping & RV
LA DORDOGNE CAMPING DE FEMMES, St.-Aubin de Nabirat, 24250 Domme, (33-5) 53 28 50 28, camping, 20 tent sites, 3 campers, 2 toilets, hot & cold showers, meeting rooms, TV lounge, many outdoor activities, convenient to shopping.

DUNKERQUE
■ Dance Bar/Disco
LE NEW AQUARIUS, 4, rue Tancrède, (3) 28 63 07 10, gay Sun from 21:00.

EPINAL
■ Dance Bar/Disco
SCOTCH CLUB, 6, quai des Bons-Enfants, (3) 29 82 50 08, 20:00-03:00, Fri & Sat till 04:00, closed Mon.

GOURIN
■ Accommodations
LA CALÉCHE, 4, rue de la Gare, (2) 97 23 40 35. Gay-friendly hotel, mostly gay on weekends.
■ Dance Bar/Disco
LE STARMAN, at La Calèche Hotel, (2) 97 23 40 35, Sat 23:00-05:00.
■ Restaurants
LA CALÉCHE, at La Caléche hotel, (2) 97 23 40 35. Daily 12:00-14:00 & 19:00-22:00, closed Wed.

GRENOBLE
■ Information
AIDS INFO, (4) 76 63 82 44.
■ Bars
LE QUEEN'S, 62, cours Jean-Jaurès, (4) 76 46 83 44, 10:00-01:00.
ORCHIDÉE BAR, 68, cours Jean-Jaurès, (4) 76 46 78 17, gay after 20:00.
RUTLI, 9, rue Etienne Marcel, (4) 76 43 21 16, 17:00-01:00 (closed Mon), bar with video area, accommodations available.
■ Saunas/Health Clubs
LE SAINT-FERJUS, 22, rue Saint-Ferjus near l'Ile Verte, (4) 76 54 13 70, 14:00-21:00, Fri till 24:00.
■ Restaurants
L'ANGE BLEU, Place de Metz, (4) 76 87 55 89, 12:00-14:00 & 19:00-01:00, closed Sun.
LE GRILL PARISIEN, 34, av Alsace-Lorraine, (4) 76 46 77 44, 12:00-14:30 & 19:30-23:30, closed Mon.
■ Erotica
SEXASHOP, 2, rue de Miribel, (4) 76 46 70 86.

HECTOMARE
■ Dance Bar/Disco
LES PLÉIADES, ask locally for address, (2) 32 35 30 83, Fri-Sun 23:00-05:00.

ILE DU LEVANT
■ Accommodations
L'EGLANTINE, Corniche l'Arbousier, (4) 94 05 92 50 (tel/fax). Rooms & apartments in a villa on a nude island in the Mediterranean, open May-30 Sept. Take ferry from Hyeres or Port de Levandou.

LA FERTE-ST-CYR
■ Bars
L'ELECTRON, Mocquebaril, Ste.-Laurent-Mouan, (2) 54 87 21 39, Fri 22:30-04:00, Sat till 07:00, videos.

LA GRANDE MOTTE
■ Bars
BAL & MASQUES, Place Paul Valéry, (4) 6756 2724, bar with restaurant.

LA MOTHE ACHARD
■ Dance Bar/Disco
LE DAMIER, Les Loges (RN 160), (2) 51 34 29 09, Fri-Sun 23:30-05:00.

LA ROCHELLE
■ Saunas/Health Clubs
L'ATLANTIS, 12, rue de l'Arsenal, near the Maaf insurance building, (5) 46 41 15 89, 14:00-21:00 (Sat 15:00-24:00), mixed gay/hetero Fri.

LA TESTE
■ Beaches
PLAGE DE LA TESTE, nude beach with many gays.

LE MANS
■ Information
AIDS INFO, (2) 43 23 96 71.
■ Bars
LA SCALA, 32, Rue des Ponts-Neufs, (2) 43 28 12 13, 22:00-04:00, closed Mon.
■ Dance Bar/Disco
LA LIMITE, 7, rue Saint-Honoré, (2) 43 24 85 54, 23:00-04:00, closed Mon.
■ Erotica
SEX SHOP 72, 72 rue du Bourg Belé, (2) 43 28 51 39.

LILLE
■ Information
ASSOCIATION DU COTE DES FEMMES, 18 rue du Cirque, women's organization, daily 14:30-18:30, contact for women's café & library info.
LES FALMANDS ROSES, 1/2, rue Denis de Pèagre, (3) 20 47 62 65, gay & lesbian cultural center, Tues from 20:00.
■ Bars
LE RAMPONNEAU, 22, square du

FRANCE

Discover Secret Corners of Europe on a Hotel Barge Cruise

Europe unfolds as you wend your way along picturesque waterways by luxury hotel barge. The scenery is ever-changing, verging from rolling hills and ancient forests to sun-drenched vineyards and lush, green fields. You'll pass chateau and lofty castles, medieval towns and timeless villages. You can disembark for part of the day and bicycle along tree-lined canals, visit wineries, or go on personally-guided tours of fascinating places, many not normally open to the public.

Accommodations are like luxury hotel rooms with well-appointed furnishings and private facilities. You'll dine on local delicacies, prepared from the freshest produce by highly-acclaimed chefs, and enjoy regional wines. One can travel by barge through France and Germany, England, Austria, Holland and Belgium.

Contact **European Luxury Barge Cruises** via Kemwell's Premier Selections, (800) 234-4000, Fax: (914) 835-5449, E-mail: premier@kemwell.com.

Ramponneau, Façade de l'Esplanade, (3) 20 74 49 80, 19:00-02:00. ♂

LE ROCAMBOLE, 11, place Jacques Louchard, Les Terrasses, Ste. Catherine, (3) 20 55 12 52, 19:30-02:00. ♂

■ Erotica
GOLDEN BOY, 33, rue des Ponts-de-Comines, (3) 20 06 34 26.

SEX CENTER, 56, rue Esquermoise, (3) 20 51 08 91.

LIMOGES

■ Bars
CAFÉ TRAXX, Place Fontaine des Barres, (5) 55 34 18 16, Mon, Wed, Sat 11:00-02:00, Sun 18:00-02:00. ♀♂

■ Dance Bar/Disco
LE BOY, 137, av du Mal de Lattre de Tassigny, (5) 55 31 19 41, Wed-Sun 23:00-05:00, videos. ♂

■ Saunas/Health Clubs
EROS, 8, rue Jean Jaures, (5) 55 32 74 48, 12:00-02:00. ♂

LOISON-SOUS-LENS

■ Dance Bar/Disco
LE CLUB 175, 175, route de Lille, (3) 21 28 05 30, Disco from 22:00 Fri & Sat, lounge open Mon-Wed & Sun from 19:00. ♂

LUNEL

■ Dance Bar/Disco
LE ZEEBOYS, Route de Nimes RN 113, between Nimes & Montpellier, (4) 67 71 02 01, Thurs-Sun from 23:00. ♀♂

LYON

■ Bars
BAR DU CENTRE, 3, rue Simon Maupin, (4) 78 37 40 18. very gay at night, daily 12:00-03:00 (weekends till 05:00). ♀♂

BROADWAY, 9, rue Terraille, (4) 78 39 50 54, from 18:00, closed Tues, videos. ♂

LE BAR DES TRABOULES, 86, Grande Rue de la Croix Rousse, (4) 78 29 20 09, daily 20:00-01:00 (closed Sun). ♂

LE CHARLESTON, 33, rue de Condé, (4) 78 42 94 14, 18:00-04:00, Sat from 21:00. ♀♂

LE QUATRE, 2-4, rue Bellecordière, (4) 78 37 89 66. Video bar, daily from 17:00. ♂

LE VERRE A SOI, 25, rue des Capucins, (4) 78 28 92 44, bar & restaurant, Tues-Fri 10:00-02:00, Sat 19:00-03:00. ♀♂

STAIRWAY CLUB, 2, rue Fernand-Rey, (4) 72 00 20 00, 18:00-02:00, closed Mon. ♂

■ Dance Bar/Disco
LA TAVERNE II, 12, rue René-Leynard, (4) 78 28 24 28, Thurs-Sun from 22:30. ♀♂

LE MYLORD, 112, Quai Pierre Scize, (4) 78 28 96 69, 22:30-04:00, closed Sun.

LE VILLAGE CLUB, 6 rue Violi, (4) 72 07 72 62, 21:00-03:00. ♂

■ Saunas/Health Clubs
LE BELLECOUR, 4, rue Simon-Maupin, (4) 78 38 19 27, 12:00-22:00, Fri till 24:00. ♂

LE MANDALA, 9, rue Boissac, (4) 78 42 74 28. Modern sauna with bar, 12:00-24:00, Fri & Sat till 06:00. ♂

OASIS CLUB, 10, quai Jean-Moulin, (4) 78 39 03 82. Open Mon-Wed, Fri & Sat 12:00-21:00, Thurs till 22:00, Sun 13:00-21:00. ♂

SAUNA & VIDEO SHOP BRICK SYSTEM, 1 Grande rue des Feuillants, at rue Violi, separate entrances for sauna & video shop, 12:00-03:00 (weekends till 05:00).

■ Restaurants
LES FEUILLANTS, 5, Petite-rue-des-Feuillants, (4) 78 28 20 50, Tues-Sat 12:00-14:00 & 19:30-22:15 (Mon only 19:30-22:15). ♀♂

TCHIN-TCHIN, 17, rue du Sergent-Blandon, (4) 78 27 20 46, 18:00-03:00, closed Mon. ♀♂

■ Erotica
BRICK SYSTEM SHOP, 1 Grande rue des Feuillants, videos, 12:00-00:30. ♂

EROS, 7, rue Comfort, (4) 78 42 39 86.

MAJOR MARTIN, 3 rue Major Martin, (4) 78 39 09 28, video sex shop.

PREMIER (1er) SOUS SOL, 7, rue Puits-Gaillot, (4) 78 29 28 87, gay cinema, 14:00-03:00 (Fri-Sat till 07:00).

MARSEILLE

■ Information
AIDS INFO, (4) 91 84 74 64.

■ Beaches
CALLELONGUE: nude beach after stop light at end of line for bus 20; Les Goudes: gay beach among the rocks opposite l'Ile Maire; Calanque de Sugiton: end of bus line 21, then follow the signs on the path; Le Mont-Rose: gay nude beach at the end of bus line 19.

■ Bars
L'EDEN, 7, rue Curiol, (4) 91 47 30 06, 16:00-02:00 (closed Mon). ♂

L'ENIGME BAR, 22, rue Beauvau, (4) 91 33 79 20, 18:30-03:00. ♂

MP BAR, 10, rue Beauvau, (4) 91 33 64 79, video bar 18:00-02:00. ♂

■ Dance Bar/Disco
NEW CANCAN, 3-5, rue Sénac, (4) 91 48 59 76, large dance bar, Wed-Sun 23:00-06:00. ♀♂

■ Saunas/Health Clubs
LE PALMARIUM, 20, rue Sénac, (4) 91 47 43 93, 12:00-20:30, Tues & Sat 12:00-24:00. ♂

LE SAUNA CLUB, 117, la Canebière, (4) 91 64 19 08, 12:00-20:30 (Mon, Fri till 01:00). ♂

MP SAUNA, 82 La Canebière, (4) 91 48 72 51, 12:00-24:00. ♂

OLYMPIC J.L., 28, rue J. Roque, (4) 91 47 35 61, 12:00-20:30, Tues, Fri, Sat 12:00-24:00. ♂

FRANCE

SAUNA CLUB SALVATOR, 20 Boulevard Salvator, (4) 91 42 99 31, 12:00-20:30. Separate women's sauna at this address. ♂
WOMEN'S SAUNA CLUB SALVATOR, 20 Boulevard Salvator, (4) 91 42 99 31, separate women's sauna at a men's sauna, 12:00-20:30. ♀

■ Restaurants
CHEZ ALEX, 43, rue Curiol, (4) 91 47 80 12, Italian cuisine, 12:00-14:00 & 18:00-24:00, closed Sun.

■ Erotica
EROS CENTER, 5 bd Garibaldi, (4) 91 92 72 30.
HOT FACTORY, 22 rue Chateauredon, (4) 91 33 44 15, gay cinema & sex shop, 12:00-01:00. ♂
SEXASHOP, 6 rue Corneille, (4) 91 33 71 91, 09:30-24:00.

MAULÉON D'ARMAGNAC
■ Dance Bar/Disco
ASSOCIATION AMAZONES, La Thébaide, (33-5) 62 09 69 55, women's disco Sat evening only in July & August. Popular with women from surrounding area. Travelers welcome. ♀

METZ
■ Dance Bar/Disco
LE CLUB, 20, rue aux Ours., (3) 87 36 08 96, 22:00-05:00, closed Mon. ♂

MONTPELLIER
■ Accommodations
CAUSSE ET LAMAS, Route de Navas, 30120 Montdardier, (4) 67 81 52 77 (tel/fax), B&B and campground with restuarant & agricultural project, 50% gay/lesbian clientele, private & shared baths, 6 tent sites, continental breakfast in B&B only.
HOTEL ULYSSE, 338 Avenue St Maur, (4) 67 02 02 30, Fax: (4) 67 02 16 50, gay-friendly hotel.

■ Bars
LA BODEGA, 27, rue du Fbg St-Jaumes, (4) 67 41 06 98, 10:30-15:00 & 19:00-01:00, closed Mon. Bar & restaurant with patio, Spanish cuisine. ♀♂
MARTIN'S BAR, 5 rue Girone, (4) 67 60 37 15, 15:00-01:00 (till 02:00 in summer). ♂

■ Dance Bar/Disco
LE ROME CLUB, in the Fréjorgues Est shopping center, Mauguio, towards the airport, (4) 67 22 22 70, large dance bar, 2 levels, Fri-Mon from 23:00. ♀♂
THT, 29, av de Castelnau, (4) 67 79 96 17, bar & disco, daily 21:00-01:00 (Fri, Sat dance bar). ♂

■ Saunas/Health Clubs
HAMMAM CLUB, 2, rue de la Merci, (4) 67 58 22 06, 14:00-19:00. ♂

LE ROME CLUB SAUNA, at Le Rome Club disco location.
SAUNA DE LA GARE, 8, rue Levat, (4) 67 58 61 42, 12:00-01:00. ♂
SAUNA ROMAIN, 5 rue de la République, (4) 67 58 70 58, 12:00-24:00.

■ Restaurants
LE COLOMBIER, 11, bd de l'Observatoire, (4) 67 66 05 99, 12:00-14:00 & 20:00-23:30, closed Mon. Seafood a specialty.
LE VOLT FACE, 4, rue des Ecoles Laïques, (4) 67 52 86 89. Restaurant & bar with garden, 17:00-23:30 (Summer also 12:00-14:00).
LES GOÉLANDS, 8, rue de la Petite-Loge, (4) 67 60 60 34, 19:00-24:00, closed Wed. ♀♂

■ Erotica
L'ARC EN CIEL, 6 bis, rue Cope Combes, (4) 67 60 64 61, 10:00-22:00, closed Sun.

MORNAC-SUR-SEUDRE
■ Dance Bar/Disco
JOY'S, Rue du Port (10km from Royan), over Dream's bar & restaurant, facing harbour, (5) 46 22 76 44, Sat 23:00-5:00. ♀♂

MULHOUSE
■ Bars
LATINO CAFE, 16 Passage du Theatre, (03) 89 66 56 52, 15:00-01:30. ♂

■ Dance Bar/Disco
LE GEMEAUX, 3 rue J. Ehrmann, (3) 89 66 19 60, from 23:00. ♀♂
LE J.H., 32 Quai du Forst, (3) 89 32 00 08, Fri-Mon 23:00-04:00. ♂

NANCY
■ Information
AIDS INFO, (3) 83 27 91 71.

■ Dance Bar/Disco
LA LUNA, 27, rue de la Visitation, (3) 83 36 51 40, 20:30-04:00 (Fri, Sat 22:30-05:00). ♀♂

■ Restaurants
LE BISTROT DE GILLES, 31 rue des Maréchaux, (3) 83 35 43 73, 12:00-14:00 & 19:00-23:30.

NANTES
■ Information
AIDS LINE, (2) 40 47 99 56.

■ Bars
LE Z, 19, quai de Versailles, (2) 40 20 07 36, 17:00-02:00. ♂

■ Dance Bar/Disco
LE TEMPS D'AIMER, 14, rue Alexandre-Fourny, (2) 40 89 48 60, 23:00-05:00, closed Mon. ♀♂

■ Saunas/Health Clubs
LE TURENNE, 8, allée de Turenne, (2) 51 82 37 02, 12:00-21:00 (Fri, Sat till 23:00). ♂

NARBONNE
■ Dance Bar/Disco
LE SAPHO, 39, av de Bordeaux, (4) 68 42 04 21, from 23:00 (closed Mon, Tues). ♂

NICE
■ Accommodations
HOTEL DU CENTRE, 2 rue de Suisse, (4) 93 88 83 85. ♀♂
HOTEL MEYERBEER BEACH, 15 rue Meyerbeer, (4) 93 88 95 65, gay-owned, gay-friendly hotel.

■ Beaches
ROCHERS DU CAP-DE-NICE, follow the path along the sea after the restaurant Coco-Beach.

■ Bars
BAR LE RUSCA, 2, rue Rusca, (4) 93 89 46 25, terrace, 17:00-02:30. ♀♂
L'ASCENSEUR, 18 bis, rue Emmanuel Philibert, (4) 93 26 35 30, American-style bar, Tues-Sun from 21:00. ♂
LE MORGAN, 3, rue Claudia, (4) 93 86 86 08, large bar, shows, 21:30-02:30. ♂
LE NAUTIQUE, 20 Quai Lunel, close to the port. ♀

■ Dance Bar/Disco
LE BLUE BOY ENTERPRISES, 9, rue Spinetta, (4) 93 44 68 24, disco, videos, 2 dance floors, 2 bars, 23:00-05:00. ♂

■ Saunas/Health Clubs
BAINS DOUCHES, 7 rue Gubernatis, (4) 93 80 28 26, 13:00-22:00. ♂
BLUE GYM'S, 7 rue Désambrois, (4) 93 80 71 11, 13:00-24:00. ♂
LE 7, 7, rue Foncet, (4) 93 62 25 02, 13:30-21:00. ♂
SAUNA DU CHATEAU, 17, rue des Ponchettes, (4) 93 85 73 91, 13:00-20:00 (Fri till 22:00). ♀♂

■ Restaurants
BARON IVRE, 6 rue Maraldi, (4) 93 89 52 13, 19:30-24:00. ♀♂
CHAT GOURMAND, 1 ruelle de la Boucherie, (4) 93 90 98 18, frequented by women, 19:30-01:00, closed Tues.
L'ESTAMINET, 21 rue Barla, (4) 93 55 41 55, 12:00-14:00 & 19:00-22:30 (Sat only 19:00-22:30, closed Sun). ♀♂

■ Erotica
SEX SHOP, 23 rue de Belgique, 09:00-24:00.
SEXA SHOP, 8 rue Descente Crotti, (4) 93 80 29 49.

NIMES
■ Information
AIDS INFO, (4) 66 76 26 07.

■ Bars
NIMES CLUB SAUNA BAR, 7, rue Fernand Pellouthier, at the Nîmes Club Sauna, (4) 66 67 65 18, daily from 12:00-24:00. ♂

EUROPE

FERRARI GUIDES' GAY TRAVEL A to Z - 18th EDITION

FRANCE

The French Tour Operator With A Different Touch

French Touch is a gay- and lesbian-owned tour company in Paris which specializes in working with your travel agent to arrange hotels, restaurants, tours and transportation in France. Tours give a panorama of the history of homosexuality in France. Did you know King Henri III or King Louis XIII were gay? Why has French law been so lenient with gays since Cambacérès wrote the Napoleonic Code? Women will enjoy a walking tour of the Paris Left Bank in the steps of the famous lesbians like Natalie Barney, Gertrude Stein, and Alice B. Toklas or Colette, while men discover the numerous gay bars and restaurants amid the 17th century mansions that line the narrow streets of le Marais.

If you prefer to travel individually, **French Touch** has contracted several gay-friendly hotels all over France and can ensure hotel bookings, plane/train reservations and ticketing.

Contact your travel agent, or ask **French Touch** to refer you to an agent. (33 01) 41 10 38 37, Fax: (33 01) 41 10 39 55.

■ Dance Bar/Disco
LULU CLUB, 10, impasse de la Curaterie, (4) 66 36 28 20, video bar, daily from 23:00 (closed Sun, Mon). ♂

MEN'S CLUB, Route de Sauve, Km 9, (4) 66 23 36 08, Fri-Sun & holidays from 23:00. ♂

■ Saunas/Health Clubs
NIMES CLUB SAUNA 7, rue Fernand Pelloutier, (4) 66 67 65 18, 12:00-24:00. ♂

■ Restaurants
OPHÉLIE, 35, rue Fresque, (4) 66 21 00 19, 20:00-23:00, closed Sun, Mon.

■ Erotica
FOLLIE'S 28, 28 Impasse de la Curaterie, (4) 66 21 33 33, Mon-Thurs 10:00-20:00 (Fri, Sat till 21:30).

HALL DU K7, 24, bd Courbet, (4) 66 36 08 12.

NIORT

■ Bars
LE FLAMAND, 12, rue Baugier, (5) 49 73 12 69, 21:00-04:00, closed Sun & Mon, rock music.

■ Dance Bar/Disco
LE DUETTO, 43, rue St-Gelais, (5) 49 24 89 19, 23:00-04:00 Thurs-Sun. ♂

ORLEANS

■ Bars
LE PETIT AMIRAL, 205 rue de Bourgogne, (2) 38 81 00 11, 14:00-03:00. ♂

■ Dance Bar/Disco
LE REFUGE, in nearby town of La Ferte-St-Aubin, 10 minutes by car south of Orleans on the RN 20, (2) 38 64 61 60, Fri & Sat from 22:30. ♀♂

■ Restaurants
LA CABANE AU CANADA, 224 rue de Bourgogne, (2) 38 81 01 08, closed Sat lunch & all day Sun.

PARIS INTRO

■ Information
ARCHIVES LESBIENNES, (1) 48 05 25 89, lesbian archives, phone Wed 16:00-20:00 or Fri 18:00-22:00 for appointment or write A.R.C.L, BP 662, 75531 Paris Cedex 11.

CANAL MIEL, lesbian info line. To receive info, call (1) 43 796 191, to give info, call (1) 43 796 607.

CENTRE GAI ET LESBIEN, 3 rue Keller (11th arrondissement), (métro: Bastille/Voltaire), (1) 43 57 21 47, Fax: (1) 43 57 27 93. Gay & lesbian group, cafe on premises, Mon-Sat 14:00-20:00, Sun Café Positif 14:00-19:00. Organizers of local gay events, information about other gay groups.

■ Accommodations
PRIVATE PARIS ACCOMMODATIONS, contact: New York B&B Reservation Center: (212) 977-3512. Rent a private, bright studio apartment in an 18th-century building on the Left Bank in St. Germain des Pres. Has high-beamed ceilings, parquet floors, modern bath and kitchenette, and is decorator-designed with a mix of modern and antique furnishings. King bed and double sofa bed. Weekly maid service, telephone, cable TV in English. The perfect alternative to hotels! Also call us for accommodations in New York City and San Francisco. See Paris ad on page 213 and our other ad under New York City. ♂

PARIS 01

■ Bars
BANANA CAFÉ, 13, rue de la Ferronnerie (métro: Châtelet/Les Halles), (1) 42 33 35 31, daily from 17:00, terrace. ♀♂

BAR DU PALMIER, 16 rue des Lombards (métro: Châtelet/Les Halles), (1) 42 78 53 53, 17:00-05:00. ♀♂

DJ CAFÉ, 87, rue St. Honoré (métro: Châtelet/Les Halles), (1) 40 26 31 92, bar & disco, 231:00-08:00.

LE BAR, 5, rue de la Ferronerie (métro: Châtelet/Les Halles), (1) 40 41 00 10, cruisy beer bar, 3 floors, a bar on each level, daily from 17:00. ♂

LE LONDON, 33 rue des Lombards (métro: Châtelet), bar & restaurant. ♂

LE TRANSFERT, 3, rue de la Sourdière (métro: Tuileries), (1) 42 60 48 42, daily from 23:00.

LE VAGABOND, 14, rue Thérèse (métro: Pyramides), (1) 42 96 27 23, bar & restaurant 18:00-03:30 (closed Mon), some women later in evening. ♂

MYTILENE BAR, 5 rue Bertin Poirée (métro: Châtelet or Pont Neuf), (1) 45 08 06 27, 14:00-02:00 (Sun from 14:30), women-only Fri & Sat 22:00-02:00. ♀

TROPIC CAFE, 66 rue des Lombards, (1) 40 13 92 62, from 16:00. ♀♂

■ Dance Bar/Disco
CLUB 18, 18, rue du Beaujolais (métro: Palais-Royal), (1) 42 97 52 13, young crowd, from 23:00 (closed Mon). ♀♂

L'INSOLITE, 33, rue des Petits-Champs (métro: Pyramides), (1) 42 61 99 22, variety of music, 23:00-05:00. ♂

LE CLUB, 14, rue Saint-Denis (métro: Châtelet/Les Halles). (1) 45 08 96 25, theme parties, younger crowd, from 23:30. ♂

■ Saunas/Health Clubs
LE TILT, 41 rue Sainte-Anne (métro: Pyramides), (1) 42 96 07 43, 22:00-08:00. ♂

UNIVERS, 20-22, rue des Bons Enfants (métro: Palais Royal), (1) 42 61 24 83, 12:00-01:00 (Fri, Sat till 02:00). ♂

■ Restaurants
AU DIABLE DES LOMBARDS, 64, rue des Lombards (métro: Châtelet), (1) 42 33 81 84,

FRANCE

restaurant & bar, American cuisine, 11:00-02:00. 🔪🍸

AU RENDEZ-VOUS DES CAMIONNEURS, 72, quai des Orfèvres (métro: Pont Neuf), (1) 43 54 88 74, 12:00-14:00 & 20:00-23:30 (Sat only 20:00-23:30). 🔪

BISTROQUET, 26, quai du Louvre (métro: Pont-Neuf), (1) 42 36 49 52, 12:00-14:15 & 20:00-04:00 (closed Mon). 🔪

CHEZ MAX, 47 rue Saint Honoré, (1) 45 08 80 13, 20:00-24:00. ♀♂

L'AMAZONIAL, 3, rue Sainte-Opportune (métro: Châtelet/Les Halles), (1) 42 33 53 13, 12:00-15:00 & 19:00-00:30 (Fri, Sat till 04:00). ♀♂

LE BON ALOI, 5, rue Sauval (métro: Châtelet/Les Halles), (1) 40 26 22 29, 19:00-24:00. 🔪

LE CHANT DES VOYELLES, 4 rue des Lombards (métro: Châtelet). 🔪

LE VAGABOND, at Le Vagabond bar location (métro: Pyramides), (1) 42 96 27 23, Tues-Sun 20:30-00:15. 🍸♂

LES PIÉTONS, 8 rue des Lombards (métro: Châtelet), restaurant & tapas bar. 🔪

■ Erotica
IEM, 4, rue Bailleul (métro: Louvre), (1) 42 96 05 74, 13:00-20:00, closed Sun.

YANKO, 54, rue de l'Arbre-Sec (métro: Louvre), (1) 42 60 55 28.

PARIS 02

■ Bars
LA CHAMPMESLÉ, 4, rue Chabannais (métro: Pyramides), (1) 42 96 85 20, one room for women, one mixed, cabaret nights, 18:00-02:00 (Thurs-Sun till later). 🎵♀

■ Dance Bar/Disco
L'ENTRACTE, 25, bd Poissonnière (métro: Rue Montmartre or Bonne Nouvelle), at Scorpion disco, (1) 40 26 01 93, Tues-Sun from 23:00, men welcome. 🍴♀

LE SCARA, 44, rue Vivienne (métro: Rue Montmartre or Richelieu-Drouot), (1) 42 33 24 89, from 23:45. 🍴♪♂

SCORPION, 25, bd Poissonnière (métro: Rue Montmartre), (1) 40 26 01 50, from 23:45 (shows start at 03:30, Fri & Sat 04:30). 🍴♪♂

■ Cafe
LE DÉNICHEUR, 4 rue Tiquetonne, (1) 42 21 31 01, everything here is for sale, coffee, snacks & even the furniture. 🔪

■ Saunas/Health Clubs
EURO MEN'S CLUB, 8-10, rue Saint-Marc (métro: Bourse or Rue Montmartre), (1) 42 33 92 63, 12:00-23:00 (Sun from 13:00). 🏊 ♂

■ Restaurants
AUX TROIS PETITS COCHONS, 31 rue Tiquetonne (métro: Etienne Marcel or Les Halles), (1) 42 33 39 69, open from 20:00, closed Mon. 🔪

BLEU-MARINE, 28, rue Léopold-Bellan (métro: Sentier), (1) 42 36 92 44, seafood, 12:00-15:00 & 20:00-22:30 (Sat only 20:00-22:30), closed Sun. 🔪

LE LOUP BLANC, 42 rue Tiquetonne (métro: Etienne Marcel or Les Halles), (1) 40 13 08 35, dinner only, Sun brunch 12:00-18:00. 🔪

LE MONDE A L'ENVERS, 35 rue Tiquetonne, (1) 40 26 13 91, 12:00-15:00 & 20:30-23:00 (Sat, Sun only 20:30-23:00), many lesbians. ♀♂

MATINÉE-SOIRÉE, 5, rue Marie-Stuart (métro: Châtelet/Les Halles), (1) 42 21 18 00, 12:00-14:30 & 19:30-22:30 (Fri, Sat 19:30-23:00). 🔪

SORTIE DES ARTISTES, 4, rue Boudreau (métro: Opéra), (1) 42 65 77 34, 12:00-15:00 & 19:00-22:30 (Sat only 19:00-22:30), closed Sun. 🔪

PARIS 03

■ Bars
BAR DE L'HORLOGE, 7 rue Brd. de Clairvaux (métro: Rambuteau), (1) 42 72 51 00. ♂

LE DUPLEX, 25, rue Michel-Le-Comte (métro: Rambuteau or Arts et Métiers), (1) 42 72 80 86, 20:00-02:00, monthly art exhibits, women welcome. ♂

ONE WAY, 28, rue Charlot, (métro: République), (1) 48 87 46 10, video bar, tapas at cocktail hour, 17:00-02:00. 🍷🔪♂

UNITY BAR, 176-178 rue Saint Martin (métro: Rambuteau), (1) 42 72 70 59, daily 15:00-02:00. ♀

■ Restaurants
AU PETIT CABANON, 7, rue Ste.-Apolline (métro: Strasbourg-St.-Denis), (1) 48 87 66 53, traditional French cuisine, open Wed-Sat evenings from 20:00, many lesbians. ♀♂

L'IMPRIMERIE, 101, rue Vieille-du-Temple (métro: Hôtel de Ville), (1) 42 77 93 80, 12:00-15:00 & 20:00-24:00 (Sun only 20:00-24:00). 🔪

MADAME SANS GENE, 19 rue de Picardie, (1) 42 71 31 71. 🔪

MOVIE'S, 15, rue Michel-le-Comte (métro: Rambuteau), (1) 42 74 14 22, cabaret nightly, 12:00-15:00 & 22:00-24:00 (Sat only 22:00-24:00), closed Sun. 🔪♪

■ Erotica
ESPACE MAN, 41 rue Volta, (1) 42 77 04 67, 10:00-19:00, closed Sun. ♂

PARIS 04

■ Accommodations
HOTEL CENTRAL MARAIS, 33 rue Vieille-du-Temple (enter from 2, rue Ste. Croix de la Bretonnerie), 75004 Paris, (1) 48 87 56 08, Fax: (1) 42 77 06 72, hotel above popular men's bar, women welcome, rooms have old-world character with modern conveniences, TV lounge, meeting room, 2 rooms & 1 shared bath per floor, private bath 5th floor (no lift), maid service. Also 2-rm apartment opposite hotel, above gay restaurant & coffee shop. ♂

■ Bars
BAR BI, 23 rue Sainte Croix de la Bretonnerie (métro: Hôtel-de-Ville), (1) 42 78 26 20 or (1) 42 78 88 89, 15:00-02:00 (Wed women only from 21:00). ♂

BAR LE CENTRAL MARAIS, 33, rue Vieille-

LE CENTRAL

EVERY DAY
14.00 - 2.00

Un authentique
Gay Singles Bar
où on n'est
jamais seul

33, rue Vieille du Temple - 75004 PARIS
Tél. (1) 48.87.99.33

HOTEL CENTRAL MARAIS PARIS

Réservations
Tél. (1) 48 87 56 08
Fax (1) 42 77 06 27

M° Hôtel de Ville

33, rue Vieille du Temple
75004 Paris

FRANCE

Cruising Paris in a Vintage Lincoln Convertible

Five minutes of burbling silkily over the cobblestones of Paris is all it takes for a gay or lesbian person to realize that: (a) A gay excursion around Paris in a 1964 vintage Lincoln Continental convertible is truly inspired "camp," and (b) It's the best way to see Paris ever invented. Have your spacious, American "boat" and courtly driver meet you (and up to 4 others) at the airport. Choose a half-day of Paris's tourist attractions...or opt for coasting around Paris by night with the top down, viewing the lighted Arc de Triumph and Eiffel Tower, etc., and a few items the mainstream city tours don't include. Short day trips outside Paris take you to famous chateaux, such as Versailles and Fontainebleau. Also nearby is France's champagne country, where you can lunch at a private chateau and drive through ancient stone villages, wonderful rolling green areas and beautiful forests.

Contact **Promenades de Style** at (33 1) 4671 7335, Fax: (33 1) 4671 6170.

---

du-Temple (métro: Hôtel-de-Ville), (1) 48 87 99 33, cruisy, 16:00-02:00. ♂

CAFÉ CHANTANT, 12, rue du Plâtre, (métro: Rambuteau), (1) 48 87 51 04, 18:00-02:00, women welcome 21:00-23:00 during karaoke hours. ♂

COX, 15 rue des Archives (métro: Hôtel-de-Ville). ♂

L'AMNESIA, 42, rue Vieille-du-Temple (métro: Hôtel-de-Ville or Saint-Paul), (1) 42 72 16 94, snacks, 12:00-02:00, women welcome. ✗♂

L'ARENE, 80 quai de l'Hôtel de Ville, (métro: Hôtel-de-Ville or Pont Marie), video bar on 3 levels, from 12:00 till late. ♂

LE MIC MAN, 24, rue Geoffroy-l'Angevin (métro: Rambuteau), behind the Pompidou Center, (1) 42 74 39 80, videos, 12:00-02:00 (Fri & Sat till 04:00), some moustaches & uniforms. ♂

LE PIANO ZINC, 49, rue des Blancs-Manteaux (métro: Rambuteau), (1) 42 74 32 42, live piano & sing-a-long. Open 18:00-02:00 (closed Tues), women welcome. ♂

LE QUETZAL, 10, rue de la Verrerie (métro: Hôtel-de-Ville), (1) 48 87 99 07, 2 bars, restaurant, 12:00-02:00 (Sat & Sun 16:00-02:00). ♂

LES MAUDITES FEMELLES, 12, rue Simon-le-Franc (métro: Rambuteau), at QG men's bar, information: (1) 48 97 92 29 or (1) 39 69 50 04, this hard-core lesbian group organizes lesbian sex parties, leather, chaps, vinyl, latex, uniform, etc. Call for schedule. ♀

LES SCANDALEUSES, 9 rue des Ecouffes, lesbian bar, 16:00-02:00. ♀

OPEN BAR, 17 rue des Archives (métro: Hôtel-de-Ville), (1) 42 74 62 60, 12:00-02:00, weekend brunch, women welcome. ♂

QG, 12, rue Simon-le-Franc (métro: Rambuteau), (1) 48 87 74 18, 17:00-02:00, sex club. ♂

SKEUD, 35 rue Ste Croix de la Bretonnerie (métro: Hôtel-de-Ville), (1) 40 29 44 40, 15:00-02:00. ♂

THERMIK BAR, 7 rue de la Verrerie (métro: Hôtel-de-Ville), (1) 44 78 08 18, 16:00-02:00. ♂

Dance Bar/Disco

L'EKIVOK, 40, rue des Blancs Manteaux, (métro: Rambuteau), (1) 42 71 03 29, daily from 23:00 (closed Mon). Women's Tea Dance Sun 17:00-23:00. Schedule varies, telephone to verify first. ♂

Restaurants

AMADEO, 19, rue François Miron (métro Hôtel de Ville), (1) 48 87 01 02, 12:00-14:00 & 19:30-23:00 (Sat, Sun only 19:30-23:00).

AU BISTROT DE LA PLACE, 2 rue Place du Marché Ste. Catherine, (1) 42 78 21 32, open daily, frequented by gays.

AU TIBOURG, 29 rue du Bourg Tibourg (métro: Saint Paul or Hôtel de Ville), (1) 42 74 45 25, closed for lunch Sat & Sun.

AUBERGE DE LA REINE BLANCHE, 30, rue St-Louis-en-l'Ile (métro: Pont-Marie), (1) 46 33 07 87, 12:00-23:30.

COFFEE SHOP, 3, rue Sainte-Croix-de-la-Bretonnerie (métro: Hôtel-de-Ville), (1) 42 74 71 52, 12:00-00:30. ♂

ECLACHE ET CIE, 10 rue St Merry.

EQUINOX, 33 rue des Rosiers (métro: Hôtel de Ville or Saint Paul), (1) 42 71 92 41, closed Mon.

FOND DE COUR, 3, rue Sainte-Croix-de-la-Bretonnerie (métro: Hôtel-de-Ville or Saint Paul), (1) 42 74 71 52, 12:00-14:00 & 19:30-23:30 (Sat only 19:30-23:30), Sun brunch.

L'EGLANTINE, 9, rue de la Verrerie (métro: Hôtel-de-Ville), (1) 48 04 75 58, traditional French cuisine, 11:30-14:30 & 19:30-22:30 (closed Sun, Mon). ♀♂

LA BERGERIE, 20, rue Beautreillis (métro: Bastille), (1) 42 72 05 84, 12:00-14:30 & 19:30-02:00, closed Sun. ♀♂

LA CANAILLE, 4, rue Crillon (métro: Quai-de-la-Rapée), (1) 42 78 09 71, 11:45-14:15 & 19:30-24:00 (Sat, Sun only 19:30-24:00). ♀

LE DIVIN, 41, rue Ste. Croix de la Bretonnerie (métro: Hôtel de Ville), (1) 42 77 10 20, 12:00-14:00 & 19:30-23:00 (Sun only 19:30-23:00), closed Mon.

LES MAUVAIS GARÇONS, 4 rue des Mauvais Garçons (métro: Hôtel de Ville), (1) 42 72 74 97, 11:45-14:30 & 19:30-23:30 (Mon only 19:30-23:30), closed Sun.

PIANO SHOW, 20, rue de la Verrerie (métro: Hôtel-de-Ville), (1) 42 72 23 81, dinner & female impersonator shows nightly from 20:30, closed Mon.

Retail & Bookstores

BOY'Z BAZAAR, 5 rue Ste Croix de la Bretonnerie, new & used clothes, leather, videos.

LE PHARMACIE DU VILLAGE, 26 rue du Temple, (1) 42 72 60 72, closed Sun.

LES MOTS A LA BOUCHE, 6, rue Sainte-Croix de la Bretonnerie (métro: Hôtel de Ville), (1) 42 78 88 30, gay & lesbian bookshop, 11:00-23:00 (Sat till 24:00, Sun 14:00-19:00), mail order available.

Erotica

PHYLEA, 61, rue Quincampoix (métro: Rambuteau), (1) 42 76 01 90.

SEX SHOP ETS COCHON, 21, rue des Lombards (métro: Châtelet / Les Halles), (1) 40 27 98 09.

TTBM, 37, rue du Roi de Sicile (métro: Hôtel de Ville), (1) 48 04 80 88.

PARIS 05

Accommodations

HOTEL DES NATIONS, 54 rue Monge (métro: Place Monge & Cardinal Lemoine), (33-1) 43 26 45 24, Fax: (33-1) 46 34 00 13. This 3-star hotel is in the Latin Quarter's picturesque

FRANCE

Mouffetard neighborhood between the Pantheon and Notre Dame and close to the Marais. Rooms have contemporary charm and the convenience of direct-dial phone, radio, TV, individual safekeeping. Parking is nearby. The bar is a congenial meeting place for your business encounters, and the lounge, with its pleasant hearthside is a cozy nook for evenings of relaxation. A buffet breakfast starts the day. Nearby are bicycle rentals, public gardens, a covered public pool, excellent restaurants, boutiques and department stores. Gay-friendly.

■ Restaurants
LE PETIT PRINCE,★ 12, rue de Lanneau (métro: Maubert Mutualité), (1) 43 54 77 26, 19:30-00:30.

■ Retail & Bookstores
LES AMAZONES, 4 rue des Grands Degrés (métro: Maubert Mutualité), (1) 46 34 25 67 (tel/fax), lesbian & women's books, by appointment only (call/fax during Paris business hours only).

LIBRAIRIE FOURMI AILÉE, 8 rue du Fouarre (métro: Maubert), feminist bookshop, lesbian periodicals.

PARIS 06

■ Bars
LE TRAP, 10, rue Jacob (métro: St-Germain-des-Près), (1) 43 54 53 53, videos, men-only, from 22:00.

■ Restaurants
LE VIEUX CASQUE, 19, rue Bonaparte (métro: St.-Germain-des-Prés.), (1) 43 54 99 46, 19:00-23:00 (closed Sun).

■ Retail & Bookstores
LIBRAIRIE DES FEMMES, 74 rue de la Seine (métro: Mabillon), (1) 43 29 50 75, personnel said not to be lesbian-oriented.

PARIS 08

■ Dance Bar/Disco
LE QUEEN,★ 102 avenue des Champs Elysées (métro: George V), (1) 53 89 08 89, from 24:00 (many lesbians Wed), call for tape of weekly programs.

■ Cafe
LORD SANDWICH, 134, rue du Fg-Saint-Honoré (métro: Miromesnil), (1) 42 56 41 68, Mon-Fri 11:00-16:00.

XAVIER GOURMET, 89, bd de Courcelles (métro: Ternes), (1) 43 80 78 22, 12:00-16:00 & 19:00-23:30.

■ Erotica
BANQUE CLUB, 23, rue de Penthièvre, (métro: Miromesnil), (1) 42 56 49 26, private men's sex club, videos, 17:00-02:00 (Sun from 14:00).

FRENCH ART VIDÉO, 64 rue de Rome (métro: Europe), 09:00-17:00.

IEM, 33, rue de Liège (métro: Liège), (1) 45 22 69 01, Mon-Sat 11:30-19:00.

VIDÉOVISION, 62, rue de Rome (métro: Europe), (1) 42 93 66 04.

PARIS 09

■ Bars
MEC ZONE, 27, rue Turgot (métro: Anvers), (1) 40 82 94 18, cruise bar with videos, 21:00-02:00 (Sun from 18:00).

MILK, 3 Cité Bergères, (métro: Montmartre), (1) 42 71 35 94, bar & disco, Fri & Sat from 00:00 & Sun from 20:30. Closed early '97, Paris gays await possible reopening.

■ Dance Bar/Disco
CHEZ MOUNE, 54 rue Pigalle (métro: Pigalle), (1) 45 26 64 64, Sun afternoon disco, lesbians-only from 16:30-20:00.

ENTRE NOUS, 17 rue Laferrière (métro: Saint-George), (1) 48 78 11 67, Fri & Sat from 23:00.

L'EGO CLUB, 50 rue de la Chausée d'Anten, (1) 42 85 20 38, Thurs-Sun 18:00-04:00 (women-only Sun from 17:00 & Thurs), Fri & Sat men welcome.

LE PALACE GAY TEA DANCE,★ 8, rue du Faubourg Montmartre (métro: Rue Montmartre), (1) 42 46 10 87, open only for gay Sun tea dance 17:00-22:30. Closed early '97, Paris gays await possible reopening.

■ Saunas/Health Clubs
IDM, 4, rue du Faubourg Montmartre (métro: Rue Montmartre), (1) 45 23 10 03, sauna & gym, 12:00-01:00 (Fri-Sun till 02:00).

LE MANDALA, 2, rue Drouot (métro: Richelieu-Drouot), (1) 42 46 60 14, sauna & gym, 12:00-01:00 (Fri, Sat till 06:00).

■ Restaurants
GILLES ET GABRIEL, 24, rue Rodier (métro: Cadet), (1) 45 26 86 26, 12:00-14:30 & 19:30-22:30 (Sat only 19:30-23:00), closed Sun.

LES COLONNES DE LA MADELEINE, 6, rue de Sèze (métro: Madeleine), (1) 47 42 60 55, 11:30-23:00 (closed Sun).

■ Erotica
JACKY JACK, 33, bd de Clichy (métro: Blanche), (1) 48 74 08 03.

YANKO, 10, place de Clichy (métro: Place de Clichy), (1) 45 26 71 19.

PARIS 10

■ Accommodations
HOTEL LOUXOR, 4 rue Taylor, (1) 42 08 23 91, Fax: (1) 42 08 03 30. Gay-friendly hotel, 50% gay/lesbian clientele, private shower/toilets, color TV, breakfast, quiet lounge, near main boulevards & northern & eastern railway stations.

■ Bars
CAFÉ MOUSTACHE, 138, rue du Faubourg St. Martin (métro: Gare de l'Est), (1) 46 07 72 70, 16:00-02:00.

■ Saunas/Health Clubs
KEY WEST, 141, rue Lafayette (métro: Gare-du-Nord), (1) 45 26 31 74, 12:00-01:00 (Fri, Sat till 02:00).

■ Restaurants
CHALET MAYA, 5 rue des Petits Hotels, (métro: Gare de l'Est or Gare du Nord), (1) 47 70 52 78, 11:30-14:00 & 19:30-01:00 (Mon only 19:30-01:00), closed Sun.

CHEZ CHAREYRE, 7, rue de l'Echiquier (métro: Strasbourg St. Denis), (1) 47 70 65 77, 12:00-14:30 & 20:00-23:00 (Sat only 20:00-23:00), closed Sun.

EXTÉRIEUR QUAI, 5, rue d'Alsace (métro: Gare de l'Est), (1) 40 35 73 79, 24hrs.

J.O.Z., 12 rue de la Fidelité, (1) 43 48 79 23, large restaurant & bar, 21:00-03:00.

LA TAVERNE DE L'EST, 72, bd de Strasbourg (métro: Gare-de-l'Est), (1) 46 07 60 64, 12:00-15:00 & 18:30-02:00 (piano bar from 21:30).

HOTEL DES NATIONS
The Latin Quarter's Comfortable Hotel
PARIS
Tel: (33-1) 43 26 45 24

PRIVATE PARIS ACCOMMODATIONS
CALL USA: (212) 977-3512
Your Own Left Bank Studio
$130/Night for Two

FERRARI GUIDES' GAY TRAVEL A to Z - 18th EDITION

FRANCE

■ Erotica

I.E.M., 208, rue Saint-Maur (métro: Goncourt or Colonel Fabien), Paris 75010, (33-1) 42 41 21 41, Fax: (33-1) 42 41 86 80. The largest gay sex shop in France. You will find a variety of videos, leathers, magazines, underwear. Open 10:00-19:30, except Sunday. Ask for our mail-order catalog. Wholesale inquiries welcomed.

RANGERS, THE, 6, Boulevard St. Denis (métro: Strasbourg St. Denis), (1) 42 39 83 30.

PARIS 11

■ Information

ARCHIVES, RECHERCHES ET CULTURES LESBIENNES ARCL, BP 362, 75526, Paris Cedex 11, (1) 48 05 25 89, Wed 16:00-20:00, Fri 18:00-22:00 and by appt.

GROUPE DES LESBIENNES FÉMINISTES, c/o Maison des Femmes, 8 Cité Prost, 75011, Paris, (métro: Charonne), (1) 43 48 24 91, lesbian feminist group.

MAISON DES FEMMES, 8 Cité Prost, (1) 43 48 24 91, women's center with different meetings & socials throughout the week.

■ Bars

LA LUNA,★ 28, rue Keller (métro: Bastille, Voltaire or Ledru Rollin), (1) 40 21 09 91, 09:00-06:00.

LE KELLER, 14, rue Keller (métro: Bastille, Voltaire or Ledru Rollin), (1) 47 00 05 39, "hard" dress code, 22:00-02:00, call for scheduled parties.

LES DOCKS, 50 rue Saint-Maur (métro: Goncourt), (1) 43 57 33 82, 17:00-02:00 (Fri-Sat till 08:00).

OBJECTIF LUNE, 19, rue de La Roquette (métro: Bastille), (1) 48 06 46 05, 18:00-02:00 (Fri, Sat till 04:00).

■ Cafe

CAFÉ HYDROMEL, 8 cité Prost, at Maison des Femmes (métro: Charonne), (1) 43 48 24 91, lesbian night Fri 20:00, presented by M.I.E.L. lesbian organization. Moving in '97.

■ Restaurants

AUX JARDINS D'ELISA, 101, rue de Charonne (métro: Charonne), (1) 43 48 79 23, 12:00-15:00 & 20:00-23:00 (Mon only 12:00-15:00), closed Sun.

MANSOURIA, 11 rue Faidherbe (métro: Faidherbe-Chaligny), (1) 43 71 00 16, women-owned Moroccan restaurant, 12:00-14:15 & 19:30-23:00 (Mon only 19:30-23:00), closed Sun.

■ Retail & Bookstores

LE FUNAMBULE, 48 rue Jean-Pierre Timbaud (métro Oberkampf or Parmentier), (1) 48 06 74 94, rare & OP books, many of homosexual themes, 14:00-19:30 (closed Sun), or by appointment.

■ Erotica

DÉMONIA, 10 cité Joly (métro: Père Lachaise), women's domination shop, books, magazines, videos, clothing, accessories, 11:00-19:00.

PARIS 12

■ Saunas/Health Clubs

BAINS MONTANSIER, 7 rue de Montreuil, in nearby Vincennes, (métro: Château de Vincennes), (1) 43 28 54 03, 12:00-20:00. ♂

■ Restaurants

CAVIAR AND CO, 5, rue de Reuilly (métro: Faidherbe-Chaligny), (1) 43 56 13 98, 12:00-14:00 & 19:30-24:30 (Sat, Sun only 19:30-24:00). ♀♂

LE TERROIR, 22, rue de Chaligny (métro: Faidherbe Chaligny), (1) 43 07 47 66, 12:00-14:30 & 19:30-23:30 (Sat only 19:30-23:30), closed Sun.

PARIS 13

■ Information

MARGUERITE DURAND ARCHIVES, 79 rue Nationale (métro: Port d'Ivry), feminist & women's studies library in existence since the late 1880's. Modern facilities & impressive resources, some personnel speak English.

■ Restaurants

LE BOEUF BISTROT, 4, Place des Alpes (métro: Place d'Italie), (1) 45 82 08 09, 12:00-14:00 & 20:00-22:30, Sat 20:00-22:30 (closed Sun).

LE VERDI, 27 rue de la Colonie, (métro: Tolbiac), (1) 45 88 30 98, 11:30-14:00 & 19:30-23:00, closed Sat, Sun.

PARIS 14

■ Dance Bar/Disco

L'ENFER, 34 rue du Départ (métro: Montparnasse), (1) 42 79 94 94, dance garage, women-only Fri & Sat from 23:30. ♀

■ Restaurants

AU FEU FOLLET, 5 rue Raymond-Losserand (métro: Gaîté), (1) 43 22 65 72, Mon-Sat from 19:15.

FAR-OUEST, 101, rue de l'Ouest (métro: Pernety), (1) 45 42 28 33, daily 19:00-05:00.

LA ROUTE DU CHATEAU, 36, rue Raymond-Losserand (métro: Pernety), (1) 43 20 09 59, 12:00-14:30 & 19:30-00:30, Mon 19:30-00:30 (closed Sun).

PARIS 15

■ Restaurants

L'ACCENT, 93, rue de Javel (métro: Charles Michel), (1) 45 79 20 26, closed Sun & Mon lunch.

L'IMPASSE, 7 rue de Cadix, (1) 40 45 09 81, restaurant & bar, frequented by women, 17:00-02:00 (closed Sun).

PARIS 16

■ Saunas/Health Clubs

SAUNA VICTOR HUGO, 109, Av. Victor-Hugo (métro: Victor-Hugo), (1) 47 04 41 24, 12:00-21:00 (Sun till 20:00). ♂

PARIS 17

■ Bars

LE GUÉPARD, 35 rue Davy (métro: Brochant,

FRANCE

Guy Moquet or La Fourche), (1) 42 28 07 09, 21:00-02:00 (closed Mon). ♂

LE MARGINAL, 2, rue Lamandé (métro: Rome), (1) 45 22 34 82, 17:00-02:00, closed Sun, frequented by gays. ⊠

■ Saunas/Health Clubs
KING NIGHT & DAY, 21, rue Bridaine (métro: Rome), (1) 42 94 19 10, 13:00-07:00. ♂

■ Restaurants
L'INSOLENCE, 66, rue Legendre (métro: Rome), (1) 42 29 57 96, 12:00-14:30 & 19:30-22:30 (Sat only 19:30-22:30), closed Sun. ⊠

WAGON 7, 7, rue Boursault (métro: Rome), (1) 42 93 41 57, Thurs-Sat jazz nights, 12:00-14:00 & 20:00-24:00 (Sat, Sun only 20:00-24:00), closed Mon. ⊠

PARIS 18

■ Bars
LES PLANCHES DOUDEAUVILLE, 36, rue Doudeauville (métro: Marx-Dormoy), (1) 42 54 12 56, beach motif, theme parties 18:00-04:00. ♂

■ Saunas/Health Clubs
SAUNA MYKONOS, 71, rue des Martyrs (métro: Pigalle), (1) 42 52 15 46, 12:30-24:00. ♂

■ Restaurants
ATMOSPHERE, 18, rue du Chevalier-de-la-Barre (métro: Lamarck-Caulaincourt), (1) 42 23 69 41, 19:00-02:00, summer 11:00-02:00. ⊠

L'ÉCHAPPÉE BELLE, 5 rue Pierre Picard (métro: Anvers or Barbès Rochechouart), (1) 42 54 61 21, Tues-Sat, lunch & dinner. ⊠

LA VILLA, 4 villa Saint-Michel (métro: La Fourche), (1) 44 85 32 71, restaurant & bar, traditional French cuisine, Mon-Fri till 22:30, Sat bar frequented by some gays. ⊠

LE PERROQUET VERT, 7, rue Cavallotti (métro: Place de Clichy), (1) 45 22 49 16, 12:00-15:00 & 18:30-23:00 (Sat only 18:30-23:00), closed Sun. ⊠

LE PIERROT DE LA BUTTE, 41, rue de Caulaincourt (métro: Lamarck-Caulaincourt), (1) 46 06 06 97, traditional French cuisine, 19:30-23:15 (closed Sun). ⊠ ♀

LE POULAILLER DE LA BUTTE, 18 rue du Bachelet (métro: Jules Joffrin), (1) 46 06 01 99, frequented by women. ⊠

RESTAURANT DU MÉTRO, 6, rue de la Fontaine-du-But (métro: Lamarck-Caulaincourt), (1) 46 06 13 40, 12:00-14:15 & 19:30-23:00 (closed Mon). ⊠

PARIS 19

■ Restaurants
LA LANTERNE, 9 rue du Tunnel, (1) 42 39 15 98, 12:00-14:30 & 19:00-23:00 (Sat only 19:00-23:00). ⊠

PAU

■ Dance Bar/Disco
LE DAIKIRI, Palais des Pyrénées, at Ave de Lattre de Tassigny & Place Clemenceau, (5) 59 27 32 44, theme parties, 24:00-04:00, closed Mon. 🍴♂

■ Saunas/Health Clubs
EROS SAUNA, 8 rue René Fournets, (5) 59 27 48 80, 14:00-02:00 (Fri till 04:00), mixed gay/hetero Tues & Thurs. ♂

SAUNA LE CENTAURE, 15, rue d'Orléans, (5) 59 27 30 41, 13:30-21:00 (closed Tues). ♂

■ Restaurants
L'ETNA, 16, rue du Château, (5) 59 27 77 94, 12:00-14:30 & 19:00-24:00. ⊠

■ Erotica
KITSCH, 13, cours Bosquet, (5) 59 27 68 67, 14:00-20:00 (closed Sun).

PERIGUEUX

■ Dance Bar/Disco
L'AN DES ROYS, 51, rue Aubarede, (5) 53 53 01 58, from 23:00 (closed Mon). Separate rooms for gays & lesbians. ♀♂

PERPIGNAN

■ Retail & Bookstores
LE FUTUR ANTÉRIEUR, 8, rue du Théâtre, 68 34 20 45, general bookstore with gay section, Tues-Sat 09:30-12:00 & 14:00-19:00 (Mon only 14:00-19:00).

■ Erotica
DÉFI, 10, av. Leclerc, 68 52 44 25.

QUIMPER

■ Bars
CARPE DIEM, 54bis Ave de la Liberation, (2) 98 90 00 21, 18:00-01:00 (closed Mon), frequented by gays & lesbians. ⊠

■ Cafe
LE COFFEE SHOP, 26, rue du Frout, (2) 98 95 43 30, younger crowd, 17:00-01:00. 🍷Y♂

REIMS

■ Information
AIDS LINE, (3) 26 49 96 10.

■ Dance Bar/Disco
LES LILAS CLUB, 75, rue de Courcelles, (3) 26 47 02 81, 22:15-04:00. 🍴♂

RENNES

■ Information
AIDS LINE, (2) 99 79 06 04.
FEMMES ENTRE-ELLES, (2) 99 59 34 07, women's group meets Wed 19:00-20:00.

■ Bars
LE PRIVILEGE, 92, rue Ange-Blaise near rue l'Alma, (2) 99 32 28 12, 20:00-01:00 (Sat, Sun from 22:00). ♂

■ Dance Bar/Disco
LE BATCHI, 35, rue Vasselot, (2) 99 79 62 27, 23:00-05:00 (closed Mon). 🍴♀♂

■ Saunas/Health Clubs
LE 16, 16, rue du Dr.-Francis-Joly, 15:00-21:00, closed Mon.

■ Restaurants
LE SHIP-SHOP, 30, rue Saint-Malo, (2) 99 79 19 89, 12:00-14:00 & 19:00-00:30 (Sat only 19:00-00:30), closed Sun. ⊠

ROUEN

■ Bars
LE KOX, 138 rue Beauvoisine, (2) 35 07 71 97, 18:00-02:00 ♀♂
LE PALACE, 40, rue Saint-Gervais, (2) 35 89 41 90, 18:00-02:00 (closed Wed), TV room & videos. ♪🍴⊠

■ Dance Bar/Disco
LE QUEEN, 2, rue Malherbe, (2) 35 03 29 36, Fri-Sun 22:00-04:00. ♪🍴♀♂

■ Saunas/Health Clubs
LE 8, 8, place Saint-Amant, (2) 35 15 06 29, 12:00-21:00 (Fri 14:00-23:00, Sat from 14:00). ♂

LE SQUARE, 39, rue St. Nicolas, (2) 35 15 58 05, 12:00-20:00 (Sun from 15:00). ♂

LES TROIS COLONNES, 4 Impasse des Hauts, Mariages, (2) 32 08 40 60, 13:00-23:00 (Fri-Sun 14:00-24:00). ♂

■ Restaurants
GOURMANDINE, 236, rue Martainville, (2) 35 71 95 13, 11:00-18:00 (Fri-Sun till 23:00). ⊠

LE BOUGAINVILLIER, 35, rue Percière, (2) 35 07 73 32, 12:00-14:30 & 19:00-22:30 (closed Sun). ⊠

ST-ETIENNE

■ Information
AIDS INFO, (4) 77 80 75 71, weekdays 13:00-19:00.

■ Bars
LE CLUB, 3, place Villeboeuf, (4) 77 33 56 25, 18:00-01:00. ♂

■ Saunas/Health Clubs
SAUNA LIBERATION, 5, av de la Libération, (4) 77 33 53 96, 13:00-19:30. ♂

ST-MALO

■ Dance Bar/Disco
ANGELUS BIS, 3, rue des Cordiers, (2) 99 40 13 20, video disco & cocktail bar 21:00-03:00. ⊠🍴

ST-MARTIN D'AUXIGNY

■ Dance Bar/Disco
LA MANDRAGORE, Vignoux-sous-les-Aix, (2) 48 64 55 76, Fri-Sat 22:30-04:00. 🍴♪♂

FERRARI GUIDES' GAY TRAVEL A to Z - 18th EDITION

FRANCE

ST-RAPHAEL

Bars
PIPELINE, 16 rue Charabois, (4) 94 95 93 98, 21:00-04:00.

ST-TROPEZ

Bars
CHEZ MAGUY, 5 rue Sibille, (4) 94 97 16 12, bar & restaurant.

Dance Bar/Disco
LE BAL, Residence du Nouveau Port, (4) 94 97 14 70, daily 23:00-06:00 (in winter Fri-Sun only).

LE PIGEONNIER, 13, rue de la Ponche, (4) 94 97 36 85, from 23:00.

Restaurants
L'ENTRECOTE 21, 12, rue du Portail-Neuf, (4) 94 97 40 02, 19:30-01:00.

LE BAR A VIN, 13, rue des Feniers, (4) 94 97 46 10, restaurant & bar, 19:00-01:00 (closed Sun).

SAINTES

Dance Bar/Disco
LE GRILLON, Courcoury, 17100 Saintes, (5) 46 74 66 98, Tues-Sun 23:00-05:00.

SPARTACUS, route de Royan, at Complexe St Vegas, (5) 46 93 42 76, Sun 22:00-05:00, 20% women.

Erotica
SEX-SHOP, 10, quai de la République, (5) 46 74 51 72.

SANARY-SUR-MER

Dance Bar/Disco
RIVE DROITE, 1111, chemin Morvemède, (4) 94 74 07 26, gay Mon & occasional Thurs, 23:00 till dawn.

SENNECEY LE GRAND

Dance Bar/Disco
LE PLAKA, Gigny / Saône, between Calon sur Soane & Tommans, A6 exit RN6 (3) 85 44 81 71, Fri & Sat 22:30-04:00.

SOUTHWEST FRANCE - RURAL

Accommodations
HILLTOP CANTEGRIVE FARMHOUSES, Bidot Haut, 24 440 St. Avit Sénieur (Bergerac), (33) 553 22 49 29, Fax: (33) 553 27 87 85. Gay-friendly & discrete, this private, centuries-old country estate is magnificently set in 50 acres (20 hectares) of field & forest 1-1/2 hours east of Bordeaux. Two self-contained, fully equipped units sleep 2-4 or 4-6 people. Modern amenities include satellite TV, fireplace & large pool. Visit prehistoric caves & fascinating châteaux, dine in quaint restaurants & participate in abundant outdoor activities. Women-oriented, but men welcome.

Women's Accommodations
LE POUY, 40190 Villeneuve-de-Marsan, (33) 58 45 30 14, Women-only retreat open July & August only, reserve well in advance, books up early, shared bath & showers, many tent sites.

MONDES, Courrensan, 32330 Gondrin, (33) 562 06 59 05. In France dial: 0562 06 59 05, women-only inn & campground, double rooms with shared baths, 20 tent sites, living room with fireplace, full breakfast buffet & gourmet vegetarian dinners.

PRAT SISTERS, Maison Prat, 32150 Cutxan, (33) 62 09 55 21, women-only retreat & campground, shared baths, 20 tent sites, breakfast.

ROUSSA, Courrensan, 32330 Gondrin, 6206 5896, fax 6264 4534, women-only guesthouse in 200-year-old renovated former farmhouse, shared baths, generous breakfast & vegetarian dinner, conference room available for rent, many group activities.

SAOUIS, Cravencères, 32110 Nogaro, (33) 62 08 56 06, women-only guesthouse, double rooms, shared showers, garden, tent sites, expanded continental breakfast, dinner.

STRASBOURG

Information
AIDS LINE, (3) 88 75 73 63, Mon-Fri 09:00-18:00.

Dance Bar/Disco
LE MAGASIN, 13 rue Wissembourg, (3) 88 75 66 88, 22:00 until dawn.

LE MONTE CARLE, 4, quai de Turckheim, (3) 88 22 35 02, 22:00-03:00, closed Mon.

WARNING BAR, 3 rue Klein, (3) 88 25 04 41, 22:00-04:00, closed Mon.

Cafe
LA LUNE NOIRE, 8, rue Metzeral, (3) 88 39 96 08, Fri, Sat 21:30-01:00, women's café with monthly dances.

Saunas/Health Clubs
OASIS CLUB SAUNA, 22, rue de Bouxwiller, (3) 88 23 03 19, 14:00-24:00.

SAUNA EQUATEUR, 5, rue de Rosheim, (3) 88 22 25 22, 12:00-24:00 (Sat 14:00-06:00).

Restaurants
AU COIN DU FEU, 10, rue de la Râpe, (3) 88 35 44 85, traditional French cuisine, 10:00-14:30 & 19:00-23:30 (Tue only 19:00-23:30), closed Mon.

TERGNIER

Dance Bar/Disco
LA PARILLA CLUB DISCO & RESTAURANT, 38, rue Démosthène-Gaucher, (3) 23 57 25 08. Disco: Fri, Sat 22:00-04:00. Bar: Tues-Sun 15:00-24:00. Restaurant: Tues-Sun 16:00-22:00.

TOULON

Information
AIDS INFO, (4) 94 62 96 23.

Beaches
PLAGES DU LITTORAL FRÉDÉRIC-MISTRAL, at Mourillons.

Bars
EQUIPE BAR, 4 Place Gustave Lambert, 2 terraces, frequented by gays, 10:00-01:00 (Sun from 17:00).

TEXAS, 1, rue de l'Humilité, (4) 94 89 14 10, 16:30-01:00 (in summer till 03:00).

Dance Bar/Disco
BOY'S PARADISE, 1, bd Pierre Toesca, across from train station, (4) 94 09 35 90, rave, from 22:30.

LE PUSSY CAT, 655, av de Claret, (4) 94 92 76 91, Wed-Sun 23:00-04:00.

Saunas/Health Clubs
AGS-CULTURO-NATURISTE INTER-CLUBS, Villa les Mouettes 87, chemin de la Pinède, (4) 94 42 38 73, daily 14:00-21:00.

TOULOUSE

Information
AIDS INFO, (5) 61 42 22 87.

Bars
BAGDAM CAFÉE, ★ 4, rue Delacroix, (5) 61 99 03 62. Cafe, restaurant & bar for women only, with theatre, exhibitions, films, concerts, lectures, discussions & women's resource center. Monthly disco, 18:00-02:00 (closed Sun, Mon). Closed for vacation mid-Aug-mid-Sept.

BEAR CAFÉ, 31 rue de Stalingrad, (5) 61 63 03 05, 16:00-02:00 (Sat 18:00-04:00).

LA CIGUE, 6, rue de la Colombette, (5) 61 99 61 87, 19:00-02:00, closed Mon.

LES DEUX G, 5 rue Baronie, (5) 61 23 16 10, 15:00-02:00.

QUINQUINA BAR, 26, rue Peyras, (5) 61 21 90 73, 08:00-22:00, Sun from 18:00.

Dance Bar/Disco
LE NEW SHANGHAI, 12, rue de la Pomme, (5) 61 23 37 80, disco in front, gay men's cruise bar with erotic videos in back, from 23:30 (Sun tea dance).

N.Y.C.★, 83, allée Charles-de-Fitte, (5) 61 59 46 45, video disco on 2 levels, from 22:00 (closed Mon).

Saunas/Health Clubs
LE CALYPSO, 16, rue Bayard, (5) 61 63 86 52, 14:00-01:00.

LE PHYSIC CLUB, 14, rue d'Aubuisson, (5) 61 62 81 29, 14:00-24:00, Fri till 02:00.

LE PRÉSIDENT, 38, rue d'Alsace-Lorraine, (5) 61 21 52 18, 11:30-19:00 (13:00-19:30).

Restaurants
L'OS A MOELLE, 14, rue Roquelaine, (5) 61 63 19 30, Mon-Fri 12:00-14:30 (Mon, Fri-Sat

GERMANY

also 19:30-22:30), traditional French cuisine. 🍽

LE PETIT SAINT-GERMAIN, 6, rue de l'Etoile, (5) 61 63 13 43, 12:00-14:00 & 20:00-24:00 (Sat, Sun only 20:00-24:00), closed Mon, traditional French cuisine. 🍽

MERE DENIS, 45 rue des Tourneurs, (5) 61 21 40 80, from 19:30.

■ *Erotica*

APHRODITE, 13, rue Denfert-Rochereau, (5) 61 62 48 82.

AUTAN X, 23, rue Denfert-Rochereau, (5) 61 63 87 90.

EROS, 22, rue Denfert-Rochereau, (5) 61 63 44 72.

SPARTACUS, 29, rue Héliot, (5) 61 63 63 59, gay shop, videos, 13:00-01:00 (closed Sun). ♂

VIDEO SHOW, 22, rue Héliot, (5) 61 62 61 45.

TOURNON-SUR-RHONE

■ *Dance Bar/Disco*

LE STAR NIGHT, Quartier du Poisson-Frais, St. Jean de Muzol, (4) 75 08 08 62, Fri, Sat from 23:00, Sun from 22:00. 🍽👠♂

TOURS

■ *Information*

AIDS INFO, (2) 47 20 16 56.

■ *Accommodations*

PRIEURÉ DES GRANGES, 37510 Savonnieres, Touraine (10-min drive from Tours), (33-2) 47 50 09 67, fax: (33-2) 47 50 06 43. Gay-friendly B&B with antique shop, luxury rooms, private baths, continental breakfast, TV lounge, phone, meeting rooms, pool on premises. 🛏

■ *Bars*

AUX VOLTIGEURS, 53 bis, rue du Docteur Fournier, 17:00-2:00, closed Tues. ♂

CHEZ NELLO, 8 rue Auguste Chevalier, (2) 47 39 12 11, 17:00-02:00. 🕺♀♂

■ *Dance Bar/Disco*

CLUB 71, 71, rue Courteline, (2) 47 37 01 54, 22:30-04:00 (closed Mon). 🕺🍽♂

■ *Saunas/Health Clubs*

LES THERMES GRAMMONT, 22, avenue Grammont, (2) 47 05 49 24, 14:00-21:00. ♂

■ *Erotica*

MIROIR DES HOMMES, 34 rue Michelet, (2) 47 37 46 46.

VALENCE

■ *Women's Accommodations*

INANNA, La Renaude, 26340 Saillans, (33-4) 75 21 50 72. Women-only retreat & campground with classes available at times, rooms & tent sites, breakfast & dinner. ♀

VESOUL

■ *Dance Bar/Disco*

LE CLUB, in nearby town of Pussy, (3) 84 76 65 90, 21:30-04:00, closed Mon. 🍽♂

VILLENEUVE-D'ASCQ

■ *Dance Bar/Disco*

ZÉNITH, 74 av de Flandre, (3) 20 89 92 29, from 23:00, closed Mon, Tues. 🍽♀♂

GERMANY
COUNTRY CODE: (49)

WHO TO CALL
For Tour Companies Serving This Destination
See Germany on page 15

AACHEN

■ *Information*

ROSALINDE LESBENTREFF, Wilhelmstr. 69 at Frauen Helfen Frauen, (0241) 902 416, lesbian meeting at Women Helping Women, 1st Sun of the month, 17:00-19:00.

■ *Bars*

BAR JEDER VERNUNFT, Promenadenstr. 43, (0241) 250 39, 22:00-03:00 (closed Tues). Women only Thurs. 🍽

HAUPTQUARTIER, Promenadenstr. 46, (0241) 231 48, 21:00-02:00 (Fri, Sat till 03:00). ♂

ZERO-EIGHT-ONE-FIVE (0815), Jakobstr. 222, (0241) 24 060, 20:00-02:00 (Fri, Sat till 03:00, Sun from 15:00). ♂

■ *Erotica*

ORION, Roermonderstr. 60, (0241) 159 117.

SEXMESSE, Gasborn.

SEXY VILLA NOVA, Heinrichsallee 2, (0241) 505 405.

ALBSTADT

■ *Cafe*

TOM TOM, Kirchgraben 38, (07431) 35 45, daily 10:00-24:00. ♂

ALTENAU

■ *Saunas/Health Clubs*

CLUB SAUNA, Breyelweg 1-3, (05328) 14 50, daily from 20:00.

ASCHAFFENBURG

■ *Information*

FRAUENZENTRUM, Herrlinstr. 26, (06021) 243 99, women's center, Lesbentreff (lesbian social) Fri from 20:00.

■ *Erotica*

ORION SHOP, Ludwigstr. 7, (06021) 25 435.

AUGSBURG

■ *Information*

AIDS HILFE, (0821) 566 93.

FRAUENZENTRUM, Haunstetterstrasse 49, (0821) 58 11 00 women's center, Lesbentreff (lesbian social) Fri from 20:30.

■ *Bars*

HOFGARTENSTÜBLE, Alte Gasse 7, (0821) 514 788, from 19:00, lesbians welcome. Lesbenstammtisch (lesbian roundtable) 3rd Thurs 20:00-01:00. ♂

POMPADOUR, Schrannenstr. 8, (0821) 51 51 21, 17:00-01:00 (Sat till 02:00).

THIRTY-FOUR (34), Hunolzgraben 34, (0821) 39 294, 18:00-01:00. ♂

UFERLOS, Konrad Adenauer Allee 19, (0821) 313 303, 16:00-01:00 (Fri & Sat till later). ♂

■ *Cafe*

CHEZ COCO, Halderstr. 14, (0821) 51 10 34, 22:00-03:00 (Sun & Wed from 20:00, Fri, Sat till 04:00). 🍽♂

■ *Retail & Bookstores*

ELISARA, Schmiedgasse 11, (0821) 15 43 03, women's bookstore.

■ *Erotica*

ORION SHOP, Leonhardsberg 17.

VIDEOWORLD, Ludwigstr. 17.

BAD KREUZNACH

■ *Bars*

BALOO, Bosenheimer Str. 158, (0671) 72 626, 20:00-01:00 (Fri, Sat till 02:00). ♂

SPARTAKUS, Rüdesheimerstr. 50, (0671) 41 535, 19:00-01:00 (Sat, Sun from 20:00). ♂

■ *Dance Bar/Disco*

CAPRI DISCO, Planingerstr. 32, (0671) 31 861, Sat from 21:00. 🍽♂

■ *Erotica*

ORION SHOP, Mannheimer Str. 206, (0671) 628 80.

BAD NAUHEIM

■ *Cafe*

BISTRO CAFE, Am Marktplatz 1, (0632) 32 719, 10:00-01:00. ♂

BAD NEUSTADT

■ *Bars*

LE BISTROT HANNES, Rossmarkstr. 8, (09771) 98509, 18:00-01:00. ♂

BAMBERG

■ *Information*

AIDS HILFE, (0951) 522 55.

■ *Bars*

ZUM PAUSEN-STÜBLE, Martin Luther Str. 4, (0951) 234 68, 11:00-01:00, Sat 19:00-02:00, closed Wed. ♂

FERRARI GUIDES' GAY TRAVEL A to Z - 18th EDITION

GERMANY

■ *Cafe*
CAFÉ ROSA, Austr. 37, Tues 16:00-18:00. ♀

BARBY

■ *Cafe*
AM COPHUS, Otto Beckmann Str. 14, 7317, 08:00-24:00. ♂

BAYREUTH

■ *Information*
AIDS LINE, 82 500, Mon-Fri 09:00-12:00 (Thurs also 14:00-17:00).

■ *Bars*
LILA, Tunnelstr. 1, close to the train station, 85 308, 20:00-01:00, closed Sun. ♂

BERLIN

■ *Information*
ARAQUIN, Bülowstr. 54, (030) 212 15 95, lesben-kultur-etage (lesbian cultural organization), Tues 17:00-19:00.
BERLINER AIDS-HILFE, (030) 883 3017 or Pluspunkt Berlin: (030) 445 86 81.
EWA FRAUENZENTRUM, Prenzlauer Allee 6, (030) 442 55 42, 442 72 57, women's center, 10:00-18:00. Lesbian group meets Wed 19:00.
FRAUEN INFOTHEK, Dircksen Str. 47 (030) 282 3980, women's info center, Mon-Fri 10:00-18:00.
FRAUENFORSCHUNGS-, BILDUNGS-, UND -INFORMATIONSZENTRUM E.V. (FFBIZ), Danckelmannstrasse 47, (030) 322 10 35, information, archives, library, gallery, cultural events for women.
GAY SWITCHBOARD (MANN-O-METER), Motzstr. 5, (030) 216 80 08, Mon-Sat 15:00-23:00, Sun 15:00-21:00, also a cafe on the premises.
LESBENBERATUNG, Kulmerstr. 20a, (030) 215 20 00, lesbian information center. Mon, Tues, Thurs 17:00-20:00.
LILA ARCHIV, c/o Uschi Sillge, Choriner Str. 9, 1054 Berlin (030) 281 29 51, women's archives.
LÄRM & LUST FRAUENMUSIKZENTRUM, Schwedenstr. 14, (030) 784 72 97, women's music center.
PELZE MULTI MEDIA, Potsdamerstrasse 139, (030) 216 23 41. Meeting place & cafe for lesbians & women to express themselves & their art in an experimental way through performances, theatre, music, lectures, workshops, etc. Opening hours change according to programme of events.
RUT, RAT UND TAT, KULTURZENTRUM, Schillerpromenade 1, (030) 621 47 53, women's cultural center, Wed-Fri 17:00-21:00.
SCHOKOFABRIK, Naunynstr. 72, (030) 615 29 99, large complex with woodworking & other workshops, 10:00-14:00 (Wed 12:00-16:00), closed Fri-Sun.
SCHWULES MUSEUM & ARCHIVE, Mehringdamm 61, (030) 693 11 72, gay museum & archive, 14:00-18:00 (Sat from 17:00).
SCHWUZ, Mehringdamm 61, (030) 693 70 25, gay center.
SPINNBODEN LESBENARCHIV, Burgsdorfstr. 1, (030) 465 20 21, lesbian archives, Wed & Fri 13:00-20:00.

■ *Accommodations*
ARCO HOTEL — NORDDEUTSCHER HOF, Geisbergstr. 30, (030) 218 2128, fax: (30) 211 3387, Hotel 2 blocks from Wittenbergplatz with breakfast buffet, private & shared baths, telephone, terrace, garden, small lounge, near gay bars, 50% gay/lesbian clientele.
HOTEL CHARLOTTENBURGER HOF, Stuttgarterplatz 14, (030) 329070, fax: 3233723, hotel with small restaurant, newsstand & hair salon, 20% gay male clientele, women welcome, mostly straight clientele, color cable TV, maid service, modern rooms, centrally located, full breakfast 5 DM extra.
PENSION NIEBUHR, Niebuhrstr. 74, (030) 324 95 95, (030) 324 95 96, Fax: (030) 324 80 21. Stay in a turn-of-the-century home in a quiet neighborhood, yet close to the well-known Charlottenburg district and the Kurfürstendamm, the popular main street of Berlin. A choice of international restaurants is nearby, as are shopping and nightlife. Our recently furnished rooms don't feel like hotel rooms. 50% hetero clientele. Most of our gay guests are men, but women are always very welcome.
TOM'S HOUSE, Eisenacherstrasse 10, 10777 Berlin, (030) 218 5544, fax 213 4464, men-only bed & breakfast predominantly for leather men, rooms with sinks, shared baths, TV lounge, refrigerator, buffet breakfast, free city map. ♂

■ *Women's Accommodations*
ARTEMISIA WOMEN ONLY HOTEL, Brandenburgischestrasse 18, D-10707 Berlin, (49-30) 873 89 05 or 873 63 73, Fax: (49-30) 861 8653. Women-only hotel with bar, 5 min from Ku-Damm, singles, doubles, suite, modern decor & soothing pastels, meeting rooms, TV lounge, art displays, lavish buffet-style breakfast. ♀

■ *Bars*
ABRICOT, Hasenheide 48, (030) 693 11 50, 19:00-01:00, closed Tues. ♂
ACTION, Lietzenburgerstr. 77, (030) 882 51 51, daily 17:00-05:00. ♂
ALBRECHT KLAUSE, Albrechtstr. 125, (030) 791 5621, 14:00-02:00 (Sat, Sun from 12:00). ♂
ALTE FEUERWACHE, Emser Str. 131, 09:00-01:00. ♂
AMSTERDAM, Gleimstr. 24, (030) 448 0792, 17:00-03:00. ♂
ANDREAS KNEIPE, Ansbacher Str. 29, (030) 218 32 57, cruise bar frequented by leather men, 11:00-04:00. ♥♫♂
ARTEMISIA HOTEL BAR, at Artemisia Hotel, a place for a quiet drink in a pleasant room with a modern decor & women's art, muted music for conversation. Open 7 days 17:00-01:00. ♀
BALLHAUS BAR, Naunynstr. 27, women-only Mon-Wed. ♫♀
BEGINE, Postdamer Strasse 139, (030) 215 43 25, Café und Kulturzentrum, with lite menu, live lesbian concerts, cabaret, readings, films, a different schedule each month. Open daily 18:00-01:00. Scheduled disco nights. ♫✕♫♀
BEI WANDA, Schaperstr. 14, (030) 883 11 02, 17:00-03:00 (Sat from 12:00), closed Sun. ♂
BESENKAMMER, Rathausstr. 1, (030) 242 40 83, 24hrs. ♂
BIERHIMMEL, Oranienstr. 183, (030) 615 31 22, 15:00-03:00. ♂
BIVALENT, Friedrichsgracht 50, (030) 309 51 80, daily from 10:00. ♂

GERMANY

BKA, Mehringdamm 32-34, (030) 251 01 12. ♂

BLIND DATE, Joachimstaler Str. 24, (030) 881 94 88. ♂

BLUE BOY BAR, Eisenacher Str 3a, (030) 218 25 18, 22:00-06:00. ♂

BREDOWSTÜBCHEN, Bredowstrasse 8a, (030) 395 29 96, 24hrs. ♂

BURGFRIEDEN, Wichertstr. 69, (030) 445 72 79, daily 19:00-04:00. ♂

CHAPEAU CLAQUE, Bergstr. 25, (030) 282 2983, from 21:00 (closed Sun). ♂

CHEZ NOUS, Marburger Strasse 14, (030) 213 18 10, shows at 20:30 & 23:00. ♂

CITY KLAUSE, Friedrichstr. 112b, (030) 282 80 87, 10:00-24:00 (Fri, Sat till later), closed Mon. ♂

CLUB 70, Ebersstrasse 58, (030) 784 17 86, cruise bar, from 21:00, Sun from 16:00, closed Mon. ♂

CLUB AMSTERDAM, Barbarossastr. 38, (030) 213 32 32, 19:00-03:00. ♂

CORDON ROUGE, Schönhauser Allee 39a, (030) 442 42 13, 22:00-06:00. ♂

COULEUR, Leykestr. 18, (030) 622 91 88, 16:00-01:00. ♂

COXX, Nürnberger Str. 17, (030) 213 6155, 17:00-02:00 (Fri, Sat 18:00-03:00, Sun from 18:00). ♂

DA CAPO, Kreutzigerstr. 8, (030) 589 20 24, daily 18:00-02:00. ♂

DANDY CLUB, Urbanstr. 64, (030) 691 90 13, from 22:00. ♂

DANEBEN, Motzstr. 5, (030) 217 06 33, 10:00-02:00. ♂

DATSCHA, Kranoldstr. 18, (030) 625 4024, 14:00-01:00. ♂

DIE KISTE, Rodenbergstr. 23, (030) 444 93 21, 21:00-03:00. ♂

DINELO BAR & CAFE, ★ Vorbergstrasse 10, (030) 782 21 85, large cafe & bar with lite vegetarian menu, Tues-Sun from 18:00. ✕ ♀

DREIZEHN, Welser Strasse 27, (030) 218 23 63, 17:00-05:00. ♂

E 116, Eisenacher Str. 116, (030) 217 0518, 20:00-03:00 (Fri, Sat till 03:00). ♂

ELDORADO, Motzstr. 20, (030) 218 25 18, 24hrs. ♂

EXTRA DRY, Pariserstr. 3, (030) 885 22 06 or 885 26 91, Bar dedicated to alcohol-free & drug-free lifestyle. No alcohol, no drugs, pool table, 11:00-23:00 (Fri, Sat till 24:00), closed Mon. ♀

FINGERHUT, Damaschkestr. 12-14, (030) 323 17 13, from 21:00, closed Wed. ♂

FLAIR, Nachodstr. 5, (030) 214 22 44, daily 06:00-05:00. ♂

FLAX, Chodowieckistr. 41, (030) 441 9856, 18:00-04:00 (Fri, Sat till 05:00). ♂

FLIPFLOP, Kulmer Strasse 20a, (030) 216 28 25, 19:00-03:00 (Sun from 11:00). ♂

FUGGER-ECK, Eisenacher Str. 3a, (030) 218 35 06, 13:00-04:00, Fri & Sat 11:00-05:00, closed Sun. ♂

GEMS, Eisenacher Str. 2, 15:00-03:00 (Sat, Sun from 10:00). ♂

HARLEKIN, Schaperstr. 12-13, 218 25 79, Mon-Sat from 16:00, Sun 14:00-01:00. ♂

KALESCHE, Knesebeckstr 56-58, (030) 881 83 16, 24hrs. ♂

KITCHEN, Fuggerstr. 34, (030) 218 87 03, 16:00-04:00. ♂

KNAST, ★ Fuggerstr. 34, (030) 218 10 26, cruise bar, 21:00-05:00. ♂

KNE-MO, Knesebeckstr. 35, (030) 883 45 47, daily 12:00-04:00. ♂

KOMMA MELINA, Fasanenstr. 40, (030) 883 1676, from 21:00. ♂

KOMMA SAFARI, Ossastr. 38, (030) 623 15 11, 16:00-02:00. ♂

KUMPELNEST 3000, Lützowstr. 23, (030) 261 69 18, 17:00-05:00.

LA VIE EN ROSE, Lise Meltner Str. 11, (030) 345 1202. ♂

LE MOUSTACHE, Gartenstr. 4, (030) 281 72 77, 20:00-03:00, closed Mon. ♂

LENZ BAR, Eisenacher Str. 3, from 20:00. ♂

LET'S GO, Hertzbergstr. 22, (030) 687 0934, from 17:00. ♂

LILLI MARLENE, Voigstr. 41, 15:00-02:00. ♂

LÜTZOWER LAMPE, Witzlebenstr. 38, (030) 321 20 97, reservations: 87 19 00, show bar Wed-Sun 22:00-03:00. ♂

M, Pfalzburger Str. 14, (030) 885 4786, from 19:00. ♂

MAURIN, Ohlauer Str. 3, (030) 612 7065, 21:00-05:00. ♂

MEMORY'S, Fuggerstr. 37, (030) 213 52 71, from 18:00. ♂

MINIBAR, Jebenstr. 9-11, (030) 315 9143, 12:00-24:00. ♂

NA UND, Prenzlauer Allee 193, at Dimitroffstr., (030) 442 89 48. ♂

NEW ACTION, Kleiststr. 35, (030) 211 82 56, from 21:00 (Sun from 13:00), frequented by some leather men. ♂

O-BAR, Oranienstr. 168, (030) 615 68 17, from 16:00. ♂

PAIRS OUT, Mittenwalderstr. 16, daily from 22:00, closed Mon. ♂

PICK AB, Greifenhagener Str. 16, (030) 445 8523, 23:00-06:00 (Fri, Sat till later). ♂

PINOCCHIO, Fuggerstr. 3, (030) 218 57 36, 24hrs. ♂

PRAGERS, Kleiststr. 7, (030) 211 7702, 16:00-02:00 (Fri, Sat till 03:00), closed Sun. ♂

PUSSY CAT, Kalkreuthstr. 7, (030) 213 35 86, 18:00-06:00, closed Tues. ♂

RIVIERA, Glasower Str. 51, (030) 625 1278, 12:00-03:00 (Fri, Sat till later, Sun from 15:00). ♂

ROLFS PUB, Ebertstr. 58, (030) 782 38 89, from 19:00 (Sun from 18:00). ♂

SCHEUNE, Motzstr. 25, (030) 213 8085, frequented by leathermen, from 21:00 (Fri, Sat from 22:00). ♂

SCHOPPENSTUBE, Schönhauser Allee 44, (030) 442 8204, 21:00-07:00. ♂

SONDERBAR, Käthe Niederk Str. 34, (030) 429 4062, 20:00-08:00. ♂

STILLER DON, Erich Weiner Str. 67, 18:00-02:00, Fri, Sat till later. ♂

TABASCO, Fuggerstr. 3, 214 26 36, 17:00-06:00 (Fri, Sat 24hrs). ♂

TOM'S BAR, Motzstr. 19, (030) 213 45 70, cruise bar frequented by leather men, 22:00-07:00, Fri & Sat till later. ♂

TONI'S HÜTTE, Mecklenburgische Str. 20, (030) 824 2545, 16:00-01:00 (closed Tues). ♂

VAGABUND KELLER, Knesebeckstrasse 77, (030) 881 15 06, 15:00-08:00. ♂

VALENTINO, Auguststr. 84, (030) 208 94 84, 18:00-03:00 (Sat from 14:00, Sun from 10:00). ♂

XL, Lychener Str. 35, (030) 441 25 60, 17:00-03:00. ♂

ZANDVOORT, Friedrich Karl Str. 15, (030) 752 20 77, from 20:00. ♂

ZUM ANHALTER BAHNHOF, Bernburgerstr. 35, (030) 261 5764, from 09:00. ♂

■ Dance Bar/Disco

ADONIS, Trautenaustr. 9, (030) 873 89 37, 18:00-02:00. ♂

AM WASSERTURM, Spandauer Damm 168, (030) 302 52 60, Wed, Sat, Sun from 21:00. ♀

BI BA BO, Pfalzburger Str. 5, (030) 883 26 85, from 16:00. ♂

BOUDOIR, Brunnenstr. 192, (030) 282 86 74, 22:00-04:00 (Sun from 20:00), closed Mon-Wed. ♂

CONNECTION BERLIN, Fuggerstr. at

PENSION NIEBUHR

NIEBUHRSTR. 74,
10629 BERLIN

(030) 324 95 95/6

Recently Remodeled
Rooms In A
Quiet Neighborhood

GERMANY

Welserstr., (030) 218 1432, Fri, Sat from 22:00. 🍸♂

DIE BUSCHE, Mühlenstr. 11-12, (030) 589 15 85, Fri, Sat 21:30-06:00; Wed, Sun 21:30-05:00. 🍸♂

E-WERK, Wilhelmstr. 43, (030) 618 10 07, Fri 24:00-10:00. 🍸♂

EWA FRAUENDISCO, Prenzlauer Allee 6, at EWA women's center, women's dance night Sat. 🍸♀

GLOBUS, Leipziger Str. 126a, (030) 609 37 02, from 24:00 (Sun 23:00-06:00), closed Mon, Tues & Thurs. 🍸♂

KLEIST CASINO, Kleiststr. 35, (030) 213 49 81, 14:00-03:00 (closed Mon, Tues). 🍸♂

LOGO DISCO, Dolziger Str. 24, 558 05 01, from 16:00. 🎵🍸♂

POUR ELLE, Kalkreuthstrasse 10, (030) 218 75 33, small bar & disco, from 21:00. Women's bar Tues & Thu-Sun, also for men on Mon, Wed. 🍸♀

SCHWUZ, Mehringdam 61, at the gay center, (030) 693 70 25, Sat from 23:00. 🍸♂

SO 36, Oranienstr. 190, Wed 22:00-06:00. 🍸♂

TOP SECRET, Jakobsohnstr. 18-20, 21:00-02:00 (closed Mon, Tues). 🍸♂

TRESOR, Leipziger Str. 126a, (030) 609 37 02, Fri & Sat from 24:00. 🍸♂

UNDERGROUND, Rochstr. 16, (030) 282 66 52, daily from 21:00. 🍸♂

ZUFALL, Pfalzburgerstr. 10, (030) 883 24 37, daily from 22:00 (closed Mon, Tues). 🍸♂

■ Cafe

ANDERES UFER, Hauptstr. 157, (030) 784 15 78, 11:00-02:00.

ARC, Fasanenstr. 81A, (030) 313 2625, 11:00-02:00 (Fri, Sat from 10:00). ♂

BERLIN CONNECTION, Martin Luther Str. 19, (030) 213 11 16, daily 14:00-02:00. ♂

BIZ CAFÉ, Rhinower Str. 8, (030) 449 75 90, fetish cafe with darkroom, 16:00-22:00 (Fri-Sat 16:00-22:00). ♂

CAFE AM MÄRCHENBRUNNEN, Am Friedrichshain 33, (030) 426 4517, 16:00-24:00. ♂

CAFE ANAL, Muskauer Str. 15, (030) 618 70 64, daily from 15:00 (from 17:00 in winter), Mon women's night. ♂

CAFE BERIO, Maassenstr. 7, (030) 216 19 46, 08:00-01:00. ♂

CAFE COUTURE, Gitschiner Str. 95, open Wed, Fri & Sat from 19:00. ♂

CAFE DOPPELFENSTER, Ackerstr. 12, (030) 208 7418, 16:00-02:00. ♂

CAFE ECKE SCHÖNHAUSER, Kastanienallee 2, 448 33 31, 12:00-05:00 (Fri, Sat from 16:00). ♂

CAFE IBIZA, Liniernstr. 134, (030) 282 49 75, 24hrs. ♂

CAFE SAVIGNY, Grolmanstr. 53-54, (030) 312 8195, 10:00-02:00. ♂

CAFE SEIDENFADEN, Dircksen Str. 47, (030) 283 2783, drug- & alcohol-free women's cafe, 11:00-21:00 (Sat, Sun till 18:00), closed Mon. ♀

CAFE SENEFELDER, Schönhauser Allee 137, 282 77 85, daily 19:00-02:00.

CAFE SUNDSTRÖM, Mehringdamm 61, from 12:00 (Fri, Sat 12:00-24:00). ♂

CAFE VOLTAIRE, Stuttgarter Platz 14, (030) 324 50 28, daily 24hrs. ♂

DAS KUCKUCKSEI, Wicherstr. 63, (030) 444 0422, from 18:00. ♂

EWA FRAUENCAFE, Prenzlauer Allee 6, at EWA women's center, Mon-Fri 16:00-23:00. ♀

FLEDERMAUS, Joachimsthaler Str. 17, (030) 883 4628, 15:00-06:00. ♂

FRAUENCAFE, Glogauer Str. 22, (030) 612 31 35, Mon-Thurs 15:00-17:00. ♀

FRAUENCAFÉ FUTURA, Hohenzollern Str. 11, (030) 801 62 61, women's cafe. ♀

HIMMELREICH, Nollendorfer Str. 27, (030) 216 56 03, 11:00-03:00 (Fri, Sat till 06:00). ♂

JIM'S, Eberswalder Str. 32, (030) 440 63 79, 08:00-05:00. ♂

LE BISTROT, Rheinstr. 55, (030) 852 49 14, 19:00-05:00.

MANN-O-METER, Motzstrasse 5, (030) 216 80 08, cafe with wine & beer, occasional films, discussions, information center mainly for men. Open Mon-Sat 15:00-23:00 (Sun till 21:00). 🍴♂

NOVEMBER, Husemannstr. 15, (030) 442 8425, from 10:00. ♂

OH-ASE, Rathausstr. 5, (030) 242 30 30, 10:00-02:00 (Sun from 14:00). ♂

SCHOKO CAFÉ, Mariannenstr. 6, (030) 615 15 61, 13:00-24:00 (closed Mon), disco last Sat. Also Hamam steam bath 13:00-22:00 (Mon from 17:00). 🍸♀

TOM'S EISCAFÉ, Düppelstr. 39a, (030) 791 65 57, 07:00-22:00 (Sat from 09:00, Sun from 10:00). ♂

■ Saunas/Health Clubs

APOLLO CITY SAUNA, Kurfürstenstr. 101, (030) 213 24 24, daily 13:00-07:00. ♂

GATE SAUNA, Wilhelmstr. 81, (030) 229 9430, 11:00-07:00.

ROMANCE, Invalidenstr. 90, (030) 282 92 06, 13:00-08:00.

STEAM SAUNA CLUB, Kurfürstenstr. 113, (030) 218 40 60, 11:00-07:00, Fri-Sun 24hrs.

TREIBHAUS, Schönhauser Allee 132, (030) 448 4503, 15:00-06:00.

■ Restaurants

ABENDMAHL, Muskauer Str. 9, (030) 612 51 70, 18:00-01:00.

ALTBERLINER BIERSTUBEN, Saarbrückenstr. 17, (030) 282 89 33, daily 12:00-02:00.

CALVADOS, Bayreuther Str. 10, (030) 213 47 79, 11:00-02:00 (Fri, Sat till 03:00), Sun 17:00-01:00.

HOFGARTEN, Regensburger Str. 5, (030) 218 18 83, bar & restaurant, 18:00-01:00, summer 17:00-01:00. 🍸

OFFENBACH STUBEN, Stubbenkammerstr. 8, (030) 445 85 02, daily 18:00-02:00.

RESTE FIDELE, Bleibtreustr. 41, (030) 881 16 05, restaurant & bar, 11:00-01:00 (Fri, Sat till 02:00). 🍸♂

RIEHMERS, Yorckstr. 84, (030) 785 27 36, 18:00-24:00, closed Sun.

SLOBO'S, Heimstrasse 8, (030) 693 09 00, 17:00-01:00, closed Wed.

■ Retail & Bookstores

BRUNO'S, Kurfürstendamm 227, (030) 882 42 90, 10:00-22:00, closed Sun.

GALERIE JANSSEN, Pariser Str. 45, (030) 881 15 90, men's art gallery, 11:00-18:30 (Sat till 14:00), closed Sun.

LILITH, Knesebeckstrasse 86, (030) 312 31 02, women's bookstore with feminist & lesbian books in German & English. Open 10:00-18:30, Sat till 14:00.

PRINZ EISENHERZ, Bleibtreustr. 52, (030) 313 99 36, gay bookstore, 10:00-18:30 (Sat till 14:00).

■ Leathers/Piercing

BEI GÜNTHER, Fredericiastr. 7, (030) 302 84 94, by appointment, closed Sun.

HAUTNAH, Uhlandstr. 170, (030) 882 3434, 10:30-18:30 (closed Sun).

■ Erotica

BAD BOY'Z, Schliemannstr. 38, (030) 440 81 65.

BEATE UHSE INT, Brunnenstr. 2; Invalidenstr. at Schw.weg; Hardenbergstr. 28; Kantstr. 5.

BLUE MOVIE KINO, Kurfürstendamm 227, (030) 882 68 98.

CITY MEN, Fuggerstr. 26, 218 29 59

CONNECTION GARAGE, Fuggerstr. 33, (030) 218 14 32.

EROTIC SHOP, Motzstr. 11, (030) 215 35 74.

GO UP, Katnstr. 117, (030) 312 30 45.

JAXX, Motzstr. 19.

MAN SHOP, Kalkreuthstr. 15, at Fuggerstr.

ORION SHOP, Leibnitzstr. 58.

PLAYGROUND, Courbierstr. 9, (030) 218 21 64.

POOL, Schaperstr. 11, (030) 214 1989.

BIELEFELD

■ Information

AIDS HILFE, (0521) 13 33 88.

FRAUENKULTURZENTRUM, FRAUENCAFE & KNEIPE, Am Zwinger 16, (0521) 686 67, women's cultural center Mon-Thurs 17:00-20:00, Frauencafé & Frauenkneipe (women's cafe & bar) Mon-Fri 16:00-24:00.

LESBENARCHIV, Am Zwinger 16, at

GERMANY

Frauenkulturzentrum, (0521) 667 13, lesbian archives, Wed 19:00-21:00.
LESBENTELEFON, (0521) 13 83 90, Wed 19:00-21:00.

Bars
MAGNUS, August Bebelstr. 112, (0521) 629 53, 18:00-01:00. ♂
MUTTI'S BIERSTUBE, Friedr. Verleger Str. 20, (0521) 61 816, 21:00-01:00 (Fri, Sat till 02:00). ♂
ROLANDSECK, Heeper Strasse 28, (0521) 622 36, daily 24:00-05:00 (Fri, Sat till 07:00). ♂

Dance Bar/Disco
FAR OUT, Niederwall 12, (0521) 175 958, gay Tues 22:00-03:00. 🍴♂

Cafe
SCHÄFERS CAFE, Artur Ladebeck Str. 5, (0521) 17 40 77, from 09:00. ♂

Erotica
NOVUM MARKT, Herforderstr. 122, (0521) 136 51 46.
SHOP INTIM, Bahnhofstr. 47, (0521) 179 550.

BOCHOLT

Bars
OLD PADDY, Franz Str. 21, (02871) 160 60, 21:00-04:00, closed Tues. ♂

Erotica
EROTIK WORLD, Münsterstr. 63.

BOCHUM

Information
AIDS HILFE, (0234) 519 10.

Dance Bar/Disco
AFTER EIGHT, Alte Bahnhofstr. 214, at Zwichenfall, (0234) 28 76 50, Sun 20:00-01:00. 🍴♂
FRAUENSCHWOOF, Langendreer, at Alter Bahnhof, women's dance night 2nd Sat. 🍴♀

Cafe
FRAUENCAFE TRA DI NOI, Oskar-Hoffmann-Str. 109, (0234) 30 91 69, kommunikationszentrum & gallerie, women's cafe, gathering place & gallery Tues-Sun 15:00-24:00. ♀

Retail & Bookstores
FRAUENBUCHLADEN AMAZONAS, Schmidstr. 12, (0234) 68 31 94, women's bookstore.

Erotica
BEATE UHSE, Kurt Schuhmacher Pl. 9.
SEXYLAND, Humboldtstr. 34, at Südring.
SHOW CENTER, Rottstr. 16, (0234) 162 71.

BONN

Information
AIDS HILFE, (0228) 21 90 21.
FRAUENMUSEUM, Im Krausfeld 10, (0228) 63 84 65, women's museum, open Mon-Sat 20:00-23:00.
LESBEN-UND-SCHWULENZENTRUM, Endenicher Str. 1, (0228) 63 00 39, lesbian & gay center, Mon 20:00-24:00, Sat 10:00-14:00, Sun 16:00-20:00. Women meet Tues from 20:00.

Bars
BOBA'S BAR, Josefstr. 17, (0228) 65 06 85, 21:00-03:00, closed Mon. ♂
LE COPAIN, Berliner Platz 5, (0228) 63 99 35, 14:00-02:00 (Fri, Sat till 03:00), Sun from 15:00). ♂
ZARAH L., Maxstrasse 22, (0228) 63 46 35, Wed, Thurs 21:30-02:00 & Fri, Sat from 22:00. Frauenabend (women's bar night) Mon. ♪♂

Dance Bar/Disco
SHARLIE, Kölnerstr. at Theaterstr., 17:00-03:00 (Sun from 15:00). 🍴♂
YSABEAU, Martinsplatz 2a, (0228) 65 16 15, Wed, Fri, Sat 21:00-05:00. 🍴♂

Retail & Bookstores
BONNER FEMINISTISCHES ARCHIV UND BÜCHEREI, Dorotheenstr. 20, (0228) 68 58 14. Feminist bookstore and archives, Tues, Thurs, Fri 14:00-18:00, Wed 14:00-20:00.
BUCHLADEN 46, Kaiserstr. 46, (0228) 22 36 08, general bookstore with a gay section, 10:00-18:30 (Sat till 14:00), closed Sun.
NORA, Kekulestrasse 35, (0228) 224 491, women's books.

Erotica
DR. MÜLLER'S, Bischofsplatz 4.
EROTIK SHOP, Aennchenplatz 7; Berliner Freiheit 18.

BOTTROP

Information
LESBENTELEFON, (02041) 635 93, lesbian line, Mon 17:00-20:00.

BRAUNSCHWEIG

Information
AIDS HILFE, (0531) 141 41.
LABRYS LESBENGRUPPE, (0531) 33 29 86, lesbian group, meets 1st Tues from 20:00. Call for details.
SPINSTERS FRAUENKULTURZENTRUM, Steintorwall 8, (0531) 124 641, women's info center.

Bars
SIR HENRY, Petersilienstr. 1-3, (0531) 434 20, 21:00-02:00, Fri & Sat till 03:00, closed Mon. ♂
WHY NOT, Echternstr. 9, (0531) 44 166, from 19:00 (Fri, Sat from 21:00). ♂

Cafe
LILITH FRAUENCAFE, Rosenstr. 6, (0531) 79 67 60, women's cafe. ♀

Retail & Bookstores
FRAUENBUCHLADEN, Magnikirchstr. 4, (0531) 407 44.

Erotica
BOUTIQUE INTIM, Friedrich Wilhelm Str. 31, (0531) 449 22.
FRANKIES EROTIK SHOP, Fallersleber Str. 27, (0531) 147 74.
ORION SHOP, Ägidienmarkt 9, (0531) 432 83.
SEX BAZAR, Wendenstr. 51, (0531) 404 40.

BREMEN

Information
AIDS HILFE, (0421) 70 2012.
BELLADONNA KULTUR, KOMMUNIKATIONS UND BILDUNGSZENTRUM, Sonnenstr. 8, (0421) 70 35 34, women's culture, communications and information center.
FRAUENKULTURHAUS, Am Krummen Arm 1, (0421) 701 632, women's center, Wed 10:00-12:00.
LESBENTELEFON, (0421) 339 9046, Fri 20:00-22:00.
RAT UND TAT ZENTRUM, Theodor Körnerstr. 1, (0421) 70 41 70, gay center, women meet Sat 17:00.

Bars
BELL'S, Auf der Brake 11, close to the train station, (0421) 32 51 44. ♂
BRONX, Bohnenstr. 1b, (0421) 70 24 04, cruise bar frequented by leather men, from 20:00. 🍴♂
DAVID, Rembertistrasse 33, (0421) 32 04 96, 22:00-06:00. ♂
FRAUENKNEIPE, Lahnstr. 37-39, at Klöntje, women's bar night Fri from 20:00. ♀
HEXENKELLER, An der Weide 24, (0421) 327 723, 21:00-02:00. ♂
LESBEN & SCHWULEN-TEESTUBE, Buchtstrasse, at the Naturfreundehaus, lesbian & gay social, Thurs from 20:00. ♀♂
MADAME LOTHAR, Kolpingstr. 6, (0421) 337 9191, 20:00-02:00 (Fri, Sat till later). ♪♂
NEW QUEENS, A.d. Schleifmühle 10, (0421) 32 59 12, from 21:00 (Fri, Sat 20:00-08:00, Sun from 17:00). ♂
ZUM RENDEZVOUS, Elisabethstr. 34, (0421) 383 159, 17:00-02:00 (Fri, Sat from 14:30). ♂

Dance Bar/Disco
FRAUENLESBEN DISCO, Thedinghauserstr. 1156, at the Jugendfreizeitheim, women's & lesbian disco, ask locally for exact dates. 🍴♀
TOM'S, A.d. Schleifmühle 49, (0421) 32 35 34, from 22:00 (closed Mon, Tues, Thurs). 🍴♂

FERRARI GUIDES' GAY TRAVEL A to Z - 18th EDITION

GERMANY

■ Cafe
CAFÉ HOMOLULU, Theodor Körner Str. 1, (0421) 70 00 07, 20:00-01:00, Sun from 15:00, closed Mon, Thurs.

FRAUEN INFO CAFE, Humboldtstr. 116, at De Colores, Tues, Thurs 15:00-19:00. ♀

FRAUENCAFE IM FRAUENKULTURHAUS, Am Krummen Arm 1, (0421) 70 16 32, women's cafe at women's cultural center. Lesbengruppe (lesbian group) meets 1st & 3rd Thurs from 20:00. ♀

■ Saunas/Health Clubs
CITY CLUB SAUNA, Humboldtstr. 144, (0421) 701 465, gay-only Tues & Sat 17:00-01:00. ♂

PERSEUS, Waller Heerstr. 126, (0421) 38 51 00, 16:00-24:00.

STEAM SAUNA WALLE, Steffensweg 157, (0421) 396 60 97.

■ Restaurants
BIENENKORB, Rembertistr. 32, (0421) 32 72 18, daily 11:00-06:00.

■ Retail & Bookstores
FRAUENBUCHLADEN HAGAZUSSA, Friesenstr. 12, (0421) 741 40, women's bookstore.

■ Leathers/Piercing
BIZZARE LUST, Herdentor Steinweg 6, 09:00-18:00, closed Sun.

H & M LEDERWERKSTATT, Neukirchstr. 18, (0421) 371 430.

■ Erotica
GAY MOVIE, An der Weide 22, (0421) 337 81 79.

MEN'S SEVEN, Am Dobben 7, (0421) 32 36 87.

SEX WORLD, Bahnhofstr. 24.

VIDEOWORLD, Rembertistr. 56, (0421) 32 58 98.

BREMERHAVEN

■ Bars
BEI JOHANN, Hafenstr. 36, (0471) 408 28, 21:00-03:00. ♂

SAND, Karlsburg 9, (0471) 41 23 40, women only 2nd & 4th Wed. ♀

WHY NOT, Körnerstrasse 33, (0471) 50 15 25, from 21:00 (Fri, Sat 22:00-05:00), closed Mon. ♂

BRUNKEN/ WESTERWALD

■ Women's Accommodations
LICHTQUELLE, FRAUENBILDUNGSHAUS, Hochstr. 11, 57539 Brunken, (02742) 715 87, women-only healing retreat, shared bath, full board, vegetarian cuisine (mainly macrobiotic), meeting rooms. ♀

BÜCKEN

■ Women's Accommodations
FRAUENFERIENHAUS ALTENBÜCKEN, Schürmannsweg 25, 27333, (04251) 7899, fax: (04251) 6291, women-only retreat with classes available, shopping, swimming & sauna nearby, single, double & dorm rooms with shared baths, groceries provided. ♀

CHARLOTTENBERG

■ Women's Accommodations
FRAUENLANDHAUS, Holzappeler Str 3, 56379 Charlottenberg, (06439) 7531, women-only bed & breakfast guesthouse with workshops, 15 rooms with single & double beds, shared baths, vegetarian cuisine, buffet breakfast, lunch, dinner. ♀

CHEMNITZ

■ Information
AIDS HILFE, (0371) 415 223.

LESBENGRUPPE, Hainstr. 34, lesbian group meets here.

LILA VILA, Kassbergerstr. 22, (0371) 326 78, Frauenbegegnungszentrum (women's info. center).

■ Dance Bar/Disco
LEBENSFREUDE, Werner Seelenbinderstr. 6, (0371) 58 45 95, gay Sat 19:00-03:00. 🔞♂

COLOGNE
SEE KÖLN.

COTTBUS

■ Bars
HAUS 23, Marienstr 23, 79 79 71, 18:30-01:00 (Fri, Sat till 03:00). ♂

LIPA, Altermarkt, city center, 252 50, 09:00-01:00. ♂

■ Erotica
ORION, Friedrich Ebert Str 15, 79 63 48.

DARMSTADT

■ Information
AIDS HILFE, (06151) 31 11 77.

■ Bars
HARLEKIN, Heinheimer Str. 18, (06151) 71 28 81, 18:00-01:00. ♂

■ Cafe
FRAUENCAFE IM FRAUENZENTRUM, Emilstrasse 10, (06151) 71 49 52, women's café in women's center, 10:00-14:00 (Thurs from 20:00). ♀

■ Erotica
ORION SHOP, Heidelberger Str. 36, (06151) 29 19 18.

VIDEO WORLD MAN SHOP & KINO, Elisabethenstr. 40.

DORTMUND

■ Information
AIDS HILFE, (0231) 52 76 37.

LESBENTELEFON, (0231) 83 19 19, lesbian line, Sat 10:00-12:00.

■ Bars
BURGTOR CLUB, Burgwall 17, (0231) 57 17 48, 13:00-01:00, Fri till 03:00. ♂

CHÉ COOLALA, Heyden Rynschstr. 2, (0231) 17 81 45, 20:00-01:00 (Sat 22:00-03:00). ♂

CLUB 64, Rheinische Str. 64, (0231) 14 32 30, daily 20:00-04:00, closed Mon. ♂

CLUB ROTE MARLENE, Humboldtstr. 1, (0231) 14 36 15, cruise bar frequented by leathermen, daily from 21:00 (closed Mon). 🔞♂

DON CLUB, Johannisborn 6, (0231) 571 676, 20:00-01:00 (Fri, Sat till 03:00). ♂

FLEDERMAUS, Königswall 17, (0231) 14 97 85, 10:00-01:00 (Sat, Sun from 07:00). ♂

KRISTAL, Ludwigstr. 14, (0231) 554 427, from 22:00 (Fri, Sat from 23:00), closed Mon, Tues. 🔞♂

LAFAYETTE, Südwall 11, (0231) 575 036, from 20:00 (Fri, Sat till 04:00), closed Thurs. ♂

NOUVELLE, Ludwigstr. 9, (0231) 57 45 40, 10:00-01:00, Fri, Sat till 03:00. ♂

SIDI CLUB, Burgwall 5, (0231) 52 55 59, daily from 20:00, closed Mon. ♂

■ Dance Bar/Disco
DAS PHANTOM, Westenhellweg 134, (0231) 914 37 01, Wed 20:00-01:00, Fri & Sat 22:00-05:00. 🔞♂

■ Cafe
CAFÉ BLU, Ruhrallee 69, (0231) 12 61 77, 18:00-01:00 (Sun from 11:00). ♂

CHAT NOIR, Alter Burgwall 2-6, (0231) 521 900, 08:00-24:00 (Fri, Sat till 03:00, Sun from 10:00).

FRAUENCAFE GERÜCHTEKÜCHE, Adlerstr 30, (0231) 14 08 21, Sun 16:00-21:00. ♀

ZAUBERMAUS, Kielstr. 32b, (0231) 81 46 49, 16:00-01:00, Fri, Sat till 03:00.

■ Saunas/Health Clubs
SAUNA AM BURGWALL, Leuthardstr. 9, (0231) 57 46 00, 15:00-23:00, later Sat.

SAUNA FONTÄNE, Gutenbergstr. 50, (0231) 52 39 99, 15:00-22:00, closed Thurs.

■ Restaurants
KITCHEN, Gerichtstr. 19, (0231) 524 442, 11:00-01:00.

■ Retail & Bookstores
LITFASS, Münsterstr. 107, (0231) 83 47 24, general bookshop with a gay section, Mon-Fri 10:00-20:00, Sat till 14:00.

■ Erotica
ADONIS CENTER, Bornstr. 14, video shop.

BEATE UHSE, Westenhellweg 51.

DRESDEN

■ Information
AIDS HILFE, (0351) 441 6142.

LESBENTELEFON, (0351) 514 70, lesbian line Wed 19:00-22:00.

GERMANY

SOWIESO FRAUENZENTRUM, Angelikastr. 1, (0351) 514 70, lesbengruppe, women's center with lesbian group meetings, lesbian disco 2nd & 4th Sat.

Bars
BUNKER, Florian Geyer Str. 3, enter from Bundschuh, (0351) 441 61 43, Dresden leather group bar night, Fri from 22:00. ♥⚤♂
CLUB 25, Fechnerstr. 2a, (0351) 569 28 83, bar & disco. Bar Wed 20:00-02:00; Disco Fri 21:00-02:00. 🍴♂
EXTRABLATT, Prager Str., (0351) 495 25 21, 09:00-01:00 (Sat, Sun from 14:00). ♂
PINK FLAMINGO, Gutschmidstr. 7, at Elypso, (0351) 441 02 58, gay Wed from 21:00, DJ. 🍴♂

Dance Bar/Disco
APOLLO, Oskar Mai Str. 3, (0351) 432 1859, 18:00-03:00, closed Mon. 🍴♂

Retail & Bookstores
FRAUENBUCHLADEN PUSTEBLUME, Martin Luther Str. 23.

DUISBURG

Information
AIDS HILFE, (0203) 66 66 33.

Bars
BLIND DATE, Realschulstrasse 10, (0203) 28 79 80, daily 20:00-02:00 (Fri, Sat till 05:00). ♂
CAFE BERLIN, An der Bleeck 40-42, (0203) 24 273, 16:00-02:00 (Fri, Sat till 03:00), closed Mon. ♀
CASANOVA, Düsseldorfer Str. 110, (0203) 229 61, daily 20:00-05:00, closed Thurs. ♂
HARLEKIN, Realschulstr. 16, (0203) 262 44, 18:00-02:00 (Fri, Sat till 03:00), closed Wed. ♂
PILSSTÜBCHEN, Hohe Strasse 24, (0203) 28 71 62, 15:00-02:00. ♂

Dance Bar/Disco
CLUB FILOU, Realschulstr. 10, (0203) 207 89, 20:00-01:00 (Fri, Sat till 04:00), closed Tues. 🍴♂

Saunas/Health Clubs
GAY SAUNA, Krummacherstr. 44, (0203) 244 10, daily 15:00-23:00.

Erotica
GAY SEX SHOP, Beekstr. 82, (0203) 274 40, cinema, 10:00-18:00 (Sat till 14:), closed Sun.
MAN SHOP, Kasinostr. 4a.

DÜSSELDORF

Information
AIDS HILFE, (0211) 726 05 26.
FRAUENBERATUNGSTELLE, Ackerstr. 144, (0211) 68 68 54, Frauenberatung (women's info), women's bar night Thurs.
LESBEN-SCHWULENZENTRUM, Kronenstrasse 74, lesbian & gay center.

Bars
BEL AIR, Oststr. 116, (0211) 161 978, 11:00-02:00 (Fri, Sat till 03:00). ♂
BISTRO INSIDER, Grupellostr. 32, (0211) 364 218, 11:00-05:00. ♂
CITY BISTRO, Luisenstr. 129, (0211) 373 973, 12:00-01:00 (Fri, Sat till 06:00). ♂
COME BACK, Charlottenstr. 60, (0211) 164 0978, 11:00-02:00 (Fri, Sat till 03:00). ♂
FIVE CLUB, Grupellostr. 5, (0211) 164 0442, 17:00-01:00 (Fri, Sat till 03:00, Sun from 15:00). ♂
HARLEKIN, Corneliusstr. 9, (0211) 37 46 28, 18:00-02:00 (Fri, Sat till 03:00, Sun from 12:00). ♂
HECKER, Lambertusstr. 10, (0211) 13 19 46, 15:00-01:00 (Sun from 11:00), closed Mon. ♂
IM GOLDENEN SPIEGEL, Ackerstr. 49, (0211) 164 02 54, from 16:00. ♂
LE CLOU, Grupellostr. 7, (0211) 36 43 65, 10:00-01:00 (Sat, Sun till 03:00). ♂
LESBENKNEIPE, Kronenstrasse 76, at the Lesben- und Schwulenzentrum, lesbian bar night at lesbian & gay center, 2nd & 4th Sat. ♀
MAU MAU, Kölner Str. 54, (0211) 358 268, 13:00-05:00. ♂
NÄHKÖRBCHEN, Hafenstr. 11, (0211) 323 0265, 18:00-01:00 (Sat 18:00-03:00), closed Mon. ♂
RABIT'S IN, Stresemannstr. 31, 18:00-01:00 (Fri, Sat till 03:00, Sun from 16:00). ♂
STUDIO 1, Jahnstrasse 2a, (0211) 37 87 43, daily 17:00-05:00. ♂
THEATER STUBEN, Luisenstrasse 33, (0211) 37 22 44, 12:00-03:00 (Mon, Wed, Thurs till 01:00). ♂
TWIST, Grupellostr. 32, (0211) 369 548, 16:00-03:00 (Sun from 13:00). ♂
VALENTINO, Bahnstr. 63, (0211) 36 29 59, 20:00-05:00, closed Mon. 🍴♀
WILMA Charlottenstr. 60, (0211) 35 17 37, daily 13:00-05:00. ♂
ZUM GOLDENEN EINHORN, Ratinger Str. 18, (0211) 32 64 06, daily 11:00-01:00 (Sun from 18:00). ♂

Dance Bar/Disco
FRAUENSCHWOOF IM ZAKK, Fichtenstr. 40, popular women's disco, 1st Fri from 22:00. 🍴♀
GAYHOUSE, Ratinger Str. 10, at Ratinger Hof, (0211) 328 777, gay Sun 23:00-05:00. 🍴♂
LESBENSCHWOOF, Oberbilkerallee 327, at Cafe Rosa Mond, Thurs from 21:00, men welcome. 🍴♀
RAMROD, Charlottenstr. 85, (0211) 35 41 01, Thurs-Sat 23:00-05:00, Sun 19:00-01:00. 🍴♂
WOMEN'S DANCE NIGHT, Kronenstrasse 74, at the Lesben-Schwulenzentrum, 4th Sat. 🍴♀

Cafe
BUCHCAFE, Bilkerstr. 23A, (0211) 323 7938, 10:00-18:30 (Sat till 14:00), closed Sun & Mon.
CAFE BERNSTEIN, Oststr. 158, (0211) 35 65 20, 09:00-01:00 (Fri, Sat till 03:00). ♂
CAFE MAILBOX, Konrad Adenauer Platz 1, (0211) 164 0553, 09:00-02:00. ♂
CAFE SPITZ, Hunsrückenstr. at Bolkerstr., (0221) 32 27 70, 11:00-01:00. ♂
CAFE WINZIG, Bagelstr. 96 (0211) 44 63 83, 11:00-03:00. ♂
EXTRA DRY, Friedrichstr. 125, (0211) 344 701, 09:00-01:00 (Fri till 03:00, Sat & Sun 11:00-02:00). ♂
LA STRADA, Immermannstrasse 32, (0211) 36 24 28, daily 10:00-01:00.
ROSA MOND CAFÉ, Oberbilker Allee 327, (0211) 77 54 42, women's café & bar night, vegetarian menu, Fri 20:00-24:00. ♀

Saunas/Health Clubs
CITY SAUNA, Luisenstr. 129, (0211) 37 39 73, daily 12:00-01:00 (Fri, Sat till 06:00).
PHOENIX SAUNA, Platanenstr. 11A, (0211) 663 638, 12:00-06:00.

Retail & Bookstores
FRAUEN-BÜCHER-ZIMMER, Becherstr. 2, (0211) 46 44 05, women's bookstore.

Erotica
BEATE UHSE, Graf Adolf Str. 79.
DR. MÜLLER'S, Graf Adolf Str. 69.
EROTIC 63, Bismarckstr. 63, (0211) 35 46 01.
GAY CENTER, Nuemarktstr. 14, Fri 10:00-01:00, Sun 12:00-22:00.
GAY SHOP, Bismarckstr. 88, (0211) 35 25 86, cinema, 09:00-01:00, Sun 12:00-22:00.
GEROTHEK, Bismarckstr. 86, (0211) 356 750.
JAVANMARDI SEXMESSE, Kölner Str. 24.

EDERTAL-ANRAFF

Women's Accommodations
FRAUENBILDUNGSHAUS EDERTAL-ANRAFF, Königsbergerstr 6, 3593, 34549 Anraff, (05621) 3218, fax: (05621) 94726. women-only retreat guesthouse with restaurant & bar, numerous classes available, double room & dorms with shared baths, groceries provided, nearby pool & lake. ♀

EGESTORF

Bars
PAPPERLA CLUB, Ahornweg 7, (04175) 1073, from 18:00. ♂

EICHSTÄTT

Cafe
FRAUENCAFÉ, Luitpoldstr. 31, (08421) 65 68, women's café, Thurs 18:00-22:00. ♀

ERFURT

Information
AIDS HILFE, (0361) 731 22 33.

Bars
CLUB 111, Zwickauer Weg 4, (0361) 646 3556, 19:00-02:00 (Fri, Sat till 04:00). ♂
UFERBAR, Boyneburgufer 3, (0361) 643 1403, from 19:00. ♂

FERRARI GUIDES' GAY TRAVEL A to Z - 18th EDITION

GERMANY

Dance Bar/Disco
ATLANTIZ, Zum Nordstrand 1, Wed-Sat 21:00-03:00. 🍴♂
LESBENDISCO, Thomas Müntzerstr. 20, (0361) 642 1383, lesbian disco last Sat of the month. 🍴♀

Erotica
BEATE UHSE, Magdeburger Allee 60.
VIDEOWORLD MAN SHOP & KINO, Schillerstr. 55.

ERLANGEN

Information
FRAUENZENTRUM & LESBENBERATUNG, Gerberei 4, (09131) 20 80 23, women's center, lesbian information center & café.

Bars
DIE INSEL, Goethestr. 12, (09131) 266 16, 18:00-01:00 (Fri, Sat till 02:00). ♂

Dance Bar/Disco
MÄNNERDISCO, Fuchsenwiese, at E-Werk, (09131) 800 50, 2nd Wed 20:30-01:00. 🍴♂

ESSEN

Information
AIDS HILFE, (0201) 236 096.

Bars
CLUB GO IN, Steeler Strasse 83, (0201) 23 61 61, 20:00-05:00. ♂
IM BÜRO, Rellinghauser Str. 6, (0201) 22 61 51, 16:00-04:00 (Sat from 18:00), closed Sun. ♂
LE CARROUSSEL, Vereinstr. 16, (0201) 23 84 85, 10:00-03:00 (Fri, Sat till 05:00, Sun from 12:00). ♂

Dance Bar/Disco
FRAUENTANZ IN DER ZECHE CARL(A), Hömannstr. 10, women's dance night, 3rd Sat from 22:00. 🍴♀
NUMBER ONE, Lindenallee 71, (0201) 23 66 82, Mon, Fri, Sat 22:00-05:00. 🍴♂

Saunas/Health Clubs
ST. TROPEZ, Am Freistein 54, (0201) 32 25 41, daily 15:00-01:00.

Erotica
GAY CENTER, Friedrich Ebert Str. 70, (0201) 20 28 27, 10:00-01:00, closed Sun.
GAY SHOP, Kastanienallee 38-40.
MAN MOVIETHEK KINO MIT BAR, Vereinstr. 22, cinema and bar.
MAX SELLER, Vereinstr. 18, (0201) 23 60 10, gay shop, 10:00-20:00 (Sat till 16:00).
ORION SHOP, Lindenallee 80, (0201) 22 63 02.

FLENSBURG

Information
AIDS HILFE, (0461) 25 599.
LESBENGRUPPE, Marienkirchof 4/5, (0461) 266 11, lesbian group, meets 3rd Mon 18:00-20:00.
LESBENTELEFON, (0461) 213 47, Tues 18:00-19:00.
LUZIE'S FRAUENZIMMER, Marianstr. 29-31, women's info center, Tues-Fri 15:00-18:00.

Bars
CLUB 69, Harrisleerstr. 71, (0461) 473 79, from 21:00, closed Mon. ♂

Erotica
BEATE UHSE, Gutenbergstr. 12.
ORION SHOP, Schäferweg 14.

FÖHR/WRIXUM

Women's Accommodations
KVINDEGARD, Ohl Dörp 52, 2270 Wrixum, Island of Föhr, (04681) 8935, women-only guest apartments with vegetarian dinner restaurant, nearby pool & ocean beach, gym, weights, sauna, steam, massage within walking distance. ♀

FRANKFURT - MAIN

Information
AIDS HILFE, (069) 43 97 04, 43 97 05.
LESBEN ARCHIV, Klingerstr. 6, at the Lesbisch-Schwules Kulturhaus (lesbian & gay cultural center), (069) 29 30 45.
LESBENINFORMATIONS UND BERATUNGSTELLE (LIBS), Alte Gasse 38, (069) 28 28 83, lesbian information center, Tues, Thurs, Fri 17:00-19:30, consultancy, seminars, info and more.
LESBISCH-SCHWULES KULTURHAUS, Klingerstr. 6, (069) 29 30 45. Lesbian and gay cultural center.
SWITCHBOARD, gay & lesbian switchboard and cafe, Alte Gasse 36, (069) 28 35 35, Tues-Thurs 19:00-24:00; Fri, Sat till 01:00; Sun 15:00-24:00.

Bars
BIRMINGHAM, Zeil 92, (069) 28 74 71, 22:00-04:00, closed Mon. ♂
CLUB LA GATA, Seehofstr. 3, (069) 61 45 81. ♀
COME BACK, Alte Gasse 33-35, (069) 29 33 45, 11:00-01:00 (Fri, Sat till 04:00). ♂
FILOU, Kornmarkt 5, (069) 297 97 86, 11:00-01:00 (Fri, Sat till 02:00, Sun from 17:00). ♂
GRÖSENWAHN, Lenaustr. 97, at Nordenstr., (069) 59 93 56, 16:00-01:00 (Fri, Sat from 02:00). ♂
HINTERHAUS, Merianplatz 9, 17:00-01:00 (Fri, Sat till 02:00). ♂
IKS BISTRO, Koselstr. 42, (069) 596 23 89, 08:00-01:00 (Fri, Sat till 02:00, Sun from 16:00). ♂
KOLIBRI, Holzgraben 11, 17:00-04:00. ♂
LA GATA, Seehofstr. 3, (069) 614 581, from 20:00. ♂
LITTLE ANGEL, Gelbehirschstr. 10, (069) 293 472, 18:00-01:00 (Fri, Sat till 02:00). ♂
LUCKY'S MANHATTAN, Schäfergasse 27, (069) 28 49 19. 12:00-01:00, Fri & Sat till 02:00, Sun 15:00-01:00. ♂
MR D GAY BAR, Alte Gasse 34, (069) 29 45 06, daily 20:00-04:00. ♂
NA UND, Klapperfeldstr. 16, (069) 29 44 61, 20:00-01:00 (Fri, Sat till 02:00), closed Mon. ♂
PARAGON, Liebfrauenberg 37, (069) 20 230, from 10:00. ♂
STALL, Stiftstr. 22, (069) 29 18 80, cruise bar frequented by leather men, 21:00-04:00. 🚭♂
STEPS, Seilerstrasse 25, (069) 29 34 66, 21:00-01:00 (Fri & Sat till 02:00, Sun 17:00-01:00). ♂
TAVERNE AMSTERDAM, Waidmannstr. 31, (069) 631 33 89, 14:00-24:00 (Sun till 23:00), closed Mon. ♂
TONIGHT, Alte Gasse 26, (069) 283 753, 20:00-04:00 (Sun from 11:00). ♂
TREIBHAUS, Elefantengasse 11, (069) 29 12 31, daily 09:00-01:00 (Fri, Sat till 02:00). ♂
UNIQUE, Baumweg 20, (069) 440 000, 10:00-01:00 (Fri, Sat till 02:00, Mon from 12:00). 🍴♀♂
ZUM SCHWEJK, Schäfergasse 20, (069) 29 31 66, 11:00-01:00, Mon from 16:00 & Sun from 15:00. ♂
ZUM WINDLICHT, Allerheiligenstr. 19, (069) 291 685, 06:00-01:00 (Fri, Sat till 02:00). ♂

Dance Bar/Disco
BLUE ANGEL, Brönnerstrasse 17, (069) 28 27 72, from 23:00 (Fri, Sat from 22:00). 🍴♂
CONSTRUCTION 5, Alte Gasse 5, (069) 29 13 56, Wed-Sat from 22:00. 🍴♂
FRAUENDISCO, Am Industriehof 7-9, at the Frauenkulturhaus, (069) 70 10 17, women's disco last Sat from 21:30. 🍴♀
PLASTIK, Seilerstr. 34, (069) 285 055, Sun only 20:00-22:30 (bistro 22:00-01:00). 🍴♂
TUNNEL, Taubenstr. 17, (069) 289 421, 21:00-04:00, closed Mon. 🍴♂

Cafe
CAFÉ LILIPUT, Neue Kräme 29 (Sandhof-Passage), (069) 28 57 27, daily 10:00-24:00 (Sun from 14:00). ♀
HARVEY'S, Bornheimer Landstr. 64, (069) 49 73 03, bar & restaurant, 09:00-01:00 (Fri, Sat till 02:00). ♂
LESBIAN CAFE, Klingerstr. 6, at the gay & lesbian Kulturhaus, Sun 15:00-19:00. ♀
TANGERINE, Stiftstrasse 39, (069) 28 48 79, 11:00-04:00 (Fri, Sat till 06:00). ♂
RENDEZVOUS, Zeil 1, (069) 28 33 27, 12:00-23:00 (Oct-Mar: 09:00-02:00), closed Tues. ♂

Saunas/Health Clubs
AMSTERDAM SAUNA, Waidmannstr. 31, (069) 631 33 71, 14:00-23:00, closed Mon.

GERMANY

CONTINENTAL BATHHOUSE, Alte Gasse 5, (069) 28 27 57, 14:00-08:00.
PALACE, Braubachstr. 1, (069) 282 852, 14:00-01:00 (Fri, Sat till 02:00, Sun from 06:00).

Retail & Bookstores
BACKDOOR, Eckenh. Landstrasse 60b, (069) 28 43 11, gay bookshop, 12:00-20:00, closed Sun.
FRAUENBUCHLADEN, Kiesstrasse 27, (069) 70 52 95, women's bookstore.
OSCAR WILDE, Alte Gasse 51, (069) 281 260, gay bookstore, 10:00-18:30 (Sat till 14:00), closed Sun.

Leathers/Piercing
LEDERSTUDIO, Rotlintstr. 11, (069) 43 91 87, Tues-Fri 10:00-18:00 (Mon from 14:00, Sat till 13:00).

Erotica
BEATE UHSE, Stiftstr. 4; Taunusstr. 38; Kaiserstr. 53 & 57; Flughafen (Halle B).
DR. MÜLLER'S & NEW MAN PLAZA, Kaiserstr. 66. Dr Müller's: Flughafen (Halle A & C).
GOOD VIBRATIONS, Eckenheimer Landstr. 60B, (069) 59 00 75.
HEAVEN, Holzgraben 9, (069) 29 46 55.
JEROME SHOP & KINO, Elbestr. 17.
ORION, Friedberger Landstr. 126.
US VIDEO SHOP, Schäfergasse 38, (069) 29 33 78.

FREIBURG

Information
AIDS HILFE, (0761) 27 69 24.
FEMINISTISCHES ARCHIV, Wilhelmstr. 15.
FRAUENZENTRUM, Schwarzwaldstr. 107, (0761) 38 33 90, women's center, lesbian group Sappho meets Tues from 20:00.
LESBENTELEFON, (0761) 38 33 90, Wed 20:00-22:00.

Bars
BELLE EPOQUE, Günwälderstr. 21, (0761) 372 00, 13:00-02:00 (Fri till 03:00, Sat 19:00-03:00). ♂
SONDER BAR, Salzstr. 13, (0761) 339 30, 13:00-01:00 (Fri, Sat till 02:00, Sun from 18:00). ♂

Dance Bar/Disco
PARABEL, Universitätsstr. 3, enter from Cafe Journal, (0761) 30 634, Sun 22:00-03:00. ♂
XTREME, Kaiser Josef Str. 264, (0761) 202 00 47, Wed 22:00-03:00, Thurs 21:00-03:00, Fri & Sat 21:00-04:00. ♂

Cafe
FRAUENKNEIPE, Wilhelmstrasse 15, at Jos Fritz bookstore location, women's café 1st, 3rd & 5th Fri. ♀
MASONERIA, Niemenstr. 8, (0761) 32 800, 11:00-01:00 (Sun from 17:00). ♂

Saunas/Health Clubs
THERMOS, Lehenerstr. 21, (0761) 27 52 39, 16:00-23:00, Sat, Sun from 14:00, closed Mon.

Retail & Bookstores
JOS FRITZ, Wilhelmstr. 15, (0761) 26 877, bookstore 09:00-18:30. Scheduled gay Fri evening, call for details.

Erotica
MANHATTAN NO. 1, Haslacher Str. 78, (0761) 49 92 21.
SEX SHOP BINOKEL, Eschholtzstr. 34.

FULDA

Dance Bar/Disco
TEMPLE OF GAY, Ruhrstr. 3, Thurs-Sat from 22:00. ♂

GARMISCH PATENKIRCHEN

Bars
BECKS STALL, Höllentalstr. 2, (08821) 5999, 17:00-01:00. ♂

GELSENKIRCHEN

Bars
FÜCHSCHEN, Idastr. 15, (0209) 452 52, 21:00-04:00, every 3rd Sun from 15:30. ♂
MIRAGE, Selhorststr. 6-10, (0209) 20 11 06, daily 21:00-05:00. ♂

Leathers/Piercing
LEDER GUMMISTUDIO, Bochumer Str. 76, (0209) 222 14, 09:00-18:30 (Sat till 14:00), closed Sun.

Erotica
GAYWORLD CENTER, Bahnhofstr. 81, (0209) 207 954.
HÖHEPUNKT, Wanner Str. 133, (0209) 255 80.
LIVE EROTIKA, Augustastr. 11.

GERA

Bars
BÜRGERSCHENKE, Plauensche Str 5, (0365) 28 614, from 21:00 (closed Mon, Tues). ♂

GIESSEN

Information
LESBENTELEFON, (0641) 314 38, lesbian line, 1st Thurs 19:00-21:00.

Bars
CLUB BONAPARTE, Liebigstrasse 66, (0641) 756 49, daily 20:00-01:00. ♂

Cafe
CAFE BISTRO LÖBERS, Löbershof 8, (0641) 387 91, 09:00-01:00. ♂
CAFE EINSTEIN, Mühlstrasse, (0641) 787 53, 08:00-01:00. ♂

GÖTTINGEN

Information
AIDS HILFE, (0551) 43735.
LESBENTELEFON, (0551) 455 10, lesbian line, Tues 18:00-20:00.

Bars
LESBENTREFF, Gronerstr. 28, enter from Nicolaistr., lesbian social 2nd Fri from 20:00. ♀

Dance Bar/Disco
FRUIT MACHINE, Weender Str. 38, at W38, (0551) 586 85, 3rd Sun from 19:00. ♂
GAY CLUB DOWNSTAIRS, Jüdenstr. 13, (0551) 48 49 43, disco Wed, Fri & Sat from 21:00; rest of week: bar. ♂

Cafe
LESBEN UND FRAUENCAFE, Geismarlandstr. 19, Tues from 20:30. ♀
SCHWESTERNBLICK, Immanuel Kant Str. 1, at the gay center, (0551) 770 1100, bar & café. ♀

Retail & Bookstores
LAURA, Burgstr. 21, (0551) 473 17, women's bookstore.

Erotica
ORION SHOP, Jüdenstr. 13a, (0551) 443 26.

HAGEN

Bars
KRÖNCHEN, Körnerstr. 47, (02331) 32 426, 11:00-01:00 (Fri 11:00-03:00, Sat 19:00-03:00). ♂

Erotica
ORION SHOP, Frankfurter Str. 62-64, (02331) 325 34.

HALLE

Information
AIDS INFO, (0345) 364 19.

Bars
BLUE VELVET, Alter Markt, (0345) 517 0359, 17:00-01:00 (Fri, Sat till 02:00, Sun till 24:00). ♂
PIERROT, Grosser Sandberg 10, 19:00-01:00 (Wed, Fri, Sat till 04:00), closed Mon. ♂

Retail & Bookstores
LITFASS, Rannische Str. 14/15, (0345) 242 63, 09:00-18:30, Sat till 14:00, closed Sun.

HAMBURG

Information
AIDS HILFE, (040) 319 6981.
HEIN & FIETE, Kleiner Pulverteich 17-21, (040) 240 440, gay information center.

GERMANY

INFOTELEFON VON LESBEN FÜR LESBEN, (040) 279 00 49, lesbian info line, Wed 17:00-19:00.

MAGNUS HIRSCHFIELD CENTRUM, Borgweg 8, (040) 279 00 69, gay & lesbian center, 15:00-24:00 (Sun from 13:00).

■ Accommodations

KÜNSTLER-PENSION SARAH PETERSEN, Lange Reihe 88, Tel/Fax: (040) 24 98 26, gay & lesbian guesthouse, 30% hetero clientele, creatively furnished rooms, B/W & color TV, shared baths, nearby lake & public pool, beverages, expanded (meatless) continental breakfast.

■ Women's Accommodations

HOTEL HANSEATEN, Dragonerstall 11, (44-40) 35 16 16, fax: (49-40) 34 58 25, hotel in central Hamburg, Café Endlich on premises, 13 rooms. ♀

■ Bars

AMIGO BAR, Spielbudenplatz 5, (040) 31 64 36, 24hrs. ♂

ANGIE'S NIGHTCLUB, Spielbudenplatz 27-28 at the Tivoli, (040) 31 12 31, Wed-Sat from 22:00. ♂

BALUGA BAR, Lincolnstr. 6, (040) 319 41 59, 22:00-04:00. ♂

BAR EXQUISIT, Spielbudenplatz 22, (040) 31 43 93, 24hrs. ♂

BAR SIR, Brennerstr. 21, (040) 24 70 45, 06:00-24:00. ♂

BEI HANNI & THOMAS, Klaus Groth Str 14, (040) 250 44 12, from 10:00. ♂

BEL AMI, Zimmerpforte 2, (040) 280 17 38, 10:00-04:00, later Fri, Sat. ♂

BLACK, Danziger Str. 21, (040) 24 08 04, cruise bar frequented by leather men, 22:00-03:00, Fri, Sat from 22:00. ♂

BLOODY MARY, Kleiner Schäferkamp 46, 430 25 90, lesbian bar Fri from 21:00. ♀

BLUE MAGIC, Rostocker Str. 12, (040) 280 90 37, 13:00-04:00. ♂

CAFÉ UHRLAUB, Lange Reihe 63, (040) 280 26 84, 08:00-02:00.

CHAPS, Woltmanstr. 24, cruise bar, Sun 15:00-02:00. ♂

CRAZY BOYS, Pulverteich 12, (040) 24 62 85, show bar, from 20:00, closed Sun, Mon. ♂

CRAZY HORST, Hein Hoyer Str. 62, (040) 319 2633, daily 22:00-08:00. ♂

DOWNSTAIRS, Ost West Str. at Brandstwiete, (040) 32 22 72, from 11:00 (Sat, Sun from 17:00). ♂

DU & ICH, Seilerstrasse 38a, (040) 31 59 69, 20:00-04:00 (Fri, Sat later), closed Wed. ♂

EXTRATOUR, Zimmerpforte 1, (040) 24 01 84, 12:00-04:00 (Sat, Sun from 06:00). ♂

FEHMARN STUBE, Landwehr 35, (040) 254 27 54, from 10:00 (Sat from 20:00), closed Sun. ♂

FLAMINGO, Kastanienallee 33, (040) 31 23 97, from 20:00, closed Thurs. ♂

FRAUENKNEIPE, Stresemannstr. 60, (040) 43 63 77, women's bar. ♀

FUNDUS, Detlef-Bremer-Str. 54, daily 12:00-04:00. ♂

IKA STUBEN, Budapester Str. 38, (040) 31 09 98, from 20:00 (Fri, Sat from 21:00), closed Mon, Tues. ♀

IM FRANZ, Steindamm 37, (040) 280 2512, 7 days, 24hrs. ♂

MEZZO, Koppel 1, (040) 280 35 39, 18:00-02:00 (Sat later, Sun 16:00-24:00). ♂

MONTE CHRISTO, Detlev Bremer Str. 144, (040) 315 206, 19:00-04:00 (Fri till 05:00, Sat 19:30-08:00). ♂

MY WAY, Brennerstr. 2, (040) 200 2209, 10:00-04:00. ♂

PARADISO, Detlev-Bremer Str. 52-54, (040) 314 988, 12:00-04:00. ♂

PICCADILLY, Silbersacktwiete 1, (040) 319 24 74, 20:00-04:00, closed Thurs. ♂

PIPIFAX, Hans Albers Platz 3, (040) 317 43 91, 18:00-02:00 (Fri, Sat till 04:00). ♂

PULVERFASS, Pulverteich 12, (040) 24 97 91, show bar, daily from 19:30. ♂

PURGATORY, Friedrichstr. 8, (040) 31 58 07, 21:00-04:00 (Fri, Sat til 06:00). ♂

ROSENGARTEN, Lange Str. 51, (040) 317 34 05, from 12:00. ♀♂

RUDI'S NIGHTCLUB, Steindamm 58, (040) 24 72 74, daily 19:00-08:00. ♂

SCHMIDT, Spielbudenplatz 24, (040) 31 12 31, show bar, daily shows at 20:00. ♂

SEAGULL, Detlev-Bremer Str. 37, (040) 310 128, from 20:00 (Sun from 15:30). ♂

SPEICHER KELLER, Hopfensack 26, (040) 321 962, 11:00-24:00 (Sat from 18:00, Sun 15:00-21:00). ♂

TIVOLI, Spielbudenplatz 27-28, (040) 311 12 31, show bar. ♂

TOOM PEERSTALL, Clemens Schultz Str. 44, (040) 319 35 23, 14:00-04:00 (Fri, Sat till later). ♂

TROCADERO, Zimmerpforte 2, (040) 24 08 28, daily 10:00-04:00. ♂

TUSCULUM, Kreuzweg 6, (040) 280 36 06, 18:00-06:00, Fri, Sat till 08:00. ♂

UNIVERSUM, Hansaplatz 3, (040) 24 07 51, 24 07 52, hotel bar, daily 12:00-04:00. ♂

UWE'S TROCA, Rostocker Str. 14, (040) 245 743, 08:00-04:00. ♂

WELCOME, Schenkendorfstr. 3, (040) 227 3686, 20:00-04:00. ♂

WILLI'S FOR YOU, Markusstr. 4, (040) 348 0388, 16:00-01:00 (Fri, Sat till later). ♂

WUNDERBAR, Talstrasse 14, (040) 317 44 44, daily from 21:00. ♂

ZUM LUSTIGEN KLEMPNER, Katharinenstr.31, (040) 374 25 93, 11:00-24:00 (Fri from 09:00, Sat from 18:00), closed Sun. ♀♂

ZUR LUSTIGE ECKE, Kaltenkirchner Platz 10, (040) 851 19 92, 14:00-02:00 (Fri, Sat till 04:00), closed Sun. ♂

■ Dance Bar/Disco

CAMELOT, Hamburger Berg 13, (040) 317 4489, lesbian disco Sat from 23:00. ♀

EDK, Gerhardstr. 3, by Hans Albers Platz, Thurs-Sun from 24:00. ♂

FRAUENDISCO, Borgweg 8, at the Magnus Hirschfeld Zentrum, women's disco 2nd Sat from 21:00. ♀

FRONT, Heidenkampsweg 32, (040) 24 21 50, Wed & Sat from 22:00. ♂

HIP TO NICE, Ost West Str. 46, at Kontor, 1st & 3rd Sun 17:00-24:00. ♂

PIT CLUB, TOM'S SALOON, Pulverteich 17, (040) 24 33 80, dance bar and saloon frequented by leather me. Dance bar: 21:00-04:00 (later Fri & Sat); Saloon: from 17:00. ♂

SPUNDLOCH, Paulinenstr. 19, (040) 31 07 98, daily 21:00-04:00, closed Mon. ♂

■ Cafe

BISTRO DES ARTISTES, Schmilinksstr. 19, (040) 246 083, 11:00-24:00.

CAFE FRADKIN, Eulenstr. 49, 10:00-24:00 (Sun from 11:00).

CAFE GNOSA, Lange Reihe 93, (040) 24 30 34, 11:00-01:00 (Fri, Sat till 02:00, Mon 18:00-02:00).

CAFE MAGNUS, Borgweg 8, (040) 2787 7800, 17:00-24:00 (Sun from 13:00). ♂

CAFE MISTRAL, Lehmweg 29, (040) 420 7702, 17:00-02:00 (Sat from 16:00, Sun from 14:30). ♂

CAFE SCHUH, Dammtorbahnhof, CCH exit, (040) 44 09 58, 17:00-01:00, closed Sun. ♂

CAFE SPUND, Mohlenhofstrasse 3, (040) 32 65 77, 10:00-24:00 (Sun till 15:00).

COSY, Beim Schlump 5, (040) 45 89 68, 10:30-02:00 (Sat & Sun from 19:00).

FRAUENCAFE VENUS, Bismarckstr. 98, (040) 420 47 48, women's cafe at the Frauenbuchladen. ♀

FRAUENCAFÉ ENDLICH, Dragonerstall 11, (040) 34 13 45, women's cafe, daily from 16:00 (Sun breakfast from 11:00). Lesbian group meets 1st Mon from 20:00. ♀

FRAUENCAFÉ, Borgweg 8, at the Magnus Hirschfeld Zentrum, women's café, Wed 15:00-18:00. ♀

TOKLAS, Clemens Schulz Str. 42, (040) 319 32 49, 17:00-02:00 (Fri till 04:00, Sat & Sun from 11:00). ♂

TOLERANCE BISTRO & BAR, Rostocker Str. 14, at Uwe's Troca bar, 08:00-04:00. ♂

TWIST, Carl von Ossietzki Platz, (040) 280 1739, 08:00-24:00.

WINTERHUDER KAFFEEHAUS, Winterhuder Marktplatz 16, (040) 47 82 00, 09:00-24:00. ♂

■ Saunas/Health Clubs

APOLLO SAUNA, Max Brauer Allee 277, (040) 43 48 11, 15:00-24:00, Sun from 13:00. ♂

GERMANY

BADEHAUS DRAGON, Pulverteich 37, (040) 240 514, 12:00-01:00 (Fri-Mon 24 hrs). ♂
MELIDISSA, Max Brauer Allee 155, 1st floor, (040) 380 96 69, 16:00-24:00 (Thurs till 02:00).
SCHWITZKASTEN, Virchowstr. 12-14, (040) 389 31 33, 13:00-01:00 (Fri-Mon 24hrs).

■ Restaurants
MESS, Turnerstr. 9, (040) 43 41 23, 18:00-01:00 (Sun from 11:00).
SCHLÖSSCHEN, Kastanienallee 2, 1st floor, (040) 3116 6117, 18:00-02:00, closed Mon.

■ Retail & Bookstores
FRAUENBUCHLADEN, Bismarckstr. 98, (040) 420 47 48, women's bookstore.
MÄNNERSCHWARM, Neuer Pferdemarkt 32, (040) 430 2650, gay bookshop, 10:00-18:30, Sat till 14:00, closed Sun.

■ Leathers/Piercing
BOUTIQUE BIZARRE, Reeperbahn 35, (040) 317 5030, 10:00-24:00.
MR. CHAPS LEATHERWORKS, Gurlittstr. 47, (040) 243 109, 10:30-18:30 (Sat till 14:00), closed Sun.
SCORPIO, Dorotheenstr. 61, (040) 270 6157, call for appointment.
SEVENTH HEAVEN, Steindamm 6, at Bizarr Shop, 09:00-01:00.

■ Erotica
BEATE UHSE, Hamburger Str. 43; Adenauer Allee 10.
CONDOMI, Ottenser Hauptstr. 10, at EKZ market, (040) 390 31 84, condoms.
DR. MÜLLER'S, Steindamm 22.
EROTIC KINO SHOP, Talstr. 2, (040) 319 37 68.
EROTICA SEX SHOP, Clemens Schultz Str. 43, (040) 31 50 68.
HENRY'S SHOW CENTER, Steindamm 7, near central train station.
HOMO KINO, Talstrasse 8, (040) 31 24 95, cinema, 09:00-06:00, Fri-Sun 24hrs.
KOOLS, Am Soldatenfriedhof 5.
NEW MAN, Pulverteich 8; Reeperbahn 63; Steindamm 16 & 21; Nobistor. 38.
ORION SHOP, Adenauer Allee 55.
SEVENTH HEAVEN, Reeperbahn 90; Steindamm 34.
SEX POINT, Steindamm 4.
SPARTA, Lange Reihe 93; Talstr. 18; Hein Hoyer Str. 5; Seiterstr. 49.

HANAU

■ Bars
PINK ELEFANT, Hanauer Vorstadt 16, (06181) 258 439, 18:00-01:00. ♂

HANNOVER

■ Information
AIDS HILFE, (0511) 32 77 71.

LESBENTELEFON, (0511) 44 05 68, lesbian line, answers Mon 19:00-21:00.
LESBENZENTRUM, Lichtenbergplatz 7 enter from Teichstr., (0511) 44 05 68, lesbian center.

■ Bars
ALCAZAR CABARET, Leonhardtstr. 11, (0511) 34 46 10, show bar, Wed-Sun 21:00-05:00. ♪♂
BACKSTAIRS, Lange Laube 24, (0511) 144 27, cruise bar frequented by leather men, 20:00-05:00 (Fri, Sat from 22:00). 🍴♂
BARKAROLE, Konkordiastr. 8, (0511) 44 53 08, 21:00-02:00 (Fri, Sat till 03:00), closed Tues. ♂
BURGKLAUSE, Burgstr. 11, (0511) 32 11 86, 18:00-02:00, Sat 13:00-03:00, closed Wed. ♂
CLUB OUI, Hallerstr. 35, (0511) 388 0333, from 15:00 (Sun from 17:00). ♂
CUP, Escher Str. 11, (0511) 161 0294, 20:00-02:00 (Fri, Sat till 03:00). ♂
HOLE, THE, Franckestr. 5, (0511) 352 3895, 21:00-02:00 (Fri, Sat till 03:00), even Sun from 18:00. ♂
LA CAGE AUX FOLLES, Kronenstrasse 4, (0511) 31 86 89, 20:00-02:00 (Fri, Sat till 03:00). ♂
MADAME ARTUR, Steintorfeldstr. 4, (0511) 341 252, 11:00-02:00 (Fri, Sat till 05:00). ♂
MEZZO, Lister Meile 4, (0511) 31 49 66, 09:00-02:00 (Fri till 03:00, Sat 10:00-03:00). ♂
ODEON, Odeonstrasse 5, (0511) 144 27, daily 20:00-05:00, summer from 21:00. ♂
SCHWULE SAU, Schauenfelderstr. 29, (0511) 700 05 25, daily from 20:00, closed Tues. ♂
VULKANO, Lange Laube 24, (0511) 137 88, Wed, Fri-Sun from 22:00. ♂
XANADU, Flüggerstr. 29 (0511) 388 5514, 17:00-02:00 (Fri, Sat till 03:00, Sun from 15:00). ♂

■ Dance Bar/Disco
FRAUENDISCO IM MUSIKTHEATER BAD, Am Grossen Garten 60, women's disco last Thurs of the month from 21:00. 🍴♀
MEN'S FACTORY, Engelborsteler Damm 7, (0511) 70 24 87, Fri, Sat from 22:00. 🍴♂

■ Cafe
CAFE CALDO, Bergmannstr. 7, (0511) 151 73, gay cafe, 09:30-02:00, Sat & Sun from 11:00. ♀ ♂
FRAUEN UND LESBENABEND IM CAFE KLATSCH, Limmerstr. 58, Linden. Women's & lesbian evening at Cafe Klatsch 2nd Mon of the month, from 20:00. ♀
OPUS MUSIK CAFE, Lange Laube 24, (0511) 138 58, daily from 15:00 (Sat, Sun from 18:00). ♂

■ Saunas/Health Clubs
VULKAN SAUNA, Otto Brenner Str. 15, entrance Haussmannstr., (0511) 151 66, daily 13:00-01:00.

■ Retail & Bookstores
BUCHLADEN ANNABEE, Gerberstr. 6, (0511) 131 81 39, general bookstore with gay & lesbian section, 10:00-18:00 (Sat till 14:00), closed Sun.

■ Leathers/Piercing
LEDER ART & DESIGN, Schulenburger Landstr. 48, (0511) 350 56 33, 11:00-18:00, closed Sat & Sun.
SW3, Herschelstr. 32, (0511) 131 72 29, 10:00-18:00 (Thurs till 20:00, Sat till 14:00).

■ Erotica
BEATE UHSE, Kleine Packhofstr. 16.
CINEMA, Am Klagesmarkt 9, (0511) 17 735.
FRANKIES EROTIK SHOP, Fernroder Str 8, (0511) 363 27 66, gay's call: 363 10 52, 12:00-02:00 (Sat 10:00-15:00).
KOOL'S KINO, Scholvinstr. 2, Am Maarstall 10.
MEN'S POINT, Goethestr. 7, (0511) 32 47 64, 10:00-24:00.
SCHAU & SPIEL, Reitwallstr. 6, (0511) 320 541.
SEX PALAST, Reitwallstr. 8, (0511) 32 87 34.
SEXYLAND, Am Maarstall 11.
VIDEO WORLD, Herschelstr. 1a, (0511) 18973.

HEIDELBERG

■ Information
AIDS HILFE, (06221) 16 17 00.

■ Bars
FRAUENCAFE, Blumenstr. 43, (06221) 213 17, women's cafe Mon 20:00-23:00, Tues till 24:00, last Wed from 19:30, Fri till 24:00, 1st & 3rd Thurs 20:00-23:00. ♀
FRAUENLESBEN FETE, Alte Bergheimerstr. 7, women's bar night, 3rd Fri. ♀

■ Dance Bar/Disco
MATA HARI, Oberbadgasse 10, (06221) 181 808, 22:00-03:00 (Fri, Sat till later). 🍴♂

■ Retail & Bookstores
FRAUENBUCHLADEN, Theaterstr. 16, (06221) 222 01, women's bookstore.

■ Erotica
SEX SHOP, Merianstr. 3, (06221) 298 99.
VIDEOWORLD MAN SHOP & KINO, Kurfürstenanlage 53.

HEILBRONN

■ Bars
QUEEN'S PUB, Gemminger Gasse 3, (07131) 816 22, 16:00-24:00, Fri till 01:00, Sat & Sun 14:00-24:00. ♂

■ Cafe
BELLADONNA FRAUENCAFÉ, Werderstr. 159, (07131) 603 50, women's café at the Frauenzentrum (women's center).

HOF

■ Bars
SCHNÜRSENKEL, Fabrikzeile 1, (09281) 446 13, 19:00-02:00, closed Wed. ♂

GERMANY

Erotica
BEATE UHSE, Brunnenstr. 2, (09281) 844 91.
SEX SHOP, Klosterstr. 30, (09281) 2931.

HOPSTEN-SCHALE

Women's Accommodations
FRAUENBILDUNGSHAUS OSTERESCH, Zum Osteresch 1, 48496 Hopsten-Schale, (05457) 15 13, Women-only retreat organised around workshops in German (some especially for lesbians) in crafts, massage, dance, feminist medicine, music, arts. Guests may stay only if attending workshop; 1 shared bath, tent sites. ♀

INGOLSTADT

Bars
PINNOCHIO, Beckerstr. 19, (0841) 910 710, 18:00-01:00, closed Mon. ♂

Erotica
AMOR & CO., Höllbräugasse 5, (0841) 32 624.
EROTIK SUPER MARKT, Dollstr. 17, (0841) 931 1265.

ISERLOHN

Bars
WHY NOT, Viktoriastrasse 1, (02371) 120 02, daily 18:00-02:00 (Fri, Sat till 03:00). ♂

ISLAND OF SYLT

Accommodations
HAUS HALLIG GUEST HOUSE, Danzigerstr 9, (49-4651) 24213, men's guesthouse & apts (Beach Club Apartments at Bötticherstr 3) with private baths, continental to buffet breakfasts, TV lounge, color cable TV, walking distance to beach, bar & sauna. ♂
HAUS KORALLE, Nordmarkstr. 5, Westerland / Sylt, 25980, (49-4651) 27315, fax (49-4651) 29866. Luxurious apartments with cable TV, phone, gardens, parking, 50% gay & lesbian clientele.

Bars
BAR NANU, Strandstrasse 23, (04651) 928 00, daily 21:00-03:00. ♂
BEACH CLUB BAR, Bötticher Str. 3, (04651) 211 91, cloudy days 14:00-03:00, clear days from 17:00. ♂
KLEIST CASINO, Elisabethstr. 1, (04651) 242 28, daily 14:00-03:00. ♂
RINGELSPIEL, Andreas Dirk Str. 2, (04651) 78 59, daily 15:00-03:00. ♂

Saunas/Health Clubs
BEACH CLUB SAUNA, at Beach Club bar, cloudy days 14:00-21:00, clear days 17:00-21:00.

KAISERSLAUTERN

Information
AIDS HILFE, (0631) 180 99.

Dance Bar/Disco
NANU, ★ Dr. Rudolf Breitscheid Str. 58, (0631) 138 12, from 21:00 (summer months from 22:00), closed Mon, Tues & Thurs. Frequented by military personnel, more women Sat. ♂
REMBRANDT'S (formerly Joy Club), Burgstr. 21, (0631) 95844, Thurs 20:00-01:00, Fri-Sat 21:00-04:00, Sun 19:00-24:00, gallery space for artists, men welcome. ♂
XTC, Burgstr. 21, (0631) 958 44, Fri, Sat 21:00-04:00. ♂

Erotica
AMOR & CO., Richard Wagner Str. 5.
SEX SHOP, Weberstr. 29, (0631) 686 89.
VIDEO WORLD MAN SHOP, Rosenstrasse 4.

KARLSRUHE

Information
LESBENTELEFON, (0721) 69 10 70, lesbian line, Fri 20:00-22:00. Ask about scheduled lesbian socials.

Bars
CAFE MIRO, Hirschstr. 3, (0721) 214 32, 10:00-01:00. ♂
ERDBEERMUND, Baumeister Str. 54, (0721) 37 42 42, 20:00-01:00, closed Tues. ♂
TREPPENHAUS, Rheinstrasse 77, (0721) 59 29 20, 22:00-05:00, closed Mon & Wed. ♂
UPS, Hirschstr. 24, (0721) 22 200, 19:00-03:00. ♂

Dance Bar/Disco
CAVE, Hirschstr. 18, (0721) 21 525, 21:00-03:00. ♂
CLUB TROPICA, Bunsenstrasse 9, (0721) 85 49 80, 21:00-05:00 (from 22:00 in summer), closed Mon. ♂
DIE ZWEI, Waldstr. 30, (0721) 21 331, daily 11:00-03:00. ♂
DIVA, Waldstr. 30, (0721) 20 55 55, Fri & Sat from 23:00. ♂
MR. SONDERBAR, Baumeister 54, Thurs-Sat 23:00 till late. ♂

Cafe
FRAUENCAFE, Rudolfstr. 17, (0721) 37 02 04, women's cafe, lesbians meet Fri from 20:00. ♀

Saunas/Health Clubs
ADONIS SAUNA CLUB, Lameystr. 12a, (0721) 55 50 51, daily 14:00-24:00.
BERNHARD SAUNA, Bernhardstr. 2, (0721) 69 67 67, 15:00-01:00, closed Tues.

Retail & Bookstores
KASSIOPEIA, Marienstr. 14, (0721) 37 02 04, women's bookstore.

Erotica
BLUE MOVIE, Kaiserstr. 33, (0721) 37 42 87.
HEINER'S VIDEO SHOP, Mathystr. 9, (0721) 358 335.
ORION SHOP, Bürgerstr. 7b.
SEX SHOP EROTIC POINT, Hardstr. 21, (0721) 55 35 75.

KASSEL

Information
FRAUENZENTRUM, Goethestr. 44, women's center with Frauenkneipe (women's bar night) 1st Fri from 21:00, Frauendisco (women's disco) 3rd Fri from 21:00.

Accommodations
HAUS LENGEN, Erzbergerstrasse 23-25, (0561) 1 68 01, fax 780 794, gay motel, gay sauna, bar & gym, singles & doubles, private WCs, 1 shared shower per floor, near train station. ♂

Bars
CAFE DESASTA, Arnold Bode Str. 6, (0561) 84235, gay Mon & Thurs 10:00-18:00 (closed Sat, Sun).
FRAUENFRÜHSTÜCK, at The Avocado, Schönfelder Str. 3, women's breakfast 1st, 2nd & 4th Sun. ♀
FRISCH & FRECH, Wilhelmshöher Allee 84, (0561) 775 252, from 18:00 (Sun from 15:00). ♂
SUSPEKT, Fünffensterstr. 14, (0561) 10 45 22, 13:00-01:00 (Fri, Sat 20:00-02:00), closed Mon. ♂
TAKE FIVE, Friedrich Ebert Str. 118, (0561) 188 54, 20:00-01:00, Fri & Sat till 02:00, closed Mon. ♂

Dance Bar/Disco
GAY NIGHT, Friedrich Ebert Str 18, at Brigoine, Sun from 21:00. ♂
R.U.K. ZUCK, Frankfurter Str. 131, (0561) 22729, Wed, Fri & Sat from 22:00. ♂

Saunas/Health Clubs
PFERDESTALL, Erzbergerstr. 23-25, (0561) 168 01, 15:30-23:00 (Fri & Sat till 01:00), closed Sun.

Retail & Bookstores
ARADIA, Pestalozzistr. 9, (0561) 172 10, women's bookstore.

Erotica
BEATE UHSE INT, Untere Königsstr. 54.
CITY SEX SHOP, Grüner Weg 10, (0561) 175 87.
ORION SHOP, Friedrichsplatz 11, (0561) 182 39.
PLEASURE, Kölnischestr. 7, (0561) 774 437.
SEX POINT, Kölnische Str. 18, (0561) 71 18 41.
VIDEO WORLD MAN SHOP & KINO, Kurfürstenstr. 2-4.

KEMPTEN

Information
FRAUENZENTRUM LILA DISTL, Hoföschle 7a, (0831) 155 86, women's center with Lesbentreff (lesbian social) 1st Mon from 20:00.

GERMANY

■ Bars
FRAUENTREFF, Stuibenweg 1, at Le Filou bar, (0831) 268 29, women's social Tue & Fri from 20:00. ♀

LE FILOU, Stuibenweg 1, (0831) 268 27, 20:00-01:00 (Sat till 03:00), closed Mon. ♂

■ Retail & Bookstores
FRAUENBUCHLADEN, Rathausplatz 9, (0831) 182 28, women's bookstore.

KIEL

■ Information
AIDS HILFE, (0431) 551 054.

■ Bars
ALHAMBRA, Herzog Friedrich Str. 92, (0431) 632 95, daily 19:30-03:00. ♂

CA VA, Holtenauer Str. 107, (0431) 854 19, daily 11:00-03:00. ♂

COMING OUT, Schuhmacherstr. 28, (0431) 94893, 18:00-05:00. ♂

HARLEKIN, Kirchhofallee 38, (0431) 636 48, daily 20:00-03:00. ♂

■ Dance Bar/Disco
FRAUENDISCO, Hass Str. 22, at Pumpe, women's disco 2nd & 4th Sat. ♀

PUMPE, Hass Str. 22, (0431) 23 17 37, 1st, 3rd & 5th Sat 21:00-03:00 (even Sat women's disco). ♂

■ Cafe
FRAUENCAFE KASSANDRA, Schasstr. 4, (0431) 67 35 36. ♀

■ Erotica
BEATE UHSE, Wall 12, (0431) 973 33.

NEW MAN IM WOS, Schumakerstr. 32; Eggerstedtstr. 11.

ORION SHOP, Winterbeker Weg 44, (0431) 68 65 59.

KOBLENZ

■ Bars
JOURNAL BAR, A.d. Liebfrauenkirche 12, (0261) 30 97 64, 17:00-01:00 (Sat, Sun till 02:00). ♂

■ Erotica
DR. MÜLLER'S, Löhrstr. 10-12.

JOURNAL SEX SHOP, at Journal Bar, A.d. Liebfrauenkirche 12, 09:30-01:00 (Sat, Sun 19:00-02:00).

PENNY SEX SHOP, Löhrstr. 65, (0261) 36 655.

KÖLN - COLOGNE

■ Information
AIDS HILFE, (0221) 20 20 30.

CHECKPOINT GAY INFO LINE, (0221) 92 57 68 68, 17:00-21:00.

LESBEN-UND SCHWULENBERATUNG IM SCHULZ, Kartäuserwall 18, (0221) 9318 8080, gay & lesbian organization with socials, daily 10:00-01:00 (Fri, Sat till 03:00). Lesbengruppe (lesbian group) meets here.

■ Accommodations
HOTEL HUBERTUSHOF, Mühlenbach 30, (0221) 217 386. Bed & breakfast with gay sauna. 60% gay & lesbian clientele, especially on weekends, expanded German buffet breakfast. ♀♂

HOTEL PLUMO, Cranachstrasse 9 at Kempenerstr, D-5000 Köln 60, (0221) 730 606, hotel, full breakfast. ♀♂

■ Bars
BACKBORD, Steinweg 4, (0221) 25 81 479, daily 11:00-01:00. ♂

BEI UDO, Vor St Martin 12, (0221) 258 23 47, 16:00-01:00 (Fri, Sat till 03:00). ♂

BEIM PITTER, Alter Markt 58, (0221) 25 64 09, cruise bar, daily 11:00-01:00. ♂

BEIM SIR, Heumarkt 27-29, (0221) 256 835, 14:00-01:00 (Fri, Sat till 03:00). ♂

BILDERSCHRECK, Königswinterstr. 1, (0221) 417 885, 17:00-02:00 (Fri, Sat till 03:00). ♂

BUSCHWINDRÖSCHEN, Buschgasse 18, (0221) 323 575, 19:00-01:00. ♂

BÖLZJE, Bolzengasse 4, (0221) 21 71 85, daily 11:00-01:00. ♂

CAFE D'OR, Kettengasse, at Friesenwall, (0221) 257 32 39, 10:00-01:00. ♂

CHAINS, Stephanstr. 4, (0221) 23 87 30, cruise bar, 15:00-02:00 (Fri, Sat till later), closed Mon. ♂

CLIP, Marsilstein 29, at Rinckelpfuhl, 20:00-02:00 (Fri, Sat till 03:00). ♂

COME BACK, Alter Markt 10, (0221) 257 76 58, 16:00-03:00 (Fri till 04:30), closed Thurs. ♂

CORNER, Schaafenstrasse 57-59, (0221) 24 90 61, from 19:00 (Sun from 16:00). ♂

ELINOR'S, Kettengasse 2, (0221) 24 57 87, 10:00-01:00 (Sun from 11:00). ♂

FILMDOSE, Zülpicher Str. 39, (0221) 23 96 43, 19:00-01:00, Fri & Sat till 03:00, closed Mon. ♂

GEORGE SAND, Marsilstein 13, (0221) 21 61 62, 19:00-01:00 (Fri, Sat till 03:00), men welcome. ♀

GIGOLO, Heumarkt 48, (0221) 256 100, 06:00-03:00. ♂

GLORIA CAFÉ & SHOWBAR, Apostelnstr. 11, (0221) 258 36 56, café: 09:00-01:00. Call 25 44 33 for show schedule. ♂

HANDS, Mathiasstr. 22, (0221) 24 35 41, cruise bar, 22:00-02:00 (Fri, Sat till 03:00). ♂

HOLLYWOOD, Heumarkt 43, (0221) 257 4219, 20:00-04:30. ♂

IM RATHÄUSCHEN, Kleine Buddengasse 7-9, (0221) 258 11 42, 17:00-03:00. ♂

KÜNSTLERKLAUSE TIMP, Heumarkt 25, (0221) 25 81 409, daily 11:00-04:00. ♂

LE CARROUSSEL, Alter Markt 4, (0221) 21 68 66, daily 19:00-05:00. ♂

LESBENABEND, Buchgasse 18, at Buschwindröschen, lesbian social Fri. ♀

MY LORD, Mühlenbach 57, (0221) 23 17 02, daily 17:00-03:00. ♂

MY WAY, Friesenstr. 47, (0221) 257 1351, 18:00-02:00 (Fri, Sat 19:00-03:00), closed Mon. ♂

PARK, Mauritiuswall 84, (0221) 21 33 57, 20:00-01:00. ♂

RATHAUSGLÖCKCHEN, Unter Seidenmacherinnen 1, (0221) 25 769 32, 11:00-01:00, closed Mon. ♂

ROTHUUSECK, Alter Markt 2, (0221) 24 25 09, 14:00-03:00 (Fri, Sat till 04:30). ♂

RÖMERSTUBEN, Mühlenbach 53, (0221) 21 64 57, cruise bar frequented by leather men, 18:00-03:00, Fri-Sun till 05:00, closed Tues. ♂

SAPPHO II, Pfeilstr. 17, (0221) 257 3085, 18:00-01:00. ♀

SCHAMPANJA, Mauritiuswall 43, (0221) 24 42 94, daily 20:00-01:00. ♂

SCHULZ BAR, Kartäuserwall 18, at the SCHULZ lesbian/gay center, (0221) 9318 8080, daily 10:00-01:00 (Fri, Sat till 03:00). Women-only 1st Sat 10:00-01:00, women's dance night 1st Sat from 21:00-02:00. ♀♂

STIEFELKNECHT, Pipinstrasse 9, (0221) 21 30 01, cruise bar, daily 22:00-02:00 (Fri, Sat till 06:00). ♂

TEDDY TREFF, Stephanstr. 31, (0221) 248 310, from 21:00 (closed Mon). ♂

VAMPIRE, Rathenaplatz 5, (0221) 240 12 11, 20:00-01:00, closed Mon. ♂

VERQUER, Heumarkt 46, (0221) 257 4810, 17:00-01:00 (Sat till 03:00), closed Mon. ♂

ZILLE, Vor St. Martin 12, Pipinstr. 5, (0221) 258 1783, 18:00-03:00. ♂

ZIPP'S, Hohe Pforte 13-17, (0221) 24 59 98, 18:00-01:00 (Fri, Sat 02:00), closed Thurs. ♂

ZUM STEINBOCK, Rheingasse 24-26, (0221) 230 247, 11:00-01:00 (Fri, Sat till 03:00), closed Sun. ♂

■ Dance Bar/Disco
DISCO, Alter Markt 4-6, (0221) 25 16 02, may change in 1997. ♂

ENTRE NOUS, at the Schulz gay & lesbian center, women's dance night, 1st Sat from 21:00. ♀

MONTE CHRISTO, Grosse Sandkaul 24, (0221) 24 48 81, 22:00-04:30. ♂

■ Cafe
CAFE PHILIPPS, Philippstr. 1, (0221) 515 333, 09:00-01:00 (Sun from 11:00). ♂

CAFÉ GO-IN, Alter Markt 36-42, (0221) 25 82 214, 11:00-03:00, Sun from 13:00.

DIX' KATTWINKEL, Greesbergstr. 2, (0221) 13 22 20, daily 11:00-01:00. ♂

HÜHNERFRANZ, Hühnergasse 2, (0221) 253 536, 07:00-01:00. ♂

GERMANY

JANUS, Schaafenstr. 51, (0221) 240 6530, 11:00-01:00. ♂

QUO VADIS, Vor St. Martin 8-10, (0221) 258 1414, 11:00-01:00, closed Tues.

RHIANNON FRAUENCAFE, Moltkestr. 66, (0221) 52 31 20, women's cafe at the women's bookstore. ♀

■ Saunas/Health Clubs

BADEHAUS AM RÖMERTURM, Friesenstr. 23-25, (0221) 25 77 006, daily 12:00-23:00.

CLUB 30, Mühlenbach 30, (0221) 21 73 86, daily 14:00-23:00.

DER FAUN, Händelstr. 31, (0221) 21 61 57, 11:00-24:00, Sat till 08:00.

PHOENIX SAUNA, Kettengasse 22, (0221) 25 73 381, 12:00-06:00, jack-off & safe sex parties.

RELAX, St. Apernstr. 20-26, (0221) 257 58 55, 12:00-01:00.

SAUNABAD VULCANO, Marienplatz 3-5, (0221) 21 60 51, 11:00-23:00, Sun till 22:00.

■ Restaurants

ANDERS EHRENFELD, Klarastr. 2-4, (0221) 510 1473, 09:00-01:00.

OSCAR'S, Sudermannstr. 12, (0221) 720 011, 12:00-01:00, closed Sun.

PEPPERMINT, Hohenstaufenring 23, (0221) 240 19 29, 10:00-03:00, Sun from 19:00.

■ Retail & Bookstores

DER ANDERE BUCHLADEN, Wahlenstr. 1, (0221) 52 05 79, gay titles.

FRAUENBUCHLADEN & CAFE, Moltkestr. 66, (0221) 52 31 20, women's bookstore.

GANYMED, Kettengasse 3, (0221) 251 110, gay bookstore, 10:00-20:00 (Sat till 16:00), closed Sun.

■ Leathers/Piercing

BOUTIQUE SECRETS, Marienplatz 1, (0221) 244 100, Tues-Fri 13:00-18:30 (Thurs till 20:30), Sat 10:00-14:00.

COSMIC WARE, Mauritiuswall 30-32, (0221) 240 1201, from 12:00 (Sat from 11:00).

DAS ATELIER, Vogelsanger Str. 286, (0221) 541 972, 12:00-18:30, closed Sun.

MODE PFORTE, Hohe Pforte 24, (0221) 247 567, 10:00-18:30 (Sat till 14:00), closed Sun.

NIMA LAPELLE, Wolfsstr. 16, (0221) 257 8315, 10:00-18:30 (Sat till 14:00), closed Sun.

PLEASURE & PAIN, Domstr. 29, (0221) 139 2642, piercing, tattoos.

■ Erotica

BEATE UHSE, Hohe Str. 158.

DR. MÜLLER'S, Hohenzollerring 32-34.

GAY SEX MESSE, Mathiasstr. 13, (0221) 24 82 17, cinema, 10:00-01:00, Sun from 12:00.

MIKE HUNTER SEXSHOP, Hohe Str 2, at Stephanstr.

ORION SHOP, Blaubach 6-8, (0221) 24 54 26.

SEX & GAY CENTER, Kettengasse 8; Mathiasstr. 23.

SEX MESSE, Breite Str. 153, (0221) 258 17 08.

SEX SHOP, Pfeilstrasse 10; Im Dam 13.

KONSTANZ

■ Bars

ABER HALLO, Kreuzlinger Str 46, (07531) 258 29, 19:00-01:00. ♂

BELLADONNA, Obermarkt. 14. ♀

EXCALIBUR, Blätzleplatz 6, Sun from 21:00. [♿]♂

FILM & VIDEOSHOP, Emmishoferstr. 4, (07531) 21 340, 21:00-02:00. ♂

HOLLYWOOD, Stadelhofgasse 1, (07531) 236 69, 19:00-01:00 (Fri, Sat till 03:00), closed Thurs. ♂

SHAKES BIER, Theodor Heuss Str. 5, (07531) 658 22, 17:00-01:00. ♂

■ Dance Bar/Disco

GAY WATCH, Spanierstr. 8, at the Rheinterasse, (07531) 560 93, Wed 17:00-02:00. [♿]♂

■ Saunas/Health Clubs

HYPERION RELAX CENTER, Gottlieb Damier Str 3, (07531) 610 61, more gays Tues & Sat 17:00-23:00, Sun 15:00-23:00.

■ Erotica

SEXOTICA, Kreuzlinger Str. 5, (07531) 220 2526.

KOPPENWIND

■ Women's Accommodations

TARA, Bergstrasse 3, 8602 Koppenwind, (09554) 481, retreat for women with seminars in a rural setting. ♀

KREFELD

■ Bars

JOGIS TOP INN, Neue Linnerstr. 85, (02151) 236 24, 21:00-03:00 (Fri & Sat till 05:00), closed Mon. ♂

PALETTE, Dionysusstr. 40, (02151) 77 23 94, 21:00-03:00 (Fri & Sat till 05:00), closed Thurs. ♂

SCHICKERIA, Westwall 33, (02151) 28 855, 20:00-05:00. ♂

SCOTCH CLUB, Westwall 30, (02151) 77 36 19, 21:00-05:00. ♂

■ Dance Bar/Disco

KÖNIGSBURG, Königsstr. 8, (02151) 80 30 71, call for scheduled gay disco nights. [♿]♂

■ Erotica

SEX MESSE, Hochstr. 11, (02151) 32 280.

LEIPZIG

■ Information

AIDS INFO, (0341) 232 31 26.

FRAUENKOMMUNIKATIONSZENTRUM, Ludwigstr. 115 (0341) 689 7903, Lesbengruppe (lesbian group), Lila Pause, meets here.

LESBENTELEFON, (0341) 123 3775, lesbian line.

■ Bars

ADVOKAT, Brühl 56, 18:00-06:00. ♂

BLACK HORSE, Ross Str. 12, (0341) 331 5267, 17:00-02:00, frequented by gays.

FILMCAFE INTERSHOP, Burgstr. 9, at Sporergasse, (0341) 960 85 04, from 14:00. ♂

HARVEY'S, Nikolaistr. 39-45, from 10:00 (Sun from 13:00). ♂

INSIDE, Dölitzerstr. 28, (0341) 391 130 91, 19:00-02:00 (closed Sun). [♿]♂

LADY LIBERTE, Rud. Breitscheidtstr. 12, (0341) 20 97 87, 22:00-01:00 (Fri, Sat till 03:00).. ♂

ROSALINDE LEIPZIG, Lindenauer Markt 21, bar & disco at gay center, Mon 20:00-01:00, Sat disco from 22:00. [♿]♂

■ Dance Bar/Disco

ESPLANADE, Richard Wagnerstr. 10, 28 23 30, Sun from 21:00, men welcome. [♿]♀

KUTSCHE, Brandenburgerstr., (0341) 211 43 74, from 19:00. [♿]♂

LEFT SIDE, Windscheidtstr. 51, room 5, (0341) 308 0142, women's disco Wed from 20:00. [♿]♀

■ Cafe

CAFE DE SAXE, Grosse Fleischergasse 4, 10:00-24:00 (Sat, Sun till 22:00). ♂

CAFÉ VISAVIS, R.-Breitscheid-Str. 33, 24hrs.

RASCHKE, Burgplatz 2, 09:00-01:00. ♂

■ Saunas/Health Clubs

CLUBSAUNA STARGYTE, call for address, (0177) 296 31 71, 14:00-02:00 (Fri, Sat till 05:00). ♂

PHOENIX, Grosse Fleischergasse 12, 14:00-24:00. ♂

■ Retail & Bookstores

TIAN-FRAUENBUCHLADEN, Könneritzstr. 67, (0341) 479 74 75, women's bookstore. Lesbenclub (lesbian group) meets here Thurs 19:30.

■ Erotica

EROTIK SHOP, Universitätsstr. 20, (0341) 28 41 44.

ORION, Bernhard Göring Str. 36.

LIPPSTADT

■ Bars

DON QUIJOTE, Am Güterbahnhof, (02941) 58 115, 20:00-01:00 (Fri, Sat till 03:00). ♂

LÜBECK

■ Information

AIDS HILFE, (0451) 725 51.

ARANAT FRAUEN-UND LESBENZENTRUM, Dankwartsgrube 48, (0451) 738 27.

GERMANY

■ *Bars*
CHAPEAU CLAQUE, Hartengrube 25, (0451) 773 71, Thurs-Sat 21:00-04:00. ♂
FLAMINGO, Marlesgrube 58, (0451) 70 48 36, daily from 17:00. ♂
PAPA GAY'S TRÄNKE, Marlesgrube 61, (0451) 721 44, 21:00-03:00 (Fri, Sat till 04:00). ♂
PETER'S KLEINE KNEIPE, Wahmstrasse 55, (0451) 741 03, from 14:00 (Sat from 18:00), closed Sun. ♂

■ *Erotica*
ORION SHOP, Ziegelstr. 232, (0451) 89 69 66.
SEVENTH HEAVEN, Lederstr. 5.
SPARTA SHOP, Hüxstr. 15.
WOS, Wahmstr. 32.

LUDWIGSBURG-EGLOSHEIM

■ *Information*
NORA FRAUENZENTRUM, Hahnenstr. 47, (07141) 343 80.

LUDWIGSHAFEN

■ *Bars*
ALTER TREFFPUNKT, Gräfenaustr. 51, (0621) 51 13 92, 21:00-01:00, Fri & Sat till 03:00, closed Sun. ♂
COME BACK, Welser Strasse 10, (0621) 51 25 51, 20:00-01:00, Fri & Sat till 03:00, closed Mon. ♂

■ *Cafe*
FRAUENCAFE, Westendstr. 17, (06210 52 84 06, women's cafe. ♀

■ *Erotica*
MIKE'S, Amtsstr. 1, (0621) 51 02 12.
ORION SHOP, Yorckstrasse 28, (0621) 58 31 21.
SEXYLAND, Ludwigstr. 10.
VIDEOWORLD MAN SHOP & KINO, Bismarkstr. 116.

MAGDEBURG

■ *Bars*
FEZ, Mittagstr. 32-33, (0391) 561 3694, 19:00-01:00 (Fri, Sat 20:00-04:00), closed Mon. ♂
GUMMIBÄRCHEN, Liebgstr. 6, 17:00-01:00 (Sat till 02:00). ♂

■ *Erotica*
ORION, Mittagstr. 28.

MAINZ

■ *Information*
FRAUENZENTRUM, Walpodenstr. 10, (06131) 22 12 63, women's center with lesbian meetings: Lesberatung Thurs 18:30-20:00 & Lesbengruppe Thurs from 20:00; Frauencafé (women's cafe) Wed from 17:00 & Fri from 19:00; and Frauenfrühstück (women's breakfast) 3rd Sun from 10:00.

■ *Bars*
CHAPEAU CLAQUE, Kleine Langgasse 4, (06131) 22 31 11, from 19:00. ♂
NOT FOR EVERYONE, Osteinstr. 7-9, (06131) 67 21 63, 20:00-01:00 (Fri, Sat till 02:00). ♂

■ *Cafe*
HINTERSINN, Gauss Str. 19, (06131) 57 16 30, 09:30-01:00, Fri, Sat till 02:00.

■ *Erotica*
CITY SEX SHOP, Grosse Langgasse 12, (06131) 22 04 79.
PINK MOVIE, Zanggasse 17, (06131) 22 62 62.
STEPHANS SEX BOUTIQUE, Dominikanerstr. 5a, (06131) 22 16 50.

MANNHEIM

■ *Information*
AIDS HILFE, (0621) 28 600.

■ *Bars*
BUTCH, S6, 21, (0621) 10 19 03, from 14:00, frequented by leathermen. ♂
CAFE KLATSCH, Hebelstr. 3, (0621) 15 610, 19:00-02:00 (Fri, Sat till 03:00). ♂
CLUB CAFE DUO, G2, 12. ♀
HEIDELBEER, Amerikanerstr. 11, (0621) 441 550, 20:00-01:00. ♂
KELLER, S6, 21, at Butch bar, cruise bar, Wed-Sun from 20:00. ♂
LE CLUB, Friedrichsring 30, (0621) 139 48, 20:00-02:00, Fri & Sat till 03:00. ♂
LE JARDIN, K2 31, (0621) 207 46. ♀
PETIT PARIS, T3, 2-3, (0621) 10 16 96, 17:00-01:00 (Sat till 05:00), closed Mon. ♂
STAGE CONNEXION, at M&S Connexion complex, Angelstrasse 33, Thurs-Sat 21:00-03:00. ♂
TOLERANT, Neckarauerstr. 85 (0621) 856 138, 16:00-01:00. ♂

■ *Dance Bar/Disco*
M&S CONNEXION, Angelstr. 33, (0621) 85 83 74, complex with café, bistro, music hall, dance bar & Stage Connexion showbar, Thurs-Sat 21:00-03:00 (Sat men-only, till 05:00). ♂
SUBWAY, T6, 14, (0621) 10 27 79, 21:00-03:00 (Fri till 05:00, Sat till 04:00). Women welcome Wed from 20:00. ♂

■ *Cafe*
FRAUENCAFE & LESBENSTAMMTISCH, C4, 6, (0621) 15 26 67, women's cafe. Lesbenstammtisch (lesbian social) Fri from 19:00. ♀

■ *Saunas/Health Clubs*
HOT HOUSE CLUB, Ladenburgerstr. 23, (0621) 73 72 60, Wed, Sat, Sun 14:00-23:00, Thurs 16:00-22:00.

■ *Retail & Bookstores*
DER ANDERE BUCHLADEN, M2, 1, (0621) 217 55, general bookshop with a gay & lesbian selection, 10:00-18:30, Sat till 14:00, closed Sun.
XANTHIPPE, T3, 4, (0621) 216 63, women's bookstore.

■ *Erotica*
BEATE UHSE, L14, 12.
SEX SHOP BINOKEL, J2, 18, (0621) 221 17.
STUDIO 7, Heinrich Lanz Str. 32, (0621) 44 93 06.
VIDEOWORLD MAN SHOP & CRUISING POINT, Mittelstr. 15.

MARBURG

■ *Bars*
HAVANNA ACHT, Lahntor 2, 234 32, Sun 20:00-01:00. ♀♂
LESBENKNEIPE, Lahntor 8, at Havanna, women's bar night, 2nd Sat. ♀
TWIST, Ketzerbachstr 23a, 648 44, from 18:00. ♂

METZINGEN

■ *Bars*
APOLLO, Dachsweg 2, (07123) 7111, Wed, Fri, Sat 21:00-01:00. ♂

MINDEN

■ *Information*
FRAUEN (LESBEN) TREFFPUNKT, Umradstr. 25, (0571) 207 02, lesbian meeting.

■ *Bars*
DELFTER STUBEN, Pionierstrasse 1a, (0571) 316 83, 21:00-04:00, closed Mon. ♂

■ *Saunas/Health Clubs*
VIKTORIA SAUNA, Viktoriastr. 22, (0571) 357 15, 15:00-23:00, closed Mon & Tues.

■ *Erotica*
NOVUM MARKT, Lübbecker Str 12; Kaiserstr. 8.
ORION SHOP, Lindenstrasse 46, (0571) 204 19.

MÖNCHEN/GLADBACH

■ *Information*
LESBENTELEFON, (02161) 219 00, lesbian line.
LILA DISTEL FRAUENZENTRUM, Lüpertzenderstr. 69, (02161) 21 900, women's center. Lesbentreff (lesbian social) 2nd & 4th Fri 20:00-22:00.

■ *Bars*
C'EST LA VIE, Gasthausstr. 67, (02161) 33 764, from 20:00, closed Wed, Thurs. ♀♂
GERMANIA STÜBCHEN, Gasthausstr. 68, (02161) 176 630, daily 20:00-03:00. ♂
TEATRO, Waldhausener Str. 86, (02161) 38 833, 20:00-02:00 (Fri, Sat till 03:00), Sun 15:00-02:00. ♂

GERMANY

FYI

New Munich Tour Operator & Travel Agent Seeks Upscale Gay Clientele

English Text

A new gay travel agency and tour operator in Europe has opened in upscale offices in the gayest part of central Munich. **Atlantis Travel** is the European representative of Atlantis Events of Los Angeles, creator of the gay Club Med resort vacations in Mexico and the Caribbean. Atlantis Travel's motto is, "Only the best is good enough for our clients." As a tour operator, Atlantis customizes packages both for Europeans going abroad and for visitors coming to Europe, whether individuals or groups.

Deutscher Text

Reisebüros gibt es wie Sand am Meer! Miesmuscheln finden Sie überall! Mit einem Urlaubs-Juwel ist das schon anders...Atlantis entdeckt es! Atlantis Travel BmbH bietet für Gays and Lesbian genau das Richtige - Erholung nach Mass, wie Sie es sich vorstellen! Es gibt keinen exklusiven Ort auf der Welt, den wir nicht für Sie entdecken! Atlantis Travel GmbH bietet persönlich zugeschnittene Traumreisen, Cluburlaub für Gleichgesinnte, Eventveranstaltungen für Anspruchsvolle, Funtravel für Singles und Businessreisen, die den Erfolg garantieren.

Atlantis Travel, Pestalozzistr. 17, 80469 München, (49-89) 23 66 60 -0, Fax: (49-89) 23 66 60-55, E-mail: tommi@atlantis-travel.de

■ *Erotica*
NEW MAN, Hindenburgstr. 201.

MÜLHEIM

■ *Bars*
CAFE LEINPFAD, Dohne 74, (0208) 380 881, 15:00-01:00. ♂

MÜNCHEN - MUNICH

■ *Information*
AIDS INFO, (089) 268 071.

FRAUENINFOTHEK, Johannesplatz. 12, (089) 48 58 75.

FRAUENKULTURHAUS, Richars Strauss Str. 21, (089) 470 5212, women's center.

KOFRA KOMMUNIKATIONS ZENTRUM FÜR FRAUEN Baaderstr. 8, (089) 2010450, women's center with cafe, groups, vast information available, library.

LESBENTELEFON, (089) 725 42 72, lesbian line.

SUB ZENTRUM, Müllerstr. 43, (089) 260 3056, 19:00-23:00 (Fri, Sat till 24:00).

■ *Accommodations*
DEUTSCHE EICHE HOTEL, Reichenbachstr. 13, (089) 26 84 77, hotel & restaurant, modest accommodation. ♂

PENSION BRASIL, Dultstrasse 1, (089) 26 3417, gay-friendly hotel above bar, shared baths, continental breakfast.

■ *Bars*
ALEXANDER'S, Utzschneiderstr. 4, (089) 260 54 98, 16:00-01:00 (Fri, Sat till 03:00). ♂

BALLHAUS, Klenzestr. 71, at Westermühlstr, (089) 201 09 92, 10:00-01:00. ♂

BAU, Müllerstrasse 41, (089) 26 92 08, 20:00-01:00, Fri, Sat till 03:00. ♂

BELL, Utzschneider Str. 12, (089) 23 60 47, daily 14:00-01:00. ♂

BISTRO MARGO, Reichenbachstr. 21, (089) 201 45 46, 12:00-01:00 (Sat from 15:00). ♂

BLUE LANE, Baaderstr 68, (089) 201 03 21, 18:00-02:00. ♂

BOLT, Blumenstr. 15, (089) 26 43 23, cruise bar frequented by leather men, daily 15:00-03:00. ♂

BYLLI'S, Kohlstr. 4, (089) 201 61 83, 12:00-01:00 (Sun from 18:00). ♂

CHIRAG'S BISTRO, Reichenbachstr. 21, (089) 201 4546, 17:00-01:00. ♂

COCK, Augsburger Str. 21, (089) 26 59 95, 20:00-12:00, Sat till 03:00. ♂

COLIBRI, Utzschneider Str. 8, (089) 260 93 93, daily 11:00-22:00. ♂

DEUTSCHE EICHE, Reichenbachstr.13, (089) 26 84 77, bar & restaurant frequented by leather men, 11:00-15:00 & 18:00-01:00, Fri & Sat till 02:00. ♂

DREI GLÖCKLEIN, Hans Sachs Strasse 8, (089) 26 61 75, daily 11:00-22:00. ♂

IWAN, Josephspitalstr. 15, (089) 554 933, 11:00-03:00. ♂

KLIMPERKASTEN, Maistrasse 28, (089) 53 76 39, daily 19:00-01:00. ♂

KUNTERBUNT, Klenzestr. 45, (089) 201 6804, 11:00-01:00. ♂

LÖWENGRUBE, Reisingerstr. 5, (089) 265 750, from 20:00 (Sun 18:00-01:00). ♂

MARKTKLAUSE, Frauenstr. 18, (089) 29 90 76, daily 14:00-01:00. ♂

MORIZZ, ★ Klenzestr. 43, (089) 201 67 76, yuppies, 19:00-02:00 (Fri, Sat till 03:00), frequented by some women. ♂

MYLORD, Ickstattstr. 2a, (089) 260 44 48, sofas & chairs, quiet music, mostly hetero, occasionally frequented by gays, lesbians, good place to meet for quiet conversation, daily 18:00-01:00 (Sat till 03:00).

NIL, ★ Hans Sachs Str. 2, (089) 26 55 45, daily 17:00-03:00 (Sun from 15:00). ♂

OCHSENGARTEN, Müllerstr. 47, (089) 26 64 46, cruise bar, daily 19:00-01:00 (Fri, Sat till 03:00). ♂

PILS STUBEN 2000, Dultstrasse 1, (089) 26 39 64, daily 16:00-01:00. ♂

PRINCE, Reichenbacherstr. 5, (089) 201 1655, 10:00-01:00. ♂

PROSECCO, Theklastr. 1, (089) 260 57 14, daily 18:00-04:00. ♂

SCHWALBE, Schwanthaler Str. 149, (089) 503 263, 09:00-01:00. ♂

TADZIO CLUB, Baldestr. 7, (089) 201 40 81, 20:00-01:00 (Fri-Sun from 19:00), closed Mon, Tues. ♂

TEDDY BAR, Hans Sachs Str. 1, (089) 260 33 59, frequented by leathermen, 20:00-01:00. ♂

TONIGHT, Detmoldstr. 2-4, (089) 351 22 33, daily 19:00-04:00. ♂

ZUR FEUERWACHE, Blumenstr. 21a, (089) 260 44 30, daily 15:00-01:00. ♂

■ *Dance Bar/Disco*
EMPIRE, ★ Thalkirchnerstr. 2, (089) 260 84 03, 20:00-01:00 (Thurs till 02:00, Fri-Sun till 03:00). ♂

FORTUNA, Maximiliansplatz 5, (089) 55 40 70, from 22:00 (closed Tues). ♂

FRED'S PUB, Reisinger Strasse 15, (089) 26 61 38, daily 18:00-01:00. ♂

NEW YORK, ★ Sonnenstr. 25, (089) 59 10 56, daily 23:00-04:00. ♂

PIMPERNEL, Müllerstrasse 56, (089) 26 71 76, 24:00-07:00. ♂

SOUL CITY, ★ Maximiliansplatz 5, enter from Max-Joseph-Str, (089) 59 52 72, 22:00-04:00 (Fri, Sat till later). ♂

TOGETHER AGAIN, Müllerstr. 1, (089) 263 469, 20:00-01:00 (Fri, Sat till 03:00). ♂

■ *Cafe*
CAFE BAADER, Baaderstr. 47, (089) 201 0638, 11:00-01:00 (Sun from 10:00). ♂

GERMANY

CAFE IM SUB, Müllerstr. 38, (089) 260 3056, 19:00-23:00 (Fri, Sat till 24:00). ♂
KLENZESTÜBERL, Klenzestr. 4, (089) 292 972, 06:00-22:00. ♂
MICHELE, Reichenbachstr. 37, (089) 201 42 94, café-style bistro, 16:00-01:00 (Sat from 19:00), closed Sun. ✗♀
PETIT CAFÉ, Marienstr. 2, (089) 29 56 72, daily 15:00-22:00.
RICK'S CAFEBAR, Augustenstr. 112, (089) 523 31 10, bistro-style café, 07:00-01:00, some hetero clientele. ✗♂
SEITENSPRUNG, Holzstr. 29, (089) 26 93 77, 10:00-01:00. ♂
SOUL CITY, ★ Maximiliansplatz 5, (089) 595 272, 20:00-04:00 (disco Thurs from 22:00). ♂
STADTCAFE, St Jakobs Platz 1, in the Stadtmuseum, (089) 26 69 49, 11:00-24:00 (Mon from 17:00).
VILLANIS, Kreuzerstr. 3b, Asamhof, (089) 260 7972, bistro-style café, 10:00-01:00 (Sun from 11:00). ✗♂
WOMEN'S CAFE, Richard Strauss Str. 21, at Frauenkulturhaus women's center, call for cafe schedule. ♀

■ *Saunas/Health Clubs*
DOM PEDRO SAUNA, Fasaneriestr. 18, (089) 129 32 76, daily 12:00-24:00.
SCHWABINGER MEN SAUNA, Düsseldorfer Str. 7, (089) 307 23 42, 15:00-01:00. ♂
TS27, Taunusstr. 27, (089) 359 7068, 14:00-01:00.

■ *Restaurants*
CAR, Rumpfortstr. 17, 11:00-01:00 (Fri, Sat till 02:00).
HEAVEN, Thierschstr. 14, (089) 298 266, restaurant & bar, 09:00-01:00.

■ *Retail & Bookstores*
LILLEMOR'S FRAUENBUCHLADEN, Arcisstrasse 57, (089) 27 21 205, women's bookstore with lesbian & feminist books in English & German and local information. Reading lounge with coffee, women only! Open Mon-Fri 10:00-18:30, Sat 10:00-14:00, closed Sun.
MAX & MILIAN, Ickstattstr. 2, (089) 260 3320, gay bookstore, 10:00-18:30, Thurs till 20:30, Sat till 14:00.

■ *Leathers/Piercing*
HARDLINE, Müllerstr. 33, (089) 260 6017, 12:30-18:30 (Sat 11:00-15:30).
RAINBOW TATTOO, Dachauer Str. 159, (089) 18 85 80, 13:00-19:00 (Sat till 14:00), closed Sun.
WALTER'S LEDERBOUTIQUE, Reichenbachstr. 40a, (089) 201 50 62, 10:00-18:30 (Sat till 13:30), closed Sun.

■ *Erotica*
APOLLO GAY VIDEO, Lindwurmstr. 21, (089) 267 438.

BEATE UHSE, Neuhauser Str. 7; Bayerstr. 7a.
BUDDY, Utzschneiderstr. 3, (089) 26 89 38.
CORNELIUS' MEN, Corneliusstr. 19, (089) 201 47 53.
EROTIC WORLD, Wohlbecker Str. 1; Hammer Str. 88.
FOLLOW ME GAY SHOP, Corneliusstrasse 32, (089) 202 12 08, 10:00-18:30 (Thurs till 20:30, Sat till 14:00), closed Sun.
LADIES FIRST, Kurfürstenstrasse 23, (089) 271 88 06, women's erotica.
ORION SHOP, Frauenstr. 20.
SEX WORLD, Sonnenstr. 12.
VIDEO WORLD MAN SHOP & KINO, Sonnenstr. 14.
WEISSBLAUER GAY SHOP, Theresienstr. 130, (089) 52 23 52, cinema, 09:00-20:00 (Thurs till 22:00, Sat till 18:00).

MUNICH
SEE MÜNCHEN.

MÜNSTER

■ *Information*
FRAUENGALERIE, Kettelerstr. 25, (0251) 27 92 56, women's art gallery.
LESBEN & SCHWULENZENTRUM, Am Hawerkamp 34, (0251) 665 686, gay & lesbian center, Mon 15:00-17:00 & Wed 17:00-19:00. Ask about scheduled lesbian socials.
LESBENTELEFON, (0251) 194 46, lesbian line, Thurs 20:00-22:00.

■ *Bars*
BERMUDA ECK, Hörster Str. 33, (0251) 562 00, daily from 20:00. ♂
CAFE MUSIK, Frauenstr. 7, (0251) 44 210, 10:00-01:00. ♂
HARDIES, Mauritzstr. 30, (0251) 568 81, daily from 18:00, closed Sun. ♂
LADYLIKE BIERCAFE, Maximilianstr. 2, (0251) 230 1097. ♀
NA UND, Sonnenstrasse 43, (0251) 430 13, daily 20:00-03:00, closed Tues. ♂
WOMEN'S BAR NIGHT, Königspassage, at Königsstrasse 14, at the Star Club, 2nd Sat & 4th Fri. 🏳️♀

■ *Dance Bar/Disco*
LE DIFFERENT, Hörster Str. 10, (0251) 51 12 39, Wed-Sat 22:00-03:00 (later Fri & Sat). 🏳️♂

■ *Retail & Bookstores*
CHRYSALIS, Buddenstr. 22, (0251) 555 05, women's bookstore.

■ *Erotica*
GEROTHEK, Mauritzstr. 20, (0251) 51 14 61.

NEUMÜNSTER

■ *Bars*
NA UND, Kieler Str. 48, (04321) 471 37, 20:00-05:00, closed Sun. ♂

■ *Erotica*
CITY SEX SHOP, Gasstr. 5, (04321) 466 99.

NEUWIED

■ *Bars*
ZUR SONNE, Marktstr. 5, (02631) 23 142, from 10:00 (Wed from 19:00). ♂

■ *Erotica*
ORION SHOP, Schloss Strasse 69, (02631) 319 65.

NÜRNBERG

■ *Information*
AIDS HILFE, (0911) 26 61 91.
FRAUENKUNST KULTURZENTRUM, Kleinreuther Weg 28, (0911) 35 19 70, women's art & cultural center, open Thurs-Sun.
LESBENBERATUNG, Fürther Str. 154, Rückgebäude, (0911) 32 82 62, lesbian info space, Tues 17:00-19:00.
LESBENTELEFON, (0911) 23 25 00, Wed 19:00-22:00.

■ *Bars*
ALT PRAG, Hallplatz 29, (0911) 243 341, 11:00-01:00 (Sun from 19:00). ♂
AMICO BAR, Köhnstrasse 53, (0911) 46 32 92, 20:00-02:00, Sat till 03:00, closed Thurs. ♂
BABEL BAR, Kolpinggasse 42, (0911) 22 36 69, daily 20:00-01:00 (Fri, Sat till 02:00). ♂
BAR TOY, Luitpoldstr. 14, (0911) 241 96 00, daily 16:00-04:00. ♂
BIER BAR SAVOY, Bogenstrasse 45, (0911) 45 99 45, 16:00-02:00, Sun from 14:00, Fri & Sat till 03:00. ♂
CHEZ ROBBY CAFE PETIT, Hinterm Bahnhof 24, (0911) 45 41 18, 15:00-01:00 (Fri, Sat till 03:00, Sun from 18:00). ♂
GRUNDMANN, Hummelsteiner Weg 80, (0911) 449 935, 10:00-01:00, closed Mon. ♂
KING'S PUB, Dr. Kurt Schumacher Str. 8, (0911) 204 784, 17:00-03:00 (Fri, Sat from 18:00). ♂
LA BAS, Hallplatz 31, (0911) 222 281, 13:00-01:00 (Fri, Sat till 03:00). ♂
LITTLE HENDERSEN, Frauengasse 10, (0911) 241 87 77, daily 18:00-03:00 (Sat, Sun from 06:00). ♂
MORRISON, Glockenhofstr. 9, (0911) 472 0383, 09:00-01:00. ♂
NA UND, Marienstr. 25, (0911) 22 73 20, 19:00-01:00 (Fri & Sat till 02:00, Sun from 15:00). ♂
PARADIES, Bogenstr. 26, (0911) 443 991, 20:15-23:00 (Fri, Sat till 00:30), closed Sun. ♪♂
SONNIGE PFALZ, Obere Kanalstr. 31, (0911) 26 23 00, 20:00-01:00 (Fri, Sat till 03:00), more women weekends, closed Mon. ♂
VICKING CLUB, Kolpinggasse 42, (0911) 22 36 69, daily 20:00-01:00 (Fri, Sat till 02:00).

GERMANY

ZUM WALFISCH, Jakobstr. 19, (0911) 22 52 70, hotel bar, 17:00-01:00, Fri & Sat 15:00-02:00. ♂

■ Dance Bar/Disco
MACH 1, Kaiserstr. 1-9, (0911) 203 030, gay 1st Sun only 22:00-04:00. ♂

■ Cafe
CAFE FATAL, Jagdstr. 16, (0911) 396 363, 09:00-01:00 (Sat from 17:00). ♂
CAFE MAX, Breitscheidstr. 18 (0911) 445 903, 17:00-01:00. ♂
CAFE WENDELTREPPE, Kleinreuther Weg 28 at Frauenkunst, Kulturzentrum, (0911) 35 19 70, women's cafe at Women's Art & Cultural Center, Thurs-Sun 20:00-01:00. ♀
CARTOON, An der Sparkasse 6, (0911) 22 71 70, 11:00-01:00, Sun from 14:00.
CHÖRLEIN, Lorenzer Str. 25, 11:00-02:00 (Sat 10:00-18:00), closed Sun. ♂
V8, Moltkestr. 2, (0911) 28 80 39, 18:00-02:00 (Fri, Sat from 19:00, Sun from 16:00). ♂

■ Saunas/Health Clubs
APOLLO SAUNA BAD, Schottengasse 11, (0911) 22 51 09, 15:00-03:00 (Fri, Sat till 06:00).
CHIRINGAY, Comeniusstr. 10, (0911) 44 75 75, 13:00-02:00, Fri-Mon 24hrs.
CLUB 67, Pirckheimer Str. 67, (0911) 35 23 46, 14:00-24:00, Fri & Sat 24 hrs.

■ Retail & Bookstores
FRAUENBUCHLADEN, Kleinreuther Weg 28 at Frauenkunst-Kulturzentrum, (0911) 35 24 03, women's bookstore.
MÄNNERTREU, Bauerngasse 14, (0911) 26 26 76, gay bookstore, 11:00-20:00 (Mon till 18:00, Sat 10:00-16:00), closed Sun.

■ Erotica
BEATE UHSE INT, Königstr. 69.
NEW MAN, Luitpoldstr. 11.
ORION, Landgrabenstr. 125, (0911) 439 78 12.
STUDIO 50, Wirthstr. 50, (0911) 44 15 20.
VIDEO CLUB 32, Tafelfeldstr. 32, (0911) 44 15 66.

OBERHAUSEN

■ Bars
CANAPEÉ, Virchowstr. 19, (0208) 889 041, 18:00-01:00 (Fri, Sat till 03:00, Sun from 16:00). ♂
FRAUENKNEIPE, Am Förderturm 27, at Druckluft, women's bar night, Thurs from 19:00. ♀
MONTPARNASSE, Helmholzstr. 7, (0208) 20 43 02, 20:00-01:00 (Sun also 04:00-12:00). ♂

■ Saunas/Health Clubs
CONDOR SAUNA, Concordiastrasse 32, (0208) 80 44 25, 15:00-24:00 (Fri, Sat till 07:00).

OFFENBACH

■ Information
FRAUENZENTRUM, Grosse Hasenbachstr. 35, (069) 81 65 57, women's center & cafe with Lesbengruppe (lesbian group) meetings.

■ Bars
VILLA KUNTERBUND, Bismarkstr. 8, (069) 88 81 52, 17:00-01:00 (Sat till 02:00). ♂

OFFENBURG

■ Bars
TABU, Hauptstr. 102, (0781) 742 43, 20:00-01:00 (Fri, Sat till 04:00), closed Tues. ♂

OLDENBURG

■ Information
AIDS LINE, (0441) 883 010, or Oldenburg Aids-Hilfe (0441) 19411.
GAY LINE, (0441) 194 46, Wed 20:00-22:00.
LESBEN- & SCHWULENZENTRUM, Ziegelhofstr. 83, (0441) 777 5990.
LESBENTELEFON, (0441) 777 5149, lesbian line, Thurs 20:00-22:00.

■ Bars
BIENENKORB, Donnerschweerstr. 50, (0441) 850 08, 21:00-02:00 (Fri, Sat till 05:00), closed Sun & Mon. ♂
FRAUENDISCO & FRAUENKNEIPE, at Alhambra, Hermannstr. 83, Frauenkneipe (women's bar night) Wed from 17:00, disco 2nd Sat of the month from 22:30. ♀
HEMPELS, Ziegelhofstr. 83, cafe at lesbian/gay center, (0441) 777 5990, Fri 20:00-24:00, Sun 18:00-20:00 (women only Thurs 20:00-24:00, men only Mon 20:00-24:00). ♀♂
LESBENKNEIPE, Ziegelhofstr. 83, at the lesbian/gay center, women's bar night Thurs 20:00-24:00. ♀
PULVERFASS, Heiligengeiststr. 12, (0441) 126 01, 22:00-02:00 (Fri, Sat till 05:00), closed Sun & Mon. ♂
ZWITSCHERSTÜBCHEN, Bahnhofsplatz 5, (0441) 177 53, 21:00-02:00, Fri & Sat till 03:00, Sun from 16:00. ♂

■ Dance Bar/Disco
DER SCHWARZE BÄR, Donnerschweer Str. 50, (0441) 885 0737, 21:00-02:00 (Fri, Sat till 05:00), closed Sun. Mon leather night with dress code. ♂
MÄNNER FABRIK, at Alhambra, Hermannstr. 83, men's disco 3rd Sat of the month from 22:00, frequented by leathermen. ♂
PINK DANCE PARTY, Baumgartenstr. 3, at Schmizz, 1st Thurs from 21:00. ♂
ROSA DISCO, at Alhambra, Hermannstr. 83, last Sat of the month from 22:00.

■ Cafe
CAFÉ AM DAMM, Damm 36, (0442) 183 30, 11:00-24:00, Sun from 10:00, Sun natural foods breakfast.
CAFÉ MACHATSCHKALA, Hauptstr. 2, Kirchhatten, (04482) 8326, vegetarian cuisine, 12:00-22:00 (Sat, Sun 09:00-19:00), closed Wed.

SCHWULES CAFÉ, Nadorster Str. 24, at the Oldenburg Aids-Hilfe center, Sun from 16:. ♂
ZUM TEESTUBEN, Staustr. 5, (0441) 156 12, 09:30-18:00 (Sun from 14:00). ♂

■ Retail & Bookstores
VIOLETTA, Lindenstr. 18, (0441) 88 30 39, women's bookstore, 10:00-18:00 (Sat till 14:00), closed Mon.

■ Leathers/Piercing
ZWEITE HAUT, Nadorstrasse 8, (0441) 88 58 31, 10:00-18:00 (Thurs 13:00-20:00, Sat till 13:00), closed Sun.

OSNABRÜCK

■ Information
AIDS-HILFE, (0541) 801 024.
FRAUENARCHIV NATALIE BARNEY, Lange Str. 26, at Laischaftstr., (0541) 875 99.
FRAUENBERATUNGSTELLE, Spindelstr. 41, (0541) 25 93 13, women's information center.
LESBENTELEFON, (0541) 85 846, Thurs 18:00-20:00.

■ Bars
BEI THEO, Pottgraben 27, (0541) 20 15 70, 20:00-02:00 (Fri, Sat till 03:00), closed Mon. ♂
BIVALENT, Johannes Str. 131 (enter on Spindelstr.), (0541) 844 88, daily from 21:. ♂

■ Dance Bar/Disco
B4, Buerschestr. 4, Wed-Sat from 22:00. ♂

■ Cafe
CAFÉ M, Bramscher Str. 23, (0541) 65 337, 18:00-22:00 (Fri, Sat till 23:00, Sun 15:00-20:00), closed Tues-Thurs. ♂

■ Retail & Bookstores
MOTHER JONES FRAUENBÜCHERCAFE, Jahnstr. 17, (0541) 437 00, women's bookstore & cafe with Lesbenstammtisch (women's meeting) Tues from 20:00.

■ Erotica
EROTIC WORLD, Hasestr. 31, (0541) 234 63.
NOVUM MARKT, Möserstr. 56; Pagenstecher Str 70.

OSTFRIESLAND

■ Women's Accommodations
FRAUENFERIENHOF OSTFRIESLAND, Zum Lengener Meer 2, 26446 Friedeburg-Bentstreek, (04) 956 4956, women-only retreat with courses & programs, shared baths. ♀

PADERBORN

■ Information
FRAUENBERATUNGSTELLE LILITH, Königstr. 64, (05251) 213 11, women's information center, meetings 2nd & 4th Thurs 17:00-19:00.

PASSAU

■ Information
LESBENTELEFON, FRAUENZENTRUM

GERMANY

UND FRAUENCAFE, Spitalhofstr. 62a, (0851) 553 67, lesbian line, women's center & cafe, line answers Thurs 19:00-20:00, women's cafe Thurs 17:30-20:00.

■ *Bars*
SMUGGLER'S, Untere Donaulände at Nagelschmiedgasse, (0851) 35 465, gay only Sun 21:00-03:00. ♂

■ *Erotica*
BEATE UHSE INT, Bahnhofstr. 2.
ORION, Franz Stockbauer Weg 1.

RECKLINGHAUSEN

■ *Bars*
AIRPORT, Grosse Perdekapstr. 21, (02361) 109 696, 20:00-02:00 (Fri, Sat till 05:00), closed Mon. ♂

■ *Dance Bar/Disco*
FRAUENSCHWOOF, Kellerstr. 10, in the Altstadtschmiede, (02361) 21 212, lesbian dance night 4th Sat. ♀

REGENSBURG

■ *Information*
AIDS-HILFE, (0941) 791 226.
FRAUENZENTRUM & FRAUENKNEIPE, Prüfeningerstr. 32, (0941) 242 59, Lesbengruppe (lesbian group) meets Thurs from 20:00. Frauenkneipe (women's bar night) Tues from 20:00.
LESBENTELEFON, (0941) 241 71, lesbian line, Tues 19:00-21:00.

■ *Bars*
ALLEGRO, Weisse Lammgasse 1, (0941) 52714, 10:00-01:00 (Fri, Sat till 02:00). ♂
JEANS, Glockgasse 1, (0941) 51 782, 18:00-01:00. ♂
NA UND, Jakobstr. 7, (0941) 56 57 55, 20:00-01:00, closed Mon. ♂
SUDHAUS, Untere Bachgasse 8, (0941) 51 946, gay Thurs 23:00-03:00. ♂

■ *Dance Bar/Disco*
JOY'S DISCO CLUB, Dr. Gessler Str. 2, (0941) 954 75, Sun from 20:30. ♀♂
SCALA, Pustet Passage, (0941) 52 293, 23:00-03:00 (Fri, Sat till 04:00), closed Mon & Tues. ♂

■ *Erotica*
BEATE UHSE, Fröhliche Türkenstrasse at Grasgasse.
ORION, Bahnhofstr. 24 at the Castra Regina Center.
VIDEOWORLD MAN SHOP & KINO, Spiegelgasse 1.

REICHENBACH

■ *Dance Bar/Disco*
FLAIR, Melanchthonstr. 22, 03765 21105 or 03746 24267, Wed 20:00-04:00, Fri & Sat from 21:00. ♂

ROSENHEIM

■ *Bars*
JÄGERSTUBERL, Nikolaistrasse 13, (08031) 346 65, 10:00-01:00, Sun from 18:00. ♂
THEATERSCHENKE, Ludwigplatz 14, at Theater am Markt, (08031) 379 73, 20:00-01:00, closed Mon. ♂

ROSTOCK

■ *Information*
AIDS INFO, (0381) 453 156.

■ *Bars*
AALGLATT, Kistenmacherstr. 17, (0381) 493 42 14, 10:00-01:00 (Sat, Sun from 20:00). ♂
ALTER HAFEN, Strandstr. 24, (0381) 342 26, 17:00-03:00 (Sun from 10:00). ♂
GERD'S BIERBAR, Schnickmannstr. 7, (0381) 493 49 61, 11:00-01:00 (Fri, Sat till 02:00). ♂

■ *Cafe*
CAFE TAUBENSCHLAG, Gerberbruch 14, at Am Windspiel bar, (0381) 490 2401, from 19:00. Tues women only. ♂

■ *Retail & Bookstores*
DIE ANDERE BUCHHANDLUNG, Wismarsche Str. 11, (0381) 492 05 13, gay titles, 09:00-18:00 (Sat till 13:00), closed Sun.

■ *Erotica*
BEATE UHSE INT, Portcenter.

SAARBRÜCKEN

■ *Information*
AIDS HILFE, (0681) 31 112.
ZENTRUM FÜR LESBEN UND SCHWULE, Bismarckstr. 6, (0681) 37 49 55, center for lesbians & gays.

■ *Bars*
ATRIUM, Schillerplatz 16, (0681) 39 88 57, 12:00-01:00 (Sat-Mon fr. 20:00), closed Sun. ♂
BOOTS, Mainzerstr. 53, (0681) 61 495, 21:00-05:00, closed Mon. ♂
FOR YOU, Mainzerstr. 110, (0681) 684 849, 21:00-01:00 (Fri, Sat till 04:00). ♂
FRAUENKNEIPE, Bismarckstr. 6, at Lesbian & Gay center (0681) 37 49 55, women's bar night Tues from 20:00. ♀
HISTORY, Obertorstr. 10, (0681) 390 8582, 15:00-01:00, closed Tues. ♂
LA BOHEME, Kronenstr. 10, (0681) 328 83, daily 15:00-01:00. ♂
MADEMOISELLE, Mainzer Strasse 8, (0681) 337 15, 19:00-04:00. ♂
TEDDY-TREFF, Mainzerstr. 57, (0681) 656 08, 20:00-03:00 (Fri, Sat till 05:00), closed Mon. ♂

■ *Dance Bar/Disco*
BIG BEN DISCO, Försterstr. 17, (0681) 358 55, from 18:00, closed Mon. ♂
FRAUENDISCO, Dudweilerstr., at Café Ultra, women's disco, Fri from 21:00. ♀

■ *Erotica*
BEATE UHSE, Bahnhofstr. 74.
CITY LIVE, Viktoriastr. 26a, (0681) 390 81 21.
ROXY KINO, Bahnhofstr. 109, (0681) 32 544.

SAARLOUIS

■ *Bars*
PAVILLION, at the Kasematten, 46 12 49, 17:00-01:00 (Sat till 04:00). ♂

■ *Cafe*
CAFE WICHTIG, Lisdorfer Str 19a, 46 01 78, 15:00-01:00 (Fri, Sat till 04:00), closed Sun. ♂

SCHLESWIG-HOLSTEIN AREA

■ *Women's Accommodations*
HAUS AM DOM FRAUENHOTEL, Töpferstr 9, (04621) 21388, women's hotel in renovated 200-year-old house, private baths, telephone, reading room, winter & flower gardens & summer house, ocean nearby. ♀

SCHÖLLNACH

■ *Accommodations*
DIE MÜHLE (THE MILL), Englfing 16, 8359 Schöllnach, (09903) 562, fax: (09903) 2614. mainly men, lesbians welcome, living room area, TV, bar, radio, record collection, shared baths. ♂

SCHWERIN

■ *Bars*
SAITENSPRUNG, Von Thünen Str 45, at Obotritenring, from 20:00. ♂

■ *Dance Bar/Disco*
CASINO, Pfaffenstr. 3, 56 10 43, 2nd Sat 21:00-03:00. ♂

■ *Erotica*
SEX SHOP, Goethestr. 62.

SIEGBURG

■ *Bars*
TÖPFERSTUBE, Tonnisbergstr. 8, 561 00, 17:00-01:00 (Sun 11:30-14:00 & 18:00-01:00). ♂

SIEGEN

■ *Bars*
DARLING, Geisweider Str. 4, (0271) 834 65, 21:00-05:00, closed Mon. ♂
INCOGNITO, Hundgasse 12, (0271) 575 23, daily 19:00-01:00 (Fri, Sat till 03:00), closed Mon. ♂

■ *Erotica*
ORION SHOP, Hagener Strasse 71, (0271) 454 08.

SIMMELSDORF

■ *Accommodations*
HOTEL SONNENHOF, Ittling 36, (49-9155)

GERMANY

823, Fax: (49-9155) 7278. E-mail: SONNENHOF.HOTEL@t-online.de. http://ourworld.compuserve.com/homepages/GAY_HOTEL/. men-only hotel with disco/bar, clothing-optional environment, gay events held throughout the year, private baths, TV lounge, buffet breakfast.

SOLINGEN

Information
FRAUENZENTRUM, Klemens Horn Str. 15, (02122) 172 29, lesbian group meets here.

Bars
CAFE COBRA, Merscheider Str. 77-79, (0212) 33 25 65, from 10:00. ♂

Restaurants
VOGELSANG, Focherstrasse 84, (0212) 531 21, 18:00-02:00 (Fri, Sat till 03:00), closed Thurs.

STUTTGART

Information
AIDS HILFE, (0711) 61 08 49.

Bars
BISTRO TORO, Eberhardstr. 65, (0711) 236 94 57, 11:00-03:00 (Fri, Sat till 05:00, Sun from 18:00). ♂

BOOTS, Bopserstr. 9, (0711) 236 47 64, cruise bar frequented by leather men, 20:00-01:00, Fri, Sat till 02:00.

EAGLE, Mozartstr. 51, (0711) 640 61 83, cruise bar frequented by leather men, daily 20:00-01:00 (Fri, Sat till 02:00).

EASTEND, Haussmannstr. 235, (0711) 286 47 02, 19:00-01:00 (Fri, Sat till 02:00). ♂

FINKENNEST, Weberstr. 11, (0711) 24 11 42, daily 06:00-01:00. ♂

HARDY'S, Lange Str 35, (0711) 226 59 10, 20:00-24:00 (Fri, Sat till 01:00). ♂

JAKOB STUBE, Jakobstrasse 12, (0711) 23 54 82, 10:00-01:00, Sat & Sun from 15:00. ♂

KELLER KÜBLE, Reuchlinstr. 12, (0711) 615 97 44, 10:00-01:00 (Fri, Sat till 02:00). ♂

LAURA'S CLUB, Lautenschlager Str. 20, (0711) 29 01 60, daily 20:00-06:00. ♂

SUSPEKT, Ludwigstr. 55a, at Hasenbergstr., (0711) 61 66 45, 18:00-01:00 (Fri, Sat till 02:00). ♂

Dance Bar/Disco
KINGS CLUB, Calwer Strasse 21, (0711) 226 45 58, 22:00-06:00, closed Mon, Tues. ♂

Cafe
JENSEITZ, Bebelstrasse 25, (0711) 63 13 03, 10:00-01:00, Tues from 18:00.

MONROE'S, Schulstrasse 3, (0711) 226 27 70, 12:00-03:00, Sun from 16:00. ♂

SARAH CAFÉ FÜR FRAUEN, Johannesstr. 13, (0711) 62 66 38, women's cafe. ♀

Saunas/Health Clubs
OLYMPUS CLUB SAUNA, Gerberstr. 11, (0711) 64 98 919, daily 14:00-24:00.

Retail & Bookstores
ERLKÖNIG, Bebelstrasse 25, (0711) 63 91 39, gay bookshop, 10:00-18:30, Thurs till 20:30, Sat till 14:00.

GOUDOU FRAUENBUCHLADEN, Schloss Str. 66, (0711) 66 11 00, women's bookstore.

Erotica
BEATE UHSE INT, Marienstrasse 24.
DR. MÜLLER'S, Alte Poststr. 2.
INSIDER VIDEO, Möhringer Str. 129, (0711) 649 4023.
SEX SHOP BINOKEL, König Karl Str. 85, (0711) 56 93 47.

TIEFENBACH

Women's Accommodations
FRAUENFERIENHAUS TIEFENBACH/SILBERSEE, Hammer 22, 93464 Tiefenbach, (09673) 499, women-only retreat & conference center, near swimming, shopping, sauna, bath hall, single, double & dorm rooms, 1 en suite & 3 shared baths, many outdoor activities. ♀

TRIER

Information
FRAUENZENTRUM, Saarstrasse 38, (0651) 401 19, women's center.
SCHMIT-Z, Mustrostr. 4, (0651) 425 14, gay center with cafe Thurs 20:00-04:00 & Sun 16:00-20:00. ♂

Bars
KULISSE, Jakobspitälchen 2-3, (0651) 727 76, from 20:00. ♂
PALETTE, Oerenstrasse 13b, (0651) 426 09, 20:00-01:00, Fri & Sat till 02:00. ♂

Dance Bar/Disco
FRAUENDISCO FAMFATAL, Wechselstrasse, at Tuchfabrik. ♀

Leathers/Piercing
BALDOS STUDIO, (0651) 28 335, piercing studio, body art.

Erotica
ORION SHOP, Metzelstr. 27.

TÜBINGEN

Information
LESBENTELEFON, (07071) 329 01, lesbian info line Fri 18:00-20:00.

Bars
ARSENAL, Am Stadtgraben 33, (07071) 51 073, Thurs from 23:00. ♂

Dance Bar/Disco
FRAUENDISCO, at Club Voltaire, Haagasse 26b, women's disco Sat from 22:00. ♀

Cafe
FRAUENCAFE, at Epplehaus, Karlstrasse 13, (07071) 328 62, women's cafe, Mon-Fri 20:00-24:00. ♀

Retail & Bookstores
THALESTRIS FRAUENBUCHLADEN, Bursagasse 2, (07071) 265 90, women's bookstore. Lesbenkontaktnetz (lesbian contact network) housed here.

ULM

Information
FRAUENZENTRUM, Hinter dem Brot 9, (0731) 67 775, women's center, lesbian group meets here.

Bars
HIT, Pfauengasse 19, (0731) 63 320, 22:00-03:00, closed Mon, Tues. ♂
PHOENIX, Sterngasse 4, (0731) 68 834, 17:00-02:00. ♂
ZUM ALTEN FRITZ, Karlstr. 9, (0731) 65 300, 17:00-02:00 (closed Mon-Wed). ♂

Dance Bar/Disco
TANGENTE, Frauenstr. 29, (0731) 65 966, Sun only 21:00-03:00. ♂

Erotica
ORION SHOP, Neue Strasse 22.
VIDEOWORLD MAN SHOP & KINO, Ulmer Gasse 7.

VILLINGEN-SCHWENNINGEN

Bars
CLUB FORTY-SIX A, Dauchingerstr. 46a, (07720) 639 09, from 21:00, closed Mon, Tues. Women's disco 2nd Fri. ♂
PFEFFERMÜHLE, Alte Tuttlinger Str. 4, (07720) 56 69, bar & sauna, closed Tues. Bar 21:00-01:30; Sauna from 16:00 (Sat, Sun from 15:00). ♂

Erotica
ORION, Hans Sachs Str. 27.

VITTE

Bars
INSEL HIDDENSEE, Süderende 166, (038300) 235, 11:00-01:00. ♂

WEIMAR

Information
FRAUENZENTRUM, Freiherr von Stein Allee 22, (03640) 850 186, women's center, lesbian group meets Wed from 20:00.

Bars
WEINSTUBE SOMMER, Humboldstr. 2, (03643) 62 257, 10:00-01:00. ♂

WESEL

Bars
RICK'S, Poppelbaumstr. 29, (0281) 310 03, from 20:00, closed Mon. ♂

GREECE

WIESBADEN

■ **Information**
FRAUENMUSEUM, Wörthstrasse 5, (0611) 308 17 63, women's museum, lesbians welcome.
FRAUENZENTRUM, Adlerstr. 7, women's center.

■ **Bars**
COURAGE, Römerberg 13, (0611) 30 46 23, 15:00-01:00 (Fri, Sat till 02:00). ♂
FRAUENLESBENKNEIPE, Marcobrunner Str. 9, at Café Klatsch, (0611) 44 02 66, women's bar night last Sun. ♀
JOY, Dotsheimer Str 37, enter from Zimmerstr., (0611) 30 75 59, from 18:00. ♂
TREND, Am Römertor 7, (0611) 304 569, 13:00-01:00 (Sat till 02:00). ♂

■ **Saunas/Health Clubs**
CLUB SAUNA, Häfnergasse 3, (0611) 30 55 74, daily 15:00-23:00.

■ **Retail & Bookstores**
FRAUENBUCHVERSAND UND -LADEN, Luxemburgstrasse 2, (0611) 37 15 15, Fax: (0611) 37 19 13, women's bookstore.

■ **Erotica**
CITY SEX SHOP, Mauritiusplatz 1, (0611) 30 48 40.
ORION, Bismarckring 44, at Wellritzstr.

WILHELMSHAVEN

■ **Information**
AIDS HILFE, (04421) 211 49.

■ **Bars**
MAI PEN LAI, Ebertstr. 128, (04421) 41 659, 21:00-02:00 (Fri, Sat till 03:00), closed Mon. ♂
ZOFF, Bismarckstr. 121, (04421) 329 78, 20:00-02:00 (Fri, Sat till 03:00). ♂
ZUR SONNE, Grenzstrasse 21, (04421) 215 02, 20:00-05:00, Fri, Sat from 18:30. ♂

■ **Cafe**
FRAUENCAFÉ BACKSTUBE, Albrechtstr. 10, women's café 1st Sat. ♀

WINTERBERG

■ **Bars**
PEPELS PUB, Neuastenbergstr. 28, 2668, 12:00-01:00. ♂

WORMS

■ **Cafe**
FRAUENCAFÉ, Friedr. Ebertstr. 20, (06241) 524 59, women's café Mon-Thurs from 15:00. Lesbenstammtisch (lesbian group) meets 1st & 3rd Wed from 20:00. ♀

WUPPERTAL

■ **Information**
FRAUENZENTRUM URANIA, Stiftstr. 12, (0202) 44 99 68, women's center.

LESBENTELEFON, (0202) 42 39 46, lesbian line, answers Mon, Tues Thurs 10:00-12:00 & 17:00-19:00, Fri only 10:00-12:00.

■ **Bars**
ADERSKELLERCHEN, Adestr. 18, (0202) 421 4408, 11:00-01:00 (Mon from 13:00). ♂
BEI ACHIM, Gathe 40, (0202) 44 14 40, 19:00-05:00. ♂
FLAIR, Gathe 34, (0202) 44 51 76, from 21:00, closed Mon. ♂
KELLER CLUB, Schlossbleiche 32, (0202) 45 55 35, 18:00-01:00 (Fri, Sat till 03:00). ♂
LESBENKNEIPE, Stiftstr. 12 at the Frauenzentrum, (0202) 44 99 68, women's bar night at the women's center, Fri from 21:00. ♀
MARLENE, Hochstr. 65, (0202) 31 64 28, 19:00-01:00. ♂

■ **Dance Bar/Disco**
FRAUENSCHWOOF, Stiftstr. 12 at the Frauenzentrum, women's dance night 3rd Sat at women's center. ⚥♀
FRAUENSCHWOOF, Viehofstr. 25, (0202) 421 081, women's dance night, last Sat from 21:00. ⚥♀
LESBENDISCO, Wiesenstr. 11, at the Autonomes Zentrum, lesbian disco 1st Sat from 21:00. ⚥♀

■ **Cafe**
CAFE CREME, Briller Str 3, (0202) 30 43 63, 08:30-01:00 (Sat, Sun from 10:00). ♂

■ **Saunas/Health Clubs**
THEO'S CLUB SAUNA, Uellendahler Str. 410, (0202) 70 60 59, 15:00-23:00 (Sat & Sun from 13:00), closed Thurs.

■ **Retail & Bookstores**
DRÖPPEL(FE)MINA, Am Brögel 1, (0202) 877 07, women's bookstore & cafe.

■ **Erotica**
ORION SHOP, City Center Passage, (0202) 44 63 00.

WÜRZBURG

■ **Information**
LESBENTELEFON, (0931) 41 26 46, lesbian line, Mon 19:00-21:00.

■ **Bars**
SONDERBAR, Bronnbachergasse 1, (09281) 543 425, 11:00-02:00. ♂

■ **Dance Bar/Disco**
GAY DISCO NIGHT, Frankfurter Str 87, at AKW, 1st Sat 21:00-03:00. ⚥♂

ZÜLPICH-LÖVENICH

■ **Women's Accommodations**
FRAUENBILDUNGSHAUS ZÜLPICH-LÖVENICH Prälat-Franken-Str 13, 53909, (02252) 6577. Women-only retreat with courses & programs, variety of rooms with private & shared baths, garden, nearby lake, groceries available. ♀

ZWEIBRÜCKEN

■ **Bars**
RENDEZVOUS, Ernstweilertal, (06332) 13 350, 20:00-03:00, closed Mon, Tues. ♂

ZWICKAU

■ **Information**
AIDS HILFE, (0375) 83 53 65.

■ **Bars**
AN DER REITBAHN, Georg Handke Str. 5, (0375) 26 271, Fri, Sat from 20:00. ♂

■ **Saunas/Health Clubs**
THERMO CLUB SAUNA, Leipziger Str 40, (0375) 29 60 10, 15:00-24:00 (Fri, Sat till 06:00), closed Tues.

GREECE

COUNTRY CODE: (30)

WHO TO CALL
For Tour Companies Serving This Destination
See Greece on page 16

NOTE ABOUT ISLAND ADDRESSES: The following Greek islands are so small that street addresses may not be necessary: Corfu, Lesbos, Mykonos, Paros, Rhodes, Samos & Santorini.

ATHENS

■ **Information**
EOK & AKOE-AMPHI, 21 Patission Str, 7th floor, (01) 52 39 017, gay & lesbian organizations.

■ **Accommodations**
ATHENIAN INN, 22 Haritos, Kolonaki. Reserve through Windmills Travel, (30-289) 23877 or 22066 (fax only November-March), gay-friendly inn.
FRANKIE'S & JOE'S IN ATHENS, (30-1) 865 4381 or (353-1) 478 3087. To open early 1997, phone for details. ♀♂
PLAKA HOTEL, 7 Kapnikareas, at Mitropoleos, Plaka. Reserve through Windmills Travel, (30-289) 23877 or 22066 (fax only November-March), gay-friendly hotel.

■ **Beaches**
ASTERIA BEACH, take the Voula bus from Zappion.
LIMANAKIA BEACH, take the Varkiza bus from Zappion (No 117), exclusively gay.

GREECE

Civilized Cycling in the Greek Islands

Imagine peddling a bicycle on the Greek island of Cephalonia. The roads are well-paved and quiet with panoramic views of the coastline. Rubber tires pass almost silently through villages unchanged since ancient times. Each afternoon brings the reward of a comfortable hotel room with balcony overlooking a fishing bay.

Such experiences have been contemplated and created by leaders John and Michel of the Peddlers bicycle touring company. Between them, John and Michel have extensive combined experience both in the tour industry and in cycling.

Morning rides are designed to accommodate even an absolute beginner to cycle touring. Some rides are a gentle downhill cruise all the way to the mid-day seashore rendezvous. Afternoons provide more challenging optional rides. Bicycles are customized to ensure the best ride, support vans are always close by, and the guide is never far away, always acting as "ride sweeper." Group sizes do not exceed 16, with two leaders.

Book through **Destinations & Adventures Int'l**, (800) 659-4599, (213) 650-7267, Fax: (213) 650-6902.

Gay Tour/Cruise Packages to Greece & Turkey

Dedicated exclusively to the gay and lesbian travel market, **Eurway Tour & Cruise Club** has more than 20 years experience in creating visionary tour/cruise packages for Greece. We specialize in off-the-beaten-path tours, and we create customized itineraries for individuals and groups. We represent exclusive villas, chateaus, hotels, and resorts, and our buying power gains preferential treatment and rates in all major Greek cruise ships and yachts. We offer yacht sharing or chartering (bare boats, sailing yachts, motorsailers, catamarans) from the largest fleet in the Mediterranean. Special packages are available with seven-day yacht cruising. Hotels and cruising in Greece are available for the value-minded, to the exclusive and epicurian.

Aegean Odyssey packages include great sightseeing opportunities at varying rates. Spend your first few days on a cruise, then several nights in Athens at a hotel of your choice. Tour Athens, then travel on to Mykonos for a few days before re-embarking for several more days of cruising. Or, choose an Athens mini citypack, which includes a three-night stay, a half-day sightseeing tour, and two transfers. You can also combine other places of interest, such as Mykonos, Santorini, Crete, and Rhodes.

Contact **Eurway** at (203) 967-1611, (800) 938-7929, Fax:(203) 969-0799.

■ Bars

ALEKOS ISLAND,★ 42 Tsakalof St, one of the oldest gay bars in Athens, popular in early evenings. ♂

BAR 21, 21 Fillia St, (01) 88 21 532, small, cozy bar open till morning, Greek music, variety of clientele. If arriving after 03:00, ring the bell. ♂

E KAI, 12 Iosef Ton Rogon, near Syngrou Ave & Gramazi bar, quiet atmosphere, Greek music. ♂

ENDEHOMENON, 8 Lembessi St, Makriyianni, (01) 92 32 849, beautiful young men, Greek music. $♂

GRANAZI, 20 Lembessi St, Makriyianni, (01) 32 44 585, cold snacks served, Greek music. ♂

MI-AR ("MR"), 39 Moschonision, Amerikis Square, (01) 86 58 872, cruise bar. ♂

PORTA, 10 Falirou St, Makriyianni, (01) 32 49 660, both Greek & foreign music. ♀

SPYROS, Vourvachi St, at Syngrou Ave, (01) 92 23 982, till late. ♀♂

STRAS PUB, 32 Odyssea Androutsou St, Koukaki, (01) 92 21 622, mostly transvestites, Greek music, dangerous area. ♂

TA PEDIA, 8 Lembessi St, below Endehomenon bar, Makriyianni. $♂

TEST ME BAR, 62 Pipinou St, (01) 82 26 029, older & younger men, Greek music. $♂

■ Dance Bar/Disco

ALEXANDER'S, 44 Anagnostopoulou St, Kolonaki, (01) 26 44 660, bar upstairs, disco downstairs, Greek music, very few lesbians. ♂

DOM, 112 Pireos St & 31 Ikarieon, Gazi, huge disco, closed Mon & Tues. ♀♂

ERECTION CLUB, 6 Trion Ierarchon, Gefira Poulopoulou, Thission, (01) 34 20 357, closed Mon, Tues. ♂

FACTORY I, Panepistimiou, at Em. Benaki, male strippers. ♂

KOUKLES, Zan Moreas, near Syngrou Ave, behind Olympic Airways, (01) 92 13 054. ♂

LAMBDA, Syngrou Ave, Lembessi, (01) 92 24 202. ♂

LIZZARD, 31 Apostolou Pavlou St, Thission Sq, (01) 34 68 670. Call first, many gay men mixed with hetero clientele, popular with lesbians. Cozy disco bar, recommended by local gay group. ♀♂

ODYSSIA, 116 Ermou St, some hetero men may be present (voyeurs). ♀

UNDERWEAR, across from Hellenikon Airport. ♂

■ Cafe

BRITANIA, Omonoia Sq, at Athineas, open all night, dangerous area.

DE PROFUNDIS, 1 Hatzimichali, Plaka, tea house.

KIRKI, 31 Apostolou Pavlou, Thission Sq,

GREECE

below Lizzard disco, Sun from 12:00, some hetero clientele. ♀

L.A., 1 Em. Benaki, mezzanine floor, at Stadiou.

MONTPARNASSE, 32 Haritos, Kolonaki, (01) 72 90 746, till 02:00 (closed Sun), reservations required.

NEON CAFE, Omonoia Sq.

OVAL CAFE, 5 Tossitsa St. near Exarchia Sq., cozy, feminist-run cafe/bar, light menu. ♀

STYLE, Kritis St, at Chiou St, Ag. Pavlou Square. ♀♂

Saunas/Health Clubs

ATHENS RELAX, 8 Xouthou St near Omonoia Sq, (01) 52 22 866, 52 28 800, 15:00-21:00, closed Sun, telephone reservations required, some hustlers among clientele.

Restaurants

FOTAERION, 74 Ippokratous St, (01) 36 22 362, excellent food & service, wide variety of teas, recommended by local gay group.

GASTRA TAVERNA, 1 Dimaki St, Kolonaki, (01) 36 02 757, excellent food, a bit expensive, closed July/Aug, reservations a must.

Retail & Bookstores

SELANA BOOKSTORE, Sina Str. 38, (01) 36 38 262, women's bookstore.

Erotica

OMONOIA, Satombriandou Str. behind Omonoia Sq, 80% gay, but hetero films shown, till 03:00.

RIVOLI, 11 Arisidou St near Klathmonos Sq, older clientele.

CORFU

Beaches

AG. IOANNIS PERISTERON, close to Benitses, mixed hetero & gay.

MYRTIOTISSA, close to Pelekas, Glyfeda, nude beach, mixed hetero & gay.

Bars

BLUE BAR, Ethnikis Antististeos, in the city center. ♂

HIPPODROME, city center, (0661) 431 50. ♂

SWEET MOVIE, Ag. Ioannis Peristeron, close to Benitses, (0661) 923 35, some hetero clientele. ♂

ISLE OF AEGINA

Women's Accommodations

MOONROCK, PO Box 237, Williamsport, OH 43164, USA reservations: (614) 986-6945, Women-only house on a Greek island (men welcome if accompanied by women), ferry or hydrofoil from Athens, double beds, shared baths, kitchen, refrig., nearby ocean. ♀

LESBOS

Accommodations

LESBOS ACCOMMODATION INFORMATION, contact Pam Taylor at (30-289) 23877 or fax (30-289) 22066.

Bars

JIMMY'S, ♀♂

Dance Bar/Disco

SARAI, some hetero clientele. ♀♂

MYKONOS

Accommodations

COSTA'S STUDIOS, above Mykonos Town, reserve through Windmills Travel, (30-289) 23877 or 22066 (fax only November-March), gay-friendly.

FLORA'S ROOMS & STUDIOS, in Mykonos Town, reserve through Windmills Travel, (30-289) 23877 or 22066 (fax only November-March), gay-friendly.

HOTEL ELYSIUM, School of Fine Arts, Mykonos Town, (0289) 23952, 24210, 24684, fax 23747. Hotel with deluxe accommodations & panoramic views of ocean & Old Town Mykonos. The 42 well-appointed rooms & 3 suites have colour satelite TV, direct-dial

EURWAY TOUR & CRUISE CLUB

Custom Itineraries
Cruise Ships, Yachts

(800) 938-7929

FYI

Mykonos Gay Reservations & 12 Gods Party

Both individual travelers looking for the right hotel and travel agents seeking professional assistance with reservations for valued clients now have a personal contact on Mykonos. Pam Taylor of **Windmills Travel** is an accommodations, transportation and excursions expert for Mykonos and Greece.

All price ranges, including first-class hotels, deluxe studios and apartments and even reasonably-priced pension rooms, can be arranged. Pam also handles airport transfer and pick-up, car, Jeep or motor-cycle rentals, plane or boat tickets and local excursions.

Excursions include guided and unguided tours of Delos archaeological sites and jaunts to Tinos. Windmills does a day excursion by fishing boat to an isolated beach, for a beach BBQ.

Windmills is the Official Tour Operator for the gay and lesbian 12 Gods Party Sept 3-7, 1997.

Contact **Windmills** at (30 289) 23877/26555/26556/26557, Fax: (30 289) 22066 (ONLY fax is operative November to March), E-mail: windmills@travelling.gr.

GREECE

Greek Sailing Charter Company

Fine, one of the most dynamic and modern companies in its field, is exclusively used by people who require holidays and yachting with personality. Since 1983, **Fine Travel and Yachting** has had extensive experience in organizing cruises and incentive trips for individual clients and groups. Members of IGTA since 1994, they organize trips for gays and lesbians as follows:

- All services in area of yachting
- Chartering yachts, motor sailers
- Scheduled Greek Island cruises
- Seminars, incentives, events
- Product promotion, presentation
- Hotels, apts., villas, car rental
- Excursions through out Greece.

Call travel agent or direct: **Fine Travel & Yachting**, (30 1) 41 22 324, Fax: (30 1) 41 70 137.

All-Inclusive Greek Sailing Vacations

Sailing the Greek islands is ideal for people with a variety of interests who seek adventure off the beaten path. **GPSC Charters** offers unique and memorable Mediterranean sailing holidays. From unspoiled villages and deserted beaches with clear, dark-blue waters to archaeological sites and sophisticated nightlife, the Med has it all.

GPSC Charters flotilla cruises are all-inclusive packages, including a large, luxurious private sailing yacht, round-trip air from New York, hotels, transfers, guide, etc., at a per-person price of just $1,950 for 14 days. GPSC also offers group and individual charters of crewed and bareboat sailing yachts, motorsailers and motor yachts from 27' to 250'. These are ideal for business, professional and casual groups who desire the luxury and privacy offered aboard a yacht.

GPSC's in-house gay travel agency is available for planning additional travel.

Contact **GPSC Charters** at (215) 247-3903, (800) 732-6786, Fax: (215) 247-1505, E-mail: corr@gpsc.com.

phones, stereo music & private baths. An American buffet breakfast is served daily. Pool on premises. Some hetero clientele.

MARIETTA'S STUDIOS, School of Fine Arts, Mykonos Town, reserve through Windmills Travel, (30-289) 23877 or 22066 (fax only November-March), gay-friendly studios.

PETINOS HOTELS & APARTMENTS, in towne & Plati Yialos, reserve through Windmill Travel, (30-289) 23877 or 22066 (fax only November-March), gay-friendly hotels & apartments.

PRESIDENT'S STUDIOS, reserve through Windmill Travel, (30-289) 23877 or 22066 (fax only November-March). Studios with double glazing, AC, color TV, kitchenette, full bathroom. In a quiet residential area of Mykonos town.

■ *Beaches*

ELIA, mixed hetero & gay men & women, nudity permitted, 2 restaurants & tabernas nearby, bus hourly from the harbor or boat from Plati Yialos.

PARANGA BEACH, a 20-minute walk from Plati Yialos, a section is becoming a gay beach area, men & women, nudity permitted, snack bar & taberna nearby.

SUPER PARADISE, mainly gay, nudity permitted. Take big boat from the harbor or bus 15 minutes to Plati Yialos, then small boat to Super Paradise.

■ *Bars*

DIVA BAR, in Little Venice, the area of Mykonos on the water, perfect for sunsets.

IKAROS BAR, Matoyianni St, over Manto bar, rooftop bar, fabulous sunset views.

KASTRO BAR, in Little Venice, the area of Mykonos on the water, (289) 23 072, sunset views & classical music.

MANTO BAR, Matoyianni St, next to Pierro's Bar, drinks and coffee.

MONTPARNASSE PIANO BAR, in Little Venice, piano bar & cafe with trendy crowd.

PORTA BAR, behind Nikos Tavern, near boats to Delos, small bar, very few women.

TAPAS BAR, at the Manto Hotel, behind Pierro's Bar, may return for 1997 season.

■ *Dance Bar/Disco*

FACTORY, ask locally for location, changes frequently.

PIERRO'S BAR, ★ Matoyianni St, popular disco, many heteros.

■ *Cafe*

ARISTOTE CAFE BAR, Matoyianni St, close to Credit Bank, upscale, trendy cafe bar with Greek & foreign music.

GREECE

Mykonos — Island of the Gods

by Pam Taylor, Windmills Travel & Tourism

Close your eyes and picture this...deep blue seas becoming turquoise along the ragged coastline dotted with sandy beaches...stark white cubed houses trimmed in blues, reds and greens...white windmills dotting the stark landscape... hundreds of red-roofed white chapels...clear blue skies...and SUN...SUN...SUN...

This is Mykonos! Located about 6 hours by ferry, 3 hours with the hydrofoil or catamaran, and only 45 minutes by air from Athens, Mykonos has, over the years, become one of the most popular of the Cycladic Islands. Since the mid-50's, the island has been the jet-set playground and artists' mecca of the eastern Mediterranean. Boasting of visits from such celebrities as Jane Fonda and her husband, Ted Turner, the late Jackie Kennedy Onassis, Brigitte Nielson, Claudia Cardinale and some of the international fashion designers like Thierry Muegler, Jean-Paul Gaultier and Valentino, Mykonos draws visitors from all over the world for stays of 1 or 2 days or 2 weeks, and even for the entire season of 6 months!

The island is very rocky and fairly hilly. It's total area is around 8.6 square kilometres (2 square miles). There are very few trees on the island, and the terrain is rough and barren. The only time one can see green is during the winter and spring, when the fields abound with wildflowers in a rainbow of colour — reds, violets, yellows.

With the coming of the hot, dry summer months, these same fields become brown, burnt by the sun and the August winds.

The weather during the summer is sunny and hot. The temperature has been known to hit 42C (107.7 Fahrenheit), and then there is the August wind, known as the Meltemi, which has been known to keep even the biggest ferry away from the island for a few days at a time!

There are only 2 towns on the island, Mykonos Town, or Chora, and Ano Mera, which is located in the center of the island, about 8km (5 miles) from the port. Ornos, Tourlos, San Stefanos, Platy Yialos, Kalafatis are not towns in the real sense, but areas where you can find hotels, pensions, apartments, tavernas and restaurants just off or close to the beaches.

The main tourist season runs from mid-April right through October, with the peak in July and August. Some tourists do venture onto the island during the winter months. The BEST time to come is during May, the first 2 weeks of June, September and the beginning of October. At these times, accommodation is more plentiful, the prices more reasonable and the beaches, restaurants and discos are not "sardine cans."

There are all types and cat-

Windmills Travel & Tourism, located at Fabrika Square, is listed in the Ferrari international gay and lesbian guides and is also a member of IGTA. Our staff will be more than happy to assist you in obtaining accommodation, etc. on Mykonos and some of the other Cycladic Islands, as well as in Athens. The agency is full-service, offering hotel, apartment and pension accommodation in all price ranges, transfer service, boat and plane schedule information, as well as all of the excursions mentioned. Contact Windmills at (30-289) 23877 or Fax: (30-289) 22066. For more information, see FYI on page 239.

Continued on next page.

GREECE

egories of accommodations, from super-deluxe hotels and studio apartments to the very basic camping sites. Here, Louis Vuitton suitcases "rub shoulders" with backpacks: There is something here for every budget and lifestyle. It is best to book your accommodation at least two months prior to your intended arrival to ensure that you get the type of room or apartment that you want, in the location you want. Since Mykonos is known as a gay-friendly or gay-oriented island, the majority of the accommodation facilities have put out the "welcome mat" for us, and many prefer to cater to the gay tourist. The Elysium Hotel, Anastasio Sevasti Hotel, Geranium Studios, Andromeda Residence Studios and Apartments, and President Studios are among many that have become popular with gays.

"What is there to do on Mykonos?" "What is there to see?" "What restaurants do you recommend?" "Where can I/we go at night for dancing or for a drink?" These are some of the questions asked during the summer.

Which Beach to Go to...

Mykonos is famous for its beaches, ranging from family-type facilities to Ornos to the famous Paradise and Super Paradise beaches. The BEST beaches are located on the southern coast of the island, with access from town by bus or taxi, or, for the more independent soul, by rented Jeep or motorbike. Beach chairs and umbrellas are available for a nominal rental fee. Snack bars and tavernas lie on the edge of the water, tempting sun worshippers with a wide variety of mouthwatering salads, sandwiches, snacks and drinks, as well as full meals of grilled fish or meat and pizzas. Sport facilities are available at most of the beaches, offering water skiing, jet skiing, windsurfing and even scuba diving. For those not afraid of "baring all," or who are not embarrassed by naturalists, then Paradise Beach (more for the younger set), Paranga Beach (near Platy Yialos), Super Paradise Beach and Elia Beach are your best bets. The latter three are the favourite "meetings places" for gays. To get to any of these beaches, you can take a public bus from the Fabrika Square end of town to Platy Yialos, where you then hop onto a caique fishing boat to the beach of your choice for a day of basking in the sun and swimming in the warm waters and, just maybe, even meeting the person of your dreams. It's been known to happen!

What to Do...

Aside from spending the day at the beach, there are many options available. Visit Delos in the morning, with or without a guide, and trace the footsteps of the ancients who had come to worship the god Apollo. Join David on a 2-hour horseback riding excursion for a very different way of seeing the island, as you wend your way to Paradise and Paranga Beaches along the numerous "goat paths" that run in a spiderweb-like network throughout the island. Sail on a caique to an isolated beach to spend the day at a beach BBQ. If the gods have blessed you with a calm day, a treat is in store for you when the caique visits the grottos of Dragonnissi Island. Go to Tinos or Santorini on a guided tour. Hire a Jeep or motorbike, and meander around the island, exploring the various nooks and crannies that are there for you to discover. Wander through the narrow streets of town with its array of tourist shops and boutiques. You are sure to find the perfect gift for everyone back home. Keep an eye out for Petros, the pink pelican and mascot of Mykonos. Careful, though. He likes to take a nip at the ladies. He's definitely not a gentleman! There are a few museums to visit in town — the Nautical, Archaeological, Folklorique, Lena's House and Boni's Windmill. Ano Mera, in the centre of the island, has a monastery and small museum, and some very good tavernas are located on the main square.

With your daylight hours taken care of...

Mykonos is famous all over the world for its varied nightlife. The only problem existing is choosing the place to go!

BUT...before you even worry about where to go for dinner or for dancing, head down to Little Venice at about 7-8 pm for a romantic pre-dinner cocktail, watching the magnificent sunset at one of the cafe bars on the edge of the water. Montparnasse Piano Bar, Kastro's and Diva are ready to serve you with a smile.

Continued on page 508

■ *Restaurants*
DELPHINE'S, Matoyianni St, homestyle Greek cuisine. ⊠
EDEN GARDEN, international cuisine. ⊠
EL GRECO RESTAURANT, international cuisine. ⊠
GATSBY'S, indoor & garden seating. ⊠
KATRINAS RESTAURANT, expensive, international cuisine.
MACCHARONI, near Lakka Square, Italian cuisine, outdoor seating. ⊠

■ *Retail & Bookstores*
INTERNATIONAL BOOKSTORE, near Pierro's disco, general bookstore with some gay & lesbian titles.

■ *Erotica*
SEXY SHOP, Zouganeli St, behind Pierro's disco.

PAROS

■ *Beaches*
LANGERI & MONASTERI BEACHES, ask locally for directions.

■ *Bars*
AUGOSTA, in the town of Naoussa, NOT a gay bar, frequented by gays.
KABARNIS, across from Christo's Taberna, rooftop garden, creperie, frequented by gays.
STAVEDO, in Parikia, frequented by gays.

RHODES

■ *Beaches*
KATO PETRES & PHALIRAKI, ask locally for directions. Phaliraki is a nude beach.

■ *Dance Bar/Disco*
BERLIN, Orphanidou 47, near Alexia hotel. 💡♂
MEDOUSSA, in city center, discreetly frequented by gays. 💡
VALENTINO, in Old Town. 💡♂
VEGGERA, in city center. discreetly frequented by gays. 💡

■ *Cafe*
NEORION, near the cathedral, NOT a gay cafe, discreetly frequented by gays.

SAMOS

■ *Beaches*
TSAMADOU, in town of Koraki, nudist beach.

■ *Bars*
BARINO, in town of Koraki. ♂
CLARY'S PUB, main square in Vathy. ♂

■ *Dance Bar/Disco*
METROPOLIS,★ trendy crowd. 💡♂
TOTEM,★ in town of Pythagoreion, (0273) 272 50. 💡♂

■ *Cafe*
MYKALI, at Mykali beach, (0273) 222 15, ask locally for directions, discreetly frequented by gays.

SANTORINI

■ *Accommodations*
GROTTO VILLAS, in Fira, reserve through Windmills Travel, (30-289) 23877 or 22066 (fax only November-March), gay-friendly villas.
MELINA HOTEL, in Fira, reserve through Windmills Travel, (30-289) 23877 or 22066 (fax only November-March), gay-friendly hotel.
NINE MUSES, in Perivolos/Emboriou, reserve through Windmills Travel, (30-289) 23877 or 22066 (fax only November-March), gay-friendly hotel.
ROCCABELLA STUDIOS & APARTMENTS, in Imerovigli, reserve through Windmills Travel, (30-289) 23877 or 22066 (fax only November-March), gay-friendly.

■ *Beaches*
AVIS, nude beach situated between Monolithos & Kamari.
MONOLITHOS, ask locally for directions.

■ *Bars*
FRANCO'S, Marinatou St, classical music. ♂

■ *Dance Bar/Disco*
CASABLANCA, younger crowd, discreetly frequented by gays.
JUST BLUE, in the main square, town of Fira, discreetly frequented by gays. 💡
TROPICAL, near Franco's bar. 💡♀♂

THESSALONIKI

■ *Information*
O.P.O.TH., (031) 85 57 06 (tel/fax), gay group with scheduled activities, publishes O Pothos magazine, airs weekly radio show Sun 12:00-14:00.

■ *Bars*
AHUDUDU, 3 Chalkis St, (031) 83 64 44. ♀♂
BACHALON, 8 Romanou St, (031) 26 86 37. 🗝♀♂
TABOO, 7 Kastritsiou St, (031) 27 91 32, may close in 1996. ♀

■ *Dance Bar/Disco*
FACTORY, 51 Proxenou Koromila St, expensive. 💡♀♂
FUNKY MOBILE, 29 Papandreu St, younger crowd, frequented by gays. ⊠

■ *Cafe*
DE FACTO, 17 Pavlou Mela St. ♀♂
STRETTO, 18 C. Diehl St. ♀♂

■ *Erotica*
VIDEORAMA VIDEO CLUB, 3 Philikis Eterias St, 1st floor.

HUNGARY

HUNGARY
COUNTRY CODE: (36)

WHO TO CALL
For Tour Companies Serving This Destination
See Hungary on page 17

BUDAPEST

■ *Bars*
DARLING, 1 Szép ut. (V), small bar, videos, 19:00-05:00, frequented by some women. U ♂
MYSTERY, 3 Nagysándor Jószef ut. (V), (1) 112 14 36, small bar, recently renovated, 21:00-04:00 (closed Sun), frequented by some women. ✕♂

■ *Dance Bar/Disco*
ACTION BAR,★ 42 Magyar ut. (V), (1) 266 91 48, cruise bar, videos, 21:00-04:00. 🎵💡 ⊠✕♂
ANGYEL, 51 Rákóczi ut. (VII), (1) 113 12 73, cruise-type bar with videos, darkrooms, hustlers, 22:00-06:00, frequented by some women. 🎵💡✕♂
LOKAL, 31 Kertész ut. (VII), 22:00-04:00 (closed Thurs). 🎵💡✕$♂

■ *Saunas/Health Clubs*
GELLERT GYOGYFÜRDO, 4 Kelenhegyi ut. (XI), at Hellert Hotel, (1) 185 35 55, not a gay sauna, discreetly frequented by gay men. Separate men's & women's sauna areas. ♨⊠
RASZ, 8-10 Hadnagy (I), (1) 175 44 49, NOT a gay sauna, discreetly frequented by gay men (more gay Sat). ♨
RUDAS, Dobrentei Ter 9 (I), (1) 156 13 22, Turkish bath, NOT gay, discreetly frequented by gays. ♨
SZECHENYI, 11 Allatkerti ut. (XIV), (1) 121 03 10, not a gay sauna, discreetly frequented by gay men. Separate men's & women's sauna areas. ♨⊠

■ *Restaurants*
FENYOGYONGYE VENDEGLO,★ 155 Szepvolgyi ut. (II), (1) 168 81 44, 12:00-24:00, some straight clientele. 🍷♀♂

■ *Erotica*
APOLLO VIDEO SHOP, 3 Terez Korut (VI).

ICELAND

Women's Journey to Mystical Ireland

Join 20 other women for a unique journey to some of ancient Ireland's pagan and goddess centres. See Ireland through the eyes of Irish women who intimately know and love their country. Mod is an archaeologist, healer and spinner of tales. Lynn, owner of Mount Bretia women's guesthouse, has a wealth of knowledge about the sites, the culture, the politics, and the women of Ireland.

We'll spend the first 4 days at Cloghroe House, a beautiful Georgian mansion outside the city of Cork, making day trips to ancient stone circles, and burial mounds and hearing about their history. While at Cloghroe, you can take long walks through achingly beautiful green meadows and misty woods to the nearby town of Blarney. Later, we'll travel by bus, staying at B&Bs and cottages, and seeing Kildare and Bridig's Well, the beautiful Dingle Peninsula and the narrow streets and old stone and wooden shopfronts of Galway, where Lynn is working on a rendevouz with Galway women.

Contact **Sounds & Furies** at (604) 253-7189, Fax: (604) 253-2191.

ICELAND
COUNTRY CODE: (354)

WHO TO CALL
For Tour Companies Serving This Destination
See Iceland on page 17

REYKJAVIK

■ Information
ALNAEMISSAMTÖKIN AIDS ORGANIZATION, Hverfisgata 16A, (1) 28586.
REYKJAVIK GAY CENTER (SAMTÖKIN 78), Lindergata 49, (354) 552 8539, Fax: (354) 552 7525, (answers Mon & Thurs 20:00-23:00), center open Mon & Thurs 20:00-23:00 with cafe, library. Very popular in winter. Open bar night Sat 21:30-02:00, Thurs cafe open till midnite, AA meetings Tues 21:00. 🏳️‍🌈

■ Accommodations
ROOM WITH A VIEW, Laugavegur 18, 6th floor, (354) 552 7262 (tel/fax), E-mail (mark all e-mail with name Arni Einarsson): mm@centrum.is. 1-bedroom apartments with kitchens, sleeping 1-4 persons, fully furnished, laundry facilities. Also on premises: coffee shop open daily 09:00-21:00 & bookshop selling gay magazines.

■ Bars
BAR 22,★ Laugavegur 22, mostly gay bar with dance floor on second floor, Thurs 23:00-01:00, Fri & Sat 18:00-03:00. 🏳️‍🌈♀♂
BIOBARINN, Klapparstig 26, 16:00-01:00 (till 03:00 Fri & Sat), very mixed, but nearly always frequented by a few gays. 🏳️

■ Dance Bar/Disco
TUNGLID, Laekjargata 2, big disco with younger crowd, frequented by some gays but not known as a gay hangout.

■ Cafe
KAFFI LIST, Klapparstig 28, 10:00-01:00 (weekends 11:00-03:00), serves soups, salads, tapas, coffee, desserts. Mostly straight clientele, but popular with gays & lesbians. 🏳️
KAFFI PARIS, Austurstrati 14, 08:00-01:00, light meals & coffee. Mostly straight clientele, but popular with gays & lesbians. 🏳️
SOLON ISLANDUS, Bankastraeti 7a, very popular with gays & lesbians, but frequented by mostly hetero clientele, many artists, serves light meals & coffee. 🏳️

■ Retail & Bookstores
MAL OG MENNING, Laugavegur 18, general bookstore with some gay books.

IRELAND
COUNTRY CODE: (353)

WHO TO CALL
For Tour Companies Serving This Destination
See Ireland on page 17

CORK

■ Information
AIDS LINE, (021) 27 66 76, Mon-Fri 10:00-17:00 (Tues also 19:00-21:00).
GAY INFORMATION & LESBIAN LINE, (021) 27 10 87, gay Wed 19:00-21:00 & Sat 15:00-17:00, lesbian Thurs 20:00-22:00.
LESBIAN & GAY RESOURCE GROUP, see Other Place listing under retail.

■ Accommodations
DANNY'S B&B, 3 St. John's Terrace, upper St. John St, (021) 50 36 06, gay & lesbian B&B. ♀♂
MONT BRETIA B&B, Adrigole, Skibbereen, (028) 33 663, B&B, some hetero clientele, shared baths, TV lounge, full breakfast, organic garden, maps of area, free bicycles, 6 mi to beach. ♀♂

■ Women's Accommodations
AMAZONIA, Coast Road, Fountainstown, Cork, (21) 831 115, women-only bed & breakfast with campsites, near shopping & swimming, double rooms & dorm with beautiful views, many outdoor activities, full breakfast. ♀

■ Bars
LOAFERS PUB, Douglas St, women only Thurs in rear bar. ♀
OTHER PLACE, at Other Place Bookstore location, (021) 31 76 60, lesbian & gay winebar Fri-Sat, women's night 1st Fri. Cafe with tea, coffee, snacks other times. 🏳️♀♂

■ Restaurants
ART HIVE, THE, McCurtain St, café & art gallery. 🏳️
OTHER SIDE CAFE, THE, 8 South Main St, (021) 27 84 70, 10:00-22:00 (Sat till 18:00).
QUAY CO-OP, 24 Sullivan's Quay, (021) 31 76 60, 09:30-22:30 (Sun from 18:00). 🏳️

■ Retail & Bookstores
OTHER PLACE, 7/8 Augustine St (beside Queen's Old Castle), (021) 27 84 70, gay & lesbian books, resource & information centre.
OTHER SIDE BOOKSHOP, 8 South Main St, (021) 27 84 70, 11:00-17:30 (closed Sun).
QUAY CO-OP, 24 Sullivans Quay, (021) 31

Iceland— Hidden Treasure of the North!

by Sue Rider Scott, l'Arc en Ciel Voyages

Mention Iceland to someone who's never been there and some may say, "Iceland— who would want to go there?" or possibly, "I've always wondered what it's like." Mention Iceland to someone who has been there, and you're likely to hear, "I loved it and can't wait to go back! It's my favorite destination!"

The name Iceland actually is a misnomer. Greenland is truly a country of ice, while Iceland is a country of green, beautifully covered with a white blanket during the winter months. Icelanders will tell you that the Vikings misnamed it on purpose to discourage others from emigrating to their beloved Iceland and encouraging trips to the barren ice fields of Greenland instead! Never typically colder than 0 degrees Fahrenheit in the winter and generally in the 60's in summer, Iceland is simply a treasure anytime of the year. In the warmer months, the bright summer nights keep locals and visitors alike enjoying the outdoors until the wee hours of the morning. When the days get shorter with the colder weather, the dark morning hours are made festive with candles and twinkling lights until everyone can enjoy the delight of a rising sun!

If you're looking for a New York City vacation, don't come here. With a population of just over 250,000 in a country about the size of Kentucky, half of whom live in the capital city of Reykjavik, this would never be considered a large city. But if you're looking for a unique, friendly and safe place to visit, Iceland is for you! City dwellers will gasp to realize that Iceland has had 39 manslaughters...in the last century! Mothers literally park their babies in their strollers—unattended—outside the local stores, while they shop! As a rule, Icelanders are very friendly people, though they may seem a bit reserved at first. Take a minute and ask for directions, or for a suggestion on a menu. Before long, your new Icelandic friend will be drawing you a map or offering to tell you everything there is to know about preparing a lamb dish!

Nowhere are the forces of nature more evident than on this island of glaciers, hot springs, geysers, active volcanoes, lava fields, waterfalls, craters and snowcapped peaks. In a world that we have tried too hard to tame, visitors to Iceland stand in awe at the mammoth Gullfoss Falls, where the river Hvitá drops 32 meters in two falls. Just down the road, others stand poised with their cameras, hoping their film is fast enough to catch the blue-rimmed bubble preceding the tremendous spouting of the Strokkur Geyser (sister to the Great Geysir for which all spouting hot springs were named). Enroute to these wonders of nature from Reykjavik, guests travel between vast deserts of lava fields left by the still-active volcanoes and reminiscent of those seen on the Big Island of Hawaii. Here, however, you'll find any number of things built in and around the lava fields, from the town of Hafnarfjördur (where lava spikes peek up between homes) to incredible Blue Lagoon. Actually not a lagoon at all, but a pale blue pool of hot water filled with silica mud, sulfur and an organic mix known to relieve psoriasis, arthritis and other ailments, the "lagoon" is the result of drilling for the Svartsengi power plant, and is now a popular spa site. A swim here can truly be an ethereal experience (especially in the winter months!) with clouds of steam rising from the delightfully hot water.

Oddly, hot water is not the expensive luxury one might expect it to be in a country named Iceland. Scalding

Continued on next page.

L'Arc en Ciel Voyages, a division of STA, Inc., specializes in custom-designed tour programs for the gay and lesbian community, and has over 35 years of group travel experience as a well-known and reputable international tour operator. They were the first to be appointed Preferred Sales Agent for the 1998 Amsterdam Gay Games, and are currently developing an assortment of group and individual programs into Iceland. Contact L'Arc en Ciel toll-free at (800) 965-LARC. See ad on page 95.

water is piped from the depths of the earth to heat 70% of the country geothermally, losing only one to two degrees along the way! This geo-thermal heating is such a part of Icelandic life that, not only is Reykjavik's gourmet revolving restaurant seated atop five geothermal hot water tanks, but outdoor swimming pools are located in every city and village and open year-round!

While one can swim comfortably year-round, it is also possible to enjoy winter sports every month of the year, as well! Skiing, while more prominent in the winter months, is available in the highland areas through June. And snow "scooting" in the mountains (with snow mobiles) is a popular activity during the warmer months. With miles and miles of mountains and wilderness, hiking is also a very popular activity here, as is horseback riding. The Icelandic horse found here is a direct descendent of horses brought to the island by the Vikings in the 9th century. (In fact, no other horses have ever been allowed in Iceland, and once a Viking horse leaves the country, it may not return!) The small, sturdy horse is very gentle and human-friendly, perfectly suited to the rough terrain, and is known for its smooth 5th gait (the tölt).

Riding expeditions of all kinds are available here, from a half-day excursion to a two-week horseback adventure for the fall sheep round-up! In fact, "adventure tours" are among Iceland's most popular, ranging from farmhouse stays to sleeping bag/hut accommodations to true tent-camping options!

Back in town, visitors will find a large assortment of shops, cafes and restaurants to keep most any guest happy. Iceland is known for its fish (especially herring, salmon, trout and haddock) as well as its sheep, which are used both for dining and for making its world-renowned Icelandic wool (for sweaters, blankets and more). Local eateries range from the deluxe Pearl to the historic Viking Restaurant to American imports, such as Pizza Hut! And, with a literary tradition going back to the sagas of the 12th and 13th centuries, Icelanders are proud that their literacy rate is an incredible 100% and almost all citizens speak English, as well as Icelandic, Danish and possibly other languages, making it very easy for visitors to get around.

Icelanders know they depend on tourists for part of their economy (70% of the gross national product comes from fishing), and while the official currency is the Icelandic Krona (about 66 to the US dollar), most hotels, restaurants, larger shops and taxis will also accept US dollars, if requested. An assortment of sightseeing tours are available from most hotels in Reykjavik, always in English. "What's on in Reykjavik," a monthly guide to entertainment, restaurants, museums and galleries in the city, can also be found in any hotel or guest house. And, yes, while a small country, Iceland boasts both a national and city theatre, symphony orchestra, opera, ballet, summer theater and a large assortment of art galleries! There is, literally, something here for everyone!

Churches are a popular site to visit on any tour abroad, and Iceland is no exception. (The "national" religion is Lutheranism). What makes Icelandic churches different, however, is their architecture! One church is built to look like a Viking ship. Another is based on the image of flowing lava! Yet a third looks from afar like it is falling into the harbor! All of the Icelandic architecture is noteworthy, however, as most has been built within the past century (due to the deterioration of earlier buildings) and almost all are topped with corrugated steel. These roofs need to be painted to avoid rust, and the Icelanders choose to do so with an assortment of colors, from reds to blues to greens, making the skyline a rainbow of color!

Gay and lesbian visitors to Iceland should feel remarkably comfortable from the moment they step off the plane and see the colorfully-lit rainbow sculpture at Keflavik Airport (actually just a coincidence). Icelanders share the same laid-back attitude seen in most Scandinavian countries, and the gay community here is considered just another part of the population. There is no "gay section" of Reykjavik, as it is deemed unnecessary. Even Reykjavik's gay bar, "Bar 22," (at 22 Laugavegur) is generally hosting heterosexual clientele, as well as homosexual. The younger gay crowd typically spends the evening at Tunglid ("The Moon" at Laekjargata 2), which is a more typical disco scene (including a hefty cover charge), but it's just as popular with straight Icelandic youth! (Be forewarned in any event...pushing your way, whether up to the bar, onto the dance floor, or wherever you're going, is not only NOT considered rude here, but is just part of Icelandic behavior. So don't be too quick to think someone is trying to start a fight. Alcohol is very expensive here. A beer can cost as much as US $10.00. So most Icelanders begin their evenings with drinks at a friend's home. Subsequently, most people turn up late at cafes, bars and

Continued on page 509

IRELAND

76 60. Bookstore with gay & lesbian sections, natural food shop, restaurant & women's centre.
WATERSTONE'S, 69 Patrick St, (021) 276 522, general bookstore with gay & lesbian section.

DERRY

■ Information
LESBIAN & GAY & FRIEND LINE, (01504) 26 312, Thurs 20:00-22:00.

■ Dance Bar/Disco
GWEEDORE BAR, Waterloo St, Thurs 22:00-01:30, frequented by gays.
MAGEE UNIVERSITY DISCO, at the Student Union, Fri. Call Friend line for hours.

■ Retail & Bookstores
BOOKWORM, 16 Bishop St, (0504) 26 16 16, general bookstore with gay & lesbian titles.

DUBLIN

■ Information
AIDS HELPLINE DUBLIN, (01) 872 42 77, Mon-Fri 19:00-21:00, Sat 15:00-17:00.
GAY SWITCHBOARD, (01) 872 10 55, Sun-Fri 20:00-22:00, Sat 15:30-18:00.
HIRSCHFIELD CENTRE, 10 Fownes St, (01) 671 09 39, lesbian & gay community centre, archive & local information, 12:00-17:30.
LESBIAN LINE, (01) 872 99 11, Thurs 19:-21:.
LOT (LESBIANS ORGANISING TOGETHER), 5 Capel St, (01) 872 7770, Tues-Thurs 10:00-17:00, women's center & library.
NATIONAL TRANSVESTITE LINE, (01) 671 09 39, Thurs 19:00-22:00.

■ Accommodations
BENTLEY'S GUEST HOUSE, 59 Lower Camden St, (1) 475 0024, luxurious rooms with en suite baths, beverage-making facilities, satellite TV, residential lounge, near to gay pubs & clubs, 50% gay & lesbian clientele.
DUNSANY BED & BREAKFAST, 7 Gracepark Gardens, Drumcondra, Dublin 9, (353-1) 857 1362, mobile: (353-88) 695 051. A warm Irish welcome awaits at this Victorian B&B with period features. A haven in a bustling city, the house is situated in a quiet cul-de-sac with a bowling green to the front and fields behind. Dublin city with its many cultural & historical sights is easily accessible by bus, car, or on foot. We offer private & shared baths, full Irish breakfast, tea & coffee all day, and a TV lounge. 50% gay & lesbian clientele.
FAIRFIELD LODGE, Monkstown Ave, Monkstown, County Dublin, (353-1) 280 3912 (tel/fax). E-mail: JSB@Indigo.ie. Studio apartment for 2 in a garden setting, 15 minutes by car from Dublin center & situated close to the sea. Bus stop outside the gate takes you into Dublin every 7 minutes.
FRANKIES GUESTHOUSE, 8 Camden Place, Reservations: (353-1) 478 3087 (tel/fax) or (353-1) 475 2182, exclusively gay, women welcome, 12 rooms with single & double beds, color TV, private & shared baths, TV lounge, full Irish breakfast, near gay venues.
HORSE & CARRIAGE GUEST HOTEL, 15 Aungier St, (01) 478 3537, Fax: 478 4010, gay-friendly hotel, near gay bars.
INN ON THE LIFFEY B&B, 21 Upper Ormond Quay, (353-1) 677 08 28 (tel/fax).

■ Bars
GEORGE, THE, 89 South Great George's St, (01) 478 29 83, complex with 3 bars & a nightclub. MSC leather group meets last Fri.
MOLLOYS LOUNGE, 4 Lower George's St, (01) 280 1238.
O'LOONEY'S, 13 High St, Christchurch.
OUT ON THE LIFFEY, 27 Upper Ormond Quay, (01) 872 24 80, 50% gays & lesbians.

■ Dance Bar/Disco
BLOCK, THE, 89 South Great George's St, above George bar, Fri, Sat 23:00-02:00.
CANDY'S CLUB, East Sussex St, at The Kitchen, Mon gay disco night.
FREEDOM AT THE MISSION, Eustace St, in Temple Bar, across from the Irish Film Centre, disco with upstairs bar, Mon from 22:30.
FRIDAZE, Sir John Rogersons Quay, at Columbia Mills, Fri from 22:30.
GET OUT, 1-2 Aston Quay, at The Furnace Club USI, 2nd Sat 21:00-01:00.
H.A.M., Old Harcourt St. train station, at POD, Fri from 23:00.
MUSCLE, D'Olier St, next to Gas Company, Thurs-Sat 22:30-02:00.
PLAYGROUND, THE, at the Temple of Sound in the Ormond Hotel, Ormond Quay, Sun from 22:30.
POWDERBUBBLE, Old Harcourt St train station, over the POD, montly gay disco, ask locally for schedule.
STONEWALTZ, at Griffith College, SCR, women's dance night, Sat 21:00-02:00.
WONDERBAR, Curved St, at Temple Bar Music Centre, gay dance nights, 1st & 3rd Sat 21:30-02:45.

■ Saunas/Health Clubs
BOILERHOUSE, 12 Crane Ln, near Dame St, 679 51 28, 18:00-05:00 (Fri, Sat till 09:00, Sun till 04:00).
GYM, THE, 14-15 Dame Lane, (01) 679 51 28.
INCOGNITO SAUNA, 1-2 Bow Lane East, (01) 478 35 04.

■ Restaurants
JUICE, South Great George's St, (01) 475 78 56, till 22:00 (Thurs-Sat till 04:00, Sun till 04:00), vegetarian cuisine.
MARK'S BROS, 7 South Great George's St, trendy coffee shop, younger crowd, 10:00-23:00.
OLDE NEW ORLEANS, 3 Cork Hill, Cajun cuisine.
SINNERS RESTAURANT, 12 Parliament St.
WELL FED RESTAURANT, 6 Crow St, at the Dublin Resource Centre, vegetarian food, 12:00-20:00 (closed Sun).

■ Retail & Bookstores
BOOKS UPSTAIRS, 36 College Green, (01) 679 66 87, gay & lesbian sections 10:00-20:00, Sat till 19:00, Sun till 18:00.
WATERSTONE'S, 7 Dawson St, (01) 679 14 15, general bookstore with gay & lesbian section.
WINDING STAIR, 40 Lower Ormond Quay, (01) 873 32 92, bookshop & cafe.

GALWAY

■ Information
AIDS HELPLINE, (091) 56 62 66, Mon-Fri 10:00-12:00.
GAY LINE, (091) 56 61 34, Tue & Thurs 20:-22:.
LESBIAN LINE, (091) 56 46 11, Wed 20:00-22:00, ask about lesbian socials.

■ Retail & Bookstores
CHARLIE BYRNE'S BOOKSHOP, Middle St, (091) 56 17 66.
PEARLS OF WISDOM, 4 Quay St, general bookstore with gay & lesbian titles.

KILKENNY

■ Restaurants
MOTTE RESTAURANT, THE, Instioge, 15 miles from city centre, (056) 586 55, limited accommodation available.

LIMERICK

■ Information
AIDS HELPLINE, (061) 31 66 61, answers Mon-Fri 09:30-17:30.
GAY SWITCHBOARD & LESBIAN LINE, (061) 31 01 01, switchboard Mon, Tues 19:30-21:30, lesbians Thurs 19:30-21:30, ask about scheduled meetings and local events.

TINAHELY

■ Accommodations
STONEYBROKE HOUSE, Ballinamanogue, Tinahely, Co. Wicklow, (353-402) 38236. Inn with restaurant & wine bar, 60 miles south of Dublin, 1-1/2 mi from Tinahely. Private & shared baths, colour TV, full breakfast, dinner. Eight entrees available from menu, including Wicklow lamb & sirloin steak, Chicken breast Stoneybroke, salmon & vegetable Kiev.

WATERFORD

■ Information
GAY LINE, (051) 87 99 07, Wed 19:30-21:30.

■ Restaurants
HARICOTS, O'Connell St, vegetarian & natural foods.

ITALY

FYI

Gay Mens' Bicycling Vacation...in Italy!

Ride a bicycle past the olive groves, vineyards and medieval castles of Tuscany, following routes used by Roman Emperors long ago. Men On Bikes has created a selection of men's biking vacations combing Italy's scenery and its rich, cultural history. You'll be linking up with gay Italian biking groups and experiencing local gay culture along the way.

Bikes are high-quality road bikes with either drop handle bars or flat ones. Trips are designed for the intermediate level. None of the trips is too difficult for an athletic beginner. Advanced bikers receive suggestions for longer, more challenging routes. You are encouraged to travel at your own pace, and the van is always along to offer support. Hotels are selected for style, quality and comfort after a day on the bike. Two bilingual guides accompany each trip. Trips include the bike, guides, van, maps and directions, accommodations, most breakfasts and dinners, picnic lunch, wines with meals, meetings and rides with gay locals, guided tours and museum entries, wine tastings, some transfers.

Sep	Syracuse-Taormina
Sep	Mantua-Venice
Sep	Rome-Capri & Pompei
Oct	San Marino-Florence

Contact **Men On Bikes** at (604) 943-9260, Fax: (604) 948-2703, E-mail: pblackman @pcg.telpress.it.

ITALY
COUNTRY CODE: (39)

WHO TO CALL
For Tour Companies Serving This Destination
See Italy on page 17

ACQUI TERME
■ *Women's Accommodations*
LA FILANDA, Red. Montagnola No. 4, (39-144) 32 39 56 (tel/fax), women-only cultural center & guesthouse in an Italian villa for female musicians & artists, music room & diverse yearly workshops, shared baths, 2 fully equipped kitchens, living rooms, video library, large garden, nearby health center, pool & river.

BARI
■ *Information*
ARCI GAY, Via Celentano 81, (080) 55 43 474, gay & lesbian organization, Tues 20:00-23:00. Women meet Wed 18:00-21:00.
CLS DESIDERANDA, Via Imperatore Traiano 28, (080) 878 8983, lesbian group with monthly Sun disco.
■ *Beaches*
PIETRA EGEA, between Cozze & Polignano.
■ *Bars*
REIFF, Lungomare, not a gay bar, discreetly frequented by gays.
TAVERNA DEL MALTESE, Via Nicolai, not a gay bar, discreetly frequented by gays.
■ *Erotica*
SALOTTINO, Via Stupelle 10, cinema.

BERGAMO
■ *Information*
ARCI GAY, Via Baschenis 9, (035) 230 959, gay organization, Mon 20:30-22:30, Sat 15:00-18:00. Gay line answers Fri 20:30-22:30.
■ *Bars*
NITE LITE, Via Baschenis 9, (035) 244 300, large bar & disco, younger crowd, some women, Thurs-Sun from 22:00.
TOO MUCH, Via Lazzaretto 2, at Via Baioni, (035) 23 26 66 or 23 23 66, not gay but frequented by gays, closed Mon.
■ *Saunas/Health Clubs*
CITY SAUNA CLUB, Via Clementina 8, (035) 240 418, 3 floors, bar, 14:00-02:00 (Fri, Sat till later), closed Tues.
■ *Erotica*
RITZ, Via G. Verdi 8, cinema.

BOLOGNA
■ *Information*
ARCI GAY NAZIONALE, Piazza di Porta Saragozza 2, (051) 644 70 54, national headquarters of Arci Gay organization.
CENTRO DI DOCUMENTAZIONE, Piazza di Porta Saragozza 2, (051) 644 68 24, library, cultural center, gay archives, open every evening.
CENTRO PER LE DONNE, Via Galliera 8, (051) 233 863, Women's organizaton with large feminist library, open daily 08:30-14:00 & 15:00-18:00 (Sat only 08:00-14:00), library Mon-Fri 08:30-14:00 (Mon & Thurs also 15:00-18:00).
GAY INFO LINE, Piazza di Porta Saragozza 2, (051) 644 68 20, answers Mon-Fri 11:00-13:00, information for all of Italy.
VISIBILIA, Via Falegnami 3c, (051) 263 592. Lesbian group & archives, Wed & Sat 20:00-23:00, holds annual film festival.
■ *Bars*
BOY BAR, Via Sampieri 2, (051) 222 571, gay Thurs only 22:00-02:00.
CASSERO,★ Piazza Porta Saragozza 2, (051) 644 69 02, parties, shows, 21:30-01:00. Sun disco 22:00-02:30.
IL SAMBA, Via Mameli, open evenings.
PACHITO CLUB, Via Polese 47c, (051) 24 39 98, cruise bar, men only, 22:30-04:00 (Fri-Sun 23:00-06:00), disco Thurs-Sun.
■ *Dance Bar/Disco*
VIPERA, Via Santa Margherita 7/2, (051) 262 912, piano bar, Wed, Fri, Sat 23:00-05:00.
■ *Saunas/Health Clubs*
COSMOS CLUB, Via Boldrini 22 int 16, (051) 25 58 90, winter: 12:00-01:30 (Fri till 02:00, Sat till 03:00); summer: 14:00-01:30 (Sat till 02:00).
NEW VIGOR SAUNA, Via S. Felice 6b, (051) 23 25 07, 14:00-02:00 (Fri, Sat till 05:00).
■ *Restaurants*
PIZZERIA DA NINO, Via Volturno 9, (051) 26 0294, gay-friendly, many gays on Sunday evenings.
PIZZERIA ZIA CATARI, Via Montegrappa, gay-friendly.
■ *Retail & Bookstores*
EDICOLE (KIOSKS), Via Zanardi; Porta S. Vitale.
LIBRERIA DELLE DONNE, Via Rosella 4 or 6, (51) 27 17 54, women's bookstore.
LIBRERIA DELLE MOLINE, Via delle Moline 3A, (051) 23 20 53, general bookstore with women's section.
■ *Erotica*
EROTIC CINEMAS: Continental (Via Emilia Ponente 221), Actor's Studio (Via Corticella 56).
MAGIC AMERICA, Via Don Minzoni 46.

ITALY

BRESCIA

■ Information
ARCIGAY ORLANDO, Piazzale ARnaldo 21, (338) 641 4316, gay group, meets Sun 15:00-18:00.
PIANETA VIOLA, Via Villa Glori 10, (030) 241 0604, lesbian group, meets Thurs 20:30-22:30.

■ Bars
RE DESIDERIO, Vicolo Lundo 11, in the old section of Brescia, closed Mon. ♂

■ Dance Bar/Disco
OUT LIMITS, Via Ugo Foscolo 2, in the town of Paderno Franciacorta, (030) 63 97 63 55, Fri-Sun 22:00-05:00, 90% men, Fri women only. ♀♂

■ Erotica
EDEN, Via Nino Bixio, cinema.
MAGIC AMERICA, Via Lamarmora 146a, (030) 349-394, 09:00-12:30 & 15:00-19:30. Second location: Via Oberdan 20c.

BRINDISI

■ Information
ATTIKA, Via Santa Chiara 6, (0831) 563 051, gay group, meets Tues & Fri 19:00-20:30. ♀♂
AVVENTATE, Via Santa Chiara 6, women's group, meets Fri 19:00-23:00.

■ Beaches
PUNTA PENNA GROSSA, 15km out of Brindisi, toward Bari at crossroad to Seranova.

CAGLIARI

■ Beaches
CALAFIGHERA, nude beach known by local gays as Calagay, near Sella del Diavolo & Calamosca.
CALAMOSCA, in Cagliari, bus 11 (end of the line).

■ Retail & Bookstores
CENTRO DI DOCUMENTAZIONE, Via Lanusei 15, (070) 66 68 82, women's center & library, Tues & Thurs 10:00-13:00 & 16:00-20:00, Wed & Fri 10:00-13:00.

CATANIA

■ Information
CIRCOLO ARCI GAY ARCI LESBICA OPEN MIND, Via Gargano 33, (095) 532 685, daily 17:00-22:00 (Mon social, Wed movies club, Sun gay youth).

■ Beaches
CAITO, near the station, nearly all gay.

■ Bars
MASTER CLUB, Via Asiago 18, bar with video games, 50% gay & lesbian.
MOON CLUB, Via Empedocle 66, zona Piazza Cavour, pub, 50% men, 50% women. ♀♂

NIEVSKY, Scalinata Alessi 13, pub, popular with gays on Fri (80% gay), otherwise mostly straight. ♀♂
SOTTO SOPRA, Via Battiato 34, women's pub. ♀

■ Dance Bar/Disco
CHARLIE BROWN, Via Martino Cilestri 19/C, (095) 53 55 19, Oct-Jun (winter) Thurs, Fri & Sun only 23:00-late, Thurs drag show. ♀♂
STARS, THE, Via Pulei 51, in village of Mascalucia, (095) 31 18 39, 7 days in summer (Jun-Sept), 50% men & 50% women. ♀♂
TOP SECRET, Via Scuto Costarelli 83, 18:00-01:00 (Fri-Sun from 23:00 till late), Sun drag shows. ♂

■ Erotica
EROTIC CINEMAS: Olimpia (Piazza Stesicoro 57), Eliseo (Via Garibaldi 271), Fiamma (Via Fischetti 2), Messina (Via Gianotta 15), Sarah (Via A. di Sangiuliano 124).

CREMONA

■ Information
ARCIGAY ARCILESBICA LA ROCCA, via Speciano 4, (0372) 20484, gay organization, meets Fri 21:30-24:00.

■ Erotica
LA MALA PROIBITA, Galleria Kennedy 12.

DESENZANO

■ Dance Bar/Disco
ART CLUB, Via Mantova, inside Centro Comerciale Garda. (030) 999 1004, gay Fri, Sat, some heteros Fri. ♀♂

FABRO SCALO - CHIUSI

■ Camping & RV
TERRADILEI, 05010 Fabro Scalo (Chiusi), Umbria, (0763) 85 241, women-only camping retreat with vegetarian restaurant, coffee bar, 1 room, trailer rental, unlimited tent space, some RV parking, inside & outside showers, nearby pool & lake, full breakfast. Open April-Oct. ♀

FIRENZE - FLORENCE

■ Information
ARCI GAY ARCI LESBICA, Via San Zanobi 54 (red number), (055) 288 126, meetings 16:00-20:00. Women meet Thurs 21:00.
L'AMANDORLA, Via degli Alfani 42, (0360) 311 058, ask for Antonella, women's group, meets Wed evening.

■ Accommodations
MORANDI ALLA CROCETTA, Via Laura 50, (055) 2344747, fax 2480954, gay-friendly guesthouse, variety of rooms with color satellite TV, AC, phone, refrigerator, private baths.

■ Women's Accommodations
B AND B, Borgo Pinti 31, 3rd floor, 50121 Firenze, 247 9654 (tel/fax) or 248 0056. Opening in April, '97, women-only B&B with 4 rooms & 2 baths (2 rooms have sinks), rooms have views of Il Duomo. ♀

■ Bars
CRISCO CLUB, ★ Via S. Egidio 43R, (055) 248 05 80, cruise bar with erotic vidoes, back room, men-only, private club, Sun, Mon, Wed, Thurs 21:30-03:30, Fri & Sat till 06:00. ♂
PICCOLO CAFFE, Via Borgo Santa Croce, open daily, usually 30% women, many women Fri evening till 01:00. ♂
SATANASSA, Via Pandolfini 26 watch for the red number, garage entrance, (055) 243 356, 22:00-03:00 (Fri, Sat till 06:00), closed Sun & Mon, Fri women's night. ♀♂
TABASCO BAR, Piazza S. Cecilia 3 (red number), (055) 21 30 00, cruising bar, 21:00-03:00 (Fri, Sat till 06:00), closed Mon. Disco only Fri-Sun. ♂

■ Cafe
PICCOLO CAFFE, Via Borgo Santa Croce, gay-friendly, day bar, closes at 01:00

■ Saunas/Health Clubs
FLORENCE BATHS, Via Guelfa 93 (red number), (055) 21 60 50, sauna & gym, 14:00-01:00 (Sat till 02:00).

■ Restaurants
TRATTORIA ANITA, Via del Parlascio 2, (055) 218 698, Mon-Sat.

■ Retail & Bookstores
EDICOLA BALSANELLI (KIOSK), Piazza S. Maria Novella.
LIBRERIA DELLE DONNE, Via Fiesolana 2/b, (055) 24 03 84, women's bookstore, 09:00-13:00 & 15:30-19:30 (closed Mon till 15:30).

■ Erotica
EROTIC CINEMAS: Arlecchino (Via de Bardi), Italia (Piazza Alinari).
FRISCO, Via F. Veracini.
MAGIC AMERICA, Via Guelfa 89/91.

FLORENCE
SEE FIRENZE.

FRASSINETO PO

■ Dance Bar/Disco
SMILE, Piazza V. Veneto 5, Frassineto Po 15040, (0330) 202 533, gay Fri, Sat 23:00-03:30. ♂

GENOVA

■ Information
ARCI GAY GENOVA, Via San Luca, 11/4, (010) 246 7506, group meets Mon 21:00-23:00, Fri 17:30-19:30.

■ Accommodations
BARABINO, Via Sanpierdarena 99, (010) 411

FERRARI GUIDES' GAY TRAVEL A to Z - 18th EDITION 249

ITALY

384, gay-friendly hotel, single & double rooms, 50% gay & lesbian clientele, more gays among large theater clientele on weekends.

MINI HOTEL, Via Lomellini 6, (010) 246 5876, gay-friendly hotel.

■ Beaches
PIEVE LIGURE, 250 km from railway station on highway to Recco.

■ Bars
LA CAGE, Via Sampierdarena, 167/R, (010) 645 45 55, Tues-Sun 22:00-04:00.

■ Saunas/Health Clubs
TOPKAPI, Via Casaregis 26/R, (010) 588 489. 15:00-24:00 (closed Tues). Moving in summer '97 to Salita Salvatore Viale 15 Rosso (red number), near Via 20 Settembre, name will change, telephone may remain the same.

■ Erotica
EROTIC CINEMAS: ABC (Via Degola 4/R), Centrale (Via S. Vincenzo 13/R, sala 1), Chiabrera (Via Chiabrera 1), Cristallo (L.go Zecca 1/R), Dioniso (Via Colombo 11), El Dorado (Via Buranello), Smeraldo (Vico Carmagnola), Alcione (Via Canevari).

MAGIC AMERICA, Via Teodosio 7r, (010) 316 783, 09:00-19:30.

SEVENTEEN, Corso Gastaldi 173-175.

ISOLA D'ELBA

■ Accommodations
CASA SCALA, Loc Filetto No 9, 57034 Marina di Campo, (0039) 565-977777, Fax 977770, cottage with workshops, women only, kitchen, refrigerator, shared baths, nearby ocean beach, continental breakfast with workshops only. ♀

LECCE

■ Information
ARCIGAY ARCILESBICA ARCOBALENO, Via Francesco Milizia 56b (0832) 312 511, Sat, Sun only 20:00-22:00.

■ Beaches
SAN CATALDO, in San Cataldo park near the lighthouse. Walk 1km around the military area.

MILANO - MILAN

■ Information
ARCI GAY CENTRO D'INIZIATIVA GAY, Via Torricelli 19, (02) 5810 0299. Gay center with archives, library, group meetings, afternoon & evening 7 days (archives Omologie/Fondo Olivari also Wed 21:00-24:00).

CDM, Via Cicco Simonetta 15, (02) 805 18 08, lesbian group, socials Sun 15:00-20:00.

TELEFONA AMICO & AMICA LINES, (02) 8940 1749, answers 20:00-24:00, gay line Mon, Tues, Thurs, Fri. Lesbian line Wed.

■ Beaches
BEACHES AROUND MILAN: Ticino (walk left at Vigevano Bridge); Cassano d'Adda (on the road to Rivolta after the RR tressle, walk the path to the river).

■ Bars
AFTER LINE,★ via Sammartini 25, (02) 669 2130, bar & disco, 17:00-02:00, closed Tues.

CICIP E CICIAP, Via Gorani 9, (02) 86 72 02, bar & restaurant from 20:00, circolo culturale e politico (cultural & political center for women), women only. ♀

COMPANY, via Benadir 14, (2) 282 94 81, 22:00-02:30 (Fri, Sat till 06:00), closed Mon, travelers welcome.

HOT LINE CLUB, Via G.B. Sammartini 23, (02) 669 884 56.

L'ELEPHANTE, Via Melzo 22, (02) 2951 8768, bar & restaurant, Sun brunch 12:00-16:00 (closed Mon). ♂

MISTER SISTER, Via Calabria 5, (02) 376 1531, 21:00-02:00, mostly women. ♀

QUERELLE, Via de Castillia 20, (02) 683 900 or 552 10359, bar run by Arci Gay organization, 21:00-02:00 (closed Mon). Third Mon of month women only.

■ Dance Bar/Disco
ARGOS CLUB, Via Resegone 1, (02) 607 2249, bar with video, dark room, disco Thurs-Sun, strippers Thurs evenings & Sun afternoons.

HD, Via Tajani 11, (02) 71 89 90, Fri-Tues 23:00-03:00.

MAN TO MAN, Viale Umbria 120, at Killer Plastic, (02) 733 996, gay only Thurs 23:00-06:00.

NUOVA IDEA,★ Via de Castillia 30, (02) 689 27 53, Thurs-Sun 21:30-02:00, women welcome.

ONE WAY, Via F. Cavallotti 204, in the town of Sesto S. Giovanni, (02) 242 13 41, dance bar Fri, Sat 22:30-03:00, Sun 15:30-19:00.

SEGRETA, Piazza Castello 1, (02) 860 307, from 22:30, closed Mon & Tues.

SOTTOMARINO GIALLO, Via Donatello 2, (02) 2940 1047, disco for women-only with 2 floors, quieter bar upstairs. ♀

ZIP CLUB, Corso Sempione, 76, (02) 331 49 04, disco & bar, private club, videos, Tues-Sun 24:00-06:00, transvestite club.

■ Saunas/Health Clubs
ALEXANDER'S CLUB & BAR, Via Pindaro, 23, (02) 255 02 20, 14:00-01:00, Fri & Sat till 03:00, bar inside. ♂

BODY GYM, via Lesmi 9, (02) 835 7029.

CLUB DELLA SAUNA, Sangallo 22, 11:00-20:00 (closed Sun).

MAGIC SAUNA, Via Maiocchi, 8, (02) 294 061 82, Wed-Mon 12:00-24:00.

TEDDY SAUNA CLUB, Via Renzo e Lucia 3, (02) 846 61 48. ♂

THERMAS, Via Bezzecca, 9, (02) 545 03 55, 12:00-24:00, closed Thurs. ♂

TRANSFER CLUB, Via Breda 158 (metro: Villa San Giovanni), (02) 2700 5565, swimming pool, dark room, videos, disco inside.

■ Restaurants
CICIP E CICIAP, via Gorani 9, (02) 86 72 02, women's restaurant & a social local for local women.

DUE AMICI, via Borsieri, 5, (metro #2, Garibaldi stop, exit to G. Pepe St.), (02) 668 46 96. Restaurant & bar with patio dining in summer, 20:00-03:00, except Wed evening.

LA RISOTTERIA, Via Dandolo 2, (02) 5518 1694, 20:00-23:00 (closed Sun).

LA VILLETTA DI ELISA, Viale Bezzi 86, (02) 498 2376, gay-friendly, expensive, 19:00-03:00, patio dining.

■ Retail & Bookstores
LIBRERIA BABELE, Via Sammartini, 23, (02) 669 2986 (tel/fax), gay & lesbian bookshop, Mon-Sat 09:30-19:30.

LIBRERIA DELLE DONNE, Via Dogana 2, (02) 874 213, women's bookstore, 9:30-13:00 & 15:30-19:00 (closed Mon till 15:30 & Sun).

■ Leathers/Piercing
BODY & SOUL, Via Vigevano 11, (02) 837 3051, piercing studio.

■ Erotica
BUSHIDO, Via Andrea Doria 48a, (02) 670 6420.

EROTIC CINEMAS: Academy (Viale Monza 101), Ambra (Via Clitunno), Argo (Viale Monza 79), Astor (Corso Buenos Aires 36), Astoria (Viale Montenero 55), Atlas (Via Sansovino 3), Aurora Pussy Cat (Via Paolo Sarpi 6), Cittanova (Via Giambellino 153), Diamante (Via Fabio Filzi 5), Donizetti (Via Masolino da Panicale 13), Embassy (Via Faà di Bruno 8), La Fenice (Viale Bligny 52), Magenta (Via R. Sanzio 23), Roxy (Corso Lodi 128), Zodiaco (Via Padova 179).

EUROPA 92, Via Sammartini, 21; Via Sirtori 24; Via Stradella 12, 09:00-19:30, leathers, videos, etc.

MAGIC AMERICA, Via Legnone 19, (02) 688 1057, 09:00-19:30. Also at: Via Bramante 20, Viale Brianza 28, Via Inama 17, Viale Umbria 50.

STUDIO KNOW HOW GAY SHOP, Piazza Duca D'Aosta, 12, (02) 6698 7085, open 7 days, 09:00-12:30 & 13:30-19:00.

MODENA

■ Bars
WOVOKA CLUB, Via Canaletto 152D, (059) 313 244, 21:00-02:00 (Tues, Fri, Sat 22:30-04:00), Sat women-only dance night.

■ Erotica
MAGIC AMERICA, Via Rua Pioppa 42.

ITALY

NAPOLI - NAPLES

Information
AIDS LINE, (081) 551 8293, answers Mon-Fri 16:00-21:00, Sat 10:30-16:00.

ARCI GAY ANTINOO NAPOLI, Vico S. Geronimo 17/20, (081) 552 8815, gay & lesbian organization, Mon-Fri 16:00-21:00, Sat 10:30-16:00. Women meet Sat 10:30-13:00.

TELEFONO AMICO, (081) 552 8815, gay information.

Bars
FERDINAND STRASSE, Piazza Porta Nova 8, (081) 206 390, gay in the evenings from 21:00, cultural discussions take place, 20% women. ♂

NIGHT & DAY, Via Matteo Schilizzi 1820, (081) 552 2266, pub, younger crowd, more gay in evening. ♂

Dance Bar/Disco
DIABOLICA, Via Nicolò Tommaseo, on 1st corner, taking Via Parenope form Piazza Vittoria, gay Sat only, 20% women. 🎵♂

KABIR, Gradini Amadeo 12, open Tues, Thurs & Sat (days change frequently). 🎵♂

MEPHYSTO, Via Medina, gay Fri only. 🎵♂

Saunas/Health Clubs
SAUNA will open in 1997, call Arci Gay for info.

Erotica
EROTIC CINEMAS: Argo (Via A. Poerio 4), Casanova (Corso Garibaldi 330), Eden (Via Sanfelice 15), Iride (A. Poerio 7), Trianon (Piazza Calenda), none are all-gay.

PADOVA

Information
ARCI GAY, Via Santa Sofia 5, (049) 875 3923, Monday 21:30-23:00.

Bars
BRIEF ENCOUNTER, Via Settima Strada 5, (049) 776 073, men-only bar & disco, backroom, 21:30-02:30 (closed Mon). 🎵♂

Dance Bar/Disco
ALCAZAR,★ Via Risorgimento 16, town of Fontaniva, on the Vicenza-Treviso road, (049) 597 0908, open Fri & Sun. 🎵♂

BLACK & WHITE DISCO BAR, Via Navigazione Interna 38/A, zona industriale nord, (049) 776 414, private club, join for 15,000 Lire or get membership to Arci Gay, 80% men, open 7 days in summer, in winter closed Mon & Tues. 🎵♂

ETIENNE BUBBLE DISCO, Zona Brusegana, Via dei Colli 19, (049) 620 156, Sat only, 22:00-04:00. Fri many women 🎵♀♂

MY TOY PRIVE, Viale Navigazione Interna 38A, (049) 776 414, Fri & Sat men & women. Women-only Wed, Thurs & Sun, closed Mon, Tues. 🎵♀♂

Saunas/Health Clubs
BLACK & WHITE, Via Pellizzo 3, (049) 776 414, 14:00-02:00 (closed Tues).

METRO, Via Turazza 19, (049) 807 5828, 20:00-02:00 (closed Mon & Tues).

OLYMPUS CLUB, Via Nicolo Tomaseo 96/A, (049) 807 5843, Mon & Tues 14:00-02:00, Wed, Sat, Sun 14:00-22:00 (closed Thurs & Fri).

Erotica
MAGIC TOP VIDEO CLUB & FLEX VIDEO BAR, via Tommaseo 96c, (049) 80 72 414.

PALERMO

Information
ARCI GAY ORLANDO, Via Genova 7, (091) 335 688, gay line, Mon, Wed, Fri 17:00-19:30 (women answer Mon).

Beaches
BARCARELLO, near Capo Gallo, nude beach.

Bars
HEMINGWAY, Piazza Ignazio Florio, 80% women. ♀

I GRILLI, Piazza Valverde, in Palermo's old section, pub, many tables outside with nice atmosphere. ♀♂

IT, Via S. Oliva 38, pub, 15,000 Lire for membership to enter, open evenings 7 days (better after 21:00), also Sun afternoons. ♂

LORD GREEN, Via Parisi, pub, 50% straight, 50% gay/lesbian.

Dance Bar/Disco
ANGELO AZZURRO, Via S. Martino, in sector called Bocca di Falco, nearly 100% men, but women welcomed if they show up. 🎵♂

Erotica
EROTIC CINEMAS: Embassy A&B (Via Mariano Stabile), Etoile (Via Mariano Stabile), Orfeo (Via Maqueda).

PALMANOVA

Bars
RAILWAY STATION PUB, Piazza Roma 8, (0432) 923 477, pub, 08:00-13:00 & 16:00-03:00 (closed Thurs). Be discreet, gay patrons mix discreetly with straight ones here.

PARMA

Beaches
SPIAGGIA DEL TARO,★ go under the bridge of Taro, the turn toward Monte; Spiaggia dell'Enza, take Via Emilia towards Reggio, descend on the left side of the Eura bridge.

Dance Bar/Disco
ANDROMEDA, Via Gramsci 5, in the town of Soragna, (0524) 597 204, Fri, Sat 22:00 till 02:00 or 03:00, 90% men. 🎵♂

Erotica
MAGIC AMERICA, Borgo del Parmigianino 31d, (0521) 206 273, 09:00-12:30 & 15:00-19:30.

RITZ CINEMA, Via Venezia 129.

PERUGIA

Information
ARCI GAY, Via Fratti 18 (Apollo 2), (075) 572 3175, gay & lesbian organization, Wed & Fri 21:00-24:00. Women meet Thurs.

Accommodations
CASA GIORGIO, CP 23, Agello PG, near town of Perugia, guest houses on a farm with horseback riding. Unverifiable spring '97. ♀♂

PESCARA

Bars
HEROES, Via E. Flaiano 21, 21:00-02:00, unverifiable spring '97. ♂

Erotica
CENTRALE, Via Trento 34, cinema.

PISA

Information
ARCI GAY, Via Calafati 3, (050) 577 540, Mon-Wed 21:00-24:00, lesbians meet Fri. Moving in June '97 to Via della Croce Rossa 7, (050) 576 420.

Bars
G.A.O., Via della Croce Rossa 7, at Arci Gay location, (050) 576 420, Thurs-Sun 21:00-01:00. ♀♂

Saunas/Health Clubs
SIESTA CLUB 77, Via di Porta A Mare 25-27, (050) 42 075, 15:00-01:00.

Erotica
MIGNON, Lungarno Pacinotti, cinema.

TENTAZIONI SEXY & GAY SHOP, Via Rosellini 13.

PONSACCO

Dance Bar/Disco
INSOMNIA, in the small town of Ponsacco, not far outside Pisa, gay-friendly disco, winter gay Fri, summer gay Sat. 🎵

RANZANICO AL LAGO

Dance Bar/Disco
IL TRIANGULO, Via Nazionale 5, (035) 811 644, more gay Sat 22:30-04:00, transvestites, patio in summer. Unverifiable spring '97. 🎵

RAVENNA

Information
ARCI GAY ANDROMEDA, Via Castel San Pietro 71, (0544) 66170, Sun & Wed evenings after 21:30.

Beaches
LIDO DI CLASSE, between Ravenna & Cervia, the gay section is near the river around the beach; Lido di Dante, nude beach near the campground on the right near dunes and pines.

ITALY

The Italian Gay Discovery Tour

On this ten-day trip through some of Italy's most important cities, you'll see significant sightseeing attractions and/or experience gay nightlife in Milan, Venice, Florence, and Rome. This tour is available for groups of 20, 30 or 40. Extensions are available at ski resorts or summer resorts. Monthly departures are available: March 8, Apr 19, May 17, Jun 14, Jul 12, Aug 9, Sep 6, Oct 11, Nov 15, Dec TBA.

MILAN: A panoramic sightseeing tour including Il Duomo, welcome dinner in a gay restaurant, evening at a gay bar & disco. Sightseeing stop in Verona on the way to Venice by bus.

VENICE: Local guide takes you to Doges' Palace and St. Mark's Square, free time to explore.

FLORENCE: View of the city from Michelangelo Square, visits to the cathedral, Baptistry and the statue of David, Uffizi Gallery, Ponte Vecchio, Signoria Square, dinner at gay-friendly restaurant, 2 evenings at different gay nightclubs. Sightseeing stop in Siena on the way to Rome.

ROME: Sightseeing at the Forum, Colosseum, Vernice Square, Quirinale Palace, Trevi Fountain, Spanish Steps, Pantheon, Via Veneto, Borghese Gardens, the Vatican, Sistine Chapel, St Peter's. An evening in a gay nightclub, one evening free. Farewell dinner, evening in Rome's newest gay nightclub.

Contact **Zipper Travel** at (39 6) 488 2730, Fax: (39 6) 488 2729. E-mail: tptravel@aconet.it

■ Erotica
EROTIC CINEMAS, Roma (Via Nino Bixio), Alexander (Via Bassa del Pignataro 8).

RIMINI - RICCIONE

■ Accommodations
GARNI CECCARINI 140 Viale Ceccarini 140, Riccione, gay friendly hotel.

■ Beaches
DELLA ROTONDA, by the Hotel Mediterraneo at the end of Viale Ceccarini in Riccione.

■ Dance Bar/Disco
CLASSIC CLUB, Via Feleto 11, Rimini, (0541) 731 113, disco & piano bar, video, 70% men; summer: 7 days 23:00-06:00, winter: Sat only 23:00-06:00.

■ Erotica
EROS CENTER, Viale Dante, 116, Riccione.
EROS CENTER, Via Vespucci 29, Rimini.
MAGIC AMERICA, Via Regina Elena 94, Rimini, 09:00-12:30 & 15:00-19:30.

ROMA - ROME

■ Information
AIDS INFO, (06) 638 0365.
ARCI GAY PEGASO, Via Primo Acciaresi 7, (06) 41 73 0752, gay & lesbian organization, answers Sat 18:00-20:00.
CENTRO ARCOBALENO (RAINBOW CENTER), (06) 581 9593, answers Mon-Fri 21:00-23:00.
CENTRO SOCIALE GARAGE, Via Gustavo Modena 92, near Piazza Sonnino, gays meet Sun, couselling & help Thurs.
CIRCOLO MARIO MIELI, Via Corinto 5, (06) 541 39 85, Mon-Fri from 18:00, bar, shows & video evenings, mostly men.
COORDINAMENTO LESBICO ITALIANO, Via S. Francesco di Sales 1/A, (06) 686 4201, lesbian organization.

■ Accommodations
HOTEL GRANDI, Via Acchile Grandi 7, for information, contact Max's Bar at 70 30 15 99.
HOTEL SCALINATA DI SPAGNA, Piazza Trinità dei Monti 17, 00187 Roma, bookings (06) 679 3006 or 699 40896, fax 699 40598, gay-friendly bed & breakfast, 20%-30% gay & lesbian clientele, rooms have modern conveniences, near Borghese Garden, 5 min to gym, steam, sauna, Jacuzzi, steps away from Spanish Steps, expanded continental breakfast.

■ Beaches
IL BUCO, on the Anzio highway near Ostia. Spiaggia Libera nude beach, Via Aurelia, km 46 marker.

■ Bars
APEIRON CLUB, Via dei Quattro Cantoni 5, (06) 482 88 20, 22:30-02:00 (closed Sun).
HANGAR,★ Via in Selci, (06) 488 13 97, video cruise bar, lite meals, Wed-Mon 22:30-02:00, closed in Aug.
IL GATTO VOLANTE, Via dei Bologna 74, Trastevere, (06) 581 3066, gay-friendly private club, bar & restaurant.
MAX'S BAR, Via Achille Grandi 3a, (06) 7030 1599, daily 22:30-02:30 (closed Mon).
MAXIMILIAN MULTICLUB, Piazza Vittorio Emanuele II 96-97, (06) 700 5931, 4 levels, 16:00-04:00, strippers.
NEW SUPERSTARS, Vicolo de Modelli 51, (06) 679 1909, 22:30-04:00 (Fri till 08:00, Sat till 06:00), closed Mon.
OFFICINA FANS CLUB, Via Ignazio Danti 20, (06) 275 3508, videos, backroom, 22:00-03:00 (Sat till 05:00).
PEGASUS, Via Arco di Ginnasi 14, (06) 6920 0138, 20:00-03:00 (closed Mon).
SHELTER, Via dei Vascellari 35, pub, 20:30-02:00, some hetero clientele.
SKYLINE CLUB, Via degli Aurunci 26/28, (06) 444 0817, American bar, videos, darkroom, disco, food buffet. Open from 22:30 (Sun 17:00-20:30 & 22:30-02:00). Arcigay group meets here Sun afternoon.

■ Dance Bar/Disco
ANGELO AZZURRO, Via Cardinal Merry del Val 13, (06) 580 04 72, 23:00-04:00 (Sat till 05:00), Fri women only.
FRUTTA E VERDURA, Via Principe Umberto 38, (06) 446 4862, 22:00-03:00.
JOLIE COEUR, Via Sirte 5, (06) 8621 5827, women's night Sat only from 22:00.
MUCCASSASSINA, Via di Portonaccio, gay Fri only 22:30-04:00.

■ Saunas/Health Clubs
APOLLION BATH, Via Mecenate 59, (06) 487 2316, 13:00-01:00.
MEDITERRANEO, Via P. Villari 3, (06) 7720 5934, 14:00-23:00.
TERME DI ROMA, Via Persio 4, (06) 718 4378, 15:00-23:00 (Fri, Sat till 04:00).

■ Restaurants
ISOLA DEL SOLE, Lungotevere Arnaldo da Brescia, (06) 320 1400, 13:00-15:00 & 20:30-24:00 (closed Mon).
PEGASUS, Via Arco de Ginnasi 14, 20:00-03:00 (closed Mon).

■ Retail & Bookstores
AL TEMPO RITROVATO, Via dei Fienaroli, (06) 654 37 49, women's bookshop & local info.
GRAND MELO, Via di Tor Millina 10-11, (06) 687 7309. General bookstore with gay & lesbian section.
LA BANCARELLA, Piazza Alessandria 2, (06) 8530 3071, gay & lesbian bookstore.
LIBRERIA BABELE, Via Paula 44, (06) 687

ITALY

66 28, gay & lesbian bookstore, Mon-Sat 9:30-19:30.

Erotica
COBRA SEX SHOP, Via Barletta 23, (06) 3751 7350; 2nd store: Via Aurelio Cotta 22/24, (06) 764 357; 3rd store: Via G. Giolitti 307/313, (06) 4470 0636.

EROTIC CINEMAS: Ambasciatori (Via Montebello 101), Aquila (Via L'Aquila 74), Blue Moon (Via Quattro Cantoni 53), Moulin Rouge (Via Corbino), Pussycat (Via Cairoli 98), Tiffany (Galleria Viminale 77), Ulisse (Via Tiburtina 372), Volturno (Via Volturno 37).

EUROPA 92, Via Boezio 96.

EUROSEX ITALIA, Via G. Bagnera 49.

EXSTASY, Via Cino del Duca 24-26.

MAGIC AMERICA, Via Marco Valerio Corvo 118.

TENTAZIONI, Via Noto 33, closed Mon.

VILLE ROUGE, Via Pigafetta 48.

TAORMINA

Accommodations
HOTEL VILLA SCHULER, Via Roma 17, I-98039 Sicily, (0942) 23481, fax 942 23522. E-mail: schuler@cys.it, http://www.cys.it/schuler. Gay-friendly bed & breakfast hotel & bar, variety of spacious guest quarters, private & shared baths, TV lounge, solarium, nearby ocean beach, expanded continental breakfast.

Beaches
ROCCE BIANCHE, 5 min by car from central Taormina, on Spisone Bay, near the autostrada exit marked "Taormina Nord."

Bars
MARENGO, Vico F. Paladini 4, (0942) 239 45, 20:00-03:00 (closed Thurs), 50% gay & lesbian.

MARRAKECH, Piazzetta Garibaldi, (0942) 625 692, 20:00-03:00 (closed Wed), patio, live music in summer, mostly gay, many heteros.

SHATULLE,★ Piazzetta Paladini 4, (0942) 211 41, 20:00-03:00 (closed Mon), 50% gay & lesbian with a large straight following.

TYKE, Piazzetta Paladini 8, 20:00-03:00 (closed Tues), 50% gay & lesbian.

Dance Bar/Disco
LE PERROQUET,★ Piazza S. Domenico 2, (0942) 244 62, cabaret, lounge, 70% men. July-Sept daily from 21:30 till late, rest of year Sat & Sun only 21:30-03:30.

Restaurants
LA PIAZZETTA, Via Paladini 5, (0942) 626 317, 12:30-15:00 & 19:30-24:00, closed Mon.

TORINO - TURIN

Information
ARCI GAY MAURICE, Via della Basilica 3/5, (011) 521 1116, gay & lesbian group, archives & library, Wed 21:00-24:00, Thurs & Sat 17:00-19:00. Women meet 1st Thurs 21:00-24:00.

INFORMAGAY, (011) 436 50 00, gay info line, AIDS info, answers Tues & Sat 17:00-20:00 & 21:00-23:00 (Fri lesbian line).

Bars
CIRCOLO BRIDGE, Via Maria Auseliatrice 46bis, (011) 436 4952, 21:00-04:00 (closed Tues). ♀

IL MALE, Via Lombardore 10, (011) 284 617, pub, 20:00-03:00, 70% men. ♂

MAIN STREET, Via Valperga Caluso 15, (011) 657 905, gay Tues only. ♀♂

Dance Bar/Disco
EPIC GAY CLUB, Via Martiri della Libertà, Località Borgaretto, (011) 358 3346, 22:30-02:00 (Sat till 04:00), 90% men. ♂

IL CENTRALINO, Via delle Rosine 16, gay Fri & Sun, 60% men, 40% women. ♀♂

QUARTIERE LATINO, Via Principessa Clotilde 82, open Sat only. ♀

Saunas/Health Clubs
ANTARES, via Pigafetta 73, (011) 501 645, open Tues-Sun 13:30-24:00. ♂

SAN MARTINO, Corso San Martino 8, Sauna, bar, gym, Wed-Mon 15:00-21:00. ♂

Retail & Bookstores
LIBRERIA LUXEMBURG, Via C. Battisti 7, (011) 561 3896, general bookstore with a small gay section.

Erotica
EROTIC CINEMAS: Cine Hollywood (Corso Regina Margherita 106), Regina (Corso Regina Margherita 123).

MAGIC AMERICA, via dell'Accademia Albertina 29, (011) 877 7007, 09:00-19:30.

TRIESTE

Information
ARCI GAY ARCOBALENO, Strade di Rozzol 7-9, (040) 941 708.

TELEFONO AMICO, (040) 941 708, gay line, Mon 18:00-24:00.

Erotica
MAGIC AMERICA, Viale Miramare 11.

TRIGGIANO

Dance Bar/Disco
WHY NOT, Via Don Peppino Patella 5, at Via Cartesio, Thurs & Sat 23:00-04:00, unverifiable spring '97. ♂

TURIN
SEE TORINO.

TUSCANY - RURAL

Accommodations
PRIELLO, 50233 Caprese Michelangelo, AR Italy, Tel/Fax: (39-575) 791 218. 1-1/2 hours east of Florence & 1-1/2 hrs west of Rimini. A b&b on a working farm on the site of an ancient monastery high in the mountains of Tuscany. Mainly gay & lesbian.

UDINE

Information
AIDS INFO, (0432) 26859.

ARCI GAY NUOVI PASSI, Via Gorghi, (0432) 454 68, gay & lesbian organization, gay line Mon & Wed 20:00-22:00.

TELEFONO AMICO, (0432) 454 68, gay line, Mon & Wed 20:00-22:00.

Dance Bar/Disco
ELEKTRA, Via Venezia 464, (0432) 233 163, Fri-Sun 23:00-05:00. ♀ ♂

Erotica
DIANA, Via Cividale 81, cinema.

MAGIC AMERICA, Via Manzini 38, (0432) 297 345, 09:00-19:30.

VENEZIA - VENICE

Information
ARCI GAY NOVE, Campo San Giacomo dell'Orio, S. Croce, (041) 721 842, gay & lesbian group, meetings Mon, Wed, Fri 18:00-24:00, Thurs 21:00-23:00.

Beaches
LIDO ALBERONI, very gay nude beach; Lido S. Nicolo, on island across from Lido Alberoni; Lido di Sottomarina, Chioggia.

Restaurants
DA CARLETTO, Calle delle Bande 5272, in Castello section, (041) 522 7944, Tues-Sun (closed Sun evening & Mon).

Erotica
ASTRO, Lido di Venezia, cinema.

VERONA

Information
CENTRO D'INIZIATIVA OMOSESSUALE PINK, Via Santa Chiara 7a, (045) 801 2854, gay & lesbian organization, Mon 21:00-23:00, Wed 16:00-19:00.

Bars
DOLCE & BANANA, Via XX Settembre 68, Mon-Sat 09:00-14:00 & 16:00-02:00, frequented by gays.

Saunas/Health Clubs
CITY SAUNA CLUB, Via Giolfino 12, (045) 520 009, closed Thurs.

ITALY

■ Erotica
EUROPA 92, Via Scarsellini 30, (045) 800 9714, 09:30-13:00 & 14:30-19:30.

MAGIC AMERICA, Via Cantarane 17a, (045) 800 5234, Tues-Sat 10:00-12:30 & 15:00-19:30.

VIAREGGIO

■ Beaches
LECCIONA, from Europa Ave walk over the beach & thru the pine forest.

■ Dance Bar/Disco
FRAU MARLEEN, Viale Europa, Torre del Lago, (0584) 34 22 82, very mixed hetero/gay, younger crowd, Sat & Sun from 23:30, hours may increase in summer.

■ Erotica
SUPERCINEMA, Lungomare Campioni.

VICENZA

■ Information
ARCI DI VICENZA, (0444) 52 28 90 or 52 31 23.

LATVIA
COUNTRY CODE: (371)

For Tour Companies Serving This Destination
See Latvia on page 19

RIGA

■ Information
AIDS INFO, 522 224.

■ Bars
EIGHT-O-ONE (801), 8 A. Kalnina St, Fri & Sat 21:00-06:00.

PURVS, 60 Matisa St, (7) 311 717, 19:00-07:00, closed Mon.

■ Cafe
CAFE OSIRIS, 31 Krisjan Barona St, (7) 243 002, 08:00-01:00 (Sat, Sun from 10:00), not a gay cafe, discreetly frequented by gays.

SYMPOSIUM, 84-1 Dzirnavu St, (7) 242 545, 11:00-01:00, not a gay cafe, discreetly frequented by gays.

LIECHTENSTEIN
COUNTRY CODE: (4175)

SCHAAN

■ Information
AIDS INFO, (075) 205 20.

LUXEMBOURG
COUNTRY CODE: (352)

For Tour Companies Serving This Destination
See Luxembourg on page 19

LUXEMBOURG

■ Bars
BIG MOON, 14, rue Vauban, (352) 43 17 46.

CAFÉ BEIM MIKE, 30, av Emile Reuter, (352) 45 32 84, videos, from 08:00.

CHEZ GUSHI, rue Eich.

CHEZ MANDA, rue Vaubon, mostly women, men welcome.

NETHERLANDS
COUNTRY CODE: (31)

For Tour Companies Serving This Destination
See Netherlands on page 21

ALDEBOARN

■ Accommodations
DE GRUPSTAL, Wjitteringswei 67, 8495 JM, Aldeboarn (FRL) 05663 1465, Fax 05663 1238, holiday retreat with special lesbian activities, mainly hetero clientele, accommodations for 45 people & camping, write for information.

ALKMAAR

■ Information
COC INFO LINE, Bierkade 14A, (072) 511 16 50, ask about scheduled bar nights.

■ Bars
DE KLEINE UNIE, 12 Koorstr., (072) 511 49 98, Sun 17:00-02:00.

SCHIPPERTJE, 'T Kanaalkade 77, (072) 515 02 92, 21:00-02:00 (Wed form 22:00), closed Mon & Tues.

ALMERE

■ Information
COC GAY ORGANIZATION, 17 L. Armstrongweg, (036) 536 40 61.

■ Bars
GAYBRIEL, 20 Botplein, 22:00-06:00 (closed Mon, Tues).

ALPHEN AAN DEN RIJN

■ Bars
LUZERN, 102 Hooftstraat, 12:00-18:00 (Thurs till 21:00, Sun till 17:00, Fri & Sat later), closed Mon.

AMSTERDAM

■ Information
AIDS LINE, (020) 685 0055.,

DORA, organization providing travel information for women of all ages traveling in Europe & overseas. Also provides contacts with women who want to share their knowledge about destinations they have visited. Write: Postbus 14735, 1001 LE Amsterdam, The Netherlands. Tel: (020) 638 0765 answers Tues 14:00-16:00, Wed 19:00-22:00.

GAY & LESBIAN SWITCHBOARD, (020) 623 65 65, 10:00-22:00.

HET VROUWENHUIS, Nieuwe Herengracht 95, (020) 625 20 66, call for opening hours.

INTERNATIONAL WOMEN'S LIBRARY, 4 O.B. Plein, (020) 624 21 34, call for opening hours.

LESBIAN ARCHIVES, Eerste Helmerstr. 17, (020) 618 58 79.

■ Tours, Charters & Excursions
VAARSCHOOL GRIETJE, Prinsengracht T/O 187, Amsterdam 1015 AZ, Tel/Fax: (31-20) 625 91 05. Sail the small canals of Holland, Belgium or France on "The Grietje." Seven-day sails are scheduled from end of July-early Sept. The vessel has a living room, kitchen & sleeps up to 4 women. There is no electricity or hot shower, but hot shower available almost daily.

■ Accommodations
AMSTERDAM HOUSE BV, Amstel 176a, 1017 AE Amsterdam, (31-20) 62 62 577, Fax: (31-20) 62 62 987, US: (904) 677-5370, (800) 618-1008, Fax: (904) 672-6659. Gay-friendly apartment hotel with houseboats. Available for short- and long-term business or leisure stays. Most apartments overlook the Amsterdam canals and both apartments and houseboats are spacious and luxuriously furnished. Accommodations include kitchen, refrigerator, telephone, color TV and private baths. Secretarial services, fax, answering machines, and photocopiers are also available. We are close to the main railway station and other transport intersections and afford

NETHERLANDS

easy access to the Amsterdam International Airport and downtown amenities.

ANCO HOTEL-BAR, Oudezijds Voorburgwal 55, (20) 624 11 26, fax: 620 52 75, hotel & bar for leathermen with rooms & dormitories, shared baths, men only. ♂

C&G BED & BREAKFAST HOUSE, (31-20) 422 7996. Private housing in two well-furnished modern houses in central Amsterdam. Continental breakfast, roof garden, near gay bars & many tourist attractions. Women welcome. ♂

CENTRE APARTMENTS AMSTERDAM, Heintje Hoekssteeg 27, Amsterdam 1012 GR, (020) 627 25 03, fax: 625 11 08, fully-furnished 2- & 3- room apartments & studios for 3, fully equipped kitchens, modern bathrooms, near Centraal Station. ♀♂

CHICO GUEST HOUSE, St Willibrordusstraat 77, (20) 675 4241. 3 rooms, 2 apartments, apartments have private baths, rooms share baths on landing, women welcome. ♂

FREELAND HOTEL, Marnixstraat 386, 1017 PL Amsterdam, (020) 6227511, fax 6267744, hotel, women welcome, private baths, full Dutch breakfast, color cable TV, telephone, meeting rooms. ♂

HOTEL "THE VILLAGE", 25 Kerkstraat, 1017 GA, (020) 626 9746, fax: (020) 625 408, centrally located hotel with residents' bar, café, restaurant, 50% gay/lesbian clientele, variety of guest quarters with private baths, Dutch breakfast.

HOTEL AERO, Kerkstraat 49, 1017 GB, (20) 622 7728, fax: 638 8531, hotel with bar & gay-sex shop, women welcome, newly-renovated rooms with modern conveniences, private & shared baths, full breakfast. ♂

HOTEL CLEMENS, 39 Raadhuisstraat, 1016 DC, (20) 624 60 89, hotel near Royal Palace, 50% gay/lesbian clientele, private & shared baths.

HOTEL NEW YORK, Herengracht 13, (20) 624 3066, fax 620 3230, bed & breakfast hotel, women welcome, private & shared baths, modern, comfortable decor, centrally located, ocean beach nearby, Dutch breakfast. ♂

HOTEL ORFEO, Leidsekruisstraat 14, 1017 RH (Centre), (20) 6231347, fax 620 2348 (confirmation only), bed & breakfast with bar, 99% male clientele, variety of guest quarters with various conveniences, TV lounge, sauna, full breakfast. ♂

HOTEL RONNIE, 41 Raadhuisstraat, (020) 624 2821, 622 6736, Fax: 638 8337, gay-friendly hotel, 25% gay/lesbian clientele, private & shared baths.

HOTEL SANDER, Jacob Obrechtstraat 69, (020) 6627574, Fax: 6796067. This attractive 4-star hotel with bar is situated 1 block from the Van Gogh Museum and the Concertgebouw and is a 10-minute walk from the Kerkstraat gay area. Rooms include colour cable TV, direct-dial phones, radio, individual safe and en suite WC & shower. Room rates include expanded continental breakfast. Mostly gay & lesbian with some hetero clientele. ♀♂

HOTEL SEVEN BRIDGES, Reguliersgracht 31, 1017 LK, (020) 623-1329, hotel with gay male following, single/double rooms, color TV, private & shared baths, full breakfast. ♂

HOTEL UNIQUE, Kerkstraat 37, 1017 GB, (31-20) 624 47 85, Fax: (31-20) 627 0164. Comfortable rooms with single through queen beds, private & shared baths, expanded continental breakfast, guests have own room keys, near gay bars. ♀♂

HOTEL WILHELMINA, Koninginne Weg 167-169, 1075 CN, (020) 662 5467, fax 679 2296, gay-friendly hotel, centrally located, variety of rooms, color cable TV, private & shared baths, full Dutch breakfast.

HOTEL/STUDIOS THE WATERFRONT, 458 Singel, 1017 PX, (020) 623 9775 or 625 5774, fax 620 7491, hotel with bar for guests, women welcome, private baths, 24-hr international direct-dial phones in-room, color TV, Dutch breakfast buffet. ♂

ITC HOTEL, Prinsengracht 1051, (31 20) 623 0230, fax (20) 624 5846, hotel with bar, in heart of Old Amsterdam, near gay nightlife of Rembrandtplein & Kerkstraat. Most rooms have private baths, and all are pleasantly furnished in a modern style. Other attractions are a late breakfast and your own front door key. Women welcome. ♂

LILIANE'S HOME, Sarphatistraat 119, (020) 627 4006 (tel/fax), guesthouse for women only, shared baths, color cable TV, breakfast, beverage-making facilities, maid & laundry service. ♀

MAES B&B, Nicolaas Maesstraat 94A, (020) 679 4496, fax 679 5595, E-mail: Maesbb94@XS4ALL.NL. bed & breakfast, expanded continental breakfast, coffee/tea-making facilities, private & shared baths, 10-20 min. walk to gay bars, some hetero clientele. ♀♂

MONOPOLE HOTEL, Amstel 60, (20) 624-6271, gay-friendly hotel, gay male following, some private baths.

QUENTIN, THE, Leidsekade 89, 1017 PN, (020) 626 2187, 627 4408, Fax: 622 0121, gay-friendly bed & breakfast hotel with 24-hr house bar, 50% gay/lesbian clientele, private baths, maid service, TV lounge.

RAINBOW PALACE HOTEL, Raadhuisstraat 33, 1016 DC Amsterdam, (31-20) 625 4317, Fax: (31-20) 420 5428.

RIVERSIDE APARTMENTS RENTALS, Weteringschans 187 E, Amsterdam, (31-20) 627 9797, Fax: (31-20) 627 9858. E-mail: geuje@worldonline.nl. Gay-friendly apartment rentals in & around Amsterdam, 50% gay/lesbian clientele, near entertainment & restaurants. Amenities vary according to type of accommodation.

RUBENS BED & BREAKFAST, Rubensstraat 38bv, 1077 MS Amsterdam, (31-20) 662 9187 (tel/fax), E-mail: rubensbb@xs4all.nl. http://www.xs4all.nl/~rubensbb. Owned & operated by 2 Dutch guys, this private apartment is in a 1930s neighbourhood, just outside the old city centre. Recently renovated, it is brought back to its original Art Deco style. The B&B's 2 rooms share a small state-of-the-art bathroom with shower & heated floor, and both rooms open up to a balcony with morning sun. Major museums & tourist attractions are within walking distance (or a few tram stops), and

FERRARI GUIDES' GAY TRAVEL A to Z - 18th EDITION

NETHERLANDS

Gay Amsterdam Experts Also Offer Worldwide Travel, European Gay Resorts

Besides their own gay resort on Gran Canaria, Los Robles, **De Gay Krant Reisservice**, a subsidiary of De Gay Krant, Holland's national gay newspaper, offers holidays to European gay resort destinations like Ibiza, Sitges, Mykonos and holidays to American destinations like New York, California and Florida. Other destination packages take you to Brazil, Costa Rica, Thailand, Kenya and the French Alps. Packages usually include lodging and transfers to and from the airport.

For those planning to visit Amsterdam, they are intimately acquainted with all the possibilities. They can arrange hotel bookings at either gay or gay-friendly, budget or luxury hotels. They also arrange city tours or tours to the typical Dutch countryside to see the windmills, wooden shoemakers or the fishing villages of Volendam and Marken, where the people still wear those costumes you see in picture postcards.

Contact **De Gay Krant Reisservice** at (31 20) 421 00 00, Fax: (31 20) 620 62 17 (in Belgium, phone: (014) 37 24 40), E-mail: reis@gayworld.nl, Web: www.gayworld.nl/reis/index.html.

Getting "INTO" Amsterdam

Rainboworld Custom Tours (RCT) gears its city tours to orienting visitors to the city so they can confidently continue to explore Amsterdam in depth on their own. In 3 hours on the Orientation Tour, you'll see sites most visitors never see and find out what it takes most visitors a week to learn...where to get the best exchange rates, good restaurants and bars to try, knowledge to help you make the most of your time in Amsterdam. RCT's Gay History Tour traces the Dutch movement toward a free, open society and visits a location where gays were once tortured and killed. Just like the locals, you'll glide swiftly through the streets on the Bicycling Tour, seeing lots of beautiful sights along the way. It's the most carefree way to see Amsterdam. RCT can also arrange tickets for events usually sold out months in advance and organize canal dinner cruises and countryside excursions (and other darker pleasures)...

Contact **RCT** at (303) 697-6956, (800) 969-2268, E-mail: rwctours@tde.com.

---

the Beethovenstraat shopping area is nearby. The exhuberant Amsterdam nightlife is not far away either. Expanded continental breakfast, 50% gay/lesbian clientele.

SINGEL SUITE — THE BED & BREAKFAST SUITES, Singel 420, 1016 AK Amsterdam, (31-20) 625 8673, Fax: (31-20) 625 8097. Overlooking one ot the prettiest canals in the heart of Amsterdam, our guests find someting better than the average hotel: luxury, comfort and privacy. Our two apartments are 17th century in style, but throroughly modern in luxury and comfort, and located near the best-known clubs and restaurants. One has a Jacuzzi-bath bathroom next to a private patio. See ad on page 255.

STABLEMASTER HOTEL & BAR, Warmoesstraat 23, (020) 625 0148, Fax: 624 8747, hotel in gay leather area, with gay bar on premises, double rooms with king & double beds, color cable TV, phone, some have stereos. ♂

SUNHEAD OF 1617, Herengracht 152, (020) 626 1809, Fax: 626 1823, bed & breakfast, some hetero clientele, some rooms overlooking canal, private baths, full breakfast, afternoon snacks, color cable TV, VCR, video tape library, phone, maid & laundry service. ♀♂

TOFFS APARTMENTS, Ruysdaelkade 167, (020) 67 38 529, fax 66 49 479, self-catering serviced apartments, 50% gay/lesbian clientele, colour cable TV, phone, kitchen, beverage making facilities, VCR on request.

TREND RENT, Standvliet 50, Amstelveen, (31-20) 641 0712, fax: (31-20) 640 5988. US agent: Clark Malcolm Custom Tours, in US (800) 688-3301, fax: (212) 262-3865. Apartments, homes, canal houses & houseboats in Amsterdam, cable TV, some accommodations with laundry facilities, near gay activites, museums, shopping & restaurants, ♀♂

WESTEND HOTEL & COSMO BAR, Kerkstraat 42, 1017 GM, (020) 624 8074, fax 622 9997. bed & breakfast with bar, women welcome, comfortable double rooms with shared baths, color TV upon request, men's bars & sauna nearby. ♂

■ Bars

AMSTEL TAVERN BAR, 54 Amstel at Halvemaansteeg, (020) 623 42 54, 15:00-01:00, popular at cocktail hour. ♂

APRIL, 37 Reguliersdwarsstraat, (020) 625 95 72, bar & café, yuppie, younger crowd, videos, popular early & late evenings & Sun afternoon, daily 14:00-01:00 (Fri, Sat till 03:00). ♂

ARGOS CLUB, 95 Warmoesstraat, (020) 622 65 95, cruise bar, backrooms, porno films, dungeon equipment, 22:00-03:00 (Fri, Sat till 04:00). ♂

BLITZ, THE, 45 Reguliedwarsstraat. ♂

CASA MARIA, 60 Warmoesstraat, (020) 627 68 48, popular with North Africans, 11:00-01:00. $ ♂

NETHERLANDS

CLIT CLUB, 472 Prinsengracht, Thurs 21:00-02:30. Location changes frequently, check locally for current address. ♀

CLUB 13, 25 Amstelstr., (020) 623 15 69, 16:00-01:00. ♂

CLUB JAECQUES, 93 Warmoesstraat, (020) 622 03 23, cruise bar, backroom, 20:30-03:00 (Fri, Sat till 04:00).

COMPANY,★ 106 Amstel, (020) 625 30 28, upstairs backroom, 20:00-02:00, Sun 16:00-02:00.

COSMO BAR, 42 Kerkstraat, (020) 624 80 74, 21:00-03:00. ♂

CUCKOO'S NEST, 6 Nieuwe Zijds Kolk, (020) 623 58 70, cruise bar with well-equipped, large basement back room, 13:00-01:00 (Fri, Sat till 03:00).

CUPIDO BAR, 7 Paardenstraat, (020) 622 17 89, in a dangerous area, 21:00-02:00. $♂

DE KROKODIL BAR, 34 Amstelstraat, (020) 626 22 43, occasional drag shows & vocalists, 16:00-01:00, till 02:00 Fri & Sat.

DE SPIJKER★, 4 Kerkstraat, (020) 620 59 19, video porn, backroom, jack-off parties 1st & 3rd Sat, 21:00-03:00.

DE STEEG, Halvemaansteeg, Dutch sing-alongs with live singers, 17:00-01:00, Fri & Sat till 03:00. ♂

DIRTY DICK'S, 86 Warmoesstraat, Fri, Sat from 24:00.

DOLL'S PLACE, 57 Vinkenstraat, (020) 627 07 90, 21:00-03:00, till 04:00 on weekends.

EAGLE, 90 Warmoesstraat, (020) 627 86 34, cruise bar, 2 bars, backroom, 22:00-04:00 (Fri, Sat till 05:00).

ENTRE NOUS, 14 Halve Maansteeg, ♂

FALCK, 3-5 Falckstraat, Mon-Fri from 12:00. ♂

FESTIVAL BAR, 15 Paardenstraat, (020) 623 12 17, in a dangerous area. Open 11:00-02:00.

G FORCE, Oudezijds Armsteeg, SM bar, 12:00-24:00.

GAIETY, 14 Amstel, (020) 624 42 71, younger crowd, popular cocktail hour, 16:00-01:00 (Fri, Sat 15:00-03:00, Sun 15:00-01:00).

HAVANA, 15 Reguliersdwarsstraat, (020) 620 8788, trendy café, 16:00-01:00 (Fri, Sat 14:00-02:30, Sun from 14:00). ♂

HEERENHUYS, 'T, 114 Herengracht, (020) 622 76 85, 11:00-05:00. ♂

HOLLYWOOD, 447 Singel, 22:00-04:00 (Sun 17:00-24:00), closed Mon-Wed. ♂

LA PORTE D'OR, 24 Rembrandtplein, 20:00-01:00 (Fri, Sat till 02:00). ♂

LA STRADA, 93 NZ Voorburgwal, 21:00-02:00. ♂

MANKIND,★ 60 Weteringstraat, (020) 638 47 55, 11:00-01:00, Fri & Sat till 02:00. ♂

MEIA MEIA, 63 Kerkstraat, (020) 623 41 29, 14:00-01:00 (Fri, Sat till 03:00). ♂

MILORD, 102 Amstel, 18:00-01:00 (Fri, Sat till 03:00). ♂

MIX CAFE, 50 Amstel, (020) 420 33 88, 20:00-03:00 (Fri, Sat till 04:00). ♀♂

MONICO, 15 Lange Niezel, popular with local women, Fri & Sat 14:00-01:00. ♀

MONOPOLE TAVERN, 60 Amstel, (020) 624 64 51, 15:00-01:00.

MONTMARTRE DE PARIS, 17 Halvemaansteeg, (020) 624 92 16, Dutch sing-alongs, drag, cabaret twice monthly, 17:00-01:00 (Fri & Sat 16:00-03:00, sun 16:00-01:00).

MUSIC BOX, 9 Paardenstraat, (020) 620 41 10, 20:00-02:00 (Fri, Sat till 03:00), closed Mon. $♂

OTHER SIDE, 6 Reguliersdwarsstraat, (020) 625 51 41. ♂

OUDE VEERHUIS, 8 Singel, (020) 624 32 81, 09:00-01:00 (Fri, Sat till 02:00). ♂

REALITY, 129 Reguliersdwaarsstraat, 20:00-03:00 (Fri, Sat till 04:00). ♂

SAAREIN, 119 Elandsstraat, 15:00-01:00 (Fri, Sat till 02:00, Mon from 20:00). ♀

SCANDAL, 303 J. van Galenstraat, 20:00-02:00 (weekends till 03:00). ♂

SECRET, 346 Kerkstraat, 20:00-02:00 (Fri, Sat till 03:00). ♂

SHAKO, 2 's Gravenlandseveer, (020) 624 02 09, younger crowd, 21:00-02:00, Sat-Sun till 03:00.

STABLEMASTER, 23 Warmoesstraat, at the Stablemaster Hotel location, (020) 625 0148, Fri & Sat jack-off parties. ♂

VAN DEN BERG, 95 Lindengracht, (020) 622 27 16, women's cafe, restaurant, bar, dancing, regular shows, gay men welcome, daily 16:00-01:00.

WEB, THE, 6 St. Jacobsstraat, (020) 623 67 58, cruise bar with roof garden, shows, parties, 12:00-02:00.

---

the leading gay escort service

home/hotel
visiting service
reliable
and discreet

020 - 662 99 90

visit our internet-site and browse our database
(pictures available) at
http://www.peoplemale.com
e-mail: info@peoplemale.com

PEOPLE™
male escorts
amsterdam

FERRARI GUIDES' GAY TRAVEL A to Z - 18th EDITION

NETHERLANDS

Women Sailing Holland's Canals

When you sail with **Vaarschool Grietje**, you'll get a different view of Holland, Belgium, and France — from the water. This summer, they'll sail through north and south Holland and Utrecht, an area of quiet, beautiful waters with old locks and bridges. At the end of July, they'll sail to France. Via Maastricht, Belgium, the French Ardennes, and Charleville, we will get to Reims.

You will have an opportunity to handle the ship, landing, departing, manueuvering through bridges, locks, and tunnels. You'll learn the "rules of the water" and even be able to receive a diploma upon satisfactory completion of the course. Register alone or with up to three other people. The vessel "Grietje" is a former freighter, built in Muiden in 1921. It's 16 meters long, and 3-1/2 meters wide. There is a kitchen, living area, and four primitive sleeping berths. Meals are not included. Cooking facilities are on board. You must bring: non-slip shoes, linens and towels.

Contact **Vaarschool Grietje** at (31 20) 625 91 05 (tel/fax).

■ Dance Bar/Disco

COC DISCO, BAR & CAFÉ, 14 Rozenstraat, (020) 623 40 79, Wed-Sun 13:00-17:00 & 20:00-24:00. Call for schedule of men's & women's disco nights.

COC VROUWENDISCO, at COC coffeeshop, 14 Rozenstraat, women's disco night. Call for scheduled Sat disco.

COCKRING, 96 Warmoesstraat, (020) 623 96 04, cruise bar, disco & upstairs video bar, backroom, 22:00-04:00.

DE BRUG, 676 Keizersgracht, disco for lesbians over 35 years, 1st Fri.

EXIT,★ 42 Reguliersdwarsstraat, (020) 625 87 88, disco & 2 bars, 23:00-04:00 (Fri, Sat till 05:00)..

HOMOLULU WOMEN'S NIGHTS, at Homolulu disco, 1st Sun/3rd Fri 20:00-01:00.

HOMOLULU,★ 23 Kerkstraat, (020) 624 63 87, disco & restaurant, ring the bell, daily 22:00-04:00, women's disco nights 1st Sun & 3rd Fri of the month.

IT, 24 Amstelstraat, (020) 625 01 11, Thurs 23:00-04:00 (Fri-Sun till 05:00).

ROXY LADY, 465 Singel, at the Roxy disco location, women's disco 3rd Sun 18:00-23:00.

ROXY, 465 Singel, Wed 23:00-04:00.

VIVE LA VIE, 7 Amstelstraat, (020) 624 01 14, 15:00-01:00, Fri, Sat till 03:00.

■ Cafe

BOLLEBEER, 38 Kloveniersburgwal, 09:00-19:00 (closed Sun).

CAFÉ GALLERY, 38 Nieuwendijk.

DE HALVE MAAN, 18 Halve Maansteeg.

DOWNTOWN,★ 31 Reguliersdwarsstraat, (020) 622 99 58, cafe, restaurant with patio, 11:00-20:00.

FRANCOISE, 176 Kerkstraat, (020) 624 01 45, cafe with light meals, 07:30-18:00.

KAFÉ VERKEERD, Brouwersgr.

LE MONDE,★ 6 Rembrandtplein, (020) 626 99 22, breakfast, lunch, dinner, patio, popular with gays & lesbians 08:00-22:00, till 24:00 during summer.

SAAREIN,★ 119 Elandsstraat, (020) 623 49 01, women-only cafe, 15:00-01:00 (Fri, Sat till 02:00, Mon from 20:00).

■ Saunas/Health Clubs

MODERN SAUNA, 311 Jacob Van Lennepstraat, (020) 612 17 12, 12:00-18:00, closed Sun.

SAUNA PARADISE, 26 Schaafstr., fr. 14:00.

THERMOS DAG,★ 33 Raamstraat, (020) 623 91 58, sauna with bar, snacks, 12:-23:.

THERMOS NACHT,★ 58 Kerkstraat, (020) 623 49 36, with full bar, movies, sunbeds, 23:00-08:00.

■ Restaurants

A ROAD TO MANILA, 23 Geldersekade, 16:00-24:00.

AMSTERDAM, 6 Watertorenplein, 11:00-01:00 (Fri, Sat till 02:00).

BALDUR, 76 Weteringschans, (020) 624 46 72, non-smoking vegetarian restaurant popular with lesbians, daily 17:00-22:00.

BISTRO CONTRA 73, 24 Karperstraat.

CAMP CAFE, 45 Kerkstraat, 11:00-01:00.

CARLITA'S CANTINA, 121 Ceintuurbaan, (020) 675 69 30, 17:00-24:00.

COSTELICK MAEL, 'T, 115 1st C. Huygensstraat, 17:00-24:00.

DE APPLEGAARD, 105 Wittenkede.

DE HUYSKAEMER, 137 Utrechtstraat.

DE JAREN, 20-22 Nieuwe Doelenstraat, (020) 625 5771.

GEMINI, 11 Thorbeckeplein, open 11:00-01:00 (Sat, Sun till 02:00).

GRIET MANSHADE, 10 Keerpunkt, from 18:00, closed Tues.

HARVEST, 25 Govert Flinckstraat, (020) 676 9995, vegetarian cuisine, Tues-Sat 17:30-22:30.

HEMELSE MODDER, 9 Oude Waal.

HET CHATEAU, 115 Fred. Hendrickstraat.

INDRAPURA, 42 Rembrandtplein, (020) 623 73 29, Indonesian cuisine.

INTERMEZZO, 28 Herenstr., 17:30-22:00 (Fri, Sat 18:00-22:30).

JARDIN PARISIEN, 30A Utrechtstraat, 16:00-24:00.

JEAN JEAN, 12 1st Anjeliersdwarsstraat, 18:00-22:30, closed Mon.

KILIMANJARO, 6 Rapenbplts., 17:00-22:00 (closed Mon).

KORT, 12 Amstelveld, restaurant & bar.

LE GARAGE, 54 Ruysdaelstraat, 12:00-14:00 & 18:00-23:00 (Sat, Sun 18:00-23:00 only).

LETO, 114 Haarlemmerdijk, 17:00-22:00, closed Mon.

LIDO RESTAURANT, 102 Leidsekade, Thurs 19:30-00:30 (Fri, Sat till 04:00).

LOMBOK, 12 Halve Maansteeg.

MAXIES BRASSERIE, 100 PC Hoofstrat, 11:00-21:30 (closed Sun, Mon).

MEMORIES OF INDIA, 88 Reguliersdwarsstr., (020) 623 5710, 17:00-23:00.

PORTUGALIA, 35 Kerkstraat, 17:-23:00.

RA KANG THAI, 29 Elandsgracht, cl. Mon.

SAY SATÉ, 26 Amstelstr., (020) 625 75 60, open till 01:00 (Fri, Sat till 02:00).

SCHOOIERTJE, 'T, 190 Lijnbaansgracht, (020) 638 40 35, Sat-Thurs 10:00-22:00.

SLUISJE, 'T, 1 Torensteeg near Spuistraat,

NETHERLANDS

(020) 624 08 13, steakhouse, 17:00-01:00 (closed Wed).

SLUIZER, 41 Utrechtsestraat, (020) 622 63 76, indoor & terrace dining 10:00-24:00.

SUKHOTHAI, 147 Ceintuurbaan, 17:30-24:00.

TEMPO DOELOE, 75 Utrechtsestraat, (020) 625 67 18, Indonesian cuisine, 18:-23:00.

TWINK, 27 Reguliersdwarsstraat, cl. Tues.

■ Retail & Bookstores

ANTIQUARIAAT LORELEI, 495 Prinsengracht, (020) 623 43 08, Tues-Fri 12:00-18:00, Sat till 17:00.

BOEKENCASA, 133 Haarlemmerdijk, (020) 622 58 92, alternative bookstore with women's section.

DESMET, 4a Plantage Middenlaan, cinema with scheduled gay movies on weekends, not erotic.

INTERMALE, 251 Spuistraat, 1012 VR Amsterdam, The Netherlands, (020) 625 00 09, Amsterdam's largest quality men's gay bookshop. Books in English, Dutch, German & French. Largest selection of men's magazines & cards. We mail order anywhere, send for catalog, Mon-Sat 10:00-18:00, Thurs till 21:00.

VROLIJK BOOKSTORE, 135 Paleisstraat, (020) 623 51 42, gay & lesbian bookshop, books in many languages, cards, art posters & magazines, Mon-Fri 10:00-18:00, Thurs till 21:00, Sat till 17:00.

VROUWENINDRUK, 5 Westermarkt near Westerkerk, (020) 624 50 03, second-hand books on women's sexuality, herstory, feminism. Most books are in Dutch, many in English, 11:00-18:00 (Mon from 13:00).

XANTIPPE, 290 Prinsengracht, (020) 623 58 54, one of Europe's largest selections of women's & lesbian books, many in English. Stop by & ask us for local info, 10:00-18:00 (Mon from 13:00, Sat till 17:00), closed Sun.

■ Leathers/Piercing

BLACK BODY MEN'S RUBBERWEAR, 292 Lijnbaansgracht, Tues-Fri 10:00-18:30 (Sat 11:00-17:00).

MASTER LEATHERS, 32 Warmoesstraat, (020) 624 55 73, full range of rubber & leather clothing, sportswear, toys, leather goods, 11:00-18:00 (Thurs till 21:00), closed Sun.

MISTER B, 89 Warmoesstraat, (020) 422 0003, 10:00-18:30 (Thurs till 21:00, Sat 11:00-17:30), closed Sun.

RIJNSPORT, 44 Rijnstr, (020) 679 94 85.

ROB AMSTERDAM, ★ 253 Weteringschans, (020) 625 46 86, leather shop & gallery of erotic art, select wines with erotic labels 11:00-18:30, Sat till 17:00, closed Sun.

ROBIN & RIK, 30 Runstraat,

WRAPPED LEERSHOP, 434 Singel, (020) 420 40 22, 10:00-18:00 (Mon from 12:00, Thurs till 21:00, Sat till 17:30), closed Sun.

■ Erotica

ADONIS CINEMA, 92 Warmoesstraat, all-male, 10:00-01:00 (Fri, Sat till 03:00).

BRONX, ★ 53 Kerkstraat, (020) 623 15 48, cinema, videos, toys, poppers, magazines, novels, leather items, big-screen, air conditioned video cinema, private booths, daily 12:00-24:00.

CHRISTINE LE DUC, Spui 6; Oudebrugsteeg 21; Reguliersdwarsstraat 107; Leidsekruisdwarsstraat 33.

DRAKE'S, 61 Damrak, (020) 627 9544, gay store with cinema.

LE SALON, 20-22 Nieuwendijk, (020) 622 65 65, videos, 10:00-24:00.

MAN TO MAN, 21 Spuistraat, (020) 625 87 97, cinemas, 11:00-01:00.

NAVIGAYTOR, 171 Korte Leidsewarsstraat, (020) 530 2125.

VIDEO AMSTERDAM, 163 Kleine Houtstraat.

APELDOORN

■ Information

COC GAY ORGANIZATION, Agricolastraat 161, (055) 355 44 25, group meets Fri from 21:00, 1st Sun 15:00-19:00.

■ Bars

CAESAR, Hoofdstr. 12, (055) 322 42 73, from 22:00.

DE SCHOUW, Spadelaan 8, (055) 341 70 35, Sun, Mon, Thurs, Fri 22:00-02:00, Wed, Sat till 04:00.

■ Saunas/Health Clubs

SAUNA FARM 63, Elburgerweg 63, in the town of Wenum, (055) 312 1430, 14:00-23:00 (Sun 12:00-18:00), closed Thurs.

■ Erotica

CHRISTINE LE DUC, Asselsestraat 131.

ARNHEM

■ Information

COC GAY ORGANIZATION, J Cremerstraat 32, (026) 442 31 61, Thurs 19:00-21:00, Sat 14:00-16:00.

IRIS, Willemsplein 21, lesbian group.

■ Bars

ENTRE NOUS, S. de Landastraat 65, (026) 445 06 52, Fri, Sat 22:00-04:00, Sun 20:00-03:00.

JOY, 4 Pauwstraat.

KELDERCAFÉ DWARS, S. de Landastr. 65, 20:00-03:00 (Fri-Sun till 04:00), closed Mon-Wed.

QUEEN'S, Velperbuitensingel 21 A, (026) 443 46 88, from 19:00 (Sun from 15:00).

SPRING, Bovenbeekstraat 5, (026) 442 50 36, 12:00-02:00 (Mon, Tues till 01:00, Sun 16:00-01:00).

■ Retail & Bookstores

HELLEVEEG, Bentinckstraat 36, (026) 451 54 31, women's bookstore, Tues-Sat 10:00-18:00 (Thurs till 21:00).

■ Erotica

CHRISTINE LE DUC, Walstr. 55.

BERGEN OP ZOOM

■ Information

COC GAY ORGANIZATION, Blokstallen 4, (0164) 2542 35, bar nights Fri 21:00-02:00, Sun 18:30-23:00, every 3rd Sat 21:00-02:00.

BEST

■ Bars

CAFÉ MANUS, Nieuwstr. 92, (0499) 3951 19, 11:30-02:00.

BREDA

■ Information

COC GAY ORGANIZATION, St. Annastraat 10, (076) 522 66 62, Sat 12:00-16:00, 2nd Sat 21:00-03:00, 4th Wed 20:30-24:00. Vrouwencafe (women's cafe) 2nd & 4th Fri from 21:00.

■ Bars

AMPFORA, Prinsenkade.

DEJA VU, 5 Haagdijk, 17:00-02:00 (Mon till 01:00), closed Tues, Wed.

FIRST FLOOR, 5 Molenstraat, (076) 521 50 05, 21:00-02:00 (closed Tues-Thurs).

HAAI BAAI, Nieuwstr 19, (076) 521 80 31, 20:00-02:00 (Sun from 18:00).

NOU EN, Molenstr. 5, (076) 521 50 05, 20:00-02:00 (Mon-Wed till 01:00, Sun from 16:00).

VENISE, Halstraat 30, (076) 521 67 02, 20:00-02:00 (Sun from 17:00).

■ Saunas/Health Clubs

LIBERTY, 1 Chassesingel, (076) 522 0976, 12:00-24:00 (Sun 13:00-20:00).

■ Restaurants

PORTO BELLO, 2 Kastelplein.

■ Erotica

CHRISTINE LE DUC, Haagdijk 14.

DELFT

■ Bars

DE KIJLEKIT, Phoenixstraat 96, from 17:

DELFT WERKGROEP HOMOSEXUALITAT BAR, Lange Geer 22, (015) 2146 893. Gay & lesbian organization with gay bar (women welcome), Sun, Wed & 3rd Thurs 20:00-01:00, Fri 21:00-02:00. Potterie lesbian evening 1st Sat of the month 21:00-02:00.

DEN HAAG - THE HAGUE

■ Information

AIDS INFO, (070) 354 1610, Tues, Thurs 19:00-21:00.

COC GAY ORGANIZATION, Scheveningseveer 7, (070) 365 90 90, bar nights Wed 17:00-00:30, Thur 20:00-00:30, Sun 15:-19:00.

FERRARI GUIDES' GAY TRAVEL A to Z - 18th EDITION

NETHERLANDS

■ *Bars*
BOKO, Nieuwe Schoolstr. 7. ♂
BOSS, THE, Rijswijkseweg 536, 22:00-01:30 (Sun from 17:00), closed Mon, Tues. ♥♫☒ ♂
DE KLAP, Koningin Emmakade 118a. ♂
DE LANDMAN, Denneweg 48, (070) 346 77 27, 16:00-01:00. ♂
DE VINK, Schoolstr. 28, (070) 365 03 57, 16:00-01:00. ♂
INTERNETCAFE, 48 Elandstraat, 17:00-01:00 (Fri, Sat till 01:30), closed Sun. ♂
STAIRS, Nieuwe Schoolstr. 11, 22:00-02:00 (Sun from 17:00). ♂
STRASS DANSCAFE, Javastr. 132, Fri & Sat 22:00-05:00. ☒♂
STRASS, 132 Javastraat, 08:00-01:00 (Sat 11:00-21:00, Sun 17:00-01:00). ♂
TRIOMFBAR, Kettingstr. 4, (070) 346 71 07, Thurs-Mon from 22:00. ♂

■ *Dance Bar/Disco*
X-TREME, Herengracht 7, from 22:00 (closed Tues, Wed). ☒♂

■ *Saunas/Health Clubs*
ELDORADO, Hogezand 92A, 13:00-24:00 (Sat till 18:00), closed Sun.
FIDES, Veenkade 20, 14:00-24:00 (Fri, Sat till 02:00).

■ *Restaurants*
DER VERLIEFDE KREEFT, Bleyenburg 9-11, 18:00-23:00. ☒
EETCAFÉ, 'T, 132 Javastraat, 07:30-01:00.
HAAGSE GRAAF, Gortstr. 12, Mon-Sat 12:00-21:00. ☒
WALONG, 286 Fred. Hendriklaan, 12:00-22:00.
WILHELM TELL, Ln. van Meerdervoort 324, 18:00-24:00 (closed Wed). ☒

■ *Retail & Bookstores*
TRIX, Prinsestraat 122, (070) 364 50 14, women's bookstore, Mon 13:00-17:00, Tues-Fri 10:00-17:30, Sat 10:00-17:00.

■ *Erotica*
CHRISTINE LE DUC, 1 Piet Heinplaats.

DONKERBROEK

■ *Women's Accommodations*
T ZIJPAD, Balkweg 8, 8435 VP, (05168) 1752, bed & breakfast guesthouse, campground, some men welcome, variety of guest quarters with modern conveniences, expanded continental breakfast for B&B only, tent sites. ♀

DORDRECHT

■ *Bars*
ANDERS, 55 Dolhuisstraat, gay bar night even Sun of the month. ♂
COC BAR NIGHTS, 4 Dolhuisstraat, Sat 21:00-01:00. ♂

EINDHOVEN

■ *Information*
COC GAY ORGANIZATION, 54 Hendrikstraat, (040) 245 57 00, bar nights Tues, Thurs, Fri 21:00-01:00, Sun 15:00-18:00.

■ *Bars*
BORSCHDIJK, 229 Borschdijk, (040) 243 9142, 17:00-02:00 (closed Mon, Tues). ♂
CHARLIE'S PUB, 36 Dommelstraat, from 17:00 (closed Mon, Tues). ♂
CLUB FUNKI BIZNIZ, Stratumsedijk 35, 19:00-02:00 (Fri, Sat 14:00-04:00, Sun 16:00-02:00), closed Mon. ☒♫♂
DANSSALON, 4 Stationsplaats, (040) 245 6377, 21:30-04:00 (Thurs till 02:00, Sun 21:00-02:00), closed Mon-Wed. ☒♂
LE PECHEUR, Stratumsedijk 37, 21:00-04:00. ☒♫♫♂
QUEENS PUB, THE, Lambertusstr. 42, (040) 244 25 06, 20:00-02:00, Sun from 16:00. ☒♫✗♦♂
RENDEZ VOUS, Stratumsedijk 14, (040) 211 83 63, 22:00-02:00 (Fri, Sat till 04:00, Sun from 20:00). ☒♫♫♂
SHAKESPEARE, Kloosterdreef 108, 20:00-02:00. ♀
TOLERANT, Stratumsedijk 103a, Wed-Sun 21:00-02:00. ♀
VAGEVUUR, 'T, Hemelrijken 18. ♥♫☒♂

■ *Saunas/Health Clubs*
JAGUAR, Ledeganckstr. 1, (040) 251 12 38, 12:00-24:00 (Sun 13:00-20:00). ♉✗
ROYAL, Stratumsedijk 23, (040) 211 08 40, 12:00-24:00 (Fri, Sat till 08:00). ♉✗

■ *Restaurants*
ANCIENNE BELGIQUE, Stratumsdijk 23-I, 11:30-22:00 (Sat, Sun from 17:00). ☒
DE PEPERMOLEN, 259 Leenderweg, 10:00-21:00.
OLD VALLEY, THE, 18 St. Antoniusstraat, 17:00-22:00 (Sun from 14:00), closed Tues.
PEACOCK, THE, 208 Heuvelgalerie, 09:00-18:00 (Fri till 21:00), closed Sun.
SALA THAI, Staringstraat 31, open Tues-Sun. ☒

■ *Retail & Bookstores*
BOEKENNEL, Grote Berg 11, (040) 243 06 39, women's bookstore.

■ *Erotica*
CHRISTINE LE DUC, Willemstr. 33.

ENSCHEDE

■ *Information*
AIDS INFO, (053) 477 82 82.
COC GAY ORGANIZATION, Walstraat 12-14, (053) 430 51 77, bar nights Thurs 20:00-24:00, Fri 20:00-02:00, Sat 16:30-20:00, Sun 16:00-22:00.

■ *Bars*
BÖLKE, 'T, Molenstraat 6-8, (053) 434 13 41, 21:00-04:00. ♂
FOR YOU, 22 Molenstraat, (053) 432 03 01, 20:00-04:00 (Sun from 16:00). ♂
POORT VAN KLEEF, Markt 14, 10:00-02:00 (Sun from 12:00). ♂
STONEWALL, Walstraat 14, (053) 431 70 14, Fri 19:30-02:00, Sat 15:30-20:30, Sun 16:00-22:00. Sat women only 21:00-02:00. ♂

■ *Saunas/Health Clubs*
BÖLKE, 'T, Molenstraat 6-8, at 't Bölke bar, 14:00-24:00 (Fri, Sat till 04:00).

■ *Restaurants*
HANS & HEINZ, Walstraat 5. ☒
LA PETITE BOUFFE, Deuringerstraat 11, 17:30-22:30, closed Mon, Tues. ☒
SAM SAM, 15-17 Oude Markt. ☒

■ *Erotica*
VIDEO CINEMA A'DAM, Molenstraat 14, 13:00-23:00.

GOES

■ *Bars*
KELDEBAR, Blauwe Steen 5, Tues, Wed 20:00-02:00, Thurs-Sat 20:00-04:00. ♂

GOUDA

■ *Bars*
CHEVY, 50 Oosthaven, Fri, Sat 22:00-04:00, Sun 20:00-02:00. ♂
COC BAR NIGHTS, 113a Spieringstraat, (0182) 524 634, Fri 21:00-01:00, Sun 19:00-24:00. ♂

GRONINGEN

■ *Bars*
DE GOLDEN ARM, Hardewikerstraat 7, 23:00-06:00, closed Mon-Wed. ♂
DE KONINGEN, O. Boteringestraat 60, (050) 314 59 62, 20:00-01:00 (Fri, Sat till 02:00), closed Sun, Mon. ♀
EL RUBIO, Zwanestr. 26, (050) 314 00 39, 16:00-02:00 (Sun from 15:00). ♂
LETO, A-Kerkstr. 20, (050) 312 22 13, 15:00-02:00, closed Tues. ♂
MAC LEATHER, Hoge der A3, Fri, Sat 23:00-03:00. ♥♫☒♂
MAC, THE, Hoge der A3, (050) 312 71 88, 23:00-03:00 (Sun from 17:00). ♂
RITS, Pottebakkersrijge 2, (050) 318 01 66, from 16:00. ♂
TOWER, Boteringeplaats 1, Fri, Sat from 22:00, Sun 16:00-19:00. ♂
WOMEN'S BAR NIGHTS, Kraneweg 56, at the COC lesbian/gay center, (050) 313 26 20, 2nd, 3rd & 4th Sat 22:00-02:00. ♀

■ *Cafe*
COC CAFÉ, Kraneweg 56, at COC lesbian/gay center, (050) 313 26 20, Fri 16:00-01:00. ♂

NETHERLANDS

■ *Saunas/Health Clubs*
PAKHUISJE, 'T, Schuitenmakersstr. 17, (050) 312 92 88, 16:00-24:00.

■ *Restaurants*
DE BENJAMIN, 33 Kl. Leliestraat, 17:30-23:00, closed Sun & Mon.
DE TWEE DAMES, 64 Zuiderdiep, from 16:00, closed Sun & Mon.
DE ZEVENDE HEMEL, 7 Zuiderkerkstraat, from 17:00.

■ *Retail & Bookstores*
TRUI, Folkingestraat 14, (050) 313 62 66, women's bookstore.

■ *Erotica*
CHRISTINE LE DUC, Ged. Zuiderdiep 88.
VIDEOTHEEK 3000, Ged. Zuiderdiep 130, (050) 314 42 21, cinema.

HAARLEM

■ *Information*
AIDS INFO, (023) 525 2530.
COC GAY ORGANIZATION, Oudegracht 24, (023) 532 54 53, bar nights Wed & Thurs 20:00-01:00, Fri 16:00-03:00, Sat 22:00-03:00.

■ *Bars*
JELTES, 15 Schagchelstraat, 16:00-02:00 (Fri, Sat till 04:00, Sun from 17:00). ♂
LA JUSLESSE, 127 Ged. Oudegracht, 17:30-01:30 (Fri, Sat till 03:30, Sun from 17:00), closed Mon. ♂
WILSONS CLUB, Ged. Raamgracht 78, (023) 532 58 54, Wed-Thurs 20:00-02:00, Fri-Sat 22:00-04:00. 🍽️🪩🎵♂

■ *Erotica*
CHRISTINE LE DUC, 17 Cronjestraat.

HEERLEN

■ *Bars*
BODY TALK, Gringelstraat 3, (045) 572 74 63, 21:00-02:00 (closed Mon.) ♂
LA PERLE, Bokstraat 47, (045) 522 69 53, from 21:00. ♂
PEPPERMILL, 90 Beitel, Fri, Sat 22:00-05:00. ♂
THEATER-KAFÉ, Honigmanstraat 2, (045) 571 73 87, Sat 15:00-18:00. ♂

■ *Restaurants*
INGENTHUN, Weltertuynstraat 31. 🍽️
LIGNANO'S, 52 Pancatiusplein, 16:00-22:00.

■ *Erotica*
CHRISTINE LE DUC, 5 Dantzenbergstraat.

HILVERSUM

■ *Information*
COC GAY ORGANIZATION, 43a Vaartweg, (035) 628 47 89, bar nights Thurs-Sat from 21:00.

■ *Bars*
SO WHAT, Noorderweg 72, (035) 683 10 03, 16:00-01:00 (Fri, Sat till 02:00). ♂

LEEUWARDEN

■ *Information*
COC GAY ORGANIZATION, Druifstreek 63, (058) 2124 908, bar night Sat 21:00-01:00. Women's bar nights 1st & 3rd Fri.

■ *Bars*
DE KANNEKIJKER, Bagijnenstraat 63, (058) 212 89 83, 16:00-24:00.
DE TUIN, Tuinen 3, (058) 213 74 87, from 20:00. ♂
INCOGNITO, Noordvliet 13, (058) 212 60 82, 22:30-04:00. ♂
MONSIEUR, 95 Nieuwe Buren, from 16:00. ♂

■ *Dance Bar/Disco*
CLUB CHEZ NOUS, 9 Gr. Hoogstraat, (058) 212 7167, 21:00-04:00, closed Mon. 🍽️♂

■ *Restaurants*
NIEUWE LIEFDE, Breedstraat 42, Wed-Mon from 17:00. 🍽️

LEIDEN

■ *Bars*
ODESSA, Hogewoerd 18, (071) 512 33 11, Thurs 22:00-01:00. ♂

MAASTRICHT

■ *Information*
COC GAY ORGANIZATION, Bogaardenstraat 43, (043) 321 83 37.

■ *Bars*
CAFE ROSE, 43 Bogaardenstraat, (043) 321 8337, gay organization bar nights, Thurs 20:00-24:00, Fri 14:00-17:00 & 21:00-02:00, Sat 21:00-02:00, Sun 20:00-02:00.
FALSTAFF, 6 Amerspl., 10:00-02:00. ♂
LA FERME, Rechtestr. 29, (043) 321 89 28, 20:00-02:00 (Fri, Sat till 03:00, Sun from 16:00), closed Tues. ♂
LA GARE, Spoorweglaan 6, (043) 325 90 90, Tues-Sun 21:00-05:00. ♂
REMBRANDT, Markt 32, (043) 321 42 18, 20:00-02:00. ♂
TRAIT D'UNION, 38 Markt. ♂

■ *Restaurants*
DE PIETERSPOORT, St. Pietersstraat 8a. 🍽️
SUKHOTHAI, Tongersestraat 54, Wed-Sun from 17:00. 🍽️

NIJMEGEN

■ *Information*
AIDS INFO, (024) 322 8556.
COC GAY ORGANIZATION & LESBIAN ARCHIVES, In de Betouwstraat 9. (024) 323 42 37, Tues, Wed, Fri 13:30-17:00. Lesbian Archives call: 323 44 59, Mon-Wed 14:00-17:00.

■ *Bars*
BAKKERTJE, 'T, 69 V. Welderenstraat, (024) 323 1348. ♂
D'END, 87 V. Welderenstraat, 12:00-02:00 (Sun from 14:00). ♂
DE PLAK, Bloemerstr 90, (024) 322 27 57, 11:00-01:00 (Thurs from 22:30). ♂
DE SPIL, 87 V. Welderenstraat, 12:00-23:00 (Sun from 11:00). ♂
DE VERJAARDAG, Van Welderenstr. 77, from 20:00. ♂
METS, Grotestraat 7, (024) 323 95 49, 12:00-02:00 (Sun from 14:00, Mon from 10:00), women welcome.
MY WAY, 2nd Walstraat 96, 20:00-02:00 (Fri, Sat till 04:00, Sun 18:00-03:00). ♂

■ *Dance Bar/Disco*
DE MYTHE, Platenmakersstr 3, (024) 322 01 55, disco & bar from 20:00 (Sat, Sun from 15:00), closed Mon-Wed. 🍽️♀♂
GAY CLUB KK, 32 Graafseweg, Fri, Sat 23:00-05:00. 🍽️♂

■ *Saunas/Health Clubs*
AZZURRA, Kerkberg 22, in Beek, (024) 684 18 08, Mon, Tues & Thurs 14:00-24:00, Fri & Sat till 02:00, Sun 15:00-24:00.

■ *Retail & Bookstores*
VROUWENBOEKHANDEL DE FEEKS, Van Welderenstraat 34, (024) 323 93 81. Women's bookstore specializing in women's literature & women's studies, with a large selection of lesbian titles in Dutch & in English. Open 10:00-18:00 (Mon from 13:00, Thurs till 21:00, Sat till 17:00), closed Sun. Ask about current local info.

■ *Erotica*
CHRISTINE LE DUC, 78 Bloemerstraat.

ROERMOND

■ *Bars*
GIGOLO, Venlosepoort 3, (0475) 315850, 20:00-02:00 (Fri, Sat till 03:00), closed Mon. 🍽️🪩🎵♂
SJINDERHANNES, Swalmerstraat 42, 21:00-02:00 (Fri, Sat till 03:00). ♂

■ *Saunas/Health Clubs*
DINGEMAN, Willem II-sngl 14, (0475) 336236, 13:00-24:00.

ROTTERDAM

■ *Information*
AIDS INFO, (010) 436 5811.
COC GAY ORGANIZATION, Schiedamsesingel 175, (010) 414 15 55, bar nights Thurs 22:00-24:00, Fri 21:00-01:00, Sat 22:00-01:00, 1st Sun 15:00-18:30.

■ *Bars*
BOY, 173 Schiedamsesingel, from 17:00. ♂
CAFÉ 'T HOK, Branderplaats 32, (010) 433 47 83. ♂
COSMO & COSMONAUT, Schiedamsesingel

FERRARI GUIDES' GAY TRAVEL A to Z - 18th EDITION

NETHERLANDS

133, (010) 412 36 68, Cosmo 20:00-02:00, Cosmonaut Thurs-Sat from 22:00. ♂
DE BAK, Schiedmasevest 146, (010) 433 47 83, 16:00-03:00. ♂
DE KANJER, 32a Maashaven O.Z., Tues-Sun 20:00-04:00. ♂
KEERWEER, 14 Keerweer, (010) 433 46 15, some heteros, 15:00-04:00, till 05:00 on weekends. ♂
KETELBINKIE, 56 Leuvehaven, 15:00-01:00 (Fri, Sat till 03:00, Sun till 02:00). ♂
KINGS & QUEENS, 12a Glashaven, 16:00-01:00 (Fri, Sat till 02:00). ♂
LOGE 90, Schiedamsedijk 4, (010) 414 97 45, 12:00-04:00 (weekends till 05:00). ♂
NEW BONAPARTE, 117a Nieuwe Binnenweg. ♂
PRINZ, 300 Maasblvd., Fri 22:00-04:00, Sat 22:00-06:00. ♂
SHAFT, Schiedamiensingel 137, (010) 414 14 86, cruise bar 20:00-01:00 (Fri & Sat 23:00-05:00). Safe Sex parties Sun, Mon & Thurs. ▼🍴🎵♂
SOLO, 23 Delftstraat, (010) 413 7108, 23:00-08:00. 🍴♂
STRANO,★ 154 Van Oldenbarneveldstraat, (010) 412 58 11, 16:00-01:00. ♂

■ *Dance Bar/Disco*
GAY PALACE DISCO,★ 139 Schiedamsesingel, (010) 414 14 86, 23:00-04:00 (till 05:00 on weekends). 🍴♪♀♂

■ *Saunas/Health Clubs*
COSMO SAUNA, at Cosmo bar location, 13:00-23:30 (Fri, Sat till 08:00).
FINLAND SAUNA, 7 Grondherendijk, (010) 429 70 29, bar inside, 13:00-23:30 (Fri, Sat till 02:00). 🧖 ♈
SPARTACUS SAUNA, 130 's-Gravendijksewal, (010) 436 62 85, bar inside, 13:00-23:30 (Fri & Sat till 08:00). ♈

■ *Restaurants*
DE MOSSELMAN VAN SCHEVENINGEN, Mariniersw. 74a, (010) 404 56 50.

■ *Erotica*
CHRISTINE LE DUC, 108 Schiew.
MASSAD SHOP, Zaagmolendrift 35-41, (010) 466 20 29, 10:00-18:00 (Fri 11:00-21:00, Sat 10:00-17:00), closed Mon.

'S-HERTOGENBOSCH

■ *Information*
COC GAY ORGANIZATION, 1st Korenstraat 5, (073) 614 16 35.

■ *Bars*
CHEZ NOUS, Vughterstraat 158, (073) 614 25 92, 22:00-03:00 (Fri, Sat till 04:00), closed Tues. 🍴♂
KINGS, Vughterstraat 99a, Fri, Sat 22:00-04:00. ♂
LE CLUB, Minderbroedersstraat 8, (073) 614 96 45, 19:00-01:00 (Tues & Thurs till 02:00), closed Mon & Wed. ♂
STAMINEEKE, 1st Korenstraat 16, (073) 614 36 46, 14:00-02:00 (Tues-Wed till 01:00), closed Mon. ♂

■ *Restaurants*
LAI THAI, Muntelstraat 12. 🌶

■ *Erotica*
CHRISTINE LE DUC, 62-64 Vughterstraat.

SCHIEDAM

■ *Bars*
DE MALLEMOLEN, 17 Vlaardingerstr., 17:00-01:00 (Fri, Sat 16:00-04:30, Sun from 16:00), closed Mon. ♂
MELODY BAR, Singel 230, 19:00-01:00 (Fri till 02:00, Sat & Sun from 16:00), closed Mon. ♂

■ *Restaurants*
CHEZ PIERRE, 429A Rotterdamsedijk, 11:00-01:00 (Fri, Sat till 02:00).

TERNEUZEN

■ *Bars*
DE UIENTUIN, 6 Nieuwstraat. ♂
PADDOCK, 25 Vlooswijkstraat, bar & restaurant, from 11:00 (Sun from 17:00), closed Mon. 🍴♂

TERSCHELLING - WEST

■ *Accommodations*
PENSION SPITSBERGEN, Burgemeester Reedekerstraat 50, (0562) 443162, B&B guesthouse, 50% gay/lesbian clientele, private/shared baths, nearby pool, lake, ocean beach, full/cont. breakfast, 3 rms have color TV.

TILBURG

■ *Information*
AIDS INFO, (013) 543 64 55.
VROUWENCENTRUM, Nieuwlandstr. 43, (013) 5421 896, women's center with scheduled socials and activities.

■ *Bars*
CAFÉ UIT, Heuvel 18, (013) 536 92 61, 10:00-02:00 (Fri, Sat till 03:00), closed Mon. ♂
COC BAR NIGHTS, Koestr. 73, (013) 535 9050, gay organization, bar nights Thurs 20:00-22:00, Fri 19:00-24:00, Sat 21:00-01:00. Women-only 2nd Sat. ♂
KANNEKE KOFFIE, Stadhuisstraat 368, 09:00-20:00, closed Sun. ♂
LA PERLE, Stadhuisstraat 366, (013) 536 30 29, 21:00-03:00 (Sat, Sun 16:00-02:00), closed Mon, Tues. 🍴♪🎵♂
MY WAY, L. van Vechelstr. 1, (013) 536 78 27, 21:00-03:00 (Sun, Wed till 02:00), closed Mon & Tues. 🍴♪🎵✖♀♂
POPCORN, Paleisring 19, (013) 543 32 18, open from 21:00. 🍴♪🎵✖♀♂

■ *Restaurants*
KHROEWA THAI, 51 Korvelseweg, (013) 544 4364, 16:00-23:00.

■ *Erotica*
GAY CINEMA CANDY, Korvelseweg 217.

UTRECHT

■ *Information*
AIDS INFO, (030) 232 29 08.
COC GAY ORGANIZATION, 221 Oudegracht, (030) 231 88 41, bar nights Thurs 20:00-01:00, Fri & Sat 21:00-02:00, Sun 20:30-02:00. 🍴♀♂
GROEP 7152, Mariaplaats 14, (030) 273 25 37, women's organization. Women's bar night 2nd Sat 21:00-01:00.

■ *Bars*
DE CONCURRENTIE, Predikherenstr. 5, (030) 234 22 69, from 16:00. ♂
NAVRATILOVA, 1 L. Bolwerk, 16:00-24:00 (Fri till 02:00, Sat 12:00-02:00, Sun 12:00-24:00). ♀
WOLKENKRABBER, 47 Oudegracht, (030) 231 97 68, bar with patio, 16:00-02:00. 🍴✖♀♂
ZEEZICHT, 2 Nobelstraat. ♂

■ *Dance Bar/Disco*
BODYTALK, 64 Oudegracht, (030) 231 57 47, mainly men with lesbians welcome, Fri-Sun from 23:30. 🍴♪♂
DE ROZE WOLK, 45 Oudegracht, (030) 232 20 66, younger crowd, 22:00-04:00, Fri & Sat till 05:00. 🍴♀♂

■ *Cafe*
BODYTALK CAFE, at the Bodytalk disco location, (030) 231 57 47, 20:00-03:00 (Fri, Sat till 05:00, Sun 16:00-04:00). ▼🍴🎵♂

■ *Retail & Bookstores*
SAVANNAH BAY, Telingstraat 13, (030) 231 44 10, women's bookstore.

■ *Erotica*
CHRISTINE LE DUC, Amsterdamsestraatweg 310.
DAVY'S EROTHEEK, Amsterdamsestraatweg 197, (030) 243 68 15.

WAGENINGEN

■ *Retail & Bookstores*
SHIKASTA, Junusstraat 1A, (0317) 4215 38, women's bookstore.

ZANDVOORT

■ *Bars*
ADONIS, T. Hiddestraat 20, Thurs-Sun 21:00-02:00. ♂
EL DORADO, Zuidstrand 6, bar on the beach. ♂
HAVANA AAN ZEE, Zuidstrand, bar on the beach. ♂
MIX, THE, Stationsstraat 17, 21:00-03:00. ♂

ZWOLLE

■ *Information*
AIDS INFO, (038) 455 1603.

■ *Cafe*
COC CAFE NIGHTS, 26 Jufferenwal, (038) 421 0065, Tues 20:00-24:00, Fri 21:00-01:00, Sat 22:00-03:00. ♂

NORWAY
COUNTRY CODE: (47)

WHO TO CALL
For Tour Companies Serving This Destination
See Norway on page 22

BERGEN

■ *Information*
LLH, 55 31 21 39, gay & lesbian organizaton. Call for current local information.

■ *Bars*
CAFÉ OPERA, Engen 24, 55 23 03 15. ♀♂
FINCKEN CAFÉ, Nygårdsg. 2A, 55 32 13 16, 12:00-00:30 (Sun from 18:00). ♂

KRISTIANSAND

■ *Information*
LLH, 38 02 00 48, gay & lesbian organization. Call for current local information.

■ *Cafe*
KAFÉ KILDEN, Rådhusgaten 11, 38 02 96 20, not a gay cafe, frequented by some gay & lesbian clientele.

OSLO

■ *Information*
AIDS INFO, 22 33 70 15, toll-free in Norway 800 34 000.
LLH (Landsforeningen for Lesbisk og Homofil Frigjoring), St. Olavs Plass 2, 22 36 19 48, center, bar and café, Mon-Fri 09:00-16:00.

■ *Beaches*
HUK, nude gay beach on the peninsula of Bygdoy. Take bus #30 to Bygdoy from central station (Jernbanetorvet), Wesselsplass just behind the Parliament bldg, or from Nationaltheatret.
LANGOYENE ISLAND, a 30-minute ferry ride from Vippetangen, then walk straight ahead until passing the ice-cream kiosk, continue to the left until you reach the nude beach.
SVARTKULP, gay beach on a small lake just north of Olso. Take the Sognsvannbanen (#13 northbound) from Nationaltheatret underground station to the terminal station Sognsvann, then ask for directions.

■ *Bars*
ANDY CAP, Fridtjof Nansens plass 5 pub, popular in evenings, Mon-Sat 11:00-01:00, Sun 15:00-23:00, mainly hetero customers.
LONDON PUB, Hambros Plass 5, downstairs,

enter from Rosenkrantz gate, 22 41 41 26, bar & restaurant, 15:00-04:00, popular weekends.
POTPURRIET, Ovre Vollgate 13, 22 41 14 40, bar & restaurant, 16:00-06:00.

■ *Dance Bar/Disco*
DEN SORTE ENKE ★ (BLACK WIDOW), Karl Johans Gt. 10, 22 11 05 60, bar, disco & restaurant daily 21:00-04:00 (restaurant from 13:00).

■ *Cafe*
CAFÉ COCO CHALET, Ostre Slotsgate 8, many lesbians. ♀

■ *Saunas/Health Clubs*
CLUB HERCULES, Stenersgate 22a, 22 17 17 35, 18:00-02:00 (Fri & Sat till 06:00).
MY FRIEND CLUB, Calmeyersgate 15, 22 20 36 67, 15:00-24:00 (Fri, Sat till 06:00).

■ *Retail & Bookstores*
TRONSMO BOKHANDEL Kristian Augustsgate 19, 22 20 25 09, left wing bookstore with gay & lesbian section.

■ *Leathers/Piercing*
MAN FASHION, Mollergaten 47, 22 36 06 03, leathers, rubber, magazines, 11:00-18:00 (Sat till 16:00), closed Sun.

■ *Erotica*
GAY INTERNATIONAL, Rostedgate 2, 22 20 37 36, Mon-Fri 10:00-19:00, Sat till 15:00.

STAVANGER

■ *Information*
LLH, Jelsagt. 34, PO Box 1502, Kjelvene 4004 S Stavanger, 51 53 14 46, gay & lesbian organizaton, Mon 18:00-20:00, Wed 19:00-22:00, youth group Fri 19:00-21:00, cafe Sat 13:00-15:00. Call for other activities.

■ *Cafe*
CAFÉ STING, Valbjerget 3, 51 53 24 40, frequented by many gays, especially on weekends.

TROMSO

■ *Information*
LLH, Stakkevollveien 24, 77 68 56 43, gay & lesbian organizaton.

TRONDHEIM

■ *Information*
LLH, Kjopmannsgata 12, 73 52 42 26, gay & lesbian organization.

■ *Dance Bar/Disco*
REMIS DISCO, at the LLH center, 73 52 05 52, Wed 20:00-01:00, Fri & Sat till 02:00. ♂

POLAND
COUNTRY CODE: (48)

WHO TO CALL
For Tour Companies Serving This Destination
See Poland on page 23

GDANSK

■ *Beaches*
NUDE BEACH, in Stogi, Gdansk. Take tram #8, get off at the last stop, walk 1-1/2 km through the woods to arrive at beach, frequented by very few women. ♂

■ *Bars*
HUBERTUS ZAPLECZE PUB, ul. Piwna 59, videos, 20:00-04:00. ♂

JELENIA GORA

■ *Dance Bar/Disco*
GALERY, ul. Wroclawska 67, at Galery restaurant, (075) 752 1694, disco & restaurant, frequented by gays, accommodation available.

KATOWICE

■ *Bars*
APERITIF BAR POLONIA, ul. Kochanowskiego, at the Polonia hotel. ♂
TROPICANA CLUB, ul. Mariacka 14, 16:00-24:00 (dance nights Fri, Sat 21:00-04:00). ♂

■ *Dance Bar/Disco*
PRIMA, ul. Weglowa 4, Fri, Sat 20:00-05:00. ♂

■ *Saunas/Health Clubs*
OLIMPIJSKA, ul. Korfantego 35, at Spodek, Tues & Thurs-Sat 12:00-20:00.

KRAKOW

■ *Information*
FUNDACJA KOBIETA (EFKA), Ponzamcze 20/6, (12) 21 93 64 (tel/fax), women's organization with hotline, counselling, annual conferences. Unverifiable, spring '97.

■ *Bars*
KLUB HADES, ul. Starowislna 60, from 20:00, disco Fri & Sat (closed Mon). ♂

■ *Cafe*
JAMA MICHALIKA, ul. Florianska, used as a meeting place by local gays & lesbians, mainly afternoons & evenings, open daily 10:00-22:00.

■ *Saunas/Health Clubs*
SPARTAKUS, ul. Konopnickiej 20. ♂

FERRARI GUIDES' GAY TRAVEL A to Z - 18th EDITION

POLAND

Intimate Experiences of Portugal, Spain, the Azores

Expatriate Americans Maggie Deffense and Joe Abdo, and their company, **Paths Less Taken**, specialize in small group tours for gays and lesbians throughout Spain, Portugal and the Azore Islands. Itineraries geared for discriminating travelers, and accommodations and restaurants are chosen for exceptional quality and charm.

The Azore Islands A part of Portugal, but sitting right in the middle of the Atlantic Ocean, between America and Europe. Island hop around four of these beautiful misty-green islands festooned with flowers and blessed with seaside villages, sapphire lakes and volcanic peaks.

Wines and Cheeses of Portugal A delightful look at a small country of surprising diversity, almost untouched by time. Its less-traveled areas are famous for their exceptional wines and cheeses. Visit whitewashed, medieval villages, fishing villages and terraced hillsides trailing green wine vines.

Moorish Memories Beautiful Andalucia, in southern Spain, was for 700 years the home of one of the world's most interesting civilizations. We follow the trail of the Moors through Cordoba, Seville and Granada for 8 nights, visiting their great monuments, sampling their cuisine and experiencing their culture.

Contact **Paths Less Taken** at (351-1) 486 2044, Fax: (351-1) 486 1409, E-mail: jcabdo@ip.pt.

LODZ

Bars
JEFFERS, ul. Bazarowa 6, (042) 54 23 05, 19:00-22:00, dance bar Fri-Sat till 04:00.

Saunas/Health Clubs
PARYS, ul. Piotrkowska 46, right-hand entrance, 303 994, 13:30-23:00 (closed Sun).

Erotica
EROTICLAND, ul. Piotrowska 48, videos.

OLSZTYN

Bars
ADONIS, ul. Na Miasteczku, at Rondo Rataje (close to final bus stop), (061) 774 227, 20:00-02:00 (disco Fri-Sun till 04:00), closed Mon.

FENDO, ul. 27 Grudnia 7, bar & cafe.

Dance Bar/Disco
QUEENS CLUB, ul. Karwoskiego 5, Fri, Sat 20:00-04:00.

POZNAN

Information
LAMBDA POZNAN, (061) 530 208, info line, group meets Fri 17:00-21:00.

Saunas/Health Clubs
AMIGO SAUNA, Os. Lecha 120, (090) 610 820, 16:00-23:00 (Fri, Sat till 02:00).
SLIM STUDIO, Osiedle Wl. Lokietka 8h, 12:00-21:00 (Sun 12:00-18:00), separate entrance fees for sauna & solarium.

SOPOT

Bars
MEZZO,★ al. Niepodleglosci 712, pub & bar, 19:00-05:00.

SZCZECIN

Beaches
LUBIEWO BEACH, nude beach, from Miedzyzdroje walk 20 minutes, more gays on left-hand side of the beach.

Bars
TO TU, ul. Wojska Polskiego 40, bar & restaurant frequented by local gays & lesbians, more gay afternoons & evenings.

Dance Bar/Disco
INCOGNITO, ul. Wojska Polskiego 20, 2nd floor, from 21:00 (closed Mon.).

WARSZAWA - WARSAW

Information
AIDS INFO, (02) 628 52 22, answers 10:00-13:00 (Mon & Thurs till 19:00, Sat 11:00-17:00).
LAMBDA WARSZAWA, Krakowskie Przedmiescie 24/26, gay organization.
RAINBOW KLUB, ul. Sniadeckich 1/15, (02) 628 52 22, gay group with current local info, Fri 16:00-22:00. Women answer Wed 18:00-21:00.

Bars
FANTOM CLUB, ul. Bracka 20a, at Fantom Centre, Sat 22:00-04:00, cruisy.
KOZLA CLUB, ul. Kozla 10/12, relaxed & intimate ambiance, open until last customer leaves bar.
LAJKONIK, pl. Trech Krzyzy, pub & cafe.
SANTOS, ul. Nowy Swiat 3.

Dance Bar/Disco
RUDAWKA,★ ul. Elblaska 53, (22) 633 1999, very popular, crowded restaurant, bar & disco with small dance floor, Fri 22:00-05:00, 80% men, 20% women (some hetero women).

Saunas/Health Clubs
GALLA, ul. Ptasia 2.
GRAND HOTEL SAUNA, ul. Krucza, 14:00-21:00, not a gay sauna, very discreetly frequented by gays.

Erotica
FANTOM CENTRE, ul. Bracka 20a, in basement of Brzozowski Palace, left gate, 3rd door. Sex shop for gays with video cabins, videocinema, darkroom, private rooms, fitness centre & sauna, very cruisy, Mon-Fri 13:00-23:00, Sat till 24:00.

WROCLAW

Information
DGGIL TECZA, (071) 364 3664, gay organization answers Mon-Fri 17:00-20:00, group meets last Sat 18:00-20:00 at Scena dance bar.

Bars
EDEN CLUB, ul. Myslowicka 31, (071) 346 6333, bar with disco Fri-Sat from 21:00.

Dance Bar/Disco
SCENA, ul. Kazimierza Wielkiego 43 (enter from ul. Franciszkanska), (071) 44 45 31, Thurs 21:00-02:00 (Fri, Sat till 04:00).

Saunas/Health Clubs
STUDIO OLIMP, ul. Teatralna 10/12, 11:00-21:00 (mixed men & women Sun, women-only Wed).

PORTUGAL

COUNTRY CODE: (351)

WHO TO CALL
For Tour Companies Serving This Destination
See Portugal on page 23

ALGARVE

■ Accommodations

CASA AMIGOS, Larga Vista, Foral, Messiness, (351-82) 56597 (tel/fax) or (44-181) 743 7417, B&B guesthouse with bar, men only, en suite baths, expanded continental breakfast, color TV, pool on premises, 20 min. drive to gay beach & clubs.

CASA MARHABA, Rua de Benagil, Alfanzina, 8400 Lagoa, (0) 82 358720, bed & breakfast with bar, women welcome, private baths, expanded continental breakfast, TV lounge, video facilities.

CASA PEQUENA, Apartado 133, Praia da Luz, Tel/Fax: (351-82) 789068 (24hrs). guesthouse with TV lounge, video, pool on premises, expanded continental breakfast, private bath adjacent to room, ocean nearby, women welcome.

CASARAO CINZENTO, Caldas de Monchique, 8550 Monchique, Algarve, Portugal, Tel. London: (81) 994-5259, luxury villa/guesthouse with bar, large, pleasantly furnished suites, private baths, TV lounge, poolside sunbeds, nearby ocean beach, full breakfast.

RUBI MAR GUESTHOUSE, Rua da Barroca 70, first floor, (082) 763 165, Fax: (082) 767 749, gay-friendly.

■ Bars

ARCO BAR, Rua Almirante Candido dos Reis 67, Tavira, (089) 235 37.

BOEMIO, Rua de Sao Jose 28, Portimao.

CHAPLIN'S, Rua Dr. Jose Antonio Santos 8365, Armaçao de Pera, Lagos.

LAST RESORT, Rua Lançarote de Freitas 30a, (082) 768 219, cocktail bar.

LUISOL, Rua de Sao Jose 21, Lagos, (082) 761 794.

PRIVILEGIO, CC Arcadas de Sao Joao, at Aveiros beach, in town of Albufeira, (089) 589 96, open 7 days.

TWICE AS NICE, Rua M. de Albuquerque, Areias de Sao Joao, in town of Albufeira, (089) 542 907, from 21:00.

■ Cafe

LA ROSE, Vila Magna, Montechor, in Albufeira, (089) 542 285.

AVEIRO

■ Bars

OPÇAO, Avda. Fernandes Lavrador 214, in town of Barra, Ilhavo, (034) 360 519.

LEIRIA

■ Bars

EÇAS BAR, Travessa da Tipografia, near Catedral Sé.

LISBOA - LISBON

■ Information

ABRAÇO, Rua da Rosa 243, AIDS organization, information & events.

AIDS INFO, (01) 603 835, (01) 395 7921 or (01) 795 8296.

ILGA-PORTUGAL, (01) 254 5383, write: Apartado 21281, 1131 Lisbon Codex.

■ Accommodations

IMPALA HOTEL APARTMENTS, Rua Filipe Folque 49, (01) 314 8914, Fax: (01) 357 5362. Gay-friendly, reasonably priced, comfortable accommodation, not fancy.

PENSAO ALEGRIA, Praça da Alegria 12, (01) 347 5522, Fax: (01) 347 8070, gay-friendly.

PENSAO LONDRES, Rua D. Pedro V 53, (01) 346 2203, gay-friendly.

■ Beaches

GAY NUDE BEACH, near Costa da Caparica, take train from Costa da Caparica, beach is at stop #18.

■ Bars

AGUA NO BICO, Rua de Sao Marçal 170, 21:00-02:00, 70% men, 30% women.

BAR 106, Rua de Sao Marçal 106, (01) 342 7373, Fax: 395 0151, E-mails: jsos@mail.telepac.pt or jsb106@esoterica.pt. Open daily 21:00-02:00, happy hour till 23:30.

HARRY'S BAR, Rua S. Pedro de Alcântara 57-61, dangerous area, but many gays go here for late-night soup after the bars close.

O DUCHE, Praça da Liberdade 33-B, in town of Costa da Caparica, outside Lisbon, 290 0431, disco bar.

PORTAS LARGAS, Rua da Atalaia.

SETIMO CEU BAR, Travessa de Espera 54.

TATOO, Rua de Sao Marçal 15, cruise bar.

■ Dance Bar/Disco

ALCANTARA-MAR, Rua da Cozinha Económica 11, (01) 363 6432, late-night disco from 04:00, mainly hetero, gays welcome (20% gay men), closed Mon.

BRIC A BAR, ★ Rua Cecilio de Sousa 82-84, (01) 342 8971, Sat 22:00-04:00, closed Tues, women welcome.

CLIMACZ, Rua Pascoal de Melo 116b, after house 07:00-noon, not gay but frequented by many gays (20-50% gay & lesbian).

FINALMENTE CLUB, Rue da Palmeira 38, (01) 347 2652, disco & showbar, till 06:00 (shows at 02:30).

FRAGIL, Rua da Atalaia 128, in the Bairro Alto, 50% gay & lesbian clientele, frequented by many gays.

KEOPS, Rua da Rosa 157, 30% gay, more gay on weekends.

KINGS & QUEENS, ask locally for address, very gay after 04:00 (50% gay & lesbian), closed Sun.

MEMORIAL, Rua Gustavo de Matos Sequeira 42-A (downstairs), (01) 396 8891, very smokey, good music.

SATYROS, Calçada da Patriacal 6-8, daily drag shows.

TRUMPS, ★ Rua da Imprensa Nacional 104-B, younger crowd, 23:00-05:00 (shows 03:00 Tues-Thurs, Sun), closed Mon, 60% men, women welcome.

■ Cafe

BRASILEIRA DO CHIADO, Rua Garret, cafe & restaurant, more gay later in the afternoon.

ESPLANADA PASSEIO DA AVENIDA, Avenida da Liberdade near Restauradores, outdoor cafe on both sides of the street, occasionally frequented by gays.

ROSSO, ask locally for address, discreetly frequented by local gays.

SUIÇA, Praça D. Pedro IV 100, Rossio, frequented by gays.

■ Saunas/Health Clubs

GINASIO SAUNA VIRIATO, Rua do Telhal 46, (01) 342 9436.

GREENS SAUNA, Rua do Telhal 77.

OASIS SAUNA, Rua do Salitre 85, (01) 352 4626.

SAUNA SPARTACUS, Largo Trinidade Coelho 2.

BAR 106
Rua de São Marçal
LISBON

OPEN EVERY DAY 21.00 - 02.00
HAPPY HOUR UNTIL 23.30
(PAY 1, DRINK 2)

RUA DE SÃO MARÇAL, 106
1200 LISBOA - PORTUGAL

TEL.: 01 342 7373   FAX: 01 395 0151
jsos@mail.telepac.pt

FERRARI GUIDES' GAY TRAVEL A to Z - 18th EDITION

PORTUGAL

Tours to Russia & the CIS Countries

Departures International arranges personal, custom-designed itineraries for travelers to Russia and the former Eastern bloc countries. With more than 50 years of experience in all aspects of the travel industry, they have the connections to arrange hotels, transfers, and sightseeing for most cities in Russia, Ukraine, Belarus, the Baltic States, and many other CIS countries.

The success of any trip, be it for pleasure or for business, always depends on how details can be addressed and experienced. Departures Int'l can arrange for all types of services for business and leisure travelers...from translators to train tickets, hired music to meeting spaces, business to beauty services, dining to dancing, and everything in between.

Departures International's operations are based in San Francisco and Moscow with additional offices in St. Petersburg and Kiev. Their staff of more than 70 is on site to serve all travelers.

Contact **Departures Int'l** at (415) 563-5959, (800) 509-5959, Fax: (415) 563-5935.

Russia's First Gay Tour Company

Have you every dreamed of discovering an unknown island? Russia is a country unknown to the rest of the world, and it has more than 10 million inhabitants. Russia's first gay tour company can personalize your arrangemetns. **Kremlin Tours** was created 5 years ago expressly to smooth the way for gay and lesbian travelers interested in getting first-hand experience of gay life in Russia, Ukraine, other C.I.S. countries, Hungary and the Czech Republic. In addition to several group itineraries each year, Kremlin provides new Russian visas (including 1-year, multi-entry business visas), special guides, centrally-located and gay-friendly hotels, accommodation in private apartments, chauffeur-driven cars. This year, they introduce De Luxe Service for businessmen, including VIP arrangements and assistance in establishing business contacts. Kremlin's young and qualified guide/interpreters familiarize you not only with the Moscow and St. Petersburg the tourists see, but also take you to the most interesting gay hangouts, gay discos and private gay parties, Russian style.

Contact **Kremlin Tours** at (7 095) 274 74 21 (tel/fax), fax: (7 095) 464 18 14, E-mail: kremln@dol.ru.

■ *Restaurants*
BOTA ALTA, Travessa da Quemada 35-37. ♀♂

CANTINHO DAS GAVEAS, Rua das Gaveas 82-84, Bairro Alto, (01) 342 6460, Portuguese cuisine, 50% gay clientele.

CANTINHO DO BEM ESTAR, Rua do Norte 46, Bairro Alto, Portuguese cuisine, 50% gay clientele.

CASANOSTRA, Travessa do Poço da Liberdade 60, (01) 342 5931, 30-40% gay clientele, closed Mon.

FREI CONTENTE, Rua de Sao Marçal 94, (01) 347 5922, Portuguese cuisine, 12:00-15:00 & 19:30-23:00 (closed Sun).

JARDIM DE SAO BENTO, Rua de Sao Bento 209, (01) 397 9118, Portuguese cuisine, closed Mon, 50% gay clientele.

MASSIMA CULPA, Rua da Atalaia 35-37, (01) 342 0121, Italian cuisine.

MATA-BICHO, Rua do Grémio Lusitano 18-20. ♂

O BICHANO, Rua da Atalaia 78, (01) 347 2546.

OS BALOES, Rua da Imprensa Nacional 116, (01) 347 44 93. ♂

PAP AÇORDA, Rua da Atalaia, Bairro Alto, 80-90% gay clientele.

POE-TE NA BICHA, Travessa da Agua da Flor 38, Bairro Alto, (01) 342 5924. ♀♂

SINAL VERMELHO, Rua das Gaveas, Bairro Alto, Portuguese cuisine, upscale dining, 50% gay clientele.

TACAO PEQUENO, Travessa da Cara 3a, Bairro Alto, 50-60% gay clientele.

TRIVIAL, Rua da Palmeira 44a, (01) 347 3552, Portuguese cuisine, lunch & dinner, 40% gay clientele.

■ *Erotica*
CONTRA NATURA, Rua dos Corrieiros.

ESPAÇO LUDICO, Rua do Conde Redondo 82a.

OLYMPIA CINEMA, Rua do Conde 13, hetero adult cinema frequented by gay men, cruisy.

PORTO

■ *Bars*
GLAM CLUB, Rua Dr. Barbosa de Castro, closed Mon, Tues. ♀♂

MOINHO DE VENTO, Rua Sá de Noronha 66, (02) 31 68 83, daily 21:30-02:00, women welcome. ♂

MY WAY, Rua do Heroismo 333, at Centro Comercial Stop, loja 145, (02) 576 739. ♂

POLL, Rua Formosa 400. ♂

SYNDICATO CLUB, Rua do Bonjardim 836, (01) 208 4383, daily drag shows. ♪♂

■ *Dance Bar/Disco*
BUSTOS BAR, Rua Guedes de Azevedo 203, 1st floor, (02) 314 876, closed Mon. ♂

Gay Russia: Winds of Change

by Igor Svetlov

The situation of gays and lesbians in Moscow is getting better and better. New gay venues, as well as the old ones, are overcrowded. The public is young and stylish. There is no gay bashing and there is no discrimination at all!

But there have been reports of some gay clubs recently being raided by the Moscow police. As it happened, a Russian justice vice minister was killed at his luxurious apartment by his 20-year-old Ukranian lover, and all Moscow police were after him. Naturally, they raided gay clubs while looking for him. If it had been a straight —instead of a gay— murder, this would not have occurred. Even this unlucky incident did nothing to spoil the generally festive atmosphere of the gay bars. As the winds of change keep blowing over Russia, there will be more and more gay bars.

The stylish Banana Disco is one of the newest. Conveniently located next to the central Baumanskaya Metro Station at 50/12 Baumanskaya U1, tel. (095) 267-4504, the disco immediately became one of the most popular gay venues in the Russian capital. Handsome waiters in Scotch kilts, their trademark, was the brainchild of the 20-year-old club's owner.

Until December, 1997, Russia always lacked a specifically gay restaurant. That's the date on which Angelico's was opened by the Swiss co-owner of the famous Teatro restaurant, a mainstream eatery popular with well-off gays for its stylish atmosphere. Designed by a well-know Moscow artist and designer, Angelico's has fine Mediterranean cuisine, very friendly service and young professional waiters, all of which attracts Moscow "tousovka," or artists, actors, writers, businessmen, cinema and video producers, etc. Angelico's, 6/1 Bolshoy Karetny Pereulok, tel. (095) 299-3696, is a must for gays visiting Moscow.

Even a few months ago, no one could imagine there ever being a lesbian club here. But now The Dyke, which is based inside another bar called the Three Monkeys, 4 Trubnaya Sq, tel. (095) 208-3341 is packing them in on Saturdays from 6:00 till 11:00pm.

That's not the only good sign of positive changes in Russia. Russian gays have entered the Internet! On December 5, 1996, Russia opened its own National Gay Website located at www.gayrussia.msk.ru, a site that even has piped in music by Tchaikovsky!

A new Russian Penal Code, which came into force January 1, 1997, is no longer discriminatory to gays. Its only specific mention of homosexuality is made in Article 132, criminalizing the rape of gays or lesbians, for which it provides the same punishment as for heterosexual rape. The age of consent is set at 16 years, regardless of sexual orientation.

But if you plan to travel to the south, take into account that the draft of the new Penal Code of the independently-minded and bellicose Chechnia,

For further information about Russia and on tours of Gay Russia, contact Kremlin Tours, the first professional gay tour company in Russia and Eastern Europe. (7-095) 274-7421 or (7-095) 454-1814 (both tel and fax).

Continued on next page

officially published in September, 1997, considers homosexuality a crime. Men who have more than twice "committed" sexual intercourse with other men are executed or sent to prison for life! Those who commit sodomy just once or twice are flogged or sent to prison for up to five years. The draft contradicts directly the Constitution of Russia and can't be enforced by Russian law, but Chechnia, now proudly calling itself Ichkeria, wants its own laws.

Fortunately, Chechnia is the only exception to a general tendency toward liberalization in the rest of Russia. The situation of gays in this country is now much more like that of gays in western countries. One big difference: There has never been a gay liberation movement in Russia, and there never will be! For some people, the most important thing about a man is his sexual orientation, but not for Russians. Private must stay private. The State has no business in a citizen's bed. Even under the communists, when homosexuality was punishable by law, it was used only as a pretext to get rid of political opponents. Many communist leaders were gay. Since there is no oppression, Russians see no need for a special political movement protecting gay rights. There is no problem about publicly "coming out" in Russia, though the general feeling is that it is nothing to be proud of. The idea of being "proud to be gay" sounds to a Russian ear the same as "proud to be straight," i.e. it's ridiculous! Even Russian drag queens, whose sexual orientation is, according to popular saying, "written on the forehead," do their best to avoid the subject in public interviews.

The same thing happens to most Russian gay venues. Very few of their owners or managers admit that their establishments are gay. You'll never see rainbow flags on facades, no rainbow stickers on car windows or bumpers. Why specify sexual orientation??? That's not how we do business here.

A co-owner of one popular Moscow disco called Chance always says that his is a club for the "intelligencia." Intellectuals are very tolerant. They just don't care. That's why his club is frequented by gays...in the owner's opinion, that is. "We welcome everybody." That's the usual phrase used by owners to save face when someone is indiscreet enough to mention that they are running a gay bar. Even though these bars average 95% gay clientele, the fiction is maintained.

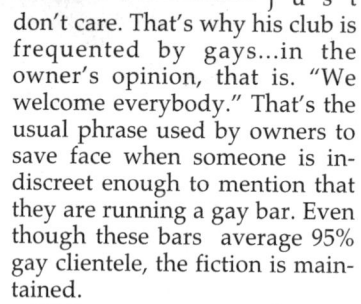

While our ways may be very different, it doesn't mean Russia is less gay than any western country. Perhaps it's even more queer here! The decent grey facades that some might find gloomy are hiding the biggest rainbow in the world. It's a whole country with a gay population of 10 million. And it's culture is almost completely unknown to the rest of the world. Come and see it!

SWING, Rua Julio Diniz, Parque Itália, (02) 609 0019.

■ *Saunas/Health Clubs*
OASIS SAUNA, Rua Guedes de Azevedo 203.

SETUBAL

■ *Cafe*
CAFE GARBO, Rua Deputado Henriques Cardoso 63, (065) 535 089, restaurant & bar. ♂

RUSSIA
COUNTRY CODE: (7)

WHO TO CALL
For Tour Companies Serving This Destination
See Russia on page 24

MOSCOW

■ *Information*
AIDS INFO, (095) 110 24 60 or 383 75 53.
MOSCOW AIDS CENTER, 14/2 8th ul. Sokolinoy Gory (metro: Semionovskaya), (095) 365 56 65, Mon-Fri 09:00-18:00.

■ *Beaches*
SEREBRIANY BOR, along the Moskva River (metro: Shchukinskaya), take any tram in the direction of the bridge ("most"), cross the bridge and descend the spiral staircase on the left and continue walking to the left. More popular in the morning.

■ *Bars*
AVANTAGE, ul. Pushkinskaya 2 (metro: Okhotny Riad), 11:00-24:00, especially popular in evening.
ELF, Zemlianoy Val 13, str. 1, 2nd level (metro: Kurskaya) (095) 917 20 14, small bar, male go go strippers. ♂

■ *Dance Bar/Disco*
BANANA,★ ul. Baumanskaya 50/12 (metro: Baumanskaya), (095) 267 45 04, disco & bar, daily 23:00-06:00.
CHANCE,★ ul. Volochaevskaya 11/15 (metro: Ploshchad Ilicha), at the DK Serp i Molot, (095) 298 62 47, disco & bar, daily 23:00-06:00, male dancers & strippers, popular disco Fri & Sat.
DYKE,★ Trubnaya Ploshchad 4 (metro: Trubnaya Ploshchad), at the Three Monkeys Club, (095) 163 80 02, very popular women-only night, Sat 18:00-23:00. ♀
IMPERIYA KINO, 33 ul. Povarskaya (metro: Barrikadnaya) at the Teatr Kinoaktera, (095) 290 37 25, Fri-Sun 23:00-06:00.
PTIUCH, 3, 5th Monetchikovsky Pereulok (metro: Paveletskaya), (095) 231 94 63, 23:00-

RUSSIA

Russia's Wild East

by Robert Hayes

Throw away all your preconceived notions about who these people are and what this place is like. The Russian Far East is far more different from Moscow than the Rocky Mountain west is from Washington, DC — and they are three times further apart.

The first thing clear on arrival in Primorye Territory is how un-oriented toward tourism this remote part of Russia is. The weekend traffic jams are caused, not by visitors, but by city dwellers rushing to or from their dachas — country houses where they grow much of their own food organically. The international airport at Artem looks more like a rundown train station than anything else...no jetways, boutiques, long lines for luggage. An ancient bus takes you one hundred yards from plane to customs, an austere waiting room with all the charm of an employee lounge at a rundown factory. Though the fixtures seem like some hold-over from a by-gone era, the officials, themselves, are far from intimidating, merely methodical with a bureaucratic love of forms. I somehow managed to fill out a form incorrectly, and was already gone with the luggage I said I didn't have. The official showed my wife how to alter her papers to say it was hers.

Under the regime of the Soviet Union, restrictions were much tighter, and foreigners were banned from the entire Russian Far East. Now, things unimaginable even under Perestroika have sprung up everywhere. Small kiosks sell newspapers, alcohol, cds, cassettes, flowers, home-raised produce, wild mushrooms. The open market offers this and everything else you need to get by.

Vladivostok blends huge Victorian structures from the late 1800s in various states of decay and restoration with austere Soviet-style apartment buildings, low-key neighborhoods with traditional wood houses and fecund gardens, three active seaports, (commercial, merchant marine, Russian Pacific fleet), and a smattering of war memorials (my favorite: Lenin with the motto "Vladivostok may be very far away, but it is ours.").

Outside of the official (read "obscenely expensive") hotels like the "Vlad," whose emblem is a pig decked out like a waiter with a serving dish, the accommodations are few and well-hidden. We stayed at the Slavyanskaya...50s decor, a 10-12 cafe/disco hidden in the basement. The difficult Cyrillic alphabet aside, advertising, signs, brochures, flyers, etc. either don't exist or are hard to come by. Restaurants are similarly scarce, as is English. On two different occasions, our conversation was interrupted by an onlooker with "What the hell are you doing in Vladivostok?" A very good question. We were on our way to run the Amur River in a remote area of the Sikhote-Alin Mountains.

We spent two surreal days on the "bus ride that would never

Robert Hayes participated in the 1996 Siberia trip operated by Hawk, I'm Your Sister, an American tour company specializing in wilderness canoe trips. Owner and guide Beverly Antaeus has years of experience leading trips in the wilderness. In 1997, Hawk will raft the Urubamba River in Peru and visit Macchu Picchu in May, hold a writing retreat in wilderness New Mexico in June, conduct a "Revisioning Personal Power" retreat in June, and revisit Rafting in Russia in September. Contact Hawk, I'm Your Sister at (505) 984-2268. or write PO Box 9109-F, Santa Fe, NM 87504.

Continued on next page

RUSSIA

end." Every bridge, and there were a lot of them, had been torn up for repairs, and a hasty detour plowed beside it. About ten minutes too late, we reached a small town where the driver intended to gas up. After protracted negotiations, the woman in charge of the pumps led us to the back of an abandoned factory, a flare shot into the air from somewhere in the middle of town, and the electricity for the pumps, and, incidentally, the entire town, came back on. We refueled, drove all night, camped in the rain, changed buses, hauled gear, drove some more. The highlight? An afternoon picnic at an unfinished building by the Sea of Japan, intended as a hostel for travelers. But Perestroika ended the funding, and this "recreation area for the people" has few visitors, most of whom prefer to camp on the beach, rather than risk the hazards of a decaying structure. We welcomed the break, reveled in the bleak seashore, and dined inside, out of the drizzle, surrounded by piles of shells and makeshift racks of drying seaweed.

We spent our first night in the taiga on the banks of the river Lagernaya: "good camping place" or "forced labor camp," take your pick. Next morning, we set out early. Almost immediately, the Lagernaya joins and becomes the Obilnaya, doubling in size. What was a stream last night where the bus drivers had diverted themselves by catching grayling on bare hooks with their long collapsible poles, now became a full-fledged river. It would double twice again.

We paddled an array of craft, all ideal for this river and all levels of skill, mostly provided by Genady, a member of a local river running club, which pools its resources and shares equipment. Genady is a "robotnik," a factory worker who now sees three days of work a week, instead of five. Things run differently now than when the Soviets were in charge, and some workers turn to free enterprise ventures, such as guiding river trips, to supplement their income. The Russian company New Impressions, with whom we collaborated to do this trip, is run by Evgeny Khramov, who occasionally works as a plumber to make ends meet.

With the exception of a few rock gardens and a six-foot waterfall, running the river mostly involves finding the open channel. We had two highly maneuverable homemade catamarans, a huge gear raft for those not wanting to paddle every day, and three inflatable canoes that are buoyant, durable, stable. Beverly Antaeus, who put this trip together, Mike, a Mainer who had run this river once before, paddled a 17-foot pack canoe that Mike brought over as luggage and assembled at riverside. I envied their ability to scoot around obstacles, go back up river, even make last-minute channel changes. In the less-maneuverable inflatable canoes, the challenge became reading the different channels, none of which I wanted to take. Since we couldn't head back up river, I wound up abandoning ship, so to speak. I warned my bow to stay put and leapt out in the shallows to reconnoiter, while still holding on. The inflatable behind us kept on going and highsided on a sweeper, a fallen tree that strained the river through its branches. Another shot off through a side channel and scraped bottom. The crew did some walking and came through okay. They stopped to help us extricate the pair stranded in the sweeper. Though not particularly dangerous, the remoteness of this run lurks on the edge of your senses.

At the waterfall on the Obilnaya, Genady told me about taimen, a Russian landlocked salmon. In spite of the fact that I could not speak Russian, and he spoke no English, I got a clear picture of what to do through hand gestures and cognates to English and Spanish: A large mouse-like fly called the Double Bunny, fished at night, cannot fail. The ubiquitous Sergei, who translated for us, was inexplicably absent. Still, I was confident that I knew what to do. That night, I didn't fight sleep, I fought the boredom and uncertainty of not really knowing what I was doing (hand gestures and cognates?). Fishing is the only sport where you never really know if the other team will show up. At times, I thought of everything but fishing...the fungi glowing along the path of the river...the roar of the waterfall below me...the diffused light of a cloud-covered moon. I recalled Genady did say total darkness, and decided to quit. Instead, I tried a rock ledge that leads out into the waterfall for a few last casts into the long current edge between channel and eddy. A solid strike and I was ready to stay up past dawn. On the next cast, I connected and set the hook on the biggest thing I've ever felt on the other end of the line. The fish ran downriver, taking all of my line and most of the backing with it, then held somewhere in the current, in the dark, 150 yards away. Fighting my ancient pack rod (it tends to come apart) and reel (it tends to loosen and fall off) and the fish until well past midnight, I finally brought him in close enough to see red fins and a silver back with my pocket flashlight. I backtracked

Continued on page 509

06:00 (closed Mon). NOT a gay disco, frequented by gays.

THREE MONKEYS (TRI OBEZIANY),★ 4 Trubnaya Ploshchad (metro: Tsvetnoy Bulvar), (095) 208 33 41 or 208 46 37, disco & restaurant with gay art exhibits, 18:00-09, membership available thru Kremlin Tours..

TITANIK, Leningradskiy Prospekt 31 (metro: Dinamo) at the Stadion Yunykh Pionerov, (095) 213 45 81, not a gay disco, but popular with upscale gays, 23;00-06:00.

UTOPIYA,★ ul. Bolshaya Dmitrovka 2 (metro: Pushinskaya / Tverskaya), at Rossiya Cinema, (095) 229 0003, not a gay disco, but popular with younger gays, 23:00-06:00.

■ Saunas/Health Clubs
BEGUEMOT,★ ul. Ivana Babushkina 20 (metro: Profsoyuznaya), 12:00-02:00, membership available thru Kremlin Tours.

NEMO, ul. Novoalekseevskaya 25 (metro: Alexeevskaya), Tues, Thurs 19:00-23:00, Sat till 22:00, cruisy.

SANDUNY, 1a Neglinny 1st Pereulok (metro: Kuznetsky Most), (095) 925 46 31, not a gay sauna, but discreetly frequented by older gay men, 09:00-22:00 (closed Tues).

■ Fitness Centers
HEALTH & SWIM CLUB, Berszhkovskaya Naberezhnaya 2, at Radisson-Slavinskaya Hotel (metro: Kievskaya), (095) 941 8020, NOT a gay gym, be very discreet. Expensive, but free for hotel guests.

■ Restaurants
ANGELICOS, Bolshoy Karetny Pereulok (metro: Tsvetnoy Bulvar), (095) 299 36 96, elegant restaurant, reasonable prices, Mediterranean cuisine, 11:30-02:00.

BANANA, at Banana disco location, 24hrs.

THREE MONKEYS (TRI OBEZIANY), at the Three Monkeys disco location, 24hrs.

■ Erotica
INTIM, 6 Zemlianoy Val (metro: Kurskaya), 29 str. 3 1st Tverskaya-Yamskaya ul. (metro: Belorusskaya), Sadovo-Kudrinskaya ul 16 (metro: Mayakovskaya).

KAZANOVA, 4, str. 3 Arbat (metro: Arbatskaya), (095) 203 54 34.

SAINT PETERSBURG

■ Information
SAFO, (812) 156 65 75, lesbian organization, for information write: c/o Natalia Ivanova, P.O. Box 113, 198096 St. Petersburg, Russia.

■ Beaches
SESTRORETSKY KURORT, on the Baltic Sea coast, about 30 mins by train from the Finlandsky Vokzal train station to Sestroretsky Kurort station, then 30 min walk to nude beach (nudistsky pliazh).

■ Bars
AMADEY, 12 Sverdlovskaya Naberezhnaya (metro: Finliandsky Vokzal), (812) 174 5120 or 112 8335, 18:00-23:00, closed Mon.

CAT, ul. Stremiannaya (metro: Mayakovskaya), (812) 311 33 77, intimate café, popular evenings, 11:00-01:00.

■ Dance Bar/Disco
AMADEY DISCO, 12 Sverdlovskaya Naberezhnaya (metro: Finliandsky Vokzal), at DK Krasny Vyborzhets, (812) 174 5120 or 112 8335, Fri, Sat 23:00-07:00.

DOMENICOS, 70 Nevsky Prospeckt (metro: Mayakovskaya), (812) 272 5717, not a gay disco, frequented by gays.

FANTOM, 23 Naberezhnaya Reki Moyki (metro: Nevsky Prospekt), Fri-Sat 23:00-06:00, cruisy. MAY CHANGE IN 1997.

MAYAK,★ ul. Galernaya 23, at the DK Mayak (metro: Nevsky Prospekt), (812) 311 43 11, Fri-Sat 23:00-06:00, male dancers.

PIRAMIDA, 3 ul. Lomonosova (metro: Nevsky Prospekt), 23:00-06:00, upscale clientele.

■ Saunas/Health Clubs
YAMSKIE BANI, ul. Dostoevskogo 9 (metro: Vladimirskaya), (812) 312 58 36, not a gay sauna, but discreetly frequented by gay men, 09:00-21:00 (closed Mon, Tues).

■ Restaurants
CAT, 24 ul. Karavannaya (metro: Nevsky Prospekt), (812) 315 39 00, 12:00-02:00.

LITERATURNOYE CAFE, 18 Nevsky Prospekt (metro: Nevsky Prospekt), (812) 312 8543, upscale, Russian & international cuisine.

■ Erotica
INTIM, 2 ul. Vosstaniya (metro: Ploshchad Vosstaniya).

KOLOS, 58 Liteiny Prospekt (metro: Mayakovskaya).

SONEKS, 1 ul. Shepetovskaya (metro: Novocherkasskaya).

SLOVAKIA
COUNTRY CODE: (42)

BRATISLAVA

■ Information
GANYMEDES BRATISLAVA, gay organization, PO Box 4, 830 00 Bratislava 3.

INFO LINE, (7) 25 38 88, information & help line, Mon, Thurs 18:00-20:00.

■ Cafe
CAFÉ AXON, Gorkého ul., Sun 09:00-02:00, some heteros.

GALERIA GREMIUM, Gorhéko ul., near National Theatre, café & art gallery, some heteros.

SLOVENIA

■ Saunas/Health Clubs
OK DELFIN, Ruzová dolina, (7) 69 497, NOT a gay sauna, but discreetly frequented by gays.

OK GRÖSSLING, Kúpelná ul., (7) 33 49 65, NOT a gay sauna, but discreetly frequented by gays.

PASIENKY, Junácka ul., (7) 279 0369, NOT a gay sauna, but discreetly frequented by gays.

KOSICE

■ Information
GANYMEDES KOSICE, PO Box G13, posta 1, 043 43 Kosice, gay organization.

PRIEVIDZA

■ Information
GANYMEDES PRIEVIDZA, Medzibriezky 10, 971 01 Prievidza, gay organization.

SLOVENIA
COUNTRY CODE: (386)

LJUBLJANA

■ Information
GALFON LESBIAN & GAY INFO LINE, (061) 132 40 89, 19:00-22:00.

ROZA KLUB, MAGNUS & LL GROUPS, Kersnikova 4, (061) 132 40 89, Fax: (061) 329 188. Three organizations are housed here: Roza Klub gay & lesbian organization, meets Tues & Thurs 12:00-14:00. Magnus gay group, publishes monthly magazine Kekec. LL lesbian group.

WOMEN'S HELPLINE, (061) 9782 or (061) 44 19 93.

■ Dance Bar/Disco
ROZA DISCO, at Roza Klub location, Kersnikova 4, dance night Sun 22:00-04:00.

■ Cafe
MAGNUS CLUB, Metelkova Sq, from 20:00, closed Thurs-Sat.

■ Saunas/Health Clubs
ZLATI KLUB, at recreacijski center Tivoli (recreational center Tivoli), not a gay sauna, but discreetly frequented by gays.

MARIBOR

■ Bars
THEATRICAL CAFE, Slomskov Trg, NOT a gay bar, discreetly frequented by gays.

PIRAN

■ Bars
PORTA CAMPO, IX Korpusa, 08:00-23:00, NOT a gay bar, discreetly frequented by gays.

SPAIN

SPAIN
COUNTRY CODE: (34)

WHO TO CALL
For Tour Companies Serving This Destination See Spain on page 26

ALICANTE

Bars
BOYS, Calle César Elguezábal 11, 21:00-03:00. ♂
ENIGMA, Arquitecto Morell 23, 20:30-03:30. ♂
JARDINETTO, Barón de Finestrat 5, (96) 521 17 36, from 19:00. ♂
MISSING,★ Calle Gravina 4, (96) 521 67 28, from 22:00. 🍴♂
MONTECRISTO, Calle Ab el Hamet 1, (96) 512 31 89, 22:00-03:00. ♂

Dance Bar/Disco
DISCOTECA ROSSE, Calle San Juan Bosco 6. ♪🍴♂
ENIGMA, Highway Villafrnqueza, direction Tangel, km 5. 🍴♂

Saunas/Health Clubs
SAUNA 26, Calle Poeta Quintana 26, (96) 521 98 25.
SAUNA YOGASAUN, Calle Marqués de Molins 34.

Erotica
COSMOPOLITAN SEX SHOP, Rafael Altamira 5, closed Sun.
QUINTANA, Calle Poeta Quintana 41.

ALMERIA

Bars
ABAKOS, Calle Dr. Araez Pacheco 8, 22:00-06:00. 🍴♪♂
PROHIBIDO, Calle General Tamayo 7, daily 21:00-03:00. ♂

BALEARIC ISLANDS IBIZA-FIGUERETAS

Cafe
MONROE'S, Calle Ramón Muntaner 3, (971) 39 25 41. ♪✗♂

BALEARIC ISLANDS IBIZA-BIZA TOWN

Beaches
GAY BEACH, (Es Cavallet), take bus from downtown to Salinas, then walk.

Bars
ANGELO, Calle Alfonso XII, 11. ♂
BRONX, Sa Carrossa 4. ♂
CAPRICHO, Calle de la Virgen 42, (971) 19 24 71. ♂
CHIRINGAY, Playa de Es Cavallet. ♂
CRISCO,★ Calle Ignacio Riquer 2, D'Alt Vila, (971) 39 34 22, 22:30-04:00, backroom. 🍴♪🎵♂
GALERIA, Calle de la Virgen 64, 21:30-03:00. 📷♂
INCOGNITO,★ Calle Santa Lucía 21-23, busy terrace. ♂
JJ, Calle de la Virgen 79, (971) 31 02 47, younger crowd. 🍴♪♂
LA MURALLA,★ Calle Sta Carrossa 3, D'Alt Vila, 22:00-04:00, well-appointed large terrace area by the city wall. ♂
LEON, Calle de la Virgen 62. ♂
MUVIE, Calle Mayor 34. ♂
SAMSARA, Calle de la Virgen 44. 🍴♀♂
TEATRO, Calle de la Virgen 83, (971) 31 22 25, 21:00-03:00. ♪♂

Dance Bar/Disco
ANFORA, Calle San Carlos 5, large disco downstairs, bar upstairs. 🍴♂

Cafe
CAFÉ ES PAS, Calle Xeringa 7, (971) 31 18 57, ♂

Restaurants
C'AN D'EN PARRA, San Rafael 3, (971) 39 11 14. 🍴
D'ALT VILA, Plaça de la Vila 3, (971) 30 55 24, 20:00-01:00 (open April-December). 🍴
EL OLIVO, Plaça de la Vila, (971) 30 06 80. 🍴
EL PORTALON, Pza. Desamparados 1-2, (971) 30 39 01. 🍴
FOC I FUM, Calle de la Virgen 55, (971) 31 33 80, bar & restaurant. 🍴

Erotica
NON STOP, Vía Romana 48.

BALEARIC ISLANDS IBIZA-JESUS

Accommodations
CASA ALEXIO, Barrio Ses Torres 16, 07819 Jesús, (71) 31 42 49, fax 31 26 19, men-only guesthouse with poolside bar, private baths, satellite TV, AC, ocean beach nearby, full German breakfast additional charge. ♂

BALEARIC ISLANDS MALLORCA-PALMA

Accommodations
HOTEL ROSAMAR, Avenida Joan Miro 74, (71) 732 723, fax 283 828, gay-friendly hotel with bar, recently-refurbished near bars & beach, single & double rooms, private baths, continental breakfast, mainly hetero clientele.

Bars
ABACO, Calle San Juan. ♂
ARIES, Calle Porras 3, (971) 73 78 99. ♂
CA'N JORDI, Plaza Mediterráneo 2-4, videos. 🍴♪♂
FINALMENTE, Calle Bartolomé Quetglas 4A, (971) 40 35 48. ♂
LA YEDRA, Avenida Joan Miró 47, (971) 73 74 93. ♂
STATUS PUB, Avenida Joan Miró 38, (971) 45 40 30. ♂
YUPPI, Avenida Joan Miró 106. videos, 22:00-08:00. ♂

Dance Bar/Disco
BLACK CAT, Avenida Joan Miró 75, 23:00-05:00. 🍴♂
CHANNA-A, Joan Miró 34. 🍴♂
OBSESION, Calle Cabo Martorell Roca 15, back room. 🍴♪♂

Saunas/Health Clubs
SAUNA ARIES, Calle Porras 3.
SPARTACUS, Santo Espíritu 8, lower level, (971) 72 50 07. 🧖

Erotica
AMSTERDAM, Avenida Argentina 34.
LIBRERIA SEXOLOGICA, Vallori 2.
SEX SHOP NON STOP, Avenida Joan Miró 30.

BARCELONA

Information
CASAL LAMBDA, Calle Ample 5, (93) 412 72 72, gay organization, 17:00-21:00 (Fri till 23:00), closed Sat, Sun.
COORDINADORA GAY Y LESBIANA, Carolinas 13, (93) 237 08 69.
K LA DONA, Gran Vía 549 4o, 1a, (93) 323 33 07, Thurs 20:00.
REVISTA LABERINT, Calle Roselló, 256, (93) 21 56 336, feminist women's magazine with current local information.
TELEFONO ROSA, toll-free in Spain (93) 900 601 601, Mon-Fri 18:00-22:00. AIDS info Fri 21:00-23:00.

Bars
BAHIA, Calle Séneca 12, 🍴♀♂
BLENDED 104, Calle Mariano Cubí 55, (93) 200 71 26, 19:00-03:00. ♪♀♂
CAFE DE COLON, Calle Paris 173, 18:30-03:00. ♀♂
CAFÉ DE LA CALLE, Calle Vic, 11, 18:00-03:00. ♀♂
DANIELS, Calle Cardona 7, at Mariano Cubí & Laforja, (93) 209 99 78, disco & bar. 🍴♀
EA3, Calle Rauric 23. ♂
ESTE BAR, Calle Consell de Cent 257, ♀♂
IMAGINE, Calle Mariano Cubí, 4, 23:00-04:00 (Sun from 19:30). 🍴♀♂
LA BATA DE BOATINE, Robadors 23. ♀♂

SPAIN

LA ROSA, Brusi 39, (93) 414 61 66. ♀♂
LUNA, LA, Avenida Diagonal, 323. ♂
MARZO, Calle Vic 19. ♀♂
MEMBERS, Calle Séneca, 3, (93) 237 12 04, ♀♂
NEW CHAPS, Avenida Diagonal 365, (93) 215 53 65, 20:00-02:30 (Fri till 03:30). ♂
PADAM PADAM, Calle Rauric 9, (93) 302 50 62. ♀♂
PUNTO BCN,★ Calle Muntaner 63-65, (93) 453 61 23, 18:00-03:00. ♂
QUE TE DIJE, Calle Riera San Miguel 55. ♂
ROMA, Alfonso XII 41. ♂
SATANASSA, Aribau 27, daily 20-02. ♀♂

■ *Dance Bar/Disco*
ARENA, Calle Balmes 32, 23:30-05:00. ♂
HEY DAY, Calle Bruniquer 59-61, (93) 450 36 75, 24:00-05:00. ♀♂
MARTIN'S★, Paseo de Gracia, 130, (93) 218 71 67, video disco, 24:00-05:00. ♂
METRO, Calle Sepúlveda 185, (93) 323 52 27, video disco. ♀♂
TALLER, México 7, videos, backroom, 21:00-02:30. ♂
TATU, Calle Cayo Celio, 7, (93) 425 33 50, large disco, video bar.
TOPXI, Calle Valencia, 358, 22:00-05:00, small disco, drag shows all in Flamenco music with Spanish dances. ♂

■ *Cafe*
CAFÉ DE LA OPERA, Ramblas, 74, outdoor café frequented by some gays.
LA ILLA, Carrer Reig i Bonet 3, Metro Joanic, lesbian cafe, 19:30-01:00 (Fri 20:00-03:00). ♀

■ *Saunas/Health Clubs*
CASANOVA,★ Calle Casanova, 57, at Diputació, (93) 323 78 60, 11:00-06:00 (later on weekends).
CONDAL, Espolsasacs 1 at Calle Condal, (93) 301 96 80. ♂
CORINTO, Calle Pelayo 62.
GALILEO, Calle Calabria 59, (93) 426 79 05.
PADUA, Calle La Gleva 34, (93) 212 16 54, 12:00-22:00 (Fri, Sat till 24:00), closed Sun.
THERMAS, Calle Diputació 46 ♂

■ *Restaurants*
CAFE MIRANDA, Calle Cassanovas 30, 21:00-01:00. ♂
LA MORERA, Plaza San Agustín 1.
LITTLE ITALY, Rec 30, at Paseo del Borne, (93) 319 79 73, Italian cuisine, 13:00-16:00 & 21:00-24:00. ♂
PATI, EL, Amargós 13, (93) 302 00 36.

■ *Retail & Bookstores*
COMPLICES, Cervantes 2, Tel/Fax: (93) 412 72 83, gay & lesbian bookshop with books in Spanish & English, mail order, 10:30-20:30 (Sat from 12:00), closed Sun.
PROLEG LIBRERIA DE MUJERES, Calle Daguería 13, (93) 319 24 25, women's bookstore with feminist & lesbian books in Catalan & Spanish, current local information avaiable here, 10:00-20:00.

■ *Erotica*
SEXTIENDA MENSTORE, Calle Rauric, 11.
ZEUS GAY SHOP, Calle Riera Alta 20. (93) 442 97 95, gay shop & current local information.

BENIDORM

■ *Bars*
AMBIGUO, Calle Santa Faz 37. ♂
CAFE KLEE, Calle del Pal 9. ♂
CHAPLIN, Calle San Vicente 9, 22:30-03:00. ♂
DAVID BAR, Calle Mayor 9, (96) 585 21 96, 22:00-04:00. ♂
EL NEW ADONIS, Calle Santa Faz 35, 21:00-05:00. ♂
EROS, Calle Santa Faz 24, 24:00-04:00. ♂
FORTYSECOND STREET, Avenida de Uruguay 8, 21:00-03:00. ♂
GARDENS, THE, Calle Alicante 18 (96) 680 42 10, 22:30-03:00. ♂
LOOK, THE, Calle Santa Faz 12, (96) 680 16 89. ♂
MISTER ME, Calle San Vicente 17, 22:00-04:00. ♂
NEIL'S, Avenida de Alcoy, at Avenida de Bilbao, (96) 680 51 09. ♂
ORPHEO'S, Plaza de la Constitución 9, late-night video bar, 23:00-05:00. ♂
PEOPLE, Calle Santa Faz 29, 22:00-04:00. ♂
PEPPERMINT, Calle San Vicente 11, (96) 586 07 89. ♂
SAN MARCOS, Avda Alcoy 6, near the beach. ♂
ZANZIBAR, Calle Santa Faz 7. ♂

■ *Dance Bar/Disco*
LA TERRAZA, Avda de la Penetración. ♀♂
VIA VENETO, Calle Martínez Oriola 18. ♂

■ *Saunas/Health Clubs*
ADONIS, Calle Venezuela 4, in Narcea Bldg., (96) 85 79 58, open 16:00-22:00.
SCORPIOS, Calle Ruzafa, in the Carrasco Bldg.

■ *Erotica*
SEX SHOP BENIDORM, Calle San Roque 10.

BILBAO

■ *Information*
EHGAM, Calle Escalinatas de Solokoetxe 4, (94) 415 07 19, gay & lesbian center, library & local information, Mon-Fri 20:00-22:00.
LAMBROA, Calle Hurtado de Amezaga 11, 1o izq, (94) 444 76 93, women's meeting place & info center.

■ *Bars*
EL CONVENTO, in the Casco Viejo (Old Town), call Lambroa women's group for details. ♀
HIGH CLUB, Calle Naja 5. ♂
OTXOA PUB, Heros 9, at Lersundi, (94) 424 18 48. ♀♂
SANTUARIO, Calle Lamana at Dos de Mayo. ♂
SPERMA, Calle Dos de Mayo 6. ♂
TEVEREE, Calle Lamana 1. ♂
TXOKOLANDAN, Calle Escalinatas de Solokoetxe 4, Fri & Sat at the EHGAM gay center, 24:00-03:00. ♂

■ *Saunas/Health Clubs*
RODAS, García Salazar 14.
SAUNA OASIS, Calle Atxuri 43, (94) 433 66 30.

■ *Erotica*
AMERICAN'S, Calle Nicolás Alcorta 5.
INTERNACIONAL, Calle Nicolás Alcorta 7.
SEX SHOP, Calle Ledesma 2.

CADIZ

■ *Bars*
AMBAR, Paseo Marítimo 30. ♂
CAFE PONIENTE, Calle Beato Diego de Cadiz 18. ♀♂
TOO MUCH, Plaza Elías Auja, in nearby town of Puerto de Sta. María. ♂

■ *Erotica*
INTERNACIONAL, Pintor Murillo 2, (956) 26 20 00, videos, 10:00-22:00.

CANARY ISLANDS
GRAN CANARIA
LAS PALMAS

■ *Accommodations*
LOS ROBLES, book through De Gay Krant Resservice, Netherlands, (31-20) 421 00 00, Fax: (31-20) 620 62 17. Men-only bungalow complex with poolside bar, color TV, private baths, kitchen, refrigerator, full or continental breakfast extra charge. ♂

■ *Bars*
BRIDGE, Mariana de Pineda 17. ♂
DERBY BAR, in the Santa Catalina Park area. ♂
METAL, Calle Miguel Rosas 37, 23:00-03:30. ♂
PUNTO DE ENCUENTRO, Calle Ripoche 22. ♂
RIO BAR, in the Santa Catalina Park area. ♂
VERTIGO, Martínez de Escobar 38. ♂

SPAIN

■ Dance Bar/Disco
COMPLICE, Calle Joaqín Costa 48, (928) 22 37 74, from 23:00. 🎵♂
FLASH, Bernardo de la Torre 86. 🎵♂
METAL, Doctor Miquel de la Rosa 37. 🎵♂

■ Saunas/Health Clubs
BRONX, Bernardo de la Torre 37-39, lower level.
SAUNA TREBOL, Calle Tomás Miller 55.

CANARY ISLANDS
GRAN CANARIA
PLAYA DEL INGLES

■ Accommodations
VILLAS BLANCAS BUNGALOWS, Gran Canaria (34-28) 141681, fax (34-28) 140539. Exclusively gay male complex. ♂
VISTA BONITA VILLAS, Gran Canaria, (44-28) 141681, fax (44-28) 140539. Fully-furnished terraced villas, mostly men with women welcome. 🏠♂

■ Bars
CENTER STAGE, Yumbo Center, 2nd floor, small, 70% men. 🎵♂
CLAXX, Yumbo Center, 4th floor. ♂
COCKPIT, Yumbo Center, 2nd floor. ♂
COME BACK, Yumbo Center, 2nd floor. ♂
COME IN, Yumbo Center, 2nd floor. ♂
CONTACT, Yumbo Center, 2nd floor. ♂
DOBLE 1, Yumbo Center, 1st floor. ♂
HUMMEL HUMMEL, Yumbo Center, 1st floor. ♂
LA CAGE AUX FOLLES, Yumbo Center, 1st floor. ♂
MYKONOS,★ Yumbo Center, 4th floor. ♂
NA UND, Yumbo Center, 1st floor. ♂
NESTOR, Yumbo Centro. ♂
SPARTACUS, Yumbo Center, 1st floor. ♂
TUBOS, Yumbo Center, 4th floor. ♂
WESTFALIA, at Cita Center, 1st floor. 🎵♂
WHY NOT, at the Yumbo Center, 4th floor. ♂

■ Dance Bar/Disco
KINGS CLUB, Yumbo Center, 2nd floor. 🎵♂
METROPOL,★ Yumbo Center, 4th floor. 🎵♂

■ Cafe
CAFE BAR BERLIN, Yumbo Center, 3rd floor. ♂
CAFE LA BELLE, Yumbo Center, 2nd floor. 🎵♂
CAFE MARLENE, Cita Center, 2nd floor. ♂
CLAUDIO'S CAFE, Yumbo Center, 2nd floor. ♂

■ Saunas/Health Clubs
MEN HOT HOUSE, Yumbo Center, 1st floor, 17:00-05:00.

NILO SAUNA, Nilo Center, 1st floor, 20:00-03:00.

■ Restaurants
AUBERGINE, Yumbo Center, 1st floor. 🍴
BEI LELO, Yumbo Center, 2nd floor. 🍴
BISTRO RESTAURANT, La Sandía Center, 2nd floor, closed Tues. 🍴
EL CHACO, La Sandía Center, 2nd floor. 🍴
VALENTIN, Yumbo Center, 1st floor. 🍴

■ Erotica
MEN GARAGE, Yumbo Center, 4th floor.
MEN'S PLAZA, Yumbo Center, 1st floor.

CANARY ISLANDS
LA PALMA - SANTA
CRUZ DE LA PALMA

■ Accommodations
APARTAMENTOS LA FUENTE, Calle Pérez de Brito 49, Santa Cruz de La Palma, (922) 415636 (tel/fax), gay-friendly self-catering apartments, maid service, color TV, telephone, central location, nearby ocean beach.

CANARY ISLANDS
TENERIFE
PUERTO DE LA CRUZ

■ Bars
ANDERSON CLUB, in the complex at Avenida Generalísimo 24, 22:30-06:00. ♂
D'ESPANTO, in the complex at Avenida Generalísimo 24, video bar. ♂
DOMINIQUE, in the complex at Avenida Generalísimo 24, 22:30-06:00. ♂
JIM'S, in the complex at Avenida Generalísimo 24. ♂
TABASCO, Avenida Generalísimo 15, video bar. ♂

■ Saunas/Health Clubs
SAUNA PUERTO, Calle Blanco 34, 13:00-22:00. ♂

CANARY ISLANDS
TENERIFE-SANTA
CRUZ DE TENERIFE

■ Information
AIDS INFO TENERIFE, (922) 24 13 54.

■ Bars
SUEÑOS AZULES, Calle San Miguel 14. ♂

CORDOBA

■ Information
LGC, (957) 47 37 60, gay organization.

■ Bars
CAFE BAR JUDA LEVI, Plaza de Judá Leví 1. ♀♂
CANTINA EL PERUANO, Calle El Reloj, 09:00-24:00. ♀♂

EL CINCO DE OROS, Calle Angel de Saavedra 4-6, daily 21:00-02:00. ♂

GIJON

■ Information
AIDS INFO, (98) 533 88 32.

■ Bars
AZUL, Calle Claudio Carreño 5. ♂
ESCALERA 7, Calle Ezcurdia 42, 20:00-08:00. ♂
LA BRUXA CURUXA, Calle Celestino Junquera 1. ♀
PIPOS, Plaza de San Augustín 2. ♂

■ Dance Bar/Disco
EROS, Calle de la Playa 17. 🎵🍴♂

■ Erotica
FANTASIAS, Calle Ezcurdia 49.
INTERNACIONAL, Linares Rivas 19; Cervantes 8.
SEX SHOP, Pablo Iglesias 20.

GRANADA

■ Information
NOS, (958) 20 06 02, gay organization.

■ Bars
ANGEL AZUL, Calle Lavadero de las Tablas 15, 22:00-06:00 (Sat, Sun till 07:00). 🎵🍴♀♂
RAYMA, Arriola 15, (958) 16 13 84, 21:00-06:00, darkroom, videos. 🎵🍴♂

■ Saunas/Health Clubs
BOABDIL, Crta de la Sierra 34, (958) 22 10 73.
ZIRIES, Calle Ziries 1, lower level, 17:00-01:00. ♂

HUELVA

■ Bars
PUB LA CASITA, Calle Villanueva de los Castillejos 13, from 20:30. ♂

ISLAS BALEARES
See Ibiza & Mallorca

ISLAS CANARIAS
See Gran Canaria, La Palma & Tenerife

JAEN

■ Bars
LA NOCHE, Avenida Andalucía 22, 22:30-04:00, closed Mon. 🎵🍴♀♂

■ Erotica
AMSTERDAM, Calle Salido 23.

LA CORUÑA

■ Bars
LABERINTO, Calle Magistrado Manuel Artime 6, video bar, back room. ♂

■ Erotica
INTERNACIONAL, Rosalía de Castro 4.

SPAIN

LERIDA

Bars
ASSIS, Carretera Comarcal 1313, (973) 29 01 52, Fri & Sat 21:00-03:00.

BRAZIL, Calle Alcalde Costa 63, 20:00-02:30.

NIDO, Calle Alcalde Costa 38, 22:00-03:00 (Sun from 20:00).

Restaurants
LA FORQUILLA, Calle Parra 2.

Erotica
SEX SHOP, Sant Real 6.

LLORET DE MAR

Bars
BAR DAVID, Calle Mediodia 53, (972) 36 23 10.

ENCUENTRO PUB, Calle de Las Flores 11.

INCOGNITO, Calle Mediodia 44.

LA BUBU, Calle Areny 33, (972) 36 71 89.

LAS CUEVAS, Calle Agustín Cabañas 21, 24:00-05:00.

TORTUGA BAR, Santa Teresa 5, (972) 37 05 69.

Erotica
LLORET SEX CENTER, Calle Sant Cristofor 7.

MADRID

Information
AIDS INFO, (91) 523 43 33.

COLECTIVO GAY DE MADRID (COGAM), Calle Espíritu Santo 37 (enter from Calle Minas), (91) 522 45 17.

CRECUL, Calle Barquillo 44, 2 izq, (091) 429 62 41, women's cultural group, publishes newsletter.

GAY INFORM, (91) 523 00 70, daily 17:00-21:00.

MSC MADRID (MOTOR SPORTS CLUB MADRID), private men's leather club. Meets 1st Thurs 24:00 at Troyans bar, for details write: MSC, Apdo de Correos 18213, 28080 Madrid.

Accommodations
HOSTAL HISPANO, Hortaleza 38, (34-1) 531 4871, Fax: (34-1) 521 8780, gay-friendly hotel, private & shared baths, color TV, telephone, laundry facilities, TV lounge, 1 block to gay bars.

HOSTAL ODESA, Hortaleza 38, 3rd floor, (34-1) 521 0338 (Tel/Fax). Hotel, private baths, color TV, some hetero clientele.

Bars
AMBIENT, San Mateo 21 (metro Tribunal), bar & restaurant, 21:00-03:00.

BAJO CUERDA,★ Calle Pérez Galdos 8 (metro Chueca), (91) 523 19 01, 19:00-03:00.

BLACK & WHITE, Calle Libertad 34, (metro Chueca), (91) 531 11 41, 20:00-05:00.

COCKRING, Cuesta de Santo Domingo 1, at Kabul disco, upstairs.

DULCE O SALAO, Calle Libertad 28 (metro: Chueca), (91) 532 49 37.

EAGLE MADRID, Pelayo 30 (metro Chueca), 18:00-02:30 (Fri, Sat till 03:30).

EL BARBERILLO DE LAVAPIES, Calle Salitre 43, (metro Lavapiés), (91) 228 18 15, bar & cafe, 80% women, men welcome.

EL CANDIL, Calle Hernán Cortés 21 (metro: Chueca), video, 20:00-03:00.

EL MOJITO, Calle del Olmo 6 (metro: Antón Martín), 21:00-03:00, some hetero clientele.

EL SUEÑO ETERNO, Calle Pelayo 37 (metro: Chueca).

EMBRUJO, Calle Buenavista 42 (metro: Antón Martin).

FP BAGATEL, Sagunto 20 (metro: Iglesias).

FRAGIL, Lavapiés 17 (metro Tirso de Molina).

HARLEY, Calle Hortaleza 43 (metro: Chueca).

HOT, Calle Infantas 9, 18:00-03:00, videos.

LA BOHEMIA, Plaza de Chueca (metro: Chueca).

LA BUBU, Recoletos 11 (metro Banco), enter from El Cid, 22:30-03:00.

LL, Calle Pelayo 11 (metro: Chueca), cruise bar, from 18:00.

LORD BYRON, Calle Recoletos 18 (metro Banco de España).

MADRID LA NUIT, Calle Pelayo 31 (metro: Chueca), video cruise bar, from 20:00.

NEW DISCO LEATHER, Calle Pelayo 42 (metro: Chueca), (91) 308 14 62, video cruise bar on 3 levels, 20:00-03:00. Frequented by some women.

RIMMEL,★ Calle Luís de Góngora 2 (metro: Chueca), video bar.

TOPXI, Calle Augusto Figueroa 16, 18:00-02:30.

TROYANS, Calle Pelayo 4 (metro Chueca), (91) 521 73 58, from 21:30, cruise bar with interesting paintings of nude men, videos. Leather group meets 1st Thurs from 24:00.

VIDEO SHOW BAR, Calle Barco 32 (metro Gran Vía), (91) 522 06 08, 16:00-24:00 (Sat till 03:00).

Dance Bar/Disco
CRUISING, Calle Pérez Galdós 5 (metro: Chueca), (91) 521 51 43, cruise bar.

DISCOTECA KABUL, Cuesta de Santo Domingo 1, daily from 23:00, 3 levels, leather bar upstairs.

GRIFFIN'S, Calle Villalar 8 (metro: Banco de España).

HEAVEN, Calle Veneras 2, (91) 548 2022.

LA ROSA, Tetuán 27, (91) 531 01 85.

MEDEA, Calle Cabeza 33 (metro Antón Martín).

REFUGIO, Calle Dr. Cortezo 1 (metro: Tiros de Molina), from 24:00.

SACHA'S, Plaza de Chueca 1 (metro: Chueca).

STRONG CENTER, Calle Trujillos 7 (metro Santo Domingo).

Cafe
CAFE LA TROJE, Calle Pelayo 26, from 15:00.

CAFÉ FIGUEROA, Calle Augusto Figueroa 17, (metro Chueca), bar & cafe, big Mardi Gras party annually.

CAFÉ GALDOS, Calle Pérez Galdós 1 (metro: Chueca), (91) 532 12 86.

Saunas/Health Clubs
ADAN, Calle San Bernardo 38 (metro: Noviciado), (91) 532 91 38, 24hrs.

ALAMEDA, Alameda 20 (metro Atocha), (91) 429 8745, 12:00-24:00.

COMENDADORAS, Plaza de las Comendadoras 9 (metro: Noviciado), (91) 532 88 92, 24hrs.

CRISTAL, Augusto Figueroa 17 (metro Chueca), (91) 531 44 89, 24hrs.

INTERNACIONAL, Calle Altamirano 37 (metro: Argüelles), (91) 541 81 98, 11:00-23:00 (Sun from 16:00).

INTERNACIONAL, Calle Maestro Arbós 23 (metro: Legazpi), enter from Valdemorillo 2, (91) 568 60 50, 12:00-07:00 (Mon till 24:00).

SAUNA PARAISO, Calle Norte 15 (metro Noviciano), (91) 522 42 32.

SAUNA PELAYO, Calle Pelayo 25 (metro Chueca), (91) 531 25 83, 15:00-08:00.

Restaurants
EL MARSOT, Calle Pelayo 6, (91) 531 07 26.

EL TRASTERO, Calle Pelayo 19, (91) 532 65 75.

ROCHI, Calle Pelayo 19, (91) 521 83 10.

Retail & Bookstores
BERKANA, Calle Gravina 11, (91) 532 13 93, gay & lesbian bookstore with books in Spanish & English.

LIBRERIA DE MUJERES, Calle San Cristóbal 17 (metro: Sol), (91) 521 70 43, women's bookstore with feminist & lesbian literature, current local information, 10:00-14:00 & 17:00-20:00.

XXX, San Marcos 8, clothing store for men.

SPAIN

■ Erotica
AMERICAN, Calle Montera 13.
CALIFORNIA, Calle Valverde 20.
CONDOMS & CO, Calle Colón 3.
FANTASIAS, Calle Orense 22; Santa Micaela 4.
FOXY LADY, Calle de la Cruz 26.
MUNDO EROTICO, Plaza del Callao 4.

MALAGA

■ Bars
AKELARRE, Calle Marblanca 4. ♂
EL CONVENTO, Madre de Dios 21. ♂

■ Erotica
AMSTERDAM, Duquesa de Parcent 1.
COSMOPOLITAN, Muelle de Heredia 12.
HAMBURGO, Casa de Campo 11.

MARBELLA

■ Bars
BOCACCIO, Calle Puerto del Mar 17, 22:00-06:00. ♂
EROS, Calle Juan Ruíz Muñoz 12. ♪♂
OJO, Calle Puerto del Mar 9, 23:00-06:00. ♂
OSCAR'S, Calle Aduar 1, bar & restaurant, from 21:00. ✗♂
PLATANO BAR, Avenida Antonio Bejón 6, 21:00-03:00. ♂

MERIDA

■ Bars
ATHOS CLUB, Calle Baños 29, from 22:00. 🎭♪♂

MURCIA

■ Information
AIDS INFO, (968) 29 88 31.

■ Bars
BACUS, Calle Isidro de la Cierva 5, videos, 20:00-03:00. 🎭♂
BLAKY, Calle San Antonio 1. (968) 21 23 36, videos, 22:30-04:30. 🎭♪♂
PISCIS DISCO BAR, Plaza Santo Domingo 8, from 22:00, frequented by some women. 🎭♪♂

■ Dance Bar/Disco
DISCOTECA METROPOL, Calle San Andrés 13, frequented by some women. 🎭♪♂
PLANET DISCO, Carretera Beniaján, kn 4, Los Zaragozos 16. 🎭♂

■ Cafe
CAFE BAR ODEON, Calle de la Fuensanta, near Blaky bar, 17:00-01:00, women welcome. ✗♂
DON CAFE, Plaza Santo Domingo 6. frequented by some women. 🎭♂

■ Saunas/Health Clubs
SAUNA NORDIK, Calle Cartagena, 72, daily 15:00-22:00.

SAUNA YELLOW, Calle Isabel La Católica, 15:00-22:00.
ULISES, Calle Madre Elisea Oliver Molina.

■ Erotica
INTERNACIONAL, Enrique Villar 7.
MASTER'S, Calle Mariano Ruiz Funes 5.

NERJA

■ Bars
BLANCO Y NEGRO, Pintada 35, (952) 252 4755. ♂

OVIEDO

■ Accommodations
CASA LORENZO, reserve through: Palo Alto Travel, c/o David Braddy, 535 Ramona #7, Palo Alto, CA 94301, (415) 323-2626, Fax: (415) 323-2684, (800) 359-3922. Gay-owned inn in the town of S. Pedro de la Ribera, a 30-minute drive northwest of Oviedo in the province of Asturias. One room, 2 suites, shared baths, expanded continental breakfast, 50% gay & lesbian clientele.

■ Bars
CHEZ NOUS, Calle Azcárraga, 2. ♂
LA SANTA SEDE, Calle Altamirano. ♀♂
TABU, Calle Alvarez Lorenzana 31. ♂
VALENTINO'S, Calle Hermanos Pidal 26-28. 🎭♂

■ Saunas/Health Clubs
SAUNA FINALMENTE, Calle Alvarez Lorenzana 22.

■ Erotica
FANTASIAS, Calle Gil de Jaz 4.
INTERNACIONAL, González del Valle 6.

PAMPLONA

■ Bars
M-4O, Calle San Juan de la Cadena 2, 22:00-05:00. ♪🎭♂

■ Erotica
AMSTERDAM SEX CENTER, Calle Virgen del Puy 9.

SALAMANCA

■ Bars
FACTORY, Calle Pinzones, lower level, from 23:00. ♪♂
SARAO, Calle Carmelitas 11-21, 23:00-04:00. ♪♂

■ Erotica
INTERNACIONAL, Bermejeros 25.

SANTANDER

■ Bars
BARBAR CAFE, Calle Santa Lucía 52. ♂
KREMLIN, Calle Casimiro Sainz. ♂
PIANOLA, Calle Alcázar de Toledo 12. ♂
SAN PETERSBURGO, Calle Andrés del Rio 2. ♂

ZONA LIMITE, Calle Tetuán 32, at Dragon disco. 🎭♪♂

■ Dance Bar/Disco
BARROCO, Calle del Carmen. 🎭♂
CUIC, Calle Panamá. 🎭♀♂

■ Saunas/Health Clubs
HADES, Calle Rosario de Acuña 4e, 19:00-22:00 (Fri till 01:00, Sat till 03:00).

■ Erotica
ARCO IRIS, Calle Arrabal 5, 1st floor.

SEVILLA

■ Information
AIDS INFO, (95) 437 19 58.
ASAMBLEA DE MUJERES DE SEVILLA, Calle Alberto Lista 16, lesbian group with feminist info for all of southern Spain.

■ Bars
CAFE BULERIAS, Calle Sánchez Barcaiztegui 3, 21:00-03:00. ♂
EL OLIVO, Calle Pelay Correa 44, near Plaza de Santa Ana (Triana section of town), from 22:00. Unverifiable spring '97. ♂
ISBILIYA, Paseo Colón 2. 🎭♀♂
LA GOLETA, Calle Riveros 7. ♂
MEMORY, Calle Fernán Caballero 6. ♂
POSEIDON, Calle Marqués de Paradas 30. ♀♂

■ Dance Bar/Disco
ITACA, Calle Amor de Dios 25, from 22:00, frequented by some leather clientele, movies. 🎭♪♂

■ Saunas/Health Clubs
SAUNA NORDIK, Calle Resolana 38, (95) 437 13 21.
TERMAS HISPALIS, Calle Céfiro 3, (95) 458 02 20.

■ Retail & Bookstores
LIBRERIA FULMEN, Calle Zaragoza 36, (95) 422 71 78, women's bookstore with current local information.

■ Erotica
INTERNACIONAL, Sierpes 48.
SEX SHOP, Gravina 86.

SITGES

■ Accommodations
HOTEL MONTSERRAT, Espalter 27, (03) 894 03 00, Fax: 894 50 50, 2-star hotel with bar, private baths, buffet breakfast, 50% gay & lesbian clientele, more gays in summer.
HOTEL ROMANTIC I LA RENAIXENCA, Carrer de Sant Isidre 33, 08870 Sitges (Barcelona), (393) 894 8375, Fax: 894 8167, Bed & breakfast hotel with bar & solarium, some hetero clientele, antique furnishings, private baths, continental & buffet breakfasts, nearby pool & ocean beach, centrally located to all gay bars. ♀ ♂

SPAIN

■ Beaches
GAY BEACH, in front of Hotel Calipulis, no nude bathing.

■ Bars
AZUL, Calle San Buenaventura, 10, small cruise bar open from 21:00.

BAR BLAU, Sant Pere 29. ♂

BOURBON'S, Calle San Buenaventura, 9, cruise bar, German style bar, from 22:30-03:00.

CHRISTOPHER'S, Santa Tecla 6. ♂

COMODIN, Tacó 4, (93) 894 50 74, 22:00-03:00.

EL CANDIL, ★ Calle de la Carreta, 9, very large cruise bar with DJ, from 22:00.

EL HORNO, Juan Tarrida 6, (93) 894 0909, 17:30-03:00.

EL SIETE, Calle Nou 7, 22:00-03:00. ♂

LORD'S, Calle Marqués de Montroig 16, (93) 894 15 22, 22:30-03:00.

MEDITERRANEO ★, Carrer San Buenaventura, 6, largest gay bar in Sitges, several bars, disco & garden bar. Open fr 22:00.

MITJA LLUNA, Santa Tecla 8, 18:-03:00. ♀♂

PARROT'S, Plaza Industria 2, 17:-03:00. ♀♂

PERFIL, Calle Espalter 7.

REFLEJOS ★, Calle San Buenaventura 19, cruise bar with DJ, Spanish-style music, from 22:30.

■ Dance Bar/Disco
TRAILER, Calle Angel Vidal, 36, large late-night disco, from 24:00.

■ Saunas/Health Clubs
SAUNA SITGES, Calle Espalter 11, (93) 894 28 63, 15:00-03:00.

TARRAGONA

■ Accommodations
MONTYMAR, Avenida Príncipe de España, Apdo 113, E-43892, Miami Playa, Tarragona, Spain, (34-77) 81 05 30. In this small village on the Mediterranean coast, between mountains and the sea, our Spanish-Moorish-style house is just 600 meters from the beach. All rooms face the quiet patio. Local restaurants feature Spanish, French and German specialties. Boat rentals are available. Day trips to Barcelona, Tarragona and Tortosa are easy by train. ♀

TORREMOLINOS

■ Bars
ABADIA, La Nogalera (local 521). ♂

CHESSA, La Nogalera (local 408). ♂

ESQUINA, La Nogalera (local 203).

MALU, La Nogalera (local 1103), 20:30-03:00, women welcome. ♂

MEN'S, La Nogalera (local 714), 22:00-05:00.

PARTHENON, La Nogalera (local 716).

POURQUOI PAS, La Nogalera (local 703). ♀♂

SOHO, La Nogalera (local 502). ♂

ZATANAZZA, La Nogalera (local 306).

■ Dance Bar/Disco
BAVARIA, Calle de la Cruz 16-27, Edificio Centro Jardín, near Rey Sol.

BRONX, Edificio Centro Jardín.

MOON, Avda Carlota Alessandri.

■ Saunas/Health Clubs
SAUNA MIGUEL, Carlota Alessandri 166 (Montemar), 16:00-24:00.

VALENCIA

■ Information
AIDS INFO, (96) 361 88 11, ext 36, Mon-Fri 10:00-14:00.

INFO ROSA, (96) 380 32 22.

LAMBDA, Calle Salvador Giner 9, (96) 391 20 84, gay & lesbian group.

■ Bars
ADN, Calle Angel Custodio 10. ♀♂

CENTRAL, Quart 57, videos, 20:00-03:00.

CONTRAMANO, Calle Murillo 12. ♀♂

LA GUERRA, Quart 47. ♂

METAL, Plaza Picadero Marqués de Dos Aguas 3. ♀♂

NORTH DAKOTA SALOON, Pza. Margarita Valldaura 1. (96) 357 52 50, western bar.

OH VALENCIA, Calle Murillo 26.

POLS, Calle Mar 45, (96) 331 09 54. ♂

STUDIO 17, Cerrajeros 17. ♂

XANDRO'S, Derechos 30. ♂

■ Dance Bar/Disco
BALKISS, Doctor Monserrat, 23.

HOTEL BABYLON, Calle San Vicente Mártir 95, Fri & Sat nights.

VENIAL, Quart 26, from 24:00 till late. ♀♂

■ Saunas/Health Clubs
MAGNUS, Avda del Puerto 27, 12:00-23:00.

OLIMPIC SAUNA, Calle Vivons 17.

■ Retail & Bookstores
SAL DE CASA LIBRERIA DE DONES, Emperador 7, (96) 352 76 98, women's bookstore.

■ Erotica
BLUE SEX FACTORY, Bailén 28.

EROS, Gil y Morte 7.

EUROPEAN SEX CENTER, Avenida Constitución 26.

EVADAN, Calle Matías Perelló 14.

HOLLYWOOD, Dr. Zamenhof 5.

MONCHO INTERNACIONAL, Dr. Zamenhof 15.

SPARTACUS, Flassaders 8, 352 56 62, gay shop.

VALLADOLID

■ Bars
ACCESO R, Alarcón 3, 19:00-03:00 (closed Mon).

■ Erotica
INTERNACIONAL, Calle San Blas 19.

VIGO

■ Bars
DORIAN'S, Calle Sombreros 6, (986) 43 94 87. ♂

■ Dance Bar/Disco
ROY BLECK, Calle Oporto 12, (986) 22 30 46.

■ Saunas/Health Clubs
AZUL, Calle Roupeiro 67.

SAUNAS CANCELEIRO, Calle Canceleiro 11, lower level, 16:00-06:00.

■ Erotica
COSMOPOLITAN SEX SHOP, Calle Príncipe 22.

VITORIA

■ Bars
DELFOS, Calle Roja 26, (945) 26 28 92, 19:00-03:00. ♂

MOET & CO, Calle Mantell 1, (945) 28 93 33, 16:00-04:00. ♀♂

■ Erotica
COSMOPOLITAN, Calle Manuel Iradier 42.

POPPERS, Calle Pintoreria 51.

ZARAGOZA

■ Bars
LA CARCEL, Calle Jusepe Martínez 7, videos, 19:00-03:30.

PUB BEAR, Calle Corso 148. ♀♂

■ Dance Bar/Disco
SPHINX, ★ Calle Madre Ráfols 2, in Edificio Aida.

■ Saunas/Health Clubs
SAUNA NORDIK, Calle A. Gurpide 4, bajo, 59 45 36, daily 15:00-22:00.

■ Retail & Bookstores
LIBRERIA DE MUJERES, San Juan de la Cruz 4, 45 26 52, women's bookstore.

■ Erotica
EL TUBO, Cuatro de Agosto 15.

PIGNATELLI, Ramón de Pignatelli 44.

SWEDEN

SWEDEN
COUNTRY CODE: (46)

For Tour Companies Serving This Destination
See Sweden on page 26

BORLÄNGE

■ Women's Accommodations
KVINNOHÖJDEN, Storsund 90, 78194 Borlänge, (0243) 223707 (tel/fax, when faxing call first). Feminist study center & guesthome in rural Sweden, room for 50 women. Week-long courses held in summer, weekend courses rest of year (most courses in Swedish, inquire about other languages). Women are expected to participate in cooking & household activities. No drugs or alcohol. ♀

GÖTEBORG

■ Information
AIDS INFO, RFSL gay centre: (031) 711 01 33, 09:00-16:00.
RFSL CENTRE, Esperantoplatsen 7, (031) 711 61 51.
WOMEN'S SPACE, Esperantoplatsen 7 (RFSL Centre).

■ Beaches
SALTHOLMEN, Tram 4 to Saltholmen beach and cafe, discreetly frequented by gays.
VALHALLABADET, Tram 4 or 5 to Korsvägen behind Svenska Mässan, sports complex with pool, sauna, steam, run by the city, discreetly frequently frequented by gays.

■ Dance Bar/Disco
BACCHUS,★ Bellmansgatan 9, (031) 13 20 43, bar, disco, restaurant, occasional shows, more gay Thurs-Sun 21:00-02:00, women welcome. 🏠♪🍸♂
TOUCH, Esperantoplatsen 7, (031) 711 14 20, disco, restaurant, bar: Wed 21:00-01:00; disco: Fri, Sat 21:00-02:00; women's disco: first Fri 21:00-02:00. 🏠✡♀♂
WOMEN'S DISCO AT TOUCH, women's disco night at Touch Disco, (031) 11 14 20, 1st Fri 21:00-02:00. 🏠✡♀

■ Cafe
CAFE HELLMAN, Esperantoplatsen 7 (RFSL Centre), (031) 711 61 51, Mon café for youth up to 26 yrs 19:00-22:00, Sun 19:00-22:00. ♀ ♂
POSITHIVA GRUPPEN, Nordhemsgatan 50, (31) 143 530, cafe & meeting place for HIV+ gay & bisexual men. ♂

■ Retail & Bookstores
ROSA RUMMET, Esperantoplatsen 7 (RFSL Centre), (031) 711 61 51, gay & lesbian bookshop, Sun 19:00-22:00.

■ Leathers/Piercing
BARBARELLA, Fjärde Långgatan 6, leather & rubber store with piercing studio.

■ Erotica
NYHAVN SEXSHOP, Lilla Drottninggatan 3, 11:00-22:00.
VIDEOLOOK, Andra Långgatan 16.

HELSINGBORG

■ Information
RFSL, Pålsgatan 1, (042) 12 35 32.

■ Bars
KOSMOS, Furutorpsgatan 73, (042) 14 16 16, 11:00-21:00. ♂

■ Dance Bar/Disco
DISCO EMPIRE (RFSL DISCO), at RFSL Centre, (042) 12 35 32, RFSL disco, pub & café. Disco: Sat 22:00-02:30; Pub: Fri 22:00-02:00; Café: Wed & Sun 19:00-22:00. Women's cafe Thurs 19:00-22:00. 🏠♀♂

■ Erotica
ERO CENTER, Järnvägsgatan 27, (042) 13 71 72, 11:00-22:00.

JÖNKÖPING

■ Information
RFSL, Västra Holmgatan 14, (036) 71 84 80, disco, bar & cafe run by gay organization. Cafe Thurs 18:00-22:00, call for disco & bar schedule.

LINKÖPING

■ Information
RFSL, Nygatan 58, (013) 31 20 22, Tues 19:00-22:00.

■ Bars
RFSL BAR NIGHTS, Nygatan 58, (013) 13 20 22, Tues 19:00-22:00, cafe: Wed, Thurs 13:00-16:00, pub: even Fri 18:00-24:00; disco: Sat 22:00-02:30 (alternate weeks women's dance night). ♀♂

LULEÅ

■ Information
RFSL, (0920) 226 166, gay organization with scheduled activities.

LUND

■ Bars
RFSL, Lilla Fiskaregatan 12, (046) 15 71 34, bar & cafe, gay center with library & bookshop, daily 19:00-22:00.
SMÅLANDS PUB, Kastanjegatan 7, hetero black & white bar with occasional gay & lesbian parties. 🏠

■ Retail & Bookstores
BOKLÅDAN, Storget 4, (046) 11 11 42, general bookstore with feminist & lesbian books, mostly in Swedish, Mon-Fri 09:30-18:00, Sat 09:30-13:30.

MALMÖ

■ Information
AIDS INFO, Noah's Ark: (040) 611 52 15; Positiva Gruppen: (040) 79 161.
MALMÖ GAY JOUR, (040) 611 99 44, gay/lesbian phone line every evening.
RFSL, Monbijougatan 15, (040) 611 99 50, gay organization with scheduled activities.

■ Dance Bar/Disco
FOUR:AN DISCO, Snapperupsgatan 4, (040) 23 03 11, Thurs 21:00-24:00, Sat 23:00-03:00, women welcome. SLM leather group meets here. 🏠♪♂
INDIGO, Monbijougatan 15, (040) 611 99 23, RFSL disco, pub & café. Disco: Fri, Sat 22:00-02:00 (women's dance night 4th Sat); Pub & café: Wed 21:00-24:00. 🏠♂

■ Cafe
GUSTAV ALBERT, Gustav Adolfs Torg 43, patio in summer. 🏠
VICTORS, Lilla Torget, bar & café, 18:00-01:00. 🏠

NORRKÖPING

■ Bars
LE CLUB (RFSL BAR NIGHT), Västgötegatan 15, (011) 23 81 50, bar held by gay organization 2nd & 4th Sat 18:00-21:00. ♀ ♂

■ Leathers/Piercing
CAFE SÄRIMNER, Stockholmsvägen 20, cafe, tattoist, piercing in a mixed, open-minded environment. Open days, organizes tattoo and fettish conventions. Unverifiable spring 1997.

NYKOPING

■ Bars
RFSL BAR NIGHT, Östra Kyrkogatan 15, (0155) 21 02 29, gay organization's cafe night, Thurs 19:00-21:00. ♀♂

ÖREBRO

■ Bars
RFSL BAR NIGHT, ORLANDO, Slottsgatan 19b, (019) 14 42 32, gay center café Mon & Fri 13:00-16:00, Tues 19:00-22:00. Disco 2nd & 4th Sat 21;00-02:00. 🏠♀♂

ÖSTERSUND

■ Information
RFSL INFO LINE, (063) 10 06 68.

■ Bars
RFSL BAR, Rådhusgatan 64, (063) 13 19 00, bar & café run by gay organizaton. Bar: 2nd Fri 20:00-24:00; Café: Wed 19:00-22:00. Scheduled parties last Sat 21:00-02:00, women-only dance nights 3rd Tues 19:00-22:00. ♂

SWEDEN

PITEÅ

Information
RFSL CENTER POLSTJÄRNAN, Aronsgatan 11, (0911) 14 440, 925 70, evening cafe and occasional parties.

STOCKHOLM

Information
AIDS LINE, (020) 78 44 14.
KVINNOHUSET (WOMEN'S BUILDING), Blekingegatan 67b, (metro: Skanstull), (08) 64 32 200, lesbian & feminist center with book café, activities.
LESBISK NU! (LESBIAN NOW! CENTRE), Kocksgatan 28 (metro: Medborgarplatsen), (08) 641 86 16, bar, café at women's centre. Café: Tues, Thurs 18:00-21:00. Bar: 2nd Sat 20:00-01:00, 2nd & 4th Thurs 21:00-24:00. ♀
NOAH'S ARK/RÖDA KORSET, Drottninggatan 61, (08) 235 060, AIDS info.
POSITHIVA GRUPPEN, Magnus Ladulåsgatan 8 (metro: Mariatorget, exit at Torkelknutssongatan), (08) 720 19 60, HIV/AIDS info, 13:00-23:00 (Fri 12:00-02:00, Sat 18:00-02:00), closed Mon, Tues. ♂
RFSL GAY LINE, (08) 31 00 18, 20:00-23:00.
RFSL HUSET, Sveavägen 57 (metro: Rådmansgatan), (08) 736 02 12, gay organization, houses RFSL library (Thurs 17:00-19:00 & Sun 13:00-15:00), Latin American cafe Wed 18:00-20:00, Bikupan bisexual cafe Tues 19:00.

Beaches
BRUNNSVIKEN, Kärsön metro to Slussen. Change to commuter train, Långholmen metro to Hornstall, Solisdan. Walk under the highway through the woods, toward the hills.
ERIKDAHLSBADET, on Gräsgatan by the underground station Skanstull. indoor & outdoor pool run by the city, discreetly frequented by gays.
FORSGRENSKA, Medborgarplatsen, indoor pool run by the city, discreetly frequented by gays. Cafe patrons can view men's locker room through a glass wall.
KÄRSÖN, over the meadow, through woods to the other side of the island.
LÅNGHOLMEN, metro to Hornstull, ask for Långholmen. Exclusively gay beach on top of a hill at the far western side, cafe on weekends.
SOLSIDAN, metro to Slussen, change to the commuter trains (Saltsjöbanan) to Solsidan.

Bars
BAREN 2 LIKE (2 OF A KIND), Wollmar Yxkullsgatan 7, daily 18:00-01:00. ♂
BITCH-GIRL CLUB, Gul Gången, Koolingsborg (metro: Slussen), (08) 720 52 05, bar & disco, Sat 21:00-02:30. ♀
BOTTLE & GLASS, Hornsgatan 136, (08) 845 610, neighborhood pub 16:00-01:00 (Sat, Sun from 14:00), frequented by some gays.
FLAP BAR, St. Eriksgatan 56, (08) 654 79 00, Wed-Sat 18:00-01:00. ♂
HJÄRTER DAM★, Polhemsgatan 23, (08) 65 35 739, private club, evenings.
KINKS & QUEENS, Kungsholmsgatan 20, at the Cavern Club (metro: Rådhuset), not a gay bar, but frequented by gays, Sat from 23:00.
KINKY BAR, same building as Hjärter Dam bar (metro: Rådhuset), (08) 65 35 739, Fri and Sat 20:30-01:00, fantasy. Bring proof of membership in a leather club.
KLUBB HÄCKTET, Hornsgatan 82, at Restaurant Bysis, (08) 84 59 10, bar & restaurant, patio in summer, gay Mon-Wed & Sun. ♀♂
SAPPHO BAR, Kocksgatan 28, at Lesbisk Nu center, (metro: Medborgarplatsen), (08) 641 86 16, women-only bar, 20:00-01:00. ♀
SLM, Wollmer Yxkullsgatan 18, (08) 643 31 00, leather, rubber, uniform, western dress code, Wed, Fri & Sat 21:00-03:00. Last Thurs of the month: meeting of LASH lesbian fetish/leather club from 20:00.

Dance Bar/Disco
GOSSIP, Sveavägen 36, entrance at metro Hötorget. Bar daily, disco disco Tues-Sat 18:00-03:00, outdoor cafe in summer. ♂
HUS 1, Sveavägen 57 (inside RFSL Huset), metro: Rådmansgatan, (08) 31 55 33, temporarily closed, may reopen in '97.
KARUSELL, Rosenlundsgatan 33, Fri, Sat 21:00-03:00, Sun women-only. ♀♂
P.L.U.S., Wollmar Yxkullsgatan 18, at SLM location (metro: Mariatorget), HIV+ disco twice a month, Sun. ♂
PATRICIA,★ Stadsgårdskajen 152 (metro: Slussen), (08) 74 30 570, gay bar nights on a boat, Sun 19:00-05:00. Variety of discos from 80's to techno, 4 different bars (5 in summer) on 3 levels with restaurant Sunday. Deck has view of Stockholm.

Cafe
CAFE FAMILIA, Sveavägen 57. at RFSL Huset, (08) 30 99 33, 11:00-21:00 (Sat, Sun 12:00-18:00). ♂
DICK FARMER, Drottningsholmsvägen 9, 09:00-20:00 (Sat 12:00-16:00), closed Sun. ♂
EKHO CAFE, Katarinavägen 19, (metro: Slussen), (08) 643 74 45, gay Christian organization café 2nd Fri 19:00-23:00.
GOLDEN LADIES, Sveavägen 57, cafe for mature lesbians at RFSL Huset, Thurs from 17:00, dinners 1st Fri,
MÄRTHA'S CAFE, Kocksgatan 28, at Lesbisk Nu center, (metro: Medborgarplatsen), (08) 641 86 16, women-only cafe Tues & Thurs 18:00-21:00. ♀
NOAHS ARK/RÖDA KORSET CAFÉ, Drottninggatan 61 (metro: Hötorget), (08) 23 50 60, AIDS center with cafe & activities.
PICCOLINO, Kungsträdgården, outdoor cafe in the central city, frequented by gays in summer.
SATURNUS, corner of Birger Jarlsgatan & Eriksbergsgatan, frequented by many gay women.
SENIORCAFÉ, Sveavägen 57, cafe at RFSL Huset for mature gay men, Wed from 15:00. ♂

Fitness Centers
MUSCLE ACADEMY, THE, Björngårdsgatan 1b (metro: Mariatorget), (08) 642 63 06, gay gym, 10:00-22:00 (Sat 14:00-20:00, Sun from 15:00).

Restaurants
BABS KÖK OCH BAR, Birger Jarlsgatan 37 (metro: Östermalmstorg), (08) 23 61 01, gay-friendly bar & restaurant attached to cinema Zita, which frequently shows gay & lesbian films from around the world, 16:00-01:00 (Sun 18:00-22:00). Unverifiable spring '97.
BAKFICKAN, Sveavägen 57, at the RFSL Huset (metro: Rådmansgatan), (08) 642 63 06, temporarily closed, may reopen in '97. ♀♂
BRASSERIE STUKET, Swedenborgsgatan 43 (metro: Mariatorget), mainly hetero clientele is mixed with gays, lesbians, transvestites & leatherham.
HANNAS KRUG, Skånegatan 80 (metro: Medborgarplatsen), gay-friendly restaurant with downstairs bar. Traditional Swedish international cuisine, open daily, popular with gays & lesbians.
LAHORE, Bondegatan 58, (metro: Medborgarplatsen), (08) 640 5281, Pakistani cuisine, daily 11:00-24:00, popular with some gays.
SPISEN, Bondegatan 54 (metro: Medborgarplatsen), restaurant & bar popular with gays & lesbians, open daily.
TEMPLE BAR, Agnegatan 39, Kungsholmen section (metro: Rådhuset), bar & restaurant, popular with gays & lesbians.

Retail & Bookstores
KVINNOBOKHANDELN MEDUSA, Wollmar Yxkullsgatan 33, (metro: Mariatorget), (08) 84 50 07, women's bookshop with women's events, 10:00-18:00 (Fri from 11:00, Sat till 14:00), closed Sun. Importers of many books from US & England.
ROSA RUMMET, Sveavägen 57 (RFSL-huset complex), (08) 736 02 15, gay & lesbian bookstore, Mon & Thurs 12:00-21:00, Fri 12:00-18:00, Sat & Sun 12:00-15:00.

Leathers/Piercing
CRIME, Borgargatan 6 (metro: Hornstull), (08) 720 6777, lesbian-owned leather/rubber shop, including specialties for women.
LÄDERVERKSTAN, Rosenlundsgatan 30 (metro: Mariatorget), (08) 668 58 69, 12:00-18:00 (closed Sat, Sun).

SWEDEN

Erotica
BASEMENT, THE, Bondeg. 1, videos, daily 12:00-06:00.
BERLIN 76, Luntmakargatan 76, 24hrs, cruisy.
HAGA VIDEO, Hagagatan 54, cinema, videos.
MANHATTAN, Hantverkargatan 49, video show.
REVOLT SHOP, Nytorgsgatan 21a, video store.
SECRETS, Tulegatan 2 (metro: Odenplan), run by women for women.
US VIDEO, Regeringsgatan 76.

SUNDSVALL

Information
RFSL, Skolhusalléen 23, (060) 17 13 30, disco, bar & cafe run by gay organization. Cafe Sun & Wed 19:00-22:00, disco Sat 22:00-02:30, bar Fri 22:00-02:30. ♀♂

UMEA

Bars
RFSL BAR NIGHT at Club Feliz, Ö Esplanaden 5, gar organization's bar & disco. Bar: Thurs 19:00-22:00, disco: 1st & 3rd Sat 21:00-01:00. 🎵♀♂

UPPSALA

Dance Bar/Disco
KLUBB 68, Svartbäksgatan 68, (018) 23 47 50, bar & disco run by gay organization, call for schedule. 🎵♀♂

VÄSTERÅS

Information
TELEFONJOUR (GAY LINE), (021) 41 80 41, Wed 19:00-22:00.

Bars
RFSL BAR NIGHTS, Stenhagsgatan 8a, (021) 11 80 41, disco, bar & café run by gay organizaton, Wed 19:00-22:00. Ask about scheduled disco & bar nights. ♀♂

VÄXJÖ

Information
RFSL HUSET, CAFE & TELEFONJOUR, Östregårdsgatan 8, (0470) 208 08, Café Sun 17:00-20:00 & Wed 19:00-22:00, parties last Sat 21:00-02:00. Gay line answers Wed 19:00-22:00.

Cafe
NOAH'S ARK/RÖDA KORSET CAFÉ & TELEJOUR, Kungsv. 66, (0470) 77 09 66, café & info line run by gay organization. Info line: Mon, Wed, Fri 10:00-12:00 & 14:00-16:00. ♂

SWITZERLAND
COUNTRY CODE: (41)

WHO TO CALL
For Tour Companies Serving This Destination
See Switzerland on page 26

AARAU

Information
AIDS HILFE, (064) 824 44 50.
FRAUENBERATUNG, (062) 822 7901, women's line.
FRAUENZENTRUM, Kronengasse 5, (062) 824 0114, Frauentreff (women's social), Thurs 19:00-23:00.

BADEN

Information
FRAUENZENTRUM, Bruggerstr. 78, (056) 22 33 50, houses many groups, scheduled bar & disco nights.

Dance Bar/Disco
FRAUENDISCO, Bruggerstr. 78, (056) 22 33 50, women's disco 2nd Sat. 🎵♀

BASEL

Information
AIDS-HILFE BASEL, (061) 692 21 22.
FRAUENBIBLIOTHEK, Rössligasse 9, (061) 641 60 62, women's library, Sat 14:00-18:00.
FRAUENZENTRUM, Klingentalgraben 2, (061) 681 33 45, women's center, Frauenbar (women's bar) Tues from 18:30. Houses Lesben Initiative Basel (LIBS), LIBS Lesbenbar (lesbian bar night) 1st Wed from 20:00, women's library Tues 18:00-21:00.
HABS INFO LINE, (061) 692 66 55, Wed from 20:00.
LESBENBERATUNG, (061) 681 33 45, lesbian info line, Wed from 20:00.
SCHWULEN & LESBENZENTRUM, Gärtnerstrasse 55, (061) 631 55 88, SchLez gay organization, Wed from 20:00, disco Fri & Sat 22:00-03:00.

Accommodations
WHITE HORSE HOTEL & BAR, Webergasse 23, CH-4005, (061) 691 57 57, fax 691 57 25, gay-friendly hotel with bar, in city centre, private showers & WCs, expanded continental breakfast, colour TV, phone.

Bars
DUPF BAR, Rebgasse 43, (061) 692 00 11. ♂
ELLE ET LUI, Rebgasse 39, (061) 692 54 79, 16:00-24:00 (Fri, Sat till 01:00). ♂
ISOLA CLUB, Gempenstrasse, 60, Fri 20:30-01:00, Sat 20:30-03:00. ♂
SCHLEZ & KEGELKINO, Gärtnerstr. 55, (061) 631 55 88, cafe & bar run by gay & lesbian organization, disco Fri & Sat from 22:00, Lesbenbar (lesbian bar) Thurs from 20:30, lesbian disco Sat 22:00-03:00, lesbian brunch Sun from 12:00. 🎵♀♂
TOWER, THE, Elsasserstr. 186b. ♂
ZISCH BAR, Klybeckstr. 1b (in the Kaserne), Tues 20:00-24:00.

Dance Bar/Disco
MATA HARI FRAUENDISCO, at the Frauenzentrum, women's disco night, 1st & 3rd Fri of the month from 21:00. 🎵♀
XQ 28, Leimgrubenweg 10, at Dreispitzareal, party group, venue changes. Ask locally for current address. 🎵♂

Cafe
CAFÉ FLORIAN, Totentanz 1, (061) 261 5754, 06:00-19:00 (Sat, Sun 08:00-18:00), frequented by gays & lesbians. 🚭

Saunas/Health Clubs
MAWI, Saint-Alban Vorstadt 76, (061) 272 23 54, 15:00-23:00. 🧖
SUNNYDAY SAUNA, Mittlerestr. 54, at Friedensgasse, (061) 261 44 07, 14:00-23:00.

Retail & Bookstores
ARCADOS BUCHLADEN & VIDEOTHEK, Rheingasse, 69, (061) 681 31 32, gay bookshop, 13:00-18:30, Sat 12:00-17:00, closed Sun, Mon.

Erotica
KIOSK 18, Schneidergasse, 18, (061) 261 19 86.

BERN

Information
AIDS-HILFE BERN, (031) 331 33 34.
FRAUENBEITZ SPINNE Langmauerweg 1 at Frauenzentrum (women's center), (031) 331 81 62, Lesbenabend (lesbian evening) Tues-Thurs from 18:00, Fri from 20:00, Sat till 00:30, disco & bar last Sat of the month 20:00-02:00. 🎵♀
FRAUENBERATUNGSTELLE, Laupenstrasse 2, (031) 381 2701, women's line, answers Mon-Tues & Thurs-Fri 09:00-12:00.
FRAUENBIBLIOTHEK, Seftigenstr. 11, at Villa Stucki, (031) 371 44 40, women's library, Wed 15:00-17:00, Sat 10:00-12:00.
FRAUENZENTRUM BERN, Langmauerweg 1, (031) 331 07 73, houses Lesbeninitiative Bern (LIB) (lesbian initiative).
HAB INFO LINE (ANDERLAND), (031) 331 63 53, Sun 20:00-22:00. AnderLand gay center located at Mühleplatz 11, 5th floor.

Bars
DIFFERENT BAR, Gerechtigkeitsgasse 50, 18:00-03:30 (Wed & Sun till 00:30), closed Mon, Tues. ♂
ISC CLUB, Neubrückstrasse 1, 20:00-23:30 (Sat till 03:00), closed Fri, Mon. ♂

SWITZERLAND

SAMURAI BAR, Aarbergergasse 35, (031) 331 66 71, 17:00-02:30 (Fri, Sat till 03:30). ♂

■ Dance Bar/Disco
ANDERLAND (SCHWULES BEGEGNUNGSZENTRUM BERN), Mühlenplatz 11, 5th floor, (031) 311 11 97 or 311 63 53, disco & bar at gay center, Sun-Fri evenings. 🏳️✗♂

URSUS CLUB, Junkerngasse 1, (031) 331 74 06, Thurs 20:00-23:30 (Fri, Sat 21:00-03:30, Sun from 17:00). 🏳️♂

■ Saunas/Health Clubs
STUDIO 43, Monbijoustr. 123, (031) 372 28 27, daily from 14:00.

SUNDECK, Länggass-Str. 65, (031) 302 46 86, sauna & fitness club, daily 12:00-23:00.

SUNSHINE, Bernstrasse 41, Zollikofen.

■ Restaurants
RESTAURANT RÖSSLI, Bernstr. 32, (031) 839 24 28, closed Mon.

■ Retail & Bookstores
FRAUENBUCHLADEN, Münstergasse 41, (031) 312 12 85, women's bookstore, 09:00-18:30 (Sat till 16:00, Mon 14:00-18:00).

■ Erotica
LOVELAND, Gerechtigkeitsgasse 39, (031) 22 45 33, 09:00-19:00 (Thurs till 21:30, Sat till 16:00), closed Sun, flicks.

BIEL

■ Information
AIDS-HILFE BIEL, Tues call: (032) 42 43 42; Fri call: (032) 41 21 41.

■ Saunas/Health Clubs
MAWI, Bahnhofsplatz 11/IV, (032) 23 88 21, daily 14:00-22:00.

SUN BEACH, Dufourpassage 12, (032) 323 23 63.

CHUR

■ Information
AIDS-HILFE GRAUBÜNDEN, (081) 252 49 00.

■ Bars
SONDERBAR, Masanserstr. 14, at The Palace, (081) 253 33 56. ♂

FRIBOURG

■ Information
AIDS INFO, (026) 426 0292.

FRAUENZENTRUM, Planche Supérieure 32, women's center.

■ Dance Bar/Disco
DISCO MACUMBA, 17 rue du Travel, Tues 21:30-02:00. 🏳️♂

GENEVE - GENEVA

■ Information
AIDS INFO, (022) 700 15 00.

CENTRE FEMMES NATALIE BARNEY, 30, av. Peschier, (022) 789 26 00, women's center & lesbian switchboard. Permanence téléphonique tous le mercredi (answers Wed) 18:00-20:30 or tape. Prêt des livres, consultation de revues, livres en anglais, français, allemand & italien (library & reading room with books in English, French, German & Italian). Bar nights Fri & Sat from 22:00. Bal (dancing) 1st & 3rd Sat of the month 22:00-03:00.

DIALOGAI GAY CENTER & INFO LINE, 11, rue de la Navigation, (022) 906 40 40, Fax 906 40 44, Wed 20:00-22:00, 90% men. Sun brunch in winter 12:00-14:00. AIDS café group 2nd & last Tues 20:00-22:00 (meal prepared last Tues by group members). Home to a library & many diverse gay groups. Info line Wed 19:00-22:00.

■ Beaches
BAINS DES PAQUIS, Quai du Mont-Blanc, open May 15th-Sept 15th, not a gay beach.

■ Bars
BAR UNDERGROUND, 22 Grand Rue, (022) 311 13 15, frequented by gays, 17:00-22:00. 🏳️

CAFE BAR LE LOFT, Quai du Seujet 20, (022) 738 28 28, 07:00-02:00 (Sat, Sun from 16:00), shows Sun-Thurs. 🏳️♂

L'INTERDIT, 18, Quai du Seujet. ♂

LA BOITE A BRIGITTE, 12, rue Prévost-Martin, 21:00-04:00. ♂

LA BRETELLE, Rue des Étuves 17, (022) 732 75 96, 17:00-02:00, dancing Fri, Sat, men welcome. 🏳️🏳️♀

LA CHAUMETTE, 11, rue des Étuves, daily 04:00-02:00. ♂

LE CONCORDE, 3, rue de Berne, (022) 731 96 80, 07:00-02:00 (Sat from 09:00, Sun from 15:00). ♂

LE TUBE 3, rue de l'Université, (022) 29 82 98, cruise bar, 17:00-02:00 (Sat, Sun from 21:30). 🏳️♂

WOMEN'S BAR NIGHT, at the Centre Femmes Natalie Barney, Fri & Sat from 22:00. ♀

■ Dance Bar/Disco
LA GARÇONNIERE, ★ 22, place Bémont, (022) 28 21 61, 2 shows each night (disco between shows), many heteros Fri & Sat for shows, daily 22:00-04:00. 🏳️♂

LE DECLIC, 28 Bld du Pont d'Arve, (022) 720 59 14. 🏳️♂

■ Cafe
CHARLES DUBOIS CONFISERIE, 49, bd Carl-Vogt, (022) 328 01 24, pastry shop, NOT gay, discreelty frequented by gays. 2nd location: 4, car. de Villeruese, Tel: (022) 736 80 64.

YVES QUARTIER, 24, rue Voltaire, (022) 44 53 21, café, patisserie, confiserie (pastry shop). 🏳️

■ Saunas/Health Clubs
SAUNA BAINS DE L'EST, 3, rue de l'Est, (022) 786 33 00, 12:00-04:00, Sat night sauna, mixed Tues & Fri.

SAUNA CLUB, Av. de Batista, Avanchet-Parc, (022) 796 90 66, 12:00-24:00 (Fri, Sat till 02:00), mixed Tues & Fri. ✗

SAUNA GÉMEAUX, 4bis, rue Prévost-Martin, (022) 20 04 63, 11:30-22:00, Sat, Sun from 15:00.

SAUNA PRADIER, 8 rue Pradier, (022) 732 28 57, 11:00-21:00, Sun 13:30-20:00.

■ Restaurants
L'ÉVIDENCE, 13 rue des Grottes, (022) 733 61 65, bar & restaurant, frequented by gays, 06:00-01:00 (Sat, Sun from 11:00). 🏳️

■ Retail & Bookstores
L'INÉDITE, 18, ave Cardinal Mermillod, Carouge, (022) 343 22 33, feminist bookshop with a small selection of lesbian books, 09:00-12:00 & 14:00-18:30 (Mon only 14:00-18:30), Sat 10:00-13:00.

■ Leathers/Piercing
BODY PEARCING YAIR, 40, rue des Maraichers, (022) 321 55 43.

JACK CUIR, 40, rue Monthoux, (022) 731 89 15, 10:00-19:00, Sat till 17:00, closed Sun.

■ Erotica
BEATE UHSE, 32, rue de Berne, (22) 738 79 92.

FLEUR DE PEAU, 20, rue de Berne, (22) 731 21 50.

MEA CULPA, 8, rue Charles Cusin, (022) 738 01 73.

INTERLAKEN

■ Saunas/Health Clubs
CLUB HORN SAUNA, Harderstr. 35, (033) 822 6002, sauna & bar, videos, Sat 14:00-24:00.

KONSTANZ

■ Dance Bar/Disco
EXCALIBUR, Augustinerplatz, gay disco Sun, women's disco 1st Tues. 🏳️♀♂

LAUSANNE

■ Information
LESBENBERATUNG, (021) 204 060, lesbian information.

SIDACTION AIDS INFO, (021) 311 11 26.

■ Bars
ART ZOO CAFE BAR, Petit Chêne 27, Les Galeries du Cinema, (021) 340 0512, 17:00-01:00. ♂

LE SPIKISI, 2 rue de Bugnon, (021) 312 4378, from 18:00 (Sat from 19:00). ♀♂

SWITZERLAND

PINK SIDE, Av. de Tivoli 1, (021) 311 33 00, 17:00-01:00 (closed Sun). ♂

■ *Dance Bar/Disco*
JOHNNIE'S DISCO, 1 rue Etraz, (021) 312 51 70, 23:00-05:00. 🍴♂
TRIXX, 23 rue de Genève, downstairs from Mad Bar, (021) 312 11 12, Sun only, 23:00-05:00. 🍴♂

■ *Saunas/Health Clubs*
NEW RELAX CLUB, Galeries St-François A, 4th floor, (021) 312 66 78, 12:00-23:00.
PINK BEACH CLUB, Ave de Tivoli 9, (021) 311 06 05, daily 12:00-23:00.
TOP CLUB, Bellefontaine 6, (021) 312 23 66, daily 14:00-23:00.

■ *Restaurants*
LE SAXO, rue de la Grotte 3, (021) 323 46 83, bar & restaurant, 18:00-01:00, closed Mon. ♂

■ *Erotica*
PINK SHOP, Av. de Tivoli 22, (021) 311 69 69.

LUZERN

■ *Information*
AIDS HILFE, (041) 410 68 48.
HALU GAY & LESBIAN GROUP, Geissensteinring 14, at Uferlos gay & lesbian center, (041) 360 14 60, meetings Wed from 20:00.
ZEFRA FRAUENZENTRUM, Mythenstrasse 7, (041) 210 73 10, women's center, library open Wed 14:00-16:00, Thurs & Fri 18:00-20:00, info office Thurs 09:00-11:00, women's bar night Fri 20:00-24:00.

■ *Saunas/Health Clubs*
DISCUS CLUB SAUNA, 26 Geissensteinring, (041) 360 88 77, 13:00-23:00 (Sat till 02:00, Sun till 22:00).
TROPICA SAUNA, Neuweg 4, (041) 23 11 50, daily 15:00-23:00.

ST-GALLEN

■ *Information*
AIDS HILFE, (071) 223 68 08.
FRAUENBIBLIOTHEK, Davidstr. 42, (071) 222 65 15, women's library, Wed, Thurs 14:00-18:00, Sat 12:00-16:00.

■ *Bars*
FRAUENBEIZ, Engelgasse 22, at Restaurant Schwarzer Engel, (071) 23 35 75, women's bar night, even Thurs from 19:30. ♀
HOPPALA BAR, Linsebühlstr. 96, (071) 222 7222, bar & restaurant with patio, from 16:00 (Sun from 18:00). ✗♂

■ *Dance Bar/Disco*
CLUB UNDERGROUND, Färberei Sitterthal, Fri from 23:00. 🍴♂
PEPPERMINT BAR, St. Jakobstr. 103, (71) 245 24 98, men-only disco, from 18:00 (Sat, Sun from 16:00). 🍴♂

■ *Saunas/Health Clubs*
OLYMPIC, Torstr. 17, (071) 245 44 24, 14:00-22:00, closed Sun.

■ *Restaurants*
RESTAURANT GUTENBERG, Hagenbuchstr. 28, (071) 244 64 68, 09:00-23:30, closed Tues. 🍴

ST-MORITZ

■ *Bars*
GRAFFITI BAR, Plazza dal Mulin 2. ♂

SCHAFFHAUSEN

■ *Information*
FRAUENZENTRUM, Neustadt 38, (053) 24 44 46, library, women's & lesbian info center, closed in July & August.

■ *Bars*
POPS, Stadthausgasse 1, 1st floor, (052) 624 1998, 18:00-01:30 (Fri, Sat till 02:30). ♂

SOLOTHURN

■ *Information*
FRAUENZENTRUM, Prisongasse 4, (032) 622 7374, women's center.

WINTERTHUR

■ *Information*
AIDS INFO, (052) 212 8141.
FRAUENZENTRUM, Steinberggasse 61, (052) 212 2650, women's center, socials Wed-Sat 14:00-18:00.

■ *Retail & Bookstores*
FRANXA FRAUENBUCHHANDLUNG, Lagerhausstrasse 15, (052) 212 3880, women's bookstore.
RAINBOW BOOKSHOP & CAFE, Spitalstrasse 11, (052) 213 8188.

ZÜRICH

■ *Information*
AIDS INFO, (01) 291 37 20, Tues, Thurs 09:00-13:00, Wed 14:00-18:00.
FRAUEN-LESBEN ARCHIVE, Quellenstr. 25, (01) 237 39 49, women's & lesbian archives, Wed 18:00-20:00, Sat 16:00-18:00.
FRAUENZENTRUM, Mattengasse 27, (01) 272 85 03, women's center. Library open Tues-Fri 18:00-20:00. Pudding Palace Frauenkneipe (women's pub) Tues-Fri 12:00-14:00 & 18:00-22:00, bar night Fri from 22:00.
HAZ INFO LINE & CENTER, Sihlquai 67, 3rd floor, (01) 271 22 50, Tues-Fri 19:30-23:00, Sun 12:00-14:00.
INFRA, (01) 272 8844, women's info line, Tues 15:00-19:30.
LESBENBERATUNGSSTELLE, (01) 272 73 71, Thurs 18:00-20:00.

■ *Accommodations*
HOTEL GOLDENES SCHWERT, Marktgasse 14, (41-1) 266 1818, Fax: (41-1) 266 1888. E-mail: hotel@gaybar.ch. http://www.gaybar.ch. Hotel with bar & disco, some hetero clientele, single, double, theme rooms & suite, all private baths. ♀♂

■ *Beaches*
STRANDBAD TIEFENBRUNNEN, take tram 2 and 4 from Seefeld to left entrance Gay-Treff.

■ *Bars*
BAGPIPER, Zähringerstrasse 11, (01) 251 47 56, daily 15:00-24:00. ♂
BARFÜSSER, Spitalgasse 14, (01) 251 40 64, bar with many outdoor tables in summer. Leather men in back bar, daily 17:00-24:00. ♥🍴✗♂
CARROUSEL, Zähringerstrasse 33, 251 64 00, after 24:00 enter thru Restaurant Johanniter Niederdorfstrasse 70, daily 14:00-02:00. ♂
CHNELLE 4, Feldstr. 108, from 16:00 (closed Mon). ♂
LES MAINS BLEUES, Kanzleistrasse 15, (01) 241 73 78, daily 17:00-24:00. ♂
LIQUID BAR, Zwinglistrasse 12, gay Sun night. ♂
PREDIGERHOF, Mühlegasse 15, (01) 251 29 85, daily 14:00-24:00. ♂
PUDDING PALACE FRAUENKNEIPE, at Frauenzentrum, Mattengasse 27, (01) 271 56 98, Tues-Fri 12:00-14:00 & 18:00-22:00 with bar night continuing Fri from 22:00. ♀
TIP TOP BAR, Seilergraben 13, (01) 251 78 22, 16:00-24:00. ♂
TRÜBLI GROTTO BAR, Zeughausgasse 67, (01) 242 87 97, daily 14:00-24:00, gay after 20:00. ♂
WUNDERBAR, Zwinglistr. 35, 14:00-24:00. ♂

■ *Dance Bar/Disco*
DJ BAR, Marktgasse 17, 18:00-02:00 (Fri, Sat till 04:00), closed Mon, Tues, Tea Dance Sun from 17:00. 🍴♂
MEDUSA FRAUENDISCO, Sihlquai 240, women's disco alternate Sat from 22:00 (address is hard to find & this disco is not held regularly). 🍴♀
PERSIL & MEGAPERLS, Sihlquai 238, Wed from 22:00. 🍴♂
PHOENIX CLUB, leather, rubber group holds theme parties & events. Call Haz infoline for times & locations. ♥🍴◆✗🍴♂
T&M DISCO, Marktgasse 14, (01) 252 59 44, 21:00-02:00 (Fri, Sat till 04:00), disco & drag shows nightly from 20:00. 🍴♦♂
ZABI, Leonhardstrasse 19, inside StuZ, disco night run by gay organization, Fri 23:00-03:00. 🍴♀♂

■ *Cafe*
CAFÉ ODEON, Limmatquai 2, (01) 251 16 50, cafe and bar frequented by many gays, especially popular late in the evening, light menu, open 07:00-02:00, Fri, Sat till 04:00. ♂
CAFÉ TABU, Josefstr. 142, (021) 272 85 86,

07:30-19:00 (Sat, Sun 10:30-17:00), closed Mon. ♂

HOT POT CAFE, Badenerstrasse 138, 06:45-22:30 (Sat 08:00-18:00), closed Sun. ♂

■ Saunas/Health Clubs

ADONIS, Mutschellenstrasse 17, (01) 201 64 16, 13:00-22:00 (in winter: Sun till 19:00).

APOLLO, Seilergraben 41, (01) 261 49 52, 12:00-23:00 (Sat, Sun from 15:00).

CITY SAUNA, Zentralstr. 45, 13:00-21:00 (Sun 12:00-18:00), closed Sun.

DAVID SAUNA, Kanzleistr. 84, (01) 241 77 87, 11:30-21:00 (Sat, Sun 14:00-20:00).

MOUSTACHE,★ Badenerstrasse 156 (blue door at Engelstrasse 4), (01) 241 10 80, 14:15-22:00.

MYLORD SAUNA, Seebahnstrasse 139, (01) 462 44 66, 14:00-22:00, closed Sun.

RENO'S RELAX CLUB, 57 Kernstr. 3rd floor, (01) 291 63 62, 12:00-23:00 (Fri, Sat till 24:00), Sun 14:00-22:00.

SAUNA PARAGON RELAX CLUB, 11 Mühlegasse, 11:30-23:00.

■ Fitness Centers

LADY FIT, Universitätstr. 33, (01) 251 9909, women's fitness center.

■ Restaurants

GROTTO, at Trübli bar location, open 14:00-24:00 7 days.

JOHANNITER, Niederdorfstrasse 70, 251 46 00, between 22:00-02:00 enter through Carrousel bar in rear. 🍽

T&M GARTENRESTAURANT, at T&M dance bar, Marktgasse 14, patio dining in summer, enter through the disco, daily 18:00-02:00. ♂

■ Retail & Bookstores

EXIT, Mühlegasse 5, (01) 262 55 05, clothing, partywear.

FRAUENBUCHLADEN, Gerechtigkeitsgasse 6, (01) 202 62 74, feminist bookstore, Mon 14:00-18:30, Tues-Fri 09:00-18:30, Sat 09:00-16:00.

SEC 52 BUCHLADEN, Josefstrasse 52, (01) 42 18 18, general bookstore with gay section.

■ Leathers/Piercing

MACHO MEN'S SHOP, Engelstrasse 62, (01) 241 32 15, leather items, toys & videos, 11:00-18:30 (Mon from 14:00), Sat 10:00-16:00, closed Sun.

■ Erotica

GAY EROTIC SHOP, Anwandstrasse 67 at Pflanzschulstrasse, (01) 241 04 41, 16:00-18:30, Sat 11:00-16:00, closed Sun.

GEROTHEK, Giesshübelstr. 66, (01) 451 2517, video rentals, sales, 11:00-20:00 (closed Sun).

MACHO CITY SHOP, Häringstrasse 16, (01) 251 12 22, 11:00-18:30 (Thurs till 21:00, Sat 10:00-16:00).

TURKEY
COUNTRY CODE: (90)

WHO TO CALL
For Tour Companies Serving This Destination
See Turkey on page 27

ANKARA

■ Bars
GRAFFITI, Farabi Sokak, in the Cankaya district, a 10 min walk from the Sheraton Hotel. ♂

KILIM, Sili Meydani, close to Airport Disco. 🍽♂

ANTALYA

■ Bars
ALWAYS BAR, in the harbour area, ask local gays for exact address, 24:00-04:00. 🍽♂

ISTANBUL

IN ISTANBUL: Take taxis from bar to bar, or go with someone trustworthy who knows the way. Although bars are close to each other, neighbourhoods may not be safe at night. Bouncers tend to be friendly & fluent in English and, when asked, will be happy to instruct taxi drivers to take you where you want to go.

■ Information
AIDS LINE, 435 2047.

LAMDA ISTANBUL, gay organization meets Sun 18:00, ask local gays for address.

SISTERS OF VENUS, write: MBE 165, Kayisdag Cadessi 99, Ziverbey, Istanbul, Turkey. Lesbian group with newsletter, local information.

■ Bars
BARBAHCE, Siraselviler Cadessi, Soganci Sok. 7, 1st floor, Taksim, bar & restaurant. ✂♂

CLUB 14, Abdulhakhamit Cadessi, Belediye Dukkanlari 14, Taksim, (212) 256 2121. Difficult to find, ask someone who knows the area how to find this bar. Busy weekends 24:00-04:00, videos. 🍽♂

DEGIRMEN BAR, Adnan Menderes Bulvari, Horhor Cadessi, Aksaray, 19:00-01:00, Turkish music. ♂

FASIL, Rihtim Cadessi, Kadikoy. ✂♂

FIVE-KAT, Siraselviler Cadessi, Soganci Sok. 7, 5th floor, Taksim, (212) 293 3774, bar & restaurant with upscale clientele, closed Sun. ✂♂

TURKEY

FYI

Private, In-Depth Tours of Ancient Lands

MOROCCO—By private, air-conditioned car with driver/guide, you'll explore the exotic kingdom where Europe meets Islam and the East, moving at your own pace. Visiting sites normally closed to the public, you'll have a chance to become acquainted with Morocco's culture, architecture and history.

SPAIN—Spain has many temptations for the gay and lesbian traveler, from its vibrant gay nightlife to its gay beach vacation resorts, Ibiza and Sitges to exquisite museums and delicious and varied cuisine. Heritage Tours provides luxury hotels, while. with rental car, you independently explore out-of-the-way places at your own pace.

TURKEY—Organized tours depart weekly. Visit Istanbul's Byzantine mosaics, Capadoccia's fairy chimneys, Ehesus and the world's most intact Roman ruins, the newly-excavated ruins of Aphrodisias, an 8-story underground city and 6th-century cave churches. Discover Istanbul's emerging gay scene and sunbathe by the pristine lagoons of the Turquoise coast.

Contact **Heritage Tours** at (212) 749-1339, Fax: (212) 749-4317.

EUROPE

FERRARI GUIDES' GAY TRAVEL A to Z - 18th EDITION

TURKEY

HAN CAFE, Cumhuriyet Cadessi, Taksim Square, bar & cafe, 09:00-02:00. ♂

HENGAME, Istiklal Cadessi, Sahne Sok. 6, Balikpazari, Taksim, transvestites, 02:00-07:00. ♂

KEMANCI MANDALA, Siraselviler Cadessi 69, Taksim, (212) 245 3048, NOT a gay bar, discreetly frequented by gays, especially on 3rd level.

PRIVE, Tarlabasi Bulvari 28, Taksim, a 5 min walk from Taksim Square, (212) 235 7999, small bar, very busy Fri & Sat 24:00-04:00, cruisy. ♂

ROXY, Siraselviler Cadessi, Arslanyatagi Sok. 9, Taksim, (212) 249 4839, NOT a gay bar, frequented by some gays & lesbians.

SAFAATHANE, Istiklal, Atlas Sinemasi Pasaji, (212) 251 2245, NOT a gay bar, discreetly frequented by gays.

■ Dance Bar/Disco

NINETEEN - TWENTY, Abdulhakhamit Cadessi, Taksim, beside Club 14 bar, 01:00-06:00.

■ Cafe

BORSA, Cumhuriyet Cadessi, Taksim Square, 09:00-24:00. ♂

CAFE PIA, Istiklal Cadessi, Bekar Sok., discreetly frequented by gays & lesbians.

KAKTUS, Istiklal Cadessi, Imam Adnan Sok. 4, Taksim, (212) 249 5979, discreetly frequented by gays & lesbians.

YELLOW CAFE, on a small side street off Istiklal, ask locally for exact address, NOT a gay cafe, discreetly frequented by gays & lesbians.

■ Saunas/Health Clubs

AQUARIUM SAUNA, Istiklal Cadessi, Ahududu Sok 29, Taksim, 24hrs. ♂

CESME HAMAMI, Voyvoda Cadessi, Cesme Sok, Karakoy, 12:00-22:00. ♂

CIHANGIR SAUNA, Cukurcuma Cadessi, Altipatlar Sok 14, Taksim, 09:00-21:00, VERY discreetly frequented by gays.

CUKURCUMA HAMAMI, Siraselviler, Cukurcuma Cadessi 57, Taksim, 15:00-22:00. ♂

■ Restaurants

DURAN SANDWICHES, in Taksim Square.

ROSA RISTORANTE, Cumhuriyet Cadessi 131, Harbiye, Italian cuisine.

■ Retail & Bookstores

MEPHISTO, Istiklal Cadessi, Taksim, general bookstore with gay & lesbian titles.

PANDORA, Istiklal Cadessi, Buyukparmakkapi Sok 3, Taksim, (212) 245 1667, general bookstore with gay & lesbian titles.

■ Erotica

EROS CENTER, Kutlu Sok. 41-43, Uygur Ishani Kat 1, Gumussuyu, Taksim, (212) 249 0701.

GUNES, Cakiraga Mah., Kurkcubasi Kulhan Sok. 5, Arkasaray, cinema.

LIPS & DELTA, Namik Kemal Cadessi, Firat Ishani 1/8, Aksaray; second location: Sehit Asim Cadessi 4/1, Koc Han Beasiktas.

MARGINAL CENTRE, Rihtim Cadessi, Resit Efendi Sok. 32/1, Ak. Ishani Kat 2, Kadikoy.

RUYA, Istiklal Cadessi 128, Taksim, cinema.

UK - ENGLAND
COUNTRY CODE: (44)

WHO TO CALL
For Tour Companies Serving This Destination
See England on page 14

This is an index to English counties and the cities within them where gay or gay-friendly places may be listed. Listings in this book are mainly organized alphabetically by city name. But, by preference, some businesses have requested to be listed directly under their county heading. Please note these differences in using this section.

AVON
Bath, Bristol, Weston Super Mare
BEDFORDSHIRE
Bedford, Luton
BERKSHIRE
Reading, Slough, Windsor
BUCKINGHAMSHIRE
High Wycombe
CAMBRIDGESHIRE
Cambridge, Peterborough
CHESHIRE
Chester
CLEVELAND
Middlesbrough
CORNWALL
Penzance
CUMBRIA
Carlisle
DERBYSHIRE
Chesterfield, Derby
DEVON
Exeter, Plymouth, Torquay
DORSET
Bournemouth
DURHAM
Durham
ESSEX
Harlow, Colchester, Southend-on-Sea, Thaxted
GLOUCESTERSHIRE
Gloucester, Cheltenham
GREATER MANCHESTER
Ashton-under-Lyne, Bolton, Manchester, Oldham, Rochdale, Stockport, Wigan
HAMPSHIRE
Basingstoke, Portsmouth, Southampton
HEREFORD & WORCESTER
Saint Albans, Worcester
KENT
Canterbury, Chatham, Folkestone, Gravesent, Herne Bay, Margate, Rochester
LANCASHIRE
Blackburn, Blackpool, Burnley, Lancaster, Preston
LEICESTERSHIRE
Leicester
LINCOLNSHIRE
Lincoln
MERSEYSIDE
Liverpool
NORFOLK
Great Yarmouth, Norwich, Wells-next-the-Sea
NORTHAMPTONSHIRE
Northampton, Wellingborough
NOTTINGHAM-SHIRE
Mansfield, Nottingham
OXFORDSHRE
Oxford
SHROPSHIRE
Shrewsbury
STAFFORDSHIRE
Stoke-on-Trent
SUFFOLK
Ipswich
SURREY
Croydon, Farnham, Richmond
SUSSEX
Brighton, Chichester, Eastbourne, Hastings
TYNE & WEAR
Newcastle upon Tyne, Sunderland
WARWICKSHIRE
Leamington Spa
WEST MIDLANDS
Birmingham, Coventry, Walsall, Wolverhampton
WILTSHIRE
Salisbury, Swindon
YORKSHIRE
Barnsley, Bradford, Doncaster, Harrogate, Huddersfield, Leeds, Sheffield, Wakefield, York

THE PHRASE "PUB HOURS" USED IN LISTINGS MEANS: 11:00-17:00 & 17:30-23:00, Sun 12:00-14:00 & 19:00-22:30. Some pubs are now open all day.

ASHFORD
■ Dance Bar/Disco
PINK CADILLACS, Woodlands Country Club, in Charing, (01233) 71 37 31, Sat 19:30-02:00.

ASHTON-UNDER-LYNE
■ Bars
BLUES FUN BAR, 213 Stamford St, (0161) 330 32 12, daily till 02:00 (closed Sun). ♂
■ Cafe
PINKIES CAFE, at Blues Fun Bar location, 19:00-23:00 (Thurs-Sat 12:30-23:00), closed Sun. ♂

AVON
■ Accommodations
LODGE, THE, Banwell Castle, Banwell, (44-1934) 823 122, Fax: (44-1934) 823 946. Bed & breakfast, women welcome, Victorian style rooms, color TV, shared baths, TV lounge, gardens, full breakfast. ♂

BARNSLEY
■ Information
AIDS INFO, (01226) 73 19 15.
■ Bars
CHARLIES BAR, Sheffield Rd, (01226) 78 16 74, gay Tues & Thurs. ♂

BATH
■ Accommodations
KENNARD HOTEL, THE, 11 Henrietta St, (01225) 310472, Fax: 460054, mostly hetero clientele, gay/lesbian following, full English breakfast, colour TV, telephone, tea/coffee-making facilities, near to gay bars.
■ Bars
DARK HORSE, 4 Northampton St, (01225) 42 59 44, pub. ♂

GREEN ROOM, THE, at The Garrick's Head bar, St John's Place, (01225) 44 88 19, pub hours. ♂

UK - ENGLAND

■ Dance Bar/Disco
SISTERS, at Sportsman, women-only dance night, last Fri from 20:00. 🏳️‍🌈♀

BEDFORD

■ Information
AIDS INFO, (01582) 48 44 99.
GAY & LESBIAN SWITCHBOARD, (01234) 21 89 90, Tues, Thrus 19:30-22:00.

■ Bars
BARLEY MOW, THE, 72 St Layes St, (01234) 35 93 55, pub hours. ♂

MATT'S PLACE, 8 Lime St, (01234) 35 23 26, jazz bar with restaurant, from 19:30. ✕♂

MENAGE A TROIS, 18-20 St Peter's, at Riviera Lights, (01234) 27 03 70, last Thurs 21:00-06:00. 🎵🏳️‍🌈♂

■ Dance Bar/Disco
CLARENCE HOTEL, 13 St. Johns St, gay Sat only, strippers. 🎵🏳️‍🌈♂

ECLIPSE, Bedford Rd, at the Saxon Club, Kempston, (01234) 34 68 38, last Fri from 19:00. 🏳️‍🌈♀

BIRMINGHAM

■ Information
AIDS LINE, (0121) 622 15 11, Mon-Fri 19:30-22:00.

FRIEND, (0121) 622 73 51, 19:30-21:30, ask about men's & women's socials.

LESBIAN & GAY SWITCHBOARD, (0121) 622 65 89, 7 days 19:00-22:00.

LESBIAN LINE, (0121) 622 65 63, Tues lesbian social nights, from 19:30.

WOMEN'S ADVICE & INFORMATION CENTRE, at the Devonshire House, High St, in Digbeth, (0121) 773 6952, Tues, Thurs 10:00-16:00.

■ Accommodations
FOUNTAIN INN, THE, 102 Wrentham St, West Midlands, B5 6QL, (0121) 622 1452, fax: (0121) 622 5387. In USA (407) 994-3558, fax (407) 994-3634, guesthouse inn with bar & pub food, women welcome, refurbished, quality rooms with coffee/tea making facilities, 10 min walk to RR Sta, shopping, entertainment, 5 min to gay pubs & discos (The Fountain), full or continental breakfast. ♂

OAK LEAVES PRIVATE HOTEL, 22 Gibson Dr, Handsworth Wood, (0121) 551 6510, fax 551 0606, visitors & guests: (021) 551 6732, private hotel, single/double rooms, private & shared baths, TV lounge, full English breakfast, near gay bars, some gay-friendly straight clientele. ♀♂

VILLAGE INN, 152 Hurst St, (0121) 622 4742, hotel with gay bar, private baths, tea & coffee making facilities, TV. ♂

■ Bars
ANARCHY, Wrottesley St, in Kotwall House, at Steering Wheel Club, Mon 22:00-02:00. ♂

BRIEF ENCOUNTER, 111 Pritchet St, Aston, pub. ✕♂

FOUNTAIN INN BAR, 102 Wrentham St at the Fountain Inn, (0121) 622 14 52, pub, 12:00-14:00 & 19:00-23:00 (Sun only 19:00-22:30), leather nights 1st & 3rd Sun. ♂

FOX, THE, 17 Lower Essex St, (0121) 622 12 10, pub with patio, 19:00-23:00 (Sun pub hours), women welcome. 🏳️‍🌈♂

JESTER, Horsefair, Hollaway Circus, Queensway, (0121) 643 01 55. ♂

PARTNERS, Hurst St, (0121) 622 47 10, pub, 15:00-23:00 (Fri, Sat from 13:00), Sun pub hours, women welcome. ♂

PELICAN BAR, 87 Bar St, Hockley Hill, (0121) 55 46 721, 19:00-23:00, men welcome. ♀

ROUTE 66, 139, 147 Hurst St, (121) 622 33 66, 12:00-15:00 & 17:00-23:00 (Sun pm 19:30-22:30), DJs. 🎵🏳️‍🌈♂

SUBWAY CITY, Livery St, (0121) 23 30 310, 7 days, Sun men only. 🎵♂

TIN TIN'S CLUB, 308 Bull Ring Centre, Smallbrook, Queensway, (0121) 643 41 29, 4th Fri till late. 🏳️‍🌈♂

VILLAGE INN, 152 Hurst St, (0121) 622 4742, 12:00-23:00 (Sun pub hours), patio. Black lesbian & gay group meets 1st Wed. ♂

■ Dance Bar/Disco
NIGHTINGALE, Kent St, at the Essex House, (0121) 622 17 18, disco, bar & restaurant complex, Mon-Thurs 22:00-02:00 (Fri, Sat from 21:00), Sun 21:00-24:00. 🏳️‍🌈♂

PEACOCKS, 311 Westcourt, Bull Ring Centre, dance bar. 🏳️‍🌈♂

■ Saunas/Health Clubs
LOOKING GLASS, Gooch St North, Kent House, unit 5, (0121) 666 7529, 12:00-24:00 (Fri till 06:00, Sat till 08:00).

SPARTAN SAUNA, 127 George Rd, Erdington, (0121) 382 33 45. ♂

■ Restaurants
OVER 18 RESTAURANT, Kent St, across from Route 66 bar, (0121) 622 6717. ♀♂

■ Leathers/Piercing
CLONE ZONE, 42 Bristol St, (0121) 666 66 40, leather, rubber, denim, books, magazines, cards.

BLACKBURN

■ Bars
C'EST LA VIE, 11-15 Market St, at the Never Never Lane, (01254) 69 18 77, Sun 20:00-24:00, Tues 21:00-02:00. ♂

BLACKPOOL

■ Information
AIDS INFO, (01253) 29 28 03.

■ Accommodations
ABBEYVILLE GUESTHOUSE, 39 High St, (01253) 752-072, bed & breakfast, gay-friendly, singles, doubles, with color TV, tea/coffee making facilities, centrally located, breakfast with optional dinner.

ASHBEIAN HOTEL, 49 High St, Blackpool, FY1 2BH, (44-1253) 26301 (tel/fax). In Sept '97: (44-1253) 626 301 (tel/fax). Small, intimate guesthouse with full breakfast, private baths. Across street from beach, near shopping, theatres & restaurants. 50% gay & lesbian clientele.

BELVEDERE HOTEL, THE, 77 Dickson Rd, (44-1253) 24733. Gay hotel with bar, private baths, TV, coffee & tea-making facilities. near other gay bars.

CHAUCER HOUSE, 59 High St, Blackpool, FY1 2BN, (44-1253) 299 099. Exclusively gay & lesbian hotel, 7 rooms, private & shared baths. ♀♂

COLINS HOTEL, 9-11 Cocker St, (01253) 20 541, hotel with bar, women welcome. ♂

CROMPTON HOTEL, THE, 20 Cocker St, (44-1253) 291 583. Hotel with bar, colour TV, coffee & tea-making facilities, concessions to Flamingo dance bar. 50% gay & lesbian clientele.

DALMENY HOTEL, 44 Palatine Rd, (44-1253) 266 60, hotel with full English breakfast, private & shared baths, concession to Flamingo gay dance bar.

GLENROY HOTEL, 10 Trafalgar Rd, (01253) 44607, hotel, 50% gay & lesbian clientele, color TV, beverage-making facilities, private & shared baths, nearby pool & ocean beach, full breakfast, dinner.

HIGHLANDS HOTEL, 46-54 High St, (01253) 752 264, fax 23179. Hotel with 24-hour disco & bar, 50% gay & lesbian clientele, private & shared baths, full English breakfast, color TV, maid service.

KINGSMEAD GUEST HOUSE, 58 Lord St, (44-1253) 24496. Hotel, exclusively gay on bank holidays, otherwise 50% gay & lesbian. ♀♂

KINGSTON PRIVATE HOTEL, 12 Cocker St, (01253) 24929, hotel with bar, 50% gay/lesbian, TV lounge, private & shared baths, concessionary pass to Flamingo club, room key with late pass key, choice of breakfast.

LEXHAM HOTEL, 14 Banks St, (01253) 271 58, private & shared baths, 5 minutes from city centre, B&B available.

LONSDALE HOTEL, 25 Cocker St, (44-1253) 21628, gay-owned licensed hotel with private baths, colour satellite TV, near gay bars, concession to Flamingo dance bar, more gay weekends.

LYNTON, THE, 53 Holmfield Rd, (01253) 51493, guesthouse, women welcome, shared baths. ♂

LYNWOOD HOTEL, 4 Trafalgar Rd, Blackpool FY1 6AW, (44-1253) 346 156, ask for Robin. Hotel with licensed bar lounge, colour TV, central heat, concessions to Flamingo dance bar, 50% gay/lesbian clientele.

OSCARS HOTEL, 23 Lord St, (44-1253) 290 700 (tel/fax), call before faxing. Gay & les-

UK - ENGLAND

Rail Europe is Gay-Friendly

Rail Europe is the leading supplier of European rail and related travel products in North America. We serve more than a million leisure and business travelers annually, with a choice of more than 44 products in 33 countries.

Among these well-known products are Eurailpass, Europass, a wide range of regional and national rail passes, Rail 'n Drive passes, as well as point-to-point tickets. Business or leisure trips can be customized to incude transatlantic air, car rental and a choice of over 1,000 hotels throughout Europe. Automated information on rail schedules and fares are available 24 hours a day via dedicated toll-free numbers.

Europe's infrastructure of high-speed rail links major cities and provides the convenience of city center to city center transportation. Rail service continues to gain appeal as the "civilized alternative" to sitting in airport traffic and checking in at least 2 hours in advance. You'll also save on the cost of ground transportation to and from airports, and won't have to worry about baggage claim delays.

Contact **Rail Europe** at US: (800) 438-7245, Canada: (800) 361-7245, Fax: (800) 432-1329.

---

bian hotel with licensed bar, private & shared baths, colour TV, near gay bars. ♀♂

PIERROTS, 45 High St, (01253) 28125, Gay-owned B&B guesthouse, shared baths, beverage making facilities, TV lounge, nearby ocean beach, full or continental breakfast. 50% gay & lesbian clientele. ♀ ♂

PRIMROSE HOTEL, THE, 16 Lord St, (01253) 22488, gay-owned hotel with bar, 60% gay / lesbian clientele, beverage-making facilities, private & shared baths, TV lounge, continental or full English breakfast, concession to Flamingo. ♀♂

ROCKLEY HOTEL, THE, 37 Hull Rd, (44-1253) 25 409. Hotel with restaurant & bar, 50% gay & lesbian clientele, exclusively gay for New Years.

ROYALE, THE, 18 Regent Road, (01253) 26623, gay-friendly guesthouse with licensed bar, private baths.

SANDOLIN GUEST HOUSE, 117 High St, (44-1253) 752 908. Gay-owned, gay-friendly hotel, tea & coffee-making facilities, 1 shared shower/WC, concessions to local clubs.

TRADES HOTEL, 51-53 Lord St, (01253) 26401 or 294 812, men-only hotel & bar, steam room, private & shared baths, full breakfast. ♂

TREMADOC GUEST HOUSE, 127-129 Dickson Rd North Shore, (01253) 24 001, guesthouse, ocean beach across road, comfortable rooms with tea-making facilities, shared baths, TV lounge, nearby exercise equipment, full English breakfast, free pass to Flamingo. ♀♂

■ *Women's Accommodations*

AMALFI HOTEL, 19-21 Eaves Street, (01253) 22971, hotel with residents' bar, full breakfast, shared baths, 95% women. ♀

■ *Bars*

BASE COFFEE BAR, 4 Springfield Rd, (01253) 29 61 96, 10:00-19:00. ♂

BASIL'S ON THE STRAND, 9 The Strand, (01253) 29 41 09, pub, Mon-Sat 12:30-00:30, Sun day & eve. 🎵✖♂

BODGERS, Church St, (01253) 29 98 06, 11:00-23:00 (Sun 12:00-22:30), many women. 🎵♀♂

FLYING HANDBAG, 170-172 Talbot Rd, opposite railway station, (01253) 255 22, 11:00-23:00. 🎵♂

LUCY'S, below Rumours straight bar on Talbot Square, (01253) 29 32 04, Mon-Sat till 01:00, Sun till 22:30. ♂

PEPES BAR, 94 Talbot Rd, (01253) 266 91, 12:00-01:00 (Sat till 02:00, Sun pub hours). ♂

■ *Dance Bar/Disco*

FLAMINGO, ★ 176 Talbot Rd, (01253) 249 01, large dance bar complex, Mon-Sat till 02:00, Sun day & eve. till late. 🎵✖📧🎵♂

■ *Cafe*

DOROTHY'S TEA SHOP, 28a King St, (01253) 29 60 52, 7 days. ♂

■ *Saunas/Health Clubs*

GALAXY SAUNA CLUB, 25 Springfield Rd, (01253) 29 46 10, 13:00-22:00 (Sat till 06:00).

■ *Leathers/Piercing*

CLONE ZONE, 11 The Strand, (01253) 29 48 50, Mon-Sat 11:00-19:00, magazines, leathers & rubber, books, cards, toys, poppers, T-shirts, jeans & fashion clothing, mail order available.

BOLTON

■ *Information*

LESBIAN LINE, (01204) 39 46 10, Thurs 19:00-22:00.

■ *Bars*

ABSOLUTELY FABULOUS, Clarence St, (01204) 39 37 05, 17:00-23:00. 🎵🎵♂

CHURCH, 174 Crook Street (01204) 52 18 56, women welcome (Thurs women-only). 🎵♂

GEORGE, 92-94 Great Moor St, (01204) 36 19 79, 11:00-23:00, women welcome. ♂

STAR & GARTER★, 11 Bow St, (01204) 259 26, pub, women welcome. ✖♂

BOURNEMOUTH

■ *Information*

AIDS LINE, (01202) 31 71 77, 24hrs.

HELPLINE, (01202) 31 88 22, Mon-Fri 19:30-22:30, or tape. Ask about women's group meetings.

■ *Accommodations*

AARON HOUSE, 18 Purbeck Rd, The Westcliff, Bournemouth BH2 5EF, (44-1202) 292 865. Gay-owned, gay-friendly hotel in a newly renovated Victorian building, all private baths, a 1-minute walk to gay nightlife, 40% gay clientele.

BEECH CRESCENT, between Shell Bay and Bournemouth, (01202) 762 092, gay guesthouse near beach, private bath, TV, hostess tray. ♂

BONDI, 43 St Michael's Rd, (01202) 554893, bed & breakfast near sea & shopping, colour TV, beverage-making facilities, shared baths, residents' lounge, color satellite TV, 50% gay & lesbian clientele.

CHINE BEACH HOTEL, 14 Studland Rd, Alum Chine, Bournemouth, (44-1202) 767 015, Fax: (44-1202) 761 218. Hotel with bar & restaurant, full English breakfast, private baths, colour TV, pool on premises. 80% gay & lesbian clientele. 🏊♀♂

CREFFIELD, THE, 7 Cambridge Rd, Bournemouth, BH2 6AE, (44-1202) 317 900. Exclusively gay late Edwardian B&B with all en-suite baths, full breakfast & two rooms with 4-poster beds. Full central heating, conservatory, large private garden & near all venues & shopping. Women welcome. ♂

HEATHER BRAE HOTEL, 19 Tregonwell Rd, West Cliff, BH2 5NR, (44-1202) 556 637. Gay-friendly hotel with full English breakfast, near gay bars, more gay in fall & winter.

UK - ENGLAND

HEDLEY HOTEL, 125 West Hill Rd, Bournemouth, BH2 5PH, (44-1202) 317 168. Gay-friendly hotel, 20%-30% gay clientele.
LEICESTER GRANGE, (01202) 760278. Men-only bed & breakfast in a large, private house, color TV, private & shared baths & continental breakfast. ♂
NEWARK HOTEL, 65 St Michaels Rd, West Cliff, (01202) 294989, gay-friendly hotel with restaurant & bar, 50% gay/lesbian clientele, color TV, private & shared baths, TV lounge, full breakfast.
ORCHARD HOTEL, 15 Alumdale Rd, Alum Chine, (01202) 767 767, hotel with full residents' liquor license, color TV, private & shared baths, TV lounge, nearby ocean beach, full English breakfast. ♀♂
RAVENSBOURNE HOTEL, 17 Westby Rd, Boscombe, (01202) 309 770, guesthouse, 50% gay/lesbian clientele, double rooms, color cable TV, shared baths, nearby ocean beach, full English breakfast, tea.
WESTOVER GARDENS HOTEL, 5-7 Westover Rd, (44-1202) 556 380 (tel/fax). Gay-owned, gay-friendly hotel with licensed residents-only bar, full English breakfast, 20% gay & lesbian clientele.

■ Bars
BAKERS ARMS, 77 Commercial Rd, (01202) 55 55 06, 11:00-23:00.
LEGENDS CAFE BAR, 53 Bourne Ave, (01202) 31 01 00, 10:00-23:00. ♂
QUEENS HALL PUB, 14 Queens Rd, Westbourne, (01202) 76 44 16, pub hours.
RENDESVOUZ, 1a Avenue Rd, (01202) 29 35 75, 10:30-23:00, bars on 2 floors.

■ Dance Bar/Disco
BOLTS, at The Academy in Boscombe, last Sun.
TRIANGLE, 30 The Triangle, (01202) 29 76 07, disco & lounge, Mon-Sat 21:30-02:00, leather club meets Fri 21:00.

■ Saunas/Health Clubs
SPA, THE, 121 Poole Rd, Westbourne, (01202) 75 75 91, 13:00-21:00 (Sun 14:00-20:00).

■ Erotica
CEREBUS, 25 The Triangle, (01202) 29 05 29.

BRADFORD

■ Information
AIDS INFO, (01274) 73 43 54.
GAY & LESBIAN SWITCHBOARD, (01274) 72 22 06, Tues, Thurs-Sat 19:30-21:30.
LESBIAN LINE, (01274) 30 55 25, Thurs 19:00-21:00, or tape.

■ Bars
BAVARIA TAVERN, Heaton Rd at Church St, (01274) 48 76 81, Mon-Thurs 19:00-23:00 (Tues lesbian social), Fri & Sat from 12:00, Sun afternoons & evenings
GUYS & DOLLS, Westgate, Bradford Centre, women-only Sun 20:00-23:00. ♀
NEW EDITION, 10 Worthington St, (01274) 49 35 49, women's nights every other Thurs 21:00-02:00. ♀

■ Dance Bar/Disco
CHECKPOINT, (01274) 49 35 49, women's dance night every other Fri, call locally for address.
SILKS, Piccadilly St, enter from back of Somewhere Else, Thurs-Sat 23:00-02:30.
SUN, THE, 124 Sunbridge Rd, (01274) 73 77 22, pub with disco Wed & Sun.

BRIGHTON

■ Information
AIDS INFO, (01273) 69 32 66, Mon-Fri 10:00-17:00.
BRIGHTON WOMEN'S CENTRE, 10 St Georges Mews, (01273) 60 21 41, Lesbian Strength social group meets 2nd & 4th Tues from 19:30.
GAY SWITCHBOARD, (01273) 69 08 25, Mon-Sat 18:00-22:00, Sun 20:00-22:00.
LESBIAN LINE, (01273) 60 32 98, Tues & Fri 20:00-22:00, ask about scheduled monthly lesbian bar nights.

■ Accommodations
ALPHA LODGE PRIVATE HOTEL 19 New Steine, Brighton, E Sussex, (01273) 609 632, fax: 690 264, guesthouse with a steam-room suite, centrally located, overlooking the sea, singles, doubles, beverage-making facilities, color TV, full English breakfast, nearby pool & beaches, women welcome. ♂
ASHLEY COURT GUESTHOUSE, 33 Montpelier Rd, (01273) 739916. B & B guesthouse, some hetero clientele, private sinks & showers in rooms, ocean beach nearby. ♀ ♂
BANNINGS GUESTHOUSE, 14 Upper Rock Gardens, (01273) 681 403, close to gay venues, private & shared baths, TV, women very welcome.
BARRINGTON'S PRIVATE HOTEL, 76 Grand Parade, (01273) 604 182. hotel with bar, 50% gay/lesbian clientele, luxury rooms, private showers, shared baths, colour TV, full English breakfast.
BRIGHTON COURT CRAVEN HOTEL, 2 Attlingworth St, (01273) 607710, hotel with bar, women welcome, showers in rooms. ♂
CATNAPS PRIVATE GUEST HOUSE, 21 Atlingworth St, E Sussex, (1273) 685 193, fax: (1273) 622 026, guesthouse, women welcome, 7 rooms, shared baths, TV lounge, nearby pool & ocean beach, full English breakfast, welcoming tea & coffee. ♂
COWARD'S GUESTHOUSE 12 Upper Rock Gardens, BN2 1QE, (01273) 692677, guesthouse, mostly men, women welcome. Ensuite bath or shower, full English or vegetarian breakfast, colour TV, near gay bars. ♂
HUDSONS GUEST HOUSE, 22 Devonshire Place, (01273) 683 642, fax 696 088, elegant, comfortable, well-equipped rooms, including tea/coffee making facilities, near shopping, restaurants, Royal Pavilion, beaches, proper English breakfast, vegetarians welcome. ♀♂
NEW EUROPE HOTEL, 31-32 Marine Parade, (01273) 62 44 62, 30 rooms, all ensuite bathrooms, colour TV, direct-dial phones, elevator, sea views, 95% men, women welcome. Sat disco, open 24hrs for residents & guests. ♂
PORTLAND HOUSE HOTEL, 55-56 Regency Square, Brighton, East Sussex, (01273) 820464, fax 746036, hotel with bar, 50% gay/lesbian clientele, rooms with modern conveniences, beverage-making facilities, full English or continental breakfast, near ocean beach.
SHALIMAR HOTEL, 23 Broad St, Marine Parade, (01273) 605 316, hotel with backroom resident's bar, women welcome, private & shared baths, colour TV, beverage-making facilities, phone, nearby ocean beach, full breakfast. ♂
SINCLAIRS GUEST HOUSE, 23 Upper Rock Gardens, (01273) 600 006, bed & breakfast guesthouse, women welcome, colour TV, beverage-making facilities, private & shared baths, full English breakfast. ♂
WHITE HOUSE HOTEL, 6 Bedford St, (01273) 626266, hotel, 70% gay/lesbian clientele, private & shared baths.

■ Women's Accommodations
ONLY ALTERNATIVE LEFT, THE, 39 St. Aubyn's, Hove, Sussex, (01273) 324739. Women-only B&B with women's non-smoking vegetarian restaurant, bar & disco, shared bath, continental breakfast buffet. Afternoon tea in the garden in summer. ♀

■ Bars
AQUARIUM, 6 Steine St, (01273) 60 55 25, cruise-type pub. ♂
BLUE MOON, 37 New England Rd, (01273) 70 90 40, Fri, Sat 19:30-23:00. ♀
BULLDOG TAVERN★, 31 St James St, (01273) 68 40 97, 11:00-23:00 (Sun pub hours), weekend piano bar. ♂
CAFE JULES & MONS BAR,, at Only Alternative Left women's hotel, 39 St Aubyns, Hove, bar & vegetarian restaurant, Fri & Sat women only. ♀
CLUN ENERGY, West St, at The Joint; or Marine Parade, at the Royal Escape. Location varies, every other Tues, ask locally for current venue location. ♂
DR. BRIGHTON'S, 16 King Rd, (01273) 32 87 65.
LEGENDS BAR, 31-32 Marine Parade, at the New Europe Hotel, (01273) 62 44 62. ♂
MARLBOROUGH,★ 4 Princes St, (01273) 57 00 28, pub, men's leather group meets 1st Wed from 21:30. ♂
ORIENTAL, THE, 5 Montpelier Rd, (01273) 72 88 08, pub, open days & evenings, Sun lunch. ♂

FERRARI GUIDES' GAY TRAVEL A to Z - 18th EDITION

UK - ENGLAND

QUEEN'S HEAD, 10 Steine St, (01273) 60 29 39, pub, women welcome.

SCHWARZ BAR, 31-32 Marine Parade, at the New Europe Hotel, Fri-Sat 22:00-02:00, cruise bar with strict dress code, leather, denim, rubber. Leather group meets Fri 22:00.

SECRETS, 25 Steine St, (01273) 60 96 72, 21:30-02:00 (Fri, Sat from 21:00), closed Sun.

VILLAGE, 74 St James' St, (01273) 62 22 60, lounge upper level, disco lower level, 20:00-02:00 (Thurs-Sat from 14:00), Sun pub hours.

ZANZIBAR, 129 St James' St, Kemptown, (01273) 62 21 00, younger crowd, Mon-Thurs 14:00-01:00, Fri & Sat till 02:00.

Dance Bar/Disco

CLUB CHEEKY, 15 King's Rd, at Zenon's, (01273) 32 68 48, women's dance night, Fri 22:00-02:00.

CLUB REVENGE, 32 Old Steine, opposite Palace Pier, (01273) 60 60 64, large dance bar, Mon-Thurs 22:30-02:00, Fri, Sat from 22:00 (Fri uniform & leather nights, upper level).

DYNAMITE BOOGALOO, 37 West St, at the Joint, Thurs.

PINK PROMOTIONS, (01903) 72 36 25, floating women's disco at various locations on the South Coast, call for exact date & location.

TRANSISTER, at Escape Club & Club Passion, gay disco every other Tues, transvestites. Ask locally for address.

WILD FRUIT, ★ 78 West St, at Paradox, (01273) 32 16 28, 1st Mon 22:00-02:00, women welcome.

Cafe

ALBATROSS CAFE, 27 Middle St, (01273) 32 94 62, 11:00-17:00 (closed Sun), call about women-only nights, some lesbian/gay nights.

RAINBOWS COFFEE BAR, 22 Preston St, (01273) 32 91 54, 10:00-19:00 (Sun 11:00-17:00).

Saunas/Health Clubs

FITNESS CAMP, 90 St. James' St, (01273) 67 44 55, 11:00-21:00.

UNIT ONE SAUNA, Seafront, in Rottingdean, (01273) 30 72 53, 12:00-22:00.

Retail & Bookstores

CARDOME, 47a St James' St, (01273) 69 29 16, gay cards, etc.

OUT!, 4 & 7 Dorset St, (01273) 62 33 56, gay & lesbian bookstore, also videos, toys, rubber, leather, etc., 10:00-18:00 (Fri, Sat till 20:00), Sun 11:00-17:00.

READ ALL ABOUT IT, 69 East St, (01273) 20 58 24, general bookstore with gay & lesbian section.

SCENE 22, 129 St James' St, (01273) 62 66 82, gay store with leather, rubber, magazines,
Mon-Fri 09:30-19:00, Sat till 18:00. Café on lower level 11:00-18:00.

Erotica

ROUGH, 36 St. James St, (01273) 27 18 08, gay store.

SIN-A-MATIQUE, 22 Preston St, (01273) 32 91 54, gay store, 10:00-18:30 (closed Sun).

WILDCAT COLLECTION, 16 Preston St, (01273) 32 37 58.

BRISTOL

Information

GAY & LESBIAN SWITCHBOARD, (0117) 942 08 42, daily 19:30-22:30.

LESBIAN LINE, (0117) 929 08 55, Thurs 19:30-22:00, ask about scheduled women's dance nights.

Bars

CLUB 49, 20 Christmas Steps, (0117) 921 11 89, Thurs-Sat from 21:00, women welcome.

CLUB LEO, 20 St. Nicholas St, (0117) 929 24 20, 22:00-02:00 (Sun 19:30-24:00), closed Mon.

ELEPHANT, THE, St Nicholas St, (0117) 949 99 01, women welcome.

GRIFFIN, THE, Colston St, (0117) 927 24 21, pub, women welcome. Leather group meets 1st Fri & 3rd Sat from 21:00.

JUST, 1 Fiennes Ct, at Fairfax St, (0117) 930 46 75, 22:00-02:00 (Sun 21:00-23:30), closed Mon. Women-only Fri.

Dance Bar/Disco

OUTWEST!, Beauley Rd, 45 Southville Centre, (0117) 983 94 45, country western dance night, last Fri 20:45.

Cafe

LILAC CAFE, Horley Rd, at St. Werburgh's Community Centre, lesbian cafe 2nd Sun 15:00-18:00.

Saunas/Health Clubs

COTTAGE, 19 West St, Old Market, (0117) 907 76 22, 24hrs.

Retail & Bookstores

GREENLEAF BOOKSHOP, 82 Colston St, general bookstore with gay & lesbian section.

BURNLEY

Bars

GARDEN BAR, 133 St James St, (01282) 41 48 95, pub hours, disco Fri & Sat.

MCNEILS, Guy St, in Padiham, (01282) 77 48 77, Sun, Mon, Thurs from 20:00.

PLANE TREE HOTEL BAR, at the Plane Tree Hotel, Westgate, (01282) 354 42, Sun 19:00-22:00.

BURTON-UPON-TRENT

Bars

BURNT GATE INN, Hopley Rd, Anslow, (01283) 636 64, Wed 19:00-23:30.

BURY SAINT EDMONDS

Information

GAY & LESBIAN LINE, (01449) 71 11 96, answers Mon-Fri 19:00-22:00.

Bars

DOG & PARTRIDGE, Newmarket Rd, Barton Mills, (01638) 71 27 61, 19:00-23:00 (Sun till 22:30). Disco 1st Sat of the month.

CAMBRIDGE

Information

CAMBRIDGE FRIEND, men call (01223) 24 60 31. Women call 321 1148.

LESBIAN LINE, (01223) 31 17 53, Fri 19:00-22:00.

WOMEN'S RESOURCE CENTRE, Hooper St, (01223) 32 11 48, lesbians meet odd Thurs 19:30.

Bars

FRUIT, (01733) 31 35 42, floating party, 1st Sun, boards at 20:30.

Dance Bar/Disco

DOT COTTON CLUB, Clifton Rd. at The Junction bar, (01223) 41 26 00, disco once a month.

SISTER ACT, Newmarket Rd, in the Harris Suite at Cambridge United, (01223) 5711 421, women's disco, scheduled one Fri per month.

TASTY, Hills Rd, at Q-Club, (01223) 51 59 57, 2nd Thurs 22:00-01:00.

CANTERBURY

Information

EAST KENT FRIEND & GAY HELPLINE, (01843) 58 87 62, Tues 19:30-22:00. Gay Helpline: (01843) 45 48 68, Wed 20:00-08:00.

LESBIAN LINE, (01227) 46 45 70, Fri 19:00-22:00, ask about scheduled lesbian disco & bar nights.

Bars

CARPENTERS ARMS, THE, Black Griffin Ln, Wed, Sat from 19:00. Disco night 2nd & last Sat.

CARLISLE

Bars

ZODIAC, THE, 161 Botchergate, (01288) 32 211, private club.

CHELMSFORD

Bars

ARMY & NAVY, Army & Navy roundabout, Parkway, Wed 19:00-23:00, Sun 19:00-22:30.

288   FERRARI GUIDES' GAY TRAVEL A to Z - 18th EDITION

UK - ENGLAND

CHELTENHAM

■ *Information*
AIDS LINE, (01242) 22 46 66, Mon, Wed 19:00-21:00.

■ *Bars*
LECKHAMPTON INN, Shurdington Rd, (01242) 52 77 63, 3 bars. ♂

PHOENIX, 36 Andover Rd, Tivoli, at the Cheltenham Spa, (01242) 52 94 17, pub, overnight accommodations available. ♂

■ *Dance Bar/Disco*
RACECOURSE DISCO, Insurance Suite, Cheltenham Racecourse, Sat 21:00-02:00. 🍸 ♂

CHESTER

■ *Information*
AIDS INFO, (01244) 39 03 00, 19:00-22:00.

■ *Bars*
RAINBOWS, St. John St, at the Marlborough Arms, (01244) 32 35 43. ✗ ♂

■ *Dance Bar/Disco*
CONNECTIONS, 39 Watergate St, (01244) 32 06 19, Mon-Sat 21:30-02:00, Sun 20:30-24:00. 🍸 ♀ ♂

■ *Saunas/Health Clubs*
PARADISE HEALTH CLUB, Welsh Rd, units 243d, Deeside Industrial Est., (01244) 28 06 66.

■ *Restaurants*
HUNGRY PILGRIM, at Connections bar, 11:00-17:00. ♀ ♂

CHESTERFIELD

■ *Information*
AIDS INFO, (01246) 55 05 50.

■ *Bars*
BASEMENT, Cavendish St, at the Bluebell Inn downstairs, (01246) 20 18 49, Wed 20:00-23:00. ♂

BRIDGE INN, Hollis Lane, (01246) 27 67 40, pub, 13:00-22:30. ✗ ♂

LA MONTMARTRE, Churchwalk, Stevensons Place, at the Queen of Clubs, (02146) 20 34 63. Wed 22:00-02:00. ♂

MANHATTAN, 50 Saltergate, (01246) 23 20 42, from 20:00. ♂

CHICHESTER

■ *Bars*
BUSH, THE,★ 16 The Hornet, (01243) 77 99 45, frequented by local gays. 🔲

COLCHESTER

■ *Information*
GAY SWITCHBOARD, (01206) 86 91 91, Mon-Fri 19:00-22:00.

■ *Bars*
DRAGOON, Butt Rd, (01206) 57 34 64, gay Mon 20:00-23:00. ♂

■ *Dance Bar/Disco*
FOX & HOUNDS, Little Bromley, Manningtree, (01206) 39 74 15, pub with gay disco nights Fri, Sat 19:00-00:30. 🍸 ♂

THELMA'S, Church St, at the Colchester Arts Centre, (01206) 57 73 01, 1st Fri 21:00-01:30. 🍸 ♀ ♂

CORNWALL

■ *Accommodations*
GLENCREE PRIVATE HOTEL, 2 Mennaye Rd, Penzance, (01736) 62026, in US (407) 994-3558, fax 994-3634. Gay-friendly guesthouse with drink license, 50% gay & lesbian clientele, private & shared baths, full breakfast, beverage making facilities, colour TV, nearby pool & ocean beach.

LONGSHIPS HOTEL, Tallan Rd, St Ives, tel/fax: (44-1736) 798 180, gay-owned hotel with restaurant & bar, open Mar-Nov, private baths, TV, nearby ocean beach, 10% gay clientele

PENRYN HOUSE HOTEL, The Coombs, Polperro, Cornwall PL13 2RG, (44-1503) 272 157. Gay & lesbian hotel with some straight clientele. ♀♂

ROSEHILL IN THE FERN, Roseworthy, Camborne, (01209) 712 573, guesthouse, some hetero clientele, spacious double rooms, private baths, colour TV, full breakfast, extra charge for evening meal. ♀♂

RYN ANNETH, Southfield Place, St Ives, (01736) 793 247, bed & breakfast, cozy, comfortable rooms, shared baths, lounge, full breakfast, nearby ocean beach. ♀♂

WOODBINE VILLA, Fore St, Grampound nr Truro, (01726) 882-005, bed & breakfast in a private home with sauna & gym, women welcome, shared baths, TV lounge with fireplace, full English breakfast. ♂

■ *Women's Accommodations*
CAPISTRANO, 1 Chy-an-Dour Square, Penzance, Cornwall TR18 3LW, (01736) 64189, women-only bed & breakfast, comfortable, homey room with sea view, color TV, beverage-making facilities, kitchen privileges, full breakfast, nearby pool & ocean beach. ♀

COTSWOLDS

■ *Accommodations*
CRESTOW HOUSE, Stow-on-the-Wold, Gloucestershire GL54 1JY, (1451) 832 129. Gay-friendly bed & breakfast in an 1870 country manor house, a 2hr drive from London. Antique furnishings, 12-foot ceilings, private baths, expanded English breakfast, colour TV, heated swimming pool. 🏊

COVENTRY

■ *Information*
AIDS LINE, (01203) 22 92 92.

COVENTRY FRIEND, (01203) 71 41 99, Mon-Fri 19:30-21:30.

■ *Bars*
MCGUIGANS, Swanswell St, near Swanswell Park, bar & disco, Thurs till 01:00, Fri & Sat till 02:00. 🍸 ♂

■ *Dance Bar/Disco*
GLAD TO BE, on the A45, between Coventry & the M45, in Stretton on Dunsmore, (01203) 54 56 04, Sat 22:00-02:00. 🍸 ♂

INDULGENCE, Lower Precinct, at Browns, gay dance night 1st Tues 21:30-01:00. 🍸 ♀ ♂

■ *Retail & Bookstores*
WEDGE BOOKSHOP, 13 High St, general bookstore with gay & lesbian section.

DERBY

■ *Information*
AIDS LINE, (01332) 29 07 66, 24hrs.
DERBY FRIEND, (01332) 349 333, Wed 19:00-22:00.

■ *Bars*
FREDDIES BAR, 101 Curzon St, (01332) 20 42 90, open evenings (closed Mon, Tues). ♂

RUBY'S AT THE GALLERY, 130 Green Ln, (01332) 36 86 52, 20:00-23:00, pub hours Fri-Sun. ✗ ♂

VINE, THE, 22 Ford St, (01322) 20 02 66, bar & disco. 🍸 🎵 ♂

■ *Dance Bar/Disco*
CURZONS CLUB, 25 Curzon St, (01332) 20 42 90, Tues-Sun. 🍸 🎵 ♂

DERBYSHIRE

■ *Accommodations*
HODGKINSON'S HOTEL & RESTAURANT, South Parade, Matlock Bath, (01629) 582 170, fax: (01629) 584 891, hotel & hairdressing salon, 50% gay/lesbian, 50% hetero clientele, 6 double rooms, private baths, tea/coffee making facilities, sauna, full breakfast.

OLD STATION HOUSE, THE, 4 Chatsworth Rd, Rowsley, Derbyshire, (01629) 732 987, bed & breakfast, some hetero clientele, 3 doubles, 1 shared bathroom, 1 toilet, TV lounge, full breakfast. ♂♀

DEVON

■ *Accommodations*
BRIDGE STREET COTTAGE, Bridge Street, Sidmouth EX10 0RU, (01395) 597 419. Thatched cottage with 3 double guest rooms in an ancient Saxon village in East Devon. ♀♂

KILDARE GUEST HOUSE, 82 North Rd East, Plymouth, (01752) 229 375, guesthouse, 50% gay/lesbian clientele, colour TV, tea/coffee makers in rooms, private baths, private key, near city centre, full English breakfast. 🔑

MAYFAIR HOTEL & YE OLDE COTTAGE INN, Lynway, Lynton, North Devon, (44-1598) 753 227, gay-friendly hotel & inn with res-

FERRARI GUIDES' GAY TRAVEL A to Z - 18th EDITION   289

UK - ENGLAND

taurant & bar, private baths, full breakfast, color TV, coffee/tea-making facilities, stunning views of N Devon coast, near National Trust Coastal Path, Exmoor & beaches, 50% gay/lesbian clientele.

POLLARDS, Yeoford, Devon, (01363) 84402. Private house, women welcome, comfortably furnished rooms, beverage-making facilities, private & shared baths, TV lounge, full English breakfast. MAY CHANGE IN 1997, CALL FIRST. ♂

TOR DOWN HOUSE, Belstone, Okehampton, (01837) 840 731, bed & breakfast guesthouse in Dartmoor National Park. Comfortable double rooms with four-poster beds, color TV, private baths, tea/coffee tray, full breakfast. ♀♂

WHITE HOUSE HOTEL, Chillington, Kingsbridge, S. Devon, (01548) 580580, fax 581124, gay-friendly hotel with restaurant in Georgian/Victorian house. private baths, color TV, video tape library, telephone, room & maid service, laundry facilities, full breakfast, 4-course dinner available, nearby ocean beach.

DONCASTER

■ *Information*
WOMEN'S CENTRE, 21 Cleveland St, social group for lesbians meets here.

■ *Bars*
VINE, THE, 2 Kelham St, (01302) 36 40 96, 12:00-14:00 & 19:00-23:00. ♂

EASTBOURNE

■ *Accommodations*
FAIRLIGHT HOTEL, 41 Silverdale Rd, Eastbourne, East Sussex, (01323) 721 770. Gay-Friendly hotel & licensed bar near town center & the sea, private baths, colour TV, full English breakfast, games room, large garden.

■ *Bars*
HARTINGTON, THE, 89 Cavendish Place, (01323) 64 31 51, 11:30-23:00, Sun 12:00-15:00 & 19:30-22:30. ♀♂

EXETER

■ *Information*
AIDS LINE, (01392) 41 16 00, Mon-Fri 19:00-22:00.

■ *Dance Bar/Disco*
BOXES,★ 35-37 The Quay, (01803) 31 39 60, gay Tues 21:00-01:00. 🍴♂
LOFT, THE, 53 Bartholomew Street West, at Bart's Tavern, (01392) 42 20 83, dance bar & pub, Mon-Thurs 20:00-24:00, Fri & Sat 21:00-01:00, Sun afternoon & evening. Gay group meets here Wed 20:30. 🍴✗♂

FARNHAM

■ *Bars*
JOLLY SAILOR, 62-64 West St, pub. ♂

■ *Dance Bar/Disco*
RALPH'S CELLAR DISCO, 33 Shortheath Rd, (01252) 71 58 44, last Sat 21:00-03:00. 🍴♂

FOLKESTONE

■ *Bars*
BOTTOMS, at the Carlton Hotel, The Leas, Thurs & Sun from 20:00. 🍴♂

GLOUCESTER

■ *Information*
GLOUCESTER FRIEND, (01452) 30 68 00, Mon, Wed, Thurs 19:30-22:00.

■ *Bars*
NEW PILOT, Southgate St, (01452) 41 09 33, pub. 🎵🍴♂

■ *Dance Bar/Disco*
HYSTERIA, at Crackers, Bruton Way, (01452) 30 02 89, gay Mon 21:30-02:00. 🍴♂

GRAVESEND

■ *Bars*
CITY OF LONDON, The Terrace 27, (01474) 56 64 68, Tues. ♀♂

■ *Cafe*
SODA STORES, 11 Perry St, (01474) 53 54 20, snack & soda shop, frequented by local gays.

GREAT YARMOUTH

■ *Dance Bar/Disco*
KINGS WINE BAR, 42 King St, (01493) 85 53 74, gays in the rear bar. 🍴♂

GRIMSBY

■ *Information*
AIDS LINE, (01472) 24 08 40, Mon, Thurs 19:30-21:30, Tues 11:00-15:00.
GRIMSBY GAY LINE, (01472) 25 18 18, Tues, Thurs 19:00-21:00.

■ *Bars*
CHEERS, Oxford St, (01472) 34 12 39, gay Mon, Wed, Fri-Sat pm & Sun lunch. ♂
EXCHANGE, Bethlehem St, Sun & every other Wed.

HALESWORTH

■ *Dance Bar/Disco*
SHADES, at the Halesworth Old Maltings Leisure Club, (01986) 87 37 37, 1st Sun 20:00-24:00. 🍴♂

HALIFAX

■ *Bars*
CUMIN ALIVE, Bull Green, at WC's wine bar, (01422) 34 73 25, Wed 19:00-22:00. ♂

HARLOW

■ *Information*
HARLOW LESBIAN & GAY SWITCHBOARD, (01279) 63 96 37, Tues, Thurs, Sun 20:00-23:00, Fri 20:00-24:00. Women answer Sun.
RUBY'S LESBIAN & GAY CENTRE, Wych Elm, (01279) 45 16 77, 20:00-23:00, Thurs till 24:00, Fri-Sat till 02:00. Call for scheduled men-only & women-only Wed.

HARROGATE

■ *Bars*
TOTO'S, 3 Kings Rd, at Jimmy's, gay night Sun. ♂

HASTINGS - E. SUSSEX

■ *Information*
AIDS LINE, (01424) 42 99 01.
HASTINGS BEFRIENDERS & LESBIAN LINE, (01424) 44 47 77, Fri 20:00-22:00. Women answer Mon 19:00-21:00.

■ *Accommodations*
SHERWOOD GUESTHOUSE, 15 Grosvenor Crescent, St Leonard's-on-Sea, (01424) 433 331, 30% gay/lesbian clientele, private & shared baths, color TV, beverage-making facilities, morning call for breakfast, near ocean beach.

HEREFORD

■ *Dance Bar/Disco*
IMPULSE, 1 St. Martins St, at the Saracens Head, (01432) 27 54 80, Sat, Sun & 1st Wed 19:30-01:00. 🍴♂

HOVE

■ *Bars*
QT'S, Seafiled Rd, across from the Seaholm Hotel, afternoon tea garden, Sun 14:00-17:00. ♂

HUDDERSFIELD

■ *Information*
AIDS LINE, (01484) 43 24 33.
LESBIAN & GAY SWITCHBOARD, (01484) 53 80 70, Sun & Tues 19:00-21:00. Ask about women's socials.

■ *Bars*
GREYHOUND, THE, 16 Manchester Rd, (01484) 42 07 42. ♀♂

HULL

■ *Information*
AIDS INFO, (01482) 32 70 60.
HULL FRIEND, (01482) 44 33 33, Mon & Thurs 20:00-22:00, Sat 19:00-21:00, ask about scheduled events.
LESBIAN LINE, (01482) 321 43 31, Mon 19:00-21:00, or tape.

■ *Bars*
EARL DE GREY, 7 Castle St, (01482) 32 49 89, Sun pub hours, accommodations available. ⚓♂
POLAR BEAR, THE, 229 Spring Bank, (01482)

UK - ENGLAND

32 39 59, frequented by gays, many women. ▨

VAUXHALL TAVERN, Hessle Rd, near the Alexander Hotel, (01482) 32 03 40. ♂

■ Dance Bar/Disco
ALEXANDRA PALACE CLUB HOTEL, 69 Hessle Rd, (01482) 32 74 55, gay dance nights Fri-Sun. ▨♂

STIMULATION, 52 Anlaby Rd, at Tower Nightclub, (01482) 32 31 21, 3rd Tues 22:00-02:00. ▨♥▨♂

■ Retail & Bookstores
CACTUS, 21 Beverly Rd, (01482) 358 84 83, gift shop.

PAGE ONE BOOKS, 9 Princess Ave, (01482) 34 19 25, general bookstore with women's & gay section.

IPSWICH

■ Information
AIDS LINE, (01473) 23 20 07, Tues, Fri 19:30-22:00.

GAY & LESBIAN SWITCHBOARD, (01473) 23 22 12, Tues & Sat 19:30-21:30.

■ Bars
BAR FONTAINE, 10-12 St Margaret's St, Wed from 20:00. ♂

ROSE & CROWN, 77 Norwich Rd, (01473) 25 81 92. ♂

■ Dance Bar/Disco
OLIVE LEAF, THE, St Helen St, (01473) 25 86 33, pub with disco Thurs-Sun. Lesbian group meets alternate Mon. ▨♀♂

ISLE OF WIGHT

■ Information
HELP LINE, (01923) 52 51 23, Wed & Sat 19:30-22:00 or tape.

■ Accommodations
EDGECLIFFE HOTEL, THE, 7 Clarence Gardens, Shanklin, Isle of Wight, PO3 6HA, (44-1983) 866 199 (tel/fax). Gay-friendly hotel with bar & small fitness room, private & shared baths, full breakfast, colour TV, coffee & tea-making facilities. Close to cliff edge walk & ocean.

■ Restaurants
COTTAGE RESTAURANT, 8 Eastcliff Rd, Shanklin Old Village, (01983) 86 25 04. ▨

LANCASTER

■ Information
AIDS LINE, (01524) 84 10 11, Mon 19:00-22:00.

GAY & LESBIAN SWITCHBOARD, (01524) 84 74 37, Thurs & Fri 19:00-21:00, ask about lesbian socials 2nd Wed.

■ Bars
ALEX NIGHTCLUB, 22 Penny St, (01524) 38 30 71, 1st Wed 22:00-02:00. ♂

■ Dance Bar/Disco
WILD DISCO, Penny St, Farmers Arms, women-only disco, last Fri from 20:00. ▨♀

LEAMINGTON SPA

■ Bars
SLUG & LETTUCE, Clarendon St, (01926) 33 93 66, women's bar night every other Sun 19:00-22:30. ♀

LEEDS

■ Information
AIDS LINE, (0113) 242 32 04.

GAY SWITCHBOARD & LESBIAN LINE, (0113) 245 35 88, 19:00-22:00. Women answer Tues 19:30-21:30.

■ Bars
C-EX CLUB, at the Corn Exchange Club, Sun from 19:00, Thurs till 02:00. ▨♂

NEW PENNY★, Call Lane, pub with shows, women welcome. ♪♂

OFF THE WALL, 153 The Headrow, 20:00-02:00 (Wed 19:00-23:00, Sun 19:00-22:30), closed Mon, Tues. ♂

OLD RED LION, Meadow Lane near Leeds Bridge, pub, women welcome. ♂

PRIMOS 2, 41-43 New York St, Westminster Buildings, (0113) 244 63 00, 21:00-02:00 (Fri, Sat till 06:00), closed Sun. ♂

QUEENS COURT, Lower Briggate, (0113) 245 9449, 21:00-02:00. ▨♪♂

RED RAW, Boar Lane, at Nato, (0113) 238 09 99, gay dance night, 1st Tues 22:00-02:00. ▨♂

TRASH, Roundhay Rd, in Astoria, (0831) 55 72 20, every other Fri 22:00-02:00, many women. ♀♂

■ Dance Bar/Disco
CONFETTIS, ★ at Primos 2 bar location, (0113) 238 09 99, 1st Tues 14:00-06:00. After hours breakfast at Primos 2 bar 02:00-06:00. ▨♂

■ Cafe
ANNARES, Corn Exchange, at The Piazza, (0113) 245 38 89, 09:00-17:30. ♂

ROOTS & FRUITS, 10-11 Grand Arcade, (0113) 293 94 03, 10:00-18:30 (closed Sun). ♂

LEICESTER

■ Information
AIDS INFO, (0116) 255 99 95.

GAY & LESBIAN LINES, (0116) 255 06 67, Mon-Fri 19:30-22:00, women answer Tues.

■ Bars
DOVER CASTLE, 34 Dover St, near Granby, pub with disco Wed, Fri-Sun, women welcome. ▨♂

LEICESTER PLACE, 24 Dryden St near Lee Circle, (0116) 251 07 85, with Crown pub & disco, Mon-Sat 22:00-24:00. ▨♂

MAGAZINE, Newark St, (0116) 254 05 23, bar, frequented by gays. Women-only evenings every other Wed. ▨

PINEAPPLE INN, 27 Burleys Way, (0116) 262 33 84, cruisy bar. ♪▨♂

■ Dance Bar/Disco
GHQ, 68 Humberstone Gate, at the Madison complex, (0116) 251 55 28, 21:00-02:00, closed Sun. ▨♀♂

KNIGHT LIFE, Burleys Way, at the Pineapple Inn, (0116) 262 33 84, Fri & Sat till 02:00. ▨♂

RATURE, Mayors Walk, at Asylum, ticket info: (0116) 223 1111, alternate Fri 21:00-02:00. ▨♂

■ Cafe
LESBIAN & GAY LINE COFFEE BAR, 45 King St downstairs from switchboard office, Thurs, Fri 12:00-14:00, Sat 10:30-17:00. Women-only Wed 12:00-14:00. ♀♂

LINCOLN

■ Information
AIDS LINE, (01522) 51 39 99, Tues & Thurs 09:00-17:30. Mon, Wed, Fri till 19:00.

LESBIAN & GAY SWITCHBOARD, (01522) 53 55 53, Thurs & Sun 19:00-22:00. Women answer Tues.

■ Bars
BIRDCAGE, Upper High St, at Falstaff Inn, (01522) 54 50 66, Wed 0:00-23:00, Fri from 20:00. ▨♂

LIVERPOOL

■ Information
AIDS LINE, (0151) 709 90 00, Mon-Wed & Fri 19:00-21:00.

LIVERPOOL FRIEND LINES, (0151) 708 95 52, Tues-Thurs 19:00-22:00.

■ Bars
BOYS BEHAVING BADLY, 18 Cumberland St, at The Pink, 20:00-02:00 (Sun till 24:00), Thurs women only. ▨♂

BRUNSWICK VAULTS, 69 Thithebarn St. ♂

CURZON CLUB,★ 8 Temple Lane, (0151) 236 51 60, private club, guests welcome, Mon-Thurs 14:00-24:00, Fri & Sat till 01:00, Sun 19:00-22:30. ♂

DALEY'S DANDELION, Dale St, (0151) 2362 905, 11:00-02:00 (Sat 19:00-02:00), closed Sun. ♂

LISBON BAR, 35 Victoria St, pub frequented by gays, more gay Sun. ▨

M BAR, 10 Cumberland St, (0151) 238 77 86, 12:00-23:00. ♂

PACO'S BAR, ★ 25 Stanley St, (0151) 236 97 37, 2 bars. ♂

Q-BAR, 41-45 Paradise St, (0151) 709 88 09, cafe: 12:00-22:30 (Sun 03:00-07:00 & 12:00-22:30); dance bar: 21:00-02:00 (Fri, Sat till 03:00), closed Sun. ▨♂

UK - ENGLAND

Gay Beach Holidays in Europe

English gays, like European gays, have for years vacationed in droves in warm Mediterranean beach locations. Places like Sitges, Ibiza, Mykonos, Torremolinos, Majorca, Gran Canaria are the European versions of America's Key West and Provincetown and the coast of Portugal hosts many gays. Accommodations are usually in gay vacation complexes or in gay-friendly apartments or hotels in the towns.

Like its numerous competitors in this market, **Sensations**, offers these destinations, plus Florida, but departs from European tradition by stressing customer service. "Sensations believes that our customers' holidays should start the moment they pick up the phone," says their promotional flyer, "and, with this in mind, our service is second to none. And, naturally, all Sensations staff are fully conversant with every single overseas property."

Sensations offers full package holidays including flights and overseas accommodations, but allows international clients to buy accommodation-only and arrange their own flights, or to fly to the UK before setting off for Europe on their Sensations holiday.

Contact **Sensations** at (44-171) 625 6969, Fax: (44-171) 625 0167.

QC'S, St John's Lane, at Le Club, (0345) 12 54 59, 22:00-02:00. ♂
TIME OUT, 30 Highfield St, (0151) 236 67 68. ♂

■ Dance Bar/Disco
FASCINATION, 62 Duke St, at Intrigue Fetish Club, Le Bateau Nightclub, lower level, 2nd Tues 21:30-02:00, dress code. ♂
FRUTIE, 28 Oliver St, at Stairways, Birkenhead, (0151) 647 65 44, gay 1st Thurs. ♂
GARLANDS, 8-10 Eberle St, (0151) 2363 946, 12:00-21:00 (Fri, Sat till 02:00), closed Sun. Women-only Thurs. ♂
LUVSTUFF, at Mount Pleasant, (0151) 2363 307, 1st Wed 22:00-03:00. ♂
PINK PALACE, 18 Cumberland St, 2 levels, Wed-Sat 22:00-02:00. ♂

■ Saunas/Health Clubs
DOLPHIN, 129 Mount Rd, Wallasey, (0151) 630 1516.

LONDON INTRO

PUB HOURS, A FREQUENTLY-USED TERM IN LONDON, MEANS A PUB is open Mon-Sat 11:00-23:00, Sun 12:00-15:00 & 19:00-22:30. Special note is made when a pub is open all day.

■ Information
AIDS INFO, (0800) 56 71 23 (toll-free national line); Body Positive (0171) 373 91 24; Nat'l Aids Trust (0171) 216 01 11; Positively Women (0171) 713 02 22.
BLACK LESBIAN & GAY HELPLINE, (0171) 620 38 85, Tues & Thurs 11:00-17:30.
GREENWICH LESBIAN & GAY CENTRE, 17 Bowater Rd, Woolwich (3rd floor), (0181) 316 59 54.
LESBIAN & GAY SWITCHBOARD, (0171) 837 73 24, 24hrs.
LESBIAN LINE, (0171) 251 69 11, Mon & Fri 14:00-22:00, Tues-Thurs 19:00-22:00.
NORTH LONDON LINE, (0171) 607 83 46.
SHAKTI, South Asian Lesbian & Gay Network, meets 2nd & 3rd Sun 15:00 & scheduled monthly socials. Call for details (0171) 837 73 41.

■ Accommodations
MANOR HOUSE HOTEL, 53 Manor Park, (0181) 318 5590, Fax: 244 4196. USA: (800) 71-ROYAL, Fax (407) 994-3634, private guesthouse, holiday apartments available, Victorian-style rooms with modern conveniences, private & shared baths, colour TV, buffet continental breakfast. ♂

LONDON EARLS COURT

■ Accommodations
BROMPTON'S GUESTHOUSE & APARTMENTS, PO Box 629, London SW5 9XF, (0171) 373 6559, Fax: 370 3923, E-mail: brompton@dircon.co.uk, men-only guesthouse & apartments, 10 tastefully decorated rooms, direct-dial phones, coffee & tea making facilities, TV, private & shared baths, in heart of gay London. ♂
EARL'S COURT APARTMENT, (44-181) 300 0035, fax: (44-181) 300 0030, self-contained mid-Victorian apartment with cable TV, VCR, stereo, telephone, fully equipped kitchen, spacious lounge, near public transportation & gay village, nearby gym & pool. ♀♂
NEW YORK HOTEL, THE, 32 Philbeach Gardens, Earls Court, London, (0171) 244 6159, Fax: (0171) 370 4961, hotel, spacious, well-decorated rooms with modern conveniences, most with en suite bathrooms, Jacuzzi, expanded continental breakfast. ♀♂

■ Bars
BALANS WEST, 239 Old Brompton Rd. ♂
BRANDED, at the Garage, upper level, across from Highbury & Islington tube, alt Fri 22:00-03:00. ♀
COLEHERNE, THE, 261 Old Brompton Rd (Earl's Ct tube), (0171) 373 98 59, cruise bar, with cafe upstairs, daily from 11:00. ♂

■ Dance Bar/Disco
BROMPTONS, 294 Old Brompton Rd, (Earl's Court tube, Warwick Rd exit), (0171) 370 13 44. Video dance bar, Mon-Thurs 22:30-02:00 (Tues Chaps leather night), Fri & Sat from 22:00, Sun C&W, 14:00-19:00 & 21:00-24:00. Not a leather bar, but there is always a contingent of clones & leathermen. ♂
BULK, at Club 180 location, Sat 21:00-02:00, dance bar night for big men & women and their admirers. Buffed-out strippers, cruisy. ♂
CLUB 180, 180 Earl's Ct Rd (Earl's Ct tube), (0171) 835 18 26, Wed-Sun from 21:00. ♂

■ Restaurants
LEATHER ATTIC, bar & restaurant above Coleherne men's pub, 261 Old Brompton Rd. open 21:00-24:00 (Sun 15:30-23:30), leather dress code. ♂
NEW YORK RESTAURANT, at the New York Hotel, (0171) 244 68 84, open 19:30-23:30.
ROY'S RESTAURANT, 234 Old Brompton Rd, (0171) 373 99 95. ♀♂
WILDE ABOUT OSCAR, at Philbeach Hotel, (0171) 373 1244, 19:00-23:00 (Fri, Sat till 24:00), closed Sun.

■ Leathers/Piercing
CLONE ZONE, 266 Old Brompton Rd, directly opposite Colherne bar, (0171) 373 05 98.

LONDON EAST

■ Information
WOMEN'S CENTRE, 109 Hoe St, (0181) 520 53 18, lesbian social odd Thurs 19:30-22:00.

■ Bars
BACKSTREET, Burdett Rd, Wentworth Mews (Mile End tube), (0181) 980 85 57, men-only,

UK - ENGLAND

strict leather dress code, live DJ, Thurs-Sat 22:00-03:00, Sun 21:00-01:00. 🍺🎵💋♂

BLACK HORSE, 168 Mile End Rd, (0171) 790 16 84, pub & cabaret 20:00 till late. 🍺🎵♂

BULL & PUMP, THE, 22 Shoreditch High St, pub. ♂

CENTRAL STATION WALTHAMSTOW, 80 Brunner Rd (Walthamstow, British Rail), (0181) 520 4836, pub with nightly cabaret, karaoke, singers, drag shows, 17:30-23:00 (Sat from 12:00, Sun 12:00-22:30). 🎵♂

COCK & COMFORT, 359 Bethnal Green Rd, (0171) 729 1090, pub & cabaret. 🎵♂

H2O, 130 Balls Pond Rd, (0171) 354 06 11, from 16:00 (Fri-Sun from 14:00). Different themes & DJs nightly, scheduled rubber, fetish & underwear nights. 🎵🍺💋♂

LONDON APPRENTICE, ★ 333 Old St (Old St tube), (0171) 739 59 49, cruise bar, leather & non-leather crowd, downstairs dance bar, Mon-Thurs 21:00-03:00, Fri & Sat till 05:00, Sun till 04:00. 🍺💋♂

OLD SHIP, THE, 17 Barnes St, Stepney, pub, cabaret on weekends. ♂

PEMBURY, THE, 90 Amhurst Rd, Hackney (0181) 985 22 05. ♂

PRIDE OF STEPNEY, 269 Stepney Way, (0171) 265 93 75, pub with 2 levels, dark, cruisy, backroom, from 20:00 (Fri & Sat till 02:00, Sat & Sun from 14:00). 🍺♂

ROYAL GEORGE, 7 Selby St, at Vallence Rd, (0171) 377 8828, bar & cabaret bar, pub hours. 🎵🍺♂

ROYAL OAK, 73 Columbia Rd (Old Street tube), (0171) 739 8204, pub with cafe, 12:00-late (Sun 08:00-24:00). 🍺♂

SHAKESPEARE, 460 Bethnal Green Rd, (0171) 739 5884, pub. 🎵♂

SHIP AND WHALE, THE, 2 Gulliver St, (0171) 394 3536, pub. ♂

SPIRAL STAIRCASE, 138 Shoreditch High St, (0171) 613 1351, 2 levels, lots of karaoke, cabaret, Wed-Thurs 20:00-02:00, Fri-Sun 20:00-04:00. ♂

WOODMAN, THE, 119 Stratford High Rd (Stratford tube), (0181) 519 8765, traditional pub, pub hours, cabaret, 70% men. 🎵♂

■ Dance Bar/Disco

BENJY'S 2000, ★ 562a Mile End Rd (Mile End tube), (0181) 980 64 27, young crowd, Sun only 21:00-01:00. 🍺♂

CLUB TRAVESTIE, 373 Commercial Rd, at the George Tavern, TV & TS dance nights 2nd & 4th Sat, call for schedule. 🍺♂

POPSTARZ, 121 Holborn, at Leisure Lounge, big gay Indian rock & pop night, Fri 22:00-05:00. 🍺♀♂

RAW, 120 Romford Rd, at The Pigeons, top 40 music, Sat 21:00-02:00. 🍺♀♂

REFLECTIONS, 8 Bridge Rd (Stratford tube), Stratford, (0181) 519 12 96, pub with cabaret & weekend disco, 21:00-02:00 (Fri, Sat till 05:00), Sun 12:00-01:00. 🍺🎵♀♂

TRADE, at Turnmills Club, 63b Clerkenwell Rd, (Farringdon tube), heavy techno dance club, late night breakfast starts at 04:00 Sun & goes till midday. 🍺❌♂

WARRIORS, at Turnmills Club, 63b Clerkenwell Rd (Farringdon tube), heavy techno dance club, Sun 14:00-06:00. 🍺❌♂

WAYOUT CLUB, 28 Minories, at Tiffany's, Sat gays, TV & TS. 🍺♂

WHITE SWAN, 556 Commercial Rd (Aldgate East tube), (0171) 791 98 70, disco nightly, male strippers, 20:00-24:00 (Fri, Sat till 02:00), cabaret till 24:00 weekdays. Sun tea dance from 17:30. 🍺💃🎵♂

■ Saunas/Health Clubs

ESSEX SAUNA & STEAM, 239 Cahdwell Heath, beside Tolgate Pub, 7 days, 11:00-23:00.

HACKNEY SAUNA CLUB, 267 Wick Rd, 7 days, 14:00-24:00.

HEALTH CLUB, 800 Lea Bridge Rd, (0181) 556 8082, 13:00-24:00, 7 days. ♂

■ Erotica

EXPECTATIONS, 75 Great Eastern St.

LONDON NORTH

■ Accommodations

ONE SIXTY REGENTS PARK RD, Primrose Hill, NW1 8XN (0171) 586 5266, elegant, Victorian bed & breakfast, some hetero clientele, rooms with antique & modern decor, color TV, private & shared baths, roof terrace, extensive English breakfast. ♀♂

■ Bars

ANGEL BAR, 65 Graham St, (Angel tube), (0171) 608 26 56, continental-style cafe & bar, open 12:00-24:00 (Sun till 11:30). ❌♂

ARTFUL DODGER, 139 Southgate Rd (Angel tube), (0171) 226 0841, pub, 17:00-24:00, Sat 15:00-24:00, Sun 12:00-23:00. 🍺❌♂

BAR 269, 269a West End Lane, West Hampstead, intimate cabaret, 18:00-23:00 (Sun 12:00-15:00 & 19:00-22:30). 🍺🎵♂

BLACK CAP, 171 Camden High St (Camden Town tube), (0171) 485 17 42. dance bar & cabaret nightly. Upstairs quiet bar (Shufflewick's), daily 12:00-02:00, Sun pub hours; Downstairs cabaret & dancing, from 21:00. 🍺🎵♀♂

CENTRAL STATION, 37 Wharfdale Road (Kings Cross tube), (0171) 278 3294, pub with quiet bar upstairs, 17:00-01:00 (Thurs till 03:00, Fri till 05:00, Sat noon-05:00, Sun noon-24:00). ❌♂

CLUB KALI, 178 Junction Rd, at Dome, South Asian club meets 3rd Fri. Arabic, Hindi & house music. 🍺♀♂

DUE SOUTH, 80 Stoke Newington High St, (0171) 249 75 43, from 16:00 (Sat, Sun from 13:00). Thurs women only. 🍺♂

DUKE OF CLARENCE, 140 Rotherfield St (Angel tube, Essex Rd BR), (0171) 226 65 26, women-only pub & patio, Mon-Fri 17:30-23:00, Sat from 19:00, Sun 19:00-22:30. ♀

DUKE OF WELLINGTON, 119 Balls Pond Rd (Dalston Kingsland BR), (0171) 249 37 29, pub, Mon-Sat 12:00-24:00, Sun pub hours, some hetero clientele. ♂

GLASS BAR, 190 Euston Rd, Euston Square Gardens at West Lodge, members club, Wed-Fri from 18:00, some hetero women. ♀

GUMMI, 130 Balls Pond Rd, strict rubber dress code, last Wed. 🍺♂

HARLEQUIN, 27 Arlington Way, in back of Sadler's Wells, (0421) 37 96 14, pub, from 11:00. ♂

KING EDWARD VI, 25 Bromfield St, (Angel tube), (0171) 704 07 45, cafe upstairs, patio, daily 12:00-24:00 (Sun till 23:30). ❌♂

KING WILLIAM IV, 77 Hampstead High St (Hampstead tube), (0171) 435 57 47, pub. 🍺♂

OAK, THE, 79 Green Lanes, use bus route, (0171) 354 2791, live bands, disco weekends, popular with women. ❌♀♂

RAM CLUB BAR, 39 Queen Head St, (0171) 154 0576. 🍺♂

SHAKTI, 178 Junction Rd, at the Dome, club for gay & lesbian Asians. 🍺♀♂

WHITE HART, 51 Station Rd, pub. 🎵♂

■ Dance Bar/Disco

CLUB EN FEMME, 388 Green Lanes, at Oasis, (01993) 700 554, 1st Fri of the month "glamour drag nite" dance party 21:00-03:00. 🍺♀

CLUB V, Highbury Corner, at The Garage (Highland & Islington tube), (0171) 607 18 18, 21:00-03:00, gay & lesbian dance night alternate Sat, Indian rock music. 🍺♀♂

GIRLZONE, 240 Amherst Rd, at Trenz, Fri 22:00-04:00. 🍺♀

MIS-SHAPES, 257-259 Pentonville Rd, at the Cross Bar, Indie pop music. 🍺♀♂

TOTALLY PUNKT, 18 Kentish Town Rd, at the WKD Club, 1st & 3rd Sat, funk, hip hop. 🍺♂

■ Cafe

SWANS AT COOLE, 22 Chalcot Rd, Primrose Hill, (0171) 722 03 54, 11:00-23:00. ❌♂

■ Restaurants

OF A FEATHER, 4 New College Parade, (0171) 722 4272, British cuisine, 12:00-15:00 & 18:00-23:30 (closed Sat, Sun).

■ Retail & Bookstores

COMPENDIUM BOOKSHOP, 234 Camden High Street (Camden Town tube), (0171) 485 89 44, general bookshop with gay & lesbian section.

GAY'S THE WORD BOOKSHOP, 66 Marchmont St (Russell Sq tube), (0171) 278 76 54. Vast collection of gay & lesbian books, magazines, newspapers, tapes from all over the world, Mon-Sat 10:00-18:00, Thurs till 19:00, Sun 14:00-18:00.

HOUSMAN'S, 5 Caledonia Rd, (0171) 837

UK - ENGLAND

44 73, radical bookshop, 10:00-18:30 (closed Sun).

KILBURN BOOKSHOP, 8 Kilburn Bridge, (0171) 328 70 71, general bookstore with gay & lesbian titles.

■ Leathers/Piercing

REGULATION, 17a St. Alban's Pl., Islington Green, (0171) 226 06 65, New & abused clothing for specialists and fetishists: leather, rubber, gas masks, plastic, military, medical, industrial & sportswear. Daily 10:30-18:30, closed Sun.

■ Erotica

SH!, 22 Coronet St, (0171) 613 54 58, erotica exclusively for women, closed Sun & Tues.

ZIPPERSTORE, 283 Camden High St (Camden Town tube), (0171) 284 05 37, gay books, magazines, leather, 10:30-18:30 (Sun 12:00-17:00).

LONDON SOUTH

■ Information

BLACK LESBIAN & GAY CENTRE, Westminster Bridge Rd, (0171) 620 38 85.

WOMEN'S CENTRE, 13 Woodside Green, Croydon, lesbian group meets Thurs 20:00.

■ Accommodations

GUYS AMERICAN STYLE HOMESTAY, 38 Baldry Gardens, Streatham, (0181) 679 7269, guesthouse, some hetero clientele, full breakfast, colour TV, beverage-making facilities, shared baths, near gay bars. Temporarily closed. To reopen in '97. Call first.

NUMBER SEVEN GUESTHOUSE, 7 Josephine Ave, London SW2 2JU, (44 181) 674 1880, Fax: (44 181) 671 6032. An exclusively gay & lesbian guesthouse, voted Guesthouse of the Year in 1994 & 1995 by readers of The Pink Paper. All rooms have private bathroom en-suite, tasteful furnishings, cable TV, and direct-dial phones. Free parking and car service available. Situated in a tree-lined avenue just five minutes' walk to gay clubs and 10 minutes by tube to the theatre district and the Soho gay village.

■ Bars

BASE BAR, 8 High St, Wimbledon, (0181) 944 6778, upscale European-style bar, gay Mon.

CASABLANCA, 28 East Dulwich Grove, cabaret bar, 18:00-01:00 (Fri, Sat till 02:00, Sun 13:00-01:00).

CHUNKKIES, 349 Kennington Lane (Vauxhall tube), at Dukes bar, (0171) 793 09 03, for large men & women.

CLOCK HOUSE, 156 Clapham Park Rd, (0171) 498 46 51, 18:00-23:00 (Sun pub hours).

DUKE'S, 349 Kennington Ln (Vauxhall tube & BR), at the Duke of Cambridge, (0171) 793 0903, late-opening pub with cabaret, big men & bears, 19:00-23:00 (Fri 21:00-02:00), closed Sun.

FATHER RED CAP, 319 Camberwell Rd,

(0171) 708 4474, cabaret, 12:00-24:00 (Fri, Sat till 01:00, Sun till 23:00). Women in upper level bar 21:00-02:00.

FORT, THE, 131 Grange Rd, (0171) 237 7742, pub hours, cruisy, underwear nights, strip parties.

GLOUCESTER, THE, 1 King William Walk, Greenwich, (0181) 858 26 66, large pub, cabaret weekly, 12:00-23:00 (Sun till 22:30).

GLP, 6 Ormond Yard & Duke of York St, at Ormonds, Mon 18:00-24:00.

GREYHOUND, 39 Lee Church St, karaoke, cabaret, Wed bears meeting.

HOIST, THE, Railway Arch 47c, (0171) 735 99 72, Fri, Sat 22:00-03:00, strict dress code, rubber, leather, uiform, 3rd Wed gay SM theme nights.

LITTLE APPLE, 98 Kennington Lane, (0171) 735 20 39, piano bar, cabaret, patio, 12:00-24:00 (Sun 13:00-23:00).

LORD PALMERSTON, THE, 141 Merton Rd, pub.

NOAH'S ARK, 68 Brigstock Rd, Thornton Heath, (0181) 240 1211, pub open late, small dance floor, 12:00-23:00 (Sun till 22:30).

PROHIBITION BAR, 2a Sunny Hill Rd, at the Greenhouse cafe bar.

QUEEN'S ARMS, 63 Courthill Rd, (0181) 318 73 05, upscale ambiance.

RED STILETTO, 108 Wandsworth Rd, (0171) 207 4944, 12:00-23:00 (Sun till 22:30), 80% men.

SUBSTATION SOUTH, 9 Brighton Terr. (Brixton tube), Brixton, (0171) 737 2095, pub with industrial motif, young crowd, large dance floor, DJs, 21:30-02:00 (Fri till 05:00, Sat till 06:00), Sun 21:00-03:00. Mon & Tues men only (Tues leather dress code).

VILLAGE AFFAIR, 8 High St, at Base Bar, (0181) 944 67 78, Mon 17:00-24:00.

VIXENS AT VAUXHALL, 372 Kennington Lane (Vauxhall tube), at the Royal Vauxhall Tavern, (0171) 582 08 33, pub dance night Fri 19:00-22:30.

YE OLDE ROSE & CROWN, Crooms Hill, Greenwich, (0181) 858 01 54, pub.

■ Dance Bar/Disco

DIAMONDS, at Jacque of Clubs, 47 Ossory Rd, near Old Kent Rd, (0171) 252 0007, Sat 21:00-03:00.

DUCKIE, 372 Kennington Lane, at Vauxhall Tavern, (0171) 582 0833, Indie rock & old pop, classic disco, Sat 21:00-02:00, a freaky, trendy dress up night.

FOUNTAIN, THE, 36 The Broadway, Deptford, (0181) 692 80 32, disco & cabaret Fri, Sat. Pub Mon-Sat 12:00-15:00 & 19:00-23:00, Sun pub hours.

FRIDGE, THE, Town Hall Parade, Brixton Hill (Brixton tube). (0171) 326 5100. men's & women's theme nights, constantly changing.

Call for current schedule. Sat Love Muscle.

IF, Douglas Way, Deptford, at the Albany Theatre & Centre, (0181) 467 19 98, 2nd Fri till 02:00.

MARKET TAVERN, Market Towers, 1 Nine Elms Lane (Vauxhall tube, Wandworth Rd exit), (0181) 622 56 55, cruise bar & dance bar, Mon & Wed leather-only in backroom, very popular Sun lunch & disco, 21:00-04:00 (Fri, Sat till 05:00, Sun 14:00-02:00).

ROYAL VAUXHALL TAVERN, 372 Kennington Lane (Vauxhall tube), (0171) 582 08 33, showbar, open Mon 20:00-01:00, Wed till 24:00, Sun 12:00-15:00 & 19:00-22:30. Women only Fri 19:00-22:30.

TWO BREWERS, THE, 114 Clapham High St (Clapham Common tube), (0171) 622 36 21, separate disco & cabaret bars, 18:00-01:00 (Fri & Sat 12:00-15:00 & 18:00-01:00, Sun 12:00-15:00 & 19:00-24:00.

WOOLWICH INFANT, 9 Plumstead Rd, cabaret & disco, pub hours, Mon women only.

■ Saunas/Health Clubs

AQUARIUS, 14 Gleneagle Rd, 3 levels, 13:00-24:00 (Fri till 02:00, Sat 11:00-06:00, Sun 11:00-24:00).

BROWNIE'S SAUNA, 14 Gleneagle Rd, Streatham. (0181) 769 69 98, daily 14:00-24:00 (Fri, Sat till 02;00). Unverifiable spring '97.

LOCKER ROOM, 8 Cleaver St, gay sauna, 7 days from 10:30.

PLEASUREDOME, 125 Alaska St (Waterloo tube), (0171) 633 91 94, 24hrs (Wed till 02:00).

STAR STEAM, 38 Lavender Hill, Battersea, (0171) 924 22 69, daily 11:00-24:00 (Sun 14:00-23:00).

STEAMING AT 309, 309 New Cross Rd, 7 days, 11:00-23:00.

■ Fitness Centers

PARIS GYMNASIUM LONDON, Goding St, Arch 73 (Vauxhall tube), (0171) 735 89 89, 7 days, 14:00-22:00 (Tues & Thurs from 10:00, Sat & Sun 15:00-20:00).

■ Restaurants

GREEN ROOM, 62 Lavender Hill, Battersea (Clapham Jct BR), (0171) 233 46 18. Vegetarian & vegan cuisine, daily 19:00-late (Sat also 12:00-16:00), live jazz Fri.

■ Retail & Bookstores

INDEX BOOK CENTRE, 10-12 Atlantic Rd, Brixton, general bookstore with gay & lesbian titles.

LONDON WEST

■ Bars

BLARNEY STONE, 48a High St, gay Irish pub, 20:00-23:00 (Fri, Sat till 01:00, Sun till 22:30).

UK - ENGLAND

CHAMPION, THE, 1 Wellington Terrace, Bayswater Rd, Notting Hill tube, (0171) 229 50 56, pub & beer garden with Ruby's basement bar, 12:00-23:00.

CITY OF QUEBEC, 12 Old Quebec St (Marble Arch tube), (0171) 629 61 59, 2 bars, 11:00-23:00 (Sun pub hours), quieter music upstairs, disco music downstairs.

EARL'S, 180 Earls Court Rd (Earls Court tube), above Club 180, (0171) 835 18 26, 16:00-24:00 (Sun from 12:00), DJ nightly.

FRIDAY'S, 305a Northend Rd, at Ted's Place, (0171) 385 93 59, Fri from 20:00.

GATE, THE, 68 Notting Hill Gate, (0171) 243 0123, small drinking club 22:00-24:00, best Fri & Sat.

GEORGE MUSIC BAR, 114 Twickenham Rd (Isleworth BR), (0181) 560 1456, traditional pub with cabaret, pub hours.

NUMBER 10'S, 10 Woodfield Rd, in back of Prince of Wales, pub, 12:00-24:00 (Fri, Sat till 02:00).

PENNY FARTHING, THE, 135 King St (Hammersmith tube), (0181) 748 70 45, pub, 12:00-23:00 (cabaret Wed-Sat), Sun pub hours, patio.

QUEEN'S ARMS, 223 Hanworth Rd (Hounslow Central tube), Hounslow, (0181) 570 9724, pub with cabaret nightly, pub hours.

QUEEN'S HEAD, 27 Tryon St (tube: Sloane Sq), (0171) 589 02 62, open pub hours, mature crowd.

REEVES, 48 Shepherd's Bush Green, at Reeves Hotel, (0181) 740 11 58.

RICHMOND ARMS, 20 The Square, near Princes St, Richmond (Richmond tube), (0181) 940 21 18, pub hours.

SHE'S OUT, 4 George St (enter from Manchester St), at Westmoreland Arms, 2nd Sat 19:30-23:00.

TED'S PLACE, 305a Northend Rd (West Kensington tube), (0171) 385 93 59, from 19:00 (closed Sun, Mon), Sat disco, many women, TV & TS. Women-only Fri from 20:00.

TED'S PLACE, 305a North End Rd, popular with transvestites.

VALE BAR, 99 Chippenham Rd, Maida Vale, 11:00-23:00 (Fri 12:00-24:00, Sun 12:00-22:00).

Dance Bar/Disco

CLUB GREYHOUND, off the A4 Colnbrook bypass, Junction 5 of the M4, just outside London, 7 days 20:00-02:00 (Fri, Sat till 03:00, Sun 19:00-24:00).

EXILIO, 2 Maxilla Walk, (0956) 983 230, call about scheduled Latin dance night every 2 weeks, 21:00-04:00, salsa, merengue, samba.

GREYHOUND, 11 High St, Guildford, disco Fri & Sat 19:00-23:00 (Sun till 22:30).

REFLEX CLUB, 200b Upper Richmond Rd, (East Putney tube), (0181) 780 28 22, large dance club, Fri, Sat 22:00-04:00.

ROYAL OAK, 62 Glenthorne Rd (Hammersmith tube), (0181) 748 27 81, pub with art deco motif, cabaret nightly, weekend disco, popular Sun lunch, Mon-Sat till 02:00, Sun 12:00-24:00.

Cafe

CAFE AU-REOLE, 233 Earls Court Rd, small cafe, 2 levels.

Saunas/Health Clubs

HOLLAND PARK SAUNA, 156 Shepherd's Bush Shopping Centre, (0181) 243 3264, 7 days, 11:30-23:00.

Restaurants

AMAZONAS, 72 Westbourne Grove, Brazilian & S. American cuisine.

BALANS WEST, 239 Old Brompton Rd, 08:00-01:00, 7 days.

LA LIBERTÉ, 32 Philbeach Gardens, at the New York Hotel, French & English cuisine.

LE GOURMET, 312 Kings Rd, 7 days.

LO SPUTINO, 130 Kings Rd, bar & restaurant.

Leathers/Piercing

ROB, 24 Wells St, near Berwick St, (0171) 735 78 93, 10:30-18:30 (closed Sun).

Erotica

X-RATED, High St, Kensington Market, 1st floor, (0181) 876 5520, rubber clothing, 12:00-18:00 (closed Thurs & Sun).

LONDON WEST END

Accommodations

CLONE ZONE LUXURY APARTMENTS, 64 Old Compton St, Soho, (44-171) 287 3530, Fax: (44-171) 287 3531. This self-contained, modern apartment is equipped with many amenities including AC, phone, fully fitted kitchen, bathroom with bath and shower and a spacious lounge. It is situated in the heart of London's lesbian & gay area, two floors above, but completely separate from, the Clone Zone shop. Women welcome.

RUSSELL LODGE GUEST HOUSE, 20 Little St, (44-171) 430 2489, fax: (44-171) 430 0755, luxury gay & lesbian accommodation in central London. Some rooms have shower & WC.

Bars

A TRULY WESTERN EXPERIENCE, 16-22 Great Russell St, at Central Club.

ADMIRAL DUNCAN, 54 Old Compton St, (0171) 433 5300, gay pub in Soho.

BACK BAR, 10 Brewer St (Picadilly Circus tube), (0171) 734 26 26, 23:00-03:00 (Sun 12:00-23:30), some hetero clientele.

BAR CODE, 3-4 Archer St, 743 33 42, 12:00-23:00, upscale ambiance, 2 levels.

BOX, THE, 32 Monmouth St, Seven Dials, (0171) 240 58 28, cafe, brasserie & bar, Mon-Sat 11:00-23:00, Sun 12:30-22:30. Sun 19:00-23:00 women only.

BRIEF ENCOUNTER, 41 St Martin's Lane (Leicester Sq tube), (0171) 240 22 21, pub, upstairs & downstairs bars, 11:00-23:00, Sun pub hours. To reopen spring '97.

COMPTON'S, ★ 53 Old Compton St (Leicester Sq or Tottenham Ct tube), (0171) 437 44 45, pub, loud music, trendy, young crowd, daily from 12:00.

DRILL HALL, THE, 16 Chenies St (Goodge St tube), (0171) 631 13 53, women only Mon 17:30-23:00, also women-only at the Greenhouse vegetarian restaurant next door, downstairs.

EDGE, THE, 11 Soho Square, Soho (Tottenham Court Rd. tube), (0171) 439 13 13, continental café & bar, 11:00-01:00 (Fri, Sat from 10:00), Sun 12:00-22:30.

FIRST OUT, 52 St. Giles High St, (Tottenham Court Rd tube), (0171) 240 80 42, cafe bar, 10:00-23:00 (Sun 12:00-22:30).

FREEDOM, 60 Wardour St (Piccadilly Circus tube), (0171) 734 0071, cafe, bar & theater, 2 floors, stylish bar serving food & fancy drinks, downstairs bar open late, 09:00-03:00 (Sun till 23:00).

GIRL BAR, Seven Dials, 32 Monmouth St, at The Box, Sun from 19:00.

HALFWAY TO HEAVEN, 7 Duncannon St. (Charing Cross tube), (0171) 930 83 12, quiet drinking bar, 2 levels, 15:00-23:00 (Sat 12:00-23:00, Sun 19:00-22:30).

JONATHAN'S, 16 Irving St (Leicester Sq tube), (0171) 930 47 70, quiet upstairs drinking bar, private club (members & guests only), 15:00-23:00.

Number Seven
Best UK Gay Hotel
7 Josephine Ave
LONDON
(44 181) 674 1880

Clone Zone Luxury Apartments
64, Old Compton St, Soho
London, W1 England
Tel Reservations: (171) 287 3530

FERRARI GUIDES' GAY TRAVEL A to Z - 18th EDITION

UK - ENGLAND

KINGS ARMS, 23 Poland St (Oxford Circus tube), (0171) 734 59 07, pub, 2 floors, open Mon-Sat 11:00-23:00, Sun 12:00-15:00 & 19:00-22:30. ✗♂

KU BAR, 75 Charing Cross Rd, (0171) 437 43 03, cocktail happy hour, 18:00-23:00 (Sun 16:00-22:30). ✗♂

KUDOS, 10 Adelaide St, (Charing Cross tube), (0171) 379 45 73, bar with brasserie, downstairs dance bar, trendy crowd.

LIMELIGHT, 136 Shaftesbury Ave, (0171) 434 05 72, Sun Tea Dance 18:00-23:00. ♂

MADAME JO-JO'S, 8-10 Brewer St (Piccadilly Circus tube), (0171) 734 24 73, showbar with major drag extravaganza mainly for hetero audience, Mon-Sat 22:00-03:00.

SEVENTYNINE CXR,★ 79 Charing Cross Rd (Tottenham Ct Rd or Leicester Square tubes), (0171) 734 0769, 13:00-02:00 (Sun 13:00-22:30), variety of gay & lesbian clientele.

SHAHARA 4-5 Neals Yard, at Euton's, (0171) 379 68 77, very upscale women-only piano bar. ♀

SUBSTATION SOHO, 1a Dean St, late-night cruise bar nightly. ♂

VILLAGE SOHO,★ 81 Wardour St (Leicester Sq tube), (0171) 436 24 68, 3 bars & cafe on 2 levels, fashionable crowd, Mon-Sat 11:30-23:00, Sun 12:00-22:30. ♂

WALTZING WITH HILDA, Great Russell St, at the Central Club Hotel, ballroom dancing, Fri 20:30-23:30 (classes 19:00-20:30). ♀

WAYOUT CLUB & PIANO BAR, 11 Kingly Ct, (0181) 363 0948, Wed 21:00-03:00, for TV, TS and their friends.

WOW BAR, Glasshouse St, Piccadilly, (0956) 514 574, Sat 20:00-23:00. ♀

YARD, THE, 57 Rupert St, (0171) 437 26 52, upstairs cruise bar with older crowd (40's), daily 18:00-23:00; stylish downstairs cafe bar, daily 12:00-23:00. ✗♂

■ Dance Bar/Disco

ACE OF CLUBS, at 52 Piccadilly, (Piccadilly tube), (0171) 408 44 57, women-only dance night Sat 21:30-04:00. ♀

CARIOCA, 49 Carnaby St, at Ruby's Dance Club, Sun ballroom dancing tea dance. ♀♂

CHROME, 4 The Plaza, at the Gardening Club, beneath Rock Garden, Tues gay night with house & hi-energy music. ♂

DTPM, 16a W Central St, at The End club, heavy techno dance club, trendy & fashionable crowd, Sun 19:00-03:30. ♂

FIST, 9 Brighton Terrace, at Substation South, S/M dance night for men & women, strict dress code leather, rubber, fetish, last Sat 22:30-05:00. ♀♂

G.A.Y.,★ 157 Charing Cross Rd (Tottenham Ct tube), at Astoria, (0171) 734 69 63, large dance bar, gay nights Mon, Thurs & Sat 22:30-04:00, trendy crowd. ♀♂

HEAVEN,★ The Arches, Villiers St (Charing Cross or Embankment tube), (0171) 930 20 20, gigantic complex with huge disco and multiple other bar venues and a changing schedule of special nights for gays & lesbians, Tues & Wed 22:30-03:00, Fri & Sat 21:30-03:00. Call for current schedule of men's, women's & mixed nights.

KITTY LIPS, 12 Sutton Row, at Mars, Fri 23:00-05:00, men welcome as guests. ♀

LA PARRANDA, 4 Wild Court, off Kingsway, at the Kulcha Kafe, gay salsa club, alternate Sat. ♀♂

LONG YANG CLUB DISCO, (0181) 397 27 37, for gay Asians & interested Westerners. Meets Sun from 20:00 at the Star Bar at Heaven (The Arches, Villiers). 樂 ♂

MUM, Villiers St, at the Soundshaft, 2nd Fri, pop, punk & Indie music. ♀♂

PHOENIX, 37 Lavendish Square, Fri & Sat disco in the basement, young crowd, top 40 music. ♂

PINK JUKEBOX, 16 Great Russell St, at Central Club Hotel, 19:30-23:00, dance lessons at 18:00. Sun afternoon dance party. ♂

QUEER NATION, at the Substation South, 9 Brighton Terrace, (0171) 836 40 52, dance night 1st Sat 22:00-05:00. ♀♂

RENEGADE RANCH, Great Russell St, at Central Club Hotel, c&w dance bar, Fri from 20:00. ♂

SALSA ROSADA, 229 Great Portland St, (0171) 837 3752, gay salsa dance club, alternate Sat 21:00-02:00, classes on Wed.

SHERBET, Hungerford Ln, at Soundshaft club, dance party Sun 11:00-20:00. ♂

TATTOO WOMEN'S NIGHT, 52 St Giles High St, at First Out, Fri 20:00-23:00, men welcome as guests. ♀

TUBE, Falconberg Court, late night club 22:00-04:00, different venues nightly. Ask locally for schedule. ♂

■ Saunas/Health Clubs

COVENT GARDEN HEALTH SPA, 29 Endell St, (0171) 836 22 36.

■ Restaurants

BALANS, 60 Old Compton St (Leicester Square tube), (0171) 437 52 12, 09:00-01:30 (Sun till 24:00). ♀♂

NUSA DUA, 11 Dean St, near Soho Square, (0171) 437 3559, Indonesian cuisine, 7 days.

ROSSANA'S, 17 Strutton Ground off Victoria St, (0171) 233 17 01, restaurant & bar, vegetarian cuisine, Wed-Fri 19:00-23:00 women-only. ♀

■ Retail & Bookstores

SILVER MOON, 64-68 Charing Cross Rd (Leicester Square tube), (0171) 836 79 06, feminist bookshop, 10:00-18:30 (Thurs till 20:00, Sun 12:00-20:00).

■ Leathers/Piercing

CLONE ZONE, 64 Old Compton St (Leicester Square tube), Soho, (0171) 287 35 30, daily 11:00-23:00.

LOUGHBOROUGH

■ Bars

RICKENBACHERS INN, Granby St, (01509) 21 62 20, hotel bar, gay Tues 19:30-23:00. ♂

ROYAL OAK, High St, (01509) 41 35 06. ♂

WOMEN'S BAR NIGHT, Fennel St, at the Labour Club, (01509) 23 56 10, even Mons 20:30. ♀

LUTON

■ Bars

GREEN DRAGON II, 202 Park St, (01582) 304 46, pub. ♂

SHIRLEY'S TEMPLE, 1 Liverpool Rd, (01582) 254 91, pub, 19:00-23:00 (Thurs-Sat from 12:00, Sun 12:00-22:30). ♂

MAIDENHEAD

■ Bars

GREEN DRAGON, 90 Moorbridge Rd, (01628) 220 42, pub. ♂

MANCHESTER

■ Information

AIDS LINE, (0161) 237 97 17.

LESBIAN & GAY SWITCHBOARD, (0161) 274 39 99, daily 16:00-22:00.

MANCHESTER GAY CENTRE, 49-51 Sidney St, (0161) 274 38 14.

■ Accommodations

CARLTON HOTEL, 153 Upper Chorlton Rd, Whalley Range M16 7SH, (0161) 881 4635, hotel, singles & doubles, color TV. ♀♂

CLONE ZONE MANCHESTER HOLIDAY APT, 39 Bloom St, (44-161) 236 1398, Fax: (44-161) 236 5178, apartment in the heart of the gay & lesbian village, 2 floors above Clone Zone store, color TV, bath/shower, kitchen, tea/coffee-making facilities, near tourist attractions & metro, bus & rail stations. ♀♂

MONROES HOTEL, 38 London Rd, (0161) 236 05 64. Gay-friendly hotel.

REMBRANDT HOTEL (THE REM), 33 Sackville St, (0161) 236 1311, hotel with 2 bars & restaurant, women welcome, shared baths, full English breakfast, color TV. ♂

ROYAL CROWN HOTEL, 37 Swan St, (0161) 8394424, hotel with bar, 20%-30% gay & lesbian clientele on weekends, color TV, minutes from clubs, pubs, full English breakfast, phone 24 hours.

SMITHFIELD HOTEL, 37 Swan St, (44-161) 839 44 24, 25% gay & lesbian clientele on weekends.

■ Bars

AUSTIN'S, 63 Richmond St, in back of New Union Pub, (0161) 236 15 47, daily 22:00-02:00, closed Sun. ♂

BRONX, THE, 98 Bloom St, (0161) 236 65 56, daily till 02:00. ♂

UK - ENGLAND

BULK, 4-6 Whitworth St, at Chains, bar night for big men & bears, last Fri from 22:00. ♂

CASTRO, Canal St, (0161) 237 91 17. ♂

CELLAR LEATHER CLUB, at Napoleon's bar, Fri from 22:30, rubber, leather. ♂

CRUZ 101, 101 Princess St, (0161) 237 15 54, private club, members only, Wed-Sat. ♂

DICKENS, 74a Oldham St, (0161) 236 51 96, Mon-Sat 22:00-02:00. ♀♂

GREEN ROOM, 54-56 Whitworth St West, (0161) 236 16 77. ♂

M.E.N., 48 Princess St, at Time, men-only fetish bar. ♂

MANTO, 46 Canal St, (0161) 236 26 67, café bar & art gallery, 12:00-23:30 (Sun 12:00-23:00). After hours breakfast Fri-Sat 02:00-06:00. ♂

MONROES HOTEL BAR, at Monroes Hotel, 38 London Rd, (0161) 236 05 64.

NEW UNION, Princess St, (0161) 228 14 92, pub, strippers & cabaret. ♂

NEW YORK, 98 Bloom St, (0161) 236 65 56, Sun brunch, open days. ♂

PRAGUE FIVE, Canal St, (0161) 236 9033. ♂

Q BAR, 28 Richmond St, (0161) 237 93 29, private club, Mon-Sat 21:00-01:00, Sun till 23:30. ♂

REMBRANDT HOTEL BAR★, 33 Sackville St, (0161) 236 24 35, 236 11 31, hotel, bar & restaurant, lesbians welcome, open daily 11:00-23:00, Sun lunch. Fri women-only upstairs bar. ♀♂

SAPPHO'S BAR, at Rembrandt Hotel (upstairs), women-only, Fri. ♀

SIN, 4-6 Whitworth St, at Chains, last Fri, fetish bar. ♂

TWO (2)KINKY, Oxford Rd, at Holy City Zoo, (0161) 237 99 24, Fri 22:00-03:00. ♂

UNIVERSAL, Canal St, below Blooms Hotel, at Village Edge, women's bar night, Sat 22:00-02:00. ♀

VELVET, 2 Canal St, (0161) 236 9003. ♂

■ Dance Bar/Disco

CENTRAL PARK, Sackville St, (0161) 236 51 96, pub & cabaret, late dance night Sun 02:30-12:00, women-only disco Fri upstairs. ♀♂

CLIMAX, 11-13 New Wakefield St, at Generation X, (0161) 236 48 99, women-only dance night, 1st Thurs 22:00-03:00. ♀

CLUB LA LA, 17 Whitworth St West, at The Venue, last Wed 03:00-08:00. ♂

GIFT, at Joshua Brooks, (0161) 237 95 49, 2nd Thurs 20:00-23:00; also 22:30-04:00. ♂

NAPOLEON'S, Sackville St at Bloom St, (0161) 236 88 00, nightly, 21:30-02:00. Leather bar downstairs. ♂

PARADISE FACTORY, 112 Paradise St, (0161) 273 5422, 4-floor dance club, Fri-Sat from 20:00, Fri women-only on top level. ♂

POPASTIC, Bloom St, below Blooms Hotel, at Village Edge, Tues. ♂

TIME, 48 Princess St, (0161) 237 99 24, Fri 22:00-03:00, Sat till 04:00, call 2 days ahead for membership. Ask about gay & lesbian dance nights.

■ Cafe

BLOOM STREET CAFE,★ 39 Bloom St, (0161) 236 34 33, Mon-Sat 09:00-18:00. ♀♂

THAT CAFE, 1013 Stockport Rd, Levenshulme, (0161) 432 46 72, cafe, Tues-Sat from 19:30, Sun 12:00-14:30.

VIA FOSSA, 28-30 Canal St, (0161) 236 81 32, 12:00-23:00 (Thurs-Sat till 02:00). ♂

■ Saunas/Health Clubs

EURO SAUNA, 202 Hill Lane in Blackley, (0161) 740 51 52. ♂

■ Restaurants

BLUE RESTAURANT, 29 Sackville St, (0161) 236 00 74, till 24:00.

■ Retail & Bookstores

CLONE ZONE, 37-39 Bloom St (opposite Chorlton St bus stn.), (0161) 236 13 98, magazines, leather & rubber, books, cards, toys, poppers, T-shirts, jeans, fashion clothing & Energize Record Shop (Hi-NRG music center). Mail order available.

FRONTLINE, 1 Newton St, radical bookstore with gay & lesbian section, 10:00-18:00 (Sat from 09:00), closed Sun.

MANSFIELD

■ Dance Bar/Disco

BLUE MONDAY, 61 West Gate, at The Yard, (01623) 2380 999, 4th Mon 21:00-02:00. ♂

MARGATE

■ Bars

NEW INN, THE, New St, (01843) 22 37 99. ♂

SCANDALS BAR, 1 Albert Terrace, (01843) 29 06 16, pub, Fri, Sat dance night. ♂

■ Erotica

PILLOW TALK, 13 Marine Dr, (01843) 29 40 69.

MIDDLESBROUGH

■ Information

AIDS LINE, (01642) 24 45 58.

LESBIAN LINE, (01642) 23 05 30.

MIDDLESBROUGH FRIEND, (01642) 24 88 88, Tues & Fri 19:30-21:30.

■ Bars

CASSIDY'S, Grange Rd, (01642) 22 12 41, 19:00-23:00, restaurant & three separate bars. ♂

NEWCASTLE-UPON-TYNE

■ Information

AIDS INFO, (0191) 232 28 55, Mon-Fri 10:00-19:00, Sat till 16:00.

LESBIAN LINE, (0191) 261 22 77, Tues 19:00-22:00.

NEWCASTLE FRIEND, (0191) 261 85 55, Mon-Fri 19:00-22:00.

■ Accommodations

CHEVIOT VIEW GUEST HOUSE, 194 Station Rd, Wallsend, NE28 8RD, (0191) 2620125, guesthouse with restaurant & bar, women welcome, private & shared baths, colour TV, full English breakfast, pool & ocean beach nearby. ♂

■ Bars

BARKING DOG, THE, 15 Marlborough Crescent, (0191) 221 0775, upstairs bar women-only Wed & Fri. ♀

HEAVENS ABOVE, Churchill St, over Courtyard bar, (0191) 232 20 37, 15:00-23:00 (Sun pub hours). ♂

POWERHOUSE, Blenheim St at Waterloo St, (0191) 261 45 07, gay Mon, Thurs-Sat 22:00-01:00, back bar men only, some hetero clientele. ♂

STRINGS, 29 Blenheim St, (0191) 232 35 30, pub, many women. ♂

TRANS-SISTERED, 29 Blenheim St, at Strings, upper level, (0191) 232 35 30, 20:00-23:00, transvestites & transexuals.

VILLAGE, THE, Sunderland St, near Powerhouse. ♂

■ Dance Bar/Disco

ROCKIES, 78 Scotswood Rd, (0191) 232 65 36, pub with disco Thurs, Sat, Sun. ♂

ROCKSHOTS, Waterloo St, (0191) 232 96 48, gay Mon, Wed, Thurs 23:00-02:00, Sat till 03:00, women welcome. ♂

■ Cafe

TYNESIDE COFFEE ROOMS, 10 Pilgrim St, at Tyneside Cinema, (0191) 261 92 91, 10:00-21:00 (closed Sun). ♂

■ Retail & Bookstores

ALLEYCAT BOOKS COOP, 46 Low Friar St, (0191) 221 17 50, radical bookstore with gay & lesbian titles.

NORFOLK

■ Accommodations

OLD CASE, THE, Fen Rd Blo'Norton Diss, (01379) 898 025, bed & breakfast, women welcome, shared bath, full breakfast, lounge with open fire, no TV. ♂

NORTHAMPTON

■ Information

GAY & LESBIAN LINES, Men (01604) 359 75, Tues 18:30-21:30. Women 397 23 or 25 08 87, Tues 18:30-21:30. Ask about socials.

LESBIAN & GAY RESOURCE CENTRE, 61-

UK - ENGLAND

69 Derngate, at Charles House, (01604) 28 986.

■ Bars
FUDGE, 39 Sheep St, at Kabana's, (01604) 78 76 41, 1st Fri.

KABANA'S, 39 Sheep St, (01604) 228 22, 20:00-01:00 (Thurs-Sat till 02:00, Sun till later), closed Mon.

LESBIAN & GAY NIGHTS, 3-7 Hazelwood Rd, 1st floor, at Junction 7, Tues: women from 18:30, men from 19:00.

■ Dance Bar/Disco
DOMINATION, 39 sheep St, at Kabana's, 3rd Thurs.

■ Cafe
ORTON'S, Roadmenders, at Ladys Lane, Sat 12:00-16:00.

NORWICH

■ Information
AIDS LINE, (01603) 61 58 16, Thurs 20:00-22:00, Sat 11:00-15:00, Sun 14:00-16:00.

NORWICH FRIEND & LESBIAN LINES, (01603) 62 80 55, Fri & Sun 19:00-21:00. Lesbian Line Tues 19:00-21:00.

■ Accommodations
LORD RAGLAN, THE, 30 Bishopbridge Rd, Norwich NR1 4ET, (44-1603) 623 304. B&B with gay bar, colour TV, 24-hr privacy access, coffee & tea-making facilities, short walk to city center.

■ Bars
CLOUDS, above 14/16 Lower Goat Lane, gay Sun from 20:00.

LOFT, 80 Rose Lane, (01603) 62 35 59, 1st Mon from 22:00 & 1st Wed from 20:00. Norwich Friend bar nights Thurs & Sat from 21:00, Sun from 20:00, younger crowd.

LORD RAGLAN, THE, 30 Bishopbridge Rd, (01603) 62 33 04, 12:00-14:00 & 19:00-23:00 (Sun pub hours).

LORD ROSEBERRY, 94 Roseberry Rd, (01603) 48 61 61, men welcome.

■ Dance Bar/Disco
FIRST OUT, King St, at The Waterfront, (01603) 63 27 17, dance bar 1st Tues 20:00-24:30.

JIGSAW CLUB, Oak St at The Talk club, Fri 22:00-02:00, men welcome.

■ Retail & Bookstores
BOOKMARK BOOKSTORE, 83 Unthank Rd, (01603) 76 28 55, general bookstore with gay & lesbian titles.

GREEN CENTRAL, 42-46 Bethel St, general bookstore with gay & lesbian titles.

JT BOOKS, Dove St, (01603) 63 06 36, general bookstore with gay & lesbian section.

NOTTINGHAM

■ Information
GAY & LESBIAN SWITCHBOARD, (0115) 941 14 54, Mon-Fri 19:00-22:00.

LESBIAN CENTRE, 30 Chaucer St, in the Women's Centre, (0115) 948 36 97, scheduled events, lesbian group meets Fri 19:30-22:00, disco 1st Fri from 21:00. Univerifiable spring '97.

LESBIAN LINE, (0115) 941 06 52, Mon & Wed 19:30-21:00.

NOTTINGHAM FRIEND, (0115) 947 47 17, Thurs 19:00-21:30, women answer Tues.

■ Bars
CAFE QUENCH, Byard Ln, Jallans, gay Sun 11:00-23:00.

CAMP, THE, 41 St Marys Gate, at the Lizard Lounge, (0115) 952 32 64, gay 3rd Wed.

CELLO'S, Meadow Lane Stadium, at the Meadow Club, (0115) 961 73 89, call for scheduled women-only night with no-smoking bar.

FORREST TAVERN, North Sherwood St, lesbian-run bar, men welcome.

GATSBY'S★, Huntingdon St, (0115) 950 53 23, 2 bars.

MGM, Greyfriar Gate, (0115) 958 05 55, 1st Mon 21:00-02:00.

STAG & PHEASANT, Lower Parliament St, (0115) 950 64 14, pub hours.

■ Dance Bar/Disco
ADMIRAL DUNCAN, 74 Lower Parliament St, (0115) 950 27 27, Sun-Wed 20:00-23:00, Thurs-Sat till 01:30. Leather group meets alternate Tues.

CARRY ON CAMPING, Station St, at After Dark club, (0115) 958 72 33, Tues 22:00-02:00.

KITSCH CLUB, 19 Greyhound St, (0115) 970 84 51, gay Fri, Sat 10:30-02:00.

REVOLUTION 2, St. James St, at the Deluxe Club, (0115) 947 48 19, gay 3rd Mon 22:00-03:00.

■ Retail & Bookstores
MUSHROOM BOOKSHOP, 10 Heathcote St, (0115) 958 25 06, general bookstore with gay & lesbian selection.

SOHO BOOKS, 147 Radford Rd, (0115) 978 35 67, gay bookshop.

NOTTINGHAMSHIRE

■ Accommodations
BATHLEY GUEST HOUSE, 101 Bathley St, Trent Bridge, (0115) 9862 463, bed & breakfast, exclusively gay, minutes from gay nightlife, women welcome, comfortable rooms, tea-making facilities, full English breakfast, concessions for admission to gay bars.

NUNEATON

■ Bars
HARCOURT, THE, 22 Princess St, (01203) 38 65 85, strippers.

OLDHAM

■ Information
GAY SWITCHBOARD, (0161) 678 94 48, Tues 19:00-21:00.

LESBIAN & GAY SWITCHBOARD, (0161) 678 94 48, Tues 19:00-21:00, ask about socials.

■ Bars
GLAMOUR, Roscoe St, at Goodfellows, (0161) 627 57 77.

■ Dance Bar/Disco
DOROTHY'S NIGHTCLUB, 171 Union St, Rhodes Bank, (0161) 652 56 62, 21:00-02:00 (Sun till 22:30).

PJ'S, 24 Lees Rd, Oldham Mumps, (0161) 624 13 25, cabaret & disco.

■ Saunas/Health Clubs
PENNINE SAUNA, 96 Rochdale Rd, Shaw, (01706) 84 20 00, gay Sun 14:00-22:00, Wed noon-22:00.

OXFORD

■ Information
AIDS LINE, (0800) 39 39 99, Mon, Wed, Fri 18:30-20:30.

GAY SWITCHBOARD, (01865) 79 39 99, 19:00-21:00.

LESBIAN LINE, (01865) 24 23 33, Wed 19:00-21:00.

OXFORD GAY & LESBIAN CENTRE (OLGC), North Gate Hall, St Michael's St, (01865) 20 00 30, gay organization with disco, café & bar. Men-only Thurs 20:00-23:00; Fri women's disco night from 20:00; Sat disco 21:00-02:00. Café: Sat 12:00-16:00. Bar: Sun 19:30-22:30.

■ Cafe
JOLLY FARMERS, Paradise St, (01865) 79 37 59, daily 11:00-23:00, Sun pub hours.

■ Retail & Bookstores
INNER BOOKSHOP, 111 Magdalen Rd, (01865) 24 53 01, alternative bookshop with gay & lesbian section, 10:00-17:30 (closed Sun).

PETERBOROUGH

■ Information
AIDS LINE, (01733) 623 34, Tues & Thurs 19:30-21:30.

GAYLINE, (01733) 70 62 92, Mon, Wed & Fri 19:30-22:00, Sat & Sun 12:00-18:00. Current local information.

PETERBOROUGH FRIEND, (01733) 614 99, Tues & Thurs 19:30-21:30, or tape.

UK – ENGLAND

■ Bars
BRIDGE, London Rd Rd, (01733) 31 21 92. ♂

WORTLEY ALMSHOUSES, Westgate, more gays Wed from 9pm.

YE OLDE BRIDGE INN, The Common, Crowland, (01733) 21 05 67, pub & restaurant, gay 3rd Fri (sometimes also last Fri). ✕ ♂

■ Dance Bar/Disco
HOP, THE, Fletton High St, at the Fleet, Fletton, gay disco night the 1st Fri of the month 21:00-01:00. ♂

PLYMOUTH

■ Information
AIDS INFO, (01752) 66 36 09.
HELP/CHAT LINE, (01752) 56 95 04.

■ Bars
SWALLOW, THE, 59 Breton Side, The Barbican, (01752) 25 17 60, pub. ✕ ♂

■ Dance Bar/Disco
FREEDOM, Mayflower St, at Powerhouse, (01752) 22 00 77, gay last Fri. ♂
ZERO'S NIGHTCLUB, 24 Lockyer St, (01752) 66 23 46, 21:00-02:00 (Sun 20:00-24:00), closed Tues. ♂

■ Retail & Bookstores
IN OTHER WORDS, 72 Mutley Plain, Devon, (0752) 663 889, general bookstore with gay & lesbian books and magazines.

PORTSMOUTH

■ Information
LESBIAN LINE, (01705) 87 69 99, Thurs 20:00-22:00.
SOLENT SWITCHBOARD, (01705) 65 50 77, Wed 19:30-22:00.

■ Bars
DD'S, 164 Twyford Ave, at The Stamshaw Hotel, lower level, women-only bar Mon, Thurs & Sat 19:00-23:00, Sun lunch (closed 2nd Sat). ♀
MARTHA'S, 227 Commercial Rd, (01705) 82 09 62, pub with disco, 22:00-02:00 (Mon, Tues till 01:00), closed Sun. ♂
OLD VIC, St Pauls Rd, (01958) 21 87 96, pub. ♂
TWO-WANDAZ, Eastgate St, at the Network Club, women's disco nights 1st & 3rd Thurs, 21:00-01:00. ♀

■ Dance Bar/Disco
FARPIES, Trafalgar Pl, Clive Rd, at the Fratton Community Centre, women-only disco, Thurs 20:00-22:00, call lesbian line for details. ♀

PRESTON

■ Information
GAY SWITCHBOARD & LESBIAN LINE, (01772) 25 11 22, men answer Tues, Thurs, Fri 19:30-21:30, women answer Wed 19:30-21:30.

■ Bars
DE TABLEY INN, Ribchester Rd, Ribchester, (01254) 87 81 38, pub, Tues 20:00-24:00. ♂
HOLLYWOOD BAR, Deepdale Rd, (01772) 25 30 80, gay Tues. ♂

■ Dance Bar/Disco
STAGE DOOR, 28 Croft St, near Marsh Ln, (01772) 25 12 75, pub, 19:30-23:00 (Sun till 22:30), disco Thurs-Sun. ♀♂

■ Restaurants
CANNONS, 37 Cannon St, (01772) 561 74, 11:00-14:00 & 19:00-23:00 (closed Sun, Mon).

READING

■ Information
AIDS LINE, (01734) 57 61 64, Mon-Thurs 17:00-21:00 or tape.
LESBIAN & GAY LINE, (01734) 59 72 69, Tues, Wed, Fri 19:30-21:30.

■ Bars
WYNFORD ARMS, 110 Kings Rd, 19:30-23:00 (Sat day & evening, Sun pub hours). ♀♂

■ Dance Bar/Disco
AWARENESS, 21 South St, 1st Fri 21:00-01:00. ♂

ROCHDALE

■ Bars
GAVAN'S D, 6 Nelson St, at Club Pazazz, (01706) 71 00 45, every other Tues 22:00-02:00. ♂

■ Saunas/Health Clubs
PENN ST. SAUNA, 1 Penn St, (01706) 52 77 86, 12:00-22:00 (Sun from 14:00).

ROCHESTER

■ Bars
SHIP INN, 347 High St, enter from Ship Lane, (01634) 84 42 64. ♂

ST. ALBANS

■ Information
AIDS INFO, (01462) 45 47 44, Mon-Fri 19:00-21:00.

■ Bars
GUYS & DOLLS, Lyre Lane, at Bricket Wood Country Club, Sun 19:00-24:00. ♂
VERULAM MSC, Redbourn Rd, at Spritzers, leather group meets last Wed 21:00. ♂

■ Dance Bar/Disco
DIVA FEVER, Redbourn Rd, at Spritzers, (01582) 79 40 53, 1st & 3rd Thurs from 20:00. ♀

SALISBURY

■ Information
GAY & LESBIAN SWITCHBOARD, (01722) 41 50 51, Wed 19:30-22:30, ask about scheduled cafe night.

■ Bars
DUKE OF YORK, 34 York Rd, (01722) 32 40 92, 7 days. ♂

SCARBOROUGH

■ Bars
BACCHUS, 7a Ramshill Rd, Fri & Sat. ♀♂

SHEFFIELD

■ Information
AIDS LINE, (0114) 275 55 00, Mon-Fri 19:00-22:00.
GAYPHONE, (0114) 258 81 99, Mon-Wed 19:30-21:30, ask about gay socials.
WOMEN'S CULTURAL CLUB, Paternoster Row, Workstation, (0114) 272 18 66, 11:00-23:00, scheduled socials, events, women's bar nights.

■ Bars
BULLDOG, 387 Altercliffe Rd, (0114) 244 21 80, Bears Club men's group meets 1st Fri. ♂
BUT & BEN, 45 Howard St, (0114) 272 28 89, pub & disco, Fri women only. ♂
NORFOLK ARMS, 195 Carlisle St, (0114) 275 2469, 2 bars. ♂
PEACH, Eyre St, at Club Uropa, 2nd Mon 22:00-02:00. ♂
RUTLAND ARMS, 86 Brown St, (0114) 272 90 03. ♂

■ Dance Bar/Disco
CAVALIERS, ★ 208 Saville St E, (0114) 278 03 83, patio. ♂
CLUB, THE, 429 Effingham Rd, (0114) 244 01 10, 22:00-02:00 (Sun 20:00-01:00), closed Mon & Tues. Women-only dance night last Wed. ♂
DELICIOUS, Charter Square at Cuba, behind Kikis, (0114) 275 45 00, Fri 22:00-02:00. ♂
QUEEN'S HOTEL 85 Scotland St, (0114) 272 69 09, hotel with scheduled women-only dance nights. ♀♂

■ Retail & Bookstores
INDEPENDENT BOOKSHOP, 69 Surrey St, (0114) 273 77 22, general bookstore with gay & lesbian titles.

SHREWSBURY

■ Bars
PEACH TREE, 21 Abbey Foregate, (01743) 35 50 55, gay Mon. ♀♂

■ Cafe
FRUIT BOWL, 1a Wyle Cop Steps, unit 3, Reilley Centre, Sat 12:00-17:00. ♀♂

SHROPSHIRE

■ Accommodations
COCKFORD HALL, Cockford Bank, Clun, Shropshire 5Y7 8LR, (44-1588) 640 327, Fax:

UK - ENGLAND

(44-1588) 640 881. Gay-friendly, luxury Georgian B&B, rural retreat on 20 acres above historic town of Clun. Full breakfast, 3-course dinner by arrangement at extra charge, all private baths.

SKEGNESS

■ Dance Bar/Disco
OBSESSION, at the Kings Head, in nearby town of Gunby, (01754) 89 06 38, bar & restaurant with a gay dance night Fri only 20:00-02:00.

SLOUGH

■ Dance Bar/Disco
GREYHOUND, Colnbrook Bypass, (01932) 68 49 20, disco with patio, Mon-Fri 12:00-16:00 & 20:00-02:00, Sat 12:00-17:00 & 20:00-02:00, Sun 19:00-24:00.

SOMERSET

■ Accommodations
BALES MEAD, West Porlock, TA24 8NX, (01643) 862565, country house B&B, private & shared baths, expanded continental or full breakfast, color TV, central heating, panoramic views of sea & countryside, 50% gay/lesbian clientele.

MANOR HOUSE FARM, Prestleigh, nr Shepton Mallet, (01749) 830 385, bed & breakfast with restaurant, private & shared baths, TV lounge, coffe/tea making facilities, full breakfast.

MODEL FARM, Perry Green, Wembdon, TA5 2BA England, (01278) 423870, guesthouse, recently renovated double rooms with historic elegance & modern conveniences, tea/coffee tray, nearby pool & ocean beach, full breakfast.

SOUTHAMPTON

■ Information
LESBIAN LINE, (01703) 40 51 11, Tues & Thurs 19:30-22:00.

SOLENT GAY SWITCHBOARD & AIDS INFO, (01703) 63 73 63, Mon, Tues & Thurs, Fri 19:30-22:00.

■ Bars
ATLANTIC QUEEN, Bugle St, (01703) 22 91 46, piano bar, women welcome.

MAGNUM, ★ 113 St Mary's Rd, (01703) 33 50 49, from 21:30, weekends till 02:00.

PINKYS, Northam Rd, Northam, (01703) 33 28 30, leather bar & 2 other bars, Mon-Sat 11:00-23:00, Sun day & eve.

ROBERT BURNS, THE, 9 South Front, (01703) 23 38 74.

SMUGGLERS ARMS, Bernard St, pub.

STRAND, Canal Walk, in back of Queensway, pub.

■ Retail & Bookstores
OCTOBER BOOKS, 4 Onslow Rd, (01703) 22 44 89, general bookstore with gay section.

SOUTHEND-ON-SEA

■ Information
AIDS LINE, (01702) 39 17 50, answers Mon-Fri 18:00-21:30.

SOUTHEND GAYLINE, (01702) 48 03 44.

■ Bars
BUZZIN, Pier Hill, at the Palace Hotel, Fri 22:00-02:00.

■ Dance Bar/Disco
CLIFF HOTEL BAR, 48 Hamlet Rd, (01702) 34 44 66, Mon-Sat 11:00-23:00, Sun 12:00-22:30, leather club meets 1st Sat 21:30.

ENIGMA, 9 Elmer Approach, at Club Art, (01702) 33 32 77, Fri 21:00-02:00.

STAMFORD

■ Bars
THREE TOWERS, 39 Broad St, (01780) 557 51, 1st Sun.

STOCKPORT

■ Dance Bar/Disco
NEW INN, THE, 93 Wellington Rd South, (0161) 480 40 63. disco Fri & Sat, pub weekdays.

PRAGUE, Turncroft Lane, Offerton, (0161) 476 36 66, gay Fri, Sat, DJs.

STOCKTON

■ Bars
CELLAR 37, Dovecote St, (01642) 61 50 68, till 02:00 (last Sun till 24:00).

STOKE-ON-TRENT

■ Information
AIDS INFO, (01782) 20 12 51, Thurs 19:00-21:30.

■ Bars
CLUB & CLUB RUBY'S, 14 Hillcrest St, Hanley, (01782) 20 18 29.

THREE TUNS, Bucknall New Rd, Hanley, pub, Sun-Wed pub hours, Thurs-Sat all day.

STRATFORD UPON AVON

■ Bars
WILD MOOR INN, Alcester Rd, (01789) 26 70 63, gay Wed only 21:30-02:00.

SUNDERLAND

■ Bars
BB'S, W. Sunnyside, (0191) 510 08 44, downstairs bar, Wed 19:00-23:30.

SUTTON-IN-ASHFIELD

■ Bars
BELL, THE, Mansfield Rd, (01623)55 97 26, last Mon 19:00-23:30.

TAUNTON

■ Dance Bar/Disco
BANANA BAR, enter from rear of The Loft, at Kingston's Nightclub, (01823) 32 70 78, 1st Sat 21:00-01:00.

TEBAY

■ Women's Accommodations
FAWCETT MILL FIELDS, Fawcett Mill Fields, Gaisgill, Tebay, Penrith CA10 3UB, (015396) 244 08. Accommodation in the town of Gaisgill, near Tebay & south of the city of Penrith, holds special women's weekends & women's events.

TORQUAY

■ Accommodations
CLIFF HOUSE HOTEL AT THE BEACH, St Marks Rd, Meadfoot Beach, (01803) 294 656, Fax: 211 983, Luxury hotel overlooking ocean with restaurant & bar, rooms have bygone elegance with modern amenities, colour TV, coffee/tea making facilities, Jacuzzi, steam room, massage, gym, full English breakfast.

OCEAN HOUSE HOTEL, Hundson Rd, (01803) 29 65 38. Hotel with bar & restaurant.

RAVENSWOOD HOTEL, 535 Babbacombe Rd, (01803) 292 900 (tel/fax), hotel & residents' bar, 20% gay/lesbian clientele, private & shared baths, full English breakfast, dinner optional, color cable TV, late night keys.

RED SQUIRREL LODGE, Chelston Rd, England, Tel/fax: (01803) 605496, gay-friendly hotel with bar, elegant Victorian rooms, colour TV, beverage-making facilities, private baths, gardens, nearby ocean beach, full English breakfast.

■ Bars
BAR ATLANTIQUE, Hundson Rd, at Ocean House Hotel, (01803) 29 65 38.

CLIFF HOUSE HOTEL BAR, at Cliff House Hotel.

DOUBLE TWO CLUB, Rock Road, (01803) 29 22 79, Mon-Sat 21:30-01:00.

IBIZA, 3-4 Victoria Parade, below Queens Hotel, (01803) 21 43 34, large bar, 20:00-24:00 (Sun 19:00-22:30), DJs Fri & Sat.

LOUIE'S WINE BAR, Torhill Rd, Castle Circus, (01803) 21 22 27, 11:00-23:00 (Sun 12:00-22:30).

MEADFOOT INN, 7 Meadfoot Lane, (01803) 29 71 12, gay pub.

■ Dance Bar/Disco
FREEDOM, Victoria Parade, Harbourside at Ritzy Nightclub, (01803) 29 50 78, gay 2nd Tues.

JUICY FRUITS, Belgrave Rd, at Judy G's, (01803) 21 11 31, 1st Tues.

MONROE'S, Victoria Rd, (01803) 29 11 49, Thurs-Sat 21:00-01:00. Leather group meets last Thurs.

TYNE - WEAR

■ *Accommodations*

STRATFORD LODGE, 8 Stratford Grove Terrace, Newcastle upon Tyne, (0191) 265 6395, bed & breakfast, shared baths, colour satellite TV, beverage-making facilities, expanded continental breakfast, massage & solarium. ♀♂

WARWICK

■ *Bars*

ANTELOPE INN PUB, Birmingham Rd, at The Antelope Inn, (01926) 49 90 35, from 19:00, 80% men, 20% women. ♂

WARWICKSHIRE

■ *Accommodations*

ELLESMERE HOUSE, 36 Binswood Ave, Leamington Spa, (01926) 424 618, Victorian bed & breakfast homestay, women welcome, spacious rooms with antique furnishings, private baths, color TV, full English breakfast. ♂

WATFORD

■ *Information*

GAY INFO, (01923) 77 35 70, 19:00-22:00.

■ *Bars*

GLOW, Local Board Rd, at the Pump House Theatre, (01923) 24 32 73, Tues 20:30-23:00. ♀♂

WELLINGBOROUGH

■ *Information*

GAY INFO LINE, (01933) 271 1871, Thurs 19:00-22:00. Ask about gay & lesbian socials.

■ *Dance Bar/Disco*

IDEAL, 17 Glenbank, (01832) 71 06 71, Fri 21:00-02:00. ♂

SAPPHO'S, The Embankment, at the Embankment Club, women's disco 1st Fri 19:30-23:30. ♀

WELLS-NEXT-THE-SEA

■ *Accommodations*

WARHAM OLD POST OFFICE COTTAGE, c/o Three Horse Shoes Free House, in Warham near Wells-next-the-Sea, Fakenham (01328) 710 547, Gay-friendly bed & breakfast with restaurant & bar near North Norfolk Coast, private & shared baths, full breakfast, TV lounge, 20% gay & lesbian clientele.

■ *Bars*

THREE HORSESHOES, Bridge Street, Warham 4 miles from Walsingham gay-friendly pub, frequented by gay men & women.

WESTON-SUPER-MARE

■ *Accommodations*

ALMOND LODGE, 42 Clevedon Rd, Weston-super-Mare, Avon, (01934) 625 113, guesthouse near beach & town centre, 50% gay & lesbian clientele, double rooms, color satellite TV, tea/coffee-making facilities, shared bath, full breakfast.

■ *Bars*

LODGE, THE, Oxford St, (01934) 62 98 44, 20:30-01:00 (Thurs-Sat till 02:00), Sun 20:00-24:00. ♂

SCALLYS, 12 Carlton St, (01934) 64 40 13, 11:00-15:00 & 19:00-23:00 (Fri 11:00-23:00), Sun pub hours. ♂

WINCHESTER

■ *Bars*

CAFE PRIDE, 25 City Rd, (01962) 84 06 74, Sun 17:30-21:00. ♂

WOLVERHAMPTON

■ *Information*

AIDS LINE, (01902) 64 48 94, Mon, Tues & Thurs 09:00-17:00, Wed & Fri till 12:00.

■ *Bars*

BABE, Temple St, at the Dorchester Club, 1st Thurs. ♀

BRIDGE 59, Bridge North Rd, Compton, (01902) 75 90 49. ♂

GREYHOUND, 14 Bond St, (01902) 209 16, pub, women welcome. ♂

KEVANS, 72-73 Darling St (enter from Clarence St), (01902) 241 12, 22:30-02:00 (Fri, Sat from 21:30, Sun 21:30-24:00). ♂

LORD RAGLAN, Great Brickkiln St, (01902) 228 87, till 02:00 (Sun till 24:00). ♀♂

MONROES, Birchills St, at the Golden Lion, Walsall, (01922) 324 29, disco & lounge, 19:30-02:00 (Sun till 23:30), many TVs. ♂

WHITE HART, ★ 66 Worcester St, (01902) 217 01, pub. ♂

■ *Dance Bar/Disco*

COTTON EYE JOE CLUB, at The Golden Lion, in Walsall, (01543) 42 44 60, country western & line dancing Thurs. ♂

GAVAN'S, at The Dorchester, (01192) 71 66 76, gay dance nights Sat, Sun. ♂

WORCESTER

■ *Bars*

POTTERS WHEEL, 42 Severn St, (01905) 72 60 88, 12:00-15:00 & 20:00-23:00 (Mon only 20:00-23:00), frequented by gays.

STRICTLY YUM, Forgate St, at Chambers Wine Bar, (01378) 64 52 39, gay Tues. ♂

■ *Dance Bar/Disco*

REFLEX, The Butts, at Images Club, Tues 21:30-01:30. ♂

YORK

■ *Information*

AIDS LINE, (01904) 63 95 95, Tues 19:00-22:00, Thurs 15:00-19:00.

GAY SWITCHBOARD, (01904) 61 28 28.

LESBIAN LINE, (01904) 64 68 12, Fri 19:00-21:00 or tape, ask about local lesbian group.

■ *Accommodations*

BULL LODGE, 37 Bull Lane, Lawrence St, (01904) 415 522 (tel/fax), guesthouse, gay-friendly, comfortable rooms with beverage-making facilities, near pool & leisure center, full English breakfast, optional evening meal.

■ *Bars*

CHURCHILL HOTEL, Bootham, (01904) 64 44 56, bar & restaurant. ✗♂

MILK & HONEY, Mickelgate, at the York Arts Centre, (01904) 62 71 29, 1st Fri 21:00-02:00. ♀♂

WHITE HORSE, Bootham St, pub. ♂

YORK ARMS, THE, 26 High Petergate near the Minster, many gays.

■ *Dance Bar/Disco*

GUPPY'S, The Old Brit, Nunnery Lane, women's dance bar twice monthly, contact lesbian line for schedule. ♀

■ *Erotica*

BLUE STAR, 1 Victoria St, near Nunery Ln, (01904) 62 49 01, open Tues-Sun.

YORKSHIRE

■ *Accommodations*

INTERLUDES, 32 Princess St, Old Town, Scarborough, (01723) 360513, fax (01273) 368597, hotel, 50% gay & lesbian clientele, well-equipped rooms, colour TV, coffee & tea-making facilities, full breakfast, ocean beach nearby.

PAULEDA HOUSE HOTEL, 123 Clifton, (01904) 634745, fax 621327, gay-friendly hotel with restaurant, gay male following, variety of rooms, private baths, colour TV, phone, choice of breakfast, optional evening meals.

SUN HOTEL, 124 Sunbridge Rd, W Yorkshire, (44-1274) 737 722, fax: (44-1274) 738 364. Hotel with gay & lesbian pub, shared baths (planning en suite facilities), English breakfast, color TV, near Lake District. ♀♂

UK - NORTHERN IRELAND

COUNTRY CODE: (44)

BELFAST

■ *Information*

AIDS LINE, (01232) 32 61 17, Mon, Wed 19:30-20:00, Sat 14:00-17:00.

CARA FRIEND, (01232) 32 20 23, Mon-Wed 19:30-22:00.

LESBIAN LINE, (01232) 23 86 68, Thurs 19:30-22:00.

■ *Bars*

PARLIAMENT BAR, Dunbar St, bar with disco. ♂

UK – NORTHERN IRELAND

■ *Dance Bar/Disco*
CROW'S NEST, Skipper St near High St. ♂

NETWORK, 11a Lower North St, (01232) 23 74 86, gay & lesbian disco Mon 21:00-01:30.

DERRY

■ *Information*
GAY & LESBIAN LINE, (01504) 26 31 20, Thurs 20:00-22:00.

■ *Retail & Bookstores*
BOOKWORM, 16 Bishop St, (01504) 26 16 16, gay & lesbian selection.

UK – SCOTLAND
COUNTRY CODE: (44)

WHO TO CALL
For Tour Companies Serving This Destination
See Scotland on page 25

ABERDEEN

■ *Information*
ABERDEEN LESBIAN GROUP, Shoe Ln, at the Women's Centre, (01224) 62 50 10, Wed 20:00-22:00.

AIDS HELPLINE, (01224) 57 40 00, or Body Positive Grampian: (01224) 40 44 08, 24hr tape.

GAY & LESBIAN SWITCHBOARD, (01224) 63 35 00, Tues 14:00-17:00, Wed & Fri 19:-22:00.

WOMEN'S CENTRE, Shoe Lane, (01224) 625 010, lesbians welcome, 09:30-14:30, Sat lunch club 12:00-14:00.

■ *Dance Bar/Disco*
CLUB CABERFEIDH, 9 Hadden St, (01224) 21 21 81, dance bar & pub, 22:00-02:00 (closed Mon).

SWEET, Triplekirks, Schoolhill, at Exodus, upper level, (01244) 624 288, Fri 22:00-02:00, DJ.

AVIEMORE

■ *Accommodations*
AUCHENDEAN LODGE HOTEL, Dulnain Bridge, nr Grantown-On-Spey, Inverness-shire, (01479) 85 347 (tel/fax). An Edwardian country hunting lodge, now an elegant, gay-friendly inn with restaurant, private & shared baths, full breakfast, furnished in antiques, with spectacular views, skiing, walking, fishing, golfing.

AYR

■ *Information*
GAY & LESBIAN SWITCHBOARD, (01292) 61 90 00, Mon, Wed, Fri 19:00-22:00, or tape.

■ *Accommodations*
ROSELAND GUEST HOUSE, 15 Charlotte Street, (01292) 283435 (tel/fax), gay-friendly bed & breakfast, variety of rooms, colour TV, beverage-making facilities, shared bath, nearby pool & ocean beach, full breakfast.

DUMFRIES – GALLOWAY

■ *Information*
LESBIAN & GAY LINE, (01387) 691 61, Thurs 19:30-21:30 or leave message, ask about schedule for lesbian & gay group meetings in local hetero bars and special disco nights.

DUNDEE

■ *Information*
AIDS INFO, (01382) 461 555, Tues 14:00-16:00, ask for Body Positive.

LESBIAN & GAY SWITCHBOARD, (01382) 202 620, Mon 19:00-22:00.

■ *Bars*
DEVA'S, ★ 75 Seagate, (01382) 2268 40, Mon-Sat 11:00-24:00, Sun 12:30-23:00, women's nights.

■ *Dance Bar/Disco*
LIBERTY NIGHTCLUB, 124 Seagate, (01382) 200 660, 23:00-02:30 (Sun from 22:30), closed Mon-Wed.

EDINBURGH

■ *Information*
BODY POSITIVE, (0131) 652 0754, answers Mon-Fri. HIV+ gay men's social Sun 14:00-18:00.

GAY & LESBIAN SWITCHBOARD, (0131) 556 40 49, 7 days 19:30-22:00.

LESBIAN & GAY COMMUNITY CENTRE, 58a-60 Broughton St, (0131) 557 26 25, 11:00-23:00 (Sun from 12:00), this centre houses several gay businesses.

LESBIAN LINE, (0131) 557 07 51, Mon & Thurs 19:30-22:00.

WOMEN'S CENTRE, 61a Broughton St, (0131) 557 3179, ask about lesbian & feminist group meetings Tues 20:00-21:30, social for lesbians over 45, first Sat 13:00-17:00.

■ *Accommodations*
AMARYLLIS GUEST HOUSE, 21 Upper Gilmore Place, EH3 9NL, (0131) 229 3292, some hetero clientele, private & shared baths, full breakfast, coffee/tea-making facilities.

ARIES GUEST HOUSE, 5 Upper Gilmore Place, (131) 229 4669. Small lesbian-owned &-run guesthouse in central Edinburgh. Private & shared baths, full Scottish breakfast, minutes to Princess Street, castle & Old Town, near gay bars. Some hetero clientele.

ARMADILLO GUEST HOUSE, THE, 12 Gilmore Pl, (0131) 229 6457, guesthouse, some hetero clientele, shared baths, color TV, beverage-making facilities, phone, laundry facilities.

GARLANDS GUEST HOUSE, 48 Pilrig St, (0131) 554 4205 (tel/fax), Non-smoking B&B with private baths, color TV, tea- & coffee-making facilities, near gay venues.

LINDEN HOTEL, 9-13 Nelson St, (0131) 557 4344, fax: (0131) 558 7170, hotel with bar & restaurant.

MANSFIELD HOUSE, 57 Dublin St, EH3 6NL (0131) 556 7980 (tel/fax), centrally located guesthouse, variety of elegantly furnished rooms, color TV, private & shared baths, continental breakfast.

REGIS HOUSE, 57 Gilmore Place, (0131) 229-4057, gay-friendly guesthouse, private & shared baths.

■ *Bars*
CC BLOOM'S, Greenside Place, (0131) 556 9331, bar with disco & restaurant, 18:00-03:00.

FOUR BBBBS CLUB, 26b Dublin St, at New Town bar, bar night for big men & Bears, 4th Fri 20:00-01:00 (members only till 22:00). ♂

FRENCH CONNECTION, 89 Rose St Lane North, (0131) 225 7561, small bar, 12:00-01:00 (Sun from 13:00).

INTENSE, 26b Dublin St, at New Town bar, lower level, Thurs 21:00-01:00.

LORD NELSON BAR, 9-13 Nelson St at Linden Hotel, (0131) 557 43 34, open till 01:00, popular Sun afternoon. ♂

NEWTOWN BAR, 26B Dublin St, (0131) 538 7775, 12:00-01:00 (Sun from 12:30).

ORANGE, 20 Calton Rd, at Calton Studios, (0131) 558 3758, alternate Sat.

ROUTE 66, 6 Baxter's Place, (0131) 556 5991, 12:30-01:00.

TOMMY THAI'S BAR, 9-13 Nelson St, at the Linden Hotel, bar & restaurant, Thai cuisine.

■ *Dance Bar/Disco*
FRUIT SHOP, 12 Shandwick Pl, at Walker's Nightclub, Sun 22:00-03:00.

INTENSE, 26B Dublin St, at the Newtown Bar, men-only dance & cruise bar, 19:00-01:00 (closed Mon-Wed). Weekends women welcome as guests.

JOY, Cowgate, at Wilkie House, (0131) 467 2551, Sat from 22:00.

TASTE, 36 Blair St, at the Honeycomb, (0131) 557 4656, 23:00-03:00, DJs.

■ *Cafe*
BLACK BO'S, 57-61 Blackfriars St, (0131) 557 6136, vegetarian cuisine.

BLUE MOON CAFE, 36 Broughton St, (0131) 557 0911, a center for gay and lesbian socializing, 09:00-01:00, women only Fri.

CAFE KUDOS, 22 Greenside Place, (0131) 556 4349, 12:00-02:00. ♂

CAFE LUCIA, 13-29 Nicholson St, at the Edinburgh Festival Theatre. frequented by gays & lesbians.

CAFE STREUSELKUCHEN, 60 Broughton St, at the Lesbian & Gay Community Centre,

UK - WALES

(0131) 478 7068, 11:00-21:00 (closed Mon).

CITY CAFE, 19 Blair St, (0131) 220 0125, 09:30-23:00 (Sun 12:00-18:00).

CYBERIA, 88 Hanover St, (0131) 220 4403, café with internet access, 10:00-22:00, frequented by gays.

OVER THE RAINBOW CAFE, 32c Broughton St, (0131) 557 8969, 11:00-01:00, frequented by gays.

■ Saunas/Health Clubs

NO. 18 SAUNA, 18 Albert Place, Leith Walk, (0131) 553 3222, 12:00-22:00 (Sun from 14:00).

■ Retail & Bookstores

BOBBIES BOOKSHOP, 220 Morrison St, (0131) 538 7069, general bookstore with gay & lesbian section, Mon-Sat 10:00-17:30.

PJ'S WATCHES & GIFTS, 60 Broughton St, at the Gay & Lesbian Center, (0131) 558 8174, 12:00-19:99 (Sun till 17:00).

WEST & WILDE BOOKSHOP, 25a Dundas St, (0131) 556 0079, gay & lesbian bookshop, 10:00-19:00 (Sun & Mon 12:00-17:00).

■ Erotica

FANTASIES, 8b Drummond St, (0131) 557 8336, 10:00-21:00 (Sun from 12:00).

FALKIRK

■ Bars

DROOKIT DUCK, Graham's Rd, (01324) 613 644, discreetly frequented by some gays.

GLASGOW

■ Information

BODY POSITIVE, (0141) 332 5010.

GAY & LESBIAN CENTRE, 11 Dixon St, (0141) 221 7203, this center houses several gay businesses, 10:00-22:00.

LESBIAN LINE, (0141) 552 3355, Wed 19:00-22:00.

WOMEN'S LIBRARY, 109 Trongate, 4th & 5th floors, (0141) 552 8345, fiction, non-fiction, postcards & information, Tues-Fri 13:00-18:00, Sat 14:00-17:00.

■ Bars

AUSTIN'S, 183a Hope St, (0141) 332 2707, Mon-Sat 12:00-24:00, Sun from 12:30, more gay in evenings.

CAFÉ DELMONICA'S,★ 68 Virginia St, (0141) 552 4803, pub, daily 12:00-24:00.

COURT BAR, 69 Hutcheson St, (0141) 552 2463, small, gay in evenings, Mon-Sat 11:00-24:00, Sun 20:30-23:00.

MADAME GILLESPIE'S, 26 Cheapside St, (0141) 221 2929, 20:30-03:00, closed Mon.

POLO LOUNGE, 84 Wilson St. ♂

SADIE FROST'S, 8-10 West George ST, (0141) 332 8005, 12:00-24:00, upscale bar with some hetero clientele. Sappho's women's bar on premises.

SAPPHO'S,★ 8-10 West George St, at Sadie Frost's bar, (0141) 332 8005, 19:00-24:00. ♀

SQUIRES LOUNGE,★ 106 West Campbell St, (0141) 221 9184, 12:00-24:00 (Sat from 12:30, Sun from 20:00), lunchtimes frequented by hetero clientele.

WATERLOO BAR,★ 306 Argyle St, (0141) 221 7359, 12:00-24:00 (Sun from 12:30).

■ Dance Bar/Disco

BENNETS DISCO★, 90 Glassford St, (0141) 552 5761, Wed-Sat 22:30-03:30.

CLUB X, 25 Royal Exchange Sq, (0141) 204 45 99, 23:00-03:00.

HATT CLUB, 228 Clyde St, (0141) 204 1404, Fri-Sun.

LOVE BOUTIQUE, Midland St, at the Arches, (0141) 221 9736, 1st Sat 22:30-03:00.

■ Cafe

CHISOLM'S COFFEE SHOP, 145 Kenmure St, 09:00-17:30, Sun 11:00-17:00.

GAY & LESBIAN CENTRE CAFE, 11 Dixon St, (0141) 204 5418, 10:00-23:00 (Sun till 17:00).

■ Retail & Bookstores

PJ'S WATCHES & GIFTS, 11 Dixon St, (0141) 226 9977, 12:00-19:00 (Sun till 18:00).

INVERNESS

■ Information

AIDS INFO, (01463) 711 585, Mon-Fri 09:00-17:00.

■ Bars

NICO'S BAR & BISTRO, at the Glen Mhor Hotel, Ness Bank, discreetly frequented by gays, more gays Wed & Fri 21:00-23:00.

ISLE OF BUTE

■ Accommodations

ARDMORY HOUSE HOTEL, Ardmory Rd, (44-1700) 502346, Fax: (44-1700) 505596, E-mail: Ardmory.House.Hotel@DIAL.PIPEX.COM. Gay-friendly hotel with restaurant & bar, 60 min. from Glasgow, 30 min. Wemyss Bay ferry, full break., dinner avail., priv. baths, garden, color TV, tele., gay male following.

KILMARNOCK

■ Bars

KAYPARK TAVERN, 27-29 London Rd, (01563) 523 623, more gays Mon (in lounge area).

STIRLING

■ Information

FORTH FRIEND, (01786) 4712 85, Mon 19:30-21:30. Ask about group meetings alternate Wed.

■ Bars

BARNTON BISTRO, 3 Barnton St, discreetly frequented by gays, younger crowd, Mon-Sat 10:15-23:00, Sun 18:30-23:00.

UK - WALES
COUNTRY CODE: (44)

WHO TO CALL
For Tour Companies Serving This Destination
See Wales on page 29

ABERYSTWYTH

■ Information

LESBIAN & GAY LINE, (01970) 62 17 18, Tues 18:00-20:00.

■ Women's Accommodations

WOMEN'S LODGINGS, (44-1974) 202 231. Women-only accommodation, 1 double room with shared bath in a private home, 9 miles south of Aberystwyth. ♀

■ Bars

BOAR'S HEAD, Queens Rd, (01970) 62 61 06, more gays Fri & Sat.

TREEHOUSE, 2 Pier St, (01970) 61 57 91, gay 2nd Tues 19:00-21:30. ♀♂

AMMANFORD - DYFED

■ Accommodations

APPLE COTTAGE, 35 New Rd, Gwaun-Cae-Gurwen, (01269) 824072, self-contained stone cottage, men welcome, fully-equipped kitchen, color TV, linens, open fire range, oil central heat, hot water, thermostatically-controlled shower. ♂

BANGOR

■ Information

GAY & LESBIAN LINE, (01248) 35 12 63, men answer Fri 19:00-21:00, women answer Tues 19:00-21:00.

BRECON BEACONS

■ Accommodations

TYBESTA TOLFRUE, Brecon, (44-1874) 611 115, B&B in the heart of Brecon Beacons National Park, full breakfast, color TV, coffee/tea-making facilities, TV lounge, maid service, nearby pool & gym. ♀♂

CARDIFF

■ Information

AIDS LINE, (01222) 22 34 43, Mon & Fri 10:00-22:00.

CARDIFF FRIEND, (01222) 34 01 01, Tues-Sat 20:00-22:00.

LESBIAN LINE, (01222) 37 40 51, Tues 20:00-22:00.

■ Accommodations

COURTFIELD HOTEL, 101 Cathedral Rd,

UK - WALES

(01222) 227 701, gay-friendly hotel with restaurant & bar, tastefully-decorated rooms with tea making facilities, private & shared baths, pool nearby, full Welsh breakfast, vegetarian cuisine available.

■ Bars
CLUB X, 39 Charles St, across from Exit Bar, (01222) 64 57 21, Wed-Sat 22:00-02:00. ♂
COURTFIELD HOTEL BAR, bar & restaurant in gay-friendly hotel, mainly hetero clientele be discreet. ⚥
KINGS CROSS, THE, Hayes Bridge Rd at Caroline St, gay pub. ♂

■ Dance Bar/Disco
EXIT BAR, 48 Charles St, (01222) 64 01 02. ⚥

■ Cafe
PRIDE CAFE, 39 Charles St, at Club X, upstairs 11:00-23:00. ♂

■ Saunas/Health Clubs
LOCKER ROOM, 50 Charles St, (01222) 22 03 88, gay sauna, 13:00-24:00 (Sat till 08:). ♂

FISHGUARD - DYFED

■ Accommodations
MERTON HALL, Dinas Cross, Newport, (01348) 811 223, gay-friendly B&B country guesthouse, 50% straight clientele, gay male following, shared baths, TV lounge, Jacuzzi, sauna, sunbed, nearby beach, full break. ⚥

LAMPETER

■ Women's Accommodations
SILVERWEED B&B, Post Office House, Park-y-rhos, Cwmann, Lampeter, Dyfed, SA48 8DZ, (44-1570) 423 254. Women-only B&B in village of Park-y-rhos, 2 miles from Lampeter. Jewelry-making courses avail., vegetarian breakfast, light lunch on course days. Cambrian Mountains nearby, 16 miles to sea. ♀

LLANDUDNO

■ Bars
BROADWAY BOULEVARD, Mostyn Broadway, (01492) 87 96 14, alternate Mon 20:30-00:30. ⚥

NEWPORT

■ Information
AIDS LINE, (01633) 22 34 56, Wed 19:30-21:00.

■ Bars
LOG BOX, High St, at the Carpenters Arms, gay in rear bar. ♂

■ Dance Bar/Disco
COTTON CLUB, Cumbrian Rd, 2nd Tues. ⚥ ♂

PONTYPRIDD

■ Accommodations
LAN FARM, Graigwen, Mid-Glamorgan, (01443) 403-606, 403-629, farmhouse bed & breakfast, single or double rooms, tea/coffee making facilities, refrigerator, private baths, sitting room with fireplace, full breakfast. ♀ ♂

POWYS

■ Accommodations
FACHWEN GANOL, Llwydiarth, Llangadfan, (44-1938) 820 595, women-only guesthouse in a 17th-century Welsh farmhouse, shared baths, full breakfast, lounge, books, games, large garden, 15 miles to Shropshire border, 10 miles to Snowdonia, 30 miles from the West Coast. ♀

SNOWDONIA NAT'L. PARK

■ Accommodations
DEWIS CYFARFOD, Llandderfel, near Bala, (44-1678) 530 243. Women's guest house, en suite baths, TV, beverage-making facilities, full or continental breakfast, art tuition available for groups or individuals, painting & sculpture also available. ♀
PENNANT HALL, Beach Rd, Penmaenmawr, Conwy, N Wales LL34 6AY, (44-1492) 622 878. Hotel with restaurant & bar, private baths, expanded continental breakfast, colour TV, Jacuzzi, ocean nearby, women welcome. ♂

■ Bars
JACK'S HYDRO, Beach Rd, at Pennant Hall, Penmaenmawr, (01492) 62 28 78, hotel bar. ♂

SWANSEA

■ Information
AIDS LINE, (01792) 45 63 03, Thurs 15:00-20:00.
LESBIAN & GAY SWITCHBOARD, (01792) 30 18 55, Tues 19:00-22:00.
LESBIAN LINE, (01792) 65 19 95, Wed 19:00-21:00.

■ Bars
CHAMPERS, 210 High St, (01792) 65 56 22, pub, discreetly frequented by some gays.
CHATTAMS BAR, High St, in the Grand Hotel, across from train station. ♂
PULLMAN BAR, 63-64 High St. ⚥

■ Dance Bar/Disco
PALACE CLUB, THE, 154 High St near the station, (01792) 45 79 77, 22:00-02:00 (Sun 19:00-22:30), ask about women's dance nights. ⚥ ♀ ♂

WHITCHURCH

■ Women's Accommodations
CEDARS GUEST HOUSE, Llangrove Road, Whitchurch HR9 6DQ, (44-1600) 890 351. Women-only guesthouse. ♀

UKRAINE
COUNTRY CODE: (380)

WHO TO CALL
For Tour Companies Serving This Destination
See Ukraine on page 27

KIEV

■ Beaches
GAY BEACH, on the Dneiper river. Take metro to Gidropark stop, exit right until crossing a small bridge. Beach is a 10 min. walk frm metro.

■ Bars
BISTRO,★ ul. Kreschatik (metro: Kreshchatik), in same bldg. as entrance to Metro Kreshchatik, 10:00-22:00, popular evenings, frequented by gays. ⚥
BUDAPESHT, ul. Leontovicha 13 (metro: Kreshchatik), at Budapesht casino, 23:00-06:00, discreetly frequented by gays. ⚥
CHICAGO,★ ul. Raisy Okipnoy 3 (metro: Levoberezhnaya), (044) 517 41 48, 19:00-06:00, discreetly frequented by gays. ⚥
DNIPRO, ul. 1/2 Kreschatik, at the Dnipro Hotel, bar & restaurant, not gay, but discreetly frequented by gays in evening, especially on weekends. ✗
GABRIELLA, Ploshchad Leninskogo Komsomola 42 (metro: Levoberezhnaya), at the Dnepr Hotel, hotel casino bar, 22:00-06:00, discreetly frequented by gays. ⚥
KRASNOYE Y CHERNOYE, Prospekt Pobedy 44 (metro: Universitet), at the Lybed Hotel, from metro take trolleybus 5 to hotel, 16:00-24:00, discreetly frequented by gays. ⚥
SPLIT, ul. Proreznaya 24 (metro: Kreshchatik), at Split casino, 23:00-06:00, discreetly frequented by gays. ⚥

■ Dance Bar/Disco
DISCO NA KIKVIDZE, ul. Kikvidze 33, at the "obshezhitiye" (hostel), irregularly held Sat disco, 21:00-05:00. Closes occasionally, ask locally for current schedule. ⚥ ♂

■ Cafe
FLAMINGO, ul. Sorokaletiya Oktiabria 70 (metro: Liebedskaya), at Hotel Mir, (044) 264 92 03, from metro take trolleybus 11, 12 or 4, 16:00-24:00, discreetly frequented by gays. ⚥

■ Saunas/Health Clubs
SAUNA, ul. Solomenskaya 4B (metro: Vokzal'naya), from metro take tram 14, 10:00-22:00, not a gay sauna, VERY discreetly frequented by gays. ⚥
SAUNA, ul. Krasnoarmeiskaya 68 (metro: Krasnoarmeiskaya), 10:00-22:00, not a gay sauna, VERY discreetly frequented by gays. ⚥

MIDDLE EAST

ISRAEL
COUNTRY CODE: (972)

WHO TO CALL
For Tour Companies Serving This Destination
See Israel on page 17

EILAT

■ *Dance Bar/Disco*
PROPAGANDA, at city entrance, across from Paz gas station. 📞♂
PROPAGANDA, at the Shalom Center, lower level, across from airport, (052) 767 449, ask for Shahar, Sat from 24:00, frequented by gays. 📞✉
TEDDY'S BAR, beside Ophira Park, frequented by gays. 📞✉

HAIFA

■ *Information*
ISHA LE ISHA, 47 Hillel St, (04) 853 0159, feminist organization, KLAF lesbian feminist group meets here, many activities & outdoor events are held.
KLAF, (04) 853 0159, lesbian feminist community meets at a feminist organization Isha Le Isha, 47 Hillel St.
LAVENDER LINE, (04) 851 0966, lesbian line, Thurs 17:30-20:30.
SOCIETY FOR THE PROTECTION OF PERSONAL RIGHTS (SPPR), 6 Nordau St, 3rd fl, (04) 8672 665, branch of main group in Tel Aviv.
WHITE LINE, (04) 8525 252, gay & lesbian helpline, Mon & Thurs 19:00-23:00.

JERUSALEM

■ *Information*
INFO & AIDS LINE, (02) 537 3906, Tues 20:00-22:00. Aids line answers Sun 20:00-22:00.
KLAF, PO Box 6360, Jerusalem 91062, (02) 625 1271, lesbian feminist community, answers Sun 19:00-21:00 or tape.
OTHER TEN PERCENT, THE, PO Box 6916, Jerusalem 91068, Israel, (02) 5818 414, student group, meets Wed at 20:15 at Mount Scopus campus of Hebrew University, Goldschmidt Bldg, room 306.

■ *Cafe*
TMOL SHILSHOM, 5 Solomon St, in pedestrian zone Nahlat Shivah, rear entrance, (02) 6232 758, coffee shop & bookstore with poetry readings, sing-alongs. 10% gay group's social Wed 23:00. ✉
ZIG ZAG, 3 Hama'alot St, (02) 625 3446, frequented by gays & lesbians. ✉

TEL AVIV

■ *Information*
AIDS HELPLINE, (03) 560 4576, Mon & Thurs 19:30-22:00.
KLAF, PO Box 22997, TA 61228, (03) 699 5606, a lesbian feminist community, meets alternate Sun at SPPR community center, publish Kelaf Hazak newsletter, many activities & outdoor events are held.
SOCIETY FOR THE PROTECTION OF PERSONAL RIGHTS (SPPR), 28 Nehmani St, lower level, (03) 629 3681, 620 4327, Sun-Tues, Thurs 19:30-22:30 (Wed 20:00 for gays & lesbians under 22 yrs). The only gay & lesbian community center in the Middle East. Organizes social & cultural events for the gay, lesbian & bisexual community in Israel, umbrella organization for various groups. Organizes disco parties, call for location. Write PO Box 37604, Tel Aviv 61375. SPPR branch in Haifa.
WHITE LINE, (03) 629 2797, gay, lesbian helpline, Sun, Tues-Thurs 19:30-23:30. Women: (03) 525 9555, Mon 19:30-23:00.

■ *Bars*
ABBIS, 40 Geulah, (03) 510 1219, daily from 20:00, 80% men. ♂
HE & SHE, 8 Hashomer, 2nd floor, (03) 510 0914, 2 bars & disco, 60% women. 📞♀♂

■ *Dance Bar/Disco*
DIP, 3 Ahuzat Bayit St, beside Shalom Tower, Sat from 21:30. 📞♂
FIFTY-FOUR SALOME, 54 Salome St, Thurs from 24:00. 📞♂
LEMON, 17 Nagarim St, at Eliphelet St, (03) 681 3313, gay Mon only. 📞♂
SHKHITUT, 146 Herzl, (03) 683 3702, gay Sat only, 80% men. 📞♂
X-PLAY, 58 Allenby St, gay Fri only. 📞♂
ZMAN AMITI, 22 Eilat St, call SPPR gay group for schedule of gay dance nights. 📞♂

ISRAEL

FYI

What to Do On Vacation In Israel?

Scuba in Eilat. Sample Bedouin hospitality. Take a camel tour. Tube or raft the Jordan River. Go rapelling in the Judean Desert. Try hands-on archaeological digging. Go boating in the Sea of Galilee. Visit a black-mud spa at the Dead Sea. Take a jeep tour in the Negev Desert. Bicycle or hike throughout Israel. Shop for fur, leather, diamonds, gold and Malakite. Enjoy the sites and sounds of historical and modern Israel. Visit biblical sites. Visit the land where Jesus walked and see Bethlehem.

All of this and more is possible with **Gay Guided Tours of Israel**. Three tour guides, each with 10 years experience and licensed by the Israeli Ministry of Tourism, are available to be your personal contact in Israel for private or group tours. Their motto: "Together we can create an Israel vacation you will never forget." Trips are mainly for women, but men are welcome.

Contact **Gay Guided Tours of Israel** at (972-2) 673 3987 (tel/fax).

FERRARI GUIDES' GAY TRAVEL A to Z - 18th EDITION

ISRAEL

■ Cafe
CAFE POSITIVE, 58 Nehmani St, at SPPR center, (03) 629 3681, cafe for PWHIV & PWAs, alternate Fri from 15:30, call SPPR for schedule. ♂

NORDAU CAFE, 145 Ben Yehuda St (at Arlozorof St), (03) 524 0134, coffee shop & restaurant, frequented by many gays & lesbians. ⊠

■ Saunas/Health Clubs
THERMOS, 79 Shlomo Hamelech St, (03) 5224202, daily from 13:00 (Fri from 24:00). ♂

■ Restaurants
BESI HATIVIYUT, 34 Yermyahu, (03) 604 2373, gay-friendly natural food & dairy restaurant with blintzes, pancakes. Open 09:00-24:00 daily.

■ Retail & Bookstores
AVI SOFFER GALLERIES, Kikar Kedumim, Old Jaffa, (03) 683 1054; 2nd location: 238 Dizengoff St, Tel Aviv, Tel: (03) 546 0184. Gay-friendly arts & crafts galleries. ⊠

BENI'S PHARMACY, 174 Dizengoff St, (03) 522 2386, gay-friendly pharmacy.

PACIFIC REGION - Australia

COUNTRY CODE: (61)

WHO TO CALL
For Tour Companies Serving This Destination
See Australia on page 9

AUS. CAPITAL TERR.
CANBERRA

■ Information
AIDS COUNCIL & GAY INFO LINE, (06) 257 28 55. Mon-Fri: AIDS council answers 09:00-17:00; Gay info line answers 18:00-22:00.

LESBIAN LINE, (06) 2478 882, Mon 18:00-20:30.

■ Accommodations
CARRINGTON OF BUNGENDORE, THE, (06) 238 1044, hotel & restaurant 30 minutes from Canberra, B&B available.

NORTHERN LODGE, Northbourne Ave, (06) 257 2599, bed & breakfast.

■ Bars
MERIDIAN CLUB, 34 Mort St, Braddon, (06) 2489 966, from 17:00 (closed Sun), DJ Fri & Sat. Women-only nights Wed. ⚣♀♂

TILLY'S, 96 Wattle Street, at Bigelow St, Lyneham, bar & cafe. ♀♂

■ Dance Bar/Disco
HEAVEN NIGHTCLUB, Garema Place, (062) 257 6180, alternative club with 20% hetero clientele, occasional male dancers, drag shows every Sat, closed Mon. ⚣♀♂

■ Saunas/Health Clubs
CLUBROOM, O'Connor Shops, Sargood Place, 12:00-01:00 (Fri 12:00-01:00 Mon).

■ Restaurants
REPUBLIC, Allara St. ⊠

■ Erotica
CHAMPIONS HEADQUARTERS, 83 Wollongong St, unit 6.

NEW SOUTH WALES
BERRY

■ Accommodations
TARA COUNTRY RETREAT, 219 Wattamolla Rd, (61) 44 641472, fax (61) 44 642265, guesthouse & campground with restaurant, bar & shops, beverage-making facilities, shared baths, TV lounge, Jacuzzi, gym equipment, nearby ocean beach, full country breakfast. 🍽⚣♀♂

BINGARA

■ Accommodations
HILL NUDIST RETREAT, THE, "The Hill", Bingara, NSW 2404, (61-67) 24 1686. Country camping retreat for nudist guys on 2500 acres, 8 hrs from Brisbane or Sydney, bushwalking & horseriding available. ♂

BLUE MOUNTAINS

■ Information
BLUE MOUNTAINS GAY LINE, (047) 821 555.

■ Accommodations
ALLENDALE COTTAGE, in Blackheath, (047) 878 270, luxury suite with private bath with sunken 2-person spa, fireplace & sun deck.

BALMORAL GUEST HOUSE, 196 Bathurst Rd, Katoomba 2780, (62-47) 822 264, Fax: (61-47) 826 008. gay-friendly B&B guesthouse with bar & restaurant, full breakfast, private & shared baths, AC, color TV, VCR, Jacuzzi, nearby pool, 30% gay & lesbian clientele.

BYGONE BEAUTYS COTTAGES, 20-22 Grose St, Leura 2780, (047) 84 3117, 84 3108, fax: 58 7257. Gay-friendly B&B cottages with restaurant, private baths, full breakfast, color TV, VCR, kitchen, refrigerator, beverage-making facilities.

CHALET, THE, 46-50 Portland Ave, Medlow Bath 2780, (047) 881 122, hotel & restaurant.

CLEOPATRA COUNTRY GUESTHOUSE, Cleopatra Street, Blackheath, (047) 878 456, fax: 876 092. Gay-friendly guesthouse with restaurant, private & shared baths.

CRABAPPLE COTTAGE, 9 Beattie St, Leura, (047) 841 899, country cottage with full breakfast, spa bath.

■ Women's Accommodations
TRILLIUM, 71 Seventh Ave, North Katoomba, (047) 826 372, B&B 1-1/2 hours from Sydney, shared shower/WCs, expanded continental breakfast, TV lounge with colour TV, men welcome. Women's healing waterhole & falls nearby. ♀

COFFS HARBOUR

■ Accommodations
SANTA FE LUXURY BED & BREAKFAST, The Mountain Way, (066) 537 700, fax: 537 050, gay-friendly B&B, 50% gay & lesbian clientele, private baths, full breakfast, colour TV, VCR, video tape library, ceiling fans, laundry facilities, pool on premises. 🍽

HUNTER VALLEY

■ Accommodations
POKOLBIN VILLAGE RESORT, in Hunter Valley vineyards area, resort & conference center, accommodation & winery tours.

NEWCASTLE

■ Bars
WICKHAM PARK HOTEL BAR, Maitland Rd, Wickham Park, pub, open daily. ♀

■ Dance Bar/Disco
ISLINGTON BARRACKS, 139 Maitland Rd, Islington, (049) 69 1848, pub with dance bar in rear, alternative, many gays & lesbians, 60% gay & lesbian.

NORTHERN NEW SOUTH WALES

■ Accommodations
RIVER OAKS B&B, c/o Bill Schreurs, 53-59 Broken Head Rd, Byron Bay, (066) 85 86 79, fax: 85 56 36, B&B with restaurant, mostly men with women welcome, private & shared baths, continental breakfast, colour TV, VCR, video tape library, heated pool on premises. 🍽♂

AUSTRALIA

■ Women's Accommodations

A SLICE OF HEAVEN RURAL RETREAT FOR WOMEN, Lot 3 Pacific Hwy, Stokers Siding 2484, (61-66) 779 276, mobile: (61-15) 590 299. E-mail: spower@medeserv.com.au. http://www.powerup.com.au/~qldq/soh.html. B&B retreat for women only, rooms in-house or in separate private accommodation, private baths, expanded continental breakfast, beverage-making facilities, TV lounge, pool on premises.

TURKEY CREEK FARM, Rosebank 2480, (066) 882 175, women-only B&B in a farmhouse on 34 acres of rainforest & farmland, swimming holes, waterfalls nearby, shared bath.

RYLSTONE

■ Women's Accommodations

STRINGYBARK FARM, PO Box 78, (063) 791 182, 2 cabins, women only, private bath.

SYDNEY

■ Information

AIDS INFO, (02) 9283 3222.

GAY & LESBIAN LINE, (02) 9207 2800, 16:00-24:00.

LESBIAN LINE, (02) 9550 0910, Fri 18:00-22:00 or tape.

LESBIAN SPACE COMMUNITY CULTURAL CENTRE, 43 Bradford St, Newtown, (02) 9519 3870, drop in Sat 11:00-17:00, drum 15:00-17:00.

NEWTOWN WOMEN'S CENTRE, 523 King St, Newtown, (02) 9550 6993.

WOMEN'S LIBRARY, Garden St, Alexandria Town Hall, Alexandria, (02) 9319 0529.

■ Accommodations

BARRACKS, THE, 164 B Bourke St, Darlinghurst, (61-2) 9360 5823, fax: (61-2) 9361 4584. Centrally located men-only B&B near Oxford St bars. Private & shared baths, coffee/TV lounge, continental breakfast & courtyard with BBQ.

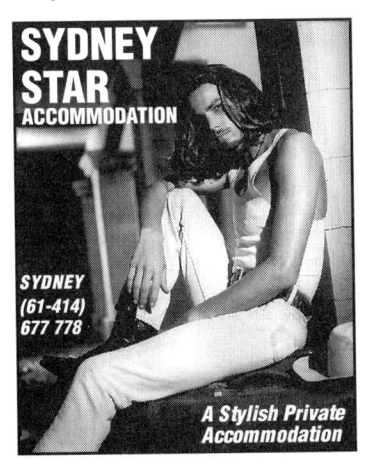

BRICKFIELD HILL BED & BREAKFAST INN, 403 Riley St, Surrey Hills, Sydney 2010, (61-2) 9211 4886 (tel/fax). Four-storey Victorian terrace house near Oxford St & the city, some rooms with balconies & views, expanded continental breakfast, private & shared baths, some hetero clientele.

COOGEE SANDS MOTOR INN, 161 Dolphin St, Coogee, (02) 9665 8588, Fax: 9664 1406, gay-friendly.

FURAMA HOTEL CENTRAL, 28 Albion St, Surry Hills, 2010, (61-2) 9281 0333, Fax: (61-2) 9281 0222. Gay-friendly, modern hotel with restaurant & bar, 128 luxurious rooms offering complete privacy & convenience. Located minutes from central train station, short walk to Darling Harbour, theatres & city centre. Amenities include private baths, indoor heated pool, colour TV, AC.

FURAMA HOTEL DARLING HARBOUR, 68 Harbour St, Darling Harbour, 2000, (61-2) 9281 0400, Fax: (61-2) 9281 1212. Gay-friendly hotel with restaurant. Located opposite Sydney Entertainment Centre, near Chinatown, short stroll to major theatres, cinemas & major tourist attractions. All private baths, AC, 24-hr room service, colour TV and more.

GOVERNORS ON FITZROY, 64 Fitzroy St, Surry Hills NSW 2010, Australia, (02) 9331 4652, Fax: (02) 9361 5094, bed & breakfast, individually decorated double rooms, private & shared baths, spa, 4 blks from heart of gay area (Oxford St), 20 min drive to ocean, full breakfast, tea/coffee.

KIRKETON HOTEL, 229-231 Darlinghurst Rd, Kings Cross 2010, Sydney, NSW, Tel/Fax: (61-2) 9360 4333. This gay-friendly, budget hotel, with restaurant and licensed cocktail bar, is in a very central position, a few minutes from Rushcutters Bay, 10 minutes from the Opera House, and a 20-minute drive to beaches. It offers convenient, around-the-corner proximity to the vibrant life of Kings Cross and is on a bus route to the city. Private &

FYI

Australia's Largest Gay Tour Company Opens Office in Seattle

To provide better service to its North American customers, **Beyond the Blue**, Australia's largest gay-owned and -operated travel agent and tour wholesaler, has opened an office in Seattle, WA (April 1997).

For those traveling to or from Australia, Beyond the Blue can provide competitive airfares, gay-specific and gay-friendly accommodations, fully-escorted tours, special events, limo transfers, adventure tours for one customer or 500. Special itineraries can be designed for specific needs. Director Phillip Amos, former President of the Australian Gay and Lesbian Tourism Association, says, "Should we not have what you want, we'll find it for you!" Both offices have the latest technology to ensure fast and accurate handling of requests. An Internet web site contains full information on BTB travel products.

Beyond the Blue are accredited tour operators for the world-famous Sydney Gay and Lesbian Mardi Gras, an offical wholesaler in Australia and North America for Man Friday Resort Fiji, and the exclusive Australian agent for Atlantis Events and Gay Games Amsterdam 1998.

Contact **Beyond the Blue** in Australia at (61-2) 9955 6755, fax: (61-2) 9922 6036, and in Seattle at 2030 Dexter Ave N #273, Seattle, WA 98109, (206) 285-8637, Fax: (206) 283-7095, E-mail: btb@msn.com.

SYDNEY STAR ACCOMMODATION
SYDNEY (61-414) 677 778
A Stylish Private Accommodation

KIRKETON HOTEL
Your Budget Hotel in Downtown Sydney
(61-2) 9360-4333

FERRARI GUIDES' GAY TRAVEL A to Z - 18th EDITION

AUSTRALIA

FYI

Devoted to Women's Travel

The above headline is the slogan of **Silke's Travel** of Sydney, Australia. An accredited Sydney Mardi Gras tour operator, they offer women's Mardi Gras packages, including event tickets. Their Cairns for Women program includes accommodations at 54 Cinderella Street, an inn that is gaining an international reputation among gay women travelers, and at Witchencroft, perhaps Australia's most famous guesthouses. A 2-week women-only resort vacation at Man Friday Resort in Fiji promises to become a legendary vacation event for lesbians worldwide. Silke will go to Macchu Picchu and Annapurna in 1997, as well as on safari in Africa.

Jun 1-14	-Trekking, Canoeing, Kimberley Mtns
Jun 22-Jul 1	-Alice with the lot-a Wildwise event
July 5-12	-Man Friday Resort, Fiji
Sep 5-26	-Peru, Macchu Picchu, Bolivia
Oct 25-Nov 13	-Annapurna, Nepal Trek
Jan 1-23, '98	-Best of East Africa

Contact **Silke's Travel** at (61-2) 9380 6244, Fax: (61-2) 9361 3729. E-mail: silba@magna.com.au.

FYI

Exclusively Gay/Lesbian Travel Arrangements for Australia

Airport pick-up to gay or gay-friendly accommodations...day tours or longer trips...sightseeing in Sydney or more distant parts of Australia...**BreakOut Tours** gay professionals handle everything from the moment you set foot on Australian soil. BreakOut

Break Out Tours

stresses personalized service, and can provide an all-gay travel experience in Australia.

BreakOut's motto: "Personal service - that's our strength. Exclusively gay every day - that's our difference. Professionally-trained gay travel staff - their our pride. Owner-operated - it's our business."

7/5/97	Fiji
9/15/97	Vietnam
10/10/97	Nepal
10/30/97	Nepal
12/20/97	Best of Australia
12/20/97	Christmas DownUnder
12/20/97	Nepal
2/3/98	Paint the (Ayers) Rock Pink!
2/20/98	Sydney Gay & Lesbian Mardi Gras
2/22/98	Best of Australia
9/3/98	Paint the (Ayers) Rock Pink!
TBA	Sydney LeatherWeek

Contact **BreakOut Tours** at (61 2) 9558 8229, Fax:(61 2) 9558 7140, E-mail: brkout@world.net, Web: http://breakout.com.au.

---

shared baths, continental breakfast, nearby swimming pool.

MANOR HOUSE BOUTIQUE HOTEL, 86 Flinders St, Darlinghurst, Sydney, 2010, (61-2) 9380 6633, Fax: (61-2) 9380 5016. Two-story terrace mansion with 18 boutique accommodations, restaurant & bar. All private baths, buffet breakfast, pool on premises. Near Oxford St and gay venues. Mostly men with women welcome.

NEWINGTON MANOR, 10-14 Sebastopol St, Marrickville, NSW (02) 9560 4922, fax: 9550 9789, guesthouse with gay male following, double rooms with private baths, color TV, phone, spa, pool, continental & expanded continental breakfast.

OBSERVATORY HOTEL, 89-113 Kent St, (61-2) 9256 2222, fax: (61-2) 9256 2233. Gay-friendly hotel with restaurant, bar, gift shop & health & leisure club, mostly straight with a gay & lesbian following, private baths, colour cable TV, VCR, video tape library, pool on premises, nearby health club.

PARK LODGE, 747 South Dowling St, Moore Park, (61-2) 9318 2393, Fax: (61-2) 9318 2513. E-mail: pklodge@geko.net.au. http://www.geko.net.au/~pklodge/. Victorian-style boutique hotel, continental breakfast, private baths, color TV, VCR rentals, telephone, refrigerator, pool & ocean nearby, 50% gay & lesbian clientele.

SIMPSON'S OF POTTS POINT, 8 Challis Ave, Potts Point, (61-2) 9356 2199, Fax: (61-2) 9356 4476. Gay-friendly boutique hotel with glass conservatory, private baths, telephone, AC, ceiling fans, color TV, near Oxford St gay venues.

SOUTHERN CROSS HOTEL, cnr Elizabeth & Goulburn Sts, (02) 9282 0987, fax: 9281 3287. gay-friendly hotel with gay & lesbian following, private baths.

SULLIVANS HOTEL, 21 Oxford St, Paddington, (02) 9361 0222, Fax: 9360 3735, gay-friendly hotel, mainly hetero clientele, private baths with shower, TV lounge, laundry facilities, nearby shops & restaurants.

SYDNEY STAR ACCOMMODATION, 275 Darlinghurst Rd, Darlinghurst, Sydney, (61-414) 677 778 (24-hr mobile phone), Fax: (61-2) 9331 1000. You'll always feel welcome. Sydney Star combines all the style and elegance of a European pensione with the service and security of a modern hotel. We're a short stroll from restaurants, cafes, galleries and boutiques. Single, twin and double suites are available, each with kitchen and colour TV. Some hetero clientele. Member AGLTA. See ad on page 307

VICTORIA COURT SYDNEY, 122 Victoria St, Potts Point, (61-2) 9357 3200, Fax: (61-2) 9357 7606, E-mail: vicsyd@ozemail.com.au(fe). Two Victorian houses, restored and modernized, comprise this gay-friendly B&B hotel. The focal point is a courtyard conservatory where free-flying birds accompany breakfasting guests. No two of the rooms are

AUSTRALIA

alike: most have marble fireplaces, some have balconies or four-poster beds. All have ensuite bathrooms, hairdryers, colour TVs, AM/FM radios, and direct-dial telephones. Located in Potts Point, the heart of Sydney's bohemian scene.

■ Women's Accommodations

HELEN'S HIDEAWAY, reservations: (02) 9810 6473, women's B&B in Sydney's city centre. ♀

VITA'S PLACE, reservations (02) 9810 5487, women's accommodation in Sydney. ♀

■ Bars

ALBURY HOTEL BAR, 6 Oxford Street, Paddington, (02) 9336 555, piano bar downstairs, restaurant above, nightly drag shows, 13:00-01:30 (Sun 14:00-01:00). ♪♂

ANNIE'S BAR, Bourke St, behind Carrington Hotel, Darlinghurst. ♂

BANANA BAR, at the Taylor Hotel, Darlinghurst, upscale cocktail bar. ♀♂

BANK HOTEL BAR, 324 King St, Newtown, from 22:00. Wed women's pool competition. ♀

BARRACKS, Patterson Lane, behind Taylor Square Hotel, Darlinghurst, pool tables.

BASE BAR, 267 Oxford St, under the Beauchamp Hotel, in basement. ♀♂

BEAUCHAMP HOTEL BAR, 267 Oxford St, Darlinghurst, 12:00-24:00 (Sat till 01:00), mainly gay. ♂

BERESFORD HOTEL BAR, 354 Bourke St, Darlinghurst, (02) 9331 1045, bar & disco, 12:00-24:00 (Thurs till 01:00, Fri & Sat till 02:00, Sun from 09:00). Alternative disco in the rear.

CAESARS BAR, 388 Parramatta Rd, behind Petersham Inn, Petersham. ♀♂

CLEVELAND HOTEL BAR, 423 Cleveland St, Redfern, alternative club with a large gay clientele. ♀

DARLO BAR, Liverpool St at Darlinghurst Rd, women's pool tourney Sat 17:00.

DOLPHIN HOTEL COCKTAIL BAR, 412-414 Crown St, Surrey Hills, (02) 9331 4800, trendy, upscale cocktail bar & pub, straight with gay & lesbian following, daily from 17:00.

G BAR, Walker at Blue St, North Sydney, cocktail bar. ♀♂

GREEN PARK HOTEL BAR, 360 Victoria St, Darlinghurst, 10:00-01:00, 60% gay clientele. ♂

LAVA BAR, 2 Oxford St, at the Burdekin Hotel, Darlinghurst, top floor cocktail bar with DJ, gay & straight crowd.

LEICHHARDT HOTEL, 126 Balmain Rd, Leichhardt, (02) 9569 1217, 10:00-24:00. ♀

LIZARD LOUNGE, 34 Oxford St, at the Exchange Hotel, 1st floor, Darlinghurst, upscale cocktail lounge, 17:00-03:00.

OXFORD COCKTAIL BAR (GILLIGAN'S), at the Oxford Hotel, upstairs Gilligan's upscale cocktail bar, downstairs is gay men's pub with DJ, Mon-Sat 17:00-02:00, Sun till 24:00. ♀♂

OXFORD HOTEL BAR,★ 134 Oxford St, Darlinghurst, (02) 9331 3467, cruise bar, 17:00-02:00 (Fri, Sat till 03:00, Sun till 24:00). ♂

RHINO BAR, 24 Bayswater Rd, Kings Cross. ♀♂

SIGNAL, Level 2, 81 Oxford St, Darlinghurst, cruise bar. ♂

■ Dance Bar/Disco

BOOTSCOOT C&W LINE DANCING NIGHTS, at the Imperial Hotel, Erskineville, (02) 9388 1236 or 9550 9937, Tues-Thurs 20:00-23:00, Sat 14:00-17:30. ♀♂

BYBLOS, 169 Oxford St, Darlinghurst, occasional gay & lesbian disco night. ♂

CLOVER CLUB, 122 Victoria Rd, Drummoyne, (02) 9812 964, dance nights for women, Fri 20:30-02:00, Sat from 20:00. ♀

DCM (DON'T CRY MAMA), 33 Oxford St, Darlinghurst, (02) 9267 7036, gay events on weeknights, gay-friendly, but mostly straight weekends, from 22:30 (Sun from 17:00).

EXCHANGE HOTEL, 34 Oxford Street, Darlinghurst, (02) 9331 1936, 2 dance bars, drag shows weekends but mostly straight, from 22:00.

FLINDERS HOTEL BAR, 63 Flinders Street, Darlinghurst, (02) 9360 4929, 20:00-03:00 (Fri, Sat 22:00-07:00, Sun 20:00-24:00). ♀♂

HELLFIRE CLUB, 111 Regent St, S/M club, 22:00 till dawn. Action-packed, call to verify night.

IMPERIAL HOTEL, 35 Erskineville Rd, Erskineville, (02) 9519 9899, from 10:00 (Fri,Sat till 08:00). Disco & cabaret in front bar where women play pool on weekends. ♀♂

KLUB KOOKIE CLUB, 77 Williams St, South Sydney, kind of bent crowd, "alternative whatever."

MIDNIGHT FACTORY, Regentville Rd at Batt St, South Penrith (far western suburbs), (047) 323 223, 19:00-01:00 (Fri, Sat from 18:00, Sun 18:00-24:00), closed Mon, Tues. ♀♂

MIDNIGHT SHIFT,★ 85 Oxford Street, Darlinghurst, (02) 9360 4319, bar & upstairs disco, from 12:00 (Sun 16:00-24:00). ♂

NEWTOWN HOTEL, 174 King Street, Newtown, (02) 9511 329, upstairs piano bar, dance bar & cabaret, 12:00-24:00. ♂

ORB, Victoria St at Kings Cross. ♂

PHOENIX,★ basement of Exchange Hotel, enter from Oxford St, East Sydney, underground, alternative, progressive music, from 22:00 (closed Mon), cruisy Thurs & Sun. ♂

SIRENS, 12-14 Enmore Rd, Newtown, (02) 9519 4270, Fri & Sat 21:00 till late. ♀

FYI

1997 Australian Gay & Lesbian Events

Provided by **Destination DownUnder**, Australia's award-winning gay and lesbian tour company

Anytime is the right time to visit the South Pacific, and your trip can be more rewarding if you plan it to coincide with an important gay event:

1/18-2/9	Midsumma Fest
1/18	Brunswisk Street Prty
1/25	Red Raw Dance Party
1/29	Sydney Mardi Gras
2/2	Stars Come Out
2/2	Midsumma Ride/Pride March
2/2	Syd Mardi Gras Sports Fest
2/9	Midsumma Carnival Day
2/10	Syd Mardi Gras Fair Day
2/11-3/6	Best of S Pacific Tour
2/13-21	New Zealand Adven. Tour
2/19-3/3	Mardi Gras Party Pkgs
2/22	Shop Yourself Stupid-Sydney
2/23-3/3	Mardi Gras Budget Buster Party Pkg
3/1	Syd Mardi Gras Parade, Party
3/3-3/8	Melbourne Queer Film Fest
5/4-11	Sydney Leather Week
5/4	Leather Week Street Fair
5/11	Leather Inquisition Party
6/7	Queen's Birthday Ball Tour
6/7	Winterdaze Dance Party
6/7	Queens B-day Ball, Brisbane
6/22-28	Sydney Pride Week
9/27	Incarceration Party
10/1-6	Sydney Sleaze Ball
11/22	AIDS Food & Wine Fest
12/23-1/2	Xmas DownUnder Tour
12/312	New Years Party Tour

Book **Destination DownUnder** tours in USA at (800) 297-2681 or (415) 284-1666, in Australia at (61-2) 92268 2188, Fax: (61-2) 9267 9733.

FERRARI GUIDES' GAY TRAVEL A to Z - 18th EDITION

AUSTRALIA

Certified Australia Specialists

Detailed custom independent gay and lesbian travel packages to Australia, New Zealand or the Pacific Islands are the specialty of **G'Day Tours**. Offices in the US, Australia and New Zealand let G'Day keep a close eye on all of your travel arrangements.

Do you want to go hot air ballooning in the Outback, enjoy the excitement of Mardis Gras in Sydney, go diving in the Great Barrier Reef off exclusive Lizard Island? How about flight-seeing around Queenstown in the Southern Alps or a romantic interlude on a secluded Fijian Island? Where some travelers see boundaries, our travel consultants see opportunities. Whatever your special interests, time restrictions, or budget, G'Day Tours will customize your land, sea, and air arrangements for any downunder destination or global hot spot.

G'day Tours is a division of Swain Travel Services, Inc., a leading five-star international destination specialist and wholesaler to Australia, the Asia Pacific, and other global destinations.

Contact **G'Day Tours** at (610) 896-9595, (800) 272-1149, Fax: (610) 896-9592. E-mail: SWAINAUST@AOL.COM.

Visiting The "Top End" of Australia

If you're planning to visit Australia and you like soft adventure, consider using Australia's "Top End" as your entry point, instead of the more usual Sydney or Cairns. The "Top End" is the northern part of Australia, site of the famous Kakadu National Park, and a place where you can commune with crocodiles, barrumundi and birdlife in the wild. Its largest city, Darwin, is actually closer to Indonesia than it is to many Australian cities, suggesting the possibility of spending some time in Bali, Timor or even Malaysia on your way to or from Australia.

There are many different types of touring, from coach tours to backpacking in the wild. Natural wonders, in addition to the Kakadu National Park, include Mataranka Hot Springs, Katherine Gorge and the little-known, but spectacular, Litchfield Park. The mystery of the indigenouis peoples of the "Top End," go back centuries, and their affiliation with the land and their paintings are in themselves a worthy subject.

Graylink tours is a one-person owner-operator who has, over the past twenty years, lived and worked in the tourist area of the Northern Territory of Australia. Graylink will work with your travel agent to arrange an interesting Top-End travel experience to enhance your visit to Australia.

Contact **Graylink** at: (61 8) 894 80089, Fax: (61 8) 894 72807, E-mail: graylink@ozemail.com.au, mail: PO Box 3826, Darwin, NT 0801, Australia.

TAXI CLUB, 40-42 Flinders St, Darlinghurst, late-night club, many transvestites, open midnight till 09:00 or 10:00.

THE OTHER SIDE,★ 383 Bourke St, at Kinselas, Darlinghurst, women's weekly dance night, Sun from 19:00. Largest running women's dance club in Sydney.

TOP GUN, 100 King St, Newtown, (02) 9519 6999, cocktail bar, disco & restaurant, usually Fri night.

■ Cafe

BETH'S PLACE CAFE, Annandale at Reserve St, Annandale, many women.

DOWNTOWN, 84 Oxford St, Darlinghurst.

GREEN IGUANA CAFE, 6 King St, Newtown, (02) 9516 3118, from 08:00.

LESBIAN LINE CAFÉ, 164 Flood St, Leichhardt, Fri 20:00-22:00.

ONE NINETY ONE CAFE, 191 Oxford St, Darlinghurst, (02) 9326 1166, frequented by gays & lesbians.

■ Saunas/Health Clubs

BODYLINE SAUNA, 58a Flinders St, Darlinghurst, (02) 9360 1006, 12-07:00.

DEN CLUB, THE, 97 Oxford St, 1st floor, Darlinghurst, (02) 9332 3402, private men's club, from 20:00 (Fri, Sat 24hrs).

KING STEAM, 38-42 Oxford St, Darlinghurst, (02) 9360 3431, 10-18.

KKK SAUNA, 83 Anzac Parade, Kensington, (02) 9662 1359, 24hrs.

NUMBERS, 95 Oxford St, Darlinghurst (upstairs), (02) 9331 6099, private men's club, from 22:00.

■ Restaurants

CITRUS, Oxford St.

EDON, 27 Victoria St, Darlinghurst.

GOODFELLAS, 111 King St, Newtown, (02) 9557 1175, from 18:30.

HARVEST VEGETARIAN RESTAURANT, 71 Evans St, Rozelle, (02) 9818 4201, vegetarian cuisine.

LIME, 420 King St, South Newtown, cl. Mon.

O CALCUTTA, 251 Victoria St, Darlinghurst, (02) 9360 3650.

SERAFIM, 389 Bourke St, Darlinghurst, (02) 9360 4959.

SIROCCO, 23 Craigend St, Darlinghurst, Morrocan cuisine.

TAPAS, 1 Burton St, Darlinghurst, (02) 9360 7027, Spanish cuisine.

TAYLOR SQUARE RESTAURANT & COCKTAIL BAR, 191-195 Oxford St, Taylor Square, Sun from 23:00.

TOTALLY CACTUS, 411 King Georges Rd, Beverly Hills, (02) 9570 8669, Mexican cuisine.

■ Retail & Bookstores

BOOKSHOP DARLINGHURST, THE, 207 Oxford St, Darlinghurst, (02) 9331 1103, wide

AUSTRALIA

selection of gay & lesbian books, magazines & cards, open Mon-Sat 10am-10pm, Sun noon-9pm.
BOOKSHOP NEWTOWN, THE, 186 King St, Newton, (02) 9514 244, gay & lesbian books, magazines & cards, open Mon-Sat 9am-9pm, Sun noon-9pm.
FEMINIST BOOKSHOP, THE, Shop 9, Orange Grove Plaza, Balmain Road, Lilyfield, 2040, (02) 9810 2666. Books by, for and about women, centre for information & resources, 10:30-18:00 (Sat till 16:00), closed Sun.
GLEEBOOKS, 49 Glebe Point Rd, Glebe, (02) 9660 2333, general bookstore with gay & lesbian section, daily 09:00-21:00. 2nd-hand books at 191 Glebe Point Rd location.

■ Leathers/Piercing
HOUSE OF FETISH, 373 Bourke St, Darlinghurst, (02) 9361 6367.
MEPHISTO LEATHERS, 112 Oxford St, 1st floor, Darlinghurst, (02) 9332 3218.
PIERCING URGE, THE, 322 Bourke St, Darlinghurst, (02) 9360 3179, piercing.
RADICAL LEATHER, 20 Hutchinson St, lower level, Surrey Hills, (02) 9331 7544.
SAX LEATHER, 110a Oxford St, Darlinghurst, (02) 9331 6105.

■ Erotica
CLUB X: Kings Cross: 26 Bayswater Rd, 78 Darlinghurst Rd, 2G Roslyn St, 380 Pitt St; Sydney: 711 George St (1st floor), 429A Pitt St.
DLC MAGNET DEPARTMENT STORE, 113-115 Oxford St, 1st floor, Darlinghurst.
GAY EXCHANGE ADULT BOOKS, 44 Park St, level 2, (02) 9267 6812.
NUMBERS, 95 Oxford Street, Darlinghurst, (first floor), (02) 9331 6099, books, videos, toys, piercing jewelry open 24hrs.
PLEASURE CHEST, 56 Darlinghurst Rd, Kings Cross, (02) 9356 3640. Other locations: 161 Oxford St, 382a Pitt St.
PLEASURE SPOT, 1/218 Crown St, Darlinghurst, (02) 9361 0433, vibrators, dildos, videos, books. ♀
PURR EFFECT, 62 Oxford St, Paddington, (02) 9332 1370, leather clothes & accessories for women.
TOOL SHED, 81 Oxford St, Darlinghurst, (02) 9332 2792, open 7 days 10am-late.
TOOL SHED, 196 King St, Newtown, (02) 9565 1599.

WOLLONGONG

■ Dance Bar/Disco
CHEQUERS, 341 Crown St (access via car park roof), at the Picadilly Shopping Centre, (042) 263 788, Thurs-Sat from 19:00.

WOODBURN

■ Accommodations
NORTH EAST NUDIST RETREAT, PO Box 108, Woodburn 2472, (066) 822 365, men-only nudist retreat. ♂

NORTHERN TERRITORY
ALICE SPRINGS

■ Information
AIDS INFO, (889) 531 118.
GAY LINE, (889) 532 844, info on social groups, monthly dances.

■ Cafe
SWINGERS CAFE, Gregory Terrace near Todd St, gay-friendly cafe with espresso & lite menu. Open evenings.

DARWIN

■ Information
AIDS INFO, 6 Manton St, (889) 411 711, Mon-Fri 10:00-17:00.

■ Dance Bar/Disco
PANDORA'S, at the Don Hotel, enter at Litchfield St, (889) 481 069, Thurs-Sat 20:00-04:00 in rear bar, DJ, occasional drag shows.

■ Restaurants
UNCLE JOHN'S CABIN, Gardiner St, gay bar with attached straight restaurant. ♂

QUEENSLAND
BRISBANE

■ Information
AIDS INFO, (07) 3844 1990.
GAYLINE, (07) 3839 3277, 19:00-22:00.
LESBIAN LINE, (07) 3839 3288, Tues & Sun 19:00-22:00.

■ Accommodations
EDWARD LODGE, 75 Sydney St, New Farm, (61 7) 3254 1078, fax: 3254 1062, B&B guesthouse. Large, comfortably furnished guest rooms with telephones, private baths, expanded continental breakfast, 24-hr tea/coffee facilities, Jacuzzi. Convenient to public transport, restaurants, cafes, gay venues and park. Women welcome. ♂

■ Bars
CLUB LIBERTINE, private fetish club with men's & women's SM parties. For info, send SASE to PO Box 5036, West End 4101 Brisbane.
RAPTOR BAR, Brunswick St, at the Brunswick Hotel, New Farm, closed Sun.
RUSSEL'S LONG BAR, 186 Brunswick St, at the Shamrock Hotel, Fortitude Valley, (07) 3252 2421, from 18:00 (closed Mon, Tues), male dancers.
SPORTSMAN HOTEL BAR, 130 Leichhardt St, Spring Hill, (07) 3831 2892, bar & hotel, daily 18:00-01:00, Sun disco 16:00-24:00. Bears 3rd Sat, leather night 1st Sat.

■ Dance Bar/Disco
KD'S, 470 St Paul's Terrace, at Jubilee Hotel, Fri women's dance night.
OPTIONS, 18 Little Edward St, Spring Hill, (around the corner from Sportsman Hotel). (07) 3831 4214, disco, showbar & good restaurant, many lesbians.
OUT NIGHTCLUB, Warner St, Wed-Sun.
PATCH, Ann St at the Waterloo Hotel, women's dance night alternate Fri.
PLAYGROUND, (07) 3257 0988, call for location.
WICKHAM HOTEL BAR, 308 Wickham St, Fortitude Valley, (07) 3852 1301, disco & good restaurant.

■ Saunas/Health Clubs
BODYLINE SAUNA, 43 Ipswich Rd, Wooloongabba, (07) 3391 4285.
DEN, 181 Brunswick St, Fortitude Valley, (07) 3854 1981, private men's club, not a sauna, till 04:00.

■ Restaurants
BOUNDARY STREET BRASSERIE, 145b Boundary St, West End, (07) 3844 3811.
CAFE BABYLON, 142 Boundary St, West End, (07) 3846 4505, dinner daily (Fri, Sun also lunch).
MORAY CAFE, at Moray St & Merthyr Rd, New Farm, (07) 3254 1342, café & wine bar, open daily.
SOUP KITCHEN, THE, 166 Hardgrave Rd, West End, (07) 3844 1132.

■ Retail & Bookstores
BRISBANE WOMEN'S BOOKSHOP, 15 Gladstone Rd, Highgate Hill, (07) 3844 6650. Women's & lesbian books, non-sexist children's books, jewelry, T-shirts, cards, music, Mon-Fri 09:30-17:30, Sat 10:00-02:00, Sun 11:00-15:00. Monthly coffeehouse in courtyard.
EMMA'S BOOKSHOP, 82a Vulture St, West End, (07) 3844 4973, general bookshop with gay & lesbian section.
RED BOOKS, Brunswick St, Fortitude Valley, general bookstore with some gay & lesbian books.

■ Leathers/Piercing
INTA LEATHER, 133 Melbourne St, (07) 3846 4946. Second location: 287 Sandgate Rd, Tel: 862 1142.

■ Erotica
SIGNAL, 191 Brunswick St, Fortitude Valley. ♂

BUNDABERG

■ Accommodations
FIELD OF DREAMS, Lot 24, Woodswallow Dr, MS 882, Gin Gin, QLD 4671, (61-71) 573 024, Fax: (61-71) 573-025, E-mail: fod@ozemail.com.au. B&B guesthouse on 25 acres of working property with gardens, chickens, some cattle. North of Brisbane & 40 minutes east of Bundaberg & coast, easy access to Great Barrier Reef, whale watching &

AUSTRALIA

FYI

Bushwalking & 4WD Touring in Queensland

A fourth-generation North Queenslander owns and manages **Witchencroft**, Australia's oldest women's guesthouse and your base for Witchencroft's outback excursions. Nearby, you can swim among crystal-clear waterfalls, explore old Aboriginal tracks in pristine "World-Heritage" rainforests, discover the spectacular "dry country" that few know about. About a half hour from Witchencroft are the Atherton Tablelands, a flat area at 2500 feet in altitude which are 60 kms inland from tropical Cairns. This area, called the "cool tropics because it lacks the heat and humidity of the coast, is uniquely placed to offer remarkably different ecosystems and microclimates.

Because of the climate, Witchencroft can virtually guarantee fine weather all year round for 4WD tours (in their new 7-seater Nissan Patrol) and on bushwalks. Accommodations are in two comfortable, private self-contained rooms set in 5 acres of gardens. Jenny Maclean of Witchencroft will customize your itinerary based on your interests and her vast knowledge of the area.

Contact **Witchencroft** at (61-70) 912 683.

FYI

Luxury Aircraft Excursions in the Food & Wine State

Don't miss South Australia on your trip Downunder. In addition to being the gateway to Ayers Rock and the Northern Territories, South Australia, the "Food and Wine State," is easily reached and has lots to attract foreign visitors. Within an hour of the capital, Adelaide, which lies just 2 hours from Sydney and an hour from Melbourne, you can sip wines, pet kangaroos and koalas, or walk amongst wild sea lions. On Kangaroo Island, visitors walk to within 15 feet of wild kangaroo, sea lions and koalas. At Cleland Wildlife Park, the kangaroos, koalas and other Australian wildlife are actually tame enough to pet. Hahndorf is an authentic German Settlement situated in the Adelaide Hills, where you can enjoy traditional German cuisine and interesting shops.

Air & Adventure Tours (AAA Tours) specializes in Adelaide and South Australia, using luxury aircraft and coaches. A variety of day and half-day tours are available, and can include Kangaroo Island with its kangaroo and sea lions, Cleland Wildlife Park, and/or AAA's Adelaide Lights Spectacular, a romantic evening in which guests sip champagne while enjoying a 1/2-hour flight over Adelaide city, followed by a city tour by mini coach for a total night experience. Tours for both individuals and groups can be arranged.

Contact **AAA Tours** at (61 8) 8281-0530, Fax:(61 8) 8281-9301, E-mail: aaatours.senet.com.au.

turtle rookeries. Some hetero clientele.

CAIRNS

■ *Information*
AIDS INFO, (070) 511 028, 24hrs.

■ *Accommodations*
EIGHTEEN TWENTY-FOUR JAMES, 18-24 James St, (61-70) 51 46 44, Fax: (61-70) 51 01 03, e-mail: 18_24james@internetnorth.com.au. Gay-owned & -operated plantation-style hotel in a tropical rainforest. Licensed restaurant & bar on premises, and complimentary tropical poolside breakfasts are served. Guestrooms feature private baths, AC, phones and TV with free in-house movies. Fully tiled salt-water pool on premises.

FIFTY-FOUR CINDERELLA STREET, 54 Cinderella St, Cairns, QLD 4878, (61-70) 550 289, Fax: (61-70) 559 383. Superb accommodation, creative cuisine & absolute beachfront at a fairy tale women-only hideaway, 10 minutes from Cairns & the airport on Reddens Island at the mouth of the Barron River on Machans Beach. Amenities at this B&B guesthouse include full breakfast, private & shared baths & color TV. Spend idyllic days in the large garden, the rock swimming pool with waterfall, or use the private beach access. Cairns offers magnificent rainforests & some of the best reef diving in the world.

TURTLE COVE RESORT CAIRNS, Captain Cook Hwy, PO Box 158, Smithfield Cairns, Far North Queensland. (61-70) 591 800, Fax: (61-70) 591 969. E-mail: turtlecove@iig.com.au. Website: http://www.iig.com.au/turtle_cove/. Beachfront resort with restaurant, bar, resort shop & private gay beach. Private baths, colour TV, in-house video, video tape library, telephone, AC, refrigerator, tropical & continental buffet breakfast, pool & Jacuzzi. Rainforest and barrier reef tours.

■ *Women's Accommodations*
WITCHENCROFT, Write: Jenny Maclean, PO Box 685, Atherton 4883, (070) 91 2683, E-mail: jj@bushnet.qld.edu.au. Women-only guesthouse on 5-acre organic farm, 2 apartments with kitchens, baths, color TV, garden, nearby rivers & lakes, vegetarian cuisine or self-cater.

■ *Dance Bar/Disco*
CLUB TRIX, 53 Spence St, (070) 518 223, open Tues-Sun.

LAKE COOTHARABA

■ *Accommodations*
LE BATEAU IVRE GUESTHOUSE & UNITS, 25 Urunga Parade, Boreen Point, (61-7) 5485 3164, (61-7) 5485 3482. Guesthouse & 2 fully self-contained units, color & B&W TV, VCR, ceiling fans. Guesthouse: expanded continental

AUSTRALIA

breakfast, shared bath. Units: private baths. Some hetero clientele. ♀♂

MALENY

■ Accommodations

ZAMAZ, Montville Rd, (074) 594 3422, fax 594 3005, gay-friendly country house with restaurant & tea rooms, 50% gay/lesbian clientele, private baths, summer house, drawing room, CD library, gardens, tennis court.

NOOSA

■ Accommodations

NOOSA COVE, 82 Upper Hastings St, (61-7) 544 926 68 (tel/fax), mobile 018 061911. Guest house & holiday apartments near national park & Alexandria nudist beach, private baths, near gay nightclub, restaurant, women welcome. ♂

NOOSA HEADS

■ Accommodations

GUYS BED & BREAKFAST NOOSA HEADS, PO Box 964, Noosa Heads, (074) 5749 322, men-only bed & breakfast, shared baths. ♂

SURFERS PARADISE

■ Accommodations

SURFERS RETREATS, (800) 060 069.

■ Dance Bar/Disco

MP DANCE CLUB, Paradise Centre, level 1, Gold Coast Hwy, Tues-Sun, male strippers, drag shows nightly.

■ Cafe

GLOBAL CAFE, 3070 Gold Coast Hwy, 92 4192, European style cafe, closed Sun.

■ Saunas/Health Clubs

CLUB R, 3 Allison St, Parkrise Bldg, basement, (07) 5539 0955, 7 days, 16:30-01:00.

TOWNSVILLE

■ Information

AIDS INFO, (077) 211 384.

■ Accommodations

SANDY'S ON THE STRAND, PO Box 193, Townsville 4810, (700) 721 193, beachfront B&B.

■ Bars

DIANA'S, at Hermit Park Hotel, upper level, (077) 214 143, Fri, Sat from 20:30.

■ Retail & Bookstores

MARY WHO BOOKSHOP, 155 Stanley St, (077) 71 38 24, general bookstore with a gay & lesbian section.

■ Erotica

SWEETHEARTS, 206A Charters Towers Rd, Hermit Park, (077) 25 1431.

SOUTH AUSTRALIA
ADELAIDE

■ Information

AIDS INFO, (08) 8232 0966.
GAYLINE, (08) 8362 3223, daily 19:00-22:00 (Sat, Sun 14:00-17:00).
LESBIAN LINE, (08) 8223 1982 or 8223 1784.
WOMEN'S RESOURCE CENTER, 64 Pennington Terrace, North Adelaide, (08) 8267 3633, women's center & library, Mon-Thurs 09:00-18:00 (Fri till 17:00).

■ Accommodations

GREENWAYS APARTMENTS, 45 King William Rd, North Adelaide, (08) 8267 5903, fax: (08) 8267 1790. Holiday apartments, mainly straight clientele, fully-furnished kitchenette apts, AC, color TV, pool 3/4 mi, close to city center, shopping, entertainment, ocean beach 15 mi.
ROCHDALE, 349 Glen Osmond Rd, Glen Osmond, (61-8) 8379 7498, Fax: (61-8) 8379 2483. Bed & breakfast, preferred gay & lesbian accommodation, private & shared baths, full cooked breakfast, TV lounge, nearby pool & ocean.

■ Bars

BEANS BAR, 258 Hindley St, (08) 8231 9614, many women, from 21:00 (Sun from 20:00), Fri women's night 17:00-21:00 (Fri, Sat over 60% women).
EDINBURGH CASTLE HOTEL BAR, 233 Currie St, (08) 8410 1211, like an English pub, 11:00-24:00 (Sun 14:00-20:00), usually 70% men. Women's night Thurs.
SEMAPHORE HOTEL BAR, 17 Semaphore Rd, Semaphore, pub atmosphere, 7 days, 60% women.

■ Dance Bar/Disco

MARS BAR, 120 Gouger St, (08) 8231 9639, Mon-Sat from 21:00, DJ, drag shows Fri, 60% men, 40% women.
PLANET, 77 Pirie St, alternative dance bar, 20% gay, more gay Wed.
Q-BAR & POOL HALL, 274 Rundle St, level one, gay only Sun 21:30-04:00.
SYNERGY/PUMP, 58 North Terrace, 3 bars, gay Fri only, 22:00-05:00.

■ Cafe

BABBETTE'S EATERY, 69a Semaphore Rd, Semaphore, (08) 8341 66 06, cafe & lite menu, 11:00-18:00 (Sat, Sun from 10:00).
CAFE ANTICO, 176 Henley Beach Rd, Torrensville, open late.
CAFE GATSBY, 143 Goodwood Rd, Goodwood.

■ Saunas/Health Clubs

PULTENEY 431, 431 Pulteney St, (08) 8223 7506.

■ Restaurants

DON'S TABLE, 136 The Parade, Norwood, (08) 8634 3488.
EXCELSIOR, THE, at Hotel Excelsior, 110 Coglin St, Brompton, (08) 8346 2521, seafood, oysters, curries, soups, beef, etc.
LIME & LEMON, 89 Gouger St, (08) 8231 88 76, Thai cuisine, lunch Mon-Fri, dinners nightly.
SWEET WATER, 187 Rundle St, (08) 8223 68 55, Thai cuisine.

■ Retail & Bookstores

IMPRINTS BOOKSHOP, 80 Hindley St, (08) 8231 4454, general bookstore with a gay & lesbian section.
MURPHY SISTERS BOOKSHOP, 240 The Parade, Norwood, (08) 8332 7508. Women's & lesbian books, journals, music with browsing section & coffee room, current local information, 09:30-05:00 (Thurs till 20:00, Sat 10:00-16:00), closed Sun.
SISTERS BY THE SEA, Shop 1, 14 Semaphore Rd, Semaphore, 314 7088, women's bookstore, open daily.

ABSOLUTE BEACHFRONT
54 Cinderella Street
CAIRNS
(61-70) 550 289

Escape to Turtle Cove
Email: turtlecove@iig.com.au
http://www.iig.com.au/turtle_cove/
Tel.: (61-70) 591 800
Fax: (61-70) 591 969

PACIFIC REGION

FERRARI GUIDES' GAY TRAVEL A to Z - 18th EDITION

AUSTRALIA

Australia's Wilder Side

Situated in the northwestern part of Western Australia is an isolated, remote, rugged and beautiful part of the country, the Kimberley. Here, in one of the world's last wilderness areas, the water is still pure enough to drink from streams. The area is home to famous wilderness areas, among them Purnululu Nat'l Park, Carr Boyd and Cockburn Ranges, and just across the border in Australia's Northern Territory is the famous Kakadu Nat'l Park.

Marian Lester is an experienced lesbian bushwalker who has lived in Kununurra in the East Kimberly Mtns since 1990, and has personally guided women's and mixed groups since 1993. She is trained in women's outdoor leadership, canoe skills and wilderness first aid. Under her company name, **Sirius Adventures**, Marian customizes bushwalking and canoe trips for lesbians and gay men, and for mixed groups to explore and discover the Kimberley and parts of the Northern Territory. By "customized," Marian means she will plan the trip according to the interests and skill levels of the participants. At day's end, she serves delicious, nutritionally-balanced meals, including home-dried vegetables and fruit, with special dietary needs catered for.

Contact **Sirius Adventures** at (61-8) 9168 2110 (tel/fax).

■ Leathers/Piercing
EAGLE LEATHER, 114 Goodwood Rd, Goodwood, (08) 8373 0088.

■ Erotica
APHRO BOOKSHOP, 49 Morphett St, 10:00-24:00.
BOX, THE, 153 Hindley St.
CLUB FEMME, 73 Hindley St, 8410 0636, men's & women's erotica, pride videos.
GOOD VIBRATIONS, Shop 2, 489 Marion Rd, South Plympton.
LOVE SHACK, 388 Port Rd, Hindmarsh, (08) 8340 7222.
RAM LOUNGE, 71-73 Hindley St, enter through Club X, (08) 8410 0444.

TASMANIA
BEACONSFIELD

■ Accommodations
YORKTOWN MANOR, PO Box 138, Beaconsfield 7270, (61-363) 834 647 (tel/fax), gay-friendly.

DEVONPORT

■ Accommodations
TRELAWNEY BY THE SEA, 6 Chalmers Lane, Devonport 7310, (61-364) 243 263 (tel/fax), gay-friendly.

HOBART

■ Information
AIDS INFO, (0362) 241 034.
GAY INFO LINE, (0362) 348 179.

■ Accommodations
FORGE, THE, Brookbank, Richmond 7025, (61-362) 602 216, Fax: (61-2) 602 699, gay-friendly.
LODGE ON ELIZABETH, 249 Elizabeth St, (61-362) 313 830, fax: (61-362) 342 566, straight clientele with a large gay & lesbian following.
MAVISTA COTTAGES, PO Adventure Bay, Bruny Island 7150, (61-362) 931 347 (tel/fax), gay-friendly.

■ Bars
BAVARIAN TAVERN, 281 Liverpool St, gay bar Sun from 20:00, gay dance night 1st Sat 21:00-03:00, occasional drag shows. ♀♂
JABLONSKI BAR, MacQuarie at Barrack St, in Bakers Bldg, upstairs, only entrance is via external stairs on MacQuarie side, gay Tues-Sat 17:00-01:00. ♀♂

■ Dance Bar/Disco
LA CAGE, 73 Liverpool St, under the Ship Hotel, Thur-Sat from 23:00. ♀♂

■ Erotica
BLACK ROSE, 108 Harrington St.

LAUNCESTON

■ Accommodations
BRICKFIELD TERRACE, 64 & 68 Margaret St, (61-363) 301 753, Fax: (61-363) 302 334. Gay-friendly terraces with private baths, expanded continental breakfast, color TV, phone, fully equipped kitchen, handmde Tasmanian fudge.
EDENHOLME GRANGE, 14 St Andrews St, Launceston 3250, (61-363) 346 666, Fax: (61-363) 343 106, gay-friendly.
NORFOLK REACH, PO Box 56, Exeter 7275, (61-363) 947 681 (tel/fax), gay-friendly.
PLATYPUS PARK FARM, 343 Brisbane St, Launceston 7250, (61-363) 561 873 (tel/fax), gay-friendly.

■ Bars
TRAMSHED BAR, at the Great Northern Hotel, mainly hetero lounge, discreetly frequented by gays (30% gay clientele). Informal gathering of gays in the bar, Wed from 20:00.

SWANSEA

■ Accommodations
COOMBEND COTTAGES, RSD 14, Swansea 7190, (61-362) 578 256, Fax: (61-362) 578 484, gay-friendly.

VICTORIA
DAYLESFORD

■ Accommodations
BALCONIES, THE, 35 Perrins St, (61-3) 53 48 1322. B&B with in-house dinner, private & shared baths, expanded continental breakfast, beverage-making facilities, TV lounge, video library, indoor heated pool (nudity permitted) on premises. ♀♂
HOLLY LODGE, Grenville St, (61-3) 53 48 3670, B&B guesthouse.
LINTON HOUSE, 68 Central Springs Rd, (61-3) 53 48 2331, gay-friendly studio-style accommodations, private bath.
VILLA VITA, Main Rd, Kingston, (61-3) 53 48 3642, B&B, mostly women with men welcome, private shower/WCs, buffet breakfast, TV lounge, VCR, video tape library, laundry facilities, nearby pool, river & lake. ♀

■ Dance Bar/Disco
SPUDS CLUB, Midland Hwy, Neewlyn, 53 45 7300, gay restaurant which becomes a dance bar Sat 22:00. ♀♂

■ Cafe
NOT JUST MUFFINS, 26-28 Albert St, 53 48 3711, 08:00-14:00 (closed Tues).

■ Restaurants
DOUBLE NUT, Howe St, 53 48 3981, variety of cuisines with a Swiss accent. ♀♂

AUSTRALIA

GEELONG

■ Dance Bar/Disco
TWO FACES, 73 Yarra St, upstairs, gay Fri. 🏳️‍🌈♀♂

WOOL EXCHANGE, 44 Corio St, (052) 242 400. 🏳️‍🌈♀♂

MELBOURNE

■ Information
AIDS INFO, (03) 9347 6099.

ALSO FOUNDATION, 35 Cato St, 1st floor, Prahran, (03) 9510 55 69, gay organization, many gay & lesbian groups meet here.

GAY & LESBIAN SWITCHBOARD, (03) 9510 5488, 18:00-22:00.

■ Accommodations
CALIFORNIA MOTOR INN, 138 Barkers Rd, Hawthorne 3122, (61-3) 9818 0281, fax: (61-3) 9819 6845, toll free in Australia (1800) 331166. Ask for Jay. E-mail: llylew@mpx.com.au. Gay-friendly motel with restaurant & bar, color TV, direct dial phones, AC, coffee/tea-making facilities, pool on premises, 50% gay & lesbian clientele.

COSMOPOLITAN MOTOR INN, 4-6 Carlisle St, St Kilda, Victoria, (03) 9534 0781, fax (03) 9534 8262, gay-friendly hotel with restaurant, bar & conference facilities across from St. Kilda Beach, color TV, AC, private baths.

FITZROY STABLES, 124 Victoria St, Fitzroy, (03) 9415 1507. Fully self-contained, fully furnished apartment, private bath, color TV, telephone, kitchen, ceiling fans. Mostly women, men welcome. ♀

GATEHOUSE, THE, 10 Peel St, Collingwood, (61-3) 9417 2182, fax: (61-3) 9416 0474. Men-only S&M guesthouse with playrooms with mezzanines, dual-purpose sling beds & eye-hooks, lights with dimmer switches, shared bath, continental breakfast, AC, public phone.

LAIRD O'COCKPEN HOTEL, 149 Gipps St, Collingwood 3067, (61-3) 9417 2832, Fax: (61-3) 9417 2109. Men-only hotel with bar & beer garden, double rooms, 3 km from city centre, shared baths, continental breakfast, additional rooms available at the hotel's Norwood annex. ♂

MELBOURNE GUESTHOUSE, THE, 26 Crimea St, St Kilda, (03) 9510 4707, men-only guesthouse, private & shared baths, continental breakfast, fresh fruit, TV lounge, laundry facilities, nearby pool. ♂

ONE SIXTY-THREE DRUMMOND STREET, 163 Drummond St, Carlton, (03) 9663 3081, guesthouse, private & shared baths, expanded continental breakfast, 24hr self-serve tea & coffee, TV lounge with colour TV, ceiling fans, laundry facilities, maid service. ♀♂

PALM COURT B&B, 22 Grattan Place, Richmond, 3121, (61-3) 9427 7365 (tel/fax), Mobile: (0419) 777 850. B&B with expanded continental breakfast, private & shared baths, women welcome. ♂

XCHANGE HOTEL, 119 Commercial Rd, (cnr Osborn St) South Yarra, (03) 9867-5144, fax (03) 9820-9603, typical pub/hotel with adequate accommodation, shared baths, budget rates, women welcome. ♂

■ Bars
CANDY BAR, 162 Greville St, Prahran, (03) 9529 6666, bar & cafe with DJ, 50% gay. No dance floor, but later in evening everyone starts dancing around wherever.

DIVA BAR, 153 Commercial Rd, South Yarra, (03) 9824 2800, bar & cafe, daily 11:00-03:00. ♪♀♂

DT'S HOTEL BAR, 164 Church St, Richmond, (03) 9428 5724, pool table, games, 11:30-01:00 (Sun till 23:00). ♂

DUKE HOTEL BAR, St Kilda Rd at Martin St, St Kilda, (03) 9534 4666, men-only, cruisy pub, from 15:00 (Sat, Sun from 12:00). ♂

GLASSHOUSE HOTEL BAR, 51 Gipps St, Collingwood, (03) 9419 4748, from 16:00, closed Mon, Tues. Call for schedule of women's nights. ♀♂

LAIRD BAR, at the Laird Hotel location, (03) 9417 2832, cruise bar, strictly men-only policy, Mon-Sat from 18:00, Sun till 24:00. Sun evening Country & Western line dancing from 19:30. ♂

MARTIN STREET BAR & CINEMA, 1-5 Martin St, St Kilda, (03) 9537 2133, theater with large screen, bar next door, men only, from 18:00. ♂

Q&A, 211 Gertrude St, Fitzroy, gay Thurs 19:00-01:00, punk, alternative grunge "Indie" crowd, dance floor. ♀♂

RASCALS HOTEL BAR, 194 Bridge St, Richmond, (03) 9429 9491, local pub with female bands, 7 days. ♀

ROYAL HOTEL BAR, 41 Spensley St, at the Royal Hotel, Clifton Hill, (03) 9489 8716, Thurs from 20:00 women's nights. ♀

RUBY LOUNGE, 141 Johnson St, Fitzroy, at The Nightcat, (03) 9531 4218, women's cabaret night 1st Sun, call for exact schedule. ♀

VM'S,★ 199 Commercial Rd, South Yarra, (03) 9827 6611, small cocktail bar with tiny dance floor & rooftop bar under the stars, open from 17:00 Wed-Sun. ♀♂

XCHANGE HOTEL BAR,★ 119 Commercial Rd, South Yarra, (03) 9867 5144, fax: 9820 9603, 12:00-01:00 (Sun till 24:00), video bar, lounge. Popular Sun afternoon beer bust. ♂

■ Dance Bar/Disco
COMING OUT, (03) 9489 8222, women's dance nights, venues change frequently, call for current locations & times. ♀

DISORDERLY, 138 Comercial Rd, Prahran, Sun from 21:00, grunge, punk, Indie music, DJ, live bands. ♀♂

GREYHOUND HOTEL BAR, 1 Brighton Rd, St Kilda, gay Sat only 19:00-01:00, dance party. ♀♂

PEEL DANCE CLUB,★ Peel & Wellington Sts,

FYI

Much to Do Around Melbourne

Melbourne is Australia's second city, an ethnically diverse mix of cultures and cuisines. Southern Discovery Tours' gay tour guide will escort you in a luxury 4WD vehicle on a City Sights tour with a gay perspective. The *Shop Til You Drop* tour takes you to factories of famous men's fashion brands, all at discount prices. *Around the Bay* visits vineyards for winetasting, a Victorian-era seaside resort and the famous Bells Beach, home of Iron Man championships, where the "scenery" can be quite delightful. The *Yarra Valley* tour acquaints you with indigenous Australian animals, lets you taste wine at the Domaine Chandon winery and tours a goldmining area known for arts, crafts, pottery and antique shops. The *Penguin Parade* is an evening tour on which you view legions of wild penguins waddling to their burrows for the night. The *Goldfields & Spa Country* tour visits a gold rush town, has lunch in gay-friendly Daylesford, explores a mineral spa and stops for winetasting at Cope-Williams winery on the way back.

Contact **Southern Discovery Tours** at (61-3) 9419 5230 (tel/fax).

FERRARI GUIDES' GAY TRAVEL A to Z - 18th EDITION

AUSTRALIA

Collingwood, (03) 9419 4762, video dance bar, daily from 22:00.

PLUSH,★ at The Lounge in Sanston Walk, Thurs gay dance nite, house music.

QUEER NATION, 19 Park St, South Melbourne.

SKIN, 19 Commercial Rd, at the Dome nightclub, S Yarra, (0418) 377 227, Sat alternative night, 50% gay/lesbian.

SNAKEPIT, 127 Fitzroy St, at The George Hotel, low.lev., St Kilda, gay Sun only.

THREE FACES, 143 Commercial Rd, South Yarra, (03) 9826 0933, Tue-Sun from 17:00, cabaret cocktail bar upstairs, dance bar & drag shows downstairs.

URANUS, Commercial Rd at Grattan St, Prahran, (03) 9534 1819, recovery bar, 02:00 Sun till Sun afternoon.

VAULT NIGHTCLUB, Vault 7, 9 Banana Alley, Flinders St, rear entrance, (03) 9629 9410, gay only alt Fri for Cruising men's or Tool Box women's nights.

■ Cafe

BLUE ELEPHANT, Commercial Rd near Izett St, South Yarra.

CAFE 151, 151 Commercial Rd, Prahran, (03) 9826 5336, daily from 12:00.

CAFE FARGO, 406 Brunswick St, Fitzroy, (03) 9416 2599, 07:00-24:00 (Fri-Sun till late).

COL'S CAFE, 70 Smith St, Collingwood.

GALLEON CAFE, 9 Carlisle St, St Kilda, (03) 9534 8934, 09:00-24:00.

RAMJET'S, Commercial Rd nr Porter St.

STRAND, THE, Commercial Rd near Porter St, South Yarra.

■ Saunas/Health Clubs

BAY CITY SAUNA CAULFIELD, 482D Glenhuntly Rd, Elsternwick, (03) 9528 2381, 18:00-02:00 (Fri, Sat 18:00-04:00).

BAY CITY SAUNA SEAFORD, 2/16 Cumberland Dr, Seaford, (03) 9776 9279, 14:00-02:00 (Fri, Sat till 04:00).

BERKELEY SAUNA, 36-42 Berkeley St, Carlton, (03) 9349 4149, 11:00-01:00 (Fri, Sat till 03:00).

CLUB 80, 10 Peel St, Collingwood, (03) 9417 2182, private men's club, 17:00-08:00 (Sat, Sun from 14:00).

LANEWAY SAUNA, 1-5 Martin St, St Kilda, (03) 9537 2177, 17:00-06:00.

PORTER STREET, 55 Porter Street, Prahran, (03) 9529 5166, 18:00-07:00, (Fri from 14:00, Sat 14:00-Mon 07:00).

R&R MEN'S CLUB, 7 Crossley St, (03) 9639 1629, private men's club, Mon-Sat 11:00-19:00.

SPA GUY, 553 Victoria St, Abbotsford, (03) 9428 5494, 17:00-01:00 (Fri-Sun fr16:00), cl. Tu.

STEAMWORKS, 279 LaTrobe Street, (03) 9602 4493, 12:00-03:00 (Wed, Thurs till 05:00).

TEN PLUS, 59 Porter St, Prahran, (03) 9525 0469, private men's club, 20:00-06:00 (Sat, Sun from 14:00).

■ Restaurants

CHINTA RIA, Commercial Rd near Izett St, Prahran, Malaysian cuisine. Second location: 94 Acland St, St Kilda. Both locations very popular with gays.

GLOBE CAFE, 218 Chapel St, Prahran, (03) 9510 8693, daily.

KING & I, 103 Lonsdale St, Thai cuisine, 7 days.

ROCOCO, 226-228 Coventry St, S. Melbourne, (03) 9696 0001, restaurant & bar, modern Australian cuisine.

SAMMY'S, 64 Acland St, St Kilda, (03) 9525 5151, pizza.

SUKHOTHAI, 490 High St, Northcote, (03) 9489 5551, Thai cuisine, daily from 17:30. Second location: 234 Johnson St, Fitzroy, 9419 4040.

THAI LOTUS, 106 Hoddle St, Collingwood, (03) 9417 4555, Thai & Australian cuisine, closed Mon.

THE ANGEL, 362 Brunswick St, Fitzroy, (03) 9417 2271, café & restaurant, vegetarian & meat dishes, mainly women, 10:00-20:00, closed Tues.

■ Retail & Bookstores

DIVERSITY FASHIONS, 196 Commercial Rd, Prahran, (03) 9521 4644, clothes for crossdressers & "clubbing."

HARES & HYENAS, 135 Commercial Rd, South Yarra, (03) 9824 0110, gay & lesbian bookshop. Second location 360 or 364 Brunswick St, Fitzroy (next to Angel Café).

LABRYS, 433 Brunswick St, Fitzroy, (03) 9417 7388. Women's jewelry, gifts & crafts, rare crystals & gemstones, open daily.

SHREW WOMEN'S BOOKSHOP, 37 Gertrude St, Fitzroy, (03) 9419 5595, books by & for women, non-sexist children's books, magazines, journals & cards, Tues-Fri 10am-6pm, Sat 10am-5pm.

THE WOMEN'S BOOK EXCHANGE, 10 Smith St, 1st floor, Collingwood, (03) 9417 7989, second-hand books for women, Tues-Sat 13:00-18:00.

■ Leathers/Piercing

EAGLE LEATHER, 118 Hoddle St, Abbotsford, (03) 9417 2100.

FLAMING GUNS, 321 Sydney Rd, Brunswick, (03) 9388 0673, tatoos & piercing.

PIERCING URGE, THE, 206 Commercial Rd, upper level, Prahran, (03) 9530 2244.

■ Erotica

BEAT, THE, 157 Commercial Rd, Prahran, (03) 9241 8748.

CLUB X, 34 Elizabeth St, (03) 9650 2047.

GEMINI ADULT BOOKSHOP, 235A Smith St, Fitzroy.

INSPIRATION BOOKSHOP, 14 Chapel St, Windsor, (03) 9510 1867.

RAM LOUNGE, many locations: Melbourne: 275 King St, 221 Russell St, 60 Spencer St, 216 Swanston St & 270 Swanston St; Kilda: 74 Acland St; Brunswick: 323 Sydney Rd; Clayton: 292 Clayton Rd; Footscray: 172 Nicholson St; Box Hill: 592 Station St.

MORNINGTON PENINSULA

■ Accommodations

CAPE SCHANCK LODGE BED & BREAKFAST, 134 Cape Schanck Rd, Cape Schanck 3939, (61-3) 598 863 95 (tel/fax). Gay-friendly B&B 1 hr south of Melbourne on the tip of the Mornington Peninsula. Popular with women looking for a peaceful retreat from the city, 2 wings allow for greater privacy. Private baths, pool, silver-service dinners on request, shiatsu massage & sauna packages, 10% lesbian following.

NEWBURY

■ Accommodations

BLUE MOUNT B&B, Kearneys Rd, Newbury (Trentham), VIC 3458, (054) 241 296. Gay-friendly B&B, 50% hetero clientele, private baths, full breakfast, beverage-making facilities, colour TV, video library, private cottage garden, nearby mineral spas, wineries, horseback riding.

STRATHBOGIE RANGES

■ Women's Accommodations

WHISPERING WINDS, PO Box 286, Euroa, (61-57) 981 608, a hand-built mudbrick, stone & timber cottage for women only, located in northeast Victoria, 2hrs from Melbourne, 1 loft bedroom (linen provided), potbelly stove heating, lovely scenery, nearby activities.

WARRNAMBOOL

■ Accommodations

KING'S HEAD, PO Box 658, Warrnambool 3280, (61-3) 5561 4569, Fax: (61-3) 5562 4085. E-mail: kinghead@ansonic.com.au. http://www.ansonic.com.au/kingshead. Good mix of gays & lesbians, priv. & shared baths.

WESTERN AUSTRALIA
BALINGUP

■ Accommodations

BALINGUP FOREST LODGE, Hay Rd, (097) 641 273, bed & breakfast.

PERTH

■ Information

AIDS INFO, (09) 429 9900.

GAY & LESBIAN LINE, (09) 328 9044, Mon-Fri 09:00-12:00 & 19:30-22:30.

■ Tours, Charters & Excursions

BEAT (BRIEF ENCOUNTERS AUSTRALIA TOURS), (61-9) 309 2982, one-day guided tours in and around Perth.

■ Accommodations

ABACA PALMS, 34 Whatley Crescent, Mount Lawley, (61-9) 271 2117, mobile (015) 089

PACIFIC REGION

New Zealand

COUNTRY CODE: (64)

WHO TO CALL
For Tour Companies Serving This Destination
See New Zealand on page 22

NORTH ISLAND
AUCKLAND

■ *Information*

AIDS INFORMATION, (0800) 802 437 (24hrs), (09) 358 00 99.
AUCKLAND GAY & LESBIAN COMMUNITY CENTRE, 44-46 Ponsonby Rd, 1st floor, (09) 302 0590. Unverifiable spring '97.
GAY & LESBIAN LINE, (09) 303 35 84, 10:00-22:00 (Sat, Sun from 17:00). Women answer evenings Mon, Wed & Sat.
PRIDE CENTRE, 33 Wyndham St, (09) 302 05 90.
WOMANLINE, (09) 3765 173, answers Mon-Fri 11:00-20:30.

■ *Accommodations*

ASPEN LODGE, 62 Emily Place, (09) 379-6698, fax: 3777-652, gay-friendly budget bed & breakfast hotel 5 min from downtown, shared baths, TV lounge, continental breakfast, complimentary tea, coffee.
BUDGET INN TALOFA, 508 Great North Rd, Grey Lynn, (09) 378 8872, gay-friendly hotel with bar & restaurant, private baths.

■ *Beaches*

LADIES BAY, just past St. Heliers Beach along the eastern waterfront. The gay section is around Achilles Point in Gentlemen's Bay. Take St. Heliers Bus #510 to shopping center, walk east up Cliff Rd and down the path to the beach.
LONG BAY, 30km north of the city in a regional park. Long Bay Bus #839. The gay area is closest to the rocks at the north end of beach.
ST. LEONARD'S, between Takapuna & Narrow Neck beaches on Auckland's north shore. Long Bay Bus #839. At low tide, walk south or drive to the end of St. Leonard's Rd. Gay area is to the left. sunbathing in the coves, below the cliffs.

■ *Bars*

BRAD'S BAR, 45 Anzac Ave (first floor), at Club Westside sauna, daily from 12:00. ♂

786, men-only B&B guesthouse with TV lounge, video library, private dining room, laundry facilities, weights & Jacuzzi, full breakfast, 20 km to gay beach.
LAWLEY ON GUILDFORD, 72 Guildford Rd, Mount Lawley, (61-9) 272 5501 (tel/fax), mobile: (015) 995 178. B&B with expanded continental breakfast, private & shared baths, color TV, AC, public phone, TV lounge, Jacuzzi, grass tennis court, enclosed conservatory, some hetero clientele. ♀♂
PENNY'S BY THE SEA, PO Box 208, 96A Stanley St, Scarborough, Sunset Coast, (09) 341 1411, fax: 245 1073, mobile: (015) 1969 30. B&B guesthouse, clean & comfortable, shared baths, continental breakfast from fresh, local produce, bowl of fruit, nearby pool & ocean beach. ♀♂
SULLIVANS HOTEL, 166 Mounts Bay Road, (09) 321 8022, Fax: 481 6762, gay-friendly hotel, private baths with showers.
SWANBOURNE GUEST HOUSE, 5 Myera St, Swanbourne, (09) 383 1981, fax: (09) 385 4595, mobile (018) 902 107. B&B guesthouse, women welcome, private & shared baths, continental breakfast, colour TV, VCR, beverage-making facilities, nearby pool, ocean, river & lake. ♂

■ *Bars*

CLICK CLUB GEREMIAH'S, William St at Milligan St, at the Orchard Hotel Complex, (09) 322 29 23. ♀♂
COURT HOTEL BAR, 50 Beaufort St, (09) 328 5292, daily 10:00-24:00 (Sun 12:00-21:00), DJ in the pub, Wed women only. ♂
DIVEBAR, 232 William St, Northbridge, (09) 328 1822, bar with snack bar. ♂

■ *Dance Bar/Disco*

CONNECTIONS, 81 James Street, Northbridge, 328 1870, 60% men, 40% women, Tues-Sat 22:00-06:00 (Tues men only, Thurs women only), Sun 20:00-24:00. ♂
DC, 105 Francis St, Northbridge, (09) 227 79 50, from 22:00, about 50% gay.

■ *Cafe*

LUKE'S CAFE, James St, Northbridge.
VULTURE'S CAFE, William St, at Francis St, Northbridge.

■ *Saunas/Health Clubs*

BEAUFORT FIVE SIXTY-FIVE, 565 Beaufort Street, Mount Lawley. ♂
CITY STEAM, 369 William St, at Forbes Rd (enter upstairs off Forbes Rd), Northbridge, (09) 328 2930. ♂

■ *Retail & Bookstores*

ARCANE BOOKSHOP, 212 William St, Northbridge, (09) 328 5073. Bookstore with lesbian, feminist & gay literature, general books, calendars, postcards, 10:00-17:30 (Sat till 17:00), Sun 12:00-16:00.

■ *Erotica*

RAM LOUNGE, 114 Barrack St, enter through Club X.

OUT! MAGAZINE

New Zealand's national Gay community magazine, covering the South Pacific area. Full of the latest local news & gay scene reports. photos, personal classifieds, book, video & magazine reviews.

AIRMAIL SUBSCRIPTION 1YR
South Pacific $45.00
Nth America & Asia $60.00
Elsewhere $70.00
Single Sample Copy $08.00

OUT!, PRIVATE BAG 92126 AUCKLAND 1
NEW ZEALAND. PH (64) (9) 3779 031

FERRARI GUIDES' GAY TRAVEL A to Z - 18th EDITION

NEW ZEALAND

FYI

Women's Adventures in New Zealand's Unspoilt Wilderness

Bushwise Women provides unique adventures for women in true, unspoilt New Zealand wilderness. Based at a Bushline lodge, near Lake Brunner on New Zealand's scenic west coast, visitors explore the rainforest, mountains and lakes, learn bushcraft skills and canoeing or

BUSHWISE WOMEN
New Zealand

goldpannning, or can simply relax. Locations are in the most beautiful part of New Zealand. Roz and Cynthia provide expert guidance in a supportive environment. Trips are for a maximum of eight women of any age. Each trip is graded "Armchair," "Easy," "Moderate" or "Fit," depending on the fitness level needed to participate. Activities include writing workshops, photography hikes, sea kayaking, cavern and cave exploring, pack and paddle, bushwalking, overnight tramping, and cross-country skiing.

When you visit Bushwise, Roz and Cynthia will pick you up in central Christchurch in their minibus. On the four-hour journey over the Southern Alps to Bushline Lodge, you'll have a change to explore dramatic landscapes along the way.

Contact **Bushwise Women** at (64-3) 332 4952 (tel/fax).

K BAR, 373 Karangahape Rd, at the Cameron Hotel, lower level, gay Sun afternoon & evening. ♂

KARAKTERS, Wallace Rd, Papatoetoe, at the St. George Tavern, (09) 277 9955, Thurs-Sat from 20:30. ♂

LATESHIFT, 25 Dundonald St, (09) 3732 657, private club, cruise bar with fully equipped backrooms, videos, 19:00-01:00 (Fri, Sat 21:00-06:00). ♂

SINNERS NIGHTCLUB, 373 Karangahape Rd, at the Cameron Hotel, upper level, gay Fri-Sun till late. ♂

STAIRCASE BAR, 340 Karangahape Rd, (09) 377 0303, Tues from 17:00. ♂

SURRENDER DOROTHY, 175 Ponsonby Rd, Shop 3, (09) 376 4460, 18:00-01:00 (Sat, Sun from 12:00). ♂

VOLT, 340 Karangahape Rd, at Staircase, upper level, private club. ♂

■ Dance Bar/Disco
KASE CLUB, THE, 340 Karangahape Rd, 3 bars, Wed-Sat from 18:00 (disco from 22:00).

LEGEND, 335 Karangahape Rd, (09) 377 60 62, from 16:00 (Sun from 14:00).

STAIRCASE CLUB, 340 Karangahape Rd, (09) 3770 303, disco Wed-Sat from 22:00. ♂

■ Saunas/Health Clubs
CLUB WESTSIDE, 45 Anzac Ave (first floor), (09) 3777 771, sauna & bar, from 12:00 (Fri, Sat 24hrs). ♂

NEW ZEALAND COUNTRYMEN'S INSTITUTE, 151 Beach Rd, Parnell, (09) 366 1781, 12:00-01:00 (Fri, Sat till 05:00). ♂

WINGATE CLUB, 76 Wingate St, Avondale, (09) 828 0910, daily from 12:00.

■ Restaurants
LET'S GET FAT CAFE, 18 Lorne St, (09) 358 0796.

RYBURN'S BAR & GRILL, North Rd, Clevedon, (09) 292 8111.

SALSA BAR & CAFE, 137a Richmond Rd, Ponsonby, (09) 378 81 58, 15:00-23:30 (closed Sun).

■ Retail & Bookstores
ONEHUNGA BOOK EXCHANGE, 163 The Mall, Onehunga, (09) 622 1766, general bookshop with new & secondhand gay titles, 09:00-17:30 (Fri till 19:00, Sat till 14:00).

THE WOMEN'S BOOKSHOP, 228 Dominion Rd at Valley Rd, Mt Eden, (09) 6307 162, feminist & lesbian books & magazines Tues-Sat from 10:00.

■ Leathers/Piercing
OTHER SIDE, 374 Karangahape Rd, at Chameleon.

VISUAL ECSTASY, 347 Karangahape Rd, (09) 3033 44 49.

■ Erotica
DEN, THE, 348 Karangahape Rd, (09) 3079 191, safe sex club. ♂

DEPOT, THE, 354a Karangahape Rd, (09) 3567 311, Wed-Sun, cruise club. ♂

OUT! BOOKSHOP, 45 Anzac Ave, (09) 377 7770, gay bookshop with videos, magazines, novelties, 11:00-23:00 (Mon, Tues till 18:00), Sun 13:00-20:00.

BAY OF ISLANDS

■ Accommodations
ORONGO BAY HOMESTEAD, Aucks Road, RD1, Russell, Bay of Islands, (64-9) 403 7527, fax: (64-9) 403 7675. Guesthouse with gourmet dining room & historic wine cellar, on 17 acres of bush, lake & lawns, sweeping views, 50-min flight from Auckland. Full breakfast with champagne, all private baths. Central to many outdoor activities, beaches & game fishing. 50% gay & lesbian clientele.

FEATHERSTON

■ Women's Accommodations
PETRA KIRIWAI FARM, RD 3, Featherston, 1 hr from Wellington airport, (06) 307 7899, women-only guesthouse on 350 acres of land, near ocean & lake, mostly lacto-vegetarian cuisine, private & shared baths, laundry facilities. ♀

HAMILTON

■ Information
AIDS INFO, (07) 838 557.

GAYLINE, (07) 854 9631, Wed 20:00-22:00.

■ Bars
NEXT DOOR BAR, 10 High St, Frankton, 17:30-03:00 (closed Mon, Tues). ♂

■ Cafe
METROPOLIS CAFE, 241 Victoria St, (07) 847 8635, gays & lesbians meet here 1st Sun from 15:00. ♀♂

■ Saunas/Health Clubs
TEN HIGH SAUNA, 10 High St, Frankton, from 17:00. ♂

■ Retail & Bookstores
BOOKSHOP 242, 242 Victoria St, gay magazines.

GOLDMINE BOOKSHOP, 312 Victoria St, general bookshop with gay section.

HUNTERVILLE

■ Beaches
VINEGAR HILL, from Christmas to the week after New Year's, large crowds of gays & lesbians. 5km north of Hunterville off State Hwy 1. Camping at the downriver end, bring a tent. Loosely-organized activities.

NAPIER/HASTINGS

■ Information
GAYLINE, (06) 8357 482, 17:00-08:00.

NEW ZEALAND

■ **Accommodations**
PROVIDENCIA GUEST HOUSE, Middle Rd, RC2, Hastings, (06) 877 2300, gay-friendly.

■ **Retail & Bookstores**
CLARK'S CIVIC CT BOOKSHOP, Station St, Napier, general bookstore with a gay & lesbian section.

STORTFORD LODGE BOOKSHOP, 1102 Heretaunga St, Hastings, gay section with books & magazines.

NEW PLYMOUTH

■ **Erotica**
NAUTI NIK NAKS, 49 Egmont St.

PALMERSTON NORTH

■ **Information**
GAYLINE & LESBIAN LINE, (06) 358 5378, 24hrs.

■ **Bars**
MANAWATU GAY RIGHTS ASSN BAR NIGHTS, (06) 358 5378, Fri from 20:00, Sat from 21:30, ask about women-only nights.

■ **Retail & Bookstores**
WOMEN'S SHOP, Square Edge, Church St, (06) 358 2644, women's bookstore & crafts, good information resource for travelling lesbians.

■ **Erotica**
BROADTOP BOOKS & TOYS, Broadway Ave.

ROTORUA

■ **Information**
AIDS SUPPORT, (03) 348 1199, ext. 8980.
GAYLINE, (07) 348 3598, Tues 19:00-21:00.

■ **Accommodations**
DEVON HOMESTAY B&B, PO Box 2438, (07) 348 0193.

TROUTBECK, 16 Egmont Rd, PO Box 242, Ngongotaha, Rotorua, (64-7) 357 4795, Fax: (64-7) 357 4780, E-mail: troutbeck@xtra.co.nz.. Homestay 5 km from Rotorua on 1/2 acre of landscaped garden on banks of Waiteti Stream, fly fish for trout Dec-May from the garden's edge. Shared baths, full breakfast & optional dinner NZ $15. Close to thermal areas, Maori culture & golf courses. Women welcome.

WELLINGTON

■ **Information**
AIDS INFO, (04) 3893 169.
GAY SWITCHBOARD, (04) 3850 674, daily 19:30-22:00.
LESBIAN LINE, (04) 3898 082, Tues, Thurs 19:00-22:00.

■ **Accommodations**
AMBASSADOR TRAVEL LODGE, 287 The Terrace, (04) 484-5697, Fax: 485-7215, bed & breakfast, centrally located, mainly straight, comfortable, clean, well-furnished, single rooms thru villas, full breakfast & dinner.

■ **Women's Accommodations**
MERMAID GUESTHOUSE, THE, 1A Epuni St, Aro Valley, Brooklyn, Wellington, (64-4) 3844511 (tel/fax), E-mail: mermaid@sans.vuw.ac.nz. Early 1900s wooden building in one of Wellington's older historical areas. Women only. Individually decorated double and single rooms, shared & private bathrooms. TV, VCR, fresh fruit, complimentary wine. Large deck, guests' lounge with pool table. Breakfast included. Great atmosphere!

■ **Beaches**
BREAKER BAY, at Wellington Harbour entrance, a pebble beach with very cold water. Bus #3 to last stop. The gay area is closest to the point.

PEKAPEKA, 80 km north of Wellington off Hwy 1, down Pekapeka Beach Rd between Waikanae and Otaki. Walk north 10 minutes past stream.

■ **Bars**
CASPERS, 120-126 Victoria St, (04) 384 1333, 11:00 till late.
CLUB WAKEFIELD, 15 Tory St, at Club Wakefield Sauna, from 12:00.
SANCTUARY, 39 Dixon St, (04) 384 1565, cruise bar, 16:00-24:00 (Wed, Thurs 20:00-02:00, Fri, Sat 20:00-06:00).
TOLEDO BAR, at The Oaks Tavern, Royal Oak Centre, Cuba Mall, (04) 385 0583, from 16:00 (closed Sun), this bar opens & closes periodically.

■ **Saunas/Health Clubs**
CLUB WAKEFIELD SAUNA, 15 Tory St, (04) 385 4400.

■ **Restaurants**
BRASSERIE FLIPP, 103 Ghusnee St, (04) 385 9493.

■ **Retail & Bookstores**
AFTERNOONS & COFFEE SPOONS, shop 6, 165 Riddiford St, Newtown. Women's shop with new & used books, videos, music, t-shirts, sarongs, jewelry, crafts, etc. Coffee, tea, muffins & cakes. 11:00-19:00 (Sun till 15:00), closed Mon.

■ **Erotica**
OUT! BOOKSHOP, 15 Tory St, (04) 3854 400, gay magazines, videos, toys, leather, 11:00-23:00 (closed Sun).

SOUTH ISLAND
CHRISTCHURCH

■ **Information**
GAY INFO LINE, (03) 3793 990, 24hrs.

■ **Accommodations**
RAINBOW HOUSE, 9 The Crescent, (64-3) 337 1438. B&B guesthouse inn with shared bath, full breakfast, TV lounge, video tape library, women welcome.

■ **Women's Accommodations**
BUSHLINE LODGE, c/o Bushwise Women, PO Box 28010, Christchurch, New Zealand. (64-3) 332 4952 (tel/fax) or (64-3) 738 0077. A women-only B&B on the West Coast of New Zealand with private & shared baths & expanded continental breakfast. Activities include bushwalking, bird watching, rafting, caving, gold-panning & year-round trout fishing. Bookings essential.

FRAUENREISEHAUS (THE HOMESTEAD), 272 Barbados St, (03) 366 2585. Women-only backpackers hostel, mostly hetero with a gay female following. Single, double & bunk rooms, shared baths, TV lounge, bedding, laundry facilities, library, bike rental, near city centre.

■ **Beaches**
NORTH NEW BRIGHTON, Effingham St. Bus No. 19 to last stop in New North Brighton, then walk north along the paths on the dunes.

■ **Bars**
UBQ SOUTHERN BOYS, 90 Lichfield St, at Ministry Nightclub, (03) 379 1821, private club for men. Public sometimes admitted, call first.

■ **Saunas/Health Clubs**
COLOMBO SAUNA, 661 Colombo St (top of stairs), (03) 3667 352, members bar, daily from 12:00.

MENFRIENDS CLUB & SPA, 83 Lichfield St, (03) 377 1701, from 12:00 (Sat, Sun from 13:00).

■ **Restaurants**
ESCAPADE, 51 Lichfield St, restaurant, bar & cafe.

■ **Retail & Bookstores**
KATE SHEPPARD WOMEN'S BOOKS, 145 Manchester St, (03) 790 784, feminist, spiritual & new age titles, also music, posters, cards & jewelry, also gay men's titles, Mon-Thur 09:00-17:30, Fri 09:00-21:00, Sat 10:00-13:00.

MENFRIENDS, 83 Lichfield St, at Menfriends Club, (03) 377 1701, gay cards, magazines.

OUT! BOOKSHOP, 661 Colombo St, at Colombo Sauna, (03) 3667 352, gay books, magazines, videos, lubes, etc.

■ **Erotica**
DAVID'S BOOK EXCHANGE, 181 High St, (03) 3662 057, magazines & videos.

DUNEDIN

■ **Information**
GAYLINE, (03) 477 2077, 24hrs, ask about coffee evenings 2nd & 4th Fri.
LESBIAN LINE, (03) 4772 077, Tues 17:30-19:30.

■ **Beaches**
ST. CLAIR & ST. KILDA, take the St. Kilda

NEW ZEALAND

bus No. 27 or the St. Clair Bus No. 7 from the Octagon.

■ *Retail & Bookstores*
ABERDEEN BOOKSHOP, 185 Hillside Rd, general book store with a gay section.
MODERNWAY BOOKS, 331 George St, general bookstore with gay section.
SOUTHERN BOOKS, 225 King Edward St, general bookstore with a gay section.

INVERCARGILL

■ *Information*
GAYLINE, (03) 216 6344, evenings, weekends.
LESBIAN LINE, 218 3877, 19:00-21:00.

NELSON

■ *Information*
AIDS INFO, (03) 546 1731, Mon-Fri 08:00-16:00.
SPECTRUM, 42 Franklyn St, (03) 548 0814, men's social group & drop-in centre, Thurs 19:30-22:30.

■ *Accommodations*
AUTUMN FARM GAY GUESTHOUSE, (03) 525 9013, write R.D.I. Takaka, 7172 Golden Bay. ♂
HENRYS & GOLDEN BAY, (03) 525 9781, gay homestays, near Golden Bay National Park & beaches. Write PO Box 209, Takaka. ♂
PALM GROVE GUEST HOUSE, Cambria St, at Tasman St, (03) 548 4645.
TE PUNA WAI LODGE, 24 Richardson St, Port Hills, (03) 5487 621, 3-storey Victorian villa with mountain & sea views.

■ *Restaurants*
RIBBETTS RESTAURANT, 20 Tahunanui Dr, (03) 548 6911.

■ *Retail & Bookstores*
REGAL MAG & TOY BOOKSHOP, 212 Hardy St, gay magazines.

WESTCOAST AREA

■ *Information*
GAYLINE WESTPORT, (03) 789 6027, Fri 19:00-20:30.

■ *Accommodations*
PYRAMID FARM, holiday farm retreat, write Private Bag, Charleston, The Buller.

PACIFIC
Pacific Islands

WHO TO CALL
For Tour Companies Serving This Destination
See Pacific Islands on page 22

COOK ISLANDS
COUNTRY CODE: (682)

RAROTONGA

■ *Accommodations*
MANUIA BEACH HOTEL, PO Box 700, Rarotonga, Cook Islands, (682) 22461, fax: 22464, on one of Rarotonga's best white-sand beaches by the lagoon, you'll stay in a Polynesian-style thatched bungalow with stylish decor, private bathroom, refrigerator, minibar and ceiling fans.
TAMURE RESORT HOTEL, PO Box 483, Rarotonga, Cook Islands, (682) 22415, fax: 24415, newly-decorated rooms overlook the lagoon and the Pacific, 100 yards from a coral reef, with patio, individual AC, private bathroom and refrigerator, tropical gardens and a cocktail bar on the premises.

FIJI ISLANDS
COUNTRY CODE: (679)

KOROLEVU

■ *Accommodations*
CRUSOE'S RESORT, PO Box 20, Korolevu, Fiji, (679) 500 185, Fax: (679) 520 666. Gay-friendly. Tropical island resort with bar, disco, & shops. Private baths, expanded continental breakfast.

NANDI

■ *Accommodations*
MELANESIAN HOTEL, PO Box 10410, Nandi, Fiji (679) 722 438, Fax: (679) 720 425. Budget hotel with restaurant & bar, pool on premises, near airport.

FR. POLYNESIA/TAHITI
COUNTRY CODE: (689)

MOOREA ISLAND

■ *Accommodations*
RESIDENCE LINAREVA, PO Box 1, Haapiti-Moorea, French Polynesia, Tel/Fax: (689) 56 15 35. At the foot of lush, green hills, is a tropical lagoon paradise with floating pub & restaurant for gay, lesbian and other visitors from faraway. Each typical Tahitian grass bungalow features deluxe accommodations with private shower-bath, kitchenette, color TV, ceiling fans & is decorated with traditional crafts. **LINAREVA FLOATING RESTAURANT,** at Residence Linareva, (689) 56 15 35, lunch & dinner daily, afternoon menu, sunset cocktails. Gay-friendly.

PAPEETE

■ *Bars*
HOTEL PRINCESSE HEIATA BAR, address not needed, 3 281 05, late-night disco popular after the other nightclubs have closed and frequently open till dawn, women welcome. ♂
PIANO BAR★, rue des Ecoles, 3 228-24, popular disco for gay men & women, drag shows featured, open till about 2am, sometimes later. ♀♂

GUAM
COUNTRY CODE: (671)

ASAN

■ *Bars*
CLUB SOPHIA, S. Marine Drive (Route 1), 477 1249, large, rustic karaoke bar, hetero sex videos, 22:00-02:00, discreetly frequented by gays.

Residence LINAREVA
Deluxe accommodations in a tropical lagoon paradise.
floating pub & restaurant
PO Box 1
Haapiti- Moorea
Tel/Fax (689) 56 15 35 • French Polynesia

PACIFIC ISLANDS

Gay and Lesbian Scuba Diving — The Urge to Submerge

by Chris Winkle

Have you wondered what it's like under the sea, where a marine world exists that cannot be believed until experienced? Have you wondered what it would be like to feel weightlessness, like the astronauts? Now's your chance to find out the answer to these and other raging questions that have been perplexing your mind. Go scuba diving!

One of the great things about diving is that it gives you the excuse to travel to remote dive sites in all parts of the world. Just as surfer dudes are in search of that "perfect wave," so are divers looking for that special, undiscovered dive spot. It can be anywhere from an island in the Florida Keys to the coral reefs of Belize, the Cayman Islands, Cozumel, idyllic South Pacific Fiji. There are endless possibilities, each with its own special cachet.

Many divers swear that Cozumel offers the best diving anywhere. This small island is located off Mexico's Yucatan Peninsula, and is part of the Mundo Maya, having originally been settled by the Mayans. It's southerly locations offer warm weather year-round, and the nature of the island's position off the coast causes powerful currents to sweep along the western beaches.

These currents are what draw divers to Cozumel - just jump in and submerge, and let the current carry you along. Diving is effortless and the sightseeing is magnificent. Why swim back to the boat, when the boat will follow you and pick you up when you're ready to ascend?

Another great dive location, convenient for those of us living in southern California, is the Sea of Cortez (Gulf of California), especially in the area of La Paz, Loreto and Cabo San Lucas. Water temperatures here vary greatly as the seasons progress, resulting in great upwellings of nutrient-rich water from the deeper depths. In the winter months, you'll see whales on every dive excursion, sometimes as many as 6 or 7 at the same time. In the summer months, lucky divers search out the elusive whale shark, the largest fish known and a gentle and peaceful filter feeder. In the autumn months, hammerhead sharks school at undersea sea mounts. These fish actually get "spooked" by divers' bubbles, and they disappear if divers come too close.

Hawaii's Kona is another top dive destination for west coasters. The intermittent flow of lava into the ocean over the millennia has created giant undersea lava formations, and swim-throughs called lava tubes. Tropical fish are abundant here, and manta rays often feed at night along Kona's coast. While the

Chris Winkle is the director of Undersea Expeditions, a gay and lesbian company dedicated to scuba diving. This feature has been intended as a survey, to let you know what's out there waiting for you. So, when you've got that urge to submerge, give Undersea Expeditions a call. They have trips planned to Truk, Fiji, Roatan (Honduras) — including an all-women's trip— and to the exotic Cocos Islands and Galapagos Islands, as well as Belize, Thailand and Cozumel in 1998. We can book you an independent vacation or on a learn-to-dive trip on your own. Contact Chris and Undersea Expeditions at (619) 270-2900, (800) 669-0310, E-mail: UnderseaX@aol.com, Web: www.mindfood.com/gaydiving.html.

Continued on next page.

PACIFIC ISLANDS

water temperatures of 75 degrees might not be equatorial, they certainly beat those at La Jolla Cove.

My personal favorites have to be in the South Pacific. The Fiji Islands, located between Australia and Hawaii, and on the 180th meridian (international dateline), are known for their stunning beaches, clear, tropical waters, mountains and incredible aquatic plant life. Most importantly, you will find the Fijian people to be some of the warmest on earth. Their openness and good nature melt the ice of even the most frigid souls.

The scuba diving in Fiji is absolutely breathtaking. Currents feed the soft coral formations, making Fiji, and Fiji's Taveuni Island in particular, the soft coral capital of the world. The Great White Wall is a stunning dive spot, an immense drop-off (underwater cliff) draped in rows of flowering soft corals. Divers here can drop off the boat, then propel themselves through an underwater tunnel, emerging at 110 feet to an unbroken wall of flowering white soft corals. The experience is absolutely mind-blowing.

The Micronesian atolls of Truk and Palau are other fabulous dive locations. Truk is known for the sunken Japanese fleet that lies 100 or more feet below the surface. These wrecks have become underwater reefs, covered with coral, anemones and sponges, and surrounded by fish and undersea creatures of all kinds. Some of these ships are over 500 feet long. You can swim their length and penetrate the ships, themselves. Inside, you'll find sake bottles, dishes and plates, telephones and more deadly items like ammunition, guns, tanks and military transport vehicles. All of these are covered with sea growth, but their outlines and deadly purposes are still recognizable. Truk is part of the Federated States of Micronesia, a US-administered area that was occupied by the Japanese during World War II. It's inhabitants are kindly, but somewhat suspicious, due to the lengthy occupation of their territory by foreign nationals.

Palau is located southwest of Truk, and what Truk is to wrecks, Palau is to drift diving. The visibility in this area is unsurpassed, often exceeding 200 feet. The best way to see Palau is on a liveaboard, i.e. a boat solely dedicated to diving. The Sun Dancer II, for example, is the newest liveaboard operating in Palau. Having a length of 120 feet, it accommodates 20 divers in maximum comfort. Using a liveaboard provides the option of up to five dives a day (as opposed to two for a land-based operation) and allows for access to remote spots unreachable on day trips.

TAMUNING

■ **Dance Bar/Disco**
CRACKERS, Chalan San Antonio, 649 6269, daytime coffee house, evening dance bar. Different music, drink specials daily. Free shuttle to & from hotels. Open nightly, more popular Fri.

KOOL WORLD/SOO JEONG, off Marine Drive, behind Guam Saving & Tic Toc, near Ace Hardware, 646 7661, open nightly, karaoke, some hetero clientele.

UNDERGROUND/CLUB PARADISE, ★ Marine Drive, near Blockbuster Video, 635 INFO (ext 888), big, trendy dance club, mostly gay clientele.

TUMON

■ **Bars**
JAKOB'S, 340 San Vitores Rd, in front of Guam Visitors Bureau, 646 9510, small karaoke lounge, 21:00-02:00, some Japanese spoken.

FYI

Around-the-World Sailing Cruise

Finish the century in beauty aboard **East-West's** magnificent Lagoon, a 55-ft catamaran which will travel around the world from January, 1997 to March, 1998. Join the entire 14-month trip (departing from Tahiti) or choose one of six legs, each lasting about two months. Don't bring your tuxedo. You will be a working crew member. Crew members will decide the itinerary but keep each arrival date.

Don't forget your walking shoes, either. You'll spend about 60% of your trip at interesting ports along the way. Scuba diving equipment, air tanks, two dinghies, and a certified instructor are on board. The price? $66,000 to sail the world, $12,000 for each stage, including meals on board, professional skipper, unlimited water skiing, scuba diving and windsurfing and emergency/repatriation insurance.

Schedule: Antilles-Galapagos 1/15-3/15, Galapagos-Tahiti 3/15-5/15, Tahiti-Salomon 5/15-7/31, Salomon-Maldives 7/31-10/15, Maldives-Greece 10/15-12/31, Greece-Antilles 12/31-3/15/98.

Contact **East-West's** Paris office at (33-1) 53 89 13 33, Fax: (33-1) 53 89 13 34.

ALBERTA

CANADA

COUNTRY CODE: (1)

WHO TO CALL
For Tour Companies Serving This Destination
See Canada on page 11

ALBERTA
CALGARY

■ *Information*
GAYLINE, (403) 234-8973. 7-10pm or tape 7 days. 24hr info line 234-9752.
LESBIAN INFO LINE, (403) 265-9458. 7:30-9:30pm Mon & Wed or tape. Information available on women's collective.

■ *Accommodations*
BLACK ORCHID MANOR, 1401-2 St NW, Calgary, AB T2M 2W2, (403) 276-2471, E-mail: lthrman@canuck.com. B&B in an Edwardian home with antique furnishings, shared baths, expanded continental breakfast, 1hour to Banff National Park & museums. ♀♂
FOXWOOD B&B, 1725-12 St SW, Calgary, AB T2T 3N1, (403) 244-6693. Edwardian character home in the heart of Calgary, shared baths, color cable TV, 2 rooms wtih VCRs, full breakfast, near gay bars, 1 hour to Olympic ski area. Some straight clientele. ♀♂
WESTWAYS GUEST HOUSE, 216 25th Ave SW, (403) 229-1758 (tel/fax). B&B private baths, women welcome. ♂

■ *Bars*
MONEY PENNIES, 130-1509 Centre St SW, (403) 263-7411. Bar & restaurant, pool table, days: 75% men, evenings 50/50.
REKROOM, 213A 10th Ave SW, at Boystown bar, downstairs, (403) 265-2028. Video cruise bar.
ROOK'S BAR & BEANERY, 112 16th Ave NW, (403) 277-1922, dance club, 90% women, men welcome.
TEXAS LOUNGE AT GOLIATHS, 308 17 Ave SW (rear), (403) 229-0911. Bar inside gay sauna. ♂

■ *Dance Bar/Disco*
BOYSTOWN/METRO & REKROOM,★ 213 10th Ave SW, (403) 265-2028. Boystown/Metro dance bar upstairs, Rekroom tavern downstairs, male strippers, men only except Wed.

DETOURS, 318 17th Ave SW, (403) 244-8537.

■ *Cafe*
MIDNIGHT CAFE, 8th St & 14th Ave SW, Dining lounge, drag shows & karaoke weekends.

■ *Saunas/Health Clubs*
GOLIATH'S, 308 17th Ave SW near 2nd St (rear), (403) 229-0911, 24hrs.

■ *Restaurants*
FOLKS LIKE US BISTRO, 110 10th St NW, at Kensington Rd, (403) 270-2241. Eclectic mix from cottage pies to veggie chilies, Middle Eastern, sandwiches, salads, some meat dishes. Women-owned.
MONEY PENNIES, 130-1509 Centre St SW, (403) 263-7411. Bar & restaurant. ♀♂
VICTORIA'S, 306 17th Ave SW, (403) 244-9991. Frequented by gays late evenings. Weekend brunches.

■ *Retail & Bookstores*
A WOMAN'S PLACE BOOKSTORE, 1412 Centre Street S, (403) 263-5256. Feminist, lesbian & gay men's titles.
RAINBOW MERCANTILE, 306-310 17th Ave SW, pride items, open Thurs-Sat evenings.

■ *Leathers/Piercing*
B&B LEATHER WORKS, 6802 Ogden Rd SE, (403) 236-7072. Custom made clothing & sub dom equipment, leather & latex.
STAIRWELL LEATHERS, 1401 2nd St NW, (403) 276-2471, www.lthrman@canuck.com.

■ *Erotica*
AFTER DARK, 7248 Ogden Rd SE, also at 13th & 1st, (403) 279-3730. Noon-8pm Mon-Sat.
LOVERS LEEP, 6806 Ogden Rd SE, (403) 236-4903.
TADS, 1217A 9th Ave SE, (403) 237-8237.

EDMONTON

■ *Information*
AIDS HELP LINE, 11456 Jasper Ave, Rm 201, (403) 488-5742.
GAY & LESBIAN COMMUNITY CENTER, #103, 10612 124th St, (403) 488-3234, info line (403) 988-4018.
GAY LINE, (403) 486-9661. Tape of local info.
WOMANSPACE & LESBIAN LIFELINE, 9930 106th St, (403) 482-1794. Lesbian meetings 2nd Tues. Monthly women's dances, lesbian library, events.

■ *Accommodations*
LABYRINTH LAKE LODGE, RR1, Site 2, Box 3, Millet, (403) 878-3301 or (403) 424-6381. Fully-equipped cabin (sleeps 12) on 160 acres of rural lesbian land with secluded lakefront. Canoes, bikes, skis & more. 50 minutes from Edmonton. Gay men welcome. ♀
NORTHERN LIGHTS GUESTHOUSE, PO Box 515, Edmonton, AB T5J 2K1, gay & lesbian guesthouse. ♀♂

■ *Bars*
BOOTS 'N SADDLES, 10242 106th St near 103rd Ave, (403) 423-5014. Private club, pub, male strippers Sat.
SHAKESPEARE'S, 10306 112th St, (403) 429-7234, DJ, darts, women-only every Fri & 1st Sat of month, men welcome one Fri per month.

■ *Dance Bar/Disco*
ROOST, THE, 10435 104th St near 104th Ave, (403) 426-3150. strippers.

■ *Restaurants*
BUDDYS, 10116 124th St, (403) 488-6636. Pub, Fri men's night. ♀♂
COOK & GARDENER CAFE, THE, 10345 106th St, (403) 421-7044. Coffee, desserts, lunch & dinner.
GARAGE RESTAURANT, 10242 106th St, attached to Boots 'n Saddles, (403) 423-5024, burgers, fries, chicken, wings, straighter crowd for lunch.
JAZZBERRY'S TOO, 10116 124th St, home cooking.

■ *Retail & Bookstores*
ORLANDO BOOKS, 10640 Whyte Ave, (403) 432-7633. General bookstore with large gay, lesbian & women's section.

■ *Erotica*
EXECUTIVE EXPRESS, 202-11745 Japser Ave, (403) 482-7480. 1pm-9pm, closed Tues.
LYONS EMPIRE, 10121 124th St, (403) 488-6915.

GRAND PRAIRIE

■ *Information*
GAY & LESBIAN COMMUNITY CENTER, (403) 539-3325. Ask about Open Closet Drop-in Center Thurs-Sat 7:30pm-9:30pm.

■ *Bars*
TOUCHÉ, 201-8502 112th St, (403) 538-9998, 9pm-2am (call to verify days open), private club. ♀♂

LETHERIDGE

■ *Information*
GAY ALLIANCE, (403) 329-4666. Socials, discussions, events, Wed 7pm-10pm.

RED DEER

■ *Information*
GAY & LESBIAN ASSN., (403) 340 2198. Wed

FERRARI GUIDES' GAY TRAVEL A to Z - 18th EDITION

ALBERTA

FYI

Evening Sails Off Vancouver, BC

Take an evening sail with Muffy and Jane of **Envision Charters** for a real ship's-eye view of one of the most photogenic cityscapes in the world. In Vancouver, an impressive skyline of tall buildings stands against a backdrop of lofty, snow-covered mountains. Between the two is a deep waterway plied by giant oceangoing freighters, container ships and cruise ships.

Join Muffy and Jane aboard the Random Wake for an evening cruise, a barbeque dinner, a commitment ceremony or weekend getaway to the Gulf Islands and the Sunshine Coast. They'll take other suggestions, too. Special events best experienced from boats include the Festival of Fire, an international fireworks competition, and the Carol Ship Parade, where folks sing Christmas Carols whilst cruising the waters around Vancouver.

Contact **Envison Charters** at (604) 688-7245, cellular: (604) 657-2893.

7pm-9pm or tape, coffee house 2nd Wed 7pm-10pm.

■ *Dance Bar/Disco*

THE OTHER PLACE (TOP), Bay 3 & 4, 55794 47th St, (403) 342-6440. 4pm-3am Tues-Sun, dance bar with DJ.

BRITISH COLUMBIA
KELOWNA

■ *Information*

OKANAGAN RAINBOW COALITION, (250) 860-8555. Scheduled Gay & lesbian dance nights, coffeehouses, potlucks, volleyball on the beach, picnics on long weekends. Coffee Mon 7pm-10pm. Lesbians meet Wed. Travelers welcome to participate.

■ *Accommodations*

FLAGS BED & BREAKFAST, THE, RR #1, Site 10, Comp 2, 2295 McKiney Rd, V1Y 7P9, (250) 868-2416. B&B, private & shared baths.

NANAIMO

■ *Bars*

NEIGHBOURS, Front St between Bastion & Church, (250) 716-0505. Video lounge, Mon-Fri 5pm-1am, Sat noon-1am, Sun noon-midnite.

SALT SPRING ISLAND

■ *Accommodations*

BLUE EWE, 1207 Beddis Rd, (250) 537-9344. Gay & lesbian inn with many female clientele.

GREEN ROSE, 346 Robinson Rd, (250) 537-9927. B&B farmhouse, 50% gay & lesbian clientele. Private & shared baths, full breakfast & nearby lake.

SUMMERHILL GUEST HOUSE, 209 Chu-An Drive, (250) 537-2727, Fax: (250) 537-4301. B&B overlooking the ocean, 50% gay & lesbian clientele. Private baths, full breakfast, many outdoor activities.

SUNNYSIDE UP, 120 Andrew Place, (250) 653-4889. Accommodations with ocean view, 50% gay & lesbian clientele.

TOFINO

■ *Accommodations*

WEST WIND GUEST HOUSE, THE, 1321 Pacific Rim Hwy, (250) 725-2224. Private cottages near beaches & Pacific Rim National Park. Telephone, hot tub, universal gym, bicycles, private covered parking.

■ *Women's Accommodations*

WIND RIDER GUEST HOUSE, Box 548, Tofino, BC V0R 2Z0, Administration: (250) 725-3230, Client Services: (250) 725-3240, Fax: (250') 725-3280. Women's guesthouse in downtown Tofino with 1 double, 2 singles, shared bath, AC, Jacuzzi, outside deck. Sunset views & view of Clayoquot Sound & Meares Island. Access to women's wilderness guide & other training.

VANCOUVER

■ *Information*

AIDS HELPLINE, (604) 681-2122. Mon-Fri 10am-9pm, Sat 10-6.

ATISH NETWORK. South Asian HIV/AIDS Awareness Project. Punjabi, Hindi & Urdu spoken. Write, Attn: Al-Qamar Sangha, Box 345-1027 Davie St, Vancouver, BC V6E 4L2.

GAY & LESBIAN CENTRE, 1170 Bute, (604) 684-5307. Helpline: (604) 684-6869. 7pm-10pm 7 days, or (800) 566-1170 (within BC).

LESBIAN CENTER, 876 Commercial Dr, (604) 254-8458. Thurs & Fri 11am-6pm, Sat noon-4pm.

■ *Accommodations*

"O CANADA" HOUSE, 1114 Barclay St, Vancouver, BC V6E 1H1, (604) 688-0555. Gay-friendly Victorian B&B with private baths, full gourmet breakfast, complimentary snack bar, short walk to beaches, 3 blocks to gay bars. Some straight clientele.

ALBION GUEST HOUSE, THE, 592 W 19th Ave, (604) 873-2287, Fax: (604) 879-5682, E-mail: hle@bht.com. B&B 5 minutes from downtown. Double rooms with private & shared baths, some with color TV or VCR & video tape library. Full breakfast, non-smoking establishment.

COLIBRI BED & BREAKFAST, 1101 Thurlow St, (604) 689-5100, Fax: (604) 682-3925. Conveniently located bed & breakfast, some hetero clientele. Airy, cheerful rooms with shared baths. Full breakfast, secure parking & nearby pool & ocean.

COLUMBIA COTTAGE GUEST HOUSE, 205 West 14th Ave, (604) 874-5327, Fax: (604) 879-4547. B&B minutes from everything, 20% gay/lesbian clientele. 1920's-style rooms with private baths & full breakfast. English country garden.

DUFFERIN HOTEL, 900 Seymour St, (604) 683-4251, fax: (604) 683-0611. Hotel with gay bar & restaurant, Private baths. 50% gay men.

HERITAGE HOUSE HOTEL, 455 Abbott St, (604) 685-7777, fax: (604) 685-7067. Guest room hotel, 3 bars, priv./shared baths.

NELSON HOUSE, 977 Broughton St, Vancouver, BC V6G 2A4, Canada, (604) 684-9793, Fax: (604) 684-4141. **No boring old B&B!** Every spacious corner guestroom suggests a different travel itinerary. Will it be Sailors, Vienna, Klondyke, or Hollywood? The third-floor studio suite, with Far Eastern ambience, a fireplace, deck, kitchen and Jacuzzi ensuite, is especially appealing. We are often complimented on our breakfast food, fun and conversation. Visit awhile. After all, Vancouver is right on the doorstep. See ad on page 327.

ROYAL HOTEL, 1025 Granville St, (604) 685-5335, Fax: 685-5351. Centrally-located hotel with gay bar, private & shared baths. We call

BRITISH COLUMBIA

Vancouver: Spectacular By Nature

by Rick Hurlbut

Perhaps it is that we are tucked so discretely into the Northwest corner of the continent, somehow removed from the rest of the world. Perhaps it is that rare and dramatic combination of ocean and mountain, which brings mild weather both summer and winter. Perhaps it is the Californian "Rest Coast" mentality which has migrated north to give Vancouver that decidedly laid back attitude. Whatever the reason, Vancouver has emerged as both a world class city and top tourist destination, replete with its own peculiar quirks and charms.

Much like other harbour cities, the natural waterfront setting is spectacular. A backdrop of rugged, forested coastal mountains to the north and the broad Fraser River delta to the south complete the scene. Outdoor activities abound, from hiking and mountain biking to sailing and sea kayaking. With all there is to do, we have the proverbial embarrassment of riches.

The region is blessed with Canada's mildest climate. Snow in winter is rare, except up on the mountains where it belongs. Summers are warm and generally sunny, although you can never guarantee dry weather in these parts. This plentiful "liquid sunshine" has given us many beautiful public gardens, lush parks and dramatic coastal rail forests. Hardy types are known to go about in shorts year round.

Three ski resorts overlook the city, offering spectacular views of the city below. In the spring you can ski in the morning, drive 30 minutes, and be sunning on the beach by afternoon. The lights for night skiing float eerily above the city, reminiscent of the landing of the giant mother ship in *Close Encounters*. Whistler and Blackcomb mountains, 90 minutes to the north, are North America's top rated ski resort five years running, and the site of the annual *Altitude* gay ski week in February, attracting some 5,000 participants.

The gay and lesbian community is concentrated in two areas: the West End between Stanley Park and downtown; and along Commercial Drive, or "The Drive", on the city's East Side. Restaurants, bistros, night clubs, book stores, boutiques and myriad other gay enterprises are found along Commercial, Davie and Denman streets.

The community is served by four newspapers. 'Angles' is published monthly by a volunteer collective, while 'Xtra! West' is a member of a Canadian chain of gay monthlies and bimonthlies. The newest two are lifestyle and entertainment

Rick Hurlbut operates Pride Enterprises Ltd., a travel marketing and promotions company. He also does freelance writing on a variety of gay community related topics, including travel.

Xtra! West is Vancouver's leading news, arts and entertainment gay & lesbian publication, with a circulation of 28,500 copies every other week. For a sample copy or a subscription, contact *Xtra! West*, 501-1033 Davie St., Vancouver BC Canada V6E 1M7. Tel: (604) 684-9696, Fax: (604) 684-9697.

Continued on next page

BRITISH COLUMBIA

magazines, 'the loop' and 'the buzz'. A number of programs are produced by Co-op Radio, including the Coming Out Show and the Lesbian Show.

Lesbian and Gay Pride has a split personality in V-town. Traditionally, the annual Pride events are celebrated the August long weekend (the first Monday in August); the date being chosen to avoid conflicting with Pride events in other cities. A parade down Denman and Pacific streets ends with a big party at Sunset Beach. Arts and cultural events, and more big parties, happen all weekend. More recently, Stonewall Day has been observed with live entertainment and a community fair at Grandview Park in the Commercial Drive area.

Founded just over a century ago, Vancouver is a fairly young city. Small until recently, the city proper has grown to just under a half million people, with another 700,000 in the surrounding Lower Mainland suburbs. Despite having our share of glass boxes, many historic buildings can still be found. A few whimsical modern structures are also worth seeing.

The old waterfront warehousing district of Gas Town is popular, with its unique steam driven clock and concentration of galleries and gift shops. A second historic district, Yaletown, is known for avant-garde clothing and home furnishing shops.

For an inexpensive overview of the city ride the Skytrain, an elevated light-rail system which passes through many of the city's suburbs and out across the Fraser River. At Waterfront Station transfer to the SeaBus, and cruise across Burrard Inlet to the North Shore and the public market at Lonsdale Quay. The view back toward the city skyline is quite dramatic.

Granville Island, one of the federal government's more successful endeavors, offers a unique mix of artisans' studios, restaurants, shops, boat rentals, an art college and farmer's market. For quick access, take one of the miniature ferries running from the West End.

The city is a favourite destination for Asian and European visitors; downtown is a veritable United Nations of languages in the summer. We are also becoming an important centre for conferences and trade shows, including the XIth International Conference on AIDS held here in July 1996, and Gay Games III in 1990.

With the recent signing of the Canada/USA open-skies agreement, and the mid-1996 completion of an expanded International Airport, Vancouver is becoming the continent's premier gateway to the Orient and Europe. Experts expect tourism to increase at a breakneck pace. Direct and nonstop flights are now available from throughout North America.

This is also the summer home of the growing Alaska cruise run, including those organized by such gay and lesbian tour operators as Our Family Abroad, Ocean Voyager, T.R.I.P. Tours, RSVP and Olivia. Some seven million tourist pass through the city annually, 600,000 being cruise passengers. One result is an excellent selection of four and five star hotels, which remain busy from May through October. Alternatively, consider staying at one of several excellent lesbian and gay Bed & Breakfasts.

Although summer season hotel rates can be steep, the current devaluation of the Canadian dollar still makes visiting Vancouver economical. In 1996, the US dollar could get you $1.35 Canadian or better. Similar results could be had for the pound, mark, yen and other hard currencies. For even better values, consider visiting in the off season, November through April.

Wreck Beach is undeniably Vancouver's worst kept secret. Located down a steep embankment below the University of British Columbia, the beach has been popular with nudists for decades. The main area features venders hawking everything from steak sandwiches to Bloody Marys. The gay section is to the left, while further south along the shoreline are smaller pockets of sand and sheltered nooks where the boys are known to gather.

Which brings us to Stanley Park. A combined natural and man-made playground, the 1,000 acre park boasts beaches, a new public swimming pool, formal gardens, a small zoo and aquarium featuring species common to the region, upscale restaurants and a magnificent coastal rain forest. The eleven kilometre sea wall is popular with cyclists, strollers, joggers and in-line skaters. Summer weekends are particularly busy and parking becomes is difficult. For the nocturnal crowd, there's also Lee's Trail, but definitely only at your own risk.

Vancouver is Canada's gateway to Asia-Pacific. In the last century, Chinese and Japanese immigrants came to help build the railways and to farm and fish. Today they are joined by Indians, Vietnamese, Filipinos and others, giving the city a diverse cultural mix, reflected in unique ethnic neighbourhoods and businesses. Both Chinatown and the Punjabi Market feature bilingual signs.

While familiar chain restaurants are abundant, Vancouver is best known for small ethnic and specialty eateries. Being on

Continued on page 510

BRITISH COLUMBIA

CANADA

ourselves a 1st-class 3rd-class hotel. Low prices, adequate accommodations for budget-minded travelers. ♀♂

RURAL ROOTS BED AND BREAKFAST, 4939 Ross Rd, Mt Lehman, (604) 856-2380, Fax: (604) 857-2380, E-mail: rroots@uniserve.com. B&B on a heather farm with gardens & orchard, Color TV, private & shared baths, full breakfast, hot tub. ♀♂

WEST END GUEST HOUSE, 1362 Haro St, (604) 681-2889, Fax: 688-8812. Gay-friendly B&B. Unique, beautiful rooms with Victorian ambiance, private & shared baths. Guest lounge, expanded continental breakfast & nearby ocean beach.

YWCA HOTEL RESIDENCE, 733 Beatty St, (604) 895-5830, Fax: (604) 681-2550; in BC & Alberta: (800) 663-1424. Hotel with international craft shop, private & shared baths, gay men welcome.

■ Women's Accommodations

HAWKS AVENUE BED & BREAKFAST FOR WOMEN, 734 Hawks Ave, Vancouver, BC V6A 3J3, (604) 253-0989. A women-only heritage townhouse in Strathcona neighbourhood. Quiet, comfortable accommodation, close (10 min) to downtown theatres, shopping and restaurants, Gastown, Chinatown and Commercial Dr. Delicious breakfast, local calls free, street parking & public transport. Reasonable rates. Non-smokers preferred. ♀

YWCA, 580 Burrard St, (604) 683-2531, Fax: 684-9171. Hotel at the YWCA. Mostly straight women with lesbians & gay men welcome. ♀

■ Bars

DENMAN STATION, 860 Denman St, (604) 669-3448. 75% men, 25% women. ♂

DUFF PUB, THE, 900 Seymour St, in the Dufferin Hotel, (604) 683-4251. Bar & restaurant in the Dufferin Hotel featuring live bands weekly drag shows, male strippers Sun. ♀♂

MS T'S, 339 W Pender St near Homer, (604) 682-8096. ♀♂

NUMBERS, 1042 Davie St near Burrard, (604) 685-4077. Music videos, dance bar & upstairs cruise bar. ♂

ROYAL HOTEL PUB, 1025 Granville at the Royal Hotel, (604) 685-5335. Afternoon pub, live bands. ♂

UNCLE CHARLIE'S BAR & GRILL & CHUCK'S PUB, 455 Abbott St at Heritage House Hotel (side entrance). Uncle Charlie's: 1st floor bar & restaurant. Chuck's is men's drinking bar. ♂

■ Dance Bar/Disco

CELEBRITIES,★ 1022 Davie St at Burrard, (604) 689-3180. Disco, DJ nightly, strippers. ♀♂

FLYGIRL, 1545 W 7, (604) 875-9907. Scheduled women's dance night (usually Sat). Tickets at the door or at Little Sisters books. ♀

LOTUS CLUB, 455 Abbott St at Heritage House Hotel, downstairs, (604) 685-7777. Tues-Sat from 8pm, Fri women-only. ♀

ODYSSEY,★ 1251 Howe St, (604) 689-5256. Trendy to the max, patio, after hours coffee house Homer's. ♂

■ Cafe

CAFE DU SOLEIL, 1393 Commercial Dr & 2096 Commercial Dr, (604) 254-1145 & (604) 254-1195.

DELANEY'S ON DENMAN, 1105 Denman, (604) 662-3344.

EDGE EXPRESSO BAR,★ 1148 Davie St, (604) 685-3417. Big with bar crowd, lots of smokers. Cruisy late evenings.

HARRY'S OFF COMMERCIAL,★ 1716 Charles St, (604) 253-1789. Coffeehouse with sandwiches.

SPUNTINO CAFFEE, 1103 Davie, (604) 688-9658. Restaurant, bakery & cafe, great lunches.

■ Saunas/Health Clubs

CLUB VANCOUVER, 339 W Pender St, (604) 681-5719. Private club, 24hrs. ♂

F212 STEAM, 971 Richards St, (604) 689-9719. Private men's spa. Also at 430 Columbia St, New Westminster, (604) 540-2117. ♂

NU WEST STEAM BATH, 553 Front St, New Westminster, (604) 526-2913, 24hrs.

RICHARDS ST SERVICE CLUB, 1169 Richards St, (604) 684-6010, 24hrs.

■ Restaurants

ALABASTER, 1168 Hamilton, (604) 687-1758.

ALLEGRO CAFE, 888 Nelson St, (604) 683-8485. Mediterranean cuisine, inspired chef, varied menu.

BEETNIX PASTA BAR, 2549 Cambie St, (604) 874-7133. Dishes like curried lamb, spring rolls, tandoori salmon.

CAFE LUXY,★ 1235 Davie St, (604) 681-9976. Italian cuisine, good food & atmosphere, large portions.

DEDE'S, 1030 Denman St, (604) 688-6264. Contemporary cuisine, lunch, brunch, dinner, & cocktails.

DELILAH'S, 1739 Comox, (604) 687-3424. Elegant, upscale continental cuisine. Trendy & excellent.

DENIRO'S BISTRO, 1007 Mainland St, (604) 684-2777. Funky with great martinis.

DOLL & PENNY'S CAFE, 1167 Davie St, (604) 685-3417.

ELBOW ROOM CAFE, 500 block of Davie St, (604) 685-3628. Brunch & lunch only. Many gays for Sat, Sun brunch.

GRASSHOPPER, 2-1600 Howe St, (604) 688-HOPP. West Coast cuisine, gay-friendly.

HAMBURGER MARY'S ("MARY'S"), 1202 Davie St, (604) 687-1293.

INSPIRING GROUNDS, 1073 W Broadway, (604) 732-1232. Sandwiches, soups, salads. Gay-friendly.

LA QUENA, 1111 Commercial Dr, (604) 251-6626. Latin-American cuisine, closed Mon.

LE VEGGIE, 1095 Denman St, (604) 682-3885. Chinese vegetarian cuisine.

MILESTONES, on Denman. Casual dining, curly fries & burgers, curry dishes.

PURPLE ONION, 15 Water St, (604) 602-9442. Healthy, gourmet, light snacks to meals, early evening till 1:30am.

QUATTRO, 4th Ave, Italian cuisine.

STEFHO'S,★ ask locally for address. Greek cuisine, gay-friendly.

TAKI'S TAVERNA, 1106 Davie St, (604) 682-1336. Greek restaurant. Gay-friendly, a "must" in Vancouver.

WAAZUBEE, 1622 Commercial Dr, (604) 253-5299. Cocktails, Asian-influenced cuisine.

■ Retail & Bookstores

LITTLE SISTER'S, 1238 Davie St, (604) 669-1753, fax: (604) 685-0252, books by mail: (800) 567-1662, E-mail: lsisters@netfinder.com. Gay & lesbian books, cards, videos.

RAINBOW'S END, 573 E Hastings St, (604) 254-6442. Thrift store & transgender boutique.

WOMEN IN PRINT, 3566 W 4th Ave, (604) 732-4128, Fax: (604) 732-4129. Feminist bookstore.

WOMYNSWARE, 896 Commercial Dr, at Venables, (604) 254-2543, Fax: (604) 254-5472, www.womynsware.com. Women's sexuality items, "vibes, dills, lubes, latex & more."

■ Leathers/Piercing

MACK'S LEATHERS, 1043 Granville St, (604) 688-MACK (6225). Ready-made and custom leather clothing, S&M accessories.

NELSON HOUSE
Vancouver
(604) 684-9793

Simply Superlative

FERRARI GUIDES' GAY TRAVEL A to Z - 18th EDITION

BRIT. COLUMBIA

The Most Spectacular Train Trip in the World

It begins in Vancouver, Calgary, Banff or Jasper and glides through the dramatic wilderness of the glacier-clad Rocky Mountains during May-October. Onboard Signature Service offers spacious, reclining seats, picture windows and a non-smoking, air-conditioned environment. Gold Leaf Service on the bi-level luxury Dome Coach seats 72 guests in a panoramic environment on the upper level. An open-air observation platform is on the lower level, and the elegant dining lounge has regional delicacies. (Smoking in designated area). An attendant provides colorful commentary and anecdotes of the regions through which you travel. On the overnight stay in Kamloops, an optional dinner theatre show features entertainment depicting life on the range in the 1880's.

Contact **Rocky Mountaineer Railtours** at (604) 606-7200, (800) 665-7245, Fax: (604) 606-7201, E-mail: rkymtn@fleethouse.com.

British Columbia's Soft Adventure Specialists

Besides being visually arresting and one of the most desireable locations for soft adventure enthusiasts, British Columbia has Vancouver, one of the world's more fascinating, cosmopolitan cities. Its active and varied gay nightlife is a nice change to come back to when you are finished with sea kayaking, rafting and canoeing, hiking, horsepacking, viewing wildlife, backpacking, rock climbing, mountaineering or bicycling, staying in remote mountain resorts, lodges or guest ranches, riding island ferries, float planes helicopters or charter boats, cruising the inside passage, journeying by rail through the Rockies, or skiing....all in breathtakingly beautiful surroundings.

Super Natural Adventures are Vancouver-based and pride themselves on their encyclopaedic knowledge of vacation options for visitors to Western Canada, including both BC and its neighboring province, Alberta. Their thick catalog is filled with color photos of the properties offered.

Contact **Super Natural Adventures** at (604) 683-5101, (800) 263-1600, Fax: (604) 683-5129.

■ *Erotica*
IMPERIAL BOOKS, 4900 block of Imperial St, Burnaby.
LOVE'S TOUCH, 1100-block of Davie St.
ULTRA LOVE, 1000-block of Davie St.
WOMYNS' WARE, 896 Commercial Dr, (604) 254-2543. Sex toys. ♀

VICTORIA

■ *Information*
AIDS HELPLINE, 733 Johnson St #304, (250) 384-4554. Mon-Thurs 9am-9pm, Fri till 5pm.

■ *Accommodations*
CLADDAGH HOUSE BED & BREAKFAST, 1761 Lee Ave, (250) 370-2816, fax: (250) 592-0228. B&B, some straight clientele, private & shared baths, hearty breakfast, Irish Milsèan confectionery, pool nearby. ♀♂
OAK BAY GUEST HOUSE, 1052 Newport Ave, (250) 598-3812, fax: (250) 598-0369. Gay-friendly B&B. Variety of rooms with private & shared baths, TV lounge, library, full breakfast, nearby ocean beach. ♀ ♂
OCEAN WILDERNESS 109 West Coast Rd RR#2, Sooke, (250) 646-2116, (800) 323-2116, Fax: (250) 646-2317. Gay-friendly B&B inn. Large, beautifully-decorated rooms, hot tub, full breakfast, wake-up coffee. Nearby ocean beach, river.
WEEKENDER B&B, 10 Eberts St, (250) 389-1688. B&B within steps of the ocean along Victoria's scenic drive. Spacious rooms with private baths, continental breakfast. ♀ ♂

■ *Women's Accommodations*
BACK HILL GUEST HOUSE FOR WOMEN, 4470 Leefield Rd, Victoria, BC V9B 5T7, (250) 478-9648. E-mail: backhill@islandnet.com. Women-only guesthouse with full breakfast, 3 rooms, 2 shared baths. Beaches & hiking nearby. ♀

■ *Bars*
BJ'S LOUNGE, 642 Johnson St at Broad, (250) 388-0505. Daily noon-1am (Sun till midnite). Piano bar & video lounge, full menu, all ages. ♪♀♂
G SPOT, 910 Store St, (250) 382-7768, bar, dancing, art gallery, run by Women's Creative Network. ♀

■ *Dance Bar/Disco*
RUMOURS, 1325 Government St near Johnson, (250) 385-0566. Dance bar, cabaret, strippers Thurs, women's nights 3rd Fri.

■ *Saunas/Health Clubs*
STEAMWORKS, 582 Johnson St, (250) 383-6623. 7pm-9am 7 days.

■ *Restaurants*
DILLETTANTE'S CAFE, 787 Forte St, (250) 381-3327. Eclectic fare, brunch, lunch.
FRIENDS OF DOROTHY, 615 Johnson St, (250) 381-2277. Restaurant with Wizard of

Oz decor, 11:30am-10pm 7 days, Sun champagne brunch 11:30am-3pm.
MILKY WAY CAFE, 560 Johnson St, Mediterranean cuisine, breakfast-dinner.

Retail & Bookstores
EVERYWOMAN'S BOOKS, 635 Johnson St near Douglas, (250) 388-9411. Women's bookstore open Mon-Sat.

WHISTLER MOUNTAIN

Accommodations
WHISTLER RETREAT, 8561 Drifter Way, Whistler, BC V0N 1B8, (604) 938-9245 (tel/fax). Discovering The Whistler Retreat, brings downhill and cross-country skiing, snowshoeing, snowmobiling, hiking, mountain biking, swimming sunbathing, golf, tennis, canoeing, and horseback riding to your doorstep. This spacious alpine home, located on a mountainside just 5 minutes north of Whistler Village, has spectacular mountain views, 3 fireplaces, queen-sized beds, an outdoor Jacuzzi, a sauna, and a pool table. We offer a full breakfast each morning which is preceded by coffee, fresh fruit and freshly-baked muffins all awaiting you when you wake up. Whistler, a world-renowned mountain resort, has been rated one of the best places in the world to ski by *Snow Country Magazine* and *SKI Magazine*.

MANITOBA
BRANDON

Information
GAYS & LESBIANS OF BRANDON & ELSEWHERE, (204) 727-4297. Monthly socials 3rd Fri. Phone line, 7pm-9pm.

WINNIPEG

Information
AIDS INFO LINE, (204) 945-2437 or (800) 782-AIDS (inside Manitoba).
GAY & LESBIAN RESOURCE CTR, 1-222 Osborne St S, office: 474-0212. Info line: (204) 284-5208.
WOMEN'S RESOURCE CENTER, 1910 Pembina Hwy, (204) 269-6836. Mon-Fri 9am-4:30pm. Call first.

Accommodations
MASSON'S B&B, 181 Masson St, (204) 237-9230 (Tel/Fax). Gay-owned & -operated B&B in a Victorian setting, shared baths, full breakfast, some hetero clientele.
TWIN PILLARS B&B, 235 Oakwood Ave, (204) 284-7590, fax: (204) 452-4925. Gay-friendly B&B, shared bath, color TV, expanded continental breakfast, 25% gay & lesbian clientele.
WINGED OX GUESTHOUSE, 82 Spence St, (204) 783-7408 (tel/fax). Smoke-free B&B, convenient downtown location, shared baths, full breakfast, some hetero clientele.

Dance Bar/Disco
CLUB 200, 190 Garry Street, (204) 943-6045. Dance bar & cabaret, restaurant, 60% men, 40% women, some straight clientele. 4pm-2am, closed Sun.
GIO'S SOCIAL CLUB, 272 Sherbrooke, (204) 786-1236. Disco & lounge, 90% men, 10% women. Private club, male strippers, travelers welcome. 9pm-2am (Fri till 3:30am). Most popular Fri.
HAPPENINGS SOCIAL CLUB, 274 Sherbrooke St near Portage (upstairs), (204) 774-3576. Nightly dance bar and lounge. Private club, travelers welcome, male strippers. On Sat for after hours, till 3:30am, 50% straight.
MS PURDY'S WOMEN'S CLUB, 226 Main St, (204) 989-2344. Disco. Men welcome Fri, closed Sun & Mon.

Cafe
PANIC CAFE, Westminster at Chestnut.

Saunas/Health Clubs
ALEXANDER & KING STEAM BATHS, 224 Alexander, (204) 943-7048, 24hrs.
OFFICE SAUNA, 1060 Main St near Burrows, (204) 589-6133, 24hrs.

Restaurants
BIG RUBY'S BISTRO, 102 Sherbrooke, (204) 775-0188.
CLUB 200 RESTAURANT, at the Club 200, 190 Garry St, (204) 943-6045. Closed Sun. Burgers, nachos, etc.

Retail & Bookstores
MCNALLY-ROBINSON BOOKSELLERS, 100 Osborne St S, (204) 453-2644, Fax: (204) 452-0749. General bookstore with coffee shop & gay section, Mon-Fri 9:30am-9:30pm, Sat 9:30am-6:00pm, Sun noon-5pm.
ZINE'S INFO CAFE, 875 Corydon Ave. Internet cafe, periodicals.

Erotica
DISCREET BOUTIQUE, 317 Ellice Ave, (204) 947-1307, Fax: 942-6516. Erotic lingerie, leatherwear, adult novelties.
UNIQUE BOUTIQUE, 615 Portage Ave, (204) 775-5435.

NEW BRUNSWICK

Information
AIDS NEW BRUNSWICK, (506) 459-7518.

FREDERICTON

Information
GAYLINE, (506) 457-2156. Tues & Thur 6:30pm-8:30pm, info on support groups and social activities, library and newsletter called Flag Mag.

Dance Bar/Disco
KURT'S PHOENIX RISING, 377 King St, (506) 453-0740. Gay bar on 2nd floor with pool table, open Tues-Sun from 8pm. 3rd fl: Alternative dance bar with 50% gay/lesbian clientele, 9pm-2am Fri & Sat. Lower level: Bona fide gay bar.

MONCTON

Dance Bar/Disco
DANS L' FOND, 238 St George St (basement of Nat'l Bank bldg). Alternative dance bar with gay/straight crowd.

SAINT JOHN

Information
AIDS SAINT JOHN, (506) 652-2437.
GAY INFO LINE, (506) 642-6969, taped event message.

Accommodations
MAHOGANY MANOR, 220 Germain St, (506) 636-8000, Fax:(506) 636-8001. E-mail: leavittr@nbnet.nb.ca. Gay-owned B&B, 50% gay & lesbian clientele, private baths, full hot breakfast.

Dance Bar/Disco
BOGART'S, 9 Sydney St, (506) 652-2004. Dance bar, Wed-Sun 8pm-2am, DJ Thurs-Sat, 60% men, 40% women. Ladies nite 3rd Fri.

NOVA SCOTIA
BEAR RIVER

Accommodations
LOVETT LODGE INN, PO Box 119, (902) 467-3917. 50% gay & lesbian clientele.

HALIFAX

Dance Bar/Disco
REFLECTIONS CABARET, 5184 Sackville St at Barrington, (902) 422-2957. Open Sat-Thurs 4pm-3:30am, Fri noon-3:30am. DJ Thurs-Sun, pool tables, live entertainment Sun with singers & live bands. 70% men, 30% women.

Whistler's Favorite Gay & Lesbian B&B

Whistler Retreat
Whistler, BC
(604) 938-9245

NOVA SCOTIA

Women's Canoeing in Canada

Five hours by car from Toronto (3 hrs from Michigan), is a riverside enclave of cozy cabins which serves as base camp for women's canoe expeditions in Ontario. Spectacular wilderness abounds throughout the area. The Temagami contains the largest stand of old-growth red and white pine in the world. The Spanish River offers unparalleled variety of wildlife. The North Channel of Lake Huron offers unlimited paddling through a channel between the La Cloche Mtns and Manitoulin Island. Killarney Provincial Park has wild landscapes and turquoise lakes. The trips vary from 3 to 7 days and accommodate the interests of both experienced and beginning paddlers, accompanied by a friendly guide.

Less demanding are the 3- to 7-day vacations at the base camp itself. These events incorporate many of the elements women love about the canoe trips, without their strenuous nature. Accommodation is in the riverside cabins. Gourmet vegetarian meals are served. A massage therapist is available on site. Swimming, paddling, cycling, campfires, sauna, and lounging by the river are the favored activities.

Contact **Wild Women Expeditions** at (705) 866-1260.

Saunas/Health Clubs
APOLLO SAUNA BATH, 1547 Barrington near Blowers, (902) 423-6549. Open Mon, Wed, Fri & Sat.

Retail & Bookstores
ATLANTIC NEWS, 5560 Morris St, (902) 429-5468. Newsstand with gay magazines.
BLOWERS ST PAPER CHASE, 5228 Blowers St, (902) 423-0750. Gay magazines.
OPEN CLOSET, (902) 422-4220, rainbow & pride items.

ONTARIO
BRIGHTON

Accommodations
BUTLER CREEK BED & BREAKFAST, RR7, Hwy 30-202, Brighton, ON K0K 1H0, (613) 475-1248, Fax: (613) 475-5267. Gay-owned B&B in the countryside halfway between Toronto & Ottawa, 15% gay & lesbian clientele.

FORT ERIE

Women's Accommodations
WHISTLE STOP, 2583 Thompson Rd, (905) 871-1265. Women's guest home & weekend retreat near the Niagara river with bicycle paths & Lake Erie beaches nearby.

GUELPH

Information
AIDS LINE, (519) 763-2255, Mon-Fri 11am-8pm, Sat 12pm-4pm.
GUELPH OUTLINE, (519) 836-4550, Sun-Wed 7pm-10pm, Thurs-Sat 4pm-7pm.

Dance Bar/Disco
GAY & LESBIAN DANCES. Call Outline for schedule.

HAMILTON

Information
AIDS LINE, (905) 528-0854, (800) 563-6919 (southern Ontario). Mon-Thurs 9-9pm, Fri 10am-7pm.

Camping & RV
CEDARS TENT & TRAILER PARK, PO Box 195, Millgrove, (905) 659-7342, 659-3655. Campground with clubhouse, 600 campsites with shared shower facilities.

Bars
CLUB 121 BAR, 121 Hughson St N, (905) 546-5258. Bar (restaurant open in summer), DJ & live bands upstairs, snack in back bar.

Dance Bar/Disco
EMBASSY CLUB, THE, 54 King St East, (905) 522-7783. High energy dance bar open 7 days, 60% men, 40% women.

Restaurants
CAFE 121 RESTAURANT, 121 Hughson St N, (905) 546-5258. Steak, chicken, Sun brunch, open summers.

Retail & Bookstores
PETTEPLACE BOOKSTORE, 27 King William St, (905) 522-9633. General bookstore with a gay & lesbian section.
WOMEN'S BOOKSTOP, 333 Main St W, (416) 525-2970. Feminist bookstore with lesbian section.

Erotica
SHOW WORLD CINEMA, 61 King St E. Non-stop erotic movies.

KINGSTON

Dance Bar/Disco
CLUB 477, 477 Princess St, (613) 547-2923. Dance bar, game room, lounge, 7 days. Winter 6:30pm-2am, Summer 4pm-2am, weekends till 3am.

KITCHENER

Dance Bar/Disco
CLUB RENAISSANCE, 24-A Charles W, (519) 570-2406. Wed-Sun 9pm-3am.
ROBIN'S NEST, in the old Farmer's Bldg near the town of Galt, (519) 621-2688. At Cambridge fairgrounds, 15 miles from Kitchener. Disco Sat, c&w dancing alt Sun afternoons. Seasonal, usually closed summers. Sat 8pm-2am. Unverifiable spring '97.

LONDON

Information
AIDS HOTLINE, 200-343 Richmond St, (519) 434-8160. Mon-Thur 9-9, Fri 9-5.
GAY LINE, (519) 433-3551. Mon, Thurs 7-10pm.

Bars
JUNCTION & TRACK 722, at Club London complex, (519) 438-2625. Junction quiet bar & Track 722 dance bar, 9pm-3am daily, Fri & Sat 2pm-3 or 5am.

Dance Bar/Disco
HALO BAR, 649 Colborne St at Pall Mall, (519) 433-3762. Private club & community center, dance bar Wed, Fri, Sat. Also Options upstairs quiet bar Sat from 9pm, coffeehouse Mon, most popular for men on Sat. Mon-Thurs 7pm-midnite, Fri-Sat 9pm-2am.
PARTNERS, 186 Dundas St, (519) 679-1255. Dance bar & restaurant with lite menu, 2pm-2am daily (after hours wknds), 50% men, 50% women (Fri 90% men, Sat 90% women).

Saunas/Health Clubs
CLUB LONDON, 722 York St near Lyle, (519) 438-2625. Private club, 24hrs.

Restaurants
BLACKFRIARS CAFE, 46 Blackfriars St, (519) 667-4930. Breakfast thru dinner, international cuisine.
EXTRA VIRGIN, 374 Richmond St, (519) 433-

ONTARIO

3988. Bar & restaurant, continental, Mediterranean cuisine.

GREEN TORONTO, 172 King St, (519) 660-1170.

MARLA JANE'S, 460 King St, (519) 858-8669.

VERANDAH CAFE, 546 Dundas.

■ Retail & Bookstores

WOMANSLINE BOOKS, 573 Richmond Street, (519) 679-3416. Feminist & lesbian bookstore, 10am-6pm (Thurs-Fri till 8pm), closed Sun.

MAYNOOTH

■ Women's Accommodations

WILDEWOOD, Box 121, Madawaska Rd, (613) 338-3134. Guesthouse with shared baths, full breakfast. The gay male owners have found that women "love the way we pamper them. They love having nothing to decide other than when to open the wine."

OTTAWA/HULL

May 1, 1997: Closing hours for bars in Ontario are 1 hour later: 2am.

■ Information

AIDS SUPPORT LINE, (613) 238-4111 or 238-5014.

GAYLINE/TELEGAI, (613) 238-1717. Mon-Fri 7:30pm-10:30pm, Sat, Sun 6-9pm.

PINK TRIANGLE SERVICES, 71 Bank St #203, (613) 563-4818. Gay & lesbian lending library, open M-Sat.

WOMEN'S CENTRE, University of Ottawa, 85 Hastey Ave, Room 08A, (613) 564-6853.

■ Accommodations

RIDEAU VIEW INN, 177 Frank St, (613) 236-9309, (800) 658-3564, Fax: (613) 237-6842, E-mail: rideau@istar.ca. http://home.istar.ca/~rideau/. B&B in a large Edwardian home built in 1907. Relax in front of the fireplace in the living room or take a walk to nearby restaurants, bars and tourist attractions. We have seven well-appointed guest rooms, two of which have private baths. In the morning, enjoy a hearty breakfast in the gracious dining room. Ours is the only gay-owned and -operated B&B in Ottawa.

■ Women's Accommodations

GABRIELLE'S GUESTHOUSE, 40 Gilmour St, (613) 237-0829 (tel/fax). Women-only B&B in downtown Ottawa, 2 doubles, shared bath, expanded continental breakfast.

LE JARDIN DES TREMBLES, 29 rue des Chardonnerets, Hull, QC (819) 595-8761, Fax: (819) 595-0515, E-mail: cw002@freenet.carleton.ca. Women-only B&B minutes from downtown Ottawa with shared bath, continental breakfast, TV lounge & video tape library.

■ Bars

CENTRETOWN PUB, 340 Somerset St West near Bank, (613) 594-0233. Video bar & restaurant with patio, 75% men.

LOOKOUT BAR & BISTRO, 41 York St, (613) 789-1624. Bar & small restaurant.

MARKET STATION, 15 George St, Ottawa, (613) 562-3540. Bar & restaurant, downstairs games room. Lunch, dinner, weekend brunch. 70% men.

SILHOUETTE PIANO BAR, 340 Somerset St West at Centretown Pub, downstairs.

■ Dance Bar/Disco

CELLBLOCK, ★ 340 Somerset St W at Centretown Pub, 2nd fl, (613) 594-0233. DJ.

CORAL REEF, 30 Nicholas St inside parking ramp, (613) 234-5118. Open Fri only, 8pm-2am.

ICON, 366 Lisgar St. Dance bar with show bar downstairs, Sat may become women's night in 1997.

PRIDE DISCO, 363 Bank St, (613) 237-0708. Drag shows Sun, 80% men, 20% women. Downstairs Camp B Tavern neighborhood bar, lunch & dinner specials.

PUB DE LA PROMENADE, 175 Promenade du Portage, Hull, (819) 771-8810. Trendy dance bar, popular with trendy gays & straights, mostly francophones.

THAT BAR, 303 Frank St, (613) 233-9195. Fireside lounge, pool tables, pinball.

■ Saunas/Health Clubs

CLUB OTTAWA, 1069 Wellington St near Merton, (613) 722-8978. Private club, 24 hours. Now serving liquor.

STEAMWORKS, 487 Louis St at Bank St. (613) 230-8431.

■ Restaurants

HOLLYWOOD CAFE RESTAURANT, 5 Jacques Cartier, Gatineau, (819) 568-7270. Seafood, steaks, fondues, many gays, some straight clientele.

LE BISTRO BIS, ★ 9 Richmond Rd. Continental cuisine with Asian flair, large gay following.

LE BOULANGER FRANCAIS/THE FRENCH BAKER, 119 Murray St, (613) 789-7941. Sandwiches, espresso.

MANGIA RESTAURANT, 121 Clarence St, (613) 562-4725. Antipasto, pasta & pizza.

URBAN BISTRO, THE, 87 Holland Ave, (613) 798-1652. Lunch, dinner, weekend brunch.

WET LOUNGE RESTAURANT, 363 Bank St, in same complex with Pride Disco. Martini lounge & coffee bar with Mediterranean cuisine.

■ Retail & Bookstores

AFTER STONEWALL, 2-105 4th Ave, (613) 567-2221. Gay & lesbian bookstore, t-shirts, cards, books galore, 10am-6pm (Fri till 9pm, Sun noon-4pm).

MAGS & FAGS, 86 Elgin St near Somerset, (613) 233-9651. Magazine shop carrying gay magazines.

MOTHER TONGUE, 1067 Bank St, (613) 730-2346. Women's bookstore with large lesbian section.

WILDE'S, 200 Dalhousie St, (613) 562-2992. Clothing, cards, t-shirts, leather, rubber, latex, pride items, etc.

■ Erotica

MARC'S SMOKE SHOP, 420 Rideau St, (613) 789-8886. Adult toys, condoms, gay XXX videos.

VARIETIES EROTIQUES, 61 Eddy, Hull, (819) 771-8994.

WILDE'S, 367 Bank St, (613) 234-5512. Rubber, latex, fetish, etc.

PETERBOROUGH

■ Information

RAINBOW SERVICE ORGANIZATION, (705) 876-1845. Men's & women's meetings & dances, Tues-Fri after 5:30pm, Mon after 8:30pm.

■ Dance Bar/Disco

FRIENDS BISTRO, 450 George St N. Dancing, pool tables, coffee lounge.

PORT SYDNEY

■ Accommodations

DIVINE LAKE NATURE'S SPORT & SPA RESORT, RR1 XD Box 3, Port Sydney, Ont, (705) 385-1212, (800) 263-6600, Fax: (705) 385-1283. Gay-friendly resort with bar, 2 lounges & restaurant, cottages & chalets. Full breakfast, fireplaces & kitchenettes available, color TV/VCR, health spa with steam/herbal sauna, massages, many outdoor activities.

SAULT STE MARIE

■ Dance Bar/Disco

WAREHOUSE DANCE CLUB, THE, 196 James St, (705) 759-1903. Hi energy dance club, lite menu, 11am-2am 7 days.

STRATFORD

■ Accommodations

BURNSIDE GUESTHOUSE, 139 William St, (519) 271-7076. Gay-friendly B&B, shared baths, TV lounge with color cable TV, VCR.

Rideau View Inn
Bed and Breakfast
Victorian Elegance in the Heart of Ottawa
(800) 658-3564
(613) 236-9309
177 Frank St
Ottawa, Ontario K2P 0X4

ONTARIO

Full breakfast, whirlpool tub. 50% gay & lesbian clientele.

MAPLES OF STRATFORD, THE, 220 Church St, (519) 273-0810. Gay-friendly B&B 3 blocks from the center of town & within walking distance of all theatres. Private & shared baths, continental breakfast. 50% gay & lesbian clientele.

SUDBURY

■ Retail & Bookstores

MARIGOLD'S BOOKS & THINGS, 5 Elgin St, (705) 675-2670. "A women's bookstore where all are welcomed." Tues-Sun, sometimes Mon.

THUNDER BAY

■ Dance Bar/Disco

HARBOR 16, 16 N Cumberland St, (807) 346-9118. Fri & Sat only 9:30pm-2am. ♀♂

■ Retail & Bookstores

NORTHERN WOMAN'S BOOKSTORE, THE, 65 S Court St, (807) 344-7979.

RAINBOW BOOKS, 264 Bay St, (807) 345-6272. Gay & lesbian bookstore with some straight titles.

TORONTO

■ Information

519 CHURCH STREET COMMUNITY CENTER, 519 Church St, (416) 392-6874. 9am-10:30pm (Sat noon-5pm, Sun 9am-5pm).

AIDS HOT LINE, (416) 392-2437, (800) 668-2437 (inside Ontario). 9am-11:30pm (Sat, Sun 11am-4pm).

KHUSH, 519 Church St at 519 Church St Community Center. South Asian gay men's group, 3rd Wed, publishes newsletter. Write: PO Box 6172 Stn A, Toronto, Ont M5W 1P6.

SOUTH ASIAN AIDS COALITION OF TORONTO, write, Attn: Kaushalya Bannerji, c/o TCCLG, 517 College St #308, Toronto, Ontario.

TEN CAWTHRA SQUARE B&B
Where The Heart Is
(800) 259-5474
TORONTO

TORONTO AREA GAYS & LESBIANS (TAGL), (416) 964-6600, 7pm-10pm Mon-Sat.

WOMEN'S CENTER, 49 St George St, (416) 978-8201. Lesbian groups, etc.

■ Accommodations

ALLENBY GUEST HOUSE, 223 Strathmore Blvd, (416) 461-7095, Fax: 923-3177. Guesthouse & apartments, private & shared baths, expanded continental breakfast. ♀ ♂

BEVERLEY PLACE, 235 Beverley St, (416) 977-0077. B&B, some straight clientele, private & shared baths. ♀ ♂

CATNAPS 1892 DOWNTOWN GUESTHOUSE, 246 Sherbourne St, (416) 968-2323, Fax: (416) 413-0485, Reservations: (800) 205-3694. Centrally-located B&B guesthouse. Color cable TV, AC, shared baths, laundry facilities & expanded continental breakfast. ♀ ♂

DUNDONALD HOUSE, THE, 35 Dundonald St, Toronto, ON M4Y 1K3, (416) 961-9888, (800) 260-7227, Fax: (416) 961-2120. E-mail: dundonal@idirect.com. http://www2.cglbrd.com/dundonald. Gay & lesbian B&B in a quiet tree-lined area of downtown Toronto. Seven bedrooms, shared baths, full breakfast, AC, hot tub, sauna, touring bikes. Near gay venues, walking distance to Yonge St. ♀ ♂

HOUSE ON MCGILL, 110 McGill St, (416) 351-1503, B&B, no smoking, no children. ♀ ♂

MANFRED'S MEADOW RESORT, RR #1, (519) 925-5306. Guesthouse, shared baths. ♀ ♂

MIKE'S ON MUTUAL, 333 Mutual St, Toronto, ON M4Y 1X6, (416) 944-2611, Fax: (416) 944-3938. Gay & lesbian B&B in a non-smoking private home, a very short walk from gay bars & shops. Shared baths, expanded continental breakfast. ♂

MOTHER'S GUESTHOUSE, 508 Eastern Ave, (416) 466-8616, TDD 652-9685. Men-only for leathermen hotel, private & shared baths. ♂

TEN CAWTHRA SQUARE B&B, 10 Cawthra Square, Toronto, ON M4Y 1K8, (416) 966-3074, (800) 259-5474, Fax: (416) 966-4494, E-mail: host@cawthra.com. Take your ease in our elegantly appointed Edwardian home, a beautiful retreat in the heart of Toronto's vibrant gay village. The salon, with fireplace and grand piano, looks out onto a quiet, tree-shaded street. Spacious guest rooms provide private terraces and a continental breakfast is served in a bright country kitchen. An inviting array of shops, restaurants, cafes & nightclubs are nearby, and theatres, museums and galleries are all at your doorstep. ♀ ♂

TWO ABERDEEN, 2 Aberdeen Ave, (416) 944-1426, Fax: (416) 944-3523, B&B with private & shared baths, full breakfast, women welcome. ♂

WINCHESTER GUEST HOUSE, 35 Winchester, (416) 929-7949, fax: (416) 928-1722. Guest house with one private and three shared baths. Open year-round. Rates: CDN $55-$110. ♀ ♂

■ Bars

BAR 501, 501 Church St. Pub. ♂

BAR BABYLON, 553 Church St, 2nd floor, (416) 923-2626. "Martini bar," fireplace, chesterfields. ♀ ♂

BARN/STABLES, 418 Church St, upstairs, (416) 977-4684. Upstairs DJ, popular after hours Fri & Sat after 2am.

BIJOU, 370 Church St, (416) 960-1272. GH bar 9pm-4am.

BLACK EAGLE,★ 459 Church St, (416) 413-1219. Hard core dress code.

BULLDOG CAFE, 457 Church St, (416) 923-3469. Casual bar & restaurant, mature crowd. ♀ ♂

BYZ, 499 Church St, (416) 922-3859. ♂

PEGASUS BILLIARD LOUNGE, 491 Church St, (416) 927-8832. Pool hall. ♂

QUEEN'S HEAD PUB, 263 Gerrard St E, above Pimbletts, (416) 929-9525. Pub & restaurant. ♀ ♂

REMINGTON'S, 379 Yonge St at Gerrard, (416) 977-2160. Strippers. ♂

SNEAKERS, Yonge St at Grosvenor. ♂

SO-BAR, 8 Gloucester ST, (416) 975-5568. "Martini bar." ♂

TANGO & CREWS TORONTO, 508 Church St, (416) 972-1662. ♀

TOOL BOX, 508 Eastern Ave, (416) 466-8616.

TRAX TORONTO,★ 529 Yonge St near Maitland, (416) 962-8729. Piano bar, cabaret, cruisy, many levels, mature crowd, neighborhood crowd. ♂

WOODY'S/SAILORS,★ 467 Church Street, (416) 972-0887. Preppie conversation bar, 70% men & lipstick lesbians. ♂

■ Dance Bar/Disco

BOOTS/WAREHOUSE, 592 Sherbourne St in the Hotel Selby bldg, (416) 921-0665, (416) 921-3142. Boots: dance bar with DJ. Warehouse levi leather bar.

CARRINGTON, 5 St Joseph St near Yonge, (416) 961-0777. After hours dance club. ♂

EL CONVENTO RICO,★ 750 College St, (416) 588-7800. Latin night club open Tue-Sun. Men's night Sun. ♀ ♂

HEAVENS, 699 Yonge St, Open Sun-Wed, strippers. ♂

PHOENIX, 410 Sherbourne St, (416) 323-1251. Scheduled gay nights. ♂

ROSE, THE,★ 547 Parliament St, (416) 928-1495. Dance bar & restaurant. ♀

STUDIO 619, 619 Yonge St, 2nd floor, in the back lane, (416) 922-3068. Dance club, lite menu, 70% men, bingo Fri & Sat. ♂

■ Cafe

CALIFORNIA BAGEL, Church & Wellesley Sts.

MOCHA JOE'S, 399 Church St, (416) 971-6356.

PAM'S TEA & COFFEE, 585 Church St, (416) 923-7267.

QUEEN MOTHER CAFE, 208 Queen St West, (416) 598-4719.

SECOND CUP, 546 Church St, (416) 727-8377. Popular after bars close.

■ Saunas/Health Clubs

BARRACKS, 56 Widmer St near Richmond, (416) 593-0499, 24hrs.

CELLAR, 78 Wellesley St E, (416) 944-3779 (tape), 24hrs.

CLUB TORONTO, 231 Mutual St near Carlton, (416) 925-9872. Private club, 24hrs.

SPA ON MAITLAND, 66 Maitland St, (416) 925-1571.

ST-MARC SPA, 543 Yonge St (top floor), (416) 927-0210. Full gym, sauna, steam room, large screen videos, rooms.

■ Restaurants

BLUE MONKEY, 890 Yonge St, (416) 944-8616. Fusion cuisine, casual funky atmosphere, live jazz.

BYZANTIUM, 499 Church St, (416) 922-3859. Mediterranean cuisine.

CAFE CALIFORNIA, 538 Church St, (416) 960-6161.

GARAGE, 509 Church St, (416) 929-7575.

LE CHAROLAIS, (416) 963-5097. French cuisine, lunch, dinner.

LIVING WELL, 692 Yonge St, (416) 922-6770.

MANGO, 580 Church St, (416) 922-6525.

NEIGHBORS, 9 Isabella St, (416) 960-1200. Bar & restaurant.

PIMBLETT'S, 263 Gerrard St E, above Queen's Head Pub, (416) 929-9525. Restaurant & bar.

PINTS, 518 Church St, (416) 921-8142. Restaurant & bar, continental cuisine, Sat, Sun brunch.

PJ MELLON'S, 489 Church St, (416) 966-3241. Lunch, dinner, Sun brunch 11:30am.

RIVOLI, Queen St near Spadina, (416) 596-1908. Bar & restaurant overlooking Queen St West.

ROSE CAFE, at Rose Cafe bar. 547 Parliament St, (416) 928-1495. Restaurant, dance bar & lounge.

SLACK ALICE, 562 Church St, (416) 962-6255, trendy.

SPIRAL, 582 Church St, (416) 964-1102. Asian continental cuisine, martini & margarita menu.

TRATTORIA IL FORNO, 459 Church St. Italian cuisine.

VOLO CAFE, 587 Yonge St, (416) 928-0008. Italian cuisine, Sat, Sun brunch, patio.

■ Retail & Bookstores

EX LIBRIS, 467 Church St, 2nd Floor, (416) 975-0580. Gay & lesbian new & used books.

GLAD DAY BOOKS, 598-A Yonge St (upstairs), (416) 961-4161. Gay & lesbian bookstore.

LEE'S GLITZ, 455 Church St, (416) 975-1343. Cards & gifts.

OMEGA CENTRE, THE, 29 Yorkville Ave, (416) 975-9086. Self-discovery bookstore with self-help resources on AIDS & an extensive alternative healing section.

OUT ON THE STREET, 551 Church St, (416) 967-2759. Cards, gifts, t-shirts & magazines.

THIS AIN'T THE ROSEDALE LIBRARY, 483 Church Street, (416) 929-9912. General bookstore with a gay & lesbian section.

TORONTO WOMEN'S BOOKSTORE, 73 Harbord near Spadina, (416) 922-8744. Feminist & lesbian bookstore in central Toronto.

■ Leathers/Piercing

DOC'S LEATHERS, 726 Queen St West, (416) 504-8888, fax: (416) 929-1849, http://www.as90.net/docs.

NORTHBOUND LEATHER, 19 St Nicholas St.

■ Erotica

NEW RELEASE ADULT VIDEO, 489 Church St, lower level, (416) 966-9815., Booths.

PRIAPE, 465 Church St, 2nd floor, (416) 586-9914, Fax: (416) 586-0150. gay store.

WARKWORTH

■ Accommodations

BAXTER'S BED & BREAKFAST, RR1, Warkworth, ON K0K 3K0, (705) 924-1230, (888) 398-6550, Fax: (705) 924-1231. E-mail: baxter@accel.net. B&B with some straight clientele, 2 rooms with 1 private & 1 shared bath.

WINDSOR

■ Information

LESBIAN & GAY HOTLINE, (519) 973-4951. 24hr tape, Mon, Thurs Fri 8-10pm. Women Tues 7:30-9:30pm.

■ Bars

SILHOUETTES, 1880 Wyandotte St East, (519) 252-0882. Bar & restaurant, "Cheers for queers." Kitchen open Tues-Sat 4-10pm, Sun brunch noon-3pm.

■ Dance Bar/Disco

HAPPY TAP, 1056 Wyandotte St E, (519) 256-2737. Nude male dancers, female exotic dancers after 11pm, 75% men, 25% women. Women's nites Wed.

■ Saunas/Health Clubs

VESUVIO STEAM BATH, 563 Brant St, (519) 977-8578. 24hrs.

QUEBEC

ACTON VALE

■ Accommodations

LE DOMAINE PLEIN VENT, 1110 Mantée de la Rivière, Upton, QC J0H 2E0, (514) 549-5831. Private campground and hotel for men only.

CHICOUTIMI

■ Bars

L'EXCENTRIQUE 95, 332 du Havre, (418) 698-5811. Bar with dancing Sat 3pm-3am.

LE VERÇO, 564 boul. Saguenay ouest, (418) 690-5354. Thurs-Sun 9pm-3am.

ROSCO PUB, 70 Racine Ouest.

GRANBY

■ Dance Bar/Disco

ZINGARO, 635 Cowei at St Jean Baptiste, (418) 777-5569. Nude dancers. May change, call first.

HULL

See Ottawa, Ontario.

JONQUIÈRE

■ Cafe

CAFE BAR 2171, 2171 St-Dominique, (418) 547-6934. Cafe & bar with many gays.

MAGOG

■ Cafe

CAFE CROUTE MAGOGUE, 299 Principale Ouest, (814) 847-3925.

MONT-TREMBLANT

■ Accommodations

VERSANT OUEST BED & BREAKFAST, 110 Chemin Labelle, Mont-Tremblant, QC (819) 425-6615 (Tel/Fax), (800) 425-6615. E-mail: verso@cil.qc.ca. B&B in mountains with walking paths & river nearby, mainly gay & lesbian clientele, full breakfast, private baths.

MONTRÉAL

■ Information

CONCORDIA WOMEN'S CENTER, 2020 rue Mackay, basement annex P-03, (514) 848-7431. Drop-in space, mainly anglophones (English-speaking). Weekday hours, scheduled evening events. Women's calendar of events available.

GAIE ÉCOUTE, (514) 521-1508. French language gay info line.

GAYLINE ENGLISH, (514) 990-1414, 6:30pm-10pm, 7 days.

■ Accommodations

ALACOQUE'S BED & BREAKFAST, 2091 St-Urbain, Montreal, PQ H2X 2N1, (514) 842-0938, Fax: (514) 842-7585. B&B in a 1900 town house with private & shared baths, full

QUEBEC

breakfast, laundry & kitchen facilities, 10 minute walk to gay bars. 50% gay / lesbian clientele.

APPARTEMENTS DORION, 1477 Dorion, (514) 523-2427. 15 rooms with TV and shower. ♂

AU BON VIVANT GUEST HOUSE, 1648 Amherst, (514) 525-7744, Fax: (514) 525-2874. B&B guesthouse in gay village, women welcome. Shared bath, TV lounge, buffet breakfast. "A fine home for the discerning traveller." ♂

AUBERGE L'UN ET L'AUTRE, 1641 rue Amherst (metro: Beaudry), (514) 597-0878, Fax: (514) 597-1430. B&B for gay men. ♂

AUX BERGES, 1070 rue Mackay, (514) 938-9393, (800) 668-6253, fax: (514) 938-1616. Men-only hotel near clubs, continental breakfast, private & shared baths. ♂

BED & BREAKFAST DU VILLAGE (BBV), 1279 Rue Montcalm, (514) 522-4771, (888) 228-8455 (US & Canada), Fax: (514) 522-7118, E-mail: bbv@total.com, Web: www.gaibec.com/bbv. Known to all our friends as BBV, we're located in the heart of Montreal's gay village. Our men-only B&B has nine cosy rooms (two with bath), a delicious continental breakfast, free private indoor parking, and the use of our sunny, spacious terrace with Jacuzzi (nudity permitted). Just a minutes' walk to bars, clubs, restaurants and the Metro. Your hosts: Alain & Shawn. ♂

BOURBON HOTEL & SAUNA, 1570-1592 Ste-Catherine Est, (514) 523-4679, 521-1419.

CHATEAU CHERRIER B&B, 550 rue Cherrier, (514) 844-0055, (800) 816-0055, Fax: (514) 844-8438. B&B in private home, some straight clientele. Rooms individually decorated in period furniture, full breakfast. Downtown near pool, quartier latin, gay village. ♀ ♂

HOTEL BOURBON, 1570-1592, Ste-Catherine Est, at La Track Complex. Men's hotel connected to La Track bar & dance complex. ♂

HOTEL DE LA COURONNE, 1029 rue St-Denis, (514) 845-0901. Hotel with private & shared baths, 50% gay and lesbian clientele.

HOTEL LE ST.-ANDRE, 1285 rue St-André, (514) 849-7070, Fax: 849-8167. Reservations: (800) 265-7071. Hotel with mini-bar, 40% gay & lesbian. Variety of rooms with private baths, continental breakfast.

HOTEL MANOIR DES ALPES, 1245 rue St-André, (514) 845-9803, reservations only: (800) 65-2929. Free parking, color TV, phone, AC & continental breakfast. ♂

LA CONCIERGERIE GUEST HOUSE, 1019 Rue St-Hubert, (514) 289-9297, Fax: 289-0845. B&B near Ste Catherine, Old Montreal & gay village, women welcome. Comfortable rooms in Victorian homes. Expanded continental breakfast. Massage by appointment, Jacuzzi, nearby gym. ♂

LE CHASSEUR GUEST HOUSE, 1567 rue St-Andre, Montréal, PQ H2L 3T5, (514) 521-2238, (514) 849-2051, (800) 451-2238. A charming European bed and breakfast, centrally located in Montréal. Gay bars, restaurants, Old Montréal, the Latin Quarter and trendy boutiques are all nearby. Our staff will provide a wealth of information and will spare no expense to make your stay easy-going and relaxing. Le Chasseur, a step in the right direction. The bed and breakfast "recommended by friends for friends." ♂

LE SECRET, 1349 rue La Fontaine, (514) 523-3991. Men-only B&B, full breakfast, private & shared baths. ♂

LE ST. CHRISTOPHE BED & BREAKFAST, 1597 St Christophe, (514) 527-7836. Guesthouse in gay village, men only. Rooms in antique or modern style, TV lounge, pool table, Jacuzzi, complete breakfast. ♂

LE STADE B&B, POB 42, Stn M, Montreal, QC H1V 3L6, (514) 254-1250, vb #1, Fax available. B&B near gay & lesbian community. Shared bath, TV lounge, small gym, fax facilities & continental breakfast. ♀♂

PENSION VALLIERES, 6562, Delorimier St, (514) 729-9552. B&B, color cable TV, ceiling fans, private & shared baths, full breakfast, 95% women, men welcome. ♀

■ Women's Accommodations

LINDSEY'S BED & BREAKFAST FOR WOMEN, 3974 Laval Ave, (514) 843-4869. Women-only B&B with private & shared baths, expanded continental breakfast. ♀

■ Bars

ADONIS, 1681 Ste-Catherine, (514) 521-1355. Nude male dancers. ♂

BAR CAJUN, 1574 Ste-Catherine Est, at La Track Complex, (514) 523-4679. Upscale bar off the lobby of the Hotel Bourbon. ♂

BARZAN, 4910 blvd St-Laurent, near Sauna 5018, (514) 847-8850. Gargoyle decor. ♂

CAFE FETICHE, 1426 Beaudry (metro: Beaudry), (514) 523-3013. S/M party with leather dress code, call for schedule. Ask for women's & men's nites. ♂

CAMPUS, 1111 rue Ste-Catherine Est, (514) 526-3616. Nude male dancers, bar for men-only. Women welcome on Sun. ♂

CITIBAR, 1603 rue Ontario est at Champlain. Tavern-like ambiance, easy parking. ♂

CLUB DATE, 1218 rue Ste-Catherine est near Montcalm, (514) 521-1242. Piano bar, Fri-Sun, karaoke nights Mon & Tues. ♂

K.O.X.,★ 1456 rue Ste-Catherine Est, (514) 523-0064. 2-level cruise bar, decor of medieval castle, younger crowd. ♂

KATAKOMBES,★ 1456 rue Ste-Catherine Est. Men-only leather bar in basement. Station C complex, mature leather crowd. ♂

L'AGORA, 1160 rue Mackay, (514) 939-1976. More anglophones. ♂

L'AIGLE NOIR,★ 1315 rue Ste-Catherine Est, (514) 529-0040. Cruise bar. ♂

L'ENTRE-PEAU CABARET,★ 1115 rue Ste-Catherine Est, (metro: Beaudry), (514) 525-7566. Show bar with large straight following. ♂

L'UN ET L'AUTRE, 1641 Amherst. Bar & restaurant, rooms for tourists by the week, mostly gay. ♂

LA RELAXE, 1309 rue Ste-Catherine Est. Taverne with big windows that open in summer. Popular with 25 yrs & older. ♂

LOUNGE, THE, 1333 rue Ste-Catherine Est above the Saloon Cafe. Live music nightly from 8pm, Sun shows at 7pm. Women's nite Sun 5-9pm. ♀♂

MAX, 1166 rue Ste-Catherine Est near Montcalm, (514) 598-5244. Cruise bar, small dance floor, young, top 40 music. ♂

METEOR, 1661 rue Ste-Catherine Est, (514) 523-1481. Cruise bar. ♂

METEORITE, 1661 rue Ste-Catherine Est, (514) 523-1481. Restuarant & bar, Sun dinner show. ♂

MYSTIQUE, 1424 rue Stanley, (514) 844-5711. Women welcome. ♂

O'SIDE,★ 4075-B St Denis (metro: Sherbrooke), (514) 849-7126. Cafe bistro with light menu, pool table, dance nights every 2 weeks, women only. Packed on weekends. ♀

SKY PUB,★ 1474 rue Ste-Catherine Est, (metro: Papineau or Beaudry), (514) 529-6969. Girls in the Sky night Thurs. ♀♂

STOCK BAR, 1278 St-André, (514) 842-1336. Nude dancers. ♂

STUD, 1812 rue Ste-Catherine Est, cruise bar. ♂

TABOO, 1950 est de Maisonneuve, (514) 597-0010. Nude male dancers. ♂

TAVERNE DU VILLAGE,★ 1366 rue Ste.-Catherine Est near Panet, (514) 524-1960. Stand-up type tavern. Building an addition in 1997. ♂

TAVERNE NORMANDIE, 1295 Amherst near rue Ste.-Catherine, erotic videos. ♂

TAVERNE ROCKY, 1673 rue Ste-Catherine Est. ♂

WESTSIDE, 1071 Beaver Hall, (514) 866-4963. Nude male dancers, women welcome Sun only if accompanied by men. ♂

■ Dance Bar/Disco

CABARET SAPHO, 217 rue Frontenac (metro: Frontenac), (514) 523-0222. Cabaret & dance bar, live singers on weekends. Slightly older crowd. ♀♂

CLUB BOLO, 960 Amherst, Fri-Sun only, C&W dancing. ♂

GROOVE SOCIETY, 1296 Amherst. Gay Thurs only. ♂

HOME, 1450 rue Ste-Catherine Est, at Station C complex. (514) 523-0064. Huge dance bar with mezzanine, 70% men. Scheduled live shows & drag shows. ♂

QUEBEC

LA TRACK COMPLEX,★ 1584 rue Ste-Catherine Est, (514) 521-1419. Rock music, pool table, daily 2pm-3am. Leather bar, basement disco, 4 restaurants: Club Sandwich, Grappa, Orient Express & Body Shop, & Hotel Bourbon men's hotel.

MISSISSIPPI CLUB, 1592 rue Ste-Catherine Est, (514) 523-4679. Wed Woolco, mixed; Fri mixed; Sat women only, Sun entertainment.

PTOWN, 1364 rue Ste-Catherine Est, above Taverne du Village, (metro: Beaudry), (514) 524-1584. Panoramic view from Terrace. Popular in summer.

SISTERS,★ 1456 rue Ste-Catherine Est, at Station C complex (metro: Beaudry), (514) 524-9947. Thurs-Sat 22:00-03:00, early 20's crowd.

SKY CLUB,★ 1474 rue Ste-Catherine Est, (metro: Beaudry or Papineau). Disco, bar, cabaret & restaurant.

Cafe

AUX DEUX MARIE, 4329 rue St-Denis, (514) 844-7246. Boutique, bistro & cafe with coffees, lunches, sandwiches, burgers, salads, desserts, imported beers.

LA BRULERIE ST-DENIS, 3967 rue St-Denis, (514) 286-9158.

Saunas/Health Clubs

AUX BERGES, at Aux Berges Hotel, 24hrs, snack bar.

BAIN COLONIAL BATHS, European sauna, straight during the day, gayer at night, Tues 1pm-10pm women only.

L'OASIS, 1390 rue Ste-Catherine Est, (514) 521-0785.

SAUNA 1286, 1286 Chemin, Chambly (Longueuil), (514) 677-1286.

SAUNA 226, 226 des Laurentides, Laval.

SAUNA 456, 456 ouest La Gauchetière near St-Alexandre, (514) 871-8341. Sauna & gym, 24hrs.

SAUNA 5018,★ 5018 St-Laurent, (514) 277-3555.

SAUNA BOURBON, 1574 rue Ste-Catherine Est, at the Bourbon Hotel, in the Track Complex.

SAUNA CENTRE-VILLE, 1465, rue Ste-Catherine est, (514) 524-3486.

SAUNA DU PLATEAU, 961 rue Rachel est, (514) 528-1679.

SAUNA PONT-VIAU, 15A des Laurentides, Laval, (514) 663-3386.

SAUNA ST-MARC, 1166 rue Ste-Catherine Est, above Max, (514) 525-8404.

SAUNA ST.-HUBERT, 6527 St-Hubert, (514) 277-0176, mostly closeted men.

SAUNA VERDUN, 5785 ave Verdun, Verdun, suburb of Montreal, (514) 769-6034, 10am-midnite, Fri 10am-11pm Sun, mostly closeted men.

Restaurants

APRÉS LE JOUR, 901 rue Rachel est near St.-André. (514) 527-4141.

BAZOU, 1271 rue Albert, (514) 526-4940. Nouvelle cuisine.

BOZ-ART, 1493 rue Amherst (metro: Beaudry), (514) 522-6144. Popular with gay women.

CAFE LES ENTRETIENS,★ 1577 Laurier est, (514) 521-2934. Healthy food, quiche, etc, 9:30am-midnite, popular with gays.

CAFE UNIVERSAL, 1030 rue Cherrier Est, (514) 598-7136. Deli.

CHABLIS, 1639 St-Hubert (metro: Berri-UQAM), (514) 523-0053. French cuisine.

CLIN D' OEIL CAFÉ, 1429 rue Amherst, (514) 528-1209. Popular Sun brunch.

CLUB SANDWICH,★ 1578 rue Ste-Catherine Est (metro: Papineau), (514) 523-4679, 24hrs.

EDEN CAFE, 1334 rue Ste-Catherine Est. Sandwiches, lite healthy menu.

KILO, 1495 rue Ste-Catherine Est. More an English-speaking crowd.

L'ANECDOTE, 801 rue Rachel est at St.-Hubert (metro: Mont Royal), (514) 526-7967. Snack bar, burgers, beer, many women.

L'ARMORICAIN, 1550 rue Fullum, (514) 523-2551. French cuisine, upscale.

L'EXCEPTION, 1200 rue St-Hubert (metro: Berri-UQAM), (514) 282-1282. Casual cuisine.

L'UN ET L'AUTRE, 1641 Amherst (metro: Beaudry), (514) 597-0878. Bar & bistro. Bar good for cocktail hour.

LA MARIVAUDE, 1652 Ontario Est, (514) 522-9897. Veal dishes a specialty, seafood daily, woman-run.

LE CRYSTAL, 1140 rue Ste-Catherine Est. 24hrs, popular after bars close.

LE RESTO BLEU, 1488 rue Ste-Catherine Est, (514) 529-8989, 80-85% gay clientele.

LE RESTO DU VILLAGE, 1310 Wolf, (514) 524-5404. 24hrs.

LE ST-CHARLES, 1799 Amherst, (514) 526-1799. International cuisine.

LE TOSTEUR,★ 950 Roy est, (514) 527-8500. Only breakfast, from 6am-8pm.

MAESTRO S.V.P., 3615 St-Laurent, (514) 842-6447; or 3017 Masson, (514) 722-4166. Steaks, oysters, shrimp & other seafood.

MOZZA, 1208 rue Ste-Catherine Est (metro: Beaudry), (514) 524-0295. Mostly pasta.

O'SIDE, restaurant in women's bar.

OGATO, 1301 rue Ste-Catherine Est, (514) 528-6222. Dessert only & only cakes.

OSIDE, 4075-B rue St-Denis, at Oside bar, (514) 849-7126. Women-only cafe bistro, lite menu, pool table, dancing Sat nite, packed on weekends.

PARYSE, LA, 302 Ontario est at Sanguinet (metro: Berri-UQAM), (514) 842-2040. Many women, closes early some evenings, call first.

PIAZZETTA, 1101 rue Ste-Catherine Est, (514) 526-2244. Square pizza.

PICCOLO DIAVOLO,★ 1336 rue Ste-Catherine Est, (514) 526-1336. Italian cuisine.

PIZZADELIC,★ 1329 rue Ste-Catherine Est (metro: Beaudry), (514) 526-6011.

PLANÉTE, LE,★ 1451 rue Ste-Catherine Est, at Plessis, (514) 526-1336. Creative, varied menu, very fine cuisine.

ROTISSERIE ST-HUBERT, 1019 rue Ste-Catherine Est, (514) 385-5555. Chicken BBQ.

SALOON CAFE,★ 1333 rue Ste-Catherine Est (metro: Beaudry), (514) 522-1333. Cafe & restaurant.

SECOND CUP, 1351 rue Ste-Catherine Est. Coffees, desserts. To open summer 1997.

Retail & Bookstores

LIBRAIRIE L'ANDROGYNE, 3636 St-Laurent, at Prince Arthur, (514) 842-4765. Gay and lesbian bookstore, with books in both French & English. Also an excellent source of local information for newcomers to Montreal. Open daily. Ask for free catalogue.

Leathers/Piercing

CUIR PLUS, 1321 rue Ste-Catherine Est, Visitation, (514) 521-PLUS (7587). Both retail and wholesale leather clothing and S & M accessories, ready-made and custom, full line of lubricants, poppers, magazines and videos.

Erotica

BOUTIQUE DE SEXE VIDEO MAG PLUS, 1243 rue Bleury, (514) 871-1653.

EROTIM, 818 rue Ste-Catherine Est & 723 rue Mont Royal Est, (514) 522-6969 or (514) 982-2534.

PRIAPE, 1311 rue Ste-Catherine Est, near Panet, (514) 521-8451. Largest gay store in Canada.

ULTRA-MAG, 11 Ste-Catherine ouest, (514) 844-1395.

WEGA COMPLEX, 930 rue Ste-Catherine Est, (514) 987-5993. Videos, cinema & arcade.

PREVOST

Dance Bar/Disco

SECRET, LE, 3029 boul Labelle, at Hotel Up-North. (514) 224-7350. Disco.

QUÉBEC

Accommodations

BED & BREAKFAST IN OLD QUEBEC, 35 Rue des Remparts, (418) 655-7685. Gay-friendly B&B. Variety of accommodations with various conveniences, private & shared baths, TV lounge, full brunch.

LE 727 GUEST HOUSE, 727 rue d'Aiguillon, (418) 648-6766, (800) 652-6766, Fax: (418) 648-1474. Guesthouse in Old Quebec with,

QUEBEC

private & shared baths, continental breakfast, women welcome. 🏳️‍🌈♂

LE COUREUR DES BOIS, 15 rue Ste-Ursule, (418) 692-1117, (800) 269-6414. An historical, early French-Canadian guesthouse within the walls of Old Québec. Seven individually furnished rooms emphasize cleanliness and comfort and share three baths. Breakfast of croissants, fresh fruit, cheese, muffins, sweet breads and assorted beverages. ♀♂

■ Bars

AMOUR SORCIER, L', 789 Côte Ste-Geneviève, (418) 523-3395. ♀

BAR DE LA COURONNE, 321 rue de la Couronne. Nude male dancers. 🏳️‍🌈♂

BAR MALE, 698 rue d'Aiguillon at Ste-Geneviève, (418) 522-6976, Men only, leather nite Sat. May change in 1997. 🏳️‍🌈♂

FAUSSE ALARME, rue St-Jean near Bloc 225. Small cruise bar. ♂

TAVERNE 321, 321 de la Couronne, (418) 522-2674. ♂

TAVERNE LE DRAGUE, ★ 815 rue St-Augustin at St-Jean. Tavern & video bar, terrace, dance bar downstairs. Sun singers, comedy, drag shows, 8pm-3am. 🏳️‍🌈♂

TAVERNE LE PUB DE CARRÉ, 945 rue d'Aiguillon at Glacis, (418) 647-9313. 🏳️‍🌈♂

■ Dance Bar/Disco

BALLON ROUGE, ★ 811 rue St-Jean at St-Augustin, (418) 529-6709. Large disco, avant garde music, terrace. 🏳️‍🌈♂

L'ÉVEIL, 710 rue Bouvier, (418) 628-0610. Pool table, men welcome. ♀

■ Saunas/Health Clubs

BLOC 225, ★ 225 rue St.-Jean. (418) 523-2562. Popular with younger body builder crowd.

SAUNA HIPPOCAMPE, ★ 31 rue McMahon at Auteuil, (418) 692-1521.

■ Restaurants

BURGER CLUB, 469 rue St-Jean, (418) 525-4766. Women-owned & -operated. 🍴

DIANA, 849 rue St-Jean. 90% gay clientele, open 7am-1am, sometimes 3am.

HOBBIT, rue St-Jean near the Ballon Rouge bar, 70-80% gay.

LE COMMENSAL, 860 rue St Jean, (418) 647-3733. Vegetarian food. 🍴

LE COUREUR DES BOIS
Within the walls of the old city of Quebec
(800) 269-6414
(418) 692-1117 • 15 rue Ste-Ursule

ZORBA, across from Diana restaurant. Popular after bars close, 90% gay.

■ Retail & Bookstores

EMPIRE LYON, 873 rue St-Jean, (418) 648-2301. Video store with cafe & books.

L'ACCRO, 845 rue St-Jean, (418) 522-9920, Fax: (418) 522-8921. Gay & lesbian bookstore.

■ Erotica

IMPORTATION DELTA, 875 rue St-Jean.

ST-CUTHBERT

■ Bars
CHEZ LINDA EN HAUT, 3189 Pointe Ste-Catherine, (514) 836-1601. ♂

ST-FRANÇOIS DU LAC

■ Camping & RV
DOMAINE GAY LURON, 261 Grande Terre, (514) 568-3634, Men-only camping. ♂

ST-GEORGES-EST

■ Dance Bar/Disco
L'IMPAK, 8450 boul. La Croix, (418) 227-5594. Small disco. ♂

SAINTE JEAN DE MATHA

■ Camping & RV
CAMPING LA CLÉ DE CHAMPS, (514) 886-0824, Fax: (514) 598-9536. Women-only camping June-Sept, 2 small year-round cottages, 17 tent spaces, 2 RV hookups. Reservations required. ♀

STE-MARTHE

■ Camping & RV
CAMPING PLEIN BOIS, 550 Chemin St-Henri, (514) 459-4646. ♂

SHERBROOKE

■ Women's Accommodations
CHEZ LA SALAMANDRE, 155 Rte 253, Sawyerville, (819) 889-2504. Women-only secluded guesthouse retreat, accommodates 1-6, 1 shared bath. Canoeing & skiing 30-45 mins away, 5 min to nearby lake, horseback riding. Professional therapuric massage available. ♀

■ Bars
LES DAMES DE COEUR, 54 rue King est, (819) 821-2217. Cafe & bar, mostly women with men welcome (Fri women only, Sat more men).

■ Dance Bar/Disco
COMPLEXE 13/12, 13-17 Bowen Sud, (819) 569-1166. Complex with sauna, disco & pub, 80% men. 🏳️‍🌈♂

TROIS RIVIERES

■ Bars
CAFE BAR LE LIEN, 1572 rue Royal, (819) 370-6492. 7 days 1pm-3am, drag shows Sun. 🏳️‍🌈♀♂

RAMSES BAR, 7375 Notre Dame. Cruise bar, 9pm-3am. ♂

■ Dance Bar/Disco
L'INTRIGUE, 1528 Notre Dame at St-Antoine, (819) 693-1979. 🏳️‍🌈♂

SASKATCHEWAN
RAVENSCRAG

■ Accommodations
SPRING VALLEY GUEST RANCH, Box 10, (306) 295-4124. gay-owned B&B & campground with restaurant, shared bath. 50% gay & lesbian clientele.

REGINA

■ Information
AIDS HOTLINE, (306) 924-8420. 9am-5pm.
GAY & LESBIAN INFORMATION LINE, (306) 525-6046. Tues & Fri 8:30pm-11:30pm. Lesbian Lavender Group (306) 586-5066 or 565-6295, dances 3rd Sat at Oddfellows Hall.

■ Dance Bar/Disco
SCARTH STREET STATION & OSCAR'S & BRIXX, 1422 Scarth St, (306) 522-7343. Disco lounge, game room with darts, pool table, cards, music theme nights, 8:30pm-2:30am, 7 days. 🏳️‍🌈♀♂

SASKATOON

■ Information
AIDS LINE, (306) 242-5005 or (800) 667-6876.
GAY & LESBIAN LINE & OUT IN SASKATCHEWAN, 241 2nd Ave S, 3rd floor, at Gay & Lesbian Health Services. (306) 665-1224, answers Mon-Wed noon-4:30pm & 7:30pm-10:30pm, Thurs-Fri noon-10:30pm, Sat noon-5:30pm & 7:30pm-10:30pm. Out in Saskatchewan: (800) 358-1833 (inside SK).

■ Dance Bar/Disco
DIVA'S, 110-220 3rd Ave S, alley entrance off 3rd Ave, (306) 665-0100. Private club, 70% men, 30% women. 8pm-2am 7 days. 🏳️‍🌈♂

■ Retail & Bookstores
CAFE BROWZE, 269-B 3rd Ave S, (306) 664-BOOK (2665). Bookstore cafe. Lunch, dinner & desserts, gay & lesbian books & magazines. Mon-Sat 10am-11pm, Sun 11:30am-11pm.

■ Erotica
OUT OF THE CLOSET, 3rd Fl, 241 2nd Ave S at Gay & Lesbian Health Services. Shop for lesbians & gay men. Magazines, pride flags, t-shirts, wet lube, etc.

YUKON
WHITEHORSE

■ Information
GAY & LESBIAN ALLIANCE, (403) 667-7857. Holds gay dances & meetings in Whitehorse, pop. 20,000.

■ Retail & Bookstores
MAC'S FIREWEED BOOKSTORE, 203 Main St, (403) 668-6104. General bookstore. Will special order gay & lesbian titles.

BRITISH WEST INDIES

CARIBBEAN ATLANTIC ISLANDS

WHO TO CALL
For Tour Companies Serving This Destination
See Caribbean on page 12

BRITISH WEST INDIES
BARBADOS

■ **Information**

INFO SERVICE, (246) 428-7635 or (246) 428-2510. Answers 8am-8pm, ask for Fran! For detailed local gay information.

■ **Accommodations**

ROMAN BEACH APTS, Oistintown Christ Church, (246) 428-7635 or (246) 428-2510, Fax: (246) 430-0406. Ten gay-friendly peaceful & private beachfront studio apartments with kitchens & private bathrooms. Not fancy, but clean and comfortable, and the price is right: US $45-$60/night winter, US $35-$50/night summer.

■ **Beaches**

ACCRA BEACH, Christ Church, NOT a gay beach, it is a public beach surrounded by hotels, restaurants, bars, but frequented by gays.

■ **Bars**

BUDDIES RESTAURANT & BAR, Worthing, Christchurch, gay-friendly bar & small restaurant. Owner, Curtis, welcomes you.

COACH HOUSE, in the St James area on west coast of island, NOT a gay bar, just one of the bars frequented by all visitors to the island Live bands.

HARBOR LIGHTS, Bay St, Bridgetown. NOT a gay bar, just one of the bars frequented by visitors to the island. Dance bar, patio & dancing under the moonlight.

SHIP'S INN, St Lawrence Gap, Christ Church on the south coast, NOT a gay bar, just one of the bars frequented by visitors to the island, live bands some nights.

■ **Restaurants**

WATERFRONT CAFE, the Wharf in Bridgetown. Restaurant & bar with entertainment nightly. NOT a gay business. One of the restaurants frequented by visitors to the island.

JAMAICA

■ **Accommodations**

HOTEL MOCKING BIRD HILL, PO Box 254, Port Antonio, (809) 993-7267, (809) 993-7134, Fax: (809) 993-7133. E-mail: mockbrd@toj.com. Elegant, charming retreat with restaurant, bar & gallery studio featuring women artists. Mixed clientele. Ceiling fans, private baths, TV lounge & pool. Hiking & tours. Nearby are rainforests, mountains and numerous waterfalls, romantic coves and beautiful beaches.

LIGHTHOUSE PARK, PO Box 3, Negril, (809) 957-4490 or (809) 957-0252. Gay-friendly seaside cabanas, a stone house & tent spaces. Double rooms, private & shared baths. House has kitchen privileges, communal kitchen available.

MUSCLE & ART B&B, 1 Denham Ave, Meadowbrook Estates, Kingston 19, Jamaica, (809) 933-1372. Gay-owned & -operated B&B in suburban Kingston offers the opportunity for social & cultural exchange in a household setting, private & shared baths, mostly men, women welcome.

SEAGRAPE VILLAS, c/o West Indies Investments, 640 Pearson #304, Des Plaines IL, (312) 693-6884, (800) 637-3608, fax: (312) 693-6889. 3 four-bdrm villas with cook & maid, gay-friendly, pier access beach available.

TINGALAYA'S, West End Rd, (809) 957-0126. 2 separate buildings with terra-cotta purple & bright green interior/exterior design, thatch roofs. Two rooms have lofts. Double beds, private baths, ceiling fans, porches overlooking garden, outside kitchen & dining area. Small rugged area on property, deep water, no beach. Good swimmers can swim there unless it's rough. Beach sand areas for private nude sunbathing. Gay-friendly.

TREASURE POINTE VILLA, mail: c/o PO Box 424, Bethany Beach, DE 19930,, (800) 442-9697, (302) 539-4003. Gay-friendly, fully-furnished & staffed villa.

ST LUCIA

■ **Bars**

PAT'S PAT, address unnecessary, NOT a gay bar, just one of the bars frequented by visitors to the island, classy bar well-known on island, discreetly frequented by gays.

FYI

A Floating Gay Resort
A Journey By Sea

Most yachts offer snorkeling, scuba diving, windsurfing, kayaking and water skiing. All include all meals and the bar. Yacht chefs are excellent, and gourmet meals are daily fare. You'll dine by candlelight in your own, private million-star restaurant. Sailing sloops have a different feel than power yachts and yachts range from 40 to 160 feet. And YOU decide the ports of call. Luxuriate in the calm waters of the Caribbean...or visit the French or Italian Riviera or the Greek islands.

Many are pleasantly surprised to discover that yacht vacations cost no more than a stay at a resort hotel. **Journeys by Sea** has been chartering yachts since 1989, offering crewed (captain and chef) and bareboat (no crew) yacht vacations worldwide and a large selection of villas in the Caribbean.

Contact **Journeys by Sea** at (954) 730-8585, (800) 825-3632, Fax: (954) 730-8586, E-mail: journeys@safari.net.

FERRARI GUIDES' GAY TRAVEL A to Z - 18th EDITION

CUBA

FYI

Cruising in Style on the Queen Elizabeth 2!

Nineteen ninety-seven is **Pied Piper Travel's** seventh year booking ever-larger gay contingents on major mainstream cruise liners like the QE2. Passengers from the gay groups get to know each other at Pied Piper "Welcome Aboard" cocktail parties and at other special events onboard. Prices average 30% off the regular brochure rates. Shares for double-occupancy can be arranged. Luxury and deluxe cabins are also available at special discount rates.

1997 Pied Piper Cruises

Feb 16-23	Eastern Caribbean
May 24-31	NCL's Norway
May 24-31	Mem'l Day-Caribbean
Jun 5-16	Mediterranean to Scandinavia
Jun 15-21	Alaska
Aug 25-Sep 1	Alaska
Aug 26-Sep 2	San Juan-NYC (Labor Day)

Contact **Pied Piper** at (212) 239-2412, (800) TRIP 312 (874-7312), Fax: (212) 239-2275.

CUBA
HAVANA

■ *Accommodations*

NEW GAY & LESBIAN GUESTHOUSE, there is a new gay & lesbian guesthouse in Havana. For information, contact Milu Tours (49-30) 217 64 88, fax: (49-30) 214 3374.

DOMINICAN REPUBLIC
CABARETE

■ *Women's Accommodations*

PURPLE PARADISE, Mail to: EPS D#184, PO Box 02-5548, Miami, FL 33102,, (809) 571-0637, Fax: (809) 571-0691. Relax on an endless sandy beach, chill out in the Jacuzzi or slide into the pool nestled in lush gardens. Our airy, Spanish-style villa on the north coast of the Dominican Republic has bright, sunny rooms, all with private baths and two with private entrances. Women only.

DUTCH WEST INDIES
BONAIRE

■ *Accommodations*

OCEAN VIEW VILLAS, Kaya Statius Van Eps 6, Bonaire, Netherlands Antilles, Tel/Fax: (599-7) 4309. Stay at these award-winning apartments in Bonaire, an arid, spartan island, surrounded by a spectacular underwater world teeming with exotic creatures. Furnished in pickled oak with pastel accents, apartments have secluded rear patios for private sunbathing & outdoor showers. Kitchens are fully equipped with all the conveniences of home. There is AC, but guests usually prefer the refreshing, cool tradewinds. Some straight clientele.

SABA

■ *Accommodations*

CAPTAIN'S QUARTERS, Windwardside, (5994) 62201, Fax: (5994) 62377, In USA: (212) 289-6031, Fax: (212) 289-1931. E-mail: sabacq@aol.com. http://saba-online.com. Sixteen-room Victorian gay-friendly guesthouse in a tropical paradise. A short 10-minute flight from St Maarten, Saba, "The Unspoiled Queen of the Caribbean," offers spectacular scuba, hiking and relaxation in a storybook setting of Dutch "Gingerbread" villages that will remind you of "Switzerland with Palm Trees." All rooms with stunning ocean views, many with antique/four-poster beds. Convenient to all diving, village shopping and the 1,064 steps to the top of Mt. Scenery & tropical rainforest. Little nightlife, less cruising, this is a perfect romantic getaway. Dive packages available.

ST MAARTEN

■ *Beaches*

CUPECOY BEACH. Beach beneath striking cliffs on the Dutch side of St Maartin island. One part of the beach (Cupecoy II) is gay.

■ *Bars*

PINK MANGO, in the Laguna Beach Hotel on French side of island in city of Marigot. Hard to find, go around the back, knock at the doo.

FRENCH WEST INDIES
ST BARTHELEMY

■ *Accommodations*

HOSTELLERIE DES TROIS FORCES, Vitet 97133, Direct: (590) 276 125, Fax: (590) 278 138. Gay-friendly inn with French & Creole restaurant & bar, private cottages with various conveniences, massage, nearby ocean beach, continental breakfast.

PUERTO RICO
AGUADA

■ *Accommodations*

SAN MAX, PO Box 1294, Aguada, PR 00602, (787) 868-2931. Guesthouse with rooms 85 miles from San Juan, studio apartment, private baths.

■ *Bars*

JOHNNY'S BAR, ask at San Max Guest House for directions. women welcome, pool table.

OCEAN VIEW VILLAS

Your Invitation to Paradise

Tel/Fax: (599-7) 4309

Bonaire

Captains Quarters

Ecotourism
Hiking
Diving

Saba
Dutch Caribbean

PUERTO RICO

AÑASCO

Bars

EL QUINQUE DE CONFE JR., in town of Añasco, past town center, a bit into the mountains, pool tables, music, open daily 3pm-1am.

BAYAMON

Dance Bar/Disco

GILLIGAN'S, Av. Betances D-18 at Hnas. Davila, (787) 786-5065. Private club, gay, daily stripper shows (Thurs male strippers), many pool tables. Popular with women, Wed women only.

BOQUERON

Bars

VILLAGE PUB CAFE, Road #110, Boqueron, pub with weekend dancing & drag shows, strippers.

CAGUAS

Dance Bar/Disco

KENNY'S, Rio Piedras to Caguas Highway, Km 232, exotic country club atmosphere on a mountaintop, swimming pool, food service, Fri-Sat.

COROZAL

Dance Bar/Disco

EXCAPE,★ Calle O'Neil 15, Corozal, huge, dancing, live performance artists, Fri & Sat only from 10pm.

ISABELA

Dance Bar/Disco

VILLA RICOMAR, Bo. Jobas, Carretera 459, Sector La Sierra, Fri-Sat from 10pm, Sun from 8:30pm, woman-owned, 70% men

Restaurants

HAPPY BELLY'S ON THE BEACH, Playa Jobos on the beach, outrageous burgers & pastas, frozen drinks. Live jazz Thurs & Fri.

LAJAS

Bars

MILAGROS PLACE, Carretera 16, Km 3.4, many pool tables, typical rural bar with large gay following.

LUQUILLO BEACH

Restaurants

KIOSKO 10, ELY'S PLACE, in Luquillo Beach, about 40 miles outside of San Juan. Oyster bar with many gay customers.

PIÑONES

Dance Bar/Disco

BEBO'S PLAYA, Carretera 187, Torruela Baja, Piñones. Wed-Sun from 5pm, Sun tea dance, 60% women.

3-Day Caribbean Cruises

Although mainly a travel agent, **Pleasure Travel...Cruise Again Too!** offers several of its own gay cruises annually. For 1997, it's a series of 3-night Bahamas cruises from Florida. These short cruises are perfect for a quick getaway, or for people who have never taken a cruise. Rates for these cruises start as low as $180.00 per person (on Dolphin) and $273.00 per person (on Majesty) for the cruise only, with air add-ons available.

June 6, 1997
Dolphin Cruise Line's "Oceanbreeze" sails from Port Everglades, Florida to Nassau and Blue Lagoon.

November 28, 1997
Majesty Cruise Line's "Royal Majesty" sails from Miami to Nassau and Key West.

December 26, 1997
Dolphin Cruise Line's "Oceanbreeze" again sets sail from Port Everglades for Nassau and Blue Lagoon.

Contact **Pleasure Travel... Cruise Again Too!** at (214) 526-1126, (800) 583-3913, Fax: (214) 526-1109.

Tie the Knot Aboard a Gay Yacht

The Robb Report has called vacations on luxury private yachts "the world's best-kept vacation secret." Much of the gay media has given yachting holidays the highest ratings. The word is out that a yacht vacation costs about the same as any other resort vacation or cruise ship. Yachts offer privacy, first-class food and accommodations, water sports and the freedom to choose your own itinerary. The Caribbean constitutes about 70% of the market, so there are many boats to choose from.

Port Yacht Charters, which matches gay clients with gay and gay-friendly captains and crews, calls yacht charters and the gay community a perfect match. They especially recommend two gay-owned yachts: The "Robert Gordon," perfect for six to ten guests, is owned and operated by a British crew of three.

"Raffles" is owned and operated by a Dutch gay couple. Philip and Abrie are wonderful hosts, and love to show just one couple the best of the Caribbean. This yacht offers a "Sailing Singles Program," which allows two guests to join others on a charter. Both captains are delighted to perform commitment ceremonies at sea, if desired. A wonderful event on the bow at sunset, complete with flowers and champagne. Fees for both yachts are all-inclusive and include gourmet meals and an open bar.

Contact **Port Yacht Charters** at (516) 883-0998 (tel/fax), (800) 213-0465.

CARIBBEAN/ATLANTIC ISLANDS

FERRARI GUIDES' GAY TRAVEL A to Z - 18th EDITION

PUERTO RICO

Authentic Tall-Ship Cruises

Described by the press as one of the most elegant of the remaining tall ships, the Sir Francis Drake is restored to meet the high standards of today's tourist. Built in 1917, this historic 165-foot schooner cruises the clear waters of the British Virgin Islands and other exotic Caribbean ports of call. From November to June, the winter itinerary departs each Saturday from Roadtown, Tortola, British Virgin Islands, on seven-night cruises. Summer itineraries vary each year, so that passengers can return to experience new island getaways.

On Sir Francis Drake you'll experience the camaraderie of only 30 fun-loving sailmates. You'll anchor in secluded coves and bays with brilliant beaches and a rainbow of tropical fish in balmy turquoise waters...visit lush, unspoiled islands with quaint local cultures. Accommodations are comfortable double- and single-berth, air-conditioned cabins, each with private bath and shower. The ship is Ideal for singles, couples, and groups. Full-ship charter rates and group rates are available. Several gay and lesbian companies book the ship for all-gay sailings.

Contact **Tall Ship Adventures** at (303) 755-7983, (800) 662-0090, Fax: (303) 755-9007, E-mail: info@tallshipadventures.com.

The Benefits of Catamarans

Space: Catamarans and trimarans have vastly more interior and deck space than most mono-hulls 10 to 15 feet longer. This translates into larger, more comfortable salons and guest cabins and room for additional heads (bathrooms). On deck, there is much more room for sunbathing and lounging. ***Comfort***: Under sail, particularly in brisk winds, multi-hulls do not heel nearly as much and tend to roll less at anchor. ***Sailing Performance***: All of Whitney's clients who tried them were surprised at the speed their multi-hulls achieved. ***Safety***: The multi-hulls' design and heavy weight make them stable. ***Other features***: Multi-hulls draw less water, making for easier navigation in shallow waters and anchoring closer to shore. Some can be taken right up to the beach. Whitney Yacht Charters, gay-friendly and in business for 35 years, knows the yachts and crews and can recommend the perfect combination for your particular group. Some of their yachts have gay crews or very gay-friendly crews that are experienced in serving gay clients. Yachts are in the Caribbean, Mediterranean and New England. Their motto: "We see every yacht we charter. We do not charter every yacht we see."

Contact **Whitney Yacht Charters** at (941) 927-0108, (800) 223-1426, Fax: (941) 922-7819, E-mail: whtney673@aol.com.

PONCE

■ *Accommodations*

MICHAEL AND SEBASTIAN'S, PO Box 221, Ponce, (787) 284-0631 (Tel/Fax). B&B with shared baths, full breakfast. Convenient to city center, shopping & dining. Beaches, mountains & other local attractions a short drive. Some straight clientele. ♀♂

■ *Dance Bar/Disco*

CAVE, THE,★ 15 Teneria, in back of Ponce Candy. Thurs-Sat, strippers, mostly salsa & merengue. Very popular, lots of drag shows, many performers from the US.

SAN GERMAN

■ *Dance Bar/Disco*

NORMAN'S BAR, Carretera 318, Barrio Maresua, San German. Salsa & marengue, lost of pool tables, 50% men, 50% women. ♀♂

WORLD,★ Carretera 360, km 9 at intersection of Carretera 2 Thurs-Sun, dancing, shows, strippers, pool tables, food.

SAN JUAN

■ *Information*

AIDS INFO, (787) 751-5858.

BREEZE DIVERS, (787) 282-7184. Social club for gays & lesbians, travelers welcome to participate.

TELEINFO GAY, metro: (787) 782-8488, island: (800) 462-9179, unverifiable spring '97.

■ *Accommodations*

ATLANTIC BEACH HOTEL, 1 calle Vendig, (787) 721-6900, Fax: (787) 721-6917, Hotel with restaurant & bar, some straight clientele. 37 double rooms, Jacuzzi, ocean beach, 10 min from historical section. Many restaurants, nightspots nearby. Mostly male clientele. ♂

BENEDICT'S BEACH HOUSE, at the Barefoot Bar, apartments & rooms for rent above gay bar. ♂

EMBASSY GUEST HOUSE-CONDADO, 1126 Calle Seaview, Condado, (787) 725-2400 or (787) 724-7440, Fax: (787) 725-2400. Guesthouse on the beach with restaurant & bar, some straight clientele. Color TV, AC, ceiling fans & private baths. ♀♂

HORNED DORSET PRIMAVERA HOTEL, PO Box 1132, Rincón, PR, (787) 823-4030, fax: (787) 823-5580. Small resort hotel in a beach town 2 hrs from San Juan, 40% gay.

L'HABITACION BEACH GUESTHOUSE, 1957 Calle Italia, Ocean Park, San Juan 00911, (787) 727-2499, Fax: (787) 727-2599. Gay & lesbian B&B on the gay Ocean Park Beach with bar & restaurant. ♀♂

NUMERO UNO GUEST HOUSE, Calle Santa Elena #1, Ocean Park, 00911, (787) 726-5010, (787) 727-5482. Guesthouse with restaurant & bar, private baths, expanded continental breakfast, AC, pool & ocean beach on pre-

PUERTO RICO

mises, near gay nightlife, 50% gay/lesbian clientele.
OCEAN WALK GUEST HOUSE, Calle Atlantic No 1, Ocean Park, (787) 728-0855, 726-0445, FAX 728-6434. Guesthouse on the beach with cafe & bar, some straight clientele in season, 50% straight off season, women welcome, variety of rooms with private baths, continental breakfast.
SEABREEZE VACATION APARTMENT RENTALS, 1505 Loiza St #277, (787) 723-1888. Studio apartments close to beach.

■ Bars
BAREFOOT BAR, 2 Calle Vendig, Condado, (787) 724-7230. Oceanfront bar & restaurant, on the beach, daily 9am-4am.
BEACH BAR, at Atlantic Beach Hotel. Outdoor bar on the beach, popular early afternoon, Sun Tea Dance.
CAFE MATISSE, 1351 Ashford Ave, gay-friendly restaurant. Bar becomes gay on Tues for Alternative night.
DOWNSTAIRS LOUNGE, at the Condado Inn.
JUNIOR'S BAR, Calle Condado 602, Parada 17 1/2, Santurce, (787) 722-5663. Small men-only cruise bar with exclusively Latin music, Salsa & Merengue. Daily from 6pm, Sun from 3pm, local crowd.
VIBRATION,★ 51 Calle Barranquitas, Condado. Cruise bar, men only, private club, till 5am, erotic videos.

■ Dance Bar/Disco
BOCCACIO, Calle Z between Avenida Ponce de Leon & Avenida Muñoz Rivera in Hato Rey. Across from fire dept, disco with outdoor patio bar and patio bar. Fri, Sat only from 10pm, $12 entry for all-you-can-drink, 50% men, 50% women.
CLUB IBIZA, Av. Ashford, at La Concha Hotel, open Fri only, trendy crowd, frequented by gays.
CUPS, Calle San Mateo 1708, Santurce, (787) 268-3570, disco.
EROS, 1257 Ponce de Leon, Parada 18, Santurce, (787) 722-1131. Wed-Sun, younger crowd, 70% men. Club kids dress up in wild costumes, all-out drag shows, real performance are, real productions.
LA LAGUNA NIGHTCLUB, Calle Barranquitas 53, Condado. Private after hours dance club with strippers & live entertainment, open Sat & Sun, from 10pm.

■ Saunas/Health Clubs
STEAM WORKS BATHS, Calle Luna 205, (787) 725-4993.

■ Restaurants
ALO BISTRO, Calle Mercado 9, Old San Juan, (787) 722-3731. Continental cuisine, popular with gays.
CAFE BERLIN, 407 San Francisco, Plaza Colon, Old San Juan, (787) 722-5202. Huge gay following.

FYI

Island Hopping Vacations

Island Hoppers Tours specializes in the Bahamas, Jamaica and Florida with a unique program that lets you choose a single island destination, or "island hop" by "adding on" other islands. You can also "add an adventure" by choosing activity-oriented itineraries. "Go Native" cultural programs provide opportunities to interact with the local people in a variety of activites. Dive programs showcase resorts that offer pristine dive sites.

You can make a Florida vacation exotic with the "Day Trips From Florida" program. A quick flight from Florida to an Island Hoppers destination will make an exotic addition to your Florida itinerary. So, you can breakfast in Key West, have lunch and dinner on another tropical island, and be back to your Florida hotel at night.

Contact **Island Hoppers** at (407) 933-4333, (800) 467-7595, Fax: (407) 933-0005, E-mail: kalikmon@digital.net

FYI

Lose yourself in the experience, NOT in the crowd!

Luxurious resorts on secluded beaches are the **Club Le Bon** trademark. No busloads of tourists and no crowds...just 30 to 100 lesbians sharing the common interest of getting away from it all amid the natural beauty of the

CLUB Le Bon

tropics. Because these trips are limited in size, you will discover an atmosphere intimate enough for two, yet large enough to mingle with other lesbians. Members enjoy the exclusive use of the finest smaller hotels in the islands, selected for privacy and spectacular views, and a multitude of inviting activities, from water sports and sightseeing to evening parties.

Club Le Bon invites you to Yucatan's, Isla Mujeres in the Caribbean, where you will enjoy endless white sand beaches bordered by turquoise waters and the finest accommodations on the island. For 1997 and 1998, for the first time ever, a lesbian all-inclusive spa vacation is being offered. Pamper yourself at this Holistic Spa Resort at an affordable price. Tea Dance and other entertainment included. Our Kool Kids Family Vacations are joined by a certified children's counselor to educate and entertain your kids while you take a break.

Contact **Club Le Bon** at (908) 826-1577, (800) 836-8687, Fax: (908) 826-1577.

CARIBBEAN/ATLANTIC ISLANDS

PUERTO RICO

FYI

The First Exclusively Gay & Lesbian Spa Vacations

Beyond Nirvana is the first company to offer a complete line of spa vacations exclusively for gays and. lesbians. Beyond Nirvana promotes a healthier lifestyle and inner relaxation in all of their packages. For those looking for a healthy new lifestyle or a jump-start on a fitness program, Beyond Nirvana has a never-ending selection of health-enhancing activity tours. Many of the offered properties include treatments such as massage, manicure, pedicure, herbal wrap, loofah scrub, facial and fango (mud) wrap. Other soul-enriching activities include yoga, Tai Chi and meditation. They also offer Amazon rainforest trips, environmental exploration, biking and hiking packages, among others.

Beyond Nirvana Planned Tours for 1997...Cuernavaca: Hotel Ville Bajar & Grand Spa (4 stars), Guadalajara: Rio Caliente (hot springs spa, cabanas, private), Jamaica: Jackies on the Reef (spiritual spa, 10 people, women-only), Belize: Maruba Resort & Spa (jungle spa, unique, private).

Contact **Beyond Nirvana** at (800) 532-0526, Fax: (503) 643-8965.

CAFE MATISSE, Av. Ashford, Condado, (787) 723-7910. Continental cuisine, live entertainment Wed.

CAFE MIRAMAR, 801 Ponce de Leon Ave, Miramar, in Hotel Excelsior, (787) 721-8955 or 721-7400. International & nouvelle cuisine, breakfast-dinner, Sun brunch 10am-3pm.

LA FONDA DE CERVANTES, Wilson Ave 1464, Condado, in Hotel Iberia, (787) 722-5380. Exotic European cuisine with Spanish influence.

LAS OLAS, 1 Calle Venedig, at Atlantic Beach Hotel, (787) 721-6900, breakfast & lunch.

LOS FAISANES, Ave Magdalena 1108, a formal-casual atmosphere, international cuisine, lunch & dinner. Rated by American Airlines as best restaurant in Puerto Rico.

OCEAN WALK RESTAURANT, at the Ocean Walk guest house.

PANACHÉ, 1126 Sea View near Vendig, Condado, (787) 725-2400. Casual southern French cuisine on the beach.

TERRACE, at Condado Inn Hotel.

■ Retail & Bookstores
SCRIPTUM, 1129 Ashford Ave, Condado. Gay bookstore.

■ Erotica
CONDOM WORLD, 353 Calle San Francisco, (787) 722-5348. 2nd location: 278-B Avd Piñero, Rio Piedras, condoms & videos.

VEGA BAJA

■ Dance Bar/Disco
EL DIAMANTE, Puerto Nuevo Rd, Carretera 686, next to Pizzeria Pagan in Vega Baja, large dance bar.

VIEQUES ISLAND

■ Accommodations
CONNECTIONS, PO Box 358, Vieques, PR 00765, (787) 741-0023, Fax: (787) 741-2022. Vacation house rentals on Vieques Island.

■ Women's Accommodations
NEW DAWN CARIBBEAN RETREAT & GUEST HOUSE, PO Box 1512, Bo Pilon, Rt 995, Vieques, (787) 741-0495. Guesthouse & campground with restaurant & bar, men welcome, some straight clientele. Variety of accommodations with various conveniences, queen beds & lofts in a 2-story wood-frame house, piano in living room, restaurant is communal, kitchen in off-season, nearby ocean beach. Specializing in groups.

VIRGIN ISLANDS BRITISH
COOPER ISLAND

■ Accommodations
COOPER ISLAND BEACH CLUB, Cooper Island, British Virgin Islands, USA office: PO Box 512, Turners Falls, MA 01376, (800) 542-4624 (USA Office), (413) 863-3162, Fax: (413) 863-3662. Experience an island 1-1/2 miles by 1/2 mile, where there are no roads, nightclubs, malls or fast-food outlets. Your principal activities will be sunning, swimming, snorkeling, reading, writing and enjoying relaxing meals. Our beachfront restaurant and bar offer dramatic sunset views. Our twelve rooms are on the beach, with open-plan living room, kitchen, balcony, bath and shower that is almost outdoors! Gay-friendly.

TORTOLA

■ Accommodations
VILLAS OF FORT RECOVERY ESTATE, Box 239, Road Town, Tortola, BVI (809) 495-4354, (800) 367-8455, Fax: (809) 495-4036, E-mail: FTRHOTEL@caribsurf.com. Gay-friendly luxury seaside villa resort & restaurant, private baths, continental breakfast, private beach, fresh-water pool on premises.

VIRGIN ISLANDS - US

■ Accommodations
RENT A VILLA, (800) 533-6863, (201) 533-6863, Fax: (201) 740-8833. Private home vacation rentals in St. Croix, St. John & St. Thomas, 1-6br, full amenities, gay-friendly.

ST CROIX

■ Accommodations
ON THE BEACH, 127 Smithfield, Frederiksted, VI 00840, (809) 772-1205, (800) 524-2018. The premier gay destination in the Caribbean. Twenty immaculate suties located directly on a beautiful white sandy beach. Two fresh-water pools. Kitchens in all units, plus free continental breakfast. Half mile to town. Exclusively gay & lesbian clientele. Member IGTA. Our 19th year!

PRINCE STREET INN, THE, 402 Prince St, Frederiksted, USVI, (809) 772-9550, (800) 771-9550. Gay-friendly inn. Suites with various modern conveniences, kitchens, private baths, 4 blocks from beach. 25% gay/lesbian clientele.

■ Bars
LAST HURRAH, King St, Frederiksted, (809) 772-5225. Bar & restaurant with Hollywood theme.

■ Restaurants
CAFE DU SOLEIL, Strand St, Frederiksted. Oceanfront continental cuisine, upstairs location with ocean view.

ARGENTINA

ST JOHN

Accommodations
OSCAR'S GUEST HOUSE, Estate Pastery 27, St John, USVI 00830, (809) 776-6193. Guesthouse in Cruz Bay, 7 rooms with queen-sized beds, full bath, daily maid service, AC, TV.

SUNSET POINTE IN ST. JOHN, 45A King St, Christainsted St Croix, (809) 773-8100. Rental house & cottage, color cable TV, fully equipped kitchen, house has pool, 50% gay/lesbian clientele.

Beaches
SOLOMON BEACH, nude beach, a 20-minute hike from Cruz Bay ferry dock. Take your own water (no facilities).

ST THOMAS

Accommodations
BLACKBEARD'S CASTLE, PO Box 6041, (809) 776-1234, (800) 344-5771, Fax: (809) 776-4321. Our tower, a national historic site, was built in 1697 to scan for pirates & enemy ships. It provides a spectacular backdrop for an oversized fresh water pond & terrace. The views are exceptional! This intimate inn's spacious, quiet guest rooms provide all the expected amenities.

Beaches
LITTLE MAGEN'S BEACH, nude beach, walk thigh-deep along rocky shore. Cars parked on the road above are sometimes broken into.

MORNING STAR BEACH. Frequented by many gays especially on Sun.

Bars
CABANA LOUNGE, on the grounds of Blackbeard's Castle hotel. Born in the aftermath of Hurricane Marilyn, Cabana Lounge is now the hottest gay bar in the Virgin Islands. Come join the party. Serving cocktails all day, dinner Tues-Sun.

Dance Bar/Disco
R & R NIGHT CLUB & LEMON GRASS CAFE, on Back Street at Baker Square. Fri & Sat only: Dining room converts to dance club about 10pm. Busy by 11pm, 80%-90% gay & lesbian.

P.O. Box 6041
St. Thomas
U.S.V.I.
00804

(809) 776-1234
(800) 344-5771

BLACKBEARD'S Castle
Restaurant Hotel Piano Lounge

Restaurants
BLACKBEARD'S CASTLE, at Blackbeard's Castle hotel. Open while rebuilding after hurricane. Come enjoy our new, intimate atmosphere.

OLD STONE FARMHOUSE, at Mahogany Run Golf Course. Rebuilding, due to reopen in 1996.

A beautiful tropical setting complimented by the only Gay-owned beachfront resort in the USVI's.

Relaxing accommodations...

Warm and friendly setting...

Two swimming pools...

Still The Hottest Spot In The Caribbean

ST. CROIX,
UNITED STATES
VIRGIN ISLANDS

(800) 524-2018
(809) 772-1205

LATIN AMERICA

ARGENTINA
COUNTRY CODE: (54)

WHO TO CALL
For Tour Companies Serving This Destination
See Argentina on page 8

BUENOS AIRES

Bars
BACH BAR, Cabrera 4390, Palermo Viejo, popular with younger crowd, from 22:00 (closed Wed).

CENTRO CLUB SNOB, Hipólito Yrigoyen 1115, (01) 384 6271, Thurs-Sat from 24:00, 50% gay & lesbian & 50% hetero clientele.

D. GALA, Paraguay 459, 50% gay & lesbian & 50% hetero clientele, more gay Wed & Sun.

EL OLMO, Santa Fe, at Pueyrredon, not a gay bar, more gay 22:00-02:30. Also after-hours café for breakfast, 07:00.

GASOIL, Bulnes 1250, strippers, from 02:00 (closed Wed), women welcome.

INCOGNITO, Scalabrini Ortiz 1721, at the Confusión bar location, small, intimate bar, open evenings.

INVITRO, Azcuenaga 1007, (01) 824 0932, 60% men, 40% women.

PIOLA, Libertad between Marcelo .T de Alvear & Avenida Santa Fe, bar & restaurant, popular with gays Wed & Sun evenings, 50% gay & 50% straight clientele.

PUERTO POLLENSA, Carlos Calvo 3778, bar & disco, 90% women.

SITDGES, Avda Córdoba 4119, Wed-Sun from 22:00.

TASMANIA, Pasaje Dellepiane 685, at Viamonte 1600.

Dance Bar/Disco
ANGELS, Viamonte 2168

BOICOT, Pasaje Dellepiane 657, women-only disco on weekends.

BUNKER, Anchorena 1170, large disco, Fri-Sun from 02:30, some straight clientele.

CLUB CANICHE, Uruguay 142, at Vampire Buenos Aires, (01) 373 2666. Wed-Sat from 24:00.

CONTRAMANO, Rodríquez Peña 1082, Wed-Sun, 90% men.

DON'T TELL MAMMA, Rodríquez Peña 1177, Wed-Sun from 23:30.

ENIGMA, Suipacha 927, in shopping center, women's disco, open only on weekends, men welcome.

TERCER MILENIO, Alsina 934, disco & restaurant, 60% men, 40% women, open Thurs & Fri.

Saunas/Health Clubs
OLIMPO, Viamonte 723, at Plaza Maipú.

Restaurants
LOCHNESS, Anchorena 1260, (01) 827 3411, fast food, pre- & post-disco crowds, 22:00-10:00.

FERRARI GUIDES' GAY TRAVEL A to Z - 18th EDITION   343

ARGENTINA

Argentina = Unusual Travel Experiences

Argentina is pampas and gaucho ranches. It's beaches. It's Andean peaks. It's the sophisticated European-style city of Buenos Aires. It's jungle trails. It's spectacular Iguaçu Falls. It's rainforest in the north and glaciers in the south. It's Tierra del Fuego.

Mix Travel, the gay arm of an established Buenos Aires travel company, has developed a range of unusual itineraries for gay travelers. You can live the gaucho life on a great colonial estancia, trek on horseback into the Andes, haunt the tango bars of Buenos Aires, hike the trails of the Spanish Conquistadores, raft, kayak or sail Argentina's lakes and rivers, and stay at exclusive resorts along the incredible, 1000-mile coastline.

Anticipating the sophisticated and eclectic tastes of gay travelers, Mix has sought to create a unique and unusual travel experience in a gay-friendly environment. Join them and see the whales off the Valdez peninsula... go cross-country skiing in July on Tierra del Fuego...sail up the Great Parana River for a look at rare and exotic wildlife. Mix specializes in individual independent travel packages, group arrangements on request.

Contact **Mix Travel** at (54 1) 312-3410, Fax: (54 1) 375-4586 or (54 1) 313 4432.

Did You Know that Argentina...

...Is known as the Europe of South America because of the looks and lifestyle of its people. ...Has a wide variety of ski resorts, and the ski season is from June to August. ...has a language which is a dialect of Spanish, with a lot of Italian influence. ...is home to

STONEWALL '69

renowned personalities like tennis player Gabriella Sabatini, top model Valeria Mazza and ballet dancer Julio Bocca, all of whom represent Argentina's X generation. ...Argentina's tango was originally danced only between men. ...is one of the few countries in the world where you can find the greatest diversity of weather and landscapes. ...Has a gay and lesbian population of 3 million brothers and sisters. ...Possesses the fourth-largest Jewish community in the world, after Israel, the USA and France.

These insights on Argentina were supplied by **Stonewall 69**, an energetic, gay-owned and -operated tour and travel company providing gay-oriented itineraries to Argentina, and a full program of worldwide travel for gay and lesbian Argentinians.

Contact **Stonewall 69** at (54 1) 394-6832, Fax: (54 1) 328-6480. Send mail to: 7891 W Flager St #54-119, Miami, FL 33144, USA.

MEMORABILIA, Maipú 761, (01) 322 7630, Wed & Sun 50% gay & lesbian & 50% hetero clientele.
NIAHI, Las Heras 4021.
PUERTO BANUS VIP BY GALA, Avenida de Mayo 1354, lower level, (01) 381 7150, enter through straight bar then go downstairs to restaurant, Thurs-Sun. ♪♂
TASMANIA, Pasaje Dellepiane 685, at Viamonte 1600, (01) 374 3177, bar & restaurant, Thurs dinner only.
TE MATARE RAMIREZ, Paraguay 4062. ✉
TERCER MILENIO, Alsina 934, at Tercer Milenio disco.

■ Retail & Bookstores
CALIBAN BOOKSTORE, Viamonte 1696, 2nd floor, #6, (01) 371 83 58, gay & lesbian bookstore with erotic literature.
LIBRERIA DE MUJERES, Paseo La Plaza, Avda Corrientes 1660. Local 3, (01) 372 7162, ext 203, women's bookstore with Argentine books & books from Spain, France, USA, Peru, Chile & Brasil about women & feminism.

■ Erotica
COMPLEMENT SEX SHOP OF ARGENTINA, Avenida Corrientes 753, 1st floor, #65, (01) 394 7581.

CORDOBA

■ Accommodations
HOSTAL DE LA LUNA, Monseñor Pablo Cabrera s/n, Cruz Chica, La Cumbre, Córdoba, (0548) 51877. Gay-friendly B&B with 5 guestrooms, color TV, phone, private baths, full gourmet breakfast & complimentary evening wine or afternoon tea. Dinner is optional. Pool on premises. ♨

■ Dance Bar/Disco
HANGAR 18 DISCO, Blvd Las Heras 116. ♫♂
LA PIAF, Obispo Ceballos 45. ♫♂
PLANTA BAJA, San Martín 666, 214 704, Wed-Sun from 24:00. ♫♂

CORRIENTES

■ Bars
CONTRAMARCHA, Paímbre 5000. ♂

LA PLATA

■ Dance Bar/Disco
BACK DISCO, Calle 35 & Calle 5, Fri & Sat. ♫♂

MAR DEL PLATA

■ Bars
CREAM BAR, Diagonal Alberdi (25 de Mayo) 2621, (023) 95 5397, from 20:00. ♂
DICROICA, Bolivar 2152, open all year.

■ Dance Bar/Disco
EXTASIS, Corrientes 2044, (023) 920 338, Fri & Sat. ♫♂
PETROLEO, Arenales 2272, Fri-Sat. ♫♂

BRAZIL

MENDOZA
■ *Dance Bar/Disco*
QUEEN DISCO, Ejercito de las Andes 656, between Dorrego & Guaymallen, (061) 316 990. 🕪♂

NEUQUEN
■ *Bars*
S.O.S., calle Rivadavia, at calle Mendoza. ♂

RESISTENCIA
■ *Bars*
PLANETA CHINO, Santiago del Estero 223. ♂

RIO NEGRO
■ *Bars*
LOS FAUNOS, calle Venezuela, at Camino de Circunvalación, in Cipolletti, ♂

ROSARIO
■ *Bars*
CONTRATO BAR, Alvear 40 bis, Thurs-Sun from 23:00. ♂
INIZIO, Mitre 1880, from 22:00. ♀♂
■ *Dance Bar/Disco*
STATION G, Avda. Rivadavia 2481. 🕪♀♂

SALTA
■ *Bars*
ESTACION TEQUILA CLUB, San Luís 648. ♂
NOSOTROS DISCO, J.M. Guemes 11, in barrio Don Emilio, (087) 224 035. ♂
■ *Dance Bar/Disco*
O'CLOCK DISCO, La Rioja, at Santa Fé, Fri-Sun. 🕪♂

SAN JUAN
■ *Dance Bar/Disco*
HENDRIX DISCO, Avda L.N. Alem Sur 209. 🕪♂

SANTA FE
■ *Bars*
TUDOR TABERNA PUB, Javier de la Rosa 325, Barrio de Guadalupe, bar with Sat disco. 🕪♂

TUCUMAN
■ *Bars*
ENIGMA PARA VOS, Monteagudo 428, bar & disco from 02:00. 🕪♂
■ *Dance Bar/Disco*
EXTASIS DISCO, San Martín 986. 🕪♂

BOLIVIA
COUNTRY CODE: (591)

WHO TO CALL — For Tour Companies Serving This Destination See Bolivia on page 10

LA PAZ
■ *Bars*
CAFE BRASIL, Avda. Héroes del Acre 1762, between Conchitas & Castrillo, in San Pedro, cruise bar with dancing on weekends, vast majority male clientele. 🕪♂

BRAZIL
COUNTRY CODE: (55)

WHO TO CALL — For Tour Companies Serving This Destination See Brazil on page 10

BELO HORIZONTE
■ *Bars*
ALIAS,★ Rua Gonçalves Dias 2217, at Santa Catarina. ♂
BAR DA ESTAÇAO, Praça da Estaçao, near train station. ♂
BAR DO LULU, Rua Leopoldina 415. ♂
BAR NACIONAL, Av. Contorno 10076, (031) 295 2525. ♂
CANTINA DO LUCAS, Av. Augusto de Lima 223/18, ♀♂
EAGLE'S BAR, Praça Clemente de Faria 100, (031) 295 5594. ♂
FRATER, Rua Levindo Lopes 18, Savassi. ♂
GAM'S, Rua Pernambuco 773. 🕪♂
ONDAS DO JEQUI, Av. Brasil 1940, (031) 261 4190, NOT a gay bar, frequented by gays & lesbians.
PACO PIGALLE, Av. Contorno 6608, (031) 127 9812, NOT a gay bar, frequented by gays & lesbians.
QUEEN SCRATCH, Rua Gonçalves Dias 2217, from 19:00, closed Mon. ↙🕪♂
■ *Dance Bar/Disco*
BIGOD'S, Rua Sao Paulo, at Rua Goitacazes. 🕪♀♂
BLOW UP, Rua Tenente Brito Mello 267, Thurs-Sun from 22:00. 🕪♀
FASHION,★ Rua Tupis 1240, near Araguari, Barro Preto, (031) 223 3352, strippers Thurs. 🕪▣↙♂
PAGA, Rua Pe Odorico 95, (031) 227 8403, 3 levels. 🕪♂
■ *Saunas/Health Clubs*
ANTARES, Av Papa Pio XII 597, Jardin Chapadao, (019) 241 6227, 18:00-23:00 (Sat 15:00-20:00), closed Sun.
ARAXA, Rua Alagoas 280, Funcionários, (031) 224 5568.
BRASIL, Av. Amazonas 315, (031) 222 2186.
CANDELARIA, Praça Raul Soares 315, (031) 212 7691.
GERMANIA, Rua Germania 221, (019) 242 1435, 15:00-23:00.
OFF, Av do Contorno 4451, Serra, (031) 221 8901.
STAR, Av Antonio Carlos 617, Lagoinha.
TEN NINETY-SEVEN (1097), Rua Guajajaras 1097, Santo Agostinho.
VAPORE, Rua Timbiras 2523, Santo Agostinho, (031) 275 2001.

BRASILIA
■ *Bars*
BEIRUTE, CLS 109, Bloco A, loja 02, Asa Sul. ♂
CAFE SAVANA, CLN 116, Bloco A, loja 04, Asa Norte, (06) 347 9403, Mon-Sat. ♂
COFFEE HOUSE, SHN, Galeria do Hotel Manhattan, loja 10. ♂
MARTINICA CAFE, CLN 303, Asa Norte, from 18:00, closed Mon. ♂
SPHAERA, CLN 203, Bloco D, loja 67-73. 🕪♂
■ *Dance Bar/Disco*
METROPOLIS, SCLN 314, Bloco A, loja 55, Thurs-Sat from 22:00. 🕪♂
NEW AQUARIUS, SDS Edificio Acropo L., Bloco N, loja 12, (06) 312 42 23, Fri, Sat from 23:00. 🕪♂
T99, SQS 203, (061) 225 2611, Fri & Sat from 23:00. 🕪♂

CAMPINAS
■ *Bars*
DOUBLE FACEM, Rua Barao de Jaguara 358, (019) 236 7361, Fri-Sun from 22:00. ↙♂
HASÉS, Av. José de Souza Campos 735, (019) 255 1552, Fri-Sun from 22:00. 🕪↙♂
■ *Dance Bar/Disco*
CLUB, THE, Rod. Campinas Mogi Mirim, km 105.5, (019) 253 6380, Fri & Sat. 🕪↙♂

CAMPO GRANDE
■ *Bars*
ELEVEN (11), Rua X de Novembro 700, (067) 382 7973, from 19:00. ♂

LATIN AMERICA

FERRARI GUIDES' GAY TRAVEL A to Z - 18th EDITION   345

BRAZIL

FYI

Tours to Brazil

Carnaval in Rio begins 40 days before Easter, but any time of the year is a good time to come to Brazil. Salvador, in the northern state of Bahia, Brazil's former capital, was founded in 1549 and made distinctive by its pastel colored houses and huge stone colonial fortresses. Manaus, a city famous for its history in the rubber trade, is on the Amazon River. Near Manaus, the muddy Amazon meets the Rio Negro, whose waters are black from dissolved jungle vegetation. Boat excursions take you to their confluence, where the colors form a straight dividing line, brown on one side, black on the other.

Fiesta Tours can take you cruising on the Amazon with jungle lodge adventure side trips. You can go scuba diving into the pristine waters of Abrolhos, Brazil's national marine park, home to the largest coral formations in the south Atlantic. Iguassu Falls, on the Argentine border, offers a breathtaking scene, as majestic as Niagara Falls. Fiesta offers custom bookings to Brazil, with itineraries like Afro-Brazilian heritage tours and healing study trips into the heart of the country, and all the insider information you need.

Contact **Fiesta Tours** at (415) 986-1134, (800) 200-0582, Fax: (415) 986-3029. E-mail: brazusa@primenet.com.

FYI

Rio de Janeiro Specialists Offer Air/Hotel Packages & Optional Amazon Tours

Call **Anderson International Tours** for tours to Rio de Janeiro. You can play and get a suntan at Copacabana, Ipanema, and Leblanc beaches, marvel at the statue of Christ the Redeemer when you visit the Corcovado Mountain, and see amazing sights just walking along the streets. Rio nightlife sizzles!

The rest of Brazil is as astonishing as Rio. Sao Paulo is elegant and its nightlife compares to that of Paris. Bahia is charming. Manaus, gateway to the Amazon Jungle, is wild and beautiful. Recife is a mixture of new and colonial. Air-and-hotel packages also offer optional tours, including one to the Amazon, that will give you real insight into what Brazil is all about. Anderson International Tours also offers all-inclusive packages to Europe.

Contact **Anderson Int'l Tours**

Anderson International Travel

at (517) 337-1300, (800) 723-1233, Fax: (517) 337-8561. E-mail: travela@pilot.msu.edu.

CURITIBA

■ Bars
CLASSIC CLUB, Av Marechal Floriano Peixoto 1635, many lesbians. ♀

NICK HAVANA BAR, Rua Francisco Torres 272, (041) 263 4884, piano bar. ♂

OPÇAO, Rua Benjamin Constant 180, (041) 322 1180. ♂

■ Dance Bar/Disco
AGNUS DEI, Rua Visconde do Rio Branco. ♂

CABARE PAGLIACCI, Rua Sao Francisco 10, (041) 272 2881. ♀♂

EPOCA, Avenida Iguaçu 560, (041) 225 2068. ♂

LA BELLE EPOQUE, Av Sete de Setembro 3453, (041) 224 8583, go go boys. ♂

LEGENDS UNDERGROUND CLUB, Rua Dr. Muricy 949, (041) 234 5134. ♂

■ Saunas/Health Clubs
CARACALA, Rua Alferes Poli 1039, (041) 232 7707, 16:00-23:30.

FIFTYNINE (59), Rua Alfredo Bufrem 59, ()41) 971 7671.

FIVE-TWENTY (520), Rua Souza Naves 520, Santo Cristo, 16:00-23:00.

OPINIAO, Rua Amintas de Barros 749, (041) 262 1982.

■ Retail & Bookstores
LILITH FEMINIST BOOKSHOP, Rua Bruno Filgueira 1921, women's bookstore.

FLORIANOPOLIS

■ Bars
FABRICA DE ARTE, Rua Nunes Machado 104, (048) 224 1102, Tues-Sat from 20:00, discreetly frequented by gays.

ORBITA, Rua Fernando Machado 64, behind the Instituto de Educaçao, (048) 223 6704, from 20:00, closed Mon. ♂

■ Dance Bar/Disco
CHANDON, Rua Felipe Schmidt 760, (048) 223 1622, Sat from 24:00. ♂

FREE BOYS, Rua Antonio Soares 65, Wed-Sat, occasional strippers. ♂

FORTALEZA

■ Beaches
JERICOACOARA, difficult to find, ask locally for directions.

■ Bars
BAR DO JOCA, Av Beira Mar 3101, barraca 205a, (085) 261 4006, 7 days. ♂

EUROTUNEL, Av 13 de Maio 2400, Benfica, closed Sun. ♂

■ Dance Bar/Disco
AXE BABA, Av. Tristao Gonçalves 1615, closed Mon. ♂

HANGAR 7 NIGHT CLUB, Av Monsenhor

LATIN AMERICA

346 FERRARI GUIDES' GAY TRAVEL A to Z - 18th EDITION

Tabosa 1101, Praia de Iracema, Fri & Sat. 🍴♂

MEDHUZA, Rua Oswaldo Cruz 46, Beira Mar, (085) 295 4127, Fri & Sat. 🍴♂

STYLE, Rua Senador Pompeu 1493, closed Mon. 🍴♂

TABU, Avenida Santos Dumont 1673, in Aldeota, Fri & Sat. 🍴♂

■ *Saunas/Health Clubs*
APOLLO, Rua Rodriques Jr. 1425, 15:00-24:00.
IRACEMA, Rua Vicente Leite 2020, Aldeota, (085) 244 1999, 14:00-22:00.

GUARULHOS

■ *Dance Bar/Disco*
CASA DO SOM, Praça dos Estudantes 174, (011) 208 0222, Fri & Sat 22:30—4:30, Sun 16:30-22:30. 🍴♀♂

MANAUS

■ *Dance Bar/Disco*
IS, Blvd. Dr. V. de Lima 33, (081) 228 6828, Fri-Sun from 22:00. 🍴♂

NOTIVAGOS, Rua Wilkes de Mattos, Thurs-Sat. 🎵🍴♂

POÇOS DE CALDAS

■ *Bars*
HALL, Rua Prefeito Chagas 23, (035) 721 8234. ♂

PORTO ALEGRE

■ *Bars*
CLAUDIO'S, Avenida Joao Pessoa, near Avenida Venancio Aires, open until very late. ♂

DOCE VICIO, Rua Vieira de Castro 32, 3 levels, bar with restaurant & terrace. ♀♂

FLY, Rua Gonçalo de Carvalho 121, frequented by gays.

INDISCRETUS, Av. Brasil 1393, strippers. 🎵♂

LOCAL HERO, Rua Venancio Aires 59, near Rua José Patrocínio, Wed-Sun. 🍴🎵♂

■ *Dance Bar/Disco*
BORDO 588, Rua Getulio Vargas 588, Fri-Sun. 🍴♂

ENIGMA,★ Rua Pinto Bandeira 485, Fri-Sun. 🍴♂

ERA UMA VEZ, Rua Pereira Franco 68. 🍴♂

FIM DE SECULO, Rua Plinio 427, gay Fri only. 🍴♂

VITRAUX, Rua da Conceiçao at Alberto Bins, Fri-Sun, many women. 🍴♀♂

■ *Saunas/Health Clubs*
HERO, Rua Visconde do Rio Branco 390, from 15:00.

LUCA, Rua Lucas de Oliveira, at 24 do Outubro.

RECIFE

■ *Beaches*
BEACHES: Galibu (Gaybu): in Cabo, 35km from city center, climb a small hill until reach Calhatas, frequented by gays. Porto das Galinhas: 90 kms from Recife.

■ *Dance Bar/Disco*
BOATO, Rua Herculano Bandeira 513, (081) 352 5300, small dance bar. 🍴♂

DAZIBAO, Rua Progresso 336, (081) 231 2492. 🍴🎵♂

RIBERAO PIRES

■ *Dance Bar/Disco*
SCHLOSS, Rua Guaracy 171, Ouro Fino Paulista, (011) 742 0168, disco, bar & gallery. 🍴♂

RIO DE JANEIRO

■ *Information*
BARRALES CULT, PO Box 37517, Rio de Janeiro 22642-970, Tel/Fax: (021) 385 2121, lesbian group.

NOSS, Rua Visconde de Pirajá 127/201, Tel/fax: (021) 227 5944, social health organization involved in HIV/AIDS issues & outreach services, publishes bi-monthly newspaper Nós Por Exemplo.

■ *Beaches*
BEACHES: Ipanema (near Rua Farme de Amoeda, in front of Alberico's Restaurante), Copacabana (in the area between Copacabana Palace Hotel & Maxim's restaurant), Praia da Barra (at Barra Tijuca, near Lokau restaurant, be discreet), Praia de Sepetiba, Praia do Bananal (on Ihla do Governador), Praia dos Cocos (in the Jardim Guanabara on Ilha do Governador, near Bicao).

■ *Dance Bar/Disco*
BATOM VERMELHO, Nova Iguaçu. 🍴🎵♂

BOHEMIO, Rua Santa Luzia 760, Cinelandia, (021) 240 7259. 🍴🎵♀♂

GAVIOTA, Rua Rodolfo de Amoedo 347, in Barra da Tijuca, Fri & Sat from 23:00, Sun from 20:30. 🍴♂

HE MAN, Rua Dr. Borman 27, Niteroi, (021) 717 9508, Fri-Mon from 23:00, go go boys. 🍴🎵✉♂

INCONTRUS, Praça Serzedelo Correia 15, Copacabana, (021) 257 6498, from 22:00. 🍴🎵♂

LE BOY, Rua Raul Pompéia 94, Copacabana, 521 0367, disco & bar, from 23:00 (closed Mon). 🍴🎵✉♂

■ *Saunas/Health Clubs*
CATETE, Rua Correia Dutra 34, (021) 265 5478, from 13:30.

CLUBE 29, Rua Prof Alfredo Gomes 29, Botafogo, from 13:00.

IBIZA, Rua Ceiqueira Campos 202, in Copacabana, (021) 235 4177, bar & sauna from 15:00.

BRAZIL

FYI

FOR TRAVELERS TO BRAZIL

Inter-Rainbow Turismo is a Brazilian supplier of vacation packages to the international gay travel industry. Prices are set to encourage inbound travel. Inter-Rainbow has built a track record as a supplier to major US gay tour companies. Fixed packages are available for Rio and São Paulo, both including gay-friendly hotel with breakfast, city sightseeing tour and an evening for nightclubbing.

FOR GAY BRAZILIANS TRAVELING ABROAD

For gay Brazilians, Inter-Rainbow has a full program of tours and cruises to destinations worldwide. One can depart any day of the week for the 10-day Miami/Orlando tour, featuring visits to Sea World, Disney World, Busch Gardens, Universal and MGM Studios. The Egypt tour visits Cairo, the Pyramids, Aswan, and Luxor, and cruises the Nile. Golden Cities of China is a 17-day trip to the major attractions of China, plus Hong Kong. The Moscow and St. Petersburg tour includes signtseeing, museums and the Moscow Circus. Gay Brazilians also can cruise the Caribbean or join a US Mardi Gras cruise out of Tampa, which visits Key West, New Orleans, Playa del Carmen and Cozumel.

Contact **Inter-Rainbow** at (55 11) 214 0380 (tel/fax).

BRAZIL

NOVA LEBLON, Rua Barao da Torre 522, (021) 287 8899, bar & sauna, 09:00-06:00.
ROGER'S, Rua Ministro Alfredo Valadao 36, in Copacabana, (021) 257 9096.
STUDIO 64, Rua Redendor 64, Ipanema, (021) 267 1138, 15:00-03:00.

SALVADOR
■ Information
GRUPO GAY DA BAHIA, Rua do Sodré 45, in Dois de Julho, city center, 243 4902.
■ Bars
ALAMBIQUE, Rua J. de Deus 25, 1st floor, (071) 322 5470, from 20:00. ♪♂
BANZO, Largo do Pelourinho. ♂
CANTINA DA LUA, Terreiro de Jesus 2, Praça da Sé, not a gay bar, discreetly frequented by gays.
CHARLES CHAPLIN, Rua Carlos Gomes 141, younger crowd. ♪♀♂
EMPORIO, Avenida 7 de Septembro 3809, in Porto da Barra, (071) 247 5881, many women. ⊞♪♀♂
QUINTAL DO RASO DA CATARINA, Av. 7 do Setembro 1370, 18:00-03:00 (closed Sun), NOT a gay bar, but discreetly frequented by gays.
SUMMER 2000, Avenida Pinto de Aguiar 25, in Patamares, (071) 231 9980, Fri, Sat from 20:00, Sun from 15:00. ♂
■ Dance Bar/Disco
BANANA REPUBLICA,★ Rua Braulio Xavier 2, in Vitoria, (071) 237 3079, disco, patio, live music, Thurs-Sun from 23:00. ⊞♪♀♂
BIZARRO DISCO DANCING, Rua Augusto França 55, in Dois de Julho, (071) 321 5373, open summers Thurs-Sun from 23:00. ⊞♂
IS KISS, Rua Carlos Gomes 30, in the city center. ⊞♪♀♂
NEW LOOK BAR, Rua Nilton Prado 24, on Gamboa, (071) 336 4949, Thurs-Sun from 23:00, go go boys, live music on 2nd level, ⊞ ♪✉♀♂
USINA DANCING, Av. Vasco da Gama 250, (071) 382 3368, some hetero clientele. ♀♂
■ Saunas/Health Clubs
CAMPUS, Rua Dias D'ávila 25, (071) 235 2247, 14:00-23:00. ✉
OLYMPUS, Rua Tuiuti 183, (071) 321 2574, 14:30-22:30. ✉
PHOENIX, Rua Prado Valadares 16, (071) 243 5495, 14:00-22:00. ✉

SANTA MARIA
■ Bars
BIG LUCAO, Praça Saldanha Marinho, (055) 221 6996. ♂
■ Dance Bar/Disco
OVER BUSY, Rua Riachuelo 244, (055) 222 7541, Thurs-Sun from 22:00. ⊞♂

REFUGIO DOS DEUSES, Rua Dr. Bozano 936, disco Fri-Sun, bar Tues-Thurs. ⊞♪♂
ZAMAH, Avenida Presidente Vargas 1030, (055) 221 4769, Fri, Sat from 24:00. ⊞♂

SANTOS
■ Saunas/Health Clubs
NUMBER ONE, Rua Conselheiro Nebias 243, (013) 233 5667, from 14:00.

SAO LEOPOLDO
■ Dance Bar/Disco
MESMORA, Rua 1 de março 61, bar & disco, strippers. ⊞♪✉♂

SAO PAULO
■ Accommodations
HOTEL RAPOSA DA MONTANHA, book through Inter-Rainbow Turismo, Rua Xavier de Toledo 264, #137, 13 andar, Sao Paulo 01048.904, Tel/Fax: (55-11) 214 0380. Nine apartments with private bath, TV, double beds. Restaurant, bar & parking on premises. ♀♂
HOTEL RAPOSA DA PRAIA, book through Inter-Rainbow Turismo, Rua Xavier de Toledo 264, #137, 13 andar, Sao Paulo 01048.904, Tel/Fax: (55-11) 214 0380. Five apartments with private bath, AC, parking, restaurant & bar. ♀♂
■ Bars
BURGER & BEER, Rua da Consolaçao 2376. ♂
CABARÉ, Rua Epitácio Pessoa 32, in Consolaçao, (011) 256 6868. ♀
CASA DA VILA, Rua Girassol 310, Vila Madalena, (011) 210 5216, gay men welcome, some hetero clientele. ♂
CHOPP ESCURO, Rua Marquês de Itù 152, in Vila Buarque, (011) 221-0872, 7 days. ✗♂
CUBE, Rua Consolaçao 2967, Jardins, (011) 932 1854, bar & restaurant, 19:00-02:00 (closed Sun). ♂
FETISH CLUB PRIVÉ, Alameda Barao de Limeira 612, (011) 223 5755, videos, private club for fetishists. ♂
HELENA, Rua Dr. Mario Ferraz 423, (011) 829 2238, bar & restaurant, 18:00-02:00. ♂
PALACIOS BAR, Av. Brigadeiro Luiz Antonio 2779, Jardins, (011) 885 2324, from 20:00, closed Mon & Tues. ♂
PAPARAZZI,★ Rua da Consolaçao 3046, (011) 881 6665. ♂
PRETA'S BAR, Rua Santo Antonio 579, Bela Vista, closed Mon. ♂
QUATRO (4) POR ACASO, Av Santo Amaro 5394, (011) 241 4907, bar & restaurant. ♀
RITZ, Alameda Franca 1088, (011) 280 6808, NOT a gay bar, discreetly frequented by gays.
TWO-SIX-SIX (266) WEST, Rua Marquês de Itú 266, (011) 222 1291. ♂
ZWEI, Rua Original 139, Vila Madalena, (011) 217 7528, bar & restaurant, from 20:00 (closed Mon, Tues), men welcome. ✗♀

■ Dance Bar/Disco
A LOCA, Rua Frei Caneca 916, Jardins, 3 levels, DJs, Thurs-Sat from 23:30. ⊞♂
BLUE SPACE, Rua Brigadeiro Galvao 723 (metrô: Marechal Deodoro), (011) 66 1616, large disco with cabaret, Sat from 23:00, Sun from 18:00. ⊞♪♂
CLUB ALIEN, Rua Fortunato 34, Santa Cecilia, Wed from 23:00. ⊞♂
COLUMBIA, Rua Estados Unidos 1572, Jardins, (011) 282 8086, from 23:00, closed Mon. ⊞♂
DREAMS, Rua Caio Prado 47, Consolaçao, 255 3939, from 18:00, closed Mon. ♪⊞♀♂
GENT'S, Avenida Ibirapuera 1911, in Moema, Fri-Sun from 22:00, go go boys. ⊞♪✉♂
KATZ, Rua da Consolaçao 3032, Jardins, Wed-Sun from 23:00. ♪⊞✗♂
MAD QUEEN, Alameda dos Arapanés 1364, Moema, (011) 240 0088, Fri-Sun from 23:00. ⊞♂
MASSIVO, Alameda Itú 1548, (011) 883 7505, Tues-Sat from 23:00. ⊞♂
NATION, Praça Roosevelt 124, (011) 256 2773, Thurs-Sat from 22:00. some hetero clientele. ⊞♂
NIGHT BOYS, Alameda Nothmann 1220, Santa Cecilia, (011) 825 9236, Fri, Sat from 23:00, Sun from 17:00. ⊞♂
NOSTROMONDO, Rua da Consolaçao 2554, Jardins, (011) 257 4481, Wed-Sun from 22:00. ♪⊞⊞♂
PROHIBIDUS, Rua Amaral Gurgel 253. ⊞♪♂
RAVE, Rua Bela Cintra 1900, Jardins, (011) 883 2133, Wed-Sun from 23:00. ⊞♂
TUNNEL, Rua dos Ingleses 355, Jardins, (011) 285 0246, Fri, Sat from 23:00, Sun from 19:00. ⊞♀♂
Z CLUB, Alameda Jaú 48, Jardins, (011) 283 0033, many women Thurs-Sun, men welcome. ⊞♀

■ Saunas/Health Clubs
ALTEROSAS, Avenida Alterosas 40, (011) 958 1712, 12:30-22:00.
AMAZONAS, Rua Gasometro 641, (011) 229 0047. 14:00-24:00 (Sat 09:00-22:00, Sun till 18:00).
ARIES MEN, Rua Guaporé 458, (011) 229 1654, from 14:00.
CARACALAS, Rua Professor Dr. José Marques da Cruz 224, (011) 240 6293, 14:00-23:00 (Fri, Sat till 02:00).
CHAMPION, Largo do Arouche 336, (011) 222 4973, 14:00-24:00 (Fri, Sat till 05:00).
CLUBE POMPÉIA, Rua Cândido Espinheira 758 (metrô: Barra Funda), (011) 873 2254, 14:00-24:00 (Fri till 05:00).
DANNY, Rua Jaguaribe 484, (011) 67 6718, 13:00-24:00.
FOR FRIENDS, Rua Morgado de Mateus 365

Costa Rica

by Rich Rubin
Reprinted with permission from *Genre* magazine

Just when I thought I'd grown too blasé, I find myself with all the symptoms: I can't concentrate, I think about my loved one all the time, I drive my friends crazy talking about it.

The object of my affections is Costa Rica. (Well, what did you think? I'm a travel writer. We fall for countries, cities, or maybe, if it's really sexy, a nice mountain range. That's the nature of the business. I can't help it.)

Why Costa Rica? Because it is, quite simply, the most beautiful country I've seen in ages. It's a haven of gay-friendliness in a part of the world not exactly known for gay-friendliness. And, last but not least, it boasts some of the world's handsomest men (so I'm only human).

What is it, exactly, that I love? Let's start at the beginning, which for me, as for most people, is San José. It's a small-scale, comfortable city. I trip down busy streets as music wafts from storefronts, vendors vaunt their piles of mangos and avocados, pastel churches appear between modern buildings, and at every turn a mountain vista opens up before my delighted eyes. "Yes, I'm in Latin America," I think with a smile, as I stumble over a huge crack in the street. (The roads here are another issue, which we'll talk about later.)

There are those who don't find San José thrilling, who treat it as a necessary evil on the way to the country's natural beauty. But I disagree. I love its irrepressible spirit, its easy layout of *avenidas* (avenues) and *calles* (streets), its abundance of shady parks. While it's not, perhaps, a world-class destination on the order of Paris or Venice, I find a wealth of fascinating sights.

My favorite area is the Mercado Central (Central Market). Cilantro scents the air, piles of yucca and chayotes spill from their crates. Bananas, limes, stark white corn, plums lascivious in their crimson ripeness, radishes as big as baseballs, mountains of pineapples, monstrously big papayas are piled high. Cheese, flowers, nuts, and herbs fight to fill your nostrils with their aromas, while coffee roasters send out their caffeinated perfume.

There are surprises lurking in every corner of this bustling city. Inside a nondescript highrise, I find the Jade Museum, a combination archaeology and gem display, the jades subtly lit from behind so they glow with

Photo by Rich Rubin

genre

Rich Rubin is a freelance writer based in New York. He has written for *Out and About*, *Saveur*, *Bride's*, *The Los Angeles Times*, *Washington Post*, *Boston Globe*, and many other publications. He is currently Travel Editor of *Genre*. *Genre* magazine is the nation's best-selling monthly magazine for gay men, covering entertainment, fashion, relationships, culture, and travel with an upscale, upbeat, irreverent voice. Featuring desirable and diverse travel destinations in every issue, *Genre* keeps you plugged into the who, what, why, and where of today's ever-expanding gay world.

Continued on next page

translucent splendor. In the Museo Nacional, I exit the exhibits on Costa Rican history into a courtyard overlooking the spires and high-rises of the city: Is it design or fortuity that allows me to emerge from a journey through the country's past to gaze at a diorama of its present?

I pass an ornate building with wrought-iron arches, curlicue moldings, pillars, railed balconies. Could it be a rococo tropical palace? No, just the post office.

I visit the Teatro Nacional, a resplendent 19th-century theater, have coffee in its charming cafe, and emerge onto Plaza de la Cultura under startling blue skies with only a hint of impending rain. I sit on one of the odd benches that look like industrial piping, and next to me a young man smiles. He's dressed in a T-shirt from New York City's Gay Pride Run. His face is a revelation. I smile back, then dart into the Café Parisien, where I sit at a plazaside table sipping yet more coffee, hoping my heart can take the strain of that smile.

Days later, I still remember his face as clearly as if he's standing there with me. Imagine my surprise, then, as I'm sitting in New Yesterday's, a friendly gay bar in the heart of the city, to see my young friend saunter in, his unmistakable smile still glowing. The young man drinks a beer with his friends, tosses me one last unforgettable smile and leaves my life forever.

Which brings us, sort of, to San José's biggest surprise: It's gay life. Who'd have expected a dozen gay bars, gay restaurants, gay guest houses, and a million, billion gay people — all in the middle of Central America? "That's because we have more gay people than most countries," claims Eduardo Guerrero Campos, owner of the popular disco Déjà Vu. "In Costa Rica, gay people are 25% of the population," he states. I'm not quite sure if he's kidding — but who cares?

We're sitting at the bar of Déjà Vu. It's Thursday night, so the place is quiet. You can hardly believe that 24 hours from now, it'll be packed to the gills (weekend nights draw over 500 people). It's one of the city's most famous spots, with its high-tech sound and light system (well, high tech for Costa Rica), male strippers and drag shows.

It's also become a landmark of local gay history, ever since a police raid a few years ago, which quickly escalated into brutality — a kind of Costa Rican Stonewall! "We denounced the police to international rights groups," says Guerrero, and, perhaps more significantly, took them to court. Their experience was illuminating.

Dora Alvarado of Way to Go Costa Rica, a US travel company that arranges tours for many gay travelers, was at Déjà Vu the night of the raid. "The government was completely supportive in the court case," she says, adding with a smile, "The police didn't know who they were dealing with. There were politicians there that night, reporters, people involved with the government."

And guess what? Déjà Vu won. In the immortal words of Harold the friendly bartender: "We said forget it, you need to respect gay people."

And indeed the gay presence, while never completely underground, has flourished since this watershed event. "There's less of a problem now," says Harold, "because we have more confidence."

Dora Alvarado agrees. "I think people were surprised by the amount of support they got, and it's made people a little braver about being open."

In turn, that openness has made for an active, sexy and appealingly diverse gay scene. I visit the popular disco La Avispa, which recently celebrated its 17th anniversary. And I can see why it has lasted: It's actually fun, in a way that such places are never fun at home anymore. While predominantly male, there's an easy mix of men and women, young and old, baseball caps and sport jackets. Outside is a palm-filled courtyard...upstairs, a bar with a video screen and pool tables. There's a feeling of camaraderie, of enjoyment. I see no *plásticos* (love that local word describing what we might call "attitude queens") standing around posing.

There's also breadth to the gay life here that's satisfying. Café Mundo, for instance, is a sophisticated restaurant - bar that's exactly the kind of place I miss in other cities — elegant but relaxed. You can have a meal in the pretty dining room or on the front porch of this renovated home, or just sip a drink with the youngish crowd of professionals. It's quiet, fun and friendly. Within minutes, I'm chatting with a couple at the small bar, and they've introduced me to a friend who's introduced me to a friend who's... That's how it works here, and I love it.

Armed with a complicated set of directions, I visit La Taberna, a long-standing local favorite. And it's worth the search: It's a low-key, welcoming spot with a sweet staff and comfortable feel.

So what exactly makes Costa Rica such a gay paradise? Alvarado attributes it, in part, to the country's high educational level (90% of its residents, she says, attend college). "There's not as much of the macho man-submissive woman thing that's com-

Continued on page 510

(metrô: Ana Rosa), (011) 570 1887, 14:00-24:00 (Fri, Sat till 01:00).

FRAGATA, Rua Francisco Leitao 71, (011) 853 7061, 14:00-24:00 (Fri till later). $

HOLIDAY, Rua Martins Fontes 295, (011) 231 2695, 14:00-24:00 (Fri, Sat till 06:00).

LAGOA, Rua Borges Lagoa 287 (metrô: Santa Cruz), (011) 571 1151, 14:00-24:00 (Sat till 05:00).

LE ROUGE, Rua Arruda Alvim 175, (011) 852 3043, 14:00-01:00 (Fri, Sat till 05:00).

■ Erotica

ARTE DOS PRAZERES, Av Sao Joao 439, 1st fl, loja 209.

ATTELIER ELIANA, Av Barao de Limeira 612.

DARME SEX SHOP, Av Ipiranga 818, 2nd fl, conjunto 21.

EROTIC CINEMAS: Cine Cairo (Rua Formosa 401), Cine G (Rua Amaral Gurgel 206), Cine Saci (Av Sao Joao 285), Nova Cine Studio (Rua Aurora 710).

PONTO G, Rua da Consolaçao 2504; Rua Amaral Gurgel 206; Av. Bernardino de Campos 300.

SEX APPEAL, Av. Miruna 18, Moema.

SAO VICENTE

■ Dance Bar/Disco

VICIUS CLUB, Alameda Julio Mesquita 67, Ilha Porchat, (013) 222 5090.

CHILE

COUNTRY CODE: (56)

WHO TO CALL
For Tour Companies Serving This Destination
See Chile on page 12

MOVILH
LIBERACION
MOVILH
CHILE
MOVIMIENTO HOMOSEXUAL

MOVILH
CASILLA 52834
CORREO CENTRAL
SANTIAGO, CHILE

TEL/FAX: (56-2)632 43 09

LA SERENA

■ Bars
FOXY BEST PUB, Balmaceda 3390, Paradero 6 1/2, La Pampa, (51) 24 26 07.

SANTIAGO

■ Information
CAPVHI (AIDS INFO), (2) 633 69 66.

CENTRO DE ESTUDIOS DE LA MUJER, Purísima 353, (2) 77 11 94, women's center & archives.

CENTRO LAMBDA CHILE, Calle Augustinas 2085, (2) 687 3595.

MOVILH (MOVIMIENTO DE LIBERACION HOMOSEXUAL), Santa Rosa 170-A, Santiago Centro, (2) 632 43 09. Gay & lesbian organization, 18:00-22:30 (Sat 17:00-21:00), active in civil & human rights causes, organizers of public marches, producers/directors of Chile's gay radio program "Triángulo Abierto," provides local information. Write: MOVILH, Casilla 52834, Correo Central, Santiago, Chile.

■ Bars
BAR DE WILLY, Paseo Las Palmas, Av. Providencia at Avda. Lyon (metro: Los Leones), Providencia, Fri, Sat 22:00-04:00.

BAR DIONISIO, Bombero Nuñez 111, Barrio Bellavista, (2) 737 60 65, 20:30-03:00 (closed Sun, Mon), Tues women's night.

DELOS, Avda Las Condes 9177, Las Condes, (02) 202 0360. Pub, piano bar & restaurant. Pub & piano bar from 18:00, restaurant from 19:30.

SEVEN-SEVEN-SEVEN (777), Alameda 777, Santiago Centro, bar & restaurant, frequented by gays.

YO CLAUDIO, Av. Santa Lucía, at Máximo Hubert, Santiago Centro.

YO YO PUB, Avenida Santo Domingo at Baquedano, at La Trianon Restaurant, Mon gay pub night.

■ Dance Bar/Disco
BUCANEROS, TELOS, new gay disco, to open Spring '97, ask locally for address.

BUNKER, Calle Bomero Nuñez 159, (2) 737 1716, Thurs 24:00-04:30, stippers, mostly gay with a large straight following.

DELOS, Avda Las Condes 9179, Las Condes, (02) 202 0360, from 23:00.

FAUSTO, Av. Santa María 0832, Providencia, (2) 777 1041, 23:30-04:00 (Fri, Sat till 06:00, Sun 21:30-06:00), closed Mon.

NAXOS, Alameda 776, Santiago Centro, (2) 639 96 29, 23:00-05:00 (closed Mon).

QUASAR, Coquimbo 1458, (2) 671 1267, Fri, Sat 23:00-06:00.

QUEEN SANTIAGO, General Santiago Bueras 128, Santiago Centro, (2) 639 87 03, disco & bar, 23:30-05:00 (Fri, Sat till 06:30, Sun from 23:00).

COSTA RICA

■ Cafe
PROSIT, Providencia 21, in front of Plaza Valledano, fuente de soda (soda fountain), not a gay cafe, frequented by gays & lesbians.

■ Saunas/Health Clubs
PROTEC, Alonso Valle 1585, sauna & gym, 10:00-22:00.

■ Restaurants
LA TRIANON, Avenida Santo Domingo at Baquedano, bar & restaurant.

■ Retail & Bookstores
LILA LIBRERIA DE MUJERES, Providencia 1652 L.3, (2) 235 81 45, women's bookstore and meeting place. Unverifiable spring, 1997.

MIMESIS, Calle Portugal 48, Torre 6, local 13, (2) 222 5321, gay & lesbian bookstore, 09:00-18:00 (Sat till 14:00).

VALPARAISO

■ Information
SOCIEDAD HOMOSEXUAL SURGENTE (SHOMOS), Independencia 2446, gay & lesbian group, AIDS info.

■ Bars
TACONES, Huito 301, at Brasil, 22:00-02:00.

■ Dance Bar/Disco
FOXY DISCO, Inpependencia 2646, Fri, Sat 23:30-05:00.

SCANDAL, Yungay 2229, (2) 59 60 83.

SOVIET, Arlegui 346, in town of Viña del Mar, Thurs-Sat 23:00-05:00.

COSTA RICA

COUNTRY CODE: (506)

WHO TO CALL
For Tour Companies Serving This Destination
See Costa Rica on page 13

ALAJUELA

■ Information
ASOCIACION TRIANGULO ROSA, (506) 234 2411, gay & lesbian community center, scheduled meetings & socials.

■ Bars
BRAMADERO TICO, across from Coope Montecillos, Wed-Sat from 19:30, many lesbians, men-only 2nd Wed, strippers, cruisy.

MARGUISS, 250 meters south of Llobet stores, city denter.

COSTA RICA

Gay & Lesbian Escorted Costa Rica Tour

Way to Go Costa Rica specializes exclusively in Costa Rica. They can custom-design itineraries according to your preferences. Adventure and ecology are offered on this tour, which explores the Tortuguero area, the northeastern Caribbean coast of Costa Rica. We'll cruise canals, relax on the unspoiled beaches of Punta Uva and experience the majestic Arenal Volcano. This escorted tour operates with a minimum of two passengers. Airfare is extra and bulk rates are available from major US cities.

Day 1
Arrival in San Jose. Overnight at the deluxe Amsterl Amon
Day 2
Transfer to the Caribbean coast to Punta Cocles Hotel
Day 3
Snorkeling and hiking at Punta Uva
Day 4
Cruise the Tortuguero Canals
Day 5
Tortuguero National Park
Day 6
Tortuguero and Arenal Volcano
Day 7
Visit Arenal Volcano and relax in hotsprings
Day 8
Return to San Jose. Free to explore gay bars and discos
Day 9
Departure

Contact **Way to Go Costa Rica** at (919) 782-1900, (800) 835-1223, Fax: (919) 787-1952, E-mail: hlasky@internetmci.com.

HEREDIA

■ Women's Accommodations

CASA YEMAYA, in the foothills of Santo Domingo, tel/fax: (506) 661 0956, e-mail: mueland@irazu.una/.ac.cr. Women-only private guestroom for 2, continental breakfast, hot water, airport transportation. Bilingual guide & driver available. ♀

LAKE ARENAL

■ Women's Accommodations

LEA'S COSTA RICA HEAVEN, Lago Arenal, two miles from town of Arenal, (011-506) 694 4093, Fax: (011) 695 5387, in USA call Lea (808) 575-2957. 1BR house overlooking lake. Private on 2 acres of land in the rainforest of north-central Costa Rica, $25 nightly, volcano views. Local swimming, kayaking, fishing, windsurfing, hot springs, nearby restaurants, men welcome.

PUNTARENAS

■ Women's Accommodations

CASA YEMAYA, write: Casa Yemaya, Apdo 258-5.400, Puntarenas, tel/fax: (506) 661-0956. Web: cybershack.com/friends/yemaya. Women-only guesthouse. Accommodations are 3 rooms with fans, and amenities include hot water, use of kitchen & laundry facilities. There is great access to the Nicoya Peninsula. We offer local trip & event planning & travel counseling. Reservations recommended. Note: Thunderstorms tend to interrupt phone service, so please try again and again. ♀

QUEPOS

■ Accommodations

COSTA LINDA, on road in back of 1st beach in Manuel Antonio, (506) 777 0304, gay-friendly youth hostel/guesthouse, 20 rooms.

HOTEL CASA BLANCA, Apdo 194, 6350 Quepos-Manuel Antonio, Tel/Fax: (506) 777-0253, E-mail: cblanca@sol.racsa.co.cr. http://bertha.pomona.edu/cblanca/. Exclusively gay & lesbian hotel & guesthouse with private baths, all rooms have ceiling fans & some rooms with A/C. Suites and apartments have kitchenette. Near gay beach.

VILLA LA ROCA, (506) 777-1349. Book through Joluva Guesthouse, San Jose, (506) 223 7961, fax: (506) 257 7668.

■ Beaches

PLAYITA MANUEL ANTONIO, at the national park, mostly gay over the rocks and north of the main beach.

■ Bars

MAMBO, on the road to the National Park, at entrance of Hotel Villas El Paque. Restaurant & bar, popular with gays for happy hour in summer.

VELA BAR, Calle Manuel Antonio, 77 04 13, bar & restaurant frequented by gays.

■ Dance Bar/Disco

ARCO IRIS, in downtown Quepos, ask locally for directions, gay crowd later in evenings after 23:00, especially weekends.

MAR Y SOMBRA, beachside disco at Playa Espadilla, not gay, but frequented by many gays, disco mostly on weekends in-season.

MARACAS, near the dock, in city center, gay crowd later in evening.

■ Restaurants

EL PLINIO, ask locally for directions, Italian & some German cuisine.

KAROLA'S, ask locally for directions, Tex Mex & seafood, closed Wed.

LA BOQUITA, in the Sansa Building, 2nd floor, city center.

SAN JOSE

■ Information

AIDS INFO, 26 8972.

■ Accommodations

APARTMENTS SCOTLAND, Avenida 1, Calle 27, (506) 223 0033, 257 4374, fax: 257 5317, gay-friendly apartment hotel, convenient to shopping, 50% gay/lesbian clientele, full 1-bedroom apartments with linens, kitchen utensils, color TVs, phones.

HOTEL COLOURS, THE GUEST RESIDENCE SAN JOSE, c/o Colours Destinations, 255 W 24th St Miami Beach, FL, (800) ARRIVAL (277-4825) or (305) 532-9341, direct: (506) 232 35 04. Hotel guesthouse centrally located, comfortable rooms with single through king beds, private & shared baths, TV lounge, guest refrigerator, expanded continental or full breakfast, swimming pool. ♂♀

HOTEL KEKOLDI, Avenida 9, Calle 3 bis, (506) 223 3244, Fax: 257 5476, E-mail: kekoldi@sol.racsa.co.cr. Gay-friendly hotel with bar & breakfast restaurant, private baths, phone, ceiling fans, TV lounge, minutes to city center & touristic points of interest.

HOTEL L'AMBIANCE, Calle 13 between Aves. 9 & 11, (506) 222 6702, elegant, small gay-friendly hotel.

JOLUVA GUESTHOUSE, Calle 3B, Avs 9 y 11 #936, Tel: (506) 223 7961, Fax: (506) 257-7668, E-mail: joluva@sol.racsa.co.cr. USA reservations/info: (800) 298-2418. B&B, women welcome, continental breakfast with tropical fruits, color cable TV, local info provided, tours/trips arranged. ♂

■ Bars

A QUIEN LE IMPORTA, between Calle 3 & Calle 5, Avda 8, (506) 221 5552.

ALFONSINA Y EL MAR, across from Kilates disco, from 19:00 (closed Sun), fast food, weekend BBQs, woman-owned.

BUENAS VIBRACIONES, Paseo de los Estudiantes, in back of Mas X Menos, city center.

HONDURAS

FACES, Avenida 10 between Calle 21 & 23, (506) 257 8664. ♀

MONTE CARLO, corner of 4th Ave & 2nd St, many gays between 1am & 4am.

PUCHOS/BARIL DORADO, 11th St between Avenidas 8 & 10, 17:00 till 10:00 next day, small bar, after midnight knock on door. ♀♂

UNICORNIO, Avenida 8 between calle 5 & 3. ♀

■ Dance Bar/Disco

DEJA VU/SINNERS,★ Calle 2 between Avenidas 14 & 16, Deja Vu: dance bar Wed-Sun; Sinners: bar, open Tues-Sun, 70% men, 30% women, many straights.

LA AVISPA,★ 834 Calle 1, between Avenidas 8 & 10, (506) 223 5343, open Tues-Sun (Tues & Sun 17:00-18:00 free entry), giant screen TV, lesbian-owned.

LOS CUCHARONES, 57 Avenida 6 between Central & 1st St, 233 5797 large dance bar with varied music, mainly working class locals, Wed-Sun from 20:00. Transvestites welcome.

NEW YESTERDAYS, Avenida 1 between Calle 5 & 7, 70% men, open Tues-Sat, male strippers Fri. Open bar Wed, Fri & Sat, all you can drink.

■ Cafe

PARISIAN, Avenida 2 between Calles 1 & 3, sidewalk cafe at the Hotel Costa Rica Grand, 24hrs, discreetly frequented by gays. ⌘

■ Saunas/Health Clubs

JANO, Calle 1 between Avenidas 4 & 6.
LEBLON, Calle 9 between Avenidas 1 & 3.

■ Restaurants

LA PERLA, Avenida 2 at Calle Central, bar & restaurant, 24hrs.

SAN PEDRO

■ Bars

LA TERTULIA, 100 meters east & 150 meters north of the church in San Pedro, (506) 225 0250, a variety of music, frequented by some men. ♀

■ Retail & Bookstores

CLARA LUNA, 150 meters south of Univ. of Costa Rica, woman-owned general bookstore with gay & lesbian titles.

SANTA ANA

■ Bars

CASA MIA, (506) 282 6077, woman-owned bar, call or ask locally for address.

TAMARINDO

■ Accommodations

CABINA MARIELLOS, (506) 653 0141, woman-owned accommodation across the street from the beach, clean rooms, kitchen facilities, turtle tour reservations.

EL SALVADOR
COUNTRY CODE: (503)

WHO TO CALL — For Tour Companies Serving This Destination — See El Salvador on page 13

SAN SALVADOR

■ Dance Bar/Disco

ESCAPE, Condominio Blvd Los Heroes, near Olimpo disco location.

OLIMPO DISCOTEC, Condominio Juan Pablo Segundo, Colonia Miramontes, dance club with show bar, Sat only.

ORACULOS, Condominio Blvd Los Heroes, 225 0427, Thurs-Sat.

■ Erotica

CINE DARIO, c/ Rubén Darío, cinema.

GUATEMALA
COUNTRY CODE: (502)

WHO TO CALL — For Tour Companies Serving This Destination — See Guatemala on page 16

ANTIGUA

■ Restaurants

GIL'S, 6a Calle Oriente #3, across from picturesque Parque Union. Authentic, hearty American cooking: lunch and dinner. Chicken and dumplings, meatloaf and mashed potatoes, roast chicken, House Specials, sandwiches, salads, iced beer. American ambience, music, and service, at Guatemalan prices. Serving travelers from all over the world. Gay-friendly. Open 10:30am.

GUATEMALA

■ Bars

ENCUENTROS, Avda 6, in city center. ♂

■ Dance Bar/Disco

METROPOLIS, Calle 6, Zona 1. ♀♂

PANDORAS BOX,★ in city center, videos. ♂

TRILOGIA, Avda 4, Zona 1. ♀♂

■ Saunas/Health Clubs

SERVIVAPORES, Avda 28, 13-20, Zona 7.

HONDURAS
COUNTRY CODE: (504)

WHO TO CALL — For Tour Companies Serving This Destination — See Honduras on page 17

PUERTO CORTES

■ Accommodations

HOTEL PLAYA, on Puerto Cortes Beach, very popular gay-friendly hotel.

SAN PEDRO SULA

■ Dance Bar/Disco

CONFETIS, Avda. Circunvalación, male strippers, 50% gay & lesbian, 50% hetero clientele.

TEGUCIGALPA

■ Information

PRISMA GAY & LESBIAN INFO, men call Juan Carlos: 327 304; women call Rosalina: 329 345.

■ Accommodations

HOTEL LA RONDA, in Barrio La Ronda, 378 151, gay-friendly hotel, 50% men, 50% women.

HOTEL PRADO, next to the cathedral in downtown Tegucigalpa, 370 121, gay-friendly hotel, 50% men, 50% women.

■ Bars

BRIK BRAK, on the pedestrian mall in city

Gil's

AUTHENTIC
NORTH AMERICAN COOKING

"Do You Miss Your Mother's Meatloaf?"

ACROSS FROM PARQUE UNION
6a CALLE ORIENTE #3
ANTIGUA, GUATEMALA

HONDURAS

Soft Adventure in Mexico

Earth Wind & Water is a gay-friendly tour operator specializing in off-the-beaten-path natural and cultural destinations. None of our itineraries require special technical skills, and all are led by expert, bilingual gay-friendly guides.

Copper Canyon A train journey into primitive, breathtaking wilderness, stopping in comfortable lodges, some on the very rims of huge canyons.

Baja Group visit the Gray Whale nurseries at Magdalena Bay. Participants camp (catered safari-style) on a remote, beautiful barrier island and watch whales from skiffs. Desert and Sea itineraries include kayaking, desert hikes, whale watching, bicycling, and snorkeling with sea lions.

Monarch Butterflies High in the mountains, in central Mexico, as many as a quarter billion Monarch Butterflies winter in alpine fir groves. Our small groups visit these unforgettable places.

Jessica and John, of Earth, Wind & Water, have nearly 30 years of professional travel experience between them to ensure your travel is interesting, fun and properly arranged.

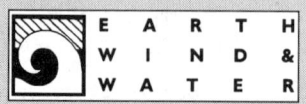

Contact **Earth, Wind and Water** at (212) 744-3177, (800) 555-0977, Fax: (212) 744-8755, E-mail: earthww@aol.com, Web: www.earthww.com.

ACAPULCO MEANS LAS PALMAS

Extraordinary Private Villa

155 Ave. Las Conchas,
Fracto. Farallon
C.P. 39690

Acapulco / Mexico

(52-74) 87 08 43
Fax: (52-74) 87 12 82

You May Visit Us On the:
www.acapulco-laspalmas.com
E-mail: bobbyjoe@acapulco-laspalmas.com

Clothing Optional

---

center, video bar & restaurant, 24hrs, discreetly frequented by gays.

EL CLOSET, Colonia El Prado, left from Krispy Chicken, open Thurs-Sat. Thurs & Sat men's cruise bar, Fri lesbian night.

ENCUENTROS,★ beside Parque Valle, in city center, 60% gay, 40% lesbian clientele.

VAQUEROS, Blvd Morazan, in La Epoca shopping center, younger crowd, 50% gay & lesbian, 50% hetero clientele.

■ *Restaurants*

PICA DELI, beside the Ministry of Finance building (Ministerio de Hacienda), open-air cafeteria, umbrella tables, live piano music, open daytime only, 20% gay clientele.

TELA

■ *Accommodations*

GRAN HOTEL PRESIDENTE, on Tela Beach in downtown Tela, 482 821, gay-friendly hotel, 50% men, 50% women.

MEXICO

COUNTRY CODE: (52)

For Tour Companies Serving This Destination
See Mexico on page 20

For much more detailed information on Mexico, watch for Ferrari Guides' GAY MEXICO coming Fall, 1997.

ACAPULCO

■ *Accommodations*

ACAPULCO LAS PALMAS, 155 Ave Las Conchas, Fracto. Farallon, C.P. 39690, Acapulco GRO, (52-74) 87 08 43, fax: (52-74) 87 12 82. E-mail: bobbyjoe@acapulco-laspalmas.com. Paradise Complete! Acapulco's newest men-only gay accommodation is a totally renovated building with deluxe hotel rooms and suites, all set in a landscape of tropical gardens which recall Colonial Mexico. Enjoy breakfast overlooking the swimming pool. Bask on the Sun Terrace, with Jacuzzi and a wonderful view of Acapulco. After exploring our 4-terrace levels of adventure, it's just a short walk to gay Condessa Beach.

CASA LE MAR, Lomas del Mar 32-B, (52-74) 84 10 22, fax: 84 68 54. B&B in a private, open-air luxury villa, patio with pool, sun deck, wet bar, private baths, full breakfast, pool on premises, women welcome.

■ *Dance Bar/Disco*

DISCO DEMAS, behind Carlos & Charlies, open daily, male strippers.

MEXICO

The Mayan World

Contributed by Mundo Maya Turquesa

CANCUN— one of the world's most important tourist resorts, welcomes the gay and lesbian community to enjoy a huge variety of activities and historical sites. Located in the Yucatan Peninsula in southeast Mexico and boasting some of the very finest beaches in the Caribbean...white, balmy sands and peerless turquoise blue waters...Cancun is an island bathed on the outside by the Caribbean Sea and on the inside by a gorgeous lagoon called Nichuite. Cancun is a strategically located place from which one may venture to numerous archaeological sites and thus get a glimpse of the mystical Mayan civilization, such as...

CHICHEN ITZA— This is the largest, best-known archaeological site of the Mayan civilization, where one may witness the splendor of its architecture and overall culture, wedged in the middle of the jungle.

TULUM— Mystical archaeological site located on the marvelous Caribbean, a mere hour and a half drive from Cancun. This was the only place the Spaniards did not manage to conquer, due to its walled-in fortifications, and ships wrecked themkselves on the barrier reef located right off the coast.

There are also archaeological sites at **COBA** and **UXMAL**. There are lovely colonial cities (Valladolid, Merida and Izamal), where old Spanish- or French-influenced buildings stand out from the rest. During the visit to these parts, one may see the small villages where the descendants of the Mayans live. They are a simple, friendly people whose physical traits proclaim their ancestry. These marvelous lands abound with underground rivers which have, through time, created endless labyrinths and awesome rock formations, or grottos, and whose air vents are called "cenotes." These cenotes are huge holes at the bottom of which a considerable amount of archaeological findings have been made, thanks to the fact that the Mayans chose such places to make their sacrifices while giving thanks to Chac, the God of Water. This area, surrounded by semi-tropical jungle, houses an infinite variety of animal species: chimpanzees, alligators, deer, flamingoes and an indescribable

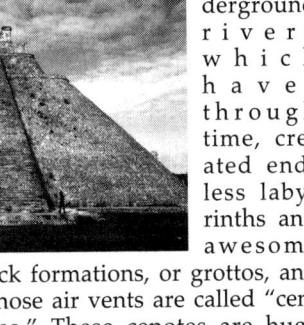

Continued on next page.

Mundo Maya Turquesa is a tour operator with experience in making arrangements for gay and lesbian visitors to Latin American destinations such as Mexico, Belize, Cuba and Guatemala. They offer private or group tours of Cancun and surrounding areas with a bilingual, mostly gay staff always willing to assist members of the gay and lesbian community. The agency is a subsidiary of Grupo Turquesa, one of Cancun's most prominent, which also boasts not only two radio stations (radio Turquesa and La Turquesita) whose transmitters reach as far as Cuba, but also Casa Turquesa, a hotel which is a member of Small Luxury Hotels of the World. The corporation now intends to build a hotel in Belize, with which Mundo Maya Turquesa will have very close ties. In addition to Cancun, the company provides air fares and tours to the rest of Mexico. Their tour to Tikal, Guatemala includes a visit to an archaeolgical site with bilingual guide for the full day. The short, 45-minute flight from Cancun is beautiful. Two- and three-night tours to Cuba are all-inclusive. Mundo Maya informs that visas are not necessary for Guatemala, just passports. In the case of Cuba, the fee for the visa is included in the package. Cuba packages include options for packages from 2 to 8 nights, staying at diversely-classified hotels and all-inclusive rates start at $316 US. The package includes round-trip air far Cancun-Havana-Cancun (a 1-hour flight), ground transportation from Havana airport to hotel and back, buffet-type breakfasts, city tour, and the fee for the Cuban visa. The Cuban visa is arranged using only copies of passports in order that original passports not be stamped, thus avoiding any future predicaments for travelers. Contact Mundo Maya Turquesa at (52-98) 87 63 21 or (52-98) 87 57 75, fax: (52-98) 87 67 78, E-mail: turquesa@cancun.rce.com.mx.

LATIN AMERICA

MEXICO

variety of other species.

Visitors not wishing to leave Cancun may enjoy this beautiful city and all the wonders in it, such as being able to take a peaceful stroll at any hour of the night or day on the main boulevard going out to the Hotel Zone (which consists of 20 kilometres of beaches, hotels and shopping malls) downtown, or even on the beaches, themselves. Cancun has a huge hotel infrastructure, luxury hotels, such as the Ritz-Carlton or the Casa Turquesa and other categories. There are also hotels particularly preferred by the gay/lesbian community, such as the Sheraton or the Villa Plaza. This heavenly place has lovely beaches on some of which both local, as well as foreign, gays and lesbians enjoy the sun and white sands, for example Delfines Beach and ChacMool Beach. There are some remains of Mayan ruins, local fun tours, fishing, snorkeling, parasailing, a 10-kilometer path for biking or skating, curio shops or flea markets and an array of activities, both daytime and nighttime. Cancun is just as lovely at night, due to the festive lights ornamenting the streets, hotels and shopping malls. If fun is on the agenda, the downtown discos will fill the order: Karamba, Picante and Quo Vadis or mixed discos, such as La Boom or Tequila Rock.

Besides Cancun, there are other islands, such as Holbox and Contoy, which are ideal for fishing, snorkeling and viewing animals in their natural habitat. These are havens left untouched and unchanged in their natural features. Considered ecological reserves internationally, they are visited by a great variety of birds which emigrate to warmer climes in order to mate and reproduce. Cozumel is the largest island in the area and is visited mostly by several cruise ships and liners.

The main acivity is diving, due to the beauty of its reef and the variety of its underwater life. Isla Mujeres is a legendary island and the spot where the Spaniards first made land on the Quintana Roo coast. It is a small fishing village offering various tourist attractions.

For snorkeling enthusiasts, there are spots of impressive beauty near Cancun, such as Xel-Ha, known as the world's largest natural aquarium, due to the fact that it is here that the warm waters of the Caribbean blend with crystal-clear water from underground rivers, resulting in an infinite variety of tropical fish.

The most gorgeous, peaceful and untouched beaches may be found all along the Cancun-Tulum strip. Sun worshippers preferring an all-over tan will find nudist beaches galore, cozy little lagoons with pristine clear waters next to the beach and beautiful towns, such as Playa del Carmen, which has made a name for itself because of its picturesqueness. The town is culturally diverse because of the arrival of many people from various countries, who have created a peaceful, friendly atmosphere here. This spot is particularly visited by gays and lesbians.

Eco-archaeological parks such as Xcaret have combined flora, fauna and culture into one Eden-like option where there are up to 18 activities to choose from, such as snorkeling, visiting zoos abounding with the area's most typical species, as well as the botanical gardens, floating down underground rivers, swimming with the dolphins, visiting the impressive aquarium and the tortoise and alligator farms, horsebackriding, enjoying a light-and-sound show portraying the most typical traits of Mayan civilization, and many others.

LA MALINCHE, in back of strip mall that's across from Fiesta Americana Hotel, male strippers.

RELAX, Lomas del Mar 4, next to La Tortuga restaurant, (74) 82 04 21, video dance bar, drag shows, male strippers.

■ **Restaurants**
LA BISTROQUET, Calle Andrea Doria 5, (074) 84 68 60. Gay-owned, gay-friendly restaurant, international cuisine.
LA TORTUGA, Lomas del Mar 5A, restaurant & bar, daily 10:00-02:00.

AGUASCALIENTES
■ **Bars**
IMPERIAL BAR, to the right of the "palacio municipal," 1 block from the Plaza de la Patria. Not a gay bar, but frequented by local gays.
LA FRONTERA BAR, Calle Cinco de Mayo. Not a gay bar, but frequented by local gays.

■ **Dance Bar/Disco**
MANDILES DISCO, Calle Lopes Mateos at Circunvalación. The hot spot for gays, some lesbians.

CABO SAN LUCAS
■ **Accommodations**
CABO SAN LUCAS ACCOMMODATIONS, contact Gay Baja Tours, (52-61) 72 8329.

■ **Bars**
RAINBOW BAR, Blvd. de la Marina 39-E, on the marina across from Planet Hollywood, next to Shrimp Bucket, (114) 87 245. Gay bar, everyone welcome, dance music, videos, Latino & techno ambiance, younger crowd, daily 20:00-03:00.

■ **Dance Bar/Disco**
TENAMPA, close to the Cabo San Lucas air strip, no official address, taxi is best. After hours, where locals go when all other bars are closed, busiest 03:00-07:00, varied clientele, gay & straight.

■ **Restaurants**
ALFONSO'S, Plaza Bonita, across marina from Rainbow Bar. (114) 320 22, daily 07:00-23:00 (off-season, call for hours), nouvelle Mexican cuisine.

CANCUN
■ **Dance Bar/Disco**
KARAMBA, Avda. Tulúm 87 altos, (98) 84 00 32, 7 days 22:00-02:00.

CIUDAD DE MEXICO
■ **Bars**
ANGEL AZUL, Universidad 1905.
ANSIA, Algeciras 26, Centro Armand, across from Galerias Insurgentes, Wed-Sat from 21:30, strippers.
ANYWAY, Monterrey 47, Zonz Rosal, daily from 21:00, strippers, some hetero clientele.

MEXICO

BARON, Insurgentes Sur 1231. ♂
BUTTERFLIES, Eje Central at J.M. Izazaga 9, Thurs-Sun till 03:00. ♂
CANTINA DEL VAQUERO, Avda. Insurgentes Sur 1231, Col. Insurgentes. ♂
CAZTZI, Carlos Arellano 4. ♂
EL ALMACEN, Florencia 37, Zona Rosa. ♂
GAB, Oaxaca 85. ♂
HOLLYWOOD BLVD, Puerto Aéreo 362, Col. Aviación Civil. ♂
LA DOLCE VITA, Orizaba 146, Col. Roma, Wed-Sat 21:00-03:00. ♂
LOS ROSALES, Pensador Mexicano 11, Col. Guerrero. ♂
PRIVATA, Avda Universitaria 1909. ♂
SALON PARIS, Donceles 3. ♂
TOM'S LEATHER BAR, Insurgentes Sur 357, 21:00-02:00 (closed Mon). ♂

■ Dance Bar/Disco
EL BARON, avenida Insurgentes Sur 1231, Col. Ins. Mixcoac. ♂
EL DON, Tonalá 79 corner of Alvaro Obregón, Col. Roma. ♂
EL TALLER, Florencia 37 (downstairs), Zona Rosa. ♂
KAOS, Queretaro 217, Col. Roma, strippers. ♂

■ Restaurants
LA CAFETERA, Rio Nazas 68-B.
MARIA BONITA, Antojería Cuernavaca 68, Condesa.
MERLIN, Culican 52.
MESON D'MISS, Tlacotalpan 18, Col. Roma.
PLATA, Juan Escutia 24, Condesa.
TABERNA GRIEGA, Algeciras 26-W-8.
THE DOORS, Monterrey 47, Col. Roma.

■ Retail & Bookstores
LAS SIRENAS, Avenida de la Paz 57, San Angel, 500 93 86, women's bookstore.

■ Leathers/Piercing
LA TIENDA DEL VAQUERO, inside El Vaquero bar.

■ Erotica
GOLD DREAMS, Ezequiel Montes 78a, Col. Tabacalera, 705 7157.

COZUMEL

■ Accommodations
LA CASA NOSTRA, 15 Avenida Sur 548, Cozumel, Quintana Roo, (987) 212 75, gay-friendly hotel inn with apartments, campground, bar & vegetarian/natural foods restaurant, almost all private baths, nearby ocean beach.

■ Dance Bar/Disco
CARLOS & CHARLIE'S, on the main strip near the pier, upstairs, dance bar & restaurant, NOT a gay bar, but discreetly frequented by visiting gays & lesbians. ♂

CUERNAVACA

■ Accommodations
CASA AURORA, Arista #12, Centro, (52 73) 18 63 94. A B&B or guesthouse with private & shared baths, continental breakfast or 3 meals. There is a small garden & each room has a terrace with a hammock. Some hetero clientele. ♀♂

■ Dance Bar/Disco
SHADEE, Avda Adolfo López Mateos, accross from gas station DIF, disco, bar & restaurant, from 21:00, occasional drag shows. ♂

ENSENADA BAJA CALIFORNIA NORTE

■ Bars
CLUB IBIS, Blvd. Costero at Avenida Sangines, discreetly frequented by gays, more gay on weekends. Same sex dancing not recommended, but it is popular for gays & lesbians to dance in groups. Good sound system with dance & stage, shows Thurs-Sun. ♂
OLA VERDE, Calle Segunda 459a, near Avenida Gastelum, gay cantina with DJs, popular very late in the evening. ♂

■ Dance Bar/Disco
COYOTE CLUB, Blvd. Costero 1000 #4 & 5, at Diamante, state-of-the-art nightclub, video bar with monitors, dance on lower level, garden patio, 9pm-3am (closed Mon, Tues), women welcome. ♂

■ Saunas/Health Clubs
BAÑOS FLORESTA, Calle Segunda 1357, near Avenida Floresta, Typical of Mexico's bathing houses, NOT a sex club, cruisy & fun, but be discreet. Sauna, steam, showers, individual & general bathing. Many workers stop by to get cleaned up on their way home.
EL DUGOUT CANTINA, Calle Segunda near Gastelum, enter from alley behind Avenida Miramar. Typical of Mexico's bathing houses, cruisy but NOT a sex club. Sauna, 2 steam bath rooms, individual rooms also available. To join the men, ask for "baños general."

■ Restaurants
MARISCOS CALIFORNIA, Calle Ruiz at Calle Segunda. Traditional Baja California seafood specialties, burritos Monterrey, seafood chili rellenos, shrimp & clams, 9am-8pm (closed Sun). ♀♂

GUADALAJARA

■ Information
GRUPO LESBICO PATLATONALLI, (3) 632 05 07, lesbian group, write: Apartado Postal 1-663, Col. Centro, C.P. 4410.

■ Bars
ARIZONAS SALON, Avda La Paz 1985, Col. Americana, gay Thurs-Sun 23:30-03:00, strippers. ♂

FYI

They Serve Great Coffee on the Beach, As the Sun Rises

Oceanwomyn Kayaking was the first women's organization to independently outfit and guide sea kayaking trips 14 years ago. Over the years, they have stuck to their specialty, offering a limited number of all-womyn, and sometimes all-lesbian, sea kayaking trips in Baja Mexico, British Columbia, the San Juan Islands and Alaska. Groups are small, warm and friendly. The pace is relaxed, non-competitive and great for beginners (no experience is necessary). OWK's lesbian guides are professional, full-time experts with many years experience in kayaking and in the womyn's community. They place great importance on providing the best of kayaking gear and instruction. And they serve excellent vegetarian cuisine in the wilderness. The memories you'll bring back from a sea kayaking expedition in Baja are of hot, sandy beaches, turquoise waters, dolphins, blowing whales, glistening kayaks on a glassy sea, desert hiking, coyotes singing on a starry night.

Contact **Oceanwomyn Kayaking** at (206) 325-3970.

LATIN AMERICA

MEXICO

Should You Retire in Mexico?

Have you considered retiring in Mexico? Many gay Americans are doing just that as they look into the retirement lifestyle that is available south of the border. As the economic realities of being retired in the US become a matter of great concern, Mexico offers a viable and attractive alternative. In fact, Mexico is now the number one relocation destination for gay retirees outside the United States.

South of the Border Tour and Travel has created an 8-day, 7-night introduction to Guadalajara and Lake Chapala, which nearly 40,000 Americans and Canadians now call home. The programs are led by Loujean La Malfa, publisher of the "Retire in Mexico Updates and Business News," a quarterly newsjournal on retirement and investment info on Mexico. Staying in traditional Mexican hotels, guests enjoy the year-round springlike climate that makes this area so desireable as a retirement location. The centerpiece of the program is a comprehensive seminar on immigration, health care, real estate, banking, investment opportunities and more from professionals, government officials and retirees. The Lakeside area is gay-friendly, and the program offers the chance to meet retired gays who share their knowledge and experiences.

Contact **South of the Border** at (707) 765-4573, (800) 922-TRAV (8728), Fax: (707) 778-1080.

Gay Baja Tours for 1997

Carnaval! Mardi Gras in Ensenada (2/7-9) Ensenada's gay clubs put on many festivities

Whale Watching in Guerrero Negro (3/2-4) Guerrero Negro is the birthing place of the Great California Gray Whales.

Gay Baja Tours

Summer Tijuana Pride! (summer) Help gays in Tijuana celebrate their third Gay Pride.

Sea of Cortez Diving (August) We dive in a marine wildlife protected zone.

Ensenada Pride at the Beach! (8/2-3) Celebrate Ensenada Gay Pride at the beach.

Ensenada, Wine Festival (September) Ensenada is the home of the 1995's Red Wine of the Year.

Palm springs Pride Weekend (11/7-9) Party passes and festival included.

Chrismas in Cabo San Lucas (12/23-26) Jet down to Land's End and celebrate with "family."

Gay Baja will customize private tours for 4 or more people.

Contact **Gay Baja Tours** at (888) 225-2429, (52-61) 76 4958, Fax:(52-61) 76 4958, E-mail: rdblack@compunet.com.mx.

Rosa Marta Knows Gay Mexico

A veteran travel professional (16 years) with close ties to the Mexico City gay community, Rosa Marta created **Gay Mexico Travel** in 1994 to customize travel itineraries for gay and lesbian visitors to Mexico. The company hired gay employees and established relationships with hotels and excursion suppliers that are gay-friendly. That list continues to grow, as Rosa Marta and her staff make contact with the growing number of Mexican companies that actively encourage gay clientele. Rosa Marta and staff can also refer travelers to local gay and gay-friendly restaurants, bars and live shows.

Call them to arrange any kind of itinerary for anywhere in Mexico. Rosa Marta, says, in her fluent English, "Just let us know what your specific needs are. We're ready to fulfill your request."

When you give Rosa Marta a call, do not be confused when someone else answers in Spanish. Just say "May I speak English, please?"

Contact **Gay Mexico Travel** at (52 5) 264 0822, Fax: (52 5) 264 2827.

For Bookings: Call travel agent or direct. Established: 1980. TAC: 10%. Payment: Checks, money orders. Member: IATA

MEXICO

PANCHOS JR. Galeana 180-A, downtown, daily 21:00-02:00. ♂
PUNTO G, Morelos 859, downtown, Thurs-Sat 21:00-02:00. ✉♂

■ *Dance Bar/Disco*
EL BOTANERO, Javier Mira, closed Mon. ♨ ♪♂
EL TALLER, Calle 66 #30, sector Reforma, men-only Wed-Sun from 21:00. ♨✉♂
LA MALINCHE, Alvaro Obregón 1230 Sector Libertad, Wed-Sun 21:00-02:00. ♪✉♂
MONICAS, Alvaro Obregón 1713, Sector Libertad. 22:00-02:00 (closed Mon, Tues). ♨♪♂
S.O.S., La Paz 1985, Sector Hidalgo, Zona Rosa, (3) 626 4179, disco & bar, 21:00-02:00 (closed Mon). ♨♪♂

ISLA MUJERES

■ *Accommodations*
VILLAS HI-NA-HA, Fraccionamiento Paraiso-Sac Bajo, Isla Mujeres, Q. Roo, (987) 706 15 (tel/fax). Six 3-bedroom/3-bath villas across from Isla Mujeres Bay with AC, kitchenette, TV, balconies, ocean views.

JALAPA

■ *Dance Bar/Disco*
LA MANSION, Fri & Sat. ♪♂

JUAREZ

■ *Dance Bar/Disco*
C&G, Lincoln 1252, daily till 03:00. ♨♪✉♂
G&G, Lincoln Ave next to El Pueblito Mexicano, restaurant, male strippers. ♪✉♨♀♂

LA PAZ

■ *Accommodations*
LA CONCHA BEACH RESORT, Kilómetro 5 Carretera a Pichilingue, in USA: (800) 999-2252, (619) 260-0991, fax (619) 294-7366, gay-friendly hotel with restaurant & gift shop, private baths, color cable TV, phone, AC, pool on premises. Condos have kitchen. 🏊

MAZATLAN

■ *Bars*
PEPE EL TORO, Avda de las Garzas 18, Dorada, (69)14 41 76, 21:00-02:00, occasional strippers & drag shows. ♪✉♨♂

MONTERREY

■ *Bars*
CHARAO'S, Zaragoza, at Isaac Garza, 22:00-02:00 (closed Sun). ✉✗♂
ESPUMA, Arteaga, at Zuazua, closed Sun. ♂

■ *Dance Bar/Disco*
BONGOLE, Avda. Constitución at Sta. Bárbara, Wed-Sat from 22:00. ♪✉♨♂
LA OPERA, Arramberri at Colegio Civil, Mon-Sat 22:00-04:00. ♨♂

MORELIA

■ *Dance Bar/Disco*
NO QUE NO, Avda del Campestre, at Rincón de los Compadres, 15 18 11, Thurs-Sun 21:00-04:00. ♪✉♨♂

ORIZABA

■ *Dance Bar/Disco*
SKY DRINK, Madero Norte 1280, Wed-Sun 21:00-03:00. ♨♪✉♂

PUEBLA

■ *Bars*
LA CIGARRA, 5 Poniente at 7 Sur. ♂

■ *Dance Bar/Disco*
JALEO'S, Reforma Sur 3121, Colonia La Paz, 3718 93, 22:00-03:00 ♪✉♨♂
KEOPS, 14 Poniente 101, San Andres Cholula (12 km from Puebla), dance & show bar, Thurs-Sun from 22:00. ♪✉♨♀♂

PUERTO VALLARTA

■ *Accommodations*
BOANA TORRE MALIBU, Amapas 328, reservations: (800) 936-3646, (415) 621-3576, Fax: (415) 621-3576. One-br suites with kitchenettes and balconies with views. Pool bar, mainly gay with some straight clientele. 🏊
CASA DE LAS OLAS, in Punta del Burro, (888) 373-3126, (52-3) 298 0060, Fax: (52-3) 298 0061. Resort overlooking beach & Banderas Bay, pool on premises. 🏊
CASA DE LOS ARCOS, PO Box 239BB, Puerto Vallarta, Jalisco, Mexico 48300, (52-322) 259 90 (tel/fax), E-mail: csarcos@tag.acnet.net. In USA: (800) 424-3434, ext. 277, ask for Ron. Our vacation villa has an incredible vista of Vallarta & the beaches of Los Muertos & El Dorado, and jungle foliage bordering our back garden provides a backdrop for colorful tropical birds. The villa accommodates up to 8 guests in two 1- or 2-bedroom suites. Amenities include AC, ceiling fans, color cable TV, on-premises pool & ocean. It can be arranged for a cook to come into your suite & prepare dinner for you. Some hetero clientele. 🏊♀♂
CASA DOS COMALES, Calle Aldama 274, (52-322) 320 42, gay-friendly B&B & apartments, private baths, AC, continental breakfast, indoor pool on premises. 🏊
CASA FANTASIA, Apartado Postal 387 Centro, Puerto Vallarta, Jalisco CP48300 Mexico. (52-322) 2 19 04, Fax: (52-322) 2 19 23, Toll-free in USA (888) 636-2539, E-mail: nenalex@aol.com. A jewel in Puerto Vallarta's gay district, this B&B guesthouse with bar & restaurant consists of 3 separate traditional Old-World-style Mexican haciendas. Common areas are elegant, yet informal, and the 8 large bedrooms have private full baths & king or twin beds. The terrace provides a staffed bar for guests & their friends adjacent to the swimming pool. Mostly men with

MEXICO

women welcome, some straight clientele. ⚓︎ ♂

CASA PANORAMICA, Apdo. Postal 114, JAL 48300, USA: (800) 745-7805, fax (808) 324-1302, direct: (52-322) 23656. E-mail: CasaPano@pvnet.com. B&B in a private 7-bedroom villa convenient to beach & downtown, breathtaking views, 2 bars, 4 dining areas, 3 terraces, full breakfast, 75% men & 25% women. ⚓︎ ♀ ♂

DOIN' IT RIGHT IN PUERTO VALLARTA, 150 Franklin #208, San Francisco, CA 94102, (415) 621-3584, USA & Canada: (800) 936-3646, Fax: (415) 621-3576. Puerto Vallarta specialists, offering 150+ properties in Puerto Vallarta with varying amenities, from basic to luxury, beachfront to jungle. We also arrange many types of gay tours — personal to corporate.

HOTEL HORTENCIA, Francisco I. Madero 336, Col. Emiliano Zapata, (322) 224 84.

LOS CUATRO VIENTOS, Matamoros 520, (52-322) 201 61, women's budget hotel. ♀

MISSION SAN FRANCISCO, Call Mike Pizza at (916) 933-0370 (tel/fax) or E-mail: mpizza@quiknet.com. Two Mexican colonial homes, gay-friendly, ocean views, accommodating 4-10 persons. Rent by the week, 6 blocks to gay beach & gay bar. Also available in Mexico City: Casita del Cielo in Zona Rosa, Mexico City: LR, DR, kitchen, one bedroom, one bath, large patio, furnished, US $800 per month. ⚓︎

PACO PACO DESCANSO DEL SOL HOTEL, Pino Suarez #583, Apdo Postal 245, Puerto Vallarta, Mexico CP 48301, (52-322) 3 02 77, Fax: (52-322) 2 67 67, E-mail: pacopaco@pvnet.com.mx. Puerto Vallarta's friendliest gay hotel is just two blocks from the beach and features a rooftop with bar, clothing-optional sunbathing and dipping pool. Suites and rooms all have private baths. Suites have kitchens and dining rooms. The hotel also organizes excursions to nearby hot springs, including an outdoor steak BBQ by candlelight. ⚓︎ ♀ ♂ See ad page 359.

PALAPAS IN YELAPA, c/o Antonio & Lucinda Saldaña Apdo 2-43, Puerto Vallarta, Jalisco, (52-322) 491 97 (tel/fax), 5 palapas (cabins), 50% gay/lesbian clientele, private showers & toilets, nearby river & ocean, Spanish & English spoken. ⚓︎

VALLARTA CORA HOTEL, Calle Pilitas 174, (52-322) 32815. Reservations: (415) 621-3576 (tel/fax), in USA/Canada (800) 936-3646. Hotel/apartment with 14 units on four floors. All units have 1 bedroom, 1-1/2 bath, daily maid service, equipped kitchens, AC or fans, and balcony. Clothing-optional pool on premises. Some lesbian clientele. ⚓︎ ♀ ♂

■ *Bars*

LA PANCHA, Lázaro Cardenas 329 near Insurgentes, 20:00-02:00. ♪ ♂

LIO'S, Ignacio Vallarta 264 at Lázaro Cardenas, C&W cantina, 10:00-02:00. May change in 1997. U ♂

■ *Dance Bar/Disco*

CLUB PACO PACO, Ignacio L. Vallarta 278, at Venustiano Corranza, (52-322) 218 99. One of the best dance bars in Vallarta, 2nd floor has pool table. 1st floor with disco nightly 20:00-06:00, drag shows & strippers on weekends. Cantina has 15:00-20:00 happy hour. Mostly men with women welcome. ♀ ♂

LOS BALCONES, Juárez 182 at Libertad, 246 71, dance bar & restaurant, ask about possible Thurs women's night.

PACO'S RANCH, Venustiano Carranza 239, male exotic dancers, Tues western nite, Thurs leather nite. ♂

ZOTANO, Morelos 101, lower level, 70's & 80's music, pool table, Wed ladies nite. ♂

■ *Restaurants*

BALAM, Basilio Badillo, 1 block east of CMQ Hospital, seafood.

BOMBO'S, Corona 327, Col. El Cerro, 251 64, upscale restaurant & bar, 16:30-23:00.

CAFE DES ARTISTES, Guadalupe Sanchez 740, 232 27, upscale dining, Mexican & French cuisine.

EL PANORAMA, J.O. Domínguez at Miramar, 21 824, taxi is best. Beautiful vistas of PV, international cuisine.

RED CABBAGE, Calle Rio Ribera 206-A, regional Mexican cuisine.

SANTOS, Fnco. Rodríquez 136, Col. Emiliano Zapata, near Playa de los Muertos, 210 84, closed Mon.

TITO'S, Playa de los Muertos, near Hotel Tropicana, beachside restaurant & bar, look for blue beach chairs & palapas. ♀ ♂

VIEJO VALLARTA, Morales 484, 3rd floor, 20 589, Mexican cuisine.

SAN MIGUEL DE ALLENDE

■ *Women's Accommodations*

BED & BREAKFAST IN SAN MIGUEL DE ALLENDE, c/o Greta Waldas Apdo #205, GTO, (52) 465 23279, women-only bed & breakfast 4 hours from Mexico city in charming colonial town with artist colony, room with private bath, friendly, safe atmosphere, much to see & do.

TIJUANA

■ *Information*

GAY & LESBIAN LINE & AIDS INFO, 88 02 67.

■ *Bars*

EL RANCHERO, Pza. Santa Cecilia, at Calle B, just off Avda Revolución, cantina, 24 hrs, very cruisy. ♂

EL TAURINO, Calle C #579 (Niños Héroes), north of Calle I, cantina, open daily (Fri, Sat till 05:00), frequented by some women. ♂

■ *Dance Bar/Disco*

EMILIO'S, Calle 3 #1810-11, enter at Parking América, 75% gay. ♪

LIGHT CLUB, on Mariscal, near the Superior straight bar on the strip, young crowd. ♀ ♂

MIKE'S, ★ Avda. Revolución 1220, near Calle 6, till 05:00 (closed Wed), occasional male. ♪ ♀ ♂

NOA NOA, Calle D (Avda Miguel Martínez), north of Calle Primera, disco & show bar. ♪ ♀ ♂

NUEVO LOS EQUIPALES, calle Séptima, south of Avda. Revolución, dance & show bar, occasional male strippers. ♪ ♂

■ *Restaurants*

LA COSTA, Calle 7 between Avdas Revolución & Constitución, seafood.

VITTORIO'S, Avda Revolución at Calle 9, Italian cuisine & pizza.

TUXTEPIC

■ *Bars*

SALON DE MACUMBA, Local 2, Conjunto Chamizal. ♀ ♂

VERACRUZ

■ *Dance Bar/Disco*

CLUB MEDITERRANEO, Avda Veracruz 927, at Mismaloya, Colonia Playa Linda, 24 01 47, Thurs-Sat from 21:00. ♀ ♂

DEEPER, Icazo 1005, between Guadalupe Victoria & Revillagigedo, 350 26 65, men-only dance bar, Thurs-Sat from 22:00. ♂

NICARAGUA

COUNTRY CODE: (505)

WHO TO CALL

For Tour Companies Serving This Destination
See Nicaragua on page 22

MANAGUA

■ *Retail & Bookstores*

GALERIA DE ARTE EL AGUILA, Carretera Sur 6 1/2 Sur, 650 524 or 650 525, art gallery.

VENEZUELA

PANAMA
COUNTRY CODE: (507)

For Tour Companies Serving This Destination
See Panama on page 23

PANAMA CITY

■ *Bars*

BOYS BAR, ask locally for address, mostly men, more women on weekends.

PERU
COUNTRY CODE: (51)

For Tour Companies Serving This Destination
See Peru on page 23

LIMA

■ *Information*

MHOL, Mariscal Miller 828, Jesús Marí, Lima 11. (1) 4 33 63 75, Fax: (1) 4 33 55 19, Mon-Fri 09:00-13:00 & 16:00-20:00. Gay & lesbian info, AIDS info, activities throughout the year.

■ *Bars*

PAULINA'S BAR, Centro Comercial San Felipe #60, (1) 4 61 90 09, women-only bar.

TWIST, Avenida Diagonal, Mira Flores, 2 blocks from Gitano disco, snack bar, 12:00-24:00, frequented by many gays.

■ *Dance Bar/Disco*

CANYU, Calle Kuilca 1, 22:00-05:00, gay & lesbian, but mostly transvestites.

CHAPS, Avenida Los Héroes, San Juan de Miraflores, Thurs-Sat from 22:00.

EL TALLER, República de Panama at Avenida Angamos, Thurs-Sat from 22:00.

GITANO,★ Calle Berlin, biggest & best disco in Lima.

IMPERIO, Avenida Girón Camaná, quadra 1, 21:00-06:00 (closed Mon), many women.

PERSEO, Avenida Aviación #2514, San Borja, 7 days, 23:00-05:00.

SAGITARIO, Avenida Garcilaso de la Vega, quadra 1, 21:00-05:00 or 06:00, very few women.

SPLASH, Los Pinos #124, Miraflores.
VOGLIA, Avenida Ricardo Palma 336, Miraflores.

■ *Cafe*

HAITI, Avenida Larco Miraflores (14) 45 05 39.

URUGUAY
COUNTRY CODE: (598)

For Tour Companies Serving This Destination
See Uruguay on page 27

MONTEVIDEO

■ *Bars*

AVANTI, Avenida Daniel Fernández Crespo at Calle Lima.

METROPOLIS, Cerro Largo 1281, bar & disco.

SPOK, San José at Santiago de Chile.

■ *Dance Bar/Disco*

EIGHT-SEVEN-FOUR (874), San Jose 874, 50% men, 50% women.

VENEZUELA
COUNTRY CODE: (58)

For Tour Companies Serving This Destination
See Venezuela on page 28

CARACAS

■ *Bars*

LA COTORRA, Centro Comercial Paseo las Mercedes, basement level, sector Las Mercedes, below and facing the Tamanaco Hotel.

LA TORTILLA, Calle San Antonio, a few meters from El Gran Cafe, Savana Grande.

PULLMAN, Avda Francisco Solano, 500m from Hotel Tampa, Savanna Grande.

TASCA DON SOL, Blvd Savana Grande, near Calle de la Puñalada.

TASCA EL GABAN, Calle San Antonio, 1 block from El Gran Cafe, Savana Grande.

■ *Dance Bar/Disco*

DISCOTECA ACERO, Avda Principal de las Mercedes, about 10 min walk from Tamanaco Hotel, sector las Mercedes, 50% men & 50% women.

ICE PALACE,★ Avda Luís Roche, next to Cine Altamira, Altamira sector, 50% men & 50% women.

LA PUNCH, Centro Comercial Cediaz, Avda Casanova near Calle de la Puñalada, street level, (1 block from Avda Savana Grande), 65% men, 35% women.

MY WAY, Avda Principal de las Mercedes, 10 min walk from Tamanaco Hotel.

ZZ, Avda Libertador, corner of Avda Las Acacias, Edificio La Linea, street level, Savana Grande, 65% men, 35% women.

MARACAY

■ *Bars*

BEER GARDEN PARK, east side of Plaza Bolivar, bar & rest., patio bar, live music, screened from the street, 65%/35%.

■ *Dance Bar/Disco*

TOWN TAVERN, Centro Comercial 19 de Abril, at corner of Avda 19 de Abril & Calle Boyacá.

MARGARITA ISLAND

■ *Dance Bar/Disco*

MOSQUITO COAST, in alley behind Bellavista Hotel.

SOUTH BEACH, Calle Malavé, between Calle Batiño & Calle Cedeño.

MERIDA

■ *Bars*

COPACABANA, Avda Lora, at Calle Carabobo, small bar with mainly local crowd.

EL SOL DISCOBAR, Calle 25 Ayacucho, between Avda Lora & Avda Independencia, gay after 22:00. No gays earlier, 99% men, but women welcome.

SAN CRISTOBAL

■ *Bars*

EL TRIGAL, Carrera 4, downtown, mainly locals.

END PUB, THE, Carrera Nueve, at Calle Nueve, downtown.

■ *Dance Bar/Disco*

PUB, THE, Centro Comercial Paseo La Villa, Avda Guayana, 90% men, 10% women.

■ *Cafe*

FUENTE DE SODA LA BOHEME, Centro Civico San Cristobal, at Carrera Séptima, not gay, but a cruisy mainstream sidewalk cafe, frequented by many gays.

VALENCIA

■ *Bars*

EL PUMA, Calle Urdaneta, between Calle Libertad Calle Independencia, 1/2 block east of the cathedral, small bar, local crowd.

■ *Dance Bar/Disco*

LOKURAS, next to baseball stadium at east side of Avda Bolivar, 50% men & 50% women.

FERRARI GUIDES' GAY TRAVEL A to Z - 18TH EDITION

ALABAMA

UNITED STATES

COUNTRY CODE: (1)

WHO TO CALL
For Tour Companies Serving This Destination
See USA on page 27

COUNTRYWIDE

■ *Information*
HIV-AIDS TREATMENT INFORMATION SERVICE, (800) HIV-0440. 9am-7pm (EST), TDD.

ALABAMA
BIRMINGHAM

■ *Information*
AIDS LINE, (205) 322-4197. Mon-Fri 9am-5pm or tape. Statewide line (800) 228-0469.
GAY & LESBIAN INFO LINE, (205) 326-8600. Mon-Fri 7-10pm.

■ *Bars*
MISCONCEPTIONS TAVERN, 600 32nd St S, (205) 322-1210, small bar, open continuously from noon Sun to 2am Sat.
SOUTHSIDE PUB, 2830 7th Ave, (205) 324-0997.

■ *Dance Bar/Disco*
BILL'S CLUB, 208 N 23rd St near 2nd Ave, (205) 254-8634. Cabaret show, country line dancing.
CLUB 21, 117-1/2 21st Street N near 2nd Ave N, (205) 322-0469. Dance & show bar, Thurs-Sat, popular Thurs, progressive crowd, 50% gay clientele (50% men, 50% women).
QUEST, THE, 416 24th St S at 5th Ave S, (205) 251-4313. Live DJ from midnight, 90% men, 10% women. Big dance floor, outdoor deck & patio open all nite. Summer patio bar.
TOOL BOX, 5120 5th Ave S, (205) 595-5120. Cruise bar & dance bar, country line dance Sat & Wed, hosts Birmingham Leather Club meetings Wed. Cruise bar in basement. 50% men/women, weekends 70% men.

■ *Restaurants*
ANTHONY'S, 2131 7th Ave S, (205) 324-1215. 2nd location: 1421 Montgomery Hwy, (205) 979-03700. Continental cuisine, gay friendly.
TWENTY-SECOND STREET JAZZ CAFE &
BREWERY, 22nd St & 7th Ave S, (205) 252-0407. Open Wed-Sat from 5pm-Til? Gay-friendly.

■ *Retail & Bookstores*
LODESTAR BOOKS, 2020-B 11th Ave South near 21st St, (205) 939-3356. Alternative bookstore with lesbian & gay books.
PLANET MUZICA, 725 29th St S, (205) 254-9303, Fax: 254-9295. General record store with jewelry, gifts & gay & lesbian magazines.

■ *Erotica*
ALABAMA ADULT BOOKS, 801 3rd Ave N, (205) 322-7323.
BIRMINGHAM BOOKS, 7610 1st Ave N.
CINEMA BLUE, 7604 1st Ave N.
DOWNTOWN BOOKS, 2731 8th Ave N, (205) 328-5525.
PLEASURE BOOKS, 7606 1st Ave N, (205) 836-7379.

DOTHAN

■ *Dance Bar/Disco*
CHUCKIE BEE'S, 100 Block S St Andrews directly across from Civic Ctr, (334) 794-0230. Three level dance & show bar with game room, Mon-Sat from 7pm, occasional male strippers.

GADSDEN

■ *Dance Bar/Disco*
NITRO, 2461 E Meighan Blvd, (205) 492-9724. A place for nighttime explosions. From 8pm Wed-Sat.

HUNTSVILLE

■ *Information*
AIDS LINE, (205) 533-AIDS.

■ *Dance Bar/Disco*
UPSCALE, 4420 University Dr, near Sparkman, (205) 837-3252. Upstairs disco, downstairs quiet bar. Pool tables, strippers, live entertainers.
VIEUX CARRE, 1204 Posey, (205) 534-5970. Dance & show bar, 60% men, 40% women. Daily from 7pm, 4pm on Sun.

■ *Retail & Bookstores*
RAINBOWS LTD, 1009 Henderson Rd #400B, (205) 722-9220. Gay & lesbian bookstore. T-shirts, jewelry, local info.

MOBILE

■ *Information*
AIDS LINE, (334) 431-5111.

■ *Bars*
BIENVILLE CRUISE PUB, 22 S Conception at Conti, 24hrs.
GABRIEL'S DOWNTOWN, 55 S Joachim St near Government St, (334) 432-4900. Neighborhood cruise bar, 7 days from 5pm, patio bar open weekends, 75% men, 25% women.
GOLDEN ROD, 13 S Joachim St, (334) 433-9175. Quiet bar, jukebox & taped music, 50% men, 50% women.
TROOPERS, 215 Conti St, (334) 433-7436, 95% men.

■ *Dance Bar/Disco*
B-BOB'S, 6157 Airport Blvd #201 near Hillcrest, West Mobile, (334) 341-0102. Hi-energy dance club, DJ, 7 days from 5pm till late, 50% men, 50% women, occasional male & female strippers. Gift shop inside.
SOCIETY LOUNGE, 51 S Conception St at Conti, (334) 433-9141. Dance & show bar, 50% men & 50% women.
SPOTLIGHT, 155 Dauphin St, (334) 438-4405. Wed-Sun from 9pm, drag shows Thurs-Sun.

■ *Erotica*
MIDTOWN CINEMA, 270 Dauphin St near S Jackson, (334) 438-9910.
NELSON'S, Royal St, between Conti & Government.

MONTGOMERY

■ *Information*
AIDS LINE, (334) 269-1002.

■ *Bars*
THIRSTIES, (334) 264-5933.

TUSCALOOSA

■ *Bars*
MICHELLE'S, in same building as Michael's bar, 2201 6th St, separate entrance on the side, Mon-Sat from 6pm.

■ *Dance Bar/Disco*
NEW MICHAEL'S LOUNGE, 2201 6th St, (205) 758-9223. 24hrs (except Sat closes 2am), closed Sun. Top billboard music hits, 50% men, 50% women.

■ *Retail & Bookstores*
ILLUSIONS, 519 College Park, (205) 349-5725. Gay & lesbian books, rainbow & pride items.

ALASKA

WHO TO CALL
For Tour Companies Serving This Destination
See Alaska on page 8

ANCHORAGE

■ Information

AIDS HELP LINE, (907) 276-4880, (800) 478-2437. Mon-Fri 9am-5pm, with person on call other times.

GAY/LESBIAN HELP LINE, (907) 258-4777. 6-11pm 7 days.

WOMEN'S RESOURCE CENTER, 111 W 9th Ave, (907) 276-0528. Weekdays 8:30am-5pm.

■ Accommodations

ARCTIC FEATHER B&B, 211 W Cook, (907) 277-3862. The charm of this B&B will warm you, as will the quiet neighborhood in which it is located. Guests are within easy walking distance of downtown while many restaurants, shops, the Anchorage Museum of History and Art, two gay bars, and three parks are close by. There's plenty to see and do. The tallest mountain in North America, Ship Creek (where 40-pound king salmon swim upstream), and 125 miles of biking/walking trails are just a few of the sights to see. Some straight clientele. ♀♂

AURORA WINDS, AN EXCEPTIONAL B&B RESORT, 7501 Upper O'Malley, (907) 346-2533, E-mail: awbnb@alaska.net. Luxurious B&B. Private baths, color TV & phones. Billiards room, TV lounge, exercise room & expanded continental or full breakfast. ♀ ♂

CHENEY LAKE BED & BREAKFAST, 6333 Colgate Dr, (907) 337-4391, Fax: (907) 338-1023, E-mail: cheneybb@alaska.net. Gay-friendly B&B on Cheney Lake, private baths, continental breakfast, color TV, VCR, phone, maid service, gay & lesbian following.

■ Bars

RAVEN, THE, 618 Gambell St at 6th, (907) 276-9672. CD juke box, pool tables, darts, pinball. ♀♂

■ Dance Bar/Disco

WAVE, THE, 3101 Spenard Rd, (907) 561-9283, Fax: (907) 563-9920. E-mail: wave@alaska.net. Dance club with coffee house upstairs, drag show Wed. 50/50 men & women, some straight clientele. ♀♂

■ Restaurants

O'BRADY'S, Dimond Center, (907) 344-8033. 2nd location: Chugach Sq, (907) 338-1080. Gay-friendly bar & restaurant.

FYI

Women Sail Alaska

Terry and Karen once sailed their 36-foot sloop down the western coast of North America, across the South Pacific for a 2 1/2-year cruise in paradise. Terry is a U.S. Coast Guard-licensed skipper, and the two have been sailing together since 1983. Now, they host women's sailing excursions in the sheltered, unspoiled waters surrounding Juneau, Alaska. Amongst the islands, there are many safe, secure anchorages with trails leading into old-growth rainforests and lakes. The waters of southeast Alaska are remarkably abundant with wildlife..seals, pods of whales, sea lions, bears, bald eagles, loons and more. There are ample opportunities for photography and beachcombing.

Taking groups of no more than 4 women, Terry and Karen teach sailing skills, boat handling, navigation, anchoring, use of electronics and safety procedures. There's always time for fishing, with both halibut and salmon to catch for dinner, and there are crab and shrimp pots to set.

Accommodations include a double berth forward, a double and single berth in the main saloon and a quarter berth aft.

Contact **Women Sail Alaska** at (907) 463-3372, (888) 272-4525.

ALASKA

FYI

Gay Charters in Alaskan Waters

A rainbow flag flies atop the M/V Sophie Lou, a 30-ft, six-passenger charter boat with fully-enclosed, heated cabin and full electronics. Over the last three years, she has carried many gay and lesbian visitors to dramatic sightseeing locations and great fishing spots in Resurrection Bay and the Kenai Fjords. The Sophie Lou is the charter boat of **Puffin Family Charters**, operated by Captain Leslie Pemberton. A veteren sailor in these waters, she'll take you to see glaciers, mountains and abundant marine life, including whales, sea lions, sea otters, eagles, porpoises, and, of course, puffins. Full day, half-day and combination trips are available. A variety of fishing adventures are available for both experienced and novice fisherpersons. Halibut, black bass, ling cod and red snapper can be caught all summer. In July and August, silver salmon abound. Captain Leslie has been operating passenger vessels in Alaska since 1979 and loves to share her knowledge.

Contact **Puffin Family Charters** at (907) 278-3346, (800) 978-3346.

UNITED STATES

FERRARI GUIDES' GAY TRAVEL A to Z - 18th EDITION 363

ALASKA

Retail & Bookstores
CAPRI CINEMA, Tudor & Dale in the mall. (907) 561-0064. Cinema plays gay films often. Coffeeshop next door is frequented by gays & lesbians.

Erotica
ADULTS ONLY BOOKSTORE, 3956 Spenard, (907) 243-0697.

SEX SHOP, LE, 305 W Dimond, (907) 522-1987.

SWINGER BOOKSTORE, 710 W Northern Lights near Arctic, (907) 561-5039.

VIDEO X, 1431 Muldoon, near Northern Lights, (907) 338-9886.

FAIRBANKS

Accommodations
ALTA'S BED AND BREAKFAST, PO Box 82290, (907) 389-2582. B&B, some straight clientele. Private & shared baths, TV lounge, Jacuzzi & full breakfast.

Dance Bar/Disco
PALACE SALOON, inside & on east side of Alaskaland Park in Gold Rush Town, near Airportway & Peeger Rd, (907) 456-5960. Gay late evening Fri & Sat, DJ.

Erotica
FANTASYLAND VIDEO, 1765 Richardson Hwy, between North Pole & Fairbanks, (907) 488-0879. Some gay & lesbian titles.

GUSTAVUS

Accommodations
GOOD RIVER BED & BREAKFAST, Box 37, Gustavus, 99826, Tel/Fax: (907) 697-2241. Spectacular Glacier Bay. Sixteen tidewater glaciers, whales, fishing, kayaking, nature walks, wilderness, and a great place to stay. Elegant log house, comfy beds, handmade quilts, fresh bread, reasonable rates. Rusic log cabin also available. Free bikes to explore unique town. Come see. 50% gay clientele.

HOMER

Accommodations
BEACH HOUSE B&B, PO Box 2617, (907) 235-5945. Gay-friendly B&B.

ISLAND WATCH B&B, PO Box 1394, Homer, AK 99603, (907) 235-2265. Gay-friendly B&B (30% gay & lesbian). Farm setting with horses & sheep, only 5 minutes from downtown. Cabin, suite & 1 handicap-accessible room. Full breakfast with fresh eggs.

JUNEAU

Information
JUNEAU SHANTI AIDS LINE, (907) 463-5665, Mon-Fri 8-5.

SOUTHEAST ALASKA GAY & LESBIAN ALLIANCE, (907) 586-GAYS (4297). Returns taped messages, monthly meetings & scheduled brunches, video nites.

KENAI

Accommodations
MOOSE HAVEN LODGE, Box 8597, Nikiski, 99635, Tel & Fax: (907) 776-8535. Gay-friendly B&B motel. Rooms & suites, color TV, telephone, private & shared baths, TV lounge, full breakfast. Closed for remodeling for 1996 season. To reopen as exclusively gay accommodation in 1997.

ARIZONA

WHO TO CALL
For Tour Companies Serving This Destination
See Arizona on page 9

BULLHEAD CITY

Bars
LARIAT SALOON, 1161 Hancock Rd, (520) 758-8479. Karaoke Fri-Sun, 60% men, 40% women, may add DJ in '97.

COTTONWOOD

Accommodations
MUSTANG BED & BREAKFAST, 4257 Mustang, (520) 646-5929. B&B with private & shared baths, continental breakfast & movie theater.

FLAGSTAFF

Information
AIDS OUTREACH, (520) 779-9498, office staffed 10am-2pm Mon-Fri.

Accommodations
CHALET IN THE PINES, PO Box 25640, Munds Park, AZ 86017, (520) 286-2417. B&B at Pinewood Country Club, 15 miles from Flagstaff, AZ. Expanded continental & full breakfast, private & shared baths, pool nearby, women welcome.

HOTEL MONTE VISTA, 100 North San Francisco St, (800) 545-3068, (520) 779-6971, Fax: (520) 779-2904. Gay-friendly hotel with restaurant & bar. Antique reproductions, color cable TV, ceiling fans, telephone and private baths.

INN AT 410 BED & BREAKFAST, THE, 410 N Leroux St, (520) 774-0088, (800) 774-2008. Gay-friendly B&B with private baths, full breakfast, AC, refrigerator, ceiling fans, coffee/tea-making facilities, maid service, nearby pool. Gay & lesbian following.

Bars
CHARLIE'S, 23 N Leroux at Aspen. NOT a gay bar. Frequented by some gays & lesbians.

MONTE VISTA HOTEL BAR, 100 N San Francisco at Aspen. NOT a gay bar! Discreetly frequented by gay men.

Retail & Bookstores
ARADIA BOOKS, 116 W Cottage, (520) 779-3817. Feminist, lesbian & gay books & local info, 10:30-5:30 Mon-Sat, closed Sun.

JEROME

Accommodations
COTTAGE INN, THE, 747 E Ave, (520) 634-0701. Gay-friendly B&B, private baths, full breakfast, gay/lesbian following.

Bars
PAUL & JERRY'S, on Jerome's main street. Not gay, but a very open atmosphere with many gays in later evenings, live bands.

LAKE HAVASU CITY

Erotica
ADULT WORLD, 3596 N London Bridge Rd, (520) 764-3066.

PHOENIX

Information
GAY & LESBIAN COMMUNITY CENTER & AIDS LINE, 3136 N 3rd Ave, (602) 234-2752. Walk-in 10am-8pm.

LESBIAN & GAY SWITCHBOARD, (602) 234-2752, TDD 234-0873. 10am-10pm 7 days.

LESBIAN RESOURCE PROJECT, at the Gay Center, (602) 266-5542.

Accommodations
ARIZONA ROYAL VILLA, 1110 E Turney Ave at 12th St, (602) 266-6883. E-mail: azroyalvil@aol.com. Rooms, junior suites & 1-bedroom apartments, all with private bath. Short or long stay. Private grounds with free parking. Pool, Jacuzzi, courtyard, color TV, laundry, continental breakfast, courtesy telephone. Central to bars and downtown.

ARIZONA SUNBURST INN, 6245 N 12th Place, (602) 274-1474, (800) 974-1474. Centrally-located, men-only B&B resort. Spacious rooms & suite with cable TV, private & shared baths, expanded contintental breakfast. Pool on premises, clothing optional.

ARROWZONA "PRIVATE" CASITAS PO Box 11253, Glendale, AZ 85318-1253, Private mini resort B&B homestay. Color cable TV, VCR, AC, Coffee/tea-making facilities, phone, refrigerator, private bath. Health Club privileges at adjacent country club. Full breakfast (continental in summer).

INNSUITES HOTEL, SCOTTSDALE, 7707 E McDowell Rd, Scottsdale, AZ 85257, (602) 941-1202, (800) 238-8851, (888) 444-HOTEL, Fax: (602) 990-7873. Located in fashionable Scottsdale, 15 minutes from the airport, we offer expanses of green grass, lakes and miles of hiking, jogging and biking trails. Studio or 2-room suites accommodate every need with refrigerator/juice, coffee- & tea-maker,

CASTLE SUPERSTORES

New Times Best of Phoenix

(800) 344-9076

Visit Our New Website:
www.castlesuperstores.com

America's Safer Sex Superstores Because We Care

• Video Sales • Video Rentals • Playful Greeting & Post Cards • Leather Goods & Apparel • Restraints • Latex Garments • Rubber Goods • Wildest Selection of Adult Toys • Gag Gifts • Novelties • Games • Condoms • Lubes • Books & Magazines • T-Shirts • Whips & Chains • Wrapping Papers • Calendars • Novels • Sensual Oils • Sexy Lingerie & more & more ...

OPEN 24 HOURS · 365 DAYS
Rediscover America's Favorite Pastime

(602) 231-9837
5501 E. Washington St.

(602) 995-1641
8802 N. Black Canyon Hwy.

(602) 266-3348
300 E. Camelback Rd.

(602) 986-6114
8315 E. Apache Trail

ARIZONA

FYI

Unusual Women's SW Adventure Visits 5 Beautiful Canyons

The Arizona Spectacular Tour by **Canyon Calling** takes you to five of the world's most beautiful canyons, while sharing the warmth and support inherent in women journeying together. Travel is by luxury 12-seater bus. Lodgings are in fine hotels and B&Bs. Two nights feature camping on soft mattresses, enjoying a view of the heavens that you won't believe! Hiking is only downhill, carrying small day packs.

The tour begins and ends in the red rocks of Sedona. Participants walk through the ancient, still-inhabited Hopi village of Walpi, tour Anasazi ruins and petroglyphs in the Navajo's Canyon de Chelly and visit with Native Americans. An experience in Monument Valley is followed by a day on motor boats at Lake Powell, exploring warm-water beaches and visiting Rainbow Bridge. Groups venture to the bottom of the Grand Canyon for swimming amongst the wonderland of waterfalls at Supai.

Contact **Canyon Calling** at (520) 282-0916, Fax: (520) 282-3586

---

hair dryer & microwave oven with popcorn. A complimentary healthy breakfast buffet and afternoon social hour are included. Other extras are a fitness center, state-of-the-art electronic security locks, heated pool & spa and more.

LARRY'S B & B, 502 W Claremont Ave, (602) 249-2974. Centrally-located B&B, women welcome, some straight clientele. Color TV, AC, private & shared baths, Jacuzzi, pool & full breakfast.

MARY CLAIRE II, 303 Patrician Dr, Tempe, (602) 967-2767 (tel/fax). B&B homestay with hot tub. Two rooms with double or single beds, shared bath.

STEWART'S B&B, 1319 E Hayward, (602) 861-2500, fax: (602) 861-0242. B&B with shared bath, expanded continental breakfast, AC/air cooler, TV lounge, video tape library, especially leather friendly, women welcome.

WINDSOR COTTAGE, 62 West Windsor, (602) 264-6309. B&B guesthouse cottages, expanded continental breakfast, private bath, color cable TV, AC, bikes & pool on premises, women welcome.

■ Bars

APOLLO'S, 5749 N 7th St at Palo Verde, (602) 277-9373. Mid 20's & up.

BS WEST, 7125 5th Ave, Kiva Mall, Scottsdale, (602) 945-9028. Video bar, popular Sun for cook out & Wed night.

COUNTRY CLUB BAR & GRILL, 4428 N 7th Ave, (602) 264-4553. Patio, hamburgers, piano bar, darts, karaoke.

CRUISIN CENTRAL, 1011 N Central Ave near Roosevelt, (602) 253-3376. Open 6am.

DURANGO'S, 1517 S Black Canyon Hwy at the Flex Complex, (602) 271-9017. Private club for use by towel crowd.

FUNDY'S, 15601 N Cave Creek Rd, (602) 493-5123.

JC'S FUN ONE LOUNGE, 5542 N 43rd Ave, Glendale, (602) 939-0528. Occasional shows, 50% men, 50% women.

JOHNNY MC'S, 138 W Camelback Rd, (602) 266-0875. Neighborhood pub, 30's & up.

MARLYS', 15615 N Cave Creek Rd, (602) 867-2463. Live bands, 50% men, 50% women.

NUTOWNE SALOON, 5002 E Van Buren St near 48th St, (602) 267-9959. From 10am, popular Tues eve & Sun afternoon, patio.

PARK, 3002 N 24th St, (602) 957-6055. Upscale electronic player piano, huge patio.

PUMP HOUSE, 4132 E McDowell, (602) 275-3509. DJ, pool, darts, etc.

ROSCOE'S ON 7TH, 4531 N 7th St, (602) 285-0833. alternative sports pub.

THREE-O-SEVEN LOUNGE, 222 E Roosevelt St near 3rd St, (602) 252-0001. From 6am except Sun 10am.

WINKS,★ 5707 N 7th St, (602) 265-9002. Show bar, yuppie types, women welcome. Lunch Mon-Fri, Sun brunch 10am. Popular happy hour.

■ Dance Bar/Disco

AIN'T NOBODY'S BIZNESS,★ (The Biz), 3031 E Indian School Rd, (602) 224-9977. Dance club, no cover charge. Variety of specials & events. Boyz night out Tues.

CASH INN, 2120 E McDowell Rd near Squaw Peak Parkway, (602) 244-9943. C&W dance bar, 70% women. Wed-Sun 4pm-1am, sun till 11pm.

CHARLIE'S PHOENIX,★ 727 W Camelback Rd near 7th Ave, (602) 265-0224. C&W dance bar, home of AZ Gay Rodeo Assn. Sun brunch, dance lessons, volleyball court.

DESERT ROSE, 4301 N 7th Ave, (602) 265-3233. C&W dance bar.

FOSTERS, 4343 N 7th Ave, (602) 263-8313. Video dance bar, Fri-Sun.

HARLEY'S 155,★ 155 W Camelback, (602) 274-8505. High energy music, popular weekend nights.

INCOGNITO LOUNGE, 2424 E Thomas near 24th St, (602) 955-9805.

NASTY HABITS, 3108 E McDowell Rd, (602) 267-8707. Dance bar with 8 music video screens, comfortable atmosphere, a variety of entertainment, open 12 noon daily. Mostly women with gay men welcome.

TRAX, 1724 E McDowell Rd near 17th St, (602) 254-0231. After hours Fri & Sat.

■ Cafe

CAFE UNIQUE/UNIQUE ON CENTRAL, 4700 N Central Ave #105, (602) 279-9691. Coffees, smoothies, desserts.

InnSuites Hotel
SCOTTSDALE
(888) 444-HOTEL
(602) 941-1202

ARIZONA

Saunas/Health Clubs

CHUTE, THE, 1440 E Indian School, (602) 234-1654. **Hottest men's club in the Southwest.** Gymnasium, steam room, showers, large-screen video room, TV lounge, specialty rooms. Cheap day rates. Sunday and Wednesday night specials. Photo ID required. Central location near all gay bars. Masculine atmosphere. Bears and leathermen especially welcome. 24 hrs.

FLEX COMPLEX, 1517 S Black Canyon Hwy at curve of fwy, (602) 271-9011. Club with full gym & rooms with private baths, 24hrs.

Restaurants

COMMON GROUND, 7125 E 5th Ave, Scottsdale. Restaurant & cafe, healthy food, courtyard dining, also desserts, gallery.

EDDIE'S GRILL, 4747 N 7th St, (602) 241-1188. Gay friendly.

POOKIE'S CAFE, 4540 N 7th Ave, (602) 277-2121. Bar & restaurant, American grill, kitchen open 11:30am-11pm, music video bar.

Retail & Bookstores

CHANGING HANDS BOOKSTORE, 414 S Mill Ave, Tempe (602) 966-0203. General bookstore with a gay & lesbian section.

OBELISK BOOKSTORE, 24 W Camelback suite A, (602) 266-BOOK (2665). Gay & lesbian bookstore.

UNIQUE ON CENTRAL, 4700 N Central Ave, (602) 279-9691. Gay & lesbian cards, gifts, books, jewelry & art gallery.

Leathers/Piercing

TUFF STUFF, 1714 E McDowell Rd near 17th St, (602) 254-9651. Men's & women's custom leather, gay magazines & videos.

Erotica

ADULT SHOPPE, 111 S 24th St, (602) 306-1130.

BARN, THE, 5021 W Indian School Rd, (602) 245-3008, Safe sex shop. Adult videos, books, novelties, 24hrs.

BOOK CELLAR DISCOUNT CENTER, 3420 S Central Ave, (602) 276-4397. Discount center, 24 hrs.

BOOK CELLARS: #2: 2103 W Camelback, (602) 433-9680; #3: 402 W Hatcher, (602) 944-3023; #5: 1421 E McDowell, (602) 252-9443; #6: 1838 Grand Ave, (602) 252-6446; #7: 6527 N 59th Ave, Glendale, (602) 939-3411; #8: 1020 S 24th St, (602) 244-8370.

CASTLE BOOKSTORE, ★ 5501 E Washington St, (602) 231-9837. Large selection of gay books, magazines, videos, and much much more. Open 24 hrs, 365 days a year. See ad on page 365.

CASTLE BOUTIQUE, 8802 N Black Canyon Hwy near Dunlap, (602) 995-1641. Large selection of gay books, magazines, videos, and much, much more. Open 24 hrs, 365 days a year.

CASTLE BOUTIQUE, 300 E Camelback Rd near Central, (602) 266-3348. Large selection of gay books, magazines, videos, and much, much more. Open 24 hrs, 365 days a year.

CASTLE BOUTIQUE, 8315 E Apache Trail, Mesa, (602) 986-6114. Large selection of gay books, magazines, videos, and much, much more. Open 24 hrs, 365 days a year.

FAR EAST BOOKS, 11405 E Apache Trail near Signal Butte, Apache Junction, (602) 986-2322.

FASCINATIONS, 10242 N 19th Ave near Peoria, (602) 943-5859. 2nd location: 16428 N 32nd St, (602) 482-3633.

INTERNATIONAL BOOKSTORE, 3640 E Thomas, near 36th St, (602) 955-2000, 24hrs.

PARADISE ADULT BOUTIQUE, 130 W Osborn, (602) 266-5896, 24hrs.

PLEASURE PALACE, 1524 E Van Buren, (602) 262-9942, 24hrs.

PLEASURE WORLD, 4029 E Washington, (602) 275-0015, 24hrs.

ZORBA'S, 2924 N Scottsdale Rd, Scottsdale, (602) 941-9891, 24hrs.

PRESCOTT

Retail & Bookstores

SATISFIED MIND, 113 W Goodwin St, (520) 776-9766. Retail bookstore with a gay & lesbian section.

SEDONA

Accommodations

COZY CACTUS, 80 Canyon Circle Dr, (520) 284-0082, (800) 788-2082, fax: (520) 284-4210. Gay-friendly B&B at foot of Castle Rock. Private baths, AC, TV lounge & continental breakfast.

HUFF 'N PUFF STRAW BALE INN, PO Box 406, Rimrock, AZ 86335, (520) 567-9066. Inn with private baths, continental breakfast, some straight clientele. Tours to indian ruins arranged.

MARTI'S GUEST RANCH, Mail: Cornville Ranch, PO Box 605, Cornville, AZ 86325, (520) 634-4842, E-mail: MartiMac@Sedona.net. Come relax and enjoy yourself in a private, rustic guest cottage located on a hsitorical 65-acre ranch beside Oak Creek. Watch the sun set as ducks, geese and heron settle for the night on the banks of cool, splashing Oak Creek. Or take a quick drive to a gaming casino or to Sedona or Old Town Cottonwood. Your cottage includes 2 bedrooms, equipped kitchen stocked with coffee, tea and condiments, cable TV with VCR and movies.

SACRED SEDONA, (520) 204-2422. Lodging with shared bath. Special diets catered to.

Women's Accommodations

PARADISE BY THE CREEK, 215 Disney Lane, Sedona, AZ (520) 282-7107, E-mail: drdeb@sedona.net. Gay-owned B&B on the shores of Oak Creek overlooked by Cathedral Rock, private & shared bath, continental breakfast, men welcome.

FYI

The Rainbow Rangers Are Your Guides

1/2-Day History & Legends of Sedona — See Sedona from four spectacular lookout points and a famous cowboy movie location.

1/2 or full-day Fine Art Gallery Tour — From western to modern fine art galleries — your choice.

Shootin On the Rocks Wild West Adventure — A helicopter whisks you to the top of a private mesa, where you will learn to fire a real six shooter. Includes 30 rounds of ammunition, with additional rounds available for purchase.

South Rim Grand Canyon Tour — Two full-day tours: #1 - Includes IMAX Theater and Nat'l Park entrance fee. Personally-escorted tour of West Rim Drive and Grand Canyon Village. #2 - Adds a scenic airplane flight into the canyon.

Contact **Sedona Rainbow Adventure Tours** at (520) 204-9967, (888) 282-9967, Fax: (520) 204-1399.

ARIZONA

UNITED STATES

PARADISE RANCH, 135 Kachina Dr, Sedona, AZ 86336, (520) 282-9769 (tel/fax). For women only. Intimate, beautiful, private guesthouse with fully equipped kitchen (coffee & tea provided). Healing center with outdoor hot tub. There is a tepee and non-traditional sweat lodge on premises. We offer hypnotherapy, star chamber experiences, transpersonal therapy, workshop facilities and specialized rituals and ceremonies. We are dedicated to spreading the light of the Goddess. ♀

SAPPHO'S OASIS, PO Box 1863, Sedona, AZ 86339, (520) 282-5679, Fax: (520) 282-1839. B&B guesthouse with continental breakfast, Jacuzzi, private baths, men welcome.

■ *Retail & Bookstores*
FLAGS, KITES & FUN, 202 Hwy 179, 86336, (520) 282-4496. Gay-friendly souvenir shop handling gay flags, windsocks, and rainbow products.

TUCSON

■ *Information*
AIDS HOTLINE, (520) 326-AIDS (2437) 9am-10pm, or call Wingspan Gay Center at (520) 624-1779.

WINGSPAN GAY & LESBIAN CENTER, 422 N 4th Ave, (520) 624-1779, 1pm-5 or 7pm.

■ *Accommodations*
ADOBE ROSE, 940 N Olsen Ave, (520) 318-4644, (800) 328-4122, Fax: (520) 325-0055. Gay-friendly B&B in an adobe house with one foot-thick walls and furniture of native lodgepole pine. Near U of A campus.

CASA ALEGRE BED & BREAKFAST INN, 316 E Speedway Blvd, (520) 628-1800, (800) 628-5654, Fax: (520) 792-1880. Distinguished 1915 craftsman-style bungalow, minutes from the University of Arizona and downtown Tucson, has private baths, TV, VCR and a decor reflecting Tucson's history. The Arizona sitting room opens onto a serene patio and pool area. A scrumptious full breakfast is served in the sun room, formal dining room, and on the patio. Shopping and dining are nearby. Gay-friendly.

CASA TIERRA ADOBE BED & BREAKFAST INN, 11155 West Calle Pima, (520) 578-3058 (tel/fax). Gay-friendly bed and breakfast inn in a remote desert setting near the Desert Museum. Great for hiking and birding. Double rooms with private baths, microwave and fridge, outdoor Jacuzzi. Full vegetarian breakfast served.

CATALINA PARK INN, 309 E 1st St, (520) 792-4541, Fax: (520) 792-0838, Reservations: (USA only) (800) 792-4885. Gay-friendly historic B&B inn. Color TV, AC, telephone, private baths. Continental breakfast delivered to your room.

DILLINGER HOUSE BED & BREAKFAST, THE, 927 N 2nd Ave, Tucson, AZ 85705, (520) 622-4306 (Tel/Fax). E-mail: DILNGR@AOL.COM. Gay-owned B&B with increasing gay & lesbian clientele, 2 self-contained guest cottages, private baths, expanded continental breakfast, Jacuzzi. Close to gay venues, museums & shops. Some straight clientele. ♀♂

HOTEL CONGRESS, 311 E Congress, (520) 622-8848, fax: (520) 792-6366. Gay-friendly hotel with cafe & bar. Double rooms with private baths, TV lounge.

MONTECITO HOUSE, PO Box 42352, 85733, (520) 795-7592. My home, not a business Mostly lesbian clientele, some gay men, some straight clientele. One double with private bath, others share. Discussions at breakfast over fresh grapefruit juice from the tree in my yard, RV parking, TV lounge. Open year-round. ♀

NATURAL BED & BREAKFAST HOMESTAY, 3150 E Presidio Rd, (520) 881-4582, Fax: (520) 326-1385. B&B with emphasis on NATURAL: maintenance of natural, non-toxic, non-chemical environment takes precedence over decor & amenities. No central AC, no shoes indoors, no aerosol deodorants, perfumes, cologne. Ceiling fans, private & shared baths, TV lounge, professional massage. ♀♂

TORTUGA ROJA BED & BREAKFAST, 2800 E River Rd, (520) 577-6822, (800) 467-6822. B&B with beautiful mountain views, on a 4-acre cozy retreat in the Santa Catalina Mountain foothills. Minutes to many hiking trails, close to upscale shopping and an easy drive to the University, gay bars and most tourist attractions. A variety of guest quarters offer modern conveniences with private baths. Some accommodations include fireplaces and kitchens. Expanded continental breakfast, pool and spa on premises. Discounts available for extended stays. ♀♂

■ *Bars*
GRADUATE, THE, 23 W University Blvd near Stone, (520) 622-9233. ♂

VENTURE-N, 1239 N 6th Ave, (520) 882-8224. Cruise bar, patio, opens 6am. ♂

■ *Dance Bar/Disco*
AIN'T NOBODY'S BIZNESS,★ (The Biz), 2900 E Broadway, (520) 318-4838. Dance club, no cover, variety of events & specials. ♀

BOOM BOOM'S, 2520 N Oracle Rd, (520) 623-6969. Dance bar, variety of music, game room, Sun BBQ, 70% men. ♀♂

HOURS, 3455 E Grant Rd at Palo Verde, (520) 327-3390. C&W dance bar, patio, 65% women, 35% men. ♀♂

IT'S 'BOUT TIME (IBT'S), 616 N 4th Ave near 5th St, (520) 882-3053. Dance bar, weekly drag shows, patio, college crowd, 75% men. ♂

STONEWALL & EAGLE, 2921 N 1st Ave, (520) 624-8805. C&W dance bar in front, the Eagle drinking bar in rear, 60% men. ♀♂

■ *Cafe*
CUP CAFE, 311 E Congress, at Hotel Congress.

■ *Retail & Bookstores*
ANTIGONE BOOKS, 411 N 4th Ave (520) 792-3715. Women's bookstore with cards, jewelry, music. Large gay men's section, too.

GIRLFRIENDS COFFEE HOUSE AND BOOKSTORE, 3540 N Oracle Rd #126, (520) 888-GIRL (4475). Enjoy our delicious gourmet coffees while you browse our great selection of lesbian books, videos, music, gifts, cards and lesbian-made crafts; or visit our New Age area and have a psychic reading. Tucson's Newest Gathering Place.

TUCSON TRUNK, 5605 E River Rd #131, (520) 529-8309. Card & gift shop with some rainbow items.

■ *Leathers/Piercing*
VENTURE N TO LEATHER, 1239 N 6th Ave (on the patio) at Speedway, (520)) 882-8224. Retail & custom levi-leather & toys for men.

■ *Erotica*
ADULT EXPECTATIONS, 2505 N Stone, (520) 623-8095.

BOOKSTORE SOUTHWEST, 5754 E Speedway, (520) 790-1550.

CAESAR'S ADULT SHOP, 2540 N Oracle (520) 622-9479.

CONTINENTAL, 2655 N Campbell, (520) 327-8402.

EMPRESS VIDEO, 3832 E Speedway, (520) 325-1072.

YUMA

■ *Bars*
TWO THIRTY-TWO CLUB, 232 S 4th Ave, (520) 782-9225. Juke box, small dance floor, covered patio. ♀♂

■ *Erotica*
BARGAIN BOX, 408 E 16th St at Arizona, (520) 782-6742, 24hrs.

ARKANSAS
EUREKA SPRINGS

■ *Accommodations*
ARBOUR GLEN VICTORIAN INN & GUESTHOUSE, 7 Lema, (501) 253-9010. B&B, 50% gay & lesbian clientele. Suites with private bath & modern amenities. Full gourmet breakfast. Lake on premises.

CEDARBERRY B & B INN, 3 King's Hwy,

TORTUGA ROJA
BED & BREAKFAST

2800 EAST RIVER ROAD TUCSON, ARIZONA 85718
(800) 467-6822   (520) 577-6822

---

368 FERRARI GUIDES' GAY TRAVEL A to Z - 18th EDITION

CALIFORNIA

(501) 253-6115, (800) 590-2424. B&B near lake & river, 50% gay & lesbian. Choice of suites, 2 with Jacuzzi. Limited kitchen privileges, full gourmet breakfast.

DAIRY HOLLOW HOUSE, 515 Spring Street, Eureka Springs, AR 74762-3032, (501) 253-7444, (800) 562-8650, Fax: (501) 253-7223. E-mail: 74762.1652@compuserve.com. Gay-friendly Ozark inn, 1 mile from downtown Eureka Springs, with restaurant & shop with books by owners. Rooms & suites with private baths, full breakfast, AC, Jacuzzi. Gay & lesbian following.

GREENWOOD HOLLOW RIDGE, Rte 4, Box 155, (501) 253-5283. B&B with double rooms & apt, Jacuzzi & full breakfast. Guests have CC privileges for golf, tennis. Near lake, Passion Play, country & western shows.

MAPLE LEAF INN B&B, 6 Kingshighway, (800) 372-6542, (501) 253-6876. B&B, private baths, 50% gay & lesbian clientele.

PEABODY HOUSE B&B, 7 Armstrong, (501) 253-5376.

POND MOUNTAIN LODGE & RESORT, Rt 1 Box 50, (501) 253-5877. Reservations only: (800) 583-8043. Gay-friendly B&B resort with stables & cabin. Suites with modern amenities, private Jacuzzi, private bath. Full buffet breakfast, pool on premises. 50% gay & lesbian clientele.

ROCK COTTAGE GARDENS, 10 Eugenia St, (501) 253-8659, (800) 624-6646. B&B, 50% gay & lesbian clientele. Cottages with private baths, full breakfast.

WOODS, THE, 50 Wall St, (501) 253-8281. 3 cottages, Jacuzzis. 50% gay and lesbian, 50% straight clientele.

Women's Accommodations

GOLDEN GATE COTTAGE, Rte 7, Box 182, Eureka Springs, AR 72631-9225, (501) 253-5291. Women-only guesthouse in a tree-shaded, peaceful setting on the lake only ten minutes from Eureka Springs. Cottage rooms with or without kitchenette. Private entrance, color TV, VCR & movie library, AC, ceiling fans, king beds, private baths, outdoor hot tub. Rates: $40-$55 (discounts for longer stays). A walking trail passes between lake and cliffs. Boat marina, with boat rentals, nearby. No children, no pets.

Bars

CENTER ST BAR & GRILLE, 10 Center St, (501) 253-8102. Caribbean & Mexican restaurant & bar. Gay-owned & -operated, live entertainment Fri & Sat.

CHELSEA'S, 10 Mountain St, (501) 253-6723, Gay-friendly pub and restaurant, closed Sun.

Restaurants

AUTUMN BREEZE, Hwy 23 South, 1/4 mile south of the 23/62 intersection, (501) 253-7734. Prime rib, rack of lamb, vegetarian stir fry, chocolate soufflé.

ERMILLO'S, ask locally for address, lunch dinner, Italian home cooking, gay-friendly.

JIM & BRENT'S BISTRO, 173 S Main St, (501) 253-7457. Eclectic American dining.

FAYETTEVILLE

Dance Bar/Disco

RON'S PLACE, 523 W Poplar St, (501) 442-3052. Dance bar 9pm-2am, private club.

Retail & Bookstores

DICKSON ST USED BOOKS, 325 W Dickson St, (501) 442-8182. General used bookstore with women's section.

PASSAGES, 200 W Dixon, (501) 442-5845. Book & gift shop with gay & lesbian books, music & jewelry.

Erotica

CURRY'S VIDEO, 612 N College Ave, (501) 521-0009.

FT SMITH

Dance Bar/Disco

LEGENDS OF ARKANSAS, 917 N A St, (501) 782-4190, Fax: (501) 471-5881. Gay-owned/operated dance club. Thurs-Sun 9pm-5am.

HOT SPRINGS

Dance Bar/Disco

OUR HOUSE, 660 E Grand, (501) 624-6868. Dance & show bar with restaurant, 50% men, 50% women. Closed Sun.

LITTLE ROCK

Accommodations

LITTLE ROCK INN, 601 S Center, (501) 376-8301. Gay-friendly hotel with bar, private baths.

Bars

FIVE-O-ONE AT THE BACKSTREET, ★ 1021 Jessie Rd, next door to Discovery III, (501) 664-2744. Private club, pool tables, dance floor. Sun-Thur 9pm-3am, Fri & Sat 9pm-5am.

PLUM'S, 601 S Center at Little Rock Inn, (501) 376-8301 ext 559. Small dance floor, singers, drag shows, etc.

SILVER DOLLAR, 2710 Asher Ave near Woodrow, (501) 663-9886. Closed Sun, men's night Mon.

Dance Bar/Disco

ANNEX/701 AT BACKSTREET, 1021 Jessie Rd, next door to Discovery III, (501) 664-2744. (Same building as 501 at Backstreet.) DJ weekends, live entertainment Fri & Sat.

DISCOVERY III, ★ 1021 Jessie Rd near River Front, (501) 664-4784. Private club, Thur-Sat 9pm-5am, huge weekend straight crowd.

MISS KITTY'S BACKSTREET, 1021 Jessie Rd, (501) 664-2744. C&W, open 7 nights.

Retail & Bookstores

TWISTED ENTERTAINMENT, 7201 Asher Ave, (501) 568-4262. Cards, leathers, videos, T-shirts.

WOMEN'S PROJECT, 2224 Main St, (501) 372-5113. Book and gift shop, lending library. Many workshops, support groups for lesbians. Monthly coffeehouse, yearly retreat.

OZARKS

Information

GLORP (GAY & LESBIAN OZARK RURAL PEOPLE), (501) 895-4959.

TEXARKANA

Information

ARKANSAS AIDS PROJECT, (501) 773-1994.

Dance Bar/Disco

GIG, THE, 201 East St (Hwy 71 S), Arkansas, (501) 773-6900. Drag shows & name entertainment, hours vary in winter & summer.

CALIFORNIA

WHO TO CALL

For Tour Companies Serving This Destination
See California on page 11

ANAHEIM - ORANGE COUNTY

Accommodations

COUNTRY COMFORT BED & BREAKFAST, 5104 E Valencia Dr, Orange, (714) 532-2802 or Fax: 997-1921. B&B near Disneyland, KnottsBerry, beaches & nightlife. All the comforts of home. Private bath, full breakfast.

ARCATA

Retail & Bookstores

NORTHTOWN BOOKS, 957 H St, (707) 822-2834. General bookstore with gay & lesbian selection.

ATASCADERO

Erotica

DIAMOND ADULT WORLD, 5905 El Camino Real, (805) 462-0404.

BAKERSFIELD

Information

GAY LINE, (805) 328-0729. Info tape & variable live staffing.

FERRARI GUIDES' GAY TRAVEL A to Z - 18th EDITION

CALIFORNIA

Outdoor Getaways for City-Weary Women

Merlyn's Journeys specializes in 3- to 4-day getaways for city-weary women to places of natural beauty (mostly in California) with options like hiking, soaking in hot tubs, swimming or just relaxing by a cozy fire. Organizer Merlyn Storm says she encourages a group atmosphere that is "joyous, nurturing and spontaneous, with a focus on group spirit, fun, learning, adventure and connection." She invites women to "laugh with us, breathe fresh air and travel out to where you can see the stars at night." Massages and yoga classes are optional. Fabulous home-cooked meals are included The more active getaways include horseback riding, sailing and walking journeys. These might be in the ancient forests of Oregon, along the Marin coastline or in Washington State's San Juan Islands. River rafting and horseback riding always take place in California.

Partial List of 1997 Trips

Apr 11-13	Wine Country	Aug 11-15	Sailing-San Juan Isl.
Apr 25-27	Santa Cruz Mtns	Aug 18-22	Hiking Oregon Forests
May 2-4	Gold Country	Aug 29-Sep 1	Point Reyes
May 12-17	Hike Marin Coast	Sep 5-6	Lake Tahoe
Jun 13-15	Carson River Raft	Sep 12-14	Dillon Beach
Jul 18-20	Horseback in Redwoods	Sep 19-20	Gold Country
July 25-27	American River Raft	Sep 26-27	Horseback in Redwoods
Aug 1-3	Camping on Navarro R.	Oct 10-13	Yosemite

Contact **Merlyn's Journeys** at (209) 736-9330, (800) 509-9330, Fax: (209) 736-4651, E-mail: merlyns@goldrush.com.

■ Bars
CASABLANCA, 1030 20th St, (805) 324-1384. 7pm-2am, 7 days.
PADRE HOTEL BAR, 1813 H St, (805) 322-1419. Piano bar, gay-friendly with 20% gay clientele.

■ Dance Bar/Disco
PLACE, THE, 3500 Wilson Rd near Wible (next to KMart), (805) 835-0494. 50% men, 50% women.

■ Erotica
DEJA VU, 1524 Golden State Ave, (805) 322-7300.
WILDCAT BOOKS, 2620 Chester Ave, (805) 324-4383.

BELL GARDENS

■ Erotica
LE SEX SHOPPE, 6816 Eastern Ave, (213) 560-9473, 24hrs.

BERKELEY

■ Accommodations
ELMWOOD HOUSE B&B, 2609 College Ave, (510) 540-5123 (Phone & Fax), (800) 540-3050. B&B 4 blocks from U of CA Berkeley, Elmwood shopping district, mostly straight clientele. Three double rooms, one triple. Continental breakfast & nearby pools.

■ Saunas/Health Clubs
STEAMWORKS, 2107 4th St near Addison, (510) 845-8992, 24hrs.

■ Retail & Bookstores
BOADECIA'S BOOKS, 398 Colusa Ave, Kensington, 1 block outside Berkeley limits, (510) 559-9184, boadbks@norcov.com. Half women's, half gay/lesbian books.
GAIA, 1400 Shattuck Ave, (510) 548-4172. Books, music, jewelry, goddess items, percussion instruments.
GOOD VIBRATIONS, 2504 San Pablo Ave, (510) 841-8986. Toys, books, videos and more for women.
MAMA BEARS CULTURE CENTER, 6536 Telegraph Ave at 66th, Oakland, (510) 428-9684, (800) 643-8629, Fax: (510) 654-2774. A full-service women's bookstore and coffee bar. It's comfortable and spacious. Open every day 10:30am-8pm, including Sundays and holidays. Centrally located 20 minutes from San Francisco. Mail order available.
SHAMBHALA BOOKSELLERS, 2482 Telegraph Ave, (510) 848-8443. Religious & metaphysical books, tapes, some cards & sacred arts.
WEST BERKELEY WOMEN'S BOOKS, 2514 San Pablo Ave, (510) 204-9399. Women's & lesbian titles. Wed-Fri 11am-6pm, Sat 9am-6pm.

CALIFORNIA

BIG BEAR LAKE AREA

■ Accommodations
SMOKETREE RESORT, 40154 Big Bear Blvd, PO Box 2801, Big Bear Lake, (909) 866-2415, (800) 352-8581. Gay-friendly B&B and cabins, set on 1-1/2 acres in the San Bernardino Mtns near Big Bear Lake, a National Forest and ski areas. The main lodge has 5 B&B suites with private baths, fireplaces and color TV. The 25 cabins vary in size from romantic, cozy 2-person accommodations up to a large 14-person abode. We have 2 pools and a Jacuzzi and are planning a meeting/TV lounge. Massage available. Continental breakfast included with B&B.

■ Women's Accommodations
BEAR PAUSE CABIN, 43345 Sheephorn Dr, lower Moonridge area, (619) 754-6747, Fax: (619) 754-8066. Secluded 2-bedroom cabin, 2 miles from Big Bear Lake, with bathroom, microwave, TV, VCR, phone, near hiking, skiing, boating, etc. ♀

BEARY MERRY MANSION, (407) 872-1286, (800) 288-6805 (answers Scott-Powell), Fax: (407) 872-3202. WALK to skiing, sledding, summer water skiing, fishing or para-sailing from your private 2-BR, 1-bath cabin with kitchen, fireplace & sun deck. Men welcome. ♀

BODEGA BAY AREA

■ Accommodations
BODEGA ESTERO BED & BREAKFAST FARM, 17699 Hwy 1, mail: PO Box 362, Bodega, CA 94922, (707) 876-3300, (800) 422-6321. B&B in a geodesic dome house on a sheep, llama & angora goat farm. Innkeepers are spinners, weavers & knitters. Instruction available & garments for sale. 4 rooms with private bathrooms, deck.

CARLSBAD

■ Accommodations
CLOISTERS OF CARLSBAD, THE, 4460 Higland Dr, (619) 720-7577, fax: (619) 720-1231 (use handset). B&B with 2 suites on a hilltop acre estate, panoramic views of the Pacific Ocean, expanded continental breakfast, private baths, color cable TV, VCR, telephone, ceiling fans, video tape library, pool on premises, commitment ceremonies can be arranged. ♀♂

CARSON

■ Erotica
KNIGHT DREAMS, 441 E Carson St #E at Grace, (310) 830-5698. Adult gift shop, books, cards, large selection of gay & lesbian videos.

CATHEDRAL CITY
See Palm Springs/Cathedral City listings

CHICO

■ Information
STONEWALL ALLIANCE COMMUNITY CENTER & AIDS INFO, 341 Broadway, 3rd fl #300, (916) 893-3336. Office: Tues-Fri 4-7pm, Sat noon-4pm. Recorded local info: 893-3338.

■ Bars
COWBOYS SOCIAL CLUB, 477 E 9th Ave, (916) 345-8073. Pool table, TV, hot tub, a bar alternative in a converted house, open evenings, coffee & juice only. ♂

■ Dance Bar/Disco
RASCALS, 900 Cherry St, (916) 893-0900, (916) 894-8809. Dance bar, top 40 & progressive music. ♀♂

CLEARLAKE AREA

■ Accommodations
SEA BREEZE RESORT, 9595 Harbor Dr (Mail: PO Box 653), Glenhaven, (707) 998-3327. Gay-friendly, lakefront resort cottages with full kitchen, color cable TV, AC & private baths. Private beach, lighted pier.

■ Camping & RV
EDGEWATER RESORT, 6420 Soda Bay Rd, Kelseyville, CA 95451, (800) 396-6224, (707) 279-0208, Fax: (707) 279-0138. Women-owned RV resort with cabins, full RV hook-ups & tent sites, clubhouse, general store, laundry facilities.

COMPTCHE

■ Accommodations
WITTWOOD, 8161 Flynn Creek Rd, (707) 937-5486. Gay-friendly retreat with gay female following, shared baths.

CONCORD

■ Erotica
PLEASANT HILL ADULT BOOKSTORE, 2298 Monument (510) 676-2962.

DAVIS

■ Information
UCD WOMEN'S CENTER, North Hall 1st fl, U of California, (916) 752-3372. Mon-Fri 8am-5pm, lesbian support groups, library.

DOWNEY

■ Women's Accommodations
CALIFORNIA INN, 7845 8th St, Downey, CA 90241, (310) 927-1212, Fax: (310) 927-4180.

EL CERRITO

■ Dance Bar/Disco
CLUB SALSA DANCE CLUB, 6401 Stockton, (510) 428-2144. Women's dance nights 2nd Sat. Salsa lessons 7:30pm, dancing 8pm-11pm. Smoke- & alcohol-free. ♀

EL MONTE

■ Bars
SUGAR SHACK, 4101 Arden Dr, (818) 448-6579. ♀ ♂

EL SERENO

■ Dance Bar/Disco
PLUSH PONY, 5261 Alhambra Ave, (213) 224-9488. Latino bar for women, men welcome.

EMERYVILLE

■ Retail & Bookstores
HEADLINES, 5719 Christie Ave in Powell St Plaza, (510) 547-3324. Clothing & gifts.

ESCONDIDO

■ Erotica
F STREET BOOKS, 237 E Grand Ave, (619) 480-6031.

EUREKA

■ Accommodations
ABIGAIL'S ELEGANT VICTORIAN B&B LODGING ACCOMMODATION, 1406 C Street, Eureka, CA 95501, (707) 444-3144, Fax: (707) 442-5594. Gay-friendly Victorian B&B, exclusively non-smoking, full breakfast, Finnish sauna.

CARTER HOUSE VICTORIANS, 301 L St, Historic Old Town, (707) 444-8062, (800) 404-1390. Gay-friendly B&B inn with dinner restaurant. Color TV, private & shared baths & full breakfast.

■ Dance Bar/Disco
CLUB WEST, 535 5th St, (707) 444-2582. Gay Sun evening only. ♂

■ Retail & Bookstores
BOOKLEGGER, 402 2nd St, (707) 445-1344. General bookstore with women's & gay books (used and new).

■ Erotica
PLEASURE CENTER, 2nd & E Sts.

FONTANA

■ Erotica
LIBERTY BOOKS & VIDEO, 15106 Valley Blvd, (909) 357-3421.

MONTANA ADULT BOOKSTORE, 14589 Valley Blvd, (909) 350-4717.

FORESTVILLE
See Russian River

FT BRAGG

■ Retail & Bookstores
WINDSONG BOOKS & RECORDS, 324 N Main, (707) 964-2050. Mostly used books, crafts, large women's section.

FERRARI GUIDES' GAY TRAVEL A to Z - 18th EDITION

CALIFORNIA

FREMONT

Erotica
L'AMOUR SHOPPE, 40555-B Grimmer Blvd, (510) 659-8161, 24hrs.

FRESNO

Information
COMMUNITY INFO & AIDS LINE, (209) 264-AIDS (2437), 8am-5pm or tape. Call for all local gay & lesbian info.

Bars
HI HO CLUB, 4538 E Belmont Ave, (209) 251-5972.

Dance Bar/Disco
EL SOMBRERO, 3848 E Belmont Ave, (209) 442-1818.
EXPRESS, THE,★ 708 N Blackstone Ave between Belmont and Olive, (209) 233-1791. Video bar, dance bar, piano bar, patio bar.
PALACE SALOON, 4030 E Belmont Ave near 11th, (209) 264-8283. Dance & show bar, 70% women, 30% men.
RED LANTERN, 4618 E Belmont Ave near Maple, (209) 251-5898. Knights of Malta home bar.

Restaurants
EXPRESS CAFE, 708 N Blackstone Ave, same building as Fresno Express men's bar. (209) 233-1791. Mon-Sat dinner 6pm-9pm, Sun brunch 10am-3pm.

Retail & Bookstores
VALLEY WOMEN'S BOOKS & GIFTS, 1118 N Fulton, (209) 233-3600. Women's, lesbian & gay books.

Erotica
ONLY FOR YOU, 1460 N Van Ness Ave, (209) 498-0284.
WILDCAT ENTERPRISE, 1535 Fresno St at G St, (209) 237-4525.

GOLD COUNTRY - SIERRA FOOTHILLS

Accommodations
RANCHO CICADA, PO Box 225, Plymouth, CA, 95669, (209) 245-4841. Clothing-optional camping resort with cabins. Tents on raised platforms, separate men/women restroom facilities with hot showers, wash basins & flush toilets. Be discreet when contacting resort.

Casa Laguna Bed & Breakfast Inn
2510 S. Coast Hwy
Laguna Beach
CA 92651
(800) 233-0449

GRASS VALLEY

Women's Accommodations
MANZANITA COTTAGE, 13571 Rhoda Rd, Grass Valley, CA 95945, (916) 272-3531 or (916) 477-2381 (message). Women's cottage & healing center on 3 acres, 1 hour from Sacramento. Fully equipped cottage includes private bath, woodstove, TV/VCR, skylight, hot tub & gas BBQ.

GUALALA

Retail & Bookstores
GUALALA BOOKS, 39145 S Hwy 1, (707) 884-4255. General bookstore with gay, lesbian and feminist sections.

GUERNEVILLE
See Russian River

HAYWARD

Bars
DRIFTWOOD LOUNGE, 22170 Mission Blvd, (510) 581-2050. DJ some weekends.
RUMORS, 22554 Main St, (510) 733-2334.

Dance Bar/Disco
RAINBOW ROOM, 21859 Mission Blvd, (510) 582-8078. DJ Fri & Sat.
TURF CLUB,★ 22517 Mission Blvd, (510) 881-9877. 70% men, summer BBQ's, patio.

Erotica
L'AMOUR SHOPPE, 22553 Main St, (510) 886-7777.
VERY VIDEO, 22523 Mission Blvd, (510) 881-0185.

IDYLLWILD

Accommodations
FERN VILLAGE CHALETS, 54821 N Circle Dr, PO Box 886, (909) 659-2869. Gay-friendly mountain resort motel in a quiet glen on the banks of Strawberry Creek. Treetop balconies, all private baths.
PINE COVE INN, THE, PO Box 2181, (909) 659-5033, Fax: (909) 659-5034. B&B, 50% gay & lesbian clientele, private baths.
WILKUM INN BED & BREAKFAST, 26770 Hwy 243, PO Box 1115, (909) 659-4087, (800) 659-4086. Gay-friendly B&B with a gay & lesbian following, private & shared baths, expanded continental breakfast.

IRVINE

Dance Bar/Disco
METROPOLIS, 4255 Campus Dr, (714) 751-1129. Sun dance party.

JULIAN

Accommodations
LEELIN WIKIUP B&B, PO Box 2363, Julian, CA 92036, (619) 765-1890, (800) 6 WIKIUP (694-5487). Gay-friendly B&B home with pet llamas on premises. 3 rooms, private baths. 1/2-day lunch llama treks available for guests.

LAGUNA BEACH

Accommodations
CASA LAGUNA BED & BREAKFAST INN, 2510 South Coast Hwy, (714) 494-2996, (800) 233-0449, Fax: (714) 494-5009. Gay-friendly B&B country inn located in Southern California's gay capital. 60 miles south of LA and 30 miles south of Disneyland, Laguna boasts scenic shorelines and crystal white beaches. The Casa offers unique accommodations in a tropical hillside setting, overlooking the Pacific Ocean. Pool and sun decks, 21 rooms, suites and cottages with kitchens. Expanded continental breakfast. Near gay bars, restaurants, entertainment.

COAST INN, 1401 S Coast Hwy, (714) 494-7588, (800) 653-2697, Fax: (714) 494-1735. 100% gay & lesbian oceanfront resort hotel with private beach, restaurant, disco, Coast Inn Cafe and the famous Boom Boom Room. One of the oldest gay establishments in the country with 5 separate businesses within a 17,000 sq. ft. location. Great weather and great views. Variety of rooms with cable color TV, private baths and sunning decks. The hotel is 15 minutes from the Orange County Airport and 2 minutes from the West Street gay beach, 15 minutes from San Onofre nude beach and 5 miles from Dana Point Harbor.

Beaches
WEST ST BEACH, opposite West St.

Bars
MAIN STREET, 1460 S Coast Hwy near Mountain, (714) 494-0056. Piano bar, 90% men, 10% women.
VICTOR VICTORIA'S, 1305 S Coast Hwy, (714) 376-8809. Bar & restaurant, piano bar, Sun brunch. 50% men & 50% women.

Dance Bar/Disco
BOOM BOOM ROOM,★ 1401 S Coast Hwy (PCH) at the Coast Inn Hotel, (714) 494-7588. Dance bar, go go dancers, theme nights.

Fitness Centers
LAGUNA HEALTH CLUB, 870 Glenneyre, (714) 494-9314. Gym, free weights.

Restaurants
COTTAGE RESTAURANT, THE, 308 N Coast Hwy, (714) 494-3023. Breakfast, lunch, dinner in a romantic setting. Sunday brunch on patio, reservations accepted.
SERRA'S BAR & GRILL, (714) 497-2566. Mediterranean cuisine, opens at 5pm.
SHAME ON THE MOON, 1462 S Coast Hwy. Bar & restaurant.
ZINC CAFE & MARKET, 350 Ocean Ave, (714) 494-2791, 494-6302. Gourmet breakfast & lunch. Dinner during the summer only.

CALIFORNIA

UNITED STATES

Retail & Bookstores
A DIFFERENT DRUMMER BOOKSHOPPE, 1294-C South Coast Hwy, (714) 497-0471. Gay and lesbian bookstore.
JEWELRY BY PONCE, 1417 S Coast Hwy, (714) 497-4154, (800) 969-7464. Gay & lesbian jewelry, watches & gifts.
UPCHURCH-BROWN BOOKSELLERS, 384 Forest Ave #15, near Coast Hwy, (714) 497-8373. General bookstore with strong gay & lesbian section.

Erotica
GAY MART, 168 Mountain. Toys, lubes, videos, t-shirts & cards.

LAGUNITAS

Cafe
LAGUNITAS SWING CAFE, 7282 Sir Francis Drake Blvd, (415) 488-1689. Women's nights Fri 6pm-11pm, soups, salads, sandwiches, espresso smoothies.

LAKE ARROWHEAD

Accommodations
SPRING OAKS B&B, PO Box 2918 (mail), 2465 Spring Oak Dr, (909) 867-7797, (800) 867-9636. Gay-friendly adult mountain retreat with guided hikes, workshops & concerts. Ceiling fans, private & shared baths, full breakfast, spa & massage.

LAKE TAHOE AREA

Accommodations
BAVARIAN HOUSE, PO Box 624507, S Lake Tahoe, 96154, (800) 431-4411, (916) 544-4411. Guesthouse with rustic, mountain decor 4 blocks from ski lift, 1 mile from Tahoe casino nightlife. Two large decks, king-sized bed, TV, VCR, private bath. Greatroom has river rock fireplace and vaulted, beamed ceiling. Separate 3-bedroom, 2-bath chalet for couples. ♀♂
INN ESSENCE, 865 Lake Tahoe Blvd, South Lake Tahoe, (800) 57 TAHOE, (916) 577-0339, (916) 577-0118. B&B guesthouse with color cable TV, VCR, telephone, Jacuzzi, shared bath. Full gourmet breakfast. ♀♂
LAKESIDE B 'N B TAHOE, Box 1756, Crystal Bay, NV (702) 831-8281, Fax: (702) 831-7329. Lakeside B&B. Private & shared baths, color TV, VCR, Jacuzzi, full breakfast.
NYVADA B & B, Box 6835, Stateline, NV, (702) 588-5559. B&B. Single rooms & apartment, TV in living room, weights, Jacuzzi, massage, full breakfast. ♀♂
SIERRAWOOD GUEST HOUSE, PO Box 11194 Tahoe Paradise, (916) 577-6073, (800) 700-3802. Guesthouse. Cozy, rustic rooms with private & shared baths, fireplace, TV lounge, hot tub, nearby lake. Full breakfast & dinner. ♀♂

Women's Accommodations
HOLLY'S, PO Box 13197, South Lake Tahoe, CA 96151, (916) 544-7040, (800) 745-7041, E-mail: hollys@oakweb.com. Vacation place for women, 2 blocks to lake, 2 miles to casinos & near all outdoor recreation. Guest rooms & cabins with private baths, kitchens, color TV/VCR, fireplaces, lofts, skylights & ceiling fans. Recreation/conference room, video library, free bikes, volleyball, barbecue grills, ping pong & horseshoes. ♀

Dance Bar/Disco
FACES, 270 Kingsbury Grade, Stateline, NV (South Lake Tahoe), (702) 588-2333. Hi-energy dance bar, DJ weekends, limited gaming, Mon-Wed from 9pm, Thurs-Sun from 5pm. ♀♂

LANCASTER

Dance Bar/Disco
BACKDOOR, 1255 W Ave I, (805) 945-2566. C&W nights Wed, DJ Fri & Sun, 50% men, 50% women. ♀♂

LEGGETT

Accommodations
BELL GLEN B&B IN THE REDWOODS & EEL RIVER REDWOODS HOSTEL, 70400 Old Redwood Hwy 101, (707) 925-6425, (800) 500-6464. Gay-friendly cottages & European-style youth hostel. B&B offers private baths, expanded continental breakfast. British-style pub, 24-hour sauna, swimming hole on premises.

LONG BEACH

Information
BEING ALIVE (AIDS INFO), 994 Redondo Ave, (562) 434-9022. Hours change. AIDS support, referral, info & drop-in.
CENTER LONG BEACH, THE, 2017 E 4th St, (562) 434-4455. 9am-10pm (Sat 10am-6pm, Sun 3pm-9pm).

Bars
BRIT, 1744 E Broadway near Hermosa, (562) 432-9742. ♂
BROADWAY, THE, 1100 E Broadway at Cerritos, (562) 432-3646. ♂
CLUB 5211 (INSPIRATION), 5211 Atlantic Ave near 52nd, (562) 428-5545. Open 24hrs Fri-Sun. ♂
CLUB BROADWAY, 3348 E Broadway, (562) 438-7700. Jukebox & pool table, 20% men, 80% women. ♂
CREST, THE, 5935 Cherry Ave, (562) 423-6650.
FALCON, 1435 E Broadway at Falcon, (562) 432-4146. ♂
MINESHAFT, ★ 1720 E Broadway near Gaviota, (562) 436-2433. DJ nightly, Tues popular Shaft night. ♂
PISTONS, 2020 E Artesia Blvd, (562) 422-1928.
SILVER FOX, 411 Redondo Ave near 4th St, (562) 439-6343. Video bar & karaoke, 30ish crowd, cruise bar. ♂
STYX, 5823 Atlantic Ave near South St, (562) 422-5997. Patio. ♂
SWEETWATER SALOON, 1201 E Broadway at Orange, (562) 432-7044. Videos. ♂
WHISTLE STOP, 5873 N Atlantic Ave near 59th, (562) 422-7927. 50% men, 50% women, pool table. ♂

Dance Bar/Disco
CLUB 740, 740 E Broadway at Alamitos, (562) 437-7705. Latin high energy & house music, 30% women. ♂
EXECUTIVE SUITE, ★ 3428 E Pacific Coast Hwy at traffic circle, (562) 597-3884. Women's dance bar open 7 days. Men's night Mon. ♀
FLOYD'S, ★ 2913 E Anaheim St near Gladys, (562) 433-9251. Mostly men except Fridays. Popular Sun BBQ, patio. Closed Mon. ♂
QUE SERA SERA, 1923 E 7th St near Cherry, (562) 599-6170. Live bands. ♀
RIPPLES, ★ 5101 E Ocean Blvd at Granada, (562) 433-0357. Videos, patio, Sun BBQ buffet. ♂

Saunas/Health Clubs
THIRTEEN-FIFTY WEST CLUB, 510 W Anaheim St at Neptune, Wilmington, (562) 830-4784. Private club, gym, sun deck, 24hrs.

Restaurants
FUNNEL & HOPS, 1800 E Broadway, (562) 590-8773. Piano bar & restaurant, deli-style dining, fine dining in evening. ♂
OMELETTE INN, 108 W 3rd St, (562) 437-5625. Breakfast & lunch.
TWO UMBRELLAS CAFE, 1538 E Broadway, (562) 435-7364. Breakfast & lunch.
WONG'S ON BROADWAY, 1506 E Broadway, (562) 432-0816. Chinese cuisine, gay-friendly.

Retail & Bookstores
BY THE BOOK, 2501 E Broadway, (562) 434-2220. Gay & lesbian bookstore.
DODD'S BOOKS, 4818 E 2nd St near St Joseph's, (562) 438-9948. General bookstore with gay & lesbian section.
HOT STUFF, 2121 E Broadway, (562) 433-0692. Cards & gifts, lubricants, adult novelties.
PEARLS BOOKSELLERS, 224 Redondo Ave, (562) 438-8875. Women's bookstore with men's section & 3rd-world women's crafts.

Leathers/Piercing
CRYPT ON BROADWAY, THE 1712 E Broadway, (562) 983-6560. Safe-sex toys, magazines, cards, gifts, sportswear, leather Fri, Sat 11am-1am.

Erotica
SOUTH SEAS ADULT BOOKS, 1567 W Pacific Coast Hwy, (562) 432-0593.

CALIFORNIA

LOS ANGELES INTRO

Information

AIDS INFO, (213) 876-2437. AIDS project LA (ALPA) (213) 962-1600. Being Alive (213) 667-3262. Shanti (213) 962-8197.

BI-LINE, BI-SOCIAL CENTER, PAN-SOCIAL CENTER, (213) 873-3700 or (818) 989-3700 (24hrs), For all ages, races, sexual orientation & gender identities.

LA GAY & LESBIAN COMMUNITY SERVICES CENTER, 1625 N Schrader Blvd, Los Angeles, (213) 993-7400.

TRIKONE, (408) 270-8776. South Asian gay groups, meets monthly, publishes quarterly magazine. Write for details: PO Box 21354, San Jose CA 95151.

WOMEN'S CENTERS, Los Angeles Metro list.

WOMEN'S REFERRAL SERVICE, (818) 995-6646. Mon-Fri 9am-5pm referrals to women professionals.

Accommodations

CARITAS BED & BREAKFAST NETWORK, (800) CARITAS, (312) 857-0801, Fax: (312) 857-0805. B&B, home-stay accommodations service. *Member: IGTA*

Dance Bar/Disco

DEDE'S WOMEN'S DANCE CLUB, (310) 433-1470. Scheduled women's dance parties. Call Hotline for current schedule & location.

FUEL, (310) 626-5659. Women's nightclub at rotating locations in LA area. Call hotline for schedule.

KLUB BANSHEE, Hotlines: (310) 288-1601, (310) 281-7358. Upscale hi-energy women's dance parties, call for location.

Retail & Bookstores

BOOKSTORES (GAY & LESBIAN), See West Hollywood.

LA HOLLYWOOD

Information

WOMEN's RESOURCES, (213) 993-7400. Housed in the Gay & Lesbian Center.

Accommodations

HOLLYWOOD CELEBRITY HOTEL, 1775 Orchid Ave, (213) 850-6464, (800) 222-7017, in CA (800) 222-7090. Gay-friendly hotel, private baths.

Bars

FAULTLINE,★ 4216 Melrose at Vermont, (213) 660-0889. Male dancers, progressive music, patio, Tues-Fri from 4pm, Sat, Sun from 2pm.

MUGI, 5221 Hollywood Blvd, (213) 462-2039. Gay Asian bar, unverifiable spring '97.

SPOTLIGHT CLUB, 1601 N Cahuenga Blvd at Selma, (213) 467-2425.

STUDY, 1723 N Western Ave near Hollywd Blvd, (213) 464-9551.

Dance Bar/Disco

ARENA, 6655 Santa Monica Blvd, (213) 462-1742.

CIRCUS DISCO, 6655 Santa Monica Blvd, (213) 462-1291. Tues & Fri only.

CLUB TEMPO, 5520 Santa Monica Blvd near Western. (213) 466-1094. Largest Latino dance club in Southern California. 2 floors, live bands. After hours Fri & Sat on rooftop deck.

LA PLAZA, 739 La Brea Ave, (213) 939-0703. 8pm-2am, 7 days, Mon women's night, drag shows nightly 10:15pm & midnight.

PROBE, 836 N Highland Ave near Willoughby, (213) 461-8301. Different format nightly, call for gay nights.

TEMPLE, 3701 Wilshire Blvd, (213) 243-5221. Call for schedule of gay nights.

Saunas/Health Clubs

FLEX COMPLEX, 4424 Melrose Ave near freeway, (213) 663-5858. Health club with full gym & pool.

HOLLYWOOD SPA, 1650 Ivar Ave near Hollywood & Vine, (800) SPA-CLUB, (213) 463-5169. 24-hr cafe, video rooms, gym, steam, sauna, Jacuzzi, no membership fee, Visa, MC, ATM, three floors of sight and sound. We play safely.

M B CLUB, THE, 4550 Melrose Ave, (213) 669-9899. NOT a health club. Men's private all-night club. Mon-Fri 8pm-4am. Sat & Sun 4pm-5am.

MEATRACK, 4621 Sta Monica Blvd near Vermont, (213) 669-9811. NOT a health club. Men's private all-night club, Sun-Thur 9pm-4am, Fri-Sat 9pm-5am.

VORTEX, THE, 1090 Lillian Way, (213) 465-0188. Not a health club. Private men's club, late nights 7 days.

Fitness Centers

HOLLYWOOD GYM, 1551 N La Brea, (213) 845-1420. 24hrs.

Restaurants

MELROSE CANTINA, 7164 Melrose Ave, (213) 937-7788. Mexican, gay-friendly.

OFF VINE, 6263 Leland Way, (213) 962-1900. Casual continental cuisine.

Erotica

CASANOVA'S EAST, 1626-1/2 Cahuenga Blvd, (213) 465-9435.

LE SEX SHOPPE, 6315-1/2 Hollywood Blvd, (213) 464-9435. Leather items.

STAN'S VIDEO & ADULT BOOKS, 1117 N Western Ave, (213) 467-1640.

LA METRO

Bars

CALIFORNIA DE NOCHE, 7810 Santa Fe, Huntington Park, (213) 581-7646.

HORIZON, Washington Blvd near 5th Ave. Cruise bar. Univerifiable spring '97.

REDS BAR, 2218 E 1st St, (213) 263-2995. Fri & Sat dancing.

Dance Bar/Disco

CATCH ONE DISCO, 4067 W Pico Blvd near Norton, (213) 734-8849 or 737-1159. Male & female exotic dancers, jazz, blues, 9pm-4am Fri & Sat, 9pm-3am Sun.

JEWEL'S ROOM, 4067 W Pico Blvd, downstairs from Catch One Disco, (213) 734-8849. Show bar & lounge, 50% men, 50% women, 3pm-2am daily. Security parking.

SCORE, 107 W 4th St near Main, (213) 625-7382. DJ Fri-Sun.

Saunas/Health Clubs

MIDTOWNE SPA, 615 S Kohler St near 6th, (213) 680-1838. Private club, 24hrs, JO shows.

LA SILVERLAKE

Bars

CASITA DEL CAMPO, 1920 Hyperion Ave, (213) 662-4255. Restaurant & bar, Mexican cuisine.

COBALT CANTINA, 4326 Sunset Blvd, (213) 953-9991. Dining room with patio, full bar. Cal-Mex cuisine, some straight clientele. Popular with women especially for women's Wednesday.

CUFFS, 1941 Hyperion Ave near De Longpre, (213) 660-2649. After hours Thurs-Sat.

DETOUR, 1087 Manzanita St near Sunset, (213) 664-1189.

GAUNTLET II,★ 4219 Sta Monica Blvd near Manzanita, (213) 669-9472.

IN TOUCH, 2538 Hyperion Ave near Griffith Park Blvd, (213) 661-4233. Bar & restaurant. Name to change in '97.

LITTLE JOY, 1477 Sunset Blvd at Portia, (213) 250-3417.

MR MIKE'S, 3172 Los Feliz Blvd near Glenfeliz, (213) 669-9640. Piano bar.

SILVERLAKE LOUNGE, 2906 Sunset Blvd, (213) 663-9636. Salsa DJ nightly, Latino bar.

Dance Bar/Disco

HYPERION, THE, 2810 Hyperion Ave near Rowena, (213) 660-1503. After hours weekends.

PLAY SAFE
ALWAYS
OPEN
WE NEVER CLOSE
toll free
800 SPA CLUB
The HOLLYWOOD Spa
two locations
1650 Ivar, Downtown Hollywood
5636 Vineland, North Hollywood

CALIFORNIA

LE BAR, 2375 Glendale Blvd near Brier, (213) 660-7595. Salsa, 75% men.
LE BARCITO, 3909 Sunset Blvd, (213) 644-3515.
SALSA CON CLASE, (818) 576-0720 or (818) 282-0330. Dance party, live bands, DJ, salsa lessons, male & female dancers. Usually 1st, 3rd & last Sat of month at Rudolpho's, 2500 Riverside Dr. Call hotline for schedule.

■ Saunas/Health Clubs
BASIC PLUMBING, 1924 Hyperion Ave, (213) 953-6731. Not a health club. Private men's club, TV lounge, films, patio area, 8pm-5am (Sat, Sun noon-5am).
NEW KING OF HEARTS (KOH), 1800 Hyperion Ave at Fountain, (213) 661-9417. NOT a health club. Private men's all-night club, from 8pm, Wed 7pm (underwear-only nite), Sun from 3pm.

■ Restaurants
CREST COFFEESHOP, 3725 Sunset Blvd at Lucile, (213) 660-3645.
ZEN RESTAURANT, 2609 Hyperion Ave, (213) 665-2929. Japanese restaurant & sushi bar, many gays on weekends.

■ Erotica
CIRCUS OF BOOKS, 4001 Sunset Blvd at Sanborne, (213) 666-1304, 7 days. Thousands of adult videos as low as $5.95. 24hrs Fri & Sat.

LA VALLEY

■ Bars
BULLET, 10522 Burbank Blvd near Cahuenga Blvd, (818) 760-9563. The only leather bar in the valley. Patio.
GOLD 9, 13625 Moorpark near Woodman, Sherman Oaks, (818) 986-0285.
JOX, 10721 Burbank Blvd near Denny, North Hollywood, (818) 760-9031. Male dancers.
MAG LOUNGE, 5248 Van Nuys Blvd, Sherman Oaks, (818) 981-6693.

OASIS, 11916 Ventura Blvd Studio City, (818) 980-4811. Piano bar.
OXWOOD INN, 13713 Oxnard St near Woodman, Van Nuys, (818) 997-9666. Friendliest bar in the Valley. Cocktails, dancing, pool, darts, DJ on weekends. Open Mon-Thur 3pm-2am, Fri-Sun 2pm-2am.
QUEEN MARY, 12449 Ventura Blvd near Whitsett, Studio City, (818) 506-5619. Show bar, mainly transvestite crowd in the back bar. 50% straight clientele.
VENTURE INN, 11938 Ventura Blvd, Studio City, (818) 769-5400. Bar & restaurant, 50% men, 50% women, Sun brunch.

■ Dance Bar/Disco
APACHE TERRITORY,★ 11608 Ventura, Studio City, (818) 506-0404. High energy dance nights, retro nights, 3pm-2am daily. Gay owned and operated.
ESCAPADES, 10437 Burbank Blvd at Strohm, North Hollywood, (818) 508-7008. 50% men, 50% women, more sophisticated clientele.
INCOGNITO VALLEY, 7026 Reseda Blvd, Reseda, (818) 996-2976. Video dance bar, 70% men, women welcome.
LODGE, 4923 Lankershim Blvd at Morrison, North Hollywood, (818) 769-7722. Different venue each night, call first.
OILCAN HARRY'S, 11502 Ventura Blvd at Berry, Studio City, (818) 760-9749. C&W dance bar Tues-Sat, 95% men.
RAWHIDE, 10937 Burbank Blvd near Vineland, North Hollywood, (818) 760-9798. C&W dance bar, ten-ft video screen, 7 pool tables, dart boards & live music.
RUMORS, 10622 Magnolia Blvd near Cahuenga, North Hollywood, (818) 506-9651. DJ weekends, Mon-Thurs 6pm-2am, Fri-Sat 3pm-2am, Sun 12pm-2am, men welcome.

■ Saunas/Health Clubs
NORTH HOLLYWOOD SPA, 5636 Vineland Ave near Burbank Blvd, North Hollywood, (800) SPA-CLUB, (818) 760-6969. 24-hr cafe, video rooms, gym, steam, sauna, Jacuzzi, sun deck, game room, no membership fee, Visa, MC, ATM. We play safely. See ad on page 375.
ROMAN HOLIDAY, 14435 Victory Blvd near Van Nuys Blvd, Van Nuys, (818) 780-1320 or (818) 997-9905. 24hrs.

■ Restaurants
OUTTAKE CAFE, Ventura Blvd & Laurel Canyon, Studio City.
VENTURE INN, 11938 Ventura Blvd, at Venture Inn bar, Studio City. Sun brunch.

■ Erotica
DIAMOND ADULT WORLD, 6406 Van Nuys Blvd, near Victory, (818) 997-3665.
LE SEX SHOPPE, 12323 Ventura Blvd, Studio City (818) 760-9352.

LE SEX SHOPPE, 4877 Lankershim Blvd, North Hollywood, (818) 760-9529.
LE SEX SHOPPE, 21625 Sherman Way, Canoga Park, (818) 992-9801.
LE SEX SHOPPE, 4539 Van Nuys Blvd, Sherman Oaks, (818) 501-9609.
TWISTED VIDEO, 10530 Burbank Blvd, North Hollywood, (818) 508-0559.
VIDEO & STUFF, 11612 Ventura Blvd, Studio City, (818) 761-3162.

LA WEST HOLLYWOOD

■ Information
JUNE MAZER LESBIAN COLLECTION, 626 N. Robertson Blvd. (2nd Floor), (310) 659-2478. Sun 12-4pm, Tues 11am-3pm, Wed 6-9pm & by appointment.
SOUTHERN CALIFORNIA WOMEN FOR UNDERSTANDING, (805) 644-7298.

■ Accommodations
GROVE GUEST HOUSE, THE, 1325 N Orange Grove Ave, (213) 876-7778, Fax: (213) 876-3170. Luxurious 1-bedroom home in quiet historical district. Full kitchen (stocked), cable TV, VCR, video tape library, gas BBQ, pool & spa.
HOLLOWAY MOTEL, 8465 Santa Monica Blvd, (213) 654-2454. Centrally-located motel with some straight clientele. Variety of rooms with color TV, AC, telephones, maid service & private baths. Walking distance to most attractions in the area and 30 minutes to major southern CA attractions. **A comfortable and convenient place to stay while in the LA area.**
LE MONTROSE SUITE HOTEL DE GRAN LUXE, 900 Hammond St, (310) 855-1115, (800) 776-0666, Fax: (310) 657-9192. Gay-friendly, European-style hotel with restaurant. Suites with modern conveniences, fireplaces, & refrigerators. Pool, Jacuzzi, video library, free bikes & free tennis.
LE PARC, 733 N West Knoll, (310) 855-8888, Reservations USA only: (800) 578-4837, Fax: (310) 659-5230. Hotel with restaurant & bar, mainly straight clientele. Suites with color cable TV, AC, telephone, kitchen & refrigerator. Gym, Jacuzzi, sauna, massage & pool on premises.
LE REVE HOTEL, 8822 Cynthia St, (310) 854-1114, (800) 835-7997, fax: (310) 657-2623. Gay-friendly boutique hotel, one block north of Santa Monica Blvd, one block south of Sunset Strip and walking distance to most gay bars. Beautiful rooftop pool and spa, room service, and well-appointed junior suites with fireplaces, multi-line telephones, refrigerators, private baths and balconies.
RAMADA HOTEL WEST HOLLYWOOD, 8585 Santa Monica Blvd, (310) 652-6400, (800) 845-8585, Fax: (310) 652-2135. Hotel with restaurant, bar & clothing shop, rooms & suites with private baths, color cable TV, AC, pool on premises. Located in the center of West Hollywood, within walking distance

---

RAMADA
West Hollywood

(800) 845-8585

CALIFORNIA

of gay bars, restaurants, shops and entertainment, 50% gay and lesbian clientele.

SAHARAN MOTOR HOTEL, 7212 Sunset Blvd, (213) 874-6700, Fax: (213) 874-5163. Motel, mostly straight clientele with gay male following. Variety of rooms with modern conveniences, private baths.

SAN VICENTE INN, 845 N San Vicente Blvd, (310) 854-6915, Fax: (310) 289-5929. Centrally located B&B inn. Color TV, AC, telephone, refrigerator, private & shared baths. Expanded continental breakfast, pool on premises.

WEST HOLLYWOOD SUITES, PO Box 691309, West Hollywood, 90069-9309, (310) 652-9600, (800) GAY-0069, Fax: (310) 652-5454. Call between 9AM-9PM PST, fax 24 hours. Small deluxe all-suite hotel in the heart of West Hollywood. Rooftop swimming pool & spa.

■ Bars

GOLD COAST, 8228 Santa Monica Blvd, (213) 656-4879. DJ nightly.

HUNTER'S, 7511 Santa Monica Blvd near Vista, (213) 850-9428.

LA PLAZA, 739 N LaBrea Ave near Melrose, (213) 939-0703. Show bar.

LUNA PARK, 665 N Robertson Blvd, (310) 652-0611. Gay-friendly bar with cabaret & restaurant, live bands

MOTHER LODE, 8944 Santa Monica Blvd near Robertson, (310) 659-9700. Best nite Sun beer bust.

MR. D'S, 2917 Beverly Blvd, (213) 721-3403.

NUMBERS, 8029 Sunset Blvd. Classy bar & restaurant, 80% men, 20% women.

RAFTERS, 7994 Santa Monica Blvd at Laurel, (213) 654-0396.

REVOLVER,★ 8851 Santa Monica Blvd at Larrabee, (310) 550-8851. Video bar, after hours weekends, variety of videos.

SEVEN SEVEN-O-TWO SM CLUB, 7702 Santa Monica Blvd, (213) 654-3336. DJ nightly, open 24 hrs Fri & Sat (not an S&M club).

SPIKE, 7746 Santa Monica Blvd at Genesee, (213) 656-9343. After hours Fri & Sat.

TRUNKS, 8809 Santa Monica Blvd near Larrabee, (310) 652-1015.

■ Dance Bar/Disco

AXIS, 652 La Peer Dr near Santa Monica, (310) 659-0471. Different venues every night, call for current schedule.

CHERRY, 657 N Robertson Blvd, above Love Lounge, (213) 896-9099. Fri night, new wave rock and alternative music from 9pm.

CLUB 7969, 7969 Santa Monica Blvd near Laurel, (213) 654-0280. Mon & Thurs drag revue, Tues: Michelle's xxx revues, call for schedule, Thurs & Sat: Hollywood Men male exotic dancers, Sun: retro alternative new wave dance club.

DIETRICHS, (213) 782-1059. Women's dance party Fri & Sat at rotating locations. Call hotline for schedule.

ESCANDALO, at Axis, 652 LaPeer Dr, (213) 882-4139. Latino dance night Thurs with salsa and old-school music.

GIRL BAR,★ women's dance party extravaganza: Fri & Sat at Axis, 652 LaPeer Dr. Sat at the Love Lounge, 657 N Robertson Blvd.

LOVE LOUNGE, different venues nightly, ask locally for exact schedule.

MICKEY'S,★ 8857 Santa Monica Blvd, (310) 657-1176. Dance bar, occasional videos, lunches, patio.

PALMS, THE,★ 8572 Santa Monica Blvd, (310) 652-6188. Dance bar, mostly women, gay men welcome. Patio, Sunday buffet.

RAGE,★ 8911 Santa Monica Blvd near Hilldale, (310) 652-7055. Video dance bar & restaurant.

■ Cafe

BUZZ COFFEE, 8200 Santa Monica Blvd, (213) 656-7460.

■ Saunas/Health Clubs

MELROSE BATHS, 7269 Melrose Ave near Poinsettia, (213) 937-2122, 24hrs.

ZONE, THE, 1037 N Sycamore, (213) 464-8881. Private members only men's club, young guys, 24hrs. JO to group action, very, very hot.

■ Restaurants

ABBEY, THE, 692 N Robertson Blvd, (310) 289-8410. Gay-owned and -operated.

BENVENUTO CAFE, 8512 Santa Monica Blvd, (310) 659-8635. Pasta, pizza, cappuccino. Delivery. Large gay & lesbian following.

CAFE D'ETOILE, 8941-1/2 Santa Monica Blvd, (310) 278-1011. Continental cuisine.

CHECCA RESTAURANT & NIGHTCLUB, 7323 Santa Monica Blvd, (213) 850-7471. French & Italian cuisine. Women's dance nights Fri & Sun in the nightclub.

FIGS, 7929 Santa Monica Blvd, (213) 654-0780. Home cooking, gay-friendly.

FRENCH QUARTER AT FRENCH MARKET, 7985 Santa Monica Blvd at Laurel, (213) 654-0898. Patio-style continental cuisine.

HEIGHTS CAFE, THE, 1118 N Crescent

WEST HOLLYWOOD CALIFORNIA

UNIVERSAL STUDIOS HOLLYWOOD • SUNSET STRIP • REVOLVER • MICKY'S • MOTHER LODE • AXIS • ABC • CBS • BILLBOARD LIVE • SPAGO • PARAMOUNT STUDIOS • CAFE LUNA • PACIFIC DESIGN CENTER • SANTA MONICA BLVD. • RODEO DRIVE • HOUSE OF BLUES • BEVERLY CENTER • PARADISE GRILL • ORSO • RAGE • ARENA • HOLLYWOOD BOWL • JACKSON'S

(800) 776-0666

MEMBER **IGTA** INTERNATIONAL • GAY • TRAVEL • ASSOCIATION

WE RUN IN VERY EXCLUSIVE CIRCLES

Le Montrose is nestled on a quiet lane just below the Sunset Strip. A stone's throw from Beverly Hills. Closest hotel to West Hollywood's hot spots.

128 charming suites, some with kitchenettes, each featuring color TV's and VCR's, individual air conditioning, multi-line telephones with voice mail, fireplace, private balcony, twice daily maid service.

Delightful private restaurant, rooftop pool & jacuzzi, lighted free tennis court, health club, tennis pro, private trainer on staff, bicycles, jogging, non-smoking, and handicapped rooms, meeting facilities, suite service. Bilingual staff, currency exchange. In-suite movies, fax machines, Nintendo.

le montrose
SUITE HOTEL DE GRAN LUXE

Internet Address: http://www.travelweb.com
Internet http://www.travel2000.com
310-855-1115
900 Hammond Street, Los Angeles, CA 90069

FERRARI GUIDES' GAY TRAVEL A to Z - 18th EDITION

CALIFORNIA

FYI

Take Mud Baths, Practice Yoga, Visit Wineries & Learn Wellness

Combine vacation activities with learning skills and strategies to help manage your stressors. Learn to work "smarter," and enhance your relationships. Learn principles of successful aging and how to incorporate wellness into your life.

Activities include gentle yoga, meditation, breathing, relaxation techniques, various styles of bodywork and Hanna somatics™. Day excursions in Napa Valley include optional gentle hikes, a visit to a geyser, mud baths, mineral water soaks at Calistoga, visits to local vineyards and wineries. Delicious gourmet meals are prepared with fresh, healthful local ingredients.

Separate times are scheduled for lesbian & bisexual women and for HIV+ men.

Contact **Destination Discovery** at (800) 954-5543, (707) 963-0543 (tel/fax).

Heights Blvd, (213) 650-9688. Breakfast, lunch, dinner.
LA MASIA, 9077 Santa Monica Blvd, (310) 273-7066. Spanish & continental cuisine.
LITTLE FRIDA'S, 8730 Santa Monica Blvd, (310) 652-6495. Cafe & gallery, sandwiches, desserts, patio.
LUNAPARK 665 N Robertson Blvd, (310) 652-0611. Bar with cabaret & restaurant, continental cuisine.
MELROSE PLACE BAR & GRILL, 650 N La Cienega, (310) 657-2227.
SILVER SPOON, 8171 Santa Monica Blvd, (213) 650-4890.
TANGO GRILL, 8807 Santa Monica Blvd, (310) 659-3663. Argentine cuisine.
YUKON MINING CO, 7328 Santa Monica Blvd, (213) 851-8833. Coffee shop, 24hrs.

■ Retail & Bookstores
A DIFFERENT LIGHT BOOKS, 8853 Santa Monica Blvd near San Vicente, (310) 854-6601. Gay & lesbian bookstore.
BOOK SOUP, 8818 Sunset Blvd, (310) 659-3110. General bookstore with gay & lesbian section.
DON'T PANIC, 802 North San Vicente Blvd, (800) 45-PANIC. Gay & lesbian T-shirts.
DOROTHY'S SURRENDER, 7985 Santa Monica Blvd, in the French Market Place, (213) 650-4111. Gift shop.
UNICORN ALLEY, 8940 Santa Monica Blvd, (310) 652-6253. Gay pride items.
UNICORN BOOKSTORE, 8940 Santa Monica Blvd, (310) 652-6253.

■ Leathers/Piercing
GAUNTLET, 8720 Huntley Dr at Santa Monica Blvd, (310) 657-6677. Piercing studio, jewelry. Closed Sun.

■ Erotica
CASANOVA'S WEST, 7766 Santa Monica Blvd, (213) 848-9244.
CIRCUS OF BOOKS, 8230 Santa Monica Blvd at LaJolla, (213) 656-6533. 6am-2am. Thousands of adult videos as low as $5.95.
DRAKE'S II, 8932 Santa Monica Blvd, (310) 289-8932. Gay & lesbian movie rentals, adult toys novelties.
DRAKE'S MELROSE, 7566 Melrose Ave near Curson, (213) 651-5600, Gay & lesbian movie rentals, 24hrs.
HIGHLAND BOOKS, INC, 6775 Santa Monica Blvd at Highland, (213) 463-0295, 24hrs.
PLEASURE CHEST, 7733 Santa Monica Blvd near Genesee, (213) 650-1022. Gay & lesbian movies, magazines & more.

WEST LA - SANTA MONICA

Also beach cities, Culver City, Mar Vista, Venice & Malibu.

■ Beaches
WILL ROGERS GAY BEACH. In Santa Monica, take Channel Rd to the tunnel under Pacific Coast Hwy, park near tennis courts.

■ Bars
FRIENDSHIP, 112 W Channel Rd near Pacific Coast Highway, Santa Monica, (310) 454-6024. Beach bar.
JJ'S PUB, 2692 S La Cienega Blvd, near Alvira, Culver City, (310) 837-7443. More gay in evenings, 30% women.
ROOSTERFISH, 1302 Abbot Kinney Blvd, Venice, (310) 392-2123. Jukebox, popular Sun BBQ.

■ Dance Bar/Disco
CONNECTION, 4363 Sepulveda, Culver City, (310) 391-6817. Big-screen TV, DJ or bands on weekends, darts, pool table, big-screen TV, men welcome.

■ Saunas/Health Clubs
ROMAN HOLIDAY, 12814 Venice Blvd near Beethoven, Mar Vista, (310) 391-0200 or (310) 397-9091. 24hrs.

■ Restaurants
TRILOGY, 2214 Stoner Ave, West LA, (310) 477-2844. Wed-Sun 6pm-10pm, drag shows nightly.
VAN GO'S EAR, 796 Main St, Venice, (310) 314-0022. 24hr coffeehouse, popular after hours.

■ Retail & Bookstores
SISTERHOOD BOOKSTORE, 1351 Westwood Blvd at Rochester, (310) 477-7300. Women's bookstore with music, cards, crafts by & about women, resource center, 10am-8pm daily.

■ Erotica
LOVE BOUTIQUE, 2924 Wilshire Blvd, Santa Monica, (310) 453-3459. Women-owned & -operated erotic store, intimate videos, small selection of lesbian & gay videos, games. We do home parties for women to display our products.
TENDER BOX, 809 Pacific Coast Hwy, (310) 318-2882.

LA SOUTH BAY

Includes Hawthorne, Redondo Beach, Inglewood.

■ Bars
ANNEX CLUB, THE, 835 S La Brea Ave, Inglewood, (310) 671-7323. Pool tables, 80% men, 20% women.
CAPER ROOM, 244 S Market Street, Inglewood, (310) 677-0403. DJ weekends, drag shows Thurs, 80% men, 20% women, mainly women on Fri ladies night.
DOLPHIN, 1995 Artesia Blvd, Redondo Beach, (310) 318-3339. Beach bar, 50% men, 50% women.
EL CAPITAN, 13825 S Hawthorne Blvd, Hawthorne, (310) 675-3436.

378 FERRARI GUIDES' GAY TRAVEL A to Z - 18th EDITION

CALIFORNIA

UNITED STATES

■ Dance Bar/Disco
CLUB BABYLON, 2105 Artesia Blvd, Redondo Beach, (310) 793-9393. Piano bar, DJ after 9pm nightly.

MARINA DEL REY
■ Accommodations
MANSION INN, THE, 327 Washington Blvd, (310) 821-2557, Fax: 827-0289, (800) 828-0688. B&B inn with courtyard cafe, 50% gay & lesbian clientele. Private baths, color TV, refrigerators, expanded continental breakfast & nearby beach.

MENDOCINO COUNTY
■ Accommodations
ANNIE'S JUGHANDLE BEACH B&B INN, 32980 Gibney Lane, Ft. Bragg, (707) 964-1415, fax: (707) 961-1473. B&B cottage in an 1880's Victorian farmhouse, private baths, full breakfast, near Jughandle State Reserve, gay & lesbian following.

INN AT SCHOOLHOUSE CREEK, THE, 7051 N Hwy One Little River, CA (707) 937-5525, (800) 731-5525. Gay-friendly inn on 10 acres of gardens, private baths, ocean views.

■ Women's Accommodations
SALLIE & EILEEN'S PLACE, Box 409, (707) 937-2028. Women-only studio cottage & guesthouse. Kitchens, fireplace in A-frame, sun decks, hot tub. Three miles to ocean & river beaches.

WILDFLOWER RIDGE, Box 685 Albion, (707) 937-3720, (510) 735-2079 for reservations. Women-only cottage, private bath.

■ Retail & Bookstores
BOOK LOFT, 45050 Main St, Mendocino, (707) 937-0890. General bookstore with women's, lesbian & gay section. Metaphysical books.

MENLO PARK
■ Retail & Bookstores
TWO SISTERS BOOKSHOP, 605 Cambridge Ave, (415) 323-4778. Women's books, cards and gifts, goddess art, jewelry, music tapes and CDs, crafts, crystals, posters, T-shirts, weekly events and workshops.

MODESTO
■ Dance Bar/Disco
BRAVE BULL, 701 S 9th St, (209) 529-6712. 50% men, 50% women, 7pm-2am.

MUSTANG CLUB, 413 N 7th St, (209) 577-9694. Est. 1966, 11am-2am summer, 2pm-2am winter, patio, drag shows Sun, ladies nite Wed & 3rd Fri of month.

■ Cafe
ESPRESSO CAFE, 3025-D McHenry Ave, (209) 571-3337. Espresso, pastas, lite menu.

■ Erotica
L'AMOUR SHOPPE, 1022 9th St, (209) 521-7987.

LIBERTY BOOKS, 1030 Kansas Ave, (209) 524-7603, 24hrs.
SUSIE'S, 100 McHenry Ave.

MONTE RIO
See Russian River

MONTEREY
■ Women's Accommodations
MISTY TIGER, 9422 Acorn Circle, Salinas, (408) 633-8808. Private room with queen bed in a contemporary home, 15 minutes from downtown Monterey & 5 minutes from the sea. Fireplace, hot tub, extensive grounds, big deck, video library. Women only.

■ Bars
EDDIE'S, 2200 N Fremont St. Straight bar with gay women's nites, probably Sat (call first).

FORMERLY TITLE IX, 281 Lighthouse, (408) 373-4488. Name to change in '97.

FRANCO'S NORMA JEAN BAR, 10639 Merritt St, Castroville, (408) 633-2090, 633-6129. Restaurant & bar, open Fri & Sat only, Ladies night Fri, house, Sat house techno, latin music & drag show.

■ Dance Bar/Disco
AFTER DARK, BACKLOT, 214 Lighthouse Ave near Reeside, (408) 373-7828. Video dance bar, 70% men, 30% women.

■ Retail & Bookstores
RAVEN IN THE GROVE, 801 Lighthouse Ave #105, (408) 649-6057. Alternative spirituality & celtic books, art & jewelry.

MORRO BAY - SAN LUIS OBISPO
■ Information
AIDS SUPPORT NETWORK, 1317-B Churro, (805) 781-3660, (800) 491-9141.

GAY/LESBIAN ALLIANCE (GALA), (805) 541-4252. Networking, dances, picnics, newsletter. They have info on numerous other local groups.

WOMEN'S RESOURCE CENTER, 1009 Morro St #201, San Luis Obispo, (805) 544-9313. For all women, meetings, network center, monthly newspaper called Women's Press.

■ Accommodations
CASA DE AMIGAS, 1202 8th St, (805) 528-3701. B&B, private bath.

■ Women's Accommodations
AMBER HILLS BED & BREAKFAST, 7720 Rocky Rd, Paso Robles, (805) 239-2073. B&B in a country setting, private bath, expanded continental breakfast, color cable TV, AC, nearby pool & ocean, men welcome.

■ Beaches
PIRATE'S COVE BEACH, on Avila Beach, Port San Luis off 101. Bear left, turn at golf course, go up the hill. Diamond Beach is down trail with a rope climb. Nude beach, NW section is more gay.

■ Dance Bar/Disco
BREEZES PUB & GRILL, 11560 Los Osos Valley Rd, San Luis Obispo, (805) 544-8010. Open Wed-Sat, dance club Thurs-Sat.

■ Cafe
LINNAEA'S CAFE, 1110 Garden St, San Luis Obispo, (805) 541-5888. Healthful cuisine, lunch.

■ Restaurants
BIG SKY MODERN FOOD, 1121 Broad St, San Luis Obispo, (805) 545-5401.

■ Retail & Bookstores
VOLUMES OF PLEASURE, 1016 Los Osos Valley Rd, Los Osos, (805) 528-5565, 528-3701. General bookstore with large gay, lesbian & women's sections & information center.

MOUNTAIN VIEW
■ Bars
DAYBREAK, 1711 W El Camino Real, (415) 940-9778. DJ Fri-Sat, Karaoke Thur & Sat. 30% men & 70% women.

NAPA VALLEY
■ Retail & Bookstores
ARIADNE BOOKS, 3780 Bel Aire Plaza, (707) 253-9402. Metaphysical, health, recovery book center with women's books & espresso bar.

OAKLAND
■ Information
GAY SWITCHBOARD & PACIFIC CENTER, 2712 Telegraph Ave, (510) 841-6224. Mon, Tues, Fri 8-10pm, Wed 4-6pm. Group meetings.

■ Bars
TOWN & COUNTRY, 2022 Telegraph Ave near 20th, (510) 444-4978. 85% men, 15% women.

■ Dance Bar/Disco
BENCH & BAR, ★ 120 11th St near Oak, (510) 444-2266.

CABEL'S REEF, 2272 Telegraph Ave, (510) 451-3777.

WHITE HORSE, ★ 6551 Telegraph Ave at 66th St, (510) 652-3820. 50% men, 50% women.

WOMEN'S COUNTRY NIGHTS, 3903 Broadway / 40th St at Masonic Hall, (510) 428-2144. Every Friday. Lessons 7:30-8:30pm, dancing 8:45-11:30pm. Smoke-free, alcohol-free, perfume-free, ages 20-70.

■ Saunas/Health Clubs
FORTY-ONE CLUB, 41 Grand Ave near Broadway, (510) 444-4141, 444-1315. Private men's club, gay & bi men & transgenderists.

CALIFORNIA

Private rooms, showers, dungeon, maze, Wed-Sun. 🏳️‍🌈♂

■ Restaurants
BRICK HUT,★ 2510 San Pablo Ave, (510) 486-1124. Selected as one of the SF Bay area's best art cafes, we are an internationally known, lesbian-owned, kid-friendly, cafe. Mon-Fri 7:30am-2pm. Sat, Sun 8:30am-3pm. Busy Fri evening & Sun for brunch. Reservations advised. ♿♀♂

■ Retail & Bookstores
MAMA BEARS CULTURE CENTER, see ad under Berkeley.

■ Erotica
HOLLYWOOD BOOKS & VIDEO, 5686 Telegraph Ave, (510) 654-1169 or 547-9077.
L'AMOUR SHOPPE, 1801 Telegraph Ave, (510) 835-0381. 2nd location: 1905 San Pablo Ave, (510) 465-4216.
XANADU, 201 Broadway, (510) 465-0374.

OCEANSIDE

■ Bars
CAPRI LOUNGE, 207 N Tremont St, (760) 722-7284. 95% men, women welcome. 🏠♂

■ Dance Bar/Disco
GREYSTOKES GRILL, 1903 S Coast Hwy, (619) 757-2955. Dance bar, DJ & piano bar Fri & restaurant with burgers, chicken sandwiches, steaks. 🎵🎶🍽️✕♀♂

■ Erotica
MIDNIGHT VIDEO, 316 3rd St, (760) 757-7832, 24hrs.

ORANGE COUNTY

See also Anaheim.

■ Information
AIDS LINE, (714) 534-0961, 10am-6pm Mon-Fri.
GAY & LESBIAN COMMUNITY CENTER, 12832 Garden Grove Blvd, #A, Garden Grove, Office: (714) 534-0862. 10am-10pm weekdays.

■ Accommodations
HUNTINGTON BEACH HOUSE B&B, 609 Main St, Huntington Beach, (714) 536-7818, Fax: (714) 960-2639. B&B & cottage with private & shared baths, full breakfast weekends, continental breakfast weekdays. Cottage has color TV, ceiling fans, kitchen, coffee/tea-making facilities. 50% gay/lesbian clientele.

■ Bars
TIN LIZZIE SALOON, 752 St Clair, Costa Mesa, (714) 966-2029. 🏠♂

■ Dance Bar/Disco
EL CALOR, 2916 W Lincoln at Beach Blvd, Anaheim, (714) 527-8873. Latino nightclub Sat till 4am, Wed-Sun from 8pm, Wed Alternative & Thurs Ladies nights, Sun live bands, male dancers, salsa music. 📺🎵♀♂
FRAT HOUSE, 8112 Garden Grove Blvd near Beach Blvd, Garden Grove, (714) 897-3431. Dance bar, opens 9pm daily, Latin nights. 🎵📺♂
HAPPY HOUR,★ 12081 Garden Grove Blvd near West St, Garden Grove, (714) 537-9079. Live bands, videos. 🎵🎶♀
LION'S DEN, 719 W 19th St at Federal, Costa Mesa, (714) 645-3830. DJ Tue, Fri-Sun. 60% men, 40% women. Sat ladies night. 🎵🎶♀ ♂
NEWPORT STATION, 1945 Placentia Ave near 19th St, Costa Mesa, (714) 631-0031. Video dance bar, gay Thur & Sat. Verify gay nights. 🎵🎶♀ ♂
OZZ SUPPER CLUB,★ 6231 Manchester, Buena Park, (714) 522-1542. Hi-energy dance bar, DJ nightly, piano lounge, cabaret, restaurant, 60% men, 40% women. Open Wed-Mon (many women Wed & Sun), Mon men's C&W & Wed ladis C&W nites, Thurs male strippers. 🎵🎶🍽️✕♀♂

■ Erotica
A-Z BOOKSTORE, 8192 Garden Grove Blvd, (714) 534-9349. 24hrs Thurs-Sun.
GARDEN OF EDEN, 12061 Garden Grove Blvd, Garden Grove, (714) 534-9805.
HIP POCKET, 12686 Garden Grove Blvd near Harbor, Garden Grove.
MIDNIGHT ADULT BOOK & VIDEO, 8745 Garden Grove Blvd, (714) 534-9823.
PARTY HOUSE, 8751 Garden Grove Blvd at Josephine, Garden Grove, (714) 534-9996, 7 days.

PALM SPRINGS - CATHEDRAL CITY

NEW AREA CODE (760), shown below, takes effect Oct 1, '97. Until Oct '97, continue to use area code (619).

■ Information
AIDS LINE, (760) 323-2118.

■ Accommodations
ALEXANDER RESORT, 598 Grenfall Rd, Palm Springs, (760) 327-6911, (800) 448-6197. Men-only Guesthouse. Double rooms furnished in desert hues, Jacuzzi, bicycles, 5-min walk to downtown. Expanded continental breakfast & light lunch. 🏨♂
ARUBA RESORT APARTMENTS, 671 S Riverside Dr, Palm Springs, (760) 325-8440 (tel/fax), (800) 84-ARUBA. Resort hotel, 50% gay & lesbian clientele. Color TV, VCR, AC, kitchens, king beds & private baths. Pool & Jacuzzi on premises. Small pets permitted, member IGTA. 🏨
ATRIUM/VISTA GRANDE/MIRAGE, 574 Warm Sands Dr, Palm Springs, (760) 322-2404, (800) 669-1069, Fax: (760) 320-1667. Men-only private resort hotels. Ask about our exotic waterfalls. 2 pools, 2 spas. Ten minutes to convention center and walk to gay restaurant, bars. 🏨📺♂
AVANTI RESORT HOTEL, 715 San Lorenzo Rd, Palm Springs, (760) 325-9723, (800) 572-2779, fax: (760) 325-4357. Exclusively male resort secluded in lush gardens at the foot of the San Jacinto mountains. Kitchens, VCRs, microwaves, video library and many other amenities. All private baths, continental breakfast. 🏨♂
CAMP PALM SPRINGS HOTEL, 722 San Lorenzo Rd, (800) 793-0063, (760) 322-CAMP, Fax: 322-5699. Men-only hotel, private baths, expanded California breakfast, pool on premises. 🏨📺♂
CANYON CLUB HOTEL, 960 N Palm Canyon Dr, (760) 322-4367, (800) 295-2582, Fax: (760) 322-4024. **Size Does Matter!** Thirty-two rooms with refrigerators, AC, cable TV and double, queen or king beds. Some with full kitchens and private patios. Large pool, Jacuzzi and dry sauna. In-house video channels, steam room. Clothing optional. Walking distance to downtown and convenient to nightspots. Men only. Rates from $59. 🏨♂
CASA ROSA, 589 Grenfall Rd, Palm Springs, (800) 322-7302, (760) 322-4143. ♂
CATHEDRAL CITY BOYS CLUB, 68369 Sunair Rd, Cathedral City, (760) 324-1350, (800) 472-0836. Studios & suites & RV spaces. 🏨♂
COLUMNS RESORT, 537 Grenfall Rd, Palm Springs, (760) 325-0655, (800) 798-0655, fax: (760) 322-1436. Men-only private resort hotel. Large, newly-decorated rooms with AC, color TV, weights, Jacuzzi & continental breakfast. 🏨📺♂
COYOTE INN, 234 Patencio Rd, Palm Springs, (800) 269-6830, (760) 322-9675. Suites iwth TV's, kitchens, AC. Near downtown, men only. 🏨♂
DESERT HANGOUT, THE, 1466 N Palm Canyon Dr, (760) 320-5984, (800) 660-5066, Fax: (760) 323-7005. Men's clothing-optional resort, locals take lockers & meet vacationers. Pool on premises, AC, color cable TV, expanded continental breakfast, weekend/holiday BBQs. 🏨♂
DESERT PALMS INN, 67-580 E Palm Canyon Dr, Palm Springs, (800) 483-6029, (760) 324-3000, Fax: (760) 770-5031. Inn with restaurant, bar & shops, women welcome. Private baths, color TV, AC, business services, Jacuzzi & pool. 🏨♂
DESERT PARADISE HOTEL, 615 Warm Sands Dr, Palm Springs, outside CA: (800) 342-7635, (760) 320-5650. A gentleman's resort of the highest caliber, representing the best the desert has to offer! Lush garden settings, majestic mountain views, attention to detail and dedication to service afford guests a truly memorable experience. Stylish accommodations include private bath, telephone, color TV, VCR, AC & kitchens. Exotic grounds, a poolside mix of music and laughter, and proximity to the excitement of Palm Springs combine to meet your every expectation. 🏨 📺♂
DESERT STARS RESORT, 1491 Via Soledad,

CALIFORNIA

(760) 325-2686. B&B inn for men, French-Mediterranean style, pool on premises. ♂

EL MIRASOL VILLAS, 525 Warm Sands Dr, Palm Springs, (760) 327-5913, (800) 327-2985, Fax: (760) 325-8931. Private baths, color cable TV, VCR, video tape library, AC, telphone, kitchen & refrigerator. Continental breakfast & lunch, Jacuzzi & 2 pools on premises. ♀♂

ENCLAVE, THE, 641 San Lorenzo Rd, Palm Springs, (800) 621-6973, (760) 325-5269, Fax: (760) 320-9535. Centrally located & close to downtown Palm Springs, complimentary continental breakfast, heated pool, Jacuzzi, BBQ area. ♀♂

FIVE FIFTY, THE, 550 Warm Sands Dr. Palm Springs, CA (760) 320-7144, (800) 669-0550. Men-only hotel, private baths. ♂

HACIENDA EN SUEÑO, 586 Warm Sands Dr, Palm Springs, (760) 327-8111, (800) 359-2007. Hotel, men only. Poolside apartments with traditional to contemporary decor, free use of Gold's Gym & Oasis, 1/4 mi from downtown. ♂

HARLOW CLUB HOTELS PALM SPRINGS CA, Palm Springs, (800) 223-4073, (760) 320-4333, (760) 323-3977, Fax: (760) 322-8534. Three deluxe resorts, women welcome. ♂

HEDY'S HIDEAWAY, (800) GAY-0069, (310) 652-9600, Fax: (310) 652-5454. B&B, private bath, full American breakfast. ♀♂

HOT DESERT KNIGHTS, 435 Avenida Olancha, Palm Springs, (760) 325-5456, (800) 256-7938. Hotel for naturist gay men with deluxe studio apartments, light breakfast. ♂

INN EXILE, 960 Camino Parocela, Palm Springs, (760) 327-6413, (800) 962-0186, Fax: (760) 320-5745. A private, gated resort. Pool, Jacuzzi, gym, daily complimentary continental breakfast, luncheon & happy hour, private direct dial telephones, TV's, VCR's, adult video tapes, room refrigerators, king sized beds, outdoor cooling mist, steam room, outdoor fireplace, indoor lounge area, and of course **clothing is always optional.** Men only. ♂

INN OF THE THREE PALMS, 370 W Arenas Rd, (760) 323-2767. In downtown Palm Springs, pool on premises.

INNDULGE PALM SPRINGS, 601 Grenfall Rd, (760) 327-1408, (800) 833-5675, fax: (760) 327-7273. Men-only inn with rooms & suites, continental breakfast, private baths, AC, color cable TV, VCR, video tape library, pool on premises. ♂

INNTIMATE, 556 Warm Sands Dr, Palm Springs, (760) 778-8334, (800) 695-3846, Fax: (760) 778-9937. Private guesthouse, women welcome. All private baths, AC & pool. ♂

INNTRIGUE, 526 Warm Sands Dr. Palm Springs, CA (760) 323-7505, (800) 798-8781, fax: (760) 323-1055. Centrally located private male resort. Private baths, color cable TV, VCR, videos, AC, kitchens, Jacuzzi & continental breakfast. ♂

MIRA LOMA HOTEL, THE, 1420 N Indian Canyon Dr, (760) 320-1178, fax: (760) 320-5308. Motel, private baths, continental (wkdays) & full (wknds) breakfast, pool on premises, 50% gay / lesbian clientele.

MOUNTAIN SHADOWS RESORT, 568 Warm Sands Dr, (760) 322-2324, (8000) 563-6646. Men's resort, poolside spa & gazebo, 1-br, studios & kitchens available. ♂

PRISCILLA'S, 528 S Camino Real, (760) 416-0168. Seven small units with 50's decor, TV, VCR, pool on premises.

SAGO PALMS, 595 Thornhill Rd, Palm Springs, (760) 323-0224, (800) 626-SAGO. Men-only resort hotel, private baths. ♂

SANTIAGO RESORT, 650 San Lorenzo Rd, (760) 322-1300, (800) 710-7729, fax: (760) 416-0347. Men-only hotel resort with rooms & suites, private baths, AC, color cable TV, expanded continental breakfast, Jacuzzi, pool on premises, outdoor pavilion with fireplace, near gay bars. ♂

TRIANGLE INN, 555 San Lorenzo, Palm Springs, (760) 322-7993, (800) 732-7555. Secluded inn resort, men only. Deluxe studios & suites, all private baths, Jacuzzi, massage, bicycles, expanded continental breakfast. ♂

VILLA, THE, 67-670 Carey Rd Cathedral City, (760) 328-7211, Reservations:. (800) VILLA OK, Fax: (760) 321-1463. Resort with pool bar, restaurant. Variety of deluxe bungalow rooms with atriums, kitchenettes, modern conveniences, fireplace lounge, sauna, Jacuzzi, massage & pool. Women welcome. ♂

■ Women's Accommodations

BEE CHARMER INN, 1600 E Palm Canyon Dr, Palm Springs, (760) 778-5883. Luxury women's hotel with 14 rooms meticulously furnished in southwestern pastels. Located in the heart of Palm Springs, minutes from clubs, restaurants, recreational venues, and attractions of the fabulous gay desert. Non-smoking rooms include private baths, color TVs, microwaves, refrigerators, phones & AC. French doors open onto a pool where continental breakfast is served every morning. ♀

■ Transportation

RAINBOW CAB CO., (760) 327-5702. Gay-owned & -operated cab company.

■ Bars

BACKSTREET PUB, 72-695 Hwy 111, A-7, Palm Desert. (760) 341-7966 Small dance floor & games, 70% men, 30% women. ♂

DATES POOLSIDE BAR, at the Villa Resort, 67-670 Carey Rd, Cathedral City, (760) 328-7211. Popular Sat & Sun brunch, Sun T dance 2pm-6pm. ♀♂

RAINBOW CACTUS CAFE BAR, 212 S Indian Ave, Palm Springs. Bar & restaurant. ♂

SPEAKEASY, 2400 Palm Canyon Dr, (760) 322-3224. Piano lounge & restaurant. ♀♂

STREETBAR, 224 E Arenas, Palm Springs, (760) 320-1266. Videos.

SWEETWATER SALOON, 2420 N Palm Canyon Dr, Palm Springs, (760) 320-8878. 11am-2am 7days, pool table, darts, pub food till midnite. ♂

TOOL SHED, 600 E Sunnydunes Rd, Palm Springs, (760) 320-3299. Pool table, videos.

WOLFS, ★ 67-625 Hwy 111, Cathedral City. (760) 321-9688. Cruise bar, full liquor.

■ Dance Bar/Disco

CC'S ON SUNRISE, ★ 1775 E Palm Canyon Dr, (760) 778-1234. Large venue, 2 dance floors, 5 pool tables. ♂

CHOICES NIGHTCLUB, ★ 58-352 Perez Rd, Cathedral City, (760) 321-1145. Complex with video bar, dance club, patio bar, theater, name

FERRARI GUIDES' GAY TRAVEL A to Z - 18th EDITION

CALIFORNIA

entertainment, theme parties. Hi-energy dance music from 9pm.

DELILAH'S,★ 68-657 Hwy 111, Cathedral City, (760) 324-3268. Disco Thur-Sun from 4pm.

SUNDANCE SALOON, 36737 Cathedral Canyon in Cathedral City, (760) 321-1233. C&W dancing.

■ Saunas/Health Clubs

CLUB PALM SPRINGS, 68-449 Perez Rd near Cathedral Canyon, Cathedral City, (760) 324-8588. Private club, 24hrs.

■ Restaurants

BLUE ANGEL, 777 E Tahquitz Canyon Hwy, Palm Springs, (760) 778-4343. Seaks.

BLUE COYOTE GRILL, 445 N Palm Canyon Dr, Palm Springs. Mexican & Southwestern cuisine. Lunch, dinner, patio dining, gay-friendly.

DAN & SWEET SUE'S CAFE, 68-955 Ramon Rd, Cathedral City, (760) 770-2760. Burgers, omelettes, pancakes, salads, breakfast-dinner, 6am-8:30pm Mon-Sat.

DATES CAFE, 67-670 Carey Rd, at Villa Hotel, Cathedral City.

GOLDEN TRIANGLES, 68-805 Hwy 111, Cathedral City, (760) 324-9113. Thai & French cuisine.

IGUANA GRILL, at Desert Palms Inn.

MAMA GLOS, 440 El Cielo Rd, Palm Springs, (760) 416-8848. Home cooking.

MICHAEL'S CAFE, 68-665 Hwy 111, Cathedral City. Gay-friendly, breakfast & lunch.

MORTIMER'S, 2095 N Indian Canyon, Palm Springs, (760) 320-4333. Upscale, elegant, expensive continental fare.

RAINBOW CACTUS CAFE, 212 S Indian Ave, Palm Springs. Bar & restaurant.

RED TOMATO, 68-784 Hwy 111, Cathedral City, (760) 328-7518. Pizza & pasta, dinner only.

RICHARD'S, 68-599 Hwy 111, Cathedral City. Continental cuisine, piano bar.

SHAME ON THE MOON,★ 69-950 Frank Sinatra Dr, Rancho Mirage, (760) 324-5515. Northern Italian, patio dining, reservations advised 2-3 weeks ahead.

SILAS ON PALM CANYON, 664 N Palm Canyon Dr, (760) 325-4776. Award-winning continental cuisine, dinner only.

SPEAKEASY,★ 2400 N Palm Canyon Dr, Palm Springs, (760) 322-3224. American cuisine.

WILD GOOSE, 67938 Hwy 111, Cathedral City, (760) 328-5775. Award-winning continental cuisine, dinner only.

■ Retail & Bookstores

BETWEEN THE PAGES BOOKSTORE, THEATRE & CAFE, 214 E Arenas Rd, (760) 320-7158. Gay & lesbian bookstore, gay theatre & cafe.

GAY MART, 305 E Arenas Rd, Palm Springs, (760) 320-0606. Cards, swimsuits, T-shirts, videos.

■ Leathers/Piercing

BLACK MOON LEATHER, 68-449 Perez Rd Cathedral City, (760) 328-7773, 770-2925. Gay department store.

■ Erotica

HIDDEN JOY, 68-424 Commercial Rd, Cathedral City, (760) 328-1694, 24hrs.

PEREZ VIDEOS & BOOKS, 68-366 Perez St, Cathedral City, (760) 321-5597, 24hrs.

PALO ALTO

■ Information

STANFORD LESBIAN, GAY, BISEXUAL COMMUNITY CENTER, (415) 723-1488 events tape, (415) 725-4222 live. Movies, discussions, socials.

■ Retail & Bookstores

STEPPING STONES—THE ARTIFACTORY, 226 Hamilton Ave, (415) 853-9685. Feminist bookstore & artist's gallery, Tues-Sat 10am-6pm.

PASADENA

■ Bars

BOULEVARD, THE, 3199 E Foothill Blvd, (818) 356-9304. Piano bar, Sun buffet at 5pm.

HOLLY ST. BAR & GRILL,, 175 E Holly St, (818) 440-1421.

NARDI'S, 665 E Colorado Blvd, (818) 449-3152. Jukebox, 70% men, 30% women, some straight clientele.

■ Dance Bar/Disco

CLUB 3772, 3772 E Foothill Blvd, (818) 578-9359. C&W dance lessons, variety bar. Men welcome.

ENCOUNTERS, 203 N Sierra Madre Blvd, (818) 792-3735. Video dance bar, 85% men, 15% women, patio.

■ Restaurants

EQUATOR COFFEE HOUSE, 22 Mills Place, (818) 564-8656. Light menu.

LITTLE RICKY'S, 39 S Fair Oaks Ave, (818) 440-0306. Mexican.

■ Retail & Bookstores

PAGE ONE, BOOKS BY & FOR WOMEN, 1200 E Walnut, Pasadena, (818) 796-8418. Feminist bookstore,

PETALUMA

■ Retail & Bookstores

BOOSHA, 125 Petaluma Blvd (behind Starbucks), (707) 773-4602. Card, gifts, jewelry.

POMONA

■ Bars

MARY'S, 1047 E 2nd St, (909) 622-1971. Bar & restaurant, 50% men, 50% women.

■ Dance Bar/Disco

ALIBI EAST,★ 225 S San Antonio Ave, (909) 623-9422. Video cruise bars (back bar is Back Alley). Patio, after-hours Fri & Sat till 4am. 20% women.

ROBBIE'S, 390 College Plaza East, (909) 620-4371. 50% men, 50% women, male, female strippers, upstairs cabaret, Sun buffet.

■ Restaurants

MARY'S, 1047 E 2nd St at Mary's bar. Dinner, soups, sandwiches.

■ Erotica

MUSTANG BOOKS, 961 N Central Ave, Upland, (909) 981-0227, 24hrs, weekends.

T 'N' A VIDEO, 2121 Foothill Blvd, Upland, (909) 985-1575. Gay-friendly bookstore, adult erotica, toys, gifts.

TOY BOX, 1999 W Arrow Route in Upland, (909) 982-9407, 24hrs.

REDDING

■ Bars

FIVE O ONE, THE, 1244 California St. DJ weekends, 60% men, 40% women.

■ Erotica

HILLTOP BOOK & VIDEO, 2131 Hilltop Dr, (916) 223-2675, 24hrs, arcade.

REDWOOD CITY

■ Bars

SHOUTS BAR & GRILL, 2034 Broadway, (415) 369-9651. jukebox, pool table, 65% men, 35% women.

■ Retail & Bookstores

B----, A PLAZA FOR WOMEN, 2209 Broadway, (415) 369-3335. Cafe, gifts, cards, women's art gallery & women's books, Tues-Sat 12pm-9pm. Name will change in '97.

■ Erotica

BACHELOR BOOKS, 2601 El Camino Real, (415) 369-2200.

GOLDEN GATE NEWS #3, 735 El Camino Real. 24hrs.

RIVERSIDE

■ Bars

MENAGERIE, 3581 University, (909) 788-8000. DJ Fri-Sun, Wed & Sun beer busts, karaoke Mon, 50% women Mon.

■ Dance Bar/Disco

V.I.P. CLUB, THE, 3673 Merrill Ave, (909) 784-2370. Hi-energy dance bar, male & female strippers, 18 & over club, after hours Fri & Sat.

■ Erotica

LE SEX SHOPPE, 3945 Market St, Riverside, (909) 788-5194, 24hrs.

CALIFORNIA

LIBRARY ONE, 623 W Baseline, (909) 889-6062.

VIDEO FANTASIES, 5327 Mission Rd, (909) 782-8056, 24hrs.

RUSSIAN RIVER

■ *Accommodations*

APPLEWOOD, 13555 Hwy 116, Guerneville, (707) 869-9093, (800) 555-8509, E-mail: stay@applewoodinn.com. B&B, mostly straight clientele. Comfortable, elegant rooms with private baths. Hot tub, massage, full breakfast & other meals on request.

FERN FALLS, 5701 Austin Creed Rd, PO Box 228, Cazadero, CA 95421, (707) 632-6108, fax: (707) 632-6216. Choose from two cottages or a suite in the main house. A curved deck looks over the on-premises creek and ravine. Amenities include color cable TV, VCR, kitchen, refrigerator, and fireplaces in the cottages. An ozonator spa is on the hill. Nearby enjoy wine tasting, horseback riding, canoeing on the Russian River, or hiking in the redwood forests.

FERN GROVE INN, 16650 River Rd, Guerneville Park, CA, (707) 869-9083, (800) 347-9083, Fax: (707) 869-2948. B&B, 50% gay & lesbian clientele. Enchanting cottages paneled in antique pine. Common room, library & expanded continental breakfast.

GOLDEN APPLE RANCH, 17575 Fitzpatrick Ln, Occidental, (707) 874-3756, Fax: (707) 874-1670. Art gallery lodge with 50% gay & lesbian clientele. Suites, apts & cottage. Phone, private baths, & most suites with satellite color TV. Continental breakfast. Nearby river & ocean beaches.

HIGHLAND DELL INN, 21050 River Blvd, Box 370 Monte Rio, (707) 865-1759, (800) 767-1759. Victorian lodge on the river, 50% gay & lesbian (sometimes more). Large, comfortable rooms with private & shared baths, TV lounge, weights, expanded continental breakfast. UNDER CONSTRUCTION. To open May '97.

HIGHLANDS RESORT, PO Box 346, 14000 Woodland Dr, Guerneville, 95446, (707) 869-0333, fax: (707) 869-0370. Inn and campground. Variety of guest quarters, 20 tent sites, TV lounge, massage, hot tub, continental breakfast.

HOUSE OF A THOUSAND FLOWERS, 11 Mosswood Circle, Cazadero, (707) 632-5571, Fax: (707) 632-6215. B&B, 50% gay & lesbian clientele. Comfortably furnished rooms with shared bath, TV lounge, Jacuzzi, massage, full breakfast. Nearby ocean & river beaches.

HUCKLEBERRY SPRINGS, PO Box 400 Monte Rio CA, (707) 865-2683, (800) 822-2683. Deluxe cottages, 50% gay & lesbian. Each residence uniquely decorated. Wood stoves, TV lounge, Jacuzzi, massage, full breakfast & nearby river.

INN AT OCCIDENTAL, THE, 3657 Church St, Occidental, (707) 874-1311, (800) 551-2292. Gay-friendly inn with restaurant. Large airy rooms, private baths & full breakfast.

JACQUES' COTTAGE, 6471 Old Trenton Rd, Forestville, CA 95436, (707) 575-1033, fax: (707) 573-8911. Cottage, women welcome.

MOUNTAIN LODGE RESORT, PO Box 169, 16350 1st St, Guerneville, (707) 869-3722, Fax: (707) 869-0556. Resort, 50% gay & lesbian clientele. Condo-style suites with modern conveniences, Jacuzzi.

PARADISE COVE, 14711 Armstrong Woods Rd Guerneville, (707) 869-270, (800) 880-2706. Resort. Luxurious, unique, double rooms with fireplaces & sun decks, wet bars, hydrotherapy spa. To reopen April '95.

RIO VILLA BEACH RESORT, 20292 Hwy 116, Monte Rio, (707) 865-1143, E-mail: riovilla@wclynx.com. Beach resort, 50% gay & lesbian clientele. Charming, spacious rooms, color/B/W TVs, outdoor fireplace, beach access. Continental breakfast on weekends. To reopen.

RUSSIAN RIVER RESORT, PO Box 2419, Guerneville, (707) 869-0691, (800) 41 RESORT (737678), fax: (707) 869-0689. Resort, restaurant & bar, private baths.

STILLWATER COVE RANCH, 22555 Coast Hwy 1, Box 5, Jenner, (707) 847-3227. Gay-friendly accommodations & restaurant, private baths.

TWIN TOWERS RIVER RANCH, 615 Bailhache Ave, Healdsburg, (707) 433-4443. Gay-friendly B&B with 2 rooms & 2 efficiency apartments built into a barn structure. Gays & lesbians especially welcome.

VILLA MESSINA B&B, 316 Burgundy Rd, Healdsburg, (707) 433-6655. A landmark bed and breakfast inn. Enjoy unsurpassed comfort and hospitality, panoramic 360 degree views from vineyards to the geysers. Twenty minutes from downtown Guerneville, yet a world away. Antiques, fine linens, TV, VCR, telephones, Jacuzzi, fireplace and superb Sonoma breakfast.

VILLAGE INN, PO Box 850 Monte Rio, (707) 865-2304. Hotel with restaurant & bar, 50% gay & lesbian clientele. Variety of rooms with private & shared baths. To reopen.

WILLOWS, THE PO Box 465, 15905 River Rd, Guerneville, (707) 869-2824, (800) 953-2828. **Bed & breakfast & camping on the river.** Double rooms with TVs, private & shared baths. Hot tub, sauna, expanded continental breakfast, coffee & tea. Canoe use, 120 tent sites, toilets & showers.

■ *Bars*

MCT'S BULL PEN, 16251 Main St, Guerneville. Sports bar.

RAINBOW CATTLE CO, 16220 Main St near Armstrong Woods, Guerneville, (707) 869-0206. 70% men, 30% women.

RIVER BUSINESS, 16225 1st St, Guerneville, (707) 869-0885, Very "LA," pool table, closed Tue.

TRIPLE R, PO Box 2419 at Russian River Resort, (707) 869-0691. Indoor & outdoor lounges, 60% men, 40% women.

■ *Dance Bar/Disco*

FIFE'S, 16467 River Rd, at Fife's Resort, Guerneville, (707) 869-0656. Disco, bar & restaurant to re-open in spring 1997.

MOLLY'S COUNTRY CLUB, 14120 Old Cazadero Rd near River Rd, Guerneville, (707) 869-0511. C&W bar & restaurant with steaks, etc, 50% men, 50% women.

■ *Restaurants*

BURDON'S, 15405 River Rd near Riverside, Guerneville, (707) 869-2615. Restaurant & bar, continental cuisine.

CHEZ MARIE, 6675 Front St, Forestville, (707) 887-7503. Sonoma County French cuisine.

FARMHOUSE INN RESTAURANT, River Rd, Forestville, (707) 887-3300. Awardwinning chef.

JOHN ASH & CO, 4330 Barnes Rd, at River Rd, Santa Rosa, (707) 527-7687.

MOLLY'S COUNTRY CLUB, 14120 Old Cazadero Rd at Molly's Country Club, (707) 869-0511.

NEW RESTAURANT AT HIGHLAND DELL, 21050 River Rd, in Monte Rio. Mediterranean cuisine.

NORTHWARD ROADHOUSE, 19400 Hwy 116, Monte Rio at Northwood Golf Course, (707) 865-2454. California cuisine.

SWEET'S RIVER GRILL, 16251 Main St, Guerneville, (707) 869-3383. Restaurant & cocktail lounge.

VILLAGE INN, PO Box 850, at Village Inn resort, Forestville, (707) 865-2304. Sun brunch.

Fern Falls

Cazadero creekside cottages
romance amidst redwoods
waterfall, fireplace
decks, spa, kitchen
pets OK, close to
Guerneville/coast

Darrel/Peter Ph (707) 632-6108
PO 228 Cazadero CA 95421

FERRARI GUIDES' GAY TRAVEL A to Z - 18th EDITION

CALIFORNIA

SACRAMENTO

■ Information
AIDS LINE, (916) 448-AIDS (2437), Mon-Fri 9am-5pm, or tape.
LAMBDA COMMUNITY CENTER, 919 20th St, (916) 442-0185.
WOMEN'S CENTER, 6000 J Street in Student Services Center, (916) 278-7388.

■ Accommodations
HARTLEY HOUSE INN, 700 Twenty-Second St, (916) 447-7829, (800) 831-5806, Fax: (916) 447-1820, E-mail: randy@hartleyhouse.com. B&B, 50% gay & lesbian clientele. Variety of rooms with colonial flavor & modern conveniences, library, full breakfast, beverages, snacks.

■ Bars
BOLT, 2560 Boxwood St, (916) 649-8420. 2pm-2am, 7 days.
JOSEPH'S T&C, 3514 Marconi Ave, (916) 483-1220. Bar & restaurant, small dance floor, lunch, dinner, 10am-2am, 7 days.
MERCANTILE SALOON, 1928 L St at 20th, (916) 447-0792.
MIRAGE, THE, 601 15th St at F St, (916) 444-3238. Sports bar, pool table, darts, popular with women, dancing Sat.
TOWNHOUSE, 1517 21st St, (916) 441-5122. Lounge, Karaoke, 90% men, women welcome.
WESTERN, 2001 K St at 20th, (916) 443-9831.
WRECK ROOM,★ 2513 Broadway near 25th, (916) 456-1181. Sunday beer & wine pig-out.

■ Dance Bar/Disco
BOJANGLE'S, 7042 Folsom Blvd, Sacramento, (916) 383-9882. 18 and over gay nightclub, live music.
BUFFALO CLUB/GARAGE, 1831 S St at 19th, (916) 442-1087. Rumored to reopen at the Garage.
FACES,★ 2000 K St at 20th, (916) 448-7798. Video, dance & cruise bar, patio bar. Women's night Wed, free BBQ Sun, C&W dancing early evening.

■ Cafe
CAFE LAMBDA, 1931 L St at Lambda Center. (916) 442-0185. Coffee & desserts Fri nights.
CAPITAL GARAGE COFFEE CO., 1427 L St, (916) 444-3633.
JAVA CITY CAFE, 1800 Capitol, (916) 444-5282. Café & bakery.
STARBUCK'S, 1401 Alhambra Blvd at N, (916) 456-9120.

■ Restaurants
ERNESTO'S, 16th & S Sts. Mexican cuisine.
HAMBURGER MARY'S, 1630 J St, (916) 441-4340.

■ Retail & Bookstores
HER PLACE, 6635 Madison Ave, Carmichael, (916) 961-1058. Metaphysical bookstore, goddess & spirituality items.
JUDY'S GIFTS & BOOKS, 2231 J Street, (916) 443-3236. Recovery bookstore with a small gay & lesbian selection.
KISS & TELL, 4201 Sunrise Blvd, (916) 966-5477. Sensuous boutique, gifts, novelties, lingerie, exotic dancewear, love toys.
LIONESS BOOKS, 2224 J St, (916) 442-4657. Feminist bookstore with gay & lesbian literature. Music, gifts & cards.
OPEN BOOK, THE, 910 21st St, (916) 498-1004. Gay & lesbian bookstore & coffeehouse, 7 days, 9am-midnight.
POSTCARDS ETC, 2101 L St, (916) 446-8049. Cards & gifts.

■ Leathers/Piercing
LEATHER SPACE, 2513 Broadway, at Wreck Room.

■ Erotica
GOLDIES BOOKSTORE & VIDEO, 2138 Del Paso Blvd, North Sacramento, (916) 922-0103.
GOLDIES BOOKSTORE & VIDEO, 201 N 12th St, (916) 447-5860. 24hrs. Also: 5644 Stockton, 453-9767.
L'AMOUR SHOPPE, 26th & Broadway, (916) 736-3467.
SUSIE'S VIDEO, corner of Florin & Franklin. Arcade. 2nd location on Auburn Blvd.

ST HELENA

■ Accommodations
INK HOUSE BED & BREAKFAST, THE, 1575 St Helena Hwy at Whitehall Lane, (707) 963-3890 or (800) 553-4343. B&B, mainly straight clientele. Rooms decorated with antique furniture. Panoramic view of NAPA Valley, expanded continental breakfast. Pool & lake nearby.

SALINAS

■ Erotica
L'AMOUR SHOPPE, 325 E Alisal St, (408) 758-9600.

SAN BERNARDINO

■ Information
GAY & LESBIAN HOTLINE, (909) 882-4488. 6:30pm-10pm, 7-days.

■ Bars
LARK, 917 Inland Center Dr, (909) 884-8770. Jukebox, pool table, opens 10 or 11am.

■ Dance Bar/Disco
PRIME TIME FOOD & SPIRITS, 127 W 40th St, (909) 881-1286. Dance bar & lounge, selection of appetizers.

■ Erotica
BEAR FACTS, 1434 E Baseline, (909) 885-9176, 24hrs, arcade.
E STREET BOOKSTORE, 304 S E St, San Bernardino, (909) 888-9040.
LE SEX SHOPPE, 304 W Highland, (909) 881-3583.

SAN DIEGO

■ Information
AIDS FOUNDATION S.D., 4080 Centre St, Hillcrest, (619) 686-5000, Linea de Español: 686-5001.
AIDS INFO, San Diego (619) 291-1400, La Mesa (619) 668-6286. Being Alive organization.
CENTER FOR WOMEN'S STUDIES & SERVICES, 2467 E St, Golden Hill, (619) 233-3088.
GAY & LESBIAN INFO LINE, (619) 692-2077. Mon-Sat 9am-10pm or tape. Center at 3916 Normal St. Info Line (619) 692-GAYS 6pm-10pm daily.
LESBIAN & GAY MEN'S COMMUNITY CENTER, 3916 Normal St, (619) 692-GAYS, 693-2077. 9am-10pm. Walk-in till 6pm.
PACTO, (619) 283-1073. Latin AIDS organiztion.

■ Accommodations
BALBOA PARK INN, 3402 Park Blvd, (800) 938-8181, (619) 298-0823, Fax: (619) 294-8070. Is the finest Bed & Breakfast Inn, located in the Hillcrest area. 26 distinctive, immaculate and beautifully appointed suites. Free continental breakfast, HBO & local calls. When you want to stay at the very best, stay with us.
BANKERS HILL B&B, 3315 2nd Ave, (619) 260-0673, (800) 338-3748, Fax: (619) 260-0674. B&B walking distance to Hillcrest. Suites available, hot tub, expanded continental breakfast.
BAYVIEW GALLERY BED & BREAKFAST, 2005 Loring St, (619) 581-3339. B&B with private & shared baths, some straight clientele.
BEACH PLACE, THE, 2158 Sunset Cliffs Blvd, (619) 225-0746. Suites for one to four people, women welcome. Accommodations include a living room, bedroom, kitchenette, private bath, closed circuit television and private deck, with a Jacuzzi in the courtyard. We are four blocks from the beach, minutes from the Hillcrest area and close to all San Diego attractions. Nightly and weekly rates.
DMITRI'S GUESTHOUSE, 931 21st St, (619) 238-5547. Enjoy San Diego's most popular gay guesthouse, overlooking downtown in one of San Diego's historic turn-of-the-century neighborhoods. We offer a variety of accommodations, heated pool & spa, continental breakfast daily at poolside. **We pride ourselves on creating a relaxed and comfortable atmosphere for the gay & lesbian traveler.** Reasonable rates, VISA, MC, reservations suggested. **Mostly men, women most welcome.**
HERITAGE PARK BED & BREAKFAST, (619) 299-6832. Gay-friendly B&B.

CALIFORNIA

HILLCREST INN, THE, 3754 5th Ave, (619) 293-7078, (800) 258-2280, fax: (619) 293-3861. Hotel, some straight clientele. Double rooms with modern conveniences, kitchenettes, patios, snack machines & nearby ocean beach. ♀♂

KASA KORBETT, 1526 Van Buren Ave, San Diego, CA 92103, (619) 291-3962, (800) 757-KASA (5272), Fax: (619) 298-9150. B&B in a 70-year-old craftsman-design home, private & shared baths, expanded continental breakfast, 4 blocks to gay bars, pool & ocean nearby. ♀♂

KEATING HOUSE, 2331 Second Ave, (619) 239-8585, (800) 995-8644, Fax: (619) 239-5774. B&B, 50% gay & lesbian. Individually decorated rooms with private & shared baths, gardens, full breakfast. Nearby ocean beach.

PARK MANOR SUITES HOTEL, 525 Spruce St, (619) 291-0999, (800) 874-2649, Fax: 291-8844. Hotel with private baths, 50% gay/lesbian clientele.

■ Transportation
SUNSET LIMOUSINES, (619) 294-9156.

■ Beaches
BLACKS BEACH, at Torry Pines State Park. Famous nude beach, gay at north end, 1/2-hr easy walk, or use semi-difficult trail down cliffs.

■ Bars
BOURBON ST., 4612 Park Blvd, (619) 291-0173. Piano lounge, nightly live entertainment, patio bar Fri-Sun.

BOURBON STREET, 4612 Park Blvd near Madison, (619) 291-0173. Piano bar, patio, Sun brunch.

CALIPH, 3102 5th Ave at Redwood, Hillcrest, (619) 298-9495. Piano bar, mature crowd.

CAPRI LOUNGE, 207 N Tremont St, Oceanside, (619) 722-7284. Pool table, some straight clientele, women welcome.

CHEERS, 1839 Adams, University Heights, (619) 298-3269. Pool table.

EAGLE, THE, 3040 North Park Way, (619) 295-8072. Cruisy.

FLICKS,★ 1017 University Ave near 10th, (619) 297-2056. Video social bar with music videos.

HOLE, THE,★ 2820 Lytton Street, (619) 226-9019. Patio, videos.

LOFT, 3610 5th Ave near Brookes, Hillcrest, (619) 296-6407. Conversation bar, pool table.

MATADOR, 4633 Mission Blvd near Emerald, Pacific Beach, (619) 483-6943. Beach bar, women welcome. Very popular Sun eve.

NUMBER 1 FIFTH AVE, 3845 5th Ave near Robinson, Hillcrest, (619) 299-1911. Darts, pool table, jukebox, patio, videos.

NUMBERS, 3811 Park Blvd near University, Hillcrest, (619) 294-9005. Video bar, patio, pool table. ♂

PECS,★ 2046 University Ave at Alabama, North Park, (619) 296-0889. After hrs Fri, Sat till 4am.

REDWING BAR & GRILL, 4012 30th St near Polk, North Park, (619) 281-8700. Patio, pool table.

SHOOTERZ,★ 3815 30th St, North Park, (619) 574-0744. Sports bar, videos, pool tournaments, 90% men, 10% women. ♂

SRO LOUNGE, 1807 5th Ave, (619) 232-1886.

TIDBITS CABARET, 3838 5th Ave, (619) 543-0300. From 6pm, 7 days, singers, drag shows, karaoke, appetizers.

WATERLOO STATION, 3968 5th Ave near Washington, Hillcrest, (619) 574-9329. Jukebox, darts, mature crowd.

WOLFS,★ 3404 30th St at Upas, North Park, (619) 291-3730. After hours Fri, Sat, pool table.

■ Dance Bar/Disco
BRASS RAIL, 3796 5th Ave at Robinson, (619) 298-2233. Dance bar.

CLUB BOMBAY,★ 3175 India St, (619) 296-6789. Very popular video dance bar, live entertainment, karaoke, patio.

CLUB MONTAGE, 2028 Hancock St, (619) 294-9590. Hi enegrgy video dance bar, 3 levels, 5 rooms, rooftop patio. Wed, Fri, Sat from 9pm, after hours till 4am Sat.

FLAME,★ 3780 Park Blvd near University, (619) 295-4163. Southern California's hottest women's nightclub. High energy dance club 7 nights a week. Three bars, large dance floor. Diverse nightly entertainment. Our exclusive Ultra Suede Lounge every Saturday. Tuesday unofficial men's night. San Diego's most popular drag review Friday nights. For a good time call (619) 295-4163.

KICKERS,★ 308 University Ave, Hillcrest, (619) 491-0400. C&W dance bar, patio, videos. Best Thurs & Sat, Hamburger Mary's restaurant on patio.

RICH'S SAN DIEGO,★ 1051 University, (619) 497-4588. Upscale dance & cruise bar, videos, male dancers, Sun tea dance 7pm-2am.

■ Cafe
DAVID'S PLACE,★ 3766 Fifth Ave, Hillcrest, (619) 294-8908. Coffeehouse, patio garden, after hours Fri & Sat. "A positive place for positive people and their friends."

EUPHORIA, 1045 University Ave, (619) 542-0445. ♀♂

LIVING ROOM, 1417 University Ave, (619) 291-8518.

STARBUCK'S, 5th & Robinson.

■ Saunas/Health Clubs
CLUB SAN DIEGO, 3955 Fourth Ave near University, Hillcrest, (619) 295-0850, 24hrs.

DAVE'S RECREATION & WORKOUT CENTER, 4969 Santa Monica near Cable, Ocean Beach, (619) 224-9011.

MUSTANG SPA, 2200 University Ave, North Park, (619) 297-1661.

VULCAN STEAM & SAUNA, 805 W Cedar St near Pacific Highway, (619) 238-1980. Jacuzzi on sun deck, 24hrs.

■ Restaurants
BAYOU BAR & GRILL, 329 Market St, (619) 696-8747. Upscale, Creole & Cajun, lunch & dinner, gay-friendly.

BIG KITCHEN, 3003 Grape St, (619) 234-5789. Breakfast, lunch. ♀♂

CALIFORNIA CUISINE, 1027 University Ave, (619) 543-0790. Expensive, beautiful presentation.

CITY DELI, 535 University, (619) 295-2747. Popular with local gays.

CREST CAFE, 425 Robinsons near 5th, Hillcrest, (619) 295-2510. Modern cafe with large gay clientele.

HAMBURGER MARY'S, 308 University, at Kickers, (619) 491-0400. Lunch & dinner. ♀♂

HILLCREST SANDWICH CO., 3780 5th Ave, (619) 293-0247.

JIMMY CARTER'S, 3172 5th Ave, (619) 295-2070. Dinner-style.

MARRAKESH, 756 5th Ave, (619) 231-8353.

TASTE OF SZECHUAN, 670 University Ave, (619) 298-1638.

■ Retail & Bookstores
BEST WISHES, 3830 5th Ave, Hillcrest, (619) 296-3234. Cards, gifts.

BLUE DOOR BOOKSTORE, 3823 5th Ave, Hillcrest, (619) 298-8610. General bookstore with strong gay & lesbian sections.

CALIFORNIA MAN, 3930 5th Ave, (619) 294-9108. Wide range of men's clothing &

BALBOA PARK INN
San Diego's Finest Bed & Breakfast
Comprised of 26 Individually Designed Suites•Fireplaces & Jacuzzis•Close to all the Action•Located in a Quiet Residential area next door to the Zoo, Balboa Park and the heart of the Hillcrest Area.
When You Care To Stay At The Very Best San Diego Has To Offer
(800) 938-8181
(619) 298-0823   Fax: (619) 294-8070

CALIFORNIA

Air Sightseeing Over San Francisco

A spectacular one-hour flight over San Francisco gives you some of the best views of the city and an opportunity to take memorable photographs. One-day air/ground tours from San Francisco to Yosemite or the Grand Canyon are also available. This option is perfect for overseas visitors who don't have time for longer visits to both San Francisco and Arizona. Yosemite tours depart daily, Grand Canyon tours are Tuesday, Thursday and Saturday. All include complimentary downtown hotel transfers in San Francisco.

San Francisco to Yosemite — Your hotel to Yosemite in 2 hours! See the valley, Bridalveil and Yosemite Falls, El Capitan, lunch stop at Ahwahnee Hotel (lunch not included), air return to SF, transfer to hotel.

San Francisco to Grand Canyon — Your hotel to Grand Canyon in 3 1/2 hours! Fly over Yosemite, Sierra Nevadas, Death Valley, Las Vegas, Lake Mead, Grand Canyon. South Rim ground tour, lunch at Arizona Room, show at IMAX, return.

Super Sights Over San Francisco — 50-minute fantastic flight over San Francisco, Golden Gate and Bay area. Free pickup and return from San Francisco's downtown hotels. $98 + tax.

Contact **Scenic Air Tours** at (415) 922-2386, (800) 95-SCENIC (957-2364), Fax: (415) 346-6940, E-mail: scenicair.com.

Off the Beaten Path into San Francisco's Victorian Neighborhoods

For a rare glimpse of San Francisco's historical past, take a **Victorian Home Walk** tour of some of her Victorian homes. You'll visit San Francisco's little-known neighborhoods, the Western Addition, Pacific Heights and Cow Hollow, each with its own unique character. This is the true heart of the city, remote from typical tourist haunts like Chinatown and Union Square. In these unexplored neighborhoods you'll view many beautiful Victorian homes of various styles, including Queen Anne, Edwardian and Italianate.

Guide Jay Gifford has extensive knowledge of the Victorian era and covers not only the architecture of San Francisco's past, but the lifestyle and history of this fascinating era. Unlike most tours, which have pre-set schedules, the Victorian Home Walk allows visitors to set their own pace and enjoy touring at their leisure.

Tours depart at 11:00 am from Union Square and last approximately 2 1/2 hours.

Contact Jay Gifford at (415) 252-9485, Fax: (415) 863-7577, E-mail: jay@victorianwalk.com.

accessories from clubwear to swimwear, ties & jeans.

GAY MART, 6th & University.

INTERNATIONAL MALE, 3964 5th Ave near University, (619) 294-8600. Retail clothing, accessories.

OBELISK THE BOOKSTORE, 1029 University Ave, Hillcrest, (619) 297-4171. Gay & lesbian bookstore with cards, jewelry & T-shirts.

■ Leathers/Piercing

CRYPT AT WOLFS, 3404 30th St, at Wolfs bar, (619) 574-1579. Leather store featuring an extensive line of leathers, lubes, safe-sex toys & magazines. Thurs-Sun 9pm-2am.

CRYPT ON WASHINGTON, 1515 Washington St in Hillcrest, (619) 692-9499. Magazines, safe-sex toys, gifts, leather repair, body jewelry, piercing, 10am-10pm (Sun 2-10pm).

HIP HAIR BODY PIERCING, 1039 Garnet Ave, Pacific Beach, (619) 270-7022.

■ Erotica

CINEMA F, 1202 University Ave near 10th Ave, (619) 298-0854.

F STREET CHULA VISTA, 1141 3rd Ave, Chula Vista, (619) 585-3314.

F STREET EL CAJON, 158 E Main, El Cajon, (619) 447-0381.

F STREET GASLAMP, 751 4th Ave near F St, (619) 236-0841.

F STREET KEARNY MESA, 7865 Balboa Ave near Convoy, (619) 292-8083.

F STREET MIRA MESA, 7998 Miramar Rd, Mira Mesa, (619) 549-8014.

F STREET NORTH PARK, 2004 University Ave at Florida, (619) 298-2644.

F STREET PACIFIC BEACH, 4626 Albuquerque St, Pacific Beach, (619) 581-0400.

F STREET SAN YSIDRO, 4650 Border Village Rd, (619) 497-6042.

F STREET SPORTS ARENA, 3112 Midway Dr, (619) 221-0075.

GEMINI ADULT BOOKS, 5265 University Ave, (619) 287-1402.

HI-LITE ADULT BOOKS/VIDEO, 3203 Hancock St, (619) 299-0601.

MIDNIGHT BOOKS, 1407 University Ave, (619) 299-7186, 24hrs. Also: 3604 Midway Dr, 222-9973; 4790 El Cajon Blvd, 582-1997; 1177 Palm Ave, Imperial Beach (619) 575-5081.

NORTH PARK ADULT VIDEO, 4094 30th St at Polk, (619) 284-4724.

SAN FRANCISCO INTRODUCTION

■ Information

BAY AREA CAREER WOMEN, (415) 495-5393. Mon-Fri 9am-5pm. Write 55 New Montgomery St, Suite 321, San Francisco, CA 94105.

**EUREKA VALLEY HARVEY MILK MEMO-

CALIFORNIA

RIAL BRANCH LIBRARY, 3555 16th St, (415) 554-9445. Comprehensive gay & lesbian collection.

WOMEN'S BATHS, see South Van Ness, Mission Area.

WOMEN'S CENTER, at Women's Bldg. See South Van Ness, Mission Area.

Accommodations

CARITAS BED & BREAKFAST NETWORK, (800) CARITAS, (312) 857-0801, Fax: (312) 857-0805. B&B, home-stay accommodations service. *Member: IGTA*

MI CASA SU CASA, PO Box 10327, Oakland, 94610, (510) 268-8534, USA toll-free (800) 215-CASA (2272), Fax: 268-0299. International and domestic home exchange and hospitality network for lesbian, gay and gay-friendly travelers. ♀ ♂

OCEANVIEW FARMS BED & BREAKFAST, 515 Bean Hollow Rd, Box 538, Pescadero, (415) 879-0698, Fax: (415) 879-0478. B&B on working horse breeding farm, women welcome. On coast halfway between San Francisco and Santa Cruz, 50 minutes by car south of San Francisco. Private baths, big country breakfast. Walk to sand beaches & rocky tide pools. ♂

Retail & Bookstores

WOMEN'S BOOKSTORES, see South Van Ness, Mission Area.

Erotica

WOMEN'S EROTICA, see South Van Ness, Mission Area.

SF WESTERN DISTRICTS
Includes Alamo Square, Haight, Pacific Hts, Fillmore areas

Accommodations

ALAMO SQUARE BED & BREAKFAST INN, 719 Scott St, (415) 922-2055, (800) 345-9888, Fax: (415) 931-1304. A unique and gracious Victorian B & B with **cozy guest rooms and luxurious, oriental-influenced suites**. All private baths, full breakfast, free off-street parking, MC, VISA, AMEX. Gay-friendly & owner-operated.

BOCK'S BED & BREAKFAST, 1448 Willard St, (415) 664-6842, Fax: (415) 664-1109. B&B, some straight clientele. Various units from plain to deluxe with beverage service & continental breakfast. Pool nearby, beach 3 miles. ♀ ♂

CHATEAU TIVOLI, 1057 Steiner St, (415) 776-5462, (800) 228-1647, Fax: (415) 776-0505. Bed and breakfast in Alamo Square district, 50% gay and lesbian. Spacious, grand rooms with fireplaces, stained glass and stunning views. Expanded continental breakfast Mon-Fri, full champagne breakfast Sat, Sun.

GOUGH-HAYES HOTEL, 417 Gough St, (415) 431-9131. Residence hotel, restaurant & bar. ♂

INN 1890, 1890 Page St, San Francisco, CA 94117, (415) 386-0486, toll-free: (888) INN-1890, Fax: 415) 386-3626. Gay-owned & -operated B&B, expanded continental breakfast, private & shared baths, 10 min. from the Castro, 50% gay & lesbian.

INN AT THE OPERA, 333 Fulton St, (415) 863-8400, (800) 325-2708. Hotel with restaurant & bar, mainly straight clientele.

METRO HOTEL, THE, 319 Divisadero St, (415) 861-5364, Fax: (415) 863-1970. Hotel with restaurant in historic district, 50% gay & lesbian. Variety of rooms with new interiors, color TVs, private showers, English garden.

RADISSON MIYAKO HOTEL, 1625 Post St at Laguna, (415) 922-3200, (800) 333-3333, Fax: (415) 921-0417. http://www.mim.com/miyako/, E-mail: miyakosf@slip.net. At the base of Pacific Heights, we're the closest luxury hotel to the Castro District. Most guest rooms are Western style with elegant Japanese touches and deep Japanese-style baths. There are also six traditional Japanese-style rooms. Several large suites have wet bars and saunas. Our emphasis on deep relaxation, superb service, and culinary creativity of Yoyo Bistro has earned the praise and loyalty of both tourists and business travelers.

RED VICTORIAN, 1665 Haight St, (415) 864-1978. Museum-like, gay-friendly B&B with Gallery of Meditative Art & Meditation Room. Economy to luxury rooms with private & shared baths & unique decor. Continental breakfast, non-smoking environment. Walk to Golden Gate Park & other nearby attractions.

Women's Accommodations

CARL STREET UNICORN HOUSE, 156 Carl St, (415) 753-5194. B&B near downtown, some straight clientele, men welcome. Rooms decorated with antiques, TV lounge, continental breakfast. ♀

ONE IN TEN, (415) 664-0748. Women-only guesthouse with kitchen privileges. In San Francisco's Sunset district across the street from the ocean, 3 blocks from Golden Gate Park. Surfing, nature trails. 1 block from streetcar. ♀

Bars

LION PUB, 2062 Divisadero St at Sacramento, (415) 567-6565. Blue jeans to businessmen. ♂

TRAX, 1437 Haight St, (415) 864-4213. Pool tables, happy hour, 75% men. ♂

Restaurants

BLUE MUSE, 409 Gough St, (415) 626-7505. Restaurant & bar. California cuisine with French influence, weekend brunch. Breakfast, lunch, dinner. ♀ ♂

CHARPE'S, 131 Gough St, (415) 621-6766. American cuisine, Sun brunch 11am-3pm. ♀ ♂

SF CASTRO AREA

Accommodations

ANNA'S THREE BEARS, 114 Divisadero St, (800) 428-8559, (415) 255-3167, Fax: 552-2959. Short-term rental B&B near The Castro, 50% gay & lesbian clientele. Luxurious apartments with antique furnishings, color cable TV, fireplaces & decks. Kitchens stocked for continental breakfast.

BECK'S MOTOR LODGE, 2222 Market St, (415) 621-8212, Fax: (415) 241-0435. Gay-friendly motor lodge, 1-1/2 blocks from Castro area. Comfortable rooms, color TVs, HBO, phones, coffee-makers. Beach 3-1/2 miles.

Visit San Francisco
(800) CARITAS
Caritas B&B Network

SAN FRANCISCO'S Opulent
Chateau Tivoli B&B
A LANDMARK MANSION
1-800-228-1647
(415) 776-5462

THE CLOSEST LUXURY HOTEL TO THE CASTRO DISTRICT
Radisson MIYAKO HOTEL SAN FRANCISCO
RESERVATIONS WORLDWIDE
• 800-333-3333 •
OR CALL YOUR TRAVEL PLANNER
1625 Post Street, San Francisco • Tel: (415) 922-3200
A Welcome Change

FERRARI GUIDES' GAY TRAVEL A to Z - 18th EDITION

CALIFORNIA

FYI

Trevor Hailey's Historical Walking Tours of San Francisco's Castro Area are Fascinating!

Since 1989, **Cruisin' the Castro** has afforded a validating experience for travelers to learn gay history in a concise and colorful format. You will be privileged to learn more gay and lesbian history than you ever knew existed.

Trevor Hailey's stream of entertaining and informative vignettes illuminate this history from 1849 to the present. You will understand the chain of events which enabled the "planets to line up" in such a fashion that the Castro emerged as its gay self. Hear the colorful history enthusiastically told in the setting where much of it took place. See Harvey Milk's camera shop and stand on the gayest four corners on earth. Tours are available year-round Tuesday-Saturday and holidays. They last from 10am to 1:30pm and include brunch for $30 per person. Reservations are required, because the tour has a four-person minimum and 16-person maximum.

Contact Trevor and **Cruisin' the Castro** at (415) 550-8110 or E-mail to: trvrhailey@aol.com.

BLACK STALLION INN, 635-635A Castro St, (415) 863-0131. Enjoy the quiet, relaxing atmosphere of our renovated Victorian flat in the Castro district, the center of the known gay universe, where streets are lined with all-gay bars, restaurants and shops. Make yourself at home by our woodburning stove. Lunch or snack in our shared kitchen or attend our private party / social club Tues-Sun (donations). Folsom St., downtown and Union Sq. shopping are nearby. Mention the exact title of this book for a special discount and gift bonus. ♂

CASTILLO INN, 48 Henry St, (415) 864-5111, (800) 865-5112, Fax: (415) 641-1321. B&B, private & shared baths, expanded continental breakfast. Mostly men with women welcome. ♂

INN ON CASTRO, 321 Castro St, (415) 861-0321. The innkeepers invite you into a colorful and comfortable environment filled with modern art and exotic plants. Meet fellow travelers from around the world over a memorable breakfast. We're just 100 yards north of the corner of Market & Castro, where the neighborhood is quiet, yet a stone's throw from the Castro Theater and dozens of bars, shops and restaurants. ♀♂

LE GRENIER, 347 Noe St, (415) 864-4748. B&B, private bath, some straight clientele. ♀♂

LEMON TREE HOMESTAYS PO Box 460424, San Francisco, CA 94146, (415) 861-4045. B&B in a Mediterranean-style home near Mission Dolores, private or shared bath, continental breakfast. ♂

RAMADA HOTEL CIVIC CENTER, 1231 Market St, (415) 626-8000, (800) 227-4747, Fax: (415) 861-1435. Gay-friendly hotel with restaurant & bar, AC, color cable TV, phone.

SAN FRANCISCO COTTAGE, 224 Douglass St, (415) 861-3220, Fax: (415) 626-2633. Very special. Very romantic. Lovely self-catering cottage and studio apartment on quiet residential street in The Castro. Both units are equipped with telephone, kitchen, cable TV, VCR and stereo. Garden patio, redwood deck and terraced garden. ♀♂

TWENTY-FOUR HENRY GUESTHOUSE, 24 Henry St, (415) 864-5686, (800) 900-5686, Fax: (415) 864-0406, E-mail: WalteRian@aol.com. Guesthouse, private & shared baths, extended continental breakfast, private phone, answering machine. ♀♂

VILLA, THE, 379 Collingwood, (415) 282-1367, (800) 358-0123, Fax: (415) 821-3995. E-mail: SFViews@aol.com. The flagship guesthouse of San Francisco Views rental services. Located atop one of the Castro's legendary hills, we offer magnificent views of the city from our double rooms and suites. Guests have the use of our fireplace lounge, complete kitchen and dining area overlooking our decks and swimming pool. Suites are equipped with TV, VCR and telephone with answering machine. Minutes from financial & shopping districts of downtown & 3 blocks from the heart of the Castro. ♀♂

WILLOWS, THE, 710 14th St, (415) 431-4770, Fax: (415) 431-5295. Your Haven within the Castro. Housed in a 1904 Edwardian, *The Willows B&B Inn* derives its name from the handcrafted willow furnishings which grace each room. Complementing these unique pieces are country antiques, willow chairs and headboards, warm earthtones, wooden shutters, fresh flowers, telephones, shared baths and expanded continental breakfast. ♀♂

■ Women's Accommodations

NANCY'S BED, (415) 239-5692. Women-only accommodations with shared bath. ♀

■ Bars

BADLANDS,★ 4121 18th St near Castro, (415) 626-9320. Live DJ 7 nites. ♂

CASTRO STATION, 456 Castro St, (415) 626-7220. ♂

DADDYS, 440 Castro St near 17th, (415) 621-8732. Patio. ♂

DETOUR,★ 2348 Market near Castro, (415) 861-6053. DJ, younger crowd, counterculture atmosphere, very cruisy. ♂

EDGE, 18th & Collingwood. 30's-50's age group, cruisy. ♂

GALLEON, 718 14th St near Church, (415) 431-0253. Piano bar, Sat & Sun brunch. ♀♂

HARVEY'S, 500 Castro St, (415) 431-4278. Gay memorabilia bar & restaurant with photos & items reminiscent of gay personalities & events. Lunch bar menu. ♀♂

MEN'S ROOM, 3988 18th St near Noe, (415) 861-1310. Mature crowd. ♂

METRO, 3600 16th St at Market, (415) 703-9750. Video bar & Chinese restaurant. Preppie, ivy-league clientele.

MIDNIGHT SUN, 4067 18th St near Castro, (415) 861-4186. Video bar, preppie crowd, everyone welcome. ♂

BLACK STALLION INN
San Francisco

A leather-levi-western bed and breakfast. Quiet, relaxed environment. Victorian house. Fireplace, sundeck, kitchen. Minutes to South of Market.

(415) 863-0131 day or night
635 Castro Street
San Francisco • 94114

— **CASTRO PARTY** —
for consenting males 18+
Hotline: (415) 863-6358

CALIFORNIA

MINT, THE, 1942 Market St, (415) 626-4726. Karaoke. ♪♂

MOBY DICK, 4049 18th St at Hartford & 18th, (415) 861-1199. Videos. 📺♂

PENDULUM, 4146 18th St near Castro, (415) 863-4441. Sports bar, opens 6am. 🏠📺♂

PILSNER INN, 225 Church St near Market, (415) 621-7058. Patio, many varieties of draft beer. 🏠♥📺♂

TRANSFER, 198 Church St at Market, (415) 861-7499. Opens 6am, drinking bar. 🏠♥♂

TWIN PEAKS TAVERN, 401 Castro St at 17th, (415) 864-9470. Mature sweater crowd. 📺♂

UNCLE BERTS, 4086 18th St near Castro, (415) 431-8616. Patio, sports bar. 🏠📺♂

■ Dance Bar/Disco

CAFE, THE,★ 2367 Market St, (415) 861-3846. Dance bar, pool table, balcony overlooking the Castro shopping area. Patio. 🏠♪♀♂

PHOENIX, THE, 482 Castro St near 18th, (415) 552-6827. Ethnic dance crowd, Latino, Asian. 🏠📺♪♂

■ Saunas/Health Clubs

EROS, 2051 Market St, (415) 864-3767, office (415) 255-4921. Sex club for men.

■ Fitness Centers

CITY ATHLETIC CLUB, 2500 Market St at 17th St, (415) 552-6680. Gym equipment, men only.

MARKET STREET GYM, 2301 Market St at Noe, (415) 626-4488. Visitors welcome, daily & weekly memberships. Bodybuilding, Jacuzzi & juice bar. Men & women. 📺

MUSCLE SYSTEM, Market near 16th St.

WOMEN'S TRAINING CENTER, 2164 Market St near Sanchez, (415) 864-6835. Weight training, free weights.

■ Restaurants

BOMBAY RESTAURANT, 2200 block of Market. 📺

CAFÉ FLORA, Market St at Noe. California cuisine. ♀♂

CHINA COURT, 19th & Castro Sts. Chinese cuisine.

COVE CAFE, 434 Castro St near Market, (415) 626-0462. Home-style diner. 📺♀♂

HOT 'N HUNKY, 4039 18th St, (415) 621-6365. Gourmet hamburgers. ♪♀♂

LATICIA'S, 2200 block of Market St, (415) 621-0441. Mexican cuisine, Sun brunch. 🍷📺

LUNA PIENA, 558 Castro St, (415) 621-2566. Lunch & dinner, Italian cuisine, patio. 📺

LUPIN'S,★ 18th St across from Midnight Sun bar. French cuisine, gay-friendly. 📺

MA TANTE SUMI, 18th St near Diamond. French with a Japanese flair, gay-friendly. 📺

METRO, 3600 16th St at the Metro men's bar, (415) 703-9750. Chinese cuisine. 🍷♀♂

NO NAME RESTAURANT,★ 2223 Market. Italian cuisine. 📺

ORPHAN ANDY'S, 3991 17th St near Castro, (415) 864-9795, 24hr burgers. 📺♀♂

PATIO CAFE, 531 Castro St, (415) 621-4640. Patio. ♀♂

PAZOLI'S, Market between Castro & Noe. Designer Mexican food with hunky waiters. Gay-friendly. 📺

SAUSAGE FACTORY, Castro St near 18th St. Italian, gay-friendly. 📺

SOUTH CHINA CAFE, 18th St near Castro. Chinese cuisine. 📺

WELCOME HOME, 464 Castro St near 18th, (415) 626-3600. Breakfast thru dinner. ♀♂

■ Retail & Bookstores

A DIFFERENT LIGHT, 489 Castro St, San Francisco, (415) 431-0891. Gay & lesbian bookstore, music, cards, videos, magazines. Open 10am-11pm & Fri & Sat till 12:00.

DOES YOUR MOTHER KNOW?, 4079 18th St near Hartford, (415) 864-3160. Cards & T-shirts.

HEADLINES FOR WOMEN, 549 Castro St, (415) 252-1280. Fashions, accessories, cards for women.

HEADLINES, 557 Castro St, (415) 626-8061. Clothing, cards, gifts.

WILD CARD, 3979-B 18th St, (415) 626-4449. Gay & lesbian erotica, cards, gifts, jewelry.

■ Leathers/Piercing

GAUNTLET, 2377 Market St at Castro, (415) 431-3133. Piercing, jewelry, crystals & periodicals, 7 days.

IMAGE LEATHER, 2199 Market St at Sanchez, (415) 621-7551, 621-6448. Custom leathers, barber shop.

LEATHER ZONE, Market near Castro.

WORN OUT WEST, 582 Castro St, (415) 431-6020. Used leather & clothes for men & women.

■ Erotica

JAGUAR BOOKSTORE, 4057 18th St, (415) 863-4777.

LE SALON, 4126 18th St, (415) 552-4213.

SF SOUTH OF MARKET

■ Bars

HOLE IN THE WALL, 8th at Folsom. Gay

INN ON CASTRO
321 castro st
san francisco
ca 94114
(415) 861-0321

SAN FRANCISCO VIEWS
THE VILLAS
- Guesthouse
- Best Castro Locations
- Short Term Rentals

(800) 358-0123
(415) 282-1367
email: sfviews@aol.com

JAGUAR
ADULT BOOKS
OBJECTS OF FINE ART

JAGUAR SAN FRANCISCO

T's Now Available
25th ANNIVERSARY

4057 18th ST. ▼ SF, CA 94114
Email: JagRon@cris.com
Phone 415-863-4777 ▼ fax 415-863-0235
Hours: Sun-Thurs 10a-11p ▼ Fri-Sat 10a-12p

FERRARI GUIDES' GAY TRAVEL A to Z - 18th EDITION

CALIFORNIA

bikers bar, hard rock & roll music, no dancing.
LOADING DOCK, 1525 Mission, (415) 864-1525. Open Thurs-Sun only. Leather, levi uniform dress code.
LONE STAR, 1354 Harrison near 10th St, (415) 863-9999. Bear bar, rock & roll, no dancing.
POWERHOUSE, 1347 Folsom, (415) 552-8689.
SAN FRANCISCO EAGLE, 398 12th St at Harrison, (415) 626-0880. Patio. Very popular on Sun afternoon.

Dance Bar/Disco
BOX, THE, 715 Harrison at 3rd, (415) 647-8258. Thurs dance night, 60% men.
ENDUP, ★ 401 6th St at Harrison, (415) 357-0827. Hi-energy club with many special dance club parties each with separate appeal. Sun T-dance.
G-SPOT AT THE ENDUP, at the Endup, 401 6th St. Largest women's dance club in San Francisco, Sat.
RAWHIDE II, 280 7th St near Folsom, (415) 621-1197.
STUD, THE, 399 9th St near Harrison, (415) 863-6623. Younger crowd, scheduled special nights. Sun: 80's music, Tues: Trannyshack transvestite dance bar with live entertainment.

Leathers/Piercing
A TASTE OF LEATHER, 317-A 10th St at Folsom, (415) 252-9166. Leather & erotica.
LEATHER ETC, 1201 Folsom at 8th St, (415) 864-7558. Leatherwear, boots, accessories.
MR S LEATHER/FETTERS USA, 310 7th St, (415) 863-7764. Complete line of leather, latex & bondage gear.
MR S LTD, 398 12th St at SF Eagle bar. Thur-Sun 9:30pm-1:30am.
ROB GALLERY, 30 Guerrero St, (415) 252-1198. Toys, equipment & clothing in leather, rubber & metals, gallery of erotic art & photography.
STORMY LEATHER, 1158 Howard St between 7th & 8th St, (415) 626-1672. Erotic boutique with leather, latex, PVC & toys. Mon-Thur 12-6pm, Fri, Sat 12-7pm, Sun 2pm-6pm.

Erotica
ARCADE BOOKS, 1036 Market St, (415) 863-7115.
CITY ENTERTAINMENT, 960 Folsom St near 5th, (415) 543-2124, 24hrs Fri, Sat. Sun till 3am Mon
FOLSOM GULCH, 947 Folsom near 5th, (415) 495-6402, 10am-3am, 24hrs Fri, Sat.
GOLDEN GATE NEWS #3, 99 Sixth St, (415) 896-9617.

SF DOWNTOWN
Includes Polk St. & Tenderloin areas

Accommodations
ALLISON HOTEL, 417 Stockton St, (415) 986-8737, Fax: (415) 392-0850. Gay-friendly budget hotel, near Union Square.
ATHERTON HOTEL, 685 Ellis St, (415) 474-5720, (800) 474-5720, Fax: (415) 474-8256. Gay-friendly hotel with restaurant & bar, near Polk St, Union Square, Civic Centre & Castro. Intimate, charming rooms, color TV, phones & private baths.
CARTWRIGHT HOTEL, THE, 524 Sutter St, (415) 421-2865, (800) 227-3844, fax: (415) 983-6244. Gay-friendly hotel with private baths, expanded continental breakfast, afternoon tea, evening wine hour, color cable TV, AC, 3 blocks to gay bars.
ESSEX HOTEL, THE, 684 Ellis St, (415) 474-4664, Fax: (415) 441-1800. Hotel, mainly straight clientele. 100 double rooms, walk to Union Square, Polk St, cable cars, Chinatown, theaters, restaurants.
GROSVENOR HOUSE, 899 Pine St, (415) 421-1899, (800) 999-9189, Fax: 982-1946. Suites with private baths.
HOTEL TRITON, 342 Grant Ave, (415) 394-0500, (800) 433-6611, Fax: (415) 394-0555. A Hit Hotel on the Bay. The Triton gives a new definition to the word "style." Each handcrafted lamp and table is a fine work of art. Rooms and suites with handpainted wall finishes have lavish comforters, fully-stocked honor bars and other amenities too numerous to mention. The location, just blocks from the financial district, is ideal for business travelers.
KING GEORGE HOTEL, 334 Mason St, (800) 288-6005, (415) 781-5050, Fax: 391-6976. Gay-friendly hotel 1 block from Union Square. Color TV, telephone, private baths. 10%-15% gay & lesbian clientele.
LELAND HOTEL, 1315 Polk St, (415) 441-5141, (800) 258-4458, fax: (415) 441-1449. Hotel, women welcome. Spacious European-style rooms. Walking distance to theatres, operas, Nob Hill, Chinatown, restaurants, boutiques, bars.
LOMBARD CENTRAL, A SUPER 8 HOTEL, THE, 1015 Geary Blvd, (415) 673-5232, (800) 777-3210, Fax: (415) 885-2802. Gay-friendly hotel with breakfast cafe, private baths, color TV, ceiling fans, complimentary wine hour weekdays 5:30-6:30 pm, 2 blocks to gay bars.
RENOIR HOTEL, 45 McAllister St, (415) 626-5200, (800) 576-3388. Gay-friendly, elegant historical landmark hotel with restaurant, bar, espresso bar & gift shop. Color TV, telephone, private bath & room service.
SAVOY HOTEL, 580 Geary St, (415) 441-2700. Elegant and romantic, this 83-room European-style boutique hotel is just 2-1/2 blocks from Union Square, located in the Theatre District.

Renovated in 1990 in a French Provençal style, it has feather beds, goose-down pillows, mini-bars, color TVs, and complimentary sherry, tea, and cookies. The Savoy Brasserie Restaurant is located in the hotel. 50% gay & lesbian clientele.
VICTORIAN HOTEL, 54 Fourth St, (415) 986-4400, (800) 227-3804. Ideally-located downtown hotel with restaurant & bar, 50% gay & lesbian clientele. Color TV, telephone, private & shared baths, continental breakfast.
YORK HOTEL, 940 Sutter St, (415) 885-6800, fax: (415) 885-2115, reservations only: (800) 808-9675. Gay-friendly hotel, private baths.

Bars
AUNT CHARLIE'S, 133 Turk St near Taylor, (415) 441-2922. Drinking bar, opens 6am.
CINCH SALOON, THE, 1723 Polk St near Washington, (415) 776-4162. Music variety, patio, open 6am, Sun BBQ & beer bust.
GANGWAY, 841 Larkin St near Geary, (415) 885-4441. Open 6am, brunch alternate Sun.
GINGER'S TOO!!, 43 6th St near Market, (415) 543-3622. 99% men, opens 10am.
GINGER'S TROIS, 246 Kearny, (415) 989-0282. Piano, Wed-Fri from 10am, upscale financial district bar, 75% gay.
GIRAFFE LOUNGE, ★ 1131 Polk St near Sutter, (415) 474-1702. Video bar, younger crowd.
HOB NOB, 700 Geary at Leavenworth, (415) 771-9866.
KIMO'S, 1351 Polk St at Pine, (415) 885-4535.
MACDONALD'S PUB, Market near 6th. Sports bar, 50% gay.
MARLENA'S, 488 Hayes, (415) 864-6672. Small neighborhood drag bar.
MOTHER LODE, 1002 Post St at Larkin, (415) 928-6006. Frequented by many transvestites.
OLD RICK'S GOLD, 939 Geary St, (415) 441-9211.
POLK GULCH SALOON, 1100 Polk St at Post, (415) 771-2022. Opens 6am, DJ.
POLK RENDEZVOUS, 1303 Polk, (415) 673-7934. Sports bar.
PS, 1121 Polk St, (415) 885-1448. Piano, small bar.
QT, 1312 Polk St, (415) 885-1114. Strippers.
REFLECTIONS, 1160 Polk St near Sutter, (415) 771-6262.
THREE-O-ONE CLUB, 301 Turk St.
WHITE SWALLOW, 1750 Polk St, (415) 775-4152. Piano bar nightly, 9pm-1am.
WOODEN HORSE, 622 Polk St near Turk, (415) 771-8063.

CALIFORNIA

■ Dance Bar/Disco
CLUB Q, 177 Townsend St at Club Townsend, (415) 647-8258. Women's dance party 1st Fri of the month.

N TOUCH, 1548 Polk St near Sacramento, (415) 441-8413.

PLEASUREDOME, ★ 177 Townsend St at 3rd St, Huge gay dance party Sun evening only.

■ Restaurants
GRUBSTAKE, THE, 1525 Pine St near Polk, (415) 673-8268. Food from 5pm till 4am, weekends from 10am.

QUETZAL, 1234 Polk St, (415) 673-4181. Indoor/outdoor cafe & restaurant, 6am-11pm 7 days.

■ Retail & Bookstores
HEADLINES, 838 Market St, (415) 956-4872. Clothing & gifts.

HEADLINES, Scott at Chestnut in the Marina, (415) 776-4466. Clothing & gifts.

■ Erotica
CAMPUS THEATRE, 220 Jones near Eddy, (415) 673-3384.

CENTURY THEATRE, 816 Larkin St at O'Farrell, (415) 776-3045.

CIRCLE J CINEMA, 369 Ellis St, (415) 474-6995, 10am-midnight.

FRENCHIES, 1020 Geary St near Polk, (415) 776-5940, 24hrs.

FRONT LYNE VIDEO, 1259 Polk St at Bush, (415) 931-9999. Videos, magazines, novelties & leather accessories.

LE SALON, 1124 Polk St near Post, (415) 673-4492.

NEW LOCKER ROOM, 1038 Polk St, (415) 775-9076.

NOB HILL ADULT THEATER, 729 Bush St near Powell, (415) 781-9468. Live shows, videos, arcade, buddy booths, 24hrs.

TEA ROOM THEATER, 145 Eddy St near Taylor, (415) 885-9887. Live shows.

WILD J'S BOOK & VIDEO, 90 Turk St near Market, (415) 567-9191, 24hrs.

SF MISSION

■ Information
WOMEN'S BLDG, 3543 18th St at Lapidge, (415) 431-1180. Resource center, meetings, events. Women's organizations meet here. Events bulletin board, closed Sun.

■ Accommodations
ANDORA INN, 2434 Mission St, (415) 282-0337, (800) 967-9219, Fax: (415) 282-2608. B&B with restaurant & bar, private & shared baths, expanded continental breakfast, some straight clientele.

INN SAN FRANCISCO, THE, 943 S Van Ness Ave, (415) 641-0188, (800) 359-0913, Fax: (415) 641-1701. Feel the years slip away, as you step through the massive, wooden doors of the *Inn San Francisco*. Each guest room is individually decorated with antiques, fresh flowers, marble sinks, polished brass fixtures and exquisite finishing touches. In the garden, under the shade of an old fig tree, a gazebo shelters the inviting hot tub. Mixed clientele with a very stong gay & lesbian following.

■ Bars
EL RIO, 3158 Mission St at Precita, (415) 282-3325. 50% gay & lesbian, patio Sun, DJ Fri, rock & roll Sat, salsa tea dance Sun afternoon.

ESPERANZA'S, 80 29th St, (415) 206-1405. Frequented by numerous gay & lesbian friends of Esperanza.

LEXINGTON CLUB, Lexington at 19th. Young crowd.

MUFFDIVE, 527 Valencia St at The Cassanova. (415) 487-6634. Sun women-only from 9pm.

WILD SIDE WEST, 424 Cortland Ave, (415) 647-3099. Gay women & straight people from the neighborhood. Patio, BBQ.

■ Dance Bar/Disco
ESTA NOCHE, 3079 16th St at Rondel, (415) 861-5757. Salsa disco Fri-Sun, after-hours, show nights, stripper nights.

■ Saunas/Health Clubs
OSENTO, 955 Valencia St near 20th St, (415) 282-6333. Women's bath, jacuzzi, massage.

■ Restaurants
BEARDED LADY, 485 14th St at Guerrero, (415) 626-2805. Vegetarian restaurant & coffeehouse. Mon-Fri 7am-7pm, entertainment mostly Sat.

CAFE COMMONS, 3161 Mission St, (415) 282-2928. Women's cafe, breakfast, lite meals, 7am-7pm daily.

EL NUEVO FRUTILANDIA, 3077 24th St near Folsom, (415) 648-2958. Puerto Rican & Cuban cuisine, closed Mon.

FIRECRACKER, Valencia & 21st. Chinese cuisine.

ROOSTER, Valencia at 22nd. European cuisine with Chinese accent.

■ Retail & Bookstores
BERNAL BOOKS, 401 Cortland Ave, (415) 550-0293. Very women-friendly general bookstore, also cards, comics, women's magazines. Closed Mon.

MODERN TIMES BOOKSTORE, 888 Valencia St. (415) 282-9246. Large gay, lesbian & feminist selections (books, mags & records), 7 days.

■ Erotica
GOOD VIBRATIONS, 1210 Valencia, (415) 974-8980. Women's erotica, videos.

MISSION NEWS, 2086 Mission at 17th St, (415) 626-0309, 24hrs.

SAN JOSE

■ Information
BILLY DE FRANK GAY & LESBIAN COMMUNITY CENTER, 175 Stockton Ave, (408) 293-4525. Gay Switchboard: (408) 293-2429. Mon-Fri 3pm-9pm, Sat noon-9pm, Sun 10am-9pm.

■ Bars
BUCK'S, 301 Stockton Ave at Julian, (408) 286-1176. 75% men, 25% women, CD jukebox. DJ Fri-Sun, small dance floor, 24hrs weekends.

MAC'S CLUB, 349 S 1st St near San Carlos, (408) 998-9535. Oldest bar in San Jose, downtown crowd.

RENEGADES, 393 Stockton Ave near Cinnebar, (408) 275-9902. Patio & fireplaces.

SIX FORTY-ONE, 641 Stockton Ave, (408) 998-1144. Dancing with DJ Fri-Sun, patio, BBQs Sun.

■ Dance Bar/Disco
A TINKER'S DAMN (TD'S), ★ 46 N Saratoga Ave near Stevens Creek, Santa Clara, (408) 243-4595. DJ nightly, summer BBQ Sun, 90% men, women welcome.

GREG'S BALL ROOM, ★ 511 Julian St across from the sports arena.

HAMBURGER MARY'S, ★ 170 W St John Street, (408) 947-1667. Dance bar, video bar, restaurant with dinner & brunch, 75% men, women welcome. DJ nightly, patio.

NEW SAVOY, 3546 Flora Vista Ave near El Camino Real, Santa Clara, (408) 247-7109, http://members.aol.com/newsavoy/ndex.html. DJ Fri-Sat, men welcome, non-smoking, micro brews, karaoke & comedy.

SILVER FOX, 10095 Saich Way near Stevens Creek, Cupertino, (408) 255-3673. CD jukebox, 80% men, 20% women.

■ Cafe
CAFE LIVITICUS, The Alameda near Julian.

■ Saunas/Health Clubs
WATERGARDEN, 1010 The Alameda at Atlas, (408) 275-1215 (tape), 24hrs.

■ Restaurants
HAMBURGER MARY'S, 170 W St John St,

The Inn San Francisco
943 Van Ness Avenue
San Francisco CA 94110
FAX (415) 641-1701
(415) 641-0188
(800) 359-0913

FERRARI GUIDES' GAY TRAVEL A to Z - 18th EDITION

CALIFORNIA

(408) 947-1667. Patio, Sun brunch, 50% men, 50% women with some straight clientele. ♀♂

Retail & Bookstores
SISTERSPIRIT, 175 Stockton Ave, at Billy de Frank Center, (408) 293-9372. Women's bookstore and coffeehouse with music, cards, journals, tee shirts, candles, posters, cards and an entire section devoted to gift items. Our coffeehouse evenings feature local artists, book signings & well-known entertainers. See our display ad for hours.

Leathers/Piercing
LEATHER MASTERS, 969 Park Ave, (408) 293-7660, (800) 417-2636. Leathers, cards, videos & erotic toys for men & women.

Erotica
BORDERLINE, 36 N Saratoga Ave, Santa Clara, (408) 241-2177, 9am-midnight.

SAN LUIS OBISPO
See Morro Bay/San Luis Obispo

SANTA BARBARA

Information
AIDS LINE, (805) 965-2925. Answering service connects you.

GAY & LESBIAN RESOURCE CENTER, 126 E Haley St, Ste A17, (805) 963-3636. ♀♂

Accommodations
GLENBOROUGH INN, 1327 Bath St, (805) 966-0589, (800) 962-0589, Fax: (805) 564-8610. Step into the past, where life was quieter and the pace relaxed. Sleep in an immaculate, old-fashioned room with fresh flowers and antiques. Enjoy hors d'oeuvres by the fireplace or indulge in the enclosed garden hot tub for private use. Gourmet breakfast delivered to your room. Take the 25-cent shuttle to the beach. Gay-owned and gay-friendly.

IVANHOE INN, 1406 Castillo St, (805) 963-8832, (800) 428-1787, fax: (805) 966-5523. Gay-friendly B&B & cottage. Variety of units, TV lounge, continental breakfast in picnic basket, welcoming wine & cheese. Nearby ocean beach. ♀♂

Bars
GOLD COAST, 30 W Cota near State, (805) 965-6701. 70% men, 30% women, small dance floor. 🎵♂

Glenborough Inn
Romantic
Intimate
Private

(800) 962-0589

1327 Bath St.
Santa Barbara CA

Dance Bar/Disco
FATHOM, 423 State St, (805) 882-2082. 🎵♂

Restaurants
CHAMELEON, 421 E Cota, (805) 965-9536. Upscale restaurant & bar. 🍷♀♂

SOJOURNER CAFE, 134 E Canon Perdido St, (805) 965-7922. Natural foods, desserts, espresso.

Retail & Bookstores
CHOICES BOOKS & CAFE, 901 De la Vina at Canon Perdido, (805) 965-5477. Gay & lesbian bookstore & cafe, light menu.

EARTHLING BOOKSHOP, 1137 State St, (805) 965-0926. General bookstore with a small section of women's, gay & lesbian titles.

Erotica
FOR ADULTS ONLY, 223 Anacapa St, (805) 963-9922, 24hrs.

RIVIERA ADULT VIDEOS, Hollister Ave near Modoc.

SANTA CRUZ

Information
LESBIAN & GAY COMMUNITY CENTER, 1328 Commerce Lane, (408) 425-5422. Noon-8pm 7 days.

Women's Accommodations
EL MAR VISTA, 5115 Ironwood Dr, Soquel, CA, (408) 476-5742. Women-only B&B overlooking Monterey Bay. Two rooms share living room & bath. ♀

GROVE, THE, 40 Lily Way, La Selva Beach, CA 95076, (408) 724-3459. Women-only country retreat. Secluded artist's mini-farm (peacocks, chickens, cats) near spectacular, uncrowded beach south of Santa Cruz. Two separate cottages with kitchen, fireplace. Shared hot tub and sun deck. ♀

Bars
DAKOTA, Pacific Ave near Lincoln. ♀♂

Dance Bar/Disco
BLUE LAGOON, 923 Pacific Ave, (408) 423-7117. Alternative dance club, many students.. 🎵♂

Retail & Bookstores
BOOK LOFT, 1207 Soquel Ave, (408) 429-1812. A used book store with separate room for women's titles.

HERLAND BOOK CAFE, 902 Center St, (408) 429-6636. Women's bookstore & cafe. Quarterly dances. 🎵

SANTA MARIA

Information
AIDS PROJECT, 2255 S Broadway, (805) 349-9947.

Erotica
DIAMOND ADULT, 942 W Main St, (805) 922-2828.

SANTA ROSA

Dance Bar/Disco
CLUB HEAVEN, 120 5th St at Davis, (707) 544-6653. Large alternative dance club, Sun 9pm-4am. 🎵♀♂

SANTA ROSA INN, 4302 Santa Rosa Ave, (707) 584-0345. 50% men, 50% women, patio. 🎵♀♂

Retail & Bookstores
COPPERFIELD'S, two shopping center locations: 2402 Magowan, (707) 578-8938, Raley's Town Center, 584-4240. General bookstore with gay section.

SAWYER'S NEWS, 733 4th St, (707) 542-1311. Gay magazines.

Erotica
SANTA ROSA ADULT BOOKSTORE, 3301 Santa Rosa Ave, (707) 542-8248, 7 days.

SEBASTOPOL

Retail & Bookstores
COPPERFIELD'S BOOKS, 138 N Main St, (707) 823-2618. General bookstore with gay & lesbian section.

MILK & HONEY, 137 N Main, (707) 824-1155. Feminist bookstore, gifts.

SONOMA

Accommodations
GAIGE HOUSE INN, 13540 Arnold Dr, Glen Ellen, CA 95442, (707) 935-0237, (800) 935-0237, Fax: (707) 935-6411. www.gaige.com. Gay-friendly 9-room inn bordered by creek & woodlands, 7 miles from Sonoma & near dozens of wineries. Two-course breakfasts, pool on premises, rooms with king & queen beds, AC, oversized towels, direct-dial phones, English toiletries.

SONOMA CHALET B&B, 18935 Fifth St West, (707) 938-3129, (800) 938-3129. Gay-friendly B&B & cottages in country setting. Fireplaces or wood-burning stoves, private & shared baths. Expanded continental breakfast, Jacuzzi & free bicycle use.

STARWAE INN, 21490 Broadway (Hwy 12), (707) 938-1374, (800) 793-4792, Fax: (707) 935-1159. Gay-friendly B&B cottages 1 hr from San Francisco & 1 hr from Russian River. Rent entire cottage or separate suites. AC, kitchen, refrigerator, private baths, expanded continental breakfast.

SONOMA COUNTY

Accommodations
WHISPERING PINES B&B, 5950 Erland Rd, Santa Rosa, CA 95404, (907) 539-0198 (Tel/Fax). B&B Sonoma/Napa wine country, private baths, full breakfast, Jacuzzi, 50% gay & lesbian clientele.

Women's Accommodations
ASTI RANCH, 25750 River Rd, (707) 894-5960, Fax: (707) 894-5658. Women-only

cottage near Russian River, 1-1/2 hr north of San Francisco. Kitchen, refrigerator, coffee/tea-making facilities, ceiling fan, private bath & continental breakfast. Non-smoking. ♀

STOCKTON

■ *Dance Bar/Disco*
CLUB PARADISE, 10100 N Lower Sacramento Rd, (209) 477-4724. 50% men & women, 7 days, 6pm-2am , Fri, Sat 5pm-2am, Sun 3am-2am.

TARZANA

■ *Erotica*
LOVE BOUTIQUE, 18637 Ventura Blvd, (818) 342-2400. Women-owned & -operated elegant erotic store, intimate lesbian & gay videos & lingerie. We do home parties for women to display our products.

THREE RIVERS

■ *Accommodations*
ORGANIC GARDENS B&B, 44095 Dinely Dr, (209) 561-0916, Fax: (209) 561-1017. Lesbian-owned, gay-friendly B&B with photo & art gallery.

UPLAND

See Pomona

VACAVILLE - FAIRFIELD

■ *Information*
GAY & LESBIAN LINE, (707) 448-1010. For Solano County, leave a message. Call here for Women Preferring Women group.

■ *Retail & Bookstores*
VACAVILLE BOOK COMPANY, 315 Main Street, (707) 449-0550. General bookstore, gay & lesbian sections. Men's meetings 2nd & 4th Tues, occasional women's meetings.

VALLEJO

■ *Dance Bar/Disco*
NOBODY'S PLACE, 437 Virginia St, (707) 645-7298. Dance bar in a Victorian building, karaoke, DJ Fri & Sat, 60% men, 40% women.

Q, 412 Georgia St, (707) 644-4584. DJ on weekend, male strippers occasionally, karaoke Thurs & Sun, 75% men, 25% women. ♂

■ *Erotica*
BOOKS ETC, 540 Georgia St, (707) 644-2935.

VENTURA

■ *Information*
AIDS INFO, (805) 643-0446, (800) 540-2437.
GAY & LESBIAN COMMUNITY CENTER, 1995 E Main St, (805) 653-1979.

■ *Dance Bar/Disco*
CLUB ALTERNATIVES, 1644 E Thompson, (805) 653-6511. Dance bar, DJ Wed, Fri & Sat, drag shows Sat.

PADDY MCDERMOTT'S, 2 W Main St, (805) 652-1071. Dance bar, DJ Fri-Sun, BBQ Sun on patio.

VICTORVILLE

■ *Bars*
WESTSIDE 15, THE, 16868 Stoddard Wells Rd, (619) 243-9600. 2pm-2am 7 days, 50% men, 50% women. Serving liquor. ♂

WALNUT CREEK

■ *Bars*
DJ'S PIANO BAR, 1535 Olympic Blvd, (510) 930-0300. Piano bar, 60% men, 40% women.

TWELVE TWENTY, 1220 Pine St, (510) 938-4550. Pool tables, live DJ weekends, 60% men, 40% women.

■ *Dance Bar/Disco*
JUST REWARDS (JR'S), ★ 2520 Camino Diablo, (510) 256-1200. Huge dance bar & lounge, 80% women (except Fri 95% men for 18 & over).

WHITTIER

■ *Accommodations*
COLEEN'S CALIFORNIA CASA, Whittier, CA (310) 699-8427. Gay-friendly B&B 8 miles from downtown LA (20 minutes from Civic Center). Private & shared baths, AC, color cable TV, phone, gay & lesbian following.

■ *Erotica*
LIBRARY ONE, 10618 Whittier Blvd, (310) 699-9458.

COLORADO

WHO TO CALL
For Tour Companies Serving This Destination
See Colorado on page 12

STATEWIDE

■ *Accommodations*
CARITAS BED & BREAKFAST NETWORK, (800) CARITAS, (312) 857-0801, Fax: (312) 857-0805. B&B, home-stay accommodations service. *Member: IGTA*

ASPEN

■ *Information*
ASPEN GAY/LESBIAN COMMUNITY, (970) 925-9249. Local gay info, mostly eves 8pm-midnight.

COLORADO

Visit Colorado (800) CARITAS
Caritas B&B Network

■ *Accommodations*
HOTEL ASPEN, 110 W Main St, (800) 527-7369, (970) 925-3441, Fax: (970) 920-1379. Centrally located gay-friendly hotel. Variety of rooms & penthouse suites, 4 with private Jacuzzi. Fireplace in common area. Expanded continental breakfast buffet, heated pool, gym & outdoor Jacuzzi.

MOLLY GIBSON'S, 101 W Main St, (970) 925-3434. Lodge with 50 rooms, some with fireplaces, Jacuzzi's. Gay-friendly.

SNOW QUEEN VICTORIAN B&B LODGE & COOPER ST LOFT, 124 E Cooper, (970) 925-8455, Fax: (970) 925-7391. Gay-friendly accommodations. Quaint Victorian lodge with a variety of rooms, private baths, 2 kitchen units & TV parlour with fireplace, plus tastefully furnished studio apartments with full kitchen, fireplaces & modern amenities. Continental breakfast.

■ *Cafe*
HOWLING WOLF, E Hopkins, (970) 920-7771. Popular after-hours cafe, gay-friendly especially Mon & Wed.

■ *Retail & Bookstores*
EXPLORE BOOKSELLERS & COFFEEHOUSE, 221 E Main, (970) 925-5336, (800) 562-READ (7323). General bookstore with small gay & lesbian section. Gourmet veget. cafe upstairs.

ASPEN AREA

■ *Accommodations*
RISING STAR GUEST RANCH, (888) GAY-RNCH (429-7624). A year-round resort for gay men and women planned for 1997 or 98.

BOULDER

■ *Information*
AIDS INFO, (303) 444-6121. Mon-Fri 8am-8pm, Sat 10am-6pm.

■ *Women's Accommodations*
BOULDER GUEST HOUSE, 1331 Marshall St, Boulder, (303) 938-8908, fax: (303) 938-8908, 11. Guest room with private bath. ♀

■ *Dance Bar/Disco*
YARD, THE, 2690 28th St Unit C (enter from Bluff St), (303) 443-1987. High energy dance bar, 50% men, 50% women (more women Sat), smoking & non-smoking sections.

■ *Cafe*
WALNUT CAFE, THE, 3073 Walnut, (303) 447-2315. Espresso, small food menu, gay friendly.

COLORADO

Retail & Bookstores

ARIA, 2047 Broadway, (303) 442-5694. Gift shop with cards & T-shirts.

BOULDER BOOK SHOP, 1107 Pearl St, (303) 447-2074. General bookstore with gay & lesbian section.

WORD IS OUT, 1731 15th St, (303) 449-1415. Women's bookstore with gifts, music, etc. Lesbian titles, some gay men's titles. Tue-Sat 10am-6pm, Sun noon-5pm, closed Mon.

Leathers/Piercing

BOUND BY DESIGN, 1119 13th St, (303) 786-7272. Tattoos, piercings, body jewelry.

Erotica

NEWS STAND BOOKSTORE, 1720 15th St, (303) 442-9515. Large gay selection, video rentals & sales.

BRECKENRIDGE

Accommodations

BUNK HOUSE LODGE, THE, PO Box 6, 80424, (970) 453-6475. Men-only B&B, shared bath. 🏳️‍🌈♂

CARBONDALE

Women's Accommodations

STARBUCK'S RANCH, 3390 Country Rd 113, (970) 945-5208. Women-only B&B cabin & rooms with mountain views. Color TV, phone, refrigerator, private & shared baths. Hot tub, deck, gazebo, stocked fishing holes, horseback riding & hiking. Breakfast in the sunroom.

COLORADO SPRINGS

Information

LESBIAN & GAY COMMUNITY CENTER & HELP LINE, (719) 471-4429.

Accommodations

PIKES PEAK PARADISE B&B, PO Box 5760, Woodland Park, CO 80866, (719) 687-7112, (800) 354-0989, Fax: (719) 687-9008, E-mail: woodlandco@aol.com. We're so happy, you might even say we're...gay! A Southern mansion with views of Pikes Peak, fireplace, queen bed, gourmet breakfast and friendly hosts eager to make you feel at home. Attractions include: US Air Force Academy, Pikes Peak Drive, Cog Railway, hiking, picnics, four-wheeling, fishing, boating, bicycling, hot air balloon rides and more. 50% gay & lesbian clientele.

Bars

MAN STOP, 512 W Colorado at Hide & Seek bar, (719) 634-9303. Game room. 🏳️‍🌈♂

Dance Bar/Disco

HIDE & SEEK COMPLEX,★ 512 W Colorado Ave near Walnut (rear), (719) 634-9303. Complex with Hide & Seek dance bar, Branding Iron country & western dance bar, Man Stop game room, Colorado Grill restaurant.

TRUE COLORS, 1865 N Academy near Palmer Park, (719) 637-0773. Wed-Fri 3pm-2am, Sat 6pm-2am. 80% women, men welcome & urged to come in.

Erotica

FANTASY BOOKS, 3425 E Platte Ave, (719) 596-6311.

FIRST AMENDMENT BOOKS, 220 E Fillmore, (719) 630-7676.

MONARCH MAGAZINE, 2214 E Platte, (719) 473-2524.

CREEDE

Accommodations

OLD FIREHOUSE NO. 1, INC, THE, Main Street (PO Box 603), (719) 658-0212. Gay-friendly Victorian B&B with restaurant & Victorian Ice Cream Parlor. Private baths, full breakfast & library lounge.

DENVER

Information

AIDS LINE, (303) 837-0166, 830-2437, (800) 333-2437, TTD. Mon-Fri 9am-5pm, or tape.

Accommodations

MILE HI BED/BREAKFAST, (303) 329-7827, (800) 513-7827. A 1910 Victorian in a quiet neighborhood. Contemporary interior, king-sized beds, VCR, TV, video library, fireplace in common area, semiprivate baths, exercise room, laundry facilities, patio and garden. Expanded continental breakfast. *Please Note: We may move. Please inquire for updated information!* ♂

P.T. BARNUM ESTATE, (303) 698-0045. B&B 1 mile from downtown, some straight clientele. Private & shared baths, TV, expanded continental breakfast. ♀♂

TWIN MAPLES BED & BREAKFAST, 1401 Madison St, Denver, CO 80206, (303) 393-1832, toll free: (888) 835-5738, Fax: (303) 394-4776, e-mail: twinmaples@boytoy.com. Our spacious rooms are richly appointed with period antiques and Queen Anne furnishings. In the European tradition, our ultra-firm beds are dressed with colorful linens and feather pillows. Expanded continental breakfast is served, baths are private or shared, and our cozy living room welcomes you to relax. We're ideally located in the Congress Park neighborhood and are close to excellent restaurants and shopping. Some straight clientele. ♀♂

VICTORIA OAKS INN, 1575 Race St, (303) 355-1818, (800) 662-OAKS (6257), Fax: (303) 331-1095. **Enjoy warmth, hospitality, and personalized services in surroundings designed for your personal comforts — a home you'd love to come home to.** We have guest rooms furnished with antiques, panoramic views, private & shared baths. Our continental breakfast is inspiring. Walk to the zoo, museum, downtown, gay clubs, and Imax Theatre. ♀♂

Bars

BJ'S CAROUSEL, 1380 S Broadway near Arkansas, (303) 777-9880. Sun Brunch 10am, restaurant from 5pm-10pm Tues-Sun.

BRICKS, 1600 E 17th Ave, (303) 377-5400.

BRIG, 117 Broadway, (303) 777-9378.

CHRISTOPHER'S UPTOWN, 1700 Logan St, (303) 837-1075.

CLUB STUD, 255 S Broadway, (303) 733-9398.

COLFAX MINING CO, 3014 E Colfax, (303) 321-6627.

DEN, THE, 5110 W Colfax Ave near Sheridan, (303) 534-9526. Bar & restaurant (dinner only), Sun brunch, 60% men, 40% women.

DENVER DETOUR, 551 E Colfax, (303) 861-1497. Bar with lunch & dinner menu, after hours Fri & Sat.

GARBO'S, 116 E 9th Ave near Lincoln, (303) 837-8217. Piano bar, cabaret & restaurant.

GRAND, THE, 538 E 17th Ave, at Pearl, (303) 839-5390. Piano bar.

HIGHLAND BAR, 2532 15th St, (303) 455-9978. DJ on weekends, 60% men, 40% women.

MIKE'S, 60 S Broadway, (303) 777-0193. Dancing, showbar.

MR BILL'S, 1027 Broadway, (303) 534-1759. Popular happy hour.

R&R, 4958 E Colfax, (303) 320-9337.

THREE SISTERS, 3358 Mariposa St at 34th, (303) 458-8926. Gay men welcome.

TRIANGLE,★ 2036 Broadway near Stout, (303) 293-9009. Outdoor deck, after hours Fri & Sat.

Dance Bar/Disco

C'S, 7900 East Colfax, (303) 322-4436. Patio.

CHARLIE'S DENVER, 900 E Colfax at

COLORADO

Trenton, (303) 839-8890. C&W dance bar, lunch & dinners.
CLUB PROTEUS,★ 1669 Clarkson, (303) 869-GODS. Hi-energy dance bar.
COMPOUND, THE, 145 Broadway, (303) 722-7977. Variety of music nights.
ELLE,★ 716 W Colfax, (303) 572-1710.
RAVEN, 2217 Welton St.
SIRENS, women's dance night at Maximillian's every Fri. NOTE: Schedule frequently changes, call first.
SNAKE PIT,★ 608 E 13 Ave, (303) 831-1234. Dance cafe with punky, tattoed, pierced crowd. Skunk Motel & Lounge parties.
TEQUILA ROSA'S,★ 5190 Brighton Blvd, (303) 295-2891. Dance club & restaurant.
TIMES TEN, 314 E 13th Ave near Grant, Hi-energy dance bar, show bar, male strippers.
TRACKS 2000, 2975 Fox St, (303) 292-6600. Hi engergy dance bar.
YE'O MATCHMAKER, 1480 Humboldt, at Colfax, (303) 839-9388. dance bar, eclectic crowd. Popular drag shows, holds pageants frequently, scheduled latino nights.

■ Cafe
ART OF COFFEE, THE, 1836 Blake St, (303) 294-0200. Coffee house.
CAFE COMMUNIQUÉ, 99 W 9th Ave, (303) 534-1199.
CITY SPIRIT CAFE, 1420 Market, (303) 575-0022.
DADS, 282 S Penn, (303) 744-1258. Bar atmosphere with coffeehouse fare, lite menu.

■ Saunas/Health Clubs
COMMUNITY COUNTRY CLUB, 2151 Lawrence St (enter through alley), (303) 297-2601. JO club with male strippers.
DENVER SWIM CLUB, 6923 E Colfax, (303) 321-9399. Private men's club, 24hrs.
MIDTOWNE SPA, 2935 Zuni St near 30th Ave, (303) 458-8902. Private club, 24hrs.

■ Fitness Centers
BROADWAY BODYWORKS, 160 S Broadway, (303) 722-4342. Weight training for men & women. Leather shop inside.

■ Restaurants
BAROLO GRILL, 3030 E 6th Ave, (303) 393-1040. Northern Italian cuisine.
AUBERGINE, 225 E 7th Ave, (303) 832-4778. Country French cuisine.
BACKSTAGE, 1380 S Broadway, at BJ's Carousel, (303) 777-9880. Casual dining in an upscale atmosphere. Daily 5pm-10pm, Sun brunch from 9am, closed Mon.
CAFE BERLIN, 2005 E 17th Ave, (303) 377-5896. German cuisine.

DEN, THE, 5110 W Colfax Ave, at The Den bar. American comfort food.
DENVER SANDWICH, 1217 E 9th Ave, (303) 861-9762.
JAN LEONE, 1509 Marion, (303) 863-8433. Restaurant & bar.
LAS MARGARITAS, 1066 Olde S Gaylord St, (303) 777-0194. Lunch, dinner, Mexican cuisine. 2nd location: 17th Ave at Downing St, (303) 830-2199.
THREE SONS, 2915 W 44th Ave, (303) 455-4366. Italian cuisine.
WHITE SPOT RESTAURANT, 800 Broadway, (303) 837-1308, coffeeshop chain.

■ Retail & Bookstores
BOOK GARDEN, 2625 E 12th Ave, (303) 399-2004, (800) 279-2426, Fax: (303) 399-6167. Colorado's complete lesbian bookstore. Large selection of books, jewelry, music, t-shirts, posters and specialty items. Phone and mail order available. A great place to visit for local information!
BOY TOY, (303) 394-4776, pride clothing, retail via the internet: www.boytoy.com.
CATEGORY SIX BOOKS, 42 S Broadway, Denver, 80209, (303) 777-0766, Fax: (303) 777-0782. Largest selection of gay men's books: literature, studies & periodicals. Hours are Mon-Fri 10am-6pm, Sat-Sun 11am-5pm.
STUDIO LITES, 333 Broadway, (303) 733-7997. card & gift shop, wigs & gowns.
THOMAS FLORAL & ADULT GIFTS, 1 Broadway #108 near Ellsworth, (303) 744-6400. Gay & lesbian T-shirts & adult gifts.

■ Leathers/Piercing
BOUND BY DESIGN, 1336 E Colfax, (303) 830-7272. Tattoos, piercings, body jewelry.
CRYPT, THE, 131 Broadway, between 1st & 2nd, (303) 733-3112. Denver's number one leather store for men & women.
FIT TO A TEE, 160 S Broadway, inside Broadway Bodyworks. Leather shop inside gym.

■ Erotica
ADULT TRADING POST, 7 S Federal Blvd, (303) 935-2901, 24hrs.
ADULT WORLD, 6600 N Federal Blvd, (303) 428-3933, 24hrs.
CIRCUS, 5580 N Federal, (303) 455-3144, 24hrs weekends.
CRYPT CINEMA, 139 Broadway, (303) 778-6584. Six XXX, all-male movies.
DOVE, 3480 W Colfax, (303) 893-0037. Cinema.
GALAXY THEATRE, 633 E Colfax, (303) 831-8319.
HEAVEN SENT ME, 482 S Broadway, (303) 331-8000. Leather, rubber, pride items.
KITTY'S EAST, 735 E Colfax, (303) 832-5140.
KITTY'S SOUTH, 119 S Broadway, (303) 733-2411.
KITTY'S TABOR, 3333 W Alameda, (303) 936-6314.

LÉ BAKERY SENSUAL, 6th Ave & Grant St, (303) 595-0055. Erotically designed cakes, cards & gifts.
ON BROADWAY VIDEO, 160 S Broadway, (303) 698-9565. General video store with adult videos.
PLEASURES ADULT ENTERTAINMENT CENTERS. Southwest: 3250 W Alameda, 934-2373; Central: 127 S Broadway, 722-5852; West 3490 W Colfax, 825-6505; North: 6970 Hwy 2, Commerce City (25 min outside Denver), 289-4606.
VIDEO LIBRARY, 1060 Broadway, (303) 831-1871.
VIDEOTIQUE, 1205 E 9th Ave, (303) 861-PINK (7465).

DURANGO

■ Information
GAY & LESBIAN ASSN (GLAD), (970) 247-7778, 7-10pm, local info.

■ Accommodations
RIVER HOUSE BED & BREAKFAST, 495 Animas View Dr, (970) 247-4775.

FLORISSANT

■ Accommodations
MCNAMARA RANCH, 4620 County Rd 100, Florissant, CO 80816, (719) 748-3466. Ride wilderness trails or climb above the timberline. We can plan overnight camping trips or return to the ranch for good food & company. Rides tailored to your stamina. You can also help move sheep from pasture to pasture, bottle-feed lambs or sheer sheep, depending on season. Lodging & horseback riding included in rate.

FT COLLINS

■ Dance Bar/Disco
CHOICE CITY SHOTS, 124 Laporte Ave, (970) 221-4333. pub atmosphere in a dance bar, dance music, retro, classic rock, etc, country

Twin Maples

**Your Bed & Breakfast
In the Heart
of Historic Denver**

Toll Free: **(888) 835-5738**
(303) 393-1832

FERRARI GUIDES' GAY TRAVEL A to Z - 18th EDITION   395

COLORADO

FYI

Hike or Ski to Cozy Shelter in the High Country

Yurts are remote, secluded shelters in the Colorado State Forest perfect for getting away from the world! Each yurt is set off by itself, at around 9500 ft. in the Medicine Bow Range of northern Colorado. Mountain scenery and wildlife viewing is bountiful...moose, elk deer, coyote and red tail hawk are regulars here! The yurts keep you warm and dry...they are comfortable, cabin-like shelters, complete with woodstove, beds, kitchen center, tables and chairs. Getting to the yurts is half the fun via skiing, mountain biking or hiking (one is reachable by car and wheelchair-accessible). Explore a seemingly endless trail system that links old logging roads and hiking trails. Most prefer to experience the yurts on their own, but several organizations offer groups, clinics and workshops utilizing the yurts. We also offer a limited guide service, so if you have special needs or would like additional trip support, just let us know.

Contact **Never Summer Nordic** at (970) 482-9411, or write PO Box 1983, Ft. Collins, CO 80522.

FYI

A Working Women's Ranch

For a real Rocky Mountain high, ride on wilderness trails seldom used by humans with the women of **McNamara Ranch**. Ride above timberline toward snowcapped peaks. Rides are tailored to your stamina. This unique vacation lets women really sample ranch life. Help move sheep on horseback and fetch them at night. In March, it's sheep shearing, April, lambing season. In May, there are usually lambs that need to be bottle fed. After a full day, starting early, you'll be hungry for dinner at the ranch house (specializing in lamb). Movies about horses are available.

The hot tub is perfect for soaking under the stars after a long ride in the saddle. A teepee is also available by the pond for camping. There's even a stocked pond full of rainbow trout! The cost is $125 per person per day and $100 per person per day for two or more people. Maximum four guests at one time. Both lodging and horseback riding are included in the rate.

Contact **McNamara Ranch** at (719) 748-3466.

---

nites, 7 days 11am-2am, sometimes later (Tues closes at midnite).

NIGHTENGALES, 1437 E Mulberry, (970) 493-0251. Hi energy music dance bar, quiet bar, game room, 50% men, 50% women.

■ *Erotica*

BOOK RANCH, 730 S College Ave, (970) 493-9404. Videos.

GRAND JUNCTION

■ *Bars*

QUINCY'S, 609 Main St, (970) 242-9633. Gay eves only, straight before 8pm, jukebox & dance floor.

GREELEY

■ *Dance Bar/Disco*

C DOUBLE R BAR, 822 9th St Plaza, (970) 353-0900. C&W & alternative mix music, open 7 days, nightly specials.

■ *Erotica*

EIGHTH AVE ARCADE, 330 8th Ave, (970) 352-9681.

PUEBLO

■ *Information*

PUEBLO AFTER 2, PO Box 1602, Pueblo, 81002, (719) 564-4004. Community outreach & networking with other statewide organizations. Organizes dances, picnics & group outings. Travelers welcome.

■ *Bars*

PIRATE'S COVE, 409 N Union Ave, (719) 542-9624. 90% men, Tues-Sat 2pm-2am, Sun 4pm-2am, best Fri & Sat, closed Mon, adding DJ in '97.

■ *Dance Bar/Disco*

AQUA SPLASH, 806 Santa Fe Dr. (719) 543-3913. Dance bar & lounge, pool table, 4pm-2am Tues-Sat, 90% women.

STEAMBOAT SPRINGS

■ *Accommodations*

ELK RIVER ESTATES, Box 5032, (970) 879-7556. B&B, women welcome, some straight clientele.

CONNECTICUT

Who To Call
For Tour Companies Serving This Destination
See Connecticut on page 13

BRIDGEPORT

Dance Bar/Disco
CAUGHT IN THE ACT, 1246 Main St, (203) 333-1258.

Restaurants
BLOODROOT RESTAURANT, 85 Ferris St, (203) 576-9168. Vegetarian restaurant, terrace. Closed Mon.

Retail & Bookstores
BLOODROOT BOOKSTORE, in Bloodroot Restaurant bldg, 85 Ferris St. Women's bookstore, closed Mon. Hours the same as Bloodroot Restaurant.

COLLINSVILLE

Retail & Bookstores
GERTRUDE & ALICE'S, 2 Front St, (860) 693-3816. Coffeehouse & general bookstore with gay & lesbian section, Wed & Thurs 10am-9pm, Fri & Sat 10am-11pm, Sun 10am-5pm.

DANBURY

Information
WOMEN'S CENTER, 2 West St, (203) 731-5200. Info & referral, travelers call first. Lesbian support group Wed 7:30pm.

Dance Bar/Disco
TRIANGLES CAFE, 66 Sugar Hollow Rd 3 miles south of Danbury Mall on Rte 7, (203) 798-6996. 5pm-1am (Fri, Sat till 2am).

Erotica
FANTASY ISLE, Mill Ridge Rd, (203) 743-1792.

ENFIELD

Erotica
BOOKENDS, 44 Enfield St, Rte 5, (860) 745-3988.

FAIRFIELD

Information
WOMEN'S MUSIC ARCHIVES, (203) 255-1348 for appointment.

GROTON

Erotica
VIDEO EXPO, 591-A Scheetz Plaza #9, (860) 448-0787.

HARTFORD

Information
AIDS LINE, (860) 247-2437, 24hrs.
HARTFORD GAY & LESBIAN COMMUNITY CTR, 1841 Broad St, (860) 724-5542. 10am-10pm Mon-Fri, gay group meetings, library. AIDS line: 278-4163.

Accommodations
EIGHTEEN NINETY-FIVE HOUSE, THE, 97 Girard Ave, (860) 232-0014, (860) 232-0594. Gay-friendly bed & breakfast. Private & shared baths, breakfast.

Bars
BAR WITH NO NAME, 115 Asylum St. Gay-friendly weekdays, futuristic decor, entertainment or drag shows Sun. Sun it's THE spot.

Dance Bar/Disco
CHEZ EST,★ 458 Wethersfield Ave, (860) 525-3243. Disco.
METRO CLUB & CAFE, 22 Union Pl, (860) 278-3333. Dance club with cafe & patio upstairs & bars downstairs, variety of atmospheres.
NICK'S CAFE & CABARET, 1943 Broad St, (860) 956-1573. Dance bar, 60% men, 40% women.
POLO CLUB, 678 Maple Ave, (860) 278-3333. Gay-owned & -operated, Sat & Sun from 3pm.
SANCTUARY, 2880 Main St, (860) 724-1277. Huge video dance bar, 80% men, 20% women. Club Lucy women's dance night one Sat per month.
TILL DAWN, 495 Farmington Ave. After hours dance bar from midnite till very late. To open April '97.

Restaurants
READER'S FEAST CAFE, 529 Farmington Ave, at Reader's Feast bookstore, (860) 232-3710. Bookstore cafe. Coffeehouse Sats, Sun brunch. Scheduled feminist meetings.

Retail & Bookstores
HILLIARD'S PRIDE, 495 Farmington Ave, (860) 523-7280. Custom gay jewelry.
METROSTORE, 495 Farmington Ave, (860) 231-8845. Videos, books, magazines, leathers, games and more. Mon, Thur, Fri 8am-8pm. Tue, Wed & Sat 8am-5:30pm. Closed Sun.
READER'S FEAST BOOKSTORE & CAFE, 529 Farmington Ave near Kenyon, (860) 232-3710. General bookstore with gay men's & lesbian sections.

Erotica
AIRCRAFT BOOK & NEWS, 347 Main St, E Hartford, (860) 569-2324.
DANNY'S ADULT WORLD, 151 W Service Rd, (860) 724-5589. Also: 35 W Service Rd, 549-1896.
RED LANTERN BOOKS, 1247 Main St, E Hartford, (860) 289-5000.

MANCHESTER

Information
WOMEN'S CENTER, (860) 647-6056. Hours irregular, best 8am-4:30pm or write MTC, PO Box 1046, Manchester, 06045-1046.

Dance Bar/Disco
ENCOUNTERS, 47 Purnell Pl, (860) 645-6688. Dance & cruise bar.

Erotica
VIDEO EXPO, 691 Main Street, (860) 649-0451.

MIDDLETOWN

Information
WESLEYAN WOMEN'S RESOURCE CENTER, 287 High St, (860) 347-9411 (ext 2669). Hours vary, library, resource files.

MYSTIC

Accommodations
ADAMS HOUSE, THE, 382 Cow Hill Rd, (203) 572-9551, In CT: (800) 553-9551, Out-of-State: (800) 321-0433. Gay-friendly colonial-style B&B with rooms & self-contained Carriage House. Private baths, TV lounge & expanded continental breakfast. Carriage House has color cable TV, VCR & sauna.

NEW HAVEN

Information
YALE WOMEN'S CENTER, 198 Elm St near College, (203) 432-0388. Mon-Fri 9am-5pm & 7-9pm.

Bars
ONE SIXTY-EIGHT YORK ST CAFE, 168 York St near Chapel, (203) 789-1915. Bar & restaurant, summer patio, women welcome.

Dance Bar/Disco
GOTHAM CITY, Crown St near Church. To open April '97.

Erotica
FAIRMONT THEATRE, 33 Main St, (203) 467-3832.
NEW HAVEN BOOK & VIDEO, 754 Chapel St, (203) 562-5867.

NEW LONDON

Information
WOMEN'S CENTER, 16 Jay St, (860) 447-0366. Lesbian group meetings.

Dance Bar/Disco
FRANK'S PLACE, 9 Tilley St next to fire station, (860) 443-8883. Dance & show bar with courtyards, 75% men, 25% women.

CONNECTICUT

Women's Sailing School

Sea Sense, the women's sailing school, was founded by women for women. That means no shouting, no embarrassment, no do-this and do-that, just an opportunity to learn and have fun in a friendly, relaxed and supportive environment. Captains Patti Moore and Carol Cuddyer share a lifetime of sailing knowledge and experience. Their instruction style is patient, perceptive and thorough. A variety of courses is available for beginners and experienced sailors. Boats are seaworthy and big enough to be easy to handle. At the end of a one-week course, you get a certificate that helps you charter boats on your own.

In summer, Sea Sense holds classes in New London, CT (Long Island Sound) and at various ports on the Wisconsin shore of Lake Michigan. The Gulf coast of Florida, Miami, the Keys and the Caribbean are used for winter classes. Locations are chosen for a wide range of challenging sailing experiences, beautiful anchorages and sun-filled, relaxing days.

Contact **Sea Sense** at (860) 444-1404, (800) 332-1404, E-mail: seasense@aol.com.

the women's sailing & powerboating school

■ Restaurants
KEEP, THE, 194 Bank St, (860) 443-8728. Coffeeshop, poet's corner, changing regional menu daily.

■ Erotica
BOOKAZINE, 116 Bank St, (860) 442-7030.

NORFOLK

■ Accommodations
LOON MEADOW FARM, 41 Loon Meadow Dr, PO Box 554, Norfolk, CT 06058, (860) 542-6085. B&B on 20 acres, 2-1/2 hours from NYC or Boston, private baths, woman-friendly. ♀♂

MOUNTAIN VIEW INN & RESTAURANT, Rt 272 South, (860) 542-6991. Gay-friendly inn & restaurant, private & shared baths.

NORWALK

■ Women's Accommodations
SILK ORCHID, (203) 847-2561. Women-only B&B in rural CT with double room, private bath, near convenient train to NYC.

STAMFORD

■ Dance Bar/Disco
ART BAR, 84 W Park Place, (203) 973-0300. Thurs & Sat alternative nights.

TWISTED, 56 W Park Place, (203) 978-1078. Gay night at Spin nightclub, Wed 9pm-1am. Unverifiable spring '97.

VERNON

■ Erotica
DANNY'S ADULT WORLD, 65 Windsor Ave, (860) 872-2125.

WALLINGFORD

■ Dance Bar/Disco
CHOICES, 8 N Turnpike Rd, exit 65 off Rte 15, (203) 949-9380. Hi-energy dance club, 60% men, 40% women. Fri Girl Twirl women's night.

WATERBURY

■ Bars
BROWNSTONE CAFE, ★ 29 Leavenworth, (203) 597-1838. Large, upscale New York-style pub, 5pm-1am Tues-Sun, Fri & Sat 5pm-2am, 50% men, 50% women. ♀♂

■ Dance Bar/Disco
MAXIE'S CAFE, 2627 Waterbury Rd, (203) 574-1629. Dance club, DJ weekends. May change in 1997.

WEST HAVEN

■ Accommodations
SEA MIST INN, 295 Beach St, West Haven, CT 06516, (203) 937-6773, Fax: (203) 933-9591. Gay & lesbian motel on the ocean. Part of huge complex with gay dance bar & restaurant.

■ Dance Bar/Disco
PIRATE'S COVE BEACH CLUB, 295 Beach St, (203) 937-8100. Dance bar & restaurant in huge complex with motel, swimming pool. Outside & inside dance bar with separate DJs, Sun tea dance 4pm, Wed ladies night, Thurs separate men's & women's rooms.

WESTPORT

■ Beaches
GAY BEACH, east end of Sherwood Island State Park.

■ Dance Bar/Disco
BROOK CAFE, THE, 919 Post Rd East, (203) 222-2233. Piano, cabaret upstairs. Patio, Sun brunch, women welcome.

WETHERSFIELD

■ Erotica
VIDEO EXPO, 1870 Berlin Turnpike, (203) 257-8663.

WILLIMANTIC

■ Retail & Bookstores
EVERYDAY BOOKS & CAFE, 713 Main St, (203) 423-3474. Alternative bookstore with a gay & lesbian selection.

■ Erotica
DANNY'S ADULT WORLD, 1110 Main St, (203) 456-3780.

THREAD CITY, 503 Main St, (203) 456-8131.

DELAWARE

DOVER

■ Dance Bar/Disco
RUMOURS RESTAURANT & NIGHT CLUB, 2206 N DuPont Hwy, (302) 678-8805. Bar & restaurant, open 7 days, male & female strippers, 60% men, 40% women. ♀♂

MILTON

■ Women's Accommodations
HONEYSUCKLE, 330 Union St, (302) 684-3284. Women-only inn & guesthouses near Rehoboth. Inn has double rooms, outdoor hot tub, massage, women's library & full breakfast. Pool on premises.

REHOBOTH BEACH

■ Information
CAMP REHOBOTH, 39 Baltimore Ave, (302) 227-5620, www.camprehoboth.com. Gay service organization & local gay information.

■ Accommodations
BEACH HOUSE, 15 Hickman, (302) 227-7074, (800) 283-4667. B&B, moderate to superior rooms, TV lounge, continental breakfast. ♀ ♂

CHESAPEAKE LANDING, 101 Chesapeake St, Rehoboth Beach, DE 19971, (302) 227-2973,

Fax: (302) 227-0301, E-mail: roccofc@aol.com. In the forest on the lake, by the sea, is Chesapeake Landing. Enjoy the hospitality of our Frank Lloyd Wright-inspired home, the area's only waterfront bed and breakfast resort. Spend lazy afternoons on the beach, half a block away, or soak up the sun beside our sparkling pool. Go fishing or explore the lake in our rowboats and paddleboats. Full gourmet breakfast, private baths, AC, cocktails poolside, on dock or by the fire. Some straight clientele.

GUEST ROOMS AT REHOBOTH, 45 Baltimore Ave, (302) 226-2400. Victorian house with private & shared baths, expanded continental breakfast, color cable TV, AC, hot tub.

MALLARD GUEST HOUSES, THE, 67 Lake Ave, (302) 226-3448. Guesthouses, 3 locations. Private & shared baths, TV lounge, bicycles. Continental breakfast.

RAMS HEAD INN, RD 2, Box 509, (302) 226-9171. Men-only B&B, color cable TV, VCR, video tape library, private & shared baths, expanded continental breakfast. Heated pool, full gym with sauna Jacuzzi & hot tub.

REHOBOTH GUEST HOUSE, 40 Maryland Ave, (302) 227-4117. B&B, variety of accommodations. Shared baths, continental breakfast & nearby ocean beach. Some straight clientele.

SAND IN MY SHOES, 6 Canal St, (302) 226-2006. B&B, private baths.

SILVER LAKE, 133 Silver Lake Dr, (302) 226-2115, (800) 842-2115. B&B guesthouse with lake and ocean view. Luxurious rooms and apartments with modern conveniences, including color cable TV, AC & private baths. Sun room, lounge, expanded continental breakfast.

SUMMER PLACE, THE, 30 Olive Ave, Rehoboth, DE 19971, (302) 226-0766, (800) 815-3925, Fax: (302) 226-3350. Newly built hotel with 5 apartments & 23 rooms on the ocean block, contemporary furnishings, mostly gay & lesbian clientele.

■ *Bars*

BLUE MOON,★ 35 Baltimore Ave, (302) 227-6515. Upscale restaurant & bar.

CULTURED PEARL, 19 Wilmington Ave, (302) 227-8493. Sushi bar.

DOS LOCOS, 42 1/2 Baltimore Ave, (302) 226-LOCO. Mexican bar & restaurant.

IGUANA GRILL, 56 Baltimore Ave, (302) 227-0948. Bar & restaurant, 75% gay & lesbian clientele.

■ *Dance Bar/Disco*

CLOUD 9, 234 Rehoboth Ave, (302) 226-1999.

RENEGADE,★ at Renegade Resort, 4274 Hwy 1 (302) 227-4713. Disco, bar, restaurant, summer T-dance, patio. Open 7 days in summer, off-season open Fri-Sun.

■ *Cafe*

DREAM CAFE, 26 Baltimore Ave, (302) 226-2233. Espresso bar & gourmet deli, lesbian-owned & -operated.

■ *Restaurants*

BACK PORCH, 21 Rehoboth Ave, (302) 227-3674. Patio, seasonal.

BLUE MOON,★ 35 Baltimore Ave, same building as Blue Moon bar, (302) 227-6515. Restaurant & bar, upscale gourmet American cuisine.

CAFE TERIA, 12 Wilmington Ave, (302) 226-2011.

CELSIUS, 50 Wilmington Ave, (302) 227-5767.

FUSION, 50 Wilmington Ave.

LA LA LAND, 22 1/2 Wilmington Ave, (302) 227-3887. Restaurant & bar.

MANO'S, 10 Wilmington Ave, (302) 227-6707.

PLANET X, 33 Wilmington Ave, (302) 226-1928. Vegetarian cuisine.

SAVANNAH'S, 37 Wilmington Ave, (302) 227-1994.

TIJUANA TAXI, 207 Rehoboth Ave, (302) 227-1986. Mexican food.

■ *Retail & Bookstores*

LAMBDA RISING, 39 Baltimore Ave, (302) 227-6969. Gay & lesbian bookstore.

WILMINGTON

■ *Bars*

EIGHT FOURTEEN, THE, 814 Shipley St, (302) 657-5730. Bar & restaurant. Small dance floor, Thurs Latin night, Fri ladies night, DJ Fri-Sun.

■ *Dance Bar/Disco*

ROAM, 913 Shipley St near 10th St above the Shipley Grill, (302) 658-ROAM (7626). Disco 7 nights, 6pm-1am, Fri 5pm-1am, 70% men, 30% women. Women welcome.

■ *Restaurants*

SHIPLEY GRILL, 913 Shipley St near 10th St,

·1836 CALIFORNIA·

A Victorian Bed & Breakfast

(202) 462-6502

Washington, DC

DIST. OF COLUMBIA

(302) 652-7797. American cuisine, lunch & dinner. Popular, large gay following. "Gay Monday" half price entrees with coupon from Roam disco.

DISTRICT OF COLUMBIA

WHO TO CALL

For Tour Companies Serving This Destination
See Washington DC on page 29

WASHINGTON

■ *Information*

GAY & LESBIAN SWITCHBOARD, (202) 628-4667. 7:30pm-10:30pm 7 days. Irregularly staffed.

LESBIAN LINE, (202) 628-4666, 7:30pm-10:30pm 7 days.

LESBIAN SERVICES OF WHITMAN-WALKER CLINIC, 1407 South St NW, (202) 939-7875, 9am-6pm Mon-Fri.

■ *Accommodations*

BRENTON, THE, 1708 16th St NW, (202) 332-5550, (800) 673-9042, Fax: (202) 462-5872. Guesthouse, women welcome. Spacious rooms furnished in antiques, art, oriental or period carpets. TV lounge & expanded continental breakfast.

CAPITOL HILL GUEST HOUSE, 101 Fifth St NE, (202) 547-1050. B&B, 50% gay & lesbian. Comfortable rooms with Victorian-era decor, refrigerator in hall, continental breakfast.

EIGHTEEN THIRTY-SIX CALIFORNIA ST, 1836 California St NW, (202) 462-6502, Fax: (202) 265-0342. Centrally-located small, elegant B&B in a 1900 Victorian townhouse. Amenities include telephone, AC, clock radios and private and shared baths. Some rooms have cable TV. Breakfasts are served family-style in the dining room. Minutes from all the capital's attractions.

EMBASSY INN, 1627 16th St NW, (202) 234-7800, (800) 423-9111, Fax: (202) 234-3309. Gay-friendly B&B on historical 16th St near restaurants and night life. Rooms with Fed-

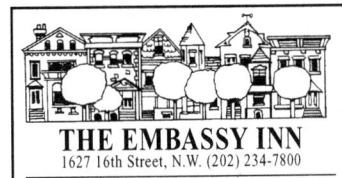

THE EMBASSY INN
1627 16th Street, N.W. (202) 234-7800

THE WINDSOR INN
1842 16th Street, N.W. (202) 667-0300

Washington, D.C. 20009 • (800) 423-9111

FERRARI GUIDES' GAY TRAVEL A to Z - 18th EDITION   399

DIST. OF COLUMBIA

eralist-style decor, private baths, telephone, color cable TV with free HBO and maid service. Continental breakfast and complimentary coffee, tea and evening sherry. **Enjoy a relaxed atmosphere and personalized service.**

GUEST HOUSE, THE, Settlers Valley Way, Lost River, WV (304) 897-5707, Fax: 897-5707. B&B, 50% gay & lesbian. Variety of spacious rooms. Private baths, TV lounge, indoor hot tub, outdoor Jacuzzi & full breakfast.

KALORAMA GUEST HOUSE AT KALORAMA PARK, 1854 Mintwood Pl NW, (202) 667-6369, Fax: (202) 319-1262. B&B, mixed straight/gay/lesbian clientele. Private and shared baths. Charming Victorian home in tree-lined downtown residential area. Walk to night spots in Dupont Circle and Adams Morgan, and the Metro. Complimentary continental plus breakfast and evening aperitif. Ten minutes to most tourist spots.

KALORAMA GUEST HOUSE AT WOODLEY PARK, 2700 Cathedral Ave NW, (202) 328-0860, Fax: (202) 319-1262. B&B, mixed straight/gay/lesbian clientele. Private and shared baths. Lovely Victorian home in tree-lined downtown residential area. Walk to the Metro and night spots in Adams Morgan and Dupont Circle. Complimentary continental plus breakfast and evening aperitif. Ten minutes to most tourist spots.

LITTLE WHITE HOUSE, THE, 2909 Pennsylvania Ave SE, (202) 583-4074. B&B, panoramic views of Capitol Dome & Washington Monument. Spacious rooms, shared baths, TV lounge & expanded continental breakfast.

TAFT BRIDGE INN, 2007 Wyoming Ave NW, (202) 387-2007, Fax: (202) 387-5019. Gay-friendly inn in a turn-of-the-century Georgian mansion, priv.& shared baths, cont. break.

WILLIAM LEWIS HOUSE, THE, 1309 R St NW, Washington, DC (202) 462-7574, (800) 465-7574, Fax: (202) 462-1608. In addition to the antique luxuries of a completely restored house, there are many modern conveniences, such as direct-dial phones with answering machines and ceiling fans in each guest room and a hot tub in the garden. We are conveniently located in the heart of the gay community very close to 17th St., Dupont Circle, Adams Morgan and The Mall. Three subway lines are within walking distance of this house, as are many of Washington's best restaurants. You are always welcome at Washington's finest bed and breakfast.

WINDSOR INN, 1842 16th St NW, (202) 667-0300, (800) 423-9111, Fax: (202) 667-4503. Gay-friendly B&B on historical 16th St. Variety of comfortable, tastefully decorated rooms and suites with modern conveniences. Cont. breakfast, comp. coffee, tea and evening sherry, color cable TV, free HBO. **Enjoy a relaxed atmosphere and personalized service.**

■ Bars

BANANA CAFE, 500 8th St SE, (202) 543-5906. Piano bar & rest. with dancing.

CIRCLE TAVERN, 1629 Connecticut Ave NW, (202) 462-5575. 3 levels: video dance bar, restaurant & tavern with terrace. Drag shows Sun.

CLUB 55, 55 K St SE, (202) 488-0555. Gay Sun only for Academy Awards of Washington drag show. Performing Sept-May, closes for the summer.

COBALT & SOL,★ 1639 R St NW, at 17th, upstairs, (202) 232-6969. Cruise bar, 2 levels with different music, upstairs more progressive music. Have non-smoking area.

D.I.K., 1635 17th St NW, (202) 328-0100. Bar & Dupont Italian Kitchen restaurant.

DC EAGLE,★ 639 New York Ave NW near 6th, (202) 347-6025.

FIREPLACE, THE, 2161 P Street NW at 22nd NW, (202) 293-1293. Men's video bar.

GREEN LANTERN, THE, 1335 Green Court NW (behind lot at 1335 L St.), (202) 638-5133. Two-level men's club, DJ weekends. Upstairs, cruise bar & techno music. Downstairs, video bar & lounge.

JR'S, 1519 17th St NW, (202) 328-0090. Video & cruise bar, popular happy hour, has non-smoking area.

LA CAGE AUX FOLLIES, 18 O St SE, (202) 554-3615. Movies & music videos, male exotic dancers.

LARRY'S LOUNGE, 1836 18th St NW, (202) 483-0097. Bar & restaurant.

MR P'S, 2147 P St NW near 22nd NW, (202) 293-1064. Video bar, live video jockey, patio, live DJ, drag shows Sun. Rainbow store upstairs.

NOB HILL, 1101 Kenyon NW at 11th NW, (202) 797-1101. Bar & restaurant, disco. Cabaret upstairs Sat. Gospel singers Sun.

OUT OF THE BLUE, 915 U St, (202) 332-7004. Small jazz club, restaurant.

PHASE I, 525 8th St SE, (202) 544-6831. Jukebox, 30's +.

TRUMPETS, 1603 17th St NW at Q St, (202) 232-4141. High-tech video bar & restaurant, patio in summer & frozen daquiri bar. Slyde - monthly women's dance parties.

WAVE BAR & LOUNGE, 1731 New Hampshire Ave, (202) 518-5011. Loungy, sofas.

■ Dance Bar/Disco

BACHELOR'S MILL, 1104 8th St SE, (202) 544-1931. Drag shows Sun, Wed ladies night, closed Mon.

BADLANDS,★ 1415 22nd St NW near P St NW, (202) 296-0505. Video cruise & dance bar. Upstairs Annex has pool table, video games & Last Chance Saloon. Young crowd.

CIRCLE, TERRACE, UNDERGROUND, PLAYROOM, 1629 Connecticut Ave NW at The Circle. (202) 462-5575. Dance & video bar & restaurant.

DELTA ELITE, 3734 10th St NE near Perry (metro: Brookland), (202) 529-0626. Private club, Sat only.

ESCANDALO & BREADBASKET CAFE, 2122 P St NW 1/2 blk from 21st St, (202) 822-8909. Video dance bar & restaurant. Lots of Latin music, salsa & merengue lessons Mon. Drag shows after hours.

HUNG JURY, 1819 H St NW near 19th St, (202) 785-8181. Open Fri & Sat, younger crowd.

OMEGA, 2122 P ST NW (rear), (202) 223-4917. Video, dance & cruise bars, game room, lounge. After-hours Thurs-Sat, drag shows Sun.

OZONE, 1214 18th St NW, (202) 293-0303, hi energy video dance bar.

REMINGTON'S, 639 Pennsylvania Ave Nr SE 6th, (202) 543-3113. Video C&W dance bar, brunches, 80% men.

TRACKS,★ 1111 1st St SE, (202) 488-3320. Giant hi-energy dance bar, patio, video, after hours, sand volleyball court. Ladies nights, black & white Sun restaurant.

WET & EDGE,★ 56 L St SE, (202) 488-1200. Big dance bar, male strippers, snack bar.

ZIEGFELD'S & SECRETS COMPLEX,★ 1345 Half St SE at O St, (202) 554-5141. Show bar with dancing. Secrets has male dancers. Drag shows late Thur & on Sun.

■ Cafe

CAFE BERLIN, 322 Massachusetts Ave NE, (202) 543-7656. German cuisine.

CUSANO'S MEET MARKET, 1613 17th St NW, (202) 319-8757.

FRANKLIN'S, 2000 18th St NW, (202) 319-1800.

FRIENDS MEETING HOUSE, 2111 Florida Ave NW, (202) 483-3310. Cafe for HIV+ people & their family & friends, Sat from 7:30pm, smoke- & alcohol-free.

POP STOP, 1513 17th St NW, (202) 328-0880. Pastries & desserts, light fare.

William Lewis House

Close to Nightlife & Restaurants of Dupont Circle

(800) 465-7574

WASHINGTON, DC

FLORIDA

■ Saunas/Health Clubs

CLUB WASHINGTON, #20 O St SE near Half St SE, (202) 488-7317. Priv. club, 24hrs, 7 days.

CREW CLUB GYM & LOUNGE, 1321 14th St NW, (202) 319-1333. Nudist gym & lounge facility, adult viewing areas, open 24hrs.

GLORIOUS HEALTH CLUB, 24 O St SE, (202) 863-2770. GH club, 24hrs.

■ Restaurants

ANNIE'S,★ 1609 17th St NW near Q, (202) 232-0395. Sat, Sun brunch.

ARIZONA, 1211 Connecticut Ave NW, (202) 785-1211. After hours gay parties & special events mainly for gay men.

CAFE LUNA, 1633 P St NW, downstairs, (202) 387-4005.

DUPONT ITALIAN KITCHEN, 1637 17th St NW.

HERB'S, 1615 Rhode Island Ave, (202) 333-4372. Restaurant at Holiday Inn, popular for Sun brunch.

JOLT 'N BOLT, 1918 18th St NW, (202) 232-0077.

LA FONDA, 1639 R St NW, (202) 232-6965.

LAS CRUCES COOK 'N CANTINA, 1524 U St NW, (202) 328-3153.

MEDITERRANEAN BLUE, 1910 18th St NW, (202) 483-2583. Restaurant & bar.

MERCURY GRILL, 1602 17th St NW. American cuisine.

MR HENRY'S, 601 Penn Ave SE, (202) 546-8412. Restaurant and bar, American cuisine.

RANDY'S CAFE, 1517 17th St NW, (202) 287-5399.

TRUMPETS RESTAURANT & LOUNGE,★ 1603 17th St NW, (202) 232-4141. Restaurant & video bar, nouvelle American cuisine with Mediterranean & Asian overtones, ladies' night Wed.

TWO QUAIL, 320 Massachusetts Ave NE, (202) 543-8030.

ZUKI MOON, 824 New Hampshire, (202) 333-3312. Noodle house.

■ Retail & Bookstores

LAMBDA RISING BOOKS, 1625 Connecticut Ave NW near R St, (202) 462-6969, Fax: (202) 462-7257. E-mail: lamdarising@his.com. Gay & lesbian books & magazines.

LAMMAS WOMEN'S BOOKS & MORE, 1426 21st St NW at P, 2 blocks from Dupont Circle, (202) 775-8218, (800) 955-2662. Lammas is DC's one-stop shop for lesbians. Books, videos, music, jewelry, sex toys, magazines and much more for today's Sapphist. Readings, events, mail order, resources, friendly staff!

PRIDE EMPORIUM, 2147 P St NW, 2nd floor, above Mr P's Bar, (202) 822-3984. Rainbow, pride items.

■ Leathers/Piercing

LEATHER RACK, 1723 Connecticut Ave NW near R St, (202) 797-7401. Clothing, accessories for men, women.

■ Erotica

FOLLIES, 24 O St SE near Half St SE, upstairs, (202) 484-0323, 24hrs. Gay films & male dancers.

PLEASURE PLACE, two locations: 1063 Wisconsin Ave NW & 1710 Connecticut Ave NW, (202) 333-8570 & 483-3297. Lingerie, accessories for men, women.

FLORIDA

WHO TO CALL
For Tour Companies Serving This Destination
See Florida on page 15

STATEWIDE

■ Accommodations

CARITAS BED & BREAKFAST NETWORK, (800) CARITAS, (312) 857-0801, Fax: (312) 857-0805. B&B, home-stay accommodations service. *Member: IGTA*

AMELIA ISLAND

■ Accommodations

AMELIA ISLAND WILLIAMS HOUSE, 103 S 9th St, Fernandina Beach, (904) 277-2328, (800) 414-9257. Gay-friendly B&B in Antebellum mansion. Color cable TV, VCR, video tape library, AC, ceiling fan, private baths, full breakfast.

BOCA GRANDE

■ Tours, Charters & Excursions

WHELK WOMEN, PO Box 1006T, Boca Grande, FL 33921, (941) 964-2027. Go day sailing and dolphin watching in beautiful Charlotte Harbor and Gulf of Mexico with us. Picnic on white sandy beaches of uninhabited barrier islands. Visit Calusa shell mounds, learn sailing techniques (chart reading and taking control at the helm), and swim, sun and relax under sail in the privacy of the open uncrowded harbor.

BOCA RATON

■ Accommodations

FLORESTA HISTORIC BED & BREAKFAST, 755 Alamanda St, (407) 391-1451. B&B near ocean beach. Double room & cottage with modern conveniences, continental breakfast.

■ Dance Bar/Disco

CHOICES, 21073 Powerline Rd, (407) 482-2195. Video bar, pool table, 70% men, 30% women. Sun-Thurs till 2am, Fri-Sat till 3am. DJ Tue (best night), Fri, Sat, Karaoke Thur.

COCOA BEACH

■ Bars

CLUB CHAOS, 610 Forrest Ave, (407) 639-0103.

■ Dance Bar/Disco

WANNA BE'S, 231 Minutemen Causeway, (407) 868-1898. 2 blocks from beach, Mon-Fri 5pm-2am, Sat-Sun 12pm-12am, 70% men, 30% women, lite menu.

■ Erotica

BEACH VIDEO, 150 Cocoa Beach Causeway, (407) 784-4756. Arcade.

DAYTONA BEACH

■ Information

AIDS LINE OUTREACH, (904) 255-0019. Mon-Fri 8am-5pm.

LAMBDA CENTER & HOTLINE, 320 Harvey Ave, (904) 255-0280.

■ Accommodations

BUCCANEER MOTEL, 2301 N Atlantic Ave, (904) 253-9678, reservations only: (800) 972-6056, fax: (904) 255-3946. Small motel, walking distance to beach & amenities, some straight clientele. Rooms with modern conveniences & complimentary morning coffee or tea in lobby.

COQUINA INN BED & BREAKFAST, 544 South Palmetto Ave, (904) 254-4969 (tel/fax), (800) 805-7533. B&B inn 7 rooms & 1 suite in Daytona's historic district. Private baths, gourmet buffet breakfast, locally-made chocolates, color cable TV, AC, ocean & pool nearby, some straight clientele.

VILLA, THE, 801 N Peninsula Dr, (904) 248-2020 (tel/fax). B&B, some straight clientele. Rooms & apts, variety of modern conveniences, library with TV lounge, continental breakfast, pool & nearby ocean beach.

■ Bars

NEW GAY BAR, 415 Main St. To open in 1997.

■ Dance Bar/Disco

BARRACKS & OFFICERS CLUB COMPLEX, 952 Orange Ave, (904) 254-3464. Complex has 4 venues. Officers Lounge: bar & lounge. NCO Club: game bar with pool table, darts, etc. Flight Deck: outdoor bar with Sun BBQ. Barracks Dance Club: 70% men, Mon-Sat 5pm-3am, Sun 3pm-3am, shows Wed, Fri-Sun, male dancers Wed, Fri, Sat.

Visit Florida (800) CARITAS — Caritas B&B Network

FERRARI GUIDES' GAY TRAVEL A to Z - 18th EDITION   401

FLORIDA

Women's Sailing Off Florida

Day sail in the beautiful waters of Florida's west coast among the dolphins and tropical birds with **Whelk Women**. Charlotte Harbor is considered one of the most beautiful sailing areas in Florida, with 200 square miles of clean water protected from the waves of the open Gulf of Mexico by a chain of barrier islands. One of these islands, Cayo Costa, is among the largest of the undeveloped barrier islands remaining in Florida. It looks much as it did 500 years ago when the Spanish arrived here greeted by the mound-building native inhabitants, the Calusa. Evidence of this 5,000-year-old culture remains in the form of shell mounds of varying heights on Cayo Costa and many of the small, mostly inhabited islands in the harbor.

Swim, sun, watch eagles, ospreys and pelicans, fish, collect shells. Stay in a rustic cabin or in a tent. You might even spot a huge loggerhead sea turtle, which sometimes visit the harbor. You need to bring your own food, bedding and towels. Camping gear is supplied.

Contact **Whelk Women** at (941) 964-2027.

BEACHSIDE CLUB, Show bar. Closed, to reopen in new location in 1997, check information for new address.

HOLLYWOOD COMPLEX & BARN DOOR, 615 Main St, (904) 252-3776. Hollywood disco & show bar, Barn Door cruise & patio bar, piano lounge, weekend shows.

SEVEN SIXTY-NINE CLUB, 769 Alabama St, (904) 253-4361. Bar & restaurant, pool tables, darts, men welcome.

■ Restaurants

CAFE FRAPPES, 174 N Beach St. Upscale American gourmet cuisine.

FT LAUDERDALE

■ Information

AIDS CENTER ONE, (954) 537-4111.

GAY & LESBIAN COMMUNITY CENTER, 1164 E Oakland Park Blvd, 3rd fl, (954) 563-9500.

■ Accommodations

ADMIRAL'S COURT, 21 Hendrick's Isle, (954) 462-5072, (800) 248-6669, Fax: (954) 763-8863. Motel near beach & Las Olas Blvd, usually 50% gay & lesbian clientele. Comfortable rooms of various sizes, private baths. Tropical gardens & private dock.

BAHAMA HOTEL, 401 N Atlantic Blvd, (954) 467-7315, (800) 622-9995, Fax: (954) 467-7319. Gay-friendly beachfront hotel with 43 rooms, 1 suite and 23 efficiency cottages. Swim in the large, heated, freshwater pool or stretch out for tanning on the sun-drenched patio. Guests enjoy 2 bars and "The Deck" restaurant overlooking the Atlantic. Friendly staff provides outstanding service. Reasonable rates.

BIG RUBY'S GUESTHOUSE, 908 NE 15th Ave, (954) 523-RUBY (7829), fax: (954) 523-7051, toll-free (888) 523-7829. Tropical Key West style guesthouse in the heart of Ft Lauderdale. Rooms & suites with private bath, cable TV. Large pool with cascading waterfall and two sun decks. Women welcome.

BLUE DOLPHIN, THE, 725 N Birch Rd, (954) 565-8437, (800) 893-BLUE, Fax: (954) 565-6015. Fort Lauderdale's largest men-only resort on the beach (1-minute walk). We offer superior hotel rooms, efficiencies and one-bedroom apartments for the discerning gay traveller. Continental breakfast included. Completely enclosed private facility. Clothing optional around our large, heated pool.

EDUN HOUSE, 2733 Middle River Dr, (954) 565-7775, (800) 479-1767, Fax: (954) 565-7812. Men-only guesthouse with private baths, continental breakfast, pool on premises.

GEMINI HOUSE, (954) 568-9791, (800) 552-7115, Fax: (954) 568-0617, E-mail: GeminiHse@aol.com. Men only, entire enclosed property is a no-clothing zone, full breakfast, shared baths, pool on premises, Jacuzzi.

KING HENRY ARMS, 543 Breakers Ave, (954) 561-0039, (800) 205-KING (5464), Fax: (954) 467-7439. Clean, quiet & congenial motel with home-like, ultra-clean rooms & private baths. Continental breakfast, tropical patio, BBQ, shuffleboard, pool on premises, beach nearby, walk to strip. Women welcome.

LA CASA DEL MAR, 3003 Granada St, (954) 467-2037, (800) 739-0009, Fax: (954) 467-7439. B&B with private baths, full American breakfast, AC, color cable TV, VCR, video tape library, pool on premises, Murder Mystery weekends, women welcome.

PALMS ON LAS OLAS, THE, 1760 E Las Olas Blvd, (954) 462-4178, (800) 550-POLO (7656), Fax: (954) 463-8544. Men only motel guesthouse. Centrally-located, private dock, 1 mile from beach. Rooms thru suites, color cable TV, AC, private baths. Expanded continental breakfast in season, heated pool.

PARADISO TROPICAL GUEST COTTAGES, 1115 Tequesta, Ft. Lauderdale, FL 33312, (954) 764-8182, (800) 644-7977, Fax: (954) 973-9722. Luxury clothing-optional accommodation for men, continental breakfast, pool on premises.

RAINBOW SUN, THE 1909 SW 2nd St, (954) 462-6035, Fax: (954) 522-2764. Men-only resort with private baths, continental breakfast, pool on premises.

ROYAL PALMS, THE, 2901 Terramar St, (954) 564-6444, (800) 237-PALM (7256), Fax: (954) 564-6443, e-mail: ryalpalms@aol.com. Men-only luxury guest suites, steps to the beach. Lush, secluded, heated pool. TV/VCR, complimentary videos, breakfast included. Personal, friendly service. Winner of the City of Fort Lauderdale "Hotel of the Year" award.

■ Women's Accommodations

INN, THE, (954) 568-5770, (800) 881-4814. Women-only B&B. Continental breakfast, pool on premises, Sun tea dance with Louise.

■ Beaches

FT LAUDERDALE PUBLIC BEACH. Public beach with many gays.

■ Bars

BILL'S FILLING STATION, 1243 NE 11th Ave, (954) 525-9403. Darts, juke box.

BOOTS, 901 SW 27th Ave at SW 9th St, (954) 792-9177. Patio, Sun BBQ & beer bust, Wed jock strap night, Fri underwear night, Sat towel night. Opens noon (Sat from 8am). Some leather.

BUS STOP, 2203 S Federal Highway, (954) 761-1782. DJ Fri-Sat, pool table.

BUSHES, THE, 3038 N Federal Hwy at Oakland Park (in shopping center), (954) 561-1724.

FLORIDA

CHARDEE'S, 2209 Wilton Dr, (954) 563-1800. Bar & restaurant, 60% men, 40% women, mature crowd.

CLUB CATHODE RAY, 1105 E Las Olas Blvd at bridge, (954) 462-8611. Preppie video bar.

CUBBY HOLE, 823 N Federal Hwy.

EAGLE, THE, 1951 Powerline Rd, (NW 9th Ave), (954) 462-6380. Patio & leather shop.

END UP, 3521 W Broward Blvd, (954) 584-9301. Open til 4am, popular late night bar.

EVERGLADES BAR, 1931 S Federal Hwy at SE 20th St, (954) 462-9165. Sat & Sun tea dance, 1/3 straight clientele.

GOLD COAST, 2471 E Commercial. Male strippers.

HIDEAWAY, THE, 2022 NE 18th Street, (954) 566-8622. Video cruise bar, drag shows, karaoke.

JOHNNY'S, 1116 W Broward Blvd, (954) 522-5931. Male dancers on stage, pool table.

LEFTY'S LOUNGE, 710 N Federal Hwy near 7th St, (954) 763-6467.

MOBY DICK'S, 3500 N Federal Hwy.

RAMROD, 1508 NE 4th Ave, (954) 763-8219. Leather inside leather shop.

SIDE STREET, 1753 Andrews Ave Extension behind Flanigans, (954) 525-2007. Patio.

VISIONS CYBER & MUSIC VIDEO BAR, 626 S Federal Hwy, (954) 523-9769. 4 on-line computers, male strippers, Sun-Thurs 5pm-2am, Fri-Sat till 3am.

WHALE & PORPOISE, 2750 E Oakland Park Blvd, (954) 572-4777. Show bar & dancing.

■ Dance Bar/Disco

CLUB 825, 825 E Sunrise Blvd, (954) 524-3333. Dance bar & piano lounge, male dancers & other entertainment, 2 pool tables.

CLUB ELECTRA, 1600 SE 15th Ave, (954) 764-8447. Male strippers, open Wed, Fri, Sat.

COPA,★ 624 SE 28th St near Fed Hwy, (954) 463-1507. Dance bar & 4 other bars, restaurant & patio. Open late, name entertainment.

CORRAL, 1727 N Andrews Ave, (954) 767-0027. Lounge & restaurant, C&W dance bar.

JR'S MINESHAFT, 3045 N Federal Hwy, (954) 561-2424. Dancing Thurs-Sat, Sun-Thurs 4pm-2am, Fri-Sat 4pm-3am. Leather dress code Fri, Fallen Angel leather shop on premises.

FT. LAUDERDALE FLORIDA
Call 1-800-833-2299 For Colorful Gay Guide
http://www.rainbow-mall.com Search: ftl

ROYAL PALMS
THE ULTIMATE TROPICAL OASIS
2901 Terramar St., Fort Lauderdale, FL 33304

- "5 Palm Award" winner from "Out & About". Rated one of the best gay accommodations in the USA.
- Luxurious Rooms & Amenities.
- A Magical Tropical Oasis.
- Steps to The Beach.

800-237-PALM
954-564-6444 • FAX 954-564-6443
e-mail: ryalpalms@aol.com
http://www: royalpalms.com
IGTA

King Henry Arms Motel
A small, clean, quiet and congenial gay motel just steps to the ocean.
- Sun-drenched, heated pool • Cable TV
- Direct dial telephone • Private baths
- Refrigerators • In-room safe • Kitchens in many units • Continental breakfast

543 BREAKERS AVENUE,
FORT LAUDERDALE, FL 33304-4129
954-561-0039 or 800-205-KING

The Palms on Las Olas
Fort Lauderdale's Finest Guest Suites
An All Male Retreat In The Most Central And Safest Location
• Tropical Waterfront Setting • Spacious, Lush Secluded Gardens •
• Nude Sundecks • Heated Pool • BBQ • Daily Maid Service •

1760 East Las Olas Blvd., Ft. Lauderdale, FL 33301
(800) 550-POLO / (954) 462-4178 / Call for a brochure.

THE BLUE DOLPHIN
THE INTIMATE HOTEL WITH A EUROPEAN FLAIR
A Premier Ft. Lauderdale Beach Men's Resort
• Private Enclosed Sundeck • Heated Pool
• Superior Accommodations • Continental Breakfast • Off Street Parking

725 North Birch Road, Fort Lauderdale, FL 33304
800-893-BLUE
954-565-8437   FAX 954-565-6015
E-Mail: 75372.1737@compuserve.com
http://www.gaywired.com/unity/bluedolp.htm

PARADISO
TROPICAL GUEST COTTAGES
Ft. Lauderdale's luxury accommodations for men in quiet central location
- Large Pool • Clothing Optional
- Special Weekly Rates • Concierge Service
- Continental Breakfast/Afternoon Social

1-800-644-7977
1115 Tequesta, Ft. Lauderdale, FL. 33312
954-764-8182 FAX 954-973-9722

FERRARI GUIDES' GAY TRAVEL A to Z - 18th EDITION

FLORIDA

Scuba, Snorkel & Fishing Excursions in the Florida Keys

Looking for water fun and adventure in the Florida Keys? **Aquatic Adventures Charter Services** will custom-design your dive or fishing vacation. They gear all their plans to the special interests of the individual, so don't be shy about telling them what interests you most.

Each charter is completely private, with specialized attention, and you'll find Aquatic's newer boat more comfortable than many charter boats in the area. Take a half day fishing and a half day diving or sightseeing...the choice is yours. Dive and fishing packages can be planned for a single day or multi-day visits in Marathon. There is no minimum number of nights to stay. Accommodations can range from economy to deluxe, according to your preference, so you don't have to be a high roller to enjoy this unique and exciting way to experience the tropics. Although primarily reef diving is available, small groups of two to six people can be taken to unexplored reefs where pelagic fish and untouched coral formations are plentiful.

Contact **Aquatic Adventures** at (305) 743-2421 or write PO Box 522540, Marathon Shores, FL 33052.

OTHERSIDE, THE, ★ 2283 Wilton Dr (NE 4th Ave), (954) 565-5538. Dance bar, men always welcome. Popular Wed & Fri.

SAINT, 1000 W State Rd 84, (954) 525-7883. Hi-energy dance bar, male strippers.

■ Saunas/Health Clubs

CLUB FT LAUDERDALE, 400 W Broward Blvd at SW 4th Ave, (954) 525-3344. Private club, 24hrs. Gym, BBQ's.

CLUBHOUSE II, 2650 E Oakland Park Blvd (954) 566-6750. 24hrs.

■ Restaurants

CHARDEE'S, 2209 Wilton Dr, at Chardee's bar. (954) 563-1800.

CORRAL RESTAURANT & LOUNGE, 1727 N Andrews Ave, (954) 767-0027. Restaurant & lounge with Southern home cooking & C&W dance bar.

COURTYARD CAFE, 2211 Wilton Dr, Wilton Manors, (954) 564-9365. Breakfast & lunch.

DECK RESTAURANT, THE, 401 N Atlantic Blvd at Bayshore in the Bahama Hotel, (954) 467-7315. Gay-friendly, breakfast, lunch & dinner.

LEGENDS CAFE, 1560 NE 4th Ave, (954) 467-2233. Innovative cuisine.

TROPICS, 2000 Wilton Dr, (954) 537-6000. Supper club, piano music, steaks, seafood, 80% men, 20% women.

VICTOR VICTORIA'S, 2347 Wilton Dr, (954) 563-6296.

■ Retail & Bookstores

CATALOG X, 850 NE 13th St, (954) 524-5050. Gay items, clothing, etc.

FALLEN ANGEL, 3045 N Federal Hwy, (954) 563-5230. Custom leather & sportswear, cards, gifts for men & women, mail-order.

LAMBDA PASSAGES, (305) 754-6900 (Miami phone #). Gay bookstore (see listing under retail in Miami, FL).

NEWS, BOOKS & CARDS, 7126 N University Dr, Tamarac, (954) 726-5544. Outrageous greeting cards, magazines, novelties.

■ Erotica

ADULT BOOKS, N Federal Hwy, next to Cubby Hole bar.

BROWARD ADULT BOOKSTORE, 3419 W Broward Blvd, (954) 792-4991, 24hrs, seasonal.

OMNI BOOK, 3334 W Broward, (954) 792-4991, 24hrs.

PRIDE FACTORY, 600 N Federal Hwy.

FT MYERS

■ Information

AIDS HOTLINE, Ft Myers: (941) 337-AIDS, Naples: (941) 263-CARE.

SUPPORT INC, (941) 332-2272.

■ Women's Accommodations

RESORT ON CAREFREE BOULEVARD, THE, 3000 Carefree Blvd, Ft. Meyers, FL 33917, (941) 731-3000, (800) 326-0364, Fax: (941) 731-3519. For women like you, who dream of a comfortable, fun community. At The Resort on Carefree Boulevard in Fort Myers, Florida, you'll find affordable luxury. Imagine tennis, swimming, fishing, spa and exercise facilities, dancing, nearby golf. Buy or rent a home that suits your lifestyle. All within easy driving distance of Sanibel and Captiva Islands. **Reserve your place in the sun.** ♀

■ Bars

OFFICE PUB, 3704 Cleveland Ave (US Hwy 41), (941) 936-3212. CD jukebox, women always welcome.

YOUR PLACE, 4261 Fowler. CD jukebox.

■ Dance Bar/Disco

APEX, 4226 Fowler St, (941) 418-0878. CD jukebox.

BOTTOM LINE, ★ 3090 Evans Ave, (941) 337-7292. Video, cruise & dance bars, 75% men, 25% women. Ladies nights, women very welcome, many straights.

■ Cafe

OASIS, 2222 McGregor Blvd, in Boulevard Plaza, (941) 334-1566. Women-owned, breakfast & lunch menus, some vegetarian meals. May change in 1997.

FT WALTON BEACH

■ Dance Bar/Disco

NEW FRANKLY SCARLET'S & CHOO CHOO'S PUB, 223 Hwy 98, 50 ft back, on right of city parking lot, next to their former address 223 Hwy 98, (904) 664-2966. Dance & lounge bars.

GAINESVILLE

■ Information

AIDS INFO, (352) 372-4370.

GAY SWITCHBOARD, (352) 332-0700, 6pm-11pm most evenings or tape.

■ Accommodations

RUSTIC INN, 3105 S Main St, High Springs, FL (904) 454-1223, fax: (904) 454-1225. Gay-friendly B&B inn 15 miles out of Gainesville, private baths, expanded continental or full breakfast, vegetarian cuisine, AC, b&w TV, ceiling fans, pool on premises, gay female following.

■ Bars

AMBUSH, 4130 NW 6th St. Open 7 days, juke box.

■ Dance Bar/Disco

CLUB DIVERSITY, Hwy 441, just outside town, 1mi S of blinking light, in town of Mickinopy 5-10 mi S of Gainesville, rainbow flags outside building. Dance & show bar, more popular after hours, large straight following.

UNIVERSITY CLUB, 18 E University Ave, entrance in rear NE 1st Ave, (352) 378-6814.

FLORIDA

Disco, 60% men, 40% women, male strippers Wed. Fri many women. Younger crowd, large straight following for the drag shows.

■ Retail & Bookstores
WILD IRIS BOOKS, 802 W University Ave, (352) 375-7477. Feminist bookstore with a gay & lesbian section.

HOLLYWOOD

■ Accommodations
CALIFORNIA DREAM INN, 300 Walnut St, (954) 923-2100, fax: (954) 923-3222. Gay-friendly hotel inn, private baths, 30% gay & lesbian clientele.

■ Bars
PARTNERS, 625 E Dania Beach Blvd, Dania, (954) 921-9893. Near the beach, DJ weekends, karaoke nites, Sun buffet, 75% women.

ZACHARY'S, 2217 North Federal Hwy, (954) 920-5479. Sports bar, occasional DJ, 75% gay women with 25% straight clientele.

■ Retail & Bookstores
ADVANTAGE RESOURCES, 1861 N Federal Hwy #319, (954) 921-1732.

■ Erotica
HOLLYWOOD BOOK & VIDEO, 1235 S State Rd 7, (954) 981-2164.

PUSSYCAT THEATRE, Hwy 441 & Sheridan, (954) 962-9955. Adult theater.

JACKSONVILLE

■ Bars
BOOT RACK SALOON, 4751 Lenox Ave, (904) 384-7090. Patio, erotic toy store inside

HMS, 1702 E 8th St, (904) 353-9200. Patio, free food Sun.

IN TOUCH TAVERN, 10957 Atlantic Blvd, (904) 642-7506. 75% men.

JAX EAGLE, 1402 San Marco Blvd, (904) 396-8551. Beer & wine bar with full-service restaurant.

JUNCTION, 1261 King St at Lydia, (904) 388-3434. Bar, patio, BBQ Sun, live entertainment weekends, 50% men, 50% women.

PARK PLACE LOUNGE, 2712 Park St, (904) 389-6616. 50% men, 50% women, full liquor.

PLACE, THE, 1746 Talleyrand Ave, (904) 358-6969. Small bar.

■ Dance Bar/Disco
BO'S CORAL REEF, 201 5th Ave N at 2nd St, Jacksonville Beach, (904) 246-9874. Dance & show bar.

METRO, 2929 Plum St, (904) 388-7192. Dance bar with Rainbow room piano bar, Boiler Room leather area with flicks, best Sat.

MY LITTLE DUDE (JO'S PLACE), 2952 Roosevelt Blvd at Willow Branch, (904) 388-9503. Dance & show bar, male & female impersonator shows, men welcome.

THIRD DIMENSION, ★ 711 Edison, (904) 353-6316. Dance, show & patio bars, drag shows Tues, Thurs-Sat, Sun buffet & beer bust 5pm-9pm, 90% men, 10% women.

■ Saunas/Health Clubs
CLUB JACKSONVILLE, 1939 Hendricks Ave near Atlantic, (904) 398-7451. Private club, 10-station gym, sun deck, 24hrs.

■ Restaurants
EUROPEAN STREET, approx. 2721 Park St, sandwiches & imported beers & teas.

■ Retail & Bookstores
BY THE CUP, 2709 Park St, (904) 389-5515. Cybershop with some gay items.

■ Leathers/Piercing
OLD KENTUCKY LEATHERWORKS, THE, 822 Lomax St, (904) 353-3770. Bondage & fetish accessories. Mon-Fri 10am-6pm, Sat 10am-5pm.

JASPER

■ Accommodations
SWAN LAKE BED & BREAKFAST, PO Box 1623, Jasper, 32052, (904) 792-2771. B&B on 78.6 acres of private wooded land 15 miles south of Georgia. Many breeds of swans, waterfowl & other animals. Shared baths, TV lounge, full breakfast, pool & Jacuzzi. Women welcome.

KEY WEST

■ Information
KEY WEST BUSINESS GUILD, (800) 535-7797. Local gay business organization.

■ Accommodations
A TROPICAL INN, 812 Duval St, (305) 294-9977. Gay-friendly guesthouse in historic Old Key West. Color TV, AC, private baths. Suites with private garden & spa. Continental breakfast in winter season.

ALEXANDER'S GUESTHOUSE, 1118 Fleming St, in Key West's Historic District, (305) 294-9919, (800) 654-9919. Tasteful gay & lesbian accommodations, an unsurpassed level of convenience & comfort with every amenity, a short walk to entertainment & attractions. Secluded & private grounds... heated pool... rooms & suites uniquely decorated in Key West "casual" style, many with private verandahs or decks. Daily complimentary continental breakfast, poolside... assistance with dining & watersport reservations. Gay-owned & -operated. Out & About Editor's Choice Award, two consecutive years.

ATLANTIC SHORES RESORT, 510 South St, (800) 526-3559, (305) 296-2491, Fax: (305) 294-2753. Ocean-front Art Deco hotel with restaurant, pool bar & grill in the heart of

Tasteful gay & lesbian accommodations

Out & About Magazine Editor's Choice Award, two consecutive years

ALEXANDER'S
GUESTHOUSE

1-800-654-9919

Fax 1-305-295-0357

1118 Fleming, Key West, FL 33040

Visit us online:
@AOL.COM/http://home.aol.com.alexghouse

FERRARI GUIDES' GAY TRAVEL A to Z - 18th EDITION

FLORIDA

KEY WEST — FLORIDA

Unparalled Service. Tropical Elegance. For Gays & Lesbians
- Large Rooms, Private Baths, Refrig., Phones
- Heated Pool. Jacuzzi.
- Continental Breakfast, Cocktail Social
- Large Screen Videos

800-459-6212
Under New Ownership/Managemnt
Colours KEY WEST
(305) 294-6977
Fax: (305) 292-9030
410 Fleming St., Key West, FL 33040

La-te-da
HOTEL • RESTAURANT • BAR
- 16 LUXURY GUESTROOMS
- TROPICAL GOURMET RESTAURANT
- TWO NOTORIOUS BARS
- LEGENDARY TEA DANCE
- CABARET SHOW NIGHTLY FEATURING KEY WEST'S PREMIERE FEMALE ILLUSIONISTS

(800) 528-3320
1125 DUVAL ST., KEY WEST
FAX (305) 296-0438
UNDER NEW OWNERSHIP
GAY OWNED & OPERATED

CURRY HOUSE
KEY WEST'S PREMIER GUESTHOUSE FOR MEN
Key West's original bed & breakfast exclusively serving men for more than 20 years.
Friendly. Elegant. Affordable.
Large Pool & Jacuzzi

(800) 633-7439
(305) 294-6777
806 Fleming St., Key West, FL 33040

Tasteful gay & lesbian accommodations
ALEXANDER'S GUESTHOUSE
1-800-654-9919
1118 Fleming, Key West, FL 33040

"Still Our Favorite" -Out & About
Secluded tropical paradise just a half block to Duval. Luxury beds and towels. Full breakfast every morning. Wine each evening. Heated pool. Wonderfully friendly. Exclusively gay.

RubyS GUESTHOUSE
409 Appelrouth La.
Key West, FL 33040-6534

1-800-477-7829 (US & CAN)
1-305-296-0281 (FAX)

Newton Street Station
Guesthouse for Gay Men.
Sun or Swim Nude
Your tropical retreat in Key West. Quiet, secluded, romantic location. All rooms with AC, TV, refrigerator. Modest rates.
Continental breakfast included.

Newton Street Station
1414 Newton St., Key West, FL 33040
800-248-2457
305-294-4288 FAX 305-292-5062

Key Lodge
LIKE STAYING WITH A FRIEND...
On Duval Street.
Friendly, Private & Mixed.
22 Rooms. TV, AC, Refrigerator & Phone.
Lushly Landscaped Pool.
Friendly Staff. Call Today...
1•800•458•1296
1004 Duval St., Key West, FL 33040
(305) 296-9915

The PINES Guesthouse
Relaxed, Friendly, Affordable
Enjoy The Best Vacation Of Your Life!

Comfortable, well-appointed rooms-- with private bath. Large pool & spa in lush tropical garden. Free continental breakfast. Welcoming the friendliest of the gay and lesbian community since 1976

305-296-7467
800-282-PINE

Call or Write For Our Color Brochure
521 United St., Key West, FL 33040
E-mail: Tomkeywest@AOL.COM

We Compete Only With Ourselves
Our exclusively-male guesthouses offer unparalled service and attention.
- Luxury accommodations, all with private bath
- Use of facilities at both resorts, including Oasis' 24-man hot tub – the largest in S. Florida
- Clothing Optional • Continental breakfast
Afternoon social • Relax & meet new friends

Coral Tree Inn & Oasis
(800) 362-7477 • (305) 296-2131
823/822 Fleming St./Key West, FL 33040
Email: OASISCT@aol.com

FLORIDA

UNITED STATES

For a Free 56-Page Color Guide, call 1-800-535-7797.
http://www.rainbow-mall.com Search: keywest

"One of Key West's most impressive & refined lodgings."
— The Advocate

THE BRASS KEY
G U E S T H O U S E
412 Frances St • Key West, FL 33040-6950
305-296-4719 • 800-932-9119
Fax 305-296-1994

LIGHTHOUSE COURT
At historic Key West Lighthouse, an exquisitely relaxed compound of cottages, rooms, suites and apartments, nestled in over a half-acre of sundecks and tropical gardens. Just a block from Duval Street bars, restaurants and shops. Heated pool, Jacuzzi, health club, cafe and bar, across from Hemingway's House.
902 Whitehead St., Key West, FL 33040
(305) 294-9588

EQUATOR RESORT
Central • Attentive • Comfortable • Tropical • Lavish
Key West's Hottest Men's Resort
Clothing Optional • Heated Pool • Hot Tub
800-278-4552
305-294-7775
818 Fleming St., Key West, FL 33040

COCONUT GROVE GUESTHOUSE FOR MEN 
Panoramic Rooftop Sundecks
• Secluded Wood Decked Pool
• Relaxed Hospitality
• Tropical Elegance
• Apartments Also Available
800-262-6055
817 Fleming St. Key West, FL 33040
(305) 296-5107 FAX (305) 296-1584

You Can Bring Your Lover, Your Mother, or Anyone Else.
1-800-452-3224
Sheraton Key West
AN ALL-SUITE HOTEL
Sheraton
IGTA
Our friendly staff will meet your every need. You'll enjoy familiar Sheraton service and quality that you've come to depend on.
All our accommodations are comfortable suites with lots of room & amenities.
2001 S. Roosevelt Blvd. Key West, FL 33040
Phone: (305) 292-9800 Fax: (305) 294-6009

Old Town, color cable TV, private baths, pool on premises, some straight clientele.

BANANA BAY RESORT KEY WEST, 2319 N Roosevelt Blvd, (305) 296-6925, (800) BANANA-1, Fax: (305) 296-2004. Adult resort with deluxe guestrooms & 1-BR suites, private sunning beach, freshwater pool.

BANANA'S FOSTER BED & BREAKFAST, 537 Caroline St, (305) 294-9061, (800) 563-4881. B&B in ideal location. Beach club privileges, everyone welcome.

BIG RUBY'S GUESTHOUSE, 409 Appelrouth Lane, (305) 296-2323, (800) 477-7829, Fax: (305) 296-0281. Guesthouse 1/2 block from Duval St restaurants, shops, bars. Thirteen immaculate rooms with sumptuous beds. Full breakfast. Dinner served major holidays. Ocean beach nearby.

BLUE PARROT INN, 916 Elizabeth St, (305) 296-0033, (800) 231-BIRD (231-2473), E-mail: bluparotin@aol.com. Hatched in 1884 and still flying high, the Blue Parrot in the heart of historic Old Town is a tropical, secluded, quiet, clean retreat just 2 blocks from famous Duval Street. Our pool is heated during the cooler months and is delightfully usable year 'round. Beaches, clubs, restaurants and shops are only a very short walk away. All water activities are nearby, including diving and snorkeling on America's only living coral reef. The atmosphere is relaxed and friendly; the music is usually classical. Brochure available. See ad page 409.

BRASS KEY GUESTHOUSE, THE 412 Frances St, (305) 296-4719, (800) 932-9119, Fax: (305) 296-1994. Key West's finest 5-star guesthouse offers attentive service and luxury accommodations in a traditional setting of wide verandahs, plantation shutters and ceiling fans. Enjoy expansive sun decks, a sparkling heated pool and a whirlpool spa set among lush, tropical gardens.

CHELSEA HOUSE, 707 Truman Ave, (800) 845-8859, (305) 296-2211, Fax: (305) 296-4822, E-mail: chelseahse@aol.com. "All welcome." This 1870 renovation (18 rooms), two blocks from Duval, has off-street parking, pool and tropical gardens on an acre of land. Complimentary continental breakfast is served from 8:30-10:30am by the pool. All rooms have refrigerators, AC, color cable television, ceiling fans, telephone coffeemaker, hairdryer and private bath. Gay-owned and -operated. See ad page 409.

COCONUT GROVE, 817 Fleming St, (305) 296-5107, (800) 262-6055. Guesthouse, women welcome. Singles thru apartments with modern conveniences, rooftop decks, gym, weights, continental breakfast. Nearby ocean beach.

COLOURS KEY WEST, 410 Fleming St, (800) 459-6212 or (305) 294-6977, Fax: (305) 292-9030. Guesthouse 1/2 block from Duval St, some straight clientele. Spacious rooms with yesteryear's charm, private & shared baths, TV lounge, expanded continental breakfast and cocktails. Nearby health club.

FERRARI GUIDES' GAY TRAVEL A to Z - 18th EDITION

FLORIDA

UNITED STATES

Gay Men's Sailing off Key West

This might be the best day of your vacation...a day on the water with a group of up to 7 other guys...a total of 6 hours sailing and visiting the reefs around Key West, where you can swim and snorkel or just relax and sun your buns, as The Clione anchors for a relaxing lunch off a beautiful coral reef. **Clione Charters** provides all equipment and instruction. The trip even includes free pick-up by a stretch limo.

The Clione is the largest schooner in Key West. In its previous life before coming to Key West, it circumnavigated the world five times. Captain Carl Nettles is the 16th owner of the Clione in the last 86 years! Interesting aspects include the original wood stove and stained glass butterfly hatches, as well as much of the original hardware. Captain Carl is US Coast Guard licensed as Master of vessels up to 100 tons. Clione exceeds Coast Guard requirements for lifesaving equipment and includes the latest in navigational electronics and communications.

Clione is available for day cruises from 12 noon to sunset. Passengers under 21 years of age are free. Daily cruises are for men only. Women-only and mixed groups can charter the entire boat.

Contact **Clione Charters** at (305) 296-1433 or (305) 745-4519.

Key West At Wholesale Prices

A large rainbow flag flies proudly outside the **"We Love the Florida Keys"** Visitor Center in Marathon, Florida. Inside, the place is filled with colorful brochures on every conceiveable Florida Keys accommodation or excursion you could think of. A member of the Key West Business Guild, the center stays totally informed on gay-exclusive and gay-friendly places to stay and activities in and around Key West. If you're already in Key West, call them for sunset sails, snorkeling, jet skiing, para sailing, glass-bottomed boat rides, scuba diving and fishing. They even make restaurant reservations! And in high season they, quite conveniently, answer calls from 8:00 am till 9:00 or 10:00 pm.

If you are trip planning and want to experience Key West during a gay or lesbian event, they can tell you what's happening when and book everything for you. Don't be surprised if their prices put a smile on your face Their exclusive contract rates apparently allow them to offer prices lower than anyone else's.

Contact **We Love the Florida Keys...** at (305) 289-1400, (800) 403-2154, Fax: (305) 289-4334.

CORAL TREE INN, 822 Fleming St, (305) 296-2131, (800) 362-7477. Men's guesthouse. 10 suites, private baths, color TV, AC, ceiling fans, refrigerator, balconies, sun decks, Jacuzzi & expanded continental breakfast.

CURRY HOUSE, 806 Fleming St, (305) 294-6777, (800) 633-7439, fax: (305) 294-5322. Men-only B&b guesthouse in the heart of Old Town, near Duval St & ocean beach. Individually decorated rooms, Jacuzzi, weights, full breakfast.

CYPRESS HOUSE, 601 Caroline St, (305) 294-6969, (800) 525-2488, Fax: (305) 296-1174. Men-only guesthouse. Luxurious, spacious rooms, TV lounge, continental breakfast & cocktail hour.

DEJA VU, 611 Truman Ave, (305) 292-1424. Bed & breakfast, 60% gay & lesbian clientele. Sauna, Jacuzzi.

DUVAL HOUSE, 815 Duval St, (305) 294-1666, (800) 22-DUVAL. Inn in center of Old Town, 50% gay & lesbian clientele. Double rooms individually decorated with wicker & antiques. Expanded continental breakfast & nearby ocean beach.

EATON LODGE, 511 Eaton St, (305) 292-2170, (800) 294-2170. Gay-friendly guesthouse. Color cable TV, VCR, AC, private baths, expanded continental breakfast. Jacuzzi & pool on premises.

EQUATOR, 818 Fleming St, Key West, FL 33040, (305) 294-7775, (800) 278-4552, Fax: (305) 296-5765. Men-only resort with deluxe suites & apartments. Spacious accommodations feature specialty lighting, Italian tile floors, wooden blinds, security access, instant hot water & climate control. Black lagoon pool, sunning decks, waterfall & monsoon whower on premises.

GARDEN HOUSE KEY WEST, 329 Elizabeth St, (305) 296-5368, Fax: 292-1160, (800) 695-6453. Guesthouse 2 blocks from Duval St, 50% gay & lesbian clientele. Variety of modestly furnished rooms, expanded continental breakfast buffet.

HERON HOUSE, 512 Simonton St, (305) 294-9227, (800) 294-1644, Fax: (305) 294-5692. E-mail: heronKW@aol.com. http://sla-keys.com/heronhouse. B&B, mainly straight clientele. Spacious, traditional, contemporary rooms. Gardens, sun decks, full breakfast. Near beach, Duval St.

ISLAND HOUSE, 1129 Fleming St, (305) 294-6284, (800) 890-6284. Men-only guesthouse, private compound with pool, sauna, Jacuzzi, cafe, private & shared baths.

ISLAND KEY COURTS OF KEY WEST, THE, 910 Simonton St (office) & 817 Catherine St, (305) 296-1148, (800) 296-1148, Fax: (305) 292-7924, E-mail: rayebv@aol.com. The only Key West guesthouse offering a special Welcome Package for Women with free gifts & a unique Key West for Women Insider's Guide. Charming guestrooms & apartment suites, very private, "Key West Casual" ambiance,

FLORIDA

in walk-to-everything Old Town. Fully equipped, private kitchens, baths, garden/patio studios, 1 & 2 bedrooms, sleeping 1-9, AC, cable color TV. Free membership to nearby beach club with pool, gym, spa, 2 restaurants, 3 bars. All-welcome policy.

KEY LODGE MOTEL, 1004 Duval St, (305) 296-9915, (800) 458-1296. Centrally located gay-friendly motel. Private baths, color TV, AC, ceiling fans, phones, refrigerator & pool.

KNOWLES HOUSE, THE, 1004 Eaton St, (305) 296-8132, (800) 352-4414, (305) 294-3273. B&B guesthouse, private & shared baths, continental breakfast, pool on premises, some straight clientele.

LA-TE-DA HOTEL, 1125 Duval St, Key West, FL 33040, (305) 296-6706, (800) 528-3320, Fax: (305) 296-0438. Hotel with restaurant & show bar, private baths, AC, phone, pool & clothing-optional sun deck. Some straight clientele.

LIGHTBOURN INN, 907 Truman Ave, Key West, FL 33040, (305) 296-5152, (800) 352-6011, Fax: (305) 294-9490. This stunning example of historical renovation has been recognized nationally and internationally as a guesthouse of outstanding quality. Each guest room has private bath, television, telephone, air conditioning and ceiling fan. Gourmet buffet breakfast is served near the pool. Two levels of decking around the pool allow plenty of space for sunning and relaxing. Lightbourn is but two blocks from Old Town's shops, restaurants and nightlife. Gay-friendly, 40% gay/lesbian clientele.

LIGHTHOUSE COURT, 902 Whitehead St, (305) 294-9588. Guesthouse with restaurant, bar, health club, men only. Variety of accommodations, beach nearby. Walk to shops, galleries, night life.

LIME HOUSE INN, 219 Elizabeth St, (305) 296-2978, (800) 374-4242, Fax: (305) 294-5858. An **island within an island,** Lime House is a centrally-located old conch mansion and the most private and friendly men-only guesthouse in Key West. Most rooms have a private bath, kitchenette, telephone and AC. All have color TV and ceiling fans. Expanded continental breakfast, pool and Jacuzzi. Nightlife and ocean beach nearby, complimentary evening cocktail hour.

MANGROVE HOUSE, 623 Southard St, (800) 294-1866, (305) 294-1866, Fax: (305) 294-8757. Men-only guesthouse, color cable TV, AC, ceiling fans, coffee/tea-making facilities & private baths. Continental breakfast, pool & Jacuzzi on premises.

MERLINN GUEST HOUSE, 811 Simonton St, (305) 296-3336, Fax: 296-3524. Guesthouse, private baths, mainly straight clientele.

MERMAID & THE ALLIGATOR, THE, 729 Truman Ave, (305) 294-1894, (800) 773-1894, fax: (305) 296-5090. Gay-friendly guesthouse, private baths.

NEWTON STREET STATION, 1414 Newton St, (305) 294-4288, (800) 248-2457, Fax (305) 292-5062. http://.travelbase.com/destinations/keywest/newton-street-station. Men-only guesthouse. Variety of individually-decorated rooms, private & shared baths, TV lounge, weights, bicycles, continental breakfast. Nearby ocean beach.

OASIS, A GUESTHOUSE, 823 Fleming St, (305) 296-2131, (800) 362-7477, Fax: (305) 296-5972. Men's guesthouse with beer & wine bar. Tastefully-appointed rooms with modern conveniences, Jacuzzi, sun decks, expanded continental breakfast. Nearby ocean beach.

ORTON TERRACE, 606 Orton Ave, Fort Lauderdale, FL 33304, (954) 566-5068, Fax: (954) 564-8646. Toll-free in USA, Canada, Caribbean: (800) 323-1142. Motel with 7 one- & two-bedroom apartments with full-sized kitchens, 27" TVs, phones, AC, color cable TV, pool on premises, steps from the beach. Some straight clientele.

PILOT HOUSE GUEST HOUSE & DUVAL SUITES, 414 Simonton St & 724 Duval St, (800) 648-3780, (305) 294-8719, Fax: (305) 294-9298. Guesthouse with private & shared baths, 50% gay & lesbian clientele.

PINES GUESTHOUSE, THE, 521 United St, (305) 296-7467, (800) 282-PINE. Key West's original gay guesthouse offers the perfect combination of congenial atmosphere and relaxation just a few minutes' walk from beaches, bars, shops and dining. Join us for continental breakfast on the patio. Spacious, tastefully-decorated rooms have private baths. Mostly men with women welcome.

RED ROOSTER, 709 Truman Ave, **Budget accommodations in Key West!** Good, clean accommodations with a very friendly staff. Centrally located.

SEA ISLE RESORT, 915 Windsor Lane, (305) 294-5188, (800) 995-4786, Fax: (305) 296-7143. Mens resort/compound, continental breakfast, private baths, color TV, AC, pool on premises, 3 blocks to gay bars.

SEASCAPE, 420 Olivia St, (305) 296-7776 (phone & fax). Gay-friendly guesthouse. Double rooms with modern conveniences, spa, nearby ocean beach, continental breakfast, 10% gay & lesbian clientele.

SHERATON KEY WEST ALL-SUITE RESORT, 2001 S. Roosevelt Blvd, (305) 292-9800, (800) 452-3224, Fax: (305) 294-6009. An all-suites resort, spacious luxury suites with extensive amenities for comfort & convenience, pool on premises, beach nearby.

SIMONTON COURT HISTORIC INN & COTTAGES, 320 Simonton St, (800) 944-2687, (305) 294-6386, Fax: 293-8446. Inn with rooms & cottages, 50% gay & lesbian. VCR's in all units, color cable TV, private baths, expanded continental breakfast. 3 pools on premises, hot tub, nearby ocean beach.

WILLIAM ANTHONY HOUSE, 613 Caroline St, (305) 294-2887, (800) 613-2276. Luxury suites & guest rooms in a quiet location. Private baths, AC, spa, breakfast & social hour.

■ *Women's Accommodations*

RAINBOW HOUSE, 525 United St, Key West, FL 33040, (800) 74-WOMYN (800-749-6696), (305) 292-1450. *Key West's Only Exclusively Women's Guest House* Our lovely accommodations include rooms, suites and kitchenettes, and feature bedrooms with queen bed, private bath, color TV, air conditioning and

---

Chelsea HOUSE

CIRCA 1870

All Adult Compound

Clothes Optional Sundeck

Luxury Accommodations

(305) 296-2211
Fax: (305) 296-4822
USA & CANADA
(800) 845-8859

707 Truman Avenue
Key West, FL 33040

BLUE PARROT INN

Heated Pool
Clothing-Optional Sundeck
Continental Breakfast
Heart of Old Town
All Adults Welcome

(305) 296-0033 • (800) 231-BIRD
916 Elizabeth, Key West, FL 33040

FERRARI GUIDES' GAY TRAVEL A to Z - 18th EDITION

FLORIDA

UNITED STATES

Bahama fans. Deluxe continental breakfast is served in our air conditioned pavilion. Massage is available. Other amenities include heated swimming pool, extensive decking for sunbathing, a shaded tropical pavilion for lazy-day lounging. Restaurants and night life are within walking distance. The shopping district is a half-block away. It's one block to the Atlantic Ocean and the southernmost point in the continental USA. Call for our color brochure.

■ Bars

BOURBON STREET PUB, 724 Duval St, (305) 296-1992. DJ.

CLUB INTERNATIONAL, 900 Simonton, (305) 296-9230. 8am-4pm.

COCKTAILS, 618 Duval St, at Donnie's Key West complex. Indoor conversation bar.

EIGHT-O-ONE BAR,★ 801 Duval St, (305) 294-4737. 2-level bar, live entertainment.

NUMBERS, 1029 Truman Ave, (305) 296-0333. Male strippers.

SOUTPAW SALOON, 7005 Biscayne Blvd, (305)759-3413. 3pm-3am 7 days.

SPURS, 422 Applerouth Ln, (305) 294-2655. C&W cruise bar, small dance floor, live C&W bands.

■ Dance Bar/Disco

EPOCH, 623 Duval St, (305) 296-8522.

LA TE DA TEA DANCE & TREETOP BAR, 1125 Duval St at La Te Da Marti, (305) 296-6706. La Te Da tea dance Sun 5pm-9pm around the pool. Treetop has nitely drag shows.

ONE SALOON,★ 524 Duval St at Appel Routh (side), (305) 296-8118. Small dance bar, male strippers, patio.

TEA BY THE SEA,★ 510 South St at the Atlantic Shores Hotel pier, (305) 296-2491.

T-dance Sun, also sunset dance Fri-Sat.

■ Restaurants

ANTONIA'S, 615 Duval St, (305) 294-6565. Northern Italian cuisine.

CAFE DES ARTISTES, 1007 Simonton, (305) 294-7100. French cuisine, patio.

CAFE MARQUESA, 600 Fleming St at the Marquesa Hotel, (305) 292-1244. New world cuisine.

CAMILLE'S, 703 1/2 Duval St, (305) 296-4811. Friendly & informal breakfast, lunch, dinner.

CRAB SHACK, 908 Caroline St, (305) 294-9658.

DIM SUM RESTAURANT, 613-1/2 Duval (in rear), (305) 294-6230. Indian, Chinese, Thai & Burmese cuisine. Closed Mon & Tues.

DONNIE'S KEY WEST COMPLEX, 618 Duval. Separate patio bar & 24hr restaurant. Popular after bars close.

DUFFY'S STEAK & LOBSTER HOUSE, Simonton St at Truman, (305) 296-4900.

EL SIBONEY, 900 Catherine St, (305) 2964184. Cuban/Spanish food in an unpretentious setting.

GATO GORDO, Southard between Whitehead & Duval. Mexican.

GODFREY'S AT LA TE DA, daily brunch 9am-3pm, dinner 6pm-11pm, except Sun.

LA TRATTORIA VENEZIA, 522 Duval St, (305) 296-1075. Italian & French cuisine.

LIGHTHOUSE CAFE, 917 Duval St, (305) 296-7837. Southern Italian cuisine.

LIGHTHOUSE COURT CAFE, 902 Whitehead St at Lighthouse Court guesthouse.

LOUIE'S BACKYARD, 700 Waddell Ave, (305) 294-1061. International & Caribbean cuisine, Sun brunch.

MANGIA! MANGIA!, 900 Southard St, (305) 294-2469. Italian cuisine.

MANGOS, 700 Duval St, (305) 292-4606. Continental cuisine, vegetarian specialties.

ROOFTOP CAFE, 310 Front St, (305) 294-2042. Famous for key lime pie, continental cuisine.

SQUARE ONE, 1075 Duval St #C12 at Duval Sq, (305) 296-4300. New American cuisine, popular happy hour.

TWO FRIENDS PATIO RESTAURANT, 512 Front St, (305) 296-3124. The Two Friends Patio Restaurant, located on Front Street across from the Conch Train depot, offers a delightful open-air garden setting, serving breakfast, lunch and dinner daily. The menu offers a variety of seafood and steaks, including clams and oysters on the half-shell. ...And while enjoying the casual atmosphere, you can listen to lively rhythm & blues every Monday through Saturday night. Entertainment varies.

■ Retail & Bookstores

FLAMING MAGGIES, 830 Fleming St at Margaret, (305) 294-3931. Gay & lesbian bookstore.

KEY WEST ISLAND BOOKSTORE, 513 Fleming Street, (305) 294-2904. General bookstore with a large gay section, opens 10am.

■ Leathers/Piercing

LEATHER MASTER, 418-A Applerouth Ln, (305) 292-5051. Custom leather clothing, accessories, toys for men & women. Call for hours.

■ Erotica

BARGAIN BOOKS, 1028 Truman Ave, (305) 294-7446.

SOUTHERN XXXPOSURE, 901 Duval St, (305) 292-2171.

LAKELAND

■ Accommodations

SUNSET MOTEL, 2301 New Tampa Hwy, (941) 683-6464. Gay-friendly motel with private baths.

■ Dance Bar/Disco

DOCKSIDE, 3770 Hwy 92, (941) 665-2590. Full liquor, Mon-Sat 4pm-2am, Sun 2pm-12am, DJ Thurs-Sun, drag shows Thurs-Sat.

ROY'S GREEN PARROT, 1030 E Main St, (941) 683-6021. Dance & show bar, male strippers, 90% men, women welcome.

MELBOURNE

■ Dance Bar/Disco

KOLD KEG, 4060 W New Haven Ave, (407) 724-1510. Dance bar, patio, DJ Thurs-Sat, shows Thurs, Sun BBQ.

LOADING ZONE, 4910 Stack Blvd, Palm Bay, (407) 727-3383. High energy dance bar, young crowd, 60% men, 40% women.

MIAMI - SOUTH BEACH

■ Information

AIDS LINE, (305) 576-1111. Health Crisis Network: (305) 751-7775.

WOMEN'S PRESERVATION SOCIETY, 4300 SW 73rd Ave, (305) 266-9480. Lesbian center with activities daily. Friday Night Women's Group meets here. Women's bar alternative.

■ Accommodations

CHELSEA HOTEL, 944 Washington Ave, Miami Beach, (305) 534-4069, Fax: (305) 672-6712. Gay-friendly hotel 2 blocks from beach. Color TV, AC, phones, fridge & private baths. 24-hour security.

COLOURS, THE MANTELL GUEST INN, 255 West 24th St, South Miami Beach, (305) 538-1821, Local Guest Switchboard, Reservation: (800) ARRIVAL (277-4825), (305) 532-9341, Fax: (305) 534-0362. Historic Art Deco hotel with over 25 studio apartments. Color TV,

---

TWO FRIENDS PATIO RESTAURANT

Breakfast • Lunch • Dinner
Seafood • Steaks • Oysters

512 Front Street • Key West
(305) 296-3124

410

FERRARI GUIDES' GAY TRAVEL A to Z - 18th EDITION

FLORIDA

UNITED STATES

AC, telephone, kitchen & private baths. Continental breakfast, pool & gym. ♀♂

EUROPEAN GUEST HOUSE, 721 Michigan Ave, Miami Beach, (305) 673-6665, Fax: (305) 672-7442. E-mail: sobegaybb@aol.com. Enjoy old world charm & beautifully-appointed rooms with modern amenities in South Beach's only gay B&B. We're 6 blocks from sandy beaches, and moonlight, balmy ocean breezes and sun-baked days are here for the taking. Rooms have AC, refrigerator, private baths & remote control cable TV. Outside, a hot tub & tropical gardens await you. Our low rates & laid-back atmosphere make your vacation most memorable. ♀♂

FAIRFAX HOTEL, 1776 Collins Ave, Miami Beach, 33139, (305) 538-7082, (800) 832-5736, Fax: (305) 673-9408. Gay-friendly hotel with a 30% gay male following, private baths.

ISLAND HOUSE, 715 82nd St, Miami Beach, (305) 864-2422, (800) 382-2422. Men-only guesthouses & cottage at 3 beach locations. Check-in at address above. Color cable TV, phones, AC, refrigerator, laundry facilities & business services. Expanded continental breakfast, Jacuzzi.

JEFFERSON HOUSE, THE, 1018 Jefferson Ave, (305) 534-5247, Fax: (305) 534-5953. B&B in the heart of South Beach, some straight clientele. 6 rooms & 1 suite with queen beds, AC & private baths. TV lounge, full breakfast & nearby pool, ocean. ♀♂

KENT HOTEL, 1131 Collins Ave, Miami Beach, (305) 531-6771, (800) 295-2788.

LILY GUESTHOUSE, 835 Collins Ave, Miami Beach, (305) 535-9900, (800) 535-9959, Fax: (305) 535-0077. In the Art Deco District, this 1936 historical building was completely remodeled in 1994. The guesthouse consists of two buildings, separated by an interior patio. Amenities include private baths, AC, color cable TV & phone. The rear building has rooms with private entrances, terraces and a common sun deck. We're 1/2-block from the beach and walking distance to nightclubs, restaurants and shopping. Some straight clientele. ♀♂

MIAMI RIVER INN, 118 SW South River Dr, (305) 325-0045, (800) 468-3589 (HOTEL 89), Fax: (305) 325-9227. Gay-friendly B&B hotel & apartments. Rooms with private baths, color cable TV, AC, ceiling fans & phones. Meeting rooms, lounge, pool, Jacuzzi & continental breakfast.

NORMANDY SOUTH, Miami Beach, (305) 674-1197. Luxury men-only guesthouse. Large, poshly-furnished rooms with modern conveniences. Jacuzzi & heated pool. Completely non-smoking inside & out. Tropical continental breakfast & nearby gay beach.

RICHMOND HOTEL, THE, 1757 Collins Ave, Miami Beach, FL 33139, (305) 538-2331, (800) 327-3163, Fax: (305) 531-9021. Gay-friendly luxury Art Deco hotel with restaurant, oceanfront location. Private baths, continental breakfast, pool & ocean on premises. Gay male following.

SHELBORNE BEACH RESORT, 1801 Collins Ave, Miami Beach, (305) 531-1271, (800) 327-8757, Fax: (305) 531-6051. Gay-friendly hotel.

VILLA PARADISO GUESTHOUSE, 1415 Collins Ave, Miami Beach, (305) 532-0616, Fax: (305) 673-5874, E-mail: villap@gate.net. Guesthouse 1/2 block from the beach, 2 blocks from gay beach. Color TV, AC, ceiling fans, telephone, kitchen, all private baths. Some straight clientele. ♀♂

WINTERHAVEN HOTEL, 1400 Ocean Drive, Miami Beach, Toll Free: (800) 395-2322, (305) 531-5571, Fax: (305) 538-3337. Hotel with

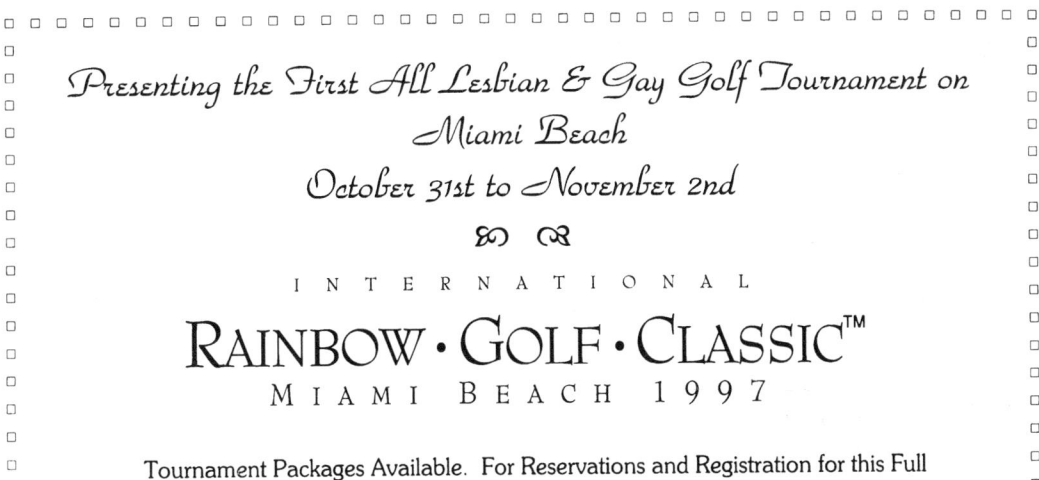

LILY GUESTHOUSE

In the Heart of South Beach

835 Collins Ave • Miami Beach

(305) 535-9900

Presenting the First All Lesbian & Gay Golf Tournament on

Miami Beach

October 31st to November 2nd

INTERNATIONAL

RAINBOW · GOLF · CLASSIC™

MIAMI BEACH 1997

Tournament Packages Available. For Reservations and Registration for this Full Handicap Competition call the Rainbow info-line, ask for Vic Ruggiero

212/206-6900 or 800/429-6969

www.worldguest.com/rainbow_golf

IGTA — we're a proud member of the International Gay Travel Association

FERRARI GUIDES

FERRARI GUIDES' GAY TRAVEL A to Z - 18th EDITION

FLORIDA

GAY FLORIDA ONLY!
Plus: Only Official Tour Operator for Gay Day at Disney

For Travelers...**Good Time Tours** has the largest inventory of gay and gay-friendly accommodations available and all must be gay-friendly, have gay employees, air conditioning, daily maid service and in-room phone. With your travel documents, you'll get a "Good Time Fun Pack" with local gay information. Never again will you waste precious vacation time searching for activities, fun or information.

For Travel Agents...Good Time Tours is dedicated exclusively to inbound gay travel to Florida. Your clients will never experience less than a gay-friendly hotel. To receive our generous prepaid commission policy and brochure, fax them on your company letterhead. They provide completely customized individual and group itineraries, on request, plus "hotels only" and will honestly answer the questions that you have about Gay Florida.

Contact **Good Time Tours** at (305) 864-9431, (888) 429-3527, Fax:(305) 866-6955, E-mail: gayfla@bridge.net

---

restaurant & bar, private baths. 50% gay & lesbian clientele.

YOUR PRIVATE ART DECO APARTMENT IN SOUTH BEACH, c/o New York Bed & Breakfast Reservation Center, Suite 221, 331 West 57th St, New York, NY 10019, (212) 977-3512, (800) 747-0868. Two private apartments together occupy the entire 2nd floor of a beautifully-landscaped Art Deco structure across from Flamingo Park in South Beach. The identical layouts include 2 bathrooms, 2 bedrooms, living room with small balcony, dining room & fully-equipped kitchen. Rooms have central AC & heat. Tennis courts & ocean beach nearby.

■ Beaches

EIGHTEENTH ST BEACH. South Beach, across from the Palace. A white-sand public beach with many gays.

TWENTY-FIRST ST BEACH, just north of the lifeguard tower. White-sand public beach, slightly older crowd.

■ Bars

BOARDWALK, 17008 Collins Ave N Miami Beach, (305) 354-8617. Male dancers nightly.

EAGLE MIAMI, 1252 Coral Way, (305) 860-0056.

EIGHT TWENTY-ONE CLUB, 821 Lincoln Rd, Miami Beach. Different venues nightly, some gay, some alternative.

HOMBRE, 925 Washington Ave, South Beach, (305) 538-STUD (7883). Male dancers, videos, patio, popular late evenings. Very popular 5-6am.

LOADING ZONE, 1426-A Alton Rd, Miami Beach. 7pm-5am daily, Leather Zone leather shop.

PARK PLACE, 17032 Collins Ave, North Miami Beach, (305) 949-4112. Many video screens.

REX, 409 Española Way, Miami Beach, (305) 534-0061. Small upscale bar with dance floor, tea dance Sun, Latin go go boys Thurs.

SUGAR'S, 17060 W Dixie Hwy, N Miami Beach, (305) 940-9887. Male dancers Sat.

TWIST,★ 1057 Washington Ave, South Beach, (305) 53-TWIST. 2 levels, patio, pool tables.

WESTEND, 942 Lincoln Rd, Miami Beach, (305) 538-WEST. 2 pool tables, male strippers, 60% men, 40% women, may change in '97.

■ Dance Bar/Disco

AMNESIA,★ 136 Collins Ave, Miami Beach, (305) 531-5535. Gay Sun only for tea dance, 70% men. Outdoor dance floor 5pm-11pm.

CLUB LIQUID, 1439 Washington Ave, Miami Beach, (305) 673-3413. Good Sun from midnite, straight other times.

HEAVEN, 245 22nd St, Miami Beach, (305) 532-9589. 2 levels, gay Fri only.

O'ZONE, 6620 Red Rd (SR 959), 1 Block off US 1, South Miami, (305) 667-2888. Male dancers, pool table, open nightly.

ON THE WATERFRONT, 3615 NW S River Dr, (305) 635-5500. Occasional name entertainment.

SALVATION,★ 1771 West Ave, Miami Beach, (305) 673-6508. Gay Sat only, 2 levels, very popular with gay men Sat evenings.

SPLASH, 5922 S Dixie Hwy, S Miami, (305) 662-8775. Dance club, patio, 2 pool tables, shows Mon, 70% men. Fri Bliss women's night.

THE 1235, 1235 Washington Ave, Miami Beach. To reopen in '97, largest dance space in N America, will have gay nights.

WARSAW,★ 1450 Collins Ave, S Miami Beach, (305) 531-4555. Large, hi-energy dance bar, strippers, 9pm-5am Wed, Fri & Sun are gay nites.

ZEN, 1208 Washington Ave, Miami Beach, (305) 673-2817. Gay Tues pm, Fri Pump men's nite.

ZEP PEPI'S, 1532 Washington Ave, between 15th & Lincoln Rd, Miami Beach, (305) 656-8411. Thurs gay nite, otherwise straight.

■ Saunas/Health Clubs

CLUB MIAMI, 2991 Coral Way near SW 30th Crt, (305) 448-2214. Private club, 24hrs. Sun cookouts, full gym, aerobics.

■ Restaurants

CHINA GRILL, 404 Washington Ave, (305) 534-2211.

DA LEO TRATTORIA, 819 Lincoln Rd, (305) 674-0350. Italian on the beach.

ELEVENTH ST DINER, 11th St at Collins Ave, Miami Beach, (305) 534-6373. Real diner food, many gays.

FLORIDA

GRANNY FEELGOOD'S, 647 Lincoln Rd, (305) 673-0408. Lighter menu. 🍴

JEFFREY'S, 1629 Michigan Ave, (305) 673-0690. ♀♂

LE BISTRO, 639 Lincoln Rd, (305) 672-1799. French cuisine. 🍴

LULU'S, 1053 Washington Ave, Miami Beach, (305) 532-6142. 🍴

LURE, 805 Lincoln Rd, (305) 538-5873. Chic & expensive. 🍴

LYON FRERES, 600 Lincoln Rd, (305) 534-0600. 🍴

MEZZALUNA, 834 Ocean Dr, (305) 674-1330. 🍴

PACIFIC TIME, 915 Lincoln Rd, (305) 534-5979. American with Asian influence. Expensive, but good. 🍴

PALACE, THE, 1200 Ocean Dr, South Miami Beach, (305) 531-9077. Bar & grill across from a gay beach & 12th St volleyball club. Patio dining. 🍴

PARAMOUNT CAFE, 1040 Lincoln Ave, (305) 535-8020. ♀♂

PETUNIA'S, 1321 Washington Ave, (305) 534-6883. 🍴

VAN DYKE CAFE, 846 Lincoln Rd, (305) 534-3600. Trendy. 🍴

■ Retail & Bookstores

GW, 720 Lincoln Rd, South Beach, (305) 534-4763. Gifts, clothing, cards, books.

LAMBDA PASSAGES BOOKSTORE, 7545 Biscayne Blvd near 75th, (305) 754-6900, 759-7141. Gay & lesbian books in English & Spanish. Cards, videos, gifts, etc.

NINTH CHAKRA, THE, 817 Linclon Rd, South Beach, (305) 538-0671. Metaphysical bookstore, Mon-Thur noon-7pm, Fri & Sat noon-8pm, Sun 2pm-6pm.

■ Erotica

ADULT VIDEO STORE, 1300 blk of Washington Ave. Movie booths.

BISCAYNE BOOKS, 11711 Biscayne Blvd.

CLOVERLEAF BOOK & VIDEO, 14907 NW 7th Ave, (305) 681-2001, 24hrs.

HOT STOP, 190 NE 167th St, (305) 956-9629. Booths.

LE JEUNE RD BOOKS, 928 SW 42nd Ave near SW 9th Terr, (305) 443-1913, 24hrs.

ONE HUNDRED SIXTY-SEVENTH ST XXX, 14 NE 167th St, (305) 949-3828.

PUSSYCAT THEATRE, 78th & Biscayne, (305) 754-2665.

STADIUM BOOKS & VIDEO, 17381 NW 27th Ave, Opa Locka, (305) 623-8933.

TRIPLEX-PLOSION, 8831 SW 40th St.

NAPLES

■ Accommodations

FESTIVE FLAMINGO, (941) 455-8833. Cozy, quiet, gay-friendly accommodation with heated pool. 15 minutes to beach, restaurants, nightlife & more.

■ Bars

GALLEY, THE, 509 3rd St, (941) 262-2808. Restaurant & lounge, breakfast to dinner, DJ Fri-Sat, shows Sat, 50/50 Fri & Sat, 80% men other times. ♀♂

■ Restaurants

CAFE FLAMINGO, 536 9th St N, (941) 262-8181. Breakfast & lunch, women-owned, Sun brunch 8am-1pm.

■ Retail & Bookstores

LAVENDER'S, 5600 Trail Blvd #4, (941) 594-9499. Gay & lesbian bookstore & pride shop. ♀

OCALA

■ Bars

CONNECTION, 3331 S Pine Ave, (352) 620-2511. About 70% men, pool table, DJ Fri & Sat, karaoke Sun, possibly drag shows Fri.

ORLANDO

■ Information

AIDS HOTLINE, (407) 841-2437. 24hrs.

GAY & LESBIAN COMMUNITY SERVICES, HOTLINE & CENTER, 714 E Colonial Drive, (407) 425-4527. 11am-9pm, Sat noon-5pm. Hotline (407) 843-4297.

WOMEN'S RESOURCE CENTER, (407) 426-7960.

■ Accommodations

A VERANDA B&B, 115 N Summerlin Ave, (407) 849-0321. B&B, 50% gay & lesbian clientele. Color cable TV, AC, telephone, private baths. Expanded continental breakfast, wedding courtyard & fax service.

GARDEN COTTAGE BED & BREAKFAST, 1309 E Washington St, Orlando, FL 32801, (407) 894-5395, Fax: (407) 894-3809. Escape to a relaxed garden atmosphere in historic Orlando's gay and lesbian neighborhood. Our private cottage is tastefully decorated, clean and comfortable featuring cable TV, VCR, movies, stereo, kitchen and more. Expanded continental breakfast. Walk to restaurants, Church Street and the heart of the city, Lake Eola. One to five miles to gay and lesbian clubs and shopping. Disney, Sea World, ect., 15-25 minutes. ♀♂

PARLIAMENT HOUSE HOTEL, 410 N Orange Blossom Trail, Orlando, (407) 425-7571, Fax: 425-5881. **World's most famous all gay resort**, 120 spacious, deluxe rooms, olympic size pool and private white sand beach on Rock Lake. 5 bars including the Power House Disco, Footlights Theatre with the Best in Female Impersonation, the Stable Western Bar with Dug Out Restaurant, open 24 hours, and the Orlando Eagle, Orlando's premier leather/levi bar.

THINGS WORTH REMEMBERING, 7338 Cabor Ct, Orlando, FL 32818, (407) 291-2127 (tel/fax), call first, (800) 484-3585 (dial code 6908). B&B with memorabilia & autographs from TV, movies, Broadway & sports. One room with queen bed, private bath, continental breakfast. ♀♂

■ Women's Accommodations

LEORA B'S ROBINSON HOUSE, PO Box 6094, Orlando, 32853, (407) 649-0009. Women-only B&B homestay in downtown historic district. Rooms range from doubles to an apartment, amenities vary, expanded continental breakfast. ♀

■ Bars

CACTUS CLUB, 1300 N Mills Ave, (407) 894-3041. Conversation bar with outside patio, 70% men, 50% men, 50% women Fri.

CLUB FUSION, 921 N Mills Ave, (407) 895-7341. Dance bar & restaurant.

CRUZ'S, 4716 S Orange Ave, (407) 850-6033. Bear bar, pool table, darts.

FULL MOON SALOON, ★ 500 N Orange Blossom Trail, (407) 648-8725. Bear bar, full moon parties, C&W music, lessons, dancing.

HANK'S, 5026 Edgewater at Lee Rd, (407) 291-2399. Cruise bar.

WYLDE'S, 3400 S Orange Blossom Tr, (407) 843-6334. Male strippers.

■ Dance Bar/Disco

CLUB AT FIRESTONE, 578 N Orange Ave, (407) 426-0005. Huge hi-energy daNce bar, gay Wed & Sat.

FACES, ★ 4910 Edgewater Dr at Lee, (407) 291-7571.

GALLERIA, 3400 S Orange Blossom Trail, (407) 422-6826. Dance & cruise bar.

PARLIAMENT HOUSE VENUES, at Parliament House Resort, 410 N Orange Blossom Trail, (407) 425-7571. Powerhouse disco, Stable western bar, restaurant breakfast thru dinner.

PHOENIX/CLUB Z, 7124 Aloma Ave, Winter Park, (407) 678-9220. Phoenix: jukebox neighborhood bar, Club Z: industrial Gothic dance bar.

SECRETS, 745 Bennett Rd. (407) 898-5603. Dance club & lounge.

SOUTHERN NIGHTS, ★ 375 S Bumby Ave, (407) 898-0424. Dance & show bar, 65% men, 35% women. Piano, patio, Fri buffet & Sun BBQ. Lesbo-A-Go Go women's night Sat.

■ Saunas/Health Clubs

CLUB ORLANDO ATHLETIC VENTURES, 450 East Compton, (407) 425-5005, Private club, 24 hrs.

FERRARI GUIDES' GAY TRAVEL A to Z - 18th EDITION

FLORIDA

UNITED STATES

Fitness Centers
NEW IMAGE FITNESS CENTER, 3400 S Orange Blossom Trail, (407) 420-9890. Gym, 24hrs. 3 day guest memberships for travelers.

Restaurants
UNION CITY TAVERN, 337 N Shine Ave, (407) 894-5778. California cuisine. ♀♂
WHITE WOLF CAFE, 1829 N Orange Ave, (407) 895-5590. Coffee shop food.

Retail & Bookstores
OUT & ABOUT BOOKS, 930 N Mills, (407) 896-0204. Gay & lesbian books, T-shirts, gifts, jewelry, cards, buttons & art gallery. Mon-Sat 11am-8pm.
RAINBOW CITY, 934 N Mills Ave, (407) 898-6096. Cards, rainbow and pride items. ♀♂

Leathers/Piercing
ABSOLUTE LEATHER, 3400 S Orange Blossom Trail, (407) 843-8168.
LEATHER CLOSET, 498 N Orange Blossom Trail, (407) 649-2011, Fax: (407) 649-4116. Custom leathers for men & women. Cards & gifts.

Erotica
MIDNIGHT NEWS, at Parliament House, 410 N Orange Blossom Trail, from 9pm.
VIDEO EXPRESS, 3400 S Orange Blossom Trail, (407) 839-0204. Till 1am daily.

PALM BEACH AREA

Information
COMPASS COMMUNITY CENTER, 1700 N Dixie Hwy, W Palm Beach, FL 33407, (561) 833-3638, Fax: (561) 833-4941. 10am-10pm (Fri 9am-5pm, Sun 4pm-9pm), Sun closed. Support & social group meetings, teen line, 24hr switchboard.

Accommodations
HIBISCUS HOUSE B&B, PO Box 2612, West Palm Beach, (561) 863-5633, (800) 203-4927. B&B, some straight clientele. Variety of rooms with modern conveniences, private baths, kitchen privileges & full breakfast. ♀♂
HUMMINGBIRD HOTEL B&B, 631 Lucerne Ave, Lake Worth, (561) 582-3224, fax: (561) 540-8817. Gay-friendly B&B hotel, continental breakfast, private & shared baths, AC, color cable TV, VCR, ceiling fans, nearby pool, ocean & lake.

Bars
BG'S, 5700 S Dixie Hwy, West Palm Beach, (561) 582-4114. ♂
H G ROOSTER'S, 823 Belvedere Rd, West Palm Beach, (561) 832-9119. Ocassionsl male dancers, patio, Sun buffet.
INN EXILE, 6 South J St, Lake Worth, (561) 582-4144. Video bar, 90% men, 10% women, many straights. ♂
K & E, 29 S Dixie Hwy, Lake Worth, (561) 533-6020. Bar & restaurant. ♀
KOZLOW'S, 6205 Georgia Ave, West Palm Beach, (561) 533-5355.
LEATHER & SPURS, 5004 S Dixie Hwy, (561) 547-1020. 01
THE 5101, 5101 S Dixie Hwy, West Palm Beach, (561) 585-2379. ♂

Dance Bar/Disco
CLUB 502, 502 Lucerne, Lake Worth, (561) 540-8881. Restaurant with Sun T dance, 70% men, 30% women. ♀♂
ENIGMA, 109 N Olive Ave, West Palm Beach, (561) 538-2430. Huge disco, mainly gay. Sun ladies night, Fri men's night. ♀♂
HEART BREAKER, ★ 2677 Forest Hill Blvd, Lake Shore Plaza, West Palm Beach, (561) 966-1590. Hi-energy laser dance bar, Wed-Sun, 70% men, women welcome. Male dancers, youngish crowd. ♂

Cafe
UNDERGROUND COFFEE WORKS, 105 S Narcissus Ave, West Palm Beach, (561) 835-4792. Coffees & limited menu, mostly vegetarian. Always gay-friendly, most popular with gays Thurs, live bands, large college crowd.

Retail & Bookstores
AMOROSO BOOKS & GIFTS, 205 N Federal Hwy, Lake Worth, (561) 533-5272. Gay pride store, Tues-Sat 10am-6pm, Sun noon-6pm. 2nd location inside Enigma bar.
ANGELIC PRIDE, 1700 N Dixie Hwy, W Palm Beach, (561) 820-0809. Pride store.
GAY BOOKS & GIFTS, 2nd at Federal. Gay & lesbian shop.
MAIN STREET NEWS, 255 Royal Poinciana Way, Palm Beach, (561) 833-4027. Gay magazines.

Erotica
CLOUD LAKE, Southern & I-95. West Palm Beach, (561) 683-4725.
PLEASURE VIDEO EMPORIUM, 464 S Military Trail, (561) 687-1424, 7 days.

PANAMA CITY

Bars
LA ROYALE, 100 Harrison Ave, (904) 784-9311. Pool tables, darts, video games, Sun T-dance, patio, 60% men, 40% women. ♀♂

Dance Bar/Disco
FIESTA ROOM, 110 Harrison Ave, (904) 784-9285. Disco, patio, 60% men, 40% women. Beer bust Wed. ♀♂

PASCO COUNTY

Bars
LOVEY'S PUB, 3338 US 19, Holiday, (813) 849-2960. Woman-owned, special events. ♀♂

Dance Bar/Disco
BT'S 7737 Grand Blvd, Port Richey, (813) 841-7900. Dance & show bar, DJ, Tues ladies night with female dancers, Thurs men's night with male dancers. Fri & Sat shows, Sun tea dances & buffet Mon. ♀♂

Restaurants
GRANDE CAFE, Grand near Main. Bistro atmosphere, fine dining.

PENSACOLA

Accommodations
MILL HOUSE INN, THE 9603 Lillian Highway, (904) 455-3400, toll free: (888) 999-4575, fax: (904) 458-6397, e-mail: TMHBB@AOL.COM. This guesthouse is a restored 1870's Victorian millhouse located on scenic Perdido Bay. All rooms have magnificent views of the bay. There is a new upper-level secluded back porch, as well as 1st- & 2nd-story verandas. It has private and shared baths, expanded continental breakfast (full breakfast weekends) and is a 10-minute drive to the white sand beaches. Women welcome. ♂

Beaches
GAY BEACH, "Gay Riviera" on Navarre Beach. Go east on Via DeLuna Dr, about 6 mi past the 2nd Circle K. Largest gay beach in the U.S. (or 2.2 mi past the sign for Gulf Nat'l Seashore).

Bars
NUMBERS, ★ 200 S Alcaniz, (904) 438-9004. Video cruise bar.
ROUNDUP, ★ 706 E Gregory St, (904) 433-8482. ♂
SEVILLE PARK PUB, Alcaniz at Government. Upscale ambiance with chandeliers & piano.

Dance Bar/Disco
CASTLE, Barrancas at Government, (904) 436-4007. Video dance bar. ♀♂
OFFICE, 1406 E. Wright St near Alcaniz, (904) 433-7278. ♀♂
RED CARPET, 937 New Warrington Rd, (904) 453-9918. 85% women. ♀
RED GARTER, ★ Main St at Palafox, (904) 433-9292. ♀♂

MILL HOUSE INN
Beautiful Sunsets Over Perdido Bay

(904) 455-3400
Toll free: (888) 999-4575
Pensacola, FL

FLORIDA

RIVIERA,★ Main St, (904) 432-1234.
Cafe
SECRET CAFE, S Palafox, enter thru Soho Gallery, (904) 444 9020. Bohemian-style alternative coffee house.
Restaurants
HALL'S SEAFOOD, 920 E Gregory, (904) 438-9019.
Retail & Bookstores
LUNAR LIBRARY, 5044 N Palafox St, (904) 470-0174. Spiritual shop, some gay & lesbian books.
PENSACOLA PRIDE, 9 E Gregory near Palafox, (904) 435-7272. Gay & lesbian superstore with pride items, books, clothing, beach wear & supplies, gifts.
SILVER CHORD BOOKSTORE, 10901 Lillian Hwy, (904) 453-6652. Alternative bookstore with gay & lesbian section.

POMPANO BEACH
Dance Bar/Disco
ADVENTURES,★ 303 SW 6th St, (954) 782-9577. C&W dance club, Fri-Sat 60% men, 40% women, lind dancing, lessons. Adventures in Dining restaurant, great buffet with prime rib to seafood Tues, Thurs-Sat.

ST AUGUSTINE
Women's Accommodations
PAGODA, 2854 Coastal Hwy, (904) 824-2970. Guesthouse in lesbian cottage community, private & shared baths.
Retail & Bookstores
DREAMSTREET BOOKSTORE, 64 Hypolita, (904) 824-8536. Metaphysical bookstore with a gay & lesbian section.

ST PETERSBURG - CLEARWATER
Information
GAY HOTLINE, (813) 586-4297, 7-11pm or tape.
Accommodations
FROG POND GUESTHOUSE, 145 29th Avenue North, (813) 823-7407 (tel/fax), Fax: (813) 620-1040. Guesthouse with garden pond, private bath, continental breakfast on arrival, color cable TV, VCR, AC, pool & ocean nearby, 50% gay/lesbian clientele.
SEA OATS BY THE GULF, 12625 Sunshine Lane, Treasure Island, (813) 367-7568, Fax: (813) 397-4157. Motel, 50% g/l clientele. Apartments with color cable TV, AC, kitchen & private baths. Ocean & Jacuzzi on premises.
Women's Accommodations
BARGE HOUSE, THE, PO Box 46526, Pass-A-Grille Beach, St. Petersburg Beach, (813) 360-0729. Private cabana or beach cottage, women only.

BOCA CIEGA BED & BREAKFAST, 3526 Boca Ciega Dr N, (813) 381-2755. Women-only B&B, private bath, continental breakfast, central AC, ceiling fans, maid service, pool on premises, minutes from beaches
Bars
BACK ROOM BAR (REAR OF SURF & SAND), 14601 Gulf Blvd at 146th, in Madeira Beach, (813) 391-2680. In back room of Surf & Sand straight bar.
DT'S, 2612 Central Ave, (813) 327-8204. Sports bar, games. 30's to 50's.
GOLDEN ARROW, 10604 Gandy Blvd, (813) 577-7774. Bear bar.
HIDEAWAY, 8302 4th St N. Men welcome.
PRO SHOP PUB, 840 Cleveland St, Clearwater, (813) 447-4259.
SPORTS PAGE PUB, 13344 66th St N, Largo, (813) 538-2430, pool, darts, sandwiches.
Dance Bar/Disco
BEDROX,★ 8000 W Gulf Blvd, Treasure Island, (813) 367-1724. Disco, beach bar, piano bar & restaurant.
FOURTEEN SEVENTY WEST,★ 325 Main St, Dunedin, (813) 736-5483. Dance & show bar, male strippers, 50% men, 50% women.
LOST & FOUND,★ 5858 Roosevelt Blvd, Clearwater, (813) 539-8903. Piano bar.
NEW CONNECTIONS, 3100 3rd Ave N, St Petersburg. (813) 321-2112. Dance bar & cafe, also cruise bar.
SHARP A'S, 4918 Gulfport Blvd South (22nd Ave S), Gulfport, (813) 327-GUYS (4897). Taped music, 70% men, 30% women, Karaoke Tue, Thur & Sun. May change in 1997.
Restaurants
FINS, 8000 W Gulf Blvd, at Bedrox bar, Treasure Island.
KELLY'S FOR JUST ABOUT ANYTHING, 319 Main St, Dunedin, (813) 736-5284. Fine dining.
Retail & Bookstores
AFFINITY BOOKS, 2435 9th St , (813) 823-3662. Gay & lesbian bookstore, Mon-Tues 10am-6pm, Wed-Fri 10am-8pm, Sat 10am-5pm, Sun noon-5pm.
BRIGIT BOOKS, 3434 4th St North #5, (813) 522-5775. Lesbian & feminist books, cards, jewelry, local info, 7 days.
Erotica
BUDDIES OF LARGO, 13801 66th St N, Largo, (813) 539-7979. Till 2am, 12am Sun.
FOURTH STREET BOOKMARK, 1427 4th St S, (813) 821-8824. Till 1am, 12am Sun, Fri & Sat till 3am.

SARASOTA
Accommodations
NORMANDY INN, 400 N Tamiami Trail,
(813) 366-8979, (800) 282-8050. Motel with xxx videos, some gay clientele.
SIESTA HOLIDAY HOUSE, 1011-1015 Crescent St, Siesta Key, (941) 488-6809, (800) 720-6885. Mail: 86 Inlets Blvd, Nokomis, FL 34275. Gay-owned with mainly straight clientele, 1- & 2-bedroom apts, steps from Crescent Beach.
Bars
H G ROOSTER'S, 1256 Old Stickney Pt Rd, (941) 346-3000. Small, quiet, after-beach bar, games, DJ Fri & Sat. Women welcome.
Dance Bar/Disco
BUMPERS NIGHTCLUB 1927,★ Ringling Blvd near Main, (941) 951-0335. Huge dance bar, Club X at Bumpers Thur & Sat gay nights. Midnight drag or strip shows, drag night 3rd Thurs.
CHRISTOPHER STREET, 6543 Gateway Ave, (941) 927-8766. Hi energy dance & video bar & piano lounge, multi-screen music videos, 4pm-2am daily.
RICKY J's 1330 Dr ML King Jr Way (27th St), (941) 953-5945. DJ weekends, shows & male dancers.
Erotica
NORTH WASHINGTON BLVD NEWS, 1038 N Washington Blvd, (813) 952-4545.
SOUTHTRAIL ADULT, S. Tamiami Trail, just south of Clark Rd.

SEAGROVE BEACH
Accommodations
MAGNOLIA MANOR & SEAVIEW, (904) 231-0254, (800) 854-9266. For gays or lesbians — two cozy beach cottages, fully furnished, comfortable and tastefully decorated, are just across the street from the quiet sugarsand beach. Seaview has an observation tower, deck, and fireplace. Both cottages have cable TV, VCR, and central heat/AC. Pets welcomed. Near exciting new town of Seaside; fabulous rest., art galleries and quaint shops close by.

Magnolia Manor & Seaview

Play on the Beach

Old Seagrove Beach, Florida

FOR YOUR PLEASURE
(800) 854-9266

FLORIDA

UNITED STATES

FYI

Nature Hikes & Kayaking for Women

It's Our Nature is a company created to provide women and girls the opportunity to explore the energy of nature through physical activity. Director Linda Taylor has over 20 years experience in the health, wellness and recreation field, and has been a naturalist all her life. Moderately-paced hikes and easy kayak paddles will take you through the often-ignored Florida eco-system in the Tampa Bay area. On some hikes, Chi Gong energy movements are taught. We move quietly through slash pine forests, beach scrub habitat, bird sanctuary shoreline, hardwood oak hammocks and bald cypress swamps. The natural history of each location is unveiled in storybook fashion.

Caladesi Island in Clearwater is the third most beautiful shoreline in the US. Honeymoon Island in Dunedin, one of the last virgin slash pine forests in Florida, is home to at least a dozen active Osprey nests. Hikes cost $15.00 to $25.00, kayaking $30.00-$50.00.

Contact **It's Our Nature** at (813) 441-2599, Fax: (813) 441-2599.

SEBASTIAN

■ Women's Accommodations
PINK LADY, THE, 1309 Louisiana Ave, (407) 589-1345. Women-only inn, 7 miles from ocean & near train tracks (formerly boarding house for railroad). Color TV, 2 rooms with microwave & refrigerator, pool on premises. Smoking outside only, pets permitted with prior permission, no credit cards.

TALLAHASSEE

■ Information
AIDS HOTLINE & INFO, (904) 656-2437.
WOMEN'S CENTER, 112 N Woodward Ave near Park, (904) 644-4007, 644-6453. M-F 1-5pm.

■ Bars
BROTHERS, 926-7 Tharpe St, (904) 386-2399. Video bar, 4pm-2am 7 days. 18 & over, shows, mostly men from 10pm, Thurs women's night.

■ Dance Bar/Disco
CLUB PARK AVE (CPA), 115 E Park Ave, (904) 599-9143. Gay Sat only, Sun urban gay night with house music.

■ Retail & Bookstores
RUBYFRUIT BOOKS, 666 W Tennessee St #4, (904) 222-2627. Lesbian & gay bookstore with large sections for both women & men. Get local info here! Closed Sun.

TAMPA

■ Information
GAY AND LESBIAN COMMUNITY CENTER OF TAMPA BAY, (813) 273-8919.

■ Accommodations
GRAM'S PLACE B&B GUESTHOUSE, 3109 N Ola Ave, Tel/Fax: (813) 221-0596, Beeper: 292-1415. B&B designed for those interested in music & the arts. Music played on request. Private & shared baths, eclectic decor, 80% gay & lesbian clientele.

■ Women's Accommodations
BIRDSONG BED AND BREAKFAST, (813) 654-8179. Women-only B&B on five wooded acres, less than an hour from downtown Tampa. Color TV, AC, ceiling fans, kitchen, private bath & expanded cont. breakfast.

■ Bars
ANGELS, 4502 S Dale Mabry Hwy, (813) 831-9980. Male strippers.
ANNEX, 2408 Kennedy Blvd W, (813) 254-4188. Male strippers.
CITY SIDE, 3810 Neptune St near Dale Mabry, (813) 254-6466. Neighborhood bar, patio.
DEUCES, ★ 2102 Highland Ave, (813) 223-3833.
KEITH'S LOUNGE, 14905 N Nebraska Ave, (813) 971-3576. Cookouts.
METROPOLIS, 3447 W Kennedy Blvd, (813) 871-2410. Noon-3am, Sun 1pm-3am, pool tables, darts, 80% men, 20% women, good for happy hour & late nite after midnite.
NORTHSIDE LOUNGE, 9002 N Florida Ave, (813) 931-3396. Summer BBQ's, Fri potluck.
RASCALS, 105 W Martin Luther King Blvd, (813) 237-8883. Bar & restaurant.
SAHARA, 4603 W Kennedy Blvd, (813) 989-3612. DJ Fri, Sat.
TAMPA EAGLE, ★ 302 S. Nebraska Ave, (813) 223-2780. 1 room has leather dress code, leather shop inside.
TWENTY-SIX-O-SIX, 2606 N Armenia Ave, (813) 875-6993. Bar with leather shop.

■ Dance Bar/Disco
CASTLE/MECCA, 16th & 9th, Ybor City (old Labor Temple Bldg). Gay night Sat, always gay-friendly.
CHEROKEE CLUB, 1320 E 9th Ave, Ybor City, (813) 247-9966. Thur-Sat from 9pm, DJ Thurs-Sat. May open Fri for happy hour in '97.
FLAVOUR, 15th & Palm Ave, Ybor City, (813) 242-8007. 70's & 80's Retro in Kaleidescope, hi energy in the Iron Arena.
SOLAR, 913 Franklin St, (813) 226-9227. Multi-level dance club, closed in early 1997, may reopen.

■ Saunas/Health Clubs
CLUB TAMPA, 215 N 11th St, (813) 223-5181, 24hrs.

■ Restaurants
RASCALS, 105 W Martin Luther King Blvd, (813) 237-8883. Restaurant & gay bar, award-winning cuisine.

■ Retail & Bookstores
MC FILM FESTIVAL, 3601 W Kennedy Blvd, (800) 445-7134. Large selection of non-erotic gay & lesbian videos.
TOMES & TREASURES, 202-1/2 S Howard, (813) 251-9368. Gay & lesbian bookstore, 12pm-9pm.

■ Leathers/Piercing
EAGLE LEATHER SHOP, 2606 N Armenia Ave at 2606 bar, (813) 875-6993.

■ Erotica
BUDDIES ADULT VIDEO, 4322 Crest Ave West, (813) 876-8083. Booths.

GEORGIA

WHO TO CALL
For Tour Companies Serving This Destination
See Georgia on page 15

ATHENS

Dance Bar/Disco
BONESHAKERS, 433 E Hancock, (706) 543-1555. Dance club, variety of music, retro to hi energy, drag shows Mon, 60% men, 40% women.

ATLANTA

Information
AIDS LINE, (404) 876-9944 or (800) 551-2728. 9am-9pm (Sat, Sun noon-5pm).

FOURTH TUESDAY, (770) 662-4353, 662-6868 (events hotline). Networking organization for lesbians.

GAY HELP LINE & GAY CENTER, 71 12th St NE, (404) 892-0661. Staffed 6pm-11pm, 24hr tape.

Accommodations
ANSLEY INN, 253 15th St NE, (404) 872-9000, Fax: (404) 892-2318, (800) 446-5416. Gay-friendly, centrally-located, elegant inn. Color cable TV, phone, wet bar, private bath with Jacuzzi. Some rooms with fireplace. Continental breakfast, pool on premises. 24hr concierge service.

BONAVENTURE, THE, 650 Bonaventure Ave, Atlanta, GA 30306, (404) 817-7024, Fax: (404) 249-9988, E-mail: friedato@mindspring.com. Victorian B&B guesthouse with private & shared baths, expanded continental breakfast, lovely private gardens & fish pond. 50% gay & lesbian clientele.

BOXWOOD HEIGHTS, 511 Toombs St, Palmetto, GA 30268, (770) 463-9966, (888) 463-0101, Fax: (770) 463-0701. B&B 25 minutes from downtown Atlanta, MARTA pulic transport 1 block. Large guest rooms, private & shared baths, antique furnishings, rocking chair porch, 9 fireplaces. 50% gay & lesbian clientele.

CANDLER PARK PATIO APARTMENT, 612 Clifton Rd NE, Atlanta, GA 30307, (404) 373-6072, (800) 392-5999, Fax: (404) 377-7637. Mediterranean-style B&B patio apartment with kitchen stocked with breakfast items, private bath, AC, color cable TV, phoone, 1 mile from Carter center, near cafes & bars.

CARITAS BED & BREAKFAST NETWORK, (800) CARITAS, (312) 857-0801, Fax: (312) 857-0805. B&B, home-stay accommodations service. *Member: IGTA*

CARUSO MANOR, Atlanta, GA (404) 875-1706. B&B with private & shared baths, continental breakfast, AC, telephone, maid service, nearby river & lake, women welcome.

GASLIGHT INN BED & BREAKFAST, 1001 Saint Charles Ave, Atlanta, GA 30306, (404) 875-1001, Fax: (404) 876-1001, E-mail: gaslight n@aol.com. http://www.gaslight.com. Extravagantly decorated craftsman-style B&B inn close to downtown Atlanta & walking distance to restaurants, shops, theaters & galleries. All private baths, expanded continental breakfast. Gay-friendly.

KING-KEITH HOUSE B&B, 889 Edgewood Ave NE, (404) 688-7330. Gay-friendly B&B, private baths, expanded continental or full breakfasts, gay male following.

MAGNOLIA STATION B&B, 1020 Edgewood Ave NE, (404) 522-3923. B&B in a Victorian colonial in Atlanta's Inman Park historical district, hearty continental breakfst.

MIDTOWN MANOR, 811 Piedmont Ave NE, (404) 872-5846, (800) 724-4381. A Victorian guesthouse in midtown Atlanta, 50% gay & lesbian clientele. Both elaborately furnished and budget rooms, breakfast and dinner restaurants 5 blocks. Walk to many gay bars and restaurants. Stay a night or two or a week or two.

TRIANGLE POINTE, Rte 4, Box 242, Dahlonega, (706) 867-6029, Fax: (706) 867-6030. B&B 70 miles north of Atlanta, with private shower/toilet, full breakfast, AC, Jacuzzi, color cable satellite TV, ceiling fans, women welcome.

TWENTY-ONE NINETEEN - THE INN & OUR HOME, 1451 Sanden Ferry Drive Decatur (Atlanta), (404) 491-0248. B&B. AC, 2 TV lounges (one smoking, one non-smoking), continental breakfast. Access to nearby gym & pool.

UPPER ECHELONS, 215 Piedmont Ave NE, (770) 642-1313. Furnished, luxury penthouse in downtown condo complex, near gay & lesbian bars. Security access gate. Please, no calls after 10 pm EST. Weekly & monthly rates available.

Women's Accommodations
ABOVE THE CLOUDS B&B, 206 Cedar Mountain Rd, Dahlonega, GA (706) 864-5211. Enjoy the quiet and privacy of a mountain getaway 70 miles north of Atlanta. Our guests occupy a large suite with its own private entrance, kitchen, deck and spa, a queen-sized bed and private bath. You can visit a local winery and a restored gold mine, shop for native crafts, hike the Appalachain Trail, canoe, ride horses, or picnic beside a waterfall in the woods. Sound Inviting? Women-only B&B.

SWIFTWATERS, Box 379-9, Rte 3, (706) 864-3229. Women-only B&B, cabins & camping. Private bath & outhouses.

Bars
ATLANTA EAGLE, 306 Ponce de Leon Ave NE, (404) 873-2453. DJ. Atlanta's only 100% leather bar.

BLAKE'S, ★ 227 10th St, (404) 892-5786. Cheers-type bar with upstairs sports bar, women welcome. Videos & patio.

BUDDIES MIDTOWN, 239 Ponce de Leon, (404) 872-2655.

BUDDIES, 2345 Cheshire Bridge Rd NE, (404) 634-5895.

BULLDOGS, 893 Peachtree St NE near 8th (rear), (404) 872-3025. Patio, Sun cookouts.

BURKHART'S, ★ 1492 Piedmont Rd NE (Ansley Square), (404) 872-4403. pub, 80% men, women welcome, patio, videos.

CHAMBER, THE, 2115 Faulkner Rd, (404) 248-1612. gay & straight S&M/fetish club.

GUYS & DOLLS, 2788 E Ponce de Leon, (404) 377-2956. Mixed gay & straight crowd, nude dancers, male & female strippers. Mostly gay crowd on Tue & Sun.

LE BUZZ, 585 Franklin Rd, Marietta, northern suburb 10 min from downtown, close to exit #112 on I-75, (770) 424-1337. Only gay bar in Cobb county, bar with espresso coffee, DJ music.

METRO, THE, 1080 Peachtree St NE, (404) 874-9869. Video bar, dancers daily.

MODEL-T, 699 Ponce de Leon, Ford Factory Sq, (404) 872-2209. Daily 9am-4pm, Sat till 3am, drag shows Sat.

MORELAND TAVERN, 1196 Moreland Ave SE, (404) 622-4650. 80% gay & lesbian.

Visit Atlanta
(800) CARITAS
Caritas B&B Network

Your Visitor's Center in Atlanta
OUTWRITE BOOKSTORE & COFFEEHOUSE
- BOOKS
- MAGAZINES
- CARDS
- MUSIC
- VIDEO
- SANDWICHES
- SWEETS
- JUICES
- COFFEE

Right on Piedmont Park
MIDTOWN ATLANTA ■ 991 PIEDMONT at TENTH
(404) 607-0082

FERRARI GUIDES' GAY TRAVEL A to Z - 18th EDITION

GEORGIA

MY SISTER'S ROOM,★ (404) 875-6699. Cozy, intimate. ♀

NEW ORDER, 1544 Piedmont Rd, Ansley Mall, (404) 874-8247. Women welcome.

OPUS ONE, 1086 Alco Street NE, (404) 634-6478. Juke box, 65% men, 35% women.

PHOENIX, 567 Ponce de Leon NE, (404) 892-7871.

SCANDALS, Ansley Square, (404) 875-5957. Open very early, drink till late.

TOWER II, 735 Ralph McGill, (404) 523-1535. Mature lesbians. ♀

■ Dance Bar/Disco

ARMORY, THE,★ 836 Juniper NE at 6th (rear), (404) 881-9280. Dance complex with showbar & late patio.

BACKSTREET,★ 845 Peachtree St NE near 6th (rear), (404) 873-1986. 80% men, women welcome, younger crowd. Patio, cabaret showe, 24hrs daily. Private club, non-members welcome.

FOUNTAINHEAD LOUNGE, 1287-D Glenwood Ave. Upscale cocktail lounge with unique architecture & intimate atmosphere. To open June '97, very gay-friendly.

HERETIC COMPLEX,★ 2069 Cheshire Bridge Rd, near Beaver Hwy, (404) 325-3061. Complex with Sanctuary dance club, Pub Room neighborhood bar, Backyard Bar outside deck, Coolers pool rooms & Heretic Leathers. Leather no-shirt dress code Wed & Sun at Sanctuary. Male strippers Thurs.

HOEDOWNS, 931 Monroe Dr, (404) 876-0001. Open daily, women welcome, patio.

LORETTA'S, 708 Spring Street NW, (404) 874-8125. DJ nightly, women welcome.

MARCH,★ 550-C Amsterdam Ave, (404) 872-6411. Voted best new dance club in Atlanta 1996, "very upscale, very New York."

MASQUERADE, 695 North Ave, (404) 577-8178. Alternative dance club with mostly straight crowd, but popular with funky gay crowd. Wed Club Fetish S&M night, Thurs Old Wave night, Fri Flash Back disco music, Sat house music, Sun swing night.

OTHERSIDE,★ 1924 Piedmont Rd, (404) 875-5238. Theme nights, shows, variety of music, open late weekends.

REVOLUTION,★ (404) 874-8455. Dance bar & restaurant, call for address. ♀

■ Saunas/Health Clubs

FLEX, 76 4th St, (404) 815-0456. Gay men's social club. 24 hrs. ♂

■ Fitness Centers

BOOT CAMP, at Ansley Mall. (404) 876-8686. Men's fitness center.

FITNESS FACTORY, 500 Amsterdam, Midtown Outlets, (404) 815-7900.

MID-CITY FITNESS, 2201 Faulkner Rd, (404) 321-6507. Fitness center & tanning salon.

■ Restaurants

AGNES & MURIEL'S, 1514 Monroe Dr, near Piedmont. (404) 885-1000.

BEE HIVE, 1090 Alpharetta St, Roswell, (770) 594-8765. ♀♂

BRIDGETOWN GRILL, 3 locations; 1156 Euclid Ave, 653-0110, 689 Peachtree St, 873-5361, 7285 Roswell Rd, (770) 394-1575. Caribbean cuisine, patio & sidewalk dining. Gay-friendly.

COWTIPPERS, 1600 Piedmont Rd, (404) 874-3751. Gay-friendly steak & rib restaurant.

CRESCENT MOON, 254 W Ponce de Leon, Decatur, (404) 377-5623. Breakfast till 3am, vegetarian, sandwiches, etc.

DUSTY'S BBQ, 1815 Briarcliff Rd, (404) 320-6264. Gay-friendly BBQ.

EINSTEIN'S,★ 1077 Juniper, (404) 876-7925. Large outdoor patio, continental cuisine, gay-friendly.

FLYING BISQUIT CAFE, 1655 McClendan Ave, (404) 687-8888. Hearty, healthy breakfast-dinner.

GREAT WESTERN BURRITO CO. 931 Monroe Dr, (404) 607-1175.

MARRA'S SEAFOOD GRILL, 1782 Cheshire Bridge Rd, (404) 874-7347. Lunch & dinner 7 days, gay following.

PRINCE GEORGE INN, 2625 Piedmont, (404) 685-8793. Pastas, seafood. ♀♂

ST. CHARLES DELI, 752 N Highland Ave, (404) 870-3354. Gay-friendly.

THAI CHILI, 2169 Briarcliff Rd, (404) 315-6750.

■ Retail & Bookstores

BOY NEXT DOOR, THE, 1447 Piedmont Ave NE, (404) 873-2664. Casual clothing, swimwear, gymwear for men.

BRUSHSTROKES, 1510-J Piedmont Ave NE, (404) 876-6567. Gay variety store, with books, magazines, videos, T-shirts, music, cards, jewelry, rainbow items.

CHARIS BOOKS & MORE, 1189 Euclid Ave, (404) 524-0304. Feminist bookstore. Program every Thurs at 7:30pm.

OUTWRITE BOOKSTORE & COFFEEHOUSE, 991 Piedmont at Tenth, (404) 607-0082. Gay & lesbian bookstore & coffeehouse. Outwrite has Atlanta's complete selection of books & magazines by, for, and about gay men & lesbians. Come in and browse in a very comfortable bookstore and have a snack in the coffeehouse. Knowledgeable, friendly staff has a great knowledge of the literature and can tell you anything you need to know about what to do and where to go in Atlanta. The new location is located right on Piedmont Park. See ad on page 417.

POSTER HUT, 2175 Cheshire Bridge Rd NE (404) 633-7491. Leather supplies, cards, books, gifts & lubes.

■ Leathers/Piercing

HERETIC LEATHERS, 2069 Cheshire Bridge Rd at Heretic Complex, (404) 325-3061. Full leather & toy shop, open Wed-Sun.

MOHAWK LEATHER, 306 Ponce De Leon Ave NE, (404) 874-4732 (87-EAGLE). Leather boutique in the Eagle bar.

■ Erotica

NINE 1/2 WEEKS: 505 Peachtree St NE, (404) 873-1612, 888-0878; 1023 W Peachtree St NE, (404) 815-9622; 2628 Piedmont Rd, (404) 262-9113; 6400 Roswell Rd, (404) 250-0428; 7855 Roswell Rd, Morgan Falls, (770) 677-9650; 850 Northside Dr, (404) 607-7176.

AUGUSTA

■ Dance Bar/Disco

WAY STATION, 1632 Walton Way, (706) 733-2603. Mon-Fri 8:30pm-3am, Sat till 2am.

CLARKESVILLE

■ Accommodations

OUTSIDER INN & GALLERY, 690 Chitwood Rd, Clarkesville, (706) 754-9260. B&B & art gallery in a hand-hewn log home in northeast Georgia, private baths, full breakfast, 50% gay & lesbian clientele.

COLUMBUS

■ Dance Bar/Disco

EXCLUSIVE, Cocita Rd.

PTL CLUB, 2nd Ave near 14th St.

■ Erotica

FOXES THEATER, 3009 Victory Drive, (706) 689-2211.

JERRY'S VIDEO, 3005 or 3011 Victory Dr. Videos & leather items.

MACA/MECCA, 3016 Victory Drive, (706) 689-2212. Til midnight.

VIDEO FANTASY, 14th St & 5th Ave, (706) 327-7987. Till midnight. Fri & Sat till 2am.

HIAWASSEE

■ Accommodations

MISTY MOUNTAIN INN, A B&B, 548 Nicholson Trail, Hiawassee, (706) 896-5619, Nov-Apr call: (770) 977-8270. B&B with local artists' work for sale, private & shared baths, expanded continental, continental or full breakfast, women welcome, some straight clientele. ♂

MACON

■ Information

GAY & LESBIAN LINE, AIDS INFO, (912) 750-8080. Rainbow Center, Mon-Thur 3pm-9pm. Fri 11am-9pm.

■ Dance Bar/Disco

CHERRY ST PUB,★ 425 Cherry St, (912) 755-1400. Big dance bar, drag shows Sat, videos, restaurant & lounge bar, large straight following. Will open Sun in '97.

HAWAII

TOPAZ, 695 Riverside Dr, (912) 750-7669. DJ, good mix of music, C&W night. Progressive, alternative club, mixed gay & straight crowd.

Retail & Bookstores
COLORS ON CHERRY, 415 Cherry St, (912) 745-7474. Gay gift shop, gay items.

MOUNTAIN CITY
Accommodations
YORK HOUSE B&B INN, PO Box 126, Mountain City, GA 30562, (706) 746-2068, (800) 231-9675, fax: (706) 746-5641. B&B inn, silver-tray breakfast, private baths, color cable TV, AC, TV lounge, hiking & jogging trails on premises, nearby river, lake & waterfalls, 50% gay/lesbian clientele.

ST. SIMONS ISLAND
Accommodations
LITTLE ST. SIMONS ISLAND, PO Box 21079, St. Simons Island, 31522, (912) 638-7472, Fax: (912) 634-1811. 10,000-acre private island resort with 7 miles of beach, unspoiled wilderness, various accommodations & family-style meals. Available to private groups, maximum 24 guests. Gay-friendly.

SAVANNAH
Information
LESBIAN & GAY INFO LINE, (912) 236-CITY (2489).

Accommodations
NINE TWELVE BARNARD B&B, 912 Barnard St, (912) 234-9121. B&B shared baths, expanded continental breakfast, walking distance to Savanna's shops, restaurants & historic Forsyth Park, 15 minutes from beaches.

Bars
CHABLIS' CABARET, made famous by movie Midnight in the Garden of Good & Evil, Lady Chablis' is opening her own show bar downtown in summer 1997. Will be open evenings & also daytimes for tourists for drag shows with Lady Chablis.

FACES, 17 Lincoln, (912) 233-3520. Noon-3am 7 days.

FANNY'S ON THE BEACH, 1613 Strand, Tybee Island, (912) 786-6109. Bar & restaurant on the beach, frozen drinks, awesome food.

Dance Bar/Disco
CLUB ONE,★ 1 Jefferson St at Bay, (912) 232-0200. Dance & show bar, 50% men, 50% women. Private club, guests welcome. Mon-Sat 5pm-3am, Sun 5pm-2am.

FELICIA'S,★ 416 W Liberty St, (912) 238-4788. Male & female strippers, drag shows Fri-Sun, restaurant.

Retail & Bookstores
DREAMWEAVER, 306 W St. Julian St, (912) 236-9003. New Age bookstore.

HOME RUN VIDEO & BOOKS, 4 E Liberty, (912) 236-5192. General bookstore with a gay & lesbian section.

Erotica
CAPTAIN VIDEO, 7 W York St at Bull, (912) 232-2951. Large selection of gay & lesbian videos, cards, 7 days.

SENOIA
Accommodations
CULPEPPER HOUSE, 35 Broad St, (770) 599-8182. Gay-friendly B&B 30 miles from Atlanta. AC, shared baths, TV lounge, fax & full breakfast. Gay female following.

STATESBORO
Accommodations
STATESBORO INN, 106 S Main St, (912) 489-8628, Fax: (912) 489-4785. Gay-friendly inn with restaurant in a 15-room Victorian.

VALDOSTA
Dance Bar/Disco
CLUB PARADISE, 2100 W Hill Ave near I-75 off-ramp, exit 4, (912) 242-9609. Mon-Sat 3pm til...

HAWAII

WHO TO CALL
For Tour Companies Serving This Destination
See Hawaii on page 16

STATEWIDE
PACIFIC OCEAN HOLIDAYS, PO Box 88245-F, Honolulu, HI 96830-8245, (808) 923-2400, (800) 735-6600, Fax: (808) 923-2499, E-mail: poh@hi.net.net. http://www.tnight.com/poh. Specializing exclusively in Hawaii vacation packages for gay travelers, widest selection of gay & gay-friendly Hawaii hotels, B&Bs, condos. Packages can be customized for length of stay, islands visited, and are offered year-round. Tours are not escorted, so sightseeing & relaxation are at one's leisure.

HAWAII - BIG ISLAND
Accommodations
HALE ALOHA GUEST RANCH, 84-4780 Mamalahoa Hwy, Captain Cook, HI 96704, (808) 328-8955 (tel/fax), (800) 897-3188, E-mail: halealoha@aol.com. Discover the "house of welcome and love" with its spacious lanais and spectacular ocean views. At 1500 ft in the lush South Kona hillside, guests will enjoy the peace and tranquillity of the 5-acre citrus and macadamia nut plantation bordering a state forest preserve. Take a stroll, get a massage, relax in the Jacuzzi or lay in the sun and read. Be more adventurous and bike, snorkel (provided free), dive or kayak. The City of Refuge and Kealakekua Bay (famous for tropical fish, sea turtles & often-present dolphins) are right down below.

Hawaii GAY VACATIONS
Pacific Ocean Holidays
Free Brochure
800-735-6600

HALE KIPA 'O PELE, PO Box 5252, Kailua-Kona, 96745, (800) LAVAGLO, (808) 329-8676. B&B with bungalow. Ceiling fans, private baths. TV lounge with theatre sound, video tape library, Jacuzzi. Bungalow has mini-kitchen, cable TV & VCR.

HALE OHIA COTTAGES, PO Box 758, Volcano, (808) 967-7986 or (800) 455-3803, Fax: (808) 967-8610. B&B & cottages, 50% gay & lesbian clientele. Private baths, continental breakfast & heated Japanese Furo.

HULIAULE'A, PO Box 1030 Pahoa, (808) 965-9175. B&B, some straight clientele. Spacious rooms with private & shared baths. Common areas, refrigerator, garden & full breakfast.

KA HALE NA PUA, PO Box 385210, Kohala Coast, HI 96738, (808) 329-2960, (800) 595-3458. Gay-friendly guesthouse on the slopes of Hualakii, on the Kona Coast. Private baths, continental breakfast.

KALANI OCEANSIDE ECO-RESORT, Box 4500, Kehena Beach, (800) 800-6886, (808) 965-7828, Fax: (808) 965-9613, E-mail: kh@ILHawaii.net. http://randm.com/kh.html. Gay-friendly eco-resort with restaurant & native gift shops. Private & shared baths, TV lounge, pool. Continental breakfast with rooms.

KEALAKEKUA BAY B&B, PO Box 1412, Kealakekua, HI 96750, (808) 328-8150, (800) 328-8150. B&B and guesthouse with private baths, expanded continetal breakfast, ceiling

Hale Aloha Guest Ranch
The Real Spirit of Aloha
(808) 328-8955
(800) 897-3188
email: halealoha@aol.com
Hawaii's Big Island

FERRARI GUIDES' GAY TRAVEL A to Z - 18th EDITION

HAWAII

FYI

Kayak Warm Waters Eat Fresh-Caught Grilled Fish on the Beach

Paddling, camping, snorkeling, and hiking or walking is the best way to explore the Big Island of Hawaii. With **Kayak Historical Discovery Tours**, you can take a half-day kayak in a stable, easy-to-paddle, sit-on-top kayak, to beautiful locations. Or you can spend 2 to 5 days kayak camping up and down the sunny leeward coast, visiting bays with names like Kealakekua or Keauhou or Kiholo. On these trips, you can snorkel reefs, see dolphins, bask in the warm water, listen to the humpback whales' epic songs, camp under the palms or relax in a hammock, enjoy fresh, grilled fish and tropical fruits. All equipment and meals are provided. The company also leases kayaks for two or more days completeley outfitted and with maps and local tips, plus a soft rack for your rental car. Owner/guide Betsy Morrigan also accompanies visitors as a guide to local sights or on walking/hiking excursions to some of the less-accessible areas, including the ancient Hawaiian sacred historical sites.

Contact **Kayak Historical Discovery Tours** at (808) 328-8911, write 87-3187 Honu Moe Road, Captain Cook, HI 96704.

---

fans, maid service, ocean nearby, 50% gay/lesbian clientele.

LA'AKEA GARDENS, RR 2, POB 4529, Pahoa, 96778, (808) 965-8164, Fax: (808) 965-9203. Two bungalows on 3 acre estate each with kitchen & bath. Decks with ocean view. Bikes & snorkel gear available to guests. 2 blocks from private black sand beach. Gay friendly.

OUR PLACE PAPAIKOU'S B&B, PO Box 469, Papaikou, HI 96781, (808) 964-5250 (tel/fax), (800) 245-5250, E-mail: rplace@aloha.net. B&B with private & shared baths, expanded continental breakfast, color cable TV, VCR, ceiling fans, river on premises, ocean nearby, 50% gay/lesbian clientele.

PAAUHAU PLANTATION HOUSE, PO Box 1375, Honokaa, HI, (808) 775-7222, (800) 789-7614, Fax: 775-7223. Gay-friendly B&B with a gay female following, private baths, color TV, ceiling fans, nearby ocean beach.

PAMALU, RR 2, Box 4023, Pahoa, (808) 965-0830, fax: (808) 965-6198. B&B country retreat, private baths, expanded continental breakfast, TV lounge, video tape library, pool on premises, nearby lagoon, some straight clientele.

PLUMERIA HOUSE, 77-6546 Naniloa Dr, Kailua, Kona (808) 322-8164. B&B, some straight clientele. Private & shared baths.

R.B.R. FARMS, PO Box 930, Captain Cook, 96704, (808) 328-9212, (800) 328-9212, Fax: (808) 328-9212. B&B, women welcome. Double rooms & cottage, private & shared baths, color TV, massage, nearby ocean beach. Full breakfast. A working macadamia nut and coffee plantation adds charm to this renovated plantation home. **Being privately owned, it retains the personal touch and attention to detail that sets us apart among outstanding B&Bs in the world.**

RAINBOW DREAMS COTTAGE, 13-6412 Beach Rd, Pahoa, HI 96778, (808) 936-9883. On the Big Island's secluded Puna Coast, you are transported back to the simple splendor of swaying palms & lulling ocean surf. This oceanfront 2-bedroom turnkey cottage is furnished in rattan tropical comfort. Sunbathe nude on a black sand beach, snorkel among coral castles, or float in a warm springs pond splashed by cool ocean surf. Some straight clientele.

RAINFOREST RETREAT, HCRI Box 5655, Keaau, 96749, (808) 982-9601, Nursery: (808) 966-7712, Fax: (808) 966-6898. Gay-friendly guest ranch. Private cottage with kitchen, full bath, color TV & hot tub on lanai, or suite with private entrance, kitchenette, color TV & full bath. Full breakfast, ocean nearby.

SAMURAI, THE, 82-5929 Mamalahoa Hwy, Captain Cook, (808) 328-9210. Inn, some straight clientele. Traditional Japanese and western-style rooms with a variety of conveniences. TV lounge, hot tub, continental breakfast. Nearby ocean beach.

VOLCANO RANCH: INN & BUNKHOUSE, 13-3775 Kalapana Hwy, Pahoa, HI 96778, (808) 965-8800. Inn & bunkhouse on 25 clothing-optional acres with steam baths & caves, forest trails, panoramic views, minutes to beach. Rooms include first-rate amenities, full bath. Separate bunkhouse with gang showers. Inndulge yourself at Hawaii's newest playground.

■ Women's Accommodations

BUTTERFLY INN, THE, PO Box 6010, Kurtistown, (808) 966-7936, (800) 54-MAGIC. Women-only B&B, shared bath.

■ Beaches

HARBOR BEACH. Nude beach between Kailua-Kona & the airport. More gay at north end.

■ Bars

MASK BAR & GRILL, 75-5660 Kopiko St, Kailua-Kona, (808) 329-8558. Karaoke, drag shows & dancing.

OTHER SIDE, 74-5484 Kaiwi St, Kailua, Kona, (808) 329-7226. Bar & cafe.

■ Restaurants

GODMOTHER, THE, 15-2969 Main St, Pahoa, (808) 965-0555. Gay-friendly restaurant with bar. New York Italian style, 7 days, breakfast-dinner.

HUGGO'S, 75-5828 Kahakai Rd, Kailua-Kona, (808) 329-1493. Fresh seafood & beef.

KAUAI

■ Information

AIDS HOTLINE, (808) 822-0878, 9am-5pm Mon-Fri.

■ Accommodations

ALOHA KAUAI BED & BREAKFAST, 156 Lihau St, (808) 822-6966, (800) 262-4652. B&B minutes from town, gay beach & many outdoor attractions. Features private & shared baths, full breakfast, sunset refreshments, pool on premises.

ANAHOLA BEACH CLUB, PO Box 562, Anahola, 96703, (808) 822-6966, (800) ANAHOLA. B&B on coconut coast. Delightful rooms with private entrances & ocean views, bunk house, TV lounge, full breakfast, complimentary cocktails.

R·B·R FARMS
Bed and Breakfast
For More Information and Reservations
Call: **1-800-328-9212**
Or Write: P.O Box 930,
Captain Cook, Hawaii 96704

HAWAII

HALE KAHAWAI, 185 Kahawai Place, Kapaa, HI 96746, (808) 822-1031, Fax: (808) 823-8220. E-mail: BandBKauai@aol.com. Conveniently located in Wailua, Kauai, Hale Kahawai has three guest rooms and one studio apartment. All guest rooms have romantic ceiling fans, queen or king mattresses and tropical furnishings. Island breakfast of local fruits, juices, cereals, breads, coffees and teas. Enjoy spectacular views of Kawaikini Peak and Mount Waialeale. End the day relaxing in the hot tub.

KALIHIWAI JUNGLE HOME, PO Box 717, Kilauea, HI 96754, (808) 828-1626 (Tel/Fax), E-mail: thomasw@aloha.net. Fully-furnished, 2-bedroom vacation rental, 50% gay & lesbian. Modern amenities, glassed-in panoramic views from each room. Nearby beach, olympic-sized pool, gym, snorkeling & windsurfing.

MAHINA KAI, PO Box 699, Anahola, Kauai, (808) 822-9451, (800) 337-1134. B&B, some straight clientele. Color TV, ceiling fans, private baths, meeting rooms & expanded continental breakfast. Lagoon pool & hot tub on premises.

MALA LANI (HEAVENLY GARDEN) GUEST HOUSE, 5711 Lokelani Rd, Kapaa, (808) 832-0422, Fax: (808) 823-0420. B&B with 2 suites, 1 studio. Cable color TV, VCR, telephone, ceiling fans, Jacuzzi.

MOHALA KE OLA B&B RETREAT, 5663 Ohelo Rd, Kapaa, (808) 823-6398 (tel/fax), toll-free (888) GO-KAUAI. http://www.hshawaii.com/kvp/mohalakeola/index.html. Escape to paradise. Wake to the sound of breeze and birdsongs. Breakfast on fresh island fruit on a private terrace. Because of the privacy provided for each of our 4 guest rooms, you'll think of Mohala Ke Ola as your own personal retreat. This gay-friendly B&B has magnificent mountain & waterfall views, private baths, TV lounge, continental breakfast, pool & hot tub. Lomi-lomi massage, shiatsu, acupuncture & Reiki are available to guests.

PALI KAI, PO Box 450 Kilauea, Kauai (808) 828-6691. E-mail: palikai@aloha.net. B&B, 3 rooms with queen beds. Private baths, 1 outdoor private shower, island-style breakfast & nearby ocean beach. ♀♂

ROYAL DRIVE COTTAGES, 147 Royal Drive Wailua, (808) 822-2321 (tel/fax). Quiet, secluded cottages, some straight clientele, nearby ocean beach. ♀♂

■ Bars

SIDE OUT, 4-1330 Kuhio Hwy near the 1st Hawaiian Bank in Kapaa, (808) 822-7330. Gay-friendly bar & restaurant.

MAUI

■ Information

AIDS INFO, (808) 242-4900. 8:30am-4:30pm Mon-Fri.

WOMEN'S EVENT HOTLINE, (808) 573-3077.

■ Tours, Charters & Excursions

MAUI SURFING SCHOOL, INC, PO Box 424, Puunene, Maui, 96784, (808) 875-0625, (800) 851-0543, Fax: (808) 875-0623. Gay-owned & -operated company. Specializing in beginners, cowards and non-swimmers! Using the world-famous "learn to surf in one lesson" technique developed by Andrea Thomas, anyone can stand up and actually catch a wave their first time out. Choose from group or private 1, 3 or 5 day sessions. Inquire about our surf camp package.

ROYAL HAWAIIAN WEDDINGS, PO Box 424, Puunene, HI 96784, (808) 875-8569, (800) 659-1866, Fax: (808) 875-0623. Gay-owned & -operated company. We arrange gay and lesbian wedding and commitment ceremonies. Packages include minister or officiant, tropical leis & bouquets, secluded beach or tropical garden setting, professional photography, champagne, limousine and many other

FYI

Matt's Big Island Kayak, Snorkel & Massage Package

Take off for a half-day island experience with writer, filmmaker Matt Link, of **Matt's Rainbow Tours**, in a three-seated kayak perfect for beginners. You'll paddle with Matt to a secluded, black-sand beach where clothing is optional. Here, you'll picnic under the palms, then snorkel and swim around a nearby coral reef thick with yellow tangs, striped angel fish, thin needle fish, multi-colored parrot fish and friendly sea turtles, who often glide right beneath you. Later, a tropical snack before professional Swedish massage therapy at Matt's hillside home overlooking the wide ocean.

This popular half-day package includes all equipment and refreshments. During heavy swell season, hiking along lava trails is substituted.

Other options vie for your attention on this island teeming with erupting volcanoes, tropical rainforests, black-lava deserts and snowcapped mountains. You can also visit coffee and macadamia nut plantations, orchid farms, ancient Hawaiian temples and deep green valley gorges.

Contact **Matt's Rainbow Tours** at (808) 328-8406 (tel/fax), E-mail: MrLinkk@aol.com.

HALE KAHAWAI
A Serene Haven
Kauai Hawaii
(808) 822-1031

Mohala Ke Ola
Escape To Paradise
Kauai, Hawaii
888-GO KAUAI
(808) 823-6398

FERRARI GUIDES' GAY TRAVEL A to Z - 18th EDITION

HAWAII

FYI

Women Dive with Lynn & Rene in Maui

Through their company, **Liquid Crystal Divers**, Lynn Allen and and Rene Umberger, both vastly experienced SCUBA divers, offer a range of underwater experiences to women visiting Maui.

Introductory Dives—You start from shore and, with minimal training, explore a shallow Maui reef ecosystem under instructor's guidance.

Diver Certification—4-day course using the PADI system.

Check-Out Dives—Perform final 4 "check-out" dives (for certification) in beautiful Maui waters.

Advanced Training—5 dives (night, deep, navigation and 2 electives).

Underwater Guided Tours—Your choice of Maui's wide variety of diving environments.

Shore Dives—View underwater marine life at Maui's best coastal sites.

Night Dives—What happens at night underwater!

Boat Dives—A skilled divermaster will cater to the skill levels and requests of each diver.

Contact **Liquid Crystal Divers** at (808) 572-4774. E-mail: aquasong@sprynet.com.

FYI

You Can Surf in ONE Lesson!

Back in 1980, Andrea Thomas invented a method of teaching people to surf in one lesson. Using a practical, easy-to-understand, and, above all, gentle method of instruction, she was able to get most students to stand up on their very first waves. Now, seventeen years later, her gay-friendly company, **Maui Surfing School**, has over 200,000 success stories to tell. Her method is so tried and true that her company advertises a 110% refund with no questions asked, if you fail to learn to surf in one lesson.

Their information flyer includes interesting quotes from satisfied customers. A 65-year-old woman called it "Some of the best teaching I've ever seen." A 39-year-old Oregon man said, "They have the you-can-do-it attitude." An 11-year-old commented, "This was the best part of my vacation."

Once you master the basics, you can continue with internediate and even advanced instruction. The company also offers custom surfing tours for those who already know what they're doing. Group and senior discounts are available.

Contact **Maui Surfing School** at (808) 875-0625, (800) 851-0543, Fax: (808) 875-0623, E-mail: andrea@maui.net

items to make a ceremony special. We can even make out-of-the-ordinary arrangements such as horseback weddings or helicopters. We offer discounts on luaus, snorkeling, and other Maui adventures. Deluxe oceanfront condo and all travel arrangements are available. ♀♂

■ *Accommodations*

ANDREA & JANET'S MAUI CONDOS, PO Box 424, Puunene, HI 96784, (808) 879-6702, (800) 289-1522, Fax: (808) 879-6430, E-mail: Andrea@maui.net. Web: http://maui.net/~andrea. Our spacious 1- and 2-bedroom deluxe oceanfront Maui condos overlook sand beaches and are surrounded by rolling green lawns and tropical foliage. Tropical rattan decor, complete kitchens, tennis courts, pool, Jacuzzi, sauna and putting green. Nearby golf, shops and dining. Gay-owned & -operated company. 50% gay & lesbian clientele.

ANFORA'S DREAMS, Attn Dale Jones, PO Box 74030, Los Angeles, CA 90004, (213) 737-0731, Reservations: (800) 788-5046, Fax: (818) 224-4312. Fully-furnished condos, 50% gay & lesbian clientele. Deluxe accommodations include color cable TV, private baths, Jacuzzi, pool & laundry facilities. Ocean & park across the road.

BLAIR'S ORIGINAL HANA PLANTATION HOUSES, PO Box 249, Hana, (808) 248-7868, (800) 228-HANA, Fax: 248-8240. Fourteen private homes in a large compound, 50% gay & lesbian. Hot tub, weights, massage, horses & nearby ocean beach.

GOLDEN BAMBOO RANCH, 1205 Kaupakalua Rd, Haiku, (808) 572-7824 (tel/fax), (800) 344-1238, E-mail: golden@maui.net. Gay-friendly plantation house suites & cottage. Color TV, VCR, phone, ceiling fans & private baths. Expanded continental breakfast. Nearby ocean & natural swimming pools.

HALFWAY TO HANA HOUSE, PO Box 675, Haiku, (808) 572-1176, Fax: (808) 572-3609. B&B, 50% gay & lesbian clientele. One room

Andrea & Janet's Maui Condos

Deluxe 1- and 2-Bedroom Oceanfront Suites

Maui

(800) 289-1522

(808) 879-6702

E-mail: Andrea@maui.net
http://maui.net/~andrea

HAWAII

Off the Map on Maui

by Barry Fried, Open Eye Tours & Photos

It's a cool, clear autumn morning on the Valley Island, so called due to the broad flat isthmus separating the two major volcanoes; Haleakala to the east, and the West Maui Mountains. Janet and Kim had heard about Open Eye Tours & Photos from Ferrari's, called for a brochure from New York, and planned this day from back home as an alternative to the more touristy sunset cruises, submarine and helicopter rides. They liked the idea that their tour would be an educational, eco-sensitive one-of-a-kind experience, as I advertise "no two tours are ever alike." They also wanted to have an experienced, qualified guide all to themselves, so that they didn't have to be on anyone else's "program," as often is the case with group tours of strangers. During our initial phone talk, they explained that they were interested in nature, culture, history, seeing the stuff most people would never get to see, swimming, and that they were vegetarians. I also determined that they were good for a few easy walks of up to twenty minutes or so throughout the day, but had no intention of doing any real hiking.

8:00 am

We meet at a convenient central location and the women recognize me by the t-shirt I chose for the day: a group of multi-racial men raising up the rainbow flag. Upon showing them a pink map of Maui and pointing out the island's abstract shape of a woman (many refer to the 'aina, or land, as "Mother Maui") I share with them a legend of Pu'u Olai and Molokini in the distance. Madame Pele, goddess of the Volcano, saved the kanaka maoli (native people) from shear disaster and ended their needless suffering. We talk of their trip from New York, the guest house and meals enjoyed on Maui thus far, as well as of the firey origin of these islands, and the arrival of the first plants and mammals.

Turning off the main road, we head towards a wildlife sanctuary in search of the Ae'o, the Hawaiian black-necked Stilt — an endangered species. Developing in isolation, I explain, this bird is its own subspecies. It's peaceful as we're the only ones there. Walking less than five minutes to the edge of this protected wetland, Kim spots one of these long red-legged birds with half black/half white plumage and the characteristic long, straight bill, which enables them to unearth snails living in the mud.

The next stop is a picnic area surrounded by graceful, shading Ironwood trees on the North Shore, with a perfect view for watching the colorful sails of the windsurfers, Maui's craze sport since the 1980's. After a colorful spread of fresh, exotic juices, tropical fruit and natural bakery items are sampled for breakfast, Janet wastes no time in getting some zoom photos of those sailboarding beauties! Kim gets her feet wet in the calm, blue water while Janet runs the fine, white silky sand through her fingers. We then try our hand at weaving palm fronds

> Barry R. Fried is the owner/guide of Open Eye Tours & Photos. He has a Master's Degree in Education and has guided visitors since 1983 in Hawaii, where he moved to from Vermont in 1982. For more information and a full-color brochure, contact him via e-mail at openeye@aloha.net at (808) 572-3483, or you can write to P.O. Box 324 Makawao, HI 96768 USA

Continued on next page

FERRARI GUIDES' GAY TRAVEL A to Z - 18th EDITION

HAWAII

before continuing on through Paia, Maui's historic plantation town (now celebrating its hundredth birthday!)

9:00 am

Colorful, eclectic Paia is referred to as the windsurfing capital of the world. We stop by the mill to learn about the importance of the sugar industry in shaping Maui, as well as the controversies facing its future.

On the way up the hill to the Kaluanui estate, we pass the Father Damien memorial, honoring the saintly Belgian who dedicated his life to helping the leper patients of Kalaupapa peninsula on nearby Moloka'i. The road is lined with Royal Poinciana red flame trees in bloom, and splashes of yellow, pink, and orange from the flowering shower trees. I stop to pick a rare night-blooming cereus fruit, magenta on the outside and clear/white on the inside, which we eat on the spot. The stately mansion of Kaluanui deserves at least the half-hour walk we do here. Standing beneath the towering Norfolk and Cook Island Pines, it's impressive that some grow as high as 100 feet with trunks 12 feet in circumference. There are several courtyards and gardens to explore with fountains and sculptures. A Hawaiian-style garden features Purple agapanthis, avocado, cup-of-gold, mulberry, red ti leaves and hapu'u ferns. I share with them uses of the ti leaf to Hawaiians, which I've learned over the years from Kupuna (elders) practitioners of La'au Lapa'au (medicinal plant healing). We stop to appreciate the Porte-cochere entry and the excellent remodeling of the interior rooms. There is currently an exhibit of printmakers' works, and again we're the only visitors here.

11:00 am

The Makawao district is our next stop. Meaning "forest beginning," I explain the main elements of the Hawaiian alphabet, pronunciation, simple vocabulary and basic sentence structure. We happen upon a few Paniolos (Hawaiian cowboys) on a small back road through a little gulch, en route to the Rodeo general store. We pass by the Po'okela church with its original thick coral foundation and stop at the famous rodeo and polo grounds and watch the practice. I stop to gather some wild anise seed for us to taste. An introduced species, it is said to help digestion and is used as a natural breath freshener. The ranch life and history comes alive before Kim and Janet's eyes as they actually get to see the locations and remnants of Maui's ranching past and present.

The mid-day sun is getting hot, and it's time for a refreshing dip in a fresh-water pool. Driving through sleepy villages and on winding roads for several miles, we turn off the main road and head towards the rugged windward shore. I describe the three main native animal creature friends inhabiting Hawaiian streams, and the benefits and threats to their existence. A short 2-minute walk reveals a lovely stream, an old, shading Mango tree, and a good-sized clear pool fed by the gentle, steady flow of a perfect waterfall. Ahhh! I take pictures for the women as they frolic and sing in the water, a rainbow circling their heads as they swim beneath the sun-streamed mist formed as the water cascades off the rocks. I collect some treats for after their bath: deliciously sweet, edible, healing, pua 'awapuhi melemele (ginger blossoms) await as they emerge giggling, nymph-like and glistening from their dip — photo-op!

It's time for one of those breath-taking views, so we find our way down to the end of a secret road for a short 3-minute walk to a panorama that includes the 10,023 ft. Haleakala crater, lush forests of the Waikamoi preserve, an uninhabited gulch, the glistening, deep blue sea below, and the Pali (cliffs) of this remote-feeling slice of heaven (we'll save the trek through the bush down to the bay for another visit — our stomachs are calling!)

2:00 pm

For lunch, it's on to gay chef Tom's cute, tucked away cafe, popular with locals. Kim orders fresh vegetable soup, corn bread, and an Asian pasta salad; Janet, the vegtarian paté garden salad, sautéed vegetables, and garlic/herb foccacia- all home-made today. Sparkling raspberry cider is the drink of choice, as is ginger-spice cake for dessert.

3:00 pm

We visit a section on the North Shore of the West Side where many Hawaiians make their home. We look at taro, a staple food source of the Hawaiian diet, growing in traditional lo'i, (irrigated terraces) as it has been grown for many centuries, and enjoy the many beautiful gardens. From a lookout we can see the sweep of earth from the mountains to the sea as we share some of the same thoughts, awe and reverence that the Hawaiians feel for this rich land of dreams.

4:15 pm

As we drive towards a Heiau, a pre-contact Hawaiian site of religious significance, I tell a story of the Polynesian triangle, the amazing voyaging canoes that brought the first Polynesians with their plants and animals here, and social structure of old Hawaii. The early Hawaiians believed that praying to their

Continued on page 511

HAWAII

with private entrance & bath, close to fresh water pools & beach, tropical breakfast.

HANAMALIA B&B, 220 Hanamalia Pl, Haiku, (808) 575-2242, Tel/Fax: (808) 871-7775. Separate one bedroom with private entrance on lower floor of private home. Kitchen available, continental breakfast. Lanai with ocean view. Non-smoking environment, gay friendly.

HUELO POINT FLOWER FARM B & B, PO Box 1195, Paia, (808) 572-1850, Fax: (808) 573-0342, E-mail: huelopt@maui.net. B&B guest cottage with kitchen, refrigerator & private bath. Color TV, Jacuzzi, & exercise equipment. Expanded continental breakfast. 50% gay & lesbian clientele.

HUELO PT. LOOKOUT VACATION RENTALS B&B, PO Box 117, Paia, Phone & Fax: (808) 573-0914. Two acre estate with 2 self-contained cottages & 1 suite with private entrance & kitchenette. Private baths, color TV, telephone, coffee & tea-making facilities, expanded continental breakfast, hot tub. 50% gay & lesbian clientele.

JACK & TOM'S MAUI CONDOS, Margaret Norrie Realty, PO Box 365, Kihei, (800) 800-8608, (808) 874-1048, Fax: (808) 879-6932. Choose between ocean and garden views for your private Maui condominium. You'll get the feeling that you're settled in and living in paradise. Each 1- or 2-bedroom condominium is within a larger complex. Color cable TV, AC, telephone, ceiling fans, kitchen & laundry facilities. Pool on premises, ocean nearby. 5-day minimum stay.

KAILUA MAUI GARDENS, SR Box 9 (Hana Hwy) Haiku, (800) 258-8588, (808) 572-9726, Fax: (808) 572-5934. Cottage & house rental, 50% gay & lesbian. Quaint to deluxe, BBQ, spas, nearby waterfall. Continental breakfast in cottages, fresh fruit.

KEIKI ANANDA, Makawao, HI (808) 573-2225 or (808) 572-8496. B&B retreat center, shared baths, vegetarian communal kitchen, yoga & meditation room & instruction, cloth-

Jack & Tom's Maui Condos

CLEAN · COMFORTABLE
FULLY EQUIPPED

(800) 800-8608
Maui, Hawaii

FYI

Plan Your Hawaiian Gay Wedding Before the RUSH!

With the coming legalization of gay marriage, Hawaii will become the gay wedding capital of the world. **Royal Hawaiian Weddings** has been coordinating gay and lesbian commitment ceremonies for a number of years, and can handle pretty much any idea you can conjure up for your special ceremony.

Most opt to have their wedding in a secluded beach setting at sunset, after which they remain on the beach for a four-course candlelit dinner. You don't have to sweat ANY of the details, because their on-site coordinators handle everything from the minister or officiant to the champagne, the cake, the photographer and musician. Although they offer wedding packages to choose from, YOUR wedding can be customized to include an airport lei greeting, a photo album or "just married" limousine service. Special requests like formal attire rentals, hair styling, witnesses, luaus, underwater or horseback weddings and even helicopters are business-as-usual for Royal Hawaiian. The company also operates a surfing school where even "beginners and cowards" discover how to handle themselves on a surfboard.

Contact **Royal Hawaiian Weddings** at (808) 875-8569, (800) 659-1866, Fax: (808) 875-0623. E-mail: andrea@maui.net.

FYI

The UNtouristy Hawaii Tour

The owner wasn't kidding when he named his company **Open Eye Tours**. One look at the photos in his brochure tells you that he is serious about showing you the best of Hawaii. The largest photo is a heartstopping view of emerald green mountainsides sloping steeply down to a valley. Another shows a couple cavorting on the lava fields, with a suggestion of volcanic steam off in the corner. A third shows variously-clad bathers in a secluded lagoon-like pool. A fourth traces inviting footpaths up a steep hillside, each hairpin turn promising new vistas.

The brochure says that, as part of the service, he will consult you before the tour to plan the experience that will most make you happy. "Never has a day with one client been repeated exactly like another," says the owner/guide, and we have reason to believe him. He asks that you tell him whether you're interested in easy walks or more challenging hikes, monuments and museums or birds in a wildlife preserve and sampling edible medicinal plants, or visiting artists' studios and unique shops the tourists haven't found, or snorkeling and swimming beneath a waterfall at a secluded ocean cove, etc. After you tell him your preferences, he prepares a notebook of relevant articles for you. In addition, there's a surprise gift for you. And he knows the best local markets or cafes for your Hawaiian lunch feast.

Contact **Open Eye** at (808) 572-3483, E-mail: openeye@aloha.net.

UNITED STATES

FERRARI GUIDES' GAY TRAVEL A to Z - 18th EDITION

HAWAII

FYI

Wahine Week-A New Lesbian Tradition

One hundred lesbians ushered in a new lesbian tradition in December, 1997 as they gathered for Wahine Week. This first-ever lesbian resort vacation week on Maui, organized by Remote Possibilities, took place at the gorgeous, five-diamond Renaissance Wailea Beach Resort.

The women stayed in the Mokapu Wing of The Renaissance, with a private lawn linking their luxury rooms to the beach. The lawn was the site of elegantly-catered social functions, including a welcome reception and a tea dance. Comedienne Georgia Ragsdale performed. The week also included a wooden boat sailing and snorkeling adventure, a dinner cruise and a full-day sail to the island of Lanai. Many women also hiked in groups to favorite grottos on Maui or rode horses into the Haleakala Crater. Beach activities at the resort included snorkeling, kayaking, wind surfing and body surfing. Capping the week was a concert featuring Holly Near.

Lesbian Ministers... Lesbian Weddings

Remote Possibilities has two licensed lesbian ministers who perform weddings, unions and commitment ceremonies year-round in secluded beach settings on Maui. Three packages with varying prices offer amenities like tropical flower leis, champagne and cake, wedding photography, musical accompaniment and edited video of the ceremony.

The Next Remote Possibility: Alaska

For 1998, Remote Possibilities is organizing two exciting programs in Alaska. Denali—Women, Wilderness & Whitewater (June 1998) will involve dramatic scenery, whitewater rafting, a visit to the terminus of a glacier, and guides who can cook gourmet food in the wilderness. Trip 2: Glacier Bay & Whales by Kayak (July 1998). Visiting lesbians will compete with local lesbians in wood splitting, running races, horseshoes and a greased pole climb. They'll also cruise Glacier Bay, see active glaciers and wildlife, paddle kayaks for five days, camping in spacious dome tents. Trip 3: The Inside Passage Wilderness Cruise (July 1998) is for those whose idea of adventure includes a warm bed and a roof over their heads. Thirty women will cruise on the M/V Wilderness Explorer, see icebergs calve, hike beaches and paddle in wilderness water, yet return to the boat each day for hot meals and a warm bed.

Fall 1997: Wahine Week #2

The second annual Wahine Week will take place in the fall of 1997.

Contact **Remote Possibilities** at (808) 875-7438, (800) 511-3121, Fax: (808) 875-4557, E-mail: remotepo@maui.net, Web: www.remotepo.com.

---

ing-optional pool on premises, ocean nearby. 50% gay & lesbian clientele.

KOA KAI RENTALS, Island Surf 401, Kihei, HI 96753, (800) 399-6058 ex. 33, (808) 879-6058, Fax: (808) 875-4274. E-mails: cloy@aloha.net or Maui4Fun@aol.com. Rental facilities throughout Maui: apartment, condos, B&Bs or houses. Some straight clientele. ♀♂

MAUI ISANA RENTAL CONDO, 515 S. Kihei Rd, (800) 414-3573, (360) 321-1069. Two-bedroom, 2-bath rental condo, color TV, phone, pool on premises, ocean across street. Condo unit is straight, Maui Isana owners rent to 50% gay/lesbian, 50% straight clientele.

MILAGROS B&B, 498 Kimo Dr, Kula, (808) 878-6110. One room cottage, great views, kitchen, continental breakfast included. Laundry facilities available. Gay friendly.

NAPUALANI O'HANA, c/o PO Box 118 Hana, (808) 248-8935 or 248-0792. Gay-friendly suites, private baths.

TRIPLE LEI, THE, PO Box 959, Kihei, HI 96753, (808) 874-8645, From Mainland: (800) 874-8645, Fax: (808) 875-7324. B&B, short drive to Makena Nude Beach, breakfast served on lanai. Pool, TV room, phone, suite has hot tub & sauna. ♂

■ Women's Accommodations

ANDREA'S B&B, Wailea, Maui, (800) 289-1522, E-mail: andrea@maui.net. Join the "Funmeister" herself, Andrea Thomas, in her Maui home. Applauded for her hospitality, Andrea offers a nicely appointed spacious & quiet bed and bath suite with TV and AC, pool and Jacuzzi spa. Wonderfully close to world-class beaches and snorkeling. If you're looking for peaceful and relaxing accommodations and don't want to feel like a stranger in Paradise, then this is for you. ♀

HALE MAKALEKA, 539 Kupulau Dr, Kihei, (808) 879-2971. Women-only B&B in garden setting. Spacious room with color TV, private bath & private entrance. Tropical breakfast. ♀

HALE O'WAHINE (HOUSE FOR WOMEN), 2777 S Kihei Rd, Kihei, (808) 874-5148, Fax: 572-0403. (800) DO-WOMYN (369-6696). Women-only B&B, private baths, expanded continental breakfast, pool. ♀

■ Beaches

LITTLE BEACH. This gay nude beach is part of Makena Beach.

■ Bars

HAMBURGER MARY'S, 2010 Main St, Wailuku, (808) 244-7776. Gay in the evenings. DJ Thurs, Fri. Ladies' night Fri. ♀ ♂

■ Restaurants

HAMBURGER MARY'S, 2010 Main St, (808) 244-7776.

■ Erotica

SKIN DEEP, 626 Front St, Lahaina, (808) 661-8531, 661-8288. Tattoos, piercing, leather, adult gifts, jewelry, Harley T-shirts & apparel.

HAWAII

OAHU - HONOLULU

■ Information
AIDS HOTLINE, (808) 922-1313.
GAY & LESBIAN COMMUNITY CENTER, 1566 Wilder Ave, (808) 951-7000, Mon-Fri 10am-2pm.
GAY INFO, (808) 926-1000, 24hr tape.

■ Accommodations
ALI'I BLUFFS WINDWARD B & B, 46-251 Ikiiki St, Kaneohe, (808) 235-1124, (800) 235-1151. B&B, some straight clientele, private baths.

HOTEL HONOLULU, 376 Kaiolu St, Honolulu, (808) 926-2766, US & Canada: (800) 426-2766, Fax: 922-3326. Hotel 2 blocks from the beach. Theme studios & suites. Next door to gay clubs, restaurants, shops.

PACIFIC OCEAN HOLIDAYS, PO Box 88245, Dept IP, Honolulu, 96830-8245, (808) 923-2400, (800) 735-6600, fax: (808) 923-2499. Hawaii accommodations in gay & gay-friendly B&B homes, resort hotels & condos.

TROPIC PARADISE, 43 Laiki Place, Kailua, HI 96734, (808) 261-2299 (tel/fax). Gay & lesbian B&B with all private baths.

WAIKIKI AA STUDIOS, 3242 Kaohinani, (808) 595-7533, (800) 288-4666, E-mail: BnBsHI@Aloha.net. Studios, hosted rentals & Statewide bed & breakfast reservation service. Gay-friendly, variety of guest quarters with a variety of conveniences.

WAIKIKI VACATION RENTALS, 1860 Ala Moana Blvd #108, (808) 946-9371, FAX: 922-9418, (800) 543-5663. Gay-friendly condominium rentals, daily thru monthly terms. Fully-furnished, budget to deluxe with modern conveniences, Jacuzzi, sauna, all with spectacular views. Nearby ocean beach.

■ Women's Accommodations
MANGO HOUSE, THE, 2087 Iholena St, Call or Fax: (808) 595-6682, (800) 77-MANGO. E-mail: mango@pixi.com. Great food, great views, great advice, great location! B&B, men welcome. Double rooms, private & shared baths and a 3-bedroom cottage, TV lounge, aloha continental breakfast, ocean view. Wake to the aroma of baking bread served with island juice, fresh fruit and Kona coffee. Host Tracey is knowledgeable about the area & can recommend the best places to visit.

■ Transportation
ISLAND PRIDE TAXI, departures: (808) 732-6518, arrivals: (800) 330-5598. Private limos, cusom tours, personal chauffeur. Gay-owned & operated.

■ Beaches
GAY & STRAIGHT BEACHES, for Queen Surf Beach, go to Kapiolani Park before the Waikiki Aquarium (gay beach is on the right side). Royal Hawaiian Hotel beach is mostly straight, but frequented by many gays. Diamond Head Beach has gay & straight areas.

FYI

Gay Honolulu Sightseeing Tours

There are plenty of driver/guide services in Hawaii, but none quite like **Dave Ambrose's Island Pride**, Oahu's only gay transportation service. Dave is a gay man who has lived in Honolulu for 25 years. He knows the ins and outs of airport pickups and is expert at arranging and escorting individualized tours that appeal to gay tourists.

Besides a "honeymoon" package that provides a romantic evening on the town, Dave escorts up to five people in his luxury van for general island tours of 3 or 5 hours. He'll also set up other itineraries, for example, gay nightlife tours.

Before starting Island Pride, Dave worked as a concierge at one of Waikiki's historic resort hotels. Because he was "out," concierges at other hotels would call him to find out about gay bars and gay-friendly restaurants. Many times, says Dave, "they'd just send their clients over to me. After awhile, it was like I had my own little gay travel desk."

Contact **Dave's Island Pride** at (808) 732-6518.

FYI

15 Years As Gay Experts on Paradise

As the first to specialize in gay vacation packages to Hawaii, **Pacific Ocean Holidays** has an established reputation as the Hawaii gay expert. They have the widest selection of gay and gay-friendly Hawaii hotels because they have continued to build on it over the years. Since they publish a quarterly gay vacation guide booklet to Hawaii, they're always up-to-date on Hawaiian gay entertainment and dining, too.

They customize unescorted vacation packages year-round, allowing you to visit one or more islands. On Oahu, Waikiki Beach packages include lodging, a flower lei greeting, airport transfers and a gay-hosted welcome and orientation to the islands. On Kauai, Maui, and Hawaii, packages include lodging and daily car rental. Air-inclusive packages are also available. All packages include a personalized itinerary, excise and hotel taxes, and Pacific Ocean Holiday's gay "Pocket Guide to Hawaii" (which is also sold separately by mail order for $5).

Contact **Pacific Ocean Holidays** at (808) 923-2400, (800) 735-6600, Fax: (808) 923-2499. E-mail: poh@hi.net, Web: http://gayhawaii.com.

FERRARI GUIDES' GAY TRAVEL A to Z - 18th EDITION

HAWAII

Follow Kalakaua Ave to Diamond Head Rd. After getting to the lighthouse, walk up footpath to beach & look for men in bikinis.

■ Bars

ANGLES WAIKIKI, 2256 Kuhio, 2nd floor, (808) 926-9766. 2nd-story patio, male strippers, pool table.

CLUB MICHELANGELO, 444 Hobron Ln, Waikiki, (808) 951-0008. Karaoke.

DIS & DAT, 1315 Kalakaua Ave, Honolulu, (808) 946-0000. Hawaiian music.

WINDOWS ON EATON SQUARE, 444 Hobron Ln, Waikiki, (808) 946-4442. Piano bar, game night Mon-Fri 11am-2am, Sun Brunch.

■ Dance Bar/Disco

FUSION,★ 2260 Kuhio Ave, Waikiki, (808) 924-2422. Hi energy dance bar till 4am nitely, male dancers.

HULA'S BAR & LEI STAND,★ 2103 Kuhio Ave, (808) 923-0669. Video dance bar & tropical patio bar, 11am-2am.

METROPOLIS, 611 Cooke St, (808) 593-2717. Dance bar, DJ, 7 days.

TRIXX, FRONT BAR & TREATS DELI, 2109 Kuhio Ave, Waikiki, (808) 923-0669. After beach cruising, Sun backyard BBQ.

■ Saunas/Health Clubs

MAX'S GYM, 444 Hobron Ln, at Eaton Sq, 4th floor. Gym & saunas, private rooms, etc.

■ Restaurants

BANANAS RESTAURANT, 2139 Kuhio Ave #125, (808) 9-BANANA. Gay-friendly cafe & bar, Thai food.

CAFE SISTINA, 1314 S. King St, (808) 596-0061. Northern Italian cuisine.

DA KINE KAFE & KATERING KO, 444 Hobron Ln at Windows on Eaton Square, Waikiki, (808) 946-4442. Lunch, evening & takeout. Deli, local & mainland dishes. Sunday brunch 11:30am - 2pm.

KEO'S THAI CUISINE, 625 Kapahula Ave, (808) 737-8240. Gourmet Thai cuisine in a casual, elegant setting.

TREATS, 2109 Kuhio Ave, at Trixx bar. Restaurant & bar.

WINDOWS ON EATON SQUARE, 444 Hobron Ln, (808) 946-4442. Cafe, bar & restaurant, lunch & Sun brunch.

■ Retail & Bookstores

C'N'N MINI MART & LIQUORS, Aiea Shopping Center, Aiea, (808) 487-2944. Gay magazines, books videos.

EIGHTY PERCENT STRAIGHT, 2139 Kuhio Ave (2nd fl), (808) 923-9996. Sportswear, cards, novelties, gay magazines.

■ Leathers/Piercing

PROVOCATION PIERCINGS, 1825 Ala Moana Blvd #201, (808) 941-2800.

■ Erotica

A VIDEO PARADISE, 767 Kailua Rd #102, (808) 261-4808.

DIAMOND HEAD VIDEO, 870 Kapahulu Ave, (808) 735-6066.

DIAMOND HEAD VIDEO-KAILUA, 25 Kaneohe Bay Dr in the Aikahi Park Shopping Ctr, (808) 254-6066. Daily 9am-midnight.

MOVIELAND, 1695B Kapiolani Blvd at Atkinson, (808) 941-1023. Sun-Thur 11am-11pm, Fri & Sat 11am-midnight.

P 10 A, 444 Hobron Ln, at Eaton Square. Pool tables, private viewing booths, private rooms.

SUZIES, Aiea Shopping Center (2nd level), (808) 486-3103. Gay & all-female videos, novelties, 10am-2am.

IDAHO

WHO TO CALL

For Tour Companies Serving This Destination
See Idaho on page 17

ASHTON

■ Women's Accommodations

FISH CREEK LODGING, PO BOX 833, Warm River, 83420-0833, (208) 652-7566. Women-only log cabin & loft with kitchen, women's library & telephone. Nearby river & lake.

BOISE

■ Information

AIDS LINE, (208) 345-2277. Mon-Fri 8am-5pm.

■ Bars

EIGHTH STREET BALCONY PUB, Capitol Terrace Bldg, 150 N 8th St #224, (208) 336-1313. Pub popular with gays, especially Sun afternoon & evenings.

PAPA'S CLUB 96, 1108 Front St, (208) 333-0074. Patio.

PARTNERS, 2210 Main St, (208) 331-3551. Open 7 days. Full liquor bar available, dance floor, bands on weekends.

■ Dance Bar/Disco

EMERALD CITY CLUB, 415 S 9th, (208) 342-5446. Progressive dance & show bar, 10am-2am, 7 days. DJ nightly, C&W Sun & Wed. Large straight following.

■ Restaurants

RICK'S CAFE AMERICAIN AT THE FLICKS, 646 Fulton St at 6th, (208) 342-4288. Gay-friendly restaurant, 5 movie theaters, video store. Triangle men's group meets here weekly.

■ Erotica

OVER 19 ADULT CENTER, 4109 Chinden Blvd, (208) 344-7532.

CALDWELL

■ Erotica

ADULT SHOP, 716 Arthur Ave, (208) 454-2422.

COEUR D'ALENE

■ Accommodations

CLARK HOUSE ON HAYDEN LAKE, E. 4550 S. Lake Hayden Rd, Hayden Lake, ID 83835, (208) 772-3470, (800) 765-4593, Fax: (208) 772-6899. Gay-friendly inn with limited restaurant, private baths, full breakfast, Jacuzzi, gay & lesbian following.

LEWISTON

■ Erotica

MAGIC VIDEO, 1026 Bryden Ave, (208) 746-7125.

MOSCOW

■ Information

WOMEN'S CENTER, U of Idaho, Line St at Idaho St (Old Journalism Bldg), (208) 885-6616, 885-6111 (switchboard). Mon-Fri 8am-5pm, library, programs and events.

■ Retail & Bookstores

BOOKPEOPLE, 512 S Main St, (208) 882-7957. General bookstore with a gay & lesbian section.

POCATELLO

■ Retail & Bookstores

SILVER FOXX, 143 S 2nd, (208) 234-2477. Gifts, novelties, large selection of adult videos.

■ Erotica

FRONT PAGE BOOKSTORE, 2nd St near Clark. (208) 233-5253.

PEGASUS UNUSUAL BOOKS, 246 W Center St, (208) 232-6493.

ILLINOIS

WHO TO CALL

For Tour Companies Serving This Destination
See Illinois on page 17

STATEWIDE

■ Information

AIDS HOTLINE, (800) AID-AIDS. Daily 10am-10pm except holidays.

ILLINOIS

AURORA

Erotica
DENMARK BOOKS & VIDEOS, 1300 Business Rte 30, (708) 898-9838.

BLOOMINGTON

Information
SAGALYNX COMMUNITY CONNECTION, 313 N Main, (309) 828-3998.

Bars
BISTRO, 316 N Main, (309) 829-2278. 4pm-1am (Fri till 2am, Sat 8pm-2am, Sun 6pm-1am).

Retail & Bookstores
ONCE UPON A TIME ALTERNATIVE BOOKS & GIFTS, 311 N Main St, (309) 828-3998, Fax: (309) 828-8879. E-mail: outbooks@outbooks.com, http://www.outbooks.com. Gay & lesbian bookstore & Out Cafe cybercafe with gourmet coffee, video rentals.

Erotica
MEDUSA ADULT WORLD, 420 N Madison St, (309) 828-2932.
RISQUE'S, 1506 N Main, (309) 827-9279.

CALUMET CITY

Bars
JOHN L'S PLACE, 335 154th Pl, (708) 862-2386. Gay & straight clientele.
MR B'S, 606 Stateline Ave, (708) 862-1221. More women later on weekends, pool table. Twice monthly entertainment.
PATCH, THE, 201 155th St, (708) 891-9854. Jukebox dancing, closed Mon.

Dance Bar/Disco
DICK'S R U CRAZEE, 48 154th Pl, (708) 862-4605.
INTRIGUE, 582 Stateline, (708) 868-5240. Pool table, nightly specials.
POUR HOUSE, 103 155th Place, (708) 891-3980.

CARBONDALE

Information
PRIDE LINE, (618) 453-5151.
WOMEN'S CENTER, 408 W Freeman, (618) 529-2324, 24hrs.
WOMEN'S SERVICES, at Southern Illinois U, (618) 453-3655.

Dance Bar/Disco
DADDY WARBUCK'S, 213 E Main. Tues or Wed-Sun.

CENTRAL ILLINOIS

Accommodations
LITTLE HOUSE ON THE PRAIRIE, THE, PO Box 525, Sullivan, IL 61951, (217) 728-4727. Gay-friendly bed & breakfast. AC, private baths, TV lounge, video tape library, full breakfast. Jacuzzi & pool on premises.

CHAMPAIGN - URBANA

Information
AIDS INFO, (217) 351-2437.

Dance Bar/Disco
CHESTER STREET, 65 Chester St, (217) 356-5607. DJ nightly, both gay & straight clientele. Becoming an alternative club, lots of college students.

Retail & Bookstores
BLUE RIDGE BOOKS, 505 E Green, General bookstore with gay section.
HORIZON BOOKSTORE, 1115-1/2 W Oregon, Urbana, (217) 328-2988. Progressive bookstore with a gay & lesbian selection. Closed Sun.
JANE ADDAMS BOOKSHOP, 208 N Neil, Champaign, (217) 356-2555. Women's bookstore and used books.

Erotica
FANTASY, N Rte 45 near Thomasboro, Urbana.
HOLIDAY THEATRE, 213 S Neil, (217) 351-8897.
ILLINI VIDEO ARCADE, 12 E Columbia, Champaign, (217) 359-8529.
URBANA NEWS, 602 N Cunningham, Urbana, (217) 384-0188, 24hrs.

CHICAGO INTRO

Information
AIDS FOUNDATION, (312) 642-5454.
HORIZONS HELPLINES, (773) 929-HELP (4357), AIDS/HIV (312) 472-6469. 6pm-10pm daily.
IN TOUCH HOTLINE, (312) 996-5535, 6pm-3am.
KINDREDHEARTS WOMEN'S CENTER, 2214 Ridge Ave, Evanston, (847) 604-0913.
SANGAT, South Asian gay group, meets 1st Fri. Write for details: Box 268463, Chicago IL 60626.

Accommodations
CARITAS BED & BREAKFAST NETWORK, (800) CARITAS, (312) 857-0801, Fax: (312) 857-0805. B&B, home-stay accommodations service. *Member: IGTA*

Beaches
BELMONT ROCKS, gay beach between Diversey Harbor & Belmont Harbor.

Retail & Bookstores
BOOKSTORES (GAY & LESBIAN), see Chicago N Halsted & Environs.
WOMEN'S BOOKSTORES, see Chicago N Halsted & Environs.

N HALSTED & ENVIRONS

Accommodations
CITY SUITES HOTEL, 933 West Belmont, (773) 404-3400, Fax: 404-3405, reservations: (800) CITY-108. Gay-friendly hotel. Comfortable, affordable, European-style singles thru suites. Lake Michigan nearby.
PARK BROMPTON INN, 528 W Brompton, (773) 404-3499, Fax: 404-3495, reservations: (800) PARK-108. Gay-friendly hotel. Rooms & suites with color cable TV, AC, phone & private baths.
SURF HOTEL, 555 W Surf, (773) 528-8400, (800) SURF-108, fax: 528-8483. Gay-friendly hotel near Lake Michigan. Variety of tastefully-appointed rooms, private baths & modern conveniences.
VILLA TOSCANA GUEST HOUSE, 3447 N Halsted, (800) 684-5755, (773) 404-2643. European-style guesthouse in the heart of gay Chicago. Private & shared baths, color TV, AC, expanded continental breakfast. Two blocks from Lake Michigan, some straight clientele.

Women's Accommodations
A SISTER'S PLACE, 3712 N Broadway, Dept 700, (773) 275-1319. Guest rooms for gay women & gay-positive women.

Bars
ANNEX 3, 3160 N Clark St, (773) 327-5969. Videos.
BERLIN, 954 W Belmont Ave, (773) 348-4975. Hi-energy video bar, patio.
BIG DADDIES BAR & RESTAURANT, 2914 N Broadway, (773) 929-0922. Cruise bar.
BUCK'S SALOON, 3439 N Halsted, (773) 525-1125. Patio.
BUDDIES', 3301 N Clark, (773) 477-4066. Bar & restaurant. 30 & over crowd. Male & female bartenders.
CLOSET, THE, 3325 N Broadway, (773) 477-8533. Small bar, popular happy hour, videos.
COCKTAIL, 3359 N Halsted, (773) 477-1420. Upscale cocktail bar, large straight following.
DANDY'S, 3729 N Halsted, (773) 525-1200.
DANDY'S, 3729 N Halsted St, (773) 525-1200.
EL TUNEL, 5553 W Belmont, (773) 282-2945.
GENTRY ON HALSTED, 3320 N Halsted, (773) 348-1053. Videos.
LITTLE JIM'S, ★ 3501 N Halsted at Cornelia, (773) 871-6116. Videos, cable.
LUCKY HORSESHOE LOUNGE, 3169 N Halsted, (773) 404-3169. Show lounge with male dancers, restaurant, game room, conversation room.

FERRARI GUIDES' GAY TRAVEL A to Z - 18th EDITION

ILLINOIS

NORTH END, THE, 3733 N Halsted St, (773) 477-7999.

SIDETRACK,★ 3349 N Halsted St, (773) 477-9189. Video bar, always crowded.

Dance Bar/Disco

CELL BLOCK, 3702 N Halsted, (773) 665-8064. "Where leathermen do hard time."

CHARLIE'S,★ 3726 N Broadway, (773) 871-8887. C&W dance bar.

CIRCUIT, 3641 N Halsted, (773) 325-2233. Videos, restaurant.

FUSION, 3631 N Halsted, Hotline: (773) 975-0660, after 9pm (773) 975-6622. Video dance bar.

GIRLBAR, 2625 N Halsted St, (773) 871-4210. Tues-Thurs 6pm-2am, Fri 3pm-2am, Sat 6pm-3am, Sun 5pm-2am.

MANHOLE,★ 3458 N Halsted St, (773) 975-9244. Popular late evening.

ROSCOE'S,★ 3354-56 N Halsted St, (773) 281-3355. Video dance bar, 2 other bars, restaurant, patio.

SPIN, corner of Belmont & Halsted, (773) 327-7711. Videos.

Saunas/Health Clubs

UNICORN, 3246 N Halsted St near Aldine, (773) 929-6080. Health club & gym, 24hrs.

Restaurants

BUDDIES, 3301 N Clark, at Buddies bar, (773) 477-4066.

JEZEBEL, 3517 N Clark. Italian, Moroccan, Greek, Spanish, French cuisines, vintage jazz music.

LAS MAÑANITAS, 3523 N Halsted, (773) 528-2109. Mexican cuisine.

MIKE'S BROADWAY CAFE, 3805 N Broadway, (773) 404-2205.

OO LA LA!, 3335 N Halsted St, (773) 935-7708.

RHUMBA, 3631 N Halsted St, (773) 975-2345. Brazilian cuisine.

STREGA NOVA, 3747 N Southport, (773) 244-0990. Italian.

WILD ONION, 3500 N Lincoln, (773) 871-5555. Pastas, Southwestern & vegetarian cuisine.

Retail & Bookstores

GAY MART, 3457 N Halsted, (773) 929-4272. Cards & gifts geared to the gay & lesbian community, daily from 11am.

HOLIDAZE, 3450 N Halsted St, (773) 327-3213. Gift store with rainbow & other gay items.

PEOPLE LIKE US BOOKS, 1115 W Belmont, 3 blocks west of the Belmont El, (773) 248-6363, fax: (773) 248-1550. Exclusively gay & lesbian bookstore.

SHIRTS ILLUSTRATED, 3315 N Broadway, (773) 871-4785. Custom-imprint & embroidery on t-shirts, hats, satin baseball jackets, bags or polo shirts.

UNABRIDGED BOOKS, 3251 N Broadway near Melrose, (773) 883-9119. General bookstore with large selection of gay & lesbian books.

WE'RE EVERYWHERE, 3434 N Halsted St, (773) 404-0590. Gay & Lesbian design T-shirts, sweats, shorts & hats. Mail order catalog available.

Leathers/Piercing

MALE HIDE LEATHERS, 2816 N Lincoln Ave near Diversey, (773) 929-0069. Leathers and accessories for men & women. Tue-Sat noon-8pm, Sun 1-5pm, closed Mon.

Erotica

ADULT FANTASY BOOKS, 2928 N Broadway, (773) 525-9705, 24hrs.

CUPID'S TREASURES, 3519 N Halsted St, (773) 348-3884. Fantasy wear for men & women. A love boutique.

NATIONWIDE VIDEO, 843-1/2 W Belmont, (312) 525-1222. Other locations: 736 W Irving Pk Rd, (773) 871-7800; 3936 N Clarendon (773) 871-1882.

PLEASURE CHEST, 3155 N Broadway, (773) 525-7151, 525-7152.

RAM BOOKS, 3511-1/2 N Halsted St near Cornelia, (773) 525-9528, 24hrs.

RJ'S VIDEO STORE, 3452 N Halsted St, (773) 871-1810.

SPECIALTY VIDEO, 3259 N Broadway, (773) 248-3434.

TABOO TABOO, 855 W Belmont, (773) 723-3739. Leather, latex, fetish store, women welcome.

CHICAGO LOOP

Bars

BATON SHOW LOUNGE, 436 N Clark St near Hubbard, (312) 644-5269. Show bar, closed Mon.

GENTRY, 440 N State. (312) 664-1033. 60% men, 40% women.

SECOND STORY BAR, 157 E Ohio at Michigan, (773) 923-9536.

STAR DUST REVUE, 440 N Halsted St, (773) 363-7827.

Dance Bar/Disco

GENERATOR, 306 N Halsted St. Wed-Sun from 9pm.

Erotica

EROTIC WAREHOUSE, 1246 W Randolph, (773) 226-5222, 24hrs.

FRENCHY'S, 872 N State St, (773) 337-9190, 24hrs.

HUBBARD STREET BOOKS, 109 W Hubbard, (312) 828-0953, 24hrs.

WELLS BOOKSTORE, 178 N Wells, (312) 263-9266, Mon-Wed, Sat till 10pm, Thurs, Fri till 11pm, Sun till 9pm.

CHICAGO NORTH

Bars

ANVIL, 1137 W Granville Ave near Broadway, (773) 973-0006. CD juke box, videos, patio.

BIG CHICKS, 5024 N Sheridan Rd, (773) 728-5511. Eclectic art bar, many straights.

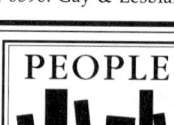

CHIPPEWA BOOTS ■ LEATHER TOYS

1972
25 YEARS
1997

LEVI 501'S ■ LEATHER PANTS ■ COCK RINGS ■ BALL STRETCHERS ■ CYCLE JACKETS & CAPS
BELTS ■ KEY CLIPS ■ HOODS ■ RUBBER WARE ■ BODY HARNESS ■ MASKS ■ TRUCKER WALLETS

Male Hide® Leathers, Inc.
2816 N. Lincoln Ave.
Chicago, Illinois 60657
773/929-0069

■ CUSTOM CHAPS ■ LEATHER VESTS ■

PEOPLE LIKE US

The exclusively gay
and lesbian bookstore
for Chicago

1115 W. Belmont Ave.
Chicago, Illinois 60657
(773) 248-6363

10 am - 9pm daily

ILLINOIS

CHARMER'S, 1502 W Jarvis Ave near Greenview, (773) 465-2811. 60% men, 40% women.

CHICAGO EAGLE, 5015 N Clark, (773) 728-0050.

CLARK'S ON CLARK, 5001 N Clark, (773) 728-2373.

DIFFERENT STROKES, 4923 N Clark St at Argyle, (773) 989-1958. Beer garden.

FRIENDS PUB, 3432 W Irving Park, (773) 539-5229. Videos, small dance floor.

LOST & FOUND, 3058 W Irving Park Rd at Albany, (773) 463-9617. Buzz to get in, closed Mon.

MADRIGAL'S BAR & CAFE, 5316 N Clark St, (773) 334-3033. Cabaret bar with piano, singers. Cafe has light meals, patio in summer.

SCOT'S, 1829 W Montrose, (773) 528-3253. Videos.

TOUCHE, 6412 N Clark St, (773) 465-7400.

TRAVELER'S REST, 1138 W Granville, (773) 262-4225. From 10am Mon-Sat, noon Sun.

■ Dance Bar/Disco

LEGACY '21, 3042 W Irving Park, (773) 588-9405. Small dance bar.

NUMBERS, 6406 N Clark, (773) 743-5772. Progressive dance, video, patio, some straight clientele.

PARIS DANCE,★ 1122 W Montrose near Broadway, (773) 769-0602. Bar, lounge, patio, till 3am weekends. Luna Park Cafe open Wed-Sun.

RAINBOW ROOM BAR & GRILLE, 4530 N Lincoln, (773) 271-4378. Sports bar with DJ & dancing Fri & Sat, grille with sandwiches.

■ Saunas/Health Clubs

MAN'S COUNTRY, 5017 N Clark St near Argyle, (773) 878-2069. Private club, 24hrs, gym equipment.

■ Restaurants

ANN SATHER, 5207 N Clark St, (773) 271-6677. Diner with Swedish home cooking. Also at: 929 W Belmont, 1329 E 57th.

JULIE MAI'S LE BISTRO, 5025 N Clark, (773) 784-6000. French & Vietnamese cuisine, steaks.

PEPPER LOUNGE, 3441 N Sheffield, (773) 665-7377. Late-night supper club, gourmet dining till 1:30am.

■ Retail & Bookstores

PAPER TRAIL, THE, 5307 N Clark St, (773) 275-2191. Alternative gift & card shop.

WOMANWILD, 5237 N Clark St, (773) 878-0300. Extraordinary art/gift gallery offering treasures by 150 women artists!

WOMEN & CHILDREN FIRST, 5233 N Clark St, (773) 769-9299. Feminist & children's bookstore with complete selection of lesbian titles and women's music. Weekly programs, large recovery, psychology & women's spirituality sections.

■ Leathers/Piercing

EAGLE LEATHER, 5006 N Clark, (773) 728-7228.

■ Erotica

BANANA VIDEO, 4923 N Clark St, 2nd Fl, (773) 561-8322. Adult bookstore.

HOWARD STREET NEWS, 7614 N Ashland, (773) 465-9431, 24hrs.

SPECIALTY VIDEO, 5225 N Clark St, (773) 878-3434.

CHICAGO NEAR NORTH

■ Accommodations

HOUSE OF TWO URNS, THE, 1239 N Greenview Ave, (773) 235-1408. Gay-friendly B&B. Eclectically furnished rooms with shared bath, TV lounge, sitting rooms, refrigerator, continental breakfast & nearby pool.

OLD TOWN BED & BREAKFAST, 1451 N North Park Ave, (312) 440-9268. This modern house is splendidly furnished and decorated with pictures and art objects from three centuries. A walled garden, a library with easy chairs, a marble bath with an oversized tub, and cherrywood sleighbeds invite rest, reflection and renewal. Lake Michigan, Lincoln Park and an urban village surround. Parking is ample. North Michigan Avenue shopping, Gold Coast mansions and fine restaurants are a short walk.

■ Bars

MANHANDLER, 1948 N Halsted St near Armitage, (773) 871-3339. Patio.

VINYL, 1615 N Clybourn, (312) 587-8469. Wed-Sun, Wed salsa & merengue, Thurs int'l dance party, Fri South Beach dance party & latin music.

■ Dance Bar/Disco

GLEE CLUB, 1543 N Kingsbury, at the Crow bar. (312) 243-2075. Gay Sun night only from 10pm, some straight clientele.

■ Restaurants

FIREPLACE INN, 1448 N Wells near North Ave, (312) 664-5264. Steaks, seafood.

■ Erotica

BIJOU THEATRE, 1349 N Wells near Evergreen. (312) 943-5397.

LESLIE'S, 738 N Clark St at Chicago, (312) 751-9672. Adult bookstore with gay & lesbian periodicals & videos.

OVER 21 BOOKSTORE,★ 1347 N Wells St near Evergreen, (312) 337-8730, 24hrs.

CHICAGO SOUTH

■ Dance Bar/Disco

JEFFREY PUB, 7041 S Jeffrey Ave near 71st, (773) 363-8555. Dance & video bar, women welcome.

CHICAGO WEST

■ Dance Bar/Disco

ESCAPADES, 6301 S Harlem, (773) 229-0886. Video dance bar till 4am.

HIDEAWAY II, 7301 W Roosevelt at Marengo, Forest Park, (708) 771-4459. Video dance bar, male dancers.

HUNTER'S, 1932 E Higgins Rd, Elk Grove, (847) 439-8840. Video dance bar, patio.

INNEXILE, 5758 W 65th Street, (773) 582-3510. Video dance bar, patio, women welcome.

NUTBUSH, 7201 Franklin, Forest Park, (708) 366-5117. Disco, videos, male strippers, women welcome.

TEMPTATIONS, 10235 W Grand Ave, Franklin Park, (847) 455-0008. Wed-Sat from 9pm.

■ Retail & Bookstores

LEFT BANK BOOKSTALL, 104 S Oak Park Ave, Oak Park, (708) 383-4700. General used bookstore with women's & gay men's section.

PRIDE AGENDA BOOKSTORE, 1109 Westgate, Oak Park, (708) 524-8429. Gay & lesbian bookstore, gifts.

■ Erotica

CIRCLE VIDEO, 7322 W Madison, Forest Park, (708) 366-1981.

CIRCLE VIDEO, 3338 N Harlem, (773) 637-7600.

DEKALB

■ Information

GAY/LESBIAN BISEXUAL COALITION, (815) 753-0584. Dances, picnics, galas, films, speakers & local info.

EAST ST LOUIS

See St. Louis, MO

OLD TOWN Bed & Breakfast

(312) 440-9268
CHICAGO

ILLINOIS

NAUVOO

Accommodations
ED-HARRI-MERE, PO Box 367, 290 N Page St, (217) 453-2796. Gay-friendly B&B, shared bath.

PEORIA

Bars
QUENCH ROOM, 631 W Main St near Sheridan, (309) 676-1079. Conversation bar, 50% men, 50% women.

Dance Bar/Disco
DJ'S TIME OUT, 703 SW Adams, (309) 674-5902. Dance & sports bar, 1pm-1am (Thurs-Sat till 2am), Thurs drag shows, 50% men, 50% women.
RED FOX DEN, 800 N Knoxville Ave, (309) 674-8013. 70% men.

Erotica
BROWN BAG VIDEO, 801 SW Adams, (309) 676-3003.
GREEN DOOR, THE 2610 W Farmington Rd near Sterling. (309) 674-4337. Videos, adult toys.
MARY'S ADULT BOOKS, 7814 N Sommer, (309) 692-7477.
SWINGER'S WORLD, 335 SW Adams, (309) 676-9275, 24hrs.

QUINCY

Dance Bar/Disco
IRENE'S CABARET, 124 N 5th St, (217) 222-6292. Dance & show bar, 50% men, 50% women.

Erotica
CHELSEA THEATRE, 5000 Gardner Expwy (217) 224-7000.

ROCK ISLAND
See Davenport, IA

ROCKFORD

Information
WOMEN'S SPACE CENTER, 3333 Maria Linden Dr, (815) 877-0118. Women's art gallery.

Bars
OH ZONE, 1014 Charles St, (815) 964-9663. Small dance floor, 50% gay clientele.

Dance Bar/Disco
OFFICE & HOT SHOTS, 513 E State St, (815) 965-0344. Mon-Fri 5pm-2am, Sat noon-2am, Sun noon-midnite, DJ Wed-Sat, 50% men, 50% women. Hot Shots is quieter basement bar with juke box, pool table, darts, Fri & Sat only.

Retail & Bookstores
BACK TO THE SOURCE CAFE & BOOKSTORE, 515 E State St, (815) 965-7611. General bookstore with a small gay & lesbian section.

WOMEN'S TIME, 2310 Charles St, (815) 227-4373. Feminist bookstore, jewelry, cards, music, t-shirts, art.

SPRINGFIELD

Bars
STATION HOUSE, 306 E Washington, (217) 525-0438.

Dance Bar/Disco
NEW DIMENSIONS, 3036 Peoria Rd near Taintor, (217) 753-9268. 90% men, closed Mon & Tues.
SMOKEY'S DEN, 411 E Washington St near 4th, (217) 522-0301. Disco, DJ wknds, 50% men, 50% women.

Retail & Bookstores
SUNDANCE BOOKSTORE, 1428 E Sangamon Ave, (217) 788-5243. Gifts, music, books, gay & lesbian jewelry, rainbow items. Tue-Fri 11am-7pm, Sat 10am-6pm.

Erotica
EXPO, 300 N 5th St, (217) 544-5145.
SELECT VIDEO, 317 E Washington, (217) 528-6037, 7 days.

INDIANA
STATEWIDE

Information
AIDS LINE, (800) 848-2437.

BLOOMINGTON

Information
GAY & LESBIAN SWITCHBOARD, (812) 855-5688. 7pm-11pm or tape.

Bars
OTHER BAR, 414 S Walnut, (812) 332-0033. Closed Sun.

Dance Bar/Disco
BULLWINKLE'S, 201 S College, (812) 334-3232. Dance & show bar, full liquor, 7pm-3am, closed Sun

Erotica
COLLEGE AVE BOOKS, 1013 N College Ave, (812) 332-5160. Arcade.

ELKHART

Information
SWITCHBOARD CONCERN, (219) 293-8761, 24hrs. Not a gay service, but will put you in touch with local gay organizations. No bar referrals.

EVANSVILLE

Information
TRI-STATE ALLIANCE, (812) 474-4853.

Dance Bar/Disco
SOME PLACE ELSE, Main & Sycamore, (812) 424-3202. Dance & show bar with Down Under Gay Pride shop.

Erotica
BOOKMART, 519 N Main St, (812) 423-2011. Arcade.

FT WAYNE

Information
AIDS INFO, (219) 744-1144. Support services, educational programs, 24hrs.
GAY OUTREACH LINE, (219) 456-6570, 24hrs.
HELP LINE & COMMUNITY CENTER, (219) 744-1199 7pm-10pm or tape.

Bars
HENRY'S, 536 W Main St at Fulton, (219) 426-0531. Not a gay bar, but frequented by some gays, lesbians.
RIFF RAFF BAR & GRILLE, 2809 W Main. Burgers, sandwiches, appetizers, entrees.

Dance Bar/Disco
AFTER DARK, ★ 231 Pearl St, (219) 424-6130. Male dancers Tues, drag shows Thurs, women welcome.
DOWNTOWN ON THE LANDING, 110 W Columbia St, (219) 420-1615. Open Thurs-Sun, many straights.
UP THE STREET, 2322 S Calhoun, (219) 456-7166. Small dance bar.

HAMMOND

Saunas/Health Clubs
SIBLEY COURTYARD, 629 Sibley Blvd, (219) 933-9604. 24hrs.

INDIANAPOLIS

Information
DIVERSITY CENTER, 1112 Southeastern Ave S of Washington St, (317) 639-4297. Gay & lesbian community center, library, archives, organized events & meetings.

Bars
BROTHER'S BAR & GRILLE, 822 N Illinois, (317) 636-1020. Bar & restaurant, American-style, daily from 4pm.
CLUB CABARET, 151 W 14th St at Capitol. (317) 767-1707. Showbar.
FIVE-O-ONE TAVERN, 501 N College Ave at Michigan St, (317) 632-2100. Hi-energy leather, levi cruise bar.
HOLLYWOOD BAR & FILMWORKS, 247 S Meridian, (317) 231 9250. Bar with movie theatre. Over 21 only.
ILLUSIONS, 1446 E Washington St at Oriental, (317) 266-0535. Showbar, ladies nite Wed, female strippers, shows weekends.
JIMMY'S, 924 N Pennsylvania near 10th, (317) 638-9039. Video bar & dinner-only restaurant. Live entertainment, 70% men, 30% women, more women on weekends.
TOMORROW'S, 2301 N Meridian at 23rd, (317) 925-1710. Pool table, darts, shows, karaoke.
UNICORN CLUB, 122 W 13th St at Illinois,

IOWA

(317) 262-9195. Members-only club, male strippers. 🏳️‍🌈♂️
VARSITY, 1517 N Pennsylvania near 16th, (317) 635-9998. Bar & restaurant 70% men, 30% women. Popular Sun brunch. 🍴✖️♂️

■ Dance Bar/Disco
METRO,★ 707 Massachusetts Ave, (317) 639-6022. Video techno dance bar, 3 bars, restaurant, patio, 90% men, 10% women. Gift shop upstairs. 🍴🎵🏳️‍🌈♂️
OUR PLACE,★ 231 E 16th St, (317) 638-8138, http://www.ourplace.net. Indy's Number One bar — 3 bars, heated patio open all winter, Country Western Wed 8pm-1am, Fri 9pm-midnight. Hi NRG dance Mon, Thurs, Fri & Sat. 🍴🎵🍸♂️
TEN, THE,★ 1218 N Pennsylvania St near 12th, (317) 638-5802. Dance & show bar, 30% men, 70% women. Closed Sun, men welcome. 🍴🎵♀️
VOGUE, THE, 6259 N College Ave, Broad Ripple, (317) 255-2828. Sun night is gay night, "Boing Night." 🍴♀️♂️

■ Cafe
ABBEY, THE, 771 Massachusetts Ave, (317) 269-8426. Mon-Thur 7am-1am, Fri-Sat 7am-4am, Sun 10am-10pm. Gay-Friendly. 🌈
COFFEE ZON, 137 E Ohio, (317) 684-0432. Gay-friendly coffee house with some art exhibits. 🌈

■ Saunas/Health Clubs
CLUB INDIANAPOLIS, 620 N Capitol Ave near Walnut, (317) 635-5796. Private club, 24hrs, sun deck, gym.
WORKS, THE, 4120 N Keystone, (317) 547-9210. 24hrs, private club, disco with videos. 🍴

■ Restaurants
AESOP'S TABLES, 600 N Massachusetts Ave, (317) 631-0055. Mon-Thus 11am-9pm, Fri & Sat 11am-10pm. Mediterranean cuisine, gay-friendly. 🌈
BROTHERS BAR & GRILLE, 822 N Illinois. ♀️♂️
JIMMY'S 924 N Pennsylvania, at Jimmy's bar. ♂️
RESTAURANT AT METRO, 707 Massachusetts Ave, (317) 639-6077. Italian menu, from 6pm on. 🍷
TOMORROW'S NEAR NORTH CAFE, 2301 N Meridian at Tomorrow's bar. (317) 925-1710. Lunch & dinner, gay after 5pm, Sun brunch 12pm-3pm. ♀️♂️
VARSITY RESTAURANT, 1517 N Pennsylvania at Varsity bar. ♀️♂️

■ Retail & Bookstores
COLOURS: GIFT SHOP, 707 Massachusetts Ave in the Metro nightclub, (317) 686-0984.
JUST CARDS, 145 E Ohio St at Delaware, (317) 638-1170. Gifts & cards. 🌈

■ Erotica
ANNEX ADULT, 6767 E 38th St, (317) 549-3522.
APOLLO ADULT BOOKSTORE, 5431 E 38th St, (317) 547-4777.
BOOKLAND, 137 W Market St, (317) 639-9864.
INDIANA NEWS, 121 S Pennsylvania, (317) 632-7680.

LAFAYETTE

■ Bars
SPORTSMAN BAR, 644 Main St, (765) 742-6321. Pool table, games, DJ Fri & Sat night. 60% men, 40% women. 🍴✖️♀️♂️

■ Erotica
ALICE'S BOUTIQUE, 604 S Earl Ave, (765) 448-9114. Clothes, accessories for crossdressers, SM equipment.
FANTASY GIFT SHOP, 2311 Concord Rd, (765) 474-2417. Second location: 119 N River Rd, (317) 743-5042.

LAKE STATION

■ Bars
STATION HOUSE, Ripley at Central, (219) 962-1017. DJ Tues, Fri-Sat, 🍴♀️♂️

MICHIGAN CITY

■ Bars
TOTAL ECLIPSE, 4960 W US Rte 20, (219) 874-1100. DJ weekends. 🍴♂️

■ Erotica
NAUGHTY BUT NICE, 104 W US Hwy 20, (219) 879-6363. Adult gift shop, 8am-midnight.

MUNCIE

■ Dance Bar/Disco
MARK III, 107 E Main St (shopping plaza), (317) 282-8273. Hi-energy dance bar, 11am-2am (Wed, Fri-Sat till 3am), 50% men, 50% women. 🍴🎵✖️♀️♂️

■ Restaurants
CARRIAGE HOUSE, 247 Kilgore Ave, (317) 282-7411. Restaurant & bar, discreetly frequented by gay men & women. 🌈🍷🍴

RICHMOND

■ Dance Bar/Disco
COACHMAN LOUNGE, 911 S Main St, (317) 966-2835. C&W & rock music. Closed Sun. Unverifiable spring '97. 🍴♀️♂️

SOUTH BEND

■ Information
AIDS LINE, (219) 287-8888. In northern IN: (800) 388-AIDS, 9am-5pm or tape.
HELP LINE, (219) 232-2522, 9am-5pm Mon-Fri.
WOMEN'S CENTER, Northside 459, Indiana U at SB, (219) 237-4494. Resources, 8am-5pm weekdays.

■ Accommodations
KAMM'S ISLAND INN/KAMM'S ISLAND, 700 Lincolnway W, Mishawaka, (219) 256-1501, (800) 955-KAMM, fax: (219) 256-1504. Inn with bar, disco, movie theatre, bistro & shops, some straight clientele. Many modern conveniences including color cable TV, AC & private baths. Continental breakfast. ♀️♂️

■ Bars
STARZ, 1505 Kendal, (219) 288-7827. Male strippers. 🏳️‍🌈♂️

■ Dance Bar/Disco
SEAHORSE II CABARET, 1902 Western Ave at Brookfield, (219) 237-9139. Dance & show bar, 50% men, 50% women. Closed Sun. 🍴🎵♂️
TRUMAN'S, 100 N Center, in the 100 Center, Mishawaka, (219) 259-2282. Dance bar with drag shows Wed. 🍴🎵♀️♂️

■ Restaurants
CENTER ST BAR & GRILL, 100 N Center St, Mishawaka, at Truman's nightclub. ♀️♂️

■ Erotica
ADULT EMPORIUM, 2715 S Main St, (219) 291-1899. Videos, gay & lesbian titles, 24hrs.
LITTLE DENMARK, 3002 W Western Ave, (219) 233-9538. 10am-9pm.
PLEASURELAND, 114 W Mishawaka Ave, Mishawaka, (219) 259-6776.

TERRE HAUTE

■ Dance Bar/Disco
R PLACE, 684 Lafayette Ave, (812) 232-9119. 🍴🎵♀️♂️

IOWA
STATEWIDE

■ Information
ACCESS OF NE IOWA, (319) 232-6805. Gay & lesbian information line.

AMES

■ Information
LESBIAN, GAY & BISEXUAL ALLIANCE, at ISU, (515) 294-2104 or 294-1020.
MARAGARET SLOSS WOMEN'S CENTER, at ISU, in the Sloss House, (515) 294-4154. 8am-5pm Mon-Fri, scheduled activities.

■ Erotica
PLEASURE PALACE II, 117 Kellogg St, (515) 232-7717. Adult & gay videos, previews, novelties. 🌈

CEDAR RAPIDS

■ Dance Bar/Disco
ROCKEFELLA'S, 2739 6th St SW, (319) 399-1623. Live DJ 7 nights, 5pm-2am, variety of shows, male & female strippers. 🍴🎵♀️♂️

■ Erotica
ADULT SHOP, 630 66th Ave, (319) 362-4939.

FERRARI GUIDES' GAY TRAVEL A to Z - 18th EDITION

IOWA

CLINTON
■ *Erotica*
ABC BOOKS, 135 5th Ave S, (319) 242-7687.

CLUTIER
■ *Accommodations*
CORNERSTONE INN, 2959 255 St, (319) 479-2268, fax: (319) 479-2288. Guesthouse on a working farm, private & shared baths, full or continental breakfast, color cable TV, AC, 20 minutes from casino, 1 hour from Amana Colonies, women welcome. ♂

COUNCIL BLUFFS
See Omaha, NE

DAVENPORT
Also includes Rock Island, IL (309).
■ *Bars*
AUGIE'S, 313 20th St near 3rd Ave, Rock Island, (309) 788-7389. 🍴♀♂
CLUB MARQUETTE, Marquette St, near Kimberley across from K's Merchandise Store. Bar & grill, sandwiches, steaks, shrimp. DJ Fri & Sat, open stage Wed, shows & male strippers, 70% men, 30% women. 🍴♂
MADISON SQUARE, 319 20th St, Rock Island next door to JR's, (309) 786-9400. Upscale decor, casual atmosphere, DJ Fri & Sat 9pm-3am. 🍴♀
■ *Dance Bar/Disco*
JR'S, 325 20th St, Rock Island, IL, (309) 786-9411. Disco Mon-Sat 3pm-3am, Sun noon-3am. Drag shows Wed & Fri-Sun, male dancers Fri, female dancers alternate months. Restaurant with sandwiches, steaks, appetizers, Mon-Thurs 5pm-10pm, Fri & Sat 5pm-2am, Sun 5pm-10pm. 🍴✕♀♂
■ *Cafe*
ALL KINDS OF PEOPLE, 1806 2nd Ave, Rock Island, IL, (309) 788-2567. Coffeeshop, books, t-shirts. Gay-friendly.
■ *Retail & Bookstores*
CRYSTAL RAINBOW, 1025 W 4th St, (319) 323-1050. Lesbian bookstore with women's spirituality section. Some gay men's titles.
■ *Erotica*
CENTENNIAL VIDEO, 20th St near 3rd, Rock Island. Booths.
T&R VIDEO, at Hickory Grove & Fairmont. Booths.

DES MOINES
■ *Information*
GAY & LESBIAN RESOURCES CENTER, 414 E 5th, (515) 281-0634.
IOWA AIDS PROJECT, 412 12th St, (515) 284-0154.
YOUNG WOMEN'S RESOURCE CENTER, 554 28th St, (515) 244-4901. 8:30am-5pm Mon-Fri. Closed 12-1pm for lunch.
■ *Bars*
BLAZING SADDLE, INC,★ 416 E 5th St, (515) 246-1299. Mon-Fri 2pm-2am, Sat & Sun noon-2am, DJ Thurs-Sun. Home of Cornhaulers levi/leather club.
FACES LTD, 416 E Walnut, (515) 280-5463. Downstairs dance bar, upstairs bar, 70% men.
■ *Dance Bar/Disco*
GARDEN, THE,★ 112 SE 4th near Vine, (515) 243-3965. Big dance bar with techno & house music, videos, patio bar. Mon-Wed 7pm-2am, Thurs-Sun 5pm-2am. 70% men.
■ *Cafe*
JAVA JOE'S, 214 4th St, (515) 288-5282. Coffees, espresso. Frequented by gays.
ZANZIBAR'S COFFEE, 2723 Ingersoll, (515) 244-7694. Non-smoking coffeeshop, frequented by gays.
■ *Restaurants*
AUNT BUTCH'S, at about 28th & Grand, (515) 244-3365. European-style bistro, lunch & dinner, frequented by gays.
OLD DOWNTOWN DELI, 418 E 5th St next door to Blazing Saddles bar. (515) 282-7041. Breakfast thru dinner, Sun brunch. Very popular late nites. To reopen in 1997.
■ *Retail & Bookstores*
BORDERS BOOK SHOP, in Watertower Square, (515) 223-1620. General bookstore with a gay & lesbian section.
CONNECTIONS BOOKSTORE, 413 Maple Valley Junction W, (515) 277-5949. New age books, tapes, cards, crystals. Closed Mon.
■ *Erotica*
ADULT EMPORIUM, 1401 Army Post Rd, behind a restaurant.
BACHELOR'S LIBRARY, 2020 E Euclid near Delaware, (515) 266-7992.
GALLERY BOOKSTORE, 1114 Walnut St, (515) 244-2916. 24hrs.
NEW BLUE NUDE, 1117 Grand Ave, (515) 244-7705. Arcade.

DUBUQUE
■ *Erotica*
GENTLEMEN'S BOOKSTORE, 306 Main St, (319) 556-9313.

FORT DODGE
■ *Erotica*
MINI-CINEMA, 15 N Fifth St, (515) 955-9756.

IOWA CITY
■ *Information*
GAYLINE, (319) 335-3251.
WOMEN'S CENTER, 130 N Madison at Market, (319) 335-1486. 10am-5pm Mon-Fri (Mon & Thurs till 7pm).
■ *Bars*
BREAKROOM, 1578 S 1st Ave, (319) 354-9271. NOT a gay bar, popular with gay women. Owner says it's just a "huge mix."
DEADWOOD, 6 S Dubuque, (319) 351-9417. Sun, Mon, Tue, Wed, mixed gay & straight crowd, 25-30% gay.
■ *Dance Bar/Disco*
SIX TWENTY, 620 S Madison near Prentiss, (319) 354-2494. Thurs-Sat 9pm-2am, 70% men.
■ *Retail & Bookstores*
ALTERNATIVES, 323 E Market St, Tel/Fax: (319) 337-4124. Lesbian owned/operated store with G&L mugs, cards, jewelery. Mon-Sat 10am-6pm, Sun noon-4pm.
MOON MYSTIQUE, 114-1/2 E College, (319) 338-5752. General bookstore with astrology books, gay, lesbian & feminist books, magazines.
PRAIRIE LIGHT BOOKSTORE, 15 S Dubuque St, (319) 337-2681. General bookstore with a gay & lesbian section.
UNIVERSITY BOOKSTORE, Memorial Union at IU, (319) 335-3179. General bookstore with a gay & lesbian section.
■ *Erotica*
ADULT MARKETPLACE, 440 Kirkwood Ave, (319) 337-7078.
JUST A BIT DIFFERENT, 116 E 9 St, Coralville, (319) 338-7978.

NEWTON
■ *Accommodations*
LA CORSETTE MAISON INN & THE SISTER INN, 629 1st Ave E, (515) 792-6833, Fax: (515) 792-6597. Two gay-friendly, elegant B&B inns, one with restaurant. Variety of rooms with French country decor & modern conveniences, private baths, full breakfast. A 25-min drive from Des Moines.

SIOUX CITY
■ *Bars*
KINGS & QUEENS, 417 Nebraska St, (712) 252-4167. DJ Fri & Sat. 🍴♂
THREE CHEERS, 414 20th St, (712) 255-8005. 70% men, 30% women, DJ Wed, Fri & Sat. ♂
■ *Erotica*
ADULT EMPORIUM, Pearl St & 4th.
FRANCIS CANTEEN, 1004 4th St, (712) 255-7363.

WATERLOO
■ *Dance Bar/Disco*
BAR, THE 903 Sycamore, (319) 232-0543. Dance & show bar, DJ weekends, male dancers.
■ *Cafe*
CUP OF JOE, 1st & Main St, Cedar Falls.
■ *Erotica*
ADULT EMPORIUM, 1507 Laporte Rd, (319) 234-9340, 24hrs.

KENTUCKY

KANSAS

KANSAS CITY
See Kansas City, MO

LAWRENCE

■ *Information*
HEADQUARTERS, (913) 841-2345. Mainstream crisis counseling, referral center, has gay information 24hrs.
QUEERS & ALLIES (Q&A) GAY INFO, (913) 864-3091, 9am-5pm, or tape.

■ *Cafe*
PARADISE CAFE & BAKERY, 728 Massachusetts, (913) 842-5199. Specialty & vegetarian cuisine.
THREE GALS COFFEEHOUSE, (913) 842-2147. Call for schedule, live music, coffee, usually 2nd Sat 8pm at Ecumenical Christian Ministries, 1204 Oread.

■ *Restaurants*
TELLERS RESTAURANT & BAR, 746 Massachusetts Ave, (913) 843-4111. Tue night "Family Night" gay night.

MANHATTAN

■ *Information*
BISEXUAL, GAY & LESBIAN SOCIETY, c/o Office of Student Act. & Services, (913) 395-2256.

MATFIELD GREEN

■ *Women's Accommodations*
PRAIRIE WOMEN ADVENTURES & RETREAT, Rural Rte Mail, Matfield Green, KS 66862, (316) 753-3465, Fax: (316) 753-3466. Be a cowhand on a working cattle ranch & perform actual chores, such as branding, vaccinating & castrating cattle. ♀

TOPEKA

■ *Information*
GAY RAP LINE, (913) 233-6558, 8pm-midnight 7 nights, or tape.

■ *Accommodations*
SUNFLOWER BED & BREAKFAST, THE, 915 SW Munson Ave, Topeka, KS 66604, (913) 357-7509. Gay-friendly B&B with 2 rooms with double beds, shared bath, full breakfast, AC, telephone, gay & lesbian following.

■ *Bars*
MARK, THE, 601 SE 8th, (913) 233-2447. Upscale lounge, 60% men. ♀♂

■ *Dance Bar/Disco*
CLASSICS, 110 SE 8th St, (913) 233-5153. Dance & show bar, 60% men, 40% women.
LYZ, 1009 S Kansas, (913) 234-0482. DJ weekends & small dance floor, 70% men. Beer garden in summer.

■ *Erotica*
ADULT BOOKSTORE, 903 N Kansas, (913) 235-6010.

WICHITA

■ *Information*
GAY COMMUNITY CENTER, 754 S Pattie, AIDS info (316) 264-2437.

■ *Bars*
DREAMERS I, 3210 E Osie, (316) 682-4461. Juke box, small dance floor, pool table, darts, Tues-Fri 4pm-2am, Sat & Sun 3pm-2am. Getting kino in '97.
SIDE STREET SALOON, 1106 S Pattie, (316) 267-0324. Pool table, juke box. ♀♂
T ROOM, 1507 E Pawnee near Ellis, (316) 262-9327. Pool tabble, darts, small dance floor, sandwhiches at lunch, 80% men, women welcome.

■ *Dance Bar/Disco*
DREAMERS II, 2835 S. George Washington Blvd, (316) 682-4490. Occasional lesbian bands, kitchen on weekends, Mon-Thurs 4pm-2am, Fri-Sat 10pm-4am, Sat-Sun 3pm-2am. ♀
OUR FANTASY COMPLEX, 3201 S Hillside at 31st, (316) 682-5494. Complex with Fantasy dance bar, South 40 C&W bar, drag shows Wed & Sun, BBQ in patio bar, swimming pool, volleyball court, 50% men, 50% women.
R & R'S BRASS RAIL, 2828 E 31st St S near Hillside, (316) 684-9009. Dance club, 60% men, 40% women, DJ. ♀♂

■ *Cafe*
RIVERSIDE PARK, 1144 Bitting, (316) 264-6464. Coffee, sandwiches.

■ *Restaurants*
UPPER CRUST, 7038 E Lincoln, (316) 683-8088. Restaurant & catering.

■ *Retail & Bookstores*
MOTHER'S, 3100 E 31st St S, (316) 686-8116. Pride store.

■ *Erotica*
ADULT ENTERTAINMENT CENTERS, 7805 W Kellogg Dr, (316) 721-3160. Also: 3721 S Broadway, 522-6409; 2809 N Broadway, 838-2817.
CIRCLE CINEMA, 2570 S Seneca, (316) 263-0587.
EXCITEMENT VIDEO, 220 E 21st St N (316) 832-1816, 24hrs. Also: 8025 S Broadway, 554-0370.
EXCITEMENT VIDEO, 1306 E Harry, (316) 269-9036, 24hrs, arcade.
TB'S BOOKS & CAMELOT CINEMA, 1515 S Oliver, (316) 688-5343, 24hrs.

KENTUCKY

COVINGTON
See Cincinnati, OH

LEXINGTON

■ *Bars*
CROSSINGS, 117 N Limestone, (606) 233-7266. Closed Sun.
JOE'S BAR, 120 S Upper near Main St, (606) 252-7946. Sun brunch & dinner Wed-Sun, 60% men, 40% women. May change in 1997. ♀♂

■ *Dance Bar/Disco*
BAR COMPLEX, THE,★ 224 E Main St at Esplanade, (606) 255-1551. Dance, lounge & show bar, younger crowd, 50% men, 50% women. After-hours Sat, closed Sun. ♀♂
CLUB 141, 141 W Vine St, (606) 233-4262. Dance bar, after hours Sat, closed Sun. ♀♂

■ *Leathers/Piercing*
RACK, THE, 117 N Limestone at Crossings bar. Fri, Sat from 10pm, or by appt.

■ *Erotica*
NEW BOOK STORE, 942 Winchester Rd, (606) 252-2093.
PHOENIX BOOKSTORE, 933 Winchester Rd near New Circle Rd, (606) 281-1228.
TWO THOUSAND FOUR VIDEO, 2004 Family Circle Rd, (606) 255-1002.

LOUISVILLE

■ *Accommodations*
ESSENCE HOUSE, (502) 458-5277, Fax: (502) 459-3414. Lodge on 30 acres of natural wooded beauty in Southern Indiana, just 25 minutes from Louisville, KY. Groups: Rent the entire lodge by day or week. Sleeps 12 comfortably. Make our place your home for your special event in any season. Pool, hot tub, tennis. ♀♂
THREE-FORTY-THREE (343) BEHARRELL, 343 Beharrell Ave, New Albany, IN 47150, 2-1/2 miles from Louisville, (812) 944-0289. Gay & lesbian B&B with comfortable rooms, private & shared baths, private deck, extensive gay & lesbian book collection on premises. Minutes to downtown Louisville & gay, lesbian & cultural attractions. ♀♂

■ *Bars*
MURPHY'S PLACE,★ 306-308 E Main St, (502) 587-8717. Piano bar, 70% men. ♂
SCORES, Market at Floyd. Sports bar. ♂
TEDDY BEAR, THE, 1148 Garvin Place, (502) 589-2619.
TINKERS II, Market St near Floyd. Women's bar in front, Rage mixed dance bar in rear. ♀
TOWN CAFE, 414 W Oak St, (502) 637-7730. Small bar with shows Wed, Fri, Sat. ♂
TRYANGLES, 209 S Preston St, (502) 583-6395.

FERRARI GUIDES' GAY TRAVEL A to Z - 18th EDITION 435

KENTUCKY

FYI

One Call Does It All

Destination Management (DMI) is a wholesale tour operator and receptive agent packaging New Orleans and the southeast region of the United States for groups and individual travelers. With affiliate companies, DMI provides a wide range of services, including everything from restaurant reservations to renting a cellular phone, from airline ticketing to hotel accommodations, and from riverboat cruises and sightseeing tours to bus charters and airport shuttle. Specialized programs for convention, corporate and incentive travel include customized group tours, theme parties, celebrity appearances, speakers, music and entertainment.

DMI supplies special event packages for the annual Jazz and Heritage Festival, Sugar Bowl, Mardi Gras. Year-round packages include the Discover New Orleans, Gourmet Classic, Romantic Getaway, Creole Family and Air-Inclusive Packages.

Individuals call: (800) 366-8882, (504) 524-5030, Fax: (504) 529-1405. Groups, agents call: (800) 471-8222, (504) 592-0500, Fax: (504) 592-0529, E-mail: info@new.orleans.com, Web: www.new.orleans.com.

Mostly men, occasional live entertainment.

■ **Dance Bar/Disco**
CONNECTION, THE,★ 120 S Floyd, (502) 585-5752, 583-1166. Hi energy dance bar & restaurant, piano, patio, show theatre.
RAGE, Market St near Floyd, behind Tinkers II bar. Dance bar.
SPARKS, 1st & Main. Alternative dance bar, 50% gay.
UPSTAIRS, THE, 306-308 E Main St, (502) 587-1432. Cozy dance & social bar, 80% men, 20% women.

■ **Restaurants**
JULIANS, 120 S Floyd, at the Connection bar, (502) 585-5752. Dinner, piano, theater. Opens 6pm nightly.

■ **Retail & Bookstores**
CARMICHAEL'S, 1295 Bardstown Rd at Longest, (502) 456-6950. General bookstore with gay & women's sections.
HAWLEY COOKE BOOKS, 27 Shelbyville Rd Plaza, (502) 893-0133. Also, 3024 Bardstown Rd in Gardiner Ln Plaza, 456-6660. General bookstores with gay & lesbian sections.
TEN PERCENT (10%) GIFTS & ACCESSORIES, 120 S Floyd St, inside the Connection nightclub. Gay novelties, magazines, guides, jewelry, etc. Open Wed-Sun 9pm-4am.

■ **Erotica**
ARCADE, THE, 2822 7th St, (502) 637-8388.
ART THEATRE, 3423 Taylor Blvd, (502) 361-8588.
BLUE MOVIES, 244 W Jefferson at 3rd, (502) 585-4627.
LOUISVILLE MANOR, 4600 Dixie Hwy, (502) 447-2440. Adult books & motel.
SHOWBOAT BOOKSTORE, 3524 S 7th St, (502) 361-0007.

LOUISIANA

WHO TO CALL
For Tour Companies Serving This Destination
See Louisiana on page 19

ALEXANDRIA

■ **Dance Bar/Disco**
UNIQUE BAR, 3117 Masonic Dr, (318) 448-0555. Hi-energy dance bar.

BATON ROUGE

■ **Accommodations**
BRENTWOOD HOUSE, PO Box 40872, Baton Rouge, 70835-0872, (504) 924-4989, Fax: (504) 924-1738. Classy home stay in park-like setting, some straight clientele, women welcome. Color TV, shared baths, hot tub, expanded continental breakfast.

■ **Bars**
BLUE PARROT, 450 Oklahoma St, (504) 267-4211. 60% men, 40% women, 2 pool tables, large patio piano bar with BBQs.
GEORGE'S PLACE,★ 860 St Louis St at South Blvd, (504) 387-9798. Jukebox & CDs, occasional male dancers. Closed Sun.
MIRROR LOUNGE, 111 3rd St near North, (504) 387-9797. 2 pool tables, closed Sun.
TIME ZONE, Main St at 7th Ave. Gay after 7pm.

■ **Dance Bar/Disco**
HIDEAWAY CLUB, 7367 Exchange Place off Wooddale Blvd near Tom Dr, (504) 923-3632. Men welcome.
TRADITIONS,★ 2183 Highland Rd, (504) 344-9291. 2-level dance bar, 75% gay/lesbian.

■ **Restaurants**
SAHARA'S, Old Hammond Hwy at Drusilla. Lebanese & Greek cuisine.
SUPERIOR GRILL, Government near Foster. Mexican cuisine.

■ **Retail & Bookstores**
HIBISCUS BOOKSTORE, 635 Main Street, (504) 387-4264. New & used gay bookstore, 7 days.

GRETNA

■ **Bars**
CHEERS, 1711 Hancock, across the Mississippi from New Orleans, (504) 367-0149.
SECRETS, 1030 Westbank Expy, on the west bank of the Mississippi, across from French Qtr. (504) 361-9995. Open from 7pm.

HOUMA

■ **Bars**
BRIDGE CORNER PUB, 1709 Havers, (504) 868-0007.
KIXX, 112 N Hollywood, (504) 876-9587.

LAFAYETTE

■ **Bars**
MOJO MONKEYS, 116 Spring St, (318) 261-9020.
QUARTER, THE, 209 Jefferson St, (318) 269-6011.

■ **Dance Bar/Disco**
IMAGES,★ 524 W Jefferson, (318) 233-0070. Huge hi-energy dance club, Wed-Sun, 60% men, 40% women.

LAKE CHARLES

■ **Bars**
RYAN ST. PUB, 723 Ryan St, (318) 436-9524.

LOUISIANA

■ *Dance Bar/Disco*

CRYSTAL'S, 112 W Broad St, (318) 433-5457. Hi-energy dance bar & lounge, 70% gay/lesbian. Lounge Mon-Sat 6pm-2am. Dance bar Fri-Sun only from 9pm.

MONROE

■ *Dance Bar/Disco*

HOTT SHOTZ, 110 Catalpa St, (318) 388-3262. Male & female strippers, shows Tues, 50% men, 50% women, 9pm-2am Tues-Sat.

NEW ORLEANS

■ *Information*

AIDS HOTLINE, (504) 944-AIDS (2437), (800) 99AIDS9, noon-10pm, 7days.

LESBIAN & GAY CENTER, 816 N Rampart St, (504) 522-1103. Info line Mon-Fri noon-6pm. Programs & weekly movies.

■ *Accommodations*

A PRIVATE GARDEN, 1718 Philip St, (504) 523-1776 (tel/fax). B&B in two self-contained apartments. Modern conveniences & expanded continental buffet breakfast.

BIG EASY GUESTHOUSE, 2633 Dauphin St, (504) 943-3717.

BON MAISON GUESTHOUSE, 835 Bourbon St, (504) 561-8498 (tel/fax). Gay-friendly guesthouse apartments & suites, private baths.

BOURGOYNE GUEST HOUSE, 839 rue Bourbon, (504) 524-3621, 525-3983. Guesthouse in heart of French Quarter, some straight clientele. Cozy studios, completely furnished suites, courtyard.

BOYS ON BURGUNDY, 1030 Burgundy St, (504) 524-2987, (800) 487-8731. B&B in heart of the French Quarter. Large rooms, cable TV, AC, telephone, coffee/tea-making facilities, private & shared baths, cont. breakfast.

BYWATER GUEST HOUSE, 908 Poland Ave, New Orleans, LA (504) 949-6381, E-mail: bywatergh@aol.com, Web: http://members.aol.com/bywatergh/. A relaxed, comfortable atmosphere in an 1872 Eastlake Victorian home located in the Bywater National Historic District, 1 mile from the French Quarter. Amenities include: served breakfast, afternoon tea and pastries, maid service, comfortable beds with feather mattresses, and a private courtyard — all within a 5-minute drive to the Vieux Carre. Visit our web site or e-mail us for more information. Mostly straight clientele with a gay & lesbian following.

CARITAS BED & BREAKFAST NETWORK, (800) CARITAS, (312) 857-0801, (312) 857-0805. B&B, home-stay accommodations service. *Member: IGTA*.

CHATEAU NEGARA, 1923 Esplanade Ave, New Orleans, LA 70116, (504) 947-1343, Fax: (504) 947-4754. Gay-friendly 1865 Antebellum guesthouse with period furnishings & ornate features, complimentary breakfast, private & shared baths, large trop. gardens.

DAUZAT HOUSE, 337 Burgundy St, (504) 524-2075. Gay-friendly hotel, private baths, 20% gay & lesbian clientele.

DEJA VU GUEST HOUSE, 1835-37 rue Rampart N, (504) 945-5912, (800) 867-7316, fax: (504) 948-6396. Guesthouse with 3 apts, 3 blocks from French Quarter gay bars, private baths, nearby gym, women welcome.

FOURTEEN TWELVE THALIA, A BED AND BREAKFAST, 1412 Thalia, (504) 522-0453, E-mail: grisgris@ix.netcom.com. Self-contained apt convenient to downtown & Conv. Center. Sleeps 2-4 people. Modern conveniences, breakfast supplies provided.

FRENCH QUARTER B & B, 1132 Ursulines St, (504) 525-3390. B&B private apartment. Large rooms, fully furnished kitchen, sleeps 6, massage available. 1/2 blk from French Quarter, 1 blk from Armstrong Pk, walk to everything. Food left in fridge, cook-it-yourself.

FRENCH QUARTER RESERVATION SERVICE, 940 Royal St #263, New Orleans, LA 70116, (504) 523-1246, (800) 523-9091, Fax: (504) 527-6327, E-mail: fqrsinc@linknet.net. *Never a fee to you."* With one call, N'awlins' oldest and largest gay reservation service can book marvelous accommodation in the French Quarter. Experience the charm and culture of New Orleans, America's most fascinating city: bars that stay open all night, great cabarets, literary tours of the city, streetcar rides, Mississippi riverboat cruises...and delicious food! Call, fax, or e-mail for information.

FRENCHMEN HOTEL, 417 Frenchmen St, (504) 948-2166, (800) 831-1781. Hotel with rest. & bar. Dbl rooms & suites.

GREENHOUSE, THE, 1212 Magazine St, New Orleans, LA 70130, (504) 561-8400, (800) 966-1303, Fax: (504) 525-1306, E-mail: SFCF11A@Prodigy.com. Welcoming gay and lesbian visitors to enjoy our Southern hospitality. This New Orleans Tropical Guesthouse, built in 1840, is conveniently located in the historic Lower Garden District. Close to the French Quarter and the Convention Center. Amenities include king-sized beds, private baths, swimming pool & spa, daily cleaning, cont. break., limited shuttle service, and free off-street parking. Some straight clientele. See ad on page 438.

LAFITTE GUEST HOUSE, 1003 Bourbon St, (504) 581-2678 (tel/fax), (800) 331-7971. Guesthouse on Bourbon St, 50% gay & les-

---

Visit New Orleans
(800) CARITAS
Caritas B&B Network

NEW ORLEANS
FOR ACCOMMODATIONS
French Quarter Reservation Service

N'AWLINS OLDEST & LARGEST GAY
RESERVATION SERVICE

"NEVER A FEE TO YOU"

1-800-523-9091

504-523-1246 • Fax: 504-527-6327   Email: fqrsinc@linknet.net   **IGTA**

FERRARI GUIDES' GAY TRAVEL A to Z - 18th EDITION

LOUISIANA

UNITED STATES

LION'S INN, 2517 Chartres St, (504) 945-2339, fax (504) 949-7321. Men-only B&B in an 1840's Edwardian, 5 blocks from the French Quarter. Private baths. bian. Modern conveniences, Victorian parlor, continental breakfast, wine, hors d'oeuvres.

MACARTY PARK GUEST HOUSE, 3820 Burgundy St, (504) 943-4994, (800) 521-2790, Fax: (504) 943-4999, E-mail: faxmehard@aol.com. Web: www.cimarron.net/usa/la/rdmacarty.html. Relax, swim, party and play in a tropical paradise. Step out of your room and go for a splash in our refreshing heated pool. Enjoy beautiful rooms and cottages in a restored New Orleans Victorian mansion furnished in antiques, reproductions, and some contemporary rooms. Private baths, cable TV, phone, breakfast, complete gym with free weights & universal. A 5-minute getaway from the French Quarter. We also have a variety of accommodations throughout the city. Reasonable rates, free parking. Some straight clientele.

MAISON BURGUNDY B&B, 1860 Burgundy, New Orleans, LA 70116-1923, (504) 948-2355, (800) 863-8813, Fax: (504) 944-8578. B&B 2 blocks from the French Quarter, walk to gay bars & restaurants. All private entrances, private parking, continental breakfast.

MENTONE BED & BREAKFAST, 1437 Pauger St, (504) 943-3019. Private suite with private entrance within walking distance of major attractions. Some straight clientele. Expanded continental breakfast.

NEW ORLEANS GUEST HOUSE, 1118 Ursulines St, (504) 566-1177, reservations only: (800) 562-1177. Guesthouse, private baths, 50% gay & lesbian clientele.

NINE TWELVE PAULINE STREET, 912 Pauline St, New Orleans, LA (504) 948-6827, E-mail: bareskin@ix.netcom.net. B&B apartment in Bywater neighborhood, private baths, continental breakfast, self-catering kitchen, private entrance. Some straight clientele.

PARKVIEW, 726 Frenchmen St, (504) 945-7875. Guesthouse, 50% gay & lesbian clientele, private baths.

REINBOWE GUEST HOUSE, 2311-15 N Rampart St, (504) 949-5815, Fax: (504) 949-5917. Guesthouse with private & shared baths, some straight clientele.

ROBER HOUSE, 822 Ursulines St, (504) 529-4663, 523-1246. Fully-furnished condos in the French Quarter, minutes from attractions. Courtyard & pool, some straight clientele.

ROYAL BARRACKS GUEST HOUSE, 717 Barracks, (504) 529-7269, Fax: (504) 529-7298. Guesthouse, some straight clientele. Rooms with modern conveniences, private baths & private entrances. Jacuzzi on premises.

RUE ROYAL INN, 1006 Rue Royal, (504) 524-3900, Fax: (504) 558-0566. From economical courtyard units to large balcony suites with Jacuzzi & wet bar.

URSULINE GUESTHOUSE, 708 rue des Ursulines, (504) 525-8509, (800) 654-2351, Fax: (504) 525-8408. In the French Quarter between Bourbon and Royal Streets, some straight clientele. Private courtyard, newly-decorated rooms with private baths.

VIEUX CARRE RENTALS, 841 Bourbon St, (504) 525-3983, Fax: 283-7777. Gay-friendly luxury condos.

■ Women's Accommodations

BYWATER BED & BREAKFAST, 1026 Clouet St, (504) 944-8438. Staying in the Big Easy? Just a bit down river from the French Quarter is a Victorian cottage in the Bywater neighborhood, near music, clubs, restaurants of French Quarter and Fauberg Marigny. Tastefully decorated with contemporary and antique furniture, and southern folk art. Shared baths, 1 private available. Continental breakfast, use of kitchen, parlors, library, TV, VCR. VISA & MC accepted. Men welcome.

OVER C'S, 940 Elysian Fields Ave, (504) 943-7166 or (504) 945-9328 (after 5 except Mon). Invite friends for coffee on your own verandah. New Orleans comfort is yours in these bright, airy & comfortable 1-bedroom apartments with private baths, cable TV, private phones, microwave & fridge. **Conveniently located above Charlene's world-famous women's club.** Walk to French Quarter attractions, the aquarium and one of the world's largest gambling casinos. Call for reservations.

■ Bars

ANOTHER CORNER & BEARS & BOOTS, 2601 Royal at Franklin, (504) 945-7006. Bears & Boots is sm. leather bar upstairs.

BIG DADDY'S, 2513 Royal, (504) 948-6288. 75% men, 25% women, congenial family neighborhood crowd.

BOURBON PUB, ★ 801 Bourbon St at St Ann, (504) 529-2107. Video cruise bar, 24hrs.

BUCKAROO'S, 718 N Rampart St at Orleans, (504) 561-0064, 24hrs, C&W music, & occasional drag shows.

BUFFAS, 1001 Esplanade Ave, (504) 945-9373. Bar & restaurant, home cooking, 70% men.

BURGUNDY ST OUTBACK, 235 Burgundy St, (504) 525-9793.

CAFE 19, 625 St Phillip St, (504) 568-1631. Bar & restaurant, breakfast through dinner.

CAFE LAFITTE IN EXILE, ★ 901 Bourbon St at Dumaine, (504) 522-8397 or 561-9248. Upstairs & downstairs cruise bar, open 24 hours.

CHARLENE'S, 940 Elysian Fields Ave at Rampart, (504) 945-9328. World-famous women's nightclub plus Over C's apartments for women.

CORNER POCKET, THE, 940 St Louis, (504) 568-9829. Male dancers Thurs-Sun, open 24hrs.

COUNTRY CLUB, 634 Louisa St near Royal, (504) 945-0742. Two bars, hot tub, swimming & sunning.

DOUBLE PLAY, 439 Dauphine, (504) 523-4517. 60% men, 40% women.

FOOTLOOSE, 700 Rampart, (504) 523-2715, (504) 524-7654. 24hrs, 70% men, drag shows weekends.

FOUR SEASONS & THE OUTBACK BAR, 3229 N Causeway, Metairie, (504) 832-0659. Large patio bar, 80% men.

FRIENDLY BAR, 2301 Chartres St, (504) 943-8929. 50% men & 50% women.

FULL MOON, 424 Destrehan, in Harvey, (504) 341-4396. Wed-Sun from 7pm, small dance floor.

GOLDEN LANTERN, 1239 Royal St near Barracks, (504) 529-2860. Mature clientele, 24hrs.

The Greenhouse
A New Orleans Tropical Guest House
(800) 966-1303
NEW ORLEANS

NEW ORLEANS

HEATED POOL • CABLE TV
PHONE • PRIVATE BATHS
GYM • BREAKFAST

MACARTY PARK GUEST HOUSE
800-521-2790
www.cimarron.net/usa/la/rdmacarty.html

MAINE

GOOD FRIENDS BAR, 740 Dauphine St at St Ann, (504) 566-7191. Two floors.

MEN'S ROOM, 941 Elysian Fields Ave, above the Phoenix bar, (504) 945-9264.

MINT, 504 Esplanade, (504) 525-2000. Show bar, 50% men, 50% women.

MRB, 515 St Philip St near Decatur. (504) 523-7764. Patio, videos, male dancers.

OUTBACK, 1000 Bienville, (504) 525-9793.

PHOENIX, THE, 941 Elysian Fields Ave at Rampart, (504) 945-9264, 24hrs.

QUEEN'S HEAD PUB, 740 Dauphine St, (504) 566-7191. Above Good Friends Sun piano bar.

RAWHIDE,★ 740 Burgundy St at St Ann, (504) 525-8106, 24hrs, good music.

ROUNDUP, 819 St Louis St near Dauphine, (504) 561-8340, 24hrs. Many drag queens.

TT'S, 820 N Rampart St near Dumaine, (504) 523-9521. Crossdressers bar, male strippers, drag shows Sat.

Dance Bar/Disco

ANGLES, 2301 N Causeway, Metairie, (504) 834-7979. Dance bar & lounge.

ATTRAXXIONS, 1734 N Galvez, (504) 947-7788. Thurs-Sun, alt. drag shows Fri.

COPPER TOP, 706 Franklin, (504) 948-2300. Gay & straight crowd, microwavable food.

OZ, 800 Bourbon St, (504) 593-9491. Huge dance bar, 2 floors, young crowd, occasional male dancers, open 24hrs.

PARADE,★ 801 Bourbon St, at Bourbon Pub, upstairs, (504) 529-2107. Dance & video bar, women welcome.

RUBYFRUIT JUNGLE, 640 Frenchmen, (504) 947-4000. DJ, live entertainment, many women. The Boy Bar Fri, Hi energy dance & drag show Sat & Sun.

WOLFENDALE'S, 834 N Rampart St near Dumaine, (504) 524-5749. Drag show Sun.

X'IS LOUNGE, 1302 Allo St, in Marrero, (504) 430-0049. Patio, 60% men, 40% women.

Cafe

CAFE MARIGNY, 1913 Royale, (504) 945-4472. Coffees, pastries, bagels & bagel sandwiches, from 7am 7 days.

ULTIMATE COFFEE CAFE, 417 Bienville, (504) 524-7417.

Saunas/Health Clubs

CLUB NEW ORLEANS, 515 Toulouse St near Decatur, (504) 581-2402. Private club, 24hrs.

MIDTOWNE SPA, 700 Baronne St, (504) 566-1442, 24hrs, videos.

Restaurants

ALBERTO'S, 611 Frenchmen, (504) 949-5952. Italian Creole, gay-friendly.

BUFFAS, 1001 Esplanade Ave, at Buffas bar.

CAFE LAFITTE RESTAURANT, 717 Orleans St, inside Bourbon Orleans Hotel, (504) 571-4655.

CAFE SBISA, 1011 Decatur St, (504) 522-5565. Gay-friendly, nouvelle American cuisine.

CLOVER GRILL, 900 Bourbon St, (504) 523-0904. 50's-style diner.

COSIMO'S, 1201 Burgundy St, (504) 586-0444.

JALAPENOS, 2320 Veterans Blvd in Metairie, (504) 837-6675. Mexican & Caribbean cuisine.

LUCKY CHENG'S, 720 St Louis, (504) 529-2045.

MAMA ROSA'S SLICE OF ITALY, 616 N Rampart, (504) 523-5546. Italian cuisine, pizza specialties.

MONA LISA, 1212 Royal St, (504) 522-6746. Pizza restaurant.

PETUNIA'S,★ 817 St Louis St, (504) 522-6440. Cajun, Creole cuisine, large gay & lesbian following.

QUARTER MASTER DELI, 1100 Bourbon St, (504) 529-1416. The nellie deli, late-night specialties.

QUARTER SCENE, 900 Dumaine at Dauphine, (504) 522-6533, 24hrs, clo. Tues night.

SEBASTIAN'S LITTLE GARDEN, 538 St Philip, (504) 524-2041.

ST ANN'S CAFE & DELI, 800 Dauphine St at St Ann, (504) 529-4421. Creole, Cajun & southern home cookin'.

Retail & Bookstores

FAUBOURG MARIGNY BOOKS, 600 Frenchmen St at Chartres, (504) 943-9875. Gay & lesbian bookstore with gay newspapers, men's magazines, 7 days.

LIMBO, 1125 Decatur St, (504) 523-3435. Leather, latex, adult novelties, lingerie, wigs.

MOORE MAGIC, 1212 Royal. Feminist bookstore.

RAINBOW FRAMING & GIFTS, 3127 Metairie Rd, Metairie, (504) 834-3064. Rainbow items for gays & lesbians.

Leathers/Piercing

GARGOYLES, 1205 Decatur St, (504) 529-4387. Leathers.

SECOND SKIN LEATHER CO, 521 rue St Phillip, (504) 561-8167. Leatherwear, accessories, novelties, books, magazines.

Erotica

AIRLINE ADULT BOOKS, 1404 26th St in Kenner, (504) 468-2931. Videos.

CONXXXION, 107 Chartres St. 1-stop sexual supermarket.

PANDA BEAR, 415 Bourbon St, (504) 529-3593.

SHREVEPORT - BOSSIER

Information

GAY & LESBIAN CENTER OF NW LA, 252 Dalzell St, Shreveport, (318) 682-4332. 24hr tape or office (318) 226-0805.

HOMOSEXUAL INFO CENTER, 115 Monroe St, Bossier City, (318) 742-4709. G/L archive, referral service, 8am-5pm Mon-Fri.

Bars

KORNER LOUNGE, 800 Louisiana, Shreveport, (318) 222-9796. Juke box.

Dance Bar/Disco

CENTRAL STATION,★ 1025 Marshall St, Shreveport, (318) 222-2216. C&W & disco, male & female dancers, name entertainers, 60% men, 40% women.

MAINE

WHO TO CALL
For Tour Companies Serving This Destination
See Maine on page 19

STATEWIDE

Information

AIDS LINE, (800) 851-AIDS. Tue, Thur-Sat 9am-5pm, Mon & Wed 9am-7:30pm.

GAY & LESBIAN COMMUNITY CENTER, 398 N Main St, Caribou (207) 498-2088. Answers Mon, Wed, Fri. Open house Wed 7pm-9pm. Newsletter, lending library, events and speakers bureau.

AUGUSTA

Accommodations

MAPLE HILL FARM, Outlet Rd, RR1 Box 1145, Hallowell, 04347, (207) 622-2708, (800) 622-2708, Fax: (207) 622-0655. Gay-friendly B&B in a Victorian farmhouse on 62 acres 5 minutes from downtown Augusta. Private & shared baths, TV lounge, full breakfast, nearby skiing, hiking & antiquing. 1 rustic campsite.

Dance Bar/Disco

PJ'S, 80 Water St near Bridge, (207) 623-4041. Tues-Sat 7pm-1am. C&W dance Wed & piano bar nights Thurs & Fri, 50% men, 50% women.

Erotica

WATER STREET ADULT BOOKS, 31 Water Street, (207) 623-0068, 7 days.

BANGOR

Dance Bar/Disco

BAR, THE, 123 Franklin St, (207) 941-8966. Wed-Sun 6pm to close, Sun 2pm to close.

BAR HARBOR

Accommodations

DEVILSTONE OCEANFRONT INN, PO Box

FERRARI GUIDES' GAY TRAVEL A to Z - 18th EDITION

MAINE

801, Bar Harbor, ME 04609, (207) 288-2933. Oceanfront B&B in a mansion on the Shore Path overlooking Frenchman's Bay. All antique decor, private baths, continental breakfast, some straight clientele. ♀♂

LINDENWOOD INN, Box 1328 Clark Point Rd, Southwest Harbor, 04679, Gay-friendly B&B with harbor views & private access to the water. Recently remodeled rooms, private baths, sitting rooms with fireplaces, full breakfast.

MANOR HOUSE INN, 106 West St, (207) 288-3759, (800) 437-0088. Gay-friendly B&B. Variety of Victorian guest quarters, TV lounge, veranda, gardens, full breakfast. Nearby pools, beaches.

BATH

■ *Cafe*

TRUFFLES, 21 Elm St, (207) 442-8474. Gay-friendly, cozy cafe, Wed-Sat breakfast & lunch, Sun breakfast only. Freshly prepared food, vegetarian offerings. ♀♂

BELFAST

■ *Accommodations*

ALDEN HOUSE BED & BREAKFAST, THE, 63 Church St, Belfast, ME 04915., (207) 338-2151. Gay-owned & -operated B&B with full breakfast, 7 doubles with single, full & queen beds, private & shared baths. 50% gay & lesbian clientele.

BETHEL

■ *Accommodations*

SPECKLED MOUNTAIN RANCH, RR 2, Box 717, Bethel, ME 04217, (207) 836-2908. B&B with guided horseback riding, full breakfast, shared baths, living room, kitchen for guests, lake & river nearby, 50% gay/lesbian clientele.

BRISTOL MILLS

■ *Accommodations*

OLD CAPE OF BRISTOL MILLS B & B, PO Box 265 Rte 130, (207) 563-8848. Gay-friendly B&B, shared bath.

BRUNSWICK

■ *Retail & Bookstores*

GULF OF MAINE BOOKS, 134 Maine St, (207) 729-5083. General bookstore with gay & lesbian section.

CARIBOU

■ *Accommodations*

WESTMAN HOUSE, PO Box 1231, (207) 896-5726. B&B, shared bath. ♀♂

COREA - ACADIA AREA

■ *Accommodations*

BLACK DUCK INN ON COREA HARBOR, THE, PO Box 39, Crowley Island Rd, Corea, ME 04624, (207) 963-2689, fax: (207) 963-7495, e-mail: bduck@acadia.net. Gay-friendly B&B in a tranquil fishing village. Private & shared baths, full breakfast, TV lounge, meeting rooms, maid service. Gay & lesbian following.

DAMARISCOTTA MILLS

■ *Accommodations*

MILL POND INN, (207) 563-8014. Gay-friendly inn, private baths.

FARMINGDALE

■ *Erotica*

FIRST AMMENDMENT BOOKS, 173 Main Ave, (207) 582-6163.

HALLOWELL

■ *Restaurants*

SLATE'S RESTAURANT, 167 Water St, (207) 622-9575. Upscale restaurant with Sun brunch. Sun brunch is popular with local gays.

KENNEBUNK

■ *Accommodations*

ARUNDEL MEADOWS INN, PO Box 1129, 04043-1129, (207) 985-377. Gay-friendly B&B near beaches, antique shops, restaurants. Cozy rooms with comfortable sitting areas. Full breakfast with afternoon tea.

KITTERY

■ *Erotica*

VIDEO EXPO, Rte 236, 2 miles north of The Circle, (207) 439-6285. Mon-Thur 10am-10pm, Fri-Sat 11am-11pm, Sun noon-8pm.

LEWISTON

■ *Dance Bar/Disco*

SPORTSMAN'S ATHLETIC CLUB, 2 Bates St at High, (207) 784-2251. 8pm-1am, 7 days. ♀♂

LOVELL

■ *Accommodations*

STONEWALL BED & BREAKFAST, RR1 Box 26, Lovell, 04051, (207) 925-1080, (800) 413-1080. 2 rooms & 2 suites in a New England farmhouse with mountain views 15 miles from New Hampshire border. All private baths, full breakfast. Hiking, cross-country skiing, boatin area. ♀♂

MID-COAST MAINE

■ *Information*

MID-COAST MAINE GAY MEN'S HELPLINE, (207) 863-2728. Call 6pm-9pm EST Mon-Fri, also gay youth info. ♂

NAPLES

■ *Accommodations*

LAMB'S MILL INN, Box 676, Lamb's Mill Rd, (207) 693-6253. Gay-owned B&B in a 19th-century farmhouse with romantic atmosphere & country charm. All private baths, full breakfast, catered dinner available. MC, VISA. ♀♂

NORTHPORT

■ *Accommodations*

SIGN OF THE OWL B & B, 243 Atlantic Hwy, (207) 338-4669. B&B with an Oriental antique shop, some straight clientele. Double/triple rooms with shared baths, TV lounge, nearby ocean beach. Full gourmet breakfast. ♀♂

OCEAN PARK

■ *Women's Accommodations*

SEAFOREST WOMEN'S RETREAT, (207) 282-1352. Women-only B&B, shared bath. ♀

OGUNQUIT

■ *Accommodations*

ADMIRAL'S INN & GUESTHOUSE, #70 US Rt 1 (S Main), PO Box 2241, (207) 646-7093. B&B, mostly straight clientele.

BEAUPORT INN AND CAFE, PO Box 1793, 102 Shore Rd, (207) 646-8680, (800) 646-8681. Centrally-located B&B with gourmet cafe, 50% gay & lesbian. AC, private baths, TV lounge, expanded continental breakfast.

HERITAGE OF OGUNQUIT, THE, PO Box 1295, (207) 646-7787, E-mail: HeritageO@cyberTours.com. http://www.one-on-onepc.com/heritage. Ogunquit is the quicker, more beautiful alternative to P-Town! Located on a quiet street near the end of the famous Marginal Way, (fabulous floral footpath on the oceans edge) this new Victorian Reproduction features a hot tub, giant cedar deck, common room with refrigerator, microwave, VCR and TV, movies and wooded privacy. All this in a hypoallergenic, **smoke free** environment only a five-minute walk to beach, town and cove. Private and shared bath, expanded continental breakfast, ample parking. 99% women, and the only lesbian-owned place in town. Off season rates & specials. Year-round!! ♀

INN AT TWO VILLAGE SQUARE, THE, 135 US Rte 1, PO Box 864, (207) 646-5779. A spacious Victorian summer home perched on a hillside. **Panoramic ocean views from rooms and sun deck.** The Inn is only a five-minute walk to beaches, shops and restaurants. Refreshing heated pool and hot tub. ♀♂

LEISURE INN, 6 School St, PO Box 2113, (207) 646-2737, Fax: (207) 646-2471. B&B, cottages, apts, 50% straight clientele. Rooms uniquely decorated to reflect old New England charm. Walk to ocean beach, restaurants, shops. Continental breakfast.

MOON OVER MAINE, PO Box 1478, 6 Berwick Rd, Ogunquit, ME 03907, (207) 646-6666, (800) 851-6837. B&B with private baths, expanded continental breakfast, Jacuzzi, color cable TV, AC, near gay bars, some straight clientele. ♀♂

OGUNQUIT HOUSE, 7 King's Hwy, Box 1883, (207) 646-2967. B&B & cottages, 50% gay & lesbian. Variety of comfortable, spacious

MAINE

rooms, some kitchens, refrigerators, TV lounge. Continental breakfast & nearby ocean beach.

TALL CHIMNEYS, 94 Main St, PO Box 2286, 03907, (207) 646-8974. B&B. Rooms & apt with private & shared baths. ♀ ♂

YELLOW MONKEY GUEST HOUSE, 168 Main St, (207) 646-9056. Seasonal. ♀ ♂

■ Bars

FRONT PORCH, Ogunquit Square at Main and Shore, (207) 646-3976. Piano bar & restaurant.

■ Dance Bar/Disco

CLUB, THE, 13 Main St, (207) 646-6655. Dance bar with upstairs cruise bar, Sun T-dance 4pm. Male dancers, preppie crowd, patio. Open April-Oct from 9pm.

■ Cafe

CAFE AMORE, 5 Perkins Cove, (207) 646-6661. Coffee & lite fare & breakfast. Woman-owned, location of many women's gatherings, popular with local women.

PEMBROKE

■ Accommodations

YELLOW BIRCH FARM, RR 1, Box 248-A, (207) 726-5807. B&B or weekly cottage rental on a woman-owned working farm. Fully-furnished two-room cottage, kitchen, outdoor hot shower, private outhouse, expanded continental breakfast. ♀ ♂

PORTLAND

■ Accommodations

ANDREWS LODGING BED & BREAKFAST, 417 Auburn St, Portland, ME 04103, (207) 797-9157, Fax: (207) 797-9040, E-mail: 74232.116@compuserve.com. A 250-year-old colonial house filled with antiques and traditional furnishings, featuring modern baths (1 with whirlpool), library, solarium, and kitchen. Continental breakfast is served on silver & china in the formal dining room. Five minutes from downtown Portland, museums, the historic Old Port, the waterfront, and the best dining in New England. Many outdoor activities, from badminton to fishing, are available. Gay-friendly.

■ Bars

BLACKSTONES, 6 Pine Street, (207) 775-2885. Fri buffet, 85% men. The CHEERS of the north. ♂

COSMOS, 117 Spring St at High. Video bar, 70% men. ♂

SISTERS, 45 Danforth St, (207) 774-1505. Game room, outdoor patio, Wed-Sun from 4pm. ♀

■ Dance Bar/Disco

UNDERGROUND, 3 Spring St, (207) 773-3315. Hi-energy dance bar, DJ Wed-Sat, male & female strippers. ♀ ♂

■ Cafe

GREEN MOUNTAIN COFFE ROASTERS, 15 Temple St, (207) 773-4475.

■ Restaurants

CAFE ALWAYS, 47 Middle St near India, (207) 774-9399. Modern American cuisine.

KATAHDIN, 106 High St, (207) 774-1740. Meat & potato menu, blue plate specials. 5pm-10pm (Fri & Sat till 11pm), closed Sun. Large gay following.

WALTERS CAFÉ, 15 Exchange St, (207) 871-9258. Regional American cuisine, open grill, exhibition-style kitchen.

WESTSIDE, 58 Pine St, (207) 773-8223. Specializing in fresh fish, from 5:30pm, closed Sun.

WOODFORDS CAFE, 129 Spring St, (207) 772-1374. Breakfast anytime, 11am-11pm. Best pies in Portland.

■ Retail & Bookstores

BOOKS ETC, 38 Exchange St, (207) 774-0626. General bookstore with a gay & lesbian selection.

CONDOM SENSE, 424 Fore St, (207) 871-0356.

DROP ME A LINE, 611 Congress St, (207) 773-5547. Progressive cards, gifts & wrap. 10am-8pm daily, Sun noon-5pm.

■ Erotica

FINE ART & THEATER II, 600 block of Congress St,

TREASURE CHEST I, 2-A Pine Street, (207) 772-2225.

VIDEO EXPO, 666 Congress St, (207) 774-1377.

SEBAGO LAKE REGION

■ Accommodations

MAINE-LY FOR YOU AT BEAR MOUNTAIN VILLAGE, RR2 Box 745, Waterford, ME 04088, (207) 583-6980. Cottages and campsites along 1800 feet of waterfront with dock and swimming float and women-only section. Climbing, ice caves, canoeing, hiking, water sports. Gay & lesbian clientele with some straights. Maine-ly for You Spring Fling and Autumn Fest women's events are for women only. ♀ ♂

STONINGTON

■ Women's Accommodations

SEA GNOMES HOME, PO Box 33, (207) 367-5076. Women-only guesthouse. Shared bath, common room, nearby ocean beach. ♀

TENANTS HARBOR

■ Accommodations

EAST WIND INN, PO Box 149, (207) 372-6366, (800) 241-VIEW. Gay-friendly B&B with restaurant & bar, private & shared baths, continental breakfast, , AC, TV lounge, mostly straight clientele.

WATERVILLE

■ Erotica

PRISCILLA'S, 18 Water Street, (207) 873-2774.

TREASURE CHEST II, 5 Sanger Ave, (207) 873-7411.

THE HERITAGE OF OGUNQUIT

"Beautiful-Place-by-the-Sea"

- 5 min. Walk to Beach
- Hot Tub. Cedar Deck
- Non-Smoking
- Private/Shared Bath
- Lesbian Owned

(207) 646-7787

PO BOX 1295
OGUNQUIT, ME 03907

www.one-on-onepc.com/heritage

email:
heritageo@cybertours.com

FERRARI GUIDES' GAY TRAVEL A to Z - 18th EDITION

MARYLAND

MARYLAND

WHO TO CALL
For Tour Companies Serving This Destination
See Maryland on page 19

ANNAPOLIS

Accommodations
TWO-ZERO-ONE, 201 Prince George St, (410) 268-8053. Gay-friendly B&B, private & shared baths, full breakfast.
WILLIAM PAGE INN, 8 Martin St, (410) 626-1506, (800) 364-4160 x34, Fax: (410) 263-4841. Gay-friendly Victorian B&B. Double rooms, 1 suite with color TV & Jacuzzi, private & shared baths.

Erotica
TWENTY/TWENTY BOOKS, 2020 West St, (410) 266-0514.

BALTIMORE

Information
AIDS INFO, (410) 837-2050.
GAY & LESBIAN CENTER OF BALTIMORE, 241 W Chase, (410) 837-5445. Meeting rooms, information.
GAY & LESBIAN SWITCHBOARD, (410) 837-8888, 837-8889, 7-10pm, 24hr tape.

Accommodations
ABACROMBIE BADGER B&B, 58 W Biddle St, (410) 244-7227, Fax: (410) 244-8415. B&B, 50% gay & 50% straight clientele. Rooms with private baths, expanded continental breakfast, AC, color cable TV, phone.
BILTMORE SUITES HOTEL, THE, 205 W Madison St, (410) 728-6550, (800) 686-5064. Urban inn, 50% gay & lesbian clientele. Private baths, expanded continental breakfast.
CHEZ CLAIRE, 17 W Chase St, (410) 685-4666, 837-0996. B&B with card shop, some straight clientele. ♀ ♂
MR. MOLE BED & BREAKFAST, 1601 Bolton St, (410) 728-1179, Fax: (410) 728-3379. 1870 Baltimore row house, 2 suites, Dutch breakfast. Mostly straight clientele with a gay & lesbian following.

Bars
BALTIMORE EAGLE, 2022 N Charles St, (410) 82-EAGLE.
CENTRAL STATION,★ 1001 N Charles St, (410) 752-7133. Upscale bar & restaurant, continental cuisine, 75% men, 25% women.
CLUB BUNS, 606 W Lexington, (410) 234-2866.

COCONUTS, 331 W Madison near Howard. ♀
DRINKERY, THE, 203 W Read St at Park, (410) 669-9820. CD jukebox.
EAGER STREET SALOON, at Hippo bar location, 1 W Eager St, (410) 547-0069. Bar adjacent to Hippo video dance bar, 80% men, 20% women. Fri women's night. ♂
GALLERY, 1735 Maryland Ave at Lafayette, (410) 539-6965. Bar & restaurant. Especially popular Sun evening. Dancing Fri, Sat & Sun.
HEPBURN'S, 504 S Haven St, (410) 276-9310. ♀
LEON'S, 870 Park Ave at Tyson, (410) 539-4993. Bar and restaurant, women welcome. Lunch, dinner & Sun brunch.
RANDY'S SPORTSMAN BAR, 412 Park Ave, (410) 727-8935.
UNICORN, 2218 Boston St at Patterson, (410) 342-8344.

Dance Bar/Disco
ALLEGRO,★ 1101 Cathedral St, (410) 837-3906. High-energy dance bar. Tues men's night, Thurs ladies' night. ♂
CLUB 1722, 1722 Charles St. After hours, open 1:45am.
CLUB ATLANTIS, 615 Fallsway, (410) 727-9099. Male dancers.
HIPPO,★ 1 W Eager St at Charles, (410) 547-0069. Hi-energy dance & video bar, 80% men, 20% women.
PORT IN A STORM, 4330 E Lombard at Kresson, (410) 732-5608. ♀
STAGECOACH,★ 1003 N Charles St, (410) 547-0107. C&W dance bar. ♀ ♂

Cafe
CITY CAFE, 1001 Cathedral St across from Hippo dance bar. Cafe with extensive menu, coffee, sandwiches, soups, desserts.

Restaurants
CENTRAL STATION RESTAURANT, at Central Station bar. ♀ ♂
CITY DINER, 911 N Charles St. Restaurant & bar, 24hrs 7 days.
GAMPY'S, 904 N Charles at Read, (410) 837-9797. Variety menu, lunch, dinner, late evening.
HENRY & JEFF'S, 1218 N Charles, (410) 727-3322. Deli.
MT VERNON STABLE, 909 Charles St. Varied menu, specialty is ribs.
STAGECOACH RESTAURANT, at Stagecoach bar. ♀ ♂
STUDIO, THE,★ 1735 Maryland Ave, at Gallery bar, (410) 539-6965. Steaks & seafood, dinner only. Closed Sun. ♀ ♂

Retail & Bookstores
LAMBDA RISING BOOKS, 241 W Chase (at Gay Center), (410) 234-0069. Gay & lesbian bookstore, 10am-10pm 7 days.

Leathers/Piercing
LEATHER STORE AT THE EAGLE, 2022 N Charles St (side entrance) at 21st & Morton, (410) 82-EAGLE. Leather goods, piercing, from 7pm.
LEATHER UNDERGROUND, 136 W Read St at Park, (410) 528-0991. Custom leather, piercings, videos, magazines, toys. Closed Sun.

Erotica
BIG TOP, 429 E Baltimore St at Gay, (410) 547-2495, Closed 4am-7am.
BROADWAY NEWS, 301 S Broadway, (410) 342-9590.
CENTER NEWS, 205 W Fayette St near Park, (410) 727-9544. 6am-10pm.
LE SALON, 18 Custom House Ave (410) 347-7555. Theater, videos, peek shows.

CUMBERLAND

Accommodations
RED LAMP POST, 849 Braddock Rd, (301) 777-3262. B&B, some straight clientele. Double rooms with shared baths, TV lounge with fireplaces, weights, nearby lake. Full breakfast, dinner for extra charge. ♀ ♂

DEALE

Women's Accommodations
CREEKSIDE B&B, 6036 Parkers Creek Drive, Deale, MD 20751, (301) 261-9438, Fax: (410) 867-1253, E-mail: mburt@ui.urban.org. Located on the Chesapeake near Annapolis and Washington, DC, we offer 2 rooms with private bath, pool, deck, pier, canoe, porch swing, hot tub, library and fireplace, old & new oak decor, and a large folk art collection. Full breakfast. "A sumptuous art-lover's, book-lover's, cat-lover's feast, 40 minutes from DC." ♀

HAGERSTOWN

Dance Bar/Disco
HEADQUARTERS, 41 North Potomac, (301) 797-1553. Daily, dancing Wed-Sun, 5pm-2am, Sun till midnight. ♀ ♂

HYATTSVILLE

Erotica
SILVER NEWS, 2488 Chillium Rd, (301) 779-1024.

SAINT MICHAELS

Women's Accommodations
LAVENDER HOUSE, PO Box 13, Claiborne, MD 21624, (410) 745-3422. Women-only B&B, shared baths, full breakfast, AC, TV lounge, video tape library, CD, books, maid & laundry service, pool on premises, beach across the street. ♀

MASSACHUSETTS

MASSACHUSETTS

WHO TO CALL

For Tour Companies Serving This Destination
See Massachusetts on page 19

STATEWIDE

■ *Information*

AIDS HOTLINE, (800) 235-2331. Youth hotline, Mass only: (800) 788-1234.

AMHERST

■ *Information*

EVERYWOMAN'S CENTER, U of Mass, Wilder Hall, (413) 545-0883. Mon, Tues, Thurs, Fri 9am-4pm. Wed noon-4pm.

U-MASS AREA WOMEN'S CENTERS, call Everywomen's Center, (413) 545-0883, for Mt Holyoke, Smith, Amherst, Hampshire.

■ *Accommodations*

IVY HOUSE B&B, 1 Sunset Court, (413) 549-7554, Fax: (413) 549-1238. B&B, 50% gay & lesbian clientele. Shared baths, full breakfast.

■ *Beaches*

CUMMINGTON BEACH, on the river 1/2 hour NW of Amherst, mostly gay.

■ *Retail & Bookstores*

FOOD FOR THOUGHT, 106 N Pleasant St, (413) 253-5432. Progressive bookstore with feminist books & music & gay men's section.

BARRE

■ *Accommodations*

JENKINS INN & RESTAURANT, THE, 7 West St, Rte 122, (508) 355-6444, (800) 378-7373. Gay-friendly B&B inn (30% gay/lesbian following), private & shared baths.

BOSTON

■ *Information*

AIDS HOTLINE, (617) 536-7733, (800) 235-2331, Youth line (800) 788-1234, TTY (617) 437-1672.

DAUGHTERS OF BILITIS, 1151 Massachusetts Ave, Harvard, Cambridge at the Old Cambridge Baptist Church, (617) 661-3633. Discussion groups weekly.

GAY & LESBIAN INFO, (617) 267-9001 (TTY & voice). Mon-Fri 4-11pm, Sat 6-8:30pm, Sun 6-11pm (irregularly staffed).

WOMEN'S CENTER, 46 Pleasant St, in Cambridge, (617) 354-8807. 10am-10pm Mon-Thurs, till 8pm Fri, 11am-9pm Sat.

■ *Accommodations*

AMSTERDAMMERTJE, PO Box 865, Boston, 02103, (617) 471-8454 (tel/fax). B&B, approx. 20-min. drive from downtown Boston, private & shared baths, color cable TV, VCR in living room, full breakfast, some straight clientele. ♀♂

CARITAS BED & BREAKFAST NETWORK, (800) CARITAS, (312) 857-0801, Fax: (312) 857-0805. B&B, home-stay accommodations service. *Member: IGTA*

CHANDLER INN, 26 Chandler St, (617) 482-3450, toll-free in USA, (800) 842-3450. Gay-friendly in-town B&B hotel in the heart of the city with a large gay & lesbian following. Walking distance to shopping, restaurants, Amtrak, bus stations and most major attractions. **One of Boston's most popular gay bars is just off the lobby.** Contemporary rooms with private baths. Continental breakfast included.

CLARENDON SQUARE B&B, THE, 81 Warren Ave, (617) 536-2229. B&B with 3 rooms, private baths, continental breakfast, 50% gay & lesbian clientele.

FOUR-SIXTY-THREE BEACON STREET GUEST HOUSE, 463 Beacon St, (617) 536-1302, Fax: (617) 247-8876. Guesthouse offering **gracious lodging in an elegant, renovated, turn-of-the century Back Bay brownstone** near Prudential/Hynes Convention Center, colleges, shopping, restaurants & nightlife. Fully-equipped kitchenettes, private baths, cable TV, AC, direct-dial telephone, electronic voice messaging service. 50% gay & lesbian clientele.

OASIS GUEST HOUSE, 22 Edgerly Rd, (617) 267-2262, Fax: (617) 267-1920, Web: www.oasisgh.com. Guesthouse with excellent Back Bay location, some straight clientele. We offer the opportunity to stay in the heart of the city and still feel at home. Our lobby, living room, outdoor decks, and accommodations are handsomely appointed with comfortable furnishings which blend with modern conveniences such as color TV, AC, and a computerized phone system. In addition to a continental breakfast, we provide evening cocktail set-ups and hors d'oeuvres in the main living room. Come experience the rewards of staying in an atmosphere that caters to your lifestyle and your budget. ♀♂

■ *Women's Accommodations*

IRIS BED & BREAKFAST, PO Box 4188, Dedham 02026, (617) 329-3514. Women-only B&B 20 minutes from downtown Boston. Non-smoking, double room with shared bath, continental breakfast. ♀

VICTORIAN BED & BREAKFAST, (617) 536-3285. Women-only B&B. Elegant & comfortable guest quarters, TV, full breakfast, soft drinks. ♀

■ *Bars*

BOSTON EAGLE, 520 Tremont St, (617) 542-4494.

BOSTON RAMROD,★ 1254 Boylston St near Park Drive, (617) 266-2986. C&W Tues, Thurs Sweat dress code dance (no shirt or wear leather), Sun buffet 8pm, Man Dance Sun after buffet. 3rd Thurs Bear meeting 7pm.

CLUB CAFE,★ 209 Columbus Ave above Metropolitan Health Club, (617) 536-0972. Three bars: Club Cafe bar in front with live piano, Moonshine cabaret becomes video bar after 9pm, Satellite Lounge has videos; Club Cafe restaurant lunch & dinner & Sun brunch 11am-3pm.

FRITZ,★ 26 Chandler St at Chandler Inn, (617) 482-4428. Sat & Sun brunch, 80% men, 20% women.

J.O.X. at the Luxor Complex, 69 Church St, (617) 423-6969. Sports bar, appetizer menu, daily from 5pm.

JACQUES, 79 Broadway St near Piedmont, (617) 426-8902. Drag bar.

LUXOR,★ 69 Church St above Mario's restaurant, (617) 423-6969. Complex with Luxor video bar, Jox sports bar & Mario's Restaurant. Luxor daily from 4pm.

ONE NINETEEN MERRIMAC, 119 Merrimac St near Staniford, (617) 367-0713.

■ *Dance Bar/Disco*

AVALON & AXIS,★ 15 Landsdowne St near Ipswich. Huge progressive alternative discos, popular Sun gay night.

BUZZ, 67 Stuart St, (617) 267-8969. Gay Sat only from 10pm.

CAMPUS AT MANRAY, 21 Brookline Ave, Cambridge, (617) 864-0400. Thurs-Sun, Sat

---

Visit Boston
(800) CARITAS
Caritas B&B Network

OASIS GUEST HOUSE
BOSTON

- Excellent Back Bay Location
- Walk to Historic Sites, Night Life, Restaurants, & Museums
- AC, TV, Tel., Continental Breakfast

22 Edgerly Rd., Boston, MA 02115
(617) 267-2262
Fax: (617) 267-1920
WWW.OASISGH.COM

UNITED STATES

FERRARI GUIDES' GAY TRAVEL A to Z - 18th EDITION

MASSACHUSETTS

& Sun are women's nite women's night. ♀♂

CHAPS, 27-31 Huntington near Dartmouth, (617) 266-7778. Annual Pride Fest block party with name entertainment.

FUSION, 212 Hampshire St, Inman Square, Cambridge, (617) 876-9330. Sun tea dance Jazz Club 5pm at Ryles. ♀

GIRL BAR 965 Massachusetts Ave, at Jungle / Coco's. Fri women's dance night upstairs in the Jungle, video bar downstairs. ♀

JOY BOY, ★ 533 Washington St, (617) 338-6999. Gay Fri only. ♂

NAPOLEON CLUB, 52 Piedmont St near Arlington, (617) 338-7547. Piano lounge daily, upstairs dance bar Fri-Sun. ♂

PARADISE, 180 Massachusetts Ave, Cambridge, (617) 864-4130. DJ nightly, upstairs pub, downstairs dance bar. Mon Latino night, Wed male strippers, other nights house music. ♂

SPOT, THE, 1270 Boylston St, (617) 424-7747. Gay dance parties Mon & Fri. ♂

■ Restaurants

BLUE WAVE, 142 Berkeley St, (617) 424-6711. California cuisine, Sun brunch. Gay-friendly.

BOTOLPH'S ON TREMONT, 569 Tremont St, (617) 424-8577. Trendy gay-friendly restaurant with nouveau Italian cuisine, beer, wine & cordials.

CLUB CAFE, 209 Columbus Ave, (617) 536-0966. Dinner with live piano & Sun brunch. Three bars feature cabaret, videos, movies. ♀

ICARUS, 3 Appleton St, South End, (617) 426-1790. Restaurant and bar, contemporary American cuisine. Jazz Fri.

JAE'S CAFE & GRILL, 520 Columbus Ave, (617) 421-9405. All-natural food with Korean accent, Thai & Sushi.

MARIO'S, 69 Church St below the Luxor bar at Luxor complex, (413) 542-3776. Italian restaurant & lounge. ♀♂

TWO TWENTY-FOUR BOSTON STREET, 224 Boston St, Dorchester, (617) 265-1217. New American cuisine, live jazz Fri, Sat.

■ Retail & Bookstores

ARSENIC & OLD LACE, 318 Harvard St #10, Brookline, (617) 734-2455. Occult store, Mon-Wed 11am-7pm, Thurs-Fri 11am-9pm, Sun noon-6pm.

GLAD DAY BOOK SHOP, 673 Boylston Street (2nd floor) near Copley Square, (617) 267-3010. Gay & lesbian bookstore.

NEW WORDS BOOKSTORE, 186 Hampshire St, Cambridge, (617) 876-5310, E-mail: newwords@world.std.com. One of the country's oldest & largest women's bookstores, offers a full, exciting selection of books by & about women, from the latest feminist bestsellers to hard-to-find small press lesbian titles. We also carry journals, music, cards, bumperstickers & jewelry, & offer community space for readings, info & browsing. Mail order services available.

WE THINK THE WORLD OF YOU, 540 Tremont St, (617) 423-1968, Fax: (617) 350-0083. Gay & lesbian bookstore.

■ Leathers/Piercing

HUBBA HUBBA, 932 Massachusetts Ave, Cambridge, (617) 492-9082.

RAMROD LEATHER SHOP, inside Boston Ramrod. Custom leather plus rubber items.

■ Erotica

ART I & II CINEMAS, 204 Tremont St at Boylston, (617) 482-4661. all-male films.

EROS BOUTIQUE, approx. 500 block of Tremont St.

GRAND OPENING, 318 Harvard St #32, Arcade Bldg, Coolidge Corner, Brookline, (617) 731-2626. Sexuality boutique especially for women.

MARQUIS DE SADE EMPORIUM, 73 Berkley St, (617) 426-2120. Videos, novelties, adult leather accessories.

VIDEO EXPO, 1258 Boylston St, (617) 859-8911. Second location: 628 Washington St, 357-8622. Gay magazines.

GREENFIELD

■ Accommodations

BRANDT HOUSE, THE, 29 Highland Ave, (800) 235-3329, (413) 774-3329, Fax: (413) 772-2908. Gay-friendly B&B in elegant Revival mansion at the foot of the Berkshires. Color cable TV, AC, ceiling fans, private baths. TV lounge, expanded continental or full breakfast.

HAVERHILL

■ Dance Bar/Disco

FRIENDS LANDING AT WATER'S EDGE, 85 Water St, (508) 374-9400. Many rooms, dance bar, karaoke bar, shows, free buffet nitely. Boatslip with space for 35 boats on Merrimac River. ♀♂

■ Retail & Bookstores

RADZUKINA'S, 714 N Broadway, (508) 521-1333. Women's gifts, cards, books, music, jewelry, crystals & stones.

HYANNIS

■ Dance Bar/Disco

DUVAL STREET STATION, 477 Yarmouth Rd, (508) 775-9835, 771-7511. Bar & Mallory Dock restaurant, lounge. Disco Thu-Sun, oldies Sun. ♀ ♂

LENOX

■ Accommodations

SUMMER HILL FARM, 950 East St, (413) 442-2057, (800) 442-2059. B&B in 200-year-old farmhouse on a 20-acre horse farm. Mainly straight, gay friendly. Country location, but near Tanglewood, restaurants and many other attractions. 6 rooms private baths, 2 with fireplaces, many antiques. Full home-cooked breakfast. Also a spacious 1-bedroom cottage in a converted barn. Lots of outdoor activities and winter sports. ♿

WALKER HOUSE, 64 Walker St, (413) 637-1271, (800) 235-3098, fax: (413) 637-2387. Gay-friendly B&B in 1804 historic building. Guest rooms with antique furnishings, private baths.

LYNN

■ Bars

JOSEPH'S, 191 Oxford St, (617) 599-9483. Viedo bar, DJ nitely, 70% men, 30% women. ♂

■ Dance Bar/Disco

FRAN'S, 776 Washington Street, (617) 598-5618. Disco, Tues karaoke, Thurs show night. ♀

MARTHA'S VINEYARD

■ Accommodations

CAPTAIN DEXTER HOUSE OF EDGARTOWN, 35 Pease Point Way, PO Box 2798, (508) 627-7289, fax: (508) 627-3328. Seasonal B&B near the harbor, ocean beach, shops & restaurants. Mainly straight clientele. Double rooms furnished with antiques, expanded continental breakfast.

MARTHA'S PLACE, 114 Main St, PO Box 1182, Vineyard Haven, MA 02658, (508) 693-0253. This stately Greek Revival overlooks Vineyard Haven Harbor, 2 blocks from village shops, restaurants and the beach. Rooms boast harbor views and are decorated with antiques, oriental carpets and crystal chandeliers. Amenities include private baths, bathrobes, Egyptian cotton linens, fireplaces and Jacuzzi. Breakfast in bed is available. Gay-owned & -operated with 50% gay/lesbian clientele and is working toward exclusively gay/lesbian clientele.

MARTHA'S PLACE
Come pamper yourself in Style!
(508) 693-0253
MARTHA'S VINEYARD

MASSACHUSETTS

NEW BEDFORD

■ Bars
PUZZLES LOUNGE, 428 N Front St, (508) 991-2306. DJ Wed-Sun, karaoke Wed, 50% men, 50% women. 🎵♀♂

■ Dance Bar/Disco
LE PLACE, 20 Kenyon St, (508) 992-8156. DJ Fri-Sun. 🎵♀♂

NORTHAMPTON

■ Information
NEW ALEXANDRIA LESBIAN LIBRARY, (413) 584-7616. National archives of lesbian herstory, appointment only.

■ Accommodations
INNAMORATA, PO Box 113, Goshen, 01032-0133, (413) 268-0300. B&B, men welcome. Shared baths, expanded continental breakfast & pool. ♀

■ Women's Accommodations
APPLE VALLEY B&B, 1180 Hawley Rd, Ashfield, MA (413) 625-6758. A women-owned Victorian paradise near Northampton, amid rolling acres of apple orchards with mountain views. The grounds are idyllic with a goldfish pond, a babbling brook and grazing cows. Each comfortable room has a cozy sitting area, the elegance of lace and the warmth of antique oak furniture. Local activities include hiking, golf, skiing, interesting restaurants and shopping. Shared bath, full breakfast, men welcome. ♀

LITTLE RIVER FARM, 967 Huntington Rd, Worthington, (413) 238-4261. Women-only, 3-room B&B in a 150-year-old farmhouse on 41 acres in the beautiful Berkshire hills. Comfortable rooms with fresh flowers, private baths. Full breakfast including homebaked breads and farm fresh eggs. Peaceful retreat in a country setting with farm animals. 1/2 hour from Northampton, Jacob's Pillow, Tanglewood and Stockbridge. ♀

OLD RED SCHOOLHOUSE, 67 Park St, (413) 584-1228. Women-only apartment with country & art deco decor. 2-bedroom, equipped kitchen, linens, etc. ♀

TIN ROOF BED & BREAKFAST, PO Box 296 Hadley, (413) 586-8665. Women's space B&B, lesbian-friendly men welcome. Comfortable double rooms with shared bath, TV in living room, porch swing, garden, expanded continental breakfast. ♀

■ Bars
PEARL STEET DISCOTHEQUE, 10 Pearl St, a very short street in downtown Northampton, (413) 584-7771. Gay Wed only. 🎵♀♂

■ Dance Bar/Disco
CLUB METRO, 492 Pleasant St, (413) 582-9898. Wed gay night.

GROTTO, 25 West St at Rt 66 & Green St, (413) 586-6900. Bar, dance club. 🎵🎵♀♂

■ Retail & Bookstores
PRIDE & JOY 20 Crafts Ave, (413) 585-0683, 584-4848. Gay & lesbian gift store with cards, original art, books, posters and more.

THIRD WAVE FEMINIST BOOKSTORE, 90 King St, (413) 586-7851, TTY/TDD. Feminist & lesbian books, music, cards, gifts. Local info, closed Mon in winter.

NORTON

■ Accommodations
DOWN BY THE BLACKSMITH SHOP BED & BREAKFAST, 102 Crane St, (508) 285-9849. B&B, 50% gay/lesbian clientele. ♀♂

PITTSFIELD

■ Information
WOMEN'S SERVICES CENTER, (413) 499-2425. Mon-Fri 9am-4pm.

PROVINCETOWN

■ Information
HELPING OUR WOMEN, 336 Commercial St, Unit 9, (508) 487-HELP (4357). Women's well-being resource center, Mon-Fri 11am-5pm. Free medical referrals.

■ Tours, Charters & Excursions
SAND FACES, Provincetown dune hikes for women, Apr 1-Oct 31. A service of The Little Inn, 31 Pearl St, (508) 487-2407.

■ Accommodations
A TALL SHIP, 452 Commercial St, (508) 487-2247, 877-5442. Beach house, some straight clientele. Rooms & apartments, private & shared baths. ♀♂

AMPERSAND GUESTHOUSE, 6 Cottage St, PO Box 832, (508) 487-0959. Guesthouse near town center, women welcome. Uniquely decorated doubles, suites, studio apartment. TV lounge with gaming table, continental breakfast, nearby ocean beaches. ♂

ANCHOR INN, 175 Commercial St, (508) 487-0432, (800) 858-2657. Inn with private bath. ♀♂

BEACONLITE GUEST HOUSE, 12 & 16 Winthrop St, (508) 487-9603 (Tel/Fax), (800) 696-9603. Call #16 Winthrop St. at (508) 487-4605 (Tel/Fax), (800) 422-4605. Guesthouse, mainly men in season. Home-like atmosphere with ever-changing decor, close to shopping, ocean beach. Gourmet continental breakfast. ♀♂

BENCHMARK INN, 6 & 8 Dyer St, Provincetown, MA 02657, (508) 487-7440, (888) 487-7440, Fax: (508) 487-7442. The Best is for You. Benchmark Inn, debuting in April 1997, promises top-notch comfort and style. Six bedrooms and penthouse suite offer a variety of luxuries including fireplaces, whirlpool baths, wet bars, private balconied entrances, stunning harborviews and a long list of deluxe amenities. ♀♂

BOATSLIP BEACH CLUB, 161 Commercial St, Box 393, (800) 451-SLIP (7547), (508) 487-1669, Fax: 487-6021. Hotel with restaurant, bar & disco. Rooms have contemporary decor & color TV. Massage available. Aerobics, sun cots & morning coffee. ♀♂

BRADFORD & SHAMROCK MOTELS, 49 Bradford St, (508) 487-1133. Motel, cottages & apartments, 50% gay/lesbian.

BRADFORD CARVER HOUSE, THE, 70 Bradford St, Provincetown, MA 02657, (508) 487-4966, (800) 826-9083, Fax: (508) 487-4966. Guesthouse with private & shared baths, expanded continental breakfast, color cable TV, AC, nearby pool, ocean & bar. Mostly men with women welcome. ♂

BRASS KEY GUESTHOUSE, THE 9 Court St, (508) 487-9005, (800) 842-9858, Fax: (508) 487-9020. Handsomely restored sea captain's house in heart of town. Women welcome. Luxury accommodations feature private bath, AC, color TV/VCR, telephone, refrigerator; some offer fireplace, king bed, whirlpool bath. Heated dip pool, enclosed sun decks, wood-burning fireplace. Open year-round. ♂

BUOY, THE, 97 Bradford St, (508) 487-3082, (800) 648-0364, Fax: (508) 487-4887. Centrally-located guesthouse, private & shared baths, continental breakfast. ♀♂

BURCH HOUSE, 116 Bradford St, (508) 487-9170. Inn, private & shared baths, continental breakfast. ♀♂

CAPE VIEW MOTEL, Rte 6, PO Box 114, North Truro, 02652, (800) 224-3232, (508) 487-0363. Hotel with fantastic views, 50% gay & lesbian clientele. Rooms & efficiencies, private baths, color cable TV, AC & pool.

CAPTAIN & HIS SHIP, 164 Commercial St, (508) 487-1850, (800) 400-CAPT. B&B, private & shared baths. ♀♂

CAPTAIN'S HOUSE, 350-A Commercial St, (508) 487-9353. Guesthouse, women welcome, continental breakfast. ♂

CARL'S GUEST HOUSE, 68 Bradford St, (508) 487-1650 or (800) 348-CARL (recorded rate/

The COMMONS

Private Balconies with Harbor & Town Views

(800) 487-0784

(508) 487-7800
Provincetown

FERRARI GUIDES' GAY TRAVEL A to Z - 18th EDITION

MASSACHUSETTS

brochure). E-mail: carlptwn@tiac.net or: http://www.tiac.net/users/carlptwn. Where strangers become friends, for **GENTLE**men of all ages. Clean, comfortable, affordable, private and shared baths, excellent location, clothing-optional sundeck. For comfort assurance, please reserve with us personally at (508) 487-1650. 🚬♂

CHICAGO HOUSE, THE, 6 Winslow St, (508) 487-0537, (800) SEE-PTOWN (733-7869), Fax: (508) 487-6212. E-mail: mongooseiv@aol.com. Guesthouse with rooms & apartments, continental breakfast, private & shared baths. ♀ ♂

COAT OF ARMS, 7 Johnson St, (508) 487-0816, (800) 224-8230. Centrally-located guesthouse, women welcome. 🍽♂

COMMONS, THE, 386 Commercial St, (508) 487-7800, (800) 487-0784. Spacious light-filled rooms, a private garden, a gourmet Bistro, and a friendly bar are just some of the features. The inn received the 1995 Best Restoration Award from the Provincetown Historical Commission. Conveniently located between downtown and the Gallery District. Our breathtaking view of Provincetown Harbor and Cape Cod Bay will make you fall in love with us. Some straight clientele. See ad on page 445. ♀♂

CROWN & ANCHOR, 247 Commercial St, (508) 487-1430. Hotel with restaurant & 3 mostly-male bars, private baths. 🍽♀ ♂

DEXTER'S INN, 6 Conwell St, (508) 487-1911, toll-free (888) 521-1999. Steeped in history, we're in the heart of downtown just a short walk to Commercial St, shops, restaurants, galleries and clubs. Our unique cluster of Cape Cod-style rooms (12 private & 3 with shared bath) allows for private entrance from deck or patio. Mornings enjoy breakfast on the garden patio or in our cozy keeping room. Relax and meet new friends on our spacious sun deck and patio. UNDER NEW OWNERSHIP. ♀♂

ELEPHANT WALK INN, 156 Bradford St, (508) 487-2543. Guest phone (508) 487-2195. Large, mission-style B&B near ocean beach & center of town. Private baths, continental breakfast. ♀♂

ELM HOUSE, 9 Johnson St, (508) 487-0793. Guesthouse. Private & shared baths. ♀ ♂

FAIRBANKS INN, 90 Bradford St, (508) 487-0386, (800) FAIRBNK, Fax: (508) 487-3540, E-mail: fairbank@capecod.net. Sensuous... Seductive...Romantic...This 18th century sea captain's house with its elegant architecture, wistful gardens, roaring fireplaces, antique-filled rooms, delectable beds, wide plank floors from the ship of the captain who built it, and a philosophy of decadence, will enchant you. "Highly recommended" by *Out & About* featured in *The Best Places to Kiss in New England*. ♀♂

FLAMINGO BAY, 27 Conwell St, (508) 487-0068, (800) FLAMBAY (352-6229), fax: (508) 487-2528. Apartments & guesthouse. Private & shared baths. ♂

FOUR BAYS GUESTHOUSE 166 Commercial St, (508) 487-0859. Guesthouse, private & shared baths, women welcome. ♂

GIFFORD HOUSE INN, 9-11 Carver St, (508) 487-0688, (800) 434-0130. Hotel with 6 bars, women welcome. ♂

GRANDVIEW INN, THE, 4 Conant St, (508) 487-9193. E-mail: gndview@capecod.net. Guesthouse, women welcome. Double rooms with private & shared baths, TV lounge, sitting room. Beverages in-season. ♂

HARGOOD HOUSE, 493 Commercial St, (508) 487-9133. 20 luxuriously-furnished condos with equipped kitchens, private beach. Some condos directly on water. Some straight clientele. ♀♂

HAVEN HOUSE, 12 Carver St, (508) 487-3031, (800) 261-2450, Fax: (508) 487-4177. Centrally-located guesthouse, women welcome. Clean, inexpensive rooms, continental breakfast. 🍽♂

HERITAGE HOUSE, 7 Center St, (508) 487-3692. Charming 19th-century sea captain's house with bay views from veranda and many rooms. Centrally-located, but in a quiet residential area. Delicious buffet breakfast with homemade muffins, yogurt, fresh fruit, granola and cold cereal. Parking and airport pick up. Good mix of gay men and women, some straight clientele, shared baths. ♀♂

HOLIDAY INN, Rte 6A, (508) 487-1711. Gay-friendly hotel with restaurant, bar & disco.

HOTEL PIAF, 3 Prince St, Provincetown, MA 02657, (508) 487-7458, (800) 340-PIAF, Fax: (508) 487-8646, http://www.tiac.net/users/ptown/piaf.html, E-mail: otelpiaf@capecod.net. This 1820's restored guesthouse in the heart of Provincetown has three rooms and one suite each with its own private full bath, telephone, and cable TV. Down comforters, terry cloth robes, European bath products, and fresh flowers are just a few of the comforts we've included. Our historic, charming facilities are not lavish and grand, but our attention to detail and our commitment to your comfort is unparalleled. Some straight clientele. ♀♂

JOHN RANDALL HOUSE, 140 Bradford St, (508) 487-3533, (800) 573-6700, fax: (508) 487-3533. Guesthouse, private & shared baths. ♀ ♂

LAMPLIGHTER INN & COTTAGE, 26 Bradford St, (508) 487-2529, (800) 263-6574, Fax: (508) 487-0079, E-mail: lamplite@lamplite.com. http://www.CapeCodAccess.com/Lamplighter. B&B guesthouse, rooms thru cottage with modern conveniences, lovely gardens, expanded continental breakfast, women very welcome. Nearby gym & ocean beach. 🚬♂

LAND'S END INN, 22 Commercial St, (508) 487-0706, (800) 276-7088. B&B, 50% gay & lesbian clientele. Private baths, continental breakfast.

LAVENDER ROSE GUEST HOUSE, 186 Commercial St, (508) 487-6648, Fax: (508) 487-6634. B&B with bar & Mexican/Southwestern restaurant, private & shared baths, AC, ceiling fans, color cable TV, continental breakfast, some straight clientele. ♀♂

LOTUS GUEST HOUSE, 296 Commercial St, (508) 487-4644. Centrally-located guesthouse, spacious rooms with private & shared baths, deck, garden. One block from ocean beach. Mostly gay & lesbian clientele. ♀♂

MONUMENT HOUSE, 129 Bradford St, (508) 487-9664, (888) 487-9664, Fax: (508) 487-3446. Charming 6-bedroom, newly remodeled 1840's home. Private and shared baths, hairdryers, queen beds, color cable TV, fresh flowers, continental breakfast, 24 hour complimentary beverages, roof deck, library, garden patio, private path to Commercial St, free parking and the most central location in

DEXTER'S INN

Open Year Round
A Traditional Cape Cod Guest House

6 Conwell Street
Provincetown, MA 02657

508-487-1911
Toll-free: 888-521-1999
Under New Ownership

SEA DRIFT INN

Guesthouse for Gay Men

(508) 487-3686

---

446   FERRARI GUIDES' GAY TRAVEL A to Z - 18th EDITION

MASSACHUSETTS

UNITED STATES

town. Brochure available. MC/Visa/Amex/Discover welcome. ♀♂

MOORS MOTEL, 59 Provincelands Rd, PO Box 601, (508) 487-1342. Motel, 50% gay and lesbian clientele. 32 comfortable double occupancy rooms with full private baths, cable TV, swimming pool & continental breakfast.

NORMANDY HOUSE, 184 Bradford St, (508) 487-1197, (800) 487-1197. Guesthouse on the hill, 3 min from Commercial St. Comfortable, immaculate rooms with modern conveniences, common room, sun porch, Jacuzzi, continental breakfast. Nearby ocean beach. 50% gay & lesbian clientele.

RANCH GUESTLODGE, THE, 198 Commercial St, Box 26, (508) 487-1542, (800) 942-1542, Fax: (508) 487-3446. men-only guestlodge, shared baths. ♂

RENAISSANCE APARTMENTS, 48 Commercial St, (508) 487-4600. Apartments, some straight clientele. ♂

REVERE HOUSE, 14 Court St, (508) 487-2292, (800) 487-2292. Guesthouse, women welcome. Charming rooms with Federal-period ambience, common lounge, continental breakfast in summer. Nearby ocean beach. ♂

ROOMERS, 8 Carver St, (508) 487-3532. Centrally-located guesthouse, women welcome. Double rooms decorated with antiques, common rooms, continental breakfast. ♂

ROSE & CROWN GUEST HOUSE, 158 Commercial St, (508) 487-3332. Guesthouse with rooms, cottage, apt, private & shared baths, sitting room, continental breakfast. Nearby pool & ocean beach. ♀♂

SANDPIPER BEACH HOUSE, 165 Commercial St, PO Box 646, (800) 354-8628, (508) 487-1928. Guesthouse near ocean beach. Variety of rooms, many with bay views. Continental breakfast in season. ♀♂

SEA DRIFT INN, 80 Bradford St, (508) 487-3686. **A Guesthouse for Gay Men,** Sea Drift is a complex with 18 double rooms with European-style shared baths. Amenities include extra beach towels, parking passes, stereo, TV/VCR with movies, and a private bar has ice, mixers & limes. Guest BBQ facilities are outside, as are a sundeck and expanded garden and patio. We serve continental breakfast and occasionally host cocktail parties. All restaurants, shops and bars are within walking distance. ♂

SHIREMAX INN, 5 Tremont St, (508) 487-1233, 487-4621. Inn, women welcome. Variety of guest quarters, TV lounge, kitchen privileges, expanded continental breakfast. Nearby ocean beach. ♂

SIX WEBSTER PLACE, 6 Webster Place, (508) 487-2266, (800) 6 WEBSTER. Centrally located guesthouse, some straight clientele. Rooms with period furnishings, modern conveniences, private & shared baths, TV lounge, weights, continental breakfast & nearby beaches. ♀♂

SOUTH HOLLOW VINEYARDS, Rte 6A, PO Box 165, North Truro, 02652, (508) 487-6200. Nestled on five picturesque acres of rolling hills and vineyards, this historic 1836 inn features private tiled baths, four-poster beds, and Jacuzzi suites. Complimentary continental breakfast. Women-owned inn and winegrape vineyard.

SUNSET INN, THE, 142 Bradford St, Provincetown, MA 02657, (508) 487-9810, (800) 965-1801. Guesthouse with garden patio & sun decks, private & shared baths, continental breakfast, 1 block from beach & 3 blocks from gay nightlife. Some straight clientele. ♀♂

SWANBERRY INN, THE, 8 Johnson St, (800) 874-7926, (508) 487-4242. Centrally-located guesthouse. Private & shared baths, TV lounge, continental breakfast & nearby ocean beach. ♀♂

THREE PEAKS, 210 Bradford St, (800) 286-1715, (508) 487-1717. East-end B&B near town beaches & shopping. Rooms & apartment with double beds, color cable TV, private baths & continental breakfast. ♀♂

TRADE WINDS INN, 12 Johnson St, (508) 487-0138, Fax: (508) 487-9484. Guesthouse, women welcome. Variety of rooms & conveniences, private & shared baths, TV lounge & continental breakfast. Nearby ocean beach. ♂

TUCKER INN AT TWELVE CENTER, THE, 12 Center St, Provincetown, MA 02657, (508) 487-0381. Something new in Provincetown! Now women-owned, the former Twelve Center Guest House has been renamed and refurbished as a romantic country inn offering a fully equipped cottage and spacious antique-filled rooms with private and shared baths, parking, cable TV and continental breakfast served on a tree-shaded patio. The inn is located on a quiet, peaceful side street, and yet is only a minute's walk from all that Provincetown has to offer. Enhance your vacation with a stay at The Tucker Inn. Some straight clientele. ♀♂

WATERMARK INN, 603 Commercial St, (508) 487-0165, Fax: (508) 487-2383. Beachfront inn, 50% gay & lesbian clientele. Private baths, color TV, telephone, refrigerator.

WATERSHIP INN, 7 Winthrop St, (508) 487-0094, (800) 330-9413, fax: (508) 487-2797. Centrally located B&B, women welcome. Comfortable rooms, expanded continental break. Nearby pool & ocean beach. ♂

WEST END INN 44 Commercial St, (508) 487-9555, (800) 559-1220, fax: (508) 487-8779. B&B & apartments, private & shared baths, some straight clientele. TV lounge, TV/VCR in apartments. Expanded continental breakfast, beaches nearby. ♀♂

■ Women's Accommodations

BRADFORD GARDENS INN, 178 Bradford St, (508) 487-1616, (800) 432-2334. Year-round B&B & cottages, 80% gay & lesbian. Beautiful oversized rooms with fireplaces & antiques, full gourmet breakfast. Ocean beach & town center nearby. ♀♂

CHECK'ER INN, 25 Winthrop St, (800) 894-9029, (508) 487-9029. A friendly, relaxing guest house for women, conveniently located on a quiet side street, yet close to all the hot spots and beaches. Our expanded continental breakfast is served in a spacious common room, featuring a fireplace, piano, library and cable TV with VCR. Enjoy our private Jacuzzi in a plant filled sun room. Relax on the decks or wander in the gardens. Cozy apartments provide all the comforts of home PLUS daily maid service! All units include free on-premises parking. ♀

DUSTY MILLER INN, 82 Bradford St, (508) 487-2213. Guesthouse with porch for people-watching, where friendships are struck on our rocking chairs. Private & shared baths, morning coffee & tea. ♀

GABRIEL'S, 104 Bradford St, (508) 487-3232, (800) 9MY-ANGEL, Fax: (508) 487-1605, http://www.provincetown.com/gabriels, E-mail: gabriels@provincetown.com. Centrally located B&B, men welcome. Doubles thru apartments with antique decorations & modern conveniences, TV lounge, library, kitchen privileges, outdoor Jacuzzi, breakfast & beverages. Nearby ocean beach. ♀

GULL WALK INN, THE, 300A Commercial St, (508) 487-9027 (tel/fax), (800) 309-4725. We are the oldest women's guesthouse in Provincetown. On quiet lane in center of town, our location ensures that you'll be near everything and yet be sheltered from hustle & bustle of town life. The inn offers five simple and clean guest rooms, two large shared baths, and continental breakfast. With its two porches (one with a distant water view), common room and large private garden, you can relax and feel at home. ♀

HALLE'S, 14 West Vine St, (508) 487-6310. **Comfortable cape-style accommodations in the West End,** one block from the beach and a five-minute walk from restaurants, shops and entertainment. Each unit has an outside entrance, soft linens, cozy comforters, deck and garden. Mostly women with men welcome. ♀

HARBOR HILL, 4 Harbor Hill Rd, (508) 487-0541, Fax: (508) 487-9804. Perched high atop dunes on quiet West End, this women's resort offers unprecedented comfort and convenience. Nearest resort to ocean beach, yet easy walk to heart of town. One and two bedroom villas are furnished from kitchens to fireplaces. Tours of the resort are available. We want to be *Your* **Lifestyle Resort.** ♀

LADY JANE'S INN, 7 Central St, (508) 487-3387, E-mail: ladyjanes@wn.net. http://www.ladyjanesinn.com. Located just steps from bay beaches and the center of town, this ideally located inn offers spacious rooms appointed with fine furnishings, private baths, remote color TV's, ceiling fans, air conditioning and outside entrances. On site parking, and complimentary continental breakfast. The inn has a large common room with a refrigerator and VCR. Open all year. ♀

FERRARI GUIDES' GAY TRAVEL A to Z - 18th EDITION

MASSACHUSETTS

MARIGOLDS, PO Box 39, North Truro, MA 02652, (508) 487-9160. Country inn, close to beaches, nature trails, birdwatching, six miles from Provincetown. Five rooms, private baths, homemade breakfasts, large common room with fireplace. Spacious yard, gardens, screenhouse for reading and relaxing. Alcohol-limited house and grounds, non-smokers, women only. ♀
PILGRIM HOUSE HOTEL, 336 Commercial St. (508) 487-6424, fax: (508) 487-6296. Hotel with restaurant. ♀
PLUMS BED & BREAKFAST INN, 160 Bradford St, (508) 487-2283. Women-only B&B **in an 1860 whaling captain's house with Victorian antiques,** (condos also available), all private baths and gourmet breakfasts. Parking, smoke-free. ♀
RAVENWOOD GUESTROOMS & APARTMENTS, 462 Commercial St, (508) 487-3203. Guestroom & year-round apartments, condo & cottage, across from harbor. Men permitted if accompanied by their women friends. Modern conveniences, patio, BBQ, nearby ocean beach, gym & Jacuzzi. Catering arranged. ♀
ROSE ACRE, 5 Center St, (508) 487-2347. A "Provincetown Classic" and women's house offering rooms, apartments and a cottage called "Rosebud." Enjoy the unhurried atmosphere of a rambling 1840 Cape House, tucked down a private drive, with decks, gardens, parking and a yard. Always open, call for brochure. Visit us where the light is bright, streets are narrow, and the minds are broad. ♀
WINDAMAR HOUSE, 568 Commercial St, (508) 487-0599, Fax: (508) 487-7505. B&B in an elegant, historical, seaside home & apts, men welcome, some straight clientele. Antique decorations, bay views, TV lounge, common room & continental breakfast. Beautiful grounds & flower gardens, nearby ocean beach. ♀

■ Bars

BACKROOM, 247 Commercial St, at Crown & Anchor Hotel, (508) 487-1430. Cabaret, dance bar, scheduled two-stepping nights.
FRONT ROOM, 247 Commercial St at Crown & Anchor Hotel. Conversation bar with fireplace. ♀♂
LARRY'S BAR,★ 177 Commercial St, at Sebastian's Rest. (508) 487-3286. ♀♂
LITTLE BAR, at the Atlantic House Hotel. ♂
MACHO BAR, 4 Masonic Place at Atlantic House. ♂
POOL BAR, 247 Commercial St at Crown & Anchor Hotel, (508) 487-1430. Poolside bar & grill with beach access. ♀♂
PORCH BAR, at Gifford House. Conversation bar. ♀♂
RED ROOSTER, 247 Commercial St, at the Crown & Anchor Hotel. Pool tables, video games, darts. ♀♂

VAULT, 247 Commercial St at the Crown & Anchor Hotel (downstairs). ♂

■ Dance Bar/Disco

AMEN, 23 Foster St, (508) 754-7742. Gothic with gargoyles, dark paint. ♀♂
ATLANTIC HOUSE, 4 Masonic Place near Commercial, (508) 487-3821. ♂
BOATSLIP BEACH CLUB,★ 161 Commercial St at Central, (508) 487-1669, (800) 451-7547. Tea dance daily 3:30pm, C&W dances, ballroom dancing. ♀♂
PIED PIPER,★ 193 Commercial (alley) near Carver, (508) 487-1527. Bar with grill on waterfront deck. After tea gay & lesbian teadance 6:30pm till? ♀
STUDENT UNION,★ at Gifford House, 9-11 Carver St, (508) 487-3490. Video & martini bar and hi-energy dance bar, women welcome. ♂
VIXEN,★ at Pilgrim House Inn. Dance bar & lounge at Pilgrim House Hotel. ♀

■ Restaurants

BOATSLIP BEACH CLUB, 161 Commercial St. at Boatslip Hotel, (508) 487-1669. ♀♂
COMMONS BISTRO, 386 Commercial St at Ocean's Inn, (508) 487-7800. Bistro cuisine, brick oven pizza, outside dining. ♀♂
FLANNERY'S, 247 Commercial St at Crown & Anchor Hotel (upstairs), (508) 487-1430. ♀♂
FRONT STREET, 230 Commercial St, (508) 487-9715. Continental cuisine. ♀♂

■ Retail & Bookstores

DON'T PANIC, 192 Commercial St #4, (508) 487-2642. Gay & lesbian gift shop, T-shirts, buttons.
NOW VOYAGER BOOKSTORE, 357 Commercial St, (508) 487-0848. A bookstore for everyone, specializing in gay and lesbian books and mysteries. Open year-round. Mail order, free catalog.
PRIDE'S OF PROVINCETOWN, 182 Commercial Street, (508) 487-1127. Gay & lesbian gift store with cards, original art, books, posters and more.
RECOVERING HEARTS BOOKSTORE, 4 Standish St, (508) 487-4875 (TTY). Women's bookstore & gift gallery. Fiction thru metaphysical, healing, recovery. Open year-round.
WOMENCRAFTS, 376 Commercial St, (508) 487-2501. CELEBRATING OUR 21ST YEAR!! A women's store with jewelry, books, music, pottery, glassware & much more, plus 5% lesbian discount! We're open year-round.

■ Leathers/Piercing

BEFORE & AFTER, 247 Commercial St, in Crown & Anchor Hotel bldg, (508) 487-9447. Drag items, clothing & accessories, makeup, nails.

RANDOLPH

■ Dance Bar/Disco

RANDOLPH COUNTRY CLUB,★ 44 Mazzeo Dr, (617) 961-2414. 20 min from Boston, 2 discos. Restaurant open Mon eve only. Swimming pool, sand volleyball court, Sun brunch. Many women Sat. ♀♂

SPRINGFIELD

■ Bars

PUB, THE, 382 Dwight St near Taylor, (413) 734-8123. Upstairs, women welcome. ♂
QUARRY, 382 Dwight St, same bldg as The Pub bar. Pool room. ♂

■ Dance Bar/Disco

DAVID'S NIGHTCLUB, 397 Dwight St, (413) 734-0566. NY-style nightclub, Wed-Sun. Shows, T-dance Thur. ♀♂
FRIENDS, 23 Hampden St, (413) 781-5878. Video dance bar, cabaret, cruise bar, 60% men, 40% women. ♀♂
OUR HIDEAWAY, 16 Bolduc Ln, Chicopee, (413) 534-6426. 5 min by car from downtown Springfield, 1/2 hr from Hartford. DJ dancing Fri & Sat. Sun tea dance 4pm-2am. Open fall, winter 7 days, summer closed Mon. Sand volleyball spring & summer, patio bar. ♀♂
PUB DISCO, 382 Dwight St at the Pub bar. Younger crowd. ♀♂

■ Restaurants

DNA ROOM, 382 Dwight St at The Pub men's bar. Video bar. ♀♂

STURBRIDGE - WARE

■ Accommodations

WILDWOOD INN B&B, THE, 121 Church St, Ware, (413) 967-7798, (800) 860-8098. Gayfriendly B&B with lesbian following. Cozy rooms with American primitive furnishings, full break., priv. & shared baths. Nearby ponds, pools, maps to book & antique shops, hot tubs, nature trails, restaurants. Near Northampton, 8 miles from Mass Pike (I-90).

WAREHAM

■ Accommodations

LITTLE HARBOR GUEST HOUSE, 20 Stockton Shortcut, Wareham, MA 02571, (508) 295-6329, (800) 515-6329. Gay-friendly guesthouse 1 hour from Boston & Provincetown, private & shared baths, continental breakfast.

WORCESTER

■ Bars

MB LOUNGE, 40 Grafton St, (508) 799-4521. Open 3pm-2am 7 days, leather night last Sat. ♂

■ Dance Bar/Disco

CLUB 241, 241 Southbridge St, (508) 755-9311. Dance & show bar, opens Thurs & Fri 6pm-2am, Sat & Sun 2pm-2am. Outdoor deck, sand volleyball court. 60% men, 40% women. ♀♂

YARMOUTH PORT

■ Accommodations

GULL COTTAGES B&B, (508) 362-8747.

MICHIGAN

MICHIGAN

WHO TO CALL

For Tour Companies Serving This Destination See Michigan on page 20

ANN ARBOR

■ Information
GAY, LESBIAN & BISEXUALS PROGRAMS OFFICE, (313) 763-4186. 8am-5pm weekdays.
WELLNESS NETWORK, (313) 572-9355. HIV & AIDS info, testing.

■ Bars
AUT BAR, 315 Braun Ct, (313) 994-3677. 7 days 4pm-2am, pool table, dinner daily, Sun Brunch 10am-3pm, upstairs bar. ♀♂
FLAME, 112 W Liberty, (313) 662-9680. ♂

■ Dance Bar/Disco
NECTARINE, THE, 516 E Liberty, (313) 994-5835. From 9pm, Tues & Fri gay nights.

■ Retail & Bookstores
COMMON LANGUAGE, 214 S 4th Ave, (313) 663-0036. Lesbian, feminist & gay bookstore with tapes, cards, jewelry, posters, non-sexist children's books. Closed Mon.
CRAZY WISDOM BOOKS, 206 N 4th Ave, (313) 665-2757. Holistic, metaphysical bookstore with a large women's spiritual section.
SHAMAN DRUM BOOKSHOP, 315 S State St, (313) 662-7407. General bookstore with a gay & lesbian section.

BATTLE CREEK

■ Dance Bar/Disco
PARTNERS, 910 North Ave, (616) 964-7276. Multi-level bar with dance bar & occasional male & female dancers, quiet bar, Mon-Sat 6pm-2am, DJ Fri, Sat. ♀♂

■ Erotica
EASTOWN CAPRI, W Michigan Ave near Angel.

BELLEVILLE

■ Bars
GRANNYS PLACE, 9800 Haggerty, (313) 699-8862. Pool table, Wed female dancers, Thurs male dancers, Fri & Sat drag shows, Wed-Sat DJ. ♀♂

DETROIT

■ Information
AFFIRMATIONS, 195 W Nine Mile Rd Ferndale, (810) 398-4297. Mon-Fri after 6pm, or tape, gay & lesbian community center.

■ Bars
ADAM'S APPLE, 18931 W Warren between Southfield & Evergreen, (313) 336-2080. Cruise bar.
BACK POCKET, 8832 Greenfield Rd near Joy, (313) 272-8374. Wide screen TV. Open nightly, after hours Wed & Sat.
CHAINS, 6228 Michigan Ave (313) 897-3650.
DECK, THE, 14901 E Jefferson at Alter, (313) 822-1991. Patio, pool table, monthly drag shows, BBQ's in summer.
DETROIT EAGLE, ★ 1501 Holden, (313) 873-6969. Open Wed-Sun. After hrs Sat.
EDGE, 1322 Conant, (313) 891-EDGE. Male dancers 6 nites.
HAYLOFT SALOON, 8070 Greenfield near Tireman, (313) 581-8913. Pool table, open 5pm daily.
MALE BOX, 3537 E Seven Mile, (313) 892-5420. Happy hour, secured parking. Open daily 2pm-2am.
NUMBERS VIDEO BAR & GRILLE, 17518 Woodward Ave, (313) 868-9145. Daily 8pm-2am, after hours Wed-Sun 2am-4am. Busy for after hours.
OTHER SIDE, 16801 Plymouth Rd near the Southfield Freeway, (313) 836-2324. 98% men, 2% women.
PRONTO VIDEO BAR, ★ 608 S. Washington, Royal Oak, (810) 544-7900. ♀♂
STINGERS LOUNGE & GRILL, 19404 Sherwood side entrance, (313) 892-1765. Open daily 4pm-2am, 50% men, 50% women.
SUGARBAKERS, ★ 3800 E 8 Mile, (313) 892-5203. Women's sports bar, softball teams, pool tables, dart boards, big-screen TV.
TIFFANY'S, 17436 Woodward Ave, near Parkhurst, (313) 883-7162. Popular Thurs, Sun.

■ Dance Bar/Disco
BACKSTREET, ★ 15606 Joy Rd at Greenfield, (313) 272-8959. Wed & Sat, preppy crowd, 90% men.
BODY SHOP, THE, 22061 Woodward Ave, S of 9-Mi Rd, Ferndale, (810) 398-1940. DJ nightly, 90% men.
GIGI'S, 16920 W Warren Ave at Clayburn, (313) 584-6525. Go go boys Mon & Fri, 80% men, 20% women.
MENJO'S SOUTH, 8120 N Dixie, Newport, (313) 586-2200. Thurs-Sun 6pm-2am, kitchen open 6pm-11pm.
MENJO'S, ★ 928 W McNichols near Hamilton, (313) 863-3934. Hi-energy dance bar, DJ Thur-Sun.
OFF BROADWAY EAST, 12215 Harper Ave at Norcross, (313) 521-0920. Male dancers weekends.
RAINBOW ROOM, THE, ★ 6640 E Eight Mile, (313) 891-1020. Dancing & entertainment, drag shows Wed, Sun, male dancers Thurs. Wed & Fri it's 50% men/women, Sat 70% women, other days 70% men.
SILENT LEGACY, 1641 Middlebelt Rd, Inkster, (313) 729-8980.
WOODWARD, 6426 Woodward Ave near Milwaukee, (313) 872-0166. CD dance bar in separate room.
ZIPPERS, 6221 E Davison, (313) 892-8120. Opens at 9pm.

■ Saunas/Health Clubs
TNT HEALTH CLUB, 13333 W 8-Mile Rd, (313) 341-5322. Private membership club open 24hrs.

■ Restaurants
PRONTO RESTAURANT, 608 S Washington, Royal Oak, (810) 544-7900. Gay bar & restaurant. ♀♂

■ Retail & Bookstores
A WOMAN'S PREROGATIVE AND CAFÉ, 175 W 9 Mile Rd, near Woodward & 9 Mile, Ferndale, (810) 545-5703. Women's bookstore with music, cards, jewelry, coffee & treats.
CHOSEN BOOKS, 120 4th Street, Royal Oak, (810) 543-5758. Gay & lesbian bookstore.

■ Leathers/Piercing
NOIR LEATHER, 415 S Main St, Royal Oak, (810) 541-3979.
RAWHIDE LEATHER SHOP, 6228 Michigan in Chains bar, (313) 897-3650.

■ Erotica
ADULT NEWS, 13705 W 8-Mile Rd, (313) 864-3361.
FIFTH WHEEL I, 9320 Michigan Ave near Wyoming, (313) 846-8613. Closed Sun.
FIFTH WHEEL II, 225 Schaefer, (313) 842-6720. Closed Sun.
IRVING ART THEATER, 21220 Fenkell near Blackstone, (313) 531-2368.
UPTOWN BOOKSTORE, 16541 Woodward Ave, (313) 869-9477. Also: 16401 W 8-Mile Rd, 836-0647.
WORLDWIDE MAGAZINES, 16140 Woodward Ave, Highland Park, (313) 866-6020.

ESCANABA

■ Dance Bar/Disco
CLUB XPRESS, 904 Ludington St, (906) 789-0140. Big party 1 weekend a month, occasional drag shows. 75% men, 25% women.

FLINT

■ Bars
CLUB MI, 2402 Franklin, (810) 234-9481. Many women in evening.

■ Dance Bar/Disco
CLUB TRIANGLE, 2101 S Dort Hwy, (810) 767-7550. 7 days.
STATE BAR, 2512 S Dort Hwy, near

UNITED STATES

FERRARI GUIDES' GAY TRAVEL A to Z - 18th EDITION

MICHIGAN

Lippincott, (810) 767-7050. 50% men, 50% women. Occasional shows, male dancers, karaoke 3 days a week.

Erotica
DEJA VU, 2200-2400 block of S Dort Hwy near the State Bar.
VELVET TOUCH, 2200-2400 block of S Dort Hwy near the State Bar.

GLEN ARBOR

Women's Accommodations
DUNESWOOD, PO Box 457, Glen Arbor, MI 49636, (616) 334-3346. A woman's resort with 12 private housekeeping rooms, nestled on 7 acres of secluded woods located in the Sleeping Bear Dunes Nat'l Lakeshore. Area activities: hiking, cross-country skiing, swimming, boating, fishing, golfing, bicycling, antiquing and great shopping, restaurants and wineries. All private baths, and a variety of cooking options. Also available is Marge & Joanne's B&B, a shared baths. Both properties are for women only, open all year, no pets. To find us on the map, look near Traverse City, MI.

GRAND RAPIDS

Information
LESBIAN & GAY COMMUNITY NETWORK, (616) 458-3511. Mon-Fri 6pm-10pm.

Bars
APARTMENT LOUNGE, 33 Sheldon NE, (616) 451-0815. English/Irish pub decor, jukebox, 90% men, 10% women.
CELL, THE, 79 S Division Ave, (616) 454-4499.

Dance Bar/Disco
CITY LIMITS, 67 S Division Ave near Weston, (616) 454-8003. Dance & show bar. Only gay bar welcoming the under 21 crowd.
DIVERSIONS, 10 Fountain NW, (616) 451-3800. Complex with dance bar, video bar & quiet atrium.

Cafe
SONS & DAUGHTERS COFFEEHOUSE, 962 Cherry St SE at Sons & Daughters Bookstore. Desserts, cappuccino, espresso. Till midnight weekdays. Three am weekends. No smoking.

Saunas/Health Clubs
DIPLOMAT HEALTH CLUB, 2324 S Division Ave at Withey, (616) 452-3754. Full gym, steam, sauna, membership required.

Restaurants
DIVERSIONS GRILL, 10 Fountain NW, at Diversions bar, (616) 451-3800. Lunch, dinner.

Retail & Bookstores
SONS & DAUGHTERS BOOKSTORE & COFFEEHOUSE, 962 Cherry St SE, (616) 459-8877. Gay & lesbian bookstore, non-smoking gallery & coffeehouse with desserts, cappuccino, espresso. Open till midnight weekdays, Fri-Sat till 3am.

Erotica
ALL STAR VIDEO, 1352 Plainfield NE, (616) 458-9047. Videos only, closed Sun.
CINA-MINI I, 1358 Plainfield NE, (616) 454-2444. Theater, closed Sun.
CINA-MINI II, 415 Bridge NW near Broadway, (616) 454-7531. Three theaters, videos, novelties.

HONOR

Women's Accommodations
LABRYS WILDERNESS RESORT, 4115 Scenic Hwy, reservations: (616) 882-5994. 4 housekeeping cabins in the Michigan woods, Lake Michigan & beaches nearby, lesbian store on premises.

Retail & Bookstores
SEEDS, Rte 1, Box 257, Honor, 49640, (616) 882-5994. Lesbian store at Labrys Wilderness Resort, featuring crafts, jewelry, artwork, cards and herbal remedies made by women on the land.

KALAMAZOO

Information
AIDS SERVICES, (616) 381-2437, for emergencies 381-4357.
LESBIAN & GAY LINE, (616) 345-7878, 7-10 pm Mon-Fri or tape.

Dance Bar/Disco
BROTHERS, 209 Stockbridge, (616) 345-1960. DJ Thurs-Sat, private club, open 7 days, male & female strippers, 50% men, 50% women.
ZOO, 906 Portage St, (616) 342-8888. Patio, 70% men, 30% women.

Retail & Bookstores
PANDORA BOOKS FOR OPEN MINDS, 226 W Lovell St, (616) 388-5656. Women's & gay & lesbian books. Tues-Thurs 11-7pm, Fri-Sat 11-6pm, closed Sun-Mon.
RAINBOW A-GO-GO, 1506 S Burdick. Pride items, etc
TRIANGLE WORLD, 551 Portage St, (616) 373-4005. Bookstore with videos, gay & lesbian cards, gifts. Noon-10pm, closed Mon.

Erotica
VELVET TOUCH, 1819 W Main, (616) 385-9304.

LANSING

Information
LESBIAN & GAY HOTLINE, (517) 332-3200, 7pm-10pm Mon-Fri, 2-5pm Sun, or tape.
LESBIAN CONNECTION, (517) 371-5257. 11am-6pm, local women's info.

Bars
ESQUIRE CLUB, 1250 Turner St, Old Town Lansing, (517) 487-5338. Pool table, 70% men.

Dance Bar/Disco
CLUB 505, 505 E Shiawasee, (517) 374-6312. DJ Wed-Sat, big screen TV, pool table, 80% women.
CLUB PARADISE, 224 S Washington Square, (517) 484-2399. Hi-energy dance bar, 60% men, 40% women, young crowd, closed Mon.

Cafe
REAL WORLD EMPORIUM CAFE, 1214-16 Turner at Real World Emporium. Cafe of queer culture.

Retail & Bookstores
REAL WORLD BOOKS EMPORIUM & CAFE, 1214-16 Turner St, Old Town Library, (517) 485-2665, Fax: (517) 485-0052. E-mail: RealWorlde@aol.com. Women's, lesbian & gay titles & performance space, noon-8pm Tues-Sun.

MARQUETTE

Retail & Bookstores
SWEET VIOLETS, 413 N 3rd St, (906) 228-3307. Women's bookstore & gift shop, feminist & spirituality books, music, pride items, cards, some gay magazines. Mon-Fri 10am-6pm, Sat 10am-5pm.

Erotica
OBSESSIONS, 215 S Front St, (906) 226-6660.

MIDLAND

Accommodations
JAY'S B & B, 4429 Bay City Rd, (517) 496-2498. Gay-friendly bed & breakfast, 50% gay & lesbian clientele.

MT CLEMENS

Dance Bar/Disco
MIRAGE, 27 N Walnut, (810) 954-1919. 7 days.

MUSKEGON

Dance Bar/Disco
R'S CLUB & DISCOTHEQUE, 3236 Hoyt St, Muskegon Hts. Unverifiable spring '97.

OWENDALE

Camping & RV
WINDOVER RESORT, 3596 Blakely Rd, Summer: (517) 375-2586, Winter: (810) 775-4066. Finest membership campground, for adult women only, in Michigan's Thumb. Large, grassy, shaded and open sites.

PONTIAC

Dance Bar/Disco
CLUB FLAMINGO, 352 Oakland Ave, (810) 253-0430. Area's largest club, 60% men, 40% women.

MINNESOTA

■ *Erotica*
FRONT PAGE BOOKS & VIDEO, 974 Joslyn Ave, (810) 334-1150.

PORT HURON

■ *Dance Bar/Disco*
SEEKERS, 3301 24th St, (810) 985-9349. Male & female strippers, patio.

SAGINAW

■ *Dance Bar/Disco*
BAMBI'S, 1742 E Genesee, (517) 752-9179. Dance & show bar, 60% men, 40% women.

SAUGATUCK - DOUGLAS

■ *Accommodations*
DOUGLAS DUNES RESORT, 333 Blue Star Highway, Douglas, (616) 857-1401, Fax: (616) 857-4052. Saugatuck/Douglas is the Key West of the north. Enjoy our wonderful beaches, boutiques, art galleries, and the beautiful people at Douglas Dunes Resort, a deluxe motel with pool, patio bar, disco, cabaret, and award-winning dining at Le Cabaret Cafe.

KIRBY HOUSE, THE, PO Box 1174 Saugatuck, (616) 857-2904 (tel/fax), (800) 521-6473. Inn, some straight clientele. Comfortable rooms with antique furnishings, kitchen privileges, BBQ, Jacuzzi, bicycles, full breakfast buffet.

MOORE'S CREEK INN, 820 Holland St, (616) 857-2411, (800) 838-5864. B&B, some straight clientele. Theme rooms with private & shared baths, TV lounge, common rooms, full breakfast. Nearby lake.

NEWNHAM SUNCATCHER INN, 131 Griffith Box 1106 Saugatuck, (616) 857-4249. B&B & separate 2-cottage suite, some straight clientele. Period furniture, shared baths, common room, TV lounge, Jacuzzi, full breakfast.

■ *Camping & RV*
CAMPIT, 6635 118th Ave, (616) 543-4335. Campground with mini-store, modern bath & shower facilities, game room, TV lounge, laundry facilities, 37 electric hookups, 30 tent sites & 30 RV spaces. Mostly men, women welcome.

■ *Women's Accommodations*
DEERPATH LODGE, PO Box 849, Saugatuck, 49453, (616) 857-DEER. Contemporary redwood lodge on 45 acres overlooking the Kalamazoo River, private baths, breakfast, 5 min drive from Saugatuck.

■ *Beaches*
GAY BEACH, follow signs to Oval Beach, then park, walk north.

■ *Dance Bar/Disco*
DOUGLAS DISCO, 333 Blue Star Hwy, Douglas, at Douglas Dunes, (616) 857-1401.

Tea-dance, Sun 4pm in summer. Open 7 days in winter.

■ *Restaurants*
LE CABARET CAFE, at Douglas Dunes Resort, 333 Blue Star Hwy, Douglas, (616) 857-1401. Fine dining, open April-Oct Wed-Sun.

SAULT SAINTE-MARIE

■ *Erotica*
OPEN MINDS BOOKS, 215 Ashmun, (906) 635-9008.

SOUTHWEST MICHIGAN

■ *Accommodations*
COZY COTTAGES/ENVOY RESORT PROPERTIES, New Buffalo, MI, (800) 44-ENVOY (36869), (312) 787-2400, Fax: (312) 787-7109. Div. of Envoy Travel, Inc, 740 N Rush St #609, Chicago IL 60611. Cozy up for a weekend getaway or crosscountry stopover just 1-1/2 hours from Chicago and 5 blocks from Lake Michigan. Walk on the beach or explore a pretty little town with fine restaurants, art galleries and jewelry shops...or cross-country ski...or visit the National & State Dunes Parks nearby. Men, women, children, small dogs — everyone is welcome. One cottage is a 2-BR with electric fireplace, the other is a 3-BR with gas fireplace. Both have full kitchens, micros, color TV and VCR, telephones and AC. Towels and linens are provided.

TRAVERSE CITY

■ *Dance Bar/Disco*
SIDE TRAXX, 520 Franklin, (616) 935-1666. Opens 6pm, 70% men, 30% women.

UNION PIER

■ *Accommodations*
WARREN WOODS INN, 15506 Lake Shore Rd, (616) 469-5880, (800) 358 4754. B&B with private baths, full breakfast, near lake & beaches, 1-1/4 hrs from Chicago Loop, gay & lesbian following.

MINNESOTA

WHO TO CALL
For Tour Companies Serving This Destination
See Minnesota on page 20

DULUTH

See also Superior, WI

■ *Information*
AURORA: NORTHLAND LESBIAN CENTER, 32 E 1st St #104 (Bldg for women), (218) 722-4903. Mon 9:15-2pm, Wed 10am-6pm, Thurs 1pm-5pm.

NORTHLAND GAY MEN'S CENTER #309 8 N 2nd Ave E, (218) 722-8585. Mon-Fri 5pm-8pm, Sat 12pm-4pm, discussion group Tues 7:30pm, Young men's discussion group cafe at 7:30pm.

■ *Accommodations*
STANFORD INN, 1415 E Superior St, (218) 724-3044, fax: (218) 724-8452. Victorian B&B with private & shared baths, sauna, full gourmet breakfast & room service coffee, some straight clientele.

HINCKLEY

■ *Accommodations*
DAKOTA LODGE B&B, Rte 3, Box 178, Hinckley MN 55037, (612) 384-6052. 50% gay & lesbian clientele. AC, private baths. 4 rooms with fireplace, some rooms with whirlpool. TV lounge, full breakfast, lake nearby.

KENYON

■ *Accommodations*
DANCING WINDS FARM, 6863 Co #12 Blvd, (507) 789-6606. B&B & campground with licensed cheesery on farmstead. Private unit with full bath, kitchen, living room, TV lounge, full breakfast, fresh goat's milk & cheese. Nearby pool.

MINNEAPOLIS - ST PAUL

■ *Information*
AIDS LINE, (612) 373-2437. Mon-Thurs 9am-9pm. Fri 9am-6pm.

CHRYSALIS, A CENTER FOR WOMEN, 2650 Nicollet, (612) 871-0118.

GAY & LESBIAN COMMUNITY ACTION COUNCIL, 310 E 38th St #204, (612) 822-0127.

GAY HELP LINE, (612) 822-8661. Mon-Fri 2pm-10pm, Sat 4pm-10pm.

QUATREFOIL LIBRARY, 1619 Dayton Ave, (612) 641-0969. Gay & lesbian library & archives.

Ahh!
★ Deluxe Rooms or Cottage Suites
★ Fine Dining at Le Cabaret Cafe
★ Disco Cabaret

Douglas Dunes Resort
(616) 857-1401
Blue Star Highway Douglas, MI 49406

FERRARI GUIDES' GAY TRAVEL A to Z - 18th EDITION

MINNESOTA

Dogsledding North of Duluth

Kathleen Anderson has been mushing for 12 years. She was the 1987 Beargrease Race Director and a racing team dog handler and has raised and trained her 28 Alaskan Huskies. It's those huskies who will "make" your trip when you join **Wintermoon** to learn to run a team of Alaskan Huskies! No experience is necessary. The huskies' enthusiasm and energy will captivate and inspire as you become part of a working team. There are miles of trails for dogsledding, skiing and snowshoeing in the area around Kathleen's 160-acre Finnish homestead, which is located 50 miles north of Duluth, Minnesota in the Superior National Forest. You'll stay in a rustic log cabin with sauna, wood heat, solar power, hand pump for well water, and outhouse. All trips include lodging, meals and instruction.

Cabin-Based Dogsledding - Dec-Mar
Sled Dog School - December
Dogsledding & Wolf Ecology - Feb

Contact **Wintermoon** at (218) 848-2442.

■ Accommodations

ABBOTTS COMO VILLA, 1371 W Nebraska Ave, St Paul, (612) 647-0471. B&B near Mall of America, 50% gay & lesbian clientele. AC, private & shared baths, TV lounge, continental (Mon-Thur) or full (weekends) breakfast.

BE YOURSELF INN, TWIN CITIES, 1093 Snelling Ave South, St. Paul, (612) 698-3571. B&B, private baths, AC, full breakfast, laundry facilities, fully-enclosed grounds.

EAGLE COVE BED AND BREAKFAST, Box 65, W4387 120th Ave, Maiden Rock, WI (800) 467-0279, (715) 448-4302. Rustic ridgetop B&B retreat 65 miles from Minneapolis, some straight clientele. Color TV, shared baths, fireplace lounge & expanded continental breakfast.

HOTEL AMSTERDAM, 828 Hennipen Ave, above The Saloon dance bar, (800) 649-9500, (612) 288-0459. Renovated hotel with restaurant & bar. Modest accommodations, Sun brunch.

■ Women's Accommodations

COUNTRY GUEST HOUSE, THE, 1673 38th St, Somerset, WI, (715) 247-3520. Two-bedroom guesthouse cottage on hobby farm along MN/WI border, men welcome. Kitchen, telephone, stereo, walking trails, row boat.

■ Bars

BRASS RAIL, 422 Hennepin Ave near 5th St, Mpls, (612) 333-3016. Karaoke.

GAY 90'S, HAPPY HOUR,★ 408 Hennepin Ave near 4th St, Mpls, (612) 333-7755. Complex with hi energy & funk dance bars, cruise bar & very large show bar, leather bar & restaurant.

INNUENDO, 510 N Robert, St Paul, (612) 224-8906. Small bar & lounge, upscale professional crowd.

NINETEEN BAR, 19 W 15th St near Nicollet, Mpls, (612) 871-5553. 60% men, 40% women.

■ Dance Bar/Disco

CHECKERS PUB & DANCE CLUB, 1066 E 7th St, (612) 776-7915.

CLUB METRO,★ 733 Pierce Butler Route, St. Paul, (612) 489-0002. Upstairs women's dance bar. Leather shop, jewelry store, restaurant, summer patio dining, volleyball court, sports & karaoke bar.

FIRST AVENUE AND SEVENTH STREET ENTRY, 701 1st Ave N, (612) 332-1775. Alternative music, gay friendly.

GAY 90'S, HAPPY HOUR,★ 408 Hennepin Ave near 4th St, Mpls, (612) 333-7755. Complex with dance bar, cruise bar, piano bar, show bar, leather bar & restaurant.

GROUND ZERO, 15 NE 4th St, Mpls, (612) 378-5115. 18 and older, gay nights like Bondage A-Go-Go, etc., call for schedule.

LOUNGE, THE, 411 N 2nd Ave N, (612) 333-8800. A pleasing mixture of straight & gay clientele (20-50% gay), jazz weedays, DJ weekends.

OVER THE RAINBOW, 249 W 7th St, St Paul, (612) 228-7180. Small dance floor.

RUMOURS, 490 N Roberts St, St Paul, (612) 224-0703. Complex with video dance bar and piano bar, 70% men, 30% women.

SALOON,★ 830 Hennepin Ave at 9th, Mpls, (612) 332-0835. Sun leather nite.

TOWN HOUSE COUNTRY, 1415 University Ave near Albert, St Paul, (612) 646-7087.

UNDERGROUND, 733 Pierce Butler Route, lower level of Club Metro women's bar. Hi energy dance club, open Wed-Sat, Thurs leather nite, Fri theme parties (mostly men), Sat mixed men & women.

■ Cafe

BLUE MOON, 3822 East Lake St, (612) 721-9230.

CAFE WYRD, 1600 W Lake, Mpls, (612) 827-5710. Coffee shop, mostly gay clientele.

CAFE ZEZ, 1362 La Salle Ave, Minneapolis, (612) 874-8477. Popular gay-friendly cafe.

CAHOOTS COFFEE BAR, 1562 Selby Ave, St Paul, (612) 644-6778.

■ Restaurants

CAFE BRENDA, 300 1st Ave N, (612) 342-9230.

METRO CAFE, 733 Pierce Butler Rd in the Club Metro, (612) 487-5909. Dinner Wed-Sun.

MINNEAPOLIS CAFE, 2730 W Lake St, (612) 920-1401. Restaurant in the Calhoun Beach Club, very popular with gays on Wed.

NICOLLET GRILLE, 1400 Nicollet Ave, (612) 874-7285.

RUBY'S CAFE,★ 1614 Harmon Pl, (612) 338-2089. Mon-Sat 7am-2pm, Sun 8am-2pm.

TIMES BAR & CAFE, THE, 1036 Nicollet Ave, (612) 333-2762. Bar & restaurant.

■ Retail & Bookstores

A BROTHER'S TOUCH, 2327 Hennepin Ave, Mpls 55405, (612) 377-6279. Gay & lesbian bookstore, records, music, cards, T-shirts, magazines. Mon, Tue 11am-7pm. Wed-Fri 11am-9pm. Sat 11am-6pm. Sun noon-5pm.

AMAZON BOOKSTORE, 1612 Harmon Pl, (612) 338-6560. Founded in 1970, Amazon Bookstore is the oldest feminist bookstore in the country. Open seven days, Amazon carries over 15,000 titles by women, women's periodicals, music, T-shirts, posters, cards & crafts.

HUNGRY MIND, 1648 Grand Ave, St Paul, (612) 699-0587. Independent general bookstore with gay & lesbian titles.

MISSOURI

RAINBOW ROAD, 109 W Grant, (612) 872-8448. Videos, gifts, cards. 10am-10pm.

■ *Leathers/Piercing*
BACK IN BLACK LEATHER INC, in same bldg as Club Metro.

■ *Erotica*
BROADWAY BOOK, 901 Hennepin Ave, (612) 338-7303.
DENMARK BOOKS, 459 W 7th St, St Paul.

MOORHEAD
See Fargo, ND

NORTH-CENTRAL MINNESOTA

■ *Accommodations*
MEADOW GROVE B&B, 13661 Powerdam Rd NE, Bemidji, MN 56601, (218) 751-9654. Gay-owned B&B with mostly straight clientele, near Concordia Language Village. In summer: lakes, fishing & outdoor recreation nearby. Isolated location appeals to artists & writers.
NORTHWOODS RETREAT, 5749 Mt Ash Dr, Hill City, MN (218) 697-8119, (800) 767-3020. We're the only resort on this lake. Two cabins, private baths, total privacy & no public access. Private lake with fishing, swimming, paddle boats. All meals included, Free use of outdoor equipment, men welcome.

ROCHESTER

■ *Information*
GAY & LESBIAN COMMUNITY SERVICES, (507) 281-3265. Office hours Mon & Wed 5pm-7pm. Call for socials, occasional dances, potlucks, contact service.

MISSISSIPPI

WHO TO CALL
For Tour Companies Serving This Destination
See Mississippi on page 20

BILOXI - GULFPORT

■ *Bars*
SANCTUARY, on Veterans Blvd, first building on the left north of the RR tracks. Small dance floor, Fri karaoke, patio.

■ *Dance Bar/Disco*
JOEYS ON THE BEACH, 1708 Beach Blvd (Hwy 90) Biloxi, (601) 435-5639. Dance club, 70% men, 30% women. Open Tues-Sun from 4pm till late, women welcome.

■ *Erotica*
ADULT BOOKS, Pass Rd near Gate 7, Keesler Airforce Base.
ADULT BOOKSTORE, 1620 Pass Rd, Biloxi.

GULFPORT

■ *Bars*
THONGS, 28th Ave. Unverifiable spring 1997, ask at bar in Biloxi.

HATTIESBURG

■ *Dance Bar/Disco*
COURTYARD, 107 E Front St, (601) 545-2714. Dance bar & lounge, 50% men & 50% women.

JACKSON

■ *Bars*
JACK'S CONSTRUCTION SITE, 425 North Mart Plaza, (601) 362-3108, 7 days, 5pm-2am.

■ *Dance Bar/Disco*
CLUB CITY LIGHTS, 220 W Amite, at Mill, (601) 353-0059. Dance & show bar open late.
POLLY ESTHER'S, 3911 Northview Dr, (601) 366-3247. Gay bar popular with straights, Wed-Thurs 8pm-2am, Fri-Sat 8pm-4am, shows Sun 8pm-2am, 50% gay, 50% straight.

■ *Erotica*
HERITAGE VIDEO, 1515 Terry Rd, (601) 354-5555.

MERIDIAN

■ *Dance Bar/Disco*
CROSSROADS, Hwy 59 South, Savoy exit, (601) 655-8415. Complex with video dance bar, cruise bar, C&W bar, deli, 50% men, 50% women, patio.

OVETT

■ *Information*
SISTERSPIRIT, INC, 203 Eastside Dr, PO Box 12, Ovett, MS 39464, (601) 344-1411 (tel/fax), sisterspir@aol.com. Women's cultural organization, camping OK, RV hookups summer '97, kitchen, meeting space, library. Women & men welcome to help us build. Looking for social justice, seeking people.

VICKSBURG

■ *Erotica*
HILL CITY NEWS, 1214 Washington St, (601) 638-4435. Closed Sun.

MISSOURI
CAPE GIRARDEAU

■ *Bars*
INDEPENDENCE PLACE, 5 S Henderson, (573) 334-2939. DJ, 50% men, 50% women, 8:30pm-1:30am, Fri-Sat 7pm-1:30am, closed Sun.

■ *Erotica*
METRO NEWS BOOKSTORE, 415 Broadway. (573) 335-8633.

COLUMBIA

■ *Information*
WOMEN'S CENTER UMC, 229 Brady Commons, (573) 882-6621.

■ *Dance Bar/Disco*
CONTACTS, 514 E Broadway, (573) 443-0281. Dance bar, open from 8pm, closed Sun.
STYX, 3111 Old Hwy 63 S, (573) 499-1828. Mon-Sat 3pm-1am, live entertainment of all kinds, 50% men, 50% women.

■ *Restaurants*
ERNIE'S CAFE, 1005 E Walnut, (573) 874-7804. Gay-friendly restaurant popular with Columbia gay community. Breakfast anytime. American fare includes burgers, steaks, chops, chicken, & wide vegetarian selection. 6am-8pm.

■ *Retail & Bookstores*
PEACE NOOK, 804-C E. Broadway, (573) 875-0539. Has some gay merchandise.

■ *Erotica*
ECLECTICS, 1122 A Wilkes Blvd, (573) 443-0873.

JOPLIN

■ *Dance Bar/Disco*
PARTNERS DANCE BAR, 722 Main St (rear) near 8th, (417) 623-9313. 50% men, 50% women. Closed Sun.
PARTNERS WESTERN LOUNGE, 720 Main St (rear), (417) 781-6453. C&W dance bar, 50% men, 50% women. Closed Sun.

KANSAS CITY
Also includes Kansas City, KS (913).

■ *Information*
GAY TALK LINE, (816) 931-4470, 6pm-midnight 7 days.

■ *Accommodations*
DOANLEIGH WALLAGH INN, 217 East 37th St, K C, MO, (816) 753-2667, Fax: (816) 531-5158. B&B between Crown Center & Country Club Plaza, mainly straight clientele. Eclectic decor, full gourmet breakfast.
INN THE PARK BED & BREAKFAST, 3610 Gillham Rd, (816) 931-0797. B&B, 50% gay & lesbian clientele. Suites, private baths, full breakfast.

■ *Bars*
BUDDIES, 3715 Main St, (816) 561-2600. Neighborhood cruise bar, best cocktail hour in the city. We welcome everyone. Open 6am-3am, closed Sun.
DAUBER'S PLACE, 1320 Washington Blvd.

MISSOURI

UNITED STATES

DB, 1922 Main at 20th St, (816) 471-2424. Small dance floor.

JAMIE'S, 528 Walnut St at 6th, (816) 471-2080. Fun bar, men welcome, DJ Wed, Fri & Sat.

MARI'S, 1809 Grand, (816) 283-0511. Bar & restaurant, burgers to steaks & seafood.

MISSIE B'S, 805 W 39th St, (816) 561-0625. Piano & cocktail lounge, mostly men. Tue & Thur Karoake, drag show Mon, Wed, Fri, Sat. 80% men, 20% women.

OTHER SIDE, 3611 Broadway, (816) 931-0501. Video bar, closed Sun, 70% men, 30% women.

UTTER HOUSE, 753 Minnesota, Kansas City, KS, (913) 321-5334. Gay & straight crowd.

VIEW ON THE HILL, 204 Orchard St in Kansas (913) 371-9370. From 4pm, women welcome.

Dance Bar/Disco

ATLANTIS, 3954 Central, 753-0112. Gay Mon & Thurs only, 70% men, 30% women. Gay-friendly other times.

CABARET,★ 5024 Main St near 50th St, (816) 753-6504. Dance & show bar, after hours till 3am Wed-Sun.

SIDE KICKS SALOON,★ 3707 Main, (816) 931-1430. C&W dance bar, closed Sun.

SOAKIE'S, 1308 Main, (816) 221-6060. R&B, rap, etc., 50% men, 50% women.

TOOTSIES NEW PLACE, 1818-1822 Main St, (816) 471-7704. Dance bar with drag shows, dinner restaurant, noon-midnight, Fri & Sat till 3am.

Restaurants

CORNER, THE, Broadway & Westport Rd. Very popular gay-friendly Sat brunch.

LATE NIGHT CAFE, at the Cabaret bar, 5024 Main St, (816) 753-6504. Lite grill menu, dinner only.

MARI'S, 1809 Grand, (816) 283-0511. Downstairs gay bar, upstairs restaurant.

SHARP'S 63RD ST GRILL, 128 W 63rd St, (816) 333-4355.

TOOTSIE'S NEW PLACE, 1818-1822 Main St at Tootsie's bar, (816) 471-7704. Sandwiches days, dinner plates.

Retail & Bookstores

HOLLYWOOD AT HOME, 9063 Metcalf at Loehmanns Plaza, Overland Park, (913) 649-9666. Books, videos, alternative newsstand.

LARRY'S GIFTS & CARDS, 205 Westport Rd, (816) 753-4757. Gay & lesbian bookstore. Music, cards, t-shirts, magazines, etc.

Leathers/Piercing

SPIKES LEATHER, 1922 Main St at DB Complex, (816) 471-2424. Clothing & accessories.

Erotica

ADRIANNE'S BOOK STORE, 3314 Troost, (816) 561-8996.

EROTIC CITY, 8401 E Truman Rd, (816) 252-3370, 24hrs.

NEWS EMPORIUM, 3325 Main St, (816) 756-0416. Arcades, magazines, videos 24hrs.

STRAND VIDEO ENTERTAINMENT CENTER, 3544 Troost. (816) 931-6452. X-rated theaters.

VALENTINE VIDEOS, 901 Westport Rd, (816) 561-3701.

VIDEO MANIA, 208 Westport Rd, (816) 561-6397.

OZARKS

Information

GLORP (GAY & LESBIAN OZARK RURAL PEOPLE), (501) 895-4959.

ST JOSEPH

Dance Bar/Disco

CLUB 705, 705 Edmond St, (816) 364-9748. Small dance bar, male & female strippers, 50% men, 50% women.

Restaurants

CABBAGE ROLL, 27th & Lafayette, (816) 233-4444. German cuisine.

JIM'S PLACE, 2110 Francis. Home cooking.

STAN & LOU'S J&J'S, 4th St near Kruzes Ave to Center. Restaurant & bar, home cooking.

ST LOUIS

Also includes East St Louis, IL (618).

Information

GAY & LESBIAN ACTION LINE & HOTLINE, (314) 367-0084. 6pm-10pm Mon-Sat.

Accommodations

A ST. LOUIS GUESTHOUSE IN HISTORIC SOULARD, 1032-38 Allen Ave, (314) 773-1016. Guesthouse, women welcome. Suites with color cable TV, VCR, ceiling fans, private baths.

BREWERS HOUSE BED & BREAKFAST, 1829 Lami St, (314) 771-1542. B&B, minutes to downtown, the Arch & river. Rooms with unusual decor, some fireplaces. Jacuzzi & steam room, continental breakfast, coffee.

NAPOLEON'S RETREAT B&B, 1815 Lafayette Ave, (314) 772-6979. B&B, 50% gay & lesbian clientele. Color TV, AC, ceiling fans, double or queen beds, private baths. Full breakfast, no smoking.

Bars

CHAR-PEI LOUNGE, 400 Mascoutah Ave near E Main, Belleville, IL (618) 236-0810. Open 7 days, 70% men, 30% women.

CLEMENTINE'S, 2001 Menard St at Allen, (314) 664-7869. Bar & restaurant. Oldest gay bar in St. Louis.

CLUB 747, 1624 Delmar, (314) 621-9030. Show bar.

CLUB METRO, 602 Belle, Alton, IL (618) 465-8687. Show bar, male dancers Fri, 50% men, 50% women.

DRAKE'S, 3502 Papin, near Grand & Chouteau, (314) 771-9445. Piano bar.

EAGLE, 17 S Vandeventer, upstairs from Outpost, (314) 535-4100.

GREY FOX PUB, 3505 S Spring near Grand, (314) 772-2150. Bar & restaurant, patio bar in summer, drag queens.

LIL'S SECOND TIME AROUND, 317 Mascoutah Ave, Belleville, IL, (618) 233-9425. 50% men, 50% women.

LOADING ZONE,★ 16 S Euclid, (314) 361-4119. Video bar, excellent happy hour, younger crowd, 50% men, 50% women. From 2pm, closed Sun.

MAGNOLIA'S,★ 5 S Vandeventer, (314) 652-6500. Complex with large dance bar, restaurant, cruise bar, leather bar & quiet bar. Women welcome.

METROPLEX,★ 657 E Broadway, E St Louis, IL, (618) 271-0558. Complex with dance bar, leather bar & drag shows.

MUSTANG SALLY'S, 408 N Euclid, (314) 367-8887.

NOVAK'S, 4146 Manchester Dr, (314) 531-3699. Bar & grill.

OUTPOST, THE 17 S Vandeventer, (314) 535-4100. THE bear club, pool table, games.

RAINBOW'S END, 4060 Chouteau, (314) 652-8790.

Dance Bar/Disco

ATTITUDES,★ 4100 Manchester, (314) 534-3858. Large dance bar, many men Fri for C&W night.

CLUB ZIPS, 3145 W Chain of Rocks Rd, Granite City, IL, (618) 797-0700. Dance bar, patio with volleyball.

COMPLEX, THE, 3511 Chouteau, (314) 772-2645. Probe dance bar & Angles restaurant

---

the CLUB ST. LOUIS

Our World Too
St. Louis's Community Bookshop
(314) 533-5322
11 S. Vandeventer, St. Louis, MO 63108

with patio, Mom's leather bar & Visions bar, outdoor volleyball.

ERNIE'S CLASS ACT, 3756 S Broadway, (314) 664-6221. Bar & informal restaurant & cabaret, live bands, comedy, etc. Closed Sun.

FACES, 130 4th St (entrance), E St Louis, IL, in E. St Louis, MO, (618) 271-7410. Complex with dance & video bar, cruise bar, show bar. More popular 3am-7am weekends, very popular Sun. Women welcome.

MAGNOLIA'S,★ 5 S Vandeventer, (314) 652-6500. Complex with large dance bar, restaurant, leather cruise bar & cabaret. Women welcome.

■ *Saunas/Health Clubs*

CLUB ST. LOUIS, THE, 2625 Sam Shepard Dr near Jefferson, (314) 533-3666. 24hrs, private club, outdoor swimming pool.

■ *Restaurants*

ANGLES, 3511 Chouteau at The Complex. American cuisine. Dinner, Sun brunch.

BALABAN'S, 405 N Euclid, (314) 361-8085. Lunch, dinner, Sun brunch.

ITALIA, 4645 Maryland, (314) 361-7010.

MAJESTIC, 49 W Laclede at Euclid, (314) 361-2011. Very popular diner.

NINER DINER, 5 S Vandeventer, at Magnolia's, (314) 652-0171. Restaurant & domino parlour. Mostly gay & lesbian crowd.

OH MY DARLING CAFE, 2001 Menard St at Clementine's men's bar, (314) 644-7869. Dinner, Sat brunch, closed Sun.

SOUTH CITY DINER, 3141 S Grand, (314) 772-6100. Popular diner open 24hrs, very gay-friendly.

SUNSHINE INN, 8-1/2 S Euclid Ave, (314) 367-1413. Lunch, dinner, Sun brunch, vegetarian menu.

■ *Retail & Bookstores*

CHEAP TRX, 3211 S Grand, (314) 644-4011. Good selection of gay & lesbian cards, gifts, boutique items.

FRIENDS & LOVERS, 3550 Gravois Ave at Grand, (314) 771-9405. Gay & lesbian novelty store.

HEFFALUMP'S, 387 N Euclid Ave near McPherson, (314) 361-0544. Gay cards & novelties.

LEFT BANK BOOKS & LEFT BANK COFFEE, 399 N Euclid Ave at McPherson, (314) 367-6731. General bookstore & coffeeshop, extensive lesbian & gay section, 10am-10pm (Sun till 5pm). Coffeeshop: from 7am (Sun from 9am).

OUR WORLD TOO, 11 S Vandeventer, (314) 533-5322. **Not just a gay and lesbian bookstore anymore!** Now, we have a great selection of gifts, music, safer-sex supplies, rainbow items, calendars, tee shirts, pink or black triangle items, awareness pins and pendants, a large AIDS selection, video rentals, magazines, travel guides, women's and feminist titles. Ask for our extensive catalog.

PAGES, VIDEO & MORE, 10 N Euclid Ave near Laclede, (314) 361-3420. Book & video rental store with large section of gay magazines, cards, books.

WHIZ BAM! 3206 S Grand, (314) 664-3663. Gay & lesbian movies, videos, magazines. Mon-Thur noon-9pm, Fri & Sat noon-10pm, Sun noon-7pm.

■ *Erotica*

A-1 BOOKS, 10204 Page, (314) 426-9088. Also ask for our 2 other locations.

ADULT BOOKSTORE, 2101 N Broadway, (314) 436-2863.

BROOKLYN BOOKS, 222-A Jefferson at Rte 3, Brooklyn, IL. (618) 271-5914.

GODFREY BOOKS, 5735 Godfrey Rd, Godfrey, IL, (618) 466-0203.

OLIVE BOOKS, 9771 Olive St.

PS ADULT BOOKS, 3419 N Lindbergh Blvd, St Ann.

SPRINGFIELD

■ *Dance Bar/Disco*

GALLERY, 424 N Boonville, (417) 865-1266. Dance floor & video bar with patio.

MARTHA'S VINEYARD, 219 W Olive St near Campbell, (417) 864-4572. DJ Fri, Sat, summer patio with outdoor dance floor.

XANADU, 1107 Commercial.

■ *Erotica*

BOLIVAR RD NEWS, 4030 N Bolivar, (417) 833-3354.

SUNSHINE NEWS, 3537 W Sunshine, (417) 831-2298.

MONTANA

WHO TO CALL

For Tour Companies Serving This Destination
See Montana on page 21

BILLINGS

■ *Retail & Bookstores*

BARJON'S, 2718 3rd Ave North, (406) 252-4398. Alternative bookstore with gay & lesbian sections.

■ *Erotica*

ADULT SHOP, 2702 Minnesota Ave, (406) 245-4293.

OTHER PLACE, THE, 2714 Minnesota Ave (406) 245-2915.

MONTANA

FYI

Outdoors Vacations in the US Far West

OutWest Adventures specializes in exclusively gay/lesbian active outdoor vacations in the American West. Both packages and custom trips take you to wilderness areas, ski resorts, working ranches, remote rivers, and national parks, always with experienced guides to smooth the way.

OUTWEST ADVENTURES

Trip Schedule
Apr 19-27
 Utah desert hiking, rafting
May 17-24
 Raft Cataract Canyon-Colo.
May 25-31, Aug 24-30, Sep 21-27
 Gay/Lesbian Ranch Week
Jun 29-Jul 5, Jul 27-Aug 2,
Aug 31-Sep 6
 Montana Big Sky Adventure
Jul 16-22
 Montana by Rail & Yellowstone
Aug 3-9
 Backpack Beartooth Wilderness
TBA '98:
 Gay Ski Tours-Montana
 XCountry Ranch Ski Week
 Contact **OutWest Adventures** at (406) 446-1533, (800) 743-0458, Fax: (406) 446-1338, E-mail: OutWestAdv@aol.com.

FERRARI GUIDES' GAY TRAVEL A to Z - 18th EDITION

MONTANA

Rafting, Biking, Backpacking

Both thrill seekers and the less adventurous will find what they're looking for at **Pangaea Expeditions**. The Missoula-based raft company offers two-hour wine and cheese float trips, half-day scenic raft trips, full-day whitewater trips, and overnight raft trips daily during the summer. These trips are for everyone. Our "Wild Women" trips take you to beautiful, far-away places and vary in length from two days to three weeks. Join our experienced guides as we spend a week navigating the challenging rapids of the Salmon River in Idaho, soaking in hot springs along the way. Or spend a more leisurely week rafting Southern Utah's San Juan River and viewing Indian archeology. Visit Alberta's quaint villages and majestic mountains on a three-week bicycle tour of the Canadian Rockies. During winter, spend 10 warm days sea kayaking in Baja, Mexico. Montana adventures include rock climbing, whitewater rafting, kayaking, mountain biking and backpacking.

Co-ed Trip Schedule 1997 - 1998

Jun 22-28	Mountain Bike, Raft Montana
Jun 14 & Aug 23	Wild Women Rafting
Jul 6-26	Bicycle Canadian Rockies
Aug 25-31	Raft Middle Fork Salmon R.
Sep 21-28	Rafting San Juan River
Jan & Feb 1998:	Sea Kayaking-Baja

WildWomen Adventures:

July 17-26, 20-26, 23-26
Aug 22-31, 25-31, 28-31

Contact **Pangaea** at (406) 721-7719, (888) 721-7719, E-mail: wildwomenz@aol.com, Web: bigsky.net/pangaea.

BOZEMAN

■ *Information*
WOMEN'S RESOURCE CENTER, Rm 15 Hamilton Hall, Montana St Univ, (406) 994-3836. Referrals to local lesbian community, Mon-Fri 9am-4pm.

■ *Women's Accommodations*
FISH CREEK LODGING, See Ashton, Idaho.

■ *Erotica*
MS KITTY'S ADULT, 12 N Wilson Ave, (406) 586-6989.

BUTTE

■ *Accommodations*
SKOOKUM MOTEL, 3541 Harrison Ave, Butte, MT 59701, (406) 494-5353. Motel with restaurant, bar & casino, private baths. ♀♂

■ *Bars*
SNOOKUMS AT THE SKOOKUM, 3541 Harrison Ave, at the Skookum Motel, where I-15 meets I-90, (406) 494-5353. Butte's "gayest" bar, casino & restaurant, 80% gay in evenings. Restaurant is a nice little place to eat, coffee shop & dinner items. In summer there's outside dining on a deck.

■ *Erotica*
ROCKY ADULT BOOKSTORE, 121 Broadway, (406) 723-7218.

HUNGRY HORSE

■ *Retail & Bookstores*
BEAR CONE TRADING POST & GENERAL STORE, in the town of Hungry Horse on the way to Galcier Nat'l Park. Old-fashioned trading post & general store with health, organic & bulk foods, crystals, Native American jewelry & artifacts, music. Mail order available.

MISSOULA

■ *Information*
AIDS HOTLINE, (406) 523-4775.

LAMBDA ASSOC, (406) 523-5567. Group meets at University of Montana.

WOMEN'S RESOURCE CENTER, UC 210, U of M, (406) 243-4153. Mon-Fri 10am-3pm, except summer.

■ *Accommodations*
FOXGLOVE COTTAGE, 2331 Gilbert Ave, Missoula, MT 59802, (406) 543-2927. Gay-owned & -operated B&B with 2 rooms, shared bath, continental breakfast, 5 min from university & downtown. Mostly gay with some straight clientele. ♀♂

■ *Dance Bar/Disco*
AM-VETS CLUB, 225 Ryman, (406) 543-9174. Gay disco Fri & Sat, friendly crowd. ♂

■ *Cafe*
CATALYST ESPRESSO, 111 N Higgins, (406)

542-1337. Mon-Fri 7am-6pm, Sat 8am-6pm, Sun 10am-5pm. Games, magazines, progressive crowd, more gays later. Some extended hours during special gay/lesbian events.

■ *Retail & Bookstores*
FREDDY'S FEED AND READ, 1221 Helen Ave, (406) 549-2127. Deli with organic food & bookstore with small, good selection of gay & lesbian titles.

UNIVERSITY CENTER BOOKSTORE, Campus Dr, University of Montana, (406) 243-4921. Good selection of gay & lesbian books.

■ *Erotica*
FANTASY FOR ADULTS ONLY (SOUTHSIDE) 2611 Brooks St, (406) 543-7510.
FANTASY FOR ADULTS ONLY, 210 E Main St, (406) 543-7760.
PEOPLE'S CHOICE, 2615 Brooks, (406) 728-5754, 7 days.

RONAN

■ *Accommodations*
NORTH CROW RANCH, 2360 North Crow Rd, (406) 676-5169. Guesthouse & campground, shared showers & toilets. ♀♂

NEBRASKA
KEARNEY

■ *Information*
GLAGN (GAY & LESBIAN ASSOC.), rdevel@itec.net. Dances, socials.

LINCOLN

■ *Information*
AIDS INFO, (402) 484-8100.
GAY & LESBIAN RESOURCE CENTER & LINE, (402) 472-5644. Youth talk line (402) 473-7932 answers evenings.
WOMEN'S CENTER, UNL Union Room 340 14th & R Sts, (402) 472-2597.

■ *Dance Bar/Disco*
"Q", 226 S 9th St, (402) 475-2269. Large, progressive, late-nite dance club, patio. Shows some Sun, occasional bands, male strippers, game area with pool table & darts, good mix of men & women.
PANIC, 200 S 18th St at N St, (402) 435-8764. Dance bar with patio, drag shows. ♀♂

■ *Erotica*
ABC LINCOLN, 921 O St near 9th, (402) 435-9323, 24hrs.

OMAHA
Also includes Council Bluffs, IA (712).

■ *Information*
AIDS INFO, (402) 342-4233.
GAY & LESBIAN INFORMATION LINE,

FYI

Rafting & Kayaking Western Montana

On any given day between April 15 and October 15, you can join a half- or full-day rafting trip in Montana with **10,000 Waves**. There are different kinds of paddling to choose from. Paddle rafting in a rubber raft with other passengers gets you involved in the action. The selfbailing rafts let you save all your energy for steering and paddling. Sit-on-top kayaks let you challenge the river on your own, after certified paddling and safety instruction. The kayaks accompany the larger rafts downriver. You can also learn how to manage a real kayak. 10,000 Waves rafts the Alberton Gorge on the Clark Fork River. This is a big-volume, big-ride river with magnificent rock formations and cliffs. On the Blackfoot, the river featured in the movie "The River Runs Through it," you can see for yourself the beauty that inspired its use as a backdrop for this artistic film.

Their goals: "Guests who feel welcome and safe, first-rate equipment and outstanding and plentiful meals."

Contact **10,000 Waves** at (406) 549-6670, (800) 537-8315.

NEBRASKA

FYI

See What Lewis & Clark Saw

The remote wild country of the Missouri River in central Montana is little changed since Lewis and Clark traversed it two centuries ago. This is one of the premier remote-country trips in the lower 48. Only one all-weather road crosses the 107-mile stretch you will canoe. This trip, by **Wild Rockies Tours**, originates in Great Falls, Montana. There is ample time — and opportunity — for hiking, birding and exploring this wild and scenic area. Like several other gay-friendly companies in Montana, Wild Rockies specializes in canoeing, offering trips on the Lower Clark Fork, Blackfoot and Yellowstone Rivers. Many trips originate in Missoula and include a soak in hot springs.

Wild Rockies also offers 3- and 4-day trips including backpacking and mountaineering in the Selway-Bitterroot Wilderness of Cherry Peak Roadless Area. The bitterroot trip offers climbs of two class-3 peaks. For the less adventuresome, canoeing, mountain biking and hiking day trips are available.

Contact **Wild Rockies Tours** at (406) 728-0566, fax coming soon.

NEBRASKA

The Gay Discount Travel King

Affordable gay Las Vegas vacation packages were pioneered in 1996 by **Players Express**, with lower hotel rates and a Las Vegas gay visitor's guide and discount coupon pack. New cities have been added to this package line for 1997: Now you can look to Players Express for discounts in Puerto Vallarta, Cancun, Hawaii and Florida.

PLAYERS EXPRESS VACATIONS

Players also reports it has discounts on major scheduled airlines of up to 20% off the lowest published fares worldwide.

Players' GROUPSTATION provides competitive group pricing, one contact through every step of the booking process, travel bonuses for groups as small as 15 and complete meeting and planning services worldwide (sales meetings, seminars, trade shows, theme parties, banquets, weddings and cruises).

In April, 1997, join Players' 11-day Greek Island Cruise/Tour vacation.

Contact **Players Express** at (702) 257-5034, (800) 458-6161 (groups: (800) 848-4877, Fax: (702) 362-5594.

(402) 341-0330. Tape 24hrs, manned 6pm-9pm weekdays, Tues, Thurs & Sat 12-6pm.

■ *Bars*
DIAMOND BAR, 712 S 16th St near Leavenworth, (402) 342-9595, 7 days.
GILLIGAN'S PUB, 1823 Leavenworth at 19th, (402) 449-9147. Bowling leagues.

■ *Dance Bar/Disco*
CHESTERFIELD,★ 1901 Leavenworth (402) 345-6889. Juke box dance bar, DJ Thurs-Sat.
CLUB JAMES DEAN,★ 1507 Farnham, (402) 341-2500. Large club with 3 rooms, large dance floor.
DC'S, 610 S 14th near Pacific, (402) 344-3103. C&W dance bar.
MAX, THE,★ 1417 Jackson at 15th, (402) 346-4110. Hi-energy video dance bar, game room, patio bar, male dancers, Stosh's leather cruise bar is inside, 60% men, 40% women.
OMAHA MINING CO., 1715 Leavenworth near 18th, (402) 449-8703. Huge dance floor, after hours weekends.

■ *Cafe*
DOWNTOWN GROUND, 1117 Jackson St in Old Market, Omaha (402) 342-1654. Coffeehouse, juice bar, food & entertainment.

■ *Restaurants*
NEON GOOSE, 1012 S 10th, (402) 341-2063. Burgers, omelettes, lunch & dinner specials.

■ *Retail & Bookstores*
NEW REALITIES, 1026 Howard St near 11th, (402) 342-1863. Specializing in gay & lesbian books & gifts. Music, new age, recovery & self-help.

■ *Erotica*
OFF-BROADWAY BOOKS, 3216 1st Ave S, Council Bluffs, (712) 328-2673, 24hrs.

SCOTTSBLUFF

■ *Information*
PANHANDLE GAY & LESBIAN SUPPORT & SERVICES, Box 1046, Scottsbluff, NE 69363, (308) 635-8488.

NEVADA

WHO TO CALL
For Tour Companies Serving This Destination
See Nevada on page 21

LAKE TAHOE
See Lake Tahoe Area, CA

LAS VEGAS

■ *Information*
AIDS HOTLINE, (702) 474-2437 OR (800) 842-AIDS, in Spanish (800) 344-7432.
GAY & LESBIAN COMMUNITY CENTER, 912 E Sahara, (702) 733-9800, 10am-8:30pm, Sat 12pm-8pm, Sun 12pm-6pm.

■ *Accommodations*
DESERT RAINBOW INN, (702) 221-4301 (recorded message/Fax), fax also to (702) 256-8052. All-male, clothing-optional motel inn with juice bar. 28 king-sized rooms, 2 suites, private baths, private courtyard, large lagoon-pool with waterfall, cable color TV with 1 adult male entertainment channel. Easy access to the Strip. OPENING OCTOBER, 1997.

LAS VEGAS PRIVATE BED & BREAKFAST, (702) 384-1129, Fax: (702) 384-1129. My home features a unique European decor with lots of amenities. Tropical plants and trees surround the pool area. Futher back are aviaries, with tropical birds and parrots. Las Vegas has 24-hr entertainment. Other activities: desert sightseeing, water sports on Lake Mead, Grand Canyon tours, Laughlin excursions, winter skiing, and hiking to hot springs along the Colorado River.

■ *Beaches*
NUDE GAY BEACH, N Lake Shore Dr to 8.0 Rd. Turn right. Follow gravel rd to water & take every left turn. Park. Walk east over 1st hill.

■ *Bars*
ANGLES-N-LACE,★ 4633 Paradise Rd at Naples, (702) 791-0100. Video bar with men's & women's sections, pool table, slots, 24hrs.

LAS VEGAS PRIVATE Bed & Breakfast
LUCKY YOU!
(702) 384-1129

NEW HAMPSHIRE

BACKDOOR, 1415 E Charleston Blvd, near 15th (rear), (702) 385-2018, 24hrs, slots.

BUFFALO, THE,★ 4640 Paradise Rd (in shop ctr) at Naples, (702) 733-8355. Slots, 24hrs, very popular beer bust 4-7pm Sun.

CHOICES, 1729 E Charleston, (702) 382-4791. Game room, slots, women welcome, 24hrs.

EAGLE/TEXAS,★ 3430 E Tropicana #47, (702) 458-8662, 24hrs, underwear nites.

SNICK'S PLACE, 1402 S 4th St at Imperial, (702) 385-9298. Slots, 24hrs.

■ Dance Bar/Disco

BACKSTREET BAR,★ 5012 S Arville, (702) 876-1844. C&W dance bar, 50% men, 50% women, beer bust 2 days a week, dance lessons.

BADLANDS SALOON, 953 E Sahara, (702) 792-9262.

FLEX, 4371 W Charleston Blvd, (702) 385-FLEX. Bar, disco & restaurant, strippers, drag shows, 24hrs. Tues & Wed many women.

GIPSY,★ 4605 Paradise Rd at Naples, (702) 731-1919. Dance & show bar, strip shows, slots, 10pm, 50% men, 50% women. Enlarging in 1997.

GOODTIMES, 1775 E Tropicana in the Liberace Plaza. (702) 736-9494. Piano bar, lounge & disco, 75% men, 25% women. THE place to be on Mon.

■ Cafe

COYOTE CAFE AT THE MGM GRAND, (702) 891-7349. Gay-friendly.

■ Retail & Bookstores

GET BOOKED, 4640 Paradise Rd, (702) 737-7780. Gay, lesbian & feminist bookstore with music, video rentals, cards & t-shirts, rainbow items.

■ Erotica

ADULT SUPERSTORE, Spring Mountain & I-15.

ADULT SUPERSTORES, Tropicana at Valleyview.

DESERT BOOKS, 4350 Las Vegas Blvd N, (702) 643-7982.

DOWNTOWN BOOKS, 516 E Fremont, (702) 386-1999.

FANTASY VIDEO PLUS, 1100 N Boulder Hwy, Henderson, (702) 565-3227.

FLICK ADULT THEATRE, 719 E Fremont at 7th, (702) 386-0250, 24hrs.

INDUSTRIAL RD ADULT BOOKS, 3463 Industrial Rd, (702) 734-7667, 24hrs.

PARADISE ADULT BOOKS, 4034 Paradise Rd, (702) 734-1591.

PURE PLEASURE, 3177 S Highland Dr, (702) 369-8044. Adult playground. Nude dancers, leather, bondage, accessories. 24 hrs.

PURE PLEASURE, 953 E Sahara #B-14, (702) 791-3288. Adult playground. Nude dancers, leather, bondage, accessories. 24 hrs.

PURE PLEASURE, 1100 N Boulder Hwy, (702) 565-3227. Adult playground. Nude dancers, leather, bondage, accessories. 24 hrs.

RANCHO ADULT CENTER, 4820 N Rancho #D N of Lone Mtn Rd, (702) 645-6104, 24hrs.

RENO

■ Bars

CLUB 1099, 1099 S Virginia St at Caliente, (702) 329-1099. videos, 24hrs, patio, pool table, slots.

FIVE STAR SALOON, 132 West St near 1st, (702) 329-2878. DJ weekends. Slots, 24hrs.

QUEST, THE, 210 W Commercial Row (702) 333-2808. DJ weekends, slots.

SHOUTS, 145 Hillcrest St, (702) 829-7667. 60% men, 40% women, popular happy hour, slots.

■ Dance Bar/Disco

BAD DOLLY'S, 535 E 4th St near Valley, (702) 348-1983. Slots, top 40's, usually 75% women late Fri & Sat.

VISIONS,★ 340 Kietzke Ln, (702) 786-5455. Young collegiate crowd, 80% men, women welcome. Big screen TV, slots.

■ Saunas/Health Clubs

STEVE'S, 1030 W 2nd St near Gardner, (702) 323-8770. Private club, 24hrs.

■ Retail & Bookstores

GRAPEVINE BOOKS & ESPRESSO, 1450 S Wells Ave, (702) 786-4869. Gay & lesbian bookstore with small general section, espresso drinks, Italian sodas, pastries. May change in 1997.

SILVER SAGE, 1557 S Virginia St, (702) 348-0022. Metaphysical bookstore with small women's section.

■ Erotica

FANTASY FAIRE, 1298 S Virginia St, (702) 323-6969. A boutique for lovers. Leather, toys, cards, gifts, lotions & potions.

SUZIE'S, 2nd at Kietzke.

STATELINE

See Lake Tahoe Area, CA

NEW HAMPSHIRE STATEWIDE

■ Information

AIDS INFO LINE, (800) 752-AIDS.

ASHLAND

■ Accommodations

COUNTRY OPTIONS, 27-29 N Main St, (603) 968-7952. B&B in a warm country style, furnished with antiques. Shared baths, mountain views, full breakfast. 50% gay & lesbian clientele.

BATH VILLAGE

■ Accommodations

EVERGREEN BED & BREAKFAST, Bath Village, (603) 747-3947. B&B near river, lake & scenic attractions, women welcome. Spacious rooms with antique furnishings & shared baths. TV lounge & full breakfast.

BETHLEHEM

■ Women's Accommodations

HIGHLANDS INN, THE, Box 118-I, (603) 869-3978. The North Country's only lesbian-owned and -operated inn. B&B inn on 100 acres. A Lesbian paradise with 20 comfortable rooms, antique furnishings, private & shared baths, TV lounge, kitchen privileges, library, heated pool, BBQ grills, hot tub, hiking, skiing and full breakfast. Rates $55-$110, weeklong & midweek discounts. Winner Out & About Editor's Choice Awards. Our sign always says "no vacancy" so please ignore it. Non-smoking rooms.

CENTRE HARBOR

■ Accommodations

RED HILL INN, Rte 25B RFD #1, Box 99M, (603) 279-7001. Gay-friendly inn with bar and restaurant. Variety of guest quarters with comfortable antique furniture, some Jacuzzis, some fireplaces. TV lounge, full breakfast, nearby lake.

FRANCONIA

■ Accommodations

BLANCHE'S B&B, Easton Valley Rd, (603) 823-7061. Gay-friendly B&B, shared baths, home-cooked breakfasts.

BUNGAY JAR, PO Box 15 Easton Valley Rd, (603) 823-7775, Fax: (603) 444-0100. Not a neighbor is visible from our private balconies. We're off the beaten path, yet near all major White Mountain attractions. Walk through the woods to a hidden stream. Meditate by the water lily pond. Relax in the library, the sauna or by the fireplace. Breakfast specialties. New Garden Suite: king bed, fireplace, 2-person Jacuzzi, kitchen/dining area, porch & mountain view. Non-smoking environment. Gay-friendly.

HORSE & HOUND INN, THE, 205 Wells Rd, (603) 823-5501, (800) 450-5501. Gay-friendly B&B inn with restaurant & lounge. Private & shared baths, TV lounge, full breakfast & nearby lake. Gay male following.

HART'S LOCATION

■ Accommodations

NOTCHLAND INN, THE, Reservations: (800) 866-6131, (603) 374-6131, Fax: (603) 374-6168. Gay-friendly inn with restaurant. Private baths, full breakfast, dinner, spa, river on premisis. No smoking environment.

FERRARI GUIDES' GAY TRAVEL A to Z - 18th EDITION

NEW HAMPSHIRE

KEENE

Accommodations
POST AND BEAM BED & BREAKFAST, HCR 33, Box 380, Centre St, Sullivan, 03445, (603) 847-3330, Fax: (603) 847-3306. E-mail: postandbeam@top.monad.net. Gay-owned B&B with gay & straight clientele, 12 min from Keene, 30 min from Brattleboro. Private & shared baths, full or continental breakfast.

MANCHESTER

Bars
SPORTERS, THE, 361 Pine at Hanover, (603) 668-9014.

Dance Bar/Disco
CLUB MERRIMAC, 201 Merrimac near Pine, (603) 623-9362. Private club.
FRONT RUNNER, 1st St near Elm behind Northend Superette, (603) 623-6477. Huge dance bar.

NEWFOUND LAKE

Accommodations
CLIFF LODGE COTTAGES, Route 3A, HC60 Box 199 Briston, NH 03222, (603) 744-8660. Old-style rustic cottages next to main house, bar & restaurant, gay & lesbian following.
INN ON NEWFOUND LAKE, THE, Rt. 3A, Bridgewater, NH 03222, (603) 744-9111, (800) 745-7990, Fax: (603) 744-3894, E-mail: inonlk@cyberportal.net. Escape to a beautiful Victorian inn sitting on one of the most pristine lakes in the country. The inn features 31 rooms and a renowned restaurant and tavern. There is a private beach, boat dock, exercise room and Jacuzzi. This year-round destination is just 2 hours from Boston, with biking, hiking, boating, skiing, snowmobiling, etc. Mention this ad for special rates. Most major credit cards. Mostly straight clientele with a gay male following.

THE INN ON NEWFOUND LAKE
NEW HAMPSHIRE
(800) 745-7990
(603) 744-9111

NORTH CONWAY - CHOCORUA

Accommodations
MT. CHOCORUA VIEW HOUSE, Rte 16 PO Box 348 Chocorua, (603) 323-8350. Gay-friendly B&B & restaurant. Shared baths, ceiling fans & continental breakfast.

PORTSMOUTH

Women's Accommodations
PAYNE'S HILL B&B, 141 Henry Law Ave, Dover, NH 03820, (603) 740-9441. B&B in a restored New Englander, walking distance to downtown Dover, 12-min drive from central Portsmouth, 3 rooms share baths, expanded cont. break.. 50% g/l clientele.

Dance Bar/Disco
DESERT HEARTS, 948 Rte 1 Bypass in Portsmouth, 3/4 mile outside Portsmouth, (603) 431-5400. Disco, Wed-Sun 8pm-1am.

Erotica
FIFTH WHEEL, Rte 1 Bypass South, (603) 436-1504. Videos.
PETER'S PALACE, Rte 1 Bypass North near Portsmouth Traffic Circle, (603) 436-9622. Videos.
SPAULDING BOOK & VIDEO, off Rte 1 traffic circle heading north. Close midnight, 2am Fri & Sat.

NEW JERSEY

WHO TO CALL
For Tour Companies Serving This Destination
See New Jersey on page 21

STATEWIDE

Information
AIDS HOTLINE, (800) 281-2437. NJ State Dept of Health, Aids Education.

Dance Bar/Disco
LADIES, (609) 784-8341. Scheduled women's dance parties throughout NJ and nearby PA.

ASBURY PARK

Information
GAY & LESBIAN COMMUNITY CENTER OF NJ, 515 Cookman Ave, (908) 774-1809. 7pm-10pm Mon-Fri, 1pm-10pm Thurs.

Bars
BOND ST BAR, 208 Bond St near Cookman, (908) 776-9766. Men welcome.

Dance Bar/Disco
DOWN THE STREET, 230 Cookman Ave, (908) 988-2163. Dance & show bar, male dancers Wed, women welcome. Outdoor deck in summer.

ATLANTIC CITY

Accommodations
ROSE'S COTTAGE, 161 Westminister Ave, (609) 345-8196. Guesthouse. Doubles or singles with shared baths, TV lounge & nearby ocean beach.
SURFSIDE GUEST HOUSE AND SUNDECK BAR, 18 South Mt Vernon Ave, (609) 347-0808, 348-3310. Men-only guesthouse.

Bars
BRASS RAIL, 12 South Mt Vernon between Atlantic/Pacific, (609) 348-0192. Cocktail lounge & Surside Six deck bar, 90% men, 10% women. Pool table, games, jukebox, 24hrs. Fri ladies night.
REFLECTIONS LOUNGE, South Carolina at Boardwalk, (609) 348-1115. Pool tables & video machines.
RENDEZVOUS LOUNGE, 137-139 S New York Ave, (609) 347-8539. 3pm-3am, Tues, Thurs & Sat male dancers (varies by season), drag show Sun.

Dance Bar/Disco
STUDIO SIX DANCE CLUB★, 12 S Mount Vernon above the Brass Rail bar, (609) 348-3310. Progressive, hi-energy video dance bar, 70% men, 30% women. Top entertainment, frequent stars, balcony bar, custom sound, 10pm-8am.

Restaurants
BRASS RAIL KITCHEN, at Brass Rail, 12 South Mt Vernon, (609) 348-3310. Dinner only.

Erotica
ATLANTIC CITY NEWS, 101 S Martin Luther King Jr Dr at Pacific, (609) 344-9444, 24hrs.
CONNIE'S NEWS 1118 Atlantic Ave, (609) 344-9813, 24hrs.

BOONTON

Dance Bar/Disco
CONNEXIONS, 202 Myrtle Ave, (201) 263-4000. Wed-Sat 8pm-closing. Fri DJ, Sat drag shows.

HOBOKEN

Dance Bar/Disco
EXCALIBUR, 1000 Jefferson St, at 10th St, (201) 795-1023. NY-style dance bar 3 min from Manhattan, Tiki Bar is outdoor patio bar. Open Thurs-Sun 9pm-2am, Sat 9pm-3am, Fri Noche Latina, drag show 1am, Sat Latin American nite.

JEFFERSON

Dance Bar/Disco
YACHT CLUB, 366 Berkshire Valley Rd, (201) 697-9780. Large Bar, 60% men, 40% women.

NEW JERSEY

JERSEY CITY

Bars
UNCLE JOE'S TAVERN, 154 1st St, (201) 659-6999. 9pm-2am, Fri & Sat till 3am, Sun 4pm-2am, DJ Fri, Sat. ♂

Dance Bar/Disco
CASTLE CLUB, 141 Bright St, (201) 413-1167. We-Su 8p-2a, DJ Fri, Sat, tea dance Sun (brunch with live jazz before tea dance).

LYNDHURST

Dance Bar/Disco
PHARAOHS, 749 Marin Ave, (201) 933-2151. Gay & lesbian Mon, Wed, Sat only.

MAYS LANDING

Dance Bar/Disco
INTERLUDE LOUNGE, 5045 Black Horse Pike, near Hamilton Mall, (609) 625-9487. From 8pm. Unverifiable spring '97.

MORRISTOWN

Information
GAY ACTIVIST ALLIANCE, (201) 285-1595. Helpline nightly 7:30pm-10:30pm or tape.

NEW BRUNSWICK - SOMERSET

Information
PRIDE CENTER OF NEW JERSEY, 211 Livingston Ave, (908) 846-CCDC (2232), 7pm-10pm, Tues 11am-1pm.

Dance Bar/Disco
DEN, 700 Hamilton St, Somerset, (908) 545-7329. Huge dance floor, beer bar & cafe, billiard room.

Restaurants
FROG & THE PEACH, 29 Dennis St, (908) 846-3216. Restaurant & bar, late-night menu.
STAGE LEFT BAR & RESTAURANT, 5 Livingston Ave, (908) 828-4444. Gay-friendly bar. Many gays & lesbians late Fri & Sat (after midnight) after gay bars close.

NEWARK - ORANGE
Also includes East Orange.

Dance Bar/Disco
MURPHY'S, 59 Edison Pl near Mulberry, (201) 622-9176. Lunch service, gay eves only. 60% men, 40% women.

PERTH AMBOY

Bars
OTHER HALF, corner of Convery Blvd (Rte 35) & Kennedy St, (908) 826-8877. DJ Fri & Sat, 85% men, women welcome.

PLAINFIELD

Accommodations
PILLARS OF PLAINFIELD BED & BREAKFAST, THE, 922 Central Ave, Plainfield, NJ 07060, (908) 753-0922 (Tel/Fax), (888) PIL-LARS (745-5277). B&B with RV hookup, 50% gay & lesbian clientele. AC, private baths, TV lounge, expanded continental breakfast & kitchen privileges.

RED BANK

Retail & Bookstores
EARTH SPIRIT, 16 W Front St, (908) 842-3855. New Age center & bookstore. Feminist literature, gay & lesbian studies.

RIVER EDGE

Dance Bar/Disco
FEATHERS,★ 77 Kinderkamack Rd, (201) 342-6410. Two floors, different music each night. Male dancers Fri, drag shows Tues & Sun. Women welcome.

SANDY HOOK

Accommodations
SEA BIRD INN, PO Box 395, 60 Bay Ave, (908) 872-0123, fax (908) 872-2476. B&B, some straight clientele, shared bath. ♀ ♂

Beaches
GAY BEACH at Sandy Hook Beach in Gateway National Park. Gay nude beach.

SAYREVILLE

Dance Bar/Disco
SAUVAGE, 1 Victory Circle, (908) 727-6619. Drag shows.

SOMERDALE

Dance Bar/Disco
LE GALAXY, 5 E Somerdale (White Horse Pike). 8pm-3am Tues-Sun, Sun drag shows, Tues ladies nite, Wed oldies & karaoke, Fri & Sat hi energy techno dance.

SOMERSET
See New Brunswick/Somerset

TRENTON

Dance Bar/Disco
BUDDIES' PUB, 677 S Broad St, (609) 989-8566. DJ Fri & Sat, 50% men, 50% women.

UNION CITY

Dance Bar/Disco
COLLEGE CLUB, 733 32nd St (Summit Ave), (201) 867-9821. Wed house music & classics from 9pm.
NITE LITE, 509 22nd St, (201) 863-9515. Bar & disco, 70% women, 30% men. Unverifiable spring '97.

WOODBURY

Information
RAINBOW PLACE OF SOUTH JERSEY, 1103 N Broad St, (609) 848-2455.

FYI

Wilderness Challenges for Women in NJ, PA and NY

Adventures for Women designs small group trips for the novice and wilderness-wise woman, with time to enjoy the surroundings, the camaraderie and the challenges. They offer cross-country ski instruction in the Adirondack Mtns of New York State and in the New York/New Jersey metropolitan area. They offer hikes throughout New Jersey, New York and Pennsylvania. They teach safe, fun-filled canoeing in all three states. Contemplation Weekends include discussion, hiking, skiing, boating and swimming. Adirondack Walking, Hiking and Canoeing includes walks in old woods, paddling the lake country, hiking the high peaks. Kayaking South Carolina's coast is for women with boating experience. It includes explorations of Charleston harbor and its barrier islands. On their Austrian Alps trip, they'll fly into Zurich, hike the Lake Constance area, visit Salzburg and fly home out of Munich. Director Betsy Thomason, a registered respiratory therapist, has been conducting The Breathing Workshop since 1987.

Contact **Adventures for Women** at (201) 930-0557 (tel/fax).

FERRARI GUIDES' GAY TRAVEL A to Z - 18th EDITION

NEW MEXICO

NEW MEXICO
ALBUQUERQUE

Information
COMMON BOND G&L COMMUNITY CTR, (505) 266-8041, helpline usually answers 6pm-9pm or tape.
WOMEN'S CENTER, 1160 Mesa Vista Hall at the U of NM, (505) 277-3716. 8am-5pm, closed Sat, Sun.

Realtors/Relocation
YOUR FAMILY REALTOR, (505) 344-9205, Fax: (505) 344-3434, at home, and email: Goldenluck@aol.com. Thinking of calling Albuquerque home? **Debbie Golden at RE/MAX Freedom Realtors** can help! From the Rio Grande River to the Sandia Mountains, Debbie knows every nook, every cranny, and every neighborhood Albuquerque has to offer. An active member of the G&L community, and Albuquerque's #1 gay & lesbian realtor, Debbie is always happy to welcome you to The Land of Enchantment. You've never met a realtor like Debbie Golden!

Accommodations
CASITAS AT OLD TOWN, THE, 1604 Old Town Rd NW, (505) 843-7479. Suites with private entrances. Private baths, AC, kitchen, refrigerator, coffee/tea-making facilities & fireplace. Minutes from Old Town. ♀♂
DAVE'S B&B ON THE RIO GRANDE, PO Box 27214, Albuquerque, 87125-7214, (505) 247-8312, Fax: (505) 842-0733, E-mail: DavesBB@Rt66.com. B&B, women welcome. Color TV, VCR, private baths & expanded continental breakfast. ♂
GOLDEN GUESTHOUSE, 2645 Decker NW, Albuquerque, NM 87107, (505) 344-5995, (888) 332-2434, Fax: (505) 344-3434, E-mail: GoldenGH@aol.com. Guesthouse casita with private bath, continental breakfast, minutes from Old Town Plaza, 1 block from Rio Grande Nature Preserve. Some straight clientele. ♀♂
HACIENDA ANTIGUA BED AND BREAKFAST, 6708 Tierra Dr NW, (505) 345-5399, (800) 484-2385, code no. 9954. Gay-friendly B&B in a 200-year-old adobe hacienda in the north valley residential area of Albuquerque. Fireplace & private bath in every room.
HATEFUL MISSY & GRANNY BUTCH'S BOUDOIR & MANURE EMPORIUM, PO Box 556, Veguita, NM 87062, (800) 397-2482, (505) 861-3328. B&B with Granny Butch's Genital Store & Art Gallery, men very welcome. Color cable TV, VCR, video tape library, ceiling fans, private baths, full breakfast. ♀
RAINBOW LODGE, THE, 115 Frost Rd, Sandia Park, (505) 281-7100. B&B located between Albuquerque & Santa Fe, private & shared baths, expanded continental breakfast, color cable TV, VCR, ceiling fans, outdoor hot tub, 50% gay/lesbian clientele.
RIO GRANDE HOUSE, 3100 Rio Grande Blvd NW, (505) 345-0120. Gay-friendly B&B 3 miles from Old Town. Single & double rooms with southwestern flavor & exotic collectibles, modern conveniences, full breakfast.
TARA COTTA, 3118 Rio Grande Blvd NW, (505) 344-9443 (tel/fax). B&B guesthouse, private bath, continental breakfast, color cable TV, VCR, swamp cooler, ceiling fans, hot tub, 50% gay/lesbian clientele.
W.E. MAUGER ESTATE, 701 Roma Ave NW, (505) 242-8755. B&B inn, 50% gay & lesbian. Variety of Victorian-style rooms with modern conveniences, TV lounge & full breakfast. Catering available, nearby river.
W.J. MARSH HOUSE VICTORIAN B&B INN, THE, 301 Edith SE, (505) 247-1001, toll-free (888) WJ MARSH (956-2774). Gay-friendly B&B inn with separate Victorian cottage & 2 in-house ghosts. Private & shared baths, AC, full gourmet breakfast in house. Cottage has full kitchen, color cable TV & ceiling fans. 50% gay & lesbian clientele.

Bars
ALBUQUERQUE SOCIAL CLUB, 4021 Central Ave SE at Montclaire, (505) 255-0887. Private club, 80% men. The Cheers of Albuquerque. ♂
CUFFS, at the Ranch bar, 8900 Central SE. Open 7 days. ♂
MARTINI GRILL, 4200 Central Ave SE, (505) 255-4111. Gay- & cigar-friendly martini bar & restaurant, 11am-2am (Sun till midnight), Sun brunch 11am-3pm, pasta, gourmet chicken dishes, steaks, 60% gay & lesbian.
PIT, THE, 7209 Central Ave NE at Albuquerque Mining Company. ♂

Dance Bar/Disco
ALBUQUERQUE MINING CO (AMC), ★ 7209 Central Ave NE at Chama, (505) 255-4022. Four bars, including The Pit, a levi/leather bar, a patio bar, open all year. We have something for everyone. All bars open at 3pm 7 days a week. 70% men, 30% women. ♂
FOXES LOUNGE, ★ 8521 Central Ave NE, near Wyoming, (505) 255-3060. Cruisiest bar on the strip! 20th year. $ ♂
LEGENDS WEST, 6132 4th St NW, (505) 343-9793. ♀
PULSE, ★ 4100 Central Ave NE, (505) 255-3334. Alternative club, hi-energy dance bar with hot bartenders, Twinky stand & model bar, underwear nights, 75% gay/lesbian. ♂
RANCH, THE, 8900 Central SE, (505) 275-1616. A man's bar. ♂

Cafe
DOUBLE RAINBOW, 3415 Central SE, (505) 255-6633. Gay-friendly coffeeshop/lunch cafe.

Fitness Centers
PRIDE GYM, 1803 3rd St NW, (505) 242-7810. Private men's health club, gay-owned & -operated, novices & travelers welcome, 6am-8pm (Sat till 6pm), closed Sun. ♂

Retail & Bookstores
FULL CIRCLE BOOKS, 2205 Silver Ave SE near Yale, (505) 266-0022. Women's, gay men's & lesbian books, jewelry, music, t-shirts. Lesbian meetings.
IN CROWD, 3106 Central SE, (505) 268-3750. T-shirts, books, fashion accessories, postcards.
MARTHA'S BODY BUENO SHOP, 3105 Central Ave NE, (505) 255-1122. Carries a selection of gay cards & gifts.

YOUR family REALTOR
Debbie Golden
(505) 344-9205

ALBUQUERQUE MINING CO.
7209 Central N.E.
(505) 255-4022
OPEN AT 3PM
4 Bars in 1
1 Dance Bar
1 Video Bar
1 Levi/Leather Bar
volleyball
Largest Patio Bar In Albuquerque
Hrs: 3pm-2am M-Sa, 3pm-12am Sun
• Ticket Tues •

ALEPOU
FOXES
8521 CENTRAL N.E.
ALBUQUERQUE, NM
(505) 255-3060
CRUISIEST BAR ON THE STRIP!

NEW MEXICO

SISTERS' & BROTHERS' BOOKSTORE, 4011 Silver Ave SE, (505) 266-7317. Lesbian, gay and bisexual bookstore.

■ Leathers/Piercing
LEATHER SHOPPE, THE, 4217 Central NE, (505) 266-6690. Largest selection of erotic leather for men & women in the Southwest. Sun-Thu noon-10pm. Fri-Sat noon-2am.

■ Erotica
BIG EYE, Jefferson at I-25.

MR PEEPERS ADULT VIDEO SALES, 4300 Edith NE, (505) 343-8063. Arcade, bondage section, theater.

NEBULA, 9132 Central SE, 1 block east of Wyoming, (505) 275-7727. Books, videos, novelties, daily 10am-midnight.

PLACE, THE, Carlisle, 1 block west of Edith.

PUSSYCAT, 4207 Central Ave NE, (505) 266-7606. Also: 4012 Central Ave SE, 268-1631.

VIEWPOINT, 620 Central SE, (505) 268-6373, dial 0 when machine picks up. Adult video store with arcade.

ESPAÑOLA

■ Accommodations
INN OF LA MESILLA, THE, Rt 1, Box 368A, (505) 753-5368. Gay-friendly B&B with private baths, full breakfast. Lesbian following with gay men welcome.

RANCHITO SAN PEDRO DE COCONO, PO Box 1849, Española, NM 87532, (505) 753-0583. B&B with 2 private rooms, kitchen (continental breakfast included), and an outdoor patio with kiva fireplace. The hostess, a watercolor professional, teaches classes on site & can suggest outings to nearby "off the beaten track" treasures. Located just off the Santa Fe-Taos Hwy 84, 18 miles north of Santa Fe at the southern edge of Española. 50% gay & lesbian clientele.

GALLUP

■ Accommodations
ZUNI MOUNTAIN LODGE, HC-62, Box 5114, Thoreau, (505) 862-7769. B&B 45 miles outside Gallup, 7 rooms with king & double beds, private baths, full breakfast, TV lounge. Some straight clientele. ♀♂

LAS CRUCES

■ Erotica
SWINGERS, 1805 W Picacho Ave, (505) 523-9050.

RED RIVER

■ Accommodations
VALLEY LODGE FAMILY MOTEL, PO Box 304, Main St, (505) 754-2262, reservations (800) 951-2262. Gay-friendly motel with suites & cabins. Color cable TV, telephone & private baths.

SANTA FE

■ Information
AIDS INFO, (505) 266-0911 or tape.

■ Accommodations
ARIUS COMPOUND, PO Box 1111, 1018-1/2 Canyon Rd, Out of Town: (800) 735-8453, Local: (505) 982-2621, Fax: (505) 989-8280. E-mail: len@ariuscompound.com. Gay-friendly Casitas, 40% gay clientele. Color cable TV, telephone, ceiling fans, kitchens, fireplace & private bath. Redwood hot tub.

CASA DE GATA, 121 E Santa Fe Ave, Santa Fe, NM 87501, (505) 995-9757, E-mail: katryn2@aol.com. Choose between romantic bedrooms, like the lavender Angel Room, the Rose Room, or two Santa Fe style casitas. Our late-Victorian home in historical Santa Fe, is within walking distance of The Plaza. The living room fireplace promises comfortable evenings by the fire. We serve an expanded continental breakfast. Restaurants and shopping are less than a block away. Lesbian owned and totally gay-friendly. 50% gay & lesbian clientele.

FOUR KACHINAS INN B&B, 512 Webber St, (505) 982-2550. Gay-friendly B&B, private baths, expanded continental breakfast.

HEART SEED B&B RETREAT CENTER & SPA, PO Box 6019, Santa Fe, 87502, (505) 471-7026. Gay-friendly accommodations. Four rooms (two with kitchenettes) on 100 beautiful acres. Large deck, full day spa with masseuse on premises. Mountain bikes available, full gourmet breakfast.

HUMMINGBIRD RANCH, Rte 10, Box 111, Santa Fe, NM 87501, (505) 471-2921. Close enough & yet far enough away from whatever it is that has brought you here to Santa Fe. 7 scenic miles from the downtown Plaza—galleries, museums, fine dining, horseback riding and our favorite, which is simply walking outside & looking up at the sky & mountains. Private & scenic accommodations. Call for reasonable rates.

INN OF THE TURQUOISE BEAR, 342 E Buena Vista St, Santa Fe, NM 87501, (505) 983-0798, (800) 396-4104, Fax: (505) 988-4225, E-mail: bluebear@roadrunner.com. Spanish-Pueblo Revival style adobe B&B inn with private & shared baths, expanded continental breakfast, some straight clientele. ♀♂

OPEN SKY B&B, 134 Turquoise Trail, (505)

Hummingbird Ranch

Private Accommodations
Santa Fe, N.M.

(505) 471-2921

FYI

Women's Wilderness Trips

Hawk, I'm Your Sister aims to teach you the language of forests, canyons, deserts, rivers, lakes, and the sea in a safe, supportive environment, without competition, women of all ages and degrees of experience. We will teach you skills that will allow you to feel at home in the wilderness...how to read the water and the sky...to camp safely and with low impact...how to cook delicious and nourishing meals in any weather. Group members share daily tasks of food preparation and clean-up, filtering water, loading and unloading and carrying canoes, and digging latrines. You will learn how to handle your craft and gear in varied weather conditions, as you discover the artistry of skillful canoeing.

Our food is good! We prepare generous, nutritious meals from the best ingredients, including bountiful fresh vegetables, fresh and dried fruits, whole grains, chicken, and fish. Vegetarian and other dietary restrictions can be accommodated when requested in advance. The aromatic creations from our Dutch ovens are delightful alternatives to the dreary dried food diet we used to expect in camping trips.

Contact **Hawk, I'm Your Sister** at (505) 984-2268.

NEW MEXICO

471-3475, (800) 244-3475. B&B, 50% gay & lesbian clientele. Double rooms, private baths, color TV, extended continental breakfast, nearby river & lake.

TRIANGLE INN-SANTA FE, THE, PO Box 3235, Santa Fe, NM 87501, (505) 455-3375. Lesbian-owned Inn, men welcome. Individually decorated adobe casitas with modern conveniences, fully-equipped kitchens, Jacuzzi, common sun deck, expanded continental breakfast. ♀♂

■ Women's Accommodations

EL PEÑASCO, PO Box 1045, Placitas, NM 87043, (505) 771-8909, E-mail: stormiep@aol.com. Enjoy the history & charm of New Mexico in this 1-bedroom casita in the picturesque Sandia Mountains midway between Albuquerque & Santa Fe. The adobe guesthouse features a kiva fireplace in the bedroom, bath with shower & tub, cable TV & a fully equipped kitchen which we stock with breakfast foods. Shopping, casinos, hiking & biking are 10 minutes away. Prefer women only, but men welcome. ♀

■ Dance Bar/Disco

DRAMA CLUB, 125 N Guadalupe, (505) 988-4374. Live bands Thurs, country & western & lessons Sun, occasional drag shows, monthly gay comedy. ♀♂

■ Cafe

GALISTEO CORNER CAFE, 201 Galisteo, (505) 984-1316. Breakfast, lunch, specialty coffees. Coffeehouse till 10pm summer weekends. ♀

■ Restaurants

COYOTE CAFE, 132 W Water St, (505) 983-1615. Nationally acclaimed modern Southwestern cuisine. Gay-friendly.

DANA'S AFTER DARK, 222 N Guadalupe, (505) 982-5225. Open after bars close, sandwiches, soups, coffees, pastries.

DAVE'S NOT HERE, 1115 Hickock St at Agua Fria, (505) 983-7060. Very popular with the lesbian community.

GERONIMO, 724 Canyon Rd, (505) 982-1500. In an adobe house, nouvelle Southwestern cuisine.

PLAZA CAFE, 54 Lincoln Ave on The Plaza, (505) 982-1664. Dinner with New Mexican & Greek items.

SANTA CAFE, 231 Washington Ave, (505) 984-1788. Restaurant & bar, popular with gays.

VANESSIE OF SANTA FE, 434 W Francisco, (505) 982-9966. Piano bar & restaurant, lobster, steaks, etc.

WHISTLING MOON, 402 N Guadalupe, (505) 983-3093. Mediterranean.

■ Retail & Bookstores

SHE SAID, 177 Paseo de Peralta, (505) 986-9196. Women's bookstore.

TAOS

■ Accommodations

MESA HOUSE, 1435 Mesa Vista Rd, (505) 751-7403. Solar adobe complex with 3 casitas, each with its own courtyard & covered portal, private baths, color TV, VCR, phone, pool & river nearby, 50% gay/lesbian clientele.

RUBY SLIPPER, THE BED AND BREAKFAST, PO Box 2069, (505) 758-0613. Seven romantic guest rooms with private entrances, private baths, fireplace or woodstove. Secluded hot tub, in-room coffee and tea. Fabulous breakfast. Predominantly lesbian & gay clientele. Rave reviews in the *Albuquerque Journal* and *Our World Magazine*. In our ninth year of fine service. Come see what everybody's been talking about! ♀♂

■ Retail & Bookstores

CORN MAIDEN, THE, 127 Bent St, 87571, (505) 751-3739. A goddess shop with books, artifacts & jewelry to honor the emerging goddess. Goddess & Green Man Festival in July. ♀

FX 18, Hwy 64, about 1 mile north of Taos. Silver, eclectic items, very interesting.

NEW YORK

WHO TO CALL

For Tour Companies Serving This Destination
See New York on page 22

ALBANY

■ Information

GAY & LESBIAN CENTER, 332 Hudson Ave, (518) 462-6138.

WOMEN'S BLDG, 79 Central Ave, (518) 465-1597. Many services, Mon-Fri 10am-4pm.

■ Bars

OH BAR, 304 Lark St, (518) 463-9004. Video bar, younger, college crowd, 90% men. Open 7 days 2pm-4am. ♂

■ Dance Bar/Disco

JD'S PLAYHOUSE, 519 Central Ave, (518) 446-1407. 2 bars, disco, Sun tea dance. ♂

LONGHORNS, 90 Central Ave near Henry Johnson Blvd, (518) 462-4862. C&W bar. ♂

POWER COMPANY,★ 238 Washington Ave, (518) 465-2556. Dance bar, Fri-Sun. ♀♂

WATER WORKS PUB,★ 76 Central Ave near Henry Johnson Blvd, (518) 465-9079. Cruise bar downstairs, dance bar upstairs, women welcome. DJ Thur-Sun. ♂

■ Cafe

RAINBOW CAFE, 332 Hudson Ave, in gay center bldg. Coffeehouse & library, 7 nites.

■ Fitness Centers

FEMALE FITNESS, 79 Central Ave, 2nd floor of women's bldg, (518) 465-1597. Women's gym.

FITNESS FOR HER, 333 Delaware Ave, Delmar, (518) 478-0237. Women's gym.

SWEAT SHOP, THE, 3 Vatrano Rd, (518) 459-6942. Gay-friendly gym.

■ Restaurants

CAFE 75, 75 Central Ave, (518) 645-6127. Short-order menu, open evenings Mon-Fri.

EL LOCO MEXICAN CAFE, 465 Madison Ave, (518) 436-1855.

MOTHER EARTHS CAFE, 217 Western Ave, (518) 434-0944. Soups, vegetarian dishes, desserts, live music nightly. 11am-11pm daily.

■ Retail & Bookstores

ART & DESIRE, 79 Central Ave, (518) 433-8909, (518) 433-7064. Women-made art & gifts. Books. Cafe.

The Ruby Slipper
A Taos Bed & Breakfast

WHY OUR GUESTS KEEP COMING BACK:
Fabulous Breakfasts ★ Seven Beautiful Guestrooms ★ Fireplaces ★ Private Baths & Entrances ★ Secluded Hot Tub ★ Lovely Grounds ★ Ideal Location ★ Casual & Friendly ★ Great Conversation

RAVE REVIEWS!
$79-104

The perfect balance of privacy and personal attention.

505-758-0613
Taos, New Mexico

NEW YORK

PEACE OFFERINGS, 33 Central Ave, (518) 434-4037. T-shirts, hats, cards, jewelry.

ROMEO'S GIFTS, 299 Lark St, (518) 434-4014. Sophisticated gift shop with some gay items.

VIDEO CENTRAL, 37 Central Ave, (518) 463-4153. Gay & lesbian video sections, 10am-midnite.

■ Leathers/Piercing
SAVAGE GIFTS & LEATHER, 88 Central Ave, (518) 434-2324. Leather chaps, vests, jackets, etc, adult toys & video library.

■ Erotica
CINEMA ART THEATER, 289 River St, Troy, (578) 274-6676. Booths.

KING VIDEO, 14 King St, Troy, (518) 272-4714. 24hrs 7 days.

ANGELICA

■ Camping & RV
JONES POND CAMPGROUND, 9835 Old State Rd, call for directions, (716) 567-8100, Fax: (716) 567-4518, E-mail: jonespond-dorin@worldnet.att.net. Men-only campground, trailers for rent, pool on premiese. Events include leather & fantasy weekends, pool/pizza parties, Christmas in July. Closed in winter.

BINGHAMTON

■ Information
GAY, LESBIAN & BI RESOURCE LINE, (607) 729-1921, in NY state (800) 287-7557. Mon-Thurs 7:30pm-9:30pm, may expand hours. Ask about gay & lesbian socials & group potlucks.

WOMEN'S CENTER, (607) 724-3462 or 785-3429.

■ Bars
SQUIGGY'S, 34 Chenango St (rear), (607) 722-2299. Pool table & conversation bar, DJ weekends.

■ Dance Bar/Disco
RISKY BUSINESS, 201 State St, (607) 723-1507. Video dance bar, occasional male dancers.

■ Retail & Bookstores
E & R GIFTS & GRAPHICS, 215 Main St, (607) 729-5305. Alternative New Age cards, books, gifts. Closed Sun.

GRACIE'S GIFTS, 201 State St, at Risky Business bar, (607) 723-1507. T-shirts, novelties.

■ Erotica
ALLIE'S BOOKSTORE EAST, 483 Court St, (607) 724-1558, 7 days.

ALLIES BLVD BOOKSTORE, 140 Washington St, (607) 724-8659.

NORTH STREET BOOKSHOP, 17 Washington Ave, Endicott, (607) 785-9606. Closed Sun.

BROOKLYN

■ Bars
CARRY NATION, ★ 363 5th Ave between 5th & 6th Sts, (718) 788-0924. Pool table, juke box.

CELEBRITY'S, 8705 3rd Ave, Bay Ridge, (718) 745-9652. Tues-Sat from 6pm, Sun from 4pm, pool table, darts.

SANCTUARY, 444 7th Ave at 15th St, Park Slope, (718) 832-9800. Lounge with bar, pool table, performance space & intimate conversation areas, live DJ Fri & Sat.

■ Dance Bar/Disco
SPECTRUM, 802 64th St, (718) 238-8213. Video dance bar Wed-Sun.

WILDFLOWER, 9235 4th Ave at 93rd St, Bay Ridge, (718) 238-6566. Mega dance bar Wed-Sun 10pm-4am, Wed men, Sun women.

■ Cafe
FLIKKER POT, 184 5th Ave, (718) 783-2136. Gay & lesbian cafe, intimate atmosphere, dinner menu.

RISING CAFE, 186 5th Ave, (718) 622-5072. Women-owned gay & lesbian cafe with social events & a pub/coffeehouse feel.

■ Retail & Bookstores
BEYOND WORDS, 186 5th Ave, (718) 857-0010. Gay & lesbian bookstore.

BUFFALO

■ Information
AIDS HOTLINE, 206 S Elmwood Ave at Chippewa, (716) 847-AIDS (2437), Mon-Fri 9am-5pm or tape.

GAY & LESBIAN COMMUNITY NETWORK, (716) 883-4750.

■ Accommodations
BEAU FLEUVE B&B, 242 Linwood Ave, (716) 882-6116.

OLD SCHOOLHOUSE GUEST HOUSE, 1148 Townline Rd Alden, (716) 683-6590. Guesthouse, women welcome. Double rooms with shared baths, color TVs, continental breakfast.

■ Bars
CATHODE RAY, ★ 26 Allen St, (716) 884-3615. Video bar, 75% men, 25% women.

LAVENDER DOOR, 32 Tonawanda St, (716) 874-1220. Patio, 30's crowd, closed Mon.

STAGE DOOR, 20 Allen St near Pearl, (716) 886-9323. Piano bar, patio.

■ Dance Bar/Disco
BUDDIES, ★ 31 Johnson Park, at Elmwood, (716) 855-1313. Hi-energy dance bar with lounge, Thurs-Sun. 80% men, 20% women.

CLUB MARCELLA, 622 Main St, (716) 847-6850. Alternative dance club, 50% gay.

COMPTON'S AFTER DARK 1239 Niagara St, (716) 885-3275. DJ Fri & Sat, patio in summer.

ROXY'S, 884 Main St, (716) 882-5009. Wed-Sun.

UNDERGROUND, 274 Delaware Ave, (716) 855-1040. Male strippers Sun from 10pm.

■ Saunas/Health Clubs
NEW MORGAN SAUNA/BULL MASTIFF, 655 Main St near Tupper, (716) 852-2153, 24hrs.

■ Retail & Bookstores
RAINBOW PRIDE GIFTSHOP, 175 Hodge St, (716) 881-6126. Rainbow items, cards, gifts & t-shirts, videos, jewelry.

TALKING LEAVES, 3158 Main St, (716) 837-8554. General bookstore with feminist, lesbian, gay section. Closed Sun.

VILLAGE GREEN BOOKS, 765-A Elmwood Ave, (716) 884-1200. General bookstore with gay, lesbian selection.

■ Erotica
ADULT BOOKS, 83 W Chippewa, (716) 856-8936, 7 days.

VILLAGE BOOKS & NEWS, 3102 Delaware Ave near Hamilton, Kenmore, (716) 877-5027, 24hrs.

CATSKILL MOUNTAINS

■ Accommodations
BRADSTAN COUNTRY HOTEL, Route 17 B, PO Box 312, White Lake, (914) 583-4114 (tel/fax). Hotel & cottages. Large gay female following, some gay men. Suites, sun deck, piano lounge, cabaret & expanded continental breakfast.

FOSTERDALE HEIGHTS HOUSE, 205 Mueller Rd, (914) 482-3369, fax: (914) 482-5346. Gay-friendly B&B inn with restaurant, private & shared baths, maid service, meeting rooms, grand piano, nearby gym, river & lake. Gay & lesbian following.

PALENVILLE HOUSE, Jct Rts 23A & 32A, PO Box 465, Palenville, NY 12463-0465, (518) 678-5649, Fax: (518) 678-9038. E-mail: palenville@aol.com. Gay-owned B&B with private & shared baths, full country breakfast, 10-person hot tub, 50% gay & lesbian clientele.

RED BEAR INN, Rte 42, West Kill, NY (518) 989-6000, (800) BEAR-INN.

STONEWALL ACRES, PO Box 556, Rock Hill, NY 12775, (914) 791-9474, NYC Metro area: (800) 336-4208. Guesthouse with 2 cottages, some straight clientele. Double rooms in main house, private baths, BBQ area, full breakfast.

■ Restaurants
CATSKILL ROSE, Rte 212, Mt Tremper, (914) 688-7100. Gay-friendly, American cuisine, dinner Wed-Sun.

NEW YORK

Gay Ski East — The Winter Games

From February 6-9, 1998, **Eclectic Excursions** will host its eighth annual Gay Ski East, The Winter Games at Lake Placid, New York, two-time site of the Winter Olympics. A weekend passport includes alpine skiing, cross-country skiing, a choice of luge or bobsled run, ice skating, admission to the Olympic ski jumps, admission to the Olympic Museum, toboggan chute, and Saturday night dance event.

The 1997 packages included the amenities below. Call for details on 1998. Choice of two - or three-night stays with breakfast and gratuities included (tax not included). Guests are free to choose from the many restaurants Lake Placid has to offer for a wonderful dinner experience at their own expense. Commissionable to travel agents for room rates only.

Participants will also have an opportunity to go for the Gold, Silver, and Bronze in the giant slalom and the "drag race."

Contact **Eclectic Excursions** at (813) 734-1111 or write to 2045 Hunters Glen Drive, Dunedin, FL 34698.

CRANBERRY LAKE

■ Women's Accommodations

AMETHYST B&B, June-Aug: PO Box 522, Cranberry Lake, NY 12927, (315) 848-3529. other times: 322 Jody way, Timonium, MD 21093, (410) 252-5990. Women-only B&B in the Adirondack Mtns of NY state, shared baths, full breakfast, many outdoor activities, lake & docks on premises. ♀

CUBA

■ Accommodations

ROCKING DUCK INN, 28 Genesee Pkwy, (716) 968-3335. Gay-friendly country B&B inn & antique shop. Variety of comfortable rooms with private baths, fireplace & TV lounge, library, full breakfast

EAST HAMPTON

■ Accommodations

CENTENNIAL HOUSE, 13 Woods Ln, (516) 324-9414, fax: (516) 324-2681. Gay-friendly B&B, full breakfast, private baths, AC, color cable TV, VCR, video tape library, pool on premises.

ELMIRA - CORNING

■ Accommodations

RUFUS TANNER HOUSE, 60 Sagetown Rd, Pine City, (607) 732-0213. Gay-friendly B&B, 50% gay & lesbian clientele. Large rooms decorated in Victorian furniture & antiques, 1 with whirlpool tub. Breakfast with homegrown maple syrup.

■ Bars

DAVID, THE, 511 Railroad Ave, (607) 733-2592. DJ Fri-Sun, 60% men, 40% women. ♀ ♂

■ Dance Bar/Disco

BODY SHOP, on Railroad Ave a block down from The David, (607) 733-6609. ♀ ♂

■ Erotica

DELUXE BOOK BARGAINS, 123 Lake St, (607) 734-9656.

FIRE ISLAND

■ Accommodations

BELVEDERE, Box 26, Cherry Grove, (516) 597-6448. Guesthouse & cottages. Stately rooms with views, private & shared baths. Gym, Jacuzzi, nearby ocean beach, restaurants & discos. Continental breakfast weekends & holidays. ♂

CAROUSEL GUEST HOUSE, PO Box 4001, Cherry Grove, (516) 597-6612. Guesthouse 300 feet from beach, mostly men. Twin & double beds, shared baths, weights & continental breakfast. ♂

CHERRY GROVE BEACH HOTEL, PO Box 537, Sayville 11782, (516) 597-6600. Hotel with restaurant, bar & disco, near ocean, private baths. ♀ ♂

DUNE POINT, Box 78, Cherry Grove, (516) 597-6261. Guesthouse on the ocean, private & shared baths. ♀ ♂

PINES PLACE, PO Box 5309, Fire Island Pines 11782, (516) 597-6162. B&B, women welcome. Private & shared baths. ♂

■ Bars

CHERRY'S, Bayview Walk, Cherry Grove. (516) 597-6820. Piano bar. ♀ ♂

TOP OF THE BAY, Dock Walk at Bay Walk, Cherry Grove, (516) 597-6699. Bar & restaurant. ♀ ♂

■ Dance Bar/Disco

ICE PALACE, Cherry Grove at the Beach hotel, (516) 597-6600. Disco daily, Sat & Sun tea dance. ♀ ♂

ISLAND CLUB, Fire Island Blvd. Dance bar. ♂

PAVILLION, ★ Harbor Walk, Fire Island Pines, (516) 597-6767. Late-night disco, busy after 1:30am. ♂

YACHT CLUB, The Pines. Days, bar with Tea dances weekends, restaurant. ♂

■ Restaurants

MICHAEL'S, Dock Walk at Bay Walk in Cherry Grove.

TOP OF THE BAY, Dock Walk, Cherry Grove at Top of the Bay bar. ♀ ♂

FLY CREEK

■ Accommodations

TOAD HALL, RD 1, Box 120, (607) 547-5774. Gay-friendly B&B with gift shop. Large, comfortable rooms with Early American ambiance, color TVs, private baths, sun deck & full breakfast.

HIGHLAND

■ Dance Bar/Disco

PRIME TIME, Rte 9W N, (914) 691-8550. Male dancers Fri & Sat. ♀ ♂

■ Restaurants

NORTHERN SPY CAFE, Rt 213 & Old Rte 213, HIgh Falls, (914) 687-7298. International cuisine.

WOULD BAR & GRILL, THE, 120 North Rd, (914) 691-9883. New American cuisine.

ITHACA

■ Information

WOMEN'S COMMUNITY BUILDING, 100 W Seneca St, (607) 272-1247.

■ Accommodations

PLEASANT GROVE B & B, 1779 Trumansburg Rd (Rte 96) Jacksonville, (607) 387-5420, (800) 398-3963. Gay-friendly B&B, 60% gay & lesbian clientele. Double rooms with private & shared baths, full breakfast. Nearby lakes & streams.

■ Women's Accommodations

SLEEPING BEAR B&B, 208 Nelson Rd, Ithaca, NY 14850, (607) 277-6220. Women-only B&B in log home, quiet setting, full breakfast, hot

NEW YORK

tub, shared bath. Jun-Dec, lesbian-owned/-run. ♀

■ *Dance Bar/Disco*
COMMON GROUND, 1230 Danby Rd (Rte 96-B), (607) 273-1505. Bar & restaurant, DJ Wed-Sat, restaurant Fri-Sun, 50% men, 50% women.

■ *Restaurants*
ABC CAFE, 308 Stewart Ave, (607) 277-4770. Alternative-style cafe & restaurant. Brunch, dinners & baked goods, brunch weekends, live music.

■ *Retail & Bookstores*
BOREALIS BOOKSTORE, 111 N Aurora, (607) 272-7752. General bookstore specializing in gay & lesbian books.

■ *Erotica*
BOOK SALE GALLERY, 103 W State St, (607) 272-9882.

JAMESTOWN

■ *Dance Bar/Disco*
NITE SPOT, 201 Windsor, (716) 483-2614. Shows Sun, DJ Wed, Fri-Sun, open daily from 7pm except in winter, 60% men, 40% women.

SNEAKERS, 100 Harrison St, (716) 484-8816. DJ Fri & Sat, many women Fri & Sat.

KINGSTON

■ *Restaurants*
ARMADILLO BAR & GRILL, 97 Abeel St, (914) 339-1550. Frozen Margaritas a specialty.

■ *Retail & Bookstores*
ALTERNATIVE VIDEO SHOP, 932 Rt 28, (914) 334-8105. Large selection of lesbian & gay videos, all denoted by rainbow stickers. 2nd location Ulster Video & Gifts, 584 Ulster Ave, (914) 331-6023.

LAKE GEORGE

■ *Accommodations*
KING HENDRICK MOTEL, 1602 State Route 9, (518) 792-0418. Gay-friendly motel. Cabins, efficiencies, modern conveniences, continental breakfast.

LONG ISLAND

■ *Information*
AIDS INFO, (516) 385-AIDS (2437).

HUNTINGTON WOMANSPACE, (516) 673-9721. Switchboard, lending library, workshops, discussions, programs, local information. No specific hours but they answer messages.

LONG ISLAND CENTER, (516) 825-0447. Gay info.

LONG ISLAND CRISIS CENTER, (516) 679-1111, 24hr straight switchboard with some gay info & peer counselors.

WOMEN'S ALTERNATIVES COMMUNITY CENTER, (516) 483-2050. Women's meetings, events & concerts, lesbian discussions.

■ *Accommodations*
COZY CABINS, Box 848, Montauk Hwy, Wainscott, East Hampton, 11975, (516) 537-1160. Cabins, motel/inn near ocean beaches. Some straight clientele. ♀♂

ONE THIRTY-TWO NORTH MAIN, 132 N Main St East Hampton, (516) 324-2246, 324-9771. Mini-resort, women welcome. Variety of accommodations with private & shared baths, TV lounge, continental breakfast, nearby ocean beach.

SAG HARBOR BED & BREAKFAST, Sag Harbor, The Hamptons, (516) 725-5945 (tel/fax), weekdays: (212) 505-7869. Country home B&B in nature preserve, gay men welcome. Three bedrooms, private baths, bicycles, full breakfast. Nearby ocean beach.

■ *Beaches*
FOWLER BEACH, on Flying Pt Rd in South Hampton. One side of the beach is gay & lesbian.

■ *Bars*
BEDROCK,★ 121 Woodfield Rd, W Hempstead, (516) 486-9516. Dancing Fri, entertainment Sat, closed Mon.

BLANCHE, 47-2 Boundary Ave, S Farmingdale, (516) 694-6906. Piano bar Fri & Sat. Opens 8pm daily, 3pm Sun.

CLUB 608, 608 Sunrise Hwy, W Babylon, (516) 661-9580. 75% men, 25% women.

CLUB PIKE, 964 Bridgehampton & Sag Harbor Tpke, Bridgehampton, (516) 537-1700.

CLUB SIX-O-EIGHT, 608 Sunrise Hwy, West Babylon, (516) 661-9580. Patio.

FANNY'S, 7 Prince Rd, Rocky Point, (516) 744-4290.

FOREVER GREEN, 841 N Broome Ave, Lindenhurst, (516) 226-9357. Jukebox dancing, DJ weekends.

LONG ISLAND EAGLE, 94 N Clinton Ave, Bay Shore, (516) 968-2750. 9pm-4am nightly.

PAL JOEY'S, 2457 Jerusalem Ave, North Bellmore, (516) 785-9301.

■ *Dance Bar/Disco*
BUNK HOUSE, 192 Montauk Hwy, Sayville, (516) 567-2865. Sun buffet, monthly parties.

CHAMELEON,★ 4020 Long Beach Rd, Island Park, (516) 889-4077. Hi energy dance club, gay Mon, Wed & especially Sat. Call for current schedule of gay nites. When gay it's 20% women.

ST MARKS PLACE,★ 6550 Jericho Tpke, Commack, (516) 499-2244. Mainly women, men welcome.

SWAMP/ANNEX, Montauk Hwy, Wainscott, (516) 537-3332. Hi-energy dance bar, patio & restaurant, Sun T-dance. Winter Thur-Sun only.

THUNDERS,★ 1017 E Jericho Tpke, Huntington, (516) 423-5241. Nightly specials & The Loft piano bar, co-ed Fri. ♂

■ *Erotica*
ADULT BOOKS, 146 A W Sunrise Hwy, Lindenhurst, (516) 226-7253, 9am-11pm 7 days.

ADULT SHOP, 6083 Sunrise Hwy, Holbrook, (516) 472-9519, 7 days.

CUPID'S VIDEO BOUTIQUE, 786-A Grand Blvd, Deer Park, (516) 586-0066. Closed Sun.

HEAVEN SENT ME, 108 Cain Dr, Hauppauge Industrial Park, (516) 434-4777 or (800) 451-0022. Private club, bar alternative, with adult books & novelties for gay men & women.

VIDEO NOVELTY, 3316 Rte 112, Medford, (516) 736-3643.

NEW PALTZ

■ *Accommodations*
CHURCHILL FARM, 39 Canaan Rd, New Paltz, NY 12561, (914) 255-7291. An 1820 Mohonk Mountain farmhouse turned into a comfortable smoke-free guesthouse 90 minutes north of New York City, and minutes away from hiking, bike trails, cross-country skiing, golf, rock climbing, bird watching, horseback riding, swimming, and antique and craft stores. Private & shared baths. Some straight clientele. ♀♂

GOLDEN BEAR FARM, THE, 1 Forest Glen Rd, New Paltz, NY 12561, (914) 255-1515. Our historic 1784 stone house is set on 12 country acres, less than two hours from New York City. Guest rooms are appointed with feather beds and antique furnishings. Weather permitting, breakfasts are served on the outdoor patio overlooking the pool, and elegant dinners are served in the candlelit dining room. Meals are prepared by the inn's owner/chefs who were trained at the renowned Culinary Institute of America. Some straight clientele. TO OPEN FALL, 1997.

Golden Bear Farm

Romantic Guest Rooms — Antique Furnishings

New Paltz, NY

(914) 255-1515

NEW YORK

FYI

Gays Sailing the East Coast

One of the more interesting ways to view the Manhattan skyline is from a boat at sunset. Most visitors who do this do it from the deck of a ferry. Gays and lesbians can do it from a private yacht in New York Harbor. **Sailing Affairs'** gay-owned yacht has conducted gay and lesbian sunset cruises of New York Harbor since 1984. They also customize sailing vacations along the eastern seaboard. In winter, they have also sailed to the Caribbean. In summer, they sail the eastern seaboard on a fixed schedule, which you can join for any number of days, although a week is highly recommended. The sailing schedule for 1997 follows:

April-May: Chesapeake Bay, Baltimore, Washington DC, Norfolk, Annapolis, Cape May, Atlantic City.

June-July: NYC, Long Island, Connecticut, New Jersey.

Aug-Sept: NYC, Long Island Sound, Mystic CT, Block Island, Newport RI, Martha's Vineyard, Nantucket, Provincetown, Boston, Maine coast.

Contact **Sailing Affairs** at (212) 228-5755, Fax: (212) 228-8512, E-mail: sailingaff@aol.com.

FYI

Insider's Tour of NYC

A truly in-depth gay- and lesbian-oriented view of New York City's architecture, theatre, fashion, music, dance and visual arts is available through **V.I.P. Tours of New York**. Your custom-designed individual or group tour can include any of the following: Private meetings with gay and lesbian actors, playwrights, opera singers, cabaret performers, classical musicians and dancers; Exclusive behind-the-scenes visits to Carnegie Hall, Lincoln Center, Radio City Music Hall, City Center Dance Theatre, NYC's oldest operating theatre and remaining movie palaces; Architectural tours with a prominent lawyer in the landmarks preservation field; Explorations of Greenwich Village, Chelsea and East Village architecture and gay nightlife; A private meeting with a Disney offical involved in restoration of an art nouveau theatre; A gay-oriented walking & luxury coach tour of NYC's architecturally fantastic neighborhoods; Private tours of major museums; A visit to one of the world's finest private corporate art collections; Art gallery tours with a gay orientation, and visits to artists' lofts.

Contact **V.I.P. Tours** at (212) 247-0366, (800) 300-6203, Fax: (212) 397-0851

■ Restaurants

LOCUST TREE INN, 215 Huguenot St, (914) 255-7888. Dating from 1759, American continental menu, casual country dining. Lunch, dinner, Sun brunch.

■ Retail & Bookstores

PAINTED WORD BOOKS & CAFE, 36 Main St, (914) 256-0825. General bookstore with gay & lesbian section, coffee, desserts & snacks.

NEW YORK INTRO

■ Information

GAY & LESBIAN CENTER & SWITCHBOARD, 208 W 13th St, (212) 777-1800 or 620-7310. AIDS info (800) 734-7104.

IDENTITY HOUSE, 39 W 14th St #205, (212) 243-8181. Events, socials, counseling, workshops.

LESBIAN HERSTORY ARCHIVES, (718) 768-3953. Call for hours.

LESBIAN SWITCHBOARD, (212) 741-2610. Mon-Fri 6pm-10pm.

SOCIAL ACTIVITES FOR WOMEN (SAL), (718) 630-9505. 24hr hotline for current lesbian events in the metropolitan NY area.

■ Accommodations

A BED & BREAKFAST ABODE LTD, PO Box 20022, NY 10021, (212) 472-2000, (800) 835-8880. Manhattan apartment rental service with a gay & lesbian following. All accommodations are fully-furnished & meet the highest standards of cleanliness & attractiveness.

BROOKLYN B & B, 128 Kent St, (718) 383-3026. Gay-friendly B&B, most with shared baths. Convenient transportation to Manhattan.

CARITAS BED & BREAKFAST NETWORK, (800) CARITAS, (312) 857-0801, Fax: (312) 857-0805. B&B, home-stay accommodations service. *Member: IGTA*

NEW YORK BED & BREAKFAST RESERVATION CENTER, THE, (212) 977-3512. A wide

FOR PERFECT ACCOMMODATIONS IN NY
B & B $60-$90

NEW YORK B&B RESERVATION CENTER
(212) 977-3512

NEW YORK

variety of bed and breakfast accommodations in New York City at prices from $60-$90 per night. Also private studios and apartments from $100/night, some less. We personally inspect all accommodations. Also see our ads and call us for accommodations in Paris & South Beach. ♂

■ Dance Bar/Disco
CHOCOLATE DREAMS & IN THE PINK ("where there's always Pink on the Inside"), (718) 783-6642. Dance parties for women of color. In the Pink is usually last Sat of month, Chocolate Dream is usually on Fri, both from 11pm till... For exact schedule call our hotline. ▦♀

SHESCAPE, (212) 686-5665. Weekly dance parties. Call 24-hr hotline for sched. ▦♀

■ Retail & Bookstores
GAY & LESBIAN BOOKSTORES, see Greenwich Village, Uptown sections.

NYC LOWER MANHATTAN
Includes SoHo, Chelsea, East & West Village, & the East Side up to 30th St.

■ Information
LESBIAN & GAY COMMUNITY SERVICES CENTER, 208 W 13th St, (212) 620-7310. Many meetings, groups, social events, women's dances, 9am-11pm, visitor's info package, local info.

SALGA (SOUTH ASIAN LESBIAN & GAY ASSOC). Meets 3rd Sun 6pm at the Lesbian & Gay Community Center, 208 W 13th.

■ Accommodations
A GREENWICH VILLAGE HABITUÉ, West Village, (212) 243-6495. Private, fully-equipped apartments, 50% gay & lesbian clientele. AC, color TV, telephone.

ABINGDON B&B, 13 8th Ave, (212) 243-5384, Fax: (212) 807-7473. Quaint West Village guesthouse with distinctively decorated rooms. Color TV, AC, private & shared baths, expanded continental breakfast, non-smoking environment. 50% gay & lesbian clientele.

CHELSEA MEWS GUESTHOUSE, 344 W 15th St, (212) 255-9174. Guesthouse, women welcome. Color TV, AC, telephone, refrigerator, private & shared baths, continental breakfast. ♂

CHELSEA PINES INN, 317 W 14th St, (212) 929-1023, Fax: (212) 620-5646, E-mail: cpiny@aol.com. B&B inn in an 1850's modernized brownstone with an Art Deco look. Women welcome. We offer clean, comfortable rooms with firm beds, private and shared baths, color cable TV, free HBO, AC, refrigerator and phone. Our continental breakfast includes homemade bread, house-blend coffee and fresh fruit. We're on the border of Greenwich Village and Chelsea and close to shopping, theatres, sights, restaurants and the nightlife of the famous Sheridan Square/Christopher St. area. Subway and bus stops at our corner make getting around the city easy and economical. ♂

COLONIAL HOUSE INN, 318 W 22nd St, (212) 243-9669, (800) 689-3779, Fax: (212) 633-1612. Conveniently-located B&B. Private and shared baths. All rooms have phones, cable TV and AC. Some have refrigerators and fireplaces. From $65. Reservations suggested. ♀♂

LA SAMANNA HOTEL, 25 W 24th St, (212) 255-5944, fax: (212) 675-3830. Gay-friendly hotel in Chelsea location.

■ Women's Accommodations
EAST VILLAGE BED & BREAKFAST, 244 E 7th St #6, (212) 260-1865. Women-only B&B, 2-bedroom apartment situated in a tasteful 2nd-floor apartment. Located in an urban, multi-cultural, multi-ethnic neighborhood close to shops, galleries and affordable restaurants. Greenwich Village, SoHo, Chinatown and other areas of interest are within easy reach. The kitchen comes complete with items for preparing your own continental breakfast. You are usually on your own in your own apartment. ♀

■ Bars
BAR, THE, 68 2nd Ave at 4th St, (212) 674-9714. ▦♂

BARRACUDA,★ 275 W 22nd St, (212) 645-8613. Drag shows, singers, DJ, 25-30 age group. ♂

BOILER ROOM, 86 E 4th St near 2nd Ave. (212) 254-7536. Pool tables, jukebox. ▦♪♂

BOOTS & SADDLES, 76 Christopher St near 7th Ave, (212) 929-9684. Opens early. ▦▨♂

BREAK, THE 232 8th Ave at 22nd St, (212) 627-0072. Video cruise bar, younger crowd, patio, martini menu. ▨♪▦♂

CHAMPS, 17 W 19th St between 5th & 6th Ave, (212) 633-1717. High tech video sports cruise bar, male dancers nightly. Open 7 days. Sun afternoon tea dance. Different themes on different nights, call for current schedule. ▦▨✕♂

CUBBYHOLE, 281 W 12th St, (212) 243-9041. 60% women. ♪♀♂

DICK'S BAR, 192 2nd Ave near 12th St, (212) 475-2071. Pool table. ▦♂

DUGOUT, THE, 185 Christopher St at Weehawken (near West St) (212) 242-9113. Sports bar & Upper Deck restaurant, Sat, Sun brunch. ▦♂

DUPLEX, 61 Christopher St, near 7th Ave, (212) 255-5438. Piano bars, cabaret, upstairs pool table. Large gay following. ▨♪

EAGLE, 142 11th Ave at 21st St, (212) 691-8451. Erotic videos. ▦♪▨♂

EIGHTY EIGHT, 228 W 10th St near Bleecker, (212) 924-0088. Piano bar, upstairs cabaret, some straight clientele, Sun brunch. Occasional name performers. ♪♀♂

FLAMINGO EAST, 219 2nd Ave (13th St), (212) 533-2860. Always gay-friendly, but gay on Wed with drag show (gay dance nite last Wed of month), lounge upstairs, restaurant downstairs. ♂

G, 223 W 19th St, (212) 929-1085. Lounge with sofas & banquettes, juice bar, coffees, power drinks, as well as full liquor & full wine list. ♂

HANGAR, THE, 115 Christopher St. (212) 627-2044. ▦▨♂

HENRIETTA HUDSON, 448 Hudson St, (212) 924-3347. Cheers for the lesbian set, bar & vegetarian restaurant, summer lite menu, men welcome. ▦♪♀

JULIUS, 159 W 10th St at Waverly, (212) 929-9672. Great burgers. ✕▦▨♂

KELLER'S, 384 West St at Barrow, (212) 243-1907. ▦▦♂

LURE, THE,★ 409 W 13th St, (212) 741-3919. 7000-foot bar with strict dress code Fri & Sat: Leather, rubber, uniforms. Leather shop inside. ▨▮♪▨♂

MARIE'S CRISIS, 59 Grove St near 7th Ave, (212) 243-9323. Piano bar, sing-a-longs. ▦♪▨♂

MEOW MIX BAR, 269 E Houston St, (212)

UNITED STATES

Visit New York City (800) CARITAS — Caritas B&B Network

NEW YORK
CHELSEA PINES INN
The Cozy Bed and Breakfast in the Heart of Gay New York

Comfortable Rooms $75 - $99
Private, semi-private or shared bath
Telephone/Color cable TV (free HBO)
Refrigerator in all rooms
Air conditioning/central heating
Expanded Continental Breakfast included
Walk to Christopher St., all bars, clubs, shops
Advance Reservations Suggested
All Major Credit Cards Accepted

317 West 14th Street, New York City 10014
Tel: 212 929-1023   Fax: 212 620-5646

Winner '94 -'95 Out & About Editor's Choice Awards

New York City
COLONIAL HOUSE INN
(800) 689-3779 · (212) 243-9669

FERRARI GUIDES' GAY TRAVEL A to Z - 18th EDITION

NEW YORK

254-1434. Dancing Fri & Sat, nite-late crowd, East Village baby dykes.

MIKE'S CLUB CAFE, 400 W 14th St at 9th Ave, (212) 691-6606. Casual, elegant bar & restaurant, 60% men, 40% women.

NUTS & BOLTS LOUNGE, 101 7th Ave South at Grove, (212) 620-4000. Video lounge bar, chic with soft chairs, tables.

PIECES & RAINBOW CAFE, 8 Christopher St, near 6th Ave, (212) 929-9291. Bar & cabaret with DJ, male dancers, drag shows, singers & cafe with lite meals. Young, trendy crowd.

RAWHIDE, 212 Eighth Ave at 21st St, (212) 242-9332.

ROME, 290 Eighth Ave, Chelsea, (212) 242-6969. Several levels, Roman forum decor, call for current theme nites.

RUBYFRUITS, 531 Hudson St, (212) 929-3343. Bar & dinner restaurant, Sun piano & singer.

SNEAKERS, 392 West St, (212) 242-9830.

SOUTH DAKOTA, 405 3rd Ave at 29th St, (212) 684-8376. Pool table.

SPIKE, 120 11th Ave at 20th St, (212) 243-9688. DJ.

SPLASH, ★ 50 W 17th St, (212) 691-0073. Large video cruise bar, Sun tea dance, Bottom Bar downstairs. The muscle-oriented in-town Fire Island crowd. Male dancers dance under a water shower on a runway.

STONEWALL, 53 Christopher St, (212) 463-0950. Videos, pool table, popular happy hour, 80% men, 20% women. Tourists & regulars.

TUNNEL BAR, 116 First Ave at 7th St, (212) 777-9232. Porno flicks, gay erotic art showings. Popular with young East Village types, West Village leather crowd, very cruisy.

TWO POTATO, 143 Christopher St at Greenwich, (212) 255-0286.

TY'S, 114 Christopher St near Bedford, (212) 741-9641.

UNCLE CHARLIE'S, ★ 56 Greenwich Ave near Perry, (212) 255-8787. Cruisy video bar, preppie crowd, DJ, male dancers, many events.

WONDER BAR, 505 E 6th St near Ave A, (212) 777-9105. Small video cruise bar, live DJ nightly.

■ Dance Bar/Disco

CLIT CLUB, ★ 432 West 14th St near 10th Ave, (212) 529-3300. Fri women's dance parties, lesbian videos. Mixed nights Tues & Sat.

CRAZY NANNY'S, 21 7th Ave S at Leroy, (212) 929-8356. DJ & dancing Sun, upstairs dance floor, men welcome.

CROWBAR, ★ 339 E 10th St, (212) 420-0670. Small dance area, different themes nightly, call for current schedule.

HERSHEE BAR, 229 W 28th St (7th / 8th Aves), (212) 631-1093. Fri only women's dance club 10pm-4am, 2 levels, DJs.

KING, 579 Sixth Ave, Chelsea, (212) 366-5464. 3 levels with upstairs dance bar & downstairs lounge. Porn performances in separate, private lounge.

LIFE, 158 Bleecker St, (212) 420-1999. Gay Sun only for Boy's LIfe hi energy dance party.

MONSTER, THE, ★ 80 Grove St near 7th Ave (Sheridan Square), (212) 924-3558. Piano bar upstairs gets older crowd, dance bar downstairs. Flashback Tues downstairs, call for current theme nite schedule.

MOTHER, 432 W 14th St, (212) 677-6060 or 366-5680. Gay on certain nights, call to confirm schedule. Fri Clit Club women's nite, Sun men's dance nite, Tues Jackie 60 (50% gay).

OPERA, 539 W 21st St between 10th & 11th Aves, (212) 229-1618. Tues: The Gathering alternative rock & roll format, gay & straight. Wed: Peak men's dance party. Call to confirm schedules.

PYRAMID, 101 Ave A near 6th St, (212) 604-4588. Gay theme nights. Call for schedule.

ROXY, THE, 515 W 18th St, at 10th Ave, (212) 645-5156. Sat night dance parties, women welcome. Tues Power Skate men's rollerskating.

SHESCAPE, (212) 686-5665. Scheduled dance parties for women. Call 24hr hotline for current schedule.

SOUND FACTORY, 618 W 46th St near 11th Ave, (718) 507-7533. Fri dance coub on 3 levels, upstairs progressive house, downstairs R&B retro 80s from 3am, 40% gay.

TWILO, ★ 530 W 27th St, (212) 268-1600. Huge dance club with after hours till 8am. Thurs Factoria Latin dance nite, Sun tea dance, call for current schedule.

WILD WEDNESDAY AT TWO I'S, 248 W 14th St near 8th Ave, (212) 631- 1093 or 807-1775. Wed women's dance party, 6:30pm-2am.

■ Cafe

A DIFFERENT LIGHT CAFE, 151 W 19th St, (212) 989-4850. Popular with the early evening before-the-bars crowd.

■ Saunas/Health Clubs

J'S/HANGOUT, THE, 675 Hudson St (upstairs) at 14th, (212) 242-9292. JO club with dancing.

MANHOLE, 28 9th Ave at 13th St, (212) 647-1726. JO club Sun 5pm-10pm, Mon-Wed 8pm-2am, +50.

VAULT, 28 10th Ave near 13th St, (212) 255-6758. Sex club, mainly straight S&M B&D club.

WALL ST SAUNA, 1 Maiden Lane (11th floor) near Broadway, (212) 233-8900. Business crowd.

WESTSIDE CLUB, 27 W 20th St, 2nd fl, (212) 691-2798.

■ Restaurants

ASTRAY CAFE, 59 Horatio St at Greenwich, (212) 741-7030. Unusual, ever-changing menu.

BLACK SHEEP, THE, 344 W 11th St, (212) 242-1010. Old-fashioned country French cuisine, Sat & Sun brunches are very gay.

BOURGO ANTICO, 22 E 13th St between 5th Ave & University Pl, (212) 807-1313. Cuisine of Tuscany, 7 days, 11:30am-midnight, Sun brunch.

BOWERY BAR & RESTAURANT, Bowery & 4th St, (212) 475-2220. Always gay-friendly, but especially so on Tues for "Beige" gay dining & socializing event.

CAFE ASEAN, 117 W 10th St, (212) 633-0348. SE Asian cuisine.

LIPS, 2 Bank St, (212) 675-7710. Drag waitresses & drag memorabilia.

LUCKY CHENG'S, 24 1st Ave, (212) 473-0516. Bar & chinese restaurant, drag queen waitresses, 75% gay.

MANATUS, 240 Bleecker St, (212) 989-7042. Open 24hrs. Sandwiches through dinners. "Manatus" was the Indian name for Manhattan.

MARY'S, 42 Bedford St, (212) 741-3387. Dinner 6pm-midnight 7 days, reservations suggested.

PARIS COMMUNE, 411 Bleecker St, (212) 929-0509. French cuisine.

RESTAURANT FLORENT, 69 Gansevoort, (212) 989-5779. French food, 24hrs.

UNIVERSE GRILL, 44 Bedford St, Chelsea, (212) 989-5621. Lunch, dinner, Sat & Sun brunch.

■ Retail & Bookstores

A DIFFERENT LIGHT, 151 W 19th St, (212) 989-4850, (800) 343-4002 (24hrs). Gay & lesbian bookstore with coffee bar, reading area. 10am-midnight 7 days.

CREATIVE VISIONS, 548 Hudson St, (212) 645-7573. Gay & lesbian bookstore.

GREETINGS, 45 Christopher St near Waverly, (212) 242-0424. Cards & gifts.

LEE'S MARDI GRAS, 400 W 14th St, (212) 645-1888, www.lmgnyc.com. Women's clothing, accessories & makeup line for crossdressers. Mon-Sat 11:30-6:30.

OSCAR WILDE MEMORIAL BOOKS, 15 Christopher St near Gay St, (212) 255-8097. Lesbian and gay books, 11:30-7:30pm daily. Sat 11:30-8:30.

RAINBOWS & TRIANGLES, 192 8th Ave, (212) 627-2166. Gay cards & gifts.

■ Leathers/Piercing

GAUNTLET, 144 5th Ave at 19th St, 2nd floor,

NEW YORK

(212) 229-0180. Piercing studio. Wed-Sun, appts recommended.

LEATHER MAN, 111 Christopher St near Bleeker, (212) 243-5339. Leather clothing, S&M accessories.

NOOSE, THE, 261 W 19th St, (212) 807-1789. Custom leather & latex bondage gear, s/m torture tools.

NOOSE, THE, 409 13th St at Lure Leather bar.

UNDERGROUND LEATHERS, 8 Weehawken St, (212) 924-0644. Wholesale mail order leather clothing, toys.

Erotica

ALL-MALE JEWEL THEATRE, 100 3rd Ave between 12th & 13th St, (212) 505-7320, 10am-3am.

ALL-MALE XXX VIDEOS, 14th St near 3rd Ave. 24hr, booths.

BIJOU 82 THEATER, 82 E 4th St.

BULL RUN, 21 Ann St, near Broadway, (212) 267-9760. Adult bookstore & all-male mini-theatre.

CHRISTOPHER STREET BOOK SHOP, 500 Hudson St at Christopher St, (212) 463-0657. 24hrs, booths.

GAY PLEASURES, 548 Hudson St, (212) 255-5756. Gay & lesbian erotica.

HARMONY, 139 Christopher St, (212) 366-9059. Videos, magazines, toys.

I.C. GUYS INTERNATIONAL, 167 W 21st St at 7th Ave, (212) 479-7786. Live dancers on stage & in private rooms. ♂

PLEASURE CHEST, 156 7th Ave South near Waverly, (212) 242-2158. Leather, S&M, latex clothing, accessories.

UNICORN ALL MALE, 277-C West 22nd St between 7th & 8th Aves, Chelsea, (212) 924-2921. All-male erotica.

NYC UPPER MANHATTAN

Includes Midtown from 31st Street, Upper East Side & Upper West Side.

Accommodations

ROSE COTTAGE, 1 Block West of Broadway, Midtown Manhattan, (212) 864-2786. Studio apartment near all amenities, 50% gay & lesbian clientele. Cable color TV, AC, telephone, kitchen, private bath & cont. breakfast.

THREE THIRTY-THREE WEST 88TH ASSOCS, 333 West 88th St, (212) 724-9818, (800) 724-9888. Unhosted B&B apartments & hosted B&B rooms in the middle of Manhattan. Color TV, AC, telephone, kitchen & private baths. Well-behaved pets & children permitted. ♀ ♂

Bars

BRANDY'S, 235 E 84th St near 2nd Ave, (212) 650-1944. Piano bar starts at 9:30pm, sing-a-long cabaret, 50% gay/lesbian crowd. ♀ ♂

BRIDGE, THE, 309 E 60 St, (212) 223-9104. Upscale video bar, East Side neighborhood crowd, patio & garden. ♂

CANDLE BAR, 309 Amsterdam Ave near 74th St, (212) 874-9155. Latino nighe Wed. ♂

CATS BAR, 232 W 48th St. After hours bar.

CLEO'S, 656 9th Ave near 46th St, (212) 307-1503. ♂

DON'T TELL MAMA, 343 W 46th St near 8th Ave, (212) 757-0788. Piano bar & cabaret with a large gay following.

EIGHT OF CLUBS, 230 W 75th St near Broadway, (212) 580-7389. Outdoor patio. ♂

GH CLUB, 353 E 53rd St near 1st Ave, (212) 223-9752. Piano bar open 4pm-1am Sun-Thurs, 4pm-2am Fri-Sat. Piano Wed-Sun usually from 8pm ♂

JOE L'S UPTOWN BAR, 4488 Broadway at 192nd St, Washington Hts/Inwood section. (212) 567-8555. Sun buffet. ♂

JULIE'S, 204 E 58th St near 3rd Ave, (212) 688-1294. DJ Wed-Sun, dance music, professional crowd. ♀

LA ESCUELITA, 301 W 39th St near 8th Ave, (212) 631-0588. Open Thurs-Sun, Sun drag shows, salsa, merengue. ♂

PEGASUS, 119 E 60th St between Lexington & Park, (212) 888-4702. Piano & cabaret. ♀ ♂

REGENTS, 317 E 53rd St, at 53rd between 1st & 2nd Ave, (212) 593-3091. Gentlemen's bar & restaurant, neat casual, piano entertainment. ♂

STELLA'S, 266 W 47th St, between 8th Ave & Broadway, (212) 575-1680. Pool table, video juke box, male dancers, weekend drag shows.

TOOL BOX, ★ 1742 2nd Ave (91st & 92nd), (212) 348-1288. Upper East Side video cruise bar, 7pm-4am. ♂

TOWNHOUSE, 236 E 58th St near 2nd Ave, (212) 754-4649. Three elegant bars, one piano bar, wee-dressed crowd. ♂

WORKS, THE, 428 Columbus Ave near 81st St, (212) 799-7365. Hi-energy video bar, younger crowd, yuppie, martini menu. ♂

Dance Bar/Disco

SHEBANG & GIRLZONE, at Octagon, 555 W 33rd St, (212) 631-1093. Sat only women's dance party. ♀

WEB, THE, 40 E 58th St near Park Ave, (212) 308-1546. DJ weekends, male dancers. 40% Asian on weekends or later in the evenings. Call for current schedule of theme nites, mainly Asians. ♂

Saunas/Health Clubs

EAST SIDE CLUB, 227 E 56th St near 3rd Ave, (212) 753-2222, 24hrs, sauna & gym.

MT MORRIS BATHS, 1944 Madison Ave near 125th St, (212) 534-9004, 24hrs.

Restaurants

MIKE'S BAR & GRILL, 650 Tenth Ave, (212) 246-4115. Bar & restaurant with eclectic cuisine.

TOWNHOUSE, 206 E 58th St, (212) 826-6241. International cuisine, supper club starting 7pm. ♀ ♂

Retail & Bookstores

EVE'S GARDEN, 119 W 57th St #420-FR, 5th/6th Aves, (212) 757-8651. Sexuality boutique by women for women & their partners. Mon-Sat noon-7pm. ♀

Erotica

COLISEUM BOOKS, 1771 Broadway at 57th St, (212) 757-8381.

COME AGAIN, 353 E 53rd St, (212) 308-9394. Erotic emporium.

EROS CINEMA, 732 8th Ave between 45th & 46th, (212) 221-2450. Live shows & movies.

GAIETY THEATER, 201 W 46th St near 7th Ave, (212) 221-8868, 391-9806.

MENSWORLD, 671 8th Ave near 42nd St, (212) 399-1096. Videos, buddy booths.

PLAYROOM, 231 W 54th St near Broadway. 24hr, buddy booths, videos.

NIAGARA FALLS

Bars

ACES, 1770 Falls St, (716) 285-1508. Open 7pm. ♀ ♂

Erotica

NINETEENTH STREET NEWS, 641 19th St near Pine, (716) 284-2214.

ONEONTA

Bars

BLACK OAK TAVERN, 14 Water St, (607) 432-9566. NOT a gay bar but gay-friendly crowd.

OTEGO

Accommodations

A WOODCHUCK'S HOLLOW, RD2 Otsdawa Rd 60A-7, (607) 988-2713. 1 bedroom efficiency on 70 acres. AC, kitchen, refrigerator & private bath. Color cable TV, telephone & maid service available upon request. 2-day minimum stay. 50% gay & lesbian clientele.

PLATTSBURGH

Dance Bar/Disco

BLAIR'S, 30 Marion St, (518) 561-9071. Dancing Fri & Sat, 50% men, 50% women. ♀ ♂

PORT CHESTER

Bars

SANDY'S OLD HOMESTEAD, 325 N Main St, (914) 939-0758. Bar & restaurant, 50% gay clientele, 50% gay women, men welcome. Private party with DJ last Sat of month is women's dance party.

POUGHKEEPSIE

Bars

CONGRESS, THE, 411 Main Mall E, (914) 486-

NEW YORK

UNITED STATES

9068 or 486-9531. Jukebox dancing, pool tables, 49th year.

■ *Erotica*
HAMILTON BOOK, 216 Hamilton St, (914) 473-1776.

QUEENS

■ *Information*
AIDS INFO, Jamaica: (718) 739-2525; Rego Park: (718) 896-2500; Far Rockaway: (718) 868-8645.

■ *Bars*
ATLANTIS, corner 37th Ave & 85th St, Jackson Hts, (718) 426-1990. Separate dance area.

BREADSTIX (BS) EAST,★ 113-24 Queens Blvd, Forest Hills, (718) 263-0300. Video bar, DJ Fri-Tues.

FRIEND'S TAVERN, 78-11 Roosevelt, Jackson Heights, (718) 397-7316.

MUSIC BOX, 40-08 74th St, Queens, (718) 429-9356. Wed drag contest & Columbian nite.

■ *Dance Bar/Disco*
EL BAR, 63-14 Roosevelt, Woodside, (718) 651-4145. Drag shows Fri, DJ nightly.

EL BOTE, Broadway & 78th St.

KRASH, 34-48 Steinway, Astoria, (718) 937-2400. Large dance club, open Mon & Thurs-Sat, 60% men, 40% women.

LUCHO'S, 38-19 69th St, Queens, (718) 899-9048.

MAGIC TOUCH, 73-13 37th Rd, Jackson Hts, (718) 429-8605. Strippers & shows.

RHEINBECK

■ *Retail & Bookstores*
HABITU, 11 Mill St, (914) 876-6652. Gay-related cards, books, gift items, Mon, Wed-Sat 11am-6pm, Sun 11am-5pm.

ROCHESTER

■ *Information*
AIDS HOTLINE, (716) 442-2200. 9am-5pm Mon-Fri.

GAY ALLIANCE & GAY SOURCE INFO LINE, 179 Atlantic Ave, (716) 244-8640 or tape. Community center Mon-Thurs 1pm-9:30pm, Fri 1pm-6pm, lending library, annual Pride parade & picnic, weekly youth group meetings, publishes Empty Closet. Women's coffeehouse 3rd Fri.

■ *Accommodations*
PARK PLACE, 1132 Park Ave, (716) 256-3389, Fax: (716) 256-2693. B&B, shared bath, continental breakfast. Mostly men, women welcome on separate nights.

■ *Bars*
ANTHONY'S 522, 522 E Main, (716) 325-1350 or 325-2060. 50% men, 50% women.

AVENUE PUB, 522 Monroe Ave at Goodman, (716) 244-4960. DJ Thurs-Sun. More women Wed, Sat.

BACHELOR FORUM, 670 University, (716) 271-6930. Leather club night 3rd Sat. Leather shop Fri, Sat from 10pm.

CHENA'S, 145 E Main St, (716) 232-7240. DJ Fri & Sat with club music.

COMMON GROUNDS. 139 State St (716) 232-9303. Pool tables, jukebox.

MUTHERS, 45 S Union St, (716) 325-6216. Bar serving burgers & wings, women's nite Fri & Sat, Tea dance Sun, DJ Fri-Sun.

TARA LOUNGE, 153 Liberty Pole Way near Andrews, (716) 232-4719. CD jukebox & games downstairs. Piano bar, cabaret upstairs. Patio, women welcome.

■ *Dance Bar/Disco*
ATLANTIS, 10/12 S Washington St. Big alternative dance bar & lounge, many straights.

CLUB MARCELLA,★ 123 Liberty Pole Way, (716) 454-5963.

■ *Saunas/Health Clubs*
ROCHESTER SPA & BODY CLUB, 109 Liberty Pole Way near Pleasant, (716) 454-1074. Sun deck, exercise equipment, 24hrs.

■ *Restaurants*
JONATHAN'S CHOICE, 122 Main St, E Rochester, (716) 248-2470. Lunch, dinner, Sun brunch. Italian-American, fresh seafood, homemade desserts, chef-owned & -operated.

SLICE OF LIFE, 742 South Ave, (716) 271-8010. Feminist vegetarian cafe.

■ *Retail & Bookstores*
GOOD COMPANY, 715 Monroe Ave, (716) 244-5719. Alternative resource, unique jewelry, cards, gifts from around the world.

PRIDE CONNECTION, 728 South Ave, (716) 242-7840. All lesbian & gay clothing, gifts, cards, books, jewelry, videos, magazines, etc. Mon-Sat 10am-9pm, Sun noon-6.

WRITERS & BOOKS., 740 University Ave, (716) 473-2590. General bookstore with some gay & lesbian titles.

■ *Leathers/Piercing*
ROCHESTER CUSTOM LEATHERS, 274 N Goodman St in Village Gate Square, (716) 442-2323, (800) 836-9047. Open 7 days, 2nd location at Bachelor Forum bar Fri, Sat evenings.

■ *Erotica*
DUNDALK NEWS, 651 State St, (716) 325-2248.

HUDSON VIDEO & NEWS, 1462 Hudson Ave, (716) 342-8310.

MONROE SHOW WORLD, 585 Monroe Ave, (716) 473-0160. Adult videos, lingerie.

NORTH END NEWS CO, 490 Monroe Ave, (716) 271-1426. Many all-male videos.

SOUTH CLINTON BOOK MART, 115 N Clinton Ave at Franklin, (716) 325-9322, 24hrs.

STATE STREET BOOK & VIDEO, 109 State St, (716) 263-9919, 24hrs.

TIMES SQUARE BOOKS, 57 Mortimer St, (716) 325-9570, 24hrs.

SCHENECTADY

■ *Accommodations*
WIDOW KENDALL, THE, 10 N Ferry St, (518) 370-5511, (800) 244-0925, fax: (518) 382-2640. Gay-friendly B&B, shared bath, 4-course breakfast.

■ *Bars*
BLYTHWOOD, THE, 50 N Jay St, (518) 382-9755, 9pm-4:30am 7 days, women welcome. 49th year.

CLINTON STREET PUB, 159 Clinton St, (518) 382-9173. NOT a gay bar, but gayer evenings, weekends.

SENECA FALLS

■ *Information*
WOMEN'S HISTORICAL SITES, National Women's Hall of Fame, 76 Fall St, 568-8060, Elizabeth Cady Stanton Home (restored), 32 Washington St, located in Women's Rights National Park (write: c/o Nat'l Park Service, US Dept. of Interior, Seneca Falls, NY 13148, 568-2991.

STATEN ISLAND

■ *Information*
LAMBDA ASSOCIATES, (718) 876-8786. Active local gay & lesbian group, annual picnic, potlucks, monthly trips, get togethers, theatrical productions. Meetings weekly. Annual gay pride dinner dance.

■ *Dance Bar/Disco*
BAY CLUB, 492 Bay St, (718) 273-7354. Wed-Sat 9pm-4am, male dancers Fri, drag shows Sat.

TUNE TOWN, 700 Van Duzer St, (718) 816-5323.

SWAIN SKI AREA

■ *Accommodations*
FAIRWISE LLAMA FARM B&B, 1320 Rt 70, Canaseraga, (607) 545-6247. Gay-friendly B&B with gift shop. Shared bath, ceiling fans, TV lounge & full breakfast.

SYRACUSE

■ *Information*
AIDS HOTLINE, (315) 475-AIDS (2437), 475-2430. 8:30am-10:30pm 7 days.

GAY PHONE, (315) 443-3599, 24hrs irregularly staffed. Socials Tues 8pm, discussion groups.

WOMEN'S INFO CENTER, 601 Allen St at

472 FERRARI GUIDES' GAY TRAVEL A to Z - 18th EDITION

NORTH CAROLINA

Harvard, (315) 478-4636 or tape. Irregularly staffed.

Bars
MY BAR, 205 N West St, (315) 471-9279. DJ Sat, 75% women.
TU TU VENUE, 731 James St, (315) 475-8888. Bar & restaurant, New Age cuisine.

Dance Bar/Disco
MR T'S, 218 N Franklin St at Herald Place (315) 471-9736. DJ Wed-Sun, 80% men, 20% women.
PLATEAU, 1203 Wilton Ave, (315) 468-9830. Wed-Sun from 7pm, DJ weekends.
RYAN'S SOMEPLACE ELSE,★ 410 Pearl St near freeway ramp, (315) 471-9499. Video dance club, 60% men, 40% women.
TREXX, 319 N Clinton St, (315) 474-6408. Alternative dance bar, many straights.

Retail & Bookstores
MY SISTERS' WORDS, 304 N McBride Street, (315) 428-0227. Feminist bookstore.

Erotica
ADULT WORLD, 2870 Erie Blvd E, (315) 446-2613, 7 days.
BOULEVARD BOOKS, 2576 Erie Blvd E near Midler, (315) 446-1595, 24hrs.
BURNET BOOKSTORE, 303 Burnet Ave, (315) 471-9230, 7 days.
SALT CITY BOOK & VIDEO, 3713 Brewerton Rd, Ponderosa Plaza, (315) 454-0629, 24hrs.

TARRYTOWN

Retail & Bookstores
RAZZMATAZZ FINE GIFTS, 35 N Broadway, (914) 631-4646.

UPPER NYACK

Dance Bar/Disco
BARZ, 327 Rte 9W, Nyack, (914) 353-4444. Dance bar, male dancers, 50% men, 50% women.

Restaurants
COVEN CAFE, 162 Main St, Nyack, (914) 358-9829. Fine dining, restaurant & bar. Gay owned & operated. All welcome, men's night Wed.

UTICA

Information
AIDS LINE, (315) 724-3921. Tape Mon-Wed-Fri 11am-2pm.

Bars
CARMEN D'S, Charlotte St across from the county office bldg, (315) 735-3964. Juke box & pool table.

Dance Bar/Disco
THAT PLACE, 216 Bleecker Street, (315) 724-1446. 7 days, patio, DJ Thurs-Sat, levi leather night 1st Sat of month, Upstate NY leather contest in Oct.

Erotica
ADULT WORLD, 319 Oriskany Blvd, Yorkville,
PLAYTIME ADULT, 400 block Oriskany Blvd, Yorkville.

WHITE PLAINS

Information
LESBIAN LINE, (914) 949-3203.

Bars
LOFT, 200 Hamilton Ave, White Plains Mall, (914) 948-9422. Unverifiable spring '97.

Dance Bar/Disco
STUTZ, 202 Westchester Ave, (914) 761-3100. Male strippers Fri & Sat, patio, summer BBQ's. 70% men, 30% women.

WINDHAM

Accommodations
POINT LOOKOUT MOUNTAIN INN, Rte 23 Box 33 East Windham, (518) 734-3381. Gay-friendly inn with restaurant, bar, fireplace lounge, gourmet food shop, gifts. Rooms with spectacular views, color TVs, fireplace lounge, expanded continental breakfast, nearby river & lake.

WOODSTOCK AREA

Accommodations
RIVER RUN BED & BREAKFAST, Main St, (914) 254-4884. Gay-owned & operated, gay-friendly B&B in an 1887 country village Victorian 35 minutes from Woodstock & 2-1/2 hours from NYC. Mostly private baths.

NORTH CAROLINA

WHO TO CALL
For Tour Companies Serving This Destination
See North Carolina on page 22

ASHEVILLE

Accommodations
ANOTHER POINT OF VIEW, 108 Weeping Cherry Forest Rd, Fairview, (704) 628-0005. Guest apartment, private bath, AC, color Cable TV, VCR, fruit & wine basket on arrival, some straight clientele.
BIRD'S NEST BED & KITCHEN, THE, 41 Oak Park Rd, (704) 252-2381. Looking for the perfect guest place with beautiful views of the Smokey Mtns and lots of privacy? This recently remodeled turn-of-the-century home is it! **Very spacious and comfortable.** Located within walking distance of downtown Asheville. Private entrance, private bath, AC, master bedroom, kitchen and sun porch. No smoking, no pets. Mostly women with men welcome.
CABIN AT WOLF LAUREL, 25 Mineral Springs Rd, (704) 254-0024. Two-story hand-hewn cabin with decks,
CAROLINA BED & BREAKFAST, 177 Cumberland Ave, (704) 254-3608. Gay-friendly B&B near downtown. Priv. baths, AC, some fireplaces. Full break., massage avail.
CORNER OAK MANOR, 53 Saint Dunstans Rd, (704) 253-3525. Elegantly-decorated, gay-friendly B&B with lesbian following. Rooms & cottages with private baths, AC & ceiling fans. Full breakfast.
INN ON MONTFORD, THE, 296 Montford Ave, (704) 254-9569, (800) 254-9569, Fax: (704) 254-9518. Gay-friendly B&B. Private baths, gym & full breakfast.
MARSHALL HOUSE B&B, PO Box 865, Marshall, NC 28753, (704) 649-9205, Fax: (704) 649-2999. Gay-friendly B&B with private & shared baths, expanded continental breakfast, 18 miles northwest of Asheville.

Women's Accommodations
CAMP PLEIADES, Summer: Rt 2, Box 250A, Hughes Gap Rd, Bakersville, NC (704) 688-9201, fax: (704) 688-3449. E-mail: starcamp @aol.com. Winter: (904) 241-3050, fax: (904) 241-3628. Winter mail: 390 Garden Lane, Atlantic Beach, FL 32233. A mountain resort for women, 60 miles north of Asheville. Explore 67 acres of private, heavily wooded property, clear-running streams, swimming pond, campfire circle, hiking trails. Enjoy sports, arts & crafts, mountain biking, horseback riding, whitewater rafting. Sleep in cozy private and group cabins. Relish wholesome family-style meals. Memorial Day to Labor Day, plus Fall Foliage Weekends. Men welcome certain times of year.
EMY'S NOOK, 248 Forest Hill Dr, Asheville, NC 28803, (704) 281-4122 (Tel/Fax). A women-only guesthouse in in-town Asheville, in a quiet, tree-lined neighborhood. Our guest space is for women wanting the convenience of a quiet, tranquil place in the city combined with easy access to mountain fun. We are only 5 minutes from Asheville's wide variety of shops, restaurants & nightlife. Amenities include shared bath, light continental breakfast, BW or color TV and ceiling fans.
MOUNTAIN LAUREL B&B, 139 Lee Dotson Rd, Fairview, NC, reservations: (704) 628-9903. 25 min. from Asheville, NC, in the heart of the Blude Ridge Mountains. Brand new home nestled in the Western NC Mts. with panoramic views. We are creating a getaway with romantic charm and gourmet hospitality, catering to lesbians and gay men. Huge rooms, king and queen beds, private baths, Jacuzzi, breakfast and dinner menus with gastronomic delights, wraparound deck. Distinctive "classy" comfort in secluded, private mountain setting.

FERRARI GUIDES' GAY TRAVEL A to Z - 18th EDITION   473

NORTH CAROLINA

FYI

Women Learn to Sail off North Carolina

If you want more from your vacation than a day at the beach, **Best of Both Worlds** offers packages to satisfy the adventurous spirit, while providing an atmosphere of relaxation. Explore the Outer Banks of North Carolina by sail on an oceangoing sloop that accommodates up to six. For three days, take the helm or relax and loll in the sun, as you sail to popular ports of call and enjoy secluded anchorages. Upon returning, spend the next four days oceanside in a condominium along North Carolina's uncrowded beaches. Great golf, restaurants, deepsea fishing, shelling, day trips to outer islands, and more are at your fingertips. Weeklong onboard sailing and navigation or pleasure cruises are also available. Overnight trips are private with only your party on board. Day trips may be mixed with other visitors. Teaching packages can take you from basic sailing all the way up to handling the boat yourself. There are more inland waters in North Carolina than any other state on the east coast.

Contact **Best of Both Worlds** at **(919) 322-5804** or write PO Box 763, Bridgeton, NC 28519.

SOPHIE'S COMFORT, (803) 787-5777 (Reservations). Women-only B&B with private bath, vegetarian continental breakfast, 20-min drive to Asheville, 10-min village of Black Mountain. ♀

TWENTY-SEVEN BLAKE STREET, 27 Blake St, (704) 252-7390. Suite with private entrance, cable TV & off-street parking. ♀

■ Bars
O'HENRY'S, 59 Haywood St (downtown), (704) 254-1891. Private club, 70% men, 30% women, C&W dances Wed, twice monthly shows & male strippers.

■ Dance Bar/Disco
HAIRSPRAY/METROPOLIS/BARBERSHOP, 38 N French Broad Ave, (704) 258-2027. Entertainment complex, 3 atmospheres in 1 location. Barbershop has patio, bar & quiet lounge. Metropolis is dance bar. Hairspray is bar with pool table.

SCANDALS, 12 Grove St, (704) 252-2838. Wed-Sat, younger crowd.

■ Restaurants
CAHOOTS, 12 Grove St, adjacent to Scandals bar, (704) 252-2838. Tues-Sat. ♀ ♂

■ Retail & Bookstores
CRYSTAL VISIONS, Hwy 25 at I-26 (exit 13), Naples (16 mi south of central Asheville), (704) 687-1193. Jewelry, crystals, metaphysical books, lifestyle resource center, 10-6 Mon-Fri, 10-5 Sat.

MALAPROP'S BOOKSTORE & CAFE, 61 Haywood St, (704) 254-6734. General bookstore with emphasis on women's issues on most subjects. Large lesbian and gay selection. Open every day.

RAINBOW'S END, 10 N Spruce St, (704) 285-0005. Bookstore with rainbow & pride items.

BAT CAVE

■ Accommodations
OLD MILL B&B, Hwy 64/7-A/9, Lake Lure Hwy, Box 252, (704) 625-4256. B&B with gift shop. Some straight clientele. Variety of rooms with modern conveniences, TV lounge, full breakfast & nearby river. ♀ ♂

BLOWING ROCK

■ Accommodations
STONE PILLAR B & B, PO Box 1881, 144 Pine St, (704) 295-4141, (800) 962-9955. E-mail: stonepillar@blowingrock.com. http:www.blowingrock.com/northcarolina/stonepillar. Gay-friendly B&B, double rooms with various conveniences, private baths, common areas with fireplaces, full breakfast. Nearby town pool.

CHAPEL HILL

■ Women's Accommodations
JOAN'S PLACE, c/o M Joan Stiven, 1443 Poinsett Dr, (919) 942-5621. B&B for women in my home. Rustic setting, secluded among trees. Share one full bath and my living room and large deck. Continental breakfast. ♀

■ Restaurants
CROOK'S CORNER, 610 W Franklin St, (919) 929-7643. Southern dining, popular Sun brunch, many gays.

WEATHERVANE, THE, Eastgate Shopping Center, (919) 929-9466. American, Southern, Int'l cuisine, lunch, brunch, dinner. Mon-Thurs 10am-10pm, Fri-Sat 10am-11pm, Sun 12pm-6pm.

■ Retail & Bookstores
INTERNATIONALIST BOOKS, 405 W Franklin St, (919) 942-1740. Progressive bookstore with gay & lesbian section.

CHARLOTTE

■ Information
AIDS HOTLINE, (704) 333-AIDS (2437). 8:30am-5pm Mon-Fri or tape.

GAY & LESBIAN SWITCHBOARD, (704) 535-6277, 6:30pm-10:30pm nightly.

■ Bars
BRASS RAIL, 3707 Wilkinson Blvd near Midland, (704) 399-8413. Large patio with bar, juke box, popular treehouse.

CHASERS, 3217 The Plaza near Pecan, (704) 339-0500. All men's club, male stripper, closed Sun.

LIAISONS,★ 316 Rensselaer, (704) 376-1617. Upscale cocktail bar in a 2-story Victorian with views of the city from the veranda. Daily 5pm-1am. ♀ ♂

■ Dance Bar/Disco
CLUB MYXX, 3110 s Tryon St, (704) 525-5001. Primarily African-American, but everyone is welcome, 3rd Fri Sistahs Night Out for women.

MYTHOS, corner of 6th & N College, (704) 375-8765. Gay Sun & Wed, drag shows Wed. Check for changes in gay nights schedule.

OLEEN'S,★ 1831 South Blvd at Worthington, (704) 373-9604. Shows Fri-Sun, 50% men, 50% women.

SCORPIO,★ 2301 Freedom Dr near Camp Green, (704) 373-9124. Huge complex with dance & show bar, C&W bar, patio, Tues-Sun form 9pm. One bar overlooks the dance bar.

■ Cafe
BRENNER WINE & COFFEE SHOP, Gay owned/friendly. Wonderful brunch. ♀ ♂

■ Restaurants
FAT CITY, 3127 N Davidson St, (704) 343-0240. Deli, bar.

THREE HUNDRED EAST, 300 East Boulevard, (704) 332-6507. Popular Sun brunch.

■ Retail & Bookstores
RISING MOON BOOKS & BEYOND, 510 E 35th St, (704) 332-7473. Gay & lesbian bookstore, Wed-Sat noon-8pm, Sun 1pm-5pm.

NORTH CAROLINA

WHITE RABBIT BOOKS, 834 Central Ave, (704) 377-4067. Gay & lesbian bookstore with erotica, leather & metaphysical items. ♀ ♂

Erotica
CAROLINA VIDEO, W.J. Harris at Albemarle.

HWY 74 VIDEO & NEWS, 3514 Barry Dr, (704) 399-7907.

INDEPENDENCE NEWS, 3205 The Plaza, 36th St, next to Chasers, (704) 332-8430.

QUEEN CITY VIDEO & NEWS, 2320 Wilkinson Blvd, (704) 344-9435.

VIDEO ADVENTURES, 3231 Wilkinson Blvd, (704) 399-7187.

CRYSTAL COAST

Accommodations
WILLIAM & GARLAND MOTEL, PO Box 204, Hwy #58, Salter Path, (919) 247-3733. Gay-friendly motel at Salter Path Dunes Nat'l Park, beach access, private baths, color cable TV, AC, kitchen, refrigerator.

DURHAM

Accommodations
MINERAL SPRINGS INN, 718 South Mineral Springs Rd, Durham, NC 27703, (919) 596-2162 (tel/fax), (888) 833-6900. Inn with private & shared baths, full breakfast, women welcome. TO OPEN SEPT 1998. ♀♂

Bars
BOXER'S, 5504 Chapel Hill Blvd at Straw Valley (15-501 & I-40), (919) 489-7678. Piano bar, 75% men, 25% women. Pool tables, big-screen TV.

Dance Bar/Disco
ALL ABOUT EVE, 711 Rigsbee Ave, (919) 688-3002. Big dance bar with deck bar. DJ Fri & Sat, men very welcome. ♀

POWER COMPANY, rear of 315 W Main St, (919) 683-1151. Wed-Sat 9pm-3am, Sun from 6pm, drag shows Fri, male strippers Sun, 65% men & 35% women.

Cafe
FRANCESCA'S, 706-B 9th St, (919) 286-4177.

MAIN STREET CAFE, 313 W Main St, (919) 682-4315.

Restaurants
PAPAGAYO'S MEXICAN CUISINE, patio dining, popular with gays.

Retail & Bookstores
REGULATOR BOOKSHOP, 720 Ninth Street, (919) 286-2700. General bookstore with strong men's and women's sections.

Erotica
ATLANTIS VIDEO NEWS, 522 E Main Street, (919) 682-7469. Videos, magazines, novelties.

DURHAM VIDEO & NEWS, 502 Lakewood Ave, (919) 489-9945. Videos, books, novelties.

FAYETTEVILLE

Bars
LYNN'S LOUNGE, 213 Hillsborough. ♀ ♂

Dance Bar/Disco
MELLENIUM 2540 Gillespie Street, (910) 485-2037. Hi energy disco, drag shows, Wed-Sun 9pm-3am, Sat male strippers.

SPEKTRUM, 107 Swain St, (910) 868-4279. Hi-energy, house, techno & rave music, 7 days 5pm-3am. Drag shows Fri-Sun, male & female strippers monthly. Patio with summer BBQ. ♀ ♂

Erotica
FORT VIDEO & NEWS, 4431 Bragg Blvd, (910) 868-9905, 24hrs.

MODERN NEWS & VIDEO, 105 Swain St.

FRANKLIN

Women's Accommodations
HONEY'S RAINBOW ACRES GUESTHOUSE/PHOENIX NEST, PO Box 37091 (704) 369-5162, weekly rentals: (704) 524-9000. Women-only guesthouse with kitchen privileges, gay/lesbian cottage with kitchen. Private & shared baths. ♀

MOUNTAIN MAGIC, (904) 231-0254, (800) 854-9266. Romantic, secluded, furnished mountain chalet with stone fireplace, sliding doors, skylights and a deck with a view. Modern conveniences, 2 bedroom, 2 baths, complimentary gourmet coffee, tea, TV, VCR. Pets & men welcome. Located 8 miles from the Appalachian Trail. ♀

GREENSBORO

Accommodations
BILTMORE GREENSBORO HOTEL, THE, 111 W Washinton Ave, (800) 332-0303, (910) 272-3474, Fax: (910) 275-2523. Urban inn, private baths, 50% gay & lesbian clientele. ♀ ♂

Dance Bar/Disco
BABYLON, 221 S Elm St, (910) 275-1006. Private club, from 9pm.

PALMS, THE, 413 N Eugene St near Lindsay, (910) 272-6307. DJ Wed-Sun, 60% men, 40% women. Private club, male strippers, lots of drag shows. ♀ ♂

WAREHOUSE 29, 1011 Arnold St, (910) 333-9333. Entertainment Sun, male strippers & drag shows, 70% men, 30% women. ♂

Restaurants
SUNSET CAFE, 4608 W Market St near Holden Rd, (910) 855-0349. Eclectic organic menu, changing daily.

Retail & Bookstores
WHITE RABBIT BOOKS, 1833 Spring Garden, (910) 272-7604. Gay & lesbian bookstore with cards, gifts, jewelry, rainbow items, T-shirts, magazines, music, videos for sale & rent.

Erotica
GENTS, 3722 High Point Rd near Holden, (910) 855-9855. Gay & lesbian videos, 24hrs.

I-40 VIDEO, NEWS & TOBACCO, 2438 Randleman Rd, (910) 378-9800.

NEW VISION, 507 Mobile St near Randleman Rd, (910) 274-6443.

TREASURE BOX, 1203 E Bessemer Ave near Lindsay, (910) 373-9849, 24hrs.

GREENVILLE

Dance Bar/Disco
PADDOCK CLUB, 1008-B Dickinson Ave, (919) 758-0990. Dance & show bar, closed Mon, Tue. Fri good night for women. ♂

HICKORY

Information
AIDS LINE (ALPHA), (704) 322-1447. 9am-5pm.

Dance Bar/Disco
CLUB CABARET, 101 N Center St, (704) 322-8103. Dance & show bar Wed-Sun 9pm-2am, male strippers Wed. Unverifiable spring '97. ♀ ♂

HOT SPRINGS

Accommodations
DUCKETT HOUSE INN, THE, Hwy 209, PO Box 441, (704) 622-7621, (800) 306-5038. B&B farmhouse in heart of Unaka Mountains on Appalachian Trail, 50% gay & lesbian clientele. Singles/doubles with shared baths. Creek, nearby river, access to hot springs. Ask about gourmet country meals.

MOREHEAD CITY

Dance Bar/Disco
SH'BOOM'S, 415 Morehead Ave, Atlantic Beach, (919) 726-7000. ♂

RALEIGH

Information
AIDS INFO, (919) 834-2437.

GAY & LESBIAN HOTLINE, (919) 821-0055, 7-10pm or tape.

Bars
FLEX, 2 S West St, (919) 832-8855. Mon-Sat 5pm-2am, Sun 2pm-2am, most days mixed crowd including leather, Fri leather dress code in The Cage (separate room), Sun buffet 6pm. ♂

Dance Bar/Disco
CC NOW, 313 W Hargett St, downtown, (919) 755-9599. 8pm-? nightly, from 4pm Sun, video dance bar, Sun shows, 18+, women welcome. ♂

LEGENDS, ★ 330 W Hargett St (919) 831-8888. Mon industrial alternative, Fri & Sat dance

NORTH CAROLINA

parties, Sun, Tues & some Fri drag shows.

■ Restaurants
BLACK DOG CAFE, 208 E Martin, (919) 828-1994. Lunch, dinner. Near galleries, gay-friendly.

FIVE EIGHTEEN WEST, 518 W Jones. Northern Italian cuisine.

IRREGARDLESS CAFE, 901 W Morgan Street, (919) 833-8898. Open for lunch, dinner and Sun brunch.

RATHSKELLER, 2412 Hillsborough St. Gay & lesbian following.

VERTIGO, 426 S McDowell St, (919) 832-4477. Late-night menu on weekends.

WICKED SMILE, 511 W Hargett St, (919) 828-2223. Fine dining.

■ Retail & Bookstores
WHITE RABBIT BOOKS, 309 W Martin St, (919) 856-1429. Gay & lesbian bookstore.

■ Leathers/Piercing
INNOVATIONS IN LEATHER, 517 Hillsborough St, (919) 833-4833.

SKIN DEEP & GUMMI, 517 Hillsborough, (919) 833-4833. Body piercing. Gummi is a latex store behind Skin Deep.

■ Erotica
ADULT BOOK, W Glenwood Ave, near Walmart.

APHRODITE'S, Rte 70 between Durham & Raleigh, near the airport.

BACHELOR'S VIDEO, 3411 S Wilmington St near Tryon, (919) 779-0995. 7 days.

CAPITOL BLVD NEWS, 2236 Capitol Blvd, (919) 831-1400.

CASTLE VIDEO & NEWS, 1210 Downtown Blvd, (919) 836-9189.

OP'S (OUR PLACE), ★ 327 W Hargett St at Harrington, (919) 833-8968. Open 7 days.

SNAPSHOTS VIDEO & NEWS, 1433 S Wilmington Street, (919) 828-2019. Gay videos, 24hrs.

SPRUCE PINE

■ Women's Accommodations
SHEPHERD'S RIDGE, (704) 765-7809. Women-only guesthouse, private bath.

WILMINGTON

■ Accommodations
ROSEHILL INN BED & BREAKFAST, 114 South 3rd St, Wilmington, NC (910) 815-0250, (800) 815-0250, Fax: (910) 815-0350. In Wilmington's Victorian Historic District, full breakfast, private baths, near dining & shopping.

■ Beaches
GAY BEACH, north end of Wrightsville Beach, 7 miles east of Wilmington.

■ Dance Bar/Disco
MICKEY RATZ, 115 S Front St, (910 251-

1289. Private club, huge patio, BBQ's. Male strippers Wed & Sat, drag shows Fri & Sun. Closed Mon & Tues.

WINSTON-SALEM

■ Accommodations
WACHOVIA BED & BREAKFAST LTD., 513 Wachovia St, (910) 777-0332. Gay-friendly B&B. AC, ceiling fans, private & shared baths, TV lounge, full breakfast.

■ Dance Bar/Disco
BOURBON STREET, 916 Burke St, (910) 724-4644. Dance & show bar. Wed-Sun shows.

CLUB ODYSSEY, 4019-A Country Club Rd., (910) 774-7071.

■ Erotica
INTOWNE VIDEO AND NEWS, 411 N Liberty St, (910) 748-9500.

NEW VISION, 1045 N Cherry St near business I-40, (910) 725-8034.

NORTH DAKOTA
FARGO

■ Information
PRAIRIE GAY & LESBIAN COMMUNITY, (701) 235-7335. A straight hotline will answer and put you in touch with the gay group.

■ Dance Bar/Disco
DECA DANCE, gay & lesbian dances. Winter-May: 1st & 3rd Fri, 9:30pm-1:30am in the banquet facility at the north end of the bowling alley, 2630 S University. In summer locations change.

■ Erotica
ADULT BOOKS AND CINEMA X, 417 NP Ave near 5th, (701) 232-9768. Videos, 24hrs.

GRAND FORKS

■ Dance Bar/Disco
JONESY'S ON THE EDGE, 10 3rd St N, near Demers Ave, (701) 772-3362. Same-sex dancing OK, 50% gay & lesbian. Some gay presence nightly, but especially popular with gays on Tues nite.

■ Erotica
PLAIN BROWN WRAPPER, 102 S 3rd St, (701) 772-9021, 24hrs.

MANDAN

■ Erotica
MANDAN BOOKSTORE, 116 Main St, (701) 663-9013. Books & videos.

MINOT

■ Erotica
RISQUE'S, 1514 S Broadway, (701) 838-2837. 7 days.

OHIO
STATEWIDE

■ Information
AIDS HOTLINE, (800) 332-2437, Spanish (800) 344-7432.

AKRON

■ Information
AIDS HOTLINE, (330) 375-2437, 24hrs.

■ Bars
ADAMS STREET BAR, ★ 77 N Adams near Upson (330) 434-9794. Video dance & cruise bar & a separate leather bar.

THREE-FIFTY-EIGHT CLUB, 358 S Main St between Cedar & Exchange, (330) 434-7788. Alternates between C&W & top 40 music, 85% men, 15% women.

■ Dance Bar/Disco
ADAMS STREET BAR, ★ 77 N Adams near Upson, (330) 434-9794. Video dance & cruise bar & a separate leather bar.

GARGOYLES NIGHTCLUB & CLUBHOUSE LOUNGE, 271 S Main St (rear entrance), (330) 384-1447. Dance bar & cocktail lounge with Sun drag shows, male strippers

INTERBELT, 70 N Howard Street, (330) 253-5700. Patio.

ROSETO CLUB, 627 S Arlington, (330) 724-4228. Dance club, volleyball court. Membership charge.

TEAR-EZ, 360 S Main, (330) 376-0011. Mostly men, women welcome.

■ Saunas/Health Clubs
AKRON STEAM & SAUNA, 41 S Case Ave at River, (330) 784-0777. Fri & Sat all night.

CLUB AKRON, 1339 E Market St at Martha, (330) 784-0309. One block east of the Goodyear Plant on the corner of Market Street & Martha, open 24 hours. Private club, membership only. Full gym, hot tub, steam room, sauna, video room.

■ Restaurants
CAFE 115, 115 E Market St.

CONNIE'S DIAMOND DELI, 378 S Main St.

SANDWICH BOARD, THE, 1667 W Market St, Sandwiches, soups, vegetarian dishes, desserts. Mon-Sat 11am-8pm.

ASHTABULA

■ Bars
LEEWARD LOUNGE, THE, 1026 Bridge St (Ohio 531), (216) 964-9935. Open daily 7pm-2:30am. Food 'til 1:30am.

ATHENS

■ Accommodations
SUSAN B. ANTHONY MEMORIAL UNREST HOME COMMUNITY, SBAMUH Box 5853, Athens, 45701, Women-only campground on

OHIO

150 woodland acres in southeastern Ohio. No electric, solar shower, outhouse. Reservation only, groups welcome.

BOWLING GREEN

■ Information
WOMEN'S CENTER, (419) 372-2281. Student group, Women For Women.

CANTON

■ Bars
FIVE FORTY CLUB,★ 540 Walnut St, (330) 456-8622.

SIDESTREET CAFE, 2360 Mahoning at Superior, (330) 453-8055. Pool room, game room, small dance floor.

■ Dance Bar/Disco
BOARDWALK, 1227 W Tuscarawas, (330) 453-8000.

■ Erotica
MARKET STREET NEWS, 440 Market St, (330) 453-1275, 7 days.

TOWER BOOKS, 219 12th St NE, (330) 455-1254, 7 days.

TOWNSHIP NEWS & BOOKS, 4445 Cleveland Ave near 44th St, (330) 966-0203.

CINCINNATI

Also includes Covington, KY (606).

■ Information
COMMUNITY CENTER, THE, 214 E 9th St, (513) 651-0040, switchboard (513) 651-0070.

WOMEN HELPING WOMEN, 216 E 9th St, (513) 381-5610. Info and referral, 24hrs.

■ Accommodations
PROSPECT HILL B & B, 408 Boal St, Cincinnati, OH (513) 421-4408. B&B on wooded hillside, 50% gay & lesbian clientele. Rooms with antique furnishings, deck, fireplace & buffet breakfast.

■ Bars
COLORS, 4042 Hamilton Ave, (513) 681-6969. Live jazz Fri & Sat, 75% gay, 25% straight.

GOLDEN LIONS, 340 Ludlow Ave near Ormond, (513) 281-4179. DJ Fri & Sat, 2 pool tables, piano.

JUNKERS TAVERN, 4158 Langland St, Northside, (513) 541-5470. Hillbilly bar.

NEW PLUM ST PIPELINE, 241 W Court St at Plum, (513) 241-5678.

ROSIE'S TAVERN, 7th & Bakewell, Covington, KY, (606) 291-9707. 40% gay & lesbian crowd. Very gay-friendly.

SIMON SAYS, 428 Walnut near 4th, (513) 381-8196. Downtown bar.

SPURS,★ 326 E 8th St near Broadway, (513) 621-2668.

SUBWAY, THE, 609 Walnut near Gano Alley, (513) 421-1294. Strippers Fri & Sat, pool tables, DJ 7 days.

■ Dance Bar/Disco
BULLFISHES, 4023 Hamilton Ave, (513) 541-9220.

CHASERS, 2640 Glendora, (513) 861-3966. Dance & show bar.

CINCINNATI DOCK,★ 603 W Pete Rose Way just east of I-75, (513) 241-LOAD (5623). Video dance bar, preppie crowd, patio. After-hours Fri & Sat.

SHIRLEY'S, 2401 Vine St, (513) 721-8483.

SHOOTERS, 927 Race St at Cort, (513) 381-9900. DJ Thur-Sat, 90% men, 10% women. Large C&W dance floor, line dancing lessons.

■ Cafe
WILD IRIS COFFEEHOUSE, Hamilton, (513) 541-4198. Ask locally for exact street address.

■ Restaurants
BOCA, 4034 Hamilton, (513) 542-2022. Restaurant & bar.

CAROL'S CORNER CAFE, 811 Main St, (513) 651-2667. Restaurant & bar with upstairs cabaret, piano & live singers.

DINER ON SYCAMORE, 1203 Sycamore.

MULLANE'S PARKSIDE CAFE, 723 Race St, (513) 381-1331.

PETERSON'S, 1111 St Gregory St, (513) 651-4777.

■ Retail & Bookstores
CRAZY LADIES BOOKSTORE, 4041 Hamilton Ave, (513) 541-4198. Women's bookstore. Lesbian support group meets here. Crazy Ladies Lesbian & Feminist Center 4039 Hamilton.

LEFTHANDED MOON, 48 E Court St, (513) 784-1166. Clothing, gifts, accessories, pride items, cards, books.

PINK PYRAMID, 36A W Court St near Race, (513) 621-7465. Gay & lesbian bookstore with cards & gifts.

■ Leathers/Piercing
ACME LEATHER & TOY, 326 E 8th St near Broadway, (513) 621-7390. Lower level of Spurs.

CLEVELAND

■ Information
GAY & LESBIAN CENTER, 1418 W 29th St, hotline: (216) 781-6736, 24hrs. Center: (216) 522-1999.

WOMEN'S CENTER, (216) 651-1450.

■ Bars
BARBARY LANE, 2619 Noble Rd, Cleveland Hts, (216) 382-2033. Sports bar, pool & dart leagues, open Mon-Fri 4pm-2:30am, Sat & Sun 5pm-2:30am.

FIVE-CENT DECISION, 4365 State Road, (216) 661-1314. Jukebox dancing, DJ Fri, country nites 1st & 3rd Fri.

HAWK, 11217 Detroit Ave near 112th, (216) 521-5443.

HI & DRY, 2207 W 11th St, (216) 621-6166. Bar & eatery with live jazz Fri, variety of music other nights. Burgers, vegetarian items, pastas, steaks, gyros. Popular with gays.

LEATHER STALLION, 2205 St Clair Ave near 23rd, (216) 589-8588. Patio.

MEMOIRS, 11213 Detroit Ave, (216) 221-8576. Conversation bar.

MJ'S PLACE, 11633 Lorain Ave, (216) 476-1970.

MUGGS AT WESTIES PUB, 3194 W 25th St, (216) 661-5365. Cocktail lounge, mellow.

OHIO CITY OASIS, 2909 Detroit Ave, (216) 574-2203. DJ Fri-Sun, C&W night Sun.

PARADISE INN, 4488 State Rd at Behrwald, (216) 741-9819. Small bar, good music. Since 1954.

REC ROOM, THE, 15320 Brookpark Rd, (216) 433-1669. Big screen TV, juke box, 2 pool tables, bowling.

ROCKIES,★ 9208 Detroit Ave, (216) 961-3115. DJ Wed-Sun, patio bar, pool room, game room. Sun tea dance.

RUDY'S, 2032 W 25th St, (216) 621-1752. A gay bistro, CD Jazz cocktail club, import beers, 70% men.

SEXX, 11213 Detroit Ave, (216) 221-8576.

■ Dance Bar/Disco
AUNT CHARLIE'S THE CAGE, 9506 Detroit, (216) 651-0727.

GRID, THE, 1281 W 9th St, (216) 623-0113. High energy dance bar and lounge, videos. 10% women except Sun 90% women from 4pm. Male strippers.

LEGENDS,★ 11719 Detroit Rd, (216) 226-1199. Karaoke.

METRONOME, 1946 St. Clair Ave, (216) 241-4663. Fri & Sat only, sometimes Sun.

NUMBERS,★ 620 Frankfort Ave, (216) 621-6900. Dance bar.

TOO'S ATTRAXXIONS, 6757 W 130th St, Parma Hts, (216) 842-0020. Very diverse suburban crowd.

U4IA,★ 10630 Berea Rd, (216) 631-7111. Dance & show bar, 80% men, 20% women. Open Fri-Sun only. After hours weekends.

VISIONS, 1229 W 6th, (216) 566-0060. Video dance bar.

■ Cafe
PHOENIX CAFE, 3750 Pearl Rd at Archwood, (216) 741-6010. Gay-friendly.

RED STAR CAFE, 11604 Detroit Ave, (216)

FERRARI GUIDES' GAY TRAVEL A to Z - 18th EDITION   477

OHIO

521-7827. Gay-friendly.

SPANIEL'S COFFEE CAFE, 2710 Lorain Ave, (216) 651-4060.

TRUFFLES, 11118 Clifton, (216) 961-7439. Pastries.

■ Saunas/Health Clubs

CLUB CLEVELAND, 1448 W 32nd St near Detroit, (216) 961-2727. Private club, 24hrs. Patio, sun deck, Sun buffet.

FLEX, 1293 W 9th St near St Clair, (216) 696-0595. Private club, gym equipment, 24hrs.

■ Restaurants

BILLY'S NORTHCOAST CAFE, 11110 Clifton, (216) 281-7722.

HARMONY BAR & GRILL, 3359 Fulton Ave, (216) 398-5052. Vegetarian, Eastern European, American & Italian cuisines.

SNICKERS, 1261 W 76th Ave, (216) 631-7555.

■ Retail & Bookstores

BOOKSTORE ON W 25TH, 1921 W 25th St, (216) 566-8897. General bookstore strong gay & lesbian sections (new & used books).

■ Leathers/Piercing

BODY WORKS, 11623 Euclid Ave, (216) 721-2248.

LAWS LEATHER, 11112 Clifton Blvd, (216) 961-0544.

■ Erotica

ADULT BOOKS, W 9th near St. Clair, (216) 861-4119, 24hrs.

ALL ADULT BOOKSTORE, 3141 W 25th St, (216) 459-1797.

AXIOM, 11829 Detroit, Lakewood, (216) 221-3013. Fetish clothing.

BANK NEWS, 4025 Clark Ave near West 41st, (216) 281-8777.

BODY LANGUAGE,★ NE crn of W 115th St & Lorain, mail to: 3291 W 115th St, (216) 251-3330. Erotic hardware and romantic software for men & women. Also cards, gifts and videos.

BROOKPARK NEWS AND BOOKS, 16700 Brookpark Rd, (216) 267-9019. Full line of gay & lesbian videos, magazines, novelties & erotica.

HOUSE OF BOOKS, 16500 Brookpark Rd, (216) 362-6800, 24hrs.

ROCKY'S ENTERTAINMENT EMPORIUM, 13330 Brookpark Rd, (216) 267-9376.

WEST 95TH STREET NEWS, 9500 Lorain Ave, (216) 631-4010.

COLUMBUS

■ Information

STONEWALL GAY & LESBIAN CENTER, 1160 N High St, (614) 299-7764. Mon-Thurs 10-7, Fri 9-5, or tape.

■ Accommodations

FIFTY LINCOLN, 50 E Lincoln, (614) 291-5056.

FIVE FOURTY TWO B&B, 542 Mohawk St, (614) 621-1741. B&B, some straight clientele. Suite with color cable TV, VCR, AC, phone, fireplace & private bath. Expanded continental breakfast.

GERMAN VILLAGE B&B, 763 S 3rd St, (614) 444-8888.

■ Bars

BLAZER'S PUB, 1205 N High St, (614) 299-1800. Pool tables, electronic darts, jukebox, Sun cookouts.

CLUB 20, 20 E Duncan St. (614) 261-9111.

CLUBHOUSE CAFE, 124 E Main St, (614) 228-5090. Coffee, desserts, pool table, movies, also drinks.

COLUMBUS EAGLE, 232 N 3rd St, (614) 228-0260 or 228-2804. Dance & cruise bar, occassional male strippers.

DOWNTOWN CONNECTION, 1126 N High St, (614) 299-4880. Gay sports bar, college crowd, pool table, darts.

EAGLE IN EXILE, 893 N 4th St, (614) 294-0069. Enforced leather dress code Fri & Sat, open Wed-Sat.

FAR SIDE, 1662 W. Mound St, (614) 276-5817. Couches, a fireplace, patio.

GARRETT'S SALOON, 1071 Parsons Ave, (614) 449-2351. Male strippers Sun, Thurs, drag shows Wed, karaoke.

HAVANA, 862 N High St, (614) 421-9697. Upscale video bar with live DJ, cigar smoking room, piano happy hour, Tues-Fri & Sun. Lots of fun parties.

REMO'S, 1409 S High St, (614) 443-4224.

SLAMMERS, 202 E Long St (614) 221-8880. Great pizza.

SUMMIT STATION, 2210 Summit St near Alden, (614) 261-9634. DJ Thurs-Sat, occasional live bands

TABU, 349 Marconi Blvd at Nationwide, (614) 464-2270. Bar & restaurant, 75% men, women welcome. Sun DJ & buffet.

TRADEWINDS II, 117 E Chestnut near 3rd St, (614) 461-4110. Closed Mon.

TREMONT, 708 S High St, in German Village, (614) 445-9365. Party bar, 70% men, jukebox dancing.

UNION STATION VIDEO CAFE,★ 630 N High St, (614) 228-3740. Upscale video bar, pool tables, darts, preppy young crowd, 70% men. Mon-Fri 4pm-2:30am, Sat 3pm-2:30am, Sun show tunes 2pm-2:30am. Good food, full-service kitchen 4pm-9pm.

■ Dance Bar/Disco

COLUMBUS EAGLE,★ 232 N 3rd St at Hickory, (614) 228-2804. Video dance bar, DJ nightly.

TRENDS/GARAGE,★ 40 E Long St near High, (614) 461-0076. Dance & quiet bars, patio bar, college crowd, 80% men, 20% women.

WALL STREET, 144 N Wall Street, (614) 464-2800. Mainly women, popular & more men Wed with progressive music. C&W Thurs.

■ Cafe

BASSO BEAN, 691 N High St, (614) 221-2326.

COFFEE TABLE, 731 N High St, (614) 297-1177.

COMMON GROUNDS,★ 2549 Indianola, (614) 263-7646. Women's coffeehouse.

CUP O' JOE, 627 S 3rd St, (614) 221-1563. Coffee, desserts.

KONA CAFE, 53 Parsons Ave.

■ Restaurants

GRAPEVINE CAFE, 73 E Gay St, (614) 221-VINE (8463). Nightclub & eatery. Closed Mon.

L'ANTIBES, 772 N High St #106, (614) 291-1666. French cuisine.

OUT ON MAIN,★ 122 E Main St, (614) 224-9510, 11am-2:30am, 7 days.

■ Retail & Bookstores

AN OPEN BOOK, 749 N High St, (614) 291-0080. Gay & lesbian bookstore.

KUKALA'S TANNING & TEES, 636 N High St, (614) 228-8337. Gay stuff & things. Cards, T-shirts, gifts & books. Tanning. Also Diablo body piercing.

TICKLED PINK, 874 N High St, (614) 488-6777. Gay & lesbian books, cards, jewelry. Tues-Fri 11-7pm, Sat 11-6pm, Sun 12-6pm. May change in '97, looking for new home.

■ Leathers/Piercing

IMRU, above Columbus Eagle.

OUTFITTERS, 636 N High St inside Kukala's, (614) 224-0448.

PIERCOLOGY, 874 N High St, inside Creativity, (614) 297-4743.

■ Erotica

DISCO BOOKS, 973 Harrisburg Pike, (614) 247-9716.

GENT'S, 245 S High St, (614) 464-1476.

LION'S DEN, 4309 Westerville Rd, (614) 663-5060.

METRO VIDEO, 848 N High St, (614) 291-7962.

NORTH CAMPUS VIDEO, 2465 High St, (614) 268-4021. Videos, magazines, 24 hours.

NU-LOOK BOOKSTORE, 3444 Westerville Rd, (614) 476-6618, 24hrs.

ZODIAC PLEASURE ZONE, 1565 Alum Creek Dr, (614) 252-0281. Videos, adult magazines, exotic leather department, erotic games & novelties. 24 hrs.

DAYTON

■ Information

AIDS LINE (513) 223-2437.

GAY & LESBIAN HOTLINE, (513) 274-1776. 7pm-11pm 7days.

OHIO

Bars
DJ'S, 237 N Main St, (513) 223-7340.

RIGHT CORNER, 105 E 3rd St at Jefferson, (513) 228-1285. Conversation bar.

STAGE DOOR,★ 44 N Jefferson near 2nd, (513) 223-7418.

Dance Bar/Disco
CITY CLUB, 121 N Ludlow.

DOWNUNDER, 131 N Ludlow, (513) 228-2520.

FOURTEEN SEVENTY WEST,★ 34 N Jefferson at Dixie, (513) 293-0066. 2-level dance complex & showbar.

JESSIE'S CELEBRITY, 850 N Main, (513) 223-2582. Hi energy dance club & show bar.

Retail & Bookstores
BOOKS & CO., 350 E Stroop Rd at Farhills, (513) 298-6540. General bookstore with gay, lesbian and women's sections.

Q GIFT SHOP, 850 N Main, inside Jessie's Celebrity. 2nd location: 1966 N Main St, (937) 274-4400. Rainbow & pride items, cards, jewelry, etc.

Erotica
CINEMA X, 2000 block of E 3rd St.

DISCOUNT BOOKSTORE, 429 E 5th St, (513) 226-1775.

EXOTIC BOOKS, 444 E 5th St, (513) 228-3584.

STATE BOOKS, 3rd at St Clair.

GLENFORD

Women's Accommodations
SPRINGHILL FARM, 5704 Highpoint Rd, (614) 659-2364. Small resort with fishing pond & trails. Variety of guest quarters with various conveniences, private baths, Jacuzzi, nearby lake. Women only.

LIMA

Dance Bar/Disco
SOMEWHERE IN TIME, 804 W North St, (419) 227-7288. Hi-energy dance bar, DJ Fri & Sat, male strippers, 50% men, 50% women.

LORAIN

Bars
SERPENT, THE, 2223 Broadway, (216) 245-6319. DJ Fri & Sat. Patio bar & dancing, 60% men, 40% women.

Erotica
CITY NEWS, 738 Broadway, (216) 246-9097. Closed Sun, Wed.

MANSFIELD

Information
LAMBDA LESBIAN & GAY HOTLINE, (419) 522-0729.

Dance Bar/Disco
ALTERNATIVES, 138 W 3rd St, (419) 522-0044. Open Tues-Sun from 7pm, Sun from 8pm. Occasional drag shows, male & female strippers monthly.

Erotica
VIDEO VISIONS, 1425 Park Ave West, (419) 529-2566, 7 days.

NILES

Erotica
NILES BOOK & NEWS, 5970 Youngstown-Warren Rd, (216) 544-3755.

SANDUSKY

Bars
X-CENTRICITIES, 306 W Water St, (419) 624-8118. Unverifiable spring '97.

SPRINGFIELD

Bars
WHY NOT III, 5 N Murray, (513) 324-9758. Women welcome.

Dance Bar/Disco
CHANCES, 1912-1914 Edwards Ave, (513) 324-0383. Dance/disco patio, male or female strippers or drag shows weekends, Wed-Mon 8:30pm-2:30am.

STEUBENVILLE

Erotica
PASSTIME ARCADE, 118 N 6th St, (614) 282-1907, 7 days.

STEUBENVILLE NEWS, 426 Market St, (614) 282-5842, 7 days.

TOLEDO

Information
TALLULAH'S, 6725 W Central, (419) 843-7707. Women's community center, Mon, Fri, Sat 11am-6pm, Tues, Wed, Thurs 11am-8pm.

Bars
BLU JEANS, 3606 W Sylvania Ave (in the shopping center), (419) 474-0690. Game room & restaurant with fine dining & extensive menu. Karaoke Tues & Thurs, usually 4pm-2:30am.

HOOTERVILLE STATION, 119 N Erie St near Monroe, (419) 241-9050.

R HOUSE, 5534 Secor Rd, (419) 474-2929, 2 floors.

RUSTLER SALOON, 4023 Monroe St at Central (rear), (419) 472-8278. We're good where it really counts!

Dance Bar/Disco
BRETZ,★ 2012 Adams Street, (419) 243-1900. Video dance bar, younger crowd, 70% men. Fri & Sat after hours 4:30am, closed Mon & Tues.

CAESAR'S, 725 Jefferson, (419) 241-5140. Dance & show bars Wed-Sun, drag shows Thurs-Sun.

Saunas/Health Clubs
DIPLOMAT HEALTH CLUB, 1313 N Summit St, (419) 255-3700. Full gym, steam, sauna, membership required.

Restaurants
ALFIE'S, 4215 Monroe.

Retail & Bookstores
THACKERAY'S BOOKS, 3301 W Central in Westgate Shopping Center. (419) 537-9259, Fax: 537-9342. General bookstore with gay & lesbian section.

Erotica
ADULT PLEASURES, 4404 N Detroit, (419) 476-4587. Movies.

G & L BOOKSTORE, THE, 1124 N Reynolds Rd, videos.

WARREN

Bars
CRAZY DUCK, THE, 121 Pine St, (330) 394-3825. DJ Fri & Sat, patio.

PURPLE ONION, 136 Pine St near Market St, (330) 399-2097. Jukebox, 80% men, 20% women. Summer patio.

Dance Bar/Disco
ALLEY, THE, 441 East Market St (enter in rear), (330) 394-9483. DJ Fri, Sat, 25% men, 75% women.

YELLOW SPRINGS

Restaurants
WINDS CAFE, 215 Xenia Ave, (513) 767-1144. Restaurant & bar, patio, bakery. Lunch, dinner Mon-Sat, Sun brunch.

Retail & Bookstores
EPIC BOOKSTORE, Dayton St near Corry, (513) 767-7997. Gay & lesbian sections.

YOUNGSTOWN

Information
AIDS HOTLINE, (330) 742-8811. Manned 8am-4pm or leave message for return call.

Bars
PHIL'S, 10 E La Clede, (330) 782-6991.

Dance Bar/Disco
SOPHIE'S II, 2 E LaClede St, (330) 782-8080. Shows Sun, 50% men, 50% women.

TROUBADOUR, 2618-24 Market St near Indianola (rear), (330) 788-4379. Shows Thurs, 60% men, 40% women.

Erotica
ADULT TOY & GIFT, 1410 Market St, (330) 752-9964.

UPTOWN BOOKS, 2597 Market, (330) 783-2533,

OKLAHOMA

OKLAHOMA
LAWTON

■ *Erotica*
INGRID'S, 1104 NW Cache Rd, (405) 353-1488.

OKLAHOMA CITY

■ *Information*
GAY, LESBIAN & AIDS REFERRAL, (405) 525-2437.
HERLAND SISTER RESOURCES, INC. 2312 NW 39th St. (405) 521-9696. Feminist bookstore, open Sat 10am-6pm & Sun 1pm-6pm. Scheduled coffee house, workshops & resources, 2 retreats per year.

■ *Accommodations*
AMERICA'S CROSSROADS, PO Box 270642, (405) 495-1111. Three private homestays close to interstates. Jacuzzi/hot tub available, full breakfast upon request. ♂
HABANA INN, 2200 NW 39th Expy, (405) 528-2221. Hotel, bar, & restaurant, women welcome, some straight clientele. Private baths.

■ *Bars*
HI LO CLUB, 1221 NW 50th St, (405) 843-1722. Quiet piano bar, shows weekends.
KA'S, 2024 NW 11. Beer bar.
KOKO LOCO, 919 N Virginia, (405) 239-2080. Unverifiable spring '97.
LEVI'S, ★ 2807 NW 36, (405) 947-LEVI.
LIDO, 2200 NW 39th Expy, inside Habana Inn complex. Quiet piano bar. ♀♂
PARK, THE, 2125 NW 39th St near Pennsylvania, (405) 528-4690. Video bar, live DJ, atrium dance floor, 70% men, 30% women.
PARTNERS 4, 2805 NW 36th, (405) 942-2199.

■ *Dance Bar/Disco*
ANGLES, ★ 2117 NW 39th St, (405) 524-3431, 528-0050. Large dance, video bar, Sun T-dance, 60% men. 40% women. Closed Mon & Tues.
COPA, ★ 2200 NW 39th Expy at Habana Inn Complex, (405) 525-0730. Hi energy dance & show bar, 60% men, 40% women. Open Wed-Sun 9pm-2am.
COYOTE CLUB, 2120 NW 39th, (405) 521-9533. Womens dance club, Thurs-Sun. ♀
FINISH LINE, ★ 2200 NW 39th Expy at Habana Inn Complex, (405) 525-0730. DJ, pool table, darts, C&W dance lessons certain nites.
TRAMPS, 2201 NW 39th St at Barnes, (405) 528-9080. Open Mon-Fri noon-2am, Sat & Sun 10am-2am.
WRECK ROOM, 2127 NW 39th, (405) 525-7610. Weekends only, after-hours juice bar,

very young crowd, large straight following.

■ *Cafe*
DIVERSITY CAFE, 2300 NW 17th.

■ *Restaurants*
GUSHER'S RESTAURANT, 2200 NW 39th Expy at the Copa bar in Habana Inn, (405) 525-0730. Dinner. ♀♂
PATIO CAFE, 5100 N Classen, (405) 842-7273. Breakfast & lunch all day.
PIZZA HAVEN, 2124 NW 39th St, (405) 557-1200.

■ *Retail & Bookstores*
JUNGLE RED, 2200 NW 39th St inside the Habana Inn, (405) 524-5733. Cards, T-shirts, leather, rainbow items, magazines, etc.
ZIGGYZ SMOKE & NOVELTY SHOPPE, 4005 N Penn, (405) 521-9999. Also S. MacArthur location. Gay magazines, cards, books & videos.

■ *Erotica*
EASTERN AVENUE, 1105 S Eastern Ave (405) 672-6459.
NAUGHTY 'N NICE, 3121 SW 29th at I 44, (405) 686-1110. Large gay selection.
RANDY'S PLAYTHINGS, 4711 S Pennsylvania.

TULSA

■ *Information*
GAY INFO LINE & PRIDE CENTER, 1307 E 38th St, (918) 743-GAYS (4297), Gay info, AIDS info, etc, 6-10pm.

■ *Bars*
BAMBOO LOUNGE, 7204 E Pine, near airport, (918) 832-1269.
NEW AGE RENEGADE, ★ 1649 S Main near 17th St, (918) 585-3405. Yuppie types, stand & model.

■ *Dance Bar/Disco*
CONCESSIONS, ★ 3340 S Peoria, (918) 744-0896. 9pm-2am Wed-Sun, male strippers Thurs, drag shows Sun, 60% men, 40% women.
LOLA'S, 2630 E 15th, (918) 749-1563. Drag bar, open 4pm-2am, drag shows Thurs-Sat.
SILVER STAR SALOON, THE, ★ 1565 S Sheridan, (918) 834-4234. C&W dance bar, dance lessons.
TNT, 2114 S Memorial near 21st, (918) 660-0856.
TOOL BOX II, 1338 E 3rd St, (918) 584-1308. Patio.

■ *Restaurants*
GRAPEVINE, S Peoria near 34th St. Fine dining in a casual atmosphere.

■ *Retail & Bookstores*
PRIDE STORE, 1307 E 38th St, (918) 743-4297. Rainbow store inside the Pride Center.

■ *Erotica*
ADULT NEWS, 21st & Memorial.
DREAMLAND, 8807 E Admiral Place, (918) 834-1051, videos.
ELITE NEWSDEN, 814 S Sheridan Rd near 11th, (918) 838-8503. Videos, 24hrs.
MIDTOWN, 319 E 3rd, (918) 584-3112.
WHITTIER NEWSTAND, 1 N Lewis, (918) 592-0767, leather goods.

OREGON

WHO TO CALL
For Tour Companies Serving This Destination
See Oregon on page 22

ASHLAND

■ *Information*
WOMANSOURCE, (541) 482-2026. Women's activities, including coffeehouse the 1st Fri of the month.

■ *Accommodations*
WILL'S RESTE, 298 Hargadine St, (541) 482-4394. B&B guesthouse, some straight clientele. Cozy, comfortable rooms with antique furniture. Self-contained cottage. Hot tub, continental breakfast & nearby pool & lake. ♀♂

■ *Women's Accommodations*
SISTERFIELDS B&B COUNTRY RETREAT, Box 1101, Ashland, OR 97520, (541) 512-0357. B&B with private bath, continental breakfast, men welcome. ♀

■ *Restaurants*
WHISTLE STOP CAFE, 258 A St #3-B, (541) 488-3354.

BROOKINGS

■ *Accommodations*
OCEANCREST HOUSE, 15510 Pedrioli Dr, Harbor, (800) 769-9200, (541) 469-9200, Fax: (541) 469-8864 (shared). Gay-friendly B&B, large detached room, private bath, color cable TV, expanded continental breakfast.
SOUTH COAST INN B&B, 516 Redwood St, (800) 525-9273, (541) 469-5557, Fax: 469-6615, E-mail:scoastin@wave.net. Surrender yourself to turn-of-the-century hospitality in a charming & spacious craftsman-style home. Centrally located in Brookings, on the rugged Oregon coast, this B&B offers gourmet breakfasts, beautiful ocean views, indoor Jacuzzi & sauna, and rooms with color TV, VCR, ceiling fans, queen beds & private baths. 50% gay & lesbian clientele.

OREGON

BURNS

Accommodations
BONTEMPS MOTEL, 74 West Monroe, Burns, OR 97720, (541) 573-2037, (800) 229-1394, Fax: (541) 573-2577. Friendly atmosphere, vintage charm and style. Suites, kitchennettes and studios have cable TV & HBO, in-room phones and double or queen beds. Continental breakfast is served, and nearby there is a restaurant & lounge. Located about 130 miles southeast of Bend, OR, our natural paradise is perfect for hunters, fishermen & rock hounds. We're south of Malheur Nat'l Forest and just north of Malheur Lake. 50% gay & lesbian clientele.

CORVALLIS

Cafe
OFF THE BEATEN PATH, 916 NW Beca Ave, (541) 753-8537. Coffees, teas, dinner Thur-Sat, breakfast Sat & Sun, lunch weekdays. Many women.

Restaurants
NEARLY NORMALS, 109 NW 15th St, (541) 753-0791. Gonzo cuisine, vegetarian.

Retail & Bookstores
BOOK BIN, 228 SW 3rd St, (541) 752-0040. Resale bookstore with gay & lesbian sections.
GRASS ROOTS, 227 SW 2nd St, (541) 754-7668. Alternative lifestyle bookstore with women's & gay men's books, women's music.

EUGENE

Information
AIDS & HIV SERVICES, (541) 342-5088. Mon-Fri 9am-5pm.

Dance Bar/Disco
CLUB ARENA, 959 Pearl, downstairs from Pass the Pepper Restaurant, (541) 683-2360. Dance & show bar from 7pm daily, 60% men, 40% women.

Restaurants
EMERALD CITY BISTRO, 525 Willamette, (541) 485-2363. Women's events some evenings.
KEYSTONE CAFE, 395 W 5th Ave at Lawrence, (541) 342-2075. Non-smoking restaurant, breakfast & lunch.
PASS THE PEPPER, 959 Pearl, (541) 683-2360. Breakfast-dinner, closed Sun.
POPPI'S ANATOLIA, 992 Willamette, (541) 343-9661. Greek & Indian.

Retail & Bookstores
MOTHER KALI'S BOOKS, 720 E 13 Ave, (541) 343-4864. Women's bookstore. Our lesbian section is the largest in the northwest. Mon-Fri 9am-6pm, Sat 10am-6pm. Free parking in basement via the alley.
PERALANDRA, 5th St by Pearl, (541) 485-4848. Metaphysical bookstore, books & music. Mon-Sat 10am-6pm.

Erotica
EXCLUSIVELY ADULT, 1166 S A St, Springfield, (541) 726-6969. Magazines, toys, gifts, lingerie, videos, 24hrs. Also: 1124-A Main St, 726-7104.
FOR YOUR EYES ONLY, 2711 Willamette, (541) 345-5065. Arcade, videos, cards & novelties.

JACKSONVILLE

Accommodations
TOUVELLE HOUSE, 455 N Oregon, (541) 899-8938, (800) 846-8422, fax: (541) 899-3992. Gay-friendly inn.

KLAMATH FALLS

Information
HIV RESOURCE CENTER, (541) 883-2437. Tape.

LINCOLN CITY

Accommodations
OCEAN GARDENS INN, 2735 NW Inlet, (541) 994-5007, (800) 866-9925. Oceanfront lodge. Rooms & suites with kitchenettes, all private baths. 50% gay & lesbian clientele.

MEDFORD

Restaurants
CADILLAC CLUB, 207 W 8th St, (541) 857-9411.

NEWPORT

Women's Accommodations
GREEN GABLES BED & BREAKFAST, 156 SW Coast St, (541) 265-9141. B&B, shared bath, men welcome.

Cafe
COASTAL COFFEE HOUSE, 433 SW Coast Hwy, (541) 265-8334.

Restaurants
COSMOS CAFE & GALLERY, 740 W Olive St, (541) 265-7511. Continental breakfast thru dinner. Specialty, vegetarian cuisine. Gay friendly.

Retail & Bookstores
GREEN GABLES BOOKSTORE, 156 SW Coast St, (541) 265-9141. Women's books & music and children's books.

O'BRIEN

Women's Accommodations
MOUNTAIN RIVER INN, PO Box 34, O'Brien, 97534, (503) 596-2392. Women's B&B and campground on 27 forested acres.

PACIFIC CITY

Cafe
WHITE MOON COW, 35490 Brooten Rd, (503) 965-5101. Cafe with all vegetarian, soups & natural food groceries. Books, jewelry. 9am-5pm daily (extended summer hours).

PORTLAND

Information
AIDS HOTLINE, (503) 223-AIDS or (800) 777-AIDS. Mon-Fri 10am-9pm. Sat & Sun noon-6pm.

Accommodations
HOLLADAY HOUSE, 1735 NE Wasco, (503) 282-3172. Gay-friendly B&B, gay female following. Shared bath, guests' choice breakfast.
MACMASTER HOUSE, 1041 SW Vista Ave, (503) 223-7362, (800) 774-9523, fax: (503) 224-8808. Gay-friendly B&B with antique shop. Color TV, AC, private & shared baths, full breakfast, pool nearby.
SULLIVAN'S GULCH BED & BREAKFAST, 1744 NE Clackamas St, (503) 331-1104, Fax: (503) 331-1575, E-mail: bbskip@teleport.com. B&B in quiet area close to everything. Private baths, ceiling fans, expanded continental breakfast. No smoking inside.
WASHINGTONIA INN, THE, 602 NW 18th Loop, Camas, WA (360) 834-7629. B&B, some straight clientele. Color TV, shared baths, TV lounge, massage & full breakfast. River nearby.

Beaches
ROOSTER ROCK STATE PARK, 22 miles E of Portland on Rt 84. Legal nude beach on Columbia River. Gay section 1/2 mile to right of parking area.

Bars
BOXXES & BRIG, 1035 SW Stark adjacent to the Fish Grotto restaurant, (503) 226-4171. Boxex Lounge: video bar with varying themes. Brig: dance bar with changing music & many straights.
BREW SISTER'S PUB, 53 NW First & Couch, (503) 274-9901. Lipstick Lesbos live music weekends, DJ on off nights, game room, pool, pinball, darts. Full lunch, dinner & hors d'oeuvres.
CC SLAUGHTER'S, ★ 1014 SW Stark St near 10th, (503) 726-0565. C&W dancing Wed & Sun, women welcome.
DARCELLE XV, 208 NW 3rd Ave near Davis, (503) 222-5338. Restaurant & cabaret features female impersonation shows for mixed audience. Shows: Wed-Thurs 8:30pm, Fri-Sat 8:30pm & 10:30pm. Dinner served only 5pm-7pm.
DIRTY DUCK TAVERN, 439 NW 3rd Ave at Glisan, (503) 224-8446.
EAGLE PDX, ★ 1300 W Burnside, (503) 241-0105. Video cruise bar.
HOBO'S, 120 NW 3rd, (503) 224-3285. Piano bar, yuppie crowd, Fri & Sat jazz, pool room in rear, lounge food, full dinners.
JOQ'S, 2512 NE Broadway near 14th, (503) 287-4210. Tavern with lite menu.
SCANDALS, 1038 SW Stark near 11th, (503) 227-5887. Darts, pool & video games.

FERRARI GUIDES' GAY TRAVEL A to Z - 18th EDITION

OREGON

SHANGHAI, Burnside & Broadway.
STARKY'S, 2913 SE Stark. Bar & restaurant, 65% men. ♀♂

Dance Bar/Disco

BRIG,★ 1035 SW Stark, adjacent to Boxx's. (503) 226-4171. Dance bar with changing music.
CHOICE'S, 2845 SE Stark St, (503) 236-4321. Downstairs top 40 disco is mainly women. Upstairs C&W dance bar is men & women. DJ Fri & Sat.
CODE BLUE, (503) 282-6979. Moveable dance parties. Location varies, call for updates. ♀
EGYPTIAN CLUB, THE, 3701 SE Division, (503) 236-8689. 7pm-2am, younger crowd.
EVOLUTION, 333 SW Park near Stark, (503) 286-1764. Mainly under 21yrs, mixed crowd, Thurs 10pm-2am, Fri & Sat 10pm-4am (after-hours till 4am Fri-Sat), alternative music disco upstairs.
SILVERADO, 1217 SW Stark, (503) 224-4493. Bar & restaurant, 9am daily. Male dancers.

Cafe

ESPRESS IT, 1026 SW Stark next door to Scandals, (503) 227-2551. Espresso bar, light meals, conversation, art.

Saunas/Health Clubs

CLUB PORTLAND, 303 SW 12th Ave at Burnside, (503) 227-9992. Private club, 24hrs.

Restaurants

BIJOU CAFÉ, 132 SW 3rd, (503) 222-3187. Breakfast & lunch, gay-friendly.
CADILLAC CAFE, 914 NE Broadway near Ninth, (503) 287-4750. Breakfast, lunch, 7 days.
CUP AND SAUCER, 3566 SE Hawthorne Blvd, (503) 236-6001. Gay-friendly restaurant.
FISH GROTTO, 1035 SW Stark, (503) 226-4171. Seafood, lunch, dinner. ♀♂
HAMBURGER MARY'S, 239 SW Broadway, (503) 223-0900.
HOBO'S, 120 NW 3rd at Hobo's bar, (503) 224-3285. From 4pm.
LAURELTHIRST PUBLIC HOUSE, 2958 NE Glisan, (503) 232-1504. Pub & restaurant.
OLD WIVES' TALES, 1300 E Burnside St at 13th Ave, (503) 238-0470. Vegetarian & special diet menu, breakfast thru dinner. Sat & Sun brunch, children's play area.
STARKY'S, 2913 SE Stark at 29th, (503) 230-7980. Lounge & restaurant, 65% men, 35% women. Fine dining, lunch & dinner.
TIGER BAR, 317 NW Broadway near Everett, (503) 222-7297. Pan-American & Asian food, dinner till midnite.
WILD ABANDON, 2411 SE Belmont, (503) 232-4458. Nouvelle American cuisine. ♀♂

Retail & Bookstores

CRIMSON PHOENIX, THE, 1876 SW 5th Ave, (503) 228-0129. Gifts, cards, incense. We honor sexual diversity.
GAI PIED, 2544 NE Broadway, (503) 331-1125. Gay bookstore.
IN OTHER WORDS — WOMEN'S BOOKS & RESOURCES, 3734 SE Hawthorne Blvd, (503) 232-6003. Women's books, videos, gifts.
IT'S MY PLEASURE, 4258 SE Hawthorne, (503) 236-0505. Women's cards, music, crafts, safe sex items, videos, feminist novelties & erotic toys.
POWELL'S BOOKS, 1005 W Burnside, (503) 228-4651. General bookstore with an extensive gay & lesbian section.
POWELL'S TRAVEL STORE, 701 SW 6th Ave, (503) 228-1108.
TWENTY-THIRD AVE BOOKS, 1015 NW 23rd Ave near Lovejoy, (503) 224-5097. General bookstore with gay & lesbian sections.

Leathers/Piercing

INFINITY TATTOO, 2138 E Burnside, (503) 231-4777. Body piercing, Tues-Sat 12-10pm, Sun-Mon 2-8pm.
LEATHERWORKS, THE, 2908 SE Belmont St near 29th St, (503) 234-COWS(2697). Tues-Sat noon-6.
SPARTACUS LEATHERS, 300 SW 12th Ave, (503) 224-2604. 10am-11pm Mon-Sat, 12-6 Sun.

Erotica

CINDY'S DIRTY BOOKS, 8 NW 4th Ave near Burnside, (503) 222-1554. Videos, 24hrs.
FANTASY FOR ADULTS ONLY, 3137 NE Sandy Blvd, (503) 239-6969. 24hrs, 7 days.
FANTASY FOR ADULTS ONLY, 6440 SW Coronado Dr, (I-5 south at Hwy 99), (503) 244-6969. 24hrs, 7 days.
FANTASY FOR ADULTS ONLY, 8445 SE McLoughlin Blvd, (503) 238-6969. 24hrs, 7 days.
FANTASY FOR ADULTS ONLY, 1512 W Burnside, (503) 295-6969. 24hrs, 7 days.
HARD TIMES WEST, 311 NW Broadway, (503) 223-2398. Gay erotica. Movies, magazines, gifts, cards, 24hrs.
HART'S VIDEO ARCADE, 330 SW 3rd Ave between Stark & Oak, (503) 224-2338, 24 hrs.
PEEP HOLE ADULT SUPERSTORE, 709 SE 122nd Ave, (503) 257-8617.
SIN CITY BOOKS, 838 SW 3rd Ave at Taylor, (503) 223-6514, 24hrs.
TIM'S HIDEAWAY, 4229 SE 82nd Ave, (503) 771-9774. Arcade.

ROGUE RIVER

Accommodations

WHISPERING PINES, 9188 W Evans Creek Rd, (541) 582-1757, (800) 788-1757. B&B retreat, some straight clientele. Variety of guest quarters with shared bath, TV lounge, Jacuzzi. Expanded continental breakfast & nearby river.

ROSEBURG

Information

GAY & LESBIAN SWITCHBOARD, (541) 672-4126, 24hrs. Answering service will patch call.
OWL, (OREGON WOMEN'S LAND TRUST), (541) 679-4655. A working women's farm. Work trade or camping & visitor fees. Write first to PO Box 1692, Roseburg, OR 97470.

SALEM

Dance Bar/Disco

SNEAKERS, 300 Liberty St SE in Pringle Park Plaza, (503) 363-0549. Dance bar with restaurant, 50% gay/lesbian, 50% straight.

Restaurants

OFF CENTER CAFE, 1741 Center St, NE, (503) 363-9245. A congenial gathering place for people of all persuasions, serving breakfast through dinner. Schedule varies.

Retail & Bookstores

ROSEBUD & FISH, 524 State St, (503) 399-9960. Alternative bookstore with gay & lesbian section, 7 days.

Erotica

BOB'S ADULT, 3815 State St SE, (503) 363-3846, 9am-4am.
HIDEAWAY, THE, 200 Lancaster Dr SE, (503) 581-6270, 24hrs.
MR PEEPER'S, 3035 Portland Rd NE, (503) 362-7953, 24hrs.

YACHATS

Accommodations

MORNING STAR B&B, 95668 Hwy 101, Yachats, OR 97494, (541) 547-4412. Gay-friendly B&B, lesbian-owned & -run, ocean views, private baths, hot tub.
OCEAN ODYSSEY VACATION RENTALS, PO Box 491, Yachats, OR 97498, (541) 547-3637, reservations: (800) 800-1915. Gay-friendly, women-owned vacation rentals in Yachats & Waldport, OR. From tri-levels to family beach cottages, some with awesome views, some on the beach.
OREGON HOUSE, THE 94288 Hwy 101, (541) 547-3329. Gay-friendly oceanfront inn with small gift shop. Accommodations vary in size (rooms thru cottages), furnishings & amenities. Some with kitchens, fireplaces, Jacuzzi, most have ocean views.
SEE VUE, 95590 Hwy 101, (541) 547-3227, Fax: (541) 547-4726. Gay-friendly motel. Variety of rooms with various motifs, modern conveniences, private baths & nearby ocean beach.
YACHATS INN, PO Box 307, Yachats, 97498, 94798, (541) 547-3456. Gay-friendly ocean-view motel units with private baths, some with fireplaces, kitchens, indoor pool.

PENNSYLVANIA

WHO TO CALL
For Tour Companies Serving This Destination
See Pennsylvania on page 23

ALLENTOWN

■ *Bars*
CANDIDA, 247 N 12th St, (610) 434-3071. Lite menu.

■ *Dance Bar/Disco*
STONEWALL, 28-30 N 10th St, (610) 432-0706 or 432-0215. Video dance bar, DJ Wed-Sun, drag shows Wed, 90% men. Second floor Moose Lounge & restaurant, lite menu.

■ *Erotica*
HAMILTON BOOKS & VIDEO, Hamilton & 11th, videos.

ALTOONA

■ *Dance Bar/Disco*
LA PIERRE HOTEL BAR, 2523 Union Ave, (814) 946-8195. 60% men, 40% women. DJ Wed, Fri & Sat. Open Mon-Sat.

BETHLEHEM

■ *Dance Bar/Disco*
DIAMONZ,★ 1913 W Broad St, (610) 865-1028. Dance club with completely separate, sound-proofed piano lounge & fine restaurant. Also separate game room, name entertainment. Fri C&W dancing. 60% women, 40% men.

BOYERS

■ *Accommodations*
CAMP DAVIS, 311 Redbrush Rd, (412) 637-2402. Gay & lesbian campground with cabins, tent sites, RV parking sites, creek & swimming hole.

BRIDGEPORT

■ *Dance Bar/Disco*
LARK, THE, 302 DeKalb St, (610) 275-8136. DJ Fri & Sat, 75% men, 25% women. Sun dinner.

DUNCANSVILLE

■ *Erotica*
ADULTS WORLD, Old 22 & Why Switches, (814) 696-4485. Call for directions. Closed Sun.

ERIE

■ *Information*
AIDS RESOURCES, (814) 456-8849, (800) 400-2437.
ERIE GAY & LESBIAN INFO, (814) 456-9833 or (814) 453-2785. Leave message. Aids info call (800) 400-AIDS.

■ *Bars*
EMBERS, 1711 State St, (814) 454-9171. DJ Wed-Sat.

■ *Dance Bar/Disco*
LIZZIE BORDEN'S PART II, 3412 W 12th St at Marshall, (814) 833-4059. 70% men, 30% women, Sat 50% men, 50% women. Closed Sun.

■ *Cafe*
AROMA'S COFFEE HOUSE, 2164 W 8th St, (814) 456-5282. Smoke-free coffees, lite menu, desserts.
COFFEERIGHT, 17 E Front St, in main concourse of library.
CUP-A-CINO, 18 North Park Row, (814) 456-1151. Live music Sat. Poetry readings & storey nights scheduled Thur.

■ *Restaurants*
LA BELLA BISTRO, 556 W 4th St, (814) 454-3616. Eclectic American cuisine, fine dining.

■ *Erotica*
EASTERN BOOKS, 1313 State St, (814) 459-7014.
FILLMORE NEWS, 2757 W 12th St, (814) 833-2667. Bookstore & theater.
MODERN NEWS, 1115 State St, (814) 453-6932.

GREENSBURG

■ *Bars*
SAFARI, 108 W Pittsburgh St, (412) 837-6614. Unverifiable spring '97.

HARFORD

■ *Accommodations*
NINE PARTNERS INN B&B, 1 N Harmony Rd, PO Box 300, Harford, PA 18823, (717) 434-2233.

HARRISBURG

■ *Information*
GAY & LESBIAN SWITCHBOARD (717) 234-0328. Mon-Fri 6pm-10pm.

■ *Bars*
NEPTUNE LOUNGE, 268 North St near 3rd, (717) 233-0581. Bar & restaurant, DJ Fri-Sun, 75% men, 25% women.
STRAWBERRY CAFE, 704 N 3rd St near Briggs, (717) 234-4228. Video bar, 80% men, 20% women (more on wknds). Closed Sun.

■ *Dance Bar/Disco*
B-TELS, 891 Eisenhower Blvd, (717) 939-1123. DJ Fri & Sat, pool tables, games, 7:30pm-1am Thurs, 7pm-2am Fri & Sat.
STALLION, 706 N 3rd St (rear), (717) 232-3060. Complex with multiple bars & Heaven restaurant.

■ *Restaurants*
HEAVEN, 706 N 3rd St, at Stallion complex. Fine dining Thurs-Sun, piano music.
PAPER MOON, 268 North St at Neptune Lounge men's bar, (717) 233-0581. Continental cuisine.

■ *Erotica*
RURAL BOOKS, Market St, downtown.

INDIANA

■ *Retail & Bookstores*
JOSEPHINE'S BOOKS, 1176 Grant St #2180, (412) 465-4469. Feminist bookstore specializing in books written by women. Large selection of lesbian titles. Also, women's crafts. Mon-Fri 11am-8pm, Sat 10am-4pm.

JOHNSTOWN

■ *Accommodations*
ROLLING STONE ACRES B&B, 1740 Frankstown Rd, (814) 539-0842. B&B with full or continental breakfast, shared bath, 50% gay/lesbian clientele.

■ *Dance Bar/Disco*
LUCILLE'S, 520 Washington St, (814) 539-4448. 70% men, 30% women, game room. From 8pm, closed Sun, Mon. Unverifiable spring '97.

KUTZTOWN

■ *Accommodations*
GRIM'S MANOR, 10 Kern Rd, (610) 683-7089. B&B, some straight clientele. Variety of rooms, private baths, TV lounge, kitchen, full homestyle breakfast.

LANCASTER

■ *Information*
GAY HELP LINE, (717) 397-0691. Wed, Thur, Sun 7pm-10pm.

■ *Bars*
SUNDOWN LOUNGE, 429 N Mulberry St near Lemon, (717) 392-2737. Quiet neighborhood bar from 8pm, Fri & Sat from 3pm, closed Sun.

■ *Dance Bar/Disco*
TALLY-HO, 201 W Orange St at Water, (717) 299-0661. 75% men, 25% women.

■ *Restaurants*
LOFT, THE, 201 W Orange St above Tally-Ho bar, (717) 299-0661. Closed Sun.

FERRARI GUIDES' GAY TRAVEL A to Z - 18th EDITION

PENNSYLVANIA

Visit Philadelphia
(800) CARITAS
Caritas B&B Network

Erotica
DEN, 53 N Prince St near Orange, (717) 299-1779.

MANHEIM
Bars
CELLAR BAR, 168 S Main St, (717) 665-1960. DJ Fri & Sat, ladies nite Wed.

MARSHALLS CREEK
Accommodations
CURT & WALLY'S, PO Box 219, Marshalls Creek, (717) 223-1395. Men-only guesthouse, private & shared baths.

MONTROSE
Accommodations
MEADOWVIEW CAMPGROUND, (717) 278-9999.

NEW HOPE
Accommodations
FOX & HOUND B & B OF NEW HOPE, 246 W Bridge St, (215) 862-5082, (800) 862-5082 (Outside of PA). B&B, 50% gay/lesbian clientele. Large rooms with antique furnishings, private baths. Near pool, river, walking distance to town center. Continental breakfast Mon-Fri, full breakfast Sun.

LEXINGTON HOUSE, THE, 6171 Upper York Rd, (215) 794-0811. B&B, private baths, some straight clientele.

RAVEN, THE, 385 W Bridge St, (215) 862-2081. Motel with restaurant & bar, private & shared baths.

Bars
RAVEN, THE, ★ 385 W Bridge St at The Raven Hotel, (215) 862-2081. Indoor & poolside bars, patio, & restaurant. Popular Sun afternoon.

Dance Bar/Disco
CARTWHEEL CLUB, ★ 437 York Rd at junction Hwy 202, (215) 862-0880. Large club with piano bar, video dance bar, restaurant, outdoor deck, drag shows Mon, male strippers Wed.

Restaurants
CARTWHEEL, 437 York Rd at Cartwheel bar. Dinner.

RAVEN, 385 W Bridge St at The Raven Hotel. (215) 862-2081. Lunch, dinner, popular Sun brunch, women welcome.

Retail & Bookstores
BOOK GALLERY, 19 W Mechanic St, (215) 862-5110. Alternative bookstore with emphasis on feminist, lesbian & gay books. Some Pride items.

EMBER GLOW, 27 W Mechanic St, (215) 862-2929. Gift shop with large selection of pride items.

Erotica
CHATEAU EXOTIQUE, 5 W Bridge St, (215) 862-3810. Wed-Mon.

GROWN UPS, 2 E Mechanic St, (215) 862-9304. Erotic store with pride items.

GROWNUPS, 93-A S Main St, (215) 862-9304.

JOY'S BOOKS, 103 Springbrook Arms, Rt 29, Lambertville, NJ, (609) 397-2907. Adult bookstore with gay & lesbian section, 10am-10pm. Across the bridge from New Hope.

NEW MILFORD
Camping & RV
ONEIDA CAMPGROUND AND LODGE, PO Box 537, (717) 465-7011 or (717) 853-3503. Guesthouse, campground & lodge with clubhouse & sauna, women welcome. Variety of guest quarters with modern conveniences, RV & tent sites, shared baths, TV lounge, library, fitness center.

PHILADELPHIA
Information
AIDS LINE, (215) 985-AIDS (2437).

GAY SWITCHBOARD, (215) 546-7100, 7-10pm, or tape.

WM. WAY LESBIAN & GAY COMMUNITY CENTER, 201 S Camac St, (215) 732-2220. 9:30am-9pm, most days. Address may change in '97.

Accommodations
ANTIQUE ROW BED & BREAKFAST, 341 South 12th St, (215) 592-7802, Fax: 592-9692. B&B & fully furnished flat, 50% gay & lesbian clientele. Private & shared baths, color cable TV, AC & full breakfast.

CARITAS BED & BREAKFAST NETWORK, (800) CARITAS, (312) 857-0801, Fax: (312) 857-0805. B&B, home-stay accommodations service. *Member: IGTA*

GASKILL HOUSE, 312 Gaskill St, (215) 413-2887. B&B guesthouse in the Society Hill District, full breakfast buffet, private baths, some straight clientele.

GLEN ISLE FARM COUNTRY INN, Downingtown, (610) 269-9100, Fax: 269-9191. Bed & breakfast inn opening spring 1994. Private & shared baths, full breakfast.

ROXBORO HOUSE, (215) 844-8122, fax: (215) 849-8197. Two well-appointed suites with private baths, claw-footed tubs, queen beds & color TV. Lovely gardens, patio, hammock. Vegetarian breakfast included. Near museums & shops. Gay friendly.

UNCLES UPSTAIRS INN, 1220 Locust St, (215) 546-6660, Fax: (215) 546-1653. B&B with gay/lesbian bar on premises, private baths, continental breakfast, color TV, AC, phone, women welcome.

Women's Accommodations
BEST NEST, THE, PO Box 23236, Philadelphia, PA 19124, (215) 482-2677. Women-only town house in a quiet residential community 5 miles from city center, continental breakfast, shared baths, nearby parks, hiking & public transportation.

Bars
BACKSTAGE, 614 S 4th St near Kater, (215) 627-9887. Restaurant & bar, continental cuisine.

BIKE STOP, ★ 206 S Quince St near Locust, (215) 627-1662. Short Stop sports bar, Top of the Stop dance bar & Pit Stop leather bar. Cafe On Quince restaurant adjacent. Variety of entertainment.

JACK RABBIT SLIMS, 602 S 2nd St, (215) 625-9533. Gay Sun only.

PORT BLUE, 2552 E Allegheny Ave at Livingston St, (215) 425-4699.

POST, THE, 1705 Chancellor St near 17th, (215) 985-9720.

RAFFLES, 243 S Camac St near Locust, (215) 545-6969. Piano bar, restaurant downstairs.

RODZ, ★ 1418 Rodman St, (215) 546-1900. Cabaret bar & restaurant with deck bar. Cabaret & piano Tues-Sun.

TWO FORTY-SEVEN BAR, 247 S 17th St, (215) 545-9779. Main floor cruisy with male erotic dancers. Upstairs piano bar, downstairs dungeony basement.

UNCLE'S, 1220 Locust St, (215) 546-6660.

VENTURE INN, ★ 255 S Camac St near Spruce, (215) 545-8731. Bar and restaurant.

WESTBURY, THE, 261 S 13th, (215) 546-5170. Bar & restaurant.

Dance Bar/Disco
12TH AIR COMMAND, 254 S 12th St, (215) 545-8088. Dance bar, lounge bar & restaurant. Restaurant open Wed-Sat & Sun brunch.

BIKE STOP, ★ 206 S Quince St near Locust, (215) 627-1662. Top of the Stop dance bar, Short Stop sports bar & Pit Stop leather bar.

CLUB UNIQUE, at Skyline, 68 N 12th St. Gay Wed-Fri, house music.

CLUB UNIQUE, at Club 1415, 1415 Locust Ave, (215) 732-6047. Gay Sun only, house music, 10pm-2am.

KEY WEST, 207 S Juniper, (215) 545-1578.

PALMER SOCIAL CLUB, ★ 601 Spring Garden St, (215) 925-5000. Private club, after hours with liquor till 3am, 20% gay.

PENNSYLVANIA

SISTERS,★ 1320 Chancellor St at Juniper, (215) 735-0735.
TWENTY-FOUR CLUB, 240 S Camac St, (215) 732-4377. Hi-energy dance bar, private club. From 10:30pm nightly. Local sponsor needed to enter.
TYZ, 1418 Rodman St at Rodz bar, (215) 546-4195. Private after-hours club, 90% men, 10% women. Guests welcome.
WOODY'S,★ 202 S 13th St at Chancellor, (215) 545-1893. Pub and separate hi-energy dance bar. Pub has lunch, Sun brunch, late-nite food. Most popular bar in Philadelphia.

■ Cafe
FRANNY'S PLACE, 203 S 13th St, (215) 790-1091.
MILLENIUM, 212 S 12th St, (215) 731-9798. Popular with gays.
PHILADELPHIA TEA PARTY, 1334 Walnut St, (215) 732-TEAS.

■ Saunas/Health Clubs
CHANCELLOR ATHLETIC CLUB, 200 S Camac St (215) 545-4098, 24hrs.
CLUB BODY CENTER, 120 S 13th St near Sansom (upstairs), (215) 735-9568, 24hrs.

■ Restaurants
ASTRAL PLANE, 1708 Lombard St near 17th, (215) 546-6230. New American cuisine, Sun brunch.
CAFE AT RODS,★ 1418 Rodman St.
CAFE EINSTEIN, 208 Race St, (215) 625-0904. Varied menu, Sun brunch.
CAFE ON QUINCE, at Bike Stop bar. Theater crowd.
CHEAP ART CAFE, 260 S 12th St.
JUDY'S CAFE,★ 627 South 3rd St, (215) 928-1968. Ecclectic menu, vegetarian available.
RAFFLES, 243 S Camac St at Raffles bar, (215) 545-6969. Continental menu, moderate prices.
VENTURE INN,★ 255 S Camac St at Venture Inn men's bar.
WALDORF CAFE,★ 20th & Lombard, (215) 985-1836.

■ Retail & Bookstores
AFTERWORDS, 218 South 12th St, (215) 735-2393. General bookstore with gay titles.
GIOVANNI'S ROOM, 345 S 12th Street at Pine, (215) 923-2960. Gay, lesbian, feminist bookstore, 11:30am-9pm (Wed till 7pm, Fri till 10pm), Sat 10am-10pm. Sun, 1-7pm.
HOUSE OF OUR OWN, 3920 Spruce St, (215) 222-1576. Women's studies, new & used.

■ Leathers/Piercing
BOTH WAYS, 201 S 13th St between Walnut & Locust, (215) 985-2344. Leatherwear & toys for men & women. Piercing by appointment.
INFINITE BODY PIERCING, 626 S 4th, (215) 923-7335.

■ Erotica
ADAM & EVE, 133 S 13th St near Sansom, (215) 925-5041. 24hrs, 7 days.
ADONIS CINEMA, 2026 Sansom St near 20th, (215) 557-9319.
SANSOM CINEMA & TOMCAT BOOKS, 120 S 13th St, (215) 545-9254. Bookstore & cinema.
SCORPIO BOOKS, 200 block of S Juniper St.
TITAN ROOM, 2132 Market St, (215) 563-4838.

PITTSBURGH

■ Information
GAY CENTER, 5808 Forward Ave, Squirrel Hill, (412) 422-0114. Answers Mon-Fri 6:30pm-9:30pm, Sat 3pm-6pm.

■ Accommodations
BREWER'S HOTEL, 3315 Liberty Ave, (412) 681-7991. Residential hotel with restaurant & bar, shared baths.
INN ON THE MEXICAN WAR STREETS, 1606 Buena Vista St, Pittsburgh, PA 15212, (412) 231-6544. Inn in a Victorian-era row house, close to downtown, private & shared baths, expanded continental breakfast, women welcome.
VICTORIAN HOUSE, 939 Western Ave, (412) 231-4948. Five min from downtown, spacious rooms.

■ Bars
BREWERY TAVERN, 3315 Liberty Ave at Herron, (412) 681-7991. 60% men.
CJ DEIGHAN'S, 2506 W Liberty Ave, Dormont, (412) 561-4044.
HOLIDAY BAR, 4620 Forbes Ave near Craig, (412) 682-8598. Collegiate crowd, year-round patio.
JAZI'S, 1241 Western Ave at Fulton, (412) 323-2721. Cruise bar, patio bar, small dance floor.
NEW YORK, NEW YORK,★ 5801 Ellsworth at Maryland Shadyside, (412) 661-5600. Piano bar & restaurant, outdoor deck, Sun brunch, 70% men, 30% women.

■ Dance Bar/Disco
DONNIE'S PLACE, 1226 Herron Ave at Ruthven, (412) 682-9869. 3 floors with bar downstairs, upstairs dance bar, basement bar with older crowd, pool table.
HOUSE OF TILDEN, 941 Liberty Ave (2nd floor), (412) 391-0804. Private club, dance bar above a straight bar, after hours till 3am. 70% men, 30% women.
IMAGES,★ 965 Liberty Ave near 10th St, (412) 391-9990. Dance & video bar, 50% men, 50% women, karaoke.
PEGASUS LOUNGE,★ 818 Liberty Ave near 9th, (412) 281-2131. Hi-energy dance bar, popular cocktail hour, male dancers. Closed Sun.
PITTSBURGH EAGLE,★ 1740 Eckert St, (412) 766-7222. 3 floors, leather cruise bar downstairs, dance bar upstairs. Leather dress code on 3rd floor.
REAL LUCK CAFE, 1519 Penn Ave, (412) 566-8988. Bar, upstairs disco, 50% men, 50% women.
TWO THIRTY-NINE ATWOOD, 239 Atwood, Oakland, ', (412) 682-9226. Dance bar & restaurant, lunch & dinner.

■ Cafe
COMMON GROUND, 5888 Ellsworth Ave, Shadyside, (412) 362-1190. Coffeehouse popular with women.

■ Saunas/Health Clubs
ARENA HEALTH CLUB BATHS, 2025 Forbes Ave near Seneca, (412) 471-8548. Private club, 24hrs. Full gym, off-street parking.

■ Restaurants
FROG POND, 223 Atwood, (412) 682-7707.
LIBERTY AVE SALOON, 941 Liberty Ave, downstairs. Lunch & dinner.
NEW YORK, NEW YORK, 5801 Ellsworth Ave at NY NY bar. (412) 661-5600. Sun brunch 11am.

■ Retail & Bookstores
A PLEASANT PRESENT, 2218 Murray Ave, (412) 421-7104, Fax: (412) 421-7105. Large selection of gay & lesbian gift items.
BOOKSTALL, 3604 5th Ave near Meyran, (412) 683-2644. Gay & lesbian selection, closed Sun.
SAINT ELMO'S OUTWORDS, 2208 E Carson Street, (412) 431-9100. Gay & lesbian bookstore within general bookstore.

■ Leathers/Piercing
LEATHER CENTRAL, 1226 Herron Ave, basement of Donnie's Place, (412) 682-9869.

■ Erotica
BLVD VIDEOS & MAGAZINES, 346 Blvd of the Allies, (412) 261-9119. Leather items, 24 hrs.

ARENA HEALTH CLUB BATHS
Friendliest Place in Pittsburgh
2025 Forbes Ave.
(412) 471-8548
24 Hrs
OFF-STREET PARKING

PENNSYLVANIA

FAIRVIEW BOOKS, 943 Liberty Ave, (412) 765-2035.

GARDEN THEATRE, 12 W North Ave, (412) 321-4262.

GOLDEN TRIANGLE NEWS, 816 Liberty Ave, (412) 765-3790, 24hrs.

VISUAL ADVENTURES, 807 Liberty Ave.

POCONOS MTN AREA

■ *Accommodations*

RAINBOW MOUNTAIN RESORT, RD #8 Box 8174, (717) 223-8484. Resort with bar, disco, restaurant. Variety of guest quarters with private & shared baths, spectacular views, color TV, outdoor activities areas, full breakfast & dinner. Outdoor Olympic-sized pool.

■ *Women's Accommodations*

BLUEBERRY RIDGE, mail to: McCarrick/Moran, RR1 Box 67, Scotrun, PA 18355, (717) 629-5036 or (516) 473-6701. Women-only B&B near Camelback ski area & Delaware Water Gap. Modern rooms, outdoor hot tub & full country breakfast.

STONEY RIDGE, mail to: P. McCarrick, RR1 Box 67, Scotrun, PA 18355, (717) 629-5036 or (516) 473-6701. Two-bedroom cedar log home, stone fireplace, beautifully furnished with antiques. Women only, nearby river & lake.

READING

■ *Bars*

NOSTALGIA, 1101 N 9th St at Robeson, (610) 372-5557. Mostly women in evenings, especially Fri, Sat.

RAINBOW, S 10th St, (610) 373-1058. Small dance floor, DJ Fri & Sat.

RED STAR, 11 S 10th St (no sign outside), (610) 375-4116. DJ Fri, Sat. Restaurant Wed-Sat.

■ *Dance Bar/Disco*

SCARAB, THE, 724 Franklin St, (610) 375-7878. Nightly, 50% men, 50% women. Closed Sun.

■ *Retail & Bookstores*

LAVENDER HEARTS, 13 North 9th St (610) 372-1828. Alternative bookstore with crystals, new age items, gay & lesbian videos.

■ *Erotica*

OVER 21 OUTLET & PENN ST NEWS, both in the 300 block of Penn St.

SCRANTON

■ *Accommodations*

WINTER PINES, RD 2, Box 25, 18822, (717) 879-2130. B&B in a restored farmhouse with 17 acres, a pond, volleyball, horseshoes & farm animals.

■ *Camping & RV*

HILLSIDE CAMPGROUNDS, PO Box 726, Binghamton NY, (717) 756-2007. Men-only campground, tent sites, trailers, RV hookups.

■ *Bars*

SILHOUETTE LOUNGE, 500 block of Linden St on Courthouse Square. Unverifiable spring '97.

STATE COLLEGE

■ *Information*

GAY & LESBIAN SWITCHBOARD, (814) 237-1950. 6pm-9pm daily or tape.

■ *Bars*

CHUMLEY'S, 108 W College Ave, (814) 238-4446. 50% men, 50% women. Popular with women for Sun evening happy hour.

■ *Dance Bar/Disco*

PLAYERS, 112 W College Ave, inside the Hotel State College, (814) 237-4350. Gay night Sun, but never all gay.

WILKES-BARRE

■ *Dance Bar/Disco*

RUMORS, between Wilkes-Barre & Plains on Rte 315, (717) 825-7300. About 1/2 mile out of Wilkes-Barre & 3/4 miles past junction of Hwys 315 & 115. Dance bar & restaurant, dinner Wed-Sun, open 7 days, 4pm-2am. 50% men, 50% women.

SELECTIONS, 45 Public Square, (717) 829-4444. DJ Fri & Sat, C&W music Thurs.

VAUDEVILLA, 465 Main St, Kingston, (717) 287-9250. From 7pm, DJ Fri, closed Sun.

WILLIAMSPORT

■ *Bars*

PEACHIE'S COURT, 320 Court St, (717) 326-3611. 1pm-2am Mon-Sat.

■ *Dance Bar/Disco*

RAINBOW ROOM, 4th St near Camel St.

YORK

■ *Information*

HELP LINE, (717) 755-1000, ask for York Support. Gay and lesbian community group providing social activities, networking, monthly meetings, newsletter.

■ *Bars*

FOURTEEN KARAT, 659 W Market St. Juke box & CDs, 80% men, 20% women. Closed Sun.

■ *Dance Bar/Disco*

ALTLAND'S RANCH, RR 6, Box 6543, Spring Grove, about 15 miles west of York off Rte 30 W, (717) 225-4479. Large dance bar, Fri & Sat only. Fri C&W, 50/50 men & women Sat.

■ *Retail & Bookstores*

HER STORY BOOKSTORE, 2 W Market St, Hallam, (717) 757-4270. Women's books.

■ *Erotica*

CUPID'S, 244 N George St, (717) 846-5029. Sun-Thurs 9am-2am. Fri, Sat till 4m.

SWINGERS BOOKS, 226 W Market St, (717) 845-9803.

RHODE ISLAND

WHO TO CALL

For Tour Companies Serving This Destination
See Rhode Island on page 24

KINGSTOWN

■ *Erotica*

VIDEO EXPO, 6772 Post Rd, (401) 885-0209.

MIDDLETOWN

■ *Erotica*

VIDEO ETC, 823 W Main Rd, (401) 847-8100, videos.

NEWPORT

■ *Accommodations*

BRINLEY VICTORIAN INN, 23 Brinley St, (401) 849-7645, (800) 999-8523, fax: (401) 845-9634. Gay-friendly B&B inn.

CAPTAIN JAMES PRESTON HOUSE, 378 Spring St, Newport, RI 02840, (401) 847-4386, Fax: (401) 847-1093. E-mail: EEXK82A@prodigy.com. Gay-friendly Victorian B&B with private & shared baths, expanded continental breakfast. An easy walk to Newport attractions, beaches & shopping. Gay & lesbian following.

HYDRANGEA HOUSE INN, 16 Bellevue Ave, (401) 846-4435, (800) 945-4667, Fax: (401) 846-6602. Gay-friendly bed & breakfast in excellent location. Rooms elegantly decorated with antiques & plush carpeting. Full breakfast. Nearby ocean beach & gym. 50 % gay & lesbian clientele.

MELVILLE HOUSE INN, 39 Clarke St, (401) 847-0640, (800) 711-7184, Fax: 847-0956, E-mail: innkeepri@aol.com. Conveniently located B&B, mostly straight clientele. Colonial decor, private & shared baths & expanded continental breakfast. Ocean nearby.

PROSPECT HILL GUEST HOUSE, 32 Prospect Hill St, (401) 847-7405. Guesthouse with art gallery, private baths, continental breakfast, some straight clientele. David's bar & disco next door.

■ *Bars*

DAVID'S, 28 Prospect Hill near Spring, (401) 847-9698. DJ Fri & Sat, patio, 60% men, 40% women.

SOUTH CAROLINA

PROVIDENCE

Information
AIDS LINE, (800) 726-3010.
GAY & LESBIAN HELPLINE, (401) 751-3322, 7-11pm Mon-Fri or tape.
SARAH DOYLE WOMEN'S CENTER, 185 Meeting St near Brown at Brown University, (401) 863-2189. Women's resources, gallery, library, programs & info.

Bars
AMBASSADOR'S CLUB, 70 Washington St, (401) 751-4241. 60% men, 40% women.
CLUB INTOWN, 95 Eddy St, (401) 751-0020.
WHEELS, 125 Washington, (401) 272-6950. 70% men.

Dance Bar/Disco
DEVILLE'S CAFE, ★ 10 Davol Square, Historic Simmons Bldg, (401) 751-7166. Nightclub with cafe, 5pm-1am Tues-Thurs, 5pm-2am Fri, 6pm-2am Sat, 6pm-midnight Sun.
GALAXY, 123 Empire St at Washington, (401) 831-9206. DJ Fri, Sat.
LOFT, THE, 325 Farnham Pike, Smithfield, (401) 231-3320. Disco with huge swimming pool. Winter: 4pm-1 or 2am. Summer: Dance parties start by the pool & end by the disco, May-Oct noon-1am.
MIRROR BAR, 35 Richmond, (401) 331-6761. Large dance bar, 70% men, 30% women.
ONE SEVENTY-ONE EAST, 171 Chestnut St. To open April, 1997. Dance bar with upscale ambiance.
UNION STREET STATION, 69 Union St, (401) 331-2291. 60% men, 40% women.
YUKON TRADING CO, 124 Snow St near Weybossett, (401) 274-4620. Male strippers.

Saunas/Health Clubs
CLUB PROVIDENCE, 257 Weybosset St near Richmond, (401) 274-0298. Private club, 24hrs.

Retail & Bookstores
DORRWAR BOOKS, 312 Wickenden St, (401) 521-3230. General bookstore with a gay & lesbian selection, closed Sun.

Erotica
JOHNSTON VIDEO CINEMA, 1530 Hartford Ave, Johnston, (401) 272-0345.
UPSTAIRS BOOKSHOP, 206 Washington St (401) 272-3139.
VIDEO EXPO, 75 Empire St, (401) 274-4477.

WARWICK

Erotica
VIDEO EXPO, 2318 Post Rd, (401) 739-3080.

WESTERLY

Accommodations
VILLA, THE, 190 Shore Rd, (401) 596-1054, (800) 722-9240, Fax: (401) 596-6268. Gay-friendly B&B, rooms & suites with private baths. Color cable TV, AC, ceiling fans, phones & expanded continental breakfast. Pool on premises.

WOONSOCKET

Dance Bar/Disco
KINGS & QUEENS, 285 Front St, (401) 762-9538. Dance & show bar, 50% men, 50% women.

SOUTH CAROLINA
ANDERSON

Dance Bar/Disco
EUROPA, 116 E Benson St. Open 7 days.

CHARLESTON

Accommodations
CHARLESTON BEACH B&B, PO Box 41, Folly Beach, 29439, (803) 588-9443. A destination for all seasons! The only gay and lesbian accommodations at the ocean between Fort Lauderdale and North Carolina. Ten miles to historic district of Charleston, America's premier walking city! Fine restaurants, cultural events and plantations. Eight rooms, affordable prices, expanded continental breakfast, social hour, spa and pool and AC.
CHARLESTON COLUMNS GUESTHOUSE, 8 Vanderhorst St, (803) 722-7341. Guesthouse. Color cable TV, AC, ceiling fans, private & shared baths, TV lounge & continental breakfast.
CRABAPPLE COTTAGE, Pine Grove Plantation, 300 Medway Rd, Goose Creek, SC 29445, (803) 797-6855, Fax: (803) 824-0435, E-mail: sccottage@aol.com. A quaint cottage in a 7000-acre wildlife preserve, 30 minutes from Charleston & adjacent to a beautiful Southern plantation property. Its rustic flavor is enhanced by ceiling beams of rich cypress, pine floors & a floor-to-ceiling brick fireplace. The completely equipped kitchenette can be stocked, per your request, for an additional fee. A complimentary bottle of wine & breakfast consumables are provided. Heated pool on premises. Some straight clientele.
EIGHTEEN FIFTY-FOUR BED AND BREAKFAST, 34 Montagu St, (803) 723-4789. B&B, some straight clientele. Suites with private baths, kitchens, color TV, private garden area & continental breakfast.

Bars
DUDLEY'S, 346 King St near Burns Alley, (803) 723-2784. Private club, 70% men, 30% women. Cd jukebox, call ahead for guest membership.

Dance Bar/Disco
ARCADE, 5 Liberty St near King, (803) 722-5656. 2 bars: country bar & hi-energy disco.
DEJA VU 2, 445 Savannah Hwy, (803) 556-5588. Shows, gay comedians, bands, Wed-Sun from 7pm, in winter from 5pm.

Restaurants
CAFE SUZANNE'S, 4 Center St, Folly Beach, (803) 588-2101. Nouvelle cuisine, seafood.
RIVER CAFE, 88 Sandbar Lane, Folly Beach, (803) 588-2255. Fresh seafood, sandwiches, full liquor.

Retail & Bookstores
HEALING RAYS, 57 Broad St, (803) 853-4499. Feminist books & gifts, closed Mon.

COLUMBIA

Information
AIDS HOTLINE, (803) 779-7257, (800) 723-7257. 9am-5:30pm Mon-Fri.
GAY & LESBIAN PRIDE MOVEMENT INFO LINE, (803) 771-7713. Tues-Fri 6pm-10pm, Sat 2pm-10pm.

Bars
AFFAIRS, 712 Huger St, (803) 779-4321. Private club.
CAPITOL CLUB, 1002 Gervais, (803) 256-6464. Private club, conversation lounge, some straight clientele. Travelers call first.

Dance Bar/Disco
ICON, 1109 Assembly, (803) 771-0121. Male strippers, drag shows Wed.
METROPOLIS, 1800 Blanding, (803) 799-8727. Thurs-Sun 10pm-3 or 4am, male strippers Fri, drag shows Thurs-Sun, 50% men, 50% women.
TRAXX, 416 Lincoln St at the railroad tracks, (803) 256-1084.

Restaurants
ALLEY CAT, 911 Lady St, (803) 771-2778.

FOLLY BEACH
See Charleston.

GREENVILLE

Information
GAY & LESBIAN SWITCHBOARD, (864) 271-4207.

Charleston Beach B&B

(803) 588-9443

P.O. Box 41
Folly Beach
South Carolina 29439

FERRARI GUIDES' GAY TRAVEL A to Z - 18th EDITION

SOUTH CAROLINA

■ Bars

CLUB 621, 621 Airport Rd, (864) 234-6767. 7pm-4am (Sat till 2am, Sun 3pm-12am), male strippers Wed, late nite drag show Fri, 90% men, 10% women.

SOUTH RAMP, 404 Airport Rd, (864) 242-0102. C&W bar, W-Sun 8pm-2am.

SPANKY'S, 1607 Laurens Rd, (864) 233-0105.

■ Dance Bar/Disco

CASTLE, THE, 8 LeGrand Blvd at Greenacre, (864) 235-9949. Dance & show bar.

HILTON HEAD

■ Bars

MOONJAMMERS (MJ'S), 11 Heritage Plaza, (803) 842-9195. 8pm-2am 7 days, 60% men, 40% women, live entertainment twice a month.

MYRTLE BEACH

■ Bars

TIME OUT, 520 8th Ave N, (803) 448-1180. Private club, daily from 5pm, 75% men, 25% women.

■ Dance Bar/Disco

ILLUSIONS, 1017 S Kings Hwy (803) 448-0421. Alternative club.

■ Erotica

BIG SIX VIDEO & BOOKS, 1474 W Hwy 501, (803) 946-9411. SC's largest selection of gay titles, 24hrs.

MAXWELL'S NEWS & VIDEO, 2027 Hwy 501, (803) 626-3140.

ROCK HILL

■ Bars

HIDE-A-WAY, 405 Baskins Rd, (803) 328-6630. Private club, live bands, Thurs-Sat 8pm-close.

SPARTANBURG

■ Bars

CHEYENNE CATTLEMEN'S CLUB, 995 Asheville Hwy, (864) 573-7304. 8pm-2am Tues-Sat, Sun 3pm-2am, occasional male strippers & drag shows.

SOUTH DAKOTA
RAPID CITY - BLACK HILLS

■ Information

BLACK HILLS GAY & LESBIAN PHONE LINE, (605) 394-8080. Mon-Sat 6pm-10pm or tape.

FACES OF SOUTH DAKOTA, 625 1/2 Main St #3, (605) 343-5577, fax: (605) 394-8962. Gay organization, office & library, Mon-Fri usually 9am-5pm, Tues 7pm-10pm, Sat 1:30pm-5pm.

■ Accommodations

CAMP MICHAEL B&B, 13051 Bogus Jim Rd, Rapid City, SD 57702, (605) 342-5590. B&B on 3 acres, 12 mi. outside Rapid City, 15 min. from Mt. Rushmore & Deadwood gambling. Three rms share 2nd floor with living & dining rm & baths. Video & book libraries.

■ Erotica

HERITAGE BOOKSTORE, 912 Main St E, (605) 394-9877.

SIOUX FALLS

■ Information

GAY & LESBIAN COALITION, (605) 333-0603.

■ Dance Bar/Disco

TOUCHÉ'Z, 323 S Phillips Ave (rear) near 12th St, (605) 335-9874. Dance bar & quiet bar areas, patio. 8pm-2am nightly, 60% men, 40% women.

■ Erotica

STUDIO ONE, 311 N Dakota Ave near 7th St, (605) 332-9316, 24hrs.

TENNESSEE
CHATTANOOGA

■ Dance Bar/Disco

ALAN GOLD'S, 1100 McCallie at National, (423) 629-8080. Dance & show bar, DJ nightly, 50% men, 50% women.

CHUCK'S II, 27 W Main St, (423) 265-5405. C&W dance bar, 60% men, 40% women.

■ Erotica

ROSSVILLE NEWS, 2437 Rossville Blvd, (423) 266-7639, 24hrs.

GATLINBURG

■ Accommodations

LAUGHING OTTER, 1321 Nobel St G, Alcoa, Tn 37701, (423) 983-9150. Fully-furnished, secluded cabin on wildlife sanctuary, 50% gay & lesbian clientele.

GREENEVILLE

■ Accommodations

TIMBERFELL LODGE, 2240 Van Hill Rd, (423) 234-0833, (800) 437-0118. Men-only resort with campsites. Deluxe rooms & baths, in-lodge bunkroom, wide-screen satellite TV, VCR, CD stereo, 10-man Jacuzzi, 20-man sauna, 20 x 40 ft pool, volleyball court, outdoor fantasy scenes, full breakfast. Levi, leather & naturalists welcome.

JOHNSON CITY

■ Dance Bar/Disco

NEW BEGINNINGS, 2910 N Bristol Hwy, (423) 282-4446. Dance bar, show bar, restaurant, Tues-Thurs, Sun from 9pm, Fri & Sat from 8pm. Closed Mon.

KNOXVILLE

■ Information

GAY & LESBIAN HELPLINE, (423) 521-6546, 7pm-11pm daily, staff permitting.

■ Dance Bar/Disco

CAROUSEL II, 1501 White Ave SW near 15th, (423) 522-6966. Dance & show bars, 50% men, 50% women.

CLOSET, THE, at Lord Lindsey bar. Alternative dance party, gay Thurs only, younger crowd.

ELECTRIC BARROOM,★ 1213 Western Ave, (423) 525-6724. Huge gay & alternative dance bar, restaurant & giftshop in a warehouse, Wed-Sun 9pm-3am.

IVANNA'S, 4541 Kingston Pike, (423) 212-3513. Disco, show bar & restaurant, Mon drag shows, 1st Sun 615 Club for men, 5pm-3am 7 days, 70% men, 30% women.

■ Retail & Bookstores

DAVIS-KIDD BOOKSELLERS, 113 N Peters Rd, (423) 690-0136. General bookstore with gay & lesbian sections.

ZEPHYR WINDS OF CHANGE BOOKSTORE, 4921 Homberg Dr #B1 & B2, (423) 588-8061, Fax: (423) 588-3228. Mainly metaphysical bookstore with gay & lesbian sections.

MEMPHIS

■ Information

FRIENDS FOR LIFE HIV RESOURCES, 24hr Hotline: (901) 278-AIDS (2437). Office, 9am-5pm, (901) 272-0855.

GAY & LESBIAN SWITCHBOARD, 1486 Madison Ave, (901) 324-4297.

■ Bars

AUTUMN STREET PUB & DELI, 1349 Autumn, (901) 274-8010. Full liquor.

CROSSROADS, THE, Jefferson at Claybrook. 75% men, 25% women, opens 11am.

DAVID'S, 1474 Madison Ave at MacNeil, (901) 278-4313. Jukebox, pool table.

FIVE-O-ONE BAR, 111 N Claybrook, (901) 726-4767. C&W bar from 1pm.

ONE MORE, Peabody & Cooper, (901) 272-1700. 80% men.

PIPELINE, 1382 Poplar Ave near Watkins, (901) 726-5263. Sun brunch & Tea dance, courtyard.

SUNSHINE LOUNGE, 1379 Lamar, (901) 272-9843.

■ Dance Bar/Disco

AMNESIA,★ 2866 Poplar Ave. Show, dance and conversation bars.

BACKSTREET, 2018 Court. After hours.

J-WAG'S, 1268 Madison Ave near Claybrook,

TENNESSEE

(901) 725-1909. Dance, show & cruise bar, patio, 24 hours.

MADISON FLAME, THE,★ 1588 Madison Ave, (901) 278-9839. We're the hottest women's bar in Tennessee! Disco on weekends, country dancing Thurs, men welcome.

N'COGNITO, 338 S Front at Vance.

WKRB IN MEMPHIS, 1528 Madison, (901) 278-9321. May change in 1997.

■ Retail & Bookstores

MERISTEM, 930 S Cooper St, (901) 276-0282. Feminist & lesbian books, music, crafts, local info.

■ Erotica

AIRPORT BOOKMART, 2214 Brooks Rd E, (901) 345-0657.

CHEROKEE VIDEO MART, 2947 Lamar, (901) 744-7494, 24hrs.

FANTASY WORLD, 1814 Winchester Rd, (901) 346-2086.

GETWELL BOOKMART, 1275 Getwell near airport, (901) 454-7765, 24hrs.

PARIS ADULT THEATER, 2432 Summer near E Parkway, (901) 323-2665, 24hrs.

TAMMY'S #1, 2857 Winchester, (901) 365-0657. Also: #2, 2220 E Brooks Rd, 396-9050; #3, 1617 Getwell, 744-4513; #4, 5937 Summer, 373-5670.

NASHVILLE

■ Accommodations

SAVAGE HOUSE INN B&B, 165 8th Ave North, (615) 254-1277. Hotel with restaurant & bar, 50% gay & lesbian clientele.

■ Bars

BOOTS, 301 S 2nd St, (615) 254-8037. Very cruisy. Moving in 1997, call for new address.

CHUTE COMPLEX,★ 2535 Franklin Rd near Horner, (615) 297-4571. Complex with Chute C&W dance bar, Silver Stirrup piano lounge, Nashville Eagle levi leather bar, hi-energy dance bars, restaurant & patio. Drag shows Wed, karaoke Thurs, 85% men, women welcome.

CRAZY COWBOY II, 2311 Franklin Rd at Mel Rd, (615) 269-5318.

GASLIGHT, 167-1/2 8th Ave N, (615) 254-1278. Piano bar, 70% men, women welcome.

RALPH'S, 515 2nd Ave S, (615) 256-9682. Pub atmosphere, small dance floor.

SILVER STIRRUP, 2535 Franklin Rd at Chute Complex. Upscale piano lounge.

TRIANGLES, 1401 4th Ave S, (615) 242-8131.

YNONAH'S SALOON, 1700 4th Ave S, (615) 251-0980. Popular for after hours, patio, bar, volleyball.

■ Dance Bar/Disco

CHUTE COMPLEX,★ 2535 Franklin Rd near Horner, (615) 297-4571. Complex with C&W, leather, hi-energy dance bars, restaurant, patio, 85% men, 15% women. Women welcome.

CONNECTION, THE,★ 901 Cowan St, (615) 742-1166. Very large gay bar, 2 dance bars, show bar, restaurant, patio, 70% men, 30% women, 50% straight.

NINE-O-NINE CLUB, 909 Church St, (615) 251-1613. Dance bar.

■ Restaurants

CHUTE COMPLEX RESTAURANT, 2535 Franklin Rd at Chute Complex men's bar, (615) 297-4571. Burgers, steaks, salads, pastries, women welcome.

TOWNE HOUSE, 165 8th Ave N, at Gaslight bar, (615) 254-1277. Steaks, seafood.

WORLD'S END, 1713 Church St. Restaurant with bar, frequented by gays.

■ Retail & Bookstores

OUT LOUD BOOKS & GIFTS, 1805-C Church St, (615) 340-0034. Gay & lesbian bookstore, rainbow items, jewelry, cards, videos, etc.

TEN PERCENT GIFTS & ACCESSORIES, 901 Cowan St at Connection nightclub. Gay novelties, magazines, guides, etc. Open Tue-Sun 10pm-3am.

■ Erotica

CAROUSEL, 5606 Charlotte Pike, (615) 352-0855. Arcade.

CLASSIC ARTS, 2702 Dickerson Rd, (615) 226-9192. Arcade, 24hrs.

MADAME X, 12th Ave S at Division.

METRO NEWS, 822 5th Ave S, (615) 256-1310, Fax: 256-4036. Huge store, adult books, videos, magazines, novelty items.

ODYSSEY BOOKSTORE, 700 Division St. (615) 726-0243.

PURPLE ONION, 2807 Nolensville Rd, (615) 256-9640. Arcade, 24hrs.

WHEEL, THE, 421 Broadway, (615) 256-4597, 7 days.

NEWPORT

■ Accommodations

CHRISTOPHER PLACE, 1500 Pinnacles Way, (423) 623-6555 (tel/fax). Inn with restaurant, 50% gay & lesbian clientele. Color cable TV, VCR, video tapes, AC, private baths, some hot tubs & fireplaces. TV lounge, game room, tanning bed, sauna & pool. Full breakfast.

OAK RIDGE

■ Retail & Bookstores

BOOKSTORE, THE, 113 Tyrone Rd, (423) 482-5286. General bookstore with a feminist section. We will special order women's or gay books.

SEWANEE

■ Accommodations

BOXWOOD COTTAGE BED & BREAKFAST, RFD #1 (Anderson Cemetery Rd), (615) 598-5912. Men-only B&B, private & shared baths.

WILD HEART RANCH, 1070 Old Sewanne Rd, (423) 837-0849. Mail: PO Box 130, Sewanee, TN 37375. A-frame cabins & lodge & campsites near 7000 acres of horse trails. Perfect for equestrian groups. Set-ups for 50-ft-long horse trailers, unlimited camping, spaces for 24 trailers, cabins & lodge sleep up to 20. Gay-friendly.

---

250 Secluded Acres
Gourmet Meals Included
Deluxe Rooms
Bunk Rooms
Pool • Jacuzzi
Clothing Optional
Open Year Round

TIMBERFELL LODGE

A Gay Men's Resort
888-TIMBERFELL • 423-234-0833
2240 Van Hill Rd. Greeneville, TN 37745

FERRARI GUIDES' GAY TRAVEL A to Z - 18th EDITION

TEXAS

TEXAS
WHO TO CALL
For Tour Companies Serving This Destination
See Texas on page 27

ABILENE

Information
AIDS HOTLINE, (915) 667-AIDS. Mon-Fri 4-10.

Bars
RAINBO BAR, 3334 E Hwy 80, (915) 670-9809. Juke box, dance floor, 75% men, 25% women.

Dance Bar/Disco
JUST FRIENDS, 201 S 14th, (915) 672-9318. Dance bar with second bar in rear.

Erotica
ADULT ETC, Bus Rte 20, east of Judge Ely Blvd.
ADULTS ETC, Rte 1, Box 8, off US 20, Merkel, (915) 928-3894.

AMARILLO

Bars
CLUB TEN, 1219 W 10th St, (806) 373-1200. noon-12am, 7 days.

Dance Bar/Disco
CLASSIFIEDS,★ 519 E 10th Ave, (806) 374-2435. Large dance bar, DJ Fri-Sun, more gay weeknites, Fri & Sat 75% straight.
RITZ, 323 W 10th St at Van Buren, (806) 372-9382. Small dance bar, patio.
SASSY'S, 309 W 6th St between Van Buren & Harrison, (806) 374-3029. 75% women.

Erotica
ADULT BOOKSTORE, E of town off I-40 in a huge white building. (806) 379-9002. Cinema, videos.
MUSIC BOX, 523 E 10th, (806) 372-0648.

ARLINGTON
See Ft. Worth/Arlington

AUSTIN

Information
AIDS SERVICES, (512) 451-2273.
CORNERSTONE COMMUNITY CENTER, 1117 Red River, (512) 708-1515.

Accommodations
PARK LANE GUESTHOUSE, 221 Park Ln, (512) 447-7460, (800) 492-8827. Cottage & guesthouse, private bath, expanded continental breakfast, AC, ceiling fans, nearby pool & lake. Cottage has color TV, VCR, kitchen. Rates: main house: single $75, double $85; cottage: double $110 ($18 each add'l person).
SUMMIT HOUSE, 1204 Summit St, Austin, TX 78741, (512) 445-5304, room with queen bed, private bath, full breakfast, mostly gay & lesbian, some straight clientele.

Bars
BLUE FLAMINGO, 617 Red River, (512) 469-0014. Mix of gays with straights, punk rock, live bands.
BOUT TIME, 9601 N I-35, on access road, just N of Rundberg St, (512) 832-5339. 2 pool tables, Wed oldies, DJ Thurs-Sat, drag shows Sat, volleyball Sun.
CHAIN DRIVE, 504 Willow Street. (512) 480-9017. Large bar with non-smoking area, Leather Chest leather shop inside. Large patio also non-smoking.
CUFF, 408 Congress. Small leather bar connected with Forum dance bar.
VICTORY GRILL / KOVAC THEATER, 1104 E 11th, (512) 474-4494. Word "grill" is misleading, actually a cabaret club with nightly entertainment & live music, mostly jazz & blues. Cafe area to open to the public in spring '97.

Dance Bar/Disco
AREA 52, 404 Colorado. Alternative bar, hi energy dance bar, ages 18 & up, opens 10:30pm, after hours till sunup. Emphasis on trendy high fashion, mostly straight.
CHARLIE'S, 1301 Lavaca Ave at 13th St, (512) 474-6481. Large bar, preppie crowd, male dancers.
EDGE, 213 W 4th, (512) 480-8686. DJ nightly.
FORUM, 408 Congress, (512) 476-2900. Male strippers nightly, drag shows Wed, rooftop patio, lots of videos, younger crowd. Open Sun-Thurs 2pm-2am, Fri & Sat till 4am, Sat & Sun from noon.
OILCAN HARRY'S,★ 211 W 4, (512) 320-8823. Upscale crowd, male dancers, 95% men.
RAINBOW CATTLE CO.,★ 305 W 5th St, (512) 472-5288. Large C&W dance bar, 60% men, 40% women.

Saunas/Health Clubs
ACI (ALTERNATIVE CLUBS, INC), 500 Chicon, (512) 472-1443. Private club for gay men, noon-9am, 24hrs weekends.
MIDTOWNE SPA, 5815 Airport Blvd, (512) 302-9696. Full gym, 24hrs.

Restaurants
KATZ'S DELI, 618 W 6th, (512) 472-2037. NY-style deli, 24hrs.
MOMMA'S DINER, 300 block of Congress Ave. 24hrs weekends.

Retail & Bookstores
BOOK WOMAN, 918 W 12th St, (512) 472-2785. Women's bookstore, cards, gifts, jewelry.
CELEBRATION!, 108 W 43rd St near Speedway, (512) 453-6207. Women's book- & giftstore, cards, gifts, ritual supplies, jewelry, beads.

Leathers/Piercing
LEATHER CLUB, 504 Willow, inside Chain Drive, (512) 478-2261.

Erotica
AUSTIN SIX, 521 Thompson Ln, (512) 385-5329. Huge 24hr theatre.
CINEMA WEST, 2130 S Congress, (512) 442-5719. Adult videos.
FORBIDDEN FRUIT, 512 Neches near 6th, (512) 478-8358. Adult toy store. 2nd location: 513 6th St.
LOBO, 3204-A Guadalupe, (512) 454-5406.
NEW VIDEO, I-35. South to Slaughter Rd exit, then north. 24hr arcade.
OASIS BOOKSTORE, 9601 N Interregional Hwy 35, (512) 835-7208, 24hrs.
PLEASURELAND, 613 W 29th at Guadalupe, (512) 478-2339.

BEAUMONT

Information
TRIANGLE AIDS NETWORK, (409) 832-8338.

Dance Bar/Disco
COPA, 304 Orleans St. Drag shows Sun, male strippers, usually 80% men, 40% women Sat.
SUNDOWNER, 497 Crockett St, (409) 833-3989. Dance & showbar, male strippers & showbar Sat.

BRYAN

Dance Bar/Disco
CLUB, THE 308 N Bryan, (409) 823-6767. Dance bar, variety of music, Tues-Sat 9pm-2am.

CORPUS CHRISTI - ROCKPORT

Information
AIDS INFO, (512) 814-2001.

Accommodations
ANTHONY'S BY THE SEA, 735 S Pearl, Rockport, (512) 729-6100. B&B near ocean beach. Private & shared baths & modern conveniences. Full gourmet breakfast, weights & Jacuzzi.

Bars
HIDDEN DOOR,★ 802 S Staples, (512) 882-5002. Cruise bar.

Dance Bar/Disco
MEMBERS ONLY, 1808 Ayers, (512) 882-3775. Small disco Wed-Sun. Moving in spring '97, call for new address.

TEXAS

MINGLES, 512 S Staples, (512) 884-8022. Tejano, dance & country music.

U B U CLUB, 511 Star St, (512) 882-9693. Alternative dance club, 18 yrs & over. Male & female strippers, 50% gay & lesbian.

ZODIAC, 4125 Gollihar, (512) 853-4077. 50% men, 50% women, DJ Wed, Fri & Sat, shows & male strippers Fri.

DALLAS

■ Information
AIDS INFO, (214) 559-AIDS (2437), 9am-9pm daily.

FOUNDATION FOR HUMAN UNDERSTANDING, 2701 Reagan St, (214) 521-5342.

■ Realtors/Relocation
UPTOWN REALTORS, DEB ELDER, (972) 623-5122. Relocating? Let me tour you through Dallas' many interesting neighborhoods. I can assist with leasing (no fees to you), buying, selling, or I can help you find a realtor wherever you relocate. Give me a call with your mailing address and I'll send an informative Welcome Wagon packet on Dallas' gay and lesbian community.

■ Accommodations
COURTYARD ON THE TRAIL, 8045 Forest Trail, Dallas, TX 75238, (214) 553-9700 (tel/fax), (800) 484-6260 pin #0465. E-mail: akrubs4u@aol.com. B&B close to downtown, yet in a country setting. Guestrooms have king-sized beds, marble baths, direct pool & courtyard access. Full breakfast, dinner by prearrangement, some straight clientele.

INN ON FAIRMOUNT, THE, 2701 Fairmount, (214) 522-2800, Fax: 522-2898. B&B inn close to gay bars & restaurants. Color TV, AC, private baths, continental breakfast, Jacuzzi.

■ Bars
DALLAS ONE, 2615 Oak Lawn, (214) 528-0454.

HIDDEN DOOR,★ 5025 Bowser Ave near Mahanna, (214) 526-0620. Opens 7am.

HIDEAWAY CLUB, 4144 Buena Vista near Fitzhugh, (214) 559-2966. More upscale, quieter crowd, piano bar in front, video bar in rear, large patio with fountains, waterfall, 75% men, 25% women. Cookouts Sun in summer.

KOLORS, 2525 Wycliff, (214) 520-2525. Neighborhood cruise bar on one side, disco on other, Mon amateur strip, Tues & Sat drag show.

MOBY DICK, 4011 Cedar Springs, (214) 520-MOBY(6629). Video cruise bar, DJ, upscale gay crowd, 20s-40s.

PUB PEGASUS, 3326 N Fitzhugh Ave, (214) 559-4663. Piano singalong Fri & Sun, slightly more mature crowd.

SIDE II BAR, 4006 Cedar Springs Rd, (214) 528-2026. Jukebox, pool table.

THROCKMORTON MINING CO, 3014 Throckmorton St near Cedar Springs, (214) 380-3808. Mid 20's & up.

TRESTLE, THE, 412 S Haskell, (214) 826-9988. Patio.

ZIPPERS, 3333 N Fitzhugh Ave, (214) 526-9519. Male dancers 7 nights, quiet bar in back with juke box, Sun BBQ in summer.

ZONE, 4020 Maple Ave, (214) 520-1366. Male dancers daily.

■ Dance Bar/Disco
BAMBOLEO'S, 5027 Lemmon Ave, (214) 520-1124. Dance & show bar, 70% men, 30% women.

BRICK, 4117 Maple Ave, (214) 521-2024. Strippers.

BUDDIES II, 4025 Maple Ave, (215) 526-0887. Mostly women.

CREWS INN, 3215 N Fitzhugh Ave near Cole, (214) 526-9510. Male dancers 7 nights, mixed-age crowd, Tues biggest night, packed by 11pm, dance floor & nightly DJ, 2 patio bars.

JR'S BAR & GRILL,★ 3923 Cedar Springs at Throckmorton, (214) 380-3808. Upscale, preppie crowd, video karaoke.

JUG'S, 3810 Congress (214) 521-3474.

METRO CLUB, 2204 Elm, (214) 742-2101. Video dance bar, open Thurs-Mon, drag shows Mon & Sun, male dancers Thurs-Sat, best Thurs.

ROSE ROOM, THE, 3911 Cedar Springs, upstairs of Village Station, (214) 380-3808. Showbar.

ROUND UP SALOON,★ 3912 Cedar Springs Rd near Reagan, (214) 522-9611. Dance lessons.

SUE ELLEN'S,★ 3903 Cedar Springs, (214) 380-3808. Video dance bar, patio, volleyball. Fri & Sat after-hours, men welcome.

VILLAGE STATION★, 3911 Cedar Springs near Throckmorton, (214) 380-3808. Video dance bar and Rose Room, Las Vegas-style show bar upstairs.

■ Saunas/Health Clubs
CLUB DALLAS, 2616 Swiss Ave near Good Latimer, (214) 821-1990. Private club, 24hrs, full gym.

MIDTOWNE SPA, 2509 Pacific near Hawkins, (214) 821-8989. Private club, 24hrs. Full gym. New mardi Gras performance room with male dancer contests Mon. Male dancers Tue-Sun.

■ Restaurants
BELLINI'S, 3102 Oak Lawn, (214) 522-7800. Italian cuisine.

BRONX, THE, 3835 Cedar Springs, (214) 521-5821. New American, Southwest & traditional cuisine, dinner only. Sun brunch.

HUNKY'S, 4000 Cedar Springs, (214) 522-1212. Lunch and dinner.

PANDA'S, next to JR's, 3923 Cedar Springs. (214) 528-3818. Oriental cuisine.

SPASSO'S PIZZA, 4000 Cedar Springs #E, (214) 521-1141. Pasta, etc.

■ Retail & Bookstores
CROSSROADS MARKET, 3930 Cedar Springs at Throckmorton, (214) 521-8919. Gay & lesbian bookstore.

NUVO, 3900 Cedar Springs, (214) 522-6886. Cards & gifts.

OFF THE STREET, 3921 Cedar Springs, (214) 521-9051. Cards, gifts & t-shirts.

TAPELENDERS, 3910 Cedar Springs, (214) 528-6344. Videos, t-shirts, magazines.

■ Leathers/Piercing
LEATHER BY BOOTS, 2525 Wycliff #124, (214) 528-3865.

SHADES OF GREY 3928 Cedar Springs, (214) 521-4739, Wed-Sun 559-4739. Opens 11am.

DENISON

■ Dance Bar/Disco
GOOD TIME LOUNGE, 2520 N Hwy 91N, (903) 463-9944. Juke box disco, male & female strippers.

DENTON

■ Information
AIDS INFO, (817) 381-1501.

■ Dance Bar/Disco
BEDO'S, 1215 E University Dr, (817) 566-9910. Private club, 50% men, 50% women. Closed Mon.

EL PASO

■ Information
AIDS INFO, (915) 543-3574, Spanish 543-3575.

LAMBDA LINE & GAY CENTER, 910 N Mesa, (915) 562-4297. Gay info line 24hrs.

■ Bars
BRIAR PATCH, 204 E Rio Grande, (915) 546-9100. 25% women.

HAWAIIAN BAR, 919 E Paisano, (915) 541-7009. Drag shows Fri & Sat, Sun Mexican food, 70% men.

WHATEVER LOUNGE, 701 E Paisano, (915)

YOUR COMMUNITY REALTOR

Deb Elder
(972) 623-5122

the CLUB DALLAS

TEXAS

UNITED STATES

FYI

IN HOUSTON: Airport Pick-up... Nightlife Tours...Even Special Itineraries

After Five Charters will customize their service to your needs, or you can choose from these packages...

The Texas Two Step
Cocktails at a piano bar in the Montrose gay area, dinner, then dancing and fun at the clubs.

Galleria Shopping Trip
A shopping trip to the famous Galleria with over 300 stores and restaurants.

NASA's Johnson Space Center
An educational tour of NASA's Texas space center.

Galveston Tour
Join the celebration in Old Galveston on the first weekend in December, with Victorian costumed characters, parades.

San Antonio Christmas Festival of Lights
An overnight visit including a cruise along the River Walk with Christmas displays, singing and other activities.

Also available: Astrodome, Six Flags, Louisiana casino runs, dog and horse track gaming.

Contact **After Five** at (800) 335-1369, (281) 444-1369, Fax: (281) 441-1275.

533-0215. 60% men, 40% women, Latin.

■ *Dance Bar/Disco*

NEW OLD PLANTATION, 219 S Ochoa St at 1st, (915) 533-6055. Dance bar, male strippers Thurs & Fri, drag shows Sun, 70% men. Open Thurs-Sun, after-hours Fri & Sat.

SAN ANTONIO MINING CO,★ 800 E San Antonio St, at Ochoa, (915) 533-9516. Summer patio, male strippers Sun, drag shows Wed, many women for Fri cocktail hour.

U-GOT-IT, 216 S Ochoa, (915) 533-9310. Open Fri only 9pm-2am, Latin & country music.

■ *Cafe*

DOLCE VITA, Cincinnati at Mesa.

SOJOURNS, San Francisco at Mills, above the San Francisco Bar & Grill. Popular with women.

■ *Retail & Bookstores*

GENERATION Q, 910 N Mesa St, at Gay Center, (915) 533-6024. Gay & lesbian books, rainbow items, videos, magazines. 2nd location inside New Old Plantation.

■ *Erotica*

EROS BOOKSTORE, 4828 Montana Ave, (915) 772-7692.

TRIX CINEMA, 2230 Texas, (915) 532-6171.

VENUS BOOKSTORE, 4812 Montana, (915) 566-8061.

FT WORTH - ARLINGTON

■ *Information*

AIDS INFO, (817) 870-7346 or 336-0066.

■ *Accommodations*

TWO PEARLS B&B, 804 South Alamo St, Weatherford, (817) 596-9316. B&B 25 miles west of Ft Worth, private & shared baths, full breakfast, AC, ceiling fans, TV lounge, video tape library, 50% gay/lesbian clientele.

■ *Bars*

CORRAL, THE, 621 Hemphill St at Cannon, (817) 335-0196.

SIX FIFTY-ONE CLUB,★ 651 S Jennings Ave near Cannon, (817) 332-0745. 70% men, 30% women.

SQUARE ROOM, 2308 W 7th St, (817) 336-1410. Live jazz, all jazz all the time, Mon-Fri 4pm-2am, Sat & Sun 6pm-2am.

■ *Dance Bar/Disco*

DJ'S, 1308 St Louis St near Magnolia, (817) 927-7321. Dance & show bar with restaurant, 60% women, 40% men.

MAGNOLIA STATION,★ 600 W Magnolia, (817) 332-0415. Male strippers.

SIX FIFTY-ONE ARLINGTON,★ 1851 W Division, Arlington, (817) 275-9651.

■ *Restaurants*

DJ'S RESTAURANT & BAR, 1308 St Louis, (817) 927-7321.

GALVESTON

■ *Information*

AIDS COALITION, 1419 Tremont, (409) 763-2437.

■ *Women's Accommodations*

RAINBOW REFLECTIONS, PO Box 3405, Galveston, TX 77551, (409) 763-2450. Women-only B&B on Galveston Island, near beach, 2 rooms, shared bath, delux continental breakfast.

■ *Bars*

LONGFELLOW'S, 2405 Postoffice, (409) 763-8800. Open 7 days 2pm-2am, drag shows Fri, 80% men, 20% women.

ROBERT'S LAFITTE, 2501 Ave Q at 25th, (409) 765-9092. Popular for drag shows.

■ *Dance Bar/Disco*

EVOLUTION, 2214 Mechanic St near 22nd St, (409) 763-4212. Video dance bar, many straights.

KON TIKI,★ 315 Tremont (409) 763-6264. Dance & show bar, 50% men, 50% women. Male & female strippers.

GROESBECK

■ *Camping & RV*

RAINBOW RANCH CAMPGROUND, Rte 2, Box 165, Groesbeck, TX 76642, (817) 729-5847. Women's campground midway between Houston & Dallas. 100 wooded acres on Lake Limestone, swimming, fishing, boating, canoeing, paddle boats, volleyball, basketball, horseshoes.

GUN BARREL CITY

■ *Bars*

MIKE'S TWO THIRTY-ONE CLUB, 602 S Gun Barrel Ln, (903) 887-2061. Pool table, patio, Sat disco with DJ, 90% men, 10% women.

HARLINGEN

■ *Dance Bar/Disco*

COLORS, 703 Ed Carey Dr, (210) 440-8663. Dance till 4am Sat.

HOUSTON

■ *Information*

AIDS HOTLINE, (713) 524-AIDS.

GAY & LESBIAN SWITCHBOARD (713) 529-3211, crisis: 228-1505.

GAY AND LESBIAN CHAMBER OF COMMERCE, (713) 523-7576.

■ *Accommodations*

LOVETT INN, THE, 501 Lovett Blvd, (800) 779-5224, (713) 522-5224, Fax: 528-6703. Lodging & catering accommodations.

---

492   FERRARI GUIDES' GAY TRAVEL A to Z - 18th EDITION

TEXAS

Guestrooms have queen sized beds, color TVs, phones, most have private baths. Pool & spa on premises.

MONTROSE INN, 408 Avondale, (713) 520-0206. "Basic & butch" all-male gay B&B, private & shared baths, full breakfast.

■ Bars

BRIAR PATCH, 2294 W Holcombe (shopping ctr) near McClendon, (713) 665-9678. Piano bar nightly from 9:30pm.

BRICKS, 617 Fairview.

CHANCES, 1100 Westheimer, (713) 523-7217. Wed either singers, live bands, dancers or drag shows.

COUSINS, 817 Fairview at Converse, (713) 528-9204. Drag shows Fri-Sun, 75% men, 25% women.

EJ'S, 2517 Ralph, (713) 527-9071.

GENTRY, 2303 Richmond near Kirby, (713) 520-1861. Male dancers, happy hour popular with yuppie crowd.

JO'S OUTPOST, 1419 Richmond Ave, (713) 520-8446. Ages 25 & above, 85% men, 15% women.

JR'S, 808 Pacific at Grant, (713) 521-2519, 521-0107. Patio, male dancers, preppies, 80% men, 20% women.

LAZY J, 312 Tuam St near Bagby, (713) 528-9343. 65% men, 35% women, drag shows Sat, Wed women's pool nite certain times of year.

MARY'S, 1022 Westheimer Rd at Waugh, (713) 527-9669. Patio open weekends, Wed happy hour prices all day & evening.

MONTROSE MINING CO, 805 Pacific at Grant, (713) 529-7488. Patio.

MS B'S, 9208 Buffalo Speedway, at The Ranch, (713) 666-3356. Quiet bar, pool table, darts, men welcome.

QT, 534 Westheimer, (713) 529-8813. Patio.

RANCH, THE,★ 9218 Buffalo Speedway, (713) 666-3464. Three bars, men welcome.

RIPCORD,★ 715 Fairview at Crocker, (713) 521-2792. Patio, after hours weekends. Leather shop inside.

SIX ELEVEN CLUB, 611 Hyde Park Ave at Stanford, (713) 526-7070. Patio, Irish pub setting, DJ weekends, burger nites most Thurs, 60% men, 40% women.

VENTURE-N, 2923 Main St near Anita, (713) 522-0000. Cruise bar, caters to leather crowd. Patio, Sun buffet, occasional cookouts.

■ Dance Bar/Disco

AK'S BERRY HILL #2, 12726 N Freeway, (713) 873-8810. Wed female dancers, Thurs male dancers, DJ Wed-Sat, live bands, 60% women, 40% men.

BRAZOS RIVER BOTTOM (BRB), 2400 Brazos St at McIlhenny, (713) 528-9192. Sun steak nights, Tues dance lessons, 75% men.

HEAVEN, 810 Pacific, at Grant, (713) 521-9123. Video dance club, younger crowd, open from 9pm.

INCOGNITO, 2524 McKinney, at Live Oak, (713) 237-9431. 9pm-2am, male & female dancers Fri & Mon, Fri boys night out, Sun drag shows, 60% men, 40% women. Patio with cookouts most Sun.

NEW BARN, 1100 Westheimer B (in rear), (713) 521-9533. C&W dance bar, 7 days noon-2am, 75% men, 25% women.

PACIFIC STREET,★ 710 Pacific St at Crocker, (713) 523-0213. Catering to the leather crowd.

RICH'S,★ 2401 San Jacinto, (713) 759-9606. Hi energy dance bar, male dancers.

XTC, same location as The Ranch bar, 9218 Buffalo Speedway, (713) 666-3464. Hi-energy dance bar, open Fri, Sat. Men welcome.

■ Saunas/Health Clubs

CLUB HOUSTON, 2205 Fannin St near Webster, (713) 659-4998. Private club, 24hrs. Pro-maximum & free weights, gym instructor.

MIDTOWNE SPA, 3100 Fannin St at Elgin, (713) 522-2379. Private club, 24hrs. Full gym. Indoor/outdoor pool. male dancers. Busy Wed & Thur, weekends.

■ Restaurants

CAFE ADOBE, Westheimer at Sheppard. Mexican cuisine. Mon after 7pm is party night.

CHARLIE'S, 1102 Westheimer, (713) 522-3332. Popular for after hours food.

CORSINI, 2411 S Shepard, (713) 524-8558.

LA STRADA, 322 Westheimer, (713) 523-1014. Italian, gay-friendly. Fantastic Sun brunch is popular with gays.

MICHELANGELO'S, 307 Westheimer, (713) 524-7836. Upscale Italian cuisine, valet parking.

RUGGLES, 903 Westheimer, (713) 524-3839. Live jazz nightly. They will serve you dinner from the restaurant next door.

■ Retail & Bookstores

BASIC BROTHERS, 1232 Westheimer Rd, 9713) 522-1626. A very gay men's clothing store with pride-, athletic- & clubwear, swimsuits, thongs, pride jewelry, Mon-Sat 10am-9pm, Sun noon-6pm.

CROSSROADS MARKET, 1111 Westheimer, (713) 942-0147. Gay & lesbian bookstore & gifts.

INKLINGS, 1846 Richmond Ave, (713) 521-3369. Gay, lesbian, feminist bookstore. Cards, t-shirts, local info. Closed Mon.

LOBO, 3939-S Montrose, suite S, (713) 522-5156. Gay & lesbian books, videos, leather, etc.

■ Leathers/Piercing

LEATHER BY BOOTS, 807 Fairview, (713) 526-2668, and inside The Ripcord, (713) 526-0444. Open 7 days.

LEATHER FOREVER, 711 Fairview, (713) 526-6940.

■ Erotica

AFTER DARK NEWS, 1431 W 18th St,

ARCADE NEWS, 5821 Hillcroft St, (713) 789-3974.

BIG CITY NEWS & VIDEO, 10105 Gulf Freeway.

DINER ADULT NEWSSTAND, 240 Westheimer, (713) 522-9679.

FRENCH QUARTER THEATER, 3201 Louisiana near Elgin, (713) 527-0782. Gay, all male cinema.

GAS LIGHT NEWS, 3519 Bellaire.

I-45 NORTH NEWS & VIDEO, 9924 North Freeway, West Road exit #59. 24hrs, 7days.

LONE STAR NEWS, 6877 S Gessner Dr, (713) 781-0288.

STUDZ 24-HOUR NEWS,★ 1201 Richmond Ave at Mt Vernon, (713) 528-1363. Arcade.

WESTHEIMER NEWS, 6427 Westheimer, (713) 522-5156.

LAREDO

■ Dance Bar/Disco

DISCOVERY, 2019 Farragut, (210) 722-9032. Dance bar.

LONGVIEW

■ Dance Bar/Disco

DECISIONS, 2103 E Marshall, (903) 757-4884. Daily 3pm-2am, disco Fri-Sun & 2nd Wed of month. Quiet bar with CD juke box pool table, games, Sun drag shows.

LIFESTYLES, 446 N Eastman Rd, (903) 758-8082. Disco & C&W bars, outdoor bar, shows Sun. 50% men, 50% women.

■ Retail & Bookstores

DREAMLAND MAGAZINE, 900 McCann Rd, (903) 238-9900. Gay & straight magazines & videos, 9-6 Mon-Sat.

LUBBOCK

■ Information

AIDS INFO, (806) 796-7068, hotline: 792-7783.

GAY HELP LINE, (806) 766-7184.

■ Dance Bar/Disco

CAPTAIN HOLLYWOOD, 2401 Main St at Avenue X, (806) 744-4222. DJ nightly, variety of music, drag shows Tues, Sun, open 8pm 7 days.

FERRARI GUIDES' GAY TRAVEL A to Z - 18th EDITION

TEXAS

MCALLEN

■ Bars
PBD LOUNGE, 2908 Ware Rd at Daffodil, (210) 682-8019. Drag shows alternate Sat, male strippers, 70% men, 30% women, patio.

■ Dance Bar/Disco
TENTH AVENUE, 1820 N 10th St, (210) 682-7131. Large dance bar.

ODESSA

■ Dance Bar/Disco
FICTIONS, 409 N Hancock.
MISS LILLI'S NITESPOT, 8401 Andrews Hwy near Yukon, (915) 366-6799. Disco, all kinds of music, open Wed-Sun.

■ Erotica
B & L ADULT BOOKS, 5890 W University Blvd, (915) 381-6855.

PORT ARANSAS

■ Accommodations
SEAHORSE INN, PO Box 426, (512) 749-5221. Self-catering guesthouse with separate entrances. We are secluded atop a sand dune, a short sandy stroll from the beach. Ocean-view units, classical antique decor. Enjoy the sun-drenched warmth and 18 miles of unobstructed white-sand beaches. We have a private, heated pool surrounded by tropical gardens. Come enjoy the sea and the wild dunes of Mustang Island and Port Aransas.

RIO GRANDE VALLEY

■ Information
GAY ALLIANCE, (210) 428-6800.

SAN ANGELO

■ Information
AIDS INFO, (915) 658-3634.

Upper Deck Hotel
Crews Quarters Bar
South Padre Island, Texas

- All rooms with private baths and TV
- Heated swimming pool and jacuzzi
- Complimentary coffee & Danish Pastry
- 1/2 block from the beach

120 E. Atol St./P.O. Box 2309
South Padre Island TX 78597
(210) 761-5953 Fax (210) 761-4288

■ Dance Bar/Disco
SILENT PARTNERS, 1819 S Harrison St, (915) 949-9041. Open Tue-Sun, DJ Thurs-Sun, drag shows monthly, 50% men, 50% women. Unverifiable spring '97.

SAN ANTONIO

■ Information
AIDS INFO, (210) 225-4715, 24hrs. Hispanic AIDS Committee: (210) 734-UNITY.
GAY & LESBIAN COMMUNITY CENTER, 923 E Mistletoe, (210) 732-4300, Switchboard: 773-7300.
LESBIAN INFO, 1136 Hildebrand, (210) 828-5472.

■ Accommodations
ADELYNNE'S SUMMIT HAUS & SUMMIT HAUS II, 427 W Summit, (800) 972-7266, (210) 736-6272, (210) 828-3045, Fax: (210) 737-8244. B&B. Rooms, suite & cottage with color TV, AC, ceiling fans, refrigerator, coffee/tea-making facilities, private baths & full breakfast.
ARBOR HOUSE HOTEL, 339 South Presa, San Antonio, TX 78205, (210) 472-2005, toll-free (888) 272-6700, Fax: (210) 472-2007. Gay-owned, gay-friendly all-suite hotel in four turn-of-the-century houses connected by a courtyard. All private baths, continental breakfast, 1-1/2 blocks from the Riverwalk.
GARDEN COTTAGE, THE, (210) 828-4539 (Phone & Fax), (800) 235-7215. Cottage, some straight clientele. Fully-furnished, modern conveniences, kitchen. Massage available, public pool nearby.
PAINTED LADY INN ON BROADWAY, 620 Broadway. (210) 220-1092. Gay-friendly guest hotel, continental breakfast, limited room services, theme rooms.
SAN ANTONIO BED & BREAKFAST, 510 E Guenther, (210) 222-1828. B&B in King William Historic Neighborhood. Color TV, AC, refrigerators, private & shared baths, meeting rooms. Use of nearby condo pool.

■ Women's Accommodations
DESERT HEARTS COWGIRL CLUB, HC-3, Box 650, Bandera, 78003, (210) 796-7446. Women-only guest ranch. Shared bath, all meals included.

■ Bars
ANNEX, 330 San Pedro at Euclid, (210) 223-6957. Male strippers.
EL JARDIN, 106 Navarro St near Nueva, (210) 223-7177. Patio, darts.
LORRAINE'S, 7834 S Presa, (210) 532-8911. DJ Fri-Sun, female strippers, BBQ Sun.
MICK'S HIDEAWAY, 5307 McCullough, (210) 828-4222. Small cocktail lounge, darts, pool table, 50% men, 50% women.
NEW PONDEROSA, THE, 5007 S Flores, (210) 924-6322.
ONE-O-SIX OFF BROADWAY, 106 Pershing, (210) 820-0906. Juke box, patio, Thurs steak nite 6pm-9pm.
PEGASUS,★ 1402 N Main, (210) 299-4222. Upscale crowd, front cruise bar with male dancers. Quiet back bar & patio bar. Sand, pool & sun deck. Cookouts alternate Mon.
REBAR, 826 San Pedro, at West Laurel, above Woody's bar, (210) 271-9663. Male strippers daily, open Tues-Sun 9pm-2am.
SPARKS, 8011 Webbles Dr (210) 653-9941. Male strippers Tues, Fri-Sat, hot oil wrestling Tues, DJ Wed-Sun, 70% men, 30% women.
STALLION, 2003 McCullough, (210) 734-7977.
TWENTY FIFTEEN PLACE, 2015 San Pedro near Woodlawn, (210) 733-3365. Small dance floor, DJ Fri-Sat, male strippers Sat-Sun, patio.

■ Dance Bar/Disco
BONHAM EXCHANGE, 411 Bonham St near Travis, (210) 271-3811. Video dance bar, 50% straight.
CHANCES, 115 General Krueger Blvd near Blanco, (210) 348-7202. DJ weekends.
EAGLE MOUNTAIN SALOON,★ 1902 McCullough Ave, (210) 733-1516. C&W dancing nightly. Your cowboy bar for the '90s.
NEXUS II, 8021 Pinebrook, (210) 341-2818. Men welcome.
SAINT,★ 1430 N Main at Evergreen, (210) 225-7330. Dance & show bar.
SANCTUARY, 1818 N Main Ave, (210) 737-2344. Hi energy dance bar, amateur strip nites Thurs. Tues-Sun 9pm-2am, Fri & Sat till 4am after hours, 70% men, 30% women.
SILVER DOLLAR SALOON,★ 1418 N Main Ave, (210) 227-2623. C&W dance bar.
SNUFFY'S, 820 San Pedro Ave, (210) 226-2620. C&W dance bar Tues-Sun 4pm-2am, 90% men, 10% women.
WOODY'S,★ 826 San Pedro, at West Laurel, (210) 271-9663. Video bar, younger preppie crowd, 2pm-2am daily, 75% men, 25% women, male strippers.

■ Saunas/Health Clubs
ACI (ALTERNATIVE CLUBS, INC), 827 E Elmira, (210) 223-2177. Noon-9am, 24hrs weekends.
EXECUTIVE SPA, 1121 Basse Rd, (210) 732-4433. Private men's club, 24hrs.

■ Restaurants
EIGHTH ST BAR & GRILL, 416 8th St, (210) 271-3227. Bar & fine restaurant with pasta, seafood, steaks. Weekends after 10:30pm turns into dance bar, mainly gay & lesbian with straights.

■ Retail & Bookstores
ON MAIN, 2514 N Main, near Woodlawn,

(210) 737-2323. Cards & gifts.

TEXTURES, 5309 McCullough, (210) 805-8398. Women's bookstore, Mon-Fri 11am-6pm, Sat 11am-5pm, Sun 1pm-5pm.

ZEBRAZ GIFTS, 1216 Euclid Ave, (210) 472-2800. Alternative gift items, 9am-9pm Mon-Fri, 11am-9pm Sat.

■ *Erotica*

APOLLO NEWS, 2376 Austin Hwy, (210) 653-3538, 24hrs.

BROADWAY VIDEO XCHANGE, 2122 Broadway, (210) 223-2034.

ENCORE, 8546 Broadway #160, (210) 821-5345. 2nd location: Encore II, 1216 E Euclid, (210) 472-3004.

SHERMAN

■ *Bars*

GOOD TIME LOUNGE, 2520 Hwy 91 N, (903) 463-9944. ♂

SOUTH PADRE ISLAND

■ *Accommodations*

UPPER DECK HOTEL, 120 E Atol, Box 2309, (210) 761-5953, Fax: (210) 761-4288. Hotel on an uncrowded beach, good mix of gay men & women. Recently renovated rooms with private baths. "Cruise Quarters" bar, located in hotel, opens onto tropical gardens. Daytime rates available for pool, hot tub, locker, game room, complimentary coffee & Danish pastry. The island is world famous for deep sea fishing. ♀♂

■ *Bars*

CREW'S QUARTERS, at Upper Deck, The first alternative bar on the island. Full liquor. ♀♂

SOUTH PLAINS

■ *Information*

AIDS INFO, (806) 796-7068, 9am-5pm Mon-Fri.

TYLER

■ *Dance Bar/Disco*

OUTLAW, 4 Miles South Loop 323 on Hwy 110, (903) 509-2248. Gay-friendly dance club. 100% gay Wed nights.

WACO

■ *Dance Bar/Disco*

DAVID'S, 507 Jefferson at North 5th, (817) 753-9189. Upper level country dance bar. Lower level dance music. BBQs, patio in summer. ♀♂

WICHITA FALLS

■ *Dance Bar/Disco*

RASCALS, 811 Indiana, (817) 723-1629. Daily noon-2am, drag shows Fri, 35% men, 65% women. ♀♂

UTAH

WHO TO CALL

For Tour Companies Serving This Destination
See Utah on page 28

STATEWIDE

■ *Information*

AIDS INFO, (800) FON-AIDS.

ESCALANTE

■ *Accommodations*

RAINBOW COUNTRY TOURS AND BED & BREAKFAST, 586 E 300 S, (801) 826-4567, (800) 252-UTAH (8824). The spectacular wilderness of the Grand Staircase Escalante National Monument surrounds you at this hilltop B&B with views of nearby mountains and slick rock. Conveniently located near a rustic town and four national parks, our modern home offers a spa, pool table, cable TV, full breakfast, and optional tours. Go off the beaten path to enjoy outdoor activities like hiking, jeep tours, horseback riding, bicycling, and campouts. Open all year. Call for a free brochure.

MEXICAN HAT

■ *Accommodations*

VALLEY OF THE GODS BED & BREAKFAST, PO Box 310307, 84531, (801) 683-2292 (tel/fax). Gay-friendly B&B in the 4-Corners Region. Private baths, full breakfast, large gay/lesbian following.

Rainbow Country Tours and Bed & Breakfast

In Grand Staircase Escalante National Monument

(800) 252-UTAH

UTAH

FYI

Gay Adventures in the American West

Discover the wilderness of the American West, while engaging in active sports and learning the tips, tricks and techniques of self-reliance in the wild, so you'll feel confident when you do it on your own. Mountain bike the best of Utah's desert and slick-rock mountain bike trails. Hike among the fantastic rock formations in the scenic canyon country. Travel by snowshoe and skis in the backcountry near Taos, New Mexico. Learn rock climbing in Colorado or desert foraging in Arizona.

Lizard Head Backcountry Tours has programs for all skill levels. If you've never hiked above treeline before, they'll walk you through it, slowly. If you've never explored a 2,000-foot-deep canyon before, they'll show you how, gently. Or, if you're already a gonzo mountain biker and want to ride the world-famous trails in Colorado or Utah, they'll take you there, show you the best riding around, and teach you a few advanced techniques.

Contact **Lizard Head** at (303) 831-7090, (888) 540-2737, Fax: (303) 831-7079, E-mail: info@lizardhead.com, Web: http://lizardhead.com.

UNITED STATES

FERRARI GUIDES' GAY TRAVEL A to Z - 18th EDITION

UTAH

Utah's Only Gay Men's River Trips

All of the following 1997 trips are operated by **Passage to Utah**, an adventure tour company for gay men. Transportation between Salt Lake City and Escalante or Salt Lake and the river launch point is included.

June 23-28 Two days Grand Staircase-Escalante with evenings in a gay B&B. Stops in Bryce Canyon and Capitol Reef Nat'l Parks, then an exhilarating 3-day ride down Westwater Canyon's exciting whitewater.

July 28-Aug 1 Desolation Canyon has stretches where the canyon is over a mile deep. Fascinating geology, history and progressively more difficult rapids make "Deso" a favorite!

August 8-11 Lodore Canyon, home of "Hell's Half Mile," is Passage to Utah's most popular and its signature trip. Lodore offers long hikes, fine fishing and abundant wildlife. A total of only 44 miles, it allows plenty of stops and time for socializing.

Contact **Passage to Utah** at (801) 582-1896, (800) 677-0553, Fax: (801) 281-1868 (faxes attn: Mike).

Exploring Canyon Country in Comfort

Narrow canyons, slick rock hills and towering sandstone formations typify the Escalante, Utah area. Here, you can explore ancient petrified forests, marvel at prehistoric Indian rock art and visit serene lakes in the Dixie National Forest. **Rainbow Country Tours** offers a combination of touring and relaxing by providing both a comfortable bed and breakfast and tours (1/2-day and full-day) of the area. Expect to see deer as you travel through the Dixie National Forest. Hells Backbone Road is one of the most dramatic stretches of road in the country, including the Historical Bridge with sheer drops on both sides. If you visit in September, you'll see the mountains turn gold as the Aspen leaves change color. Rainbow Country Tours will customize a tour to fit your hiking abilities and the weather. For those preferring to hike alone, they provide trail shuttle service which gets you 4 miles further in than most vehicles can take you.

Contact **Rainbow Country Tours** at (801) 826-4567 (tel/fax) or (800) 252-8824 (tel/fax).

MOAB

■ *Accommodations*

MT. PEALE B&B COUNTRY INN, PO Box 366, LaSal, UT 84530, (801) 686-2284 (tel/fax), mobile: (801) 260-1305. B&B & cottages with private & shared baths, buffet breakfast, near Canyonlands & Arches Nt'l Parks, 50% gay & lesbian clientele.

OGDEN

■ *Dance Bar/Disco*

BRASS RAIL, 103 27th St, at Wall, (801) 399-1543. Dance bar, private club, open 7 days.

PARK CITY

■ *Retail & Bookstores*

A WOMAN'S PLACE BOOKSTORE, 1890 Bonanza Dr, (801) 649-2722. General bookstore with special emphasis on women's studies.

SALT LAKE CITY

■ *Information*

AIDS FOUNDATION, (801) 487-2323.

GAY HELP LINE, (801) 533-0927, 24hrs.

STONEWALL CENTER, 770 S 300 W, (801) 539-8800. Community center, 1pm-9pm Mon-Sat.

■ *Accommodations*

AARDVARK'S BED & BREAKFAST, (801) 533-0927. B&B, some straight clientele, singles & doubles. Catering for private parties.

ANTON BOXRUD B&B INN, 57 South 600 East, (801) 363-8035, (800) 524-5511, Fax: (801) 596-1316. Centrally-located gay-friendly B&B. Private & shared baths, TV lounge, full breakfast & Jacuzzi.

■ *Bars*

RADIO CITY, 147 S State St near 100 S, (801) 532-9327. Cruise bar, pool tables.

■ *Dance Bar/Disco*

BRICKS, 579 W 2nd S, (801) 328-0255. Private liquor club, disco, male dancers, 60% men, huge patio bar, 7 days.

DEER HUNTER, 636 S 300 W near 6th S, (801) 363-1802. Large private liquor club, patio, dance floor, pool room.

KINGS, 108 S 500 West, (801) 521-5464. Private liquor club, show bar with small dance floor, large stage.

PAPER MOON, 3424 S State, (801) 466-8517. Private liquor club, dance bar.

SUN,★ 200 S 700 W at 2nd South, (801) 531-0833. Private liquor club, dance bar, patio, 50% men, 50% women.

TRAPP, THE,★ 102 S 600 W, (801) 531-8727. Private liquor club, video bar, 90% men, small dance floor, Sun buffet.

VORTEX, 32 Exchange Place, (801) 521-9292. Private liquor club. Alternative club with hi-energy dancing, large trendy college crowd. Scheduled gay nights Thurs, dress-up bar. 🏳️‍🌈 ♂

Saunas/Health Clubs
FOURTEENTH ST GYM, 1414 W 200 South, (801) 363-2023. Private health club.

Restaurants
BACI TRATTORIA, 134 W Pierpont Ave, (801) 328-1500. Italian cuisine, gay friendly. 🏳️‍🌈

CAFE PIERPONT, 122 W Pierpont Ave, (801) 364-1222. Mexican cuisine, gay friendly. 🏳️‍🌈

DODO, THE, 680 S 900 E, (801) 328-9348. American cuisine, gay friendly. 🏳️‍🌈

FRUGGLES, 367 W 2nd South, (801) 363-7000. Great selection of salads, pastas. Gay-friendly. 🏳️‍🌈

MARKET STREET BROILER, 260 S 1300 E, (801) 583-8808. Gay-friendly restaurant near U of U. Cocktails available with membership. 🏳️‍🌈

MARKET STREET GRILL, 48 Market St, (801) 322-4668. Gay-friendly restaurant. Fresh seafood, daily specials, prime businessman's lunch. Cocktails available with membership. 🏳️‍🌈

Retail & Bookstores
A WOMAN'S PLACE BOOKSTORE, 1400 Foothill Dr, (801) 583-6431. 2nd location: 4835 Highland Dr, (801) 278-9855). General bookstore with special emphasis on women's studies & a gay & lesbian section.

BOB'S MAGAZINES, 777 S State, (801) 364-1133. Gay magazines. 🏳️‍🌈

CAHOOTS, 878 E 900 South, (801) 538-0606. Cards, gifts, leather & rubberware, adult novelties.

FERTILE GROUND, 274 E 900 S, (801) 521-8124. Women-oriented new-age store & art gallery.

GYPSY MOON EMPORIUM, 861 E 900 S, (801) 521-9100. Mythology & folklore, feminist & women's books.

KING'S ENGLISH, 1511 S 1500 E, (801) 484-9100. General bookstore with gay & lesbian titles.

MISCHIEVOUS, 559 S 300 W, (801) 530-3100. Selection of gay & lesbian cards, guides, adult section (adult chocolates), balloons, 7 days.

NEW PATHWAYS, 3159 W 5400 S, suburb of Kearns, (801) 966-8352. Unique gifts, New Age music, herbs & supplies.

OASIS BOOKS & CAFE, 213 E 300 St, (801) 322-0404. New age books, cafe. 🏳️‍🌈

Erotica
BLUE BOUTIQUE, 2100 S 1100 E, (801) 485-2072. Lingerie, toys, accessories, gay friendly.

MAGAZINE SHOP, 267 S Main, (801) 359-3295.

SOUTH CENTRAL UTAH
Accommodations
SKYRIDGE, A BED & BREAKFAST INN, near Capitol Reef National Park, Torrey, UT (801) 425-3222 (tel / fax). **4-Diamond Rating AAA & Guest-Rated One of the Top Inns in Utah's State B&B Assoc.** This artist-owner designed inn on 75 acres has unparalleled views of multicolored cliffs, domes & forested mountains. Each of the 5 rooms has a queen-sized bed, private bath, TV / VCR & phone. Rooms with patio, deck, Jacuzzi or hot tub available. Elegant full breakfast. Experience this spectacular park — cooler than Arches / Zion in the summer & less crowded than both!

ZION NATIONAL PARK
Accommodations
RED ROCK INN, 998 Zion Park Blvd, PO Box 273, Springdale, (801) 772-3139. Gay-friendly motel cottages near Zion National Park. Color cable TV, AC, refrigerator, coffee & tea-making facilities & private baths. Nearby pool & river.

VERMONT

ANDOVER
Accommodations
INN AT HIGHVIEW, THE, East Hill Rd, (802) 875-2724, Fax (802) 875-4021. Gay-friendly inn. Fabulous views, all private baths, TV lounge, pool, sauna, game room & full breakfast. 🏳️‍🌈

ARLINGTON
Accommodations
CANDLELIGHT MOTEL, Rt 7A, PO Box 97, (802) 375-6647, (800) 348-5294. Mixed clientele. **Located in historic Arlington, VT, the home of Norman Rockwell.** We are a short drive to major ski areas, outlet and specialty shops, antique shops and fine restaurants. Fireside lounge, continental breakfast. Special group packages.

HILL FARM INN, RR 2 Box 2015, (802) 375-2269, (800) 882-2545, fax: (802) 375-9918. Gay-friendly inn. Private & shared baths.

BENNINGTON
Information
BENNINGTON AREA AIDS PROJECT, (802) 442-4103. 7pm-10pm daily.

Women's Accommodations
GYPSY LADY, RD 2, Box 56W, N Bennington Rd, Hoosick Falls, NY, (518) 686-7275. B&B, private baths, some straight clientele, men welcome. ♀

BRATTLEBORO
Information
AIDS PROJECT, (802) 254-4444, 10:30am-3pm Mon-Fri. Hotline (800) 882-2437.

Restaurants
COMMON GROUND, 20 Elliot St, across from Colors on Harmony parking lot, (802) 257-0855. Natural foods, no smoking. 🏳️‍🌈

Retail & Bookstores
EVERYONE'S BOOKS, 23 Elliot St near Main, (802) 254-8160. Alternative bookstore with lesbian & gay section. ♿

BURLINGTON
Accommodations
HOWDEN COTTAGE, 32 N Champlain St, (802) 864-7198. B&B, mainly straight clientele. Cozy rooms, continental breakfast. Lake nearby, pool at YMCA. Convenient to Marketplace shopping complex, Lake Champlain, restaurants, theatre, concerts.

Dance Bar/Disco
ONE THIRTY-FIVE PEARL, 135 Pearl St at Elmwood, (802) 863-2343. 1st Fri women's nite 5pm-9pm with buffet. 🏳️‍🌈 ♀♂

Retail & Bookstores
CHASSMAN & BEM BOOKSELLERS, 81 Church St Market Place, (802) 862-4332. General bookstore with a gay & lesbian selection.

CENTRAL VERMONT
Accommodations
AUTUMN CREST INN, Box 1540 Clark Rd, (802) 433-6627, (800) 339-6627. Gay-friendly inn with restaurant & bar. Large, handsome rooms, 1 fireplace suite, library, tennis, horseback riding, hiking. Full breakfast. 🛏️

COLCHESTER
Erotica
VIDEOTOWN, 33 Jasper Mine Rd, (802) 893-1502. Adult bookstore, no arcades.

DUMMERSTON
Dance Bar/Disco
RAINBOW CATTLE CO., Rte 5, East Dummerston. Dance bar & quiet bar, occasional drag shows, 8pm-2am Wed-Sat, 7pm-2am Sun. 🏳️‍🌈 ♀♂

EAST HARDWICK
Women's Accommodations
GREENHOPE FARM, RFD 1, Box 2260, (802) 533-7772. Woman-only guesthouse since 1982, in Vermont's Northeast Kingdom. Open year-round. Six cozy guest rooms in a spacious post-and-beam house on a mountainside, with our six saddle horses and dairy goats grazing outside your windows. Join in the life of our farm or retreat to one of many secluded spots on our scenic, private acreage. Cross-country ski from our door on limitless miles of groomed trails. Skinny dipping nearby, hike or canoe. Delicious gourmet vegetarian cuisine. No smoking. Photo brochure available. Special summer rates and group discounts. ♀

VERMONT

FAIR HAVEN
■ *Accommodations*
MAPLEWOOD INN, Route 22A South, (802) 265-0839, (800) 253-7729, Fax: (802) 265-8210, E-mail: maplewd@sover.net. Gay-friendly B&B. Rooms & suites with color cable TV, AC, fireplaces & private baths. Expanded continental breakfast, nearby lake.

MONTGOMERY CENTER
■ *Accommodations*
PHINEAS SWANN B&B, PO Box 43, The Main Street, (802) 326-4306 (tel/fax). Country inn central to everything, 50% gay & lesbian clientele. Private & shared baths, ceiling fans, TV lounge, full gourmet breakfast & afternoon tea.

MONTPELIER
■ *Information*
COALITION OF LESBIANS & GAY MEN, PO Box 1125, (802) 454-8552.

■ *Restaurants*
HORN OF THE MOON CAFE, 8 Langdon St, (802) 223-2895. Vegetarian natural food, 7 days. Good mix of clientele.

■ *Retail & Bookstores*
BEAR POND BOOKS, 77 Main St, (802) 229-0774. General bookstore with small gay & lesbian section.

ST JOHNSBURY
■ *Women's Accommodations*
HIGHLANDS INN, THE, Box 118-I, Bethlehem, NH, (603) 869-3978. B&B inn on 100 acres. **A Lesbian paradise** with 20 comfortable rooms, antique furnishings, private & shared baths, TV lounge, kitchen privileges, library, heated pool, BBQ grills, hot tub, hiking, skiing and full breakfast. Rates $55-$110, weeklong & midweek discounts. Winner Out & About Editor's Choice Awards. Our sign always says "no vacancy" so please ignore it. Non-smoking rooms.

Buccaneer Country Lodge
Comfortable Lodgings in the Ski Capital of the East
(800) 543-1293
STOWE, VERMONT

SHAFTSBURY
■ *Accommodations*
COUNTRY COUSIN, RR 1, Box 212, Old Depot Rd, (802) 375-6985, (800) 479-6985. B&B, private baths, TV lounge, music room, hot tub, full breakfast.

STOWE
■ *Accommodations*
ARCADIA HOUSE, PO Box 520, Hyde Park, VT (802) 888-9147. B&B with queen-sized bed, private bath, expanded continental breakfast. 25 acres of grounds with orchard and vegetable & herb gardens. Within 1/2 hour of Stowe, Smuggler's Notch & Jay Peak skiing areas.
BUCCANEER COUNTRY LODGE, 3214 Mountain Rd, (802) 253-4772, (800) 543-1293. Lodge with breakfast cafe. Varied rooms & suites, near lake, village, mountain, nightlife & recreational activities. Full breakfast except in spring, complimentary hot soup & mulled cider during ski season. Enjoy gay skiing events and parties during Igloo Weekend annually in early March. Gay-friendly hosts are avid skiers. **READER COMMENT:** "Building in immaculate condition, grounds well landscaped, pool well maintained, pleasant dining room, owners pleasant and helpful." — Peter, Seattle, WA.
FITCH HILL INN, RFD 1 Box 1879, Hyde Park, 05655, (802) 888-3834, (800) 639-2903, Fax: (802) 888-7789. Enjoy friendly, country-English elegance at an affordable historic inn, built in 1794, in a mountain setting ten miles from Stowe, where year-round activities abound. The five rooms share baths and are attractively decorated with antiques. Hearty breakfast included. MC & VISA, mostly straight clientele.
HONEYWOOD COUNTRY LODGE, 4527 Mountain Rd, Stowe, VT 05672, (802) 253-4124, (800) 659-6289. Gay-friendly B&B motel on 4 acres, private baths, continental-plus breakfasts, in winter cross-country ski from front door, nearest AAA 3-Diamond lodging to Stowe Mtn. Resort.

WATERBURY-STOWE AREA
■ *Accommodations*
GRÜNBERG HAUS BED & BREAKFAST, RR #2, Box 1595, Route 100 South, (802) 244-7726, (800) 800-7760. B&B guesthouse, mainly straight clientele. Individually-decorated rms furnished with antiques. Jacuzzi, sauna, tennis court, library, full breakfast, many complimentary items. River & lake nearby.

WOODSTOCK AREA
■ *Accommodations*
MAITLAND SWAN HOUSE, THE, Happy Valley Rd, PO Box 105, Taftsville, 05073, (802) 457-4435 (tel/fax), (800) 959-1404. B&B,

---

mixed clientele of straight, gay & lesbian. 3 rooms & a cottage with private baths, color cable TV.
SOUTH VIEW BED & BREAKFAST, PO Box 579, Rowe Hill Rd Brownsville, (802) 484-7934. Gay-friendly B&B with lesbian following, shared baths.

VIRGINIA

ARLINGTON
■ *Information*
GAY ALLIANCE, (703) 522-7660 (tape).

CAPE CHARLES
■ *Accommodations*
CAPE CHARLES HOUSE B&B, 645 Tazewell Ave, (804) 331-4920. Gay-friendly B&B on Virginia's Eastern shore, just 40 minutes from Norfolk. Five rooms with private baths & sitting area. Gourmet breakfast included. Swimming, water sports, wildlife preserve all nearby.
WILSON-LEE HOUSE BED & BREAKFAST, 403 Tazewell Ave, Cape Charles, VA 23310, (757) 331-1954, Fax: (757) 331-8133, E-mail: WLHBnB@aol.com. Gay-friendly B&B with private baths (1 with whirlpool), full breakfast, steps to the beach, sunset cruises arranged.

CHARLOTTESVILLE
■ *Camping & RV*
INTOUCH WOMEN'S CAMPING & EVENT CENTER, Rt 2, Box 1096, Kent's Store, (804) 589-6542. A women's camping and event center near Fernville, VA, INTOUCH is 100 acres of **almost heaven** with a 7-acre lake. 50 campsites and cabins, hiking and mountain bike trails, outdoor showers, sand volleyball court, playing field, stage, and pavilion. Reservations required for non-members.

■ *Bars*
EASTERN STANDARD, 102 Old Preston Ave, (804) 295-8668. ES Cafe: casual bar & restaurant; Eastern Standard: fine dining upstairs. Discreetly frequented by gays later in the evenings. About 40% gay.

■ *Dance Bar/Disco*
CLUB 216, 216 Water St, (804) 296-8783.

CHESAPEAKE
■ *Retail & Bookstores*
CURIOUS GOODS, 2981 S Military Hwy. New age supplies, wiccan, pagan, druid, etc.

LEXINGTON
■ *Accommodations*
INN AT UNION RUN, RR 3, Box 68, (703) 463-9715, (800) 528-6466, Fax: (703) 464-3526. Gay-friendly country inn near Roanoke, full breakfast, private baths, Jacuzzi, AC, nearby lake & river.

VIRGINIA

LURAY

Accommodations
CREEKSIDE: A COUNTRY GUEST COTTAGE, Route 1, Box 338, (540) 743-5040. Gay-friendly cottage a 90-min drive from Washington, DC. Private bath, color TV, AC, fresh-water stream on premises.

NELLYSFORD

Accommodations
MARK ADDY, THE, 56 Rodes Farm Dr, (804) 361-1101, (800) 278-2154. Gay-friendly 1884 country inn located between the Blue Ridge Mountains & Charlottescille. Private baths (1 with double whirlpool bath), bountiful breakfast, AC, down comforters.

Restaurants
BISTRO 151, Hwy 151, in the Valley Green Center, in downtown Nellysford, about 30 mi SW of Charlottesville. Upscale restaurant & bar, seafood & Italian cuisine with jazz music.

NEW MARKET

Accommodations
A TOUCH OF COUNTRY, 9329 Congress St, (540) 740-8030. B&B near caverns & historic points of interest, 50% gay/lesbian clientele. Double rooms decorated with a country flavor. Full breakfast.

NEWPORT NEWS

Bars
CORNER POCKET, 3516 Washington Ave, (757) 247-6366. Pool table.

NORFOLK - VIRGINIA BEACH

Accommodations
CORAL SAND MOTEL, 2307 Pacific Ave, Virginia Beach, (757) 425-0872, (800) 828-0872. Guesthouse & motel **located in the heart of the resort strip,** near a gay beach. Mostly men, women welcome. Rooms with various modern conveniences, in-room telephones, cable color TV, some kitchens, private & shared baths, continental breakfast and a friendly atmosphere. A fun place in the sun. ♂

Beaches
GAY BEACH, between 21st & 24th Sts & 83rd St. Mostly gay.

Bars
AMBUSH,★ 2838 Virginia Beach Blvd, Virginia Beach, (757) 498-4301. Bar & restaurant, pool tables, karaoke, 70% men, women welcome.

DANNNY'S PLACE, 2901 Baltic Ave, Virginia Beach, (757) 428-4016. Restaurant & bar. ♀♂

GARAGE, THE & THE OTHER SIDE,★ 731 Granby St Norfolk, (757) 623-0303. Bar & restaurant, C&W bar, breakfast & lunch. Pool tables on one side, the other side is a dance floor.

MS. P'S, 5401 Tidewater Dr, (757) 853-9717. DJ, pool tables, mostly women, men welcome.

Dance Bar/Disco
CHARLOTTE'S WEB, 6425 Tidewater Dr, Norfolk, (757) 853-5021. Men's night Tue.

CLUB RUMOURS, 4107 Colley Ave, Norfolk, (757) 440-7780.

HERSHEE BAR,★ 6117 E Sewell's Pt Rd (rear entrance) Norfolk, (757) 853-9842. Bar & restaurant.

LATE SHOW,★ 114 E 11th St, Norfolk, (757) 623-3854. Bar & restaurant. Private after-hours dance bar midnite till 8am & boutique. Non-members, ask other bars entrance requirements, or call first.

LEATHER & LACE, 149 E Little Creek Rd, (757) 583-4334.

NUTTY BUDDYS, 143 E Little Creek Rd, Wards Corner, (757) 588-6474. Bar, restaurant & pub. Attic upstairs bar is quiet lounge, 70% men.

PRIVATE EYES, 249 W York St, (757) 533-9290. Open 7 nights for dinner, 90% men.

Retail & Bookstores
LAMBDA RISING BOOKS, 9229 Granby St, Ocean View, (757) 480-6969. Gay & lesbian books, cards, magazines & gifts.

PHOENIX RISING EAST, 808 Spotswood Ave, Norfolk, (757) 622-3701. Gay & lesbian bookstore with cards, magazines & gifts. Call (800) 719-1690 for mail order catalog.

TWO OF A KIND BOOKS, 6123 Sewells Pt Rd, inside Hershee Bar, (757) 857-0223. Women's bookstore.

Erotica
BEACH BOOKS, 1789 Virginia Beach Blvd, Virginia Beach, (757) 425-7830.

FIRESIDE NEWS, 3115 Pacific Ave, Virginia Beach, (757) 425-7271.

SEVENTEENTH ST BOOKS, 325 Virginia Beach Blvd, Virginia Beach, (757) 428-1816.

PORTSMOUTH
See Norfolk/Virginia Beach

RICHMOND

Information
AIDS LINE, (804) 358-6343. Mon-Fri 10am-9pm or tape.

GAY INFO LINE, (804) 967-9311. Recorded information.

Accommodations
BELLMONT MANOR B&B AND SILVER ROOSTER ANTIQUES, 6600 Belmont Rd, (804) 745-0106. Gay-friendly B&B with antique shop, 20 minutes from downtown Richmond. Country gourmet breakfast, air conditioning, private & shared baths, 50% gay & lesbian clientele.

Bars
BROADWAY CAFE, 1624 W Broad St, (804) 355-9931. Lounge & restaurant, 90% men, 10% women, women welcome.

CASABLANCA, 6 E Grace St, (804) 648-2040. Bar, lite menu, 75% men, 25% women.

CLUB COLORS, 534 N Harrison St, (804) 353-9776. Younger crowd, gay Fri-Sun. Call for schedule of women's nites, drag shows & dance nites.

Dance Bar/Disco
BABES OF CARYTOWN, 3166 W Cary St near Auburn, (804) 355-9330. Bar & restaurant, more gay evenings. Patio, DJ Fri & Sat, many men Sun for Sun brunch. C&W dancing Tues, alternative music Thurs.

FIELDEN'S,★ 2033 W Broad St, (804) 359-1963. After hours private club, progressive dance club. Travelers welcome.

RUMORS II, 1008 N Boulevard, (804) 355-9822.

SANCTUARY & CHAPLIN'S GRILL, 2001 E Franklin St, (804) 643-7520. Hi-energy dance club.

Cafe
CAFINE'S, 401 E Grace St, (804) 775-2233. Lunch cafe Tues-Fri. Fri nite mainly straight with live bands, Sat dance club 70% gay & lesbian, 30% straight.

Retail & Bookstores
CARYTOWN BOOKSTORE, 2930 W Cary St at Sheppard, (804) 359-4831. General bookstore with women's & gay selections.

PHOENIX CENTRAL, 19 N Belmont Ave, (804) 355-7939. Gay & lesbian bookstore. Call (800) 719-1690 for mail order catalog.

ROANOKE

Bars
BACKSTREET, 356 Salem Ave, (540) 345-1542. Pool table, dart board, pinball, 7 days. ♀♂

Dance Bar/Disco
CLUB 1919, 434 Church, (540) 343-1919. Dance bar & restaurant.

PARK, THE, 615 Salem Ave SW, (540) 342-0946. Video dance bar, lounge, 70% men, 30% women. Wed, Fri-Sun. Sun drag shows

Restaurants
MAGNOLIA'S, 434 Church, (540) 343-9443. ♀♂

Retail & Bookstores
OUT WORD CONNECTION, 114-A Kirk Ave SW, (540) 985-6886. Gay & lesbian bookstore.

Erotica
ADULT BOOKS, Orange Blvd & Williamson Rd.

CLASSIC VIDEOS, Williamson Rd, about a mile N of Orange.

FERRARI GUIDES' GAY TRAVEL A to Z - 18th EDITION

WASHINGTON

WASHINGTON

WHO TO CALL
For Tour Companies Serving This Destination
See Washington on page 29

BELLINGHAM

■ *Information*
AIDS SUPPORT, (360) 671-0703, crisis center 734-7271.

■ *Accommodations*
MARC-JAMES MANOR, 2925 Vining St, Bellingham, WA 98226, (360) 738-4919. A contemporary interpretation of an English manor house, situated on two acres in the Highland Heights district of Bellingham. The guest suite has a private entrance off a semi-secluded courtyard, queen-sized bed, private bath, wet bar, wood-burning fireplace, and private bath. Relax in the hot tub. Located one hour south of Vancouver and 90 minutes north of Seattle. Some straight clientele. Our specialty: gay & lesbian commitment ceremonies, we arrange for catering. ♀♂

■ *Dance Bar/Disco*
RUMORS, 1317 1/2 N State St, (360) 671-1849. DJ Wed-Sat, opens noon-2am 7 days. ♀♂

■ *Retail & Bookstores*
RAINBOW BRIDGE, 304 W Champion, (360) 715-3684. Gay & lesbian bookstore with coffee & pastries, video rentals, cards, novelties.

■ *Erotica*
GREAT NORTHERN BOOKS, 1308 Railroad Ave near Holly, (360) 733-1650.

MARC-JAMES MANOR
A contemporary interpretation of an English manor house
Commitment ceremonies a specialty
Bellingham WA
(360) 738-4919

CHELAN

■ *Accommodations*
MARY KAY'S ROMANTIC WHALEY MANSION INN, 415 Third St, (509) 682-5735, (800) 729-2408 in USA. Gay-friendly B&B. Elegant Victorian-style rooms with modern conveniences & 5-course candlelight breakfast.

EVERETT

■ *Bars*
EVERETT UNDERGROUND, 1212 California St, (206) 339-0807. DJ Tues & Thurs-Sat, dancing 11am-2am, karaoke Wed & Sun, great Italian food. ♀♂

■ *Retail & Bookstores*
ORION AT TWILIGHT, 2934 B Colby Ave, (206) 303-8624. Books & gifts.

INDEX

■ *Accommodations*
WILD LILY RANCH, PO Box 313, Index WA, (360) 793-2103. B&B, tropical bath house, some straight clientele, women welcome. ♂

KENT

■ *Bars*
SAPPHO'S, 226 1st Ave S, (206) 813-2776. Bar & restaurant. DJ & dancing Fri & Sat. ♀♂

■ *Retail & Bookstores*
NEW WOMAN BOOKS, 326 W Meeker, (206) 854-3487. Feminist & lesbian books.

LA CONNER

■ *Accommodations*
HERON, THE, 117 Maple Ave, PO Box 716, La Conner, WA 98257, (360) 466-4626, 9 rooms & 3 suites in a Victorian-style home, all private baths, expanded continental breakfast.

WHITE SWAN GUEST HOUSE, 1388 Moore Rd Mt Vernon, (360) 445-6805. Gay-friendly B&B. Variety of guest quarters including private cottage. Kitchen privileges, lounge, garden, sun deck, expanded country continental breakfast.

LOPEZ ISLAND

■ *Accommodations*
INN AT SWIFTS BAY, Lopez Island, WA 98261, (360) 468-3636. A Small Inn with a National Reputation...we've gained national recognition as one of the finest accommodations in the beautiful San Juan Islands of Washington State. This elegant country home sits on 3 wooded acres with a private beach nearby. The inn has 5 quiet and romantic guest rooms, 3 with private baths and fireplaces. The hot tub is at the edge of the woods...we provide the robes and slippers. Gay-owned with mix of gay/lesbian and straight clientele.

LUMMI ISLAND

■ *Accommodations*
RETREAT ON LUMMI ISLAND, (360) 671-6371, ask for Mary Ellen or Marie. E-mail: okeefe@pacificrim.net. First-floor of home with 2 bedrooms, kitchen, bath, large living & dining spaces & spectacular views. Plenty of hiking, biking & spectacular views. ♀♂

MARYSVILLE

■ *Accommodations*
EQUINOX INN, 13522 12th Ave NW, Marysville, WA (360) 652-1198. B&B on 2-1/2 acres in the woods on Tulilap Indian reservation, private baths, full breakfast, many outdoor activities, 15- to 30-min drive to casino. Some straight clientele. ♀♂

MORTON

■ *Accommodations*
ST HELENS MANORHOUSE B&B, 7476 Hwy 12, (360) 498-5243. Gay-friendly B&B with gift shop, shared baths.

OCEAN PARK

■ *Accommodations*
SHAKTI COVE COTTAGES, PO Box 385, (360) 665-4000. 10 cottages with private baths, color TV, 5-minute walk to beach, some straight clientele. ♀♂

ORCAS ISLAND

■ *Accommodations*
SWEET CEDAR RETREAT, Rt 1 Box 1238, Eastsound, Phone & Fax: (206) 376-5444. Fully-furnished 1-bedroom cottage, sleeps 4. Color cable TV, telephone, full kitchen. Pool, ocean & lake nearby. ♀♂

■ *Women's Accommodations*
ROSE COTTAGE, Rt 2, Box 951, Eastsound, 98245, (360) 376-2076. Fully-furnished efficiency unit, men welcome. Private bath, ocean beach on premises. ♀

INN AT SWIFTS BAY
A Small Inn with a National Reputation
LOPEZ ISLAND
(360) 468-3636

WASHINGTON

PORT TOWNSEND

■ Accommodations

GAIA'S GETAWAY, 4343 Haines St, (360) 385-1194. Large studio apartment with queen bed, private bath, color cable TV & fully-equipped kitchen. Gay-friendly with a gay & lesbian following.

RAVENSCROFT INN, 533 Quincy St, (360) 385-2784, Fax: (360) 385-6724, (800) 782-2691. Welcome to paradise, your room is ready.... Enjoy colonial hospitality in a Victorian seaport. The Ravenscroft Inn, whose photogenic breakfast room was featured on the front cover of *Inn Places-1994*, looks forward to welcoming you to our special corner of the world: the captivating Olympic Peninsula.

SEATTLE

■ Information

LESBIAN RESOURCE CENTER, 1808 Bellevue Ave E #204, (206) 322-3953, 2pm-7pm Mon-Fri.

■ Accommodations

BACON MANSION, 959 Broadway East, (206) 329-1864, (800) 240-1864, Fax: (206) 860-9025. B&B guesthouse, 40% gay and lesbian clientele. This English Tudor house is in the Harvard-Belmont district on Capitol Hill, one of Seattle's most exciting neighborhoods for dining, sightseeing, nightlife and boutiques. Choose from well-appointed moderate rooms, suites and even a carriage house. Eight rooms have private baths. We have immense, beautifully-decorated day rooms and a large, private patio. Don't miss it!

BED & BREAKFAST ON BROADWAY, 722 Broadway E, Seattle, WA 98102, (206) 329-8933, (888) 329-8933, Fax: (206) 726-0918. B&B with private baths, private baths, expanded continental breakfast, collection of original paintings & artwork by Northwest artists. 50% gay & lesbian clientele.

BELLEVUE PLACE B&B, 1111 Bellevue Place East, Seattle, WA (206) 325-9253, (800) 325-9253, Fax: (206) 455-0785. This 1905 storybook house with leaded glass and Victorian charm is located in the Landmark District of Seattle's Capitol Hill close to restaurants & shops. Three rooms have queen beds, cotton bedding, down comforters and share 2 baths. Full breakfast includes fruits, pastries, pancakes, meats, egg dishes. Parking is available and public transportation is two blocks away. 50% gay & lesbian clientele.

CAPITOL HILL INN, 1713 Belmont Ave, (206) 323-1955, (206) 322-3809. Lavishly furnished 1903 Victorian on Capitol Hill with antiques, fireplaces, brass beds, private baths, full breakfast, non-smoking.

CHAMBERED NAUTILUS, 5005 22nd Ave NE, (206) 522-2536, Fax: (206) 528-0898. Gay-friendly B&B. Private & shared baths, full breakfast, nearby lake.

COUNTRY INN, 685 NW Juniper St, Issaquah, (206) 392-1010, fax: (206) 392-9110. B&B in the middle of 5 acres, 50% gay & lesbian. Rooms with private baths, refrigerator, AC & maid service. Expanded continental breakfast.

GASLIGHT INN, 1727 15th Ave, (206) 325-3654, Fax: (206) 238-4803. Guesthouse minutes from downtown, some straight clientele. Comfortable & unique double rooms with modern conveniences. Living room, library, continental breakfast, beverages, fruit. Smoke-free indoors.

HILL HOUSE BED & BREAKFAST, 1113 E John St, (206) 720-7161, (800) 720-7161, Fax: (206) 323-0772, E-mail: http://uspan.com/hillhouse. Experience the Romance! Gay-owned B&B in a recently restored 1903 Victorian home on Capitol Hill, minutes from downtown attractions, dining, shopping and nightlife. 50% gay and lesbian clientele. **Five romantically decorated rooms with down comforters,** a variety of color schemes, private and shared baths and private entrances. Full gourmet breakfast, off-street parking. Non-smoking environment.

ISLAND WITHIN BED & BREAKFAST, THE, PO Box 2241, (206) 567-4177. B&B cottage, men welcome, some straight clientele. Accommodates up to 10. Kitchen, washer & dryer, private yard & garden. With or without full breakfast.

LANDES HOUSE, 712 11th Ave E, (206) 329-8781, (888) 329-8781, Fax: (206) 324-0934. B&B, some straight clientele. Private & shared baths, hot tub, expanded continental breakfast.

ROBERTA'S B&B, 1147 16th Ave E, Seattle, WA 98112, (206) 329-3326, Fax: (206) 324-2149. E-mail: robertasbb@aol.com. Gay-friendly B&B with private baths, full "wild-west-sized" breakfast, near Volunteer Park & Broadway.

SCANDIA HOUSE, 2028 34th Ave S, (206) 725-7825, Fax: 721-3348. B&B with lake & mountain views, 50% gay & lesbian clientele. Color TV, phone, king bed & private bath. Expanded continental breakfast.

■ Transportation

FIRST CLASS LIMOUSINE, (206) 329-5395, (800) 225-6717, www.limo.com. Woman drivers.

■ Bars

C.C. ATTLES, 1501 E Madison, bar: (206) 726-0565, grille: (206) 323-4017. Bar & restaurant with full liquor, intimate veranda bar. ♂

CHANGES, 2103 N 45th St, Wallingford, (206) 545-8363. Video bar. ♂

CRESCENT, THE, 1413 E Olive Way. Horseshoe bar, jukebox & pool table. Sun piano bar. ♂

CUFF, 1533 13th Ave, (206) 323-1525. Leather, levi bar, pool table. Big for Sun beer bust! ♂

DOUBLE HEADER, 407 2nd Ave, (206) 464-9918. Oldest gay bar in Seattle. ♂

ELITE II, 1658 E Olive Way, (206) 322-7334. Pool table, darts, micro brews, good mix of men & women.

ELITE TAVERN, ★ 622 Broadway Ave E at Roy, (206) 324-4470. Popular daytime bar. ♂

HAMBURGER MARY'S, ★ 1525 E Olive Way, (206) 324-8112. Bar & restaurant, 60% men, 40% women. ♀ ♂

HANA'S RESTAURANT & LOUNGE, 1914 8th Ave near Greyhound terminal, (206) 340-1591, (206) 340-1536. ♂

JADE PAGODA, 606 Broadway, (206) 322-5900. Lunch & dinner, stiff drinks & average Chinese food. ♂

MADISON PUB, 1315 E Madison, (206) 325-

Bacon Mansion
Seattle's Finest B & B 
(800) 240-1864

HILL HOUSE
Bed & Breakfast
http://uspan.com/hillhouse
(206) 720-7161 • (800) 720-7161
1113 E. JOHN ST., SEATTLE, WA.

Bellevue Place B&B
A 1905 Storybook House
(800) 325-9253
(206) 325-9253
SEATTLE

FERRARI GUIDES' GAY TRAVEL A to Z - 18th EDITION

WASHINGTON

Women's Sailing Adventures

Izarra and her women crews have sailed to SE Alaska, Vancouver Island and throughout the San Juan Islands off the coast of Washington State. In this beautiful area, when hiking and exploring ashore, days are filled with sightings of dolphin, whales, eagles and numerous sea birds, and you'll often encounter traces of early Native American culture. Izarra cruises using wind and current and anchors in protected coves, or docks at picturesque towns. Izarra is a smoke-free environment.

Izarra holds four women and their Coast Guard licensed skipper. Delightful, healthy meals feature fresh seafood. All skill levels are welcome, and everyone participates in a supportive atmosphere. You'll learn helmswomanship, navigation, anchoring and docking, rules of the road, handling lines and knots, trimming the sails. Each voyage is divided into 2-week legs. Women can sign on for the whole voyage, or one or more legs. A cruise amongst Australia's Whitsunday Islands and the Great Barrier Reef is planned for Sept 24-Oct. 8, 1997.

Contact **Izarra Cruises** at (206) 789-2175.

6537. Darts & pool table, beer imports.

R PLACE, 619 E Pine St, (206) 322-8828. Sports bar, 3 levels, games, micro brews, sweater queens.

SEA WOLF SALOON, 1413 14th Ave near Union, (206) 323-2158. Darts & pool tables. A bit of the Leather Daddy crowd. May change format in '97.

SEATTLE EAGLE, 314 E Pike St, (206) 621-7591. Late-nite bar (after midnite).

SONYA'S BAR & GRILL, 1532 7th Ave near Pike, (206) 624-5377. Opens 6am, full liquor.

SPAGS TAVERN, 1118 E Pike, (206) 322-3232. Bear bar.

THUMPER'S, 1500 E Madison, (206) 328-3800. Video bar and restaurant, upscale clientele.

WILDROSE, 1021 E Pike at 11th, (206) 324-9210. Beer, wine & espresso, non-alcoholic drinks, desserts, smoke-free area.

Dance Bar/Disco

EASY, THE, 916 E Pike, (206) 323-8343. DJ Thurs-Sat, darts & pool table. Full-service restaurant.

KID MOHAIR, 1207 Pine at Melrose, (206) 625-4444. Modern East Village type bar, dance bar with beer, wine, music, closed Mon.

MR PADDYWACK'S, 722 E Pike St near Harvard. Male strippers continuously & table dancers, open Sun-Thurs 8pm-3am.

NEIGHBOURS,★ 1509 Broadway near Pike (enter rear alley), (206) 324-5358. High tech dance & cruise bar, younger crowd. Buffet Fri & Sat, 90% men, 10% women.

RE-BAR,★ 1114 Howell St, (206) 233-9873. Always gay-friendly. Thurs Queer Night, very popular, Sat Queen's nite out. Gay comedy most weekends. Women's dance last Sat of month.

TIMBERLINE,★ 2015 Boren Ave, (206) 622-6220. C&W dance bar, 60% men, 40% women, straight following. Closed Mon.

Cafe

BATTERY CAFE, 2331 2nd Ave, (206) 441-9240. Outdoor seating, micros, wine. Breakfast, lunch, dinner.

BEYOND THE EDGE CAFE, 703 E Pike, (206) 325-6829. Daily specials, art shows.

ROSEBUD ESPRESSO & BISTRO, 719 E Pike, (206) 323-6536. Espresso/cappuccino cafe with desserts. Lunch, dinner Sat, Sun brunch.

Saunas/Health Clubs

BASIC PLUMBING, 1104 Pike near Boren, (206) 682-8441. Private club. Mon-Thurs from 7pm, Fri from 6pm, Sat & Sun 1pm-4am.

CLUB SEATTLE,★ 1520 Summit Ave, (206) 329-2334. X-rated videos, 24hrs.

CLUB Z, 1117 Pike St near Boren, (206) 622-9958. Private club, opens 4pm.

SOUTH END STEAM BATHS, 115-1/2 1st Ave S at Pioneer Square, (206) 223-9091. Heated pool, wet steam.

Restaurants

CADILLAC GRILLE, 1501 E Madison at CC Slaughter's bar, (206) 323-4017. '50's Grandma cooking, take-out bakery, hand-packed ice cream.

GIORGINA'S ITALIAN KITCHEN, 131 15th Ave E, (206) 329-8118. Pizza, sandwiches, pasta, espresso.

GLO'S, 1621 E Olive Way, (206) 324-2577. Breakfast & lunch, gay-friendly.

HAMBURGER MARY'S, Olive Way at Denny, (206) 324-8112. Bar & restaurant.

JACK'S BISTRO, 405 15th E, (206) 324-9625. Dining patio.

NIKKO, 1900 5th Ave, (206) 322-4641.

RHODODENDRON, 1006 Spring St, (206) 223-7654.

SIMPATICO, 4430 Wallingford Ave N, (206) 632-1000. Italian bistro.

TANGIER, 1556 E Olive Way, (206) 324-1808. Moroccan & Mediterranean cuisine.

THUMPER'S, 1500 E Madison at Thumper's bar, (206) 328-3800. Restaurant & bar, patio dining area, Sun brunch 10am-4pm.

VILLA MARIETTA'S, 345 15th Ave E, (206) 325-8911.

Retail & Bookstores

BAILEY-COY BOOKS, 414 Broadway E near Harrison, (206) 323-8842. General bookstore with gay & lesbian section.

BEYOND THE CLOSET BOOKSTORE, 518 E Pike St, (206) 322-4609. Gay & lesbian bookstore, Sun-Thurs 10am-10pm, Fri & Sat 10am-11pm.

PINK ZONE, 211 Broadway East, (206) 325-0050. Gay & lesbian gift shop. Body piercing.

RED & BLACK BOOKS, 432 15th Ave E, (206) 322-7323. General bookstore with small gay & lesbian section.

Leathers/Piercing

CRYPT, THE, 1310 E Union St near 14th, (206) 325-3882. Safe-sex toys, video sales & rentals, magazines, lubes, lotions.

ONYX LEATHER, 1605 12th Ave #8, (206) 328-1965. By appointment.

PLAYSPACE LTD., 1512 11th, (206) 329-0324. Body piercing, scarification, branding.

TATOO YOU, 1017 E Pike St, (206) 324-6443. Tattoo studio, Tue-Sat 1pm-8pm.

Erotica

ADULT ENTERTAINMENT CENTER (AEC), 120 Pike St, upstairs, (206) 622-9984.

BLUE VIDEO, 4210 Aurora North, North Seattle, (206) 632-9886.

WEST VIRGINIA

CHAMPS ARCADE, 1510 1st Ave, (206) 624-1784.
FANTASY UNLIMITED, 102 Pike St corner of 1st, (206) 682-0167.
JERRY'S ADULT, 120 Pike St.
SPANKY'S, 3276 California Ave SW, West Seattle, (206) 938-3400.
TABOO VIDEO, 1012 1st Ave, (206) 622-7399. Also: 1012 First Ave, 622-7399. Arcades.
TOYS IN BABELAND, 711 E Pike St, (206) 328-2914. Adult toys, etc, for women.
WORLD WIDE VIDEO, 1585 Pacific Coast Hwy at SEA TAC airport, (206) 244-2291. Also: 12700 Aurora Ave N, 363-0768; 7830 Bothell Way NE, 485-0838.

SPOKANE

■ *Dance Bar/Disco*
DEMPSEY'S BRASS RAIL, W 909 1st St, (509) 747-5362. Disco & restaurant, 50% men, 50% women.
HOUR PLACE, W 415 Sprague at Hour Place bar, (509) 838-6947. Dance bar & restaurant.
JS PUMPS!!, W 4 Main, (509) 747-8940. 50% men, 50% women (Fri 60% women).

■ *Retail & Bookstores*
AUNTIE'S BOOKSTORE, 313 W Riverside, (509) 838-0206. General bookstore with a gay & lesbian section.

■ *Erotica*
MISS KITTY'S, 6311 E Sprague Ave, (509) 535-2378.
PARADISE BOOKSTORE, 12122 E Sprague Ave, (509) 926-7931.
SPOKANE ARCADE, 1125 W 1st Ave, (509) 747-1621.

TACOMA

■ *Information*
TACOMA LESBIAN CONCERN (TLC), (206) 472-0422. Charitable support group, monthly newsletter, resource list, social group. Travelers welcome.

■ *Accommodations*
CHINABERRY HILL, 302 Tacoma Ave, (206) 272-1282. B&B in a Victorian home, near waterfront shops & theaters.

■ *Dance Bar/Disco*
GOLD BALL TAVERN, 2708 6th Ave, (206) 627-0430. Full liquor, patio, gambling, 80% women, dancing weekends.
SEVEN THIRTY-THREE, 733 Commerce St. Restaurant, bar, disco, full liquor, DJ Fri & Sat, 70% men, 30% women.
TWENTY-FOURTH ST TAVERN, 2409 Pacific Ave, (206) 572-3748. Dance, show & cruise bar, DJ Fri & Sat.

■ *Erotica*
ELMO'S BOOKSTORE #2, 5440 S Tacoma Way, (206) 474-9871.
ELMO'S BOOKSTORE #5, 3922 100th St SW, Lakewood, (206) 582-3329.
JERRY'S ADULT BOOKSTORE, 12626 Pacific Hwy SW, Lakewood, (206) 588-7668.
JERRY'S MECCA THEATER, 755 Broadway, (206) 272-4700. Magazines, videos.

VANCOUVER

■ *Dance Bar/Disco*
NORTH BANK TAVERN, 106 W 6th St, (360) 695-3862. Juke box dancing, patio, lite menu, open 7 days 12pm-2am, 60% men, 40% women.

WHIDBEY ISLAND - LANGLEY

■ *Accommodations*
GALITTOIRE, 5444 S Coles Rd, Langley, (360) 221-0548. Gay-owned, gay-friendly contemporary guesthouse in the woods. TV lounge, video tape library, business services, full breakfast. Ideal for executive retreats, weddings & union ceremonies, 35% gay/lesbian clientele.
GALLERY SUITE, PO Box 458, Langley, (360) 221-2978. B&B on the waterfront, 50% gay & lesbian clientele. Private apartment with kitchen, continental breakfast, snacks & nearby gym.

WEST VIRGINIA STATEWIDE

See also **District of Columbia.** Some locations close to Washington, DC, are listed there instead of under their WV cities.

BERKELEY SPRINGS

■ *Erotica*
ACTION BOOKS, VIDEOS, Route 522 S, (304) 258-2529, 24hrs.

CHARLESTON

■ *Bars*
TAP ROOM, 1022 Quarry at Broad, (304) 342-9563. Mostly gay clientele.

■ *Dance Bar/Disco*
BROADWAY, THE, 210 Broad Street, (304) 343-2162. Mon-Thurs 4pm-3am, Fri 4pm-4am, Sat 1pm-3am. DJ Wed-Sun, patio, Sun tea dance 4pm-8pm. 75% men, 25% women.
GRAND PALACE, 617 Brooks St near Smith, (304) 345-0377. Disco & show bar. DJ 7 nights, videos, patio, 50% men, 50% women.

■ *Restaurants*
LEE ST. DELI, Lee St near Broad St.

ELKINS

■ *Accommodations*
RETREAT AT BUFFALO RUN, 214 Harpertown Rd, (304) 636-2960. Gay-friendly B&B. Double rooms with shared baths, common rooms, large porch, full breakfast. Nearby lakes & mountain streams.

HUNTINGTON

■ *Bars*
BEEHIVE, 1121 7th Ave above the Driftwood bar, (304) 696-9858. Show bar, Beehive dance bar open Fri-Sun, 60% men, 40% women.

■ *Dance Bar/Disco*
DRIFTWOOD, 1121 7th Ave near 12th St, (304) 696-9858. 60% men, 40% women.
POLO CLUB, 733 7th Ave (rear), (304) 522-3146. Drag shows Sat & Sun, DJ Wed, Fri, Sat, Sun (opens early Sun).
STONEWALL, 820 7th Ave, (304) 528-9317.

■ *Erotica*
BOOKMARK VIDEO, 1119 4th Ave near 11th St, (304) 525-6861.
HOUSE OF VIDEO, 1109 4th Ave, (304) 525-2194. Theater & bookstore.

HUTTONSVILLE

■ *Accommodations*
RICHARD'S COUNTRY INN, US 219, Rte 1, Box 11-A-1, Huttonsville 26273, (304) 335-6659, (800) 636-7434. In the Potomac Highlands of rural West Virginia just 4-1/2 hours from Washington, DC. Gay-friendly B&B inn and cottage with restaurant and bar in a restored pre-Civil-War mansion. Private and shared baths, TV lounge, full breakfast. Close to state parks, national forest and many outdoor activities such as mountain bike tours, horseback riding, cave exploration, hiking, trout fishing, whitewater rafting and golfing. Public pool and river nearby.

MARTINSBURG

■ *Accommodations*
BOYDVILLE, THE INN AT MARTINSBURG, 601 S Queen St, (304) 263-1448. Gay-friendly B&B, private baths.

Richard's Country Inn
4½ HRS FROM DC
(304) 335-6659
Huttonsville, WV

FERRARI GUIDES' GAY TRAVEL A to Z - 18th EDITION

WEST VIRGINIA

MORGANTOWN

■ *Erotica*
VARIETY BOOKS, VIDEO, 255 N Queen St, rear entry, (304) 263-4334, 24hrs.

■ *Information*
GAY & LESBIAN HELPLINE, (304) 292-GAY2 (4292). Irregularly staffed eves & weekends or tape.

■ *Bars*
PINK FLAMINGO, 1301 University Ave.

■ *Dance Bar/Disco*
CLASS ACT, 335 High St (rear), (304) 292-2010. occasional male & female strippers, 10% alternative straight crowd, 50% men, 50% women.

PINK TRIANGLE, 417 Holland Ave, Westover, (304) 292-6722. Mixed, but slightly more women, especially Sat.

■ *Erotica*
OTHER BOOKSTORE, THE, Spruce St at Walnut.

SELECT VIDEOS, Walnut St near Spruce. Arcade.

PARKERSBURG

■ *Bars*
DIFFERENT STROKES, Market St, (304) 485-5113.

WHEELING

■ *Dance Bar/Disco*
DREAM HARBOR, 1107 Main St, (304) 232-9822. Occasional buffets, strippers & comedy artists, pool table, video games. Open Thurs-Sat 6pm-3am

TRICKS, 1429 Market St (rear) behind Market St News, (304) 232-1267.

■ *Erotica*
MARKET ST NEWS, 1437 Market St, (304) 232-2414, 24hrs.

WISCONSIN

WHO TO CALL
For Tour Companies Serving This Destination
See Wisconsin on page 29

APPLETON

■ *Bars*
RASCALS BAR & GRILL, 702 E Wisconsin Ave, (414) 954-9262. Cocktail lounge, quiet conversation. Outdoor bar & picnic area, BBQs, pig roasts, lite grill menu.

BELOIT

■ *Cafe*
UNCOMMON GROUNDS CAFE, 414 E Grand, (608) 362-0773.

■ *Retail & Bookstores*
A DIFFERENT WORLD, 414 E Grand Ave, (608) 365-1000. Women's & children's books, gifts, boutique items, arts, crafts & mail order. Women's groups meet here. Closed Sun.

■ *Erotica*
NAUGHTY BUT NICE, 3503 E County Rd S, (608) 362-9090, 24hrs.

DELAVAN

■ *Accommodations*
ALLYN MANSION INN, THE, 511 E Walworth Ave, (414) 728-9090, Fax: (414) 728-0201. Gay-friendly B&B in award-winning restored mansion with authentic Victorian antique furnishings. Shared baths, AC, some working fireplaces, full breakfast. Strictly a no smoking environment.

EAGLE RIVER

■ *Accommodations*
EDGEWATER INN MOTEL AND RESORT, THE, 5054 Hwy 70 West, (715) 479-4011 (tel/fax, call first), Toll-free: (888) EDGEWTR (334-3987). E-mail: edgewater@edgeinn.com. Gay-friendly motel, inn & resort with cottages, near lakes. Private baths, color cable TV, coffee/tea-making facilities, phones, fax, maid, & laundry service, 50% gay & lesbian clientele.

EAU CLAIRE

■ *Information*
AIDS INFO, (715) 836-7710.

■ *Bars*
SCOOTERS, 411 Galloway, (715) 835-9959.

WOLFE'S DEN, THE, 302 E Madison St, (715) 832-9237. 75% men, 25% women.

■ *Dance Bar/Disco*
TRADING COMPANY, THE, 304 Eau Claire St, (715) 838-9494. Dance bar & restaurant, restaurant open Fri & Sat till 4am. DJ Fri & Sat, male dancers & drag shows monthly. Opens 9pm, Tues-Thurs 7pm-2am, Fri & Sat 9pm-2:30am.

■ *Erotica*
ADULT BOOK & NOVELTY, 129 N Barstow, (715) 835-7292.

VIDEO UNLIMITED, 1518 Bellinger St, (715) 834-3393. Closed Sun.

GREEN BAY

■ *Information*
AIDS INFO, (414) 437-7400 or tape. In WI, outside of Green Bay (800) 675-9400. Mon-Thurs 8:30am-4:30pm, Fri till 12:30pm.

AIDS PROJECT, (414) 733-2068.

■ *Bars*
BRANDY'S II, 1126 Main Street. 70% men.

JAVA'S, 1106 Main St, (414) 435-5476. Lounge with Za's dance bar.

NAPALESE LOUNGE 515 S Broadway near Clinton, (414) 432-9646. Closed, may reopen.

SASS, 840 S Broadway, (414) 437-7277. Women's sports bar, videos, pool table, foosball, darts.

■ *Dance Bar/Disco*
ZA'S, 1106 Main St near Webster, (414) 435-5476. Video dance & show bar, 50% gay, 50% straight. Java's lounge is inside Za's.

■ *Erotica*
FANTASY WORLD, 163 N Broadway, (414) 432-6577.

MAIN ATTRACTION, 1614 Main, (414) 465-6969, 24hrs, motel in rear.

MOVIELAND, 836 S Broadway, (414) 433-9640. 24hrs.

PARADISE, 1122 Main St near Webster, (414) 432-9498.

HAYWARD

■ *Accommodations*
LAKE HOUSE BED & BREAKFAST, N 5793 Division Rd (on the lake), Stone Lake, WI 54876, (715) 865-6803, 80% gay & lesbian clientele, private baths.

LA CROSSE

■ *Bars*
RAINBOW'S END, 417 Jay St, (608) 782-9802. Small dance floor, pool tables.

■ *Dance Bar/Disco*
CAVALIER, THE, 114 5th Ave N, (608) 782-9061. DJ Fri, Sat, 60% men, 40% women.

■ *Retail & Bookstores*
RAINBOW REVOLUTION BOOKSTORE, 122 5th Ave S, (608) 796-0383. Gay & lesbian bookstore. Fiction, non-fiction, metaphysics, alternative spirituality.

■ *Erotica*
BEST BUYS BOOKSTORE, 314 Jay Street, (608) 784-6350, 7 days.

PURE PLEASURE, 407 South 3rd Street, (608) 785-1912.

LA FARGE

■ *Accommodations*
TRILLIUM, Rte 2, Box 121, (608) 625-4492. Gay-Friendly B&B cottage.

LAKE GENEVA

■ *Accommodations*
ELEVEN GABLES INN ON THE LAKE, 493

WISCONSIN

Wrigley Dr, (414) 248-8393, (800) 362-0395. Gay-friendly B&B, private baths, expanded continental breakfast (wknd/holiday: full breakfast), color cable TV, ceiling fans, AC, lake on premises.

LAKE MILLS

Bars
CROSS ROADS BAR, W 664d Hwy B, (414) 648-8457. Tues-Sun 1pm till late (later Fri & Sat), 50% men, 50% women.

MADISON

Information
APPLE ISLAND, meets at 953 Jennifer St, The Wilmar Center, (608) 258-9777. Women's cultural & events space, dances Sat. Travelers welcome.

CAMPUS WOMEN'S CENTER, at Univ of Wisconsin, 710 University Ave, Rm 202, (608) 262-8093. Lesbian groups meet here.

GAY & LESBIAN PHONE LINE, (608) 255-4297, 255-8582, 255-0743. Mon-Fri 9am-9pm or tape.

WI AIDS HOTLINE, (800) 334-2437 in Wisconsin only.

Accommodations
CHASE ON THE HILL BED & BREAKFAST, 11624 State Road 26, Milton, (608) 868-6646. Farmhouse B&B, 50% gay & lesbian clientele. 3 rooms with double or queen beds, private & shared baths. TV lounge, full breakfast & nearby lake.

PRAIRIE GARDEN B&B, W 13172 Hwy 188, Lodi, WI 53555, (608) 592-5187, (800) 380-8427. B&B on a farm 1/2 hour north of Madison, near canoeing, fishing & nude beach.

Beaches
MAZOMANIE BEACH, west of Madison on the Wisconsin River. Nude beach, more gay at west end.

Bars
GERALDINE'S, 3052 E Washington, (608) 241-9335. 2 bars: Men's Room men's cruise bar & a women's dance bar. Patio with volleyball court, Sun BBQs in summer. Also restaurant with sandwiches & steaks.

MAD BAR, 150 S Blair St (same building as Manouvres), (608) 258-9918. Pool, darts, videos.

SCANDALS, 119 Main St, (608) 251-1030.

SHAMROCK, 117 W Main St, (608) 255-5059. Bar & grill. More gay evenings.

Dance Bar/Disco
CARDINAL, 418 E Wilson St at Franklin, (608) 251-0080. Alternative hi-energy dance bar, gay night Thurs.

MANOEUVRES, 150 S Blair St, (608) 258-9918, manoeu9918@aol.com. Video dance bar, DJ Tues-Sun, shows Sun, open 7 days, 80% men, 20% women.

Restaurants
RAY'S CAFE, 3052 E Washington Ave, inside Geraldine's gay bar, (608) 241-9335. Serving till 4am.

Retail & Bookstores
A ROOM OF ONE'S OWN, 317 W Johnson St near State, (608) 257-7888. Women's books and gifts and information center.

MIMOSA COMMUNITY BOOKSTORE, 212 N Henry, (608) 256-5432. General bookstore with gay & lesbian sections.

PIC-A-BOOK, 506 State Street, (608) 256-1125. General bookstore with gay & lesbian selections.

RAINBOW BOOKSTORE CO-OP, 426 W Gilman, (608) 257-6050. Feminist bookstore with men's section.

WE ARE FAMILY, 524 E Wilson, (608) 258-9006, wfam9006@aol.com. Gay & lesbian gift shop with espresso served. Rainbow items, jewelry, books, videos, t-shirts, open Tues-Sun.

Erotica
FOUR STAR VIDEO HEAVEN, 315 N Henry St, (608) 255-1994. Items for gay men & women.

RED LETTER NEWS, 2528 E Washington, (608) 241-9958, 24hrs.

STATE STREET ARCADE, 113 State St, (608) 251-4540, 24hrs.

MAUSTON

Camping & RV
CK'S OUTBACK, W5627 Clark Rd, (608) 847-5247. Campground and 3-bedroom guest house on 77-1/2 acres of Womyn-Only land with trails throughout the property. Campsites set high on a wooded ridge. For winter fun we have x-country ski trails and miles of snowmobile trails. Downhill skiing nearby. Social gatherings and activities available. Boys allowed up to age 10.

MILWAUKEE

Information
AIDS LINE, (414) 273-AIDS (2437). Mon-Thur 9-9. Fri 9-6 or tape.

GAY INFO LINE, (414) 444-7331. Irregularly staffed, but frequently available.

LESBIAN ALLIANCE METRO MILWAUKEE, (414) 264-2600. Tape, calls are returned.

Accommodations
SILVER MAPLE INN, THE, 2927 South 31st St, Milwaukee, WI 53215, (414) 389-1595. B&B with shared baths, full breakfast, AC, near St Luke's Medical Center, 50% gay & lesbian clientele.

Bars
B'S, 1579 S 2nd St, (414) 672-5580.

BALLGAME, 196 S 2nd St at Pittsburgh, (414) 273-7474. Women welcome.

BOOT CAMP SALOON, ★ 209 E National at Barclay, (414) 643-6900. Patio.

C'EST LA VIE, 231 S 2nd St near Oregon, (414) 291-9600. Cruise bar, younger crowd.

FANNIE'S, ★ 200 E Washington Ave at Barclay, (414) 643-9633. DJ on Sat. Patio, men welcome.

IN BETWEEN, 625 S 2nd St, (414) 273-2693.

KATHY'S NUT HUT, 1500 W Scott, (414) 647-2673. Occasional live entertainment.

M & M CLUB, 124 N Water St at Erie, (414) 347-1962. Piano bar, popular cocktail hour, Sun brunch. 70% men, 30% women.

MAMA ROUX, 1875 N Humboldt, (414) 347-0344. Burgers, soups, Creole items.

RENE'S COZY CORNER, 3500 W Park Hill, (414) 933-7363. DJ weekends, 70% men, 30% women.

S. WATER ST. DOCKS, 354 E National, (414) 225-9676. Front & back bar.

STATION 2, 1534 W Grant, (414) 383-5755. Patio in summer, slightly more mature crowd, men welcome.

TEN PERCENT CLUB, 4322 W Fond du Lac Ave near Sherman, (414) 447-0910. Darts, jukebox with Jazz music, 70% gay (50/50 men & women), 30% straight clientele.

THE 1100 CLUB, 1100 S 1st, (414) 647-9950.

THIS IS IT, 418 E Wells St, (414) 278-9192.

TRIANGLE BAR, ★ 135 E National Ave at Barclay, (414) 383-9412. Videos, patio, mixed ages.

ZIPPERS, 819 S 2nd St, (414) 645-8330. From 3pm, Sat & Sun from 2pm.

Dance Bar/Disco
CLUB 219, ★ 219 S 2nd St near Oregon, (414) 271-3732. Upstairs dance bar, 50% men, 50% women. Downstairs cruisy video bar.

JUST US, 807 S 5th St, (414) 383-2233. DJ Fri & Sat. Sat 50% men, 50% women.

LA CAGE & DANCE DANCE DANCE, ★ 801 S 2nd St at National, (414) 383-8330. Dance, video & show bar, 70% men, 30% women (sometimes more), Grubb's Pub has after hours food.

Cafe
CAFE KNICKERBOCKER, 1030 E Juneau Ave, (414) 272-0011.

Restaurants
CAFE MELANGE, 720 N Old World (3rd) near Wisconsin, (414) 291-9889. Lunch, dinner, cabaret, gay-friendly.

GRUBB'S PUB, 801 S 2nd St at La Cage bar, (414) 383-8330. After hours restaurant.

LA PERLA, 734 S 5th, (414) 645-9888. Mexican cuisine.

FERRARI GUIDES' GAY TRAVEL A to Z - 18th EDITION   505

WISCONSIN

FYI

Trail Riding for Women

Bar H Ranch conducts individualized horse pack and trail riding trips into the wilderness areas and high country of Wyoming's Grand Tetons.

Trail Riding in the Tetons Explore two hundred miles of trails from a comfortable base camp. Enjoy remote back country and majestic views of peaks and glacial lakes. Campfire cooking and equipment furnished, except sleeping bags.

Ranch Riding & Loft Accommodations Spend a week at the ranch in deluxe loft accommodations for two with fully-equipped kitchen. Saddle your own horse for daily ranch riding. Check fences. Move cattle. Take a privately-guided trail ride into the high country. Or relax, hike, fish, read, drive to nearby Yellowstone Park.

Tipi Experience Your genuine Sioux tipi is made of canvas and set in a private wooded pasture. The location is surrounded by willows and aspens. The tipi is large enough to accommodate 4 people, with nearby private bath, dressing room, kitchen and sunny deck. Ranch activities are easily accessible.

Contact **Bar H Ranch** at (800) 247-1444 or wite PO Box 297, Driggs, ID 83422.

M&M CLUB RESTAURANT, 124 N Water St at M & M bar. Lunch & dinner, Sun brunch, 80% men.

MAMA ROUX BAR AMERICAIN & GRILL, 1875 N Humboldt.

WALKER'S POINT CAFE, 1106 S 1st Street, (414) 384-7999. Open 10pm-5am only, popular after-hrs restaurant.

WILD THYME CAFE, 231 E Buffalo, (414) 276-3144. Lunch & brunch only.

■ *Retail & Bookstores*

AFTERWORDS, 2710 N Murray Ave, (414) 963-9089. Gay & lesbian bookstore with espresso bar. Mon-Thur 10am-10pm, Fri & Sat 10am-11pm, Sun noon-6pm.

DESIGNING MEN, 1200 S 1st St, (414) 389-1200. Exclusive gay & lesbian gift & jewelry store.

■ *Erotica*

J & R NEWS, 831 N 27th St, (414) 344-9686, 24hrs.

LIBRA ADULT BOOKS, 2945 S 13th St, (414) 647-9090, 24hrs.

PARADISE VIDEO, 227 Water St near Wisconsin, (414) 278-8900. Rentals only, 7 days.

POPULAR NEWS, 225 N Water St, (414) 278-0636, 7 days.

NORWALK

■ *Women's Accommodations*

DOE FARM, c/o WWLC, Rt 2 Box 150, Norwalk, 54649, (608) 269-5301. Women-only lodge & camping.

OGDENSBURG

■ *Tours, Charters & Excursions*

QUIET TRAILS, PO Box 85, Ogdensburg, WI 54962, (414) 244-7823. Day canoe trips with shuttle, extended canoe camping (3-5 days) & canoes for rent. Mostly women, men welcome.

OSHKOSH

■ *Erotica*

PURE PLEASURE, 1212 Oshkosh Ave, (414) 235-9727.

SUPREME VIDEO, 945 N Washburn, (414) 235-2012, 24hrs.

RACINE - KENOSHA

■ *Bars*

WHAT ABOUT ME?, 600 6th St, (414) 632-0171. 60% women, 40% men.

■ *Dance Bar/Disco*

CLUB 94, 9001 120th Ave (Hwy 194 & Hwy C, exit 345), Kenosha, (414) 857-9958. DJ wknds, videos, 60% men, 40% women, closed Sun & Mon.

JODEE'S INT'L, 2139 Racine St at 22nd St, (414) 634-9804. Dance & show bar, DJ wknds, summer BBQs, 60% men, 40% women. From 7pm.

■ *Erotica*

CROSSROADS, 9230 120th Ave near I-94, (414) 857-2771, 24hrs.

RACINE NEWS & VIDEO, 316 S Main St near 3rd, (414) 857-7773. 7 days.

SUPERB VIDEO II, 6005 120th Ave, Kenosha, (414) 857-9922.

SHEBOYGAN

■ *Bars*

BLUE LITE, 1029 N 8th St, (414) 457-1636. Lounge with upscale atmosphere, 70-80% men, good late-nite crowd 11pm-2:30am. Open Sun-Thurs 2pm-2am, Fri-Sat 2pm-2:30am.

■ *Restaurants*

TRATTORIA STEFANO, 522 S 8th St, (414) 452-8455. Italian cuisine.

STURGEON BAY - DOOR COUNTY

■ *Accommodations*

CHANTICLEER GUESTHOUSE, 4072 Cherry Rd, (414) 746-0334. Inn in a turn-of-the-century farmhouse 40 minutes from Green Bay, 50% gay & lesbian clientele. All rooms have private baths & fireplaces. Heated pool, sauna, expanded continental breakfast.

SUPERIOR

■ *Bars*

TRIO, 820 Tower Ave, (715) 392-5373.

■ *Dance Bar/Disco*

JT BAR & GRILL, 1506 N 3rd, (715) 394-2580. Dance bar & restaurant with burgers & pizza, 50% men, 50% women, DJ Fri & Sat, karaoke Thurs.

WASCOTT

■ *Women's Accommodations*

WILDERNESS WAY RESORT & CAMPGROUND, PO Box 176, (715) 466-2635. Women-only resort campground on lake. Fully-furnished cabins with private baths, 6 electric hookups, 20 tent sites, showers & restrooms, common room with fireplace. Boat & canoe use with cabin rental.

WATERLOO

■ *Information*

MODE THEATER 121 S Monroe St, (414) 478-9632, (800) 280-9632, Fax: (414) 478-9630. Gay & lesbian art shows, theater, concerts. Planning a center for commitment ceremonies.

WAUKESHA

■ *Retail & Bookstores*

BY THE LIGHT OF THE MOON, 880 N Grand Ave, (414) 574-7651. Bookstore specializing in books by women authors & on women's health, Tues & Wed 10am-5pm, Thurs & Fri 10am-6pm, Sat 10am-4pm.

WYOMING

GOOD EARTH, 340 W Main St, (414) 521-0664. New age & spirituality books.

MARTHA MERRELL'S BOOKSTORE, 228 W Main St, (414) 547-1060. General bookstore with women's studies & feminist selections.

WAUSAU

■ *Dance Bar/Disco*

MAD HATTER, 320 Washington, (715) 842-3225. 70% men, 30% women. DJ Sat. ■♂♂

WYOMING

WHO TO CALL
For Tour Companies Serving This Destination
See Wyoming on page 29

CHEYENNE

■ *Erotica*

CUPID'S, 511 W 17th St, (307) 635-3837.

ETNA

■ *Information*

BLUE FOX STUDIO & GALLERY, 107452 Hwy 89, (307) 883-3310. 1 hour outside Jackson on the main hwy between Cheyenne & Jackson. Gay-owned jewelry & pottery studio. Ask for Tony or Wayne for gay info on Jackson area.

JACKSON

■ *Accommodations*

REDMOND GUEST HOUSE, Box 616, (307) 733-4003. Self-contained apartment with private entrance, private bath, color cable TV, fireplace & kitchen. 50% gay & lesbian clientele.

■ *Women's Accommodations*

BAR H RANCH, Box 297, Driggs, ID 83422, (208) 354-2906. One bedroom deluxe loft with kitchen, unique bath & woodstove. Nicely furnished, TV, VCR, decks, mountain views, horses & trail riding. Stay in a genuine Sioux teepee made of canvas, set in a private pasture surrounded by willows and aspens. Accommodates 4 people. Private bath, kitchen, dressing room & sunny deck nearby. Mostly women with men welcome. ♀

FISH CREEK LODGING, See Ashton, Idaho.

■ *Retail & Bookstores*

GRAND BASKET, 140 N Cache, (307) 739-1139. Gourmet food gifts & gift baskets. We ship anywhere in the US & specialize in Wyoming-made products.

VALLEY BOOKSTORE, 125 N Cache, (307) 733-4533. General bookstore with a good gay & lesbian section.

RIVERTON

■ *Restaurants*

COUNTRY COVE RESTAURANT, (307) 856-9813. Gay-friendly family restaurant, breakfast & lunch & steaks & seafood at dinner, 7:30am-3pm & 5pm-9pm, closed Sun. Candle & giftshop next door. ■

THERMOPOLIS

■ *Accommodations*

OUT WEST B&B, 1344 Broadway, Thermopolis, WY 82443, (307) 864-2700. B&B in 1908 Queen Anne home, overlooks Owl Creek Mtns. Shared baths, full breakfast, world's largest mineral hot spring in town's state park, 136 miles to Yellowstone Nat'l Park, 84 miles to Cody, WY. 50% gay/lesbian clientele.

HONG KONG - THE MERRY WIDOW

Continued from Page 178

than a just a few years before - with unofficial gay bars, cruising in public parks, and Western ideas about homosexuality flooding in. Few see an all-out crackdown on "Western sexual bourgeois" lifestyles, but all it takes is one hard-liner in high power to bring down swift penalties for "anti-social" behavior. With China's infamous track record on human rights, at times it doesn't look very promising.

But it's not as if Hong Kong gays have had a history of rights themselves. Homosexuality was erased from the Hong Kong books as an offense punishable by imprisonment only in the late 1980's! Now, homosexual acts between males is legal for those over 21. Lesbianism, in true Victorian fashion, was never officially addressed, leading one to assume it has always been wholeheartedly legal.

There is still gay life in Hong Kong, and no doubt it will survive one way or another. Most gay establishments are in and around the nightlife party centers of Lan Kwai Fong and Wan Chai, both on Hong Kong Island. The few square blocks of Lan Kwai Fong is chock full of trendy cafes, bars, and eateries, although most tend to be straight with gays interspersed. The two big gay bars for men, Propanganda and Yin-Yang are in this vicinity, with Yin-Yang also drawing the largest crowds of lesbians. Most local Chinese are warm towards foreigners in gay establishments, and speak good English, but there are some who prefer fellow Chinese and aren't comfortable conversing with foreigners. And this is not Thailand: local boys do not need your money - they have their own investment portfolios! If you are non-Asian, watch out, you may be preyed upon by a "potato queen" - the Asian reverse of a "rice queen". Also, whites are usually referred to as a gweilo, which is not really a derogatory term, but it does mean "foreign devil." You'll feel the British presence in most gay bars and pubs, though recently there has been some anti-British sentiment among locals; but for the most part, the gay world is friendly and glad to exist!

For more nightlife, check out the other lively area of town - Wan Chai. This district used to be where American G.I.s would hunt for their own personal Suzy Wong during the Vietnam War. Even now, sailors with buzzed heads still carry on the tradition of stumbling down to the girlie bars where Filipinas in thongs entertain them. Wan Chai is still a lot more presentable than its North American red-light district counterparts, with great restaurants and fine British pubs. It may be worth the trip only to be mesmerized by the millions of neon lights and colored signs overlapping each other, vying for space above the streets. There are a couple of gay saunas nearby and a gay pub - check *Contacts Magazine*, available at most gay establishments, for current listings and addresses. (Another good paper to see what's up is

Continued on next Page

UNITED STATES

the *HK Weekly*, highlighting arts and entertainment, with some gay personals in the back.)

Of course, on your nightly outings, you'll probably run into one Hong Kong staple: the Karaoke bar. You see them everywhere, identifiable by the letters OK on their marquee. Hong Kongers can go on for hours, days at Karaoke bars. If locals invite you out for Karaoke, be prepared for a marathon. They pass the mike around between drinks and you can warble your way along to tacky videos in Chinese or English into the next day. The usually public-shy locals metamorphose in front of your eyes into an Anita Mui or Jackie Cheung or one of the many "Canto-pop" celebs, famous Asia-wide. Karaoke is a must for every traveler looking for the quintessential Hong Kong experience.

Karaoke also curiously dominates the gay bath scene as well. Bath houses in Hong Kong tend to be a lot more social than in other countries, with full bars and private Karaoke rooms. This is probably due to the absence of plentiful gay bars, or places for gays to meet in general. What Hong Kong may lack in bars, it makes up for with gay bathhouses, numbering over a dozen scattered throughout the small colony. Most tend to be revamped flats - small and cozy. Sex is not always the main theme, as much as is informality and intimacy. Saunas are probably one of the only places in Hong Kong where you can watch a gay porno movie.

For gay beaches, try Repulse Bay, on the south side of Hong Kong Island. Surrounded by million dollar apartments, the southern-most end of this beach is where you'll find a wonderfully garish temple and statue of the Chinese goddess of the sea, *Tin Hau*. But it's on the northern end of the beach where you may find local gay goddesses laying out on the sand. The water's fairly dirty as is most of the ocean around Hong Kong. Hike up the road heading south from Repulse Bay towards Chai Wan beach, and you will find outcroppings of rugged rocks where many gays congregate and cruise. Worth a look on a sunny day, but not on Sundays - most Hong Kongers work six days a week, and Sundays are a nightmare as every last family floods the island, taking their youngsters out. A day to be avoided at the beach or in town! (And don't forget Hong Kong is very humid in the summer, cool and wet in the winter. The best months to visit would be September-October or March-April.)

And lastly, a word about the language of Hong Kong: Cantonese. It's spoken in Hong Kong and adjoining provinces in China, and is not to be confused with Mandarin, which is the official language of Taiwan and the People's Republic of China. Most foreigners learn Mandarin, as it has easier pronunciation and only five tones to the words, as compared to Cantonese's nine! Learning Cantonese is like banging your head against a wall, because the subtle pitches and tones can completely alter the literal definition of words. But Hong Kongers love it when you try to speak Cantonese, mainly to laugh at you, I guess. The Chinese have a saying that a Chinese and a foreigner having a conversation is like a chicken and a duck trying to talk to each other. After spending some time in China and Hong Kong, you'll know what they mean.

MYKONOS - ISLAND OF THE GODS

Continued from page 242

Ready for Dinner?

There are restaurants to please every palate and wallet — French, international, Chinese, Thai, Tex-Mex, Italian, Greek, and even fast food snack bars with gyros, souvlakis (many have vegetarian dishes on their menus. Keeping in pace with the late nightlife routine, most people eat dinner late, starting around 9-10 pm, after having had their "siesta" to help recover from the day at the beach. Some restaurants to consider: Alefkandra, on the waterfront at the beginning of Little Venice, for Greek cuisine. Gatsby's, in the centre of town (near the beginning of Matoyianni Street), offers a garden setting and international cuisine. Dynasty, for Chinese or Thai. La Mexicana for Tex-Mex. Maccheroni, near Lakka Square for Italian. Delphine on Matoyianni Street, serves "homestyle" Greek cooking. Eden Garden, at Cleopatra's Pool, for international cuisine served at your poolside table. Mykonos is filled with restaurants. To try each and every one, whether it be a proper restaurant or fast-food snack bar, you would have to be here at least a month or eat good-sized meals twice a day! Try a different one each night that you are here. It's vacation time. You can go on a diet when you get back home.

After a leisurely dinner, head down quay-side for a stroll. It might help to settle that delicious dinner you just ate. Stop for a coffee and brandy at one of the many cafes lining the harbour front Head back to Little Venice, or go to one of the cafes located "inland." Then, it's off to the bars and discos.

And What a Choice!

All types of music and venues await you, from techno/rave to 60's, 70's, 80's to soft, relaxing "pop," to classical to "live" cabaret-style. Mykonos has something for literally everyone. You might want to return to Montparnasse Piano Bar to enjoy the live piano and Broadway-caliber singer., or back to Kastro's to enjoy the soothing tones of classical music. Diva, located next to Alefkandra Restaurant, is owned and run by Evangelina (last seen at Pierro's) and her brother. Be sure to stop in. Porta Bar, near Nilo's Taverna, is in a small cul-de-sac and offers a relaxing atmosphere. Or just dance the night away at Pierro's, Factory, Manto Bar or Icaros.

All the bars/discos mentioned are gay-oriented or gay-owned. Sorry, girls, there are no specific women-only venues. As yet, all are mixed. But don't misunderstand: Mykonos is not just for the guys. It's for everyone, and you may find some straight couples at some of the night spots. Keep in mind that even though a bar or disco may be open when you get there, the real action doesn't really start until about midnight or later.

ICELAND - HIDDEN TREASURE OF THE NORTH!
Continued from page 246

discos, which are often almost deserted until 11:00 or 12:00 at night! These late evenings also make taxi hailing an Olympic-style sport when the bars close at 3:00am. So your best bet may be to walk from the city center to the taxi stand at the east end of Laekjargata, to avoid taxi competition.

The gay community is so assimilated here that our sources could only think of one place they would consider a "gay" restaurant—Jömfruin at 8 Laekoargata. There is one gay bed and breakfast, A Room With a View, aptly named, as it sits on the 6th floor of a major shopping street (Laugavegur 18), overlooking all of the buildings, giving it a gorgeous view of the city and the mountains behind it. The city does have a gay community center (Samtökin 78, founded in 1978) at Lindergata 49, which houses a library, cafe and an assortment of group meetings throughout the week. Gay Pride is celebrated each June 27th, and an exciting Country Ball is always planned the weekend closest to that date. The gay community here is very proud of the fact that partnership legislation has been passed in Iceland, and that the gala celebrating the legalization of same-sex marriages was attended by the country's president. It is anticipated that anti-discrimination laws will be in place in the very near future.

If you're looking for something new...if you want the chance to enjoy the bounties of nature...if you seek a place to vacation safely and comfortably...then set your sights on Iceland. You'll soon see for yourself why its guests return year after year, having discovered the hidden treasure of the north.

RUSSIA'S WILD EAST
Continued from page 270

along the rock ledge to shore, passed the rod around a tree jutting from the bank and crunched up and down a gravel bar trying not to lose this taimen in the shallows. No one woke, even when I scooped him up on the gravel between two tents. Angela, our Russian cook, made the most delicious salmon crepes for us, and two more meals for nineteen from this one 32" fish.

After the falls, the river soon joins the Amur and doubles in size. One day, we paddled in dense fog, reading the river by sound, alone, listening for rapids and then paddling between them and the shore. We camped among bear and sable tracks, beneath the nests the bears build in treetops, then abandon after a night.

The last camp on the Amur held many surprises. I could not overcome the sensation of Russian soldiers singing, perhaps the ghosts of Arsenyev's group celebrating a day on the river's shore after slogging through a nearly impenetrable forest for some obscure survey, led by a Goldi native named Dersu, quite at home in this land. Beverly, as drawn to raptors as they are to her, sighted an immature Imperial eagle, the subject of much discussion among the birders of our group and Sergei, who claimed the book says they don't exist in this part of Primorye. The next morning, early, Mike saw a mother tiger and yearling cub come down to the river for a drink. Every step I took away from that camp and the next, I could swear some tiger was watching.

After a week in the wilderness, a hunting camp with cabins and banya (the Russian version of sauna) loom large. We steamed, jumped in the river, steamed, flailed each other with Manchurian oak leaves, sat on the deck, steamed, washed, shampooed!, rinsed from a barrel of river water, drank limonyik, a tea brewed from liana vines.

That evening, Andrei, a local fisherman, took me and two women from our group to fly fish for Linook, another type of Russian landlocked salmon. Marcy declared this to be her finest fishing trip ever. Candy, with advice from Marcy, hooked and landed a 22-incher, her first fish ever on a fly. We all had such good luck catching 18-24" fish that I taught Andrei our method, lent him my pole, and he hooked one the very first cast, but lost it. When I showed him how the barb was pinched down, he understood how the fish got away, but it was not until the next day with Sergei to interpret, that he found out I intentionally do this to all my flies. I did leave the barbs on the flies I traded to him for his own hand-tied specials.

The Amur joins the Bolshaya Ussurka to form a broad river that braids itself through rolling green hills and the first farms and homesteads we had seen in a week. Our river journey ended at Dalnykut, "faraway place." Our presence was rare enough to start a procession of children, bicycles, cats and dogs, and locals who show us their gardens, mushrooms gathered from the forests, wonderful complexities of the simple life, all in a pastoral setting festooned with outrageous wildflowers, sheep, geese, sleek horses and rare butterflies like the iridescent Maack's swallowtail.

We returned to Vladivostok in a sleeper car on the luxurious Trans-Siberian Railway, and relished the wood interiors, hot-and-cold running water, hot tea in glass and pewter cups, the early-morning beauty of Amur Bay. Our last night in Russia, we celebrated at Evgeny's apartment with our new Russian friends, a feast of seafood, chicken, vegetables of all kinds, fern salad, many desserts, and innumerable champagne toasts.

This is the way to travel.

VANCOUVER: SPECTACULAR BY NATURE

Continued from page 326

the ocean, fresh seafood is plentiful. Given the large Asian community, Chinese, Thai, Sushi, and Indian restaurants are plentiful. Italian, Portuguese and Greek bistros are most prevalent along Commercial Drive. You could easily dine out every evening for two weeks and never visit the same country twice.

We blame Seattle for our favourite obsession: coffee. Beans from around the world arrive in North America through our U.S. neighbour. Having the pick of the crop has resulted in a regional fascination with the brew. Coffee bars, complete with biscotti and flavoured syrups, are all the rage, and have become the gay community's afternoon alternative to the bars.

Another neighbour is Victoria, the provincial capital, situated at the southern tip of Vancouver Island. While it's possible to fly, the more scenic route is by government-operated BC Ferries, (604) 669-1211. Recommended as an overnight trip, historic Victoria features a beautifully refurbished old town, the stately Empress Hotel and the neo-classical Legislative Buildings. The gay community, like the city itself, is smaller, with the nightclubs and eateries within easy walking distance of the tourist district.

Between the mainland and Vancouver Island are a number of smaller Gulf Islands, which are accessible only by ferry and seaplane. Rustic and isolated, Salt Spring Island offers an honest get away from the big city hustle. Several fine gay and lesbian guest houses bring a sense of sophistication to this pastoral setting, best known for its artisans and bohemian atmosphere.

For more information contact BC Tourism at (604) 663-6000 or 1-800-663-6000, or write: Ministry of Tourism, #802, 865 Hornby Street, Vancouver, BC V6Z 2G3. The Vancouver Travel Information Centre can be reached at (604) 683-2000, or write: #201, 200 Burrard Street, Vancouver, BC V6G 3L6.

For more detail on the lesbian and gay community, surf the Internet to "http://www.glba.org/", sponsored by the Gay & Lesbian Business Association of Greater Vancouver, or "http://www.f212.com/Vancouver%20Comm.html".

COSTA RICA

Continued from page 350

mon in other Latin American countries," she says, "so it's much more gay-friendly."

Another contributor to tolerance may be that the Catholic church seems to have less of a stranglehold on its citizens here than elsewhere. Indeed, I constantly hear rumors (though, typically, none of the sources will allow me to quote them directly) that even a highly-placed Costa Rican Catholic official is himself gay. Then there's the legendary friendliness of the Ticos, as Costa Ricans call themselves, which also must have something to do with the welcome given to gay visitors.

"In many ways, Costa Rica is different from most of Latin America," says Rodolfo Gómez, the incredibly knowledgeable guide Way To Go provides for our stay in the countryside. Indeed, the fact that my group of seven queens — just call us Priscillas of the rainforest — are comfortably and openly touring the environs seems to illustrate the point.

We're bumping across a landscape of rolling green hills that looks more like my image of Switzerland or Devonshire than Central America while Gómez speaks of the country's free-thinking tradition. Costa Rica has long held democratic elections, unusual in this dictatorial region, and there is, to this day, no army, he states with pride as we dodge a pothole as big as my apartment. *(No need for an army, I think. What invader would want to deal with these roads?)*

I ask Julio, our driver an the only straight man in the crew, if he felt uncomfortable at the prospect of this group. "Why should I feel uncomfortable?" he replies matter-of-factly. "I have respect for other people." Which gives me pause: In Gringolandia (as they call the U.S.)

people speak of tolerance. In Costa Rica, they speak of respect. I'm about to tell him this when he careens around a pothole the size of San José and I decide to leave him to his driving.

We pass placidly grazing cows and fields of shiny coffee plants, towering Guanacaste trees and stately cedars 'til we arrive at Manual Antonio National Park, one of Costa Rica's most popular beauty spots and perhaps the gayest area outside the capital. There's a gay beach here (turn right at the park's entrance, walk toward a group of rocks, climb over them, look for naked men). I remember the words of the bartender at Déjà Vu: "La Playita (The Little Beach)? Gay, gay, gay." Wait 'til low tide if you don't want to be trapped there for hours — though I suppose there are worse fates in the world.

I can see why Manuel Antonio Park is so beloved. Jungle and sea collide in a devastating display of lushness: wild ginger with blazing torches of blossom, heliconia dangling in sensual scarlet masses, mushrooms lining an overturned tree trunk like multicolored moths. Iguanas dart through the woods under the lazy eye of overhanging sloths, monkeys chatter, and a neon blue butterfly alights on a flaming red flower. A parade of leaf-cutter ants marches its green scraps across the road (I even see one macho ant literally stagger under his overambitious load) as the deafening cacophony of cicadas duels with the ocean's roar.

The beach, with its dark sands and stunning turquoise waters, is too picture-postcard to be true. A tree-covered islet sits serenely in the pounding surf. Snorkelers float in an isolated cove A long-nosed coatimundi snuffles through a swimmer's satchel, carrying off a bag of fruit. Indeed, you can't leave your things unattended, or the monkeys might steal them.

This is only one of many natural wonders we discover. There's Poás National Park, overlooking one of Costa Rica's nine active volcanoes. Here, in the heart of the cloud forest, our guide points out bromeliads sprouting from tree branches, "poor man's umbrellas" unfolding their protective foliage, pagoda trees among ferns as thick as green molasses. In the distance, the fine mist lifts from Poás's charred crater, as the volcano belches forth a rivulet of steam.

But this is nothing compared to the nightly fireworks of Arenal, the country's most active volcano. As we head for Tabacón Hot Springs, a luxuriously landscaped series of natural waters heated by the volcano, we see cars lined up by the side of the road, their occupants eager in anticipation. Later, while I luxuriate in a steamy spring, a distant roar signals curtains-up on a display of fiery splendor that continues several moments before the volcano subsides into complacence.

More delights can be found in charming towns like Grecia, with its metal cathedral (the previous church, which took 18 years to build, was destroyed by an earthquake in 35 seconds); Sarché the handicrafts center, where I go wild in a woodworking shop; Zarcero, whose photogenic church is fronted by an amazing topiary garden. And there are still other enchantments I can't wait to explore, from the unspoiled Caribbean coast to the fascinating Guanacaste region in the west.

But in the end, it's back to San José, where I head straight to Plaza de la Cultura to sit over a coffee and watch the world stroll by. Within ten minutes, I've seen five of the handsomest men in history. My friend in the Gay Pride Run shirt is nowhere to be seen, but it doesn't matter: He's moved into the realm of legend now, just one more delight to recall from a country whose delights overflow in my memory like water spilling from a maracas plant.

OFF THE MAP ON MAUI
Continued from page 424

gods would help and protect them, as the gods were always watching over them. We walk about a quarter mile to the stones of this temple mount and sense the presence of Spirit here and now, as well as from other times past. Thanks go to Kane, god of life, fresh water, forests and sunlight, for this exquisite day with which we've been blessed.

5:00 pm

The end of a glorious day! One gift left with Janet and Kim is a cassette of fine Hawaiian music, including Ki ho'alu (slack key). Played throughout their tour, it will provide them with fond memories of this excursion. I also leave them with a thick folder complete with write-ups, articles, stories, pictures, a map, information on the subjects covered, places visited, and much more. And of course, suggestions as to where to eat, dance, shop, play during the rest of their visit. They're already wondering what they'd like to experience their next trip to Maui. I have plenty of ideas... Aloha a hui hou ia olua, 'o Janet a me 'o Kim! Farewell to you both, Janet and Kim! Until we meet again!